International Council on System Engineering 2000

Minneapolis, Minnesota, USA
16 - 20 July 2000

Volume 1 of 2

ISBN: 978-1-5108-6245-6

Printed from e-media with permission by:

Curran Associates, Inc.
57 Morehouse Lane
Red Hook, NY 12571

Some format issues inherent in the e-media version may also appear in this print version.

Printed by Curran Associates, Inc. (2018)

For permission requests, please contact John Wiley & Sons
at the address below.

John Wiley & Sons
111 River Street
Hoboken, NJ 07030-5774

Phone: (201) 748-6000
Fax: (201) 748-6088

info@wiley.com

Additional copies of this publication are available from:

Curran Associates, Inc.
57 Morehouse Lane
Red Hook, NY 12571 USA
Phone: 845-758-0400
Fax: 845-758-2633
Email: curran@proceedings.com
Web: www.proceedings.com

TABLE OF CONTENTS

VOLUME 1

SECTION I: SYSTEM ENGINEERING APPLICATIONS

HEALTH CARE APPLICATIONS 3

VEHICLES/TRANSPORTATION 2

INFRASTRUCTURE SYSTEMS ENGINEERING APPLICATIONS

ENVIRONMENTAL SYSTEMS

LEGAL AND PUBLIC INTEREST

SECTION II: MODELING AND SIMULATION

TOOLS

MODELING 2

MODELING 3

SYSTEMS

SECION III: SYSTEM ENGINEERING MANAGEMENT

MANAGEMENT 1

MANAGEMENT 2

MANAGEMENT 4

REQUIREMENTS

RISK 2

SECTION IV: SYSTEM ANALYSIS/PROCESS

ARCHITECTURE

METHODS 2

VOLUME 2

METHODS 3

METHODS 4

LIFE CYCLE 1

LIFE CYCLE 2

SECTION V: MEASUREMENT

CAPABILITY ASSESSMENT 1

CAPABILITY ASSESSMENT 2

ANALYSIS 2

PROCESS 1

SECTION VI: EDUCATION/STANDARDS

EDUCATION AND RESEARCH 1

EDUCATION AND RESEARCH 2

STANDARDS 2

STANDARDS 3

COMMERCIAL AVIATION APPLICATIONS 2

SECTION VII: SUPPLEMENTAL PAPERS

RESERVE/POSTER PAPERS

A Systems Engineer's Approach to Brain Surgery

Dr. William F. Mackey
8800 Teresa Ann Court
Alexandria, VA 22308

Abstract. What can a patient do when faced with a critical health challenge that might be body disabling or life threatening? This author when diagnosed with a brain tumor decided to apply the principles of systems engineering. As a result of applying a reasonable constraint at the early stages of evaluation, the solution to the challenge resulted in two relatively noninvasive cranial procedures, rather than the conventional craniotomy recommended by three of the five neurosurgeons consulted.

The approach elected by this author included several systems engineering processes such as developing a concept for the operation, a key requirement(s) definition, a tradeoff analysis of neuroradiosurgery systems, a risk analysis, and even an evaluation of the mission during medical follow-up. Such medical procedures could not have been conducted successfully as few as 10 to 15 years ago.

The thesis of this paper is that patients can affect the outcome of the medical procedures to be conducted on them, and the approaches of the systems engineering discipline are extremely useful when appropriately applied to healthcare challenges.

COMPARING THE MEDICAL PROCESS WITH SYSTEMS ENGINEERING

The role of the medical staff and patient in developing a medical diagnosis and preparing for an operation or medical procedure is not unlike that of a systems engineer. The medical staff and patient use a medical process life cycle to develop a treatment in a similar way as a systems engineering team uses a system development life cycle to develop a system (Table 1). The medical staff usually participates in the entire process from the beginning of medical case definition through implementation to the medical resolution.

The systems engineer identifies and validates the concept and requirements for a system; the medical staff with the patient's assistance identifies and validates the symptoms of a case, creates a diagnosis that fits the symptoms and develops a concept and requirements for treating the illness. Just as the systems engineer creates a system design, the medical physician develops a design for the operation or medical procedures to be followed after a thorough evaluation of all the options. The system implementation has a corollary in the preparation for the operation and/or medical treatment initiation. The systems engineer finds out during system integration and test whether the system design actually validates the requirements. The medical staff conducts the medical operation and/or procedures and finds out after the operation whether the medical process has produced the desired results or has caused any of the risks to materialize. The acceptance of the system is very much like the recovery and the medical resolution. Finally, just as the systems engineer must be prepared to maintain the system for the remainder of the life cycle, the medical staff must be prepared to follow-up any medical side-effects and evaluate the success of the medical treatment.

Systems Engineering Phases	Medical Process Corollary
1. System Concept and Requirements Definition	1. Client discussions regarding symptoms, diagnosis, and medical requirements
2. System Design	2. Medical evaluations and medical procedures development
3. System Implementation	3. Preparation for the operation and/or medical procedures
4. System Integration and Test	4. Conduct the operation and/or medical procedures
5. System Installation and Acceptance	5. Recovery and medical resolution
6. System Operation and Maintenance	6. Medical follow-up and mission success evaluation

Table 1. Corollary Life Cycles of the Medical Staff and the Systems Engineer

There are some differences between the medical and systems engineering processes in the individuality with which every patient in the medical process is treated because of age, general health, and the risks that each physician and patient are willing to take. However, there are clearly more similarities than differences. The use of technology in the medical processes over the past 50 years has expanded responsibility for the success of any operation or procedure to the entire medical support industry that develops and delivers systems and products unforeseen even a few years ago.

INTRODUCTION AND BACKGROUND OF THE CHALLENGE

The Challenges of Youth. It was almost 41 years ago on a June morning in the summer of 1959, but I remember that day as if it were yesterday. I had just completed my second year at the United States Naval Academy, and my dreams were beginning to become all I had ever hoped they would be. I had been on the Superintendent's Honor List (the highest honor role at USNA), standing 23 in a class of about 1140 midshipmen who were all mentally, morally, and physically fit. Having come from a low- to middle-income family in a small town in western Pennsylvania, I had begun to achieve things I had not thought possible 2 years before. I was a member of one of the finest drum & bugle corps in the nation and because of my class standing and leadership skills would likely become its commander when I became a Firstclassman (a senior). I was one of a few coxswains on the USNA crew-racing team that would later represent the United States at the 1960 Summer Olympics in Rome. During the previous month, I was given the opportunity and honor, along with a small cadre of classmates, to lead the indoctrination of the new class of plebes who would be entering USNA in a few weeks. I would also be the Drum & Bugle Corps Commander for the yet to be formed Plebe D&B Corps. The only challenge facing me was whether to become a naval aviator and strive to become an astronaut (of the first seven astronauts chosen, two were USNA graduates; and the USNA has produced at least 46 astronauts to date) or join Admiral Hyman Rickover's nuclear submarine corps.

After finishing a month's leave, I awoke early on that June morning. As I carried my suitcases down the hall of my parent's home, I collapsed into unconsciousness for no apparent reason. The family doctor came to our home, told me to take it easy, and gave me some pills to take for the summer. I arrived in Annapolis and, as planned, began to indoctrinate, drill, and teach the plebes how to become midshipmen and made them ready to join the brigade when the upperclassmen returned in the fall. There were no more periods of unconsciousness that summer, but I did notice a severe left-arm quiver almost every morning and that my arm became limp during morning exercise.

As the academic year progressed, I continued to have the left-arm problems in the mornings and on two occasions in formation collapsed into unconsciousness. A few tests, including EEGs, in the Navy hospital, revealed nothing. In late November 1959, we had congregated in formation in Bancroft Hall court about 4 a.m. to board buses to Philadelphia, PA, for the biggest day in the year for any midshipman . . . the Army vs. Navy football game! I again collapsed and was rushed to Bethesda Naval Hospital in what would become the initial recognition of a neurological concern and the end of my promising military career.

Evaluating the Neurological Concern. I was admitted to the Bethesda Naval Hospital and watched on TV as my classmate Joe Bellino had an outstanding football game that would eventually win him the Heisman Trophy. I also watched and listened to the USNA Drum & Bugle Corps as they played the march I had arranged earlier in the year. I was in good company in the hospital with an ensign named Bruce who was 2 years older than I and had graduated from Amherst a year or two earlier, and a USNA plebe named Lenny who was 2 years younger than I. We all had similar symptoms. Both Bruce and Lenny were diagnosed with significant brain tumors and ultimately had to have craniotomies. As a young man, it was difficult to watch these other young men have their lives altered in such a dramatic way and to recognize that I too was heading down the same path. I learned later that Bruce had an inoperable malignant brain tumor and would pass away 6 months later. Lenny fared a bit better, but his military days were over. I lost track of Lenny, but I truly hope he is alive and living a productive life.

After numerous tests including arteriograms, pneumoencephalograms, and more puncture wounds than I wish to recall, a simple X-ray focused attention on an intracranial calcification deposit about the size of a marble (1.5 cm) on the right side of my brain resting above the corpus collosum, "a 1.5 cm fairly well circumscribed stipped calcific density within the right parietal lobe." It was believed that sometime in my life, either in my youth or as a midshipman, a significant headblow had caused a small hemorrhage and the calcium deposit to form in response to the body's natural healing functions. Whatever the cause, I wanted the neurosurgeons to get that calcium deposit out of my brain so I could get on with becoming a naval aviator or a submariner. There was no way that a bump on the head was going to crush my dream!! Fortunately, the physicians were more objective than I and decided that medication could probably control any symptoms. I could live a normal life without surgery.

Unfortunately, the potential for future periods of unconsciousness meant I would never pilot a Navy plane or command a nuclear submarine. In short, my naval career was coming to an end. Even worse, they were recommending separation from the Naval Academy. This devastated me! I had done nothing wrong and had been the best midshipman I could be. I would not give up that easily. For more than 2 months in the hospital, I studied on my own and returned to the Naval Academy to take semester final exams in January 1960. My diligence paid off. My grades were good enough to make the Superintendent's Honor List again. My classmates were very supportive, and my Company

Officer wrote recommendations on my behalf. I appealed to my Congressman and wrote official memoranda to the Chief of Naval Operations and the Secretary of the Navy. I reasoned that if I could not fly a plane or dive a submarine, I would become the best Navy engineer to ever join the Civil Engineering Corps. I requested I be allowed to finish the remaining year and a half to graduation. The Navy saw it differently and, although I was permitted to finish my third year, I would have to leave Navy in June 1960. And so I did.

The Change of a Career. I experienced all the disappointment and normal depression that comes with a difficult life-altering experience. In addition, I did not know what the future held. To be only 20 years old and contemplating the possibility of death or severe restrictions on the type of life I would lead was very difficult. Was I born with this condition? Could this condition be controlled with medication or would it get worse? Would I ever get married or raise children? Would I ever find a career that offered the possibilities of my previous dreams? How could someone who was frequently tested and found to be in wonderful physical condition be suddenly in such difficulty? All of these questions bothered me for months and years to come.

I immediately decided to attend the University of Pittsburgh and study physics and mathematics. The medication seemed to be working just fine and I had few, if any, noticeable symptoms. I briefly considered medicine as a career, but had not taken the prerequisite courses for medical school entrance and still did not know whether I might place possible patients in danger if I chose that profession. After graduation with honors from the University of Pittsburgh, I attended graduate school at Rensselaer Polytechnic Institute and completed a Masters degree in physics. During one summer, I had the opportunity to work in a nuclear reactor facility near Pittsburgh. In the summer of 1963, I was chosen to be a student intern at the NASA Marshall Space Flight Center. What a thrill it was to be working in the same building as Werner von Braun who was the architect and spokesman for the U.S. Space Program. Before I graduated from the University of Pittsburgh, I met a beautiful and caring young woman whom I would marry in 1964 and with whom I would father and raise three great children. In 1965, I decided to begin my career in the aerospace program.

The aerospace company I worked for in Philadelphia allowed me to complete my Ph.D. in the scientific or engineering field of my choice. I decided to try the emerging new field of "systems engineering," which would combine my earlier desire to contribute to medicine by studying biomedical electronic engineering and my recently acquired skills in computing, electrical engineering, and aerospace systems. While I was completing my studies at night at the University of Pennsylvania, all three of my children were born; I helped to start a small company in oil exploration and aerospace consulting; and I became internationally recognized as an expert on a supercomputer called the "array processor." The emerging energy crisis in the early 1970s enabled me to travel to geophysical companies, power generation utilities, and energy systems organizations throughout the world and try to assist them. Indirectly, my work with the array processor began to benefit medical science. The array processor is used by hospitals to process CATSCAN and Magnetic Resonance Images (MRIs). Without the array processor to perform the image computations, the development of such devices would have been uneconomical and perhaps impossible for many years.

In 1975, I moved my family to Virginia to continue work in resolving the energy crisis at the Federal level. By this time, I had experimented with reducing and eliminating the medication I had taken since the early 1960s. I did not seem to need it, and other than minor left-arm limpness on occasion, I skied, snorkeled, sailed, rappelled off cliffs, camped, swam, bicycled, fished, traveled, played ice hockey and did far more activities with my family than most fathers in our community. In short, I had developed a zest for life that could not be diminished by some easily defeated health challenge. Along the way, I completed a law degree at night and was briefly considered for president of two major universities. I currently support NASA on unmanned missions development and with my sons have developed some concepts for intelligent transportation systems (automated automobiles and highways). I am also an Adjunct Professor at the University of Maryland and have a small law practice.

Why am I telling this story? Because somewhere out there is a young reader or some parents who fear that the first signs of a brain tumor may permanently destroy their hopes and dreams. Somewhere out there is someone who needs the encouragement to overcome a neurological disorder and regain the zest for life that I presently feel. While I surely could have lived without my early discouragement, perhaps I would not have realized the value of living a full life that I gained in overcoming my health challenges. Although I have had a wonderful learning experience and a career in several disciplines, I have never lost the importance of having a family and was always able to focus on the pleasure of raising three wonderful and talented children. If my story ended here, I would never have written this article, so please read on.

Accepting a New Life Challenge. In 1993, I drove with my younger son and daughter from our home in Virginia to Alaska. My son had graduated from West Point the year before and had recently undergone paratrooper school and ranger training. Out of a sense of adventure, I guess, he chose Alaska as his first duty assignment. Having done extremely well at West Point, he could have chosen virtually any assignment he wanted. My daughter had just completed her first year at the University of Virginia and would spend the summer working in Alaska and living with her brother. After completing the 6500-mile drive to Fairbanks, Alaska with my children, I set out on my own to see some of the most pristine and beautiful parts of our country. I signed up for a 24-glacier cruise and left for Portage, about 75 miles south of Anchorage. Unfortunately, I could find no hotels and spent the summer night sleeping in the car beside Explorer Glacier. It gets pretty cold at night beside a glacier and because I enjoyed the glaciers on that all-day cruise, the cold wind caused me to get a severe case of bronchitis. Over the following weeks, the bronchitis created an inner ear infection, which in turn caused ringing in the right ear. When it didn't go away, I recalled that the calcification was also on the right side, so out of caution I got a neurological examination. The neurologist suggested an MRI/MRA to determine whether auditory nerves were being affected. It was the first time that I had any brain images created since that X-ray in 1959.

The MRI/MRA images now revealed not only the 1.5-cm calcification, but also an adjacent complex cystic lesion of 2.5 cm (slightly smaller than the size of a golf ball) including the calcification. It couldn't be determined whether the cyst was there in 1959, because X-rays would not provide such granularity. The findings suggested a cystic calcified neoplastic process such as a low-grade astrocytoma or oligodenroglioma. The neurologist decided that the formation did not cause the ringing in the ear, but deserved tracking over time. It was the first time in 34 years that I had reason to be cautious.

Four years later in 1997, I began to notice unusual fatigue and a slight limp that caused me to sometimes trip going up stairs. I obtained treatment for a back problem, without much satisfaction. During a summer family outing, I suddenly noticed several strange symptoms: an inability to throw a frisbee, a very weak tennis forearm, and a loss of function in the left arm. I also noticed that my left leg would collapse when stopping on a bicycle, I could not keep up with the other bicyclists, and the limp continued. I wrote all of these symptoms down and presented them to my family doctor with the admonition that I didn't think I had a back problem. I returned to the neurologist who again requested another MRI/MRA. The images now showed a 5-cm well-defined cystic lesion (about the size of a hen's egg) that had grown 5 to 8 times in volume in the previous 4 years. If it kept growing, I would continue to lose function. I had to take action and immediately scheduled an appointment with a neurosurgeon.

APPLYING SYSTEMS ENGINEERING PRINCIPLES TO THE HEALTHCARE CHALLENGE

The systems engineering principles were a clear benefit in addressing this challenge. The key steps follow and are discussed in subsequent paragraphs:

1. Developing a medical treatment concept including a medical constraint by which to proceed
2. Establishing the key requirement(s) for selection of medical procedures
3. Evaluating the therapy procedures including the selection of the radiation devices
4. Selecting the neurosurgery team and the medical facility
5. Conducting the stereotactic aspiration procedure
6. Conducting the Gamma Knife radiosurgery procedure
7. Evaluating risks and actually encountering them
8. Evaluating the mission success and lessons learned

Developing a Medical Treatment Concept and the Requirements. Faced with such a challenge, I decided to apply all the principles of systems engineering I had learned to address the challenge and find the correct solution. I first decided to develop a concept by which I would evaluate all that I was about to be told.

The concept consisted of the following four primary elements:

1. Since this lesion had been part of me for 38 years, I believed it must be benign or I probably would have been dead years before.
2. I would use the history of the illness to my advantage and take the time to do the necessary research.
3. I would NOT panic, no matter what I was told.
4. I would look for the least invasive procedures that would allow me to regain full function and retain my high quality of active life. **This constraint turned out to be the key element in forcing a solution beyond the procedures usually suggested for treating this cranial problem.**

By the time I finished getting the information I needed and understood my challenge in-depth, I had consulted with five very reputable neurosurgeons at a local hospital, the University of Virginia, Johns Hopkins University, the University of Chicago, and the University of Maryland. All of the neurosurgeons were objective and professional and all gave me their best advice. Three of the five recommended a craniotomy. Each neurosurgeon provided some new insight that built on the previous consultations. I will always be grateful for the advice received from each of these physicians. Two of the neurosurgeons, Dr. Edward Laws of the University of Virginia and Dr. Lawrence Chin of the University of Maryland, stood out in their approach to my concerns.

I met Dr. Laws as the second consult. Dr. Laws listened to my history and the one constraint of desiring the least invasive procedures. He was very personable and suggested a full craniotomy only as a deferred option, preferring instead two procedures: a stereotactic aspiration to reduce the size of the cyst followed by radiosurgery using the Gamma Knife system to stop the creation of the fluid. By this time, I had already begun to search libraries for brain tumor information and to surf the Internet for additional insights. I went away from this consultation excited that a noninvasive procedure existed. Dr. Laws gave credence to my belief that the tumor with high probability was benign and that I would probably regain full function quickly if I had the suggested procedures. I only had to await the decision of the physician who controlled access to the Gamma Knife machine that I was an appropriate patient for such a procedure. However, that physician said no unless I had a biopsy to satisfy his concerns.

Realizing that my initial concept for a medical procedure or procedures was possible, my initial constraint now became a requirement for me. *I would consent to only the least invasive procedures that would still permit me to regain full function and retain the high quality of active life that I enjoyed for 58 years, unless I was convinced beyond a shadow of a doubt that a craniotomy was absolutely necessary.*

Evaluating the Therapy Procedures and Conducting Tradeoff Analyses. I concluded that the stereotactic aspiration was the correct first procedure and, surfing the Internet using two keywords, "radioneurosurgery" and "Gamma Knife," I discovered that there were at least four machines that could perform the radioneurosurgery: Proton Beam, Linac, Peacock, and Gamma Knife. Which one should be used?

I began to evaluate the tradeoffs for each machine (refer to Table 2). Each machine generates accelerated proton beams or gamma rays either from the photoelectric effect or from the radioactive decay of a cobalt source. There were two proton beam machines, one at Mass General Hospital in Boston, MA, and one in Loma Linda, CA. The ability to target high-energy proton beams with accuracy was appealing in such a machine. However, if I had to eventually have a major operation (I discounted that possibility, but never ruled it out), both of those facilities were far from home. Some neurosurgeons suggested that the Linac or the Peacock (a Linac fitted with a special cranial device for directing gamma rays) had the energy level necessary to bombard the cells that surrounded the calcification.

However, the more I learned about the Gamma Knife, the more I became convinced that it was the correct system. I reasoned that the Linac was a single-beam device that incrementally moved and directed the beam from different angles one beamshot at a time. Even with the Peacock adapter, the process of moving the Linac machine relative to the patient would inherently create a less-accurate targeting process. The data shows that the Gamma Knife is accurate to within 0.1 mm and the Linac is accurate to within 0.3 mm. In addition, I preferred to have 201 low-energy beams converging on a target, being in effect magnified 201 times at the target site rather than a higher energy beam being used multiple times. I reasoned that all cells, including the healthy ones encountered by the gamma ray beam on the way to the target site, would be affected in some way by the radiation. I would prefer the low-energy beams of the Gamma Knife to interact with those healthy cells rather than the higher energy beams of the Linac.

About this time, I came upon a reference to the International Radiosurgery Support Association (IRSA) and called to discuss my evaluations. Their representatives directed me to the University of Chicago and the University of Maryland for their consult. The University of Chicago had three of the four radiosurgery devices, the Linac, the Peacock, and the Gamma Knife. In my case, Dr. Helenowski of the University of Chicago indicated that if I were to proceed with radioneurosurgery, he would recommend the Gamma Knife because of its accuracy. I concluded that stereotactic aspiration followed by stereotactic radioneurosurgery using the Gamma Knife system was probably the correct therapy for me.

Selecting the Neurosurgery Team and the Medical Facility. I met with Dr. Lawrence Chin of the University of Maryland in mid-October, and was extremely impressed with him. He listened intently as I told him my story and the evaluations I had performed to date. After I finished, he presented three options.

The first option was to wait and examine the growth of the cyst over time. Because of the cystic calcification was with high probability benign, I could the afford time to consider what I really wanted to do. However, this option had the disadvantage of allowing my body to lose function over time, possibly creating damage that could not be repaired. The second option was to have a full craniotomy to remove the cystic calcification lesion. The advantage of this option was that I would be rid of the lesion forever. The disadvantage was that if bleeding began during the operation, I could possibly lose function before the bleeding could be stopped; the recovery time from such an operation could also be significant. The third option was to have the stereotactic aspiration to reduce the size of the cyst and thereby relieve the pressure that had begun to cause the loss of left-side function. Shortly thereafter, Dr. Chin would perform the stereotactic radioneurosurgery using the Gamma Knife system. The advantage of this option was that except for the small

	Proton Beam	Linac	Peacock (Type of Linac)	Gamma Knife
External Beam Radiation Technique	Accelerated proton beam (Cyclotron)	Gamma rays from linear accelerator	Gamma rays from intensity-modulated radiation therapy	Gamma rays from cobalt -60 delay
Energy Level	Single high-energy proton beam	Single high-energy gamma beam	Low-energy (10 Mv) 20 pencil beams	201 low-energy collimated beams
Accuracy (approx.)	"Bragg Peak" region	0.3 mm	0.1–0.3 mm	0.1 mm
Number of machines (As of January 2000)	2 in U.S., 14 worldwide	At least 100 in U.S.	53 in U.S., 59 worldwide	54 in U.S., 132 worldwide
Date of Invention Introduced in U.S.	1954 in U.S.; 1990 at LLUMC	Mid-1960s in U.S.	1986 in U.S. 1991 in U.S.	1967 in Sweden 1980 in U.S.
Advantages (Author's Perception)	• Extremely accurate • Conformal radiation • Useful for irregular shaped and small deep-seated tumors	• Limited accuracy • Intended initially for body cancer therapy	• Used with Linac for conformal radiation • Intended for brain tumors	• Extremely accurate • Low-energy beam • Intended for brain tumors
System/ Manufacturer	• LLUMC/Proton Treatment Center and Fermilab • Northeast/Proton Treatment Center	• Clinac 600/Varian • Novalis/Brainlab • XKnife/Radionics • Peacock/NOMOS • Cyberknife/Accuray • SRS 200XK/Elekta	• Peacock/NOMOS	• Gamma Knife/ Elekta • Rotating Gamma System (RGS)/ OUR Scientific Int

Table 2. Tradeoff Analysis of Radiation Therapy Systems (Conducted by author/patient. Medical accuracy is not guaranteed)

burrhole to aspirate the cyst, the two procedures would be noninvasive and I would have a reasonably quick recovery. The disadvantage was that it would require two brief hospitalizations rather than one and in the end there was no guarantee that the two procedures would work. Some neurosurgeons had cautioned that the cyst might be a mass not amenable to aspiration. In addition, the possibility remained that the tumor was actually malignant and I would have to have the more radical craniotomy. I could be losing time in that case.

It did not take more than a few minutes to decide. Dr. Chin was Director of the Gamma Knife facility. He needed no additional consult to schedule the facility. If the tumor turned out to be malignant, he would also be able to perform the neurosurgery with his assistants at a later time. I reasoned that should the stereotactic aspiration followed by the radiosurgery not work or should the tumor be malignant, I could then proceed with the full craniotomy. If I proceeded with the removal of the cystic calcification, I could never back up to perform the less invasive procedures. I decided that stereotactic aspiration followed by stereotactic radioneurosurgery using the Gamma Knife system was the correct therapy and that Dr. Chin and the UMD Neurosurgery Team were the correct team to perform the procedures and with whom to entrust my future.

Although my conviction was firm and I felt I had made the correct decision, I told Dr. Chin that it still was a difficult decision for me. His reassurance that he would have made the same decision and that the UMD Neurosurgery Team had performed many such procedures was helpful. We scheduled the stereotactic aspiration for the next Friday, pending confirmation that my children could travel to Maryland to be with me during the operation. Terri Biggins, the Gamma Knife Nurse Coordinator, then showed me the Gamma Knife facility and the stereotactic frame and explained with care all that would take place in the next week. She reassured me that the hospital had an excellent neurosurgery intensive care unit should it be needed.

Conducting the Stereotactic Aspiration Procedure. During the next week, I did all the preparation that was necessary for the operation. I had done all of my research well and was glad I had taken the time to be thorough and confident in my decision. All along I had expected the very best and had the opportunity to reflect on my life. I held a deep belief in God, who had been preparing me for many years for this event. Fortunately, at this time, I could look back on my life with very little regrets. I had raised three wonderful children who were not only successful in their educational and career pursuits, but are wonderful people as well. They know that being their father has been the most wonderful experience of my life. In addition, I've had the best education at the most prestigious universities. My career has been excellent with a smorgasbord of opportunities. I worked on the Saturn IVB that helped send man to the moon, I was involved heavily in the energy crisis during the 1970s, and I've worked on the evolution of computing technology from 1965 to present. Even the array processor that I helped develop for oil exploration and that was the foundation for my Ph.D. dissertation is the very same technology that permits radiologists to obtain the medical images that just might save my life. God had been good and had been directing my life much of the way. I was prepared for whatever lie ahead. Knowing that this event was someday highly probable allowed me to take advantage of each day. Anyone who knew me also knew of my zest for life.

I had also prepared over the last few months for the very worst. My last will and testament, living will, power of attorney, proposed distribution of my possessions, and burial plans were all intact. I had written my closest friends that, "before I get too involved in so many things in the next few weeks, I just want each of you to know that you played a wonderful positive role in my life. I now need your prayers and support. I hope when all of this is over, we will still be able to squeeze the last enjoyment out of living life together. God bless each of you and the people you hold dear." Life had been good and I was indeed ready.

I played with my grandchildren on Thursday; had a delightful dinner with my family and played Trivial Pursuit with my children; slept very peacefully and arrived at the hospital with my children early on Friday, October 24. After joking with the nursing staff and attending physicians, I was fitted with the stereotactic frame. Interestingly, this procedure turned out to be the most difficult part of the day because the frame has to be rigidly fixed to the skull to ensure accurate placement of the burrhole and catheter. By the time I said my good-byes to my children and was wheeled off to the operating room, I was pretty groggy. The burrhole was carefully positioned to ensure that the catheter would puncture no vessels and the catheter was centered in the cyst. An Ommaya Reservoir was attached to the catheter and placed under the skin so that future aspirations could be conducted without reentering the brain. During the operation, 18 cc of cystic fluid was removed and I was sent to recovery. That evening, I felt fine for someone with a new hole in his head. I joked with my brother and my children.

The next morning, I was aspirated through the Ommaya Reservoir again, but blood appeared in the 1 cc of cyst fluid extracted and the procedure was stopped. I was sent home with medicine to prevent swelling and a caution to be aware of strange sensations and possible dizziness. I walked out of the hospital that Saturday with no limp and all symptoms gone.

Conducting the Gamma Knife Radiosurgery Procedure. I recovered extremely well from the insertion of the catheter, suffering virtually no ill effects. I had noticed immediate improvement from all symptoms and over the next few weeks was aspirated on successive Fridays. Because Dr. Chin was very sensitive to the psychological effects of such an operation, he removed only a small amount of hair around the incision. There were virtually no signs of an operation and persons who did not know me intimately had no clue that I had undergone any procedure at all.

The laboratory tests on the cyst fluid had returned and did indeed reveal the fluid was benign. No biopsy had been made of the tissue surrounding the calcification due to the possibility of hemorrhage, but I presume that if there had been cancerous cells they would have been found in the fluid tested. The diagnosis was a benign pilocytic astrocytoma.

Alas, we had avoided the risks! The cyst was not a mass that would prevent aspiration; the mere pressure of the large cyst had been causing all the symptoms and once even 19 cc had been removed all symptoms disappeared. The organic cell process was indeed benign and if the fluid production could be slowed or stopped by the Gamma Knife treatment, I would have no need for a craniotomy. One problem had arisen, however; the cyst had actually dented the corpus collosum and when the pressure was released, the cyst decompressed from the bottom causing the catheter to touch the bottom of the cyst and partially shut off the withdrawal of fluid. The last two aspirations had yielded only 3 cc and 2 cc of fluid, respectively. The phenomenon is much like pressing a straw to the bottom of a glass of soft drink and trying to drink through the straw ... it won't work. The catheter would have to be recentered.

I was scheduled for the Gamma Knife treatment to be followed with recenter of the catheter. I entered the hospital on Thursday, November 20, 1997. Again, I was fitted with the stereotactic frame fixed to the skull to ensure accurate targeting of the gamma rays. The Leksell Gamma Knife System consists of six components: the radiation unit, individual collimator helmets of four different beam diameters, the patient couch, the hydraulic bed subsystem, the control console, and the treatment-planning computer subsystem. I lay prone on the patient couch and the stereotactic frame was locked into the collimator helmet selected for my treatment. I was given head receivers so that the physicians could speak to me during the procedure and I could select music I liked to hear.

When the neurosurgeons had chosen the target carefully from the MRI conducted that morning and were ready for the radiation to commence, they initiated the program from the control console and the treatment-planning computer subsystem started. The patient couch was moved by the hydraulic bed subsystem into radiation "igloo" and the cobalt-60 sources sent the gamma ray beams through the 201 collimators in the helmet to the target site. I felt no sensation from the beams whatsoever and I just listened to the music and actually dosed off. In 20 minutes, the radiation was complete and I was ready to be sent to the operating room to have the catheter recentered. I had agreed to have my picture taken for a nursing journal, so Dr. Chin, Medical Director of the Gamma Knife Center, Terri Biggins, the Gamma Knife Nurse Coordinator, and I posed while they removed the frame.

The catheter was recentered successfully and 20 cc of cyst fluid was removed. On Friday morning, 10 cc more of fluid was removed, bringing the accumulation of fluid aspirated to 54 cc. I went home that morning in excellent condition and took my son and his friend out to dinner that evening. On Saturday, my son and I replaced rain guttering on the front and rear of my home that we had removed for painting. And on Sunday, after my son departed, I vacuumed up leaves from my lawn and cut small tree limbs for Monday refuse pickup. In short, I outworked all of my neighbors that weekend, and I was the one that had brain radiosurgery on the Thursday before! While I don't advocate that kind of activity level for everyone who undertakes such a procedure, it does illustrate how easy such procedures have become for patients over the past 10 years since the introduction of the Gamma Knife to the United States in 1987.

Over the next 2 weeks, 17 cc more of cystic fluid were aspirated, bringing the accumulation of fluid aspirated to 71 cc. Because 1cc is equivalent to 1 milliliter of fluid by volume and there are 355 ml in a 12-oz can of soda, the amount fluid extracted to the point that the cyst by CATSCAN was shown to be virtually collapsed was about one-fifth a 12-oz can of soda. The only remaining issue was, had the Gamma Knife treatment worked? Would the targeted cells stop or slow in their production of cystic brain fluid?

Evaluating the Risks and Mitigating Those Encountered. With every medical operation or procedure there are risks which with some probability may be encountered. An important issue to be remembered is to attempt to avoid the high-cost risks and be prepared to mitigate those that are encountered. The choice of medical procedures, instruments and medical systems, and even the medical staff that will carry out the medical operation or procedures are each important in minimizing the risks. Every patient must also recognize that each physician and patient has an individual view of the risk, and the patient has a right to be included in the evaluation.

An open-skull operation such as a craniotomy has risks of infection and the possibility of bleeding that can damage brain tissue. The medical instruments that are used to remove harmful brain cells can also remove good brain cells resulting in loss of function or even death. These kinds of risks are direct and any losses of function or to life are usually known within 24 to 48 hours after the operation. There are also indirect risks such as the length of recovery time. I viewed these kinds of risks as too high for the challenge that I faced.

The risks of surgery using radiation are less subtle and are not known for several months. Radiation damages and even destroys good brain cells on its path to the target area. Such damage is termed necrosis and edema. Necrosis is defined as the pathologic death of living plant or animal tissue. Edema is the abnormal accumulation of fluid or inflammation of the tissues. In order to mitigate the effects, the radiation levels must be high enough to damage the cells creating the abnormal activity, but not too high to cause necrosis or edema to the surrounding healthy cells. In addition, the radiation device must be extremely accurate in targeting the abnormal cells. I elected the Gamma Knife for its very high accuracy. I also elected these procedures for the rapid recovery time.

Nevertheless, about 8 months after the radiation treatment, I began to experience cramping in the left leg. An MRI/MRA revealed that I had experienced a mild case of necrosis and a more significant case of edema (or inflammation of the tissue surrounding the target site). The mitigation treatment was to take steroids to reduce the swelling of the surrounding brain tissue for about 3 months. After this period, the MRI/MRA revealed very little effects of either necrosis or edema and the risks had been mitigated.

Evaluating the Success of the Mission. As an engineer, I am expected to evaluate the success of each mission in which I participate. We evaluate such success against some acceptance criteria. *The mission as I saw it was to consent to only the least invasive procedures, that would still permit me to regain full function and retain the high quality of active life that I enjoyed for 58 years.* The stereotactic aspiration and the Gamma Knife treatment were minimally invasive and anyone who wasn't told what had happened could not easily determine that I had any operation or procedures at all. I had missed only 6 days of work spread over 2 months and my projects never got behind. I had missed fewer days than some employees who get the flu. I could have even reduced those days to three if I had chosen to be less cautious. Clearly, all symptoms had disappeared, allowing me to regain full function and I had already demonstrated that I was ready for increased activity. Could I now declare success?

The acceptance criteria for success of the Gamma Knife treatment and long-term full recovery depend on whether the cells slow in their production of cystic brain fluid. If they did not, the symptoms would slowly begin to reappear as the fluid built up and again caused pressure on the brain tissue. Ideally, the complete cessation of fluid production and the removal of the Ommaya Reservoir would be the best outcome. Having fluid aspirated once or twice a year would be very tolerable; doing it every few weeks would not be good.

By December, the cyst had virtually collapsed. I began monitoring the fluid aspirated at each visit to Dr. Chin and the days elapsed between aspirations. Each aspiration takes about 15 minutes. Applying the conservative assumption that the accumulation of 40 cc of cyst fluid would cause me to experience some symptoms, I could calculate how much time it would take until I was back in the same condition. The data from December 12, 1997 (the cyst was demonstrated to have collapsed as of December 5) to the most recent aspiration on October 1, 1999, is shown in Table 3.

Date	Fluid Aspirated (in cc)	Days Elapsed (in days)	Average Production Rate (in cc per day)	Days Until Symptoms Reappear (40 cc accum.)
12/12/97	5.0	7	0.71	56
12/23/97	4.5	11	0.41	98
01/05/98	4.2	13	0.32	124
01/23/98	3.0	18	0.17	240
02/20/98	3.4	28	0.12	329
03/20/98	3.2	28	0.11	350
05/15/98	2.2	56	0.04	1018
07/17/98	2.2	63	0.035	1145
09/11/98	1.2	56	0.021	1867
10/23/98	0.8	42	0.019	2100
12/18/98	1.2	56	0.021	1867
03/26/99	0.4	98	0.004	9800
10/01/99	2.6	189	0.014	2908

Table 3. Aspiration Procedures for Brain Cyst

Note that in that period, the average production rate has, with some minor fluctuations, continually dropped from 0.71 cc per day to 0.014 cc per day. This means that cell activity has steadily decreased, and the days until symptoms would again appear has been expanded from 56 days in December 1997 to 350 days (1 year) in March 1998 to a dramatic 2,908 days (almost 8 years) in October 1999 (refer to Figure 1). Although the ultimate outcome is yet to be determined, if the fluid production begins to level off at 0.01 cc per day, I will need to be aspirated less than once or twice a year. Even if the Gamma Knife radiosurgery does not achieve complete cessation of fluid production, the mission can now be declared a success.

LESSONS LEARNED AND THE FUTURE

My hope is that my life experiences in this matter can benefit others who are just beginning to encounter the fears and decisions that I have already encountered. What lessons have I learned from these experiences that are repeatable in the lives of others?

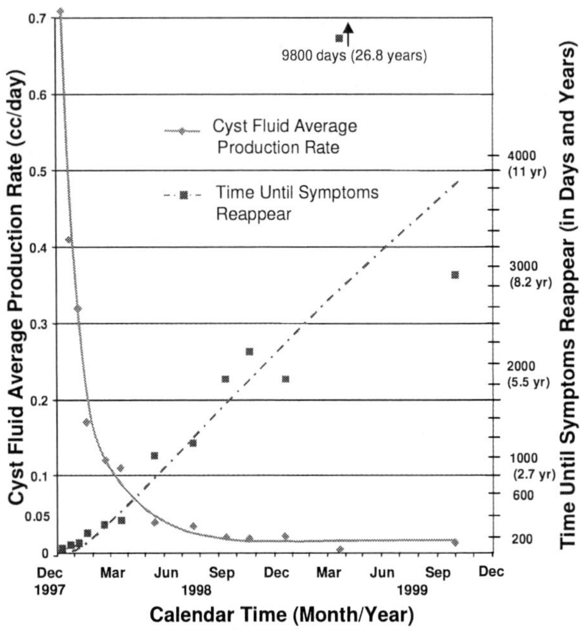

Figure 1. Evaluation of Radiation Therapy Success

1. **Develop a plan to understand and assist in the solution of your own problem.** Do that for at least two reasons. It will assist you in understanding the therapies that the physicians are recommending; and it will actually reduce the anxiety you experience because you will focus on the possible solutions and positive results rather than on the potential gloomy outlook that can prevail in these circumstances.
2. **Do your research.** Use all the library and computer resources at your disposal. Many solutions arise out of sheer need. Should anyone doubt their capacity to achieve such a solution, just rent the movie video "Lorenzo's Oil" which is a true story of a family in need and the measures they took to find the solution to their son's medical challenge. Set a reasonable time limit on the amount of research that you will perform before you will take action; but do take that time.
3. **NEVER yield to panic.** It is easy to say, but difficult to achieve. In my case, I had learned to comfortably live with my challenge for 38 years before it began to cause symptoms that had to be addressed. Not everyone will have had such a long history. However, if you panic, you will be tempted to cut short the necessary research and probably accept the first advice given.
4. **Don't assume that the first few consults represent the final answer.** My experience indicates that one needs to discuss the options with several skilled physicians before the correct solution will become apparent. Not all physicians have the same learning experience. For example,

only a few neurosurgeons have a Gamma Knife system available, while all have surgery experience. I was fortunate to meet three internationally recognized neurosurgeons early who also had a background with the Gamma Knife system. Also, three of the five neurosurgeons consulted, concluded that a craniotomy was the preferred answer. Had I agreed with the majority vote, I would have proceeded with a more invasive approach than I eventually elected.

5. **Evaluate your own risks.** The physician's view and a patient's view of the risks can be quite different. Without exception, each neurosurgeon with whom I consulted gave excellent professional opinions. I was prepared to make assumptions and assume risks that some neurosurgeons were not. I was willing to assume that the tumor was not malignant and also consisted of fluid that could be aspirated. I based my assumptions on a long history of living with the tumor and the imaging that showed a well-bounded cyst formation. I could have been wrong, but my assumptions proved to be correct. Had I been incorrect, I could have proceeded with the more invasive approach. I believe I risked only the time necessary to perform the less-invasive procedures.
6. **Try not to allow fear to consume a valuable and productive life.** Work toward a positive result and prepare for the worst outcome should you not achieve the most positive result. After all, each of us will ultimately lose to a life threatening illness or to an accident. That reality should not lessen the enjoyment or diminish the beauty of living a productive life. I believe that my life has reached a higher level of fulfillment because I have had these experiences. My original dream was to travel into space, to journey where few had gone before and return safely to Mother Earth. Instead, I recently underwent neurosurgery procedures that few persons ever attempt, have returned safely to excellent health, and now have the opportunity to encourage some of you on your prospects of returning safely from a similar journey.
7. **The discipline of systems engineering is extremely useful when appropriately applied to challenges such as those of healthcare.** The scientific method was of little assistance in addressing this medical concern. Although I did hypothesize that the brain tumor probably was benign, the scientific approach may have still led to the more conventional result of a full craniotomy. It was the mission constraint of selecting the least invasive method that required the neurosurgeons to suggest the two procedures: the stereotactic aspiration of the cyst followed by the stereotactic radioneurosurgery.

What will the future bring? The jury is still out on whether fluid production will drop to absolute zero; however, full recovery with careful monitoring is already assured. I owe my present good health and rapid recovery to the skills of Dr. Lawrence Chin of the UMD. He has become more than the physician who cured me; he has become my very good friend. The UMD medical staff has my deepest gratitude for making a potentially difficult life experience a relatively simple and painless one.

The present radiosurgery techniques will undoubtedly be improved in the coming years so that the procedures will be easier to perform. On the way to the operating room, I discussed with Dr. Chin the possibility of using satellite-positioning technology to build a case for a new stereotactic frame. We continue to discuss this possibility each time we meet. Some patients could have a significant reaction to the application of the frame, and might even request that the procedure should be stopped, not realizing that it represents the most difficult part of the procedure. I believe that a new frame could be developed that provides even more accurate positioning without the rigid attachment to the skull. As time permits, I am evaluating that possibility.

For those of you who are about to begin evaluation for a significant medical concern such as brain tumor for yourself, relative, or friend, I hope this article has been of benefit. Should you need to have additional advice from the point of view of a patient, please do not hesitate to contact the author.

REFERENCES

Haye, Andrew H. and Edward R. Laws, Jr., Brain Tumors: An Encyclopedic Approach. 1995

Mackey, W. F., "Engineer Chartered Own Course for Treatment of Cyst," *Another Perspective*, The Publication of the International Radiosurgery Support Association, Volume 3, No. 3, 1998

AUTHOR'S BIOGRAPHY

William Mackey, Ph.D., J.D., a Senior Consulting Engineer of CSC, is an attorney in both the District of Columbia and the State of Virginia Legal Bars. He is a professor teaching telecommunications and systems engineering at the University of Maryland University College. Dr. Mackey attended the U. S. Naval Academy and has B.S. and M.S. degrees in Physics from the University of Pittsburgh and the Rensselaer Polytechnic Institute. He received his Ph.D. in Systems Engineering from the University of Pennsylvania and his J.D. degree from the Washington College of Law, American University. He has a career in law, scientific research, systems engineering, and management applied to aerospace, telecommunications, transportation, and energy.

10046359-O97

Intelligent Agent Technology in the Health Care Environment

Desiree. J. Simons
University of Maryland University College
5018 Kenilworth Avenue
Edmonston, MD 20781

Abstract. Most people think of intelligent agent technology and the Internet as being connected because of the awareness brought to search engines by the public's use of the Internet. However, agent technology has always been in existence, as for example in the banking environment where an agent might be the alert agent for detecting when a stock price reaches a certain point. Unfortunately, many of today's Internet agents are not considered "intelligent" mainly because they are incapable of defining their area of search and as such, their applications are somewhat limited. Efforts to make agents work more efficiently have led to the emergence of a new technology called "filtering" which makes use of the speed of computers and the ability of networks to communicate. This paper examines the factors that are driving the development of filtering as well as the role of agent technology in the ever-changing landscape of computer systems development. Finally, the impact that this kind of technology will have on medical professionals and patients in our future health care environment is illustrated by a description of the Patient Advocate system being developed by Stanford University.

In the sixties, the book A Space Odyssey by Arthur C. Clarke was written about a computer named HAL (Heuristically Algorithmic Computer). HAL was given human-like intelligence by its creator, and in preparation for a long and difficult space mission, was subjected to rigorous training along with his human counterparts. The computer, however, had the advantage of being able to absorb more information at a faster rate than his colleagues did and never requiring any sleep. Its responsibilities included monitoring the spaceship's life-support systems, as well as checking the oxygen, pressure, temperature and all other factors that the humans relied on for survival. In time, HAL became so sophisticated that he usurped the control of the space ship from his human colleagues. (Murch, Johnson 8)

From the limited information given about HAL the computer, we can deduce that it was a robot with the ability to think, reason and perform repetitive and tedious duties. If we define an intelligent agent as software that performs delegated tasks without human intervention, then Hal was really an intelligent agent. Simply put, an intelligent agent is software that knows how to do things that we humans could probably do if we had the time.

It is said that fiction has a habit of becoming fact. This is reflected in our present-day society where software agents are not only replacing human agents in almost every area of the service industry but are also beginning to pattern themselves after the concepts and actions of HAL the robot. For example, in almost every gas station in the world, the automated gas pump systems have replaced attendants, who originally were responsible for pumping gas into a car's gas tank.

Characteristics and Functions of Intelligent Agents

Intelligent software agents, however, have special characteristics or attributes that distinguish them from other software packages and commercial programs and they are as follows:

Adaptability: An agent should simultaneously be able to function on multiple platforms, networks and software operating systems and resolve any technical problems by itself.

Mobility: An agent should possess the ability to freely roam networks and the Internet based on decisions made by itself.

Transparency and accountability: An agent can must be able to produce on demand, information pertaining to where it has been, what it has done, whom it contacted, and when.

Ruggedness: It should be able to deal with a variety of conditions and resolve each one as it crosses different types of networks.

Self-starters: An agent should be able to determine when to start/stop, when to deliver its results and what interface to deliver.

In essence, an intelligent software agent is similar to a human being in that it is reactive, flexible, autonomous, and adaptive, has character, is purposeful and can learn from experiences.

Unfortunately, many of the today's Internet agents are not considered "intelligent" mainly because they are incapable of defining their area of search, thereby extending their choices. Their primary functions consist largely of retrieving data from large databases and predicting future selections by examining the activity trails of past selections. The following example shows that while these agents are helpful their applications are somewhat limited. In 1997, an experimental agent called "Bargain Finder" was developed by Andersen Consulting, to allow users to shop for the best price of a CD on the Internet. In the same year, another agent called "Roboshopper" was created by RobboShopper, Inc., to offer a similar service but for many more items, such as cigars, computers, electronics, books, games etc. Shopping by these agents was however limited to internal lists of places such as Amazon, Barnes and Noble, and perhaps a few other sites, but new companies with the same offerings were ignored.

The computer has undergone many changes and functions from the 1970's to the present. In the beginning, it was mainly used by data processing departments to perform calculations that would have required whole departments of staff to accomplish. In the 1980's, with the advent of screens, the focus changed to data capture at the source or "information systems" (IS), resulting in timelier information. The improved quality of the screens in the 1990's- the age of the Graphic User interface (GUI)- coincided with lower computer production costs and this allowed each staff to have a powerful computer on his or her desk. These personal computers were then linked together to create networks, which are playing an important role in this "Information Technology" period or IT, by allowing database companies to correlate and access information in new and innovative ways.

There have also been changes in the area of general computer systems development and in fact, some experts are claiming that we have entered our First Generation of Agents. The development of computer languages can also be traced through four generations, beginning with machine code, which utilized hard coded commands directly on specific machines. The second and third generations were characterized by command functions, indirect retrieval of data from separate storage devices, data manipulation, call routines and the ability to run on a wide range of hardware from different manufacturers. The fourth generation can be identified by the use of language and tools which allow one to access information by issuing powerful language constructs which do not require a lot of detail coding, e.g., Structured Query Language (SQL). Thus the ever-changing landscape of computer systems development has been moving from environments to objects and as such, has provided a background for the development of agents.

Object orientation and Intelligent Agent Technology Development

Before we look at how Object Oriented principles can be used to produce agent systems let us briefly define objects and the elements of an object system:

Object: An object is a person, place or thing and is generally defined within a class.

Abstraction: Abstraction focuses on the important functions of the system.

Encapsulation: Encapsulation refers to the concealment of the source code from the users.

Modularity: Modularity allows objects to be made up of other objects.

Hierarchy: Hierarchy is the concept that objects in the same class or subclass bears the same characteristics. (Murch, Johnson 192)

The elements of an object model are identified and retrieved from the requirements specification, which contains information about objects, attributes, methods, inheritance, polymorphism and relationships between objects. In fact, agent technology is based on the concept of objects because agents are in fact "encapsulated packages of functionality and data"-the very definition of objects. Modern agent-development environments are also object oriented and the infrastructures that support distributed computing are designed with objects in mind, for example, CORBA. (Knapik, Johnson 52)

Objects can be used to represent any or all aspects of a system or an application, as for example, scheduling agents, human interface agents and search agents. There are many benefits to developing objects as components in the object oriented environment, primarily because the programmer does not have to begin from scratch. Over the past fifty years, computing has been based on the implementation of specific algorithms that process known ranges of data and produce predictive outputs. But the ever-increasing ability of machines and software to recognize patterns, reason under uncertainty, learn and plan has brought them closer to humans in terms of intellectual capabilities.

Achieving human characteristics, however, requires the development of agents that incorporate fuzzy systems, artificial neural networks, and evolutionary processes such as genetic algorithms. Fuzzy systems are an extension of Boolean logic, which handles degrees of truth, and this technology has been used in a wide range of application areas, such as production scheduling and loan analysis. This trait of agent development is generally used when the agent has to reason with incomplete or imprecise information. The structure of artificial neural networks are similar to neurons in one's brains in that they are composed of groups of interconnected processing elements. The objective of this second characteristic of network of neurons is to learn patterns, predict trends and improve performance over time. The final feature gives agents the ability to evolve their reasoning and behavior by using genetic algorithms and other evolutionary techniques and is particularly useful in a market place environment with a multitude of buyers and sellers. (Walkowiak 23)

Intelligent Agents in the Health Care Field

Only recently has the potential for significant contributions by intelligent agents in different domains and industries been realized, and the Health Industry is one of the categories to which intelligent agent technology could be applied. We can simplify the process of medical diagnosis and treatment of disease by classifying it into the following categories:

- Diagnosis- the analysis and identification of the problem.
- Treatment- set of corrective actions for the ailment diagnosed.
- Recuperation-recovery from the treatment and diagnosis.
- Follow-up- procedures carried out after treatment and recuperation to ensure a successful outcome.
- Administration-managing all the steps from diagnosis to follow-up, including payment for them.
- Education- learning about illness, new procedures, treatment, and so on.

There are however, limitations in current medicine and they include its tools and understanding, and a lack of integration. A description of the various elements making up the group of support services, each with its own needs, will highlight these deficiencies.

- Insurance companies and Medicare/BlueCross/BlueShield make payments to hospitals in addition to focusing on issues such as fraud detection and pattern recognition.
- Pharmacies have their own needs such as inventory management.
- Hospitals and clinics use computers for medical records, billing, testing and diagnosis.
- Doctors and specialists often have a simple PC for tasks such as scheduling, patient records and billing software package.
- Laboratories that carry out screening and testing have systems for reporting details, statistical analysis of trends and billing.
- Health centers regularly collect information that is not filtered back to health professionals.
- Government agencies such as child support track their own workload.
- World bodies such as World Health Authority are primarily interested in the number of diseases and the statistical signs of health in nations.

It is clear that health care is rich in information. However, it is also cost intensive and as such, poor or less-educated patients cannot afford the expense for adequate preventive care, early interventions and clinical observations. Some of the future challenges for medicine will include high-quality health care at low cost and complete care coverage from hospital to home. However, the systems that were introduced in recent years were built to support health care providers and not the consumers of health care, namely, the patients. How therefore, can agent technology be of assistance to the patient in the healthcare field? In the next section we will present a prototype of a system that is being developed to meet the challenge of focusing on the individual patients' demands and needs.

Patient Advocate

This system, developed by Stanford University, is called the Patient Advocate and uses multiple types of intelligent agents that communicate with each other and across the Internet, performing tasks for the doctors/patients. The purpose of the project is to create a system supported by cooperative technologies, for patients' management of their own health-related behavior on a day-to-day basis at home.

In this manner, patients will be assisted when complying with physician's advice and recommendations, and checking themselves for danger signs related to specific conditions.

The Patient Advocate is being designed to provide three kinds of functions. First, it will assist the patient in controlling ongoing conditions, for example chronic problems such as diabetes, special normal conditions such as prenatal care, and wellness issues such as diet, exercise, and stress. Second, it will provide health-related information by allowing the patient to interact with the on-line health-care information network and scan media resources to suggest information of interest. Third, it will coordinate patient-relevant information such as reminding the patient when a visit to the clinic is indicated. The following figure 1 summarizes the several resources administered by the Patient Advocate and Figure 2 shows the agent's system organization and its interactions.

Figure 1: Several resources administered by the Patient Advocate project

Figure 1.

Figure 2. The agent's system organization and its interactions

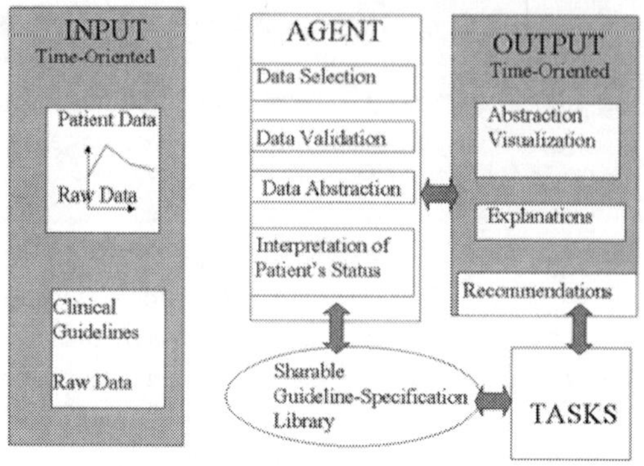

Figure 2.

The requirements for such a system include the provision of a user interface according to the patients' needs and abilities and a vocabulary tailored to the patients' level of education. In addition, the system should be able to perform various reasoning processes and have the ability to provide connections to resources and facilities even though it is used at home.

The first phase of the Patient Advocate project was implemented to investigate the scenario of gestational diabetes mellitus (GDM). The test requirements were high-risk pregnancy in an early stage, measurable parameters that could also be monitored and monitoring a pregnant woman at home as an alternative to staying in the hospital. In preparation for the implementation of the monitoring and consulting functionality of the system, information was gathered from consulting meetings between the medical professionals and patients and used in the creation of the knowledge database and graphical user interface.

A mock-up of the graphical user interface of the Patient Advocate's monitoring and consultation component is displayed as figure 3. Note that the first three windows reflect the observed data and a fourth window displays recommendations. The windows display the medical screening which is executed in conjunction with medication, nutrition management, observation of the mother's body weight gain, stress management, fetal evaluation and women's exercise. By grouping the parameters in separate windows, the patients are provided with multiple views of the observed data so as to get a clearer insight into their clinical conditions. The lower part illustrates the interactions with several resources (e.g. connection to nurse, appointment scheduling, medical libraries).

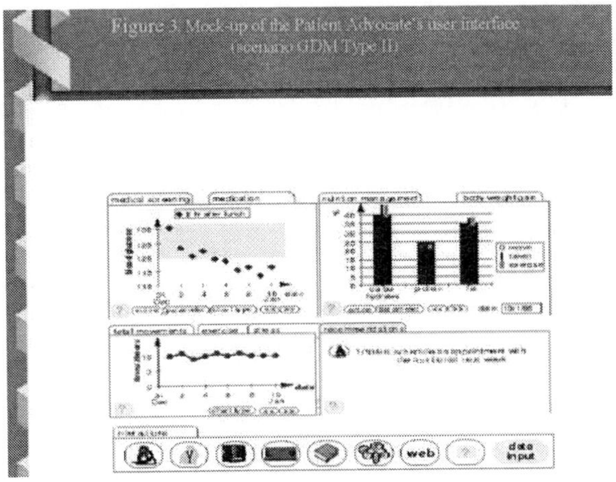

Figure 3.

Conclusion

This paper has taken the reader on a short journey across the ever-changing landscape of computer systems development, which has provided a background for the development of intelligent agents. A non-technical explanation of how these agents work and how they are being used to simplify the world was also presented. The many ways in which the health care environment could benefit from the application of agent technology were examined by analyzing the state of current medicine and the elements making up its support services. Potential solutions to the deficiencies inherent in the current health care systems are addressed by describing a prototype of the Patient Advocate project. In closing, we see that the application of intelligent agent technology holds much promise in the health care environment, particularly in the automation of monitoring, analysis and control of disease.

REFERENCES

1. S. Miksch, K. Chang, & B. Hayes-Roth. An Intelligent Assistant for Patient Health Care. Knowledge Systems Laboratory, 1996.
2. Miksch, S.; Cheng, K.; Hayes-Roth, B.: An Intelligent Assistant for Patient Health Care, in Johnson, L.W. (ed.), The First International Conference on Autonomous Agents (AA-97), ACM Press, New York, pp. 458-465, 1997.
3. Knapik, Michael, and Jay Johnson. Developing Intelligent Agents: for Distributed Systems. New York: McGraw-Hill Companies, Inc. 1998.
4. Murch, Richard, and Tony Johnson. Intelligent Software Agents. New Jersey: Prentice-Hall, Inc. 1999.
5. Walkowiak, Diane. "Your own personal Web Sleuths: Intelligent Agents Do The Work Of Ferreting Out Information You Want." Smart Computing July 1999: 22-25.
6. Strauch Joel. "This is the Web on Broadband; Faster Internet connections will change Media Use and More." Smart Computing September 1999: 90-92.
7. Watson, M. Programming intelligent Agents for the Internet. New York: McGraw-Hill Companies, Inc. 1996.
8. Halfhill, T.R. "Agents and Avatars" Byte, February 1996.
9. Miksch, S.; Horn, W.; Popow, C.; Paky, F.: Context-Sensitive Data Validation and Data Abstraction for Knowledge-Based Monitoring, in Cohn A.G. (ed.), Proceedings of the 11th European Conference on Artificial Intelligence (ECAI-94), Wiley, Chichester, UK pp. 48-52, 1994.
10. Miksch, S.; Horn, W.; Popow, C.; Paky, F.: Intensive Care Monitoring and Therapy Planning for Newborns, in Kohane, I.S. et al.(eds.), AAAI 1994 Spring Symposium: Artificial Intelligence in Medicine: Interpreting Clinical Data, AAAI Working Notes, Menlo Park, CA, 1994.
11. Chen, H., A Houston, J. Nunamaker, and J. yen. "Toward Intelligent Meeting Agents". IEEE Computer August 1996: 62-70.
12. Browning J. "Agents and Other Animals." Scientific American, February 28, 1996
13. Fodor, J. The Language of Thought. Thomas Y. Crowell. New York: 1975
14. King, J.A. "Intelligent Agents: Bringing Good Things to Life." AI Expert, February 1995: 17-19.
15. Wayner, P. "Agents Unleashed." AP Professional. Boston, MA: 1995.
16. Woelk, D., et al. "Uncovering the Next Generation of Active Objects." Object Mag. July-August 1995
17. Eliot, L. "Intelligent Agents are watching you." AI Expert August 1994: 9-11.
18. Maes, P. Intelligent Software." Scientific American, Vol. 273, No. 3, September 1995: 84-86
19. Y. Lashkari, M. Metral, & P. Maes. Collaborative Interface Agents, Proceedings of AAAI '94 Conference, Seattle, Washington, August 1994.
20. CiteWeb: "Research on architectures for intelligent agents at URL: http://www.cs.bham.ac.uk/~axs/cogaff.html".

BIOGRAPHY

Desiree J. Simons, has a B.A. degree in Mathematics from the University of Guyana and is employed as a systems analyst at Westat (An Employee-Owned Research Corporation). She is currently attending the UMUC in pursuit of a Master's in Software Engineering (MSWE)

Desiree Simons migrated to the U.S.A. in 1986 and has worked in various capacities –programmer/analyst, data manager, systems analyst- on tax-related financial and accounting, and health survey systems.

The Application of Systems Engineering to Telemedicine

Stephen J. Chorley
BAE SYSTEMS
Grange Road
Christchurch
Dorset
BH23 4JE

Abstract. A case study is presented of the application of the systems engineering process of BAE SYSTEMS to a telemedicine project for South Africa. It is an example of the successful transfer of technology from the defence to the civilian sector and shows how the company's systems engineering practices were effectively applied in this field. The conclusion reached is that a good systems engineering process should be adaptable and effective and that technology transfer is an ideal benchmark test for any such process.

INTRODUCTION

This paper takes the form of a case study describing the work undertaken in relation to a consultancy agreement with the South African government for a telemedicine project. Involvement in social programmes of this nature is part of the company philosophy of BAE SYSTEMS as a means of forging stronger links with customers and maximising the benefits of high technology. Our principal role in the programme is to provide project management and systems engineering expertise.

The programme of work is currently in its early stages. The paper describes our activities to date which have been an initial system design study and evaluation of a pilot programme. Our involvement from an early stage is crucial in being able to influence the programme and apply best systems engineering techniques.

TELEMEDICINE

What is Telemedicine? Literally, medicine practised at a distance. Telemedicine is not a new technique and has used whatever communications technology has been available at a particular time in history. Radio transmissions were used as early as the 1920's sending Morse code messages to ships. Video was used as early as the 1950's but it is not until comparatively recently with the advent of video conferencing and compression technology that telemedicine has become practicable on a large scale.

The core applications of telemedicine are diagnosis, treatment and education.

Diagnosis. This is by far the most common application of telemedicine. The doctor/patient situation lends itself to the benefits of video conferencing. There is a need to preserve as much of the "face to face" feel as possible.

Treatment. This is not really practicable with current technology. There have been limited experiments by the US military on pigs using remotely controlled surgical instruments.

Education. There are many examples from broadcast television networks to live video links between operating theatres in teaching hospitals and university lecture theatres. A common feature of these applications is high quality video transmitted over high bandwidth links.

BACKGROUND

This is one of a number of socio-economic programmes being instigated by the South African government.

The end of the apartheid era sees the South African government embarking upon a far reaching political agenda with a need to deliver quickly on some of the reforms it has promised. There is a need to redress the balance between the advantaged and disadvantaged sectors of society and, not surprisingly, healthcare features highly on the list of priorities. The major health related problems in the country are infant mortality and sexually transmitted diseases - especially AIDS. Telemedicine is seen as a means of bridging the divide between poor rural areas and more affluent suburbs.

Despite these numerous social problems the government also has a need to continue military spending. The government views industrial participation agreements of this kind as a solution to fulfilling both needs. BAE SYSTEMS has a long and successful history of being involved in education, development and training programmes providing support and consultancy to organisations world-wide. This programme fits well into this portfolio.

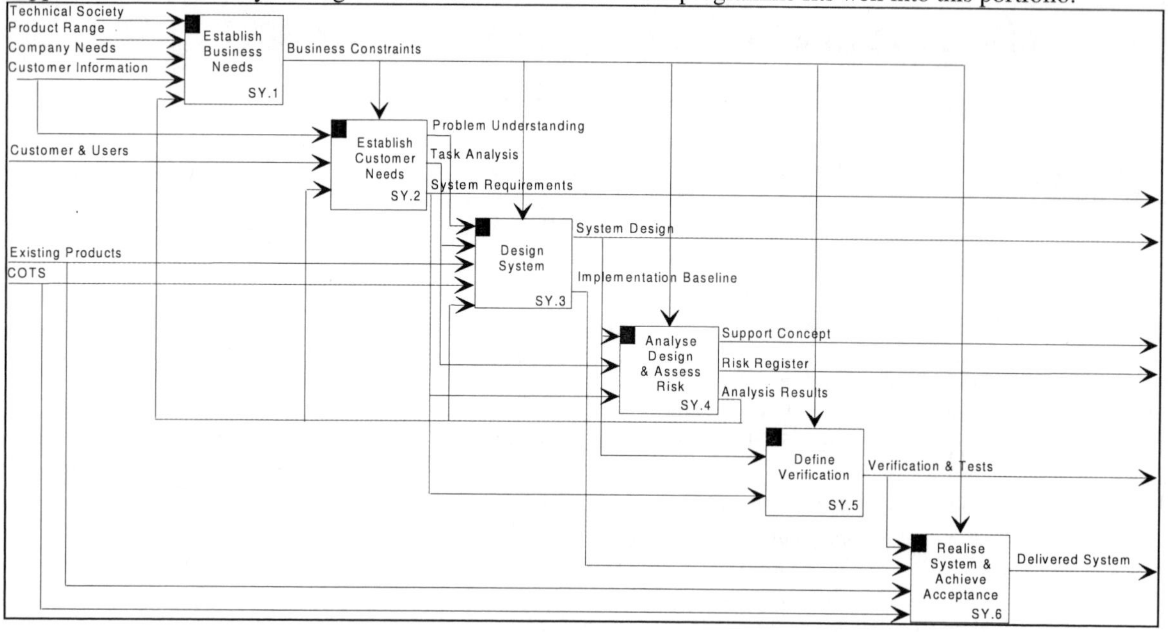

Figure 1. The Systems Engineering Process of BAE SYSTEMS

THE PROCESS

BAE SYSTEMS has developed over the years a systems engineering process to deal with the analysis, evaluation and solution of complex technical problems. This is illustrated in figure 1.

The key elements of the process are listed below:

Establish business needs
Establish customer needs
Design system
Analyse design and assess risk
Define verification
Realise system and achieve acceptance

The process has been developed through, sometimes painful, experience to address typical problems experienced by different groups such as:

The user. The performance is not what I expected.

The customer. The sub-systems don't work together. The delivered technology is already obsolescent.

Companies. System integration is where we lose money. Why do programme slips become visible near the end of the programme?

Equipment suppliers. Why are so many changes needed? The kit was working when we shipped it.

Note that each group has a different perspective of the programme. Not all businesses believe in objectively reconciling them, as does BAE SYSTEMS.

Many of the comments are related to surprise at the state they found themselves in at a particular time. "If we had known about this earlier we could have suggested X", is often the comment.

The other major cause for concern is sub-systems not working when put together.

The remainder of this section looks at the key elements of the process in more detail in relation to how they were applied on this programme and how the problems listed above were (or will be) avoided.

Establish Business Needs. The immediate business need in this case is the fulfilment of the company's aims for developing industrial participation agreements. Another aim is the growth of a generic capability for other contracts and pull- through back into the defence sector. Our main role is the provider of project management and systems engineering expertise.

BAE SYSTEMS operates a system of value-based management where the success of the company is judged against five core values. This programme is to be judged against two core values – partnerships in the community and people.

Establish Customer Needs. The government level customer needs were as follows:

1. The provision of clinical services to remote rural communities.
2. Medical research education and training of rural healthcare providers.
3. Improved efficiency and cost effectiveness in the delivery of rural healthcare services.
4. The delivery of education and other social services to rural communities.

Our initial in-country visit has established good reasons for suggesting that a telemedicine network could succeed and be effective in South Africa. One is that there is a shortage of healthcare professionals. Another is the distribution of facilities. There are centres of high quality healthcare located in major cities (tertiary centres in medical terminology) and disadvantaged rural communities (primary health care centres in medical terminology). The connection of the two is an obvious solution.

Sitting below these top level ministerial objectives was a detailed specification for a telemedicine terminal to be installed in a series of pilot networks. A general purpose PC was specified which can connect to a wide variety of specialist medical equipment. Our initial concerns were that this was bottom-up engineering with no obvious justification or connection between the low level and high level requirements.

This concern was further fuelled on our site visit when we found an ophthalmology department struggling to find a use for a terminal delivered with a selection of endoscopes.

Design System. Our first task was to produce a strawman system design architecture. We identified the key components which are shown in figure 2 and are listed below:

Medical equipment
Conference terminal
Communications networks
Network management system
Information system

Although a simplified figure it does show the number of diverse technical disciplines involved and indicates the need for a strong systems engineering process. Each component is described below.

Medical Equipment. This comprises the specialist equipment that produces the medical images and includes X ray scanners, ultrasound scanners, endoscopes, slit lamps for ophthalmology etc etc. Mandating standards for the connectivity of this equipment will be an important task.

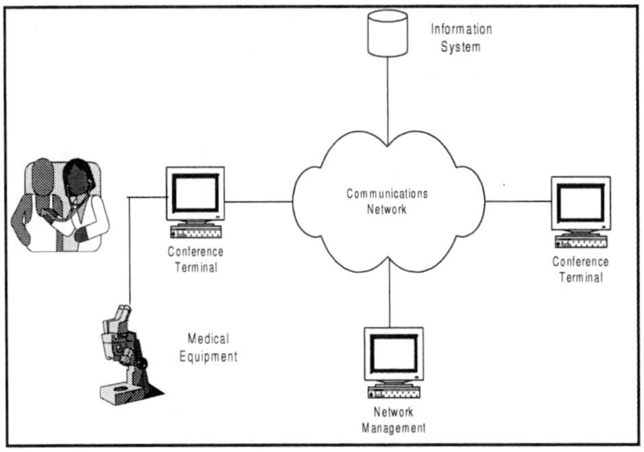

Figure 2. Simplified System Architecture

Conference Terminal. This contains the video conference equipment providing the core functionality of video compression technology for the transmission of real time video. It also includes all other HMI and user facilities.

Communication Networks. These provide the means for the transport of the communications. Again, standards are important and ISDN, ATM, IP, GSM, TETRA or satellite technologies are all possibilities.

Network Management. This is important for large networks and includes the provision of a helpdesk, call logging, billing, security features etc. Most telemedicine systems in use today are small scale on a point to point basis so do not require such features. Network management becomes much more important as the system grows and is key to future-proofing the design.

Information System. Whilst not strictly a core telemedicine feature it is an important innovative feature of our system. Medical information systems are used mainly for the recording, storage and retrieval of patients' medical records. One view that became clear early on in our work was that when a consultation is over there is no record unless notes have been taken. By combining a medical information system with traditional telemedicine a powerful additional benefit could be realised in that information would be recorded as a mater of course and would be available for later retrieval.

The information system becomes the glue which holds the whole system together. It provides the means for the effective use and sharing of information. There are strong similarities and synergies in this respect to military systems. Information superiority is key to military thinking and has a parallel here.

The information system also provides other opportunities for technology transfer. One is the use of distributed data base technology. This is essential in military systems for survivability but is not usually employed in medical systems. Its adoption in medical systems has the potential for greatly improving performance, reliability and access times for information.

The security of patient records could also benefit from technology transfer. There have recently been adverse comments made about the security of the UK NHS network.

The next step in the design process was to consider the key video conference technology and assess the capability of current technology.

We first conducted a market survey and found the market to be separated into high end, high performance (and high cost) systems provided by traditional video conference manufacturers and low end, low video performance (and low cost) systems provided by other specialist manufacturers.

The latter systems are termed "store and forward" systems which recognises their technical limitations. They do not attempt to transmit high quality full motion images. Instead they offer lower real time quality but maintain reasonable performance on still images.

There was a need to do a cost/performance analysis in order to assess the suitability of these cheaper systems bearing in mind the customer's pilot network specification and budget.

We did this in conjunction with our consultants at the Institute of Telemedicine in Belfast. For each medical application we considered the following key requirements:

1. Still image transmission of output of medical instrument
2. Moving image transmission of output of medical instrument
3. Real time interaction between medical professionals at either end of the link
4. Real time interaction between doctor and patient

Of these, only the fourth and sometimes the second place critical demands on motion quality.

By considering these four key requirements we determined which applications required true real time performance and therefore could not be successfully implemented with low cost equipment.

Application	Description	Req 1	Req 2	Req 3	Req 4	Comments
Radiology	Production of X-ray images. Traditionally hard copy but more commonly data files.					Classic store and forward application
Ophthalmology	Eye examinations. Main output is the video image from the slit lamp.					Still images more critical than real time images
Ultrasound	Foetal examination.					Motion critical
Pathology	Examination of tissue samples on microscope slides.					Real time aspects not essential
Dermatology	Examination of the skin. Main output is the video image from the dermascope.					Still images more critical than real time images
Endoscopes	Internal examinations with video cameras.					Still images more critical than real time images
Psychiatry	Doctor/Patient meeting application.					Classic video conference meeting application
A+E	Accident and emergency. Main uses are initial patient assessment and triage.					Good results obtainable with low cost links
Neurology	Examination of the patient's nervous system. Reflex testing critical to the process.					Motion critical
Vital Signs	Remote monitoring of heart monitoring, pulmonary monitoring equipment etc.					Outputs from monitoring equipment low bandwidth

Table 1: Summary of Performance Analysis

The findings of this review were, surprisingly, that only two disciplines required full motion high quality video. Table 1 summarises the findings.

However, we still had many reservations about using an exclusively PC-based approach. One was the ease of use and reliability of PCs. The considerations of the user featured very highly in our work because of the stressful nature of the working environment. Another was the video performance of the PC - both real time and for still images.

A bespoke solution combining a PC with separate integrated video conferencing equipment and other facilities for producing high quality still image files was recommended.

Analyse Design and Assess Risk. A preliminary risk analysis has been carried out covering technical and non-technical areas.

The main technical risks identified were as follows:

Communications Networks - Capabilities, Costs. The cost of bandwidth is falling all the time opening up new possibilities for telemedicine (an issue rather than a risk). The programme is reliant on progress in establishing ISDN communication networks.

Standards. Standards issues are important for any system whose primary purpose is communication. Applicable standards are in the medical, video conferencing and communications networks fields.

Confidentiality. Confidentiality of patient records is important as is the trusted reliable transmission of the records.

Video technology. This has been discussed above.

New technology eg. VR. In assessing the impact of the pace of technological change and potential equipment obsolescence, a technology forecasting exercise was carried out. On the positive side, new technologies especially VR and robotics could open up the way for new applications, especially for treatment.

In addition to the technical issues there are a wide range of other issues including:

Acceptance by the medical community. Equipment must be easy to use and effective. It should be as "transparent" as possible ie. interfere and change as little as possible the normal way of working.

Legal issues. What are the legal implications of a false diagnosis over telemedicine? Few insurance companies currently provide cover.

Assessment of benefits. In pilot schemes an accurate assessment of benefits is important.

Cost effectiveness. There is difficulty in quantifying all the benefits.

Define Verification. How do you judge, quantify and measure the effectiveness of the system? This has been recognised above as a major issue.

The direct evidence of the cost effectiveness of telemedicine is still scarce. This is due to most systems being small scale pilot systems. There are few large scale self-sustaining applications in existence.

Some benefits are easy to quantify such as reduced travel costs (patients and staff) and savings in hospital accommodation. Others are more difficult. How do you quantify a better quality of healthcare or an improvement in teaching and learning opportunities?

It is envisaged that the adoption of our company's values-based approach to measuring effectiveness would be beneficial. In this way the wider benefits over and above pure economics can be captured and evaluated.

The realisation of a planned and extensive programme of system trials with accurate and thorough data collection supported by detailed reports is essential. This will be developed further as the programme evolves and will have a high priority.

Realise System and Achieve Acceptance. This is another very important area.

There is still much work to be done here. In putting together our plans from our initial studies we consider the adoption of a phased gradual introduction of systems very important.

The importance of gaining the acceptance of the users and main players has already been discussed. The work done early on in assessing the capabilities and limitations of the equipment and its applicability to different applications will be invaluable in managing the expectations of the users and shaping the system trials. Without buy-in from the user community the undertaking is doomed to failure.

It may also be possible to target quick-win, low cost, high benefit applications early in the programme. One potential example is in the area of reducing infant mortality. Low cost video links installed in local maternity clinics could prove very effective.

A LOOK TO THE FUTURE - 2020 VISION

This programme has the potential to become the largest implementation of telemedicine in the world to date and if successful will have great implications both for our company and the telemedicine industry at large.

Shrinking military budgets and the need to justify military spending against social programmes mean that this way of working could become more commonplace in the future. Technology transfer in both directions both from the military sector to the commercial sector and vica versa can have many benefits and our systems engineering process has shown itself applicable to both sectors.

CONCLUSIONS

The application of the systems engineering process on this programme has demonstrated many benefits. In particular, the system engineering process:

Ensures a structured design approach. The customer's original documentation demonstrated a bottom-up equipment based approach which we have been able to develop and improve.

Encourages innovation. An early system-wide design review helps identify innovative solutions.

Reduces costs. By assessing COTS capabilities, maximising its use and advocating bespoke development only where necessary.

Ensures success. By determining realistic and achievable performance and success criteria for the equipment at an early stage. This is future-proofing the programme.

Ensures the connectivity of all equipment. By the selection of appropriate standards and mandating standards for connectivity.

Maintains the programme schedule. By early assessment and identification of risk.

Ensures success. By making all parties buy-in to the programme and by managing the customer's expectations.

Ensures success. The importance of the trials programme was realised early and it will incorporate the results of the equipment performance analysis to ensure its success.

Above all, our systems engineering process has proved itself adaptable and effective in this new sphere of activity for our company.

BIOGRAPHY

Stephen Chorley works in the Combat and Radar Systems division of BAE SYSTEMS Christchurch. A graduate of Southampton University, Stephen has twenty years experience working in systems engineering in the electronics industry both in the civil and military sectors. His civil experience includes broadcast engineering at the BBC and air traffic management. His military experience includes communication and C4I systems.

Predictive Performance Analysis and System/Software Architecture

Yves Lacerte
Architecture Technology Corporation
P. O. Box 24859
Minneapolis, MN 55424

Abstract. The development of long-lived real-time embedded software-intensive systems face unique challenges. It is critical that sound architectural principles be applied toward the development of such complex systems. An essential architectural element in a real-time system is performance.

Predictive evaluation techniques can be effectively applied as part of the architecture design process. These techniques enable the estimation of performance of a given implementation on a given hardware configuration without having to actually execute it. In addition, it allows the architect to evaluate individual application modules during development instead of waiting for the application to be completely developed before assessing its performance.

PROBLEM STATEMENT

Introduction. Software development of real-time distributed systems is a non-trivial process. A thorough understanding of the application and system architecture is required. Resource utilization and performance must be optimized in order to ensure adequate system growth and longevity without having to do major surgery to the architecture.

During the architecture design phases, it is important to have the ability to predict resource utilization given a hardware and software configuration. It is also important to have the ability to automatically determine an optimal allocation of software to hardware, especially when the set of design alternatives is large. Prediction models and tools are needed to assess expected system performance before any implementation takes place. Redesign at the later stages of development is costly.

Several types of models and tools exist, each with their advantages and disadvantages. Analytical techniques lead to large evaluation times. Simplifying analytical models make them less accurate. Monitoring techniques are not feasible when a new complex system is in the development stages. Even when there are developed components, evaluating alternatives is often impractical.

Context. The following abstracted system is representative of the class of problem that requires predictive performance analysis when the system and software architectures are elaborated.

The electronics system may consist of a large number of sensors, devices, motors and computers, driven by sophisticated command and control software to support the users as they perform a defined mission. Software size may be in excess of one million lines of code. It is likely that several computers, and several VME card cages will be needed. A local area network (LAN) will be needed to interconnect each computer. In addition to main processing computers, each VME card cage is likely to hold additional cards performing a variety of functions such as Digital Signal Processing (DSP), Analog/Digital converters, graphics processing, I/O functions, network interface, etc.

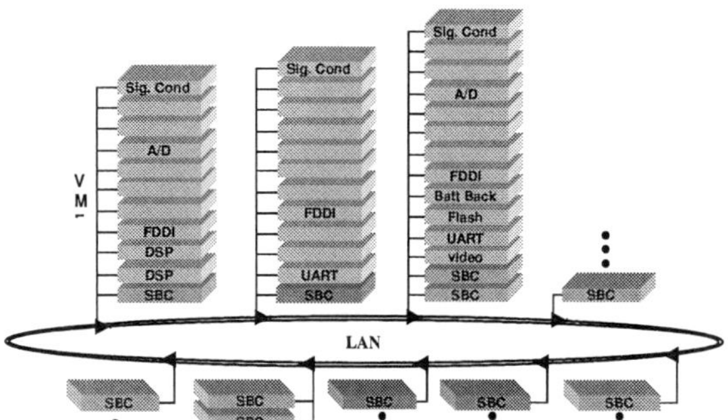

Figure 1. A Notional Electronics Architecture

A fundamental challenge during the software architecture design phase is to map software functionality to a given set of computing nodes such that performance requirements are met. In addition, there may be several competing system architectures (each system architecture being composed of a set of computing nodes).

Given the scope of the above problem, assessing the design in terms of performance is complex. Assessing each design alternative is non-trivial given the large number of design alternatives.

SOFTWARE ARCHITECTURE

Introduction. Sound architectural principles must be applied toward the development of complex real-time distributed systems. A visual modeling language such as UM to bring together the design vision of all of the key stakeholders becomes essential for building complex systems. It is the visual modeling language of choice for building object-oriented and component-based systems. The software architecture method applied to capture the general principles used throughout the design is described in Kruchten. The real-time application design is drawn from Douglas.

The 4 + 1 model describes software architecture using five concurrent views. The following four of the five views are relevant to performance analysis.

Use Case View. The Use Case View is the architectural view used to investigate the dynamic behavior of the system. Interaction diagrams and collaboration diagrams are used to visualize dynamic behaviors. An example of an interaction diagram is shown in Figure 2.

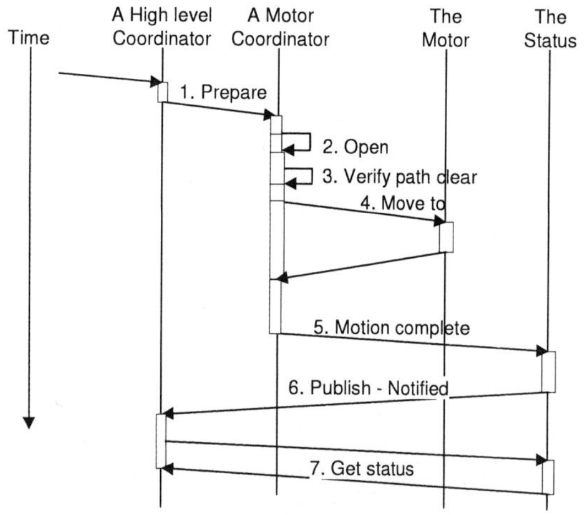

Figure 2. A Notional Use Case View

Logical View. The Logical View describes the design's object model. Definition of the Logical View is part of functional analysis. The Logical View is defined by decomposing the system into a set of key abstractions, taken mainly from the problem domain. An example is shown in Figure 3.

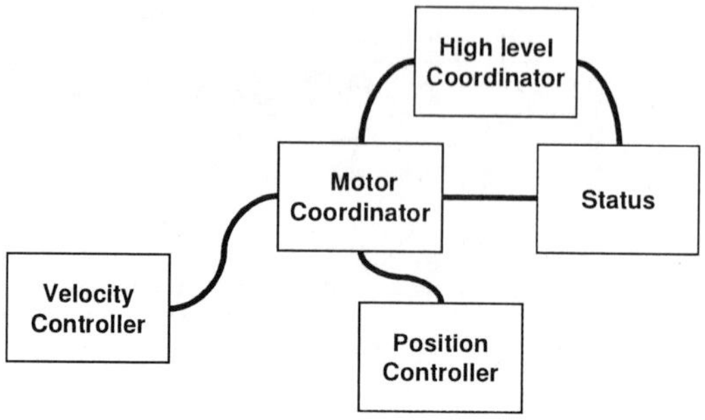

Figure 3. A Notional Logical View

Component View. The Component View describes the design's concurrency and synchronization aspects. An example is shown in Figure 4.

The Component View addresses concurrency and distribution. It specifies which thread of control executes each operation of each class identified in the logical view.

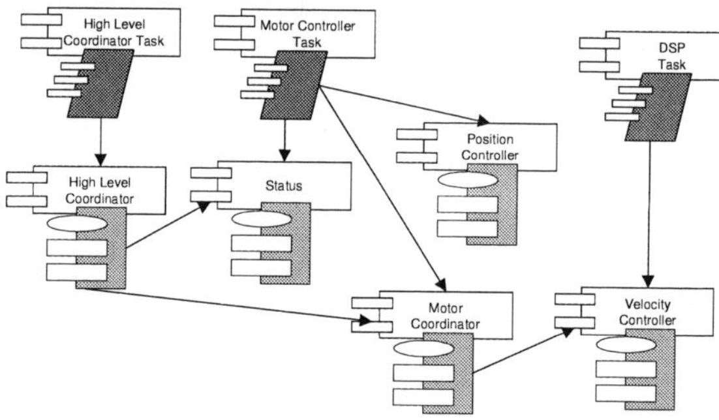

Figure 4. A Notional Component View

Deployment View. The Deployment View describes the mapping of software to computing nodes and reflects its distributed aspect. An example is shown in Figure 5.

The Deployment View takes into account performance, throughput, and scalability. The mapping of the software to the nodes needs to be flexible since several different physical configurations may be used.

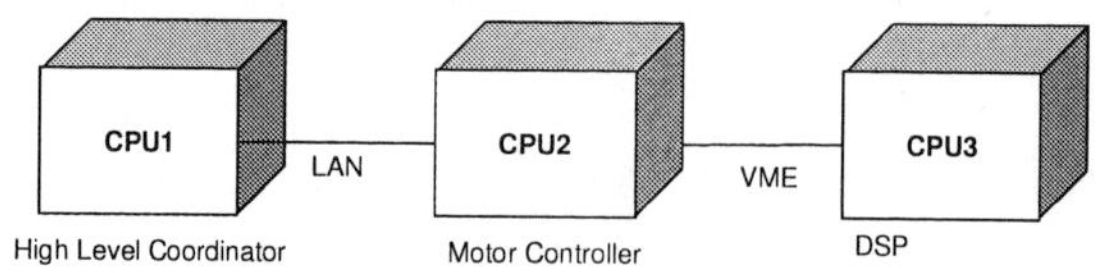

Figure 5. A Notional Deployment View

ANALYSIS APPROACH

Introduction. The analysis approach is depicted in Figure 6. Each step is detailed in the following paragraphs.

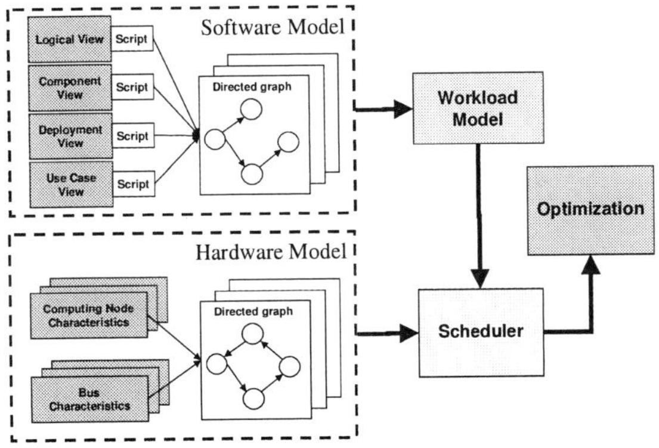

Figure 6. Predictive Performance Analysis

Software Model. Relevant interaction diagrams are extracted from the software architecture model and are transformed into a set of acyclic directed graphs, one for each major software component being modeled. Simple scripts can be used to extract data from tools such as Rational ROSE.

Each node on a graph represents a thread of control. Each arc may represent an event, the invocation of an operation on the destination process, or the flow of data.

Associated with each node is the expected number of executed source lines of code (accounting for iterations) for that operation. This parameter is used to estimate CPU requirements. Associated with each arc is the expected size of the data flowing on the arc. This parameter is used to estimate communications requirements.

Since interaction diagrams are based on cooperating objects, every object is assumed to have its own thread of control. Some rough estimates can be derived directly from cooperating objects. This may not a practical implementation due to the associated computing overhead.

As a refinement to the software model, multi-tasking can be introduced; i.e. each activity has a "virtual" processor, called process. A process has its own address space that is logically distinct from the address space of other virtual processors. When concurrency and synchronization aspects of the design are available (i.e. component view), cooperating objects can be easily rolled up into cooperating processes.

Upon completion of a pass at identifying processes, the allocation of processes to computing nodes can proceed. The allocation to a few computing nodes based on performance considerations can be simple. Extending the analysis to tens of processors and hundreds of processes quickly becomes a difficult problem.

Hardware Model. The hardware model is a directed graph. Each node on the graph represents a bus or a computing node. Each arc is unidirectional and represents a connection between nodes on the graph. Connections are CPU – CPU, bus – bus, CPU – bus, and bus – CPU.

Each node on the graph consists of a description of the associated computing node or bus.

Minimal computing node attributes are DRAM size, CPU clock speed and the number of instructions per CPU cycle. Assumptions can be made regarding cache hit rates, and cache miss latencies.

Minimal bus attributes are inherent latencies, and bus throughput. Specific delays can be introduced when more details about the buses and the LAN are known.

An example of the hardware model is shown in Figure 1.

Workload Model. The workload model, derived from system performance requirements, represents end-to-end system behaviors. Performance requirements should dictate the maximum allowable execution time of these behaviors.

The workload model consists of a well-defined sequence of events that stimulate the appropriate processes defined in the software model, and at the appropriate time(s). The source of the stimulus (process, processor, and time) is specified.

The workload model allows system evaluation under various conditions such as loads and resource contentions. The workload model allows varying degrees of abstractions so that alternatives can be quickly assessed, i.e. end-to-end system behaviors can be fined grained (low abstraction) or coarse-grained (high abstraction). Finally, the workload allows scalable system evaluation, i.e. performance analysis between pairs of processors, with a subset of the application, to the complete system.

Workload Scheduler. The Workload scheduler merges the workload model and the hardware model and simulates activities resulting from the workload. Activities include CPU and Bus loading. Scheduling, with peak loading and latency are output.

During simulation when tasks are assigned to CPUs, the message traffic loading and timing is computed by determining all the busses traversed by each message being sent between tasks. Bus scheduling conflicts are resolved so that one message at a time is sent over each bus.

Optimization. An optimization algorithm can be used to provide an optimum mapping of software processes onto processing nodes. The analysis of what constitutes a "good" candidate architecture is determined by the architect by applying weighted priorities to each design characteristic.

The attributes to minimize may be a weighted combination of the following:

- CPU load balancing minimizes the maximum CPU loading or the standard deviation of the CPU loads.
- Busload balancing is similar to CPU load balancing. By itself, this is not useful since minimum bus loading occurs when all tasks are in one CPU.
- Latency involves setting latency time constraints from start-to-end of the software model, and then running simulations until all latency constraints have been met. CPU preemptive scheduling and bus scheduling can be performed. End-to-end delays including all scheduling conflicts are calculated.

CONCLUSION

Effective integration of capabilities of modeling, analyzing, and predicting the performance of computing systems into the hardware and software design process can help in the early discovery of a workable system and software architectures.

The use of UML in an automated environment such as Rational ROSE, coupled with a scalable and flexible performance framework such as the one described herein, provides an integrated suite of capabilities that can lead to building long-lived systems with performance as a key architectural parameter.

REFERENCES

Douglas, Bruce, *Doing Hard Time*, Addison-Wesley, Reading, Mass., 1999.

Krutchen, Philippe, "Architectural Blueprints–The '4+1' View Model of Software Architecture," IEEE Software, November, 1995.

Unified Modeling Language Specification. Object Management Group, Framingham, Mass., 1998.

BIOGRAPHY

Yves Lacerte is a consulting systems engineer. He is a member of the International Council of Systems Engineering (INCOSE). He holds a BS and MA in Applied Mathematics from California State University.

Modular Vehicle Architectures: A Systems Approach

Gary J. Rushton
Visteon Automotive Systems
Visteon Technical Center – Allen Park
16630 Southfield Road
Allen Park, MI 48101 USA

Armen Zakarian
The University of Michigan - Dearborn
2320 Engineering Complex
Dearborn, MI 48128 USA

ABSTRACT

Modular systems provide the ability to achieve product variety through the combination and standardization of components. In this paper, a methodology that combines the Hatley/Pirbhai system model, integration analysis, and optimization techniques for development of modular electrical/ electronic vehicle systems is presented. The approach optimizes integration and interactions of the electrical/ electronic system elements and creates functional and physical modules for the vehicle. The paper illustrates importance of system modeling in developement of modular products. Discussion on how to make the system modeling more attractive to the industry is also presented.

INTRODUCTION

Modular systems provide the ability to achieve product variety through the combination and standardization of components. Potential benefits of modularity include (Ulrich 1991):

- Ecomomies of scale
- Increased ease of product/component change
- Increased product variety
- Reduced time to market
- Easier product diagnostics, maintenacnce, and repair.

To develop modular systems, well defined techniques and methodologies are required to assist the product development process. A classical product development process includes six phases shown in Figure 1.

This research focuses on the design phase of the product development process. Several studies have shown that product cost, quality, and time to market are most affected in the product design phase. For example, a study conducted at Ford Motor Company shows that only 5% of the manufacturing costs of a car are for design activities. However, the decisions made during the design phase affect 70% of the manufacturing costs. In a similar study, Xerox attributed 50% of the final product cost to the results of the design phase. Furthermore, 75% of the manufacturing costs are committed by the end of the preliminary design phase (Ullman 1992). These studies give a good indication of the impact of the design on the product cost.

This paper focuses on the modeling, analysis, and design of systems and illustrates the importance of system modeling in development of modular vehicle systems. The approach presented in this paper creates modular systems and optimizes integration and interactions of the system elements. The application of the approach is illustrated with an industrial example from the automotive industry, i.e., design of an instrument panel (cockpit). The Hatley/Pirbhai methodology is used for modeling functional requirements of the cockpit system of a vehicle. The Hatley/Pirbhai requirements model defines the interfaces (interactions) to support the functions of a cockpit system. Once the interfaces among the functions are identified, integration (cluster) analysis techniques are used to group the functions in the cockpit of a vehicle, and create electronic modules. The integration analysis approach uses analytical techniques to optimize interactions between system functions and group them in such a way that inter-cluster interactions are minimized (Pimmler 1994). A Hatley/Pirbhai architecture model is developed to represent the system design. The completed Hatley/Pirbhai system model, i.e., requirements and architecture, represents the functional requirements and the physical structure of the entire system. The overall system design process is shown in Figure 2.

SYSTEM DESIGN

In this section, different phases of the system design processes shown in Figure 2 are discussed.

Requirements Analysis. In this phase, the functional decomposition and a detailed system requirements model for the cockpit is developed. The Hatley/Pirbhai methodology is used for modeling the cockpit system. First, a top level system context diagram is constructed (see Figure 3). Once the cockpit system boundaries and external entities are established, the interactions between the cockpit system and the external entities are identified. The external entities in the context diagram are represented as terminators (rectangles).

The electrical/electronic functions of a cockpit system may be decomposed into six main functions (processes) shown in Figure 4:

1. Protect Occupants and Cargo
2. Provide Vehicle Motion
3. Provide Information, Communication, and Entertainment
4. Provide Visibility
5. Provide Interior Comfort
6. Control Power Distribution

All possible features of the cockpit system can be logically grouped into one of the six main processes presented above. Figure 4 is the child diagram of the context process shown in Figure 3 and presents the interactions among the six functions of the cockpit system. Each process in Figure 4 is further decomposed to the lowest level processes, i.e., primitives (PSPECs).

The functional decomposition and system modeling allows one to identify the functional elements of the system and their relationships. The system model represents the flow, processing, and transformation of data, energy, and material within the system. Once the Hatley/Pirbhai requirements model is constructed and the relationships between the functional elements (primitives) are identified, a function-function incidence (interaction) matrix for the cockpit system is developed (discussed next).

Integration Analysis. The Hatley/Pirbhai requirements model developed in the requirements analysis phase, identifies all the functional elements of the cockpit system and defines the interactions (interfaces) between the elements to support the functions of a cockpit system. Once the interactions among the functions are identified, a function-function interaction matrix of the interfaces is developed. A function-function interaction matrix $[a_{ij}]$ includes "1", "blank" entries (see Figure 5), where an entry "1" indicates the information, material or energy link (signal flow) between functions i and j, and the direction of the link (flow) is from $j \rightarrow i$.

A function-function interaction matrix in Figure 5 can be restructured using integration (cluster) analysis techniques to obtain the clusters in the binary interaction matrix and create functional modules (see Figure 6). Cluster analysis is concerned with the grouping of objects into homogeneous clusters (groups) based on the objects features. The application of cluster analysis techniques to the product design problem leads to the grouping of product functions and components (Kusiak 1998). In this research, the Extended Cluster Identification (ECI) algorithm is used to group the cockpit functions into modules (Kusiak 1987). Improvement steps for the ECI algorithm is developed to maximize functional integration and minimize the interaction between the system functional modules. The application of the ECI algorithm and the improvement steps is explained next.

The ECI algorithm is an extension of the cluster identification algorithm (Iri 1968). The cluster identification algorithm identifies mutually separable clusters in the function-function interaction matrix. The ECI algorithm first checks for the existence of mutually separable clusters in the interaction matrix and if such a solution does not exist, heuristically solves the problem by randomly removing the bottleneck functions/interactions from the interaction matrix. A function (interaction) is considered a bottleneck, when it does not allow the decomposition of the function-function interaction matrix into mutually separable clusters.

In the modularity matrix $[a_{ij}]$, two types of bottleneck functions are possible: upper diagonal and lower diagonal (see Figure 7). Each bottleneck function, i.e., entry $x_{ij} = 1$ in matrix $[a_{ij}]$ not belonging to any cluster (module) in the matrix $[a_{ij}]$, interacts with only two clusters (modules), i.e., m(1) and m(2) in matrix $[a_{ij}]$. The improvement steps developed in this research moves the bottleneck function (interaction) $x_{ij} = 1$ to module m(1) or m(2) if such an assignment improves the functional modularity of the system, i.e., maximizes interactions within the modules and minimizes interactions between the modules.

The two steps performed in the integration analysis phase are as follows:

1. Construct function - function interaction matrix

The Hatley/Pirbhai requirements model identifies the relationships between the functional elements, primitives. In essence, the model can be thought of as a huge network of primitive processes linked together by their flows (Hatley 1987). Once the system functions and their relationships are obtained, a function – function interaction matrix for the system is constructed.

2. Construct modularity matrix

Apply the ECI algorithm and the improvement steps to obtain the modularity matrix.

Design Analysis. In this phase, the system design is completed. The Hatley/Pirbhai architecture model is developed to allocate the functional requirements and interactions from the Hatley/Pirbhai requirements model to the modules identified in the modularity matrix of cockpit system.

The application of the ECI algorithm and the improvement steps resulted in seven functional modules for the cockpit system (see Figures 8 and 9). The seven modules are shown in the cockpit architecture flow diagram (AFD) in Figure 8 and as follows:

1. Locking module
2. Climate Control module
3. Lighting module
4. Driver Information module
5. Entertainment module
6. Power pedal module
7. Ignition module

Each of the data flow lines shown in Figure 8 represent an interaction between functions contained within a module from the cockpit modularity matrix. For example, the entertainment module has an interaction with the locking module known as "RADIO PRESENT" and is represented as a data flow line in Figure 8.

Figure 9 shows the cockpit architecture interconnect diagram (AID). The AID represents the communication channels that exist between the cockpit architecture modules shown in Figure 8. The AID in Figure 9 has the same architecture modules as the AFD and shows the physical means by which the cockpit modules communicate (channels).

DISCUSSION

Today's systems are too complex to depend on the ability of a few overworked engineers to keep the various subsystems consistent. Systems have reached a point at which the interactions between the systems/subsystems are at least as complex as the subsystems themselves (Hatley 1987). Therefore, system models should be used to represent information that is gathered about the system in the requirements and design analysis phases.

The TurboCase/SYS software tool from Structsoft, Inc. was used for the development of the Hatley/Pirbhai requirements and architecture models. The TurboCase/SYS tool facilitates the allocation of functional elements in the requirements model to physical entities in the architecture model. System modeling tools can become even more attractive to the industry by integrating integration analysis techniques (i.e., ECI algorithm and improvement steps). The latter should allow the user, i.e., product developement engineers, to automatically determine the optimal number of modules and allocation of functions into each module.

CONCLUSION

This research developed a methodology that combined the system modeling, integration analysis, and optimization techniques for development of modular electrical/electronic systems. The approach optimized integration and interactions of the system elements and created functional and physical modules for the cockpit system.

The approaches presented in literature concentrate in partitioning simple products into physical modules without considering functional requirements of the system. This research demonstrated the importance of functional decomposition and system modeling of a complex system. The component analysis is very valuable at the detailed design phase. However, focusing on the functional analysis of the system allows one to develop several different system architecture and partitioning alternatives.

REFERENCES

Hatley, D. J. and Pirbhai, I. A. (1987), "*Strategies for Real-Time Specification*", Dorset House, New York.

Iri, M. (1968), "On the Synthesis of the Loop Cut Set Matrices and the Related Problem", *RAAG Memoirs*, Vol. 4, pp. 376-410.

Kusiak, A. and Chow, W. S. (1987), "Efficient Solving of the Group Technology Problem", *Journal of Manufacturing Systems*, Vol. 6, No. 2, pp. 117-124.

Kusiak, A. (1998), "Group Technology", *University of Iowa*, Working Paper Version 8-25.

Pimmler, T. U. and Eppinger, S. D. (1994), "Integration Analysis of Product Decomposition", *Design Theory and Methodology – DTM*, DE-Vol 68, ASME.

Ullman, D. G., (1992), "*The Mechanical Design Process*", McGraw-Hill, New York, NY.

Ulrich, K. and Tung, K. (1991), "Fundamentals of Product Modularity", DE-Vol. 39, *Issues in Design Manufacture/Integration*, ASME.

BIOGRAPHY

Gary Rushton has over 15 years of commercial and military electrical/electronic systems engineering experience. He has an MS in Automotive Systems Engineering from the University of Michigan. He is currently working as a systems engineering technical speicalist with Visteon Automotive Systems, an enterprise of Ford Motor Company. At Visteon he has worked on audio software, subsystem product development/design, diagnostics, vehicle system architectures and design, and cockpit systems design. Previously, with General Dynamics, he worked on avionics systems for the F-16 and vehicle electronics systems for the Abrams M1A2 tank. (grushton@visteon.com).

Armen Zakarian received his B.S. degree in mechanical engineering from Yerevan Polytechnic University, Yerevan, Armenia, his M.S. degree in industrial and systems engineering from the University of Southern California, Los Angeles, California and his Ph.D. degree in industrial engineering from The University of Iowa, Iowa City, Iowa, in 1997. He is an Assistant Professor of Industrial and Manufacturing Systems Engineering at the University of Michigan - Dearborn. He taught at both undergraduate and graduate levels at The University of Iowa and has held a visiting faculty position at the American University of Armenia. He has published papers in jounals sponsored by IEEE and IIE societies. His research interests include development of products and systems, reliability and risk analysis of process models, and modeling and analysis of manufacturing systems. (zakarian@umich.edu).

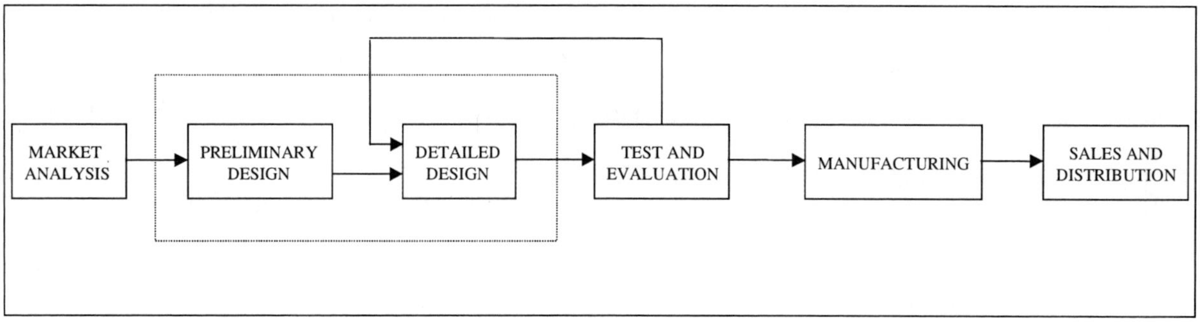

Figure 1: Phases of Product Development Process

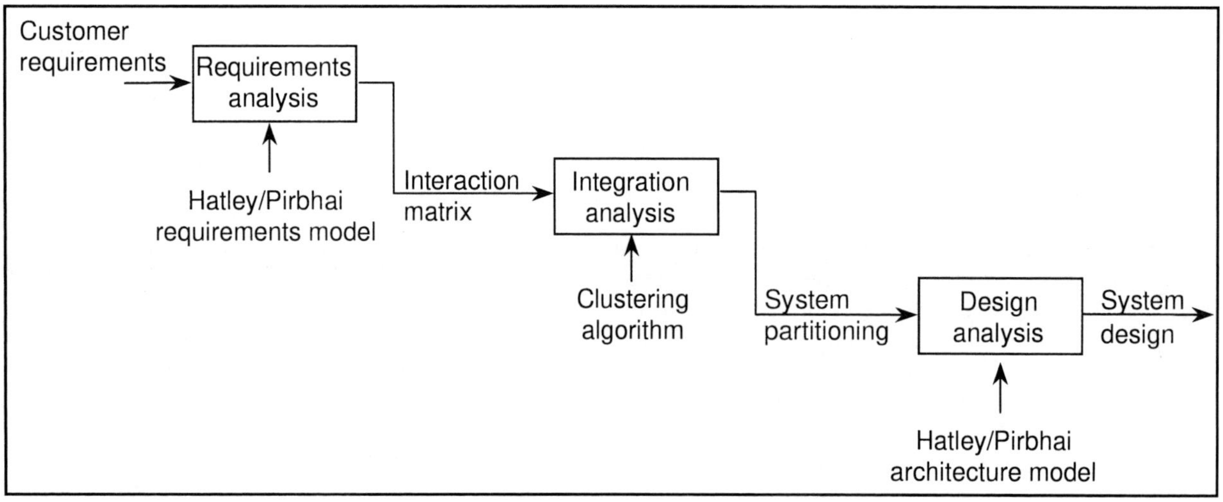

Figure 2: System Design Process

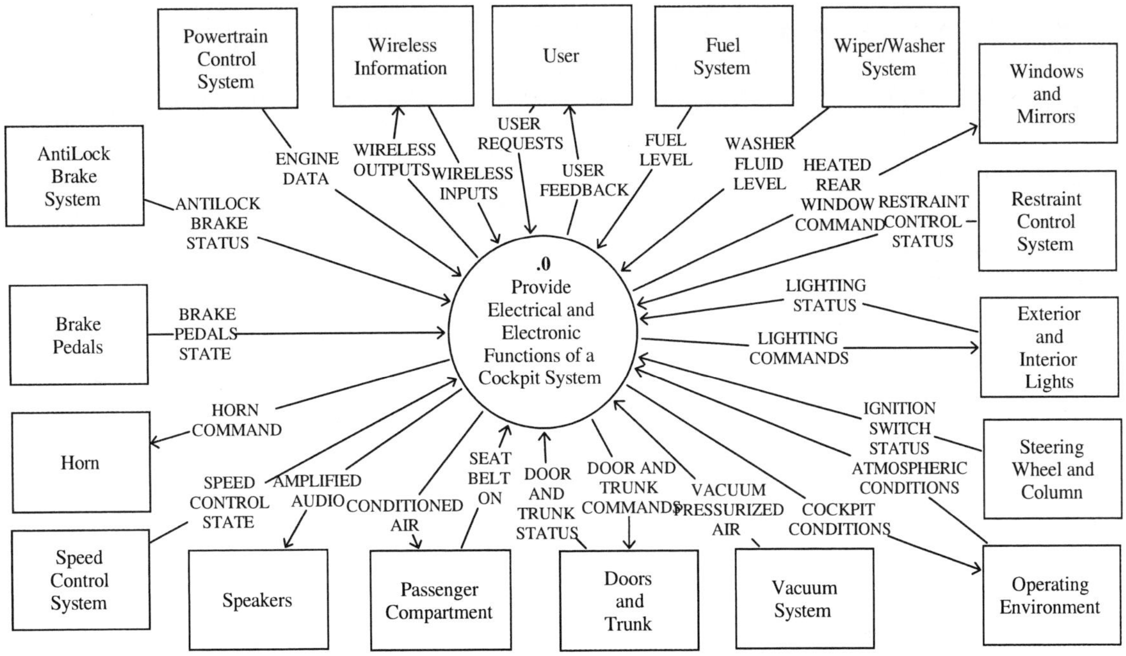

Figure 3: Cockpit System Context Diagram

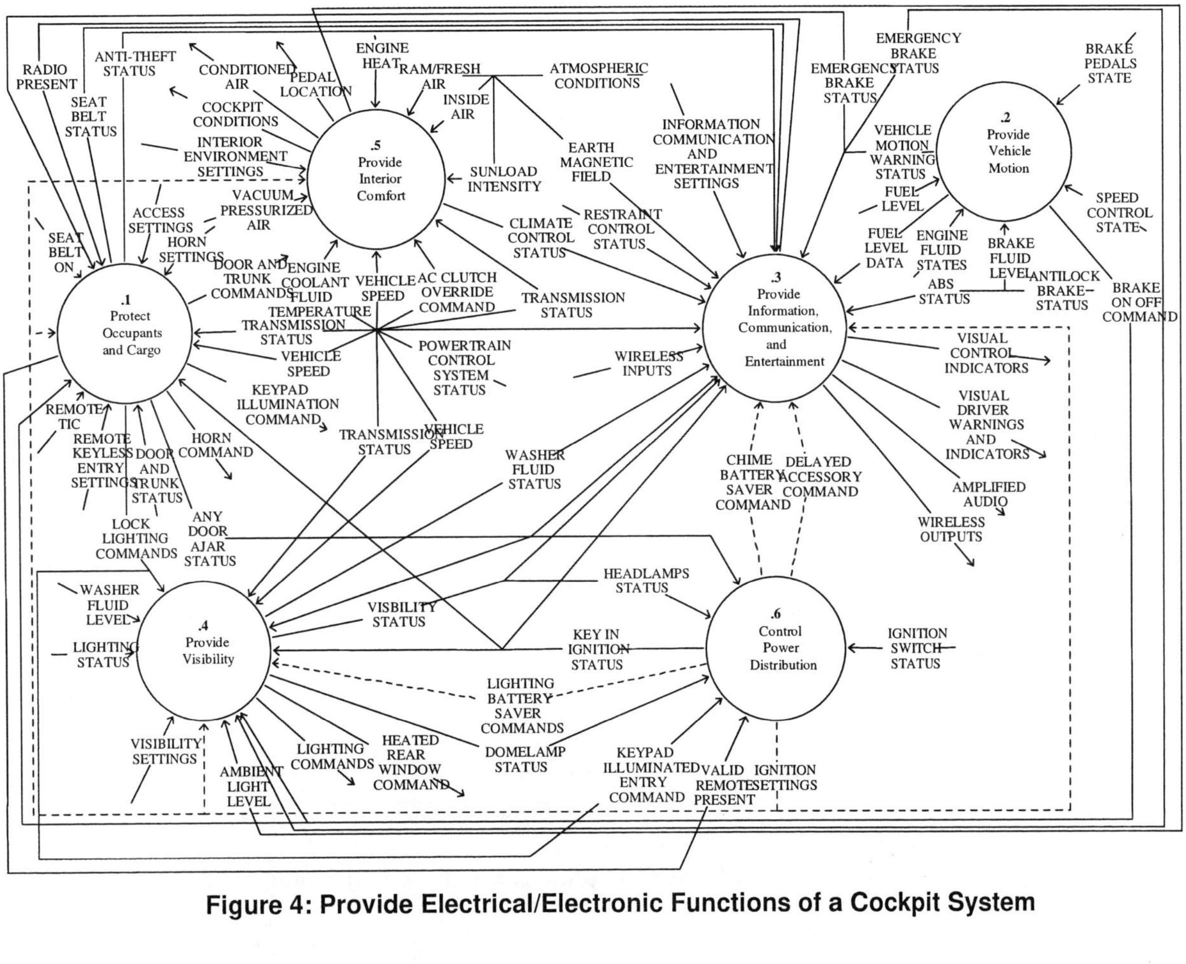

Figure 4: Provide Electrical/Electronic Functions of a Cockpit System

Function

Function	1	2	3	4	5	6	7	8	9	10	11	12	13	14
1	1													
2	1	1							1		1			
3			1											
4				1										1
5			1		1									
6						1								1
7							1							
8			1			1		1						
9				1	1			1	1	1				
10			1							1				1
11							1				1			
12												1		
13													1	
14						1								1

Figure 5: Function- Function Interaction Matrix

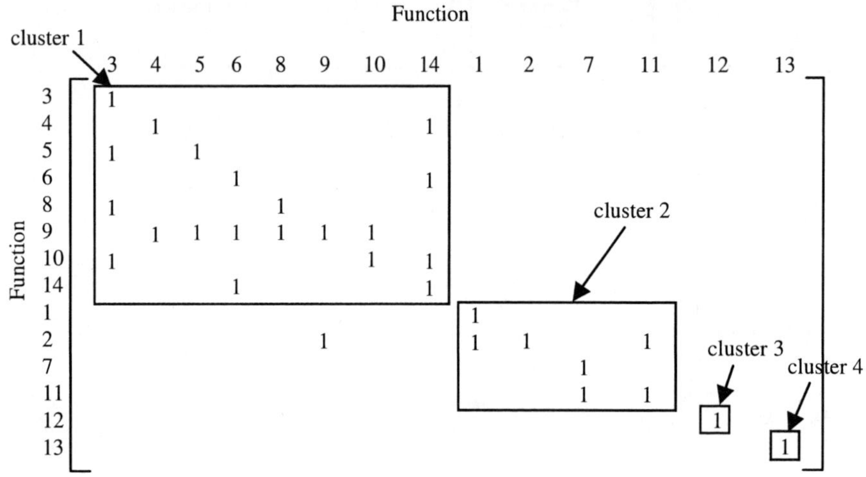

Figure 6: Modularity Matrix

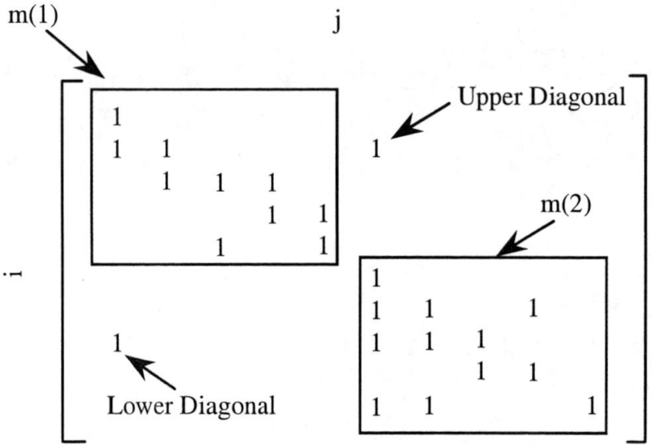

Figure 7: Upper/Lower Diagonal Bottleneck Functions

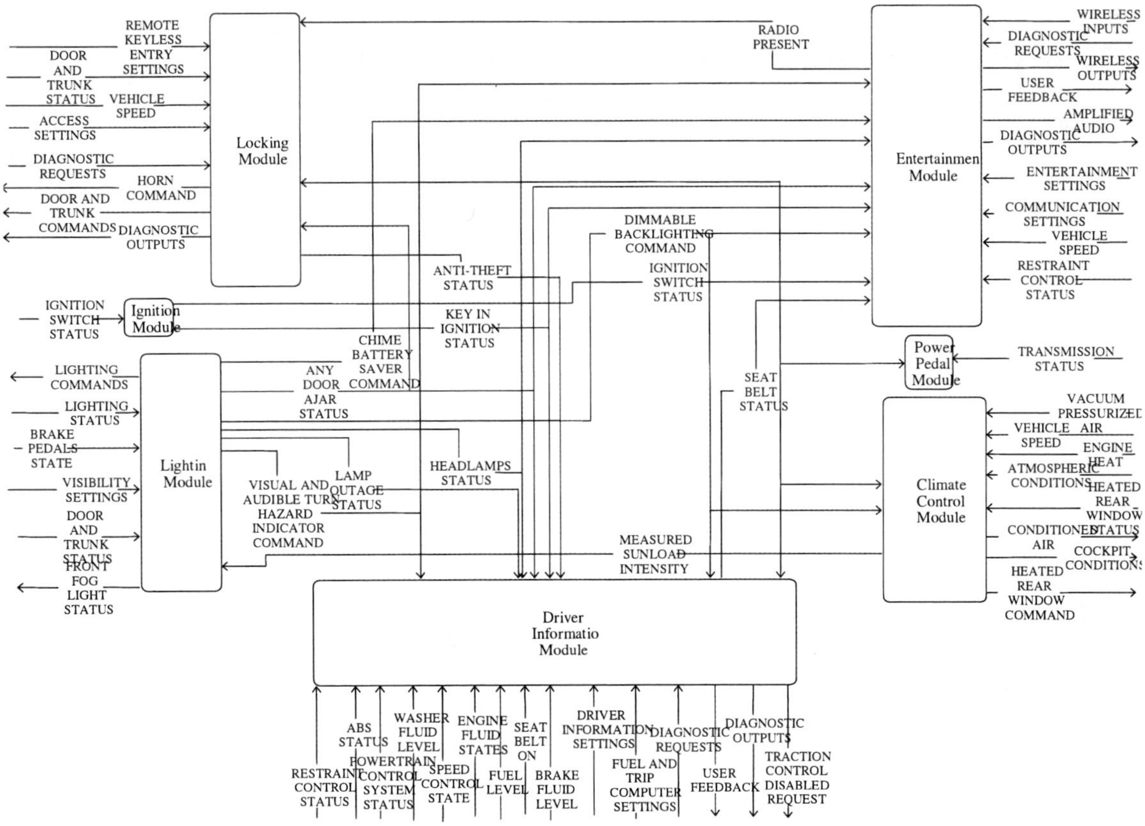

Figure 8: Cockpit Architecture Flow Diagram

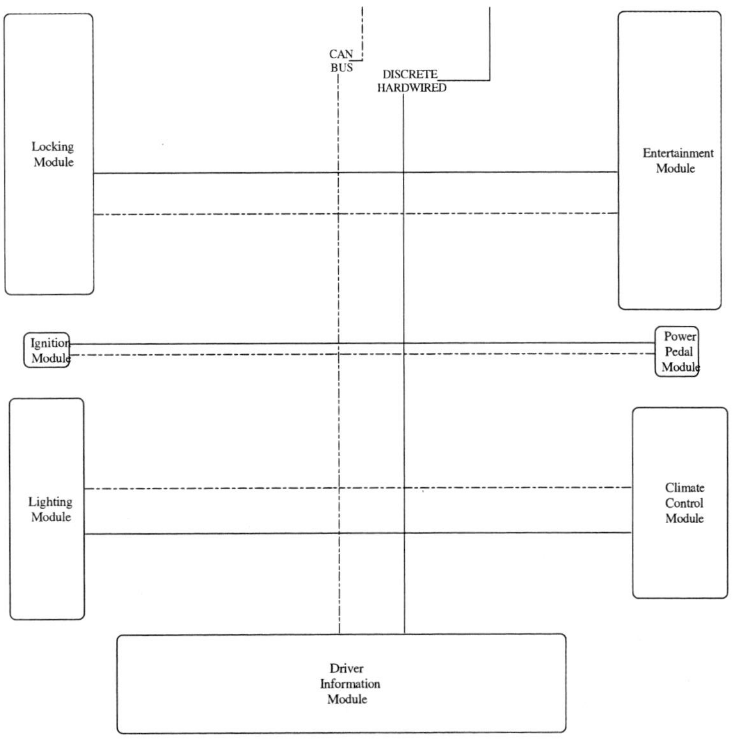

Figure 9: Cockpit Architecture Interconnect Diagram

Chances for Systems Engineering in Road Transport and Traffic Telematics

J. N. Hadderingh
CMG-Public sector, Division ATG
Lange Voorhout 3
Den Haag
The Netherlands

Abstract. This paper highlights some of the possibilities for applying Systems Engineering in the field of Road Transport and Traffic Telematics (RTTT). Although large and often complicated systems are or will be applied in this field, they are often specified, developed, designed and commissioned without employing Systems Engineering (SE). This has resulted in long and cumbersome procurement processes and sub-optimal solutions. Even more severe problems may occur with the need for further integration of these often stand alone systems. Applying SE may be a way to solve some of these problems. But it will require the use of this methodology in a field that is not (yet?) ready for it. This paper gives examples of some RTTT systems, shows what SE could do for them and gives a few suggestions for achieving these benefits.

ROAD TRANSPORT AND TRAFFIC TELEMATICS

Road Transport and Traffic. Our modern society has become more and more critical dependent on transport of people and goods over roads networks. Modern production methods like "just in time" would be impossible without a reliable and efficient road transport system. But increased demand has resulted in the use of the existing road network beyond its capacity. The classical solution of building more roads is often no or an extremely costly option.

Telematics. The use of telematics is seen as one of the more promising ways to overcome the current problems with road transport and traffic. Intelligent vehicles and intelligent road infrastructure should offer a saver, more efficient and environmental friendly transport system. But this comes at a price. Our modern society has become more and more dependent on these RTTT systems. Could they in the past be considered "nice to have" in the near future they will be "mission critical". But the procurement, design and development, installation and operation of such mission critical RTTT systems can no longer be done with methods of the past. SE will be essential for a successful introduction of these RTTT systems. In an earlier paper (Mackey, 1994) SE is proposed for highway design. It concludes by mentioning the advent of RTTT systems. Here we will elaborate on applying SE for the design of RTTT systems.

CURRENT SITUATION

Introduction. To clarify some of these problems a few examples will be given of RTTT projects. The examples are taken from Electronic Fee Collection (EFC), Traffic Management systems, Electronic Vehicle Identification (EVI) and Road Use Charges.

Electronic Fee Collection. Classical toll collection systems force the users to stop and pay with cash. The increasing use of toll roads has resulted in large toll plaza's. These classical toll systems are a major investment and require a lot of space. See figure 1.

Figure 1, a classical toll plaza

With the introduction of EFC it became possible to substantially increase the throughput of the lanes of the toll plaza's or even get rid of them. See figure 2 for an example of such an EFC system.

Figure 2, example of an EFC system

This has reduced the cost of toll collection and increased the service to the public. But people that where accustomed to build toll plaza's are now confronted with buying large telematic systems. This has caused and still causes lots of problems by the operators that have to acquire such systems. That these problems may be severe is shown in the Melbourne example. It has taken much longer than planned to get the system operational resulting in substantial loss of income. In those circumstances where SE methods and concepts has been (partially) introduced substantial improvements in both the design and development and in the procurement process have been achieved. The major problems to overcome where:

- Gain acceptance for the introduction of concepts which where considered cost drivers. "We are not a defence organisation".
- The operators had no personal with a background in SE. So it was often difficult to explain why certain in there view superfluous or complicated steps where necessary.

Traffic Management Centres. This is a typical example of uncontrolled growth resulting in a large collection of independent monitoring and control systems. (Koningsbruggen 1999). Each with its own man-machine interface and proprietary technology. This collection has become very expensive to maintain and hard to control. There is a need to integrate these systems. The investments in these centres are such that the simple solution of equipping them with new systems is to expensive. So a gradual upgrading to an integrated system is required.

Figure 3, example of a traffic control centre

This turns out to be quite a challenge from a SE point of view. Again the operators often lack a SE background resulting in complicated situations when introducing SE. But the complexity of the task seems to make it a mission impossible without applying SE techniques and tools.

EVI. In several European countries plans exist to equip vehicles with a unique electronic identification, the EVI (Electronic Vehicle Identification). This would imply that each vehicle should be equipped with a tag. There are several applications that would require or benefit from such a tag. But the architectural and organisational difficulties are substantial. (Hadderingh, 1998). Here again SE could be of great value in assisting solving these architectural and organisational difficulties.

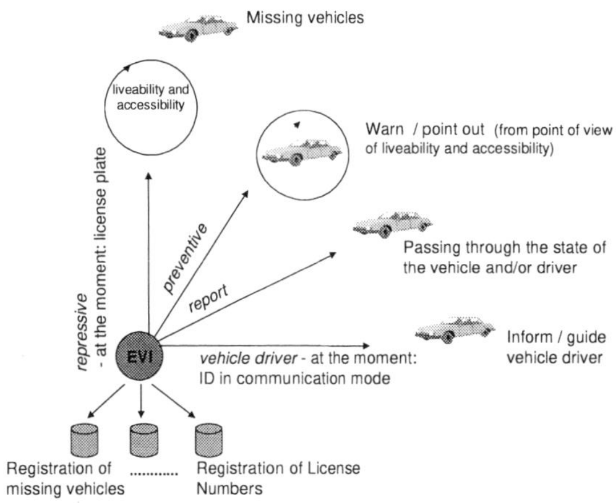

Figure 4, scope of the EVI

Road Use Charges. There is a trend to charge the road users for the costs they are causing to the society in relation to their usage of the road network. This requires charging systems where parameters like distance travelled, time, place and vehicle category are determined and the fee is calculated based on these parameters. Depending on the extent to which changes in these parameters need to be determined the resulting in-car equipment can be quite complicated. The equipment should not only measure these parameters but should do this in such a way that the drivers are unable to fraud the system. Intelligent vehicles will have such measuring devices among others for navigation purposes but if they will fulfil the requirements for road use charges is an open question. (Buitenhuis, 1999). The relations between the different applications as they appear in this example is one of the reasons for studying the integration of RTTT applications. But for this integration the same holds as in the EVI example, the architectural and organisational difficulties are substantial.

SYSTEMS INTEGRATION

Systems Integration. Road transport telematics is still in the phase of island automation. Lots of systems are introduced but independent of each other. These systems are based on proprietary solutions that cannot be connected to each other. This causes several problems:

- To the public, no uniformity in service. At different places the same service is provided with a different interface or different quality.
- To the operators, higher operational costs.
- To the manufacturers, a scattered market.

On the other hand the social developments will force towards integration. This is already shown in the examples Traffic management centres, EVI and road use charges. The promises RTTT brings in providing saver, more reliable and efficient traffic and transport systems can never come true without integration of today's stand alone systems. Intelligent vehicles have to co-operate with intelligent road-infrastructure to exploit both to the maximum extent.

The question arises, how such an integration could be achieved. Some steps are already taken but they make the need for SE even more obvious. The first examples of so called "ITS architectures" have appeared. (ITS-America, 1997) Intelligent Transport Systems (ITS), is a public private co-operation all over the world that aims at the introduction of RTTT. But the same examples of ITS architectures made it also clear that a large gap exists between the transport policies and the software engineering approach used for the ITS architectures.

ANALYSYS OF THE EXAMPLES

Motivation. The idea is to investigate if some commonality can be found in the problems mentioned in the examples before going into discussing the SE aspects and the solutions they might bring in solving some of the RTTT problems.

Trend. The examples have at least one thing in common. The systems are large distributed systems consisting of a combination of hardware, software and procedural solutions to provide the required services. In principle is the technology available. Bottlenecks are architectural, organisational and economical difficulties. Design and development of such systems is typically the domain of SE. But the people that procure or design such systems have often little background in SE. The problem is sometimes even worse due to the fact that even a background in telematics is missing.

Future. The trend emerging from the examples will appear even stronger in the near future. The need for further integration will alleviate discussions on the allocation of functionality to subsystems. The different stakeholders will have different views on the optimal allocation of functionality. The non functional requirements will reduce the freedom of the stakeholders in the allocation of the functionality. Because we have apart from functional requirements non-functional requirements with respect to reliability, maintainability, security, safety, expandability and last but not least the question of gradual introduction and graceful degradation. This in itself makes it already a SE challenge.

Current practice. The solutions for the technical problems mentioned above are further complicated by the organisational situation. A problem that needs to be solved by a RTTT system has a lot of stake holders. Each has its own ideas on what the new system should do for them. Sometimes these ideas can be seen as something that could be considered an operational concept. If it is decided to go ahead with the new system parties are made responsible for aspects of the system but in most cases there is not such a thing as a systems engineer. A RTTT system is a combination of hardware, software and procedures solving a problem. This implies that allocation of system requirements to hardware, software and procedures requires a system design phase. Simply making parties responsible for system aspects or sub systems without performing an explicit system design phase results in a lot of co-ordination problems due to lacking or insufficient interface specifications. Unfortunately this is happening quite often. One of the drives behind this is a desire for a concurrent engineering approach to speed up the process. But the co-ordination problems result often in substantial delays. This is one area where the introduction of SE could be beneficial.

IDEAL SITUATION

Ideal Situation. The ideal situation would be to make the current implicit concurrent engineering approach an explicit concurrent system engineering approach.

Prerequisites. The current situation does not explicit take the step of "designing" the interaction between the involved parties. Today the structure is often the result of incidents or an existing structure not optimised for the problem at hand. Designing the optimal structure is in itself a SE task. The "soft" system should be designed in such a way that the cohesion within the organisational units is maximal and the interaction between the organisational units in minimised.

Role of the ITS architectures. ITS architectures could play an important role in getting to this ideal situation. The upper levels of these architectures give an inventory of the different stakeholders, their policies and the RTTT applications. The question is whether this inventory is just an inventory of the current situation or a well designed structure that fulfils the SE requirements for a good architecture. The lower levels give inventories of telematic services. Thus the ITS architectures relate the stakeholders with the technology and form as such an ideal base for studying the reasons behind interactions between systems. Knowledge of these reasons is the first step towards controlling the interactions and thus managing the complexity. But it requires that the ITS architectures really try to provide this link between transport policies and systems.

SYSTEM ENGINEERING PRACTICES

Requirements Management. Due to the growing complexity of RTTT systems the need for requirements management has appeared. The problem is alleviated by the fact the lots of parties are involved in the procurement of such systems. Only systematic requirements management can assure that all the needs are taken into account in the new system.

Modelling and Simulation. It is often hard to specify the required performance for RTTT systems. And once it is specified it is hard to prove that the proposed design meets the specifications. Modelling and simulation are tools to assist in this area. For several EFC projects modelling and simulation has been used with encouraging results. (Meijer, 1998)

Acceptance Testing. The current practice of accepting a systems by performing a test once it is installed is insufficient for complex RTTT systems. Qualification procedures are required that start by approval of the design up to acceptance testing via several steps that assure that a project phase has been successfully completed. In this way problems are encountered in early phase of the project where they can be corrected cheaper.

Concurrent Engineering. Concurrent Engineering does not only take place at top level. It often takes place at almost each level in realising an RTTT application. But the problem is that this is not recognised. Therefor a lot of interactions emerge during the realisation process that either could have been circumvented or could have be steered instead of "just happening" as is often the case.

HURDLES TO BE TAKEN

What are major hurdles. What is preventing the RTTT world from being in the ideal situation. Some major hurdles are:

- No tradition is SE
- Lack of critical mass
- Explicit approach

No tradition in SE. For many people in the RTTT field issues like complexity and interaction are more or less considered acts of God and not something that is designed into the system. A great faith in the possibilities of modern technology makes things worse. It is hard to explain that complex interactions remain complex in an automated system. So there is a drive towards complicated requirements. Long procurement processes combined which are often political

Critical mass. Due to the many stakeholders each contribution to the solution is quite small. This makes it difficult for these organisations to motivate a substantial investment in SE training and tools. Especially tool development can be so costly that this can never be achieved within the scope of a single project. And without successful examples there is not much drive to invest. But there won't be many successful examples without tools and training.

A possible way out of this dead lock is to make products of these tools and services. This would enable sharing costs between many projects. An example of such a product is the ADSSIM simulation environment for EFC systems.

Explicit approach. SE offers a explicit approach from missions and threats to operational systems. When applied correctly it offers tracebility from the system to its goals. It makes clear why the system is as it is, what the system is supposed to do and how it is done. But often there exists in the RTTT world quite a difference between the "official" and the "real" missions of the system. And sometimes the political decision making process creates a lot of hesitation to be explicit about the threats or other aspects of the project because that might endanger the acceptance of the project. The large number of stakeholders with often partly conflicting interests adds an additional dimension to this complex situation. Getting things realised in such an environment might ask for translation of SE concepts and methods into something that can work in such a complicated political oriented environment without compromising the essential elements of the SE concepts and methods. Of course the ultimate challenge for SE would be to consider the realisation of such type of projects as a SE project of an organisational system.

CONCLUSIONS

RTTT offers an interesting opportunity for applying SE. But some hurdles need to be taken. The first is that the field is hardly familiar with SE so that a lot of education is required. The second is that the principles and concepts of SE need to be translated in the language of transport engineers. And last but not least the road traffic and transport world has to become aware of the consequences of the massive introduction of telematic systems. That does not mean that the field should refrain from the introduction of such systems. On the contrary, the problems facing the transport community are such that they have no other option than large scale introduction of such systems with the use of SE as an enabler. But awareness of the consequences could prevent disappointments and may result in realistic expectations of what SE can bring to the field.

REFERENCES

Reference list.

Mackey,William F.,jr, Mackey,William F., *A Systems Engineering Approach to Highway Design,* Proceedings of the Fourth Annual International Symposium of the National Council on Systems Engineering , San Jose CA 1994.

Buitenhuis-Vermeij,Y., Hadderingh,J.N., Postema,R.J., Rutten,B.J.C.M., *Verkenning van de Technische Haalbaarheid van Kilometerheffing,* CMG Public Sector B.V. 1999.

ITS-America, *Executive Summary of the National Architecture,* ITS-America 1997.

Hadderingh,J.N., Koningsbruggen,P.H.van, Vieveen,J, *EVI in relatie tot de ontwikkelingen in en rondom het voertuig,,* CMG Public Sector B.V. 1998.

Meijer,G.R., Hertzberger,L.O., Wijk,D.P.van, "Design and Operation of ERP by Simulation". *Proceedings of the International Conference on Tranportation in the Next Millenium* (Singapore , September 9-11, 1998). pp 197-222.

Koningsbruggen,P.H.van, Mozes,A., Zon,C.B.M.van, Hommes,R., *Towards a new architecture for traffic management systems in traffic control centres,* CMG Public Sector B.V. 1999.

ACKNOWLEDGEMENT

The author wants to thank the people in the RTTT team of CMG ATG for the interesting discussions on the subject. He also wants to acknowledge the anonymous reviewer who made him aware of some literature, an example and gave some good suggestions to improve the concept.

BIOGRAPHY

Hans Hadderingh is team manager of the RTTT team of CMG ATG. He has 10 years experience with applying SE in the road transport telematic field. Before joining CMG he worked for 12 years in the defence industry where he gained experience in the application of SE on large systems. He was among others involved in the introduction of MIL STD 490A in the company he worked for.

Traceability in A Unified Systems Engineering Framework for A High-Speed Railway System

Young Won Park, Hae Sang Song*, and Heung Chae Chung**
Ajou University, Institute for Advanced Engineering*, Korea Railroad Research Institute**
YONGIN P.O. BOX 25, KYONGGI-DO, 449-860, KOREA

Abstract. This paper presents results from a computer-aided systems engineering application to a high-speed railway system technology development project, called KHST(Korea High Speed Train). RDD-100 version of ALC Inc. was used in this work. The framework adopted in the study takes a unified approach to the system design and the process management associated with it, thereby coherent and full traceability between them is maintained. Conventional system engineering process supported by the tool is adopted in the KHST system design; however, some modification is inevitable because of a late introduction of the tool on the project. On the other hand, the same tool is also used to the systems engineering management to get full traceability between system design data and engineering management data. It is greatly helpful in managing many sub-contractors in the sense that the traceability can help identify the sub-project responsibility as well as the objectives of the project in coordination with interface requirements. We conclude with the advantage and limits of our unified approach.

INTRODUCTION

High-speed rail system represents a typical example of large-scale multi-disciplinary system, consisting of train, electrical hardware, electronics, control, information, communication, civil technology etc., that must exercise configuration and requirement management. Not only the requirements dictate the contracts with the suppliers but also becomes the basis of the project execution, system integration, and testing. It provides the basic specification of development activities. This paper summarizes the results of using **RDD-100®**, a systems engineering tool, to establish requirement traceability and development process management in performing next-generation high-speed train technology development program.

As a result of the study, the segmented systems engineering data including requirements, component information, WBS, projects, and organization information etc. that existed with minimal documentation were organized into a reusable form of RDD-100 database with traceability among data. Additionally, new data model and schema was proposed and built along with a management framework.

THE UNIFIED SYSTEMS ENGINEERING FRAMEWORK

Why unified framework? KHST program that manages and oversees various subsystem suppliers and performs systems engineering activities needed the visibility and traceability of the contracted work and systems requirements as well as of the system design and project management data. Accordingly, the purpose of the study was to develop a unified systems engineering data concept and structure that use a single tool to manage both system design results and development processes.

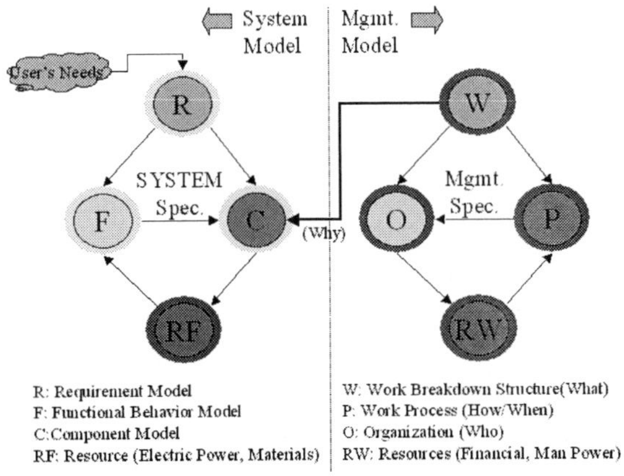

Figure 1. Abstract data model of the unified systems engineering

Systems Engineering Data Model. Figure 1 represents a single systems engineering data model built to organize KHST program and system design data using **RDD-100®** computer aided systems engineering software. The left-hand side of the picture depicts system-level design data model while the right-hand side shows the systems engineering management related data model in a symmetric form. System model divides into four elements of System Requirement (R), Functional Behavior (F), Component Model (C), and Resources for Function (RF) consumed or produced during the execution of each function.

Systems engineering management data model demonstrates a similar form of WBS (W), Organization (O), Process (P), and Resources for work (RW) needed to perform each task.

This data model provides element-level mutual interrelationship since all high-speed rail system design data can be traced each other. Finally the resultant database serves as *"systems engineering knowledge base"* essential for enterprise knowledge management and *reusability*.

Systems Engineering Process. Systems engineering process in this study signifies the sequence of development activities to produce system specifications and process specifications. A reverse engineering approach was used to determine system specification since the KHST program develops only the train system portion of the improved high-speed railway system and the tool was introduced to the program about the completion of the system architecture selection. The process specification was obtained based on the system specification. An iterative process at each hierarchy level of the system produced a gradually detailed model. More detail is given in the following sections.

SYSTEM-LEVEL DESIGN FRAMEWORK

System-level Design Data Model. System design data model is an abstract model for various data obtained from *systems design activities.*

The data structure of RDD-100 implementing system design data model depicted in Fig. 1 is called a data schema shown in Fig. 2. Data schema consists of data element types and relationships as well as directional links and reverse links. For example, requirement elements have the data structure to describe a tree-structured system requirements showing the relationship between the requirements of upper-level and lower-level using "incorporates" link (ALC 1996).

Requirement Model (R). In KHST systems engineering project, in spite of the established systems engineering process, it was discovered that the requirement management and traceability task could not be performed easily without improving the process. Because of the evolutionary development nature of the railroad industry, a reverse systems engineering process was required to retrieve the upper-level system requirements from the top-level system design specifications. As a result, several hundred of leaf-requirements were obtained and many incomplete requirements that were not addressed by the system design specifications were also discovered during the process. These requirements were classified as critical issues requiring further attention and special review.

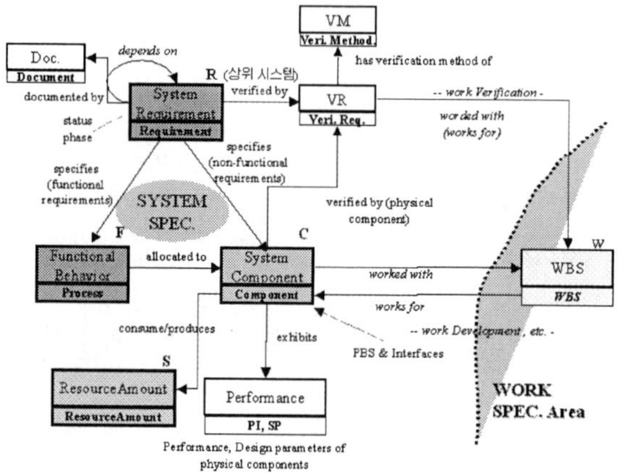

Figure 2. Brief schema of the design elements and its relation to WBS element.

Functional Behavior Model (F). The most significant area of behavior analysis in KHST was in electrical signal subsystem area. The increased speed of the next generation high-speed rail system stresses the safety issues greatly and the electrical signal subsystem deserves extensive behavior analysis for optimal design. The system level safety requirements needs to be decomposed into several subsystems areas. Many safety issues are subject to further study.

Component Model (C). Component objects are used to represent system architecture model. Due to its top-down modeling approach, the component architecture demonstrates a tree structure. Based on the identified components and the associated interfaces, the component model was built. Several hundred components were identified through a reverse engineering process of the train subsystem for KHST program. A complex model was built by considering the interfaces surrounding the train subsystem that includes the electrical supply subsystem and rail subsystem

Using the system design model and schema as described above, the requirement model (R), the function model (F), the component model (C) were obtained and managed through RDD-100 tool.

Reverse Systems Engineering. As shown on the right hand side of Fig. 3, RDD-100 supports the forward engineering process of iterating requirements analysis, functional analysis, and architecture synthesis. (Martin 1997).

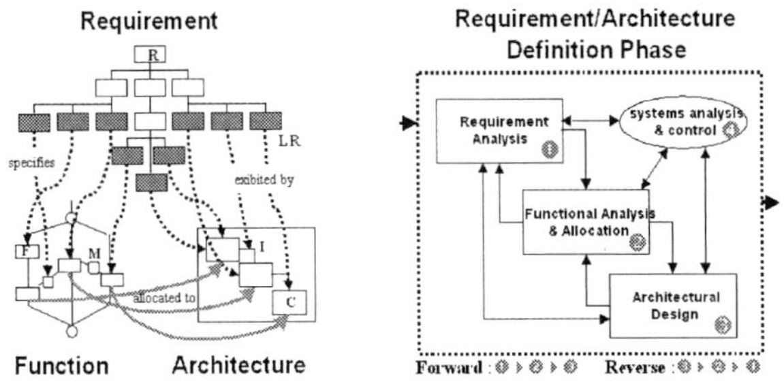

Figure 3. Forward and reverse engineering process for KHST(right) and final form of the system-level design database (left)

Since other than the train system to be improved to handle 350Km speed, the rest of the subsystems mainly remain unchanged from the imported French high-speed rail system. For this reason and the evolutionary nature of the mature railway industry, the entire system level requirements were not available to the KHST technology development program. Therefore, the system level requirements and the engineering processes were retraced from the results of the detailed design adopting a reverse engineering process (Martin 1993, Park 1999).

Accordingly, a reverse engineering process of bottom-up approach was performed utilizing system specification document and PBS to retrieve system architecture and subsystem interfaces. Functional and performance requirements were obtained subsequently from this process as shown in the design database of Fig. 3 (left).

Benefit. The main advantages of the database obtained from this study are the requirements and configuration management with traceability, the reusability of the database, and the report generation capability provided by the tool which exhibits a great deal of productivity and convenience upon design changes and improvements.

SYSTEMS ENGINEERING MANAGEMENT

Engineering Management Data Model. Since Many subsystem contractors support the KHST program, data models were established to support the suppliers' activities and to consistently manage those tasks in pursuing to meet the prescribed system requirements. As mentioned earlier, the process management model demonstrates a *symmetric* structure of the system data model (recall Fig. 1).

Fig. 4 shows more details of the RDD-100 core schema relevant to the process management data briefly shown in Fig. 1. Both organization and workflow models as well as the resource model surround the WBS that has attribute defined as project information. Each WBS is assigned to a work team and the project information specifies the resource assigned to the WBS. Upon the completion of each WBS task the assigned resource is consumed. WBS can be traced from either a system requirement or from an architecture component.

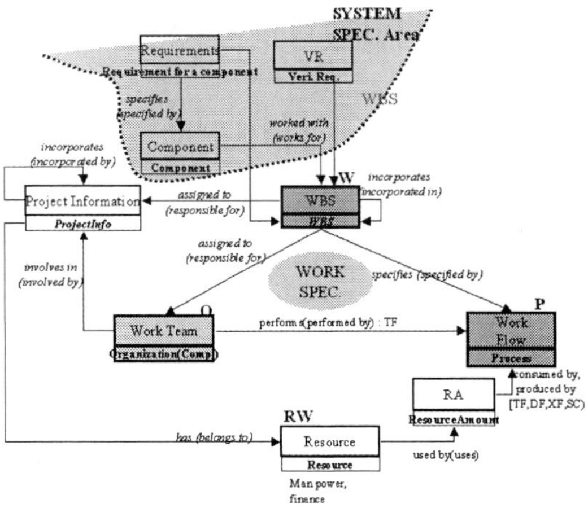

Figure 4. Core schema of engineering management data and its relation to the design data.

WBS-Centered Project Management (W). Those activities performed within a WBS are justified by their contribution toward the objective of the WBS. Each WBS has justification why it needs to be performed. Therefore, each WBS must have traceability within the system model to answer to the question of 'why '. In the process management model, the traceability serves as the link between WBS and the system component model.

Fig. 5 represents a process of defining work from the system specification. Since the systems engineering process is to define the system design specification, as the system specification gets more concrete the iteration activity gets in more detail to define the needed tasks.

In KHST program, since the database building was performed after both SEMP and the system design specification were available, the WBS was generated based on existing data. Most of the work was divided by projects according to each project's schedule using RDD tool.

Workflow Management (P). While the WBS shows what task must be accomplished, the workflow defines the input, the sequence of work steps, and the output information. The details of work within a WBS item gets described in natural language while the workflow model represents its behavior in a mathematical form. The modeling for the sequence of work and schedule utilizes the Behavior diagram of RDD-100.

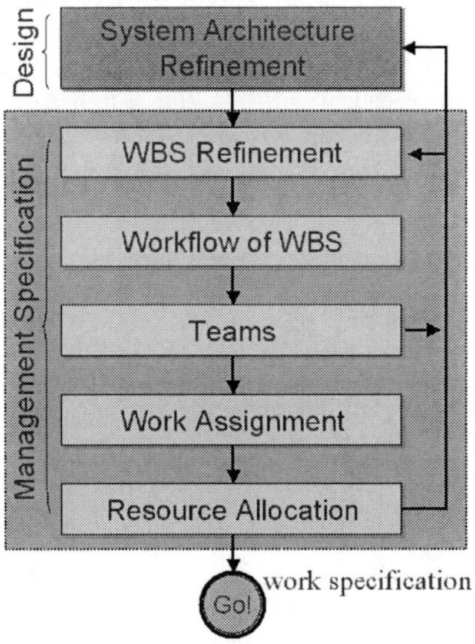

Figure 5. Engineering management specification process in KHST.

The advantage of using the workflow model is to express the sequence of work and the input and output relationship that is unavailable from the WBS model. Additionally, through the use of Dynamic Verification Facility (DVF), one can exercise 'what-if' analysis, which can simulate the overall schedule change scenarios when there is work delay problem in a critical path.

Fig. 6 shows the relationship between a WBS element and the workflow example. There must be one-to-one matching relationship between the tasks of a WBS element and the workflow model. Furthermore, an output obtained from a task within WBS becomes an input to another task.

As a task is modeled in a hierarchy the work sequence, input and output, and the execution time can be retrieved if the workflow model is examined in detail.

Organization (O). Organization describes the responsible party executing each task defined in the WBS element. It uses the component modeling facility in RDD-100 with some modifications. In KHST application the decomposition was accomplished up to the team level of each subsystem WBS leaving the further details to the responsibility of the subsystem WBS.

Resource for Work (RW). Resource is required to model the allocated budget, manpower, and facilities when a WBS element was assigned to a responsible organization. Initial allocation of the resource gets re-allotted to perform each task. The resource model can be used to analyze the budget using the dynamic simulation facility of RDD-100.

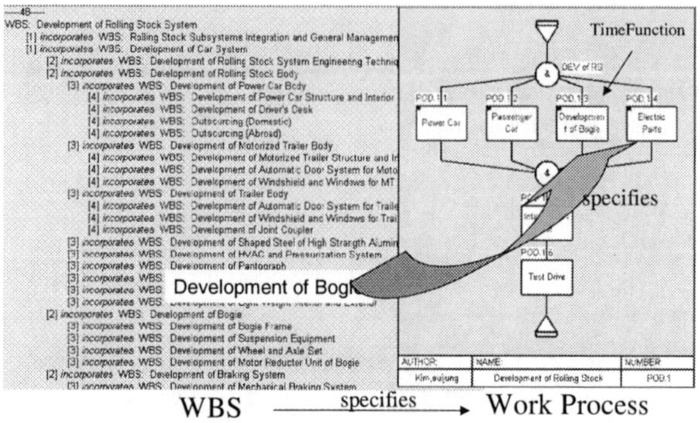

Figure 6. Example of traceability from WBS to the workflow

Project Management. Those tasks within a WBS element relevant to the total system acquisition must be performed to execute the work process in a single batch of process, work authority, and needed resource. This unit was defined as a project. As a large-scale system, KHST project is unable to accomplish all required tasks within a single WBS element. Several lower-level WBS elements were used to accomplish the overall task. For example, the systems engineering task deserves as a single WBS element that can be assigned to a project. Accordingly, some task under a WBS element can be performed as a lower-level allocated task item.

DISCUSSION

Merits. The most advantage achieved by an integrated management of both systems design data and process management data comes from the ability for easy traceable management and the reusability of the database. Additionally, all of the system design data could be collected and captured by using the tool and the data model presented in the study. The benefit of the database to support the future configuration management for improvements and routine maintenance is incalculable. Furthermore, it provides the foundation to facilitate any changes in the specification can be analyzed and reflected.

Limits. The application of the process management data for detailed project schedule management using RDD-100 may not be advantageous over the use of other specialized schedule management tool such as MS-Project that provides various options in data display. However, it was sufficient for the kind of need to manage only the top-level schedule in KHST program applications.

CONCLUSION

An application of the systems engineering tool using a unified data framework to manage both system design data as well as the development process data demonstrated a successful management of KHST program data. Much of the system level program data existed in many different forms were collected, captured, and organized in a traceable form of single database. As a result, the traceability for system requirements was established and an efficient development process was setup for KHST program.

It was learned that a reverse engineering process was more appropriate to build the system design database in the case of the evolutionary nature of the railway system development. RDD-100, a system design tool, was successfully applied to organize the top-level program control data.

The data model framework and the database built from the study will play a significant role in performing system interface management, integration, and verification work to follow later.

ACKNOLEDGEMENT

This study is a part of the project G7 conducted at the Korea Railroad Research Institute. The authors are grateful to the support and help extended to this work.

REFERENCES

ALC Training Course 101: *Intro. RDD-100 Student Workbook,* Ascent Logic Co., 1996.

Blanchard, B. S., and Fabrycky, W.J., *Systems Engineering and Analysis,* Chapter 17, Prentice-Hall, Feb. 1998.

Carroll, John M. Ed., *Scenario-Based Design*, John Wiley & Sons, Inc., 1995.

IEEE Computer Society, *IEEE Standard for Application and Management of the Systems Engineering Process, IEEE Std 1220-1998,* IEEE, Jan 1999.

Martin, James N. "Reverse Engineering a System Using Life Cycle Modeling", *proc. INCOSE*, 1993.

Martin, James N., *Systems Engineering Guidebook,* CRC Press, 1997.

Park, J.S, et. al., *System-level Requirement Management Using a Systems Engineering Tool,* 99F02-MR-99.01, IAE, 1999.

Song, H. S, et. al., *Modelling Paradigm of a Systems Engineering Tool,* 98D05-MR-99.01, IAE, 1999.

Tim, C.R., *Systems Engineering Handbook,* INCOSE, Jan. 1998.

Zeigler, B.P., Multifaceted Modelling and Discrete Event Simulation, Academic Press, 1994.

BIOGRAPHY

Youngwon Park is a Professor of Systems Engineering at the Ajou University in Yongin, Korea. He worked at the Institute for Advanced Engineering and McDonnell Douglas Aerospace in GN&C, avionics, and software systems engineering and development.

Hae Sang Song is a Senior Engineer for Institute for Advanced Engineering. He has a B.S. and an M.S. in Electrical Engineering and is a candidate for PhD in electrical engineering from Korea Advanced Institute of Science and Technology. His area of interest is in Systems Modeling and Simulation.

Heung Chae Chung is a Principal Research Engineer for the High-Speed Rail Engineering Department at Korea Railroad Research Institute. He has a PhD in mechanical engineering and his area of interest is in energy systems and in railroad systems development.

Information modelling and systems re-engineering– an efficient approach to assessing complex current Norwegian natural gas transport operations

by
Hans J. Dahl, Statoil
Center for Energy and Environmental Policy Research
Massachusetts Institute of Technology
Cambridge, MA 02139-4307
HJD@mit.edu

Abstract. This paper presents the use of *information models* as tools for systematically assessing existing Norwegian natural gas transport operations. The models, integral parts of a *systems re-engineering process* to analyze the entire transport operation, consist of a requirement traceability model, a system architecture model, a behavior model, and a context model. These models not only consistently define existing operations, but also verify how well the operations meet *effectiveness measures* that have been identified for the operations.

Systems re-engineering and the models derived from it are shown here to reduce the asymmetry in information that is typically present in this industry between principals and their agents (e.g., authorities vs. system owners, system owners vs. system operators, and shippers vs. shippers' dispatching representatives). Further, information modelling of an existing system is shown here to differ from the more traditional application of information modelling: to bring a new system into being.

Models provide a scientific framework for evaluating how a changing business environment impacts existing operations. New legislative requirements and economic measures can be tested with models, which also allow new operational services and business opportunities to be identified and evaluated prior to implementation in actual operations.

INTRODUCTION

The Norwegian natural gas industry is exposed to a changing business environment due to the introduction of the European Union (EU)'s Gas Directive. The European Union approved the directive on the 11th of May, 1998, and member states must implement it into their national legislations by summer of the year 2000.[1] The directive suggests a new regulatory regime, which may impact the industry in any of a number of different ways.

One cardinal question, among several others, is how the Gas Directive impacts Norwegian "dry gas" (i.e., natural gas at sales quality) transport operations. Little research focusing on this issue is available, and limited documentation exists clarifying the potential impacts. In 1997, therefore, Statoil initiated a research program[2] to explore the new regulatory regime and suggest operational approaches and new business opportunities.

In order to address this issue, decisions must be made regarding scientific methods to be applied and the scope of inquiry. In Dahl[3], a *master strategic approach*[4] is suggested addressing the choices. The approach, broadly speaking, has two components. The first is an assessment of all relevant information regarding current operations. Based on this information, and by applying systems theory and a *systems re-engineering process*, current operations are consistently defined. The systems re-engineering process yields *information models*, which convey information about operations' context and behavior, the system structure, and requirement traceability.

The second component of the master strategic approach is an assessment of available information about the future regulatory regime. Based on this information, plausible test-case scenarios will be developed and introduced to considerations of the future system. A *systems engineering process* will then be carried out (much like the systems re-engineering process) and the system response studied. By means of systems engineering principles, *gas-flow theory,* and *microeconomics,* new methods and recommendations for future operations will then be designed and tested.

[1] White Paper #46 (1997-98).

[2] i.e., the author's doctoral program.

[3] See Dahl (1999).

[4] The term "master strategic approach" is not applied in Dahl (1999). This term is, however, used in the present paper to refer to the earlier paper's main points of discussion.

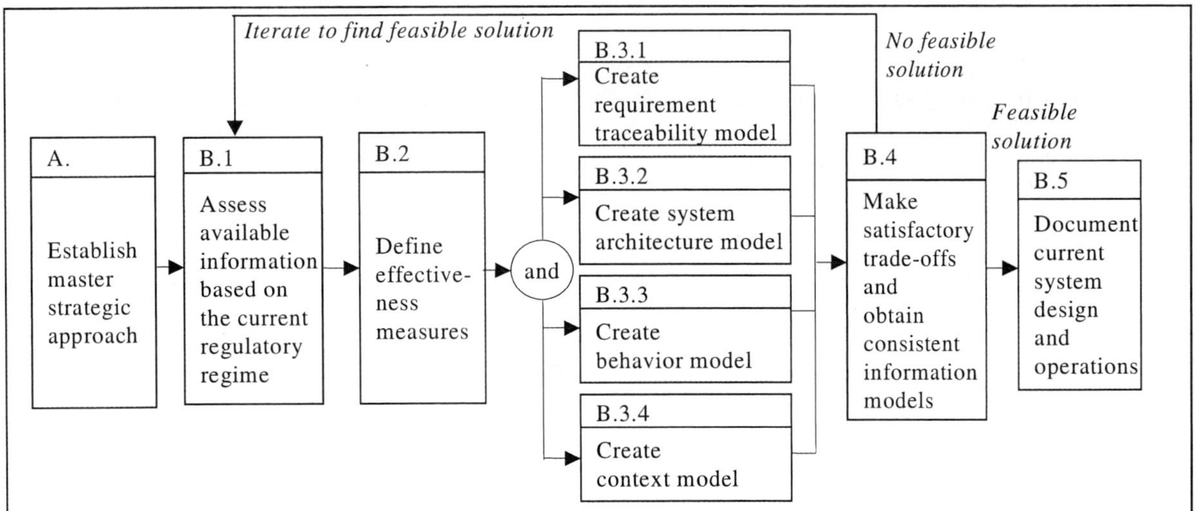

Fig. 1 The systems re-engineering process

The present paper offers a synthesis of the author's work on the first component of the master strategic approach. It focuses on information models and the process that led to their development, then discusses how they were developed and how they can be used to make inferences about existing operations.

The work presented here is based on systems engineering theory and principles. Several recent books and papers offer particularly relevant discussions of systems engineering processes and information modelling[5]; the present paper utilizes the conceptual thinking and principles outlined in documents such as Oliver[6] and Purves.[7]

It is the author's hope that lessons learned in this project will be shared with other individuals, companies, and industries working on complex, multidisciplinary tasks. Information models are useful tools for complex industries subject to a regulatory regime in transition, or otherwise in need of a holistic, systematic assessment of entire systems or operations.

THE SYSTEMS RE-ENGINEERING PROCESS

According to Oliver, information modelling is often conducted as work tasks incorporated into the systems engineering process. INCOSE[8] defines the systems engineering process as: "a logical, systematic process devised to accomplish systems engineering tasks." A systems engineering process is often applied in connection with creating a *new* complex system from the very beginning. In this research however the system in concern is *already built*, is operated for many years, the operations personnel perform their tasks according to an established organization model and the operations functions and the system's performance are defined. The systems engineering process as applied in this work is thus a kind of "*re-engineering*" or "*reverse*" engineering activity.

Before proceeding, the following question must be answered: Why spend time and effort re-engineering the existing transport system operations? Several reasonable answers can be given. First, nowhere are the current operations analyzed and documented as a whole. Because transport capacity has been added almost continually during the last 15 years, operations today are considered to be complex, multidisciplinary, and difficult to document. To model the system and document results thus has intrinsic value. Secondly, the re-engineering process offers opportunity to verify and document compliance with requirements, and to reveal critically important aspects of the operations. Thirdly, as already mentioned, the process yields models that are needed later in this research. Lastly, the systems re-engineering process systematically guides assessment, enabling discussions and conclusions about Norwegian dry gas transport operations to be validated.

The systems re-engineering process considered here can be illustrated by a functional flow block diagram (FFBD), following the conceptual thinking of Blanchard[9] and Oliver (see Figure 1). In Figure 1, five activities are identified, each accomplishing specific tasks. The first activity (B.1) assesses available information about how the system is designed and operated. This activity consists of a documentation review and in-depth interviews with selected stakeholders. The next activity (B.2) consists of defining effectiveness measures derived from the first activity, to specify whether or not operations are successful. The third activity (B.3.*i*, *i*=1,4) is creation of the information models. These provide a static communication mechanism, completely specifying the system and its operations. The fourth activity (B.4) indicates the iterative activity that takes place in order to consistently improve the models and effectiveness

[5] See for example: Bahill et al. (1997), Stevens et al. (1998).
[6] Oliver et al. (1997).
[7] Purves et al. (1998).
[8] INCOSE (1998).

[9] Blanchard et al. (1990).

measures during modelling. The last activity (B.5) covers the reporting and documentation.

This systems re-engineering process structured the following overall hypothesis (B.0), on which this work was based: *"It is possible to develop a systems re-engineering process for assessing, specifying, and documenting current operations in a holistic manner."* The remainder of this paper presents experiences and lessons learned from the process, describes related activities, and tests the above hypothesis.

INFORMATION ASSESSMENT

The first activity (B.1) of the FFBD was formulated in this study as the following hypothesis: *"Major stakeholders will provide empirical descriptive data regarding their needs and systems requirements."* In order to test this hypothesis, scientific methods for qualitative research such as those described by King[10] and Ilstad[11] were applied. Specifically, representatives of selected stakeholders were interviewed in depth, based on questionnaires issued to them well beforehand. Methods were chosen to minimize the risk of bias in the results. The information assessment also included a comprehensive review of documentation identified by stakeholders.

A seemingly overwhelming amount of raw data was collected during this activity, and the need for classifying the information became apparent. Dahl[12] originally suggested hardware, software, and bioware as appropriate information classes. These were further disaggregated into the following eight main classes (which were then divided into subclasses) through an iterative process (the B.4 activity) to better organize the information:

- *Source and lower-tier documents*
  All documents containing requirements.
- *Requirements*
  All specifications of functions, decisions, and components relating to the dry gas transportation system and its operations.
- *Functions*
  All actions allocated to stakeholders.
- *Input/output*
  All discrete or time-related input/output from functions that are "passive" and may cause an effect, e.g., oral or written instructions and criteria defined to enable decision-making.
- *Stakeholders*
  All personnel and other actors who perform one or more functions within the system or who have a right to impose requirements on the system as a whole or on any of its operations.
- *Dry gas transportation system*
  All "main facilities" of the Statoil-operated dry gas transportation system, as defined in the Transportation Agreements, which themselves are decomposed into "components" such as valves, pipes, and the dry gas itself.
- *Communication and support systems*
  All systems that support the transfer of technical data and other information (oral, electronic, or written) among stakeholders and components.
- *Context systems*
  All physical components of external systems that affect dry gas transport in any way.

EFFECTIVENESS MEASURES

Activity (B.2) of the FFBD was expressed in this study as the following hypothesis: *"It is possible to define effectiveness measures for the prevailing operations."* The result was the establishment of effectiveness measures: criteria that separate success from catastrophe, as observed by Oliver. The measures were classified into three groups, covering authorities', licensees', and transport and production field operators' operations, as follows:

Authorities' measures:

- Operations shall [JVS1]help optimize the exploitation of Norwegian petroleum resources.
- Operations shall utilize the Norwegian natural gas transport system in a socioeconomically optimal manner.
- The regulatory regime must be designed with incentives, which aim to ensure that a company's optimal economic adaptation to the regime coincides with the socioeconomically optimal solution for the Norwegian people.
- The assignment of gas sales contracts to contractual fields, the allocation of delivery requirements to supply fields, and the development of new transport capacities must support the optimization of transport operations as a whole.

Licensees' measures:

- Sales-, transport-, and upstream-support agreements shall be negotiated and agreed upon by parties in such a manner that the agreements support transport operations, and vice versa.
- Operations shall be conducted in a "reasonable and prudent manner," with due attention to safety and the environment.
- Gas buyers must act in accordance with sales agreements.

Production field and transport system operators' measures:

[10] King et al. (1994).
[11] Ilstad (1998).
[12] Dahl (1999).

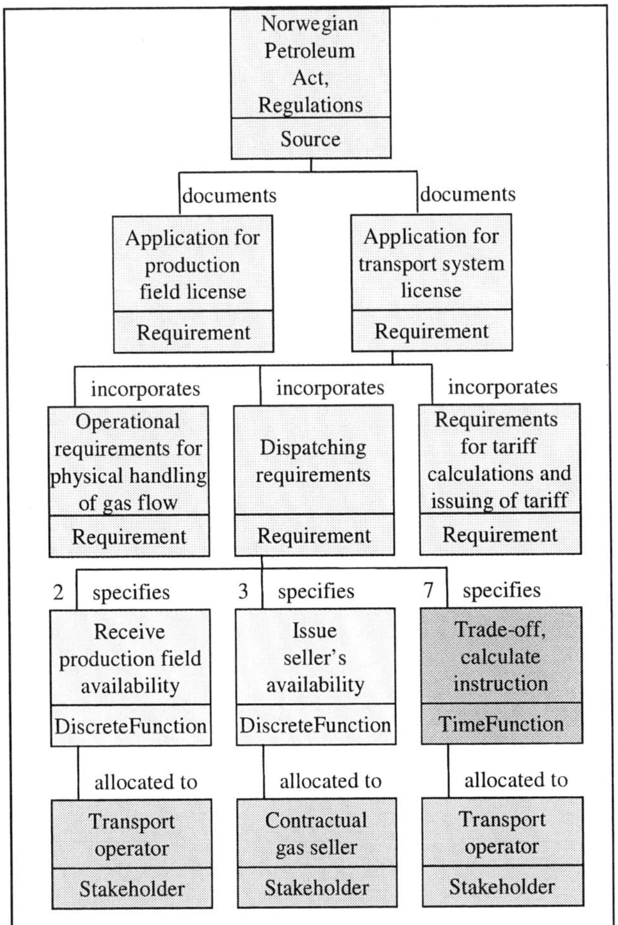

Fig. 2 The requirement traceability information model

- Dry gas transport system deliveries shall be made to gas buyers with 100% regularity.
- Dry gas transport system deliveries shall meet gas quality specifications at all times.
- Transport operators shall correctly produce and issue tariffs to shippers in a timely manner.
- Communications and support systems shall never shut down.
- Natural gas producers must deliver gas of the agreed-upon quality in a timely fashion, according to the specified delivery instructions.

The present work showed that authorities' and licensees' measures, unlike operators' measures, are not directly measurable; these therefore had to be decomposed to lower-tier requirements in order to permit testing. Each of these groups' effectiveness measures was thus decomposed to successively lower-level requirements, eventually reaching "leaf-node"-level (the lowest level in a branched structure) requirements, which are consistently defined and utilized in the information models. In this manner, the way in which operations fulfill the above-noted twelve measures is easily documented.

INFORMATION MODELS

Requirement traceability information model. The modelling work for the present study was expressed as the following hypothesis (B.3.*i*, *i* = 1,4): *"It is possible to create information models that unambiguously specify the system."* The first model developed, the requirement traceability information model, is based on the conventional Entity-Relationship-Attribute (ERA) information diagram concept as described by, for example, Purves et al.[13] The ERA diagram offers a basic understanding of interactions among entities. The main purpose of the requirement traceability model is to show the flow of requirements from initial source documents to appropriate entities.

All requirements start somewhere. They may be derived, for example, from a stakeholder's expressed need, or from a document. The model identifies relationships between documents and requirements. High-level requirements typically give rise to lower-level documents, which themselves bring about even lower-level requirements. Each "leaf-level" requirement allocates one and only one function to any given stakeholder. Figure 2 presents a schematic of the requirement traceability model developed in this project.

The three source documents identified for this model are *public* documents, easily available in the public domain. The next lower level of documents is classified as *licensee's* documents, covering agreements between parties. These documents are subject to the Royal Norwegian Ministry of Petroleum and Energy's acceptance, and are confidential in nature. *Company* documents, such as working procedures and instructions, constitute the lowest level of documents.

Approximately ten types of licensee's documents were identified for the requirement traceability model, and ten types of company documents. Approximately 50 leaf-level requirements, total, specify functions.

System architecture information model. Figure 3 schematically illustrates the Norwegian dry gas transportation system. Borders are defined such that the system consists of two treatment terminal facilities (Kollsnes and Kårstø), two riser platform facilities (Sleipner riser platform, or SLR, and Draupner riser platform, or Dr), four shore terminal facilities on the European continent, and 11 pipelines. Belonging to external systems are two production fields (Sleipner and Oseberg) and a number of production fields upstream from the treatment terminals (not shown). Customer facilities downstream from the shore

---

[13] Purves et al. (1990).

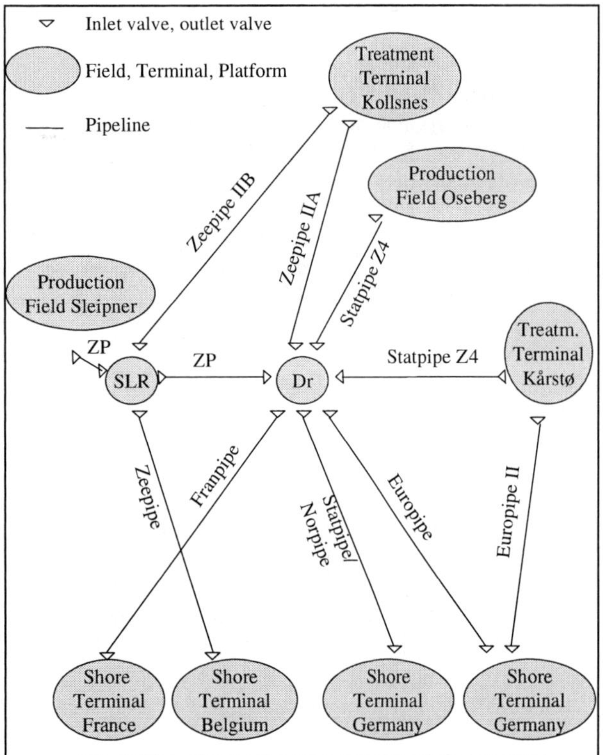

Fig 3 The physical components of the system

terminals also belong to the external system (not shown).

At each facility, a gas input and/or output valve is installed; between the output valve at one facility and the input valve at another facility, a pipeline is installed, connecting the facilities. This fairly obvious observation has significant implications guiding subsequent modelling and later research. First, the pipeline's configuration (length, diameter, internal coating condition, etc.) unambiguously defines its gas-flow capacities. Knowledge of these capacities and of how to optimize flow in the total pipeline network will be vital later in this research.

Secondly, many economic topics relating to the transport owner's tariffs are linked to gas flow in each pipeline.

Thirdly, from an operational point of view, the most interesting actions focus on the *set point values of flow and pressure* at each valve: in fact, all operational behavior eventually devolves to decisions about how to set each valve's gas pressure and gas flow values. Such implications were carefully considered in this research project's subsequent modelling of the system architecture and behavior.

According to INCOSE (1998), a system may be disaggregated to lower levels of systems and components. The top level, defined as *the system,* consists of "an integrated set of elements to accomplish the defined objective." Intermediate levels are defined, and the lowest level, each member of which is termed a *part,* is defined as "the lowest level of separately identifiable items." Figure 4 displays schematically the system architecture modelled for this project.

Behavior information model. Behavior can be understood at its most basic level in terms of functions, inputs and outputs to functions, ordering of functions, and how inputs trigger functions. In order to capture the different types of behavior occurring in transport operations, leaf-node requirements need to be grouped into classes.[14] Two classes were chosen for the present study: *behavioral requirements* and *nonbehavioral requirements.*[15]

Behavioral requirements specify the functions of a system, the operations, *inputs/outputs,* and all interfaces; behavioral requirements specify *what* a system or operation does. Behavioral requirements are disaggregated into three subclasses: *Preoperational* requirements concern planning, negotiating, and so on. *Operational* requirements relate to actual day-to-day operations. *Postoperational* requirements relate to the "day after"; for example, tariff requirements and requirements for issuing gas invoices to customers. Nonbehavioral requirements specify physical components and stakeholders.

The model identifies several *processes* that order the functions. Three main processes are modelled: *the dispatching process,* comprising four subprocesses; *the optimization process,* comprising six subprocesses; and the *handling of physical gas process.* Figure 5 illustrates a simplified extract from the part of the

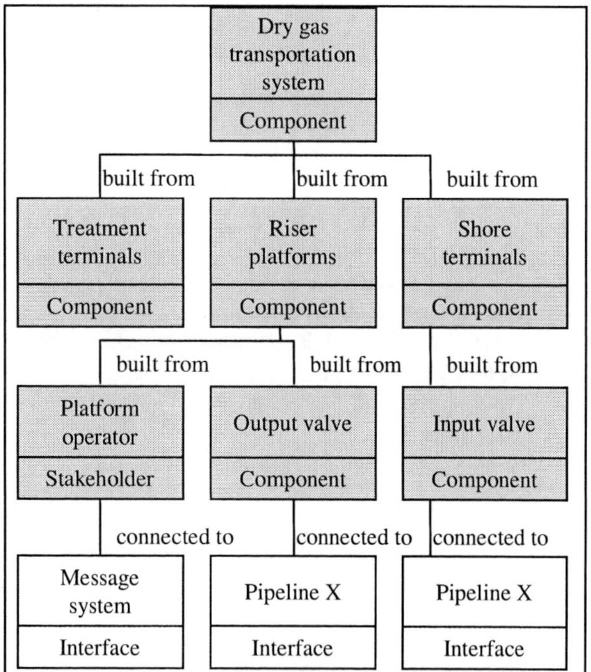

Fig. 4 The system architecture information model

[14] Asbjørnsen (1992).

[15] See also RDD-100 User Manual.

behavior information model dealing with the dispatching process.

The final behavioral model arose from several attempts; it did indeed result from iterative, creative activity (activity B.4).

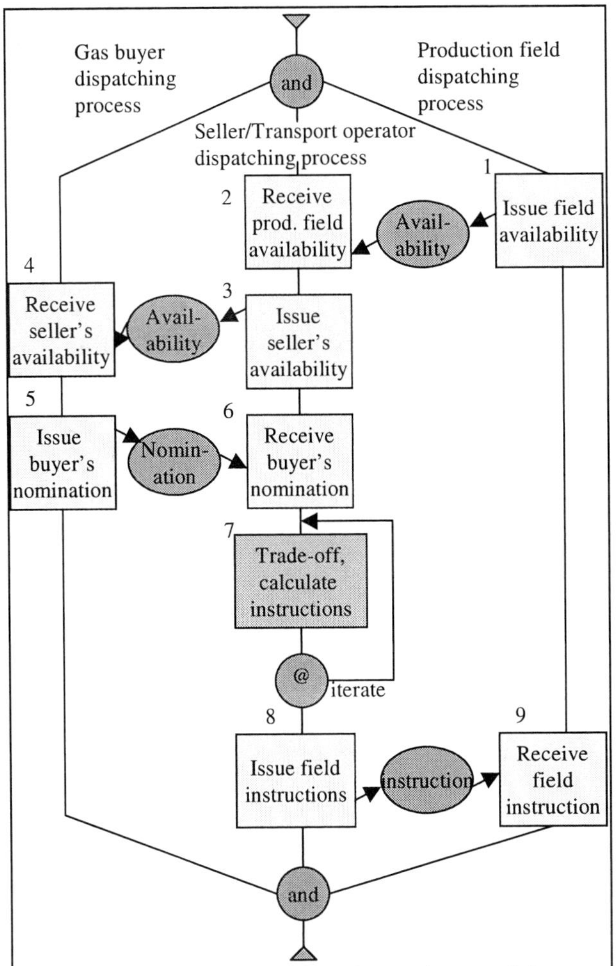

Fig. 5 The behaviour information model of the gas dispatching process

Context information model. The last conceptual model, the context information (or "interface") model, identifies the system's interfaces with surrounding systems and the environment. Figure 6 illustrates an extract of the context information model applied in this research project.

THE NEED FOR COMPUTER TOOLS

To model the available information, the author applied a specialized systems engineering computer tool (ALC's RDD-100[16]), for many reasons:[17] First, the information collected must be verified for accuracy. This requires neat and thorough work that, for practical reasons, ought to be computerized. If the work is done manually, errors are easily introduced. A computer program, on the other hand, first checks data for completeness and consistency.

An equally important feature of a systems engineering computer tool is its capability to develop information models. Each model specifies different aspects of the system. The important step of mapping models onto each other to verify consistency among them can also be done easily by a systems engineering computer tool, once data has been entered into the computer database. One example of this mapping feature is illustrated in Figures 2 and 5. These figures represent two models, both of which trace the same functions, numbered 2, 3, and 7.

Trade-offs and iterations (activity B.4) were performed with the computer program, and the program also "forced" data to be entered according to defined rules, helping the author to think logically, systematically, and holistically, as well as creatively. Results from the computer program were immediately visible, the data it accepted were accurate, and it performed consistency checks regularly. The author believes that the same level of data accuracy and creativity would have been very difficult (or at least time consuming) to achieve, had the work been done manually.

DISCUSSION

Primary reasons for re-engineering systems, as in this work, are to reduce the asymmetry in information typically present in this type of industry[18] and facilitate multidisciplinary communication.[19] The Storting (parliament) determines the framework for natural gas transport operations, the Norwegian state is a principal owner, and the Ministry has direct involvement as the approval body for agreements governing the licensees'

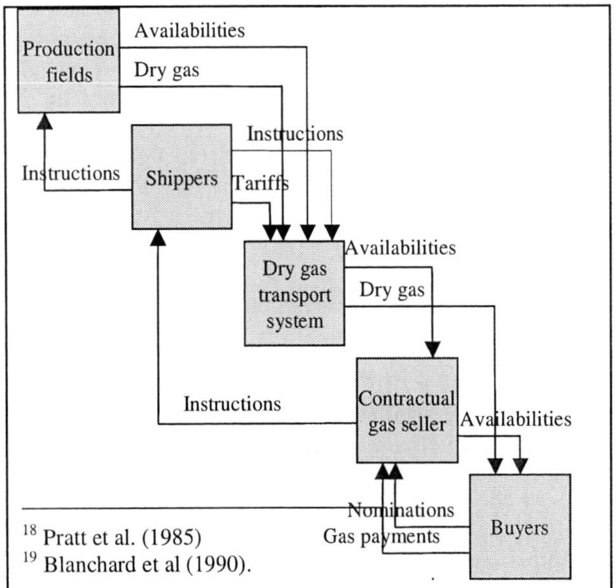

Fig. 6 The context information model

[16] RDD-100 User Manual (1996).

[17] See also Malcolm et al. (1993).

[18] Pratt et al. (1985)

[19] Blanchard et al (1990).

main activities. This industry thus involves several tiers of principal–agent relationships, and efficient information flow between principals and their agents is imperative, especially during transition periods.

The information models presented here are believed to offer one means for improving this type of information flow. Practitioners of different professions can "enter" the models at whatever point they feel confident, and from there, work into areas in which they are less knowledgeable.

Further, the dry gas transportation system has the characteristics of a natural monopoly, and legislative requirements must be aligned carefully with economic considerations and microeconomic theory.[20] Several of the effectiveness measures established by this work address such considerations, in general terms. The measures thus provide a framework for fully discussing such considerations.

The author would also like to emphasize, from a systems engineering point of view, a critical assumption underlying this work: that the systems re-engineering process and information modelling as presented in this paper distinctly differ from modelling work typically done to engineer new complex systems. The first difference, which is the main focus of this work, is that in this systems re-engineering process, stakeholders' actions are enhanced, whereas in traditional systems engineering, information models are utilized to engineer physical systems, as well. In a traditional engineering process, information models guide development of subsequent activities, such as the development of technical specifications and acquisition documents, and production, testing, and so on.

Another distinct difference is that constraints as applied in this work differ from those applied in modelling a new system. The models must accurately specify existing behavior, rather than suggest optimal behavior, which is a prime objective when designing a new system.

Finally, the models developed in this work are based on documentation assessment and interviews of select individuals. The collected information base is somewhat asymmetrical, as some relevant stakeholders were not interviewed. It is believed, though, that most major issues were covered, and that the models can be corrected easily if misunderstandings or discrepancies are identified.

CONCLUDING REMARKS

The following section offers some industry-related conclusions in order to show the level of inferences that can be drawn from knowledge obtained through information modelling.

The hypothesis (B.0) proved to be true. Systems engineering theory was applied to Norwegian dry gas transport operations, and systems re-engineering resulted in four types of information models and 12 effectiveness measures.

The models specify operations and trace relationships between documents, requirements, components, stakeholders, and behavior; they also show how well the success criteria specified by the effectiveness measures are complied with. A specialized systems engineering computer tool tested each information model in order to increase the accuracy of the results and the coherence of the models.

The models document that Norwegian natural gas transport operations are integrated, and that services to customers are bundled. Operations aim to simultaneously meet many overall requirements, among which resource management, socioeconomic utilization, and high regularity in gas delivery are prominent. The current regulatory regime is based on the Norwegian Petroleum Act, which requires the Royal Norwegian Ministry of Petroleum and Energy to accept all agreements entered into between licensees, except for the lowest-level company procedures.

One observation made is that vital features of operations optimization are based on requirements stated in documents issued at company levels, but higher-level documents only briefly specify relevant requirements. This asymmetry in information complicates external bodies' assessment of transport operations' optimization, and limits understanding of the nature of bundling services currently being provided. This work, however, has modelled the optimization process conceptually, thus clarifying the matter.

Analysis of the behavior models has identified three major trade-offs being made in day-to-day operations. The first relates to prioritizing requirements for gas-upstream arrangements relative to requirements for buyer nominations. The second trade-off evaluates various possible means to utilize operational flexibility and "linepacking" (i.e., adjusting a pipeline's gas inventory) in order to optimize operations. The final trade-off of note involves a consideration of contractually identified preferences in light of the actual physical handling of gas streams in the pipeline system.

REFERENCES

Asbjørnsen, O.A. (1992), "Systems engineering principles and practices," *Department of Thermal Energy and Hydro Power*, Norwegian University of Science and Technology (NTNU), Trondheim.

Bahill, A.T., and Dean, F.F. (1996), "What Is Systems Engineering? A Consensus of Senior Systems Engineers," *Proceedings of the Sixth Annual International Symposium of the International Council on Systems Engineering (INCOSE)* (Boston, USA, July), vol. I, pp. 503-508.

Blanchard, S.B., and Fabrycky, W.J. (1990), "Systems

[20] IEA (1994)

Engineering and Analysis," *Prentice Hall,* Englewood Cliffs, New Jersey, USA.

Dahl, H.J. (1999), "Systems engineering and Statoil natural gas transport operations," *Proceedings of the Ninth Annual International Symposium of the International Council on Systems Engineering (INCOSE)* (Brighton, UK, June), vol. II, pp. 791-798.

Fact Sheet (1999), "Norwegian Petroleum Activity," *Ministry of Petroleum and Energy*, Oslo. See <http//odin.dep.no/oed/eng/>.

Hitchins, D.K., Boarder, J.C., Moore, and Borgan, I. (1999), "Guide to the Practice of Systems Engineering," *Structured Software Systems*, Henley-on-Thames, UK.

International Energy Agency (IEA) (1994), "Natural gas transportation, organization and regulation," *OECD,* Paris, France.

Ilstad, S. (1998), "Lecture in Methodology," Course: "Psychology in organisation and management." *Department of Industrial Economics and Technology Management,* Norwegian University of Science and Technology (NTNU), Trondheim.

INCOSE (1998), "Systems Engineering Handbook," Release 1.0, January 1998, *San Francisco Bay Area Chapter,* USA.

King, G., Keohane, R.O., and Verba, S. (1994), "Designing Social Inquiry: Scientific Inference in Qualitative Research," *Princeton University Press*, Princeton, New Jersey, USA.

Malcolm, N., and Alford, M. (1993), "Systems Engineering: Its Roots, Its Future," *Ascent Logic Corporation*, San Jose, USA.

Oliver, D.W., Kelliher, T.P., and Keegan, J.G. (1997), "Engineering Complex Systems with Models and Objects," *McGraw-Hill,* New York, USA.

Oliver, D.W. (1999), "Concept Analysis: Modelling and Organisation Transformation," *Proceedings of the Ninth Annual International Symposium of the International Council on Systems Engineering (INCOSE)* (Brighton, UK, June), vol. II, pp. 1445-1451.

Pratt, J.W., and Richard, J.Z., (1985), "Principal and Agents: The Structure of Business," *Harvard Business School Press*, Boston, USA.

Purves, B., and Baker, L. (1998), "Information Models as a Prerequisite to Software Tool Interoperability," *INCOSE Insight*, Fall 1998, Vol. 1, Issue 3, Seattle, Washington, USA.

RDD-100 User Manual (1996), "ALC Training Course 101, Introduction to RDD-100, Student Workbook, version 1.3," *Ascent Logic Corporation*, San Jose, USA.

Selvig, E. (1995), "Petroleum Law," *Sjørettsfondet*, University of Oslo (in Norwegian).

R. Stevens, P. Brook, K Jackson, and S Arnold (1998), "Systems Engineering: Coping with Complexity," *Prentice Hall Europe*, London, UK.

Thome, B. (1993), "Systems Engineering: Principles and Practice of Computer-based Systems Engineering," *Wiley,* Chichester, UK.

White Paper No. 46 (1997-98), "Olje- og gassvirksomheten," *Ministry of Petroleum and Energy*, Oslo (in Norwegian). See <http//odin.dep.no/nou/>.

ACKNOWLEDGEMENTS

The author would like to thank Statoil for its kind and generous support during this study.

BIOGRAPHY

Hans Jørgen Dahl received a MSc in mechanical engineering from the Norwegian Institute of Technology (NTH) in Trondheim in 1977 and is currently working on a doctoral thesis (Dr.ing) at the Norwegian University of Science and Technology (NTNU), Trondheim. He has worked in the Norwegian oil and gas industry since 1979: with Det Norske Veritas for eight years, the Kværner group for two years, and Statoil for the past 11 years. Mr Dahl has held various senior engineer and management positions in Norway and abroad. His latest positions in Statoil were as operations manager, heading the Bygnes Transport Control Center for five years, and as project manager for transport and business development the following 18 months. Dahl is currently a visiting researcher for one year at the Center for Energy and Environmental Policy Research at MIT in Cambridge, Massachusetts. From summer 2000, his contacting information will be:

Bygnes Transport Control Centre, Statoil
P.O. Box 308, N-5501 Haugesund, NORWAY
HJD@Statoil.com

Effective Control in Peopled Systems

Jack Ring
Kennen, Inc.
32712 N. 70th St.
Scottsdale, AZ

Abstract. This paper suggests approaches to and guidelines for installing, instilling and inspiring control in peopled systems. These guidelines apply to mission systems, to the projects that produce mission systems and to organizations which determine the competencies and culture of the project teams. With the right control peopled systems can be highly efficient and highly innovative, simultaneously.

A REVIEW OF CONTROL TERMINOLOGY

James Watt's simple flyball governor has been cited as the trigger of the industrial revolution. Later, Norbert Weiner's cybernetics triggered an era of increasingly larger and more effective information and control systems. Although abundant literature exists for designing systems composed of hardware and software not much literature exists regarding control in, of, and by systems that depend on people. The people factor is significant because non-peopled systems are generally state-determined and predictable whereas peopled systems can exhibit quite surprising behavior.

For context, Figure 1 illustrates the ontology of control for regarding the scope of this paper.

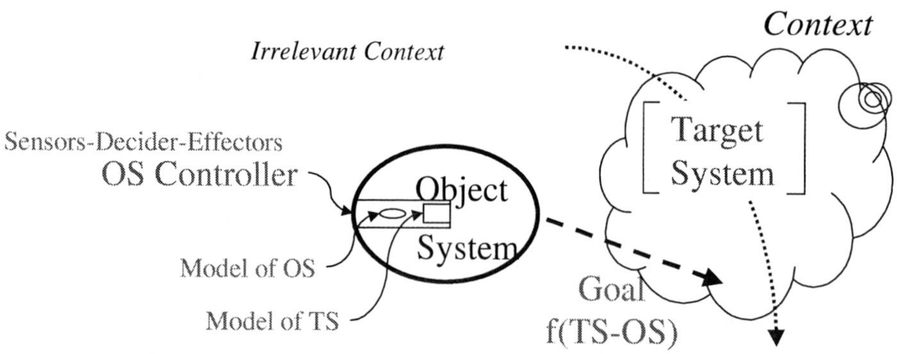

OS	Goal	TS
Missile	Intercept	Aircraft
Aircraft	Safe transit	Airspace
Salesman	Sell Aircraft	Airline
Proj. Mgr.	Reward	Project Completion
SE	Reward	System Effectiveness

Figure 1. Ontology of Control

A Target System, TS, is moving through a coordinate system. The coordinate system may be spatial, temporal, gravitational, or any combination of these and other forms. An Object System, OS, located in the same coordinate system, seeks to achieve a specified relationship with TS. This relationship specification is the OS Goal that the OS seeks to achieve. For example, the goal may be to detect the TS or to describe the TS or to measure the TS or to shadow, pace, intercept, displace or collide with the TS. In addition to pursuing a relationship with respect to the TS the Goal may be concerned with causing the OS to morph into a different form or structure such as increasing the rate of OS operation, mimicing the TS or becoming invisible to the TS.

The OS has Context which consists of the TS and of other pertinent relationships and entities including distubances to both TS and OS. The OS has Other_Context which consists of all the stuff that doesn't make any difference to achieving the Goal. Finally, the OS has Control in the form of one or more controllers which may be within, partially within or outside the OS. The purpose of the Control is to achieve the goal regarding either the TS-OS relationship or the OS content, structure or behavior.

MODEL-BASED CONTROL

Higher performance controllers contain a model of the system to be controlled. For example, the operators of an crude oil refinery use a process control system to maximize refinery output. Such process control system measures temperatures, pressures and flows at more than 150 locations throughout the refinery. The control system then decides which situations need to be adjusted and makes the adjustments in the right sequence. This occurs several times per minute. The control system contains a model of the refinery that consists of several hundred equations which represent what happens to crude oil under a program of temperature and pressure with specific catalysts present. The process control system, by solving these equations often enough, can control the proportion of gasoline, kerosene, heating oil, and other products extracted from each barrel of crude. Further, when the market changes the demand for gasoline vs. home heating oil, management can easily respond to by changing the set points in the process control system. The system, in turn, will cause the desired ratio of output products to change.

.Note that real process control focuses on results as well as the process that produces the results. Although the process is the subject of control the results are the object of control. This is an important distinction because much current literature regarding management, business process reengineering, systems engineering standards and capability maturity emphasizes process without relating process to results and outcomes adequately.

So much for an oil refinery. How does a manager make an organization highly efficient and highly innovative? By bringing that organization under control, toward specific goals, with a controller that contains a model of the organization as a system. Such controller will measure orders, inventory, employee enthusiasm, resource utilization levels, inventory levels, cash and numerous other variables. It will decide which are mutually consistent and which are out of bounds. It will make adjustments to the business rules to bring the organization to a state that causes its outputs to meet expectations.

Bringing a team, project or organization under control requires a mental model of; work products, events; and activities as well as a model of how activities are supposed to transpire and the roles, responsibilities, and authorities for making it all happen. Additionally, that model must have high fidelity with the real world. Quality management guru, Phil Crosby summed it up best, "As the organization grows the leader finds it harder to know what is going on and nearly impossible to know what is not going on." In fact, the only way a leader can detect what is not happening is by having an *a priori* model of expectations and a report-by-exception scorecard. And hueristics indicate that these become pertinent by the time the team reaches as few as fifteen people.

Dynamic Stability: Helicopters and hummingbirds are instructive examples. Both have dynamic stability. When aerodynamicists declared that the hummingbird could not fly they had not yet understood dynamic stability even though many of them had been riding bicycles for years. Like a hummingbird a helicopter is both stable and maneuverable because it has a very effective control system. In fact, a high proportion of the cost of a helicopter is the cost of its controls.

Dynamic stability applies in peopled systems, as well. Under a control system capable of producing dynamic stability peopled system can achieve high levels of stability and maneuverability simultaneously. A dynamically stable project can outperform ad hoc projects or rules-driven projects or competitor-mimicing projects which emphasize benchmarking and best practices. Further, the project can progress from seeking tactical goals to seeking strategic goals to seeking self improvement goals. Some even achieve the ability to perform as distributed, virtual, collaborative projects.

Controller Content: A controller is made up of four basic subsystems (Bateson 1993):

1. **Sensor.** Measures and reports state of assigned variables.
2. **Evaluator.** Collects sensor data and, using its OS-TS model, interprets all sensor reports for maximum likelihood representation of the TS-OS situation. Selects appropriate criteria for mission/objective/goal of OS because the applicable

criteria may depend on the perceived situation. Performs mensuration or applies judgement to ascertain degree of gaps between situation and criteria

3. **Decider**. Assesses significance of gaps. Performs Root Cause Analysis to identify the sources of and/or reasons for the gaps. Decides what changes may be transpiring in the TS. Decides what changes are desired in the TS-OS relationship. Decides what changes are desired in the OS. Selects most appropriate effectors of the changes. Updates the TS-OS model. Commands a scenario of effector actions. Actions scenarios are limited by design -- primarily to minimize cost. Typical action scenarios are; bang-bang (as in the household thermostat), proportional or PID (as in HVAC and most industriall process control) and Goal-seeking (as in air-air missiles, orchestras, race teams and agile enterprises.)
4. **Effector.** Make and verify changes to the variables each control. Does not verify that desired OS-level behaviors resulted. That must await the next cycle of sense-evaluate-decide.

Effectiveness factors: If more resources are dedicated to control of operations then the operations may become more efficient and more maneuverable. However, there are limits. The expense of added control begins to offset the value of incremental improvements in system performance.

The initial and on-going cost of control is largely determined by the competency of the control system developer when designing the system. At least five factors must be balanced: objective of control, variety of behavior exhibited by the TS, method of maintaining the OS-TS model, inertia of the OS (due to size, complexity, and fear), contextual disturbances and disturbances internal to the controller, such as failures.

The factors affecting the effectiveness vs. cost gradient are:

1. **Model Fidelity:** The controller is not dealing directly with the physical world but with a model of the physical world. Accordingly, the performance and even integrity of control is directly dependent upon the fidelity of the TS-OS model relative to the real world OS and TS. Although obvious in electromechanical control systems, this fundamental is often overlooked in peopled systems. Hardly any organization has a high fidelity model of their business development process, system design process, development process, etc.
2. **Acuity:** The degree to which the process control system can sense or know about all the events and conditions throughout the system under control. Design decisions must include granularity, discrimmination, and coverage
3. **Latency:** The time delay between and event and the control system cognizance of that event. The dramatic effect of latency is described in (Senge 1994). For example, businesses are making current investments in systems for Data Warehousing, Data Mining and Balanced Scorecards. Although many of these investments produce previously unknown and sometimes startling facts about the users market, customers, production, people, etc. these reports are using data that was true 30 to 90 days earlier. As W. Edwards Demming remarked, "That is like trying to drive through Tokyo in rush hour using only your rear view mirror."
4. **Accuracy:** means how closely the process control system can adjust the outcomes to the desired conditions. A significant factor in accuracy is the fidelity of the model contained in the process control system software relative to the real world it is supposed to represent. This is why model fidelity is a measure of management effectiveness.
5. **Power:** The power level of effectors vs. inertia of the system being controlled.
6. **Distance:** The separation, in time and space, between the actual operation and the controller. Distance may be secondary but greatly affects acuity, latency, and the accuracy of situation assessments.

CHOICES OF CONTROL OBJECTIVE

The control systems engineer must be very clear on the objectives of control. Beyond open-loop or ballistic systems in which no control is exercised after the system is put into operation there are at least five distinct categories of control objectives.

Homeostatic: Seeks to maintain a variable at a constant state despite changes in other variables. Model is simple and static. An examples are: human body (OS) temperature at 98.6 regardless of external ambient temperature (TS). House thermostat set at X. Customer is always right. Featherbedding by unions. The relative cost is Low.

Pursuit: Seeks to achieve a specified relationship to a target system regardless of changes in the relative location of the target system. Model of TS is simple and of OS a little more comprehensive. Model must be updated as often as the situation changes. Examples are: dog chasing car, smart bomb, house "setback" thermometer, and new product/process development team. Relative cost is Medium

Goal-seeking: Seeks to improve performance in the OS pursuit of a TS and simultaneously direct the evolution of the OS into a more effective pursuer. Model is more comprehensive than in the pursuit case and is updated in strucuture and well as situational data. Examples are: variable suspension on automobiles, aircraft changing speed or altitude during turbulence, staffing a project based on the risks to be mitigated instead seniority, and changing your normal persona when talking to your boss. Relative cost is High.

A Goal-seeking System, GSS, consists of; a **goal** that orients the system or gives it purpose, a **trigger** that causes the system to function, **.competency** that informs the system on what to do, **energy** that enables the sysstem to do it at the required rate, **statusing** that objectively assesses the gap between the system state and its goal and **feedback** (acutally, feedforward) that causes the system to direct its competencies and energy toward closing the gap (Livingston).

A GSS goes beyond Pursuit control by additionally changing OS structure and content. A GSS can even change the context that the OS will acknowledge in the future. Two subtypes of GSS that are emerging with the complex, adaptive systems movement are:

Autopoietic: Seeks to expand envelope of control by changing internal structure of OS to better cope with dynamics of TS and intertia of OS. Examples are: factory changeover for new model year, adding objectives for supplier satisfaction and employee satisfaction in addition to customer satisfaction, changing design team makeup as new challenges are uncovered during a project, and open book management. Relative Cost is Very High but trending to to Low

Autocatalytic: Seeks improved performance of OS mission through proactive collaboration with other systems. Includes modularizing and distributing the OS for multiple but orchestrated interaction with the TS. Examples are: formation flying (vs. solo dog fighting), a wolf pack, a kieretsu, a clique or a club. The more advanced forms of web-enabled eBusiness, beyond eCommerce, tend toward autocatalytic. Relative cost is Very High but trending to Low.

TRI-PURPOSE CONTROL

Peopled, goal-seeking systems embody a tri-purpose controller in order to accommodate the variability of the TS system as well as the content, structure and behavior of the OS. These three purposes are Operations Control, Supervisory Control and Alignment Control.

Alignment Control sets the stage and all three collaborate to follow the rules for sustaining dynamic stability or for ringing the alarm when the behavior of the TS gets outside the OS's envelope of operational capability. Supervisory control coordinates or orchestrates the individual operations controllers which are concerned primarily with nulling variances from planned operations.

A peopled GSS involves double-loop learning. It not only learns how to pursue the goal even if the TS is evasive or the OS is recalcitrant but also learns how to learn. This is important to peopled systems in general and to those desiring to perform world-class systems engineering in particular. For example, a practitioner (lawyer, doctor, or musician) is not marked solely by his domain of knowledge but also by his ability to apply ascending levels of behavior to the needs of his clients, in this case the TS. (Schon 1987). An advanced practitioner has two kinds of knowing; objectivist and constructivist (world making) and excels not only in familiar situations, marked by the routine application of facts, rules, procedures, but also in unfamiliar situations, marked by the the practitioner not only recognizing givens but also discerning "what is going on, here."

Design Reviews: The well known activity of a design review makes a good frame of reference for putting all the foregoing into one picture. There can be several ways of doing a design review (when or how often? how thorough? against what checklist? with formal discrepancy reports,? is complete when the discrepancies are found or when they are closed?). The "best" flavor may be different for each project. But above the level of accomplishing some flavor of design review there are further considerations.

After the discrepancies are found and communicated, some companies take the trouble to reflect and learn from Design Reviews. They ask the question "What was the root cause of each discrepancy?" and require the answer before moving on to the next phase of the project (because the answer typically reveals a systemic problem which discovery can be used to find other errors that even the Design Review missed.) At this level, there may be very little difference between which style of review is best for one project vs. another.

At an "action learning" level, a Design Review Team, as they begin to see a pattern of discrepancies, modifies their own checklist or their allocation of time and effort to pay more attention to "weak spots" in the design. Clearly, this is the most effective team behavior for any project, providing, of course that it doesn't cost more than the value of the outcomes it produces.

At the "reflection in action" level a Design Review Team would discover their own errors (both Type 1 and Type 2), as well as the designers' errors. Also, they would discern why they were making errors, and change their competency mix or change their allocation of time and effort to preclude such errors. Once again, this is the most effective team behavior for any project, providing, of course that it doesn't cost more than the value of the outcomes it produces..

CONTROL SYSTEM ARCHITECTURES

It is now appropriate to turn to the topic of how the tri-purpose control can be architected and how the architecture will determine the effectiveness of mission pursuit and accomplishment. Five forms of control are pertinent; Authoritarian, Oversight, Process Office, Embedded and the Systemic.

The Systemic mode will show about 100X better acuity and responsiveness than Authoritarian but can be harder to install and sustain in peopled systems. On the other hand if done right the cost of systemic control can be less than all the other styles.

The **Authoritarian** form of controller needs little introduction. This style allows no action that is not directed from "Headquarters" through Policies, Procedures, Rules -- and dismissals. Typically it uses the bang-bang scenario and seeks stasis in order to "keep on keeping on" even while the enterprise becomes non-competitive.

The **Oversight** Committee controller reviews past events, actions and outcomes and discerns which were appropriate and which not and then recommends new rules or guidance for such situations if they reoccur. An oversight controller typically is located some distance in space and time from the real action, thus usually several months behind the real world events. Examples are an oversight committee in the U.S. Congress or an annual CMM® Assessment of your organization. Oversight control has built in limitations in acuity, model fidelity and latency. It is the less expensive control architecture when only the cost of the controller is considered but may be very expensive if the cost of inaccurate control of outcomes is considered.

A Process Office, a recent invention of the organizational psychologists, is similar to an Oversight Committee but is closer to the action thus does not suffer the time delays and chances of mis-information endemic to Oversight. However, the Process Manager not directly involved in producing the deliverable work products of the the organization. In the "ham and eggs" analogy of commitment, the production manager is the pig and the process manager is the hen.

The **Embedded** style is woven into the OS at the scene of the action. Relative to Oversight the time delays are further reduced, model fidelity is futher improved and the decision rules are more likely to be updated when business objectives change. Autonomous vehicles rely on embedded control. When people are involved they become invested in the outcomes of the project even though their primary responsibility is for the methods of producing the outcomes.

The final form, called **Systemic** control, is quite different. In this form instead of one controller which contains the model of the OS and TS and to which all the data flows there are "N" controllers which are interconnected for collaborative control. This style of control does not work well until each of the controllers has a mutual model of the TS-OS and consistent goals for their aspect of the OS. But once each controller has these, systemic control is far more performant at far less cost than other forms. In people terms, each individual is brought to an understanding of enterprise Mission, Market, Strategy, Structure, Objectives and Process all ensured by shared Values. No model of the effectors is required because each person is the action system. The systemic form of control seeks "control from within" or, as coined by Peter Senge, "control without controlling." In this form, a manager ensures (by role modeling) that sufficient shared values (principles) and vision (purpose and meaning) exist and that each element has the fundamental behavior patterns needed to survive (plan, organize, integrate and measure is an upper level pattern and plan, do, check, adjust is a lower level pattern). Finally, the manager facilitates and ensures the setting of standards in terms of goals and objectives at a level that will ensure success in the face of competition, shortage of resources, and other adversities.

This form of controlling peopled systems has been around since the Halls of Montezuma and the Shores of Tripoli and modern management writers are re-describing it in the terminology of chaos theory and complex-adaptive systems. The power and promise of this is illustrated by the BOIDS simulation which Craig Reynolds demonstrated in 1987. BOIDS may not have completely explained the complexity of the flight patterns exhibited by a flock starlings as fascinated the poet, Colerige, in 1799 (Whyte 1994), but close enough.

The key to success in this form of control is the consistency and coherency of the rules and goals "instilled" in each individual. In the BOIDS simulation there was not a problem because each BOID followed identical rules. But in the world of systems which contain humans we have no such assurance. In fact, one of the often mentioned "truisms" is that one group of people will invariably act in a way that optimizes their domain and inevitably degrades the system of which they are part. In system dynamics literature this is called the Tragedy of The Commons. However, (Wymore 1997) has shown that there are conditions under which this is not true -- that a system performs optimally when each of its subsystems performs optimally. For this condition to be met the individuals do not have to have identical goals but they do have to have goals which are complementary (coherent) and consistent. This has been further explored and elucidated in (Axelrod 1997).

SYSTEMIC CONTROL IS FREE

It started 2,500 years ago. In 508 B.C. a Greek philosopher articulated an astounding idea -- that people are capable of governing themselves with laws devised by themselves.

It continues today. The author has frequently experienced that people can a) perform a task while b) operating as part of a process, while c) operating at the level of principles. And most people are most happy, thus most productive, innovative and collaborative, when operating on all three levels simultaneously.

Clearly, we have a lot of learning to do about what to install, instill and inspire in the individuals who comprise control. But the point is, systemic control, by avoiding the deleterious time delays and misinformation of an external controller, is the right way to go and is more compatible with the way people work, think and feel.

Systemic control, like quality, is free. It is not cheap nor easy to attain but pays back far more that it costs. And it is largely achieved by appropriately modeling the TS-OS and architecting a GSS. Consequently, a leader's challenge is to put his/her energy into establishing meaningful and

Each style of control is a tradeoff in cost vs. performance. The Authoritarian style produces minimum levels of both. The Customer Oversight style (typical of government procurements) produces a higher level of dynamic stability and can produce very high levels of productivity at the expense of maneuverability and vise versa. Higher levels of dynamic stability are produced by the Process Office, whether it be in the form of a GSE/TD contractor on government projects or the Process Management office in commercial enterprises. Goal-seeking Workgroups are even better. These are not to be confused with "self-managed teams" which all too often have unclear purpose and insufficient authority. Goal-seeking Workgroups do not yield the best dynamic stability, however, because each group has a distinct purpose (as in subsystem) which still invokes delay and ambiguity during collaboration among the groups. Not until the goal-seeking workgroups are brought to a level of mutual understanding and purpose, where each workgroup is both a system and a part of a larger system, does system dynamic stability occur and "control without controlling" become possible.

OUR OPPORTUNITY

Think of your own responsibilities and what happens when you can't be everywhere at all times. What happens to your acuity, latency and decider? What would happen if your responsibilities were doubled? What if your team just knew what to do in every situation?

Given that we now know about how to create emergent behavior by installing rules locally in the elements of the system, the question becomes whether we are smart enough to write the "rules for managers." Also, it is clear that an optimizing organization, to the degree it means 'neat and orderly,' is not a desirable sufficient goals instead of trying to exercise corrective control. Improving and optimizing, in the adaptive sense, are not enough. The preferred behavior is 'exploring and recouping.' As Prof. Azides has pointed out (Adizes 1988), the non-innovating organization is near death.

Figure 2 shows the characteristic functions of cost effectiveness for the three main choices of control..

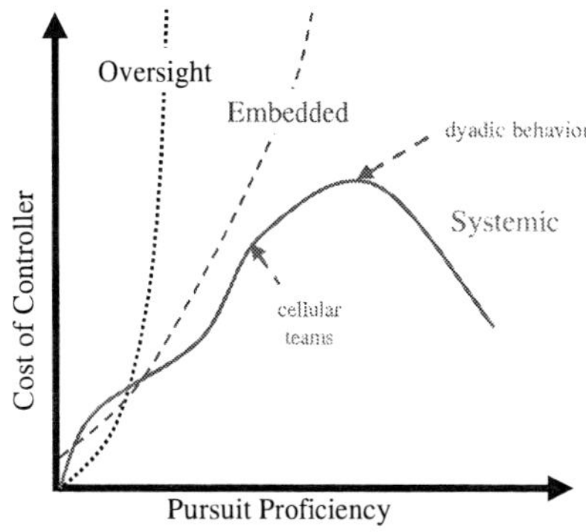

Figure 2. Cost Effectiveness of Choices

Oversight control is low cost but cannot cope with any but trivial pursuit. Embedded control can achieve higher levels of pursuit proficiency but gets more costly and evenutally limits regardless of cost. Systemic control costs more than the others even for modest pursuit proficiency because more participants have to be involved and have common purpose, goals and mental models of their roles in the process. But as this community of thought takes hold, higher levels of pursuit proficiency are achieved. A maximum is reached when the team learns to learn. Subsequently, increased pursuit proficiency can be had at decreasing cost of control.

Those wanting to explore systemic control in peopled systems should pay close attention to four heuristics:

MYOB - Model Your Own Business: Just as model fidelity is critical to TS-OS control it is equally critical when the TS is a yet-to-be-created system design and the OS is your team and their work context. You must lead the modeling of your own business and remember that the model must be available to and understood by all.

Treat your (part of the) organization as a system: Select the type of control and the control architecture based on the possible (not probable) future behaviors of the TS. Understanding the possibilities in the Problem Space is mandatory.

Use only the best components -- People who can: dialog, innovate (because continuous improvement is not sufficiently robust to deal with the punctuated equilibrium of your TS), and can establish meaningful and sufficient goals instead of trying to exercise corrective control.

Tend your fences: Left to itself a peopled system drifts toward spending an increasing proportion of its energy in random behaviors that are not aligned with the system's purpose. People, the sole source of software bugs, are also the source of "organizational noise." A good controller must be vigilant at detecting and nulling variances, both what is going on that should not be and what is not going on that should be.

SUMMARY

An organization can be controlled toward meaningful and mutually consistent goals. Organizational objectives can range from "make no errors" to "follow the rules" to "make the rules" to "zero defects." The principle of requisite variety demands that the method of control, whether oversight, embedded or systemic, must be consistent with the objectives and the dynamics of the situation. The controller must contain a model of the organization context, content, structure and behavior. Several variables must be considered when designing a controller. Designing the cheaper controller may result in wasting dramatically more money nf undesirable system outcomes. The best models of organizations are built by members of the organization. The finest models should be expected from systems engineering organizations.

REFERENCES

Adizes, I,, "Corporate Lifecycles." pg 87-88, Prentice Hall, 1988

Axelrod, R., "The Complexity of Cooperation." Princeton University Press, 1997

Bateson, R., "Introduction to Control Systems Technology." 1993

Livingston, W. "Friends in High Places." FES Publishing, Stuart, FL, 1982

Schon, D. "Educating the Reflective Practitioner." Jossey-Bass, 1987

Senge, P. et al, "The Fifth Discipline Fieldbook." pg173, Doubleday, 1994

Whyte, D., "The Heart Aroused." pg 215, Currency Doubleday, 1994

Wymore, A. Wayne, 1997, *Subsystem Optimization Implies System Suboptimization: Not!,* see www.sie.arizona.edu/faculty/wymore.html

BIOGRAPHY

Jack Ring earned his undergraduate degree in physics from Emporia State College, Kansas. He used his twenty years with GE, ten with Honeywell and ten as a coach to high tech executives as a learning laboratory about systems, people and management. He continues coaching regarding strategy, process, organization and innovation by treating the business enterprise as a complex, adaptive. Jack especially enjoys working with organizations of less than 200 people -- because they can still be helped.

Assessment of Systems Engineering Compliance in a Facilities Environment*

R. R. Matty
Sverdrup Technology, Inc.
678 2nd Street
Arnold Air Force Base, TN 37389-4401
rosemary.matty@arnold.af.mil

Abstract. The test facilities at Arnold Engineering Development Center are unique and complex, involving many different engineering disciplines. Recently, formal systems engineering methodologies have been applied to projects to upgrade, maintain, and repair these facilities. This paper describes a method to evaluate how well project teams are adhering to systems engineering techniques.

ARNOLD ENGINEERING DEVELOPMENT CENTER

Located in middle Tennessee, the Arnold Engineering Development Center (AEDC) has helped ensure American aerospace superiority since 1951. AEDC is one of the world's largest complexes of highly versatile test facilities comprised of wind tunnels, propulsion test cells, space chambers, and hyperballistic ranges and tunnels. Figure 1 is an aerial view of AEDC. AEDC's mission is to support the development of aerospace systems, both public and private, by testing hardware in these facilities.

The U. S. Air Force owns and manages the infrastructure. Sverdrup Technology, Inc., AEDC Group is under contract to operate and maintain the test facilities. Although AEDC belongs to the U.S. Air Force, it runs like a business in that it depends upon test customers to provide a portion of operating and maintenance costs. Reduced defense budgets and fewer new DOD aerospace programs have driven AEDC to aggressively seek new ways, such as a formal Systems Engineering (SE) program, to become more efficient and effective.

Although AEDC had been using some SE from its inception, the SE process was first formalized in 1995 by *AEDC-STD-SE-1, Systems Engineering*. AEDC has been successful in obtaining Air Force funding for projects to upgrade and modernize essential test facilities, which will improve throughput, increase capabilities, and reduce future costs. Other projects involve the maintenance and repair of these unique facilities. Managing these facilities-related projects in compliance with the SE techniques in *AEDC-STD-SE-1* is crucial to AEDC's future.

As our SECM office trained the project managers and engineers, we found that while many of them were receptive to formalized SE, some did not necessarily welcome the thought of added paperwork. The SE office needed a way to determine how well *AEDC-STD-*

Figure 1. Aerial View of Arnold Engineering Development Center

* The research reported herein was performed by the Arnold Engineering Development Center (AEDC), Air Force Materiel Command. Work and analysis for this research were performed by personnel of Sverdrup Technology, Inc., AEDC Group, technical services contractor for AEDC. Further reproduction is authorized to satisfy needs of the U. S. Government.

SE-1 was being applied to projects.

AEDC's facilities are divided into three business areas corresponding to the primary types of services provided by each facility group: Aeropropulsion, Aerodynamic, and Space and Missiles. We decided to develop a process to assess each of these business areas for SE compliance as they managed their investment projects.

DEVELOPING THE SE ASSESSMENT PROCESS

Consistency was one of our major concerns in developing this process. Since different systems engineers in the office would be assessing each business area, the process needed to be as objective as possible.

We followed a multistep approach for developing the assessment criteria. The first step was to determine which areas of systems engineering would be used as indicators. The team chose the use of the Integrated Master Plan (IMP) and the conduct of Design Reviews as two fundamental areas that could reflect the SE status of each business area.

The second step was to define the standards for assessing these indicators. Because AEDC has used rating systems based on color for other contractual evaluations, the team adopted a similar system. We chose the following color ratings to use in this process:

- Blue is outstanding.
- Green is satisfactory.
- Yellow indicates improvement is needed.
- Red indicates an unacceptable level of conformance.

INTEGRATED MASTER PLAN/INTEGRATED MASTER SCHEDULE (IMP/IMS)

The IMP is a compilation of important accomplishments, each with measurable criteria, requiring successful completion to pass identified events. Events include technical reviews and audits, demonstration milestones, and decision points. Accomplishments include major and critical tasks, activities, and demonstrations. Accomplishment criteria are measurable indicators of successful completion of the associated accomplishment; they can include completed work efforts and demonstrations of technical performance. The IMP is event-based and not calendar-based.

The Integrated Master Schedule (IMS) is the detailed, time-dependent, task-oriented schedule of the work required to accomplish the complete, integrated effort and its relationship to the events, accomplishments, and accomplishment criteria identified in the IMP. The IMS shows detailed progress of the work efforts, including tasks for the continual assessment of the technical parameters.

Each project has a unique IMP/IMS. In essence, the combination of IMP and IMS defines and documents how the Project Manager and the Project Team apply SE practices described in *AEDC-STD-SE-1* to a particular project. However, the process for developing an IMP/IMS should be consistent for all projects. The team broke the IMP/IMS development process into four tasks to evaluate.

The first task is to complete the IMP by considering all tasks described in *AEDC-STD-SE-1* and to document that they have been considered. Doing no IMP at all would be unacceptable and would earn a red rating. Putting forth a minimal or cursory effort in the IMP would merit a yellow rating indicating a need for improvement. Displaying an understanding of SE would earn a green, or satisfactory rating. To earn the highest rating, blue, the project team would have to use the SE principles to overcome obstacles and improve the project.

The second task in the IMP/IMS area is to consider how a project fits into the long-range plan for the business area. If the project failed to take long-range planning into account, it would get a red. If only a minimum amount of long-range planning was considered on a superficial level, the project would get a yellow. A green score would be granted if an acceptable level of long-range planning was evident. If AEDC business area long-range planning for the project was considered and applied, the project would be rewarded with a blue rating.

Since Sverdrup Technology, Inc., AEDC Group is under contract to the U. S. Air Force, the contractor team members must work closely with Air Force counterparts on each project. The third task, Air Force concurrence, would rate a green if it were evident that the project team and the Air Force Project Manager had communicated on the project and agreed on the direction the project was taking. A red rating would indicate that there had been no communication between the Air Force Project Manager and the project team.

The last task considered the actual execution of the IMP/IMS. If the majority of the planned IMP/IMS criteria were not completed, the score would be red. If it appeared that the IMP/IMS was followed, but not documented, the score would be yellow. If the majority of the IMP/IMS was worked and documented, the score would be green. Finally, if all the planned IMP/IMS criteria were worked and documented, the score would be blue.

Because developing and executing the IMP/IMS were the two tasks most crucial to the success of a project, the team gave the first and last tasks the highest weighting factor of 10. Long-range planning and working with the Air Force counterpart were next in importance, so these two tasks have a weight factor of seven.

TECHNICAL REVIEWS

Technical reviews are a series of system engineering activities by which the technical progress of a program is assessed relative to its technical or contractual requirements. These reviews are conducted at logical transition points in the developmental effort to reduce risk of failure by identifying and correcting problems or issues resulting from the work completed before the program is disrupted or delayed. These reviews provide a method for the performing activity and integrated product team to determine if the development of a system and/or configuration item and its documentation meet contract requirements.

The technical content of each design review will vary with the project. However, all reviews should be conducted in the same manner. The team chose to evaluate five characteristics that the team members felt all reviews should demonstrate.

First, the participants must be prepared. This would include having pertinent documents distributed to the participants before any design review meeting.

Second, the meeting should be a *review of progress*, not a design meeting. The product design should be accomplished outside of the review.

Third, the Project Manager, or a technically qualified representative, should present and follow an agenda for the review.

Fourth, the review should be run in an organized and orderly manner.

The review should end with the review team members signing a document that lists status of review completion.

Each of the above will earn either a green or a red score, depending on whether or not the characteristic is evident during the reviews.

The final evaluation criterion is that all the essential people should be present at the review. This would include, but not be limited to, the review team members, project team members, the AF Project Manager, Quality and Safety representatives (as applicable), customer representatives, and shop representatives. A green is earned if all these people are present; a yellow means that most of the people are present; and a red is given if any essential players are absent.

The team next assigned weight factors to the review tasks. The following tasks have a weight factor of seven:

- Being prepared
- Having the proper attendees
- Running the review in an organized and orderly manner
- Ending the meeting with a signed deficiency list that includes a suspense date and the person responsible for addressing each deficiency

The two tasks with a weight factor of five are:

- Conducting a review as opposed to a design meeting
- Distributing and following a written agenda

COMBINING THE SCORES

After assessing each project for each of the tasks under IMP/IMS and Technical Reviews, the team had to devise a way to combine the scores into an overall SE score. Scores for each project needed to be combined to provide an overall score for each section. To accomplish this, color scores for each task were given a numerical value:

- blue = 3
- green = 2
- yellow = 1
- red = 0

These task scores were then to be multiplied by the weight factors, averaged together, and converted back into a color to provide an overall score for each section. In addition, the two sections' scores would next be combined to get an overall score for the project. The team planned to assess each business area on a monthly basis. Within a business area, there was likely to be more than one project with a review. Therefore, the scores for all of the projects for a given month were to be averaged to get a monthly business area score.

A Microsoft® Excel® spreadsheet (Fig. 2) automatically performs all of these calculations. The person doing the assessment enters the color for each task; the spreadsheet performs the arithmetic and assigns the proper color scores for both the individual project and the business area.

SYSTEMS ENGINEERING OVERALL SCORE **RED**

Business Area:	TURBINES
Project Name:	Sample 1
Project Number:	xxx1
Date:	8-Mar-00

Type of Review: SSR

Use a separate form for each project. Use TAB key to move between data entry areas. Make sure unused forms are left blank. Include comments for red or blue scores.

1

Score Criteria

A.1. Blue: Follows SE Principles/Processes & overcomes obstacles
Green: Displays understanding of SE
Yellow: Minimum effort/reviews
Red: No IMP planning
A.2. Blue: AEDC/BA/LRP considered & applied
Green: LRP considered--acceptable
Yellow: Minimum LRP considered--improvement required
Red LRP not considered
A.3. Green: yes
Red: No
A.4. Blue: Work all planned IMP/IMS criteria
Green: Work majority of planned IMP/IMS criteria
Yellow: Undeterminable
Red: Did not work the majority of planned IMP/IMS criteria
B.1. Green: yes
Red: No
B.2. Green: yes
Red: No
B.3. Green: All
Yellow: Most
Red: Minimum
B.4. Green: Yes
Red: No
B.5. Green: Yes
Red: No
B.6. Green: Yes
Red: No

SE SCORE FOR THIS PROJECT		GREEN
	Task Score	Section Score
A. IMP/IMS		YELLOW
1. IMP Planning completed and All Tasks Considered/Documented	GREEN	
2. Long Range Planning Considered (viability/efficiency evaluated)	YELLOW	
3. Air Force Concurrence	GREEN	
4. IMP/IMS Execution	RED	
B. Conduct Reviews		GREEN
1. Prepared: SvT PM, AF PM, Customers (Documents distributed beforehand	GREEN	
2. Review vs. Design Meeting	GREEN	
3. Proper Attendees--Review Team, AF, Quality, Safety, Customers, Shop R	YELLOW	
4. Agenda	GREEN	
5. Form 1683 with Defieincy List with Responsible Persons and Suspense D	GREEN	
6. Organized and Orderly	GREEN	

Project Name:	Sample 2
Project Number:	xxx2
Date:	25-Mar-00

Type of Review: CDR

Use a separate form for each project. Use TAB key to move between data entry areas. Make sure unused forms are left blank.

2

Score Criteria

A.1. Blue: Follows SE Principles/Processes & overcomes obstacles
Green: Displays understanding of SE
Yellow: Minimum effort/reviews
Red: No IMP planning
A.2. Blue: AEDC/BA/LRP considered & applied
Green: LRP considered--acceptable
Yellow: Minimum LRP considered--improvement required
Red: No IMP planning
A.3. Green: yes
Red: No

SE SCORE FOR THIS PROJECT		GREEN
	Task Score	Section Score
A. IMP/IMS		BLUE
1. IMP Planning completed and All Tasks Considered/Documented	BLUE	
2. Long Range Planning Considered (viability/efficiency evaluated)	GREEN	
3. Air Force Concurrence	GREEN	
4. IMP/IMS Execution	BLUE	

Figure 2. Microsoft® Excel® Worksheet

CURRENT ASSESMENTS

As of this writing, we have only a few months of assessments. However, most of these assessments show green scores in most areas. In the near future, we plan to focus on the areas that are not green by providing more training and working with the project managers. Once the systems engineering attitude is firmly established we hope to be able to document progress with our projects management in terms of cost, schedule, and requirements compliance.

BIOGRAPHY

Rosemary R. Matty is a systems engineer for Sverdrup Technology, Inc., AEDC Group at Arnold Engineering Development Center in middle Tennessee. She holds a B.S. in Engineering Science from the University of Virginia and an M.S. in Mechanical Engineering from Texas Tech University. She has over 18 years of experience working with test facilities and facility-related projects.

Systems Engineering and Supportability Analysis: Technology Refreshment for COTS-Intensive Systems

Dinesh Verma, Ph.D.
Systems/Supportability Strategist
Lockheed Martin Naval Electronics and
Surveillance Systems, Manassas, VA 20110
Phone: (703) 367-6888
Email: dinesh.verma@lmco.com

Galen Plunkett
Chief Technologist
Lockheed Martin Naval Electronics and
Surveillance Systems, Manassas, VA 20110
Phone: (703) 367-4855
Email: galen.plunkett@lmco.com

Abstract. The desire to integrate supportability issues in product and system design has long been articulated within the systems engineering community [Asimow, 1964; Ostrofsky, 1977; Pugh, 1980]. However, there has often been a lag between this intent and its execution. Supportability and serviceability analysis (traditionally, also referred to as ILS in the aerospace industry) is often relegated to a reactionary mode during detailed system design. At least partially, a contributing factor to this reality has been a hazy definition of supportability and serviceability parameters. This inhibits quantitative "dovetailing" of supportability parameters into the design and architecture synthesis activity.

The application of a systematic and integrated development approach must contend with the prevailing business realities. These include increased international competition, resource constraints, evolving system requirements and customer expectation, along with an imperative to get the system to market expeditiously. Furthermore, there is an increasing emphasis on assessing systems and products from a total ownership cost perspective. This mandates explicit inclusion of supportability and serviceability issues into system design. The requirement becomes even more urgent with the emphasis on commercial-off-the-shelf system elements (COTS) in the development of complex, distributed, and multi-functional systems. This emphasis on COTS technologies and elements has already resulted in significant, relatively immediate, reduction in system development and production costs, as reflected in Figure 1.

These benefits and cost reductions notwithstanding, an emphasis on utilizing COTS system elements results in unique challenges from a systems and supportability engineering standpoint. Proactive refreshment of COTS system elements becomes a key component within the overall system supportability and serviceability strategy. Furthermore, any technology refreshment strategy must be tailored to account for the system operational concept, its availability and accessibility, the business strategy, and the system maintenance concept. This is necessary if reductions in development and production costs are to be extended into an overall reduction in system ownership costs.

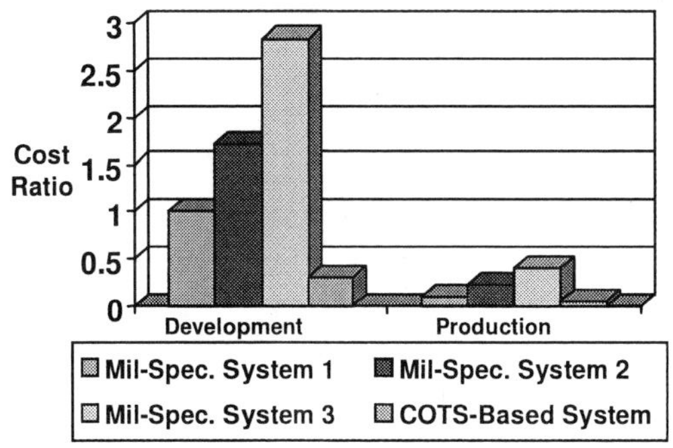

Figure 1. System Development and Production Cost Reduction

ADAPTED SYSTEMS ENGINEERING

Experience on recently completed and on-going COTS-intensive programs reaffirms the need for an adapted system engineering process as shown in Figure 2. In order to ensure an affordable and effective configuration, this process must be robust in its active consideration and involvement of system supportability.

Accordingly, an adapted supportability engineering process, dovetailed with the early top-down design synthesis phases of the system engineering process, is shown in Figure 3. A significant step in these systems and supportability engineering processes pertains to the assessment and selection of COTS products and technologies within the context of a technology refreshment strategy. This is depicted in both Figures 2 and 3. Lockheed Martin has developed a software template, CAST™, based on the Analytic Hierarchy Process (AHP) to facilitate execution of this step.

COMMERCIAL TECHNOLOGY ASSESSMENT, SELECTION, AND REFRESHMENT

It is a system engineering objective to facilitate the translation of a need or an operational shortfall into a system architecture. Another objective is to strike a balance between effectiveness (function of performance/readiness) and life-cycle cost during this translation. When addressing COTS-intensive systems, the fundamental objectives still apply. However, the architecture and functional packaging concepts need to be developed with an explicit consideration of available commercial technologies. In this regard, an early systems engineering and supportability analysis practice pertains to the assessment of available COTS technologies and products. Thereafter, a strategy for providing effective and affordable refreshment of the system configuration needs to be formulated and executed. These issues are addressed in the following sections.

COTS ASSESSMENT AND SELECTION

Given the influence of early COTS assessment decisions on the architecture, its supportability, and ultimately life-cycle cost, Lockheed Martin has developed a methodology and a tool to impart necessary rigor and discipline to this activity.

The methodology relies on Quality Function Deployment (QFD) to identify the assessment parameters traceable to customer requirements, followed by the Analytic Hierarchy Process (AHP) to compute parameter priorities and to conduct a comparative assessment of COTS alternatives.

In addition to performance and functionality, system-level concerns relating to commonality, compliance with OSA standards, and supportability are explicitly considered, as depicted in Figure 4.

The selection criteria address inherent design characteristics along with the vendor and technology environment (which can impact timely and cost effective procurement of spare/repair parts).

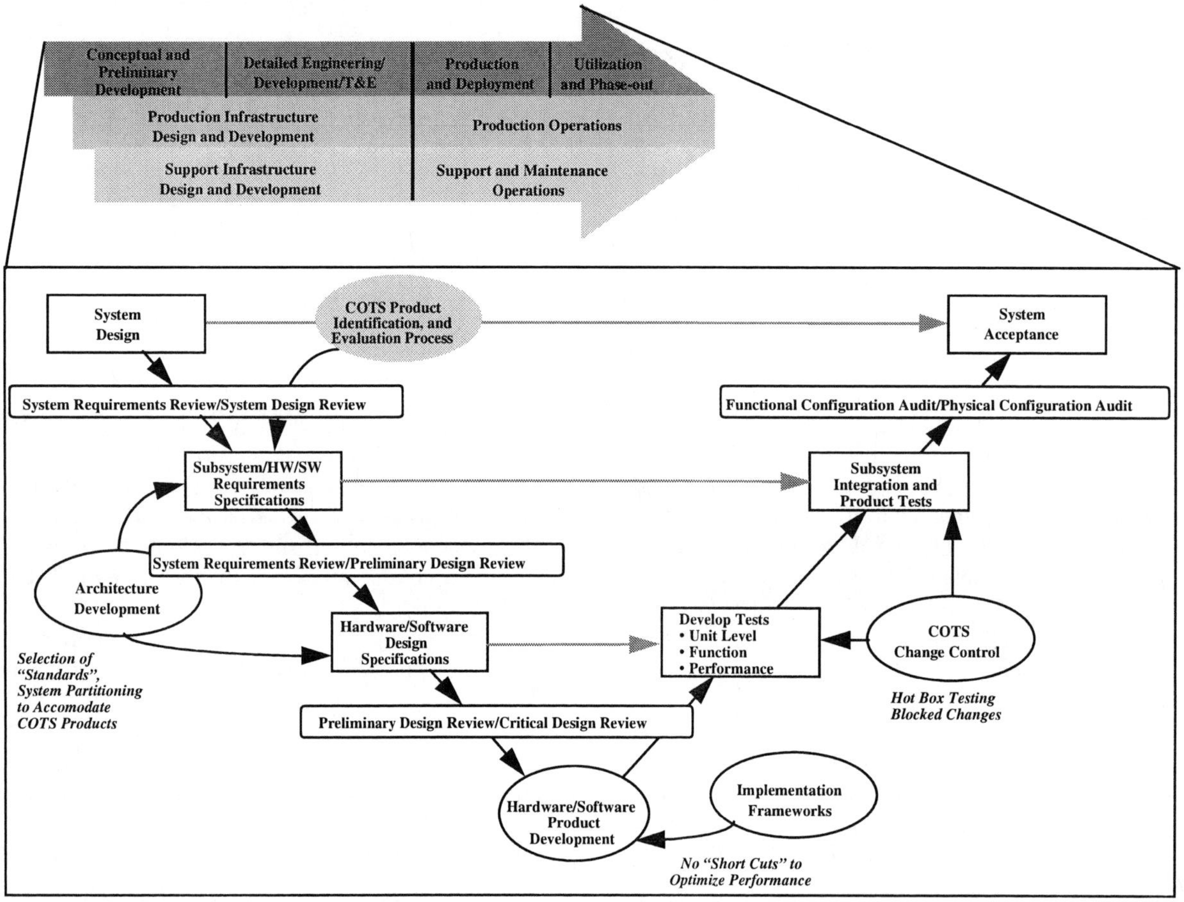

Figure 2. Tailored systems engineering process for COTS Intensive design & development effort.

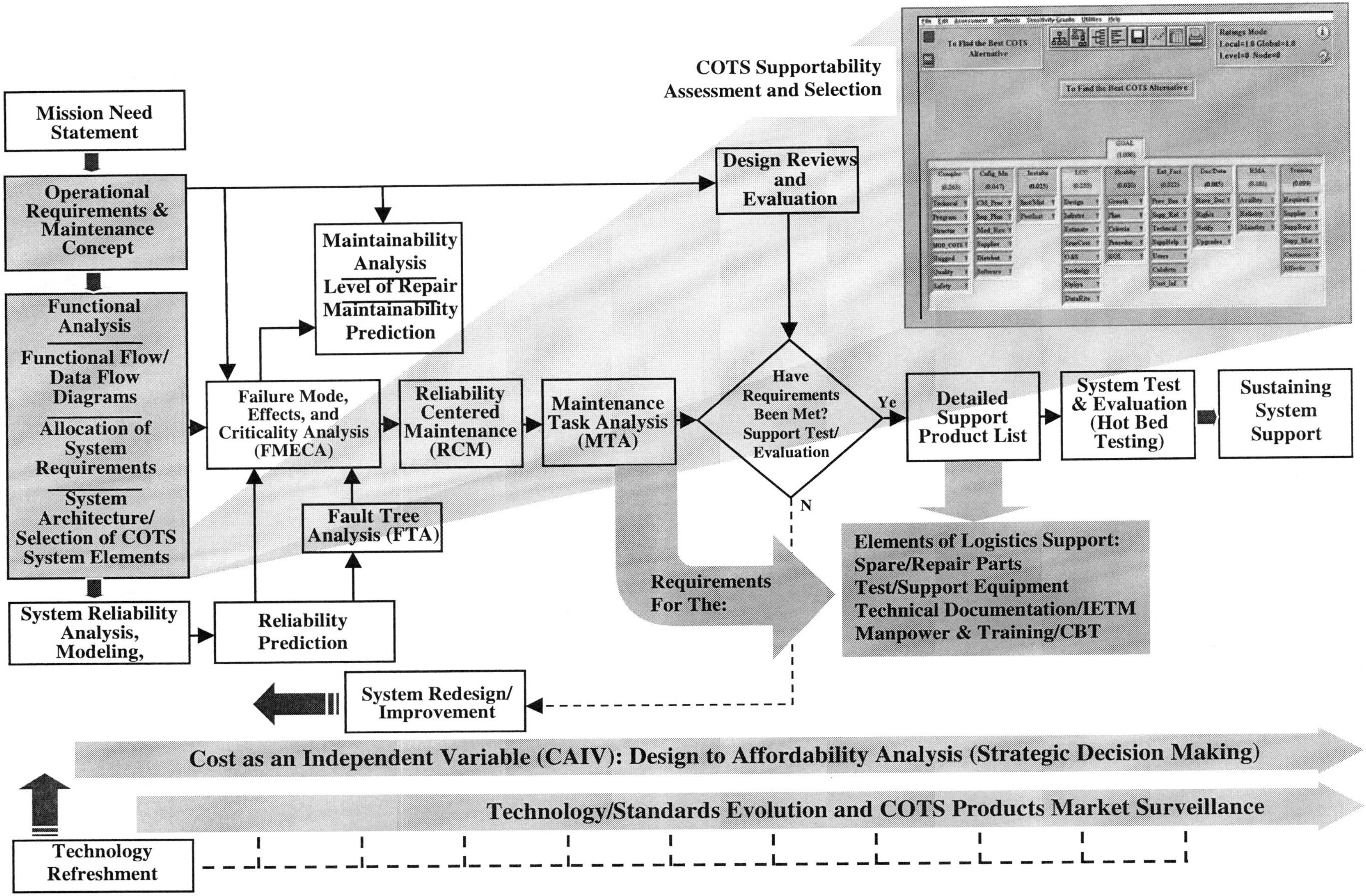

Figure 3. An Adapted System Supportability Engineering Process

This makes the selection robust allowing the formulation of a maintenance concept that evolves with technology and leverages the commercial support infrastructure to the extent possible. A detailed discussion of the underlying assessment and selection model is included in [Verma, et. al., 1996]. The methodology has been implemented within a software template, CAST™, which itself resides within a commercial AHP Shell, Expert Choice.[1]

The CAST™ software template initially guides the analyst to a particular COTS technology segment, as shown in Figure 5 (a). Thereafter, alternatives are assessed with regard to relevant open systems standards and profiles, as shown in Figure 5 (b). Subsequent to this, the evaluation focuses on assessing commercial alternatives from a supportability and vendor standpoint. Screen shots of an assessment attribute hierarchy within the CAST™ template are shown in Figure 6.

The initial emphasis on open system standards and profiles, and system supportability, decreases dependence on a single source and/or a proprietary technology that might suggest risk. This in turn enhances the logistics planning activity from a cost and efficiency perspective.

Metrics have been developed to provide guidance on identification of system elements that are good technology refreshment candidates.

TECHNOLOGY REFRESHMENT STRATEGY

A COTS based open system architecture approach must contend with the rapid pace in technology evolution and the short life of commercial products (production and OEM support). The historic and exponential growth in processor performance continues today, with processor performance doubling every 18 to 20 months, continually facilitated by innovations like copper interconnects and the EPIC architecture.

This is depicted in Figure 7. In order to address and exploit this fast pace of technology evolution, most commercial vendors have a development phase (product requirements definition to initial delivery) of approximately 6 to 15 months, followed by a production phase (new production and market development) of 6 months to 3 years. Subsequent to production, a product is often supported for 2 to 5 years by the commercial vendors, as a function of their business strategy.

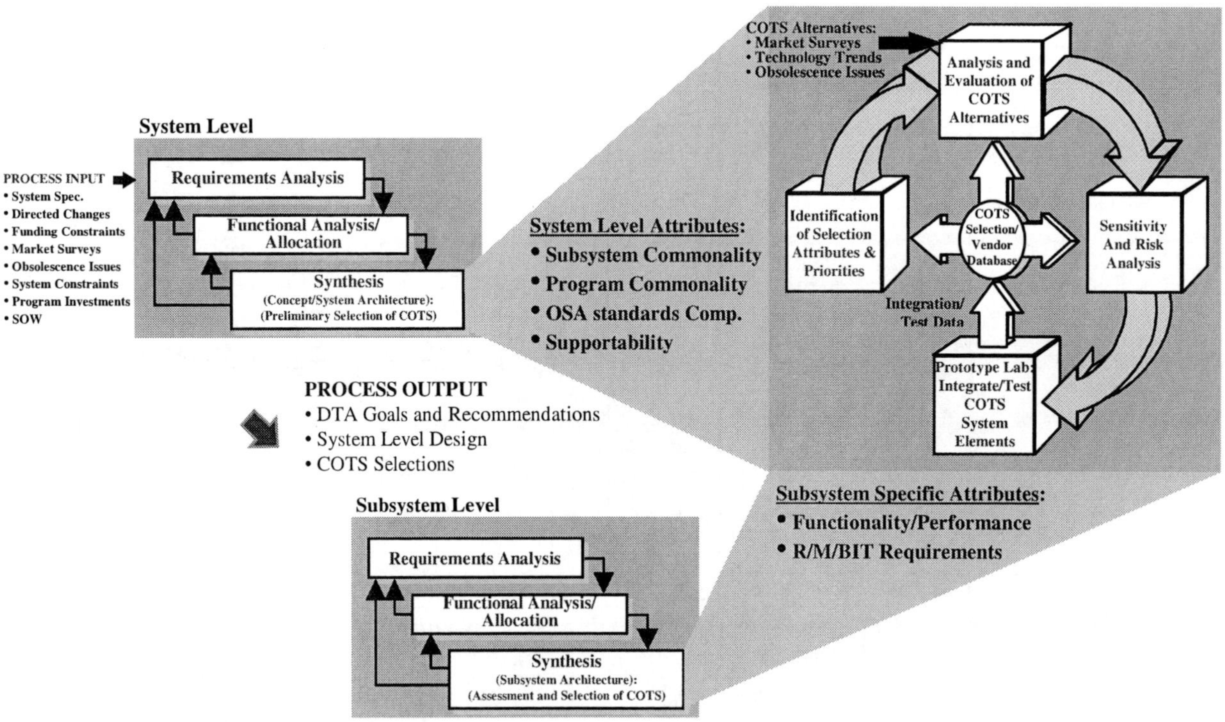

Figure 4. COTS Assessment and Selection Process.

1. Expert Choice® is a Registered Trademark of Expert Choice, Inc.

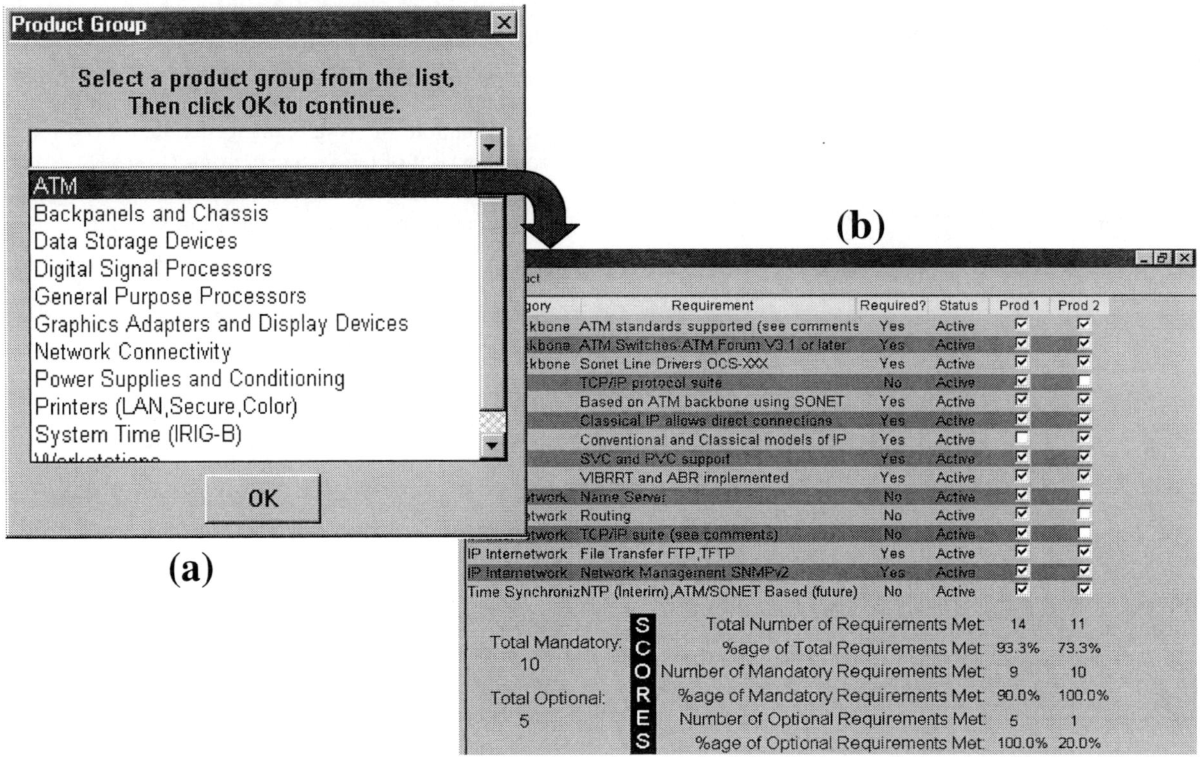

Figure 5. COTS Assessment and Open System Standards.

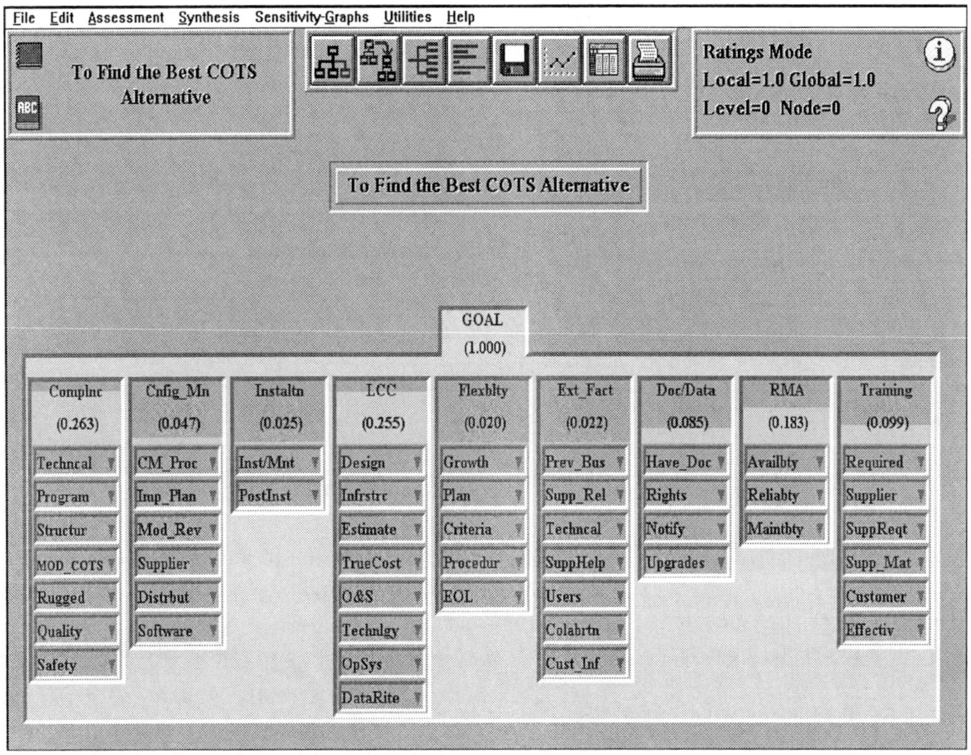

Figure 6. Supportability Parameters in the COTS Assessment Process.

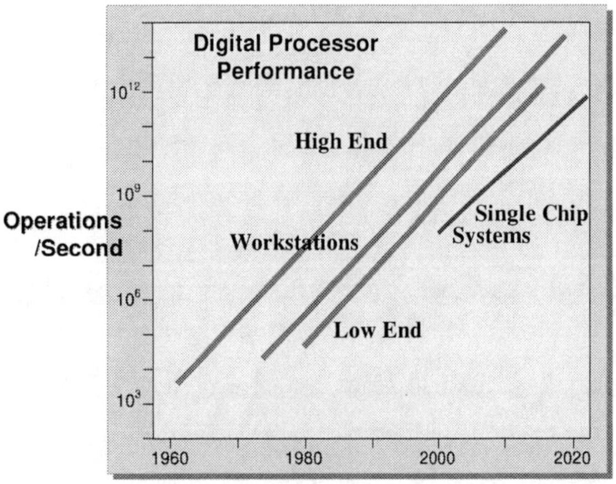

Figure 7. Processor Performance Evolution.

Thereafter, selected commercial products often go into an extended support phase, lasting 1 to 3 years, when support is limited to providing spares from the existing, and fast depleting, inventory. This "life cycle" for a COTS element is depicted in Figure 8. It is during the extended support phase that a system element is flagged as a support risk item.

In the presence of such rapid and asynchronous COTS element evolution, systems with long operational use profiles must establish and execute a technology refreshment strategy to leverage advancements and investments in commercial technology while also exploiting the commercial support infrastructure. The objective of this strategy is to avoid technology obsolescence and product incompatibility. Given this objective, key triggering mechanisms need to be implemented which facilitate identification of system elements that need to be refreshed out of the system configuration.

Thereafter, a design to affordability analysis is conducted to evaluate all feasible technology migration paths from a holistic perspective. Lockheed Martin NE&SS-Manassas has developed metrics that provide the design and supportability engineering team insight into the technology maturity of key system elements within the configuration, as shown in Figure 9. In the context of this discussion, a low rating (1,2,3) suggests an immature or state-of-the-art technology or product. This rating may qualify the item for evaluation in the prototype laboratory, it further suggests that the technology is not mature enough to be fielded.

A high rating (8, 9, 10) suggests that the item is in its extended support phase and is therefore nearing technology obsolescence or potential end-of-life risk, and would trigger technology refreshment. This information is included in the optimization of logistics and support resources for fielded systems, while simultaneously providing input to the technology refreshment catalog. The tools, methods, and metrics discussed in this section are embedded within an overall technology refreshment process as reflected in Figure 10.

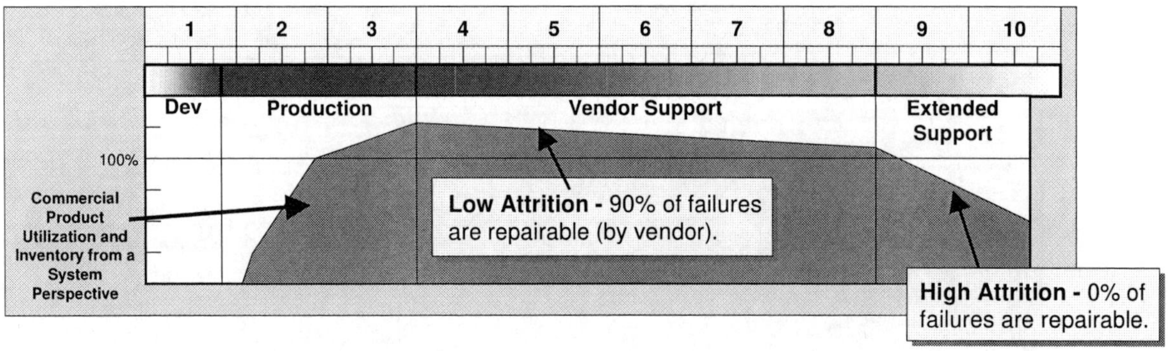

Figure 8. Typical COTS Availability Profile and Schedule.

CONCLUSIONS

Affordable support strategies for COTS based open system architectures mandate a technology refreshment plan. This is necessary to ensure readiness at reduced system ownership costs. The technology and vendor landscape must be understood and leveraged. Traditional supportability engineering and logistics processes and methods must be adapted. A discussion in this regard is included in [Verma, et. al., 1997a; and Verma, et. al., 1997b].

REFERENCES

[Asimow, 1964] Asimow, Morris, Introduction to Design, Prentice Hall, Inc., Englewood Cliffs, New Jersey, 1964.

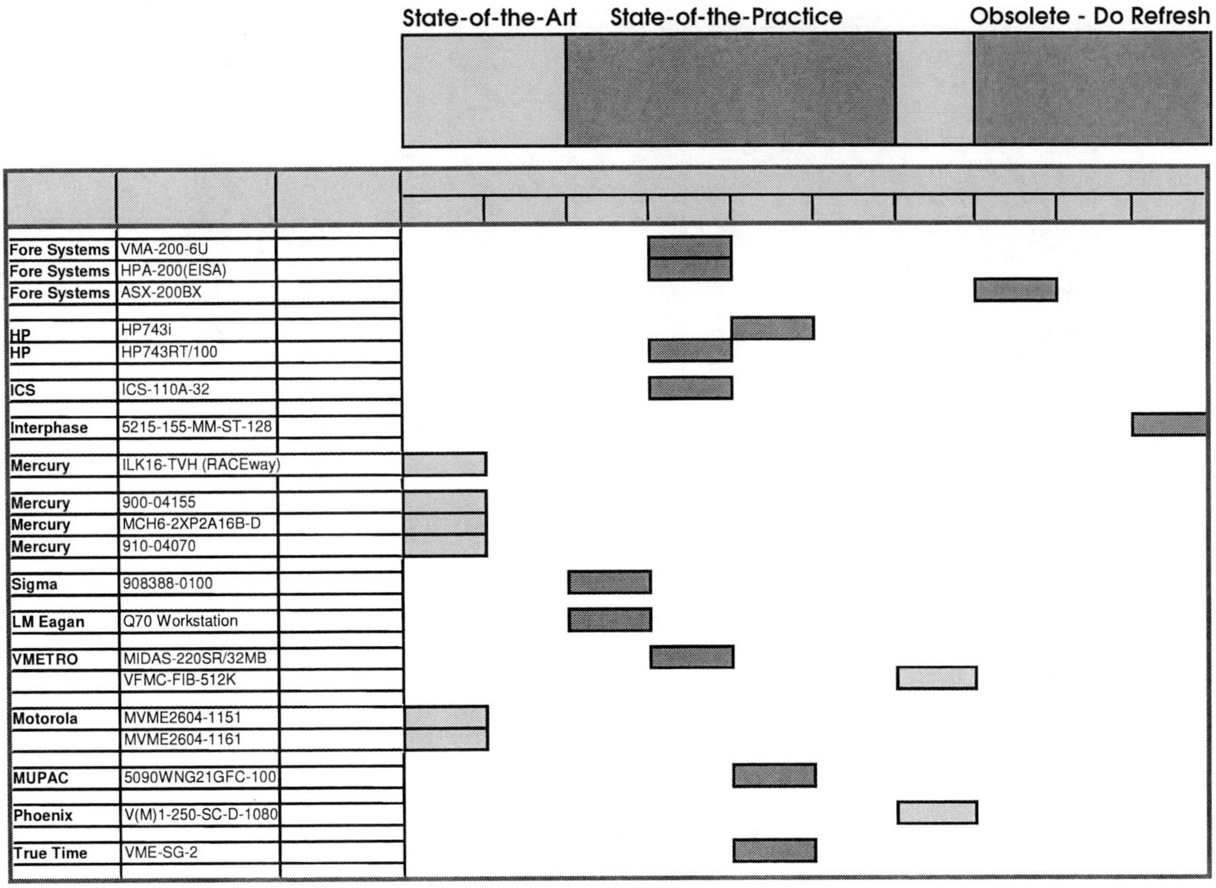

Figure 9. Technology maturity metric.

[Pugh, 1990] Pugh, S., Total Design: Integrated Methods for Successful Product Engineering, Addison-Wesley, Inc., New York, 1991.

[Ostrofsky, 1977] Ostrofsky, B., Design, Planning, and Development Methodology, Prentice Hall, Inc., Englewood Cliffs, New Jersey, 1977.

[Verma, et. al., 1997a] Verma, D., T. Herald, and J. Knezevic, *Integration of Supportability Considerations into the System Engineering Process through Focused Modeling and Simulation*, 2nd Modeling, Simulation, and Virtual Prototyping Conference, Arlington, Virginia, November 1997.

[Verma, et. al., 1996] Verma, D., B.S. Blanchard, R.G. Giffin, D.V. VanBuskirk, R. Webb, "*COTS Assessment and Selection Methodology*", Annual Symposium, (INCOSE), July 1996, Boston, MA.

BIOGRAPHICAL SKETCHES

Dinesh Verma received the Ph.D. and the M.S. in Industrial and Systems Engineering from Virginia Tech. He is the Systems and Supportability Strategist at Lockheed Martin NE&SS, in Manassas, Virginia, while concurrently serving as a Research Fellow at the University of Exeter, United Kingdom.

Prior to joining Lockheed Martin, Verma worked as a Research Scientist at Virginia Tech and managed the University's Systems Engineering Design Laboratory. While at Virginia Tech and afterwards, Verma served in a consulting capacity with numerous companies to include Eastman Kodak, United Defense, PSI, and Motorola.

Verma has authored over 75 papers, monographs, and co-authored two textbooks: *Maintainability: A Key to Effective Serviceability and Maintenance Management* (Wiley, 1995), and *Economic Decision Analysis* (Prentice Hall, 1998).

Galen Plunkett has over 30 years experience in systems architecture design and development. He started his career with IBM, and is currently the Chief Technologist at Lockheed Martin NE&SS-Manassas. In this role he has been responsible for the development of COTS-based system architectures for various applications including New Attack Submarine (C31) System and for devising common architectural solutions for a number of Naval platforms.

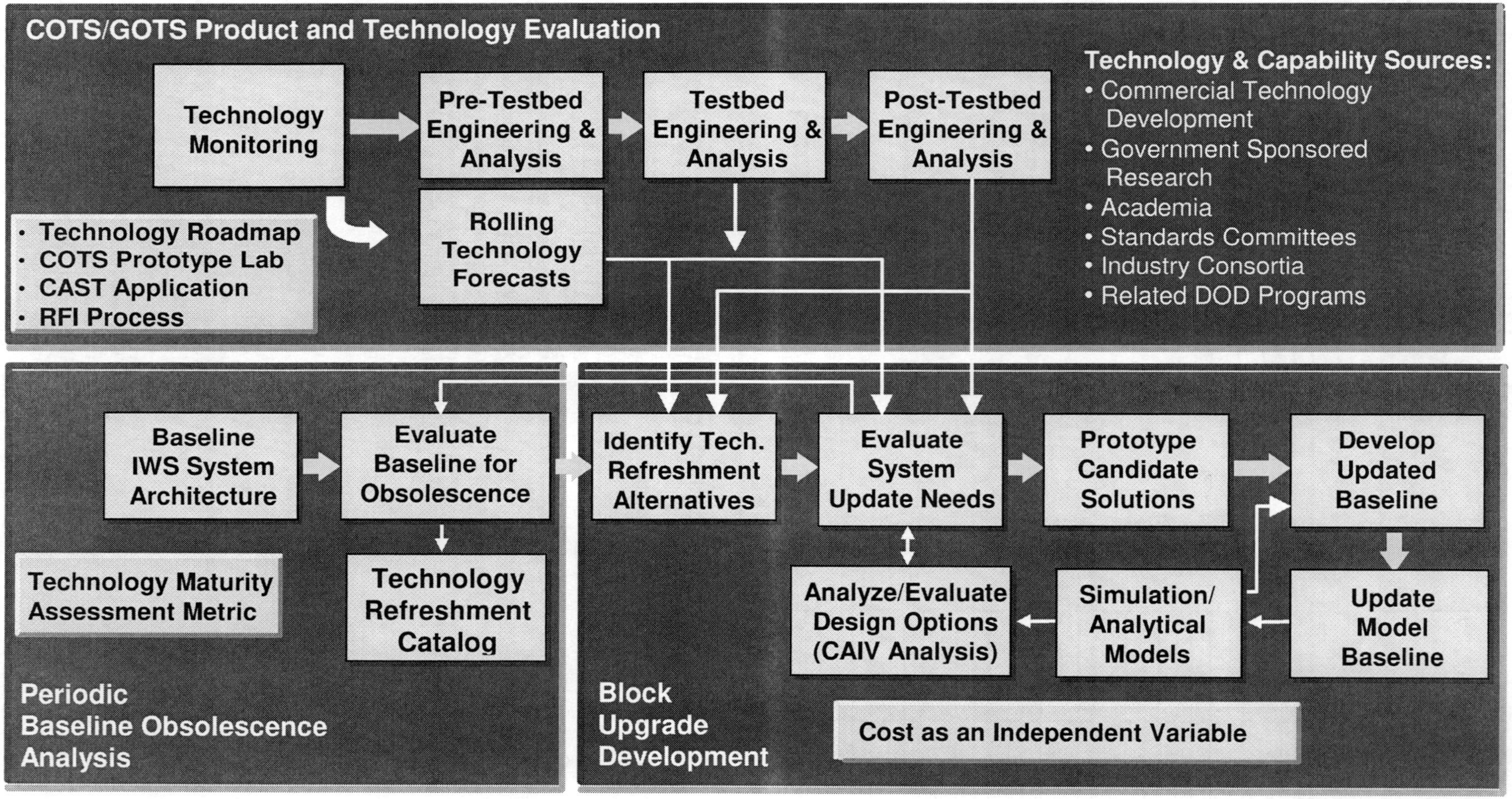

Figure 10. Technology Refreshment Procedure, Anchored with Best Practices.

The Telecommunication Domain - a Challenge for INCOSE

Ruediger Kaffenberger
Marconi Communications
Marconi Communications GmbH
Gerberstrasse 33
D-71522 Backnang

Abstract. The telecommunication sector harbours the true giants among the artificial systems. Telecommunication systems have the largest physical size of man made systems, they have the most users and the largest commercial value. Telecommunication systems have even outpaced the automobile in respect to its impact onto society. However, despite these facts and despite humankind relies on the availability and effectiveness of telecommunication systems, one finds only few contributions from individuals or organisations of the telecommunication industries to the science of systems engineering. In this paper, the outline of an alternative systems engineering profile of the telecommunication domain will be presented. This profile will be used to illustrate why systems engineering in the telecommunication domain is different and why INCOSE should be interested in it.

INTRODUCTION

They were alive, and they had the most dangerous weapon known to man - a radio.

Tom Clancy in Red Storm Rising (Clancy 1986)

Long History. The hunger for new knowledge is one of the distinguishing traits of humankind. This can be seen from people's desire to travel and to gain new experiences by this. However, even more valuable for the individual are news - the precise report of distant events. Both desires - that for experiences and that for news have driven the minds of many inventors. The use of artificial means for the speedy transport of news - that is the use of telecommunication systems - has a long history. Homer tells in his Iliad of a chain of beacon fires that, around 1200 BC, Clytemnestra and Aegisthus had arranged, with the aim to learn of the return of Agamemnon's fleet in time to arrange the assassination of Agamemnon (Holzmann 1994). There are more records of the use of beacon fires to signal events or warnings. For example in 427 BC, beacon fires signalled the Spartan fleet an attack by Athenian vessels and as early as 150 BC Polybius designs a system for torch telegraphy (Holzmann 1994). While fires worked only during the dark, reflected sun light and smoke were used during the daytime. This optical telegraphy prevailed until the electrical current took over.

Huge Dimensions. The idea of a telecommunication system is, that it transports information over long distances in a time as short as possible. The result is that the individual elements of telecommunication systems can be very distant from each other - the most distant are the transmitters aboard of spacecraft that travel to the edge of or solar system.

In respect to another dimension, telecommunication systems are giants too: the number of pieces of equipment installed. In 1998, there were 838,000,000 main telephone lines, one for 14 of every 100 inhabitants of Earth. Nearly each of these lines is equipped with some terminal device, mostly telephone receivers. Virtually any of these main lines can be connected to any other.

Equally astonishing is the growth rate in some areas. For example, from 1997 to 1998 the number of cellular telephones has risen by 48% on world average.

Perhaps the best measure for the special position of the telecommunications industry is the commercial value. In 1998, the cumulated revenue of the telecommunication operators for telephone and data services was $744,781,000,000. The cumulated revenue of the telecommunication equipment vendors in 1998 was $260,000,000,000. These numbers account for telephone and data transport services only. For a full view of the commercial position of the telecommunication domain, the revenues of broadcast services like radio and television have to be added. (Source: `http://www.itu.int/ti/industryoverview/at_glance/KeyTelecom99.htm`)

Coverage by INCOSE. In the proceedings of the past ten international symposia of INCOSE, I found one or two papers each year from authors that belong to the telecommunication domain outside space or military applications. Appendix I of (Mackey 1999) shows seven entries for the years form 1993 to 1998. This is a far too small number for such large an industry and products of such high a complexity as will be shown later.

INCOSE does not ignore the telecommunication domain. There is a telecommunication working group that is actively working on an revised systems engineering profile for the domain and this paper is intended to be a part of this effort.

The Contents of this Paper.

- A sketch of an alternative systems engineering profile will be presented.

  The current systems engineering profile (Mackey 1999) is in parts very specific and in parts rather vague. This is caused by the very broad spectrum of systems that is covered by the term "telecommunication application domain". The vague parts of the profile do not carry a distinctive message and the specific parts are in the permanent danger to become outpaced by the technical development. Systems engineering practitioners with backgrounds from all aspects of the telecommunication domain will have to participate in the effort to produce a true profile of the domain.

  My approach to the profile is a more generic one than that of the current profile and consequently its statements are not as technology dependent but still it can not cover the full spectrum of the domain.

- The essential statements of (Martin 1999) will be used to verify the profile.
- Some motivation for INCOSE to work on a better incorporation of the telecommunication domain (and other similar domains) will be given.

THE TELECOMMUNICATION DOMAIN'S PROFILE

A High Degree of Regulation and Standardisation.

Regulation. Information is not only valued high by individuals but especially by governments and the military. All new telecommunication systems have been expensive, because of their large size and the sophisticated technology involved and the initial expenditures had to come from these public parties. Consequently most telecommunication systems are initially in the hands of governments or the military and the access to the telecommunication systems has always been restricted in some way by the governments. The nature and use of the systems was and is subject of tight regulations. Virtually every country has a national regulation body like the Federal Communications Commission (FCC) in the US that develops the regulations and eventually enforces them.

Standardization. Another point is the tendency of telecommunication systems to cross national borders. The lines of optical telegraphs build by Claude Chappe (Holzmann 1994) in France soon crossed the borders to the neighboring countries and the wireless systems of our days can not be stopped at the borders. This situation requires additional regulations to ensure minimal interference between local services on either side of a border and some compatibility if the information shall cross the border successfully.

These problems have been solved even during times like the cold war by international standardization organizations like International Telecommunications Union (ITU), the former CCITT and CCIR. Interference free coexistence and exchange of information between different and similar telecommunication systems is ensured by thousands of recommendations and standards. Usually the national regulation bodies enforce the adherence to the standards.

Different Kinds of Telecommunication. Clearly there are two different kinds of telecommunication: The communications between a closed group of individuals, as in a telephone conversation, and the communication to an open group of individuals, like the broadcast of a television program.

Broadcast Communication. In the latter case, the communication is one-way, from a single transmitter to as many receivers as possible. The transmitter can be very powerful and expensive, while the receivers should be simple and inexpensive. It is to be expected that the demand for receiver equipment can not be satisfied by a single source. The specification of the transmitted signal has to be open, for the different receiver equipment to be compatible. Examples for this kind of telecommunication are the traditional wireless television broadcasts and cable television. Encrypted broadcasts like pay television are used to limit the reception of the broadcasts to a large closed group. Except from the subscription, there are no special prerequisites necessary for a user, to take part in a broadcast communication as a receiver.

Individual Communication. In contrast to broadcast communication, individual communication takes place between a closed group of communication partners. This kind of communication is usually interactive; that is, all partners send and receive information. The are many different telecommunication systems in use for this kind of communication, the most common is the telephone system. Before an individual communication can take place, the group of participants must be assembled. This is done by establishing connections between the group members. It requires a connection establishment procedure that has to be known to all members of the group.

Data Communication. Data communication is a relative new form of individual communication. The traditional individual communication was between men. Data communication is between computers. Because of the success of the Internet, this is the section with the most rapid growth. The characteristic of data communication differs substantially form that of human communication. Computers need very elaborate connection establishment protocols and a very reliable data transport. The reason for this is that computers do not have the intelligence and flexibility of the human brain to compensate for errors in the transmitted information. While humans are good in dealing with errors, they are very impatient and can not comprehend the transmitted information if there are large delays between successive packages of speech information. For a successful voice transmission, there has to be a continuous and steady stream of information elements. In contrast, for a computer it is acceptable that the information arrives in bursts with arbitrary pauses in-between but it can compensate errors only in the limited way that has been designed into the protocols used.

Different Businesses in the Telecommunication Domain.

As can be seen from the television example, in a communication relation there are several rolls. Someone transmits a television program and many receive the program. Both parties need some equipment that facilitates the communication and of course there has to be a party the supplies the program content. Similar rolls can be found in all kinds of communication.

Network Elements. Every kind of telecommunication requires some means to send, transport, and receive the information. These means are called network elements. Figure 1 shows the typical architecture of a telephone or computer network.

The network elements at the periphery of the network (the squares in Figure 1), the end terminals like television sets of telephone receivers, are deployed in huge numbers - that is in millions. They have to be very low cost, easy to use by every one, and the products of competing suppliers have to be interchangeable. They have to follow trends in fashion also, the design of the housing and the set of features changing from year to year or even faster.

The profile of the network elements in the center of a network (the bold circles in Figure 1) differs substantially form that of the peripheral devices. Examples for such network elements are the large switches, employed in the central exchange offices of telephone networks, or the head stations of a

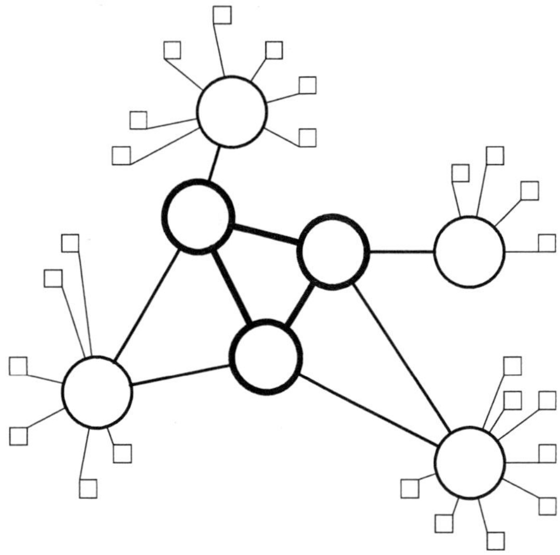

Figure 1. A Telecommunication Network

broadcaster. This kind of devices is built in numbers of a few thousands only. They are used and maintained by highly skilled personal. The failure of such a network element can result in very high costs for the owner because it may disrupt the whole communication in a network. Therefore, this kind of equipment has to be extremely reliable. Devices that are large and reliable consequently are very expensive and the purchasers expect a long usable lifetime in return to their high investment. The specifications for this kind of networks have to be such that they stay valid for at least two decades.

The rapid growth of the traffic generated by individual communication, especially by data communication like Internet access has forced a more decentralized processing of the information streams. This trend has been enabled by the rapid growth of the capability of computers and transmission circuitry that is at the core of all network elements. This decentralised equipment (the light circles in Figure 1) has to handle many communication links too and must have a reliability comparable to that of the elements at the centre of a network. On the other side, often the devices will not be installed in maintained offices but in the basements of buildings or at the curb of streets. Production volumes are rather high but so is the pressure by technical innovation.

Telecommunication Networks. The network elements have to be linked together, to establish a means for communication. This can be done wireless by free electromagnetic radiation or through wires, cables or glass fibers that guide the electromagnetic waves. The network elements in conjunction with their links are called the transport network.

The communication links usually travel over or through the estates of different owners and telecommunication is regarded as vital for the functioning of community. This is the reason why the establishment and the use of communication links is almost everywhere regulated by some public organisation, that issues licenses to those that want to build and maintain a telecommunication network. A telecommunication network requires big investments to acquire the required licenses and to buy the needed equipment. Key to a successful network operation is a careful planning of what network elements to use where to deliver the best performance to the users at the lowest cost for the operator, now and in the future. The network may not interfere with other installations in the same area and may not pose a hazard to anyone.

Telecommunication Services. In the beginning of modern telecommunications, networks and services were one. The telephone network had been build for the only purpose of transporting telephone calls. Until a few years ago this was true for virtually every network, but by and by each of those networks was used for applications it was not built to. For example, the telephone network carries data traffic and data networks like the Internet are used for telephony. To do this, special adaptations are necessary, that are but not part of the network. There is the universal tendency to separate the telecommunication network from the services that use it. The service becomes a business of its own.

Not all services are as simple as the pure telephony. Intelligent networks offer very complex services that require extensions like database systems or additional communication links to work.

Telecommunication Applications. Telecommunication services themselves produce not enough value to justify the huge investments in telecommunication networks. The real drivers are the applications. The ultimate user of a telephone network has an aim he or she wants to achieve. The same is true for the different parties that supply a television program. One party for example wants to educate the public and some other party presents entertainment or news as a vehicle for commercial advertising. These are different applications of the same service. Complex applications like multi media presentations use several different services at the same time.

There is a strong interrelation between the capabilities of the telecommunication services and the applications. Many applications become feasible only with the advent of certain services but at the same time desired applications drive the development of the services that enable them. The applications do most strongly interfere with the life of people. The introduction of novel telecommunication applications can have a heavy impact on the social and economical system.

Hierarchies. In the telecommunication domain, hierarchies play an important roll. The individual levels of a hierarchy are often called layers. Typically, layers are used to designate domains where different rules apply. A classical telephone network for instance consists of at least three levels of networks: The subscriber lines connect the users to network elements that bundle the low-capacity information streams. This is the lowest level of the network hierarchy. The intermediate level of the network connects the local offices and the local offices to the offices that handle the long distance traffic. The connections between the long distance offices have the largest transport capacity. They are represented by the top level of a network hierarchy.

As shown in the previous section, the telecommunication domain includes four different businesses. Each business relies on the services provided by another business. At the lowest level telecommunication networks rely on the services provided by the network elements they use. Telecommunication services use one or more telecommunication networks to transport the service's information elements. The user of a service does not see the transport network but he sees a service network. This structure repeats for applications. Applications use the services of the service networks. This is a different kind of a hierarchy of networks. Figure 2 illustrates a simple two-layer hierarchy.

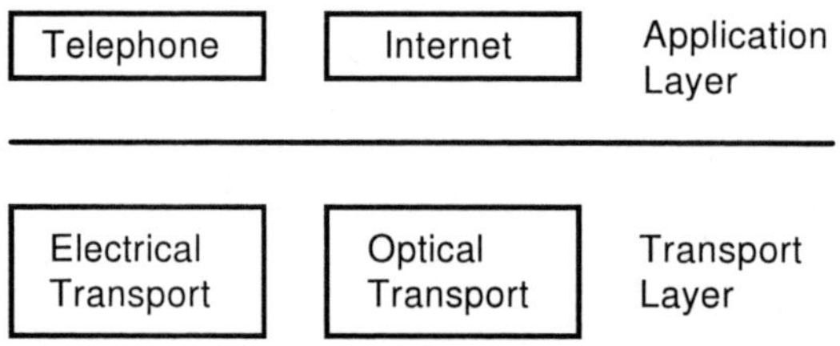

Figure 2. A Two-Layer Network Hierarchy

Protocols. The client-server-principle as exemplified in the previous paragraph can be found everywhere in the telecommunication domain. It is most pronounced in the area of telecommunication protocols. For a successful transmission, it is necessary the all partners involved have some knowledge about the other partners. In the telecommunication domain, this knowledge is called a protocol. Information processing instances of a telecommunication network that belong to a common level in the network's hierarchy have to share a common protocol. Ideally, a protocol specifies everything that is needed for the communication at a given level of the hierarchy independently of the protocols used by the underlying (server) layers.

Figure 3 illustrates this principle with a small protocol stack.

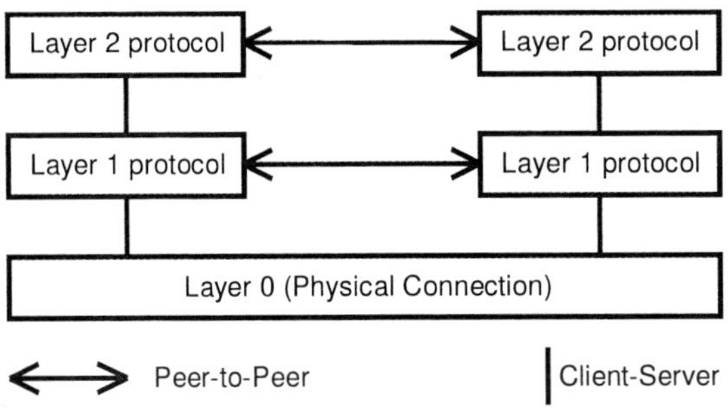

Figure 3. A Small Protocol Stack.

SYTEMS ENGINEERING IN THE TELECOMMUNICATION DOMAIN

From the preceding profile, it can be seen the telecommunication domain has to employ systems engineering principles unless it was not as successful as it is. New telecommunication systems usually are right on the edge, of what is technological possible. This was true for the first telephone systems and is still true for the multi gigabit per second data-highways of today. Optimal transmission speed and reliability is only achievable if all components of the system interface without a single gap. This requires factoring in the limitations of the human beings that are part of the system beside all the other components.

Differences between Systems Engineering in the Telecommunication Domain and the Defence domain. To investigate why this systems engineering is not as visible in INCOSE as it is expected to be, one has to look at the differences between the telecommunication domain and other domains that are more prominent in INCOSE.

In (Martin 1999) the differences between systems engineering practice of the telecommunication domain and the defence domain have been contrasted. The findings of (Martin 1999) will be matched with the profile presented above:

Four key differences have been isolated:

- Aestethics,
- Regulatory Constraints
- Development Cost
- Services.

Aestethics. While in the defence domain the functionality and behaviour dominate all considerations, the developer in the telecommunication domain has to be concerned about the look of his system too. As the profile tells us a large portion of the telecommunication equipment designed - the terminal network elements - will be sold to individuals that will use it in their daily life. How important design considerations are can be seen from the fact that there are exchangeable, differently coloured, shells for cellular telephones.

Regulatory Constraints. In the defence domain, there are many regulations but they originate from a moderate number of sources. In contrast, in the telecommunication domain there is at least the same number of regulations that originate from a vast number of sources. As the profile shows, there are international, national and even regional regulations.

An additional and essential difference is what is governed by the regulations. In the defence domain, many regulations state how the development has to be performed and what quality has to be achieved. The regulations in the telecommunication domain state the minimum of functionality that has to be provided and the minimum performance of the associated functions.

Development Cost. As the profile shows the telecommunications market is huge. Especially the equipment for the individual user is produced in very large numbers. To gain a reasonable profit in this volume production sector it is reasonable to spend a large development effort with the aim to cut the production cost of the items. When developing services and applications a big development effort will pay back too if the product is used by millions of users every day.

Services. While the defence business primarily deals with equipment the profile of the telecommunication domain show that a large part of the business are services and applications.

WHERE IS THE SYSTEMS ENGINEERING HIDDEN?

- The sophisticated services and applications are based on information technology systems. The associated engineering problems are covered by the software engineering community.
- For volume production items, the most development effort is spent for production engineering. The systems engineering effort, though it may be considerable in relation to other domains, looks negligible in comparison.
- The many standards and recommendations for telecommunication systems specify functionality and the associated performance. They are a compilation of the systems engineering works of all parties that have contributed to the standards - equipment suppliers, network operators, service

suppliers, governments, users etc. Because these systems engineering results are publicly available, they will be reused repeatedly.

- The applicable standards and regulations as well as most of the customers do not force the telecommunications industry to use predefined development processes. There is no necessity to demonstrate that there is a systems engineering step in the process. Consequently, there is no need to distinguish systems engineering from the other engineering steps.
- Telecommunication systems have a long history. During this time several problem domains associated with telecommunication systems have spawned distinct branches of science and engineering that do not show up in the systems engineering context any more.

WHY IS THIS A CHALLENGE FOR INCOSE?

The Situation for Telecommunications Industry Will Change. Telecommunication networks are growing rapidly and likewise grows the complexity of the equipment. The network operators are forced to do big investments in new equipment but due to the complexity of the purchased systems, they loose the ability to control the quality and adequacy of their purchases themselves. To compensate this inability the network operators demand that the suppliers are able to demonstrate the quality of their products and an adequate quality assurance program for example through an ISO9000 certificate. One step further in this direction is the "TRILLIUM Model for Telecom Product Development & Support Process Capability" of Bell Canada (Coallier 1994). ISO9000 as well as TRILLIUM require a well-defined engineering process that includes at least requirements engineering steps. Formal systems engineering will have to be demonstrated in the near future. INCOSE is able to provide the systems engineering methodologies and the scientific background that would put the telecommunication industry in a position where it can demonstrate engineering excellence over the full scale of disciplines.

The Telecommunications Industry uses Interesting Methods. The Telecommunications industry uses various highly effective methods that have system scope especially in the domain of mathematical modelling of systems. These methods could be of high value to the general systems engineering community.

What is to be done? The challenge for INCOSE is to attract more practitioners from the telecommunication domain to explore the possible synergies between the telecommunication domain and other domains.

The principles of systems engineering, processes and activities like those described in (INCOSE 1998) are universally applicable. They have to be tailored for the use in the different industries. Regarding the telecommunications industry this tailoring differs considerably from the tailoring described in (INCOSE 19998). The way how engineers in the telecommunications domain analyse a system and the vocabulary they use differs from that of other, younger, domains. The ideas about tailoring systems engineering processes and activities have to be broadened if they were to be easily used in the telecommunications domain.

Engineers in the telecommunications industry are not attracted to the benefits of systems engineering because they often do not find their problems reflected by the systems engineering community. This is not because the systems engineering community would not cover those problems but again results form the cultural difference. INCOSE should steer the systems engineering research community into looking more at the traditional engineering domains. How do they analyse the systems and how do the describe them?

REFERENCES

Clancy, Tom, *Red Storm Rising*. G. P. Putnam's Sons, New York, 1986.

Coallier, François, Trillium Model for Telecom Product Development & Support Process Capability, Bell Canada Acquisitions, 1994

Holzmann Gerard J. and Björn Pehrson, *The Early History of Data Networks*, IEEE Press, 1994.

INCOSE, Systems Engineering Handbook -A "How To" Guide For All Engineers, 1998

Mackey, William F. et al., Systems Engineering Applications Profiles. Version 2.0a, 1999. (http://www.incose.org/seatc/seap2a-1.pdf, http://www.incose.org/seatc/seap2a-2.pdf)

Martin, James N., "Telecom and Defense Systems: Exploring Differences in the Practice of Systems Engineering." *Proceedings of the Ninth International Symposium of the International Council on Systems Engineering*. INCOSE 1999, pp 1191-1198.

BIOGRAPHY

Ruediger Kaffenberger works as a systems engineer since 1992. He is now with the Optical Networks Division of Marconi Communications, where his responsibilities include the definition of the architecture of future SDH systems. In previous positions Ruediger Kaffenberger developed the requirements for application specific integrated circuits, designed single board computers, multi-processor systems, and hard real-time software.

Ruediger Kaffenberger received a M.S. degree in Electrical Engineering from the Universität Stuttgart. He is a founding member of the INCOSE German Chapter, a member of the IEEE and the IEEE Computer Society.

A Systematic Approach to Environmental Legislation

Catherine M. Plowman, David W. Nipper, Bradley M. Gardner
Idaho National Engineering & Environmental Laboratory
P.O. Box 1625
Idaho Falls, Idaho 83415-3750

Introduction and Background. Environmental legislation in today's world presents a difficult challenge. Much time may pass between the documentation of the original legislative needs and the actual attempts at fulfilling that legislation. In the ensuing years, political sensitivities, technical solutions, and public opinions are all subject to change. Yet the original legislation is often written so tightly as to be literally "fixed in concrete". The specific approach, tightly defined in legislation, may be so inflexible that to accommodate new technologies, opinions, sensitivities, etc., can not only drive the cost of implementation far higher than originally estimated, but also limits the end users ability to implement the newest and best technologies. By adapting systems engineering techniques, legislated processes can be made more adaptable. As a result, some pitfalls of legislatively prescribed solutions can be avoided by concentrating on the desired result and specifying the goals with measurable values. By modifying the methods by which environmental legislation is created, we hope to provide significant cost savings realized at the time the work is actually performed. At the same time, legislation thus created may allow executive agencies the latitude they need to respond appropriately to changing conditions. The method we will define and discuss here is called "A Systematic Approach to Environmental Legislation".

METHODOLOGY

General Systematic Approach. When discussing a 'systematic approach', the underlying technology belongs to the discipline of Systems Engineering. When a major engineering effort is undertaken, such as the design of a new skyscraper, vehicle, or cellular phone, there is usually a detailed planning phase. In this phase, the requirements for the system are defined, and the process by which the system will be designed is defined. The Systems Engineering (SE) method defines a process of designing to requirements, first to top-level requirements, with top-level functions, then the requirements for those functions, and the smaller functions that will satisfy them, and so on. Each piece of a system needs measurable requirements, and each piece is designed and tested to those requirements. When Boeing lined up the first 777 for takeoff, they knew it would fly, and land, and meet airline needs, and be maintainable, and many other things. They knew this because they determined the requirements of the customers (the airlines, the passengers, the air traffic system, etc.) in advance. They designed each system and sub-system to a set of customer needs that added up to a complete and verified aircraft system.

At the Idaho National Engineering & Environmental Laboratory (INEEL), our Systems Engineering process is based on both traditional applications of SE and on the tailored application of SE within the DOE environment. The result is a cyclic and recursive model that is applied at different levels of rigor depending on the type of program or project involved. This adaptation has been the subject of much study, and a college course has been prepared on the subject (now available through the University Of Idaho). Figure 1, below, graphically depicts one cycle of this tailored SE process, and is followed by a summary outline of the model. While many cycles of the SE process typically occur during the course of a project, each cycle covers the same basic steps:

Systems Engineering Planning

Assess the complexity and risks of the problem, and decide the level of rigor required in the engineering process. Plan the activities and products for the duration of the effort. Document all of these as a part of the overall management plan.

Mission Analysis

Analyze the problem and determine that a solution is possible and desirable. Clearly state the goal or end result to be achieved. Identify the boundaries of the system that is involved. Define and document the specific requirements that apply, in measurable terms.

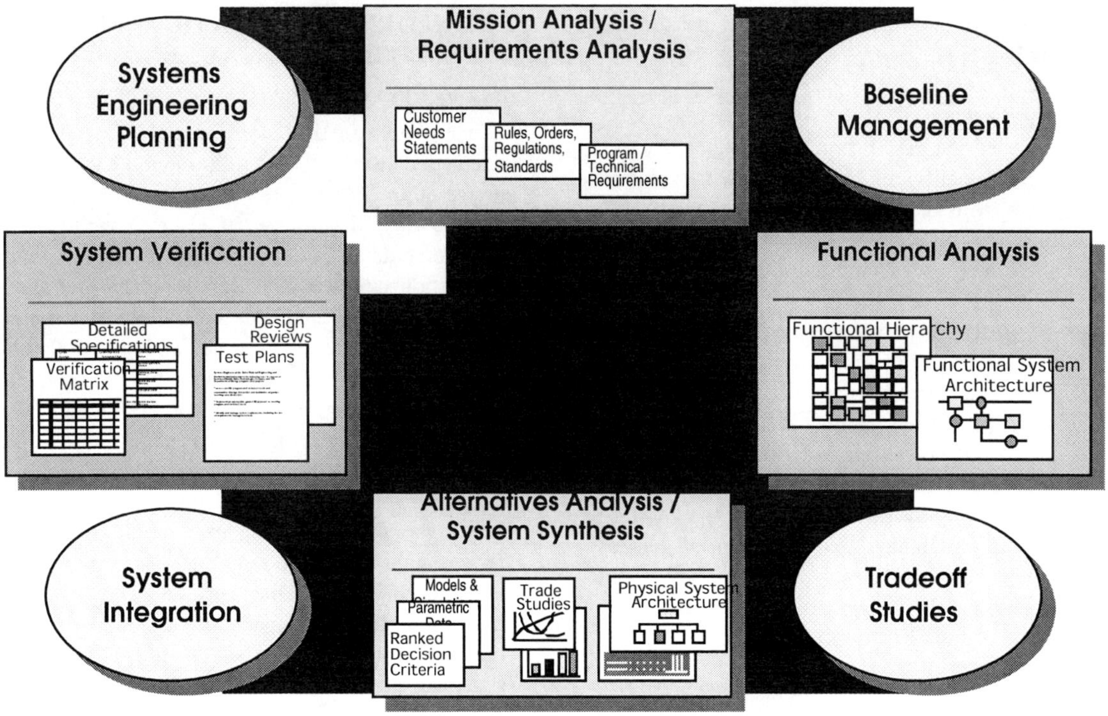

Figure 1: One Cycle of a Standard Systems Engineering Process

Requirements Analysis

Identify the customers and stakeholders, their expectations, requirements, issues, constraints, assumptions and assertions. Study these thoroughly, and document your understanding of them. Organize these requirements by type and scope, such as those that apply directly to the entire system (the aircraft shall carry 500 passengers). Those requirements that apply to and imply a specific function (the aircraft shall have nose-wheel steering), and those that apply to the system indirectly (aircraft operation will be expected to result in no more than 1 death per 1,000,000,000 miles flown). Combine these into a set of specific and measurable requirements. Document the work with the concurrence of the customer.

Baseline Management and Change Control

Identify system and project elements which must not be allowed to change without management agreement and communication to all affected parties (i.e., the aircraft is now going to carry 700 passengers instead of 500). Place these items under "Configuration Control", a process that documents, communicates, and controls changes to documents, drawings, and other design and system elements. Review these documents regularly to ensure that they are consistent with the ongoing effort.

Functional Analysis

Turn system functional requirements into generic system functions (the aircraft is made up of fuselage, wings, tail, landing gear, and engines). Assign the applicable known requirements to each function, defining sub-functions (landing gear have tires, wheels, axles, brakes, controls) and requirements for these. Document this functional architecture and control these new details of the design.

Tradeoff Studies

Decide which requirements are most critical in each function. Determine a method to weigh conflicting requirements. Identify different ways to accomplish the functions. Test the alternatives to each function and determine the levels of performance against the critical requirements. Document all results for further analysis.

Alternatives Analysis

Develop and document a set of alternative system concepts, weighing them against the various modes the system will encounter (four turbojets, 3 fan-jets, or two large fan-jets, considered while parked, taxiing, taking off, cruising, and landing). Test, simulate, model, or estimate the performance of each alternative in each mode. Organize and analyze the results, then make and document a decision as to the best alternative.

System Synthesis

Assign the generic system functions to actual physical components of the preferred solution (engines: 3 Rolls-Royce fan jets, model X-99, mounted on the fuselage). Document the design. This is called the physical architecture.

System Integration

Review the functional and physical architectures and define the interfaces between the parts (tires must fit wheels, wheel-to-tire seal must hold air at 200 PSI, braking heat must not exceed 180 degrees Celsius). Optimize these interfaces, and the interfaces outside the system under study (the plane must use existing gates at airports). Obtain agreement from all parties and document the interfaces. Manage the design process to maintain the integrity of these interfaces.

System Verification

Plan to verify that the requirements are met by the design. Hold reviews and audits at designated points in the process. Provide corrective feedback from reviews and audits to the design, and follow up.

A TAILORED SYSTEMATIC APPROACH FOR ENVIRONMENTAL LEGISLATION

The INEEL Systems Engineering process, as shown above, is designed to start from a customer's mission need and top level requirements and objectively arrive at an end state that meets those original needs. Key to this SE process is a set of well-understood requirements and goals. Where these exist, and new legislation is under consideration, a proper statement of quantifiable user needs will allow implementation which can be revised as times and situations change. In some existing cases, quantifiable requirements are not extant. Prior legislation or decisions may have hidden the underlying needs under an established solution or end-state. In these cases, it may be possible to reverse the SE process and reduce the existing "solution" into a set of requirements. These requirements can be the starting point for new legislation provides the latitude necessary to meet future conditions while ensuring that the original intent is enforced. In essence, this is reversing the standard SE cycle and doing it backwards as demonstrated in Figure 2 below.

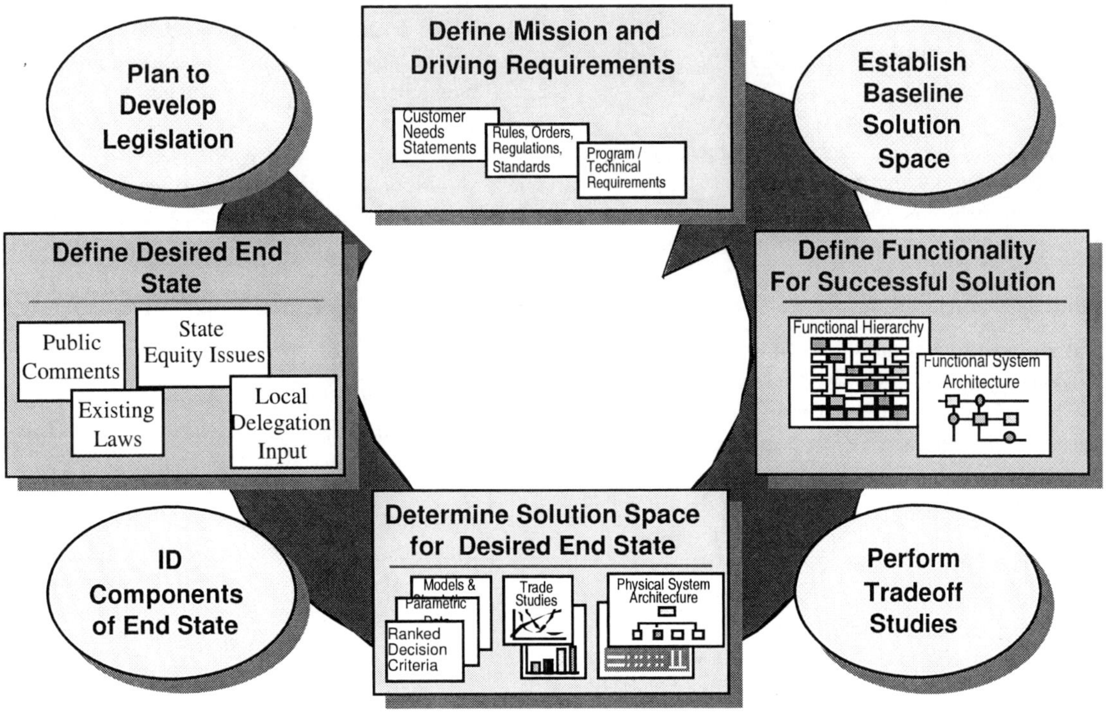

Figure 2: Tailored Systematic Approach to Environmental Legislation

Steps of the Reversed SE Process.

Plan to Develop Legislation

Study and understand the need for the legislation. Estimate the level of difficulty in establishing the underlying mission and requirements. Plan an effort to arrive at a defensible derivation of the requirements.

Define Desired End State

Analyze the existing legislation or solution and determine the result of its application in the context in which it was created. Determine, where possible, the details of that context, including existing law, stakeholder interests, political climate, technological capabilities, etc.

Identify Potential Components of Desired End State

Divide the resulting end state system into manageable components. Identify resulting systems, sub-systems, processes, products, etc, and organize them logically. This is the original physical architecture.

Determine Feasible Solution Space for Desired End State

Considering the conditions as understood at the time, in the original context, expand a model of the possible solutions that may have been considered. This is the original feasible solution space.

Perform Tradeoff Studies on Potential Components

Reverse the process that resulted in the original solution, arriving at the weighting factors and models that were used to arrive at the original solution. This will establish the priority of the original requirements.

Define System Functionality for a Successful Solution

Create generic statements of the functional requirements that led to the originally selected solution. Simplify these into a system functional architecture.

Establish Baseline of Successful Solution Space

Analyze the functional architecture and devise alternatives that may have been considered. The solutions that were rejected under the original context establish the requirements and relative ranking of values that pertained at the time.

Define Mission and Driving Requirements for Performing Organization

Combine the available knowledge of the context, including existing laws, stakeholder interests, political climate, technological capabilities, etc., with the derived requirements and values from the analysis above. Create a unified statement representing the mission, vision, and goals of the original creators of the legislation or solution.

Demonstration of Methodology. This approach creates legislation that defines "what" is to be done, rather than "how" it is to be done. The implementing agencies are given requirements that establish the intent of Congress, but they are free within the solution space to create the best solution possible given the political sensitivities and technology available at the time of implementation.

The example described below is limited to addressing contact handled Transuranic Waste (TRU). The remote handled TRU will be shipped in a system as yet undefined, but this process could be applied to remote handled waste as easily as to contact handled waste. In order to develop this example it was necessary to estimate the intent of Congress on the transportation of TRU waste to the Waste Isolation Pilot Plant (WIPP). This was done by an analysis of the existing legislation. All statements or requirements relating to transport were isolated into a list of specific requirements. These requirements were reduced into a general design, and the overall requirements were estimated. Detailed requirements for emergency training, for instance, were consolidated into the more general "Waste shall be transported safely". These are the resulting general requirements:

1. Transport waste to WIPP as soon as it is safe to do so.
2. Transport waste to WIPP safely.
3. Waste transported shall be authorized waste.
4. Comply with all existing laws and settlement agreements.

These requirements are not well stated or clearly defined. They must be refined further, and tied to a functional model of the overall "Waste-to-WIPP" solution. A little thought (and imagination) provided a view of the "Congressional Intent". While we can only estimate their intent, the concept here is a tool for the Congress, and when applied they will know their own intentions. For now, we will assume that the intent was as follows:

1. To reduce the risk to the public and environment presented by the continued storage of TRU waste in diverse locations of questionable suitability.
2. To reduce the costs of TRU storage.

A legislative approach to the overall "Waste-to-WIPP" problem might be limited to the highest level requirements, but in practice it will probably be designed down to the top-level functions and requirements. While the Congress will need to address the entire solution, in this example we will only address a portion of the problem. We will assume that the solution system has several functions, such as: Identification, Extraction, Preparation, Staging, Transportation, Disposal, Security, Monitoring.

This overall system solution would be outlined in the legislation, accompanied by a set of system and first-level sub-system requirements. To simplify this example, only one sub-system will be addressed: the transportation sub-system function. The function will be called "Transport Waste to WIPP", and we postulate only the following Congressionally mandated requirements:

1. The cost of the system shall be minimized.
2. The risk to the public shall be at or below that of the existing system (the "No Action" baseline).
3. Existing Federal, State, and Tribal laws governing this sub-system and related operations must defer to this legislation but shall not be unnecessarily waived.

[Note: this does not call for the minimization of risk and cost. It minimizes cost while establishing a ceiling for risk. This avoids the questionable situation where money is traded for lives at equal priority. An alternative requirement might call for a cost ceiling with minimized risk. This is rejected because the alternative might result in the ceiling cost having only high-risk alternatives. The selected option does not increase risk to the public, but it accepts the possibility that it will result in high cost.]

The current legislated solution for transporting TRU waste to WIPP requires the use of specially designed and constructed transports and containers. This required point solution has driven WIPP-related costs exceedingly high and stretched out the schedule due to the high costs and limited availability of the designated transports and containers. If, instead, the legislation carried need-based requirements as stated above, then the organization responsible for transporting waste to WIPP (DOE) has the opportunity to devise and explore numerous alternatives, show creativity, and to "think outside the box". To complete the demonstration, we will outline a small number of potential solutions available when requirements-based legislation is provided and show an estimate of savings or risk reductions that might result.

1. The "No Action" solution. Leave the waste where it is, secure and monitor it for as long as necessary. This approach will meet the risk requirement by definition. The cost of this alternative must be compared to the other alternatives that can meet or improve upon the risk requirement.

2. The current solution defined by DOE, which calls for contact handled TRU to be shipped over the highway on specifically designed and constructed tractor/trailer transporters with the waste over-packed in TRUPACT II containers. This alternative is well documented.

3. A modification of Alternative 2, where qualified contact handled TRU is shipped in Department of Transportation (DOT) approved low specific activity (LSA) (strong tight container) packages. Shipments are made with highly qualified, trained drivers using new or near new conventional equipment and utilizing existing HAZMAT/emergency personnel and procedures, the TRANSCOM tracking system, and other measures developed for use with the TRUPACT II. This alternative allows for twice as many containers of qualified waste to be shipped per truck. Consequently, only half as many shipments are needed which in turn reduces the number of road miles to roughly one half of the current plan. Since the number of deaths incurred is more directly related to road miles than to waste container rupture, the deaths per container shipped would be significantly reduced. Consequently, both the cost and risk of shipping waste would be reduced by about one half. The schedule also would be reduced and become far more flexible due to the use of conventional resources. Conventional trucks are available in quantity and at lower cost than the specifically designed transporters. And there are many more LSA containers available than TRUPACT II containers.

4. A completely new alternative in which the standard for shipping containers is changed to a new DOT standard. This DOT standard would be designed specifically for this task, mandated by Federal law, and would allow the waste to be shipped for the most part as it is stored at this time. The waste drums and boxes would be nested, banded and wrapped in the WIPP storage configuration (14 drums/two boxes) prior to being loaded on the conventional vehicles. Safety concerns would be met be means other than "accident-proof" containers, using procedures akin to military convoys. These procedures would mandate having emergency crews, security personnel, cleanup equipment, and inspectors included with the shipments. This alternative reduces the payments to States and Tribes for emergency preparedness, since it provides for this to be on site at all times during transport. It further reduces risk by removing competing traffic from the roads while the convoy is passing. Security personnel would limit vulnerability to sabotage and public disturbances as well. Costs of supporting personnel would be minimized if convoy sizes were large. This would reduce the number of convoys per year, resulting in lower inconvenience to the public.

5. Alternative # 4 above with the modification that the nested 55 gal DOT approved drums and boxes are shipped via rail and the convoy described above (emergency/hazmat/ waste/security) be housed in rail cars to accompany the waste.

CONCLUSIONS AND RECOMMENDATIONS

This study illustrates how application of the Systems Engineering process leads to development of legislation that ultimately defines "what" is to be done, rather than "how" it is to be done. By concentrating on the desired result, and by specifying the goals with measurable values, some potential pitfalls in legislatively prescribed solutions can be avoided. The examples in this study were developed from the set of all options which meet requirements, rather than being confined to a single pre-determined solution. As further advances in technology are developed, or as other conditions change, these advances and changes can easily be used to add to or refine existing options, and to re-direct efforts to the best option. Working in a verified, requirements-based solution space (rather than towards a pre-determined solution) ultimately provides latitude to the end user to utilize new innovative technologies and reduce overall cost and schedule constraints, without adversely affecting the accepted risk.

Recommendations. Systems engineering is widely practiced and accepted in many agencies of the government and in commercial settings that deal with complex designs and critical products. The SE process is a highly effective tool that can be adapted to successfully deal with the complexities involved in designing environmental legislation. This paper, and any extensions or derivatives, should be forwarded through channels to the appropriate State and

National legislative bodies, as well as to those regulatory agencies which produce quasi-legislative rules and policies in the Environmental arena. Citizen's groups and other stakeholders may also find this approach useful in understanding the processes that affect them.

Follow on tasks recommended for this adaptation of the SE process include further refinement of the "reverse SE process" as it applies to design of environmental legislation. This refinement could be accomplished through an in depth study of carefully selected corollary subjects. The study should including workshops involving SE professionals, subject matter experts from the areas to be evaluated and environmental law professionals who participate in rule or law making. The result would be a verified product that could then be documented in a "how to" procedure to be presented to legislative and other bodies for future implementation.

REFERENCES

Defense Authorization Act of 1979 (PL 96-164)

Department of Energy National Security and Military Applications of Nuclear Energy Authorization Act of 1980 (Pub. L. 96-164; 93 Stat. 1265)

Nuclear Waste Policy Act of 1982 (PL97-425)

Stipulated Agreement between the DOE and the State of New Mexico (07/01/1981) and its various attachments, appendices, and supplements, as amended.

The Solid Waste Disposal Act (42U.S.C.6901 et seq.)

The Toxic Substances Control Act (15 U.S.C. 2601 et seq.)

The Toxic Substances Control Act (15 U.S.C. 2601 et seq.)

The Comprehensive Environmental Response, Compensation, and Liability Act of 1980 (42U.S.C.9601 et seq.)

Title XIV of the Public Health Service Act (42U.S.C.300f et seq.; commonly referred to as the "Safe Drinking Water Act")

U.S. Congress. Waste Isolation Pilot Plant Land Withdrawal Act. (P.L. 102-579).

U.S. Congress. Waste Isolation Pilot Plant Land Withdrawal Amendments Act. National Defense Authorization Act for Fiscal Year 1997, Subtitle F. (P.L. 104-201), September 23, 1996.

U.S. Department of Energy. "Waste Acceptance Criteria for the Waste Isolation Pilot Plant." (DOE/WIPP-069, Rev. 5), DOE Carlsbad Area Office, Carlsbad, NM, April 1996.

U.S. Environmental Protection Agency. 40 CFR 191. Environmental Radiation Protection Standards for Management and Disposal of Spent Nuclear Fuel, High-Level and Transuranic Radioactive Wastes; Final Rule. (Federal Register, Vol. 58, No. 242), December 20, 1993.

U.S. Environmental Protection Agency. 40 CFR 194. Criteria for the Certification and Re-Certification of the Waste Isolation Pilot Plant's Compliance with the 40 CFR Part 191 Disposal Regulations. (Federal Register, Vol. 61, No. 28), February 9, 1996.

40 CFR 261-264

42 USC Secs. 2014, 6924, and 10101

BIOGRAPHY

Catherine Plowman has worked at the Idaho National Environmental & Engineering Laboratory since 1995. She is leading the Systems Sceinces Group and has managed DOE's Partnership in Systems Engineering Excellence. Prior to that, she worked at NASA's Johnson Space Center in Houston, Texas developing Space Station simulations and providing Systems Engineering expertise to organizational development initiatives. She holds a B.S. in Aerospace Engineering and a B.S. in Computer Science from Texas A&M University and has been working as a Systems Engineer since 1985.

David W. Nipper has been a scientist and engineer for the Idaho National Engineering and Environmental Laboratory for over ten years. He has worked with command and control systems, sensor systems, unique radio antenna designs, database systems, and internet-based information systems. This second career follows a full career as an Air Force officer in the fields of information systems, tactical communications engineering, and research [and development test. He has a bachelor's in chemistry from San Diego State, and a Master's in Public Administration from Golden Gate University.

Bradley Gardner is employed by Bechtel BWXT Idaho, LLC at the Idaho National Engineering and Environmental Laboratory as a Staff Engineer in the Environmental Technology Planning and Integration Department. Mr. Gardner has over 15 years of professional experience spread over the following disciplines: Systems Engineering, Project

Management, Communications, and Technical Leadership in the areas of Transportation, Waste Technology Development, Robotics, Insitu Waste Remediation and other Environmental Restoration projects for the U. S. Department of Energy. Brad is the lead inventor on five patents for a devise and method for Insitu Waste Barrier Apparatus and Construction. Four of the patents have been issued, and one is pending. Brad received his Bachelors Degree in Waste Management from the University of Idaho, in May 1995.

Abatement Of Nonpoint Source Pollution: A Systems Engineering Model

Bahador Ghahramani, Ph.D., P.E., CPE,
Bassam Elmaimani
Tito Pope
Engineering Management Department
School of Engineering
University of Missouri-Rolla, Rolla, MO 65409-0370
Tel: (573) 341-6057, Fax: (573) 341-6567
E-Mail: ghahrama@umr.edu

ABSTRACT

Nonpoint source pollution prevention management, primarily consisting of education and regulatory efforts, has met little success to date. Indeed, nonpoint pollution is getting worse, not better, and the Environmental Protection Agency rates it as the leading cause of water quality problems. We must deal with the problems through a systems approach to achieve workable, feasible solutions. Unlike point source input, where the levels, quantities, and consistency of loading are known, nonpoint source pollution must be modeled as an environmentally open system that is constantly changing. Successful nonpoint pollution management requires a systems approach for applying general land management practices to specific unique watersheds focusing on identifying the specific objectives, increasing participation of the affected people in the development process, and applying continuous refinements and improvements once the watershed' s management system is implemented. This paper proposes a more holistic approach that will result in robust methods for modeling, implementing, and assessing the control and abatement of nonpoint source pollution.

INTRODUCTION

Nonpoint Source (NPS) pollution has been identified as one of the primary threats relative to our nation' s water and environmental quality. The Environmental Protection Agency (EPA) states that nonpoint source contamination is the main reason that approximately 40 percent of our lakes, rivers, and estuaries are not clean enough to meet basic uses such as fishing or swimming (EPA website). It is pollution that does not emanate from any one source and is, therefore, much more difficult to manage and control. It is the result of every individual who spills oil that is washed down the gutter or who improperly applies environmentally harmful fertilizers and pesticides to his lawn or farmland that eventually reaches ground and surface water supplies.

The Environmental Protection Agency (EPA) and other government regulatory bodies attack all forms of pollution, including nonpoint sources of contamination, through a three-tiered approach. The EPA seeks pollution control through legislative regulations imposed on possible producers, application of Best Management Practices (BMP) to abate the effects, and education. Controlling pollution through water quality standards such as the Clean Water Act has worked quite successfully for controlling and regulating point sources of pollution, but falls short when dealing with nonpoint source pollution. Although the EPA has come to realize the benefits of a watershed or drainage basin based approach, it needs to assume a more holistic view to solve the problems associated with nonpoint source pollution.

Regulations can be easily monitored and enforced for point sources of pollution such as municipal sewage treatment facilities that produce discharge from a single outlet. However, attempting regulatory enforcement of innumerable minute sources from constantly changing locations is nearly impossible. Furthermore, Best Management Practices must be tailored for the specific watershed for which it is to be implemented. There are too many factors that go into development and implementation of conservation and pollution management practices for any one general approach to work everywhere. Factors leading to water contamination differ in different locations due to characteristics such as soil types and average rainfall amounts. Even the goals and desired end-state of an area can be different due to social and economic factors. Education must go beyond pollution prevention to include more technical training and empowerment to enable communities not only to prevent pollution activities, but also develop watershed-based management procedures for themselves. It will be the individual farmers who become the "scientist" implementing and adjusting the methods and procedures for controlling nonpoint source pollution on their land.

To proactively combat the decentralized and profuse environmental problems related to nonpoint sources we must take a more decentralized systems engineering approach to problem solving. This will enable us to better define and address nonpoint source pollution management, identify critical areas of concern on which to focus, and develop and assess implementation methods for better control and management of these areas. In many cases, these plans will result in economic benefits through the associated costs of reduced tillage and the better utilization of fertilizers and pesticides that create a win-win situation for the producer and for water quality.

DEFINING NONPOINT SOURCE POLLUTION

Nonpoint source pollution can be categorized into three major producers: agricultural activities, residential/ urban runoff, and construction/ mining operations. Nonpoint source pollution by its very nature is widespread, and focusing on any single producer will have negligible effects on its reduction. The EPA states that two-thirds of the nation's rivers are affected by agricultural nonpoint source pollution resulting from crop production and animal tending (EPA website). Manure runoff from feedlots and runoff from fields containing fertilizers, pesticides, organic compounds, and soil itself cause major problems with the quality of our water supplies. These runoff events can be due to rainfall, snowfall, or in large part, to irrigation practices. The latest National Water Quality Inventory indicates "agriculture is the leading contributor to water quality impairments nationwide, degrading 60 percent of the impaired river miles and half of the impaired lake acreage surveyed by states, territories, and tribes." At the same time, urban nonpoint source runoff is the largest source of water quality impairments to surveyed estuaries (Figure 1). With this emphasis on the effects and criticality of nonpoint source pollution, control and abatement strategies have received ever-increasing emphasis in the last decade.
Point source pollution can be cleaned and controlled at its effluent point (i.e., a municipal or industrial wastewater treatment plant) thereby minimizing environmentally harmful effects. On the other hand, nonpoint source pollution must be proactively managed. It is not feasible to attempt control of every possible effluent point in a watershed or enforce regulatory actions against every single individual who may contribute to nonpoint pollution. Therefore, means must be developed to monitor and control nonpoint source pollution before it reaches and contaminates ground and surface water supplies. It must be managed specifically for each topographical area that defines the natural course of runoff events or watershed.

The primary sources of agricultural nonpoint source pollution are well documented. They include soil erosion from cropland; nutrients and pathogens that are released from improperly stored animal feeding operations or from the over-application of manure to cropland; over-application of fertilizers and pesticides; poorly managed grazing operations; and sub-optimal irrigation practices. It should not be surprising that agriculture exerts such a large influence on our aquatic resources; after all, it is the dominant feature of our national landscape. Almost 400 million acres of land are actively managed to grow crops in the United States every year. Even greater acreage supports grazing activities. The direct and inevitable association between land use and nonpoint source pollution creates challenges for the agricultural community and those of us who work with this community.

In "Disasters Aren't the Problem--The Real Environmental Catastrophe Is the Slow Creep of Crud, " author Michael Parfit argued that "ruination" proceeds from "small events—the spraying of lawns; the dumping of oil; the demand for wormless apples, beachfront cottages, shrimp, and layers of packaging—in which we all partake." It is these small events, which accumulate into the major problems and risks that nonpoint source pollution poses to us today.

CHARACTERISTICS OF NPS POLLUTANTS

One of the first steps in developing measures to control the problem of pollution from nonpoint sources is to identify the various types, characteristics, attributes, and methods in which pollutants affect the environment. It is only from this point that a logical and comprehensive plan can be implemented to control and abate nonpoint source contamination of our nation's water resources.

The EPA states that 6 billion tons of soil are lost from farmlands each year deteriorating our farmlands and clogging our rivers and waterways. We then spend $300 million per year dredging silt out of our waterways. The General accounting Office (GAO) has reported that soil losses from poor erosion control are 25% worse than soil loss conditions in 1934 during the "Dust Bowl" days. This loss of soil cover is a huge problem in itself and what it carries with it compounds the problem even more.

A large amount of nutrients resulting from the application of fertilizers and untreated livestock sewage either erode with the soil or leach into the subsoil and subsequently the ground water. Runoff of nutrients such as phosphorus and nitrates has been increasing since the 1950's and poses numerous threats to the environment. These fertilizers work in aquatic environments just as they do on land and stimulate growth of algae and moss, which in turn can choke waterways and damage aquatic life. As recently as the July 28 edition of U.S. News and World Report, an article entitled "The Cell from Hell" was written concerning the toxic algae Pfiesteria that is killing fish and marine life along the coasts of the United States. This alga thrives on the nitrate and phosphorous pollutants from biological wastes entering the rivers and estuaries. In North Carolina and Maryland recent outbreaks led to so many dead fish on the beach that it took bulldozers to clear them. The principle culprit is the nonpoint runoff of sewage wastes from industrial-scale hog farms in North Carolina.

Another example of environmental waste is the high nitrate levels, which have been recorded throughout the Corn Belt states of the country. This contamination has resulted in many wells exceeding safe levels of nitrate contamination due to sorption and leaching. More than 50% of the wells in Kansas were deemed contaminated in 1989, which can lead to methemoglobinemia or "blue baby disease" in infants and possibly contribute to some types of cancer (Pitt, Clark, Farmer, & Field, 50, 55).

Pesticide contamination is another nonpoint source area of concern. Most of these chemicals are water-soluble and, as a result, easily carried with water runoff or adsorbed into the soil. Many of these chemicals dissipate from the soil to the point where no obvious pesticide properties remain within a year with the exception of a few, such as Atrazine, which can stay suspended much longer. Pesticides are often assumed to degrade at a rate proportional to the amount present and, thus, the EPA usually refers to the pesticide's half-life when considering its dissipation period. The relation of the soil type and the chemical type will determine the adsorption, solubility, and infiltration characteristics affecting the method and speed in which the chemicals reach ground or surface water sources. The greatest pesticide mobility occurs in areas with coarse-grained or sandy soils without a hardpan layer, having low clay and organic content and high permeability. At the same time, basic (pH>7) pesticides become more mobile in soils having high pH values and vice-versa (Pitt et al., 60). The health risks posed by these chemical contaminants include possible linkages to cancer, nervous system disorders, birth defects, and other systemic disorders.

Organic compounds that enter our water resources primarily from livestock operations pose additional threats to the environment. Industrial and urban areas also contribute heavily to the organic load in our water as a result of storm water runoffs collecting petroleum-based (organic carbon) products off roads and streets that are subsequently carried into our water supply. There are three principle characteristics leading to the removal and dissipation of organics:

1) Volatilization is the dissipation of organics into the atmosphere.
2) Sorption is bonding of the organic molecules to other molecules and can take the form of several types of bond.
3) Decomposition through degradation is the process in which the organic is chemically or biologically broken down. It includes hydrolysis and photo-degradation as well as degradation from biological microorganisms (Pitt et al., 69-70). This method accounts for the majority of organic decomposition and there are many additional factors that contribute to this process. Organics can stay suspended in water for long periods before settling, which increases the related environmental hazards.

Along with organic compounds and often associated with organics are pathogenic microorganisms. Many factors affecting their ability to contaminate water supplies and their removal (See Figure 2). Viral and bacterial pathogens pose great risk of disease to humans ranging from salmonella to viruses causing hepatitis and meningitis.

Metals and minerals pose another primary risk to the environment from nonpoint sources such as mining operations. Mineral salts can dissolve in water and rapidly infiltrate into water resources. Heavy metals can leach into the ground water from various nonpoint sources bonding with water molecules under certain conditions. Many metals are known to have harmful effects on fish, animal, and human populations while salts can "kill" the ground it accumulates in and prevent any plant or crop growth.

These major types of nonpoint source pollution are dependent on many factors. The problem of nonpoint source pollution is difficult to encompass. Yet one can begin to relate specific attributes to the different causes of contamination, which in turn allows for developing models and measures for control.

APPLYING A SYSTEMS APPROACH

A general framework for improving the management of lands and reducing the delivery of pollutants should involve efforts to (1) maintain and enhance soil quality, (2) improve the precision and efficiency of inputs, including nutrients and crop and lawn protection products, and (3) reduce the urban and agricultural delivery of sediment, nutrients, and pathogens due to erosion, runoff, and drainage. Still, the specific strategies that are most effective at achieving these goals will depend upon the site-specific soil, landscape, and hydrologic characteristics of each farm and watershed. No single management practice is a "cure" for nonpoint source pollution and each watershed presents an entirely different system containing an entirely different problem to be solved.

One must identify the critical area (i.e., watershed or basin) to be managed, develop and select means with which to control or lessen the unforward effects in that critical area, and develop a comprehensive plan for implementing measures area wide in order to have lasting real effects. The control measures and proposals must be developed with the social and economic benefits in mind since the best means for ensuring successful implementation of environmental stewardship is to relate the problem directly to the people and give them ownership of the solutions. The immense scale and dynamics associated with the different characteristics and parameters of nonpoint source pollution demands a more holistic, systems approach.

THE MODEL DESCIPTION

The first step using a systems approach to problem solving is problem formulation and needs analysis. The selected system principles and strategies and methods confirm an open system architecture concept due to the environment (dynamic, diverse and tremendous amounts of inputs). Selected principles influence the selection of the process strategies and methods, which intern will dictate the appropriate tools. Additionally, these tools must be supported by the system's environment as shown in Figure 3. Nonpoint pollution must be identified in relation to the types of topography, economy, and possible pollutant producers. A hog farm in Iowa surrounded by acres of corn will have entirely different solution needs than an apple orchard in Washington of the same dimensions. The critical area must be defined since the viability of a project is defined in terms of the entire watershed and not any single source of contamination. At the heart of this are extensive research and documentation of water quality problems and their sources in order to develop a well-defined baseline with which to begin.

Next, the setting of objectives and an overall project plans must begin. Specific project objectives and goals must be defined in terms of short and long-term environmental goals as well as social, economic, and geographic goals. Furthermore, management must "power-down" to the potential participants and community members involved. It will be the individual stewards of the land conducting the research and implementing management practices. The Snyder Evaluation Model (Alien) is an evaluation process which lends itself to involving participants as co-evaluators through a three-stage process of evaluation: process, outcome, and short-cycle (Figure 3). This involves the concept of "learning by doing" since initial objectives and procedures are likely to result in both intended and unintended effects. While the unintended effects are to be minimized, the project is developed with a long-term, idealistic focus for refinement and continuous improvement.

At the same time, funding must be secured and the roles of agencies such as the EPA must be clarified to ensure adequate delineation of responsibilities. A critical phase of project development is model building. One must design a data-collection, monitoring, and evaluation model that enable studying the critical area as well as continuous revision and improvement once systems are emplaced. This can be done with geographic information system (GIS) tools, simulation, and measuring devices. The specific characteristics of the primary pollutants identified in problem analysis can be related to the system attributes that will drive criteria development. These attributes are the methods in which contamination by the major pollutants occurs: runoff, sorption, bonding, leaching, solubility, half-life, degradation, and/ or relation to atmospheric conditions. Thus, the variables (PPM contaminants in water) and model parameters (runoff events) can be associated with the accumulation of nonpoint source pollution and the pre-defined environmental thresholds (EPA standards) for such pollutants.

Data collection can now take place to measure the current environment's water quality and potential threats. This information process will, in turn, lead to verification and validation of the problem analysis and modeling process. Should the data not verify and validate the model, the problem, goals and model can be adjusted and refined as necessary since the system is a continually improving process. Since the model is a continuous quality improvement process, one must modify the selection of the principles, strategies and methods, and tools in order to meet the system's performance and design objectives. Altering the objectives is another alternative to the system's performance improvement. The process of reevaluation contributes to the two proposed modifications since it provides one with added knowledge about the principles, strategies, tools, and the system's environment and the robust interactions among these components.

Once the model and system achieve validity, an experimental design can be created. It can be based on the general land treatment and Best Management Practice (BMP) approaches, but will also apply a much more holistic approach based on the specific watershed system that has been constructed. Efforts can also be concentrated and exercised more efficiently. For example, if only a small portion of the watershed produces a wide majority of the pollution, management practices can be tailored to this area. It is much more feasible and cost effective to achieve this than a 100% solution which would be impossible to design given the constantly changing state of nonpoint pollution. Should the experimental design meet the project objectives and attain the intended effects, full-scale implementation can then occur along with documentation of results. This will allow for performing continuous assessment and improvement to the system parameters (See Figure 4). This systems approach results in the most efficient and productive means of managing nonpoint source pollution since it accounts for all factors within the specific watershed or basin.

CONCLUSIONS

Conservation efforts have shown limited success in implementing the general soil control practices such as terracing, improved tillage methods, and use of settling basins, but sedimentation from runoff is still the leading source of water quality impairment. This is primarily because specific watersheds need specific treatment and control procedures. Much more needs to be done in environmental management to ensure that all areas contributing significant runoff to water quality problems are addressed. Furthermore, any individual occurrence of nonpoint source pollution is negligible and environmental management must take this into account. In order to achieve this, an individualized, systems approach to watershed management must be adopted that involves all participants with the design, development, and implementation of the control and abatement procedures. These procedures must be robustly tailored specifically for the needs and requirements of the watershed's principle uses, topography, and stated objectives in order to maximize effectiveness. Otherwise, control of nonpoint source pollution will remain where it is today— tied up in bureaucratic policy procedures that attempt regulation, not functional management.

REFERENCES

Blanchard, Benjamin S., and Fabrycky, Wolter J., "System Engineering and Analysis", Englewood Cliffs, New Jersey, Prentice-Hall, 2d ed., 1990.

Bosch, O.J.H., Alien, W.J., and Gibson, R.S., "Monitoring as an Integral Part of Management and Policy Making", Manaaki Whenua- Landcare Research, 1997. Available at URL: wm/landcare.cri.nz.

Curtis, D.S., Memorandum from Deputy Secretary Curtis to Field Offices 1/25/96; includes the Interim Safe Storage Criteria as an attachment, January 1996.

Dalton, H.F., Memorandums dated September 12, 1996 and November 1, 1996 issued by H.F. Dalton, DOE Rocky Flats Field Office, subject: Rebaselining of Residue Elimination Project, 1996.

DOE, 1995a, DOE's DNFSB Recommendation 94-1 Implementation Plan, dated February 28, 1995.

DOE, 1995b, DOE Order 4301, "Life Cycle Assets Management", August 4, 1995. Available through the web at http://www.doe.gov/.

DOE, 1996a, DOE-STD-3013-96, "Criteria for Preparing and Packaging Plutonium Metals and Oxides for Long-Term Storage", U.S. Department of Energy, Washington, DC, September, 1996.

DOE, 1996b, DOE-GPG-FM-003, Tradeoff Studies, Department of Energy Office of Field Management Good Practice Guides, Washington, D.C., March 1996. Available on the web at http://www.doe.gov/.

DOE/WIPP-069, "Waste Acceptance Criteria for the Waste Isolation Pilot Plant", Rev. 4.0, 1996.

DNFSB, Recommendation 94-1 to the Secretary of Energy, May 1994. Available from DNFSB at http://www.dnfsb.gov/.

Gale, J. A., Osmond, D. L., Line, D. E., Spooner, J., and Arnold, J. A. "Planning and Managing a Successful Nonpoint Source Pollution Control Project", North Carolina Cooperative Extension Service, North Carolina State University College of Agricultural and Life Sciences, 1995.

INFL-96/0427, "Integration of Transuranic and Mixed Low Level Waste Activities Across the Department of Energy Complex", Technical Report, December, 1996.

Loehr, R. C., Haith, D. A., Walter, M. F., and Martin, C. S., "Best Management Practices for Agriculture and Silviculture", Ann Arbor, MI: Ann Arbor Science Publishers, 1979: 98-114.

Murphy et al., "Development of the Environmental Management Integration Baseline at the Idaho National Engineering Laboratory Using Systems Engineering", INCOSE Paper, Lockheed Martin Idaho Technologies Company, 1997.

Parfit, M., "Disasters Aren't the Problem—The Real Environmental Catastrophe Is the Slow Creep of Crud", Office of Water Nonpoint Source News/ Notes. Available at URL: www.epa.gov/owow/info/NewsNotes.

Pitt, R., Dark, S., Parmer, K., and Field, R., "Groundwater Contamination from Stormwater Infiltration. Chelsea, MI: Ann Arbor Press Inc, 1996.

Plowman et al., Adopting Classical Systems Engineering to Department of Energy (DOE) Needs", Technical Report INEL-96-0262, INCOSE Paper, Lockheed Martin Idaho Technologies, 1996.

RFETS, 1996b, DOE Order 5480.23, Nuclear Safety Analysis Reports, April 10, 1992, and DOE Order 5480.21, Unreviewed Safety Questions, December 21, 1991.

Satchell, M., "The Cell from Hell", U.S. News and World Report 28, pp. 26-28, July 1997.

U.S. Congress, Resource Conservation and Recovery Act (RCRA), Public Law 42 USC section 6901 et seq. As amended by the Hazardous and Solid Waste Amendments of 1984, and the Federal Facility Complaisance Act of 1992.

U.S. Environmental Protection Agency, Office of Water Nonpoint Source Control Branch. "Managing Nonpoint Source Pollution from Agriculture", EPA841-F-96-004F. Available at URL: www.epa.gov/owow/nps.

U.S. Environmental Protection Agency, Office of Water Nonpoint Source Control Branch. "Nonpoint Source Pollution The Nation's Largest Water Quality Problem". Available at EPA841-F-960 0 4A)(URL: www.epa.ffov/owow/nps.

U.S. Environmental Protection Agency, Office of Water Regulations and Standards, Perspectives on Nonpoint Source Pollution, Proceedings of a National Conference: Kansas City, Missouri, 1985.

ACKNOWLEDGMENTS

Support of the NJK grants throughout this research is greatly appreciated and acknowledged. The authors wish to thank the Bell Laboratories System Engineering group and IBM Watson Center engineers for their valuable collaboration in support of this project. Also, appreciation is given to graduate assistance and Ph.D. candidate Ahmet Tugrul Ozdemir of the Engineering Management Department at the University of Missouri-Rolla, for his help in the preparation of this paper.

Three Leading Sources of Water Quality Impairment

Rank	Rivers	Lakes	Estuaries
1	Agriculture	Agriculture	Urban runoff
2	Municipal point source	Municipal point source	Municipal point source
3	Stream/ habitat changes	Urban runoff	Agriculture

Source: Water National Quality Inventory, 1994

Figure 1. Primary Sources of Water Quality Impairment

FACTOR	PATHOGEN	EFFECT
pH	Bacteria	Shorter survival in pH5 & below (acidic)
Moisture content	Bacteria & entervirus	Longer survival in moist soils
Temp.	Bacteria & viruses	Longer survival at low temp.
Sunlight	Bacteria & viruses	Shortens survival at soil surface
Organic matter	Anaerobic bacteria & viruses	Longer survival & possible regrowth if enough organic present

Figure 2. Source: Crites, 1985

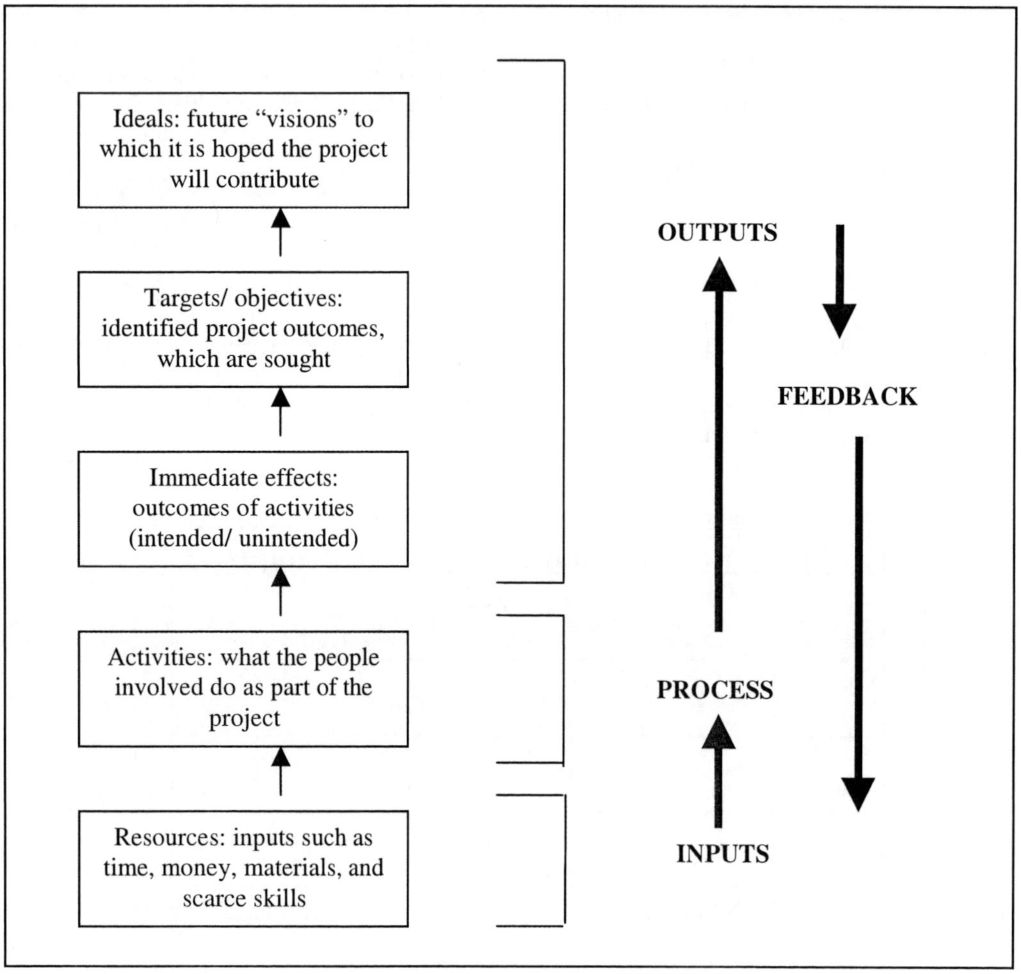

Figure 3. Snyder Evaluation Model

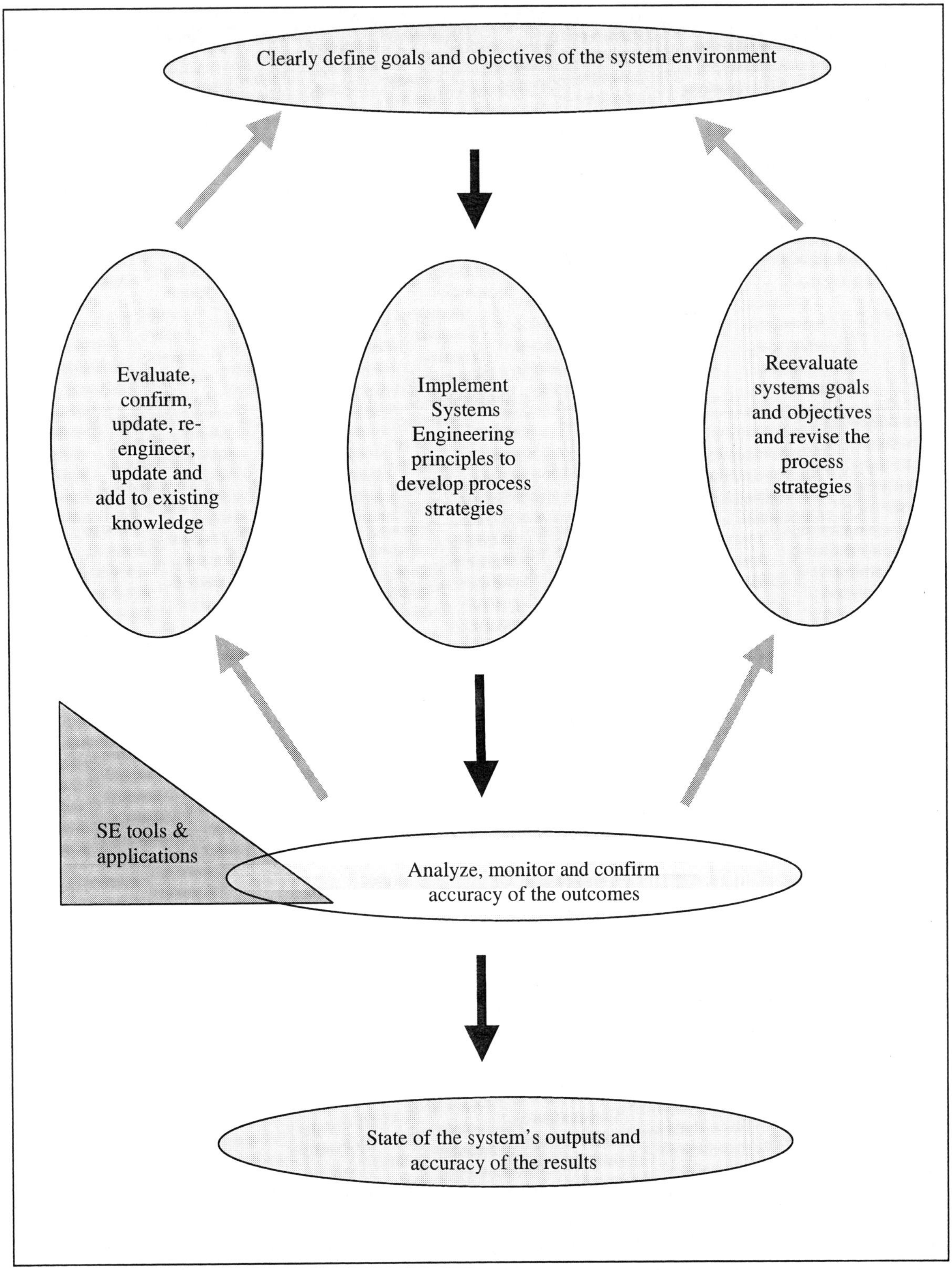

Figure 4. The Systems Engineering Approach Used

Radioactive Material Transportation Requirements for the Department of Energy

Thane W. Bolander
Global Technologies Incorporated
2265 East 25th Street
Idaho Falls, Idaho 83404

Mark E. John
Bechtel BWXT Idaho, LLC
PO Box 1650
Idaho Falls, Idaho 83415

Rick L. Fawcett
Bechtel BWXT Idaho, LLC
PO Box 1650
Idaho Falls, Idaho 83415

Abstract. The Department of Energy (DOE) created the National Transportation Program (NTP) whose goal is to ensure the availability of safe, efficient, and timely transportation of DOE materials. The Integration and Planning Group of the NTP, assisted by Global Technologies Incorporated (GTI), was tasked to identify requirements associated with the transport of DOE Environmental Management (EM) radiological waste/material. A systems engineering approach was used to identify source documents, extract requirements, perform a functional analysis, and set up a transportation requirements management database in RDD-100. Functions and requirements for transporting the following DOE radioactive waste/material are contained in the database: high level radioactive waste (HLW), low-level radioactive waste (LLW), mixed low-level radioactive waste (MLLW), nuclear materials (NM), spent nuclear fuel (SNF), and transuranic waste (TRU waste). The requirements will be used in the development of standard transportation protocols for DOE shipping. The protocols will then be combined into a DOE Transportation Program Management Guide, which will be used to standardize DOE transportation processes.

INTRODUCTION

DOE made 13,000 shipments of hazardous materials in 1998, 5,000 of which were radioactive material shipments. The DOE radioactive material shipments account for 0.17% (5,000 out of 3 million) of all radioactive material shipments made in the United States (US) in a year and 0.001% (5,000 out of 300 million) of all hazardous material shipments (DOE 1999). However, DOE shipments account for about 75% of the total curies shipped in the US. The number of radioactive material shipments made by DOE will increase as the sites begin cleaning up contaminated areas and as Foreign Research Reactor (FRR) SNF is shipped back to the US.

This paper describes the process used to develop the transportation requirements management database and possible future work that can be done to enhance the database.

OBJECTIVES FOR DEVELOPING THE REQUIREMENTS DATABASE

The primary objectives for developing the transportation requirements management database include:

1. Identify all hazardous material requirements associated with the transport of DOE EM radioactive waste/material (HLW, LLW, MLLW, NM, SNF, and TRU waste).
2. Categorize the requirements according to transportation function, waste/material stream {including any specific site/project [e.g., FRR, Waste Isolation Pilot Plant (WIPP)]}, and transportation mode [highway, rail, vessel, or air (The air transportation mode was not part of the project. However, air transport requirements were recorded as they were encountered)].
3. Develop a comprehensive set of requirements that can be used to support the DOE Standard Transportation Protocol development and the Transportation Program Management Guide, which will help to standardize the way DOE transports their hazardous material.
4. Identify ways to reduce the cost of transporting DOE EM radioactive waste/material without affecting operational safety by associating costs to each function.

SYSTEMS ENGINEERING APPROACH

A systematic approach was used to identify and manage the requirements associated with transporting DOE radioactive material. Hazardous material transportation requirements affecting DOE have been established by the Department of Transportation (DOT), the Nuclear Regulatory Commission (NRC), DOE, other federal and state agencies, and stakeholders.

A systems engineering approach has been used in managing the requirements. Source documents have been identified, requirements extracted, and a functional analysis has been performed. The data is now available to assist in developing a standardized DOE transportation process. In addition, internal and external derived requirements imposed on DOE can easily be identified (these would be requirements imposed on DOE but not on commercial transporters of radioactive waste/material).

RDD-100, a systems engineering software package developed by Ascent Logic Corporation, has been used to manage the data. Using RDD-100 has helped to develop the interrelationships between the requirements, functions, and documents.

SOURCE DOCUMENTS

Over 127 documents were identified that may apply to transporting DOE radioactive material. Fifty-three were determined to be relevant to the project and classified as source documents. The source documents have been categorized as: regulatory, internal, or external.

Regulatory documents. Regulatory documents are defined as documents that have been issued by federal and state agencies and international organizations. They do not include any document generated or issued by DOE or their subcontractors. They may include: the Code of Federal Regulations (CFR), ANSI standards, etc.

The NRC and DOT share primary responsibility for the control of radioactive material transport in the US, based on a Memorandum of Understanding (MOU 1979). In general, DOT regulations (Section 49 of the CFRs) are more detailed. They cover all aspects of transportation, including packaging, shipper and carrier responsibilities, documentation, and all levels of radioactive material from exempt quantities to very high levels. The NRC regulations (10 CFR) are primarily concerned with special packaging requirements for high level radioactive materials (e.g., HLW, SNF, NM). NRC regulation 10 CFR 71.5 requires NRC licensees transporting radioactive material to comply with the DOT hazardous material regulations.

Internal documents. Internal documents have been prepared and issued by DOE and/or their support contractors. They may include: DOE Orders, Records of Decision, Environmental Impact Statements, Implementation Plans, etc. These documents contain requirements that DOE has agreed to follow during the transportation process.

External documents. External documents are those that have been published by organizations outside of DOE and the regulatory agencies. They may include documents published by the Western Governors Association or other stakeholders.

REQUIREMENTS

Source documents were reviewed and requirements extracted and input into RDD-100. Each requirement is documented according to the source document it was extracted from.

The requirements have been categorized as follows (based on the document categorization):

- External requirements – Those extracted from regulatory documents that, if not followed, would lead to illegal operations and possible fines.
- Internal derived requirements – Those extracted from source documents produced and issued by DOE and its support contractors. These are DOE self-imposed requirements.
- External derived requirements – Requirements extracted from source documents that are not regulatory in nature or from DOE (e.g., stakeholder requests). DOE has an option to follow these requirements; however, justification for non-compliance will be required from the organization issuing the document.

The goal was to write each requirement as a single stand-alone requirement that is defendable and measurable. Each requirement is a summary of the verbatim text extracted from the source documents. For example: 49 CFR 173.22(c) states the following:

> "Prior to each shipment of fissile radioactive materials, and Type B or highway route controlled quantity packages of radioactive materials (see §173.403), the shipper shall notify the consignee of the dates of shipment and expected arrival. The shipper shall also notify each consignee of any special loading/unloading instructions prior to his first shipment."

This verbatim statement has been summarized into nine separate requirements three are presented below that deal with transporting highway route controlled quantity (HRCQ) materials. The six other requirements are worded the same as the ones below but the material has been changed to Type B and fissile materials.

1. Pre-shipment notification for HRCQ materials shall include special loading/unloading instructions prior to the first shipment.
2. The shipper shall notify the consignee of the shipment dates prior to transporting HRCQ material.
3. The shipper shall notify the consignee of the expected arrival date prior to shipping HRCQ material.

The focus of the project has been to identify those requirements that deal specifically with transporting hazardous material. Therefore, requirements that apply to all transportation activities (e.g., domestic goods, commercial transport, hazardous materials, radioactive waste/material) were not included.

Currently there are over 5,400 requirements in the database. Each requirement was recorded and sorted by waste/material type (HLW, LLW, MLLW, NM, SNF, TRU waste), transportation mode (highway, rail, vessel, air), and the topical areas identified in Table 1. Sorting the requirements as they were extracted has saved time during the functional analysis portion of the project because it was easier to work with a smaller set of requirements when dealing with a specific function.

The DOE Senior Executive Transportation Forum has undertaken an initiative to evaluate DOE shipping practices and recommend standardization of those practices where appropriate. The topical areas designated with a "•" in Table 1 are protocol areas that the DOE Senior Executive Transportation Forum is currently standardizing. The other topical areas (designated with a "-" in Table 1) are transportation functions that are followed during the transportation process. The database has been used to identify specific functions and requirements for each protocol area, which is being used in the standardization process.

Pre-Shipment	– Loading
• Notification	– Inspections
• Inspections	– Exclusive use shipments
• Security	– Communication
• Public Information	– Mechanic qualifications
• Routing	**Accidents/Incidents**
• Training	• Notifications
• Emergency Planning	• Emergency Response
• Carrier/Driver Requirements	• Communications
– Other	• Remediation
– Categorize by DOT material category	**Post-Shipment**
– Package Material	• Inspections
– Safety	• Radiological Survey
– Mark Packages	– Other
– Label Packages	– Receive Material
– Placard/mark Vehicle	– Unload Transporter
– Prepare shipping documents	– Record Keeping
– License/Registration	– Communication
– Transporter qualifications	**General Transportation Requirements**
– Determine transportation mode	– Follow hazardous material regulations
Shipment	– Costs
• Transportation Operational Contingencies	– Quality Assurance
• Safe Parking/Safe Haven	– Export
• Tracking	– Import
– Other	– Exemption
– General Shipping requirements	

Table1: Topical areas.

FUNCTIONAL ANALYSIS

A hierarchy of high level functions necessary to perform transportation was developed. Creating a function for each of the topical areas listed in Table 1 developed the hierarchy. Additional sub-functions were created under each of the topical area functions that address specific requirements associated with a transportation mode, waste stream, and/or site/project.

This is illustrated in Table 2, which shows the general shipping function (1.2.4.1) and related sub-functions. The general shipping function is specified by requirements that apply to all shipments of radioactive waste/material by all transportation modes. The first four sub-functions (1.2.4.1.1 – 1.2.4.1.4) apply to all shipments of radioactive waste/material and a specific transportation mode. Those sub-functions that apply to a specific radioactive waste/material stream and all transportation modes are then listed (1.2.4.1.5, 1.2.4.1.6, 1.2.4.1.7, 1.2.4.1.8, and 1.2.4.1.9). Additional sub-functions are developed under each of the specific radioactive waste/material stream sub-functions that deal with a specific transportation mode (1.2.4.1.5.1, 1.2.4.1.7.1, and 1.2.4.1.7.2) and/or a specific project (1.2.4.1.8.1 and 1.2.4.1.9.1). Therefore, the shipping functions and associated requirements that would apply to transporting NM by air would include (from Table 2): 1.2.4.1, 1.2.4.1.1, 1.2.4.1.7, and 1.2.4.1.7.1.

The function number (the number preceding the function name as shown on Table 2) indicates the position of the function on the functional hierarchy. The first number in the sequence indicates the type of hazardous material the function is associated with (1-radioactive waste/material, 2-all other hazardous waste). The second number in the sequence indicates the transportation phase (1-pre-shipment, 2-shipment, 3-accident/incident, 4-post-shipment, and 5-general). The protocol area is indicated by the third number in the sequence (the numbers vary according to the transportation phase). The remaining numbers do not represent specific items but relate to the waste/material stream, transportation mode, and site/project specific functions.

The functions are grouped according to the transportation phase: pre-shipment, shipment, accident/incident, post-shipment, and general. The pre-shipment phase includes all functions that are performed prior to allowing the radioactive waste/material on public thoroughfares. The shipment phase deals with the actual transport of the material. The accident/incident functions deal with notification of, responding to, and cleaning up a radioactive release that has happened during transport. The post-shipment phase is associated with activities that are performed once the shipment has been received at the destination site. The last grouping, general, is not a transportation phase but is a section for those functions and requirements that do not fit one specific phase.

1.2.4.1 Follow general shipping requirements
1.2.4.1.1 Follow general air shipping requirements
1.2.4.1.2 Follow general highway shipping requirements
1.2.4.1.3 Follow general rail shipping requirements
1.2.4.1.4 Follow general vessel shipping requirements
1.2.4.1.5 Follow HLW shipping requirements
1.2.4.1.5.1 Follow HLW rail shipping requirements
1.2.4.1.6 Follow LLW/MLLW shipping requirements
1.2.4.1.7 Follow NM shipping requirements
1.2.4.1.7.1 Follow NM air shipping requirements
1.2.4.1.7.2 Follow NM vessel shipping requirements
1.2.4.1.8 Follow SNF shipping requirements
1.2.4.1.8.1 Follow FRR SNF shipping requirements
1.2.4.1.9 Follow TRU waste shipping requirements
1.2.4.1.9.1 Follow WIPP TRU waste shipping requirements

Table 2: General shipping function and sub-functions.

The interrelationship between the source documents, the requirements, and the functions are illustrated in Figure 1. A source document is reviewed for leaf level requirements (those requirements that summarize a verbatim statement taken from the source document). The leaf level requirements are grouped together into higher level requirements (these were developed at the request of the NTP Integration and Planning Group manager based on input from the protocol working groups). The requirements are associated with a function by specifying all functions that relate to a requirement. Requirements that are repeated in more than one document (e.g., R2 and R7 in Figure 1) are incorporated into the highest level document. For example: a requirement from an external document would be incorporated into the requirement from a regulatory or internal document, a requirement from an internal document would be incorporated in the requirement from a regulatory document. This way there are no duplicate requirements specifying a function or sub-function.

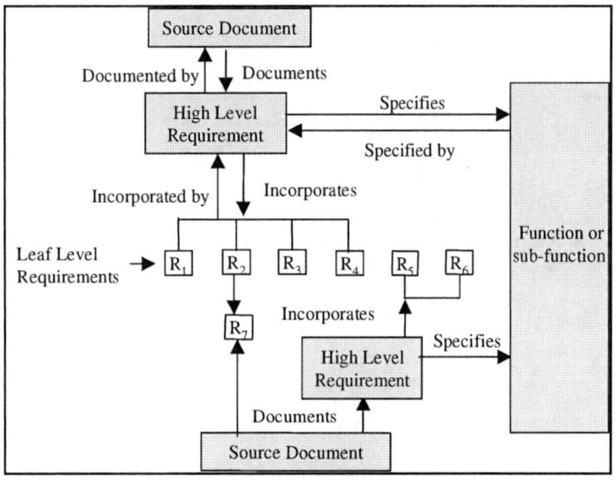

Figure 1: Interrelationships between source documents, requirements, and functions.

FUTURE ENHANCEMENTS

"Transportation" must be defined. In other words, at what point in the treatment and transfer of radioactive waste/material from one facility to another does transportation begin and end. Establishing when one operation ends and transportation begins, and when transportation ends and another operation begins, will aid in determining the cost of transportation. For example, is loading material into a transportation package considered part of the transportation phase of a project? In order to ensure the material is properly packaged for transport it needs to be characterized and categorized according to DOT regulations. The categorization will determine the type of shipping package that should be used. This may be a very simple process and easily incorporated into the transportation phase (e.g., for DOE purposes SNF is packaged in Type B containers). However, it could be a very complicated procedure that would not be included within the scope of transportation (e.g., some of the TRU waste being shipped to WIPP needs to be characterized prior to loading into the transport package).

Requirements. The transportation requirements management database has been specifically designed to identify hazardous material requirements dealing with the transport of DOE radioactive waste/material. It can be expanded to include the transportation of other hazardous and non-hazardous materials. It presently models less than 1% of all transportation activities. However, this 1% is highly visible and often very controversial with the public because it deals with transporting radioactive waste/material.

The air transportation mode has not been fully developed because it was not part of the project scope. However, when air requirements were encountered while reviewing the source document they were recorded and sorted into the functional hierarchy. All air transport requirements can be included in the database.

The requirements have been reviewed and agreeded upon by the NTP Integration and Planning Group. However, to be an effective tool that can be used by all transporters of radioactive waste/material, the requirements should be presented to and agreeded upon by other transportation organizations and regulatory agencies.

Functional analysis. Currently the database contains only high level functions. The high level functions need to be broken down into the lowest level of system behavior that can be observed. This will assist in future comparisons. It will also make it easier to identify specific functions that need to be accomplished during the transportation process.

Cost analysis. The source document "documents" a requirement, which "specifies" a function, that "consumes" a resource. The resource is generally monetary in the case of transportation. Therefore, in order to determine where costs can be reduced the lower level functions will need to be identified and then costs associated with them.

Internet access. The NTP Integration and Planning Group is currently working on putting the database on the Internet. This would allow transporters of DOE radioactive waste/material to have the regulations readily available on their computer broken down by functions and requirements. This will add in helping to standardize the DOE transportation procedures.

CONCLUSION

A systems engineering process has been used to develop a transportation requirements management database. The process is in the beginning stages (only the requirements and functional analysis has been performed).

The database has been set up to collect, organize, and present all hazardous material transportation requirements established to regulate the transport of DOE EM radioactive waste/material. It is currently being used to review DOE protocol standardization procedures. At the present time the database shows the interrelationships between high level requirements, high level functions, and source documents.

Further enhancements to the database would allow transporters of all materials to determine proper procedures, functions, and requirements they are required to follow to be in compliance with DOT, NRC, international, and other federal and state regulatory transportation requirements. In addition, adding cost information to the database would allow transporters to more accurately estimate the cost of transporting goods.

REFERENCES

The following references have been cited in the paper:

Code of Federal Regulations, 1999 revisions.

MOU, 44 Federal Register 38690, "Transportation of Radioactive Materials; Memorandum of Understanding," July 2, 1979.

US Department of Energy National Transportation Program, "Transporting Radioactive Materials Answers to Your Questions," June 1999.

BIOGRAPHICAL SKETCH OF AUTHORS

THANE W. BOLANDER

Biography: Mr. Bolander has fifteen years experience in systems engineering, safety and risk assessment, hazard analysis, probabilistic risk assessment, and reliability. He has assisted in: identifying requirements for several Department of Energy (DOE) programs, writing safety analysis reports conforming to DOE regulations; performing various types of risk, hazard, and vulnerability assessments; and developing computerized databases for DOE environmental management and systems engineering. He assisted the Department of Defense perform facility hazard assessments and develop reliability models of several missile programs.

MARK E. JOHN

Biography: Mr. John has experience in hazardous waste transportation, treatment, and disposal, and in Systems Engineering. He assisted in the development and management of a transportation requirements baseline for the Department of Energy (DOE) complex. He has experience identifying characterization and transportation requirements for hazardous, PCB, and industrial waste disposal, and has assisted in development and implementation of waste transportation, treatment and disposal strategies.

RICK L. FAWCETT

Biography: Mr. Fawcett is recognized as a national leader in Transportation Systems Engineering and Stakeholder Involvement Strategies and has a unique blend of experience and education in industrial safety, systems engineering and environmental management. Mr. Fawcett has developed public and industrial safety programs for fixed facilities and transportation campaigns. He also has extensive experience in hazardous materials transportation both as a safety professional, a systems engineer and as an operations manager.

Identifying and Modeling Safety Hazards

Jesse Daniels
A. Terry Bahill, Fellow of INCOSE
Systems and Industrial Engineering
The University of Arizona
Tucson, AZ 85721-0020
danielsj@engr.arizona.edu
terry@sie.arizona.edu

Paul W. Werner
High Consequence Surety Engineering
Department 12331
Sandia National Laboratories
Albuquerque, NM 87185-0490
pwwerne@sandia.gov

Abstract. The Hazard Model described in this paper is a risk management tool that is intended to aid in tracking and evaluating risks. The model is a new application of old systems engineering tools, i.e., tradeoff studies. However, the model is not intended to be directly integrated into the SE process. Rather, it should be implemented as an ongoing evaluator of key attributes as required by the system under study. The Hazard Model is designed to accept data from distributed databases, evaluate the data, and provide as output a numerical representation of the system's state, called the *Hazard Index*. The Hazard Index may be interpreted as a traveler's advisory. A *Hazard Object* template is used to ensure that all necessary descriptors for each condition that may potentially contribute to hazardous circumstances are collected in a standardized format. Three methods for combining hazard data are presented and compared. These three methods serve as the "engine" for our Hazard Model. Interactions among hazard stimuli are also investigated. Three methods are presented for handling three different types of interactions between the Hazard Objects.

INTRODUCTION

A major concern of the Federal Aviation Administration (FAA) is creating and maintaining a safe operating environment for the airlines and the flying public. Recent events have prompted more rigorous analysis of hazards and their impact on airline safety. This paper describes a risk management model that is intended to aid FAA inspectors in the detection and analysis of aviation-related hazards. However, the modeling technique is general and our techniques should have an intuitive and straightforward interpretation for systems engineers in most fields.

Currently, information pertaining to conditions present in an aviation operating environment is gathered and stored in various databases. This information may include data relating to weather, training, maintenance, etc. We intend to extract appropriate data from such databases and input the data into our model for evaluation. The model will accept this data as input and provide as output a numerical designation representing the state of the aviation system under observation from a hazard viewpoint. An indirect goal of employing such a model is determining which data are beneficial in assessing the impact of hazards on airline safety, i.e., the model can help decide where to allocate resources so that pertinent data are collected and frivolous data are ignored.

Another advantage in using the model is that hazards can be quickly identified, described, categorized and archived for future reference. This provides a basis for which a consensus among experts can be attained. Thus, ambiguity associated with interpreting attributes of the hazards will be reduced. In order to ease the archiving process we have defined a convenient format called a *Hazard Object* in which all necessary information about a specific hazard can be captured. We will introduce the concept of Hazard Objects in a later section and explain how they are useful in evaluating hazardous conditions.

THE HAZARD MODEL

The *Hazard Model* is a risk management tool with an underlying structure that is based on tradeoff analysis concepts used in the systems engineering (SE) process (see http://www.sie.arizona.edu/sysengr/pinewood/ for an example), however, it is not intended to be directly integrated into the SE process. Rather, it should be implemented as an ongoing evaluator of conditions and attributes that are of significance to the system under study.

The Hazard Model is hierarchical in its structure. Hazard Objects serve as the atomic level components handled by the Hazard Model. A Hazard Object hierarchy is arranged by partitioning the Hazard Objects into categories that together span the possible areas in which hazards may occur. Example high-level categories might be Human Factors, Physiology, Weather, Physical Components, etc. The category structure is also partitioned in a hierarchical fashion in which top-level categories are broken up into finer and finer segments as necessary for ease of communication and to eliminate certain computational difficulties. We will address this later in more detail. The Hazard Objects reside in the lowest level categories.

In order to make it possible to combine and evaluate hazard data from diverse sources, each Hazard Object includes a *scoring function* as part of its definition. The purpose of the scoring function is to transform the raw input data associated with a particular Hazard Object into a normalized, quantitative *score* that represents the relative preferences as assigned by the stakeholder for the possible input values for the Hazard Object.

The scores for each hazard are rolled up by applying some combining algorithm to form a score for their respective category. Similarly, the scores for sub-categories are combined to generate scores for their respective super-category. Finally, the top-level categories are combined to form an overall score, called the *Hazard Index*, which functions as the quantitative measure indicative of how hazardous the situation is. The Hazard Index may be interpreted as a sort of traveler's advisory and may be accompanied by a list of Hazard Objects that contribute most to the Hazard Index. A fragment of a typical hazard hierarchy and simple weighting combination algorithm is shown in Figure 1.

Hierarchically partitioning the hazards allows us to evaluate contributions of the individual hazards to the main category and each main category to the overall hazard assessment: the Hazard Index. The hierarchical structure also helps in dealing with dependence issues between hazards. Since hazards in a category are intrinsically related, dependence between them remains isolated in that specific category and will not directly affect the overall evaluation. This feature establishes a sort of *encapsulation* between categories.

HAZARD OBJECTS

Figure 2 shows an example of a hazard object that we will use to describe the details of hazard objects.

First, we give the hazard a descriptive *Title* so it can be easily and unmistakably identified. In this case, we are attempting to model the effects of "Pilot Recurrent Training" on safety. The next entry contains a Description of the hazard. This was done to ensure a consistent and agreed-upon definition for each hazard. The Units of measure are included to indicate how the quantity is to be measured and how it is presented in graphical representations, such as the Hazard Object's scoring function. In this example, we chose to define the units of measure to be the number of hours of recurrent training in the current year.

The Scoring Function is given next as a chart on the hazard object as shown in Figure 2. Scoring functions (Wymore, 1993) are used to subjectively ascertain the severity of a hazard given the state of nature. Specific data on each identified hazard object is input into the scoring function and the score is given as output. The scores are combined to generate the overall appraisal of the situation.

The scoring function chart is set up such that the input values (in the units of measure defined earlier) are displayed along the horizontal axis, and the output value (always between 0 and 1) is presented along the vertical axis. The function itself is defined so that the more hazardous the input value, the higher the output score will be. This is apparent from looking at the example since as the number of recurrent training hours in the current year diminishes, a higher score is output indicating a greater hazard.

A researcher will poll experts in the field where the hazard applies to get appropriate units of measure, reasonable ranges for input values, the scoring function shape and other characteristics of the scoring function. This captures the expert's perception concerning the hazard. There has been extensive research in developing a robust array of mathematical equations to represent standardized scoring functions useful in such characterization. Examples of this will be given later.

The *Category* field initiates the hierarchical decomposition process. Categories are the subdivisions of the hazard space. It is here where we package hazards of similar characteristics such as environment-related hazards or human performance issues, etc. The Recurrent Training Hazard Object falls under the category Human Performance.

Next, we have the subcategory field that further refine the categories into a finer granularity. Currently, we have only two levels of decomposition: category and subcategory. For example, in the Human Performance category, we may include subcategories such as Psychology, Physiology, Communication etc. Recurrent training is part of the Training subcategory of Human Performance in the above example.

We include a field called *Phase of Flight* because most hazards are most important during specific phases of flight, such as takeoff or taxiing. Thus, when a new Hazard Object is defined the researcher must consider

Category							Input value	Weight	Input times weight
1. **Human Performance**							0.34	0.50	0.17
2. **Environment**							0.87	0.50	0.435
2.1 **Weather**							↑		
	Qualitative weight	Normalized weight	Input value	Scoring function	Score	Score times weight			
2.1.1 **Air Temperature**	10	0.50	120°F	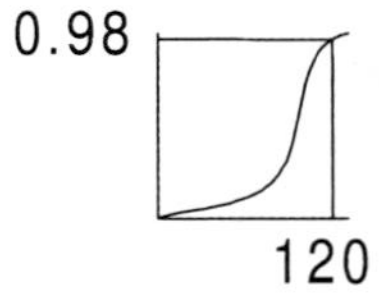	0.98	0.49			
2.1.2 **Visibility**	5	0.25	1 Mile	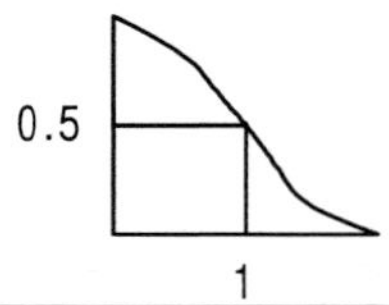	0.50	0.13			
2.1.3 **Relative Humidity**	5	0.25	100%	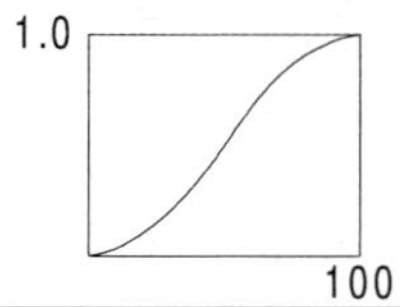	1.00	0.25			
Sum						0.87 →			0.605

Figure 1: Hazard Model Layout

Hazard Object

Title: Pilot Recurrent Training

Description: The number of hours the pilot has spent in flight training in aircraft and approved simulators concerning specified maneuvers and procedures (e.g., CRM, wind shear, etc.)

Units: Hours in Current Year

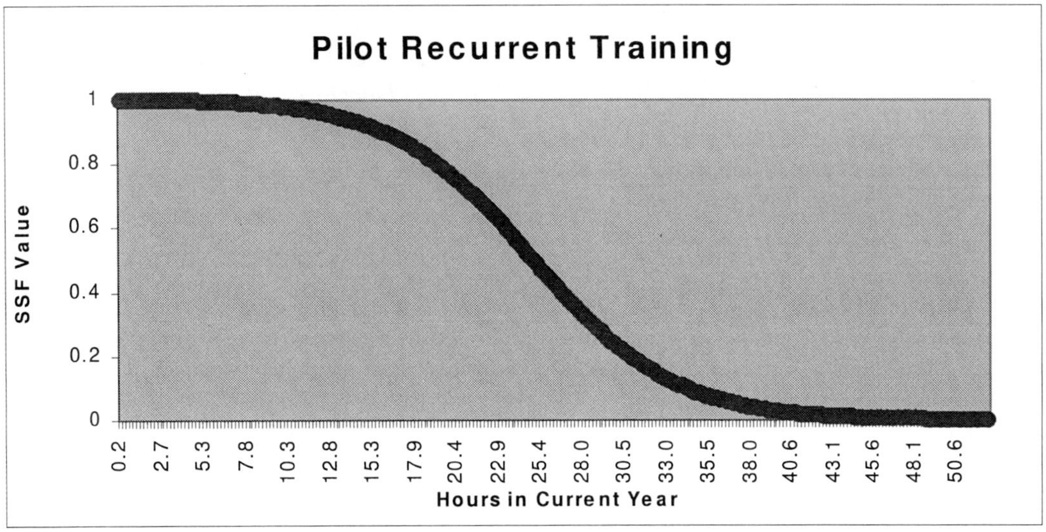

Category:	Human Performance
Subcategory:	Training
Phase of Flight:	All
Interactions:	N/A
Qualitative Weight:	6
Default Input Value:	5 hours in current year
FAR:	121.427
Aircraft Specific?	Yes
Direct or Latent?	Latent
Source of Data:	Human Resources
Owner:	Paul Werner
Date Approved:	3 Sept. 1999, Meeting, The University of Arizona
Notes:	Regulatory minimum = 25 hours per year

Figure 2: Hazard Object Example

the interaction between the hazard and the phases of flight. In the example, we decided that all phases of flight are affected by the pilot's recurrent training. Therefore, we entered (rather arbitrarily) "All" in the Phase of Flight field.

A more general field called *Interactions* allows the researcher the freedom to document all other interactive phenomena that transpire between hazards. An example of this would be the interaction between air temperature and relative humidity. This interaction exists because the relative humidity does not become a hazard unless (A) the air temperature is cold enough to (1) reduce visibility due to the formation of fog, (2) cause icing (either on aircraft or on the ground), (3) reduce radar and laser propagation, or (4) impact radio communications, or (B) the air temperature is hot enough to adversely affect aircraft performance.

Next, we include a *Qualitative Weight* field. The qualitative weight is a numerical entry given by experts indicating the relative importance the expert believes the hazard has on safety. The qualitative weight is a value between 1 and 10, with a 1 meaning the hazard is minimally detrimental to system safety and a 10 denoting that if the hazard is present, it can severely impact system safety. In the example, we have assigned a qualitative weight of 6 for the hazard, indicating that the hazard rates 6 out of a possible 10 in overall consequence on airline safety.

The *Default Input Value* field helps handle missing data. If there are inconclusive or missing data or if good guesses for the inputs are not available, the Hazard Model will automatically revert to the default values. In most cases, we have set up the default values to be the worst possible. This was done in part to motivate the acquisition of the necessary data, and also to promote a "better safe than sorry" safety philosophy. In the example, the default input value was chosen to be 5 hours in the current year. This is not an attractive input value and generates an undesirably high score for the hazard.

Links between hazards and the Federal Aviation Regulations (FARs) will be useful in providing a solid reference to the hazards and recognized mitigation procedures. Therefore, we have included a *FAR* field for the particular hazard. If there is a FAR relating to the hazard, it should be listed here. If there is no FAR pertaining to the hazard, then this might spur an investigation as to why and whether one should be created. This cross-referencing between the FARs and the hazards will establish traceability between regulations put in place to eliminate or mitigate hazards and the hazards themselves. It will also be useful in uncovering inadequacies or gaps in the FARs. Such is the case when a hazard is identified that is not attended to in the regulations.

The next field, *Aircraft Specific?* is a yes/no question used for indicating whether a hazard is specific to certain aircraft. Some hazards are common to all aircraft while some concern specific aircraft. This field will allow the researcher to illustrate such discrimination. In the example, it seems reasonable that pilot recurrent training may very well relate to the specific aircraft the pilot flies, and therefore will receive a "yes" in the "Aircraft Specific?" field.

We shall classify Hazard Objects into two classes: *Direct* and *Latent* hazards. Some hazards directly affect the overall hazard severity of the situation at hand such as cross-winds or crew fatigue. These hazards will be classified as direct hazards. Some hazards indirectly influence the overall safety of the system. We call these indirect hazards or latent hazards. The Latent class of hazards include areas such as safety culture, business success, complaints, ongoing scheduling issues, etc. These represent more of the *programmatic* hazards. The Hazard Object template contains a field titled *Latent or Direct?* to help establish which of the two classes the hazard belongs to. The Hazard Model addresses the issue of latent hazards by increasing the baseline for the Hazard Index. This means that instead of starting from a "zero" hazard state, the direct hazards will begin to accumulate from a higher baseline starting state. This feature allows us to model the situation in which direct hazards that might normally have a minimal effect on the Hazard Index may have a more significant impact with a heightened baseline due to latent hazards.

The inputs for the scoring functions will be collected from numerous sources, so it is important to state where the data will come from. Therefore, we have provided a field to account for such information: *Source of Data*. Examples of entries to this field could be databases, experts, reports, etc.

The owner of a hazard object is the person or group ultimately responsible for ensuring the accuracy and correctness of the information presented in a hazard object. The *Owner* field is provided so that if there are any discrepancies, questions or updates for information on the hazard object, the responsible party can be contacted. Typical entries here will include a name and telephone number.

The *Date Approved* field should show the date when a final consensus was reached and the Hazard Object was admitted into the Hazard Model. This field will also reference the source of the expertise: For example it will state whether the information in a hazard object came from a FAR, a book, one expert, two experts, a consensus of experts, a specific meeting, etc., along with the physical location when the decision was made. In this case, the Hazard Object was created during a meeting at The University of Arizona on September 3, 1999.

Finally, the *Notes* field is included to catch any information not addressed in the other fields. This may include explanations for information or special cases.

RESOURCE OBJECTS

We note that all of the data submitted for analysis to the Hazard Model is data leading to a decrease in safety or an increase in risk. However, it may be beneficial to consider data that combats hazards and lowers risk. We call such data *Resource Objects*. Possible resources that may be "pumped" into the system to reduce risk may include: extra fuel, change in route, removal or re-distribution of cargo, fresh crew, backup crew, crew rest facility, schedule consideration, etc. Each of these resources may reduce one or more hazards.

To bring the full analysis into perspective, we propose the following fundamental relationships:

Hazards - Resources = Risk; and
Risk + Safety Margin ≤ Acceptable Risk

Where the safety margin represents a "safety buffer" resulting from precautious actions that aid in the mitigation of unforeseen risks. A more thorough treatment of Resource Objects is an objective of future endeavors and is beyond the scope of this discussion.

METHODS FOR COMBINING DATA

In this section, we explore three different methods for combining data to calculate the Hazard Index, which is a single numerical designation representing the state of system safety. The combining techniques described here are used at all levels of the system decomposition. At the lowest level when we are dealing with individual Hazard Objects, the scores are derived from the scoring function for each hazard object and normalized qualitative weights, which are based on expert opinion. These scores are used to comprise the hazard's subcategory score.

When we move to the next level and are dealing with higher-level categories, the scores are no longer directly derived from scoring functions, but are taken as the scores for each of the subcategories contained in a super-category. The weights at this level may be evenly divided between super-categories unless there are obvious reasons to consider some super-categories more significant than others. Combining the data at the top category level yields the Hazard Index. The three data-combining methods are outlined next.

Linear Combination. The linear method of combining data is the simplest method of the three. It is useful when the output is not computed until the whole data set is available and when missing data are unlikely. The data combining process is as follows: Suppose there are *n* reasonably independent constituents to be combined. We assign a qualitative weight to each of the *n* constituents and then normalize the weights so they add up to 1. The score (valued from 0 to 1) from the scoring function associated with each constituent is then multiplied by the corresponding weight. The final result is the summation of the weight-times-score for each element. This process is commonly used, for example, when computing a grade point average for a student at a university. This technique is shown in Table 1.

The equation defining the process mathematically is given as:

$$f = \sum_{i=1}^{n} w_i \cdot x_i ,$$

where *n* is the total number of elements to be combined, w_i represents the normalized weight and x_i represents the score for the ith constituent. An extensive example of such rolling-up of figures of merit is given at http://www.sie.arizona.edu/sysengr/pinewood/.

Soft Aggregation. Arlin Cooper of Sandia National Labs developed the soft aggregation method discussed in this section (Cooper, 1999). The application of soft aggregation techniques is effective when incorporating uncertainty into the models and when the output is to be updated with each new input.

The soft aggregation model presented here attempts to combine information nonlinearly to obtain a single numeric output that characterizes the state of system attribute(s) (in this case the system attribute is safety). In particular, the aggregation is accomplished by utilizing an exponential combining function. The exponential technique was favored in part since the effects of combining such measures responds less and less to additional inputs hence the "soft" nature of this combining method.

The original model incorporates two families of information, those that lead to an increase in safety and those that lead to a decrease in safety. In the Hazard Model, we only consider those that increase hazards, and thus decrement safety.

The function that serves our needs for a soft aggregation calculi is given as

$$f = 1 - e^{-\sum_{i=1}^{n} k w_i x_i}$$

The w_i indicate weights between 0 to 1 that suggest the significance of the measure with respect to increases in the overall hazard level for the situation. The x_i are scoring function scores affiliated with the ith hazard. The k is a scaling constant used to further manipulate the results to match the requirements necessary for accurate evaluation. Note that if k=1 the output of this model will range from 0 to 0.63.

Certainty Factors. Certainty Factors (CFs) have been used successfully in the expert system arena for many years (Buchanan and Shortliffe, 1984). The underlying theory surrounding CFs is based on axiomatic probability theory and has survived thorough mathematical scrutiny. Thus, a vast knowledge base has developed for CFs and a great deal is known about their properties and uses. As in the soft aggregation technique, the CF method is useful when the output is incrementally updated with each input and may also be used effectively when missing data or uncertain data cannot be avoided.

The initial CF data points are derived from the weights and scores for the hazard objects as follows: $CF_i = w_i * x_i$, where w_i is the weight (0 to 1) and x_i is the score (output of the scoring function) corresponding to the ith hazard object. The CFs for the hazard objects are then combined to create a score for the associated subcategory. When we move to the next level up, the x_i's and w_i's become the weights and scores for the subcategories, and are combined to form a main category score.

An advantage to using CFs is that the weights do not have to be normalized. This means each time a new constituent is introduced, be it a new hazard object, subcategory, or super-category it is not necessary to re-normalize the weights. This artifact eases necessary computation consideration and resources. The weights must still be between 0 and 1, however.

The recursive formula for computing CFs is given as:

$$CF_{Aggregate} = CF_{Old} + (1\text{-}CF_{Old}) * CF_{New},$$

where CF_{New} is the certainty factor for the new piece of evidence to be combined with the existing set and CF_{Old} represents the CF for the existing data set. $CF_{Aggregate}$ is the cumulative outcome from combining the data. At the highest level, this becomes the Hazard Index as with the other combination methods. In our system, the CFs are restricted to the range [0, 1].

INDEPENDENCE & INTERACTIONS

As an example of independence and interactions, consider modeling the hunting behavior of lions in Africa. First, consider independence. It would be incorrect to use both weight and sex of the lions to predict success, because these measures are dependent.

Next, consider interactions. If one lion chases a Thompkins Gazelle, it has a one in eight likelihood of catching the gazelle. If another lion chases another gazelle, it has a one in eight likelihood of catching it. We expect a *linear addition* for the two hunting sprints, which gives a one in four likelihood of success. Now consider two lions simultaneously chasing one gazelle. They have a one in two likelihood of catching it. *Cooperation* gives a greater likelihood of success than linear addition. Next, suppose a cheetah is chasing a gazelle and a lion joins in the chase. The likelihood of success becomes about one in twelve. *Interference* decreases the likelihood of success below that of linear addition.

In terms of hazards when the effect of two hazards is greater than that obtained by linear addition, such as mixing Clorox and Sani-Flush™ producing chorine gas, we call the effect an *amplifying interaction*. When the effect of two hazards is less than that obtained by linear addition, such as the presence of flammable liquids and a temperature below freezing, we call the effect an *attenuating interaction*.

When selecting components for the hazard model, the components should be as independent as possible. It is more difficult to analyze systems when the metrics depend on one another. However, when analyzing complex systems this is almost unavoidable.

In the Hazard Model, we propose to handle the interaction issue in two ways. For attenuating interactions, the final score for the first measure is the product of the original score for the first measure and the score for the second. This technique allows us to model phenomena where if one constituent of the interactive relation is close to zero, then the hazard is close to zero. A good example is the relative humidity – air temperature interaction. If the temperature is below freezing, then high humidity increases the chance of icing or fog and therefore increases the hazard. However, at 70°F high humidity is no hazard at all.

Amplifying interactions involves metrics in which there is a synergistic effect. That is, when two metrics are present the hazard from the combination is greater than the hazard resulting from the weighted, linear sum of the two metrics. For such amplifying interactions we use an equation from reliability theory: $H_{Overall} = 1\text{-}[(1\text{-}H_1)(1\text{-}H_2)]$. In this equation, $H_{Overall}$ represents the resulting score after the interaction effect has been accounted for. H_1 and H_2 are the original scores for the first and second hazards, respectively. This equation gives us the synergistic effect desired. An example of an amplifying interaction is consumption of alcohol and barbiturates. The combined effect of the alcohol and barbiturates is greater than the effects modeled by the linear sum. Another example is chopsticks: a pair of chopsticks performs much better than the linear sum of two individual chopsticks.

CONCLUSIONS

The Hazard Model realizes a new application of an old SE tool, i.e., tradeoff studies. The Hazard Object template and hierarchical structure make categorizing and referencing complex data manageable. The Hazard Object template that was presented in this paper would be a good template to use in any database. The field for *Units* is particularly important: it may seem obvious, but experience has shown that it is often omitted.

Combining diverse data to extract useful results is a goal of the Hazard Model. We showed three methods for combining the data. Interactions among hazard data were also regarded since it is difficult for humans to deal with interactions between stimuli, but it is easy for computers (i.e., the Hazard Model) to do so. We have presented three types of interactions: linear addition, amplifying and attenuating. We gave examples of each and presented a mathematical treatment of each.

The output of the Hazard Model, or the Hazard Index, is intended to be interpreted as a traveler's advisory. The relative magnitude of the Hazard Index is subject to interpretation as well. In other words, how do we know how high the Hazard Index has to be in order to call the situation "unsafe"? This is a focus of collaborative future efforts with possible users of the system.

ACKNOWLEDGEMENTS

The authors gratefully acknowledge the support of the Federal Aviation Administration (AAR-424). This paper is based on work done at The University of Arizona and Sandia National Laboratories. Sandia is a multiprogram laboratory operated by Sandia Corporation, a Lockheed Martin Company, for the United States Department of Energy under Contract DE-AC04-94AL85000.

REFERENCES

Cooper, J. A., "Soft mathematical aggregation in safety assessment and decision analysis," *Proceedings of the 17th International System Safety Conference,* August 16-21, 1999, Orlando, FL.

Buchanan, B. G. and Shortliffe, E.H., (Eds.) *Rule-Based Expert Systems*, Addison-Wesley, Reading, MA, 1984.

Wymore, A. W., *Model-Based Systems Engineering*, CRC Press, Boca Raton FL, 1993.

AUTHOR BIOGRAPHIES

Jesse Daniels is a graduate student at the University of Arizona in the Systems and Industrial Engineering Department. He received his B.S. and M.S. in systems engineering in 1999 and 2000 from the University of Arizona.

A. Terry Bahill is a Professor of Systems Engineering at the University of Arizona in Tucson. He received his Ph.D. in electrical engineering and computer science from the University of California, Berkeley, in 1975. He holds a U.S. patent for the Bat Chooser™, a system that computes the Ideal Bat Weight™ for individual baseball and softball batters. He is Editor of the CRC Press Series on Systems Engineering. He is a Fellow of the Institute of Electrical and Electronic Engineers (IEEE) and of the INCOSE. He is the chair of the INCOSE Fellows Selection Committee.

Paul W. Werner is a Principal Member of the technical staff at Sandia National Laboratories. He works with the High Consequence Surety Engineering Department. He received his Ph.D. in electrical engineering from the University of New Mexico in 1991. He is also a Commander and a Naval Flight Officer in the U.S. Naval Reserve.

Systems Engineering and the Legal Profession – Revisited

William F. Mackey, Esq.
Computer Sciences Corporation
7700 Hubble Drive
Lanham-Seabrook, MD 20706

Abstract. This paper explores some of the similarities of the approaches taken by attorneys to a complex litigation case and those taken by engineers to a complex system development problem. The system development life cycle used in systems engineering has a direct corollary in the process of developing a legal case. Furthermore, the identification of technical, management, and legal risks; mitigation of those risks; and allocation of responsibility for them are of common interest to attorneys and engineering managers. This paper explores how attorneys can best assist engineers in the development process and how engineers can begin to address the problems of the litigation process.

Selected topics concerned with the invention and patent process, the systems development life cycle, and the criminal justice system are also examined in this paper. These topics are evaluated to determine some of the ways the systems engineer and the attorney can improve the people, the process, and the tools used in these two professions. The thesis is that many of the problems to come in the 21st century can be solved by the collaboration of systems engineers and attorneys.

INTRODUCTION

SYSTEMS ENGINEERING—WHAT IS IT?

One definition of systems engineering that might meet with universal agreement has several components: (1) it is an interdisciplinary engineering approach for establishing a sound system concept, (2) it defines and validates clear and concise system requirements, (3) it creates an effective system design or solution, and (4) it ensures that the developed system meets client and user objectives and needs in an operational environment. This definition focuses on efforts of the Systems Engineering Team (SET) in the early phases of the system development life cycle (SDLC), and ensures their participation throughout the SDLC.

The discipline of systems engineering may have been developed in the communications industry to meet the networking challenges of the 1950s. It grew in the space, defense, and computer industries during the 1960s and into the 1990s in response to the hardware and software system integration complexities of that period. By 1965, the Department of Defense (DOD) mandated Military Standard for Systems Engineering, MIL-STD-490, for the development of all military systems using a systems engineering approach (DOD 1965). The National Aeronautics and Space Administration (NASA) and the Department of Energy (DOE) soon followed with systems engineering guidelines for the civilian aerospace and energy programs of the 1970s.

New horizons for application of the systems engineering discipline in the 21st century will be to nontraditional engineering and even nonengineering disciplines. Nothing in the definition of systems engineering is limited to communications, space, defense, energy, or computer development. Much of the national interest in the early 21st century may focus on other engineering areas that can benefit from the systems approach, such as mass transportation, housing, infrastructure renewal, and environmental systems. In addition, areas such as the criminal justice process, drug abuse prevention, medical evaluations, and economics are fertile subjects for the application of systems engineering in the 21st century.

The systems engineering community has already begun structuring the major aerospace programs to address interests of the international scientific community and to focus on the environmental concerns of the planet. As large numbers of international scientific investigators are permitted to provide near-real-time feedback to orbiting sensors and to direct the information-gathering efforts from their workstations, the more stochastic the whole system will become. Such stochastic systems are more like the people-intensive criminal justice system. As systems engineers learn to design these more complex stochastic systems where people continually alter the outcomes, the engineering community will become more useful in applying itself to nonengineering disciplines with the challenges of nonlinear, probabilistic, and multivariable inputs, processes, and outputs.

WHY IS THE LEGAL PROCESS A SYSTEM?

In approaching the legal process as a system and analyzing it on a consistent basis, the three main components—input, process, and output—of a traditional system with feedback response are useful. The ease with which the systems engineering concept can be applied to the legal process and the obvious ability for communicating legal issues to an engineering community in familiar terms are two advantages to this approach (Figure 1).

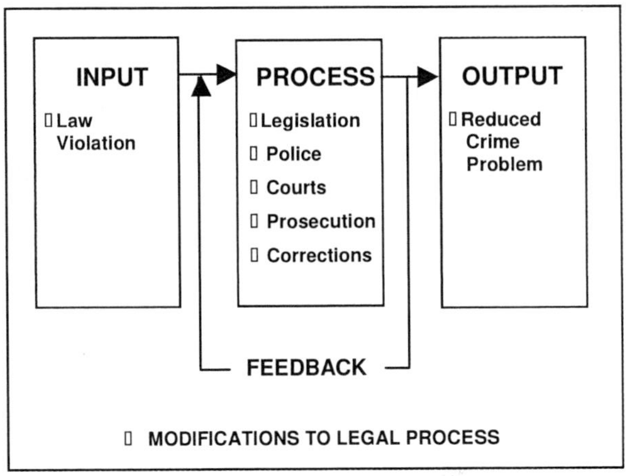

Figure 1. The Legal Process as a Traditional Linear System With Feedback Response

Distinguishing the major elements of the criminal justice system in terms of input, process, and output is a useful example of systemizing the legal process (Figure 2). The civil procedures, contract negotiations, and corporate formation processes could be analyzed in a similar way. Input to the criminal justice system is individual violations of the law. The process of the system refers to the many activities of police, attorneys, judges, probation and parole officers, and prison staff. The process of the criminal justice system is the most familiar and visible portion of the system to us. Output of the criminal justice system may be described as the success or failure of society to cope with crime. The feedback response is useful in changing input to effectively provide the desired output, i.e., a reduction in the amount of crime.

The role an attorney plays in developing a legal case and preparing for the eventual trial and/or negotiation is not unlike that of a systems engineer. The systems engineer determines and validates the requirements of a system and creates the system architecture for SDLC implementation. The legal team also has a legal process life cycle just as the SET must conform to an SDLC (Table 1).

The systems engineer identifies and validates the requirements of a system, and the lawyer identifies and validates the issues of a case. Just as the systems engineer creates a system design, the lawyer develops a design for the case using legal research and a discovery process. The system implementation has a corollary in the pleadings preparation and lawsuit initiation. The systems engineer finds out during system integration and test whether the system design actually verifies the requirements. The attorney finds out during the trial or negotiations whether the case presentation has been based on the correct issues. The acceptance of the system is very much like the verdict of a jury or the acceptance of the settlement by the opposing counsel. Finally, just as the systems engineer must be prepared to maintain the system for the remainder of the life cycle, the attorney must be prepared to enforce the judgment or verdict decree after the trial is over.

Apparent differences exist between the legal and systems engineering processes in the individuality with which every input to the legal process is treated and the judgment and discretion that the large number of persons responsible for executing the legal process may use. For example, in the criminal justice system, one person who commits a crime may do so for motivations that are quite different from those of another person who commits the same crime. Similarly, a police officer, who exercises judgment daily, has a range of discretion that determines whether the criminal justice process is invoked against an individual. Among the factors accounting for this discretion are a large volume of violations, the limited resources of the police, the overgeneralizing legislative enactments that define criminal conduct, and various local pressures reflecting community values and attitudes (Coffey et al. 1974).

In systems that are well designed and engineered, output is usually predictable—given a specified input. However, technically sophisticated systems can also be subject to a range of probabilistic outcomes. How safely an aircraft is operated, given unpredicted circumstances, or whether a weapons system actually hits a target often depends on the individuals that exercise discretion at the controls.

In this century, the systems engineering community will be called on to specify and develop more complex systems involving multiple users. These systems will need to support larger portions of the population. Also,

System Engineering Phases	Legal Process Corollary
1. System concept and requirements definition 2. System design 3. System implementation 4. System integration and test 5. System installation and acceptance 6. System operation and maintenance	1. Client discussions and issue identification 2. Legal research, discovery process, and case development 3. Pleadings preparation and/or law suit initiation 4. Negotiations and/or trial 5. Verdict or settlement 6. Enforcement of judgment or verdict decree

Table 1. Corollary Life Cycles of the Lawyer and the Systems Engineer

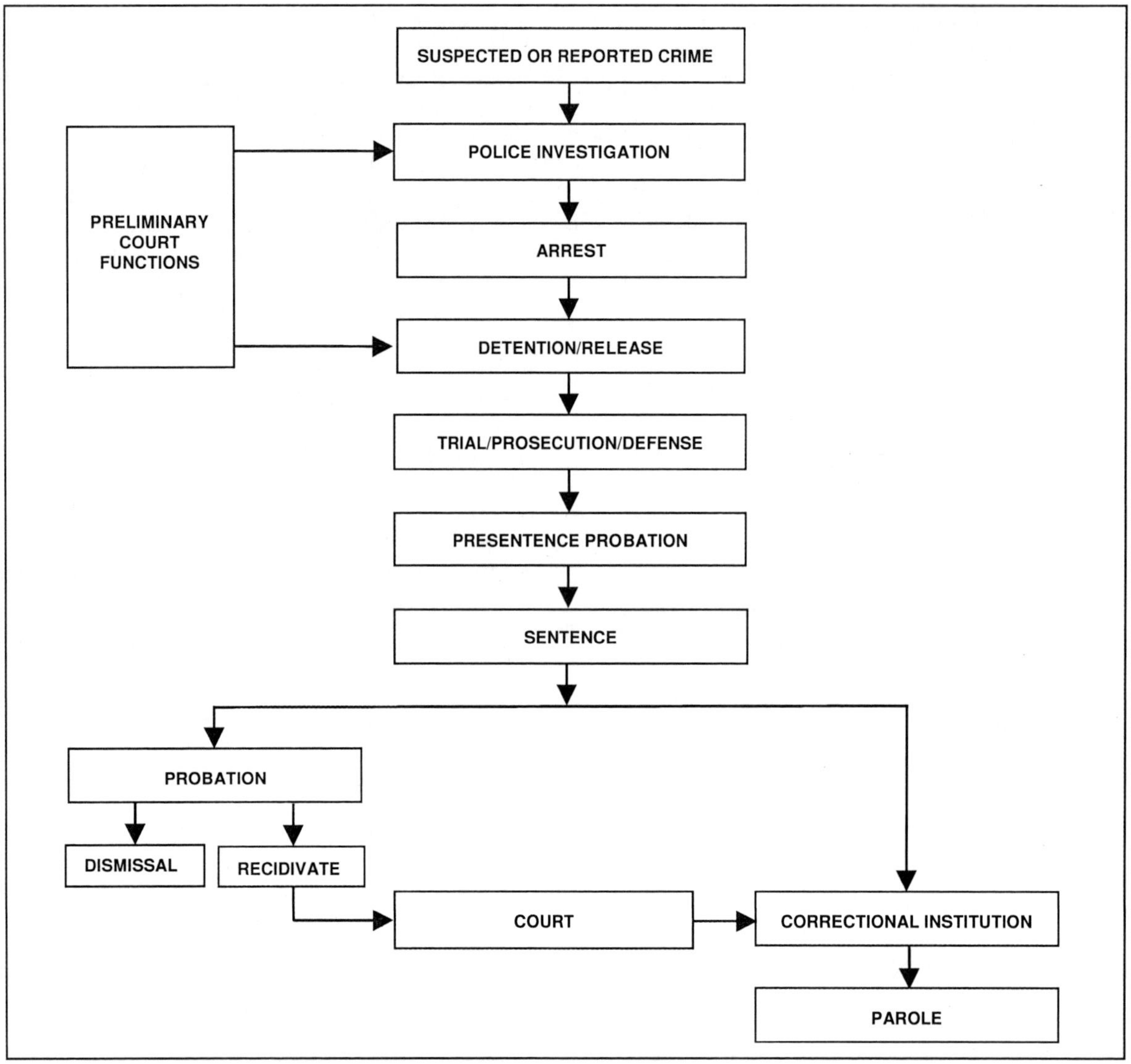

Figure 2. Major Elements of the Criminal Justice System

the legal community cannot continue to maintain an ineffective criminal justice system, but must address improvements to serve the interests of the people. Both communities must seek out areas of mutual interest and work together to meet the challenges of the new century.

AREAS OF MUTUAL INTEREST

An attorney can assist the engineering process in this century through participation in the following activities:

- Understand the SDLC by creating contracts that focus on risk mitigation during development and participate in the engineering process to ensure mutual agreement and an equitable outcome
- Revitalize the intellectual property protection mechanisms, i.e., patents, copyrights, and trade secrets, with the objectives of stimulating creativity and reducing infringement of property rights
- Apply principles of regulation to achieve the goals of regulating while providing incentives to achieve desired results.

Likewise, a systems engineer can assist the legal process in this century through participation in the following activities:

- Understand the criminal and civil legal processes, apply allocation of resources, and optimize techniques so processes might run more efficiently
- Provide simulation models for the criminal justice system and legal enforcement process so criminals can be identified easily and quickly brought to justice to achieve a thorough satisfaction of judgment against them in an environment of limited resources
- Identify appropriate tradeoff analyses and prototyping efforts to ensure regulations enacted by the legal community, balance diverse interests (for

example, the environment versus the economy), while providing incentives for advancing the technologies of society.

Table 2 lists some actions that both the engineering and legal communities might take to better train and provide incentives for the people in those professions. It also lists activities to improve the processes with which each profession operates and the tools of each profession. Several of these topics are discussed more fully in the remainder of this paper.

Rather than providing definitive answers to all the issues presented, this paper is intended to initiate a dialogue between the legal and the engineering communities on how best to address some of the pressing issues of this century.

	Engineering	Law
People	Participation in the educational community	Participation in the educational community
	Stimulating development of systems engineering textbooks	Joint MS/JD degree programs
	Incentives and recognition for the engineering profession	Incentives and recognition for the legal profession
Process	Adversarial process for concept development	Evolution of intellectual property protections
	Self-assessment of the systems engineering process	Participation in the SDLC
Tools	Automation of the systems engineering process	Simulation models for the criminal justice process

Table 2. Selected Activities for Improving People, Process, and Tools of the Profession

PROCESS: IMPROVING THE SYSTEMS ENGINEERING AND LEGAL PROCESSES

USE OF THE ADVERSARIAL PROCESS FOR CONCEPT DEVELOPMENT

The first task of a competent systems engineer or a SET is to conduct a meaningful system concept definition phase for a potential mission. The primary goals of this phase are to

- Rigorously define a system concept that will meet mission requirements and external user and system operations needs
- Assess the technical and economic feasibility of the system

After completing this phase, the system concept should provide the initial top-level description of the system. This description is used to assess the end-to-end system scope and the feasibility of proceeding with the development effort. The identification of potential risks and high-cost areas are also important results of this phase.

Tradeoff analyses, cost-benefit analyses, and even prototyping are useful methods for weighing one concept against another. With well-trained engineering minds performing these analyses, one would expect a solid system concept to emerge with most of the high-risk questions answered. How is it possible then that in the last 30 years significant technical and management lapses have occurred in many of the systems of the 20th century? Examples could include the virtual collapse of the nuclear reactor steam supply system industry, loss of a space shuttle, and chemical process systems that foul our water supplies and destroy our environment.

Several factors influence the outcomes of these system concepts, which have led to undesirable results. The public certainly has become more averse to risk. The lack of economic resources has limited the amount of tradeoff studies, as has the limited understanding of complex systems, such as ecology. Also, the desire to meet schedules permits risks to be accepted when they should be evaluated more carefully. This author submits that engineers are not completing the system concept definition phase of the life cycle very well and, in many cases, the tradeoff analyses and other critical analyses that would uncover many of the risks are not in fact being performed.

Most of us have noticed in our careers that, once an effort gets some funding, there is great impetus to move the development process along. Any views that might slow the process or risk the loss of future funding for one's company or agency are unlikely to be expressed. The debates that should occur in technical forums often do not happen. The important tradeoff analyses that should appear in technical journals are also lacking. As a result, the tough questions get asked in public forums and congressional committees, and the technical bodies are unprepared to answer them.

For the 21st century, the author believes that the engineering community and the SETs should structure a debate process, particularly for the system concept definition phase, with forums, such as the International Council on Systems Engineering (INCOSE), where all facets of the system can be examined. These forums could ensure that valid tradeoff analyses have been conducted, that technical evaluation criteria include social and economic values, and that advocates for most views have been heard. While such forums are more familiar to the legal community, they could greatly benefit the technical community by identifying and addressing the system risks and by permitting eventual convergence on a system concept that can be supported by users in the scientific and engineering communities and the and general public.

Self-Assessment of the Systems Engineering Process

The Need for Self-Assessment. As a result of the difficulties experienced by DOD in the 1970s and 1980s in obtaining embedded software of uniform quality for tactical weapons systems and its delivery on time within cost, the Software Technology for Adaptable and Reliable Systems (STARS) program was initiated. One of the facets of the STARS program was the creation of the Software Engineering Institute (SEI), whose primary objective was to improve the software development process that defense contractors use to design and implement software for DOD.

Systems Engineering Maturity Model. The creation of a systems engineering maturity model was initiated by INCOSE following the Seattle Symposium in 1992. At that time, the author recommended the development of such a model (Mackey 1992) and was honored to participate in the development of the first version of the Interim INCOSE Model, denoted Interim Model Version 1.00, which was completed in February 1994 (E. R. Widmann, et al. 1995). CSC was one of the first to conduct a Systems Engineering Process Assessment (SEPA) using this model and integrally participated in the subsequent development of Versions 1.10, 1.20, 1.30, and 1.40 of the Interim Model in 1994. The INCOSE Model and the later developed EPIC Model provide a basis for evaluating an organization's systems engineering process and are in the late stages of merger under the EIA. These models may result in a valued addition to the discipline of systems engineering. Such models directly or indirectly address the agreements on systems engineering nomenclature, system hierarchy, organization, life cycle, and the management process used to improve the performance of systems engineering.

By adopting and using such models, improvements may be witnessed within the systems engineering process during the 21st century. The question is, "How could the legal profession add value to such models?" In some respects, the code of ethics of the legal profession might well be incorporated into the maturity model as one evaluation factor. As some state jurisdictions move in the direction of licensure of systems engineers, a code of ethics may become a valued addition to such assessment models.

Evolution of Intellectual Property Protections

During the past several years, there have been significant changes in the intellectual property protection mechanisms of patents and copyrights. The percentage of patents issued by the U. S. Patent Office is no longer dominated by submissions from U.S. inventors. As a result of the International Bern Convention in 1989, notices are no longer required for copyrights. Further, an evolution is underway to permit patents to protect software as well as hardware and copyrights to protect hardware as well as software. The legal area of intellectual protection could benefit from the interaction of systems engineers and attorneys both to stimulate the invention process in the United States and to assist in creating the most meaningful protection mechanisms. A little history of the traditional domains of copyrights and patents illustrates the evolution that has been taking place in the law relating to the core of every system, the computer (i.e., computer law).

Traditional Domain of Patents. The traditional domain of patents has been hardware and hardware function. If *function* is the objective of protection, the *patent* is the mechanism of choice. To acquire a patent, an invention must pass the tests of patentability, which include novelty, nonobviousness, and utility (35 U.S. Code Sections 101–103). The invention must also pass the test of no prior disclosure to the public in the year prior to patent application. The patent submission consists of three parts: (1) the specification, (2) claims that define the boundaries of ownership rights and (3) any drawings. The advantage of a patent is that it provides sole rights to inventors for 17 years; a high percentage (e.g., 80 percent of patents recently being litigated) is being held valid. A patent protects function regardless of whether the infringer copied the protected hardware or software. The disadvantages of patents are that the registration process is relatively complex and therefore expensive, and there is a long patent-pending timeframe of 18 to 27 months (Mackey 1991a).

Traditional Domain of Copyrights. The traditional domain of copyrights has been documentation and more recently computer software. If *expression* is the objective of protection, the *copyright* is the mechanism of choice. To obtain a copyright, an author needs only to document the expression on some media. No formal registration or public notice is required; however, it is desirable to register a copyright with the U.S. Copyright Office because the registration establishes the right to sue in case of infringement; it also establishes prima facie evidence of ownership. The advantages of copyrights are (1) they are inexpensive to register, (2) the copyright is immediate upon putting pen to paper, and (3) the registration process is simple. The disadvantages of copyrights are that they are perceived to provide protection at a lower level than patents and that there is limited public disclosure.

A third intellectual property mechanism is the trade secret. Businesses, such as Coca-Cola and Kentucky Fried Chicken, have used this method successfully.

The advantages of this method are that (1) it can be controlled by business management, (2) it sometimes is less expensive, and (3) at times it can be combined with the protective mechanisms of copyrights and patents. Disadvantages of the trade secret mechanism are (1) the need to maintain secrecy may constrain the technical team, (2) it can be hard to implement and enforce, and (3) it does not protect from reverse engineering.

Evolution of Software Patent Protection. Intellectual property protection with regard to computers has been possible only since the 1970s and 1980s. In 1969, the courts established that natural, mathematical, and mental processes could not per se be claimed in a patent (in re *Prater* vs. *Wei*, on rehearing, 1969). Also in the same year, the court held that programmatic changes to machines may be patentable (in re *Bernhardt* vs. *Fetter*, 1969). Again, the courts upheld that some computer processes are patentable (in re *McIlroy*, 1971) while a year later, in *Gottschalk* vs. *Benson*, 1972, the ruling was that computer programs are not patentable (Siegel, et al. 1989). In 1981, in *Diamond* vs. *Diehr*, 1981, it was ruled that processes embedded in computer programs are patentable. While the final word has not established the precise boundaries of a patent, the trend of the U.S. Patent Office from 1971 to the present has permitted most software that passes the patent tests of novelty, nonobviousness, and utility to be patented.

Evolution of Hardware Copyright Protection. Copyrights were initially applied to software in the early 1980s. In *Apple Computer* vs. *Franklin Computer Corp.*, 1983, the Third Circuit Court established that software (source code and object code) is copyrightable. In addition, screen displays were deemed copyrightable under the "look-and-feel" decision stated in *Midway Mfg. Co.* vs. *Arctic Int'l Inc.*, 1982. The copyright was ruled to extend beyond the literal program to the sequence, structure, and organization in *Whelan* vs. *Jaslow*, 1983. In 1989, in *NEC Corp.* vs. *INTEL Corp.*, the courts held that microcode is similar enough to software to warrant copyright protection (Siegel, et al.).

Evolution of the Computer Control Unit and Software Program Storage. From the late 1950s through the 1970s, the computer control unit and the manner in which software programs are stored in the computer have changed significantly. The computer control units in the earliest machines were wire patch panels with vacuum tubes, followed by discrete logic units, (e.g., transistors, diodes, resistors, capacitors, AND gates, and OR gates).

In the late 1960s, these same units used integrated circuitry microprogramming; in the 1970s and 1980s, the computer control unit became very large-scale integrated (VLSI) circuitry. Program storage in the first-generation machines was accomplished by the manner in which patch panels were wired, which evolved to software stored in the main memory of the computer. By the third-generation computers, control storage read-only memory (ROM) microinstructions were added, followed by writeable, control store, programmed logic arrays (PLAs). In summary, the intellectual property mechanisms of patents protecting hardware and copyrights protecting software have evolved during the 1970s and 1980s. Also during this period, computer engineers complicated the situation by storing computer programs first in hardware patch panels, then in software code, and more recently in microcode firmware. Microcode firmware is defined as a multilevel instruction set that can be implemented in hardware or software (or both) and provides the logic sequences to activate the hardware elements.

State of Case Law on Software and Microcode. Figure 3 illustrates the evolution of the case law on software and microcode. If one views a computer system as a vertical continuum of hardware to software, there is a gray boundary, somewhere near microcode and programmed logic arrays, where hardware ends and software begins. This boundary will not remain static in the coming years. The illustration shows that, from 1971 to 1981, the patent protection of function evolved from hardware to some software. During the 1980s, the copyright protection of expression was in the process of evolving from software to microcode. Several questions remain unanswered: "Will copyright evolve to protect hardware?" "Has engineering created a gray area where something historically called hardware has now taken on the characteristics of something historically called software?"

How the Systems Engineer Can Assist the Invention Process. The patent attorney and those who regulate the patent process could benefit from the assistance of professional systems engineers who would be willing to study the invention and intellectual property processes for the purpose of improving the effectiveness of these processes. Yet, other questions remain: "Are there ways to increase the numbers of patents that American inventors will create by reducing the costs of protection?" "Is there a way to provide incentives to the creative scientist or engineer in a large corporation so that they gain significant rewards from a successful invention without making the royalties paid too burdensome for the corporation?" "Shouldn't we encourage the creation of millionaire inventors, such as those of the early 20th century (Thomas Edison, the Wright Brothers, and Henry Ford)?"

The engineering community could also advise the legal profession on technology forecasting. Questions to be answered include: "Is the present evolution of patents from hardware to software and copyrights from software to hardware a good result?" "Is not copyright

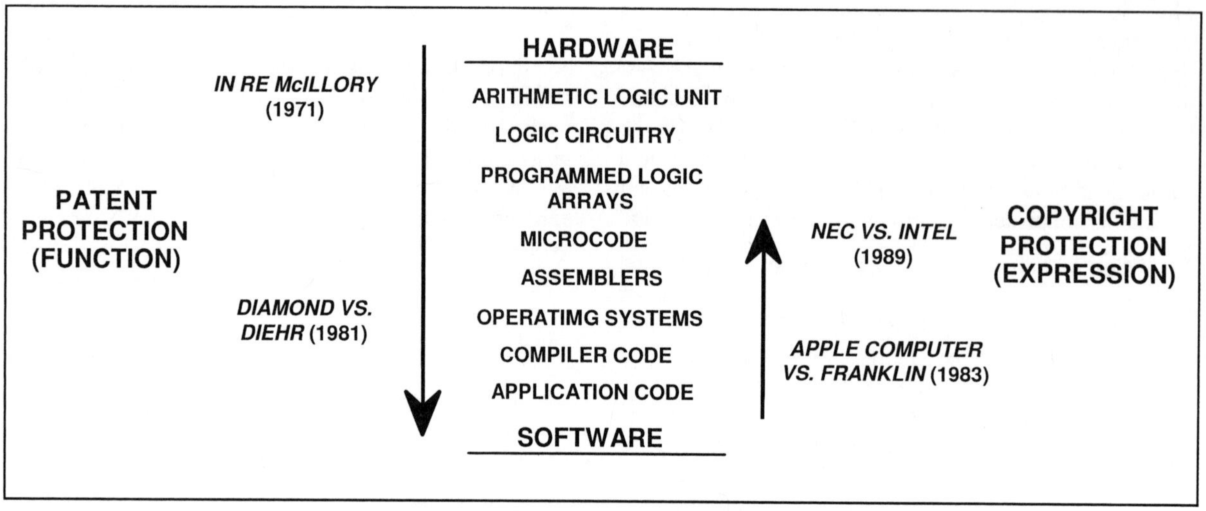

Figure 3. The Evolution of "Hardware" Copyright Protection: State-of-Case Law on Software and Microcode

protection of software and microcode implemented in ROM/PLA form simply a "backdoor patent" way of gaining protection for hardware inventions?" "Does not the 'look-and-feel' decisions for copyright protection, if extended to microcode, offer more protection to hardware than could be achieved through specific claims in any hardware patent?" "Would not the copyrighting of ROM-based software and microcode become a major deterrent to clone manufacturing?"

There are many avenues of mutual interest to attorneys and engineers in the intellectual property protection arena.

LEGAL PARTICIPATION IN THE SYSTEM DEVELOPMENT LIFE CYCLE

The systems engineer is very familiar with the activities of the SDLC. A well-managed SDLC requires the complete cooperation of the project management team, the SET, and all other line organizations. Often forgotten in the project organization are the legal advisors. Usually, the legal advisors are called upon to draft the contract and subcontract documents and then fade into the background until the project encounters difficulty. This event could occur early in the contract or, more likely, in several months or even years after contract initiation. At that point, the project is so interwoven with actions taken by contractor and client that it is often difficult to determine how to allocate those losses that result from the realized risks.

The most significant risks involved in large projects are usually related to the development of initial system concepts, ensuring specificity and the agreement of system requirements and design, and in the management of the SDLC to achieve the desired implementation (Mackey 1991b). A competent legal counsel can add value to the activities of the project organization. A legal advisor should therefore be involved in the project to ensure that the interests of the organization are being monitored.

A legal advisor can assist the project management team in the following activities:

- Participate in all project reviews where binding technical and management agreements are reached
- Assist in identifying and allocating the risks
- Ensure all requirements in the system requirements specification are written to be easily understood by persons skilled in the appropriate subject
- Monitor the completion and proper transfer of all contract deliverables
- Ensure that all appropriate contract requirements are passed on to individual subcontractors
- Assist in identifying system changes that impact the contract and are out of scope from the contract's original intent

In summary, the legal counsel can be invaluable to the project without understanding all the technical details. Such counsel can assist the project manager and the line managers in managing the SDLC and mitigating potential risks.

PEOPLE: IMPROVING THE SYSTEMS ENGINEERING AND LAW PROFESSIONS

PARTICIPATION IN THE EDUCATIONAL COMMUNITY

Currently, there is great concern about the status of learning in all subjects. The current willingness of both high school and college students to study science, mathematics, and engineering is causing the most concern because these subjects will determine the innovations that stimulate growth of the economy.

Recent American Institute of Aeronautics and Astronautics (AIAA) conferences and the INCOSE conferences have made education and training major segments of focus.

Because we can learn more from those who have intensive experience with the educational system, I will confine my comments to those of us who practice engineering or law on a daily basis. Having worked extensively with organizations, such as the Boy Scouts of America and many students in our high schools, I am more optimistic about the prospects for the future than the statistics we see on television and in the newspapers every day. I have found students who are open and willing to give up their weekends if the opportunity to learn appears worthwhile. In addition, I have found that scientists, engineers, and lawyers are willing to volunteer to relate their experiences to youth if given the right forum. I would like to relate two examples of how we can participate in stimulating technical education in our own neighborhoods without becoming professional teachers.

Case Study 1: Boy Scouts of America. A few years ago, I had two sons who wanted to become Eagle Scouts. I agreed to become an assistant scoutmaster for the troop and conducted campouts like many of the other fathers who were heavily involved. I quickly became aware of the merit badge process and the multitude of subjects that the process covered. As the young men got well into high school, their interests began to shift from outdoor activities and campouts to girls, college, and career preparation. I decided to take the opportunity to assist them in college and career preparation by touring all the major college campuses in two states over a period of 3 years on the weekends when they could enjoy college football, basketball, and lacrosse games as part of the tour. Using the very well written Boy Scouts' merit badge books, we studied different careers and visited laboratories and conducted creative classrooms. We also made trips to TV studios, chemical plants, hospitals, laser labs, judges' chambers, and prisons. The scouts studied subjects such as atomic energy, computers, communications, engineering, energy, environmental science, space exploration, law, architecture, aviation, first aid, and so forth. I found the county, state, military, and industrial facilities not only open to participate, but also often willing to dedicate a portion of their weekend to these efforts.

As a result, all of those young men went to colleges and schools such as the Massachusetts Institute of Technology (MIT), the University of Virginia, Virginia Tech, Virginia Commonwealth University (VCU), Cornell, the U.S. Military Academy, the U.S. Air Force Academy, the U.S. Naval Academy, College of William & Mary, Harvard University, Duke University, and many more. They majored in technical subjects, including computer science, electrical engineering, aerospace engineering, environmental engineering, architecture, mathematics, law, medicine, pharmacy, and veterinary medicine. Most of those who graduated from college are pursuing careers in the military or in scientific, engineering, medical, or legal professions. In summary, the cost per youth in developing these interests was only a few pennies because the merit badge books were already developed and inexpensive, the tours were free, and all the labor and materials were volunteered. By volunteering our efforts to youth, each of us can have a major impact on many of our young people over a period of a few years.

Case Study 2: District of Columbia Legal Bar. While I was Chairman of the District of Columbia Bar Computer Law Section, the committee decided to examine how to improve the image of the legal profession and promote the interests of computer law. We decided to develop a training session that could be taught in 1 hour to high school students taking computer science. The session introduced the subject of intellectual property and how to protect it using the current mechanisms in law. The students were asked to simulate a new business, i.e., creating and marketing a new piece of software such as "Desert Storm" or "Recovering From a Recession." The class was divided into software development, marketing, and legal teams. The students estimated the costs for developing and manufacturing the software, packaging and marketing the product, and developing legal and business strategies for protecting the company from bankruptcy if potential customers illegally copied the software.

Long-term results are not yet available, but our efforts have continued over the past few years. Several attorneys have taken time off from their regular work each year and dedicated a day to teaching this session to all computer science classes at prearranged high schools within the Washington, D.C., Maryland, and Virginia metropolitan area. More than 20 such sessions have already taken place. The regular teachers without exception welcomed the opportunity for the attorneys to share their experiences. Most feel that the image of the legal profession was improved at very little cost, the impact of computer software piracy was understood, and perhaps one day students will choose to become computer scientists or computer lawyers.

In addition to these kinds of initiatives, the professions need to work on improving the image of engineering and law as professions. College graduates must be shown that a technical education represents a key to a rewarding and exciting career. If professional societies and individual volunteers take action, there will be less need for government involvement and far less cost to each taxpayer.

STIMULATING THE COLLEGE CURRICULUM

Stimulating Development of Systems Engineering Textbooks. In his paper on automating the discipline of systems engineering, M. Alford points out that each DOD prime contractor had its own internal systems engineering education program (Alford 1992). However, he noted that no professional society in systems engineering existed before INCOSE, no conferences on systems engineering occurred, and no journal of systems engineering to record research results was published. By the mid-1980s, only a few textbooks and some internal company documents still in print described the systems engineering process. Furthermore at that time, no widespread research activity explored the adaptation of computerized tools to service the systems engineering market. Fortunately, in the 1990s, members of INCOSE have written several excellent textbooks and have closed this gap.

If systems engineering is to continue to grow as a discipline, such growth must occur in most of the engineering colleges of the nation's universities. Organizations such as INCOSE must continue to stimulate professional activities in systems engineering and give some direction to the development of systems engineering textbooks.

Joint MS/JD Degree Programs. Many universities now offer systems engineering at the graduate level. Some universities, including all of the military service academies, offer systems engineering as an engineering major at the undergraduate level, often under the Department of Electrical Engineering. Perhaps more than any other engineering discipline, the study of systems engineering requires an engineering mind capable of adopting a more global view. For that reason, combined programs in business, economics, and law are fertile areas for training the systems engineers of the future. Many universities with both business and law schools offer combined programs with an MBA/JD joint degree. Some universities, such as the University of Pennsylvania, which offered the first systems engineering degree, have met with some success in offering a combined program in engineering and business, resulting in an MS/MBA degree. As we prepare to solve the social problems of the 21st century, it would be appropriate to have systems engineers with a broad understanding of both law and engineering. A combined program in engineering and law with an MS/JD joint degree might be appropriate.

INCENTIVES FOR THE ENGINEERING PROFESSION

Initiatives for Technical Education. This paper has previously referred to the great concern for the status of education in the United States. *The Washington Post* stated that 13 percent of American students leave school lacking minimal reading skills versus only 4 percent in Europe and 1 percent in Japan (Wolff 1992). The report states, "Poorly prepared and inadequately trained workers hurt productivity growth and tilt the overall economy toward low-end, unskilled tasks. Indeed, the United States has now become a source of relatively cheap labor for Japan and Europe." While these statistics are disturbing, the statistics for American students pursuing technical degrees are likely to be of greater concern.

What has caused this lack of desire for a technical education among American students? First, obtaining a technical education has always been difficult. The diligence required to become skilled in mathematics and science has always been one of the most significant in education. During the space race of the 1960s and, to a lesser degree, the energy crisis and computer expansion of the 1970s, a graduating engineer could expect multiple job offers upon receipt of his/her degree. More recently, America's investment in itself, in scientific and industrial research and development, in roads and communications, and in new factories and equipment is the smallest among all modern nations, save only for Ireland. Only 17.1 percent of U.S. gross domestic product (GDP) is invested in assets that produce wealth. This investment compares with the 30.6 percent of GDP in Japan that is put back into productive investments. This lack of investment in America translates into lack of opportunity for both new science and engineering graduates and for mature professionals. The effort required to pursue a technical education has therefore become less attractive as technical career and job opportunities diminish in the United States.

Improving the Image of Engineering and Law. In addition to a fluctuating presence of opportunities for scientists and engineers in America, there is a need to improve the image of the engineering and legal professions. The engineering profession often lacks visible rewards for a job well done while the legal profession often is the butt of unkind jokes. The entertainment and sports communities have learned the lessons that the scientific, engineering, and legal communities have yet to understand. The present heroes of American youth are the sports figures, singers, musicians, and actors/actresses who are viewed daily on television in most homes. While TV occasionally portrays medical doctors, attorneys, scientists, and engineers, these youths admire the stage figure, not the actual person being portrayed. In the 1990s, many of these very visible entertainment figures have parlayed their public visibility into major political positions. In a highly technical society, shouldn't scientists and engineers be best equipped to make many of the political decisions?

Weekly television spectaculars honor performers with Oscars, Emmys, Grammys, Tonys, and so on. These honors are funded by the industries that benefit from the images these honors create. Sports figures are similarly honored in all-star appearances, superbowls, most valuable player awards, or Olympic performances. Rather than discontinuing these honors, I would like to recommend the receipt of similar awards by members of the scientific, engineering, and legal professions.

Visible Awards for Science and Engineering. I believe, we should support the attempt to stimulate the desire to obtain a technical education by honoring those who have contributed most to chemistry, mechanical engineering, mathematics, and other disciplines on an annual basis. I submit that it could be done with all the flair and elegance of an Academy Awards presentation. It could be interesting, informative, and uplifting. Music, dance, and visual effects could all be combined to make these presentations a pleasure to watch. We would need the support of those industries from which many of the award winners would arise to fund a National Academy of Sciences and Engineering. We, as scientists and engineers, would also have to be willing to fund such an organization. The rewards for doing so would present an opportunity to provide visible awards for science and engineering, improve the image of our profession, and stimulate a desire in our youth to study science and engineering.

TOOLS: IMPROVING THE TOOL SET

AUTOMATING THE SYSTEMS ENGINEERING PROCESS

M. Alford's paper also discussed the need and required characteristics for automation of the systems engineering process (Alford 1992). It describes systems engineering as the last engineering discipline to be automated. This author refers the interested reader to the Alford paper to gain historical perspective on why this discipline was initially slow to automate.

Trends Inhibiting Automation. M. Alford states that at least four trends have historically hindered automation of systems engineering:

- Early success of systems engineering during which many of the principles were codified and there seemed little more to do
- Lack of professional societies and publications caused by systems engineers leaving the aerospace industry after the aerospace crash of 1969
- Emergence of document-driven design that resulted in a deemphasis of solid systems engineering design processes and emphasis on the documents themselves
- Lack of funds for workstations, tools, and training in the systems engineering discipline

Trends Supporting Automation. In more recent years, several trends have emerged to support the use of tools in systems engineering, including

- Advances in workstation technology
- Increasing system complexity, which could not be managed by the old manual methods
- The desire for increased quality at the early requirements and design specification levels
- The need to maintain a database of engineering design decisions made while going from customer requirements to a proposed design
- The desire to improve the systems engineering process itself
- The emergence of systems engineering tools, which provide integrated capabilities
- A resurgence of interest in the systems engineering discipline

Often, systems engineers have learned from software engineers and have adapted their tools, such as computer-aided software engineering (CASE) and structure analysis tools.

Many of us are pleased with the emergence of automation in systems engineering in the 1990s, and the refocusing of systems engineers from the clerical to the engineering tasks. INCOSE must continue to stimulate these efforts.

SIMULATION MODELS FOR THE CRIMINAL JUSTICE SYSTEM

Components of the Criminal Justice System. The criminal justice system is an apparatus society uses to enforce the standards of conduct necessary to protect individuals and the community. If prosecution and defense are viewed as separate entities from the court, the criminal justice system has four separate organized parts: the police, the court prosecution, the defense, and corrections, each with its own distinct activities (Coffey 1974).

The police are concerned with control, apprehension, and support for the criminal justice system. The role of the police in the administration includes

- Prevention of crime
- Detection of crimes that have been committed
- Identification of the person(s) responsible for crimes
- Apprehension of the person(s) responsible for crimes
- Detention of the person for processing by the judiciary
- Presentation of the evidence to the prosecutor

The court includes the roles of prosecutor and defense as two distinct interrelated phases of the administration of justice. The key administrative officer in the processing of cases is the prosecutor. The prosecutor's decisions significantly affect the arrest practices of the police, the volume of cases in courts, and the number of offenders cleared through the correctional system. Thus, the prosecutor is in the most favorable position to bring about the needed coordination among the various law enforcement and correctional agencies in the community. The important role of defense counsel is to provide clients with the right to be heard and achieve the most appropriate disposition of clients. The right of a criminal defendant to be represented by counsel is a fundamental protection for individual liberty in our system of criminal justice.

Corrections involves implementing the orders that the court gives to probation departments or parole agencies and institutions. Corrections includes America's prisons, jails, juvenile training schools, and probation and parole machinery.

CONCLUSION

How Can the Systems Engineer Help? The systems engineer can help by perceiving that the criminal justice system with its component hierarchy could be modeled just as any other probabilistic system might be. Therefore, the opportunity exists for simulating the criminal justice system at any level. Figure 4 shows a typical model of the criminal justice system with estimates of offenders and operating costs (in 1965 dollars) for index crimes in the United States (President's Commission 1967). The dated flow does not diminish the value of the concept.

Modeling the criminal justice system could be useful in many ways. Determining whether a new statute or other measure might be effective in reducing crime or the numbers of persons convicted of a particular crime could be modeled and understood before the measure was implemented. Evaluating corrections methods or courts processes could be simulated to evaluate their efficiency. Evaluating the fairness of sentences according to a defendant's level of education, race, and income could be examined in much more detail. Reduction of the court load, prison population, and resources spent on maintaining the criminal justice system could be measured and optimized.

Understanding the criminal legal processes and applying the allocation of resources and optimization techniques so that those processes might run more efficiently could all be enhanced with simulation models built by systems engineers with a background in law. By providing simulation models for the criminal justice system and the legal enforcement process, criminals might be more easily identified, quickly brought to justice, and judgment against them satisfied in an environment of limited resources.

REFERENCES

Alford, M., "Systems Engineering: The Last Engineering Discipline To Be Automated." AIAA Space Programs and Technologies Conference, March 1992, Huntsville, AL.

Coffey, Alan, Eldefonso, Edward, and Hartinser, Walter, *An Introduction to the Criminal Justice System and Process.* Prentice-Hall, Englewood Cliffs, NJ, 1974.

Department of Defense, MIL-STD-490, Military Standard for Systems Engineering, 1965.

Mackey, W. F., "The Evolution of Hardware Copyright Protection." Presentation at the D.C. Bar Winter Meeting, February 1991.

Mackey, W. F., "Technical Issues in Computer Contracting." Presentation at the Intellectual Property Symposia, Marco Island, FL, March 1991.

Mackey, W. F., "Systems Engineering and the Legal Profession." Presented at the NCOSE 2nd Annual Symposium, Seattle, WA, July 20–22, 1992.

The President's Commission on Law Enforcement and the Administration of Justice, "The Challenge of Crime in a Free Society." U.S. Government Printing Office, Washington, D.C., 1967.

Widmann E. R., B. A. Andrews, and W. Mackey, *"An Improved NCOSE/CAWG Interim Model for the Capability Assessment of Systems Engineering and Supporting Documents"*, Proceedings of the Fifth Annual International Symposium of the National Council of Systems Engineering, July 22–26, 1995, St. Louis, MO, Volume II, p. 97.

Wolff, M., "Walking Small at Munich: Why George Bush Won't Be Signing Any Autographs at the Summit." *The Washington Post*, July 5, 1992.

Siegel, D., and R. Laurie, "Beyond Microcode: Alloy vs. Ultratek—The First Attempt to Extend Copyright Protection to Computer Hardware." *Computer Lawyer*, April 1989.

AUTHOR'S BIOGRAPHY

William Mackey, Ph.D., J.D., is a Senior Consulting Engineer of CSC. He is an attorney and a member of both the District of Columbia and the State of Virginia Legal Bars. He is also a professor teaching telecommunications and systems engineering at the University of Maryland University College. Dr. Mackey attended the U. S. Naval Academy and has B.S. and M.S. degrees in Physics from the University of Pittsburgh and the Rensselaer Polytechnic Institute. He received his Ph.D. degree in Systems Engineering from the University of Pennsylvania and his J.D. degree in law from the Washington College of Law, American University. He has a long career in scientific research, engineering, and management applied to aerospace, transportation, energy, systems integration, and law.

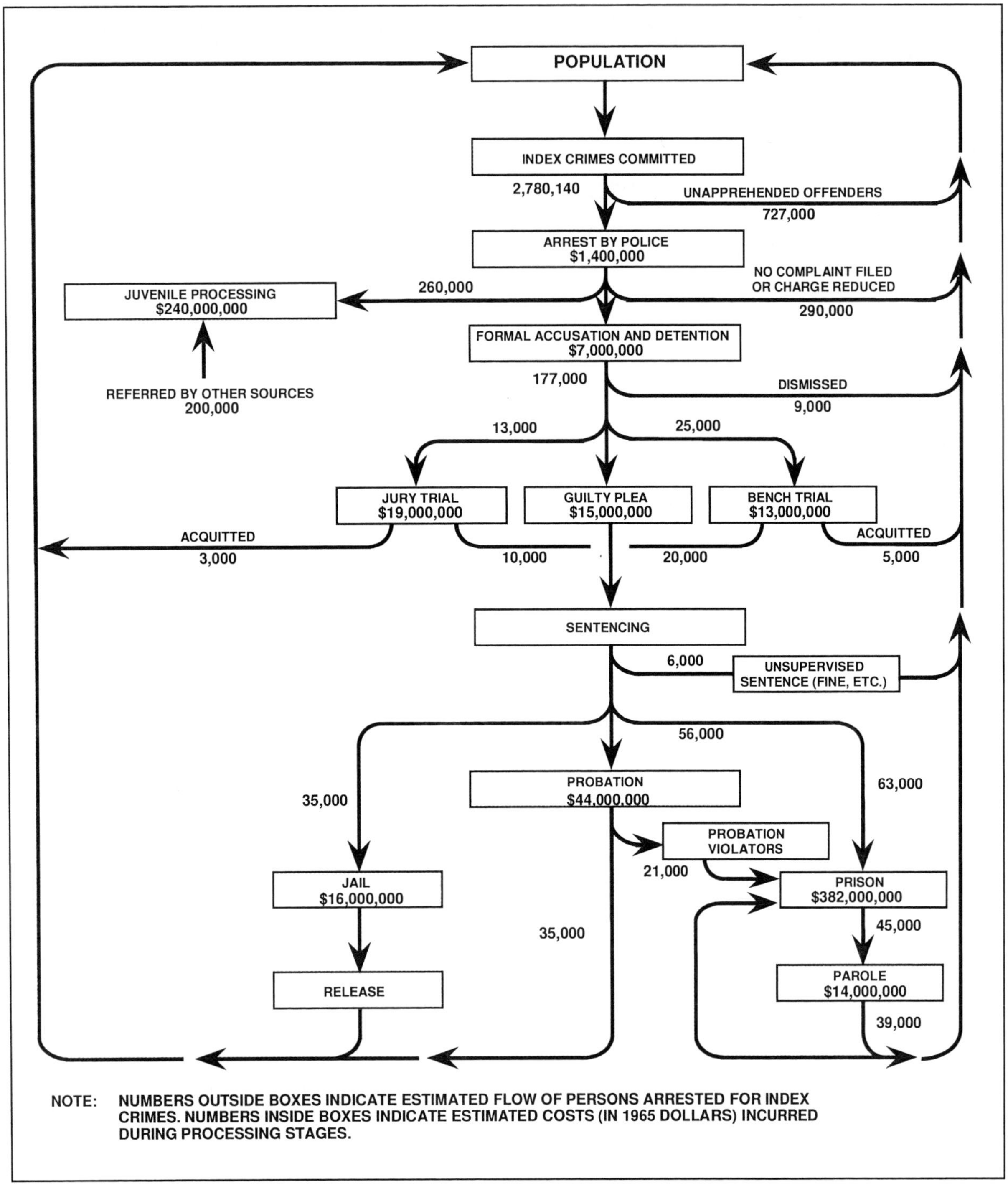

10046257-O97

Figure 4. Criminal System Model (President's Commission, 1967)

Systems Engineering in a Public Interest Project: Providing a Web Based Communications Capability

Janet Villa Roberson
Enterprise Information Systems Company
P.O. Box 3504, Sunnyvale, CA 94088-3504
jan.roberson@lmco.com

Gerald C. Bauknight
Lockheed Martin Space Systems Company
P.O. Box 3504, Sunnyvale, CA 94088-3504
jerry.bauknight@lmco.com

Abstract. This paper describes an application of the systems engineering process in a public interest project. The purpose of the project was to support the Salinan Native American Nation in an unobtrusive way that was important to the nation. This goal was identified through action research discussions with a Salinan Nation leader and the tribal council. The chosen project was to develop a web based communications system for this virtual nation. The authors selected the INCOSE "How To" Guide as a process to develop this project. The project is outlined through its planned completion and lessons learned from this project are considered for similar future projects.

INTRODUCTION

This study was based on a basic definition and mission statement that is familiar to many in the systems engineering community. INCOSE (International Council on Systems Engineering) is an international organization formed to develop, nurture and enhance the systems engineering approach to multi-disciplinary system product development (Robertson, 1999). The traditional Mission Statement is, "INCOSE shall foster the definition, understanding, and practice of World Class Systems Engineering in industry, academia, and government." Because today's managers and professionals find themselves in environments of great change and turbulence, the traditional methods and processes must be modified and used in many different and innovative ways. Systems engineers are required to work in areas of law, health care, education, and civic action, just to name a few domains. They are pressured by the world marketplace, and are dealing with many constantly changing situations around the globe with persons of different cultures and languages. It may be necessary to not only learn better techniques, but to become "mindful inquirers" in approaching our systems engineering work (Bentz and Shapiro, 1998).

WORKING WITH THE SALINANS

The people of the Salinan Nation

For thousands of years, the Salinan people, known as the people of the Oak Trees, lived in the coastal area of central California. In the late 1700's, the early explorers from Europe and Mexico began to arrive in California and life was never the same for the Salinan people. Since California's unwritten solution to dealing with their native people was annihilation, those Native Americans who would survive "went underground" and attempted, at least outwardly, to blend into society (Eargle, 1996).

About 20 years ago, the Salinan people, who remembered and treasured their heritage (and despite their innate distrust for government), began to come forward to formally re-establish the tribe. The U. S. Government's requirements for recognition are monumental. It has been a long and arduous process that is far from over. All participation and work has been carried out by a small core group of volunteers. Monthly planning meetings are ongoing. Yearly tribal gatherings are held in the area of California that is considered their homeland. A museum was established to display the few remaining examples of life before the destruction of the tribe. Reliable and regular communication within the tribe was hampered by the diverse locations of all tribal members, the limited time the volunteers had to accomplish the numerous tasks required for Federal recognition, and the minimal budget that they had available.

Volunteering to do Systems Engineering
The first written record of the lead author's connection with the Salinan Nation occurred in the late 1760's when her ancestor, Rafael de Jesus Villavicencia, traveled from Baja, Mexico, with Father Junipero Serra and founded several California missions, including the Mission San Antonio (Crosby, 1981). Rafael's marriage to a local Salinan girl in 1773 at this Mission was the second recorded marriage in California (Brusa, 1992). They started their family in Cayucos, California, on a land grant provided by the King of Spain (Crosby, 1994). It was in this general area of California where the author grew up.

Over the years, the author had been aware of the tribe, but seldom participated in the work being done to obtain Federal recognition for the tribe. Two years ago, a Web page was found that had been set up for the Salinan tribe from another tribe's home page. This page had dated material that had not changed in over a year and a half later. The page still showed an invitation to an event that had occurred more than a year before. The author decided at this time to volunteer both time and talent to provide their own Web page. In the process of doing this task, both authors began a collaboration of mutual interest. This project was the application of the systems engineering process to a project related to a Public Interest domain. The first task was to really find out what the Salinan Nation considered to be its important interfaces with "the outside world." What is important in delivering system performance and what is not? Making that judgment call is "one of the earliest and most dangerous decisions" at the outset of a project (Rechtin, 1999).

SELECTING THE PROCESS

The authors decided, after reviewing the many appropriate standards and references, that it would be best to use the INCOSE Systems Engineering Process to accomplish the job. The specific set of INCOSE process steps came from the "Systems Engineering Process Activities: A 'How To' Guide," originally prepared by the INCOSE San Francisco Bay Area Chapter (Robertson, 1999).

The handbook states, "The basic engine for systems engineering is an iterative process that expands on the common sense strategy of (1) understanding a problem before you attempt to solve it, (2) examining alternative solutions (do not jump to point design), and (3) verifying that the selected solution is correct before continuing the definition activities or proceeding to the next problem." It is this basic philosophy that the authors decided to follow.

The Process Steps
The list (Table 1) of process steps in the INCOSE handbook provided the necessary guidelines for the study.

Basic Step	Process
Define the system objectives	User Needs
Establish performance requirements	Requirements Analysis
Establish the functionality	Functional Analysis
Evolve design and operations concepts	Architecture Synthesis
Select a baseline	Through Cost/Benefit Trades
Verify the baseline meets requirements	User Needs
Iterate the process through lower level trades	Decomposition

Table 1. Basic Steps to Follow

Using the process for the Web page design
The first task "Define the System Objectives" appeared on the surface to be an easy task. The lead author recounts her initial thoughts and mental steps: "I knew what my needs were as a user of the Web page and I defined them from my personal perspective as a member of the (Salinan) community. Basically, my needs were to have access to timely news about the tribe and

to receive notices of upcoming events with plenty of time to plan to attend. As soon as I had what I thought were the needs of the community of users, I set up a meeting with the Salinan Tribal Council Leader to go over these potential requirements. It was quite a shock to me to come away from this meeting with a completely different set of needs. First, the Council Leader told me I had not considered the fact that few of the tribal members have computers. Therefore, the primary requirement today would not be for communication between members of the tribe. In addition, it became evident during the discussion that there were several layers of importance and urgency to the different needs that we eventually identified."

Some of the needs, both future and current, identified during this meeting included:

- Communicate tribal events to tribal members.
- Provide the tribe with information on the ongoing Federal recognition process.
- Minimize time and cost of providing information.
- Provide information about the tribe to people and organizations outside the tribe.
- In order to eliminate time intensive correspondence, provide information to schoolchildren who need to write reports on California Missions.

The second process step, "Establish Performance Requirements" occurred when those identified needs were transformed into requirements. It was also during this stage that a prioritization level was assigned to each of the requirements.

The third task of "Establish the Functionality" required little time, as most of the requirements became rather self evident and easily satisfied. The depth of this project's requirements was at such a lower level of functionality that little technical research was necessary.

The fourth task of "Evolve Design and Operation Concepts" was by far the most enjoyable and conversely the most frustrating. The fun came in the designing and identifying ways to meet the requirement needs. The frustration came from realizing the constraints did not allow the authors, as systems engineers, to do everything just the way they wanted. For example, the necessary font size to make the page readable left the designer with fewer words than she had wanted to put on the page. It became a time of give and take between the constraints and the requirements.

The fifth task was "Select a Baseline". The risks that were identified during this step included:

- The Web site may be unavailable to most of the tribe because of the lack of computer systems or lack of computer literacy.
- Material may quickly become outdated.
- Dealing with insulting racist remarks if there is a discussion box or area for comments (e.g., the problem of operating in a political environment).
- The downloading "waits" if there are extensive graphics of the Salinan Nation's homeland.

Taking these risks into consideration, the finally selected baseline is, in essence, the first phase of the Web page deployment. Few trade studies were necessary for this start, but more extensive ones will be considered during the next two phases of deployment. All three required phases will be discussed in the following section.

The sixth step is "Verify the Baseline Meets Requirements" or is commonly known as "where the rubber meets the road." This task was accomplished by notifying the Tribal Council at completion of phase one and receiving comments back through the Tribal Leader. Unfortunately, because of the lack of computers, not all the council members were able to view the site and they had to rely on others for communication by word of mouth.

The seventh and last step, "Iterate the Process Through Lower Level Trades", has begun and will continue through the last two phases.

Table 2 shows the seven INCOSE steps with the resulting actions and products of this project.

Basic Step	Process	Action	Product
Define the system objectives	User Needs	Determine the tribe's needs	Preliminary list of needs
Establish performance requirements	Requirements Analysis	Document and prioritize requirements	Preliminary requirements
Establish the functionality	Functional Analysis	Evaluate the feasibility of the requirements	Workable requirements
Evolve design and operations concepts	Architecture Synthesis	Identify the page designs and content	Initial design
Select a baseline	Through Cost/Benefit Trades	Identify risks to be resolved	Documented risks
Verify the baseline meets requirements	User Needs	Obtain Tribal Council approval	Approved Phase 1 web pages
Iterate the process through lower level trades	Decomposition	Start Phase 2 of website development	A continuously improving website

Table 2. Basic Steps of Process

The Three-Phased Approach

The varying levels of urgency of the different requirements have led to three phases of implementation. The first phase was designed to meet the urgent need to post the notice of an upcoming yearly tribal gathering. This requirement was satisfied in time for the gathering on 25 September 1999. The second phase addresses the need to provide information to the tribe as well as "the rest of the world." The last phase will address the "wish list" of things that will be nice to have, but those requirements may lack the urgency and importance of the other needs of the Nation.

Prioritization of requirements by phase

The goal of Phase 1 was to get the flyer on the tribal gathering on the Web as the time element was short and this task had the highest priority. This first phase included a front page with links to the flyer.

Phase 2 included a front page with a picture of an Oak tree, the symbol of the Salinan Nation (See Figure 1), and a menu to more information. This page also contains a contact link to the Tribal Leader for more information and the Web Master for Web page problems and comments.

The bullets, which link to other pages, will be listed on the front-page menu are:

- Tribal Council: This connecting page will have an organizational chart, a picture of the tribal council members and links to each member's biography. This section is planned for Phase 3, but work begins with the organizational chart when it is available.
- Events: In Phase 1, this page links to the flyer on the tribal gathering. In Phase 2, it will also inform the people that there is a Tribal Council meeting on the second Sunday of each month. In Phase 3, this page will connect to a calendar of tribal events and information on each event.
- Links: URL addresses will be linked to related pages such as other Native American tribes. This bullet is scheduled to start in Phase 2, but it will be updated continuously.
- Newsletters: Phase 2 will include the latest newsletter. Phase 3 will maintain a history file of past newsletters.
- Sign-up Forms: During Phase 3, this site will provide sign up forms for events, tours, work parties, and other more routine activities.
- History: During Phase 2, this page will include the three handouts currently available for distribution. During Phase 2 and Phase 3, more information will be written and added to the page.
- Culture Center: During Phase 2, this site will show hours, location, and a map to the center. During Phase 3, this site should be expanded to discuss content of the Cultural Center's museum.
- Guest Book: In Phase 3, this site will allow people to record

comments and information about themselves.

Current state of this page
Phase 1 was completed in June of 1999. The site has been available since that time and has received many favorable comments related to content and design. (See the site at salinan-nation.com.)

Phase 2 has been started and information is being processed for posting on the site. For example, the tribe is just starting to receive permission to list the links that they want to include on the pages. Also, several documents on the history of the people are being written and need to be reviewed for clarity and accuracy.

Phase 3 is still in the planning stage, but this phase is being developed in a thoughtful and logical manner. A few more trades will be necessary, as the tribe approaches the planned implementation. Those studies will not be done until "the last minute" to take advantage of any new technology or software that may be released.

Vision for future use of this site
The authors see two main goals for this site, speaking from the perspective of the Salinan Nation. The first and most important goal today is to function as a source of information to be released to the outside world (i.e., that world external to the tribal environment). In time, the authors expect this goal to become minor compared to the second, longer-term goal that is envisioned for this site. The second goal is that this page becomes a vehicle to bind together the Virtual Salinan Nation through communication and sharing of common belief systems and ideals with each other. That goal will foster the Nation's higher goal of recognition and re-establishment of the tribe as the "caretaker" of its sacred sites and homeland.

LESSONS LEARNED

The authors have developed a list of five distinct Lessons Learned as follows:

- Assumed requirements may not be actual requirements and all requirements must be verified with the user.
- Determining which requirements are actually desirements will avoid problems later because desirements may not get funding in money or hours.
- Failure to clearly describe the benefits of features to obtain buy-in may result in lack of participation
- Time line schedules tend to stretch out when inputs are needed from other individuals not directly involved in the project
- Failure to clearly describe project closure results in a never-ending project.

What may be interesting to the System Engineers reading this paper is that these Lessons Learned appear to be typical and are often seen on other kinds of projects. The authors are left wondering if these lessons are not universal issues for all systems engineering projects.

The authors feel that the communications capability of the Salinan website was improved through the use of the INCOSE requirements process and the later work of the authors. The Salinan tribal leaders appear to agree! Perhaps there were high hopes on the part of the authors of doing more, but the users had their perceived needs, which were respected. Was this the first time that systems engineers were surprised during the requirements process? Certainly not! Will the project lead to more challenging and complex projects in the future? The authors surely hope so and are looking forward to that future!

Figure 1. An oak tree, the symbol of the Salinan Nation

Currently, the lead author is in discussions with parties to take on a new project with similar challenges. This next project would support a native tribe in Alaska, studying the possible development of a computer network that would link all of their members with various services. The authors expect to incorporate the Lessons Learned here to better serve this Native American tribe.

CONCLUSIONS

The INCOSE process, although not developed for this specific purpose, has worked very well in the application of sound Systems Engineering for a significant project in the domain of Public Interest. The SE Handbook provided clear guidance for the steps needed to organize a project of this type and to establish a Web site, as the primary requirement came to be. It was ideally suited to the development of a Web based communication resource for a Virtual Native American Nation. Currently, the authors are using what they have learned in this experience to visualize future projects that will contribute to improved communication for communities of different cultures.

REFERENCES

Bentz, V., and Shapiro, J., *Mindful Inquiry in Social Research*, Sage Publications, 1998.

Brusa, B., *Salinan Indians of California and Their Neighbors*, Naturegraph Publishers, 1992.

Carey, P., *Creating Web Pages with HMTL*, International Thomson Publishing Company, 1999.

Crosby, H., *Antigue California*, University of New Mexico Press, 1994.

Crosby, H., *Last of the Californios*, Copley Press, 1981.

Eargle, D., *The Earth Is Our Mother, A Guide to the Indians of California, Their Locales and Historic Sites*, Trees Company Press, updated March 1996.

Moore, F. *Considerations for Getting Traffic to Your Web Site*, (Online) Available: http://www.topten.org, 1999.

Rechtin, E., *Systems Architecting of Organizations: Why Eagles Can't Swim*, CRC Press, 1999.

Robertson, T., ed., et al, *Systems Engineering Process Activities, A "How To" Guide.* Seattle, Washington: International Council on System Engineering, 1999.

Taylor, D., *Creating Cool HTML Web pages*, IDG Books Worldwide, Inc., 1997.

Web Site Development, (Online) Available: http://www.royal-web.com/develop.htm, 1999.

Willians, J., Clark, J., Clark, C. & Noe, J., *What a Tangled Web: The Legal and Public Relations Dangers of Operating a Web Site. Information Strategy: The Executive's Journal*, Spring 99, Vol. 15, Issue 3, 1999.

BIOGRAPHY

Jan Roberson is a Senior Computer Support, Staff person at Enterprise Information Systems Company, Sunnyvale, CA. She has received a BS in Mathematics and a second BS in Computer Science, both from California State University, Hayward, and a MS in System Management from College of Notre Dame, Belmont, CA. She is presently pursuing a PhD in Human and Organizational Systems from The Fielding Institute. Her work experience has included Systems Engineering and Quality Management at Lockheed Martin Space Systems, Sunnyvale, CA. She is a member of the San Francisco Bay Area Chapter of INCOSE and the Resource Management Working Group.

Jerry Bauknight is a Systems Engineer, Staff, in Engineering Process, Training, Tools, and Assessments, at Lockheed Martin Space Systems, Sunnyvale, CA. He performed in key technical design and systems engineering roles during a career in the U.S. Air Force, including instructor in the Department of Aeronautics, U.S. Air Force Academy. He has worked in launch system integration and systems engineering positions with Martin Marietta Corporation, UltraSystems, and Lockheed Martin Corporation. He has received a BS in Mechanical Engineering from the University of South Carolina, a MS in Aeronautics and Astronautics from Purdue University, and a MS in Counseling and Guidance from Troy State University. He is presently pursuing a PhD in

Human and Organizational Systems from The Fielding Institute. He enjoys active roles in INCOSE, including work in the Systems Engineering Applications Technical Committee and co-chairing the Resource Management Working Group and the Commercial and Public Interest Working Group.

Applying Engineering Principles to Human Components in Complex Systems

Harold Kurstedt
Director of Systems Engineering
Virginia Tech
231 New Engineering Building
Blacksburg, VA 24060

Abstract. Systems engineers must understand the workings within and the relationships among human as well as non-human subsystems in the larger systems they're engineering. To be systems thinkers, we must easily and comfortably integrate human subsystems into complex systems. A key to approaching the human subsystems is to incorporate solution-focused thinking that is based on circular and mutual causality rather than cause and effect. However, systems engineers can quite well apply their engineer's laws of physical science to human subsystems. The fundamental building block for systems that include humans is the dyad (two people). When anxiety rises in a dyad, the two people will attract a third human or non-human subsystem to form a triangle. We can diagram dyads and triangles to better analyze, design, and implement complex systems containing human subsystems.

INTRODUCTON

As systems engineers dealing with complex systems, we tend to focus mostly on physical mechanical, electrical/electronic, materials, or chemical subsystems. We focus less on the conceptual economic, managerial, or aesthetic subsystems. We tend not to give the same level of attention to human subsystems as we do non-human subsystems. And the human subsystems provide the glue to all these other subsystems. (Kurstedt, 2000) For human subsystems, we design using their tangible attributes and functions; we often ignore their intangible attributes and functions.

Humans play three roles in systems: 1) System functioning—humans function as components or subsystems of the systems we're responsible for, 2) System engineering—humans analyze, design, and implement systems, and 3) System use—humans use the systems we're responsible for. I'm focusing on the system functioning role. However, many of the concepts, skills, and techniques I'll present apply to the other roles.

In designing with the human-machine interfaces in our systems, we work to integrate the human subsystems into the system. We perform the integration by finding ways the human can be more machine-like. For example, we train pilots to function similar to the non-human subsystems they interact with. We also work with the non-human subsystems to provide sensory presentations that are more perceptible to the pilots. In short, we tend to dehumanize the human subsystems.

We dehumanize the pilots by focusing on their physical, sensory, and mental functions. We pay much less attention to their emotional and social functions. Humans have attributes of imagination, creativity, motivation, and conscience other subsystems don't have. When we dehumanize the human subsystems, we reduce the full value of these special attributes to the functioning of the larger system.

As engineers, we shy away from understanding the human subsystems in our larger systems. That's because we have little or no education in how humans function together or how humans function in relation to non-human subsystems. My point is an issue of our lack of knowledge and understanding of the internal functioning of the human subsystems. I recognize the engineer's dedication in focusing time and energy when we're confronted with a problematic relationship.

The bottom line to this entire discussion is that a systems thinking systems engineer must 1) consider human subsystems within the larger system, 2) must understand how human subsystems work as subsystems, and 3) must design how human subsystems relate to the other subsystems in the larger system. My emphasis is on identifying the lack of and need for true systems thinking as we do systems engineering.

In this paper, 1) I'll argue for the importance of dealing with human components in systems thinking—an approach we systems engineers need to incorporate into our work, 2) I'll show the use of many engineering principles that work effectively in dealing with human subsystems, 3) I'll illustrate the use of solution-focused thinking in systems engineering, 4) I'll apply the engineer's laws of physical science to human subsystems, and 5) I'll include ways to construct representations of human subsystems interacting with other humans or other non-human subsystems that are useful in analyzing or designing complex systems.

SYSTEMS THINKING VERSUS SYSTEMS ENGINEERING

Good systems *engineers* need to be good systems *thinkers*. In systems *engineering*, we know about and implement systems, the engineering process, and systems modeling. In systems *thinking*, we approach the world differently. In systems *thinking* we see patterns of connection where others see only components, their attributes, and relationships among components or where others see only isolated events. We understand the essence or meaning of the system. We recognize the relationship of each system component to the whole. We learn about a system's functioning by generalizing lessons learned from other systems. We include everything that affects the system's aim, functioning, and result. We understand the context of the system. We know how the system came to be.

In systems thinking, we see the roles, functioning, and interactions of as many of the system components at one time as possible. We need to see all subsystems that are instrumental to the larger system meeting its aim. In short, without understanding the human subsystems of the larger system, we don't know the system. Without knowing human relationships, we can't be systems thinkers.

I used to think that my background in civil, mechanical, and nuclear engineering meant that I was a systems thinker. I saw enough different types of systems and I saw the absolute consistency of mother nature across these types of systems. Then, I focused on organizational systems—largely from a measurement and data perspective, as in total quality management. This additional focus surely would make me a systems thinker. I don't think so now.

I believe that, before we can be systems thinkers, we have to deal with biological, ecological, sociological, or family systems in addition to the engineering systems we're used to. I believe we have to deal with these kinds of systems because we're more apt to confront the roles and characteristics of humans in these systems. We have to deal with humans as subsystems and how the intangible components within the human subsystems relate to components in our other subsystems. We need profound and intimate knowledge of human subsystems, individually and as a type of system component. And, ultimately, humans hold the systems we engineers deal with together.

A systems thinker easily and comfortably integrates human components as subsystems in complex systems. Integrating human subsystems requires understanding how human subsystems work emotionally and socially as well as physically and mentally. The key to effectively integrating humans is in analyzing, designing, and implementing relationships between and among human subsystems. We must engineer relationships between human subsystems as well as between humans and non-human components and subsystems.

HUMAN EMOTIONAL AND SOCIAL RELATIONSHIPS WITH NON-HUMAN SUBSYSTEMS

Humans do have emotional and social relationships with non-human subsystems. We now have these relationships by accident. The question is: Can we design these types of relationships into larger systems so the larger systems will function more effectively? The larger systems will function more effectively because we'll harness more of the human potential energy into the functioning of the system.

But, what about human subsystems having human-like relationships with non-human subsystems? Notice this different focus from human subsystems having non-human-like relationships with non-human subsystems. Probably the best example of a human-like relationship is the relationship we have with our computers. This human-computer relationship can be quite emotional. In fact, a worry in family therapy is the issue of men or women (stereotypically men) having affairs with their computers. Men or women (stereotypically women) also have affairs with their telephones, and men or women have affairs with their automobiles. We use the term "affairs" because these relationships between humans and non-human subsystems are dysfunctional. The relationships are dysfunctional in that they form triangles that are destructive to the functioning of the family system. These affairs beget jealousy, anger, and retaliation. The examples are extensive, including the TV set's role in the relationships between children and their parents.

In the workplace, we find people so attached to their computer or telephone that their relationship behavior detracts from their functioning within the organizational system. In human-machine interfaces in complex systems, we worry about the human's bias toward the mechanical or electrical subsystem the human is most comfortable with and has the most trust in. Notice how we naturally have a more human-like relationship with the computer or phone than we do with a carburetor simply because of the language-oriented connection we have between human subsystems and the computer or phone subsystems. However, try to tell some people they don't have a human-like relationship with their car.

ENGINEERING PRINCIPLES APPLIED TO HUMAN SUBSYSTEMS

We can effectively apply our engineering thinking to human relationships. We can look at the effect of focusing on a person's strengths from the point of view of nuclear physics. And we can look at why people have trouble behaving according to their intent from the point of view of thermodynamics. From these vantage points, we can transfer our understanding of the basic laws of nature to human relationships. In understanding and improving the effects of our actions in human relationships, we have to put Newtonian physics in its place and focus on vision, or aim, rather than cause.

My point is that as engineers, we're equipped to include human subsystems in our systems design, development, implementation, and in our systems problem solving. We must integrate, not separate, the human subsystems and the non-human subsystems in our larger systems. Furthermore, we must integrate, not separate, our competency in human relationships and emotions with our competency in technical relationships and constraints. These ideas are important when considering successful performance of any human-made system that has humans involved in its design, development, or implementation. These ideas are also important when considering the success of the people involved in their roles in a system, at work, and in life. A person-made whole system ultimately depends on humans for its design, construction, and operation.

We can look at systems from two approaches: 1) Blanchard and Fabrycky (Blanchard, 1998) define a system as a physical thing, including the system's components, their attributes, and their relationships; 2) Gerald Weinberg (Weinberg, 1975) defines a system conceptually, as a way of thinking. Considering either approach, a system depends on its human subsystems and especially on the relationships among those human subsystems.

If we're to be systems thinkers and systems doers, our success depends on our understanding of humans and their relationships. From the Blanchard and Fabrycky perspective, we must understand all subsystems of a system and the relationships among the subsystems. As engineers, we're good at the non-human subsystems, fair at integrating the non-human subsystems for system effectiveness, poor at the human subsystems, and terrible at integrating the human subsystems for system effectiveness.

A NON-NEWTONIAN WAY OF LOOKING AT HUMAN SUBSYSTEMS

In dealing with the relationships among human subsystems, the successful approach is to build on solution-focused thinking. A solution focus emphasizes looking forward rather than backward. Regardless of Newtonian Physics and cause-and-effect diagrams in total quality management, as engineers, managers, or leaders of systems, we'll be most effective working solutions toward the aim of the system or of the relationship. With human relationships, searching for the cause usually consumes our energy ineffectively and distracts us from the aim of the system and solutions to get to that aim. A solution-focused leader recognizes and gathers the strengths and resources of others and moves those collective strengths and resources toward a shared vision, or aim.

When looking at the non-human subsystems in systems, we engineers naturally build on our Newtonian physics foundation. For example, we rest on the idea that to deal with the effect, we must first understand the cause. We know that for every action, there's an equal and opposite reaction. Those involved in management and total quality management have learned about cause-and-effect diagrams, or Ishikawa Diagrams (Brocka, 1992). Logically, to solve the problem, we first find the cause. Then we fix the cause and the problem won't happen again. Those experiences have served us well in dealing with materials, equipment, and manufacturing lines. They don't serve us well in dealing with people.

For people, there's still a cause for every effect. However, humans are more complicated than machines. So, tracking down the cause (the blame) for why a person acts, reacts, or interacts the way he or she does usually requires a lot of time and doesn't often yield a helpful answer.

In Newtonian physics, we learn of linear causality; and, in organizational systems, when we practice total quality management (or whatever buzzword you prefer at the moment), we carry our thinking of cause and effect into our work and management processes. Linear causality is useful for describing and acting on a nonliving world of objects and forces. Linear causality isn't useful for describing and acting on systems with living things, because it neglects to account for communication and human relationships in addition to force. (Kurstedt, 2000)

When one or more of the components of the system is human, that component carries a predisposition based on its expectation to reciprocate. That is, at any time, the human component can change its reaction given the same precipitator. In fact, "reciprocity is the governing principle of [human] relationships." (Nichols, 1998)

Reciprocity in humans gives rise to circular and mutual causality. When human subsystems are part of a system, non-human subsystems are often brought into dyadic and triadic relationships with the humans. Circular causality is in a dyadic relationship between two human subsystems. The point is that a human subsystem's action toward or interaction with another subsystem depends on and reciprocates to that other subsystem's action or interaction. For more than two human subsystems, we deal with mutual causality.

The human subsystems respond reciprocally to forces outside themselves, but also initiate forces with imagination, abstract reasoning, creativity, memory, desire, and a wide range of emotion (types and intensities of energy). We can see human subsystems as playing roles dictated by function within the larger system as do non-human subsystems. But, it's the human subsystems that must act to bring about change in the system. Most systems fail to meet their aims because they are unable to adjust to changing circumstances. The human subsystems spell the difference between system success and failure.

Here's another example of applying physical science laws to human relationships within a system. The First Law of Themodynamics has to do with the conservation of energy and The Second Law has to do with entropy. Considering The First Law, synergy isn't getting more out of a group of people than you put in. The whole isn't greater than the sum of its parts. Synergy is converting energy—converting friction among people (energy loss) and physical energy into motivational energy. Considering The Second Law, our desired behavior in interacting with humans both at work and home degrades over time because of entropy. As engineers, we know we counteract entropy by adding energy. We turn around degrading organizational effectiveness at work and deteriorating marriage at home by adding positive energy.

The bottom line is that there are natural laws that govern complex systems. We tend to think the laws govern only the technical components. In reality, they govern the human components too. As engineers, we can extend our understanding in ways and in places we've not dared to go before.

AN EXAMPLE OF SOLUTION-FOCUSED THINKING RELATED TO SYSTEMS ENGINEERING

As engineers, we tend to bypass the critical issue of relationships between two human subsystems, even though significant system failures can usually be traced to difficulties in these relationships. As engineers, I believe we need a solution-focus for starting with the principles we're competent and confident in applying to technical needs and transferring those principles to human relationship needs.

Solution-focused thinking is based on six principles: 1) Because we get what we focus on, we should focus on the positive. 2) Because the other person has the strengths and resources to solve his or her own problem, we should recognize, affirm, and appreciate those strengths. 3) Because there are exceptions to every issue, we should draw on strengths and resources displayed in exceptional moments. 4) Because change is happening all the time, we should recognize that people can change too and we should amplify positive change. 5) Because small changes in the right place make big differences, we should look to accumulate doable-but-surprising positive new behaviors in our human interactions to get large improvements in our relationships. 6) Because to resolve an issue in human relationships we don't have to know the details or the cause, we should focus on our vision and solutions to get us to that vision.

I'll specifically illustrate several of the solution-focus principles in relation to systems engineering. However, I'll address the question of cause and effect in the sixth principle now for those of us who either use cause-and-effect diagrams in our work or have difficulty letting go of using Newtonian physics for every situation. The bottom line is that people are much more complex than machines or work processes. We can understand how Newtonian physics relates to cause-and-effect in machines. We can't always understand why our pet dog will love us when we scold or punish the dog when they happily meet us at the front door and we see the mess they've made in the room behind them. We can't understand the cause for our dog's behavior because dogs are much more complex than machines or work processes. Consider how much more complex humans are than dogs and you understand the dilemma. Humans have imaginations and can envision and have consciences and can feel guilty. Machines and dogs can't do that. The important point is that looking for causes in human interaction ends up being blame; and we're not likely going to blame the right thing.

Newtonian Physics has to do with cause and effect. Finding the cause is relatively straight forward in building bridges and improving work flow in manufacturing plants. A nuclear engineer determines the thermal effect based on the nucleonic cause in the nuclear reactor by trying to solve the Boltzmann equation. We can only solve the Boltzmann equation piecemeal. For four variables for neutrons (space, time, energy, and angle) and their relationships, the nuclear engineer develops dozens of models, each varying one parameter while assuming the others constant. Each of the many models is imperfect, but taken together and using the Gestalt of the human brain we can solve the problem. Now, consider variables for humans and their relationships. Even though we believe cause and effect relationships exist, for the vast majority of situations, we just can't find enough time and resources to make anything approaching a definitive determination of cause (O'Hanlon, 1989). Therefore, we abandon a search for cause and instead focus on, and get, our aim for the human relationships or the human system and spend our time and resources to work solutions toward that aim. I've now illustrated the sixth principle of solution-focused thinking that I defined earlier.

APPLYING THE ENGINEER'S NATURAL LAWS TO HUMAN SUBSYSTEMS

I'll illustrate the first solution-focused principle using an engineering analogy. I'll apply that principle and that analogy to humans in an organizational system.

As a nuclear engineer, I learned that a subatomic particle will be what we perceive, or observe, it to be. The particle is mass when we consider it to be mass and energy when we consider it to be energy. Between the Heisenberg Uncertainty Principle and the Schroedinger Wave Equation, we discover that both the particle changes and our perception of it changes.

Stephen Covey (Covey, 1990) argues that each person has a paradigm, the filter through which he or she sees the world and he or she sees himself or herself within the world. Covey further argues that how we perceive, or observe, a person both changes the person and how we relate to the person. When we consider how a human subsystem works within the subsystem itself, we find we can have significant effects as systems engineers when we analyze, design, and implement larger systems containing humans.

What happens within the human subsystem is that, as humans, we live up to what is expected of us. We live up to what is expected of us by others (the Pygmalion effect) and expected of us by ourselves (the Galatea effect). When we focus on a person's strength, we place expectation for that strength. In simple terms, when we design a system around the strengths of a single person or around human strengths in general, we get the strengths our design expects. When we design a system around weaknesses, we get weaknesses. We'd never admit we design a system around human weaknesses. What do we mean when we say, "I'll design this system to be foolproof."? How do we balance safety and creativity in systems that include human subsystems?

Here's an organizational example of the first principle. Unlike me, my administrative doesn't focus on attention to detail. Her weakness is difficulty with meticulosity. However, as I point out errors in the details, she's agreeable, helpful, and flexible in tending to the errors. Her strength is a positive attitude. When I focused on my administrative assistant's weakness, I got more and more of that weakness; and, when I changed my focus to her strength, I got more and more of her strength. The issue is both my choice of perception and my focus. She changed and my perception of her changed. I got more than her most; I got her best.

Another organizational example of this solution focus principle relates to W. Edwards Deming's eighth point of this fourteen points, "Drive out Fear" from the organization (Deming, 1982). We have trouble responding to how to drive out fear. I attended all three of Deming's different workshops; and, even though frequently questioned on this point, he couldn't operationalize the point sufficiently to satisfy the questioner. The reason is that we can't drive out fear. We can't drive out fear because it violates solution-focused thinking's first principle: You get what you focus on. When you work to drive out fear, you focus on fear, and you get fear.

A basic technique of solution-focused thinking is called the miracle question. The miracle question goes something like this: If you go to sleep tonight and while you're asleep a miracle happens such that fear is gone from your organization, what will you first see or hear in the morning that will tell you the fear is gone? If you answer the miracle question, you say something like, "I'll see optimistic, self-confident people with joy who feel safe in interacting with one another to get the job done." In short, there will be trust in the workplace. So, the answer to the issue of Deming's eighth point is "Drive in Trust."

When you work to drive in trust, you're supporting solution-focused thinking's first principle. When you drive in trust, you focus on trust, and you get trust. I'll bet you can operationalize driving in trust quite handily. For example, I believe we help drive in trust when we act with integrity. We act with integrity when we meet our commitments. I meet my commitments when I say, "I'll have the report on your desk by 5:00 pm Friday, I'll make sure it's there just as I said it would be." By living out the behavior related to meeting my commitments, I focus on trust and help drive in trust. (For whatever it's worth, fear is one of the four fundamental emotions in all cultures in the world: 1) mad, 2) glad, 3) sad, and 4) afraid. Trust is a decision—a choice.)

Let's consider Deming's first point: Constancy of Purpose. (Deming, 1982) Just how powerful is vision? Once you have the vision, the vision is only as powerful as your diligence in focusing on the vision. When in the batter's box, Mark McGuire stares two holes into the ground by focusing on his imagination and envisioning each and every step and nuance of going to the plate, receiving a pitch, and hitting that pitch out of the ball park. He's programming his unconscious brain that will dictate what his conscious brain does half a second before the fact. His vision comes true because he focuses on the vision.

According to Heisenberg and Mark McGuire, we get what we focus on. So, in solution-focused thinking, we focus on the aim of the system and on the solutions to move us toward that aim. We don't focus on cause.

SYSTEMS INCLUDING HUMAN RELATIONSHIPS START WITH DYADS

The fundamental building block of human relationships is the dyad—two people—from either an organizational perspective or a complex defense system perspective. When in tension, human dyads will draw in or attract a third component, or subsystem, and form a triangle—the most robust configuration of components. Teams are complex groupings of dyads and triangles, and so is society. Leadership results from working through effective dyads and triangles.

Leadership results from working through effective dyads. As engineers, we must learn how to build, improve, and repair human relationships in which we are one part of the dyad. Then, we must learn how to build, improve, and repair human relationships between other humans where we aren't part of the dyad. The skills for building and improving human relationships include communication, understanding interpersonal cycles, and recognizing the dynamics of systems of people.

In solution-focused thinking, we can use four techniques for building or improving relationships among the human components, or subsystems, in our larger system: 1) diagramming interpersonal cycles, 2) surfacing and planning the right resources, 3) changing personal paradigms in systemic misunderstanding, and 4) developing information transfer for effective decisions.

In diagramming interpersonal cycles, we recognize the logic and power of the cycle or pattern of interaction between the human subsystems, and we act on our control points in the cycle. We turn our attention toward the aim of the system or the aim of the relationship and away from past performance that got the relationship into the difficult condition it's in. We want to change patterns of attitude and behavior to improve performance of the dyad and of the system. Because the dyad is embedded in the system, a change in behavior of one person in relation to the dyad will affect other people outside the dyad and other relationships in the system. I'll give more detail for this technique shortly.

In surfacing and planning the right resources, we concentrate on the strengths, resources, and experiences of the person who's responsible to make decisions and take action. In dyads, we often impose solutions to system problems based on our own strengths, resources, and lessons learned. Those solutions often fail because the person responsible to resolve the problems has an entirely different set of strengths, resources, and lessons learned. Human resources are different from the non-human resources we're used to. Human resources include strengths such as courage, patience, and inner security. These human resources can make or break our system. Through information transfer, we can identify the strengths that fit the solution to the problem and the person implementing the solution.

In changing personal paradigms, we realize exceptions that change our frame of reference. We each see reality through a filter Thomas Kuhn (Kuhn, 1962) calls our paradigm. Kuhn studied scientists observing experimental data. This filter makes certain data invisible to our observation powers. Recognizing the effect of our own filter on data collection helps us value the differences in observation among different people experiencing the same action.

An issue related to Kuhn's research is that we can portray information in ways we believe will help a human subsystem. However, the human may not perceive the information in helpful ways, and not in the ways we intended. Let's return to our example of the pilot. Two pilots with different paradigms will perceive the same information differently. We train the pilots because we want to get consistent and expected paradigms leading to consistent and expected information transfer. The trouble is that training doesn't make a new paradigm. Training adds to the two different existing paradigms in the two pilots. So, by definition, two pilots after training will have different paradigms with similar tendencies based on their similar training. Their paradigms dictate what information they receive, how they receive the information, and what information is invisible to them.

In developing information transfer, we focus on bridging the information portrayal/information perception interface. Portrayal and perception are as two projections on a common screen. When the projections match, information transfer is effective and efficient. When the projections don't match, information transfer can be impossible or difficult.

These four techniques, only when applied with a caring and positive attitude, can significantly change dyadic relationships and improve the system performance in terms of its human subsystems. As systems engineers, if we're working on systems in the true sense of the word, we must accept the challenge of building and improving effective relationships among the human subsystems of the system.

WE CAN USE DIAGRAMS OF OUR RELATIONSHIPS TO IMPROVE SYSTEMS.

I'm expanding on the technique for diagramming interpersonal cycles because I believe engineers like the usefulness of pictorial representations inherent in diagramming techniques. First, select a dyad—two people. Then, identify a pattern of behavior, or interpersonal cycle, between the two people that is negatively affecting the relationship. This negative pattern is a vicious cycle. Write down the aim, or vision, for how we want the relationship to work if a miracle happened and the vicious cycle went away. We've completed our identification of the two people in the cycle, what the cycle is about, and our goal for the relationship. For simplicity, we've pulled the dyad out from the complex system. It's like a model based on varying one variable in an equation while holding the others constant.

We'll now draw a diagram. See the example in Figure 1. Draw the symbol of one person on the left of the page and the other person on the right, showing an arc from each person to the other. Write the names of the each of the two people in the appropriate symbol. Between the two arcs, we write the issue of the vicious cycle. Above the top arc, which is directed to the right, we write from left to right across the page the thoughts, the resulting feelings, and the resulting actions of the person on the left side of the page relating to the issue of the vicious cycle. Below the bottom arc, which is directed to the left, we write from right to left across the page the thoughts, feelings, and actions of the person on the right side of the page. The diagram is complete.

Figure 1 shows the flow of sensory data through the person's paradigm, or filter. The comparison of the sensory data to the paradigm generates the thoughts and feelings that lead to actions affecting the other person. Notice 1) the steps of the cycle are logical, implying the cycle controls the people involved; 2) the thoughts, feelings, and actions of each person make sense to that person but carry the person away from his or her vision for the relationship; 3) each person has no control over the thoughts, feelings, and actions of the other person, even though that's where each person has been focusing his or her energy for changing the cycle; and 4) each person only has control over his or her own thoughts, feelings, and actions.

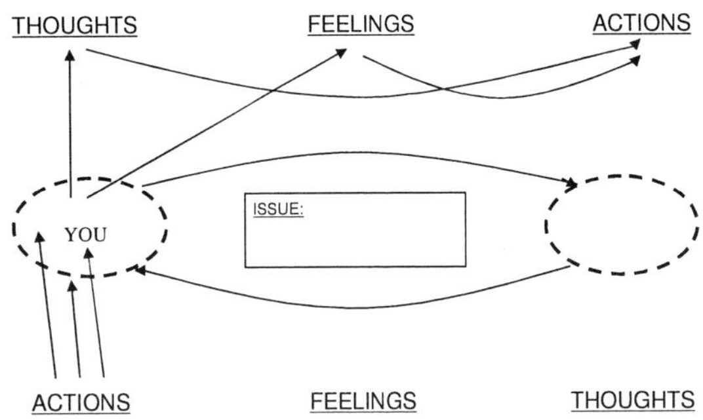

Figure 1. You Can Improve an Interpersonal Cycle.

Obviously, the only way to have control or influence on the cycle is to change our own thoughts, feelings, or actions. The dyad is a system within a larger system of people. Your change will change the state of the system; and the other human components of the system must change to find equilibrium. That's the only way you can purposefully move toward your aim for the system.

TRIANGLES

Since we have a clear understanding or systems, we realize that the dyad doesn't exist in a vacuum. The next, more complex configuration is the triangle. As we know, triangles are the strongest, most robust configuration. We started with dyads because dyads are much simpler.

Here's an example of a triangle involving two human components and one technical component. Consider the two human components to be me and my boss. The relationship between me and my boss is a dyad. We have characteristics of that relationship—some of which are issue dependent. Let's say my boss and I have an issue around switching to a new computer system. The new computer system is the technical component. My boss and I disagree about the old computer system. I like the system; he doesn't. I've tried to convince my boss for a long time that the system is what we need and I try to help him like the system more. I'm trying to control his relationship with the computer system. But, he's the boss. So, we get the new computer system that I don't like.

My boss wants and likes the new system. So, we consider that relationship to be a good one. I don't like the new system. I much prefer the old system and I'm not switching my allegiance as fast as my boss wants. We consider my relationship with the computer system to be a bad one. What happens is that my boss tries to convince me to get into the new system and I try to poison my boss toward that system. My boss thinks I'm stonewalling and I think my boss is wrong and unreasonable. The relationship between me and my boss is deteriorating.

How do I deal with the triangle. The bottom line is: 1) Don't try to fix the boss's relationship with the computer system, 2) Work on my relationship with the boss, 3) Concentrate on my vision for my relationship with my boss, and 4) Determine whether what I'm saying, doing, or deciding moving me closer to or farther from my vision.

CONCLUSION

The point is that human subsystems in some ways are similar to the non-human subsystems they interact with; and we design for those similarities. Human subsystems are in many ways quite different from non-human subsystems; and systems engineers have understandings of natural laws that can help design for those differences also. To design for the differences, we must be systems thinkers and design complex systems that incorporate the laws of social science. However, some of our understandings of natural laws typically involving physical science need expansion to include social science laws. The social science laws govern the emotions, thoughts, and behaviors of the human subsystems. This paper points out some of these natural laws.

REFERENCES

Blanchard, Benjamin S. and Wolter J. Fabrycky, *Systems Engineering and Analysis*. Third Edition, Prentice Hall, NJ, 1998, p. 2.

Brocka, Bruce and M. Suzanne Brocka, *Quality Management*, Richard D. Irwin, Inc, IL, 1992, p. 77.

Covey, Stephen R. (1990), *Principle-Centered Leadership*, NY, Simon & Schuster, p. 58.

Deming, W. Edwards (1982), *Out of Crisis*, MA, MIT Press, p. 59.

Goleman, Daniel, *Working with Emotional Intelligence*, Bantam Books, NY, 1998.

Kuhn, Thomas S. (1962), *The Structure of Scientific Revolutions*, Chicago, the University of Chicago Press.

Kurstedt, Harold A. (2000), *Are You Forgetting the Glue in Your Systems? (Without Effective Relationships among Your Human Components, Your System is Impotent.)*, Proceedings of INCOSE MARC 2000, 2000, pp. 13.3-1 – 13.3-7.

Nichols, Michael P. and Richard C. Schwartz, *Family Therapy: Concepts and Methods*. Allyn and Bacon, Boston, 1998, p. 11.

O'Hanlon, William Hudson and Michele Weiner-Davis, *In Search of Solutions: A New Direction in Psychotherapy*, W.W. Norton and Company, Inc., NY, 1989, pp. 40-41.

Weinberg, Gerald M., *An Introduction to General Systems Thinking*. John Wiley & Sons, Inc., NY, 1975, p. 52.

BIOGRAPHY

Harold Kurstedt is the Hal G. Prillaman Professor of Industrial and Systems Engineering and is director of Virginia Tech's systems engineering program. He developed Virginia Tech's management systems engineering program. Harold has been searching for the secrets of good management for 30 years. Good systems engineering requires understanding all system components and mostly understanding, designing, and implementing good relationships among the components, including the human components. Harold recognizes that successful engineers and organizations must improve their relationship competence to the level of their technical competence and must do more coaching than problem solving or the human components in our systems will under-perform.

Military and civil logistic support of humanitarian relief operations

M. W. Ludema
Delft University of Technology
Jaffalaan 5
2600 GA Delft
The Netherlands

H.B. Roos
Erasmus University Rotterdam
Burg. Oudlaan
3000 DR Rotterdam
The Netherlands

Abstract. As a result of a higher frequency of crisis situations, and due to the fact that societies become more and more vulnerable, the expenditures for humanitarian relief operations are growing. The currently available knowledge concerning humanitarian relief operations and relief logistics can be used more effective. Much knowledge is available in the humanitarian relief society and in military organizations involved in relief operations in crisis situations. The current base of knowledge is not interrelated or evaluated enough in respect to relief system effectiveness. If knowledge concerning humanitarian relief operations would be reengineered following a systems engineering, system logistics, and a more coordinative approach, humanitarian relief operations might be more effective for the same or even less money. One solutions that could benefit from integrated civil and military relief logistics knowledge and coordination of civil and military relief operations is the establishment of several relief-hubs for one the Netherlands might prove a good location.

THE GROWING NEED FOR RELIEF LOGISTICS

The growing need for humanitarian relief can for instance be derived from the following three parameters:

- The total tonnage of emergency food shipped by the World Food Programme (WFP) has grown from 250,000 tons in the mid seventies, to 600.000 tons in the mid eighties, 1.4 million tons in 1991, to 2.2 million tons in 1992. The expenditures were $ 1.2 billion in 1995.

- The expenditures of UNICEF (United Nations Children's Fund) for humanitarian relief have increased by a factor seven in the years 1982 to 1992 from $ 35 million to $ 240 million. This has grown to the number of $ 300 million in 1995.

- The expenditures of the UNHCR (United Nations High Commissioner for Refugees) for humanitarian relief have seen an eighty fold increase from $ 12 million in the beginning of the seventies, to $ 360 million in the beginning of the eighties first, to $ 880 million in 1991, and more than $ 1 billion à year in the period 1992 to 1995.

One of the reasons of this immense growth is the increase of the number of conflicts situations and natural disasters. Another cause is the fact that political climate in the world has changed significantly and made more civil and military humanitarian relief operations possible. A major third cause of the growing need for humanitarian relief is (and possibly will continue to be) natural causes, as a result of the greenhouse effect, the erosion and diminishing fertility of land, as a consequence of deforestation and predatory cultivation of land, which may lead to flooding and local climate changes, and subsequently to growing streams of environmental refugees. Another major cause is the declining supply of clean drinking water. If this shortage is accompanied by a malfunctioning infrastructure for drinking water and drains, the number of victims of diseases will definitely grow, as will the number of diseased itself. The ever growing world populations leads to a larger vulnerability of human societies in the near future.

Statement 1: Decreasing the vulnerability of human societies is more effective than increasing the expenditures for humanitarian relief operations. This through life management approach needs a completely different mindset than is currently used. More effort should be placed on studying the system dynamics of relief operations for vulnerable human societies to prevent growing expenditures on humanitarian relief operations in the future.

A TYPOLOGY OF RELIEF OPERATIONS

Humanitarian relief more and more includes all types of

humanitarian relief operations, varying form elementary humanitarian relief operations to rehabilitation relief operations, both during and after peace operations where military organizations are involved. Joint military and civil operations are more preferred than solemn civil operations. It is applied that warfare related conflict situations require a different type of organization of relief logistics than is required for natural disasters.

One can distinguish between four different types of humanitarian relief operations: emergency relief, rehabilitation relief, development relief, and elementary relief, see for example "(Roos et al. 1994)", "(Dutch Ministry of Foreign Affairs 1993)", and figure 1.

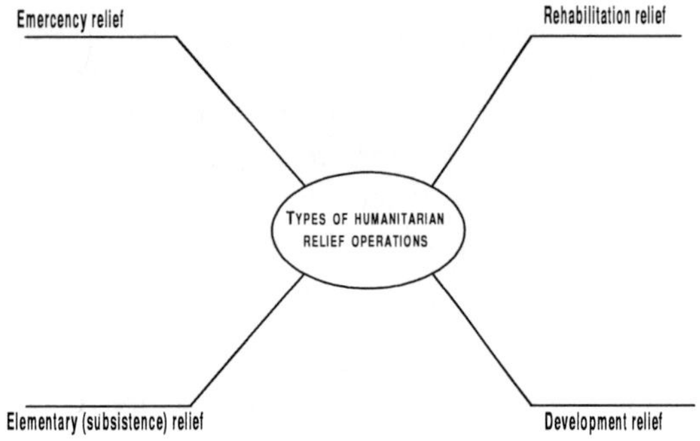

Figure 1: Four types of relief operations

1 emergency relief operations:

These are the kind of relief operations that are characterized by a short response time, and a low frequency of occurrence. During emergency relief operations the effects of disasters such as floods, droughts, emergency feeding program, transportation calamities, etc. are opposed within the shortest possible time frame.

2 rehabilitation relief operations:

These are the kind of relief operations that are aiming at the restoration of everyday life after a natural or man-made disaster. Rehabilitation relief operations may consist of e.g. renovations of infrastructure, and basic teaching activities. Characteristic for rehabilitation relief is the long response time, that it is non-incidental, so has a more structural basis. In many initiatives a rehabilitation relief operation is preceded by an emergency relief operation.

3 development relief operations:

Like rehabilitation relief operations, development relief operations are characterized by a long response time, a lengthy operation, and a structural basis. Development relief operations are aimed at the improvement of human systems (societies) without necessarily restoring the previous situation. This is often achieved by installing several facilities not available in the past.

4 elementary (subsistence) relief operations:

Elementary relief operations are concerned with the supply of basic goods such as food, and other subsistence goods such as tents, shelters and housing facilities. Characteristic of elementary relief operations are a long response time, and a lengthy operation to withstand the effects of a disaster. Elementary relief operations are often complimentary to rehabilitation relief operations, by filling in the remaining gaps.

Statement 2: More structural rehabilitation relief operations lead to less vulnerable societies and as a consequence this will lead to a diminishing need for emergency and elementary relief operations. In the short term and medium term this will likely not be enough to decrease the growing need for emergency and elementary relief operations. One should not forget that a natural disaster itself is not the factor that may lead to escalation of the disaster into a even more serious disaster situation, but the fact that a society is vulnerable and unable to cope with the natural disaster. Emphasis therefor should be placed on the smooth transition from one type of relief operation to another. This leads to a reengineering approach for every new situation. The humanitarian relief society could benefit largely form the basic procedures such as that found within the field of systems engineering.

THE PRESENT ORGANISATION OF RELIEF LOGISTICS

It is interesting to take a closer look at the organizations and institutes involved in humanitarian relief operations and its logistics support. They include: financiers, initiators, and executive organizations e.g. manufacturers, logistics service providers and, several in the disaster area operational civil and military organizations. One should make a distinction here between the organizations that have and that do not have a military component in natural disasters and conflict situations.

In conflict situations, the agencies of the United Nations and the non-governmental organizations (NGO's) such as the Red Cross and Médecins sans frontières play an important role. These NGO's initiate and organize the humanitarian relief operations in areas with a limited and for these organizations acceptable chance of violence. This type of relief operation can be either an emergency operation or a rehabilitation operation.

The actual humanitarian relief operations in conflict situations are really not that different from those in situations caused by natural disasters. Relief material is only slightly adapted to the war situations. Though the goals of a humanitarian relief operation may not affect the neutrality principle of the NGO's, this directive can not always be followed in detail when air transport is the only type of transport available. The closure of the air space for civil airplanes will make military air transport the only type of transport available. In this case, the role of the logistics service provider is often represented by military organizations. For several logistics services private companies are approached, especially when air transport of civil and military personnel is concerned.

The need for humanitarian relief is always first investigated by the departments of several NGO's, that are specialized in humanitarian relief. These departments analyze the alternatives for the supply of the necessary goods. Médecins sans frontières has several specialized toolkits (relief boxes) that proved useful in specific relief situations, see for example "(Andriesse 1993)". The contents of these toolkits can be acquired from all over the world and obtained with the use of military or civil means of transportation. In the case of a combined military and civil humanitarian relief operation the final leg of transport often is under military escort.

The end of the Cold-War has increased the possibility of organizations such as the United Nations to provide relief on a broader basis. The United Nations, and other organization such as WEU, NATO, CVSE, and EU eventually may play a growing role in the international security politics. Due to several economic and political transformation processes securities are difficult to achieve and due to the high risk for more ethnical conflicts the need for relief is growing. Ethnical mostly violence-related conflicts often take place in urban areas, rather than on the battlefield. As a consequence a lot of civilians are involved in these conflict situations.

An increase in the number of violence-related conflicts results in more military involvement. Humanitarian relief organization have to address the question whether military input, such as military protection, in their operations, may jeopardizes the desired independence of their organization.

Phasing of UN-relief operations. On the basis of the earlier-mentioned phasing, the possible involvement of civil and military organizations in humanitarian relief operations for natural disasters and conflict situations can be indicated and partly planned in advance. In the event of natural disasters the logistics support of humanitarian relief operations is controlled and executed by civil organizations. Sometimes food distributions from the air are performed by military airplanes as a supplement of a humanitarian relief operation. Clearly humanitarian operations are often of combined military and civilian nature.

The United Nations use a lot of military equipment for the logistics support of their humanitarian relief operations. The own UN-military forces (blue helmets) are employed by the United Nations. The dynamic phasing of the logistics support in UN-relief operations is recorded in the so called "Agenda for peace" of the Secretary General of the United Nations. In the peace-enforcing phase, control and execution is performed by the military. When the chance of violence is diminished a transition takes place from the peace-enforcing phase to peace-keeping phase. In the peace-keeping phase the executing of humanitarian relief is more and more hand over to civil organizations like the UN-organizations and the NGO's. In the peace-building phase the violence threat has completely disappeared or is insignificant. In this last phase all military equipment is withdrawn and the actual relief logistics is completely executed by civil organizations.

Transportation. On average 8% of the total costs of an humanitarian relief operation is caused by the logistics support of this operation. In 1992 the total expenditures for logistics support for humanitarian relief operations paid by the Netherlands where as large as $320 million.

A useful definition of relief logistics is: Relief logistics is the total logistics support required for humanitarian relief operations performed by dedicated military and civil organizations. Air transport is often vital for a successful organization of the relief logistics of a humanitarian relief operations; although the real contribution of air transport can vary considerable. When speed is required and alternative modes of transport are not available, air transport is the only option. This is especially true for most emergency relief operations. In the case of normal air transport services use can be made of airline companies that already have regular scheduled flights into or nearby the disaster areas. Otherwise charters are a good alternative. Large parts of the transportation activities are outsourced to large specialized logistic service providers, see for example: "(Javad et.al 1991)" and "(Roos 1994)".

One can differentiate between transport to the disaster area, and transport within the disaster area. Both segments have well-defined demands. Transport from Europe and the United States of America towards a disaster area in Africa, the Middle-East, or Asia is carried out by means of air or sea transport, depending on the emergency. Often large commercial charters or scheduled flight airlines are used, with special rates. The whole circus looks very much like a military operation, such as the operation Desert Shield in the early days of what would become the Gulf War "(Pagonis, et.al 1992)".

Transport within the disaster area is generally controlled by the humanitarian relief organization itself by means of road transport, and (often rented) air transport. Supplies are transported from an airport or a seaport to the disaster area. Because of a lack of basic facilities and reliable means of transportation, this transportation within the disaster area is often the bottleneck in the logistics support of humanitarian relief operations.

Statement 3: Relief logistics can benefit from a better coordination in the supply chain from the suppliers all over the world to the disaster of crisis areas. Because air transport is very expensive it should be minimized as much as possible. If air transport is involved airplanes should have the possibility to land as close as possible in the area of the disaster or crisis area. If frequent flight are expected a temporary airport or airstrip might be an alternative. Several military organizations have experience with these kind of emergency airports. Involvement of military organizations can guard the supplies from theft and robbery. Humanitarian relief operations and the necessary logistics can benefit from planning these operations upfront and coordination during the relief operations itself, as a joint civil and military effort.

RELIEF OPERATIONS EFFECTIVENESS

There is a relation between the sequence of the type of humanitarian relief operations needed in time, the effectiveness-efficiency ratio, and the associated costs. The same relation is found within the logistics support necessary for the other types of humanitarian relief operations. When humanitarian relief logistics is needed immediately, high demands are made on the effectiveness of these operations. In this phase the effectiveness of an emergency humanitarian relief operations is subordinate to the expected expenses. The actual costs of these operations are often very high. The use of foreign military resources in relief operations, especially military flight operations can be very costly. A striking quotation is *"It has been calculated that each flight costs as much as purchasing one food truck plus fuel to run for six months."* Emergency relief operations are often provided by means of air transport because speed is of vital importance and the disaster areas often are badly accessible by land.

When humanitarian relief has less an emergency character and is not immediately necessary, there is much more emphasis on the efficiency of the logistics support of the humanitarian relief operations. The duration of these humanitarian relief operations such as these is quite long. Although the humanitarian support could be of incidental nature, cost control stays always of great importance.

After a while there can be a transition from the provision of international relief supplies to the provision of regional and local relief supplies. Air transport is only deployed when the accessibility is low in a certain disaster area because of a defectively infrastructure. In the end the humanitarian relief operations will be more of the rehabilitation type. The ratio between effectiveness and efficiency of humanitarian relief operations and its logistics is of extreme importance. The way it changes over time related to the costs is shown in figure 2.

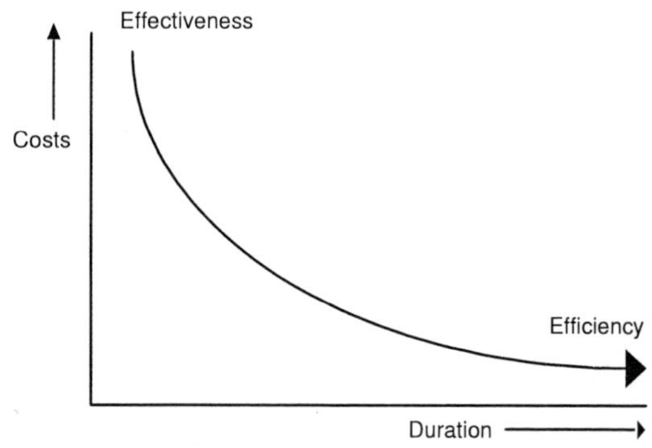

Figure 2. The dynamics of humanitarian relief operations and logistics

Local businesses should be involved as much as possible for the supply of goods and services. If these local businesses are not involved, they may go out of business as a consequence of the humanitarian relief operations, and this will destabilize the local society ones more, so more and frequent relief will be necessary in the future. For examples "(Roos 1992)" argues, that it is better to pay and use local transportation companies and provide wheat instead of bread to keep the bakeries and their distribution network intact. International and regional (air) transport should be limited to incidental flights for water and food supplies. This sound obvious, because higher layers can only established when lower structures are in place. First the roads than the trucks, and first the wheat than the bread, and first the essentials than the niceties and other complex systems. Hutchinson makes this clear in "(Hutchinson 1987)" with a pyramid view point of logistics, see also figure 3, indication the following three layers of logistics:

1 Subsistence Logistics: Subsistence logistics provides the necessities of live. This type of logistics consists out of the gathering of basis materials such as food, clothing, and shelter to support the continuation of live. Subsistence logistics can and does exist as an independent activity.

2 Operational Logistics: Operational logistics can only exist on the foundation the layer of subsistence logistics. It is concerned with providing us with the niceties of live by movement of materials into, through, and out of the firm. Basic involvement of society in need for operational logistics is the ownership transfer of products.

3 *System Logistics:* System logistics can only exist on a foundation of subsistence and operational logistics. The life cycle of products and structures, repair, management and the necessary training and tools necessary to do so belong to this type of logistics. Support subsequent to ownership transfer becomes crucial.

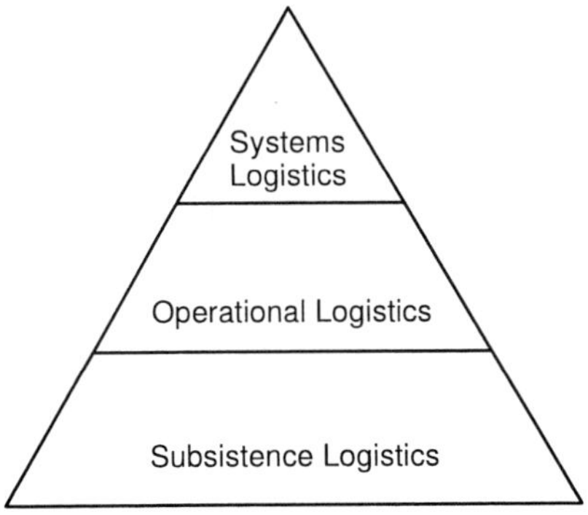

Figure 3: Logistics as a Pyramid of Subsets, from "(Hutchinson 1987)"

Hutchinson states that this pyramid view point of logistics shows that each sub-set or type of logistics is supported by the lower-level logistic subsets. It is this viewpoint the humanitarian relief society should adopt within their policies, planning and operations. It is more or less the same view point authors like Blanchard "(Blanchard 1992)" take when they discuss the integrated logistic support of durable systems

Statement 4: The effectiveness of humanitarian relief operations and relief logistics can be improved if the different layers of logistics, the time-phasing and the transition between the different types of relief operations would be pre-formatted from a systems engineering and systems logistics point of view. Such point of view should be developed bringing in the combined knowledge and by the joint effort of civil and military organizations. It would be beneficial if a set of procedures for the planning of operations and the management of these operations would be established out of such an effort.

CURRENT MALFUNCTIONS OF HUMANITARIAN RELIEF OPERATIONS

In two reports of the Dutch Ministry of Foreign Affairs "(Dutch Ministry of Foreign Affairs 1992)" questions have been raised concerning the effectiveness and efficiency of humanitarian relief operations in general. Some of the identified problems were:

1 The coordination of humanitarian relief operations and logistics support both show large deficiencies. There is no central and collective date-base of the total available (international) physical relief logistics capacity. An effective planning in the preliminary phase of a humanitarian relief operation is, due to this incompleteness of data, not possible. Another problem is the inadequate cooperation between NGO's in order to achieve economies of scale, for example in purchasing goods, as a result these economies are not always exploited. Priorities given to aspects such as: being first on site, or the first in front of the camera, and paying a lot of attention to the financiers, are seldom of interest of the humanitarian relief operation itself.

2 The overall organization involved in humanitarian aid is extensive. Only 50% of all funding of the United Nations is directly available for the actual operation. This percentage is much higher when NGO's are concerned. For example Médécins sans frontières, one of the best for money performers have spends 15% of the total costs of humanitarian relief operations on support tasks and fund raising; 85% is spend on the actually humanitarian relief operation.

3 In conflict situations a large proportion of the total international available relief capacity is not ready for action. Several NGO's only want to operate if the local authorities approve the humanitarian relief operation or a UN-mandate is available, or their neutrality is not at stake, and the situation is not to dangerous for the personnel or the volunteers that are employed by these organizations. The number of conflict situations compared to natural disasters, and the scarcity of the available capacity makes several humanitarian relief operations unfeasible, or to some degree ineffective.

4 A supply chain breaks always at its weakest link. The transport of relief goods to the actually disaster area is often the weakest link, due to banditry and sometimes unreliable local transport organizations.

Statement 5: Coordination between humanitarian relief organizations can be improved considerable. Collaborative engineering of humanitarian relief operations might prove worth a try, and might also keep the costs of overhead within limits.

TOWARDS A MORE EFFICIENT DEFENCE-CIVIL COOPERATION OF RELIEF LOGISTICS

For the coordination of logistics support of humanitarian relief operations the United Nations has establish the United Nations Office for Coordination of Humanitarian Affairs (OCHA) formerly know as the Department of Humanitarian Affairs (DHA). The OCHA did publish a handbook that consolidates a part of the available knowledge. This handbook though is not a tool for the implementation of the necessary coordination between humanitarian relief organizations, see for example: "(http://www.reliefweb.int)".

The European Union has established the European Community Humanitarian Office (ECHO) in 1992. To enforce the Dutch humanitarian relief work the Disaster Relief Agency (DRA), an initiative of Hivos, Novib, and SNV was been established. This agency concentrates its attention on mediation, planning, advising and execution of humanitarian relief organization that lack these relief capabilities.

Most initiatives are directed towards the improvement of emergency relief operations by means of general coordination of activities. A problem with these coordinating organizations is emphasis on the actual execution of the relief operations instead of the coordination itself. This may in time create an unwanted extra administrative layer. Another problem is the lack of specific knowledge needed to add the intended contribution to humanitarian relief operations and their logistics support.

In the field of logistics support of humanitarian relief operations there is room for several initiatives where specific organizational and knowledge concerning coordination of aligned processes between organizations is integrated in the planning and management of logistics supply chains. By way of combining knowledge and organizational efforts on the subject of logistics support, economies of scale can be accomplished, and the individual character of the humanitarian relief operations can be maintained. Suchlike facilitating organizations can increase their efficiency of humanitarian relieve operations without decreasing the effectiveness. One of the key projects of the OCHA that focuses on an increased effectiveness of humanitarian relief operations is the ReliefWeb, see for example: "(http://www.reliefweb.int)", a premier online source of information that ensures a comprehensive base of information to subscribers and others.

Notes on the Dutch situation. The Dutch defense organization pays attention to the (logistics) support of humanitarian relief, such as military protection of humanitarian transports by assignment of the United Nations. Besides this logistics support the military have defined there own tasks, including the formation of deployable units and the procurement of means of amphibical sea transport and the increase of the air transport capacity. The Dutch defence organization is mainly concentrating on the operational tasks.

The Dutch defence organization is often involved in humanitarian relief operations needed as a result of natural disasters. In the past this contribution to humanitarian relief was not on a structural basis. Nowadays the Dutch defence organization concentrates more on humanitarian relief with military protection. Readiness during humanitarian relief operations with a military component are currently of the main interest of the Dutch defence organization.

Military involvement in relief logistics. Humanitarian relief operations in crisis areas are strongly related and not easily separated from humanitarian relief operations in disaster areas. An other basis for an extra emphasis towards contribution in humanitarian relief operations is the training of military personnel with material in real situations. Finally, the work of defense forces in relief operations is contributing towards the image of the army in general. When subsistence facilities are not available, such as local and regional transport in certain areas, a defense organization can provide these facilities relatively easy. Conceivably the following organization for the transport component of relief logistics can be represented:

- long distance or global transport;
- regional transport;
- local transport.

Global transport of supplies is often large scale by nature, and can easily be performed by (sea) liners, scheduled (air) services or military transport. Regional distribution of supplies on medium-range distances can be performed by military or civil means of transport dependent of the size of possible threat. Local distribution or supplies can be done by military transport, e.g. trucks or helicopters. This cooperation's can have advantages on the civil side as well on the military side of a humanitarian relief operation during these humanitarian relief operations in crisis situations.

Though the military contribution in relief operations can have a negative influence on the aimed neutrality of NGO's. In particular in cross-border-operations where a differentiation between war-victims is contradicting to the neutral intends of NGO's. In such cases the military can be quite clear about their purpose to persuade the refugees to go home to there own country, though the aid agencies are usually more concerned with the issue of meeting the basic needs and ascertaining whether or that the refugees want to go back to there country in the actual situation. When such a situation is leading to a conflict the intended cooperation's could be endangered. A second restraint are costs. Usually, military operations are more costly than civil operations. These cost are charged to the civil organizations or to the donor countries. A good starting-point is to first give priority to civil organizations if possible, and to include military organizations only when the civil organizations do not suffice. The Dutch government prefers not to let military and civil organizations compete for humanitarian relief activities. Military involvement is always connected with a mandate of the Minister of Defense that is tested against the intended tasks of the defense organization itself. Furthermore, the relief receiving country must agree on the intervention of militaries in the crisis situation. These conditions can all limited a prosperous civil-military cooperation.

The OCHA performed a study on the world wide availability of relief supplies. This study identified, that the Netherlands are a good candidate for one of five world wide Air Rescue Supply Depots. These locations will turn into humanitarian transport hubs, where a broad assortment of available means of transportation for the transport towards disaster areas can be held in storage and ready for action. These hubs may also be the preferable location for the emergency supplies for humanitarian relief operations. Besides excellent facilities, these hubs should be equipped with and provide for the capacity and knowledge for the organization and coordination of the requested logistics support.

Statement 6: The OCHA is probably the right institution for an establishing the necessary coordination between the humanitarian relief organizations. For the involvement of the military component a joint platform needs to be formed where for instance NATO and OCHA can coordinate their activities and learn from each other. From a research point of view it is recommended to engineer a knowledge framework containing set of procedures worthwhile to follow and the appropriate access to all civil and military existing data on previous humanitarian relief operations.

CONCLUSIONS

General. In the situations where military personnel is deployed for logistics support during humanitarian relief operations it may be advised to let civil organizations cooperate with the military at the same time or at an other time during the operation. Deployment at the same moment can be the case if the military can not bear the full responsibility for there duties in relation to the crisis situation for organizations, for example in cross-border situations. In the case of parallel deployment the emphasis is on the cooperation of joint actions in the disaster area and the necessary logistics support. Sequential deployment will take place during peace-operations if a peace-enforcing phase transits towards a peace-keeping phase. In this case the emphasis is on an easy transition from military to civil support where such a civil deployment is possible and desirable. An other form of cooperation can be in the world wide organization and coordination's of supplies of goods readily available for humanitarian relief operations.

Concluding remarks from the statements:

- Decreasing the vulnerability of human societies is more effective than increasing the expenditures for humanitarian relief operations.
- More structural rehabilitation relief operations lead to less vulnerable societies and as a consequence this will lead to a diminishing need for emergency and elementary relief operations
- Emphasis should be placed on the smooth transition by constant reengineering the relief operation system from one type of relief operation to another.
- The humanitarian relief society could benefit largely form the basic procedures such as that found within the field of systems engineering.
- Relief logistics can benefit form a better coordination in the supply chain from the suppliers all over the world to the disaster of crisis areas.
- Humanitarian relief operations and the necessary logistics, such as the establishment of emergency airports can benefit from planning these operations up-front and coordination during the relief operations itself, as a joint civil and military effort.
- The effectiveness of humanitarian relief operations and relief logistics can be improved if the different layers of logistics, the time-phasing and the transition between the different types of relief operations would be pre-formatted from a systems engineering and systems logistics point of view.
- Coordination between humanitarian relief organizations can be improved considerable. Collaborative engineering of humanitarian relief operations might prove worth a try, and might also keep the costs of overhead within limits.
- For the involvement of the military component a joint platform needs to be formed where for instance NATO and OCHA can coordinate their activities and learn from each other.
- From a research point of view it is recommended to engineer a knowledge framework containing set of procedures worthwhile to follow and the appropriate access to all civil and military existing data on previous humanitarian relief operations.

Some recommendation. The suggestions of establishing several 24-our humanitarian relief hubs (one in the Netherlands), that can grow into specialized logistics support center where all necessary facilities are available or can be obtained just in time is worthwhile to investigate. Specialized logistics service providers, humanitarian aid organizations and military support units can facilitate the effectiveness and efficiency of emergency humanitarian relief operations. Such a relief hub should also be the place to integrate and consolidate all available knowledge on humanitarian relief operations to provide the proper coordination with the humanitarian relief society.

REFERENCES

Andriesse, F,G., "Artsen zonder grenzen: Logistiek zonder grenzen, Tijdschrift voor Inkoop en Logistiek, jrg.9, 1993/3,p.8-12 (in Dutch).

Blanchard, B.S., "Logistics Engineering and Management", 4th edition, Prentice-Hall, New Jersey, 1992.

Dutch Ministry of Forein Affairs, "Humanitaire hulp tussen conflict en ontwikkeling", Ministerie van Buitenlandse Zaken, november 1993 (in Dutch).

Hutchinson, N.E., "An integrated approach to logistics management", Prentice-Hall, New Jersey, 1987.

Javad, S., and D. Weeks, "International contract logistics case study", Annual Conference Proceedings, Vol.II, Council of Logistics Management, 1991, p.123-133.

Pagonis, W.G., and J.L. Cruikshank, "Moving Mountains, Lessons in Leadership and Logistics from the Gulf War", Harvard Business School Press, Boston, Massachusetts, 1992.

ReliefWeb: Mandate and Objectives, http://www,reliefweb.int/mandate.html.

Roos, H.B., "Onbeschrijfbare Logistiek?", rede, Koninklijke Militaire Academie, Breda, 1992. (in Dutch)

Roos, H.B., D.H. van der Laan & E. Altena, "'Relief Logistics', Mogelijkheden voor een effectievere organisatie", Universiteit van Amsterdam, 1994. (in Dutch).

BIOGRAPHY

Marcel W. Ludema (1963) studied architecture at the Delft University of Technology. In 1989 he graduated on the development of an expert and decision support system for housing and facility management decisions for the Dutch Government. After his military service he joined the TNO Laboratory of Electronics and Physics and developed a life cycle management procurement procedure for the Dutch Ministry of Defense. Form 1993 to 1997 he joined the Faculty of Economics of the Erasmus University of Rotterdam and gave lectures on logistics management. He participated in several commercial research projects of a broad variety of logistics subjects. In preparation of his Doctoral thesis he wrote several research papers At the moment he hold an educational position at the Faculty of System Engineering & Policy Analysis of the Delft University of Technology, and is performing several commercial research activities.

Hugo B. Roos (1945) studied spacial economics at the formerly Dutch Economic Academy (at the moment the Erasmus University) in Rotterdam. After his graduation in 1972 he worked for four year at the faculty of Transport- and Port Economics at the same University. In 1977 he worked at the Verkeersakademie Tilburg. In 1986 he was a marketing consultant distribution and logistics at Bull Nederland NV. He finished his PhD in 1987. He was a member of the Town council in Gilze from 1974 till 1978. In 1988 he worked at the Royal Military Academy in Breda as a professor in Transport Economics. During this period he worked at KPMG Klynveld Management Consultants. From 1989 till 1994 he was professor in air transport economics at the University of Amsterdam. In 1992 until now he is professor in Logistics Management at the Erasmus University Rotterdam.

Realizing Complete Traceability With An Integrated Systems Engineering Environment (ISEE)

Scott A. Hyer
The Johns Hopkins University
Applied Physics Laboratory
Laurel, Maryland 20723

Mark W. Jones
Naval Surface Warfare Center
Dahlgren Division
Dahlgren, Virginia 22448

Abstract. The development of any major system involves a dynamic atmosphere of ideas, people, and information. Traceability (from requirements to functions to physical architecture) grounds a system and all its confusing details to the founding ideas that are critical to its success. Documenting the process (i.e., decision rationale, considered and discarded alternatives, changes, approvals, etc.) is as important as documenting the system requirements, concept, and design themselves. As chronicled in this paper, the US Navy has undertaken an effort using RDD-100® to provide such traceability with an Integrated Systems Engineering Environment (ISEE) for the Navy Theater Wide Theater Ballistic Missile Defense (NTW TBMD) Program. The NTW ISEE is used to centrally locate all technical information related to the engineering development of the NTW TBMD system. It supports critical activities such as specification development, concept definition, and certification by utilizing critical database capabilities. Such an information management environment has become a necessity in developing large systems.

INTRODUCTION

The U.S. Navy has taken on a new mission as part of the larger plan for Theater Missile Defense (TMD). TMD, a joint mission shared by each branch of the US military, gained a large share of its current visibility from the Iraqi Scud missile attacks during the Persian Gulf War in 1991. The latest resurgence comes after a decade of ups and downs which can traced back to the Strategic Defense Initiative (SDI) initiated under the Reagan Administration in the mid-1980s.

Shipboard NTW capabilities will be developed using elements that build upon, and go beyond, existing anti-air warfare (AAW) technologies. To do this, a rigorous systems engineering approach will be undertaken by multiple organizations. A cornerstone of this approach will be complete traceability from the highest-level mission requirements down to the actual system implementation. Figure 1 illustrates the traceability path as it applies to the information supporting the NTW TBMD program. Such traceability is absolutely necessary to the US Navy in order to maintain visibility into the multitude of efforts supporting the system development. This paper will illustrate how the ISEE supports this critical need for traceability.

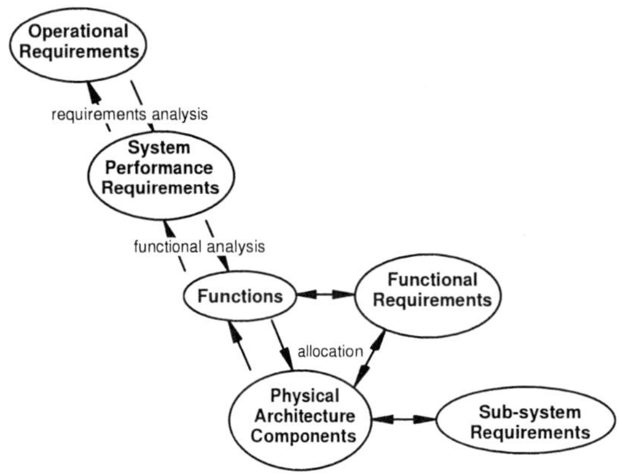

Figure 1. The traceability chain covers every step of a system's decomposition

ISEE STRUCTURE

The ISEE consists of a Computer Aided Systems Engineering (CASE) tool acting as a database management system containing engineering information and governed by processes with which the database is developed and used. Figure 2 shows the NTW ISEE broken down into its five major processes (depicted by slices in the upper level pie):

- Requirements
- Functional Behavior
- Physical Architecture
- Verification Methodology
- Cost

Each process represents a different perspective of the system under development. It is important that these different perspectives be linked together as a database such as the ISEE allows. Each process consists of information and the structure by which it is arranged.

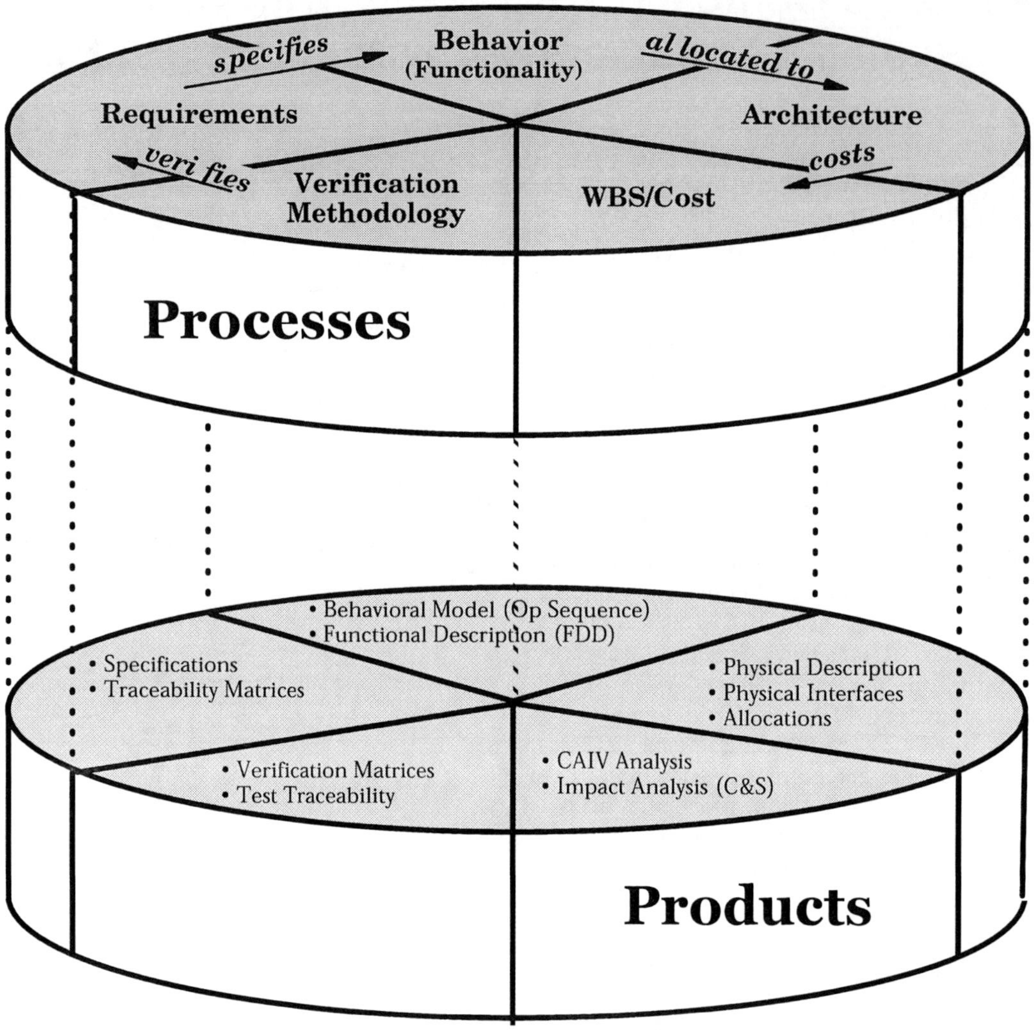

Figure 2. ISEE database contents and major relations between these contents support necessary engineering data products

Each process also corresponds to one or more products (shown in the lower level pie) that are critical to various events in the development life cycle.

Requirements. There are many requirements contained within the NTW TBMD specifications that are captured, traced, and managed. These include operational requirements, system performance requirements, functional requirements, and subsystem requirements. These requirements act as the "anchor" for the database. They form the beginning of the traceability chain and, as such, the basis for all problem decomposition and solution definition that follows. Given complete traceability, any portion or feature of the system, no matter how small, can be traced to an operational need at the user's level. Conversely, every operational need can be traced down to some part or parts of the system to show how it is being satisfied. The ISEE facilitates the traceability of NTW TBMD requirements in one central location giving them the visibility and control necessary for their proper development.

Requirements related products from the ISEE include specifications and traceability matrices. Specifications can be produced from the information contained in the database allowing the ISEE to play a direct role in producing requirements and not just tracking them. Traceability matrices are key to providing the NTW system organization with the insight to derive system impacts brought about by lower level changes.

Functional Behavior. System performance requirements are statements describing a desired capability. The first step in realizing that capability is to describe the desired behavior of a system that can satisfy the stated requirements. System functions are a collection of system behaviors, arranged in a manner that supports a desired operational sequence. As part of the traceability chain, functions are specified by requirements and thus can be formed, or linked, to the system performance requirements. This is done through the process of functional analysis. Functional analysis reinforces system performance requirements and serves to derive lower level or functional requirements.

Function related products include a functional description complete with block diagrams. Block diagrams show interconnections that are necessary to define the operational sequence. Timing diagrams or some alternative form of functional flow diagram can then represent the operational sequence.

Physical Architecture. A system is ultimately realized with tangible parts including hardware, software, personnel, and procedures. Such tangible parts are referred to as the physical architecture. The physical architecture must clearly relate to the system's desired behavior represented by its functionality. Thus, functions defined during functional analysis are allocated to parts of the physical architecture. Allocation defines where and how desired behaviors are to be physically realized. The functional and physical perspectives once joined and consistent make up the system concept.

Products related to the physical architecture would be highlighted by a system concept description that would include an allocated block diagram showing functions mapped to the physical architecture. Other products would include component and interface descriptions.

Cost. Developing a system demands resources (e.g., time and money). Estimation of the necessary resources is an ongoing task that must stay ahead of the actual development activities to allow for sound planning. The ISEE allows costs, schedule constraints, and other management information to be linked to any element in the database.

Products addressing resource utilization include Cost As An Independent Variable (CAIV) studies, and a work breakdown structure (WBS) to estimate time and manpower necessary to address every task associated with the development effort.

Universal Attributes. The database allows for a universal set of attributes to be associated with any of the major ISEE processes. These universal attributes include risk, critical issues, and decision rationale. As an example (see Figure 3), satisfying a requirement may be associated with a risk identified as "high." In the mitigation of that risk, a particular functional and physical design are selected based on a tradeoff analysis. The rationale for the selection is then associated with the functional and physical components that are also linked to the original requirement. The result is a traceable record of the actual engineering process that so often goes uncaptured. In fact, the only place such information is usually preserved is in the mind of the specific person doing the analysis or making the decision. Thus, lose the person and you have lost that information, be it critical or not.

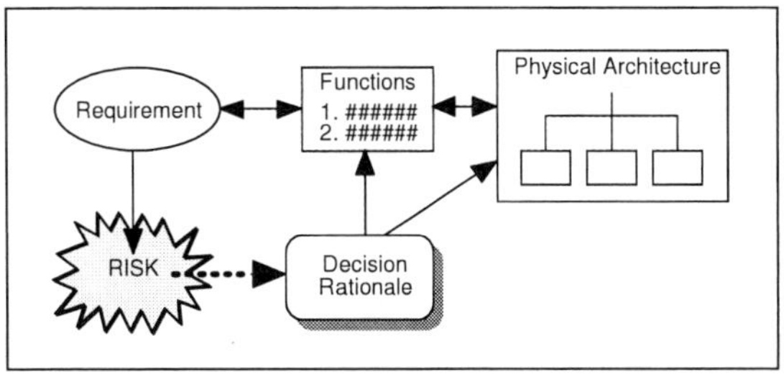

Figure 3. Example of Information Traceability through the ISEE database

ISEE WORKING GROUP

The success of any database such as the ISEE described herein is critically dependent on the team of persons who develop and maintain it. The ISEE Working Group (ISEEWG) for NTW TBMD is a multi-organizational team comprised of representatives from both mission and product engineering organizations involved in the system development as shown in Figure 4. The ISEEWG is the technical lead for the ISEE and is responsible for developing the database and managing the information. Each ISEEWG member focuses on a unique part of the database while also helping to define its overlying structure.

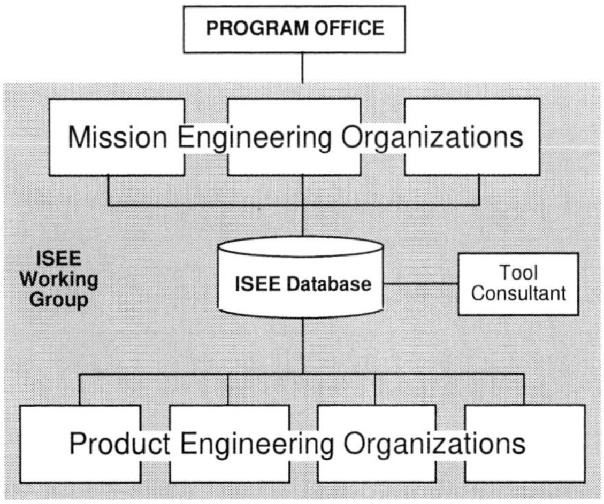

Figure 4. Members of the ISEEWG each uniquely contribute to the database

Specifics on the experiences of the NTW TBMD ISEEWG follow in order to convey both the accomplishments and the difficulties encountered.

Why was the ISEEWG formed? Key individuals in both the NTW TBMD Program Office and mission engineering organizations recognized the need for efficient information management. One of the mission engineering organizations already had experience in the use of Computed Aided Systems Engineering (CASE) tools and they spearheaded the formation of the ISEEWG. Other related Navy efforts (in particular, the Navy Area TBMD Program) utilized CASE tools in their effort to manage requirements. This experience was leveraged as much as possible.

How was the ISEEWG formed? Once support was established, each organization was asked to assign individuals to the ISEEWG based on experience and interest. The ISEEWG then went through a formation period in which members discussed their "visions" and a set of objectives were agreed to in forming a charter.

A CASE tool platform for the ISEE was then chosen (RDD-100®), training of the core team commenced, and the effort to develop the database structure, its user procedures, and populate it with information gained momentum.

How does the ISEEWG operate? Each organization contributes information and data to the ISEE given their specific roles and responsibilities and their areas of expertise. A database of this size requires a "divide and conquer" approach to build it up and maintain it efficiently. However, the division of labor also presents challenges that must be addressed. These challenges are discussed in the section on ISEE operation.

Applying the "divide and conquer" approach, the ISEEWG maintains a master database that contains all information under firm control. This information has been agreed to by all organizations represented and can only be changed by unanimous agreement from those organizations. Each organization uses working copies of the database derived from the master and then modified through their focused activities. Periodically (one a month on average), the working databases are presented and reviewed by the ISEEWG. If there is unanimous approval to accept the newly offered information, it is merged into the master database to form an updated master database. This process repeats and acts to build and update the database as the program proceeds.

As previously mentioned, the divide and conquer approach also presents challenges the ISEEWG must deal with. Each person on the ISEEWG has a unique vision of what the ISEE should be. Thus, when various contributions are brought together, they often do not readily fit the database structure or they may be inconsistent with information already residing in the database. This requires frequent ISEEWG meetings at which these topics are addressed and resolved through database modifications and adjustments that are proposed and then agreed to by the core group. In most cases, problems are identified through trial and error. Another problem is the review and approval of information entered into the database. Given the amount of information that must be captured and the personnel limits of the ISEEWG, each member is expected to get review of their material by their organization prior to entry into the database. Then, before the information is accepted into the master database, each organization represented in the ISEEWG reviews it with the option to either approve it, suggest modifications to it before approval, or reject it.

The dual hat role played by the ISEEWG members is also a constant challenge. Qualified ISEEWG members must understand the NTW TBMD system in terms of its operating principles and driving technical issues as well as be proficient in the use of RDD-100®. While either of these activities could constitute a full time job, ISEEWG members must perform both. Practically speaking, this calls for ISEEWG members to specialize in a particular sector of the database. They must then tie into the NTW TBM working groups and activities that affect that area of specialization. The difficulty of this "juggling process" cannot be understated and the proficiency by which it is accomplished directly impacts the quality and usefulness of the ISEE database.

What has the ISEEWG accomplished? Since the formation of the ISEEWG, its accomplishments include the following:

- A case was made to the NTW TBMD program office to make an initial investment of approximately $200k to license the mission engineering organization to use RDD-100®. The program office responded by granting the proposed funding request. The need for maintenance funding was also presented and this is revisited on an annual basis.

- Introductory RDD-100® training of 15 people was implemented. Advanced training of 5 people on more advanced skills took place approximately 14 months into the effort.

- The ISEE database was built up with the following information:
  - Operational Requirements
  - System Requirements (performance & verification)
  - Mission Level Functions
  - Test and Evaluation Plans (top level)

- The capability to generate specialized reports directly form the database was mastered by a couple of selected ISEWG members. The reports are generated from scripts which extract specific information for purposes of analysis, documentation, or management use. Examples include:

- Traceability between Operational Requirements and System Requirements
- Relation of System Requirements to Mission Functions
- Relation of Test and Evaluation Activities to Mission Functions

• Designed and tailored the database schema (database structure and rules of operation) to suit the needs of the NTW TBMD program. The database schema consists primarily of elements (e.g., requirements, functions, components, etc.) and relations (e.g., specifies, allocated to, verifies, etc.). RDD-100® allows the schema to be tailored for specific uses. The ISEEWG has designed the database schema primarily through expert consultation with Ascent Logic Corporation and trial and error (discovering what works and what doesn't work by trying ideas out for a period of time and assessing the usefulness).

• Two major documents were produced directly from the database through the RDD-100® document facility. Before the ISEE was established, work began to write a Systems Requirements Document (SRD) for the NTW TBMD program. Eventually, the capability to print the SRD directly from the ISEE database was established. However, the ISEE was not used to develop the SRD. A conscious decision was made to maintain separation between the SRD development and the ISEE. This was because the ISEE was in the process of being formed and would present to high a risk of failure to the critical SRD effort. The effort required to allow the ISEE to keep pace with the SRD development was significant. Ideally, if the ISEE had been established earlier, it could have been the single development platform for the SRD and much duplication of effort could have been avoided. A Functional Description Document (FDD) for the NTW TBMD system was also produced directly from the ISEE database. The FDD describes the relationship between the system requirements and the mission functions. Subsequently the mission functions are broken down and allocated to components of the system residing in the major system products.

• The ISEEWG crafted a process to control and manage the engineering information in the ISEE. This process, described in an Information Management Plan (IMP) is part of the NTW TBMD Program's greater Configuration Management Plan.

CULTURAL CHALLENGES

Regardless of any case that can be made for the efficient management of critical engineering information, there is always a degree of organizational and cultural "inertia" that must be overcome.

The initial hurdle was to have strong support and understanding from the program manager and his supporting staff. This was a painstaking process of two-way communication between those that had experience with database tools and methods and the program office. Given inherent insight on the part of the program manager and staff and the benefit of related examples from other Navy programs close at hand, the decision was made to move ahead with development of an ISEE.

Establishment of the ISEEWG was only the first step to successful implementation. The ISEEWG now had to prove itself by producing useful products. A strong cornerstone was established by the efforts to establish the requirements in the database and produce a series of reports, traceability matrices, and eventually a copy of the Systems Requirements Document.

As well as the external challenges described to this point, life within the ISEEWG was by no means void of difficulties. Each member had different visions of how the database should operate and these visions sometimes conflicted. At these times, revisiting the groups overall objectives was necessary to draw priorities and subsequently remedy such conflicts. Even without conflicts, a great deal of effort was necessary to identify issues and communicate enough across the members' various perspectives to reach a decision that everyone could work with. The bottom line is one that has been stated many time: Good people (not just tools) are the key to an effective information management process.

SUMMARY

Any large development project needs to efficiently manage its technical information given the critical activities and decisions that revolve around it. The shear volume and diversity of this information has come to dictate an approach involving the use of CASE tools to aid the human effort to manage this information. The concept of an Integrated Systems Engineering Environment (ISEE) was explained and its implementation on a current US Navy project was provided as an example. The key to successful management of project information is to provide the capability of timely traceability from top to bottom and from bottom to top. Every decision made should have logical rationale. Every aspect of a system's design should have a purpose directly related to the user's mission. With this ability to manage information, a project's leaders can chart and incrementally navigate a course more likely to lead to success.

ACKNOWLEDGEMENTS

The authors would like to recognize many others who have contributed to the material expressed in this paper:

James Leary, JHU/APL
Jim Doerr, NSWC Dahlgren Division
JM Gallier, NSWC Dahlgren Division
Paula Khoe, NSWC Dahlgren Division
Michael Ryan, NSWC Dahlgren Division
Max Kovel, Boeing

REFERENCES

EIA Interim Standard – 632 (EIA/IS-632) Systems Engineering, Electronic Industry Association, Washington, D.C., December 1994

Navy Theater Wide Defense Program Systems Engineering Management Plan, February 1999

PEO(TAD) Systems Engineering Directorate Operations Manual, PEO(TAD)-SE, January 1998

Systems Engineering Plan (SEP) for NTW TBMD (draft) Volume I – System Requirements Engineering, Naval Surface Warfare Center / Dahlgren Division, November 1997

AUTHORS' BIOGRAPHIES

Scott A. Hyer is a member of the Senior Professional Staff at the Johns Hopkins University Applied Physics Laboratory where he is involved in the analysis, development, and improvement of surface ship combat systems. He has 19 years of engineering experience on a variety of large miltary systems. He earned a B.S. in electrical engineering from Rutgers University, an M.S. in Electrical Engineering from The Johns Hopkins University, and an M.S. in Technical Management from The Johns Hopkins University. He also currently teaches Systems Engineering at the Johns Hopkins University Whiting School of Engineering. A member of INCOSE since 1991, he has served as both President and Technical Director for the INCOSE Chesapeake Chapter located in Maryland.

Mark W. Jones is a systems engineer for the Naval Surface Warfare Center in Dahlgren Virginia where he is involved in the corporate development of systems engineering processes and procedures and has responsibilities for requirements engineering. He has been involved in systems engineering and development of collaborative environments for several Navy projects. He has a BS in Electrical Engineering from the University of Akron. He has been a member of INCOSE since 1997 and has been a member of IEEE since 1980.

Engineering of Complex Adaptive Systems using OpEMCSS

John R. Clymer
Applied Research Center for Systems Science
California State University Fullerton
Fullerton, CA 92834

Abstract. A graphical discrete event simulation library is proposed for the engineering of complex adaptive systems. This library works with EXTEND (Imagine That Inc), an inexpensive yet capable and easy to use simulation software package, and it is called Operational Evaluation Modeling for Context-Sensitive Systems (OpEMCSS). Context-Sensitive Systems (CSS) is a systems theory, based on finite state machines, that can assist a system designer in understanding and evaluating complex adaptive systems, represented as communicating concurrent (parallel) processes. CSS theory can be expressed using the OpEM graphical modeling language. Thus, OpEMCSS is a graphical simulation library that can model systems based on CSS theory and the OpEM language. As an example, an OpEMCSS model is discussed such that each of two intelligent agents learn rules that maximizes their average reward in the prisoner's dilemma game.

INTRODUCTION

Simulation has become, in the last few years, a mandatory part of the systems engineering process, especially as applied to the engineering of complex adaptive systems. Large military, manufacturing, and transportation systems are too complex and costly to be designed and evaluated without the use of simulation. Business organizations are currently being re-engineered, and simulation is a natural tool to design and evaluate them. OpEMCSS is a graphical Discrete Event Simulation (DES) library that works with EXTEND, a relatively inexpensive yet powerful software product of Imagine That Inc located in San Jose, CA ("http:\\www.imaginethatinc.com"). OpEMCSS has been applied successfully in each of these application areas and many more.

It is useful to put OpEMCSS in perspective by comparing it with other DES views such as queuing models, Petri nets, and functional flow models. A more comprehensive review of alternative system modeling views, including OpEMCSS, can be found in (Bahill 1998).

Queuing Models. In a queuing model, transactions flow through a network of queues and servers. If queuing processes operate without any interactions or communications that modify their behavior, other than transaction flow, they are called context-free processes in this paper. In contrast, if transaction flow in one queuing process depends on what is happening in another queuing process, they are called context-sensitive processes. For example, the EXTEND DES library is based on context-free queuing processes. To apply this library to model context-sensitive process interactions in surface ship combat, attribute sharing and process synchronization blocks had to be added to the library. The SLAM graphical simulation language (Pritsker 1986) also describes transactions flowing through a network of queues and resources.

Petri Nets. In a Petri net model, tokens flow from place to place as defined by transitions. The significance of tokens can be as varied as the change of state in a process or data flow. One of the early goals of Petri net developers was to be able to predict mathematically, model characteristics such as consistency and deadlock. Since then, the Petri net model has been expanded to model process timing, and what tokens can represent has also been expanded by allowing tokens to have "Color." With these additions, the Petri net modeling approach has lost the ability to predict model characteristics mathematically and has evolved from an analytical to a simulation based method. Petri nets are capable of expressing moderately context-sensitive process interactions.

Functional Flow Models. In a functional flow model, transactions flow in a network of functional blocks. Each block receives transactions (i.e., data, knowledge, energy, and material) from other blocks, transforms input transactions into output transactions which are then sent to other blocks. Functional flow models are usually developed from the top-down, forming a hierarchy of models. OpEMCSS supports hierarchical functional flow models by using EXTEND's hierarchical blocks. In context-free systems these transformations do not adapt. If these transformations do adapt based on what other functions are doing, then such a system model is context-sensitive. Complex Adaptive Systems (CAS) are context-sensitive systems that have an emergent behavior for the overall system that cannot be achieved by any proper subset of the system.

Overview. The concept of a parallel process is discussed first because this concept is key to understanding Context-Sensitive Systems (CSS) theory and thus Complex Adaptive Systems (CAS). A Finite State Machine (FSM) modeling view, that is based on transition rules, is presented next to explain CSS theory and the parallel process concept. The FSM modeling view is presented because this model has a formal basis in computation theory (Yeh 1976). In the FSM modeling view, the form of the transition rules determines if a system is context-free or context-sensitive and, thus, provides a formal definition of these concepts. Different kinds of transitions are possible which allow modeling of systems operation, functional flow, and architecture as they affect systems effectiveness. A FSM expressed using transition rules, although instructive, is not easy to understand or communicate to others. Therefore, a graphical description of FSM transitions is presented using the OpEM language in the remainder of the paper.

OpEM graphical language, that is an expression of FSMs and the parallel process concept, and OpEMCSS library blocks, that implement the OpEM language, are proposed as a basis for simulation-based engineering of complex adaptive systems. A simulation of the prisoner's dilemma that is built using these blocks is discussed as a simple example of an OpEMCSS model. The prisoner's dilemma model is an example of an evolutionary, CAS where each agent adapts its decision making rules to achieve its goals. The agents discover that collaboration leads to the maximum payoff. The paper concludes with a discussion of OpEMCSS as one tool that can be applied during the simulation-based engineering (design and evaluation) of complex adaptive systems.

PARALLEL PROCESS

Considering the three modeling views that are used for systems design and evaluation, discussed above, the functional flow model is probably the one most familiar to systems engineers. In particular, the IDEF0 model is a popular example of the functional flow modeling view. In this view, a system is decomposed into a hierarchy of interconnected functional blocks where each block explicitly defines inputs, controls, outputs, and mechanisms (Buede 1999).

However, the blocks at the bottom of the IDEF0 hierarchy can open to a different view, the process view of modeling. In this view, process flow for a functional block is described, and resource contention, communication, and activity synchronization interactions among concurrent or parallel processes are represented. Process flow describes the execution of functional activities during a period of time. For example, consider an Anti-Air Warfare (AAW) missile firing function that is executed by performing a sequence of activities: pre-fire evaluation, missile flight, and post-fire evaluation. Several of the system functions could be executing concurrently. Concurrent operation could result in sharing of AAW workstation, missile launcher, and missile Fire Control System (FCS) resources. If permission to fire is required from the ship command function, activity synchronization of the AAW missile firing function with a ship command function must also occur. The concurrent operation, including interactions and communications, for all functions in the model can be described as a parallel process.

A parallel process is defined as the collection of all possible sequences of system states and events that represent process flow and interactions for a system or organization. For example, suppose that three processes describe a system where the weapon (WPN) process is in the "PreFire Evaluation" state, the Fire Control System (FCS) process is in the "Tracking" state, and the Launcher (LNCH) process is in the "Aim" state. When the LNCH process goes to the "Ready" state, a message is sent to the WPN process that causes a transition of the WPN process to the fire weapon "Fire" state. Each system state of a parallel process model includes the discrete state of each parallel sub-process. For example, FCS Tracking, LNCH Ready, and WPN Fire comprises a system state for the three process model discussed above. Thus, discrete states represent periods of time where either (1) each function activity is being performed by a resource(s) or (2) each function activity is waiting for a specified logical condition to be satisfied before it can continue, as discussed above. Also part of the system state are zero or more state variables for each sub-process. State variables have values that identify conditions, other than what activity is currently being performed, such as parameters that are used to control execution of the process activities. For example, a state variable of the launcher process is how many weapons are remaining in the magazine. Events define points in time where a change of system state occurs.

A Finite State Machine (FSM) is defined as a set of states and a set of transitions between these states. For example, DEVS (Zeigler 1999) uses a FSM model to describe the operation of each system component such that components can communicate with each other and can be formed into hierarchies. FSM models are often expressed either in terms of state transition tables, sets of transition rules, or using state transition graphs. We will use transition rules in the following discussion because the form of these rules determines whether a system is context-free or context-sensitive (Yeh 1976). Each of these rules we use describes the operation of a subset of FSMs where each FSM in the subset represents one sub-process. Thus, a rule can describe one FSM as Zeigler does or several FSMs operating together. This allows us to explicitly describe both context-free operation and context-sensitive interactions among concurrent sub-processes using our transition rules.

In the FSM modeling view discussed next, system operation is represented by a set of concurrent processes where each sub-process is a FSM. Thus, each sub-process or process instance in the set requires a discrete state dimension and zero or more state variable dimensions as discussed above. A process instance occurs each time that a subprocess is duplicated one or more times as discussed below. Dimensions for one or more process instances can form subsets of the system state vector ($D_1D_2...D_N$) that contains dimensions for all process instances currently in the system model. Thus, size of the system state vector changes as process instances are created and destroyed.

Let ($D_iD_j...D_k$) dimensions be a subset of system state and event sequence $E_aE_b...E_n$, implementing a transition, indicate value changes in these dimensions. A system transition is described by the rule:

$$(D_i\ D_j...D_k) \rightarrow E_aE_b...E_n\ (D'_i\ D'_j...D'_k)$$

This rule indicates that a transition from subset dimensions ($D_iD_j...D_k$) to new values ($D'_iD'_j...D'_k$) occurs after event sequence $E_aE_b...E_n$ is executed. Each event E_i is associated with an individual process instance, and it may cause a change in one or more dimensions of the subset. The dimensions of each sub-process are grouped together, and one or more sub-processes can be represented in a rule. An event occurs and persists for zero time; a state may persist for a non-zero time. The transition rule notation is commonly used in computation theory (Yeh 1976) to define formal languages or finite state machine behavior as strings of symbols.

For the operational view, state transitions provide a parallel process model of operation for the overall system. The OpEM graphical language and it's OpEMCSS implementation describe the behavior of parallel processes, as they interact in time, and the dependence of each process instance execution on subsystem attributes and data flow.

For functional flow and architectural views, subsystem behavior is described by a collection of one or more processes. Here, a state dimension containing a state variable can also represent transactions. Flow of transactions from one subsystem to another in the network is also governed by transition rules.

Context-Sensitive Systems (CSS) are systems with at least one transition rule based on a context involving two or more process instances. For example, a system becomes context sensitive when the subset dimensions ($D_iD_j...D_k$) forming the left side of a transition rule represent two or more process instances. This definition permits many context-sensitive interactions, which may include:

- A transition for a single sequential process that depends on state dimensions of two or more process instances and results in a change in discrete state. A process is permitted to adapt its behavior based on data or knowledge (facts used by the Classifier block) from other processes. The OpEMCSS alternate action block models this interaction.
- A synchronized transition for two or more process instances that depends on discrete state dimensions of each process instance and results in a change of discrete state for each process instance. Processes can coordinate begin and end of tasks using the OpEMCSS split action and assemble event blocks to model this interaction. These blocks allow one subprocess to split into one or more subprocesses; further, each subprocess in the split can be duplicated forming multiple concurrent process instances.
- Functional flow transition rules that can depend on state variable dimensions (data or control) for one or more process instances and result in a change in one or more state variable dimensions for one or more process instances. These rules model the functional transformations of transaction flows found in the functional-flow model. OpEMCSS context-sensitive, message, memory, local, and global event action blocks model this interaction.

Because of the split action and assemble event pairs in a system process model discussed above, process instances can come into and out of existence as a function of time. Such variable instantiation of process instances is similar to the Object-Modeling Technique (OMT) where instances of object classes are created and deleted as the program executes (Rumbaugh 1991).

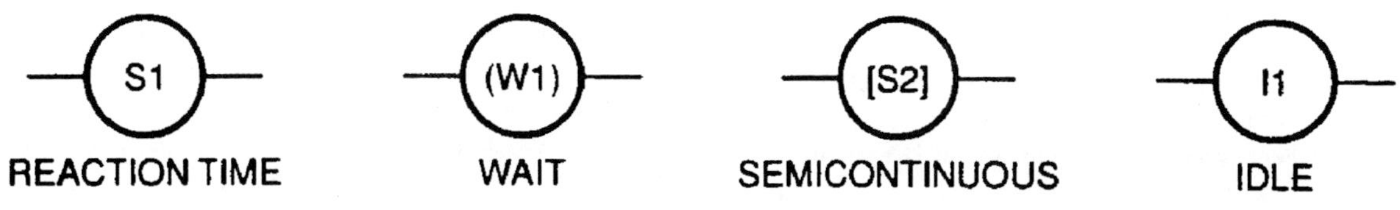

Figure 1. Four Kinds of Discrete States

OpEM DIRECTED GRAPH LANGUAGE

Use of the OpEM directed graph language to develop a model and analyze a problem requires an in-depth understanding of the parallel process language. In this section, each language element is defined and rules for combining elements to form processes are provided.

System State. A parallel process is the set of all sequences of system states and events that represent system operation. The system state is the discrete state of each process instance and the value of each state variable. Discrete states of parallel processes represent periods of time and are circles on a directed graph. There are four kinds of discrete states: (1) reaction time, (2) wait, (3) semi-continuous, and (4) idle. These are shown in figure 1.

A reaction time state represents the length of time a resource is performing a particular functional activity. Often a random variable generator computes a reaction time. Data to determine the distribution of the random variable may be determined by field observation or experimentation.

A wait state represents the time a system component waits for a logical condition to be satisfied in order to perform a functional activity. Logic that activates the event may be in the event itself or elsewhere. If in the event itself, the state itself is identified with the logic on the graph. If 'passivated', awaiting external logic to be satisfied the event following the wait state is identified as a direct execution path. Events are depicted as "< >" in a model. The two kinds of wait states are shown in figure 2.

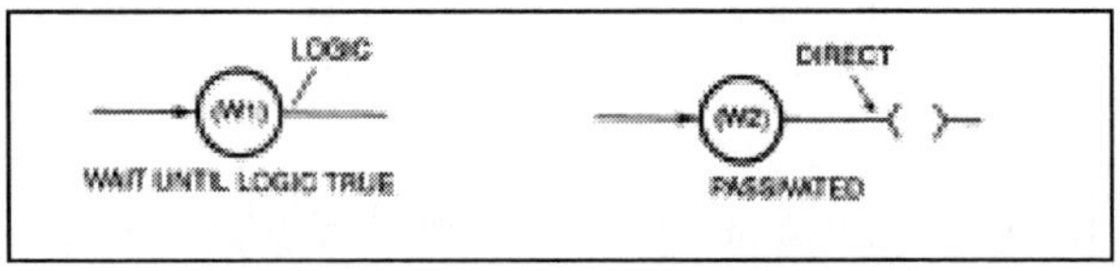

Figure 2. Two Kinds of Wait States

If the logic is located internally, logic usually is tested at each discrete time in the simulated sequence of states and events until it is satisfied. Logic can involve values of both discrete and continuous state variables. In a detailed model it is sometimes necessary to compute values of state variables prior to testing logic.

A more efficient technique, from the point of view of computer time required, is to use the 'passivated' event approach. Logic is checked by another process instance only when necessary and the wait event is executed by this process instance, using a direct execution path, when this logic is satisfied.

A semi-continuous state approximates the continuous behavior of a detailed model of system operation. State variables associated with this kind of state are updated repeatedly with a constant time step to model a process that varies continuously. In contrast, discrete time events occur at irregular time intervals. Combined discrete event and continuous processes often occur in hardware-in-the-loop simulations. A semi-continuous state is shown in figure 3.

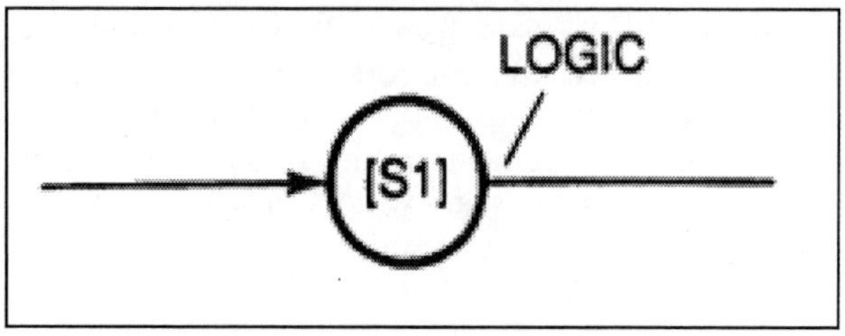

Figure 3. A Semi-Continuous State.

A semi-continuous state is indicated by square brackets around the state name inside the circle. A detailed model that updates state variables is a part of the logic associated with the event following the state. The logic decides when the continuous process ends.

An idle state represents a period of time a subprocess is waiting for one or more other subprocesses to be completed before an assemble event can occur. Some of these subprocesses may be duplicated into multiple process instances. An assemble event combines one or more subprocesses and process instances into a single subprocess. The idle state will be discussed further in the context of the assemble event.

State Variables. State variables represent data, knowledge facts used in inferencing, process control variables, entity position and velocity, and many other useful model attributes. In general, they represent process conditions other than the discrete states discussed above.

Events. Events signify changes in system state, and are represented by directed line segments connecting the states in a directed graph model (figure 4). Near the center of the line segment is a pair of brackets "< >." Below these brackets is the event name, a short description of the event. To the left of the brackets is the 'occurrence path' that connects the event to the prior state. To the right is the 'action path' that connects the event to the following state. As discussed above, an event represents a change in one or more subprocess dimensions of the system state vector. Event action implements state vector dimension changes, controls process flow, directly executes events in other subprocesses, and collects simulation report data.

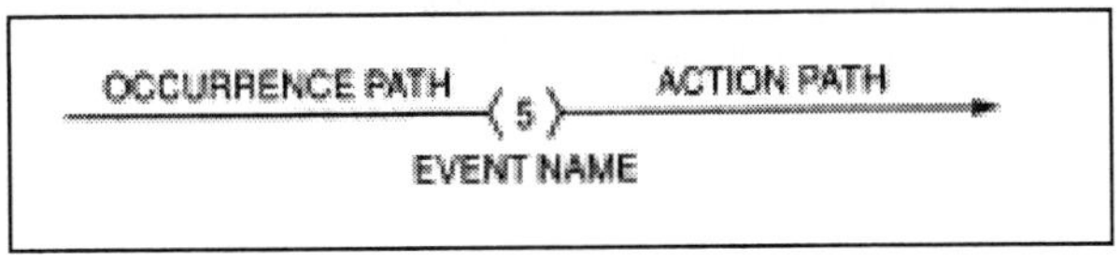

Figure 4. Events are shown as Directed Line Segments.

Figure 5 shows an exit event from a wait state. The event has two alternate occurrence paths. Path 1 has logic specified and path 2 is a direct execution path from another event. An event may have alternate action paths as well.

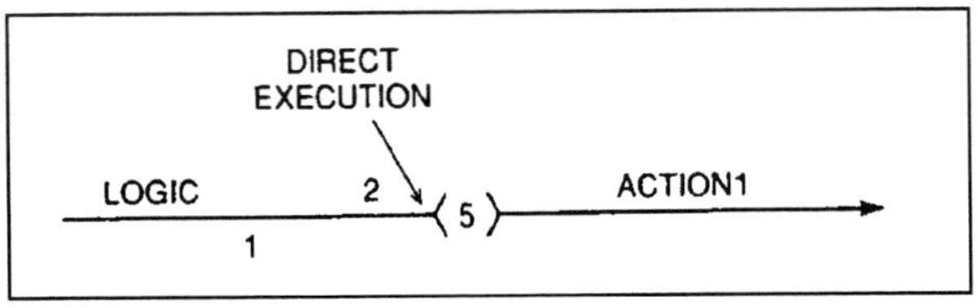

Figure 5. A Wait State Event having Alternate Occurrence Paths.

Figure 6 shows an event having two action paths. Only one path can occur each time that the preceding event is executed. ACTION1, associated with either path, is executed first, then logic chooses the action to perform. In the example shown, if LOGIC is true action two is performed, otherwise action three occurs.

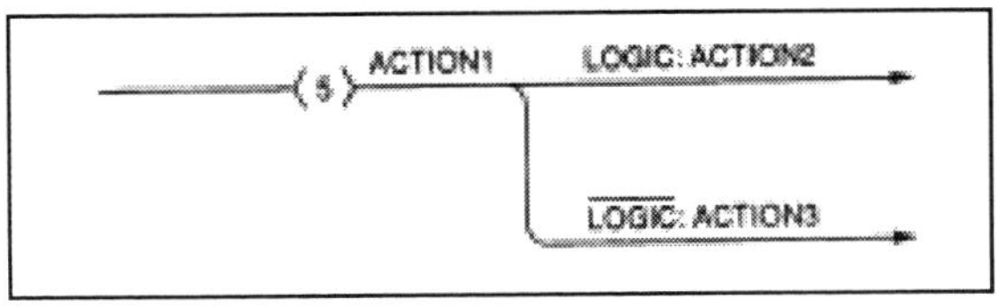

Figure 6. An Event that has two Action Paths.

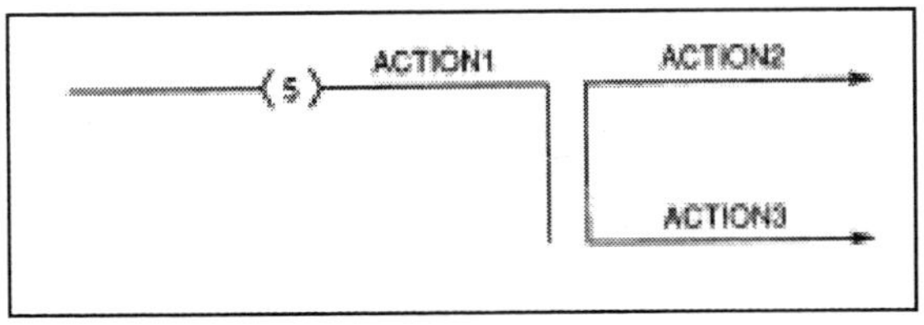

Figure 7. A Split Event.

Two parallel vertical lines to the right of the brackets "< >" indicate a split event (figure 7). Action one, preceding both parallel paths, is performed first. The subprocess then splits into two parallel subprocesses, both action two and three being performed.

Multiple process instances can occur two ways: (1) a split event creates multiple subprocesses and process instances as discussed above or (2) a generator process can create process instances and directly execute each process start event as discussed in the space factory example.

An assemble event (figure 8) has two parallel vertical lines preceding the brackets "< >." Assemble logic is specified to the left of the brackets next to the parallel lines. The numbers below each occurrence path to the left of the parallel double lines are path numbers that define the path that has been completed.

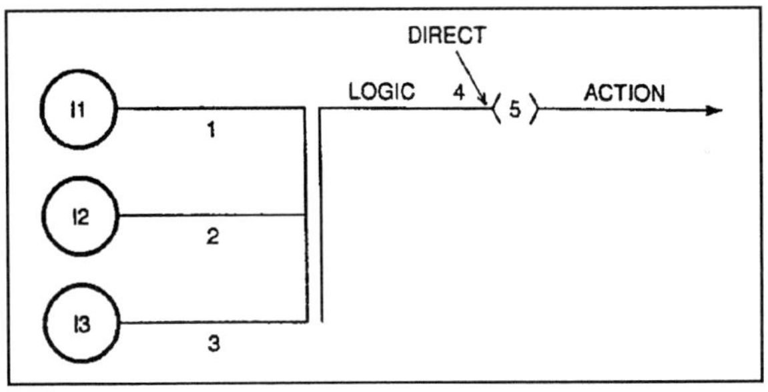

Figure 8. An Assemble Event.

When a subprocess ends, assemble logic is tested. The path number associated with the occurrence path determines that the process that has been completed. The event "<5>" occurs only when the assemble logic is satisfied. An example of assemble logic is (1 * 2 * 3). The * is a logical AND. This means that subprocess paths one and two and three must be completed before these processes are assembled. Another example logic is ((1 * 2) + 3) which means that subprocess paths one and two or three must complete before these processes assemble since the + is a logical OR.

When assemble event "<5>" occurs, the three subprocesses and associated process instances are destroyed and a single subprocess continues. In comparison, assemble logic that includes a logical OR is very difficult for Petri nets to model because some process instances must be found and destroyed. However, the OpEMCSS assemble block can model OR logic easily and automatically destroys the required subprocesses and process instances.

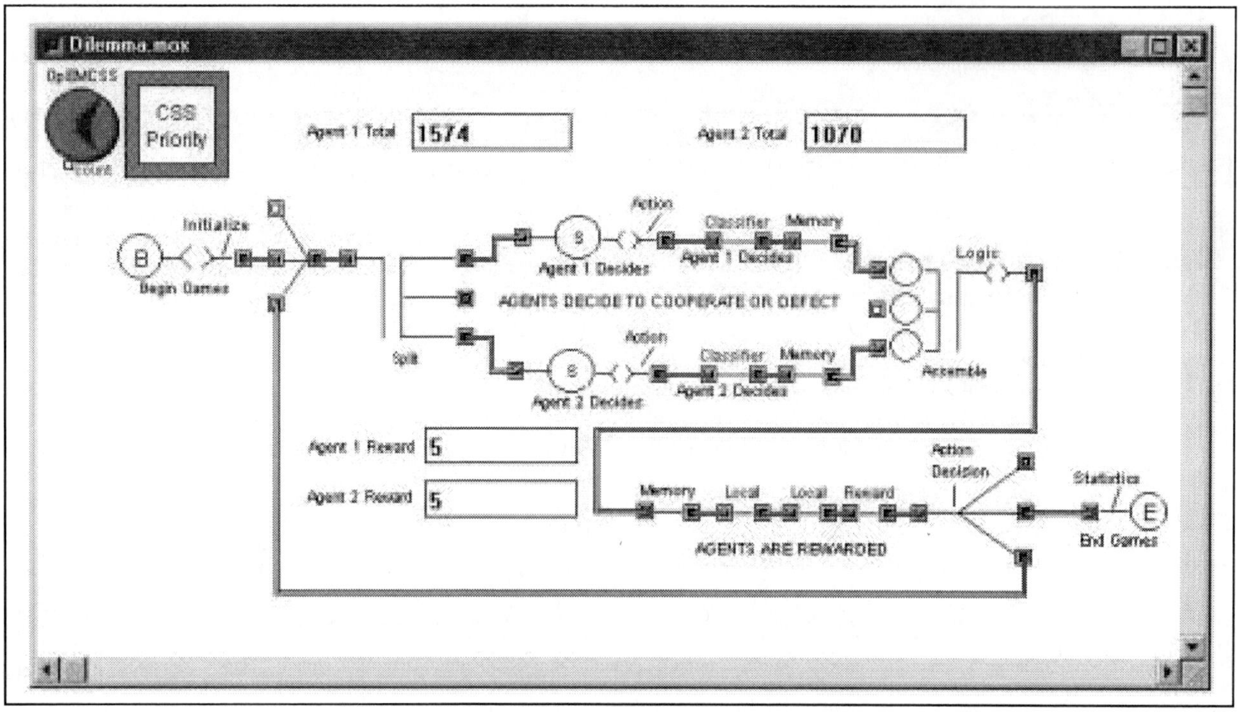

Figure 9. Prisoner's Dilemma Model.

PRISONER'S DILEMMA

The Prisoner's Dilemma model (AxelRod 1984) is shown in figure 9, and it is comprised of OpEMCSS library blocks. The ExecutiveS block, in the upper left-hand corner, controls the sequence of events in the model, and updates agent position if motion blocks are included. Next to the ExecutiveS block is a Context-Sensitive Priority block that can update the priority of each process instance currently in the model at every discrete time. This block also works with the ExecutiveS block to produce the state-trace when the model is in trace mode.

The first block in the model is the Begin Event block that creates a process instance item, a record that is passed from block to block to model process flow, and initializes some state variables, called attributes in EXTEND, that are of the form "AttributeName = NumericalValue." Attributes "Agent1" and Agent2" are initialized to one, and they are used to define the current play of each agent (1-cooperate, 2-defect). Attributes "Past1" and Past2" are initialized to one, and they are used to define the past play of each agent (1-cooperate, 2-defect). Also initialized to zero are two counters, "Agt1Totals" and "Agt2Totals," that are used to accumulate the total payoff of each agent in the game. The attribute "CountGames" is initialized to zero, and the attribute "MaxGames" is initialized to the maximum number of games for a simulation run. The model is executed for multiple runs in order to compute Measures of Effectiveness (MOE) statistics.

The Begin Event block passes the process instance item to a Event Occurrence(3) block that increments the attribute "CountGames" and that provides for multiple paths into the Split Action block that follows.

The Split Action block receives a single item and splits the sequential process into two concurrent process instances where each process instance represents an intelligent agent playing the game. The top and bottom sub-process diagrams shown in figure 9 consist of a Reaction Time Event block followed by a Classifier Event Action block and a Memory Event Action block. The Reaction Time Event block represents a period of time spent in a discrete state and also sets "PastX" equal to "AgentX," for sub-process X, to remember the agent's previous play.

The Classifier Event Action block contains a forward chaining, inference engine that uses condition-action rules to transform condition attributes into action attributes. The condition attributes are obtained from a process instance item passing through the block. After inferencing is complete, action attributes are added to the process instance item passing through the block before the item is sent to the output connector. The initial rules used by agent1 are as follows:

Rule1:IF
  Agent2=Cooperate,
THEN
  Agent1=Defect,CF=50%

Rule2:IF
  Agent2=Defect,
THEN
  Agent1=Cooperate,CF=50%

The rules used by agent2 are similar. Attributes "Past1" and "Past2" are also allowed as conditions in the rules.

If several different actions are implied by the condition attributes (i.e., several rules are eligible to fire in a context), the best action is selected based on either the maximum BID value or a probability. The BID is a function of rule strength (CF), specificity, and condition support such that a more specific rule has a higher BID. The rule selection probability is a function of rule strength and specificity such that a more specific rule has a higher probability of being selected to fire. Probability of rule selection is required for rule learning, but the maximum BID can be used once all rules have been determined. The Classifier Event Action blocks in both sub-processes have been set up for rule learning discussed below.

The parallel sub-processes both connect to an Assemble Event block that produces a single process instance as its output. The Memory Event Action blocks, that are placed before and after the assemble, store and retrieve attributes in a global memory named "Dilemma." The Memory Event Action block and the Message Event Action block allow process instances to communicate either through global memory or message passing; respectively. A third option in OpEMCSS is to use a set of blocks to send and receive message items in a hierarchical functional flow model such as an IDEF0 model discussed in (Buede 1999).

Following the Memory Event Action block that retrieves attributes for both agents, two Local Event Action blocks use the rules of the prisoner's dilemma game to determine each agents reward based on current play and then accumulates the total reward for each agent. The Reward Event Action block, dialog shown in figure 10, computes the payoff for each of the Classifier Event Action blocks.

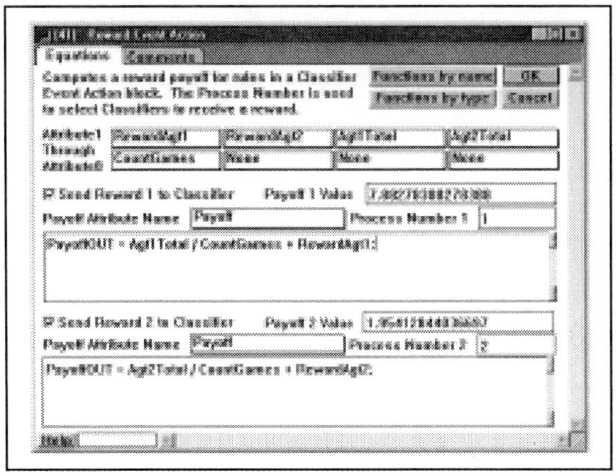

Figure 10. Reward Event Action block dialog.

The classifier blocks always converge to the following rules:

Agent1:

Rule1:IF
  Agent1=Cooperate AND
  Agent2=Cooperate AND
  Past1=Cooperate,
THEN
  Agent2=Cooperate,CF=100%

Agent2:

Rule1:IF
  Agent2=Cooperate AND
  Past2=Cooperate AND
  Agent1=Cooperate,
THEN
  Agent1=Cooperate,CF=100%

Therefore, the agents start out playing the "zero sum game" strategy that is win-lose, defined by the initial rules, and end up playing a win-win rule strategy that maximizes their total reward. However, it is interesting that if one agent is locked into the "zero sum game" strategy of win-lose through its reward payoff equation and the other agent's strategy remains win-win, the heterogeneous agents can only adapt to a win-win rule strategy if the rule learning rate is balanced. If both agents play the "zero sum game" strategy of win-lose due to their reward payoff equations, the game converges to lose-lose.

If you watch the model operate, you will observe that before the rules converge to complete cooperation, the agents play a "tit-for-tat" strategy (Axelrod 1984). The rules are: 1) if you cooperate then I cooperate and 2) if you defect then I punish you and defect, cooperating with you at a later time.

SUMMARY AND CONCLUSIONS

The prisoner's dilemma model is an example of applying the OpEMCSS library to model a simple process. Even for complex models, it is easy to place the blocks on the screen and connect them. Just click your mouse on an output connector (little box with a black interior) and drag the mouse symbol to an input connector (little box with a white interior) of the next block. Next, you double click your mouse on a block icon and the block dialog, such as shown in figure 10, appears. You set up the dialog for proper block action, click your mouse on "OK," and the dialog closes. A model like the prisoner's dilemma model can be built in less than an hour.

How do we use OpEMCSS in the engineering of complex adaptive systems? Engineering of complex systems is accomplished using the systems engineering process: (1) dialog with the customer, (2) requirements analysis, (3) functional decomposition, (4) architectural design, and (5) write systems specification. Two kinds of systems engineering tools are typically applied to support the engineering of complex systems and the systems engineering process: (1) tools that produce a design capture data-base such as CORE (Buede 1999) and (2) tools that are used for concept exploration and discovery such as OpEMCSS.

A design capture tool is used for complete automation of the systems engineering process from design team entry of requirements until generation of systems specification documents occurs. Such a tool allows a central design data-base to be accessed by members of a design team and design description information to be entered and shared. Design modeling is provided to check the consistency of the design and assure that system performance and other requirements are met. A design capture tool can be used to map the functional model onto a system architecture, and it can generate systems specification documents.

A concept exploration tool, such as OpEMCSS working in EXTEND, allows rapid motion through problem space to examine system design problems. It facilitates "out-of-the-box" thinking to discover the best system concepts that solve system design problems without focusing on a point design too soon. As each problem is solved, the solution is entered into the system design database.

Development of OpEMCSS is a continuing process, and inputs from OpEMCSS users are highly desired to determine when additional block features or new blocks are needed.

See **"http//ecs.fullerton.edu/~jclymer/"** to download the OpEMCSS and OpEMAUX libraries and benchmark models for your evaluation.

REFERENCES

Axelrod, R.M., *The Evolution of Cooperation*, New York, NY: Basic Books, Inc., 1984.

Buede, D.M., *The Engineering Design of Systems: Models and Methods*, Wiley-Interscience, 1999.

Bahill, A.T., et al, "The Design-Methods Comparison Project," IN *IEEE Transactions on Systems, Man, and Cybernetics-Part C Applications and Reviews*, Volume 28, Number 1, February 1998.

Clymer, J. R., *Systems Analysis Using Simulation and Markov Models*, Englewood Cliffs, NJ: Prentice-Hall Inc, 1990.

Clymer, J. R., "Expansionist/Context-Sensitive Methodology: Engineering of Complex Adaptive Systems", IN *IEEE Transactions on Aerospace and Electronic Systems*, April 1997 issue, Volume 33, Number 2, pages 686-695.

Clymer, J. R., "Simulation-Based Engineering of Complex Adaptive Systems", IN *Simulation*, San Diego, CA: The Society of Computer Simulation International, April 1999 issue, Volume 72, Number 4, pages 250-260.

Pritsker, A.A.B., *Introduction to Simulation and SLAM II*, New York, NY: John Wiley and Sons, 1986.

Rumbaugh, J. et al, ***Object-oriented Modeling and Design***, Englewood Cliffs, NJ: Prentice-Hall Inc., 1991.

Yeh, R. T., *Applied Computation Theory: Analysis, Design, and Modeling*, Englewood Cliffs, NJ: Prentice-hall, 1976.

Zeigler, B.P., and H. Praehofer, *Theory of Modeling and Simulation*, 2nd edition, Academic Press, 1999.

BIOGRAPHY

JOHN R. CLYMER is a professor of electrical engineering at California State University Fullerton (CSUF) and consults in the area of systems engineering, simulation, and artificial intelligence. In addition to consulting, he presents intensive short courses at various locations around the United States and abroad. His teaching assignments have included computer engineering, system control, continuous systems simulation, operational analysis and DES simulation, optimization and mathematical programming, and artificial intelligence (fuzzy logic and control, neural networks, and expert systems). Dr. Clymer's current research interests are focused in the area of intelligent, complex adaptive systems, applying integrated simulation, artificial intelligence, and evolutionary programming methods to study such systems. He is a founding member of the Applied Research Center for Systems Science at CSUF. He is a member of IEEE, SCS, and INCOSE.

Web-based Aerospace System Evaluation Software:
The Development and Assessment of Conceptual Space Missions

B.J. Makins and D.W. Miller
MIT Space Systems Laboratory
77 Massachusetts Avenue
Cambridge, MA 02139

Abstract. The conceptual design of aerospace missions occurs when resources are at minimum, the trade space is vast, and experts are distributed. GINAware provides a quantitative methodology to evaluate vastly different mission architectures and offers a collaborative environment to share resources. This paper outlines the GINAware methodology: a model driven system engineering design process that develops, assesses, compares and optimizes conceptual space based missions. The process utilizes some established design tools, information technology and applies the Generalized Information Network Analysis (GINA) framework. Together, these tools help the end-user systematically define the design, capability, and performance metrics of a mission. This process has been published on the World Wide Web in an effort to encourage collaboration and to foster productivity. A case study of NASA's Terrestrial Planet Finder mission is developed to illustrate the process.

INTRODUCTION

To thrive in an increasingly competitive business, aerospace organizations are urgently streamlining their system design, development, and implementation processes. To this end, these organizations are often found collaborating on projects. The National Aeronautics and Space Administration (NASA) strategic plan for cost cutting calls for the "Increasing leverage of NASA's research and development investments in commercial partnerships with industry ... to develop new technologies and processes to enhance research and make aeronautics and space programs more affordable and to develop affordable technologies..." (NASA Strategic Plan, 1998)

This paper outlines the GINAware methodology: a model driven system engineering design process that develops, assesses, compares and optimizes conceptual space based missions. This process utilizes some established design tools, information technology, and applies the Generalized Information Network Analysis (GINA) framework. GINAware has been published on the World Wide Web to encourage collaboration and to foster productivity. It allows geographically distributed systems engineers and expert designers to construct mathematical models, update a system model, and then recognize its immediate effect on cost and performance. GINAware enables engineers to better design to system objectives and provides better access to experts, thus reducing unnecessary travel and role redundancy.

With regularly updated models, GINAware can be a valuable tool throughout the design process: in the comparison of conceptual designs, the development of preliminary designs, and the validation of design modifications. GINAware simulations may be run synchronously or asynchronously, enabling experts from around the world to share their work, safely, and at their leisure.

MOTIVATION

"NASA has undergone a 25% reduction in work force within the past 6 to 7 years. In the same time period, the Agency has focused its technical capabilities in way that distributes the primary technical competency across the agency." (Monell, 1999) As a result, NASA is streamlining the early stages of mission design, as well as facilitating remote collaboration, through programs and facilities such as the Integrated Synthesis Environment (ISE) and Product Development Centers (PDCs).

The MIT Space Systems Laboratory (SSL) has developed the Generalized Information Network Analysis (GINA) methodology to organize and foster conceptual design trades using physical models to derive quantifiable and comprehensive metrics. Quantifiable metrics enable the comparison of life-cycle cost to the lifecycle mission productivity and thereby provide a common comparison between seemingly different architectures. Comprehensive metrics avoid degenerate designs based solely on minimum cost or maximum performance. The development of these metrics is particularly difficult to implement during the conceptual design phase when resources are at a minimum, the trade space is vast, and experts are distributed. What GINA currently lacks is accessibility to the experience base resident throughout the research community. This is the motivation behind the GINAware project.

The framework of GINA and the web implementation of GINAware are generic and can be applied to any space system, commercial or otherwise.

In fact, GINA has been tested and validated on many civil and commercial programs, including sparse aperture synthesis for astronomy (Jilla-a, 1999), space-based radar, Broadband Communication, and GPS. (Shaw, 1999) GINA has also been specifically validated in NASA missions, including some Code-Y studies and the Terrestrial Planet Finder Mission (Miller et al., 2000).

The web implementation itself is generic enough to be applied to any distributed system, and is especially useful when model integration is a challenge. However, the GINA analysis engine makes it especially useful in the study of space missions where considerably different architectures are equally viable.

OUTLINE

There are two major themes to this paper: an aerospace systems methodology and the subsequent web-based implementation. Specifically, this paper:

1. Provides a step-by-step description of the GINA-based space systems methodology, and
2. Describes the web-based implementation of this process, showcasing how it fosters collaboration.

A case study that has been successfully implemented in GINAware, NASA's Terrestrial Planet Finder (TPF) Mission, will be used to illustrate these themes. The background for this mission is included at the conclusion of this paper.

CONCEPTUAL DEVELOPMENT OF GINAWARE

Step-1. Define the Mission Capability Metrics. The first step in the GINAware process is to translate the science objectives into a quantifiable set of system capability requirements.

The Generalized Information Network Analysis methodology, which was developed to analyze and trade fundamentally different mission architectures, is founded on the belief that distributed satellite systems are information disseminators that can be represented as an information transfer network; (Shaw, 1998) because the goal of any space-based science satellite can be simplified to the collection of data and the subsequent transfer of that information to the scientists. Similarly, the goal of any communication satellite constellation can be simplified to the transfer of data from one user to another.

In the GINA methodology, the capability of an information system is characterized by four "Quality of service" parameters that relate to the quantity, quality, and availability of the information that is processed through the network. (Shaw, 1998) These four parameters serve as the minimum instantaneous capability requirements a mission must satisfy.

1. *Isolation*: Isolation refers to the ability of a system to isolate and distinguish information signals from different sources within the field of view.
2. *Rate*: Rate measures the speed at which the system transfers information between the sources and the sinks in the network.
3. *Integrity*: Integrity is a measure of the quality of the information being transferred trough the network.
4. *Availability*: Availability characterizes the instantaneous probability that information is being transferred through the network at the required level for the above three parameters.

GINAware supports the conceptual development of each capability metric, but more importantly it necessitates a quantitative input. These requirements define the minimum capability acceptable for a successful mission, which helps build the GINA-assessment module. The capability requirements for the TPF case study are summarized in Table 1.

Capability Metrics	Key Factors	Quantitative Requirement
Isolation	Angular Resolution	< 1 milli-arcsecond
Integrity	SNR Signal-to-Noise	>5 for detection >10 for planet characterization
Rate	Imaging Rate	Capable of detecting more than 150 star systems and capable of characterizing 50 planets
Availability	Operational Overhead	

Table 1: TPF Capability Metrics

Step-2. Identify different mission architectures and down select to a reasonable set. The second step in the GINAware process is to identify the top-level architecture trades that drive the system design.

There are usually several architectures that can be implemented to satisfy a single set of requirements. For example, a communications network may consist of a monolithic satellite (Hughes 601) or as a constellation of distributed satellites (Iridium). These architecture trades have a great deal of impact on model design and on the mission itself. All missions are imposed with manpower and budgetary constraints, so architecture options are limited to a reasonable set.

This architecture down select, perhaps the most important decision in any mission, should be well thought out. GINAware offers a systematic approach, comparing each architecture by its effect on the capability and system metrics. The system metrics - performance, cost per function, and adaptability - are the quantitative means by which each feasible mission architecture is evaluated and compared.

1. *Performance*: Performance measures how well an architecture satisfies the demands of the network over the entire life of the mission. To calculate this quantity, all possible component failures, their likelihood, and effect on the system must be taken into account.
2. *Cost Per Function*: Cost per function measures the cost of an architecture versus its performance. It is a measure of the cost to achieve a common level of performance and includes expected development, launch, failure compensation, and operation costs.
3. *Adaptability*: Adaptability is a measure of how flexible an architecture is to changes in design assumptions and mission requirements. Adaptability may be thought of as the sensitivity of the cost per function to incremental changes in design variables, assumptions, or requirements.

The system requirements for the TPF case study are summarized in Table 2. Establishing these metrics, gives a performance basis to compare system architectures.

Step-3. Identify the key design variables. The third step in the GINAware process is to identify the design variables that drive the architectural design. This is the cornerstone of the GINAware approach because it establishes the relationship between the trade space and the metrics by which competing architectures are judged. GINAware sets up a qualitative and quantitative comparison of the capability metrics to the key design variables.

System Metrics	Description
Performance	Total images collected over the system lifetime, considering failures
Cost per Function	Lifecycle cost per Image
Adaptability	The time it takes to transition between mission phases

Table 2: TPF System Evaluation Metrics

For example, a metrics matrix tool helps identify the attributes that distinguish individual architectures. Figure 1 shows the metric matrix used throughout the TPF case study. If any design variable, denoted by column, does not show a clear effect on the capability metrics, then it should be removed. Non-essential design variables are set constant - based on some reasonable assumption – and remain unchanged from model to model. These constants can be changed if necessary. Once a preliminary model has been put in place, sensitivity analyses (adaptability metric) offer a systemic method for determining the significance of each constant assumption.

The fewer key design variables, the smaller the trade space and the simpler the model. In practice, it is best to keep the model as simple as possible.

Trades / Metrics	Heliocentric Orbital Altitude (1 to 6 AU)	Aperture Maintenance (SCI vs. SSI)	Number of Apertures (4 to 12)	Size of Apertures (1 to 4 m)
Isolation (Angular Res.)	N/A	SSI allows more freedom in baseline tuning	Fine tuning of transmissivity function	N/A
Rate (Images/Life)	Noise reductions increase rates; Operation delay changes	SSI power and propulsion requirements highly sensitive	Increased collecting area improves rate	Increased collecting area improves rate
Integrity (SNR)	Different local zodiacal emission and solar thermal flux	SCI: passive alignment but complex flexible dynamics	Tuning of transmissivity for exo-zodiacal suppression	Smaller FOV collects less local zodiacal noise
Availability (Variability)	N/A	Different safing complexity and operational events	Different calibration and capture complexity	N/A

Aperture GINA Operations Controls Environment S/C Bus

Figure 1. TPF Metrics Matrix, which compares key design variables to the GINA metrics

Step-4. Subsystem definition. The fourth step in the GINAware process is to define the major subsystems and recognize how they relate to one another. If the metrics matrix was filled out in detail, most of the major design relationships should be identified. The key coding at the bottom of Figure 1 shows how the TPF metrics matrix was used to identify major systems; each color refers to a unique subsystem. Some examples of typical subsystems are:

- *Orbital Analysis*: The orbit analysis system should include orbital element calculations, and if necessary provide thermal and environmental look-up tables. The orbit may well be a design variable, and not necessarily a subsystem.
- *Mission science*: The mission science system should quantify the capability of the mission, and should set requirements for supporting subsystems. The mission science system is usually highly dependent on the design variables.
- *Payload*: The payload system should size the sensors and actuators to meet the mission science requirements.
- *Spacecraft bus*: The spacecraft bus system should size the power, thermal, communication, propulsion, structural, attitude and control subsystems to meet the mission science requirements at a minimum mass, power consumption.
- *Operations*: The operations system should calculate the cost of developing an operations concept, and to operate the spacecraft over its lifetime. Operational issues are traditionally relegated to the tail end of a spacecraft design process and they rarely influence the decision criterion of the system trades they directly affect. GINA has offered a unique opportunity to include operations in the conceptual design phase. A generic modeling framework that captures the key functional relationships of space operations, including autonomy and complexity trades, has been developed at MIT (Girerd et al, 1999). This framework has been implemented in a modular software format using Matlab™ functions, which can be utilized in future GINAware models.
- *Launch*: The launch system should fit the system to an appropriate launch vehicle, and to determine the cost for the vehicle and its support.
- *GINA-Assessment*: The GINA assessment module should compute the minimum capability requirements, capture overhead and spacecraft costs, and quantify the system degradation as a function of time.

This is a generic list of spacecraft subsystems and is of course subject to change. A salient benefit of GINAware is that it can support the specific needs of any space mission.

WEB IMPLEMENTATION OF GINAWARE

Step-5. Develop subsystem modules and control their integration. The fifth step in the GINAware process is to code subsystem modules and to integrate them according to each systems inputs and outputs. Design Structure Matrix methods have been developed for similar model integration problems; GINAware uses such a technique and leverages work from several sources.

Various tools for the sequencing and monitoring of multidisciplinary design processes have been developed at NASA Langley Research Center (LaRC). In most cases, the Design Structure Matrix (DSM or the N-squared diagram) has been used to represent the interaction of the design space, and as a means of configuration control. (Rogers, 1998)

Design Structure Matrices have also been used to develop environments that integrate user defined, specialized applications. For example, a Distributed Object based Modeling Environment (DOME) framework has been developed in the MIT CAD lab. (Pahng, 1998) On a much grander scale, NASA is implementing the Collaborative Engineering Environment (CEE) as the infrastructure for the upcoming Intelligent Synthesis Environment (ISE). The CEE has been designed to manage a distributed set of state of the art applications and video conferencing tools, among other utilities, for NASA's PDCs. The next generation of CEE will include rapid simulation and risk management tools, and lifecycle integration and validation technologies. (Monell, 1999) Alternatively, GINAware will focus on the sharing of a specific application (Matlab™) to systematically evaluate different design architectures with a set of quantifiable and comprehensive metrics. (These metrics encompass lifecycle costs and risk effects.) GINAware distinguishes itself from typical collaborative environments because it is useful during both the conceptual and preliminary design stages, where extensive modeling of multiple architectures in specialized applications is impractical.

The DSM, originally formulated by Steward, provides a visual representation of flow through a model, and is used to sequence dependent processes into a workable order. (Steward, 1981) The DSM is simply an N-by-N matrix whose main diagonal represents system modules (Orbit, Operations, etc.). The inputs to a given module are recorded on its column, where the outputs are recorded along its row.

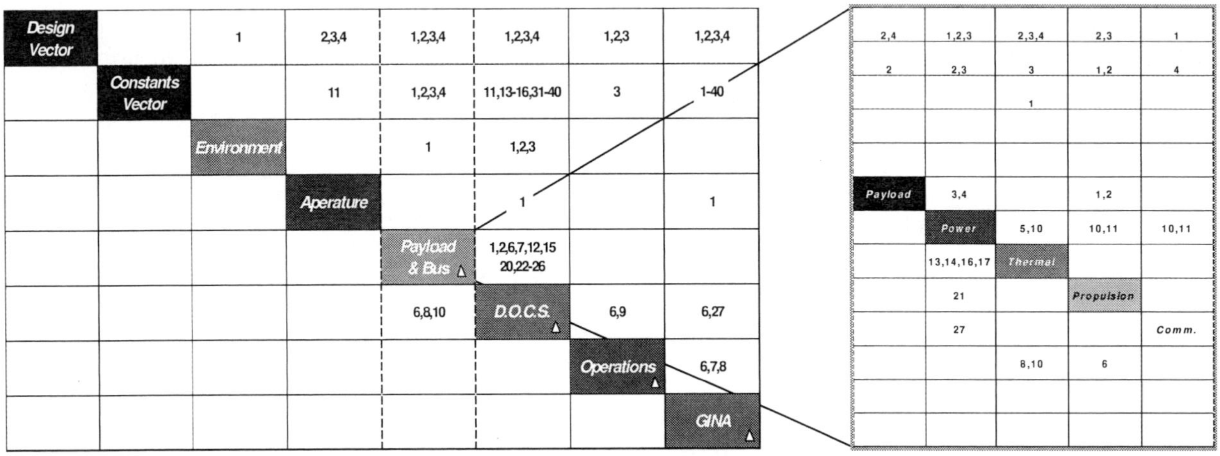

Figure 2. TPF Multi-tiered, Design State Matrix

Figure 2 shows the DSM used throughout the TPF case study. The inputs and outputs of the TPF DSM are encoded, but the general flow of information is clearly demonstrated. GINAware provides a DSM applet; this applet displays the current module inputs and outputs – which is absolutely necessary if remote collaborators are going to provide working modules.

Multi-tiered DSM approaches, which enable users to pinpoint the interdependency of their tasks at their desired complexity level, have been designed at the MIT Center for Innovation in Product Development. (Sabbaghian, 1998) GINAware uses a similar multi-tiered approach to organize and manipulate its design processes. The left sub-figure of Figure 2 shows the top level systems interaction for the TPF case study, which is necessary for system engineering and integration; the right sub-figure of Figure 2 displays the lower level interaction of the spacecraft bus, which aids subsystem engineers during the design and update of their models. Note that there are entries below the diagonal in the Spacecraft Bus system. This indicates variable feedback, a local optimization, about which, only bus engineers will be considerably concerned.

The integration of subsystem modules in GINAware requires a robust interface. The DSM applet required the design of an amenable graphical user interface, a utility to allow changes to the inputs and outputs of user defined models, immediate identification of unresolved variables and feedback loops, the capability to run individual modules or partial models, and a script to translate these options into Matlab™ code. The true challenge is to capture the transient nature of conceptual design; but once all the components are in place, the update of user-defined models within the DSM interface is straightforward.

Once a final model is assembled, the DSM applet is translated into a master Matlab™ m-file script. This script calls the subsystem modules in the appropriate order, applying the noted inputs. By defining the interfaces at the outset of the design problem, concurrent engineering and development are accessible throughout the design process. For convenience, a DSM will be made available in standard spreadsheet formats. (This template will encourage offline design.) When the user is ready, the template will be uploaded and automatically translated into GINAware.

Step-6. Update and iterate the model over the Internet. The sixth step in the GINAware process is to test, run, and update the baseline model.

GINAware's modular approach allows for the rapid evaluation and comparison of different system architectures. If a particular module becomes antiquated, it can be removed, re-coded, or replaced, if it maintains the same inputs and outputs. (See Figure 2) This step, where various engineers and experts tweak the subsystem models, was the primary driver in creating a web-based tool. This is clearly an iterative process that requires collaboration. An example HTML form used for model iteration during the beta testing of GINAware is shown in Figure 3.

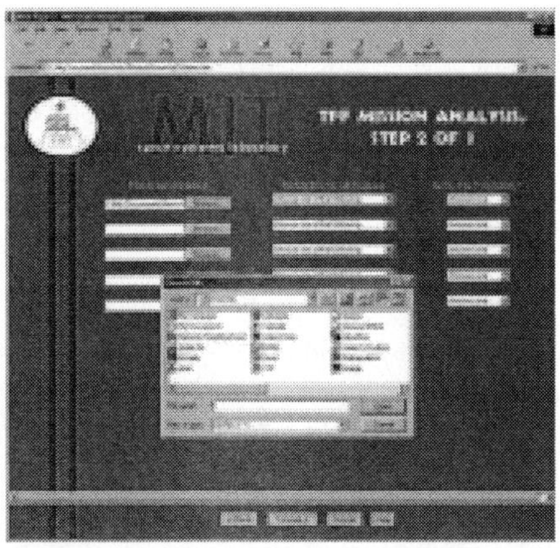

Figure 3. HTML form for updating TPF

The GINAware module update process is simple and intuitive; a description is included below:

1. The user logs-in -- providing their user name, affiliation, and password. The login procedure encourages user responsibility and permits the traceability of all test runs.
2. The user specifies a set of design variables
3. The user chooses what modules will be used in this iteration. The default modules will be set automatically for each organization, as agreed to in advance. If the user has a module to update, he or she simply chooses "Upload In-house Module".
4. The user uploads the appropriate files (e.g. a spacecraft bus update or an alternate orbit analysis) All uploads and downloads use 128-bit encryption.
5. The user indicates whether it is a preliminary, proprietary or public file. If the file is public, it will be available as a choice in the next test run to all users. If it is proprietary, it will be available as a choice to all members of matching affiliation.
6. The test run is sent to the server, while selected output and debugging information is returned through an applet.
7. At completion, an output (.mex) data file will automatically download to the user. The session history, user information and the results file will be archived as well. This serves as a backup and helps identify user specific problems.

To be successful, this tool must ensure the author's ownership of the modules. To protect each users investment, a security system will be set in place. All internal models are the sole property of the creator, but the results from each test run are the joint property of this institution and the submitter's affiliate. To ensure the intellectual property of the user, all files shall be uploaded in executable form. Executable m-files cannot be edited or viewed, they are essentially a black box that takes a set of inputs and provides a set of outputs.

In GINAware, a message board, a set of frequently asked questions (FAQ), and a tutorial are all available as aids to the user. This helps facilitate communication between the program manager and the technology contributors. The FAQ and tutorial exclusively focus on how to use GINAware. But the message board can be used a forum to discuss technical issues regarding the mission of interest. Once the security and usability of the system are established, GINAware will foster productive collaboration of remote users. Any registered user can contribute, safely, at their leisure. An industry expert could provide a proprietary module; a university program could share cutting edge research; and eventually NASA could provide technology databases and look-up tables.

Step-7. Optimization. Once completed, a GINAware model is not just an end-to-end simulation tool. GINAware is flexible enough to explore widely varied trade spaces, enabling the application of architectural optimization.

Four separate multi-disciplinary optimization techniques – Taguchi methods, simulated annealing, single-axis searches, and pseudo gradients – have been demonstrated in GINAware. In fact, simulated annealing algorithms found particularly good conceptual design solutions with a high degree of confidence. (Jilla-b, 1999)

Several generic optimization modules will be made available in GINAware, but the framework is flexible enough to allow user defined optimization packages and the refinement of the generic set. Multi-disciplinary design optimization work is currently under development at the MIT SSL.

QUALITITATIVE ASSESSMENT

The Software Engineering Institute (SEI) at Carnegie Mellon University has identified a set of technical challenges that must be met, and some typical contributions that are present in successful process automation tools. (Barbacci, 1997) These findings were used to preliminarily appraise GINAware as a design tool.

Throughout the beta test cycle, the productivity of GINAware will be evaluated using the following SEI metrics: reliability, security, sensitivity, availability, throughput, dependability, and customizability. Reliability, security, and availability will be measured with Internet statistics; where customizability, dependability, and sensitivity will be measured qualitatively with user feedback. (Florac, 1992) Figure 4 shows how the original GINAware design considered security, reliability, customizability and its ease of use.

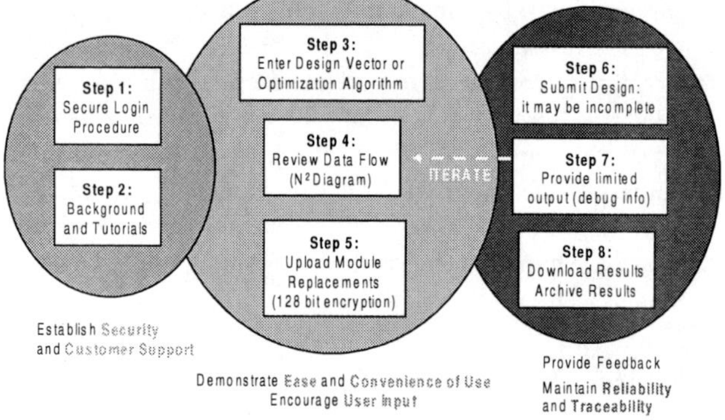

Figure 4. How GINAware meets SEI requirements

SUMMARY

The conceptual design of aerospace missions occurs when resources are at minimum, the trade space is vast, and experts are distributed. GINAware provides the quantitative methodology to evaluate vastly different mission architectures and offers a collaborative environment to share resources. This environment allows distributed engineers and experts alike to contribute to a project at their leisure, while recognizing its immediate effect on cost and performance.

To this end, the GINAware approach embodies more than an average end-to-end simulation tool.

- It enables experts from all around the world to collaborate on the development of conceptual space missions.
- It provides a quantitative systems engineering methodology that can be used to compare different mission architectures.
- It considers system operations, which is a major contributor to cost in most space missions, at the forefront of the design process.

The GINAware process has been validated, as illustrated throughout this paper, for the TPF conceptual design. Only by exercising GINAware in this manner will its shortcomings be identified and remedied. Thus, the beta testing of GINAware continues in selected civil and commercial programs, including the upcoming TPF industrial study.

CASE STUDY BACKGROUND

The TPF mission is to directly detect the existence of Earth-like planets orbiting near-by stars. This space-borne telescope will directly detect and characterize exo-solar planets by collecting and interfering their light, while suppressing the light from their parent star. For more information visit the TPF web page: `http://tpf.jpl.nasa.gov/`

ACKNOWLEDGEMENTS

The authors would like to thank the members of the ASTRO design team for implementing the GINAware approach. The authors would also like to thank Cyrus Jilla for his insight into the GINA framework and his invaluable feedback.

REFERENCES

"NASA Strategic Plan - NASA Policy Directive (NPD)-1000.1", The National Aeronautics and Space Administration, 1998.

Barbacci, M. R., Klein, M. H., and Weinstock, C. B., "Principles for Evaluating the Quality Attributes of a Software Architecture," Technical Report, SEI-96-TR-036, May 1997.

Florac, W. A., Park, R. E., and Carleton, A. D., "Practical Software Measurement: Measuring for Process Management and Improvement," Technical Report, SEI-97-HB-003, April 1997.

Girerd, A., Brenize, M., Chase, J., Chueng C., Faust A., Ferris, D., Jilla C. D., Makins B. J., Munson, J., Proulx, G., Rea, J., Saleh, J., Shchmidt, P., Steare, D., Thomas, S., and Wood, B., "Conceptual Operations Design Evaluator (CODE): Software and Methodology Manual," Optimization Methods for Space Operations Class Report, 1999.

Jilla, C.D., and Miller, D.W., "Separated Spacecraft Interferometry System Architecture Design and Optimization on the Basis of a Cost Per Function Metric," *Proceedings of the 3rd International Symposium on Reducing the Cost of Spacecraft Ground Systems and Operations*, MP-3, Tainan, Taiwan, March 1999.

Jilla, C.D., Sedwick, R.J., and Miller, D.W., "Application of Multidisciplinary Design Optimization Techniques to Distributed Satellite Systems," *Proceedings of the AIAA 1999 Space Technology Conference*, Paper AIAA-99-4632, September 1999.

Miller, D. W., Curtis, A., de Weck, O., Frazzoli, E., Girerd, A., Hacker, T., Jilla, C. D., Kong, E. M., Makins, B. J., and Pak, S., "Architecting the Search for Terrestrial Planets and Related Origins (ASTRO)," *Proceedings of the SPIE UV Optical, and IR Space Telescopes and Instruments Conference*, Paper 4013-74, SPIE, Munich, Germany, 2000.

Monell, D. W. and Piland W. M., "Aerospace Systems Design in NASA's Collaborative Engineering Environment," *50th International Astronautical Congress*, October 1999.

Pahng, F., Bae, S., and Wallace, D., "A Web-based Collaborative Design Modeling Environment," *Proceedings of the Seventh IEEE International Workshops on Enabling Technologies; Infrastructure for Collaborative Enterprises Conference*, 1998.

Rogers, J. L., Salas, A. O., and Weston, R. P., "A Web-Based Monitoring System for Multidisciplinary Design Projects," AIAA-98-4706, 1998.

Sabbaghian, N., Eppinger, S., and Murman, E., "Product Development Process Capture and Display Using Web-Based Technologies," *Proceedings of the IEEE International Conference on Systems, Man, and Cybernetics*, 1998.

Shaw, G.B., "The Generalized Information Network Analysis Methodology for Distributed Satellite Systems," PhD Thesis. MIT Department of Aeronautics and Astronautics. 1998.

Shaw, G. B., Miller, D. W., and Hastings, D. E., "Development of the Quantitative Generalized Information Network Analysis (GINA) Methodology for Satellite Systems," accepted to the *AIAA Journal of Spacecraft and Rockets*, Aug. 1999.

Steward, D. V., *Systems Analysis and Management, Structure, Strategy and Design*. Petrocelli Books, Inc., New York / Princeton, 1981.

BIOGRAPHIES

Brian Makins is a research assistant in the MIT's Space Systems laboratory. Mr. Makins served on the ASTRO design team that implemented the Generalized Information Network Analysis approach to NASA's Terrestrial Planet Finder mission. Mr. Makins is currently on educational leave from Hughes Space and Communications, pursuing a Masters Degree in Aeronautics and Astronautics. His research interests include distributed satellite systems, optimization algorithms, software design techniques, and spacecraft operations design.

Dr. David Miller, Assistant Professor of Aeronautics and Astronautics at the Massachusetts Institute of Technology, is the Director of MIT's Space Systems Laboratory. Dr. Miller's research areas include distributed satellite systems, modular and multifunctional spacecraft design, and space-based interferometry. Dr. Miller has served as a co-principal investigator on several space flight projects, including the Middeck Active Control Experiment (STS 67) and the Middeck 0-G Dynamics Experiment (STS 48 and STS 62). Dr. Miller received his Doctor of Science degree in Aeronautics and Astronautics from the Massachusetts Institute of Technology.

A Web-Enabled, Collaborative Solution for Product Development: The Enterprise Process Analysis Toolkit for Affordability (*e*PATA)

Roger D. Moulder
Bruce R. Reed, Jr.
James Gregory Associates, Inc.
4615 Hilton Corporate Dr.
Columbus, OH 43232-4151

Abstract. The virtual enterprise is becoming a reality. With the advances in communication and computer technology, organizations now have the capability to conduct *real* business over the Internet. From weekly staff meetings to actual product design and services, it is now possible to sit in the comfort of your own office and collaborate with your colleagues electronically. These advances are especially advantageous to those companies involved in the design and manufacture of new products. The focus of this paper is to present the progress made in developing software tools to support the Air Force Research Laboratory's Science and Technology (S&T) Integrated Product and Process Development (IPPD) process. The IPPD process applies a systems engineering approach to the research and development phase of system design using modified six sigma methods to provide a measurable way to evaluate and decide among competing design approaches. This measurement-based approach involves an Integrated Product Team (IPT) comprising experts from every aspect of the project. They determine customer requirements and candidate technologies that may answer those requirements, then apply a series of metrics to analyze the technologies for performance, producibility, cost, schedule and risk tradeoffs to arrive at the best value design. Early research efforts indicated several tools would be needed to support the activities of the process. From requirements management to workflow, a suite of tools would provide program managers, scientists, engineers, cost analysts, etc. with the capability to effectively carry out their various duties in an integrated environment.

The enterprise version of PATA is appropriately named Enterprise PATA or *e*PATA. Implemented in JAVA, *e*PATA will run on any computer platform that provides an Internet connection and an appropriate Web browser. Besides such benefits as ease of maintenance and support, this type of implementation provides an enterprise capability for product development. That is, *e*PATA offers the capability to conduct systems engineering activities in a Web-enabled, virtual enterprise environment. By way of review, we first present the S&T IPPD Process background. Next, we cover the first iteration of the tools to support the process—PATA. Finally, we discuss *e*PATA, its architecture, and functionality.

BACKGROUND

Integrated Product and Process Development. In its quest to achieve more affordable weapon systems, the U. S. Air Force has researched and invested in Integrated Product and Process Development (IPPD). The research began in 1994 in a seminar hosted by the Air Force Materials Laboratory, other Air Force agencies, and thirty industry participants. The result of the seminar was a consensus that IPPD should be applied in the Science and Technology (S&T), or research and development, environment. The decision was thus made to see if IPPD, which had proven to be so successful in industry production, could indeed be beneficial in the research and development of new products. The result was the development of the S&T IPPD Process. (See Figure 1.)

At last year's INCOSE Symposium, Dr. James Brink of James Gregory Associates presented a paper entitled, "Managing Research and Development Projects: A Systems Engineering Approach in the Early Stages of Design." The basis of this presentation was that Integrated Product and Process Development (IPPD) could indeed be applied early, even in the initial stages of system design. In fact, the U. S. Air Force is implementing the Science and Technology (S&T) IPPD Process on many of its Advanced Technology Demonstration (ATD) programs. The presentation delineated the activities of the S&T IPPD process and introduced several tools (in differing stages of development) to support the process. Figure 1 shows the S&T IPPD Process Model as presented by Dr. Brink.

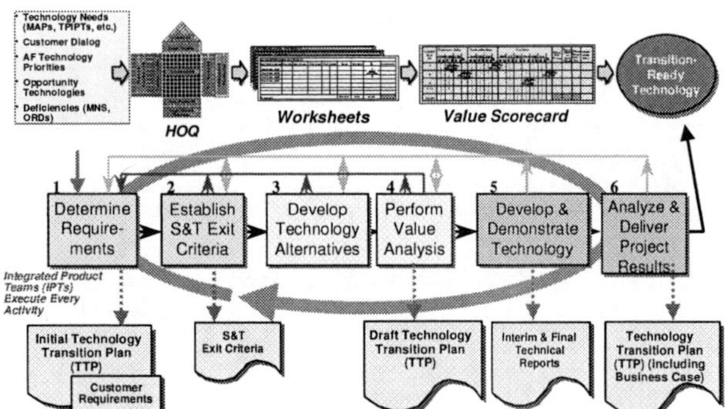

Figure 1. S&T IPPD Process Model

The six activities of the process are supported by several tools and methods indicated by the artifacts at the top of the figure. There are also several outputs of the process represented by the boxes at the bottom of the figure.

A central tenet of IPPD is that Integrated Product Teams (IPTs) perform all of the activities associated with the project. Often in business today, IPTs are formed to solve all kinds of problems including: 1. process definition, 2. process improvement, and 3. systems engineering.

Once an organization has a process in place and has formed IPTs to tackle a problem, tools and methods are needed to support the teams in successfully and efficiently accomplishing their tasks.

PATA

Tools and Methods. Research into tools and methods to support the S&T IPPD Process revealed that the unique requirements of the Air Force S&T environment required a set of tools and methods that were not commercially available. James Gregory Associates, working under U.S. Air Force sponsorship, thus researched and developed a suite of tools and methods to support the S&T IPPD Process. This suite of tools, the Process Analysis Toolkit for Affordability (PATA) has been used by several Air Force research programs over the past year and a half. The PATA supports IPTs by providing comprehensive data capture and analysis capability throughout the S&T IPPD Process.

The suite of tools in PATA is as follows:

- Requirements management
- Desirability curve generation
- Expert estimation
- Risk calculator
- Technology worksheets
- Scorecards

In combination, these tools give the user an end-to-end analysis capability for determining which technology alternatives will best answer customer requirements.

PATA offers the capability of capturing and analyzing customer requirements, defining and quantifying customers' satisfaction, or desirability indices for those requirements, measuring how well different technology alternatives satisfy requirements in terms of desirability, and the risk associated with meeting requirements. In essence, the PATA offers the user an integrated approach to conducting a value analysis during system design. Value Analysis is the process of quantitatively estimating the desirability, performance, producibility, cost, and risk of one or more technologies, processes or design concepts. The result is a *Value Scorecard* that contains values for all of these factors that are traceable back to the original requirements. The Value Scorecard gives the decision-maker a quantitative, informed way to compare and choose among competing solutions to meet customer needs.

The initial version of PATA was a stand-alone application implemented in Microsoft Excel using macros, Visual Basic, and Microsoft Access for data storage. This version of the PATA has been and is being used extensively in several Air Force programs as well as Navy, Army, and commercial projects. During the time that these programs have used the PATA, it has become increasingly clear that teams need a version of the tool that can be used in a distributed/dispersed environment. Further, the nature of IPPD and IPTs is such that the need for anytime/anyplace communication and collaboration is vital.

Collaboration. Collaboration is a process of participation through which people, groups and organizations work together to achieve desired results. In his book, *Shared Minds*, Michael Schrage describes collaboration as "the process of *shared creation*: two or more individuals with complementary skills interacting to create a shared understanding that none had previously possessed or could have come to on their own." Schrage continues that the goal of collaboration is the creation of value, not merely value as the sum of individual efforts but, more importantly, value born from the exponential product of the collective interactions among the collaborators. Collaboration describes a process of value creation that our traditional structure of communication and teamwork cannot achieve.

To achieve true collaboration, participants must be able to share ideas and information, resolve conflict, and reach consensus. These kinds of activities are a challenge even when people can meet face-to-face on a regular basis. In today's environment of dispersed teams, the challenges and difficulties of collaborating effectively are magnified. These challenges require both technical and organizational solutions. Managers must provide teams with the necessary tools to effectively share information and meet as needed. Recognizing that collaboration is necessary in implementing the S&T IPPD Process, the U.S. Air Force has invested in the research necessary to extend the capabilities of the PATA from the desktop to the Word Wide Web.

ENTERPRISE PROCESS ANALYSIS TOOLKIT FOR AFFORDABILITY (ePATA)

Motivation. Creating a design or a plan for a product requires that customer representatives, planners, designers, and other experts from many disciplines work together throughout the process. In today's virtual workplace, widely distributed teams are formed, often across enterprises. Keeping the customer involved throughout the design process and collecting and managing requirements and other technical information calls for a Web-enabled solution. All IPT members need to have an up-to-date view of a project, access to tools and data, and the capability to work at any time from their offices, homes, or hotel rooms.

PATA Enterprise (a.k.a. *e*PATA) was developed to meet these needs. *e*PATA (www.epata.com) is a Web-based, multi-user collaborative implementation of the single user PATA toolset. It utilizes a central database and delivers all the PATA tools over the Web with run-time generated graphics and real-time data. For example, customers can work with planners and engineers to specify and negotiate their needs from their own offices. Meanwhile, other IPT members can define technology approaches and gather and post performance, cost, and producibility data. Throughout a project, IPT members can watch the progress and impact of their own as well as others' inputs to the IPPD process through Web-based views and tools that are specific to each step of the S&T IPPD Process.

In Figure 1, notice that the S&T IPPD Process is iterative. Specifically, as a team investigates design alternatives and as more information becomes clear on how a technology performs against a set of requirements, and how much the estimated cost will be, the customer has the opportunity to redefine requirements in a tradeoff mode, illustrated by the radar charts in Figure 2[1]. This, in turn, will likely drive

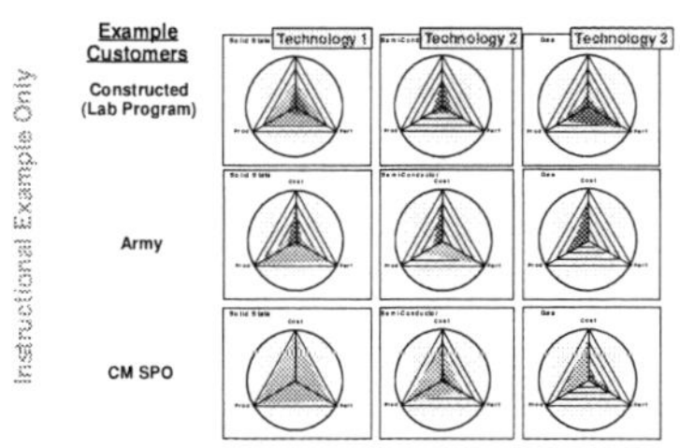

Figure 2. Balancing Customer Tradeoffs

[1] These charts are generated from the Value Scorecard and represent how alternative solutions will meet customer requirements in terms of desirability (green) and risk (red).

changes in design. As the process is iterated, *e*PATA provides the analysis tools for performing individual tasks and is also the central repository for all decisions and actions taken in the IPPD process.

Platform Independence. IPT members travel frequently and often have meetings or telecons in which they need to work on project data. IPT members, may include users of Windows, Macintosh, and Unix machines. *e*PATA runs in standard Web browsers on all platforms. Each IPPD project's data resides in a central database so the IPT members can simply enter a URL in their favorite browsers, launch *e*PATA, and access shared tools and data. Hosting the application on a central Web server has the additional benefit of providing the latest version of the tools without the overhead of local installation. Software and databases can be migrated in synchronization without burdening the user. The only system requirements for running *e*PATA are a Web connection and a browser.

Real-time Collaboration and Centralized Data. *e*PATA supports synchronization of shared data so that multiple team members can work on an IPPD project at the same time. In the IPPD process, the same data can be used or viewed at different steps in the process. Much of the data is interdependent so that any change to an element can propagate changes in values throughout the process. *e*PATA has a unique solution to synchronizing data and views across all its tools simultaneously. While other tools available on the Web allow multiple users to run the same application synchronizing the same display across browsers, *e*PATA synchronizes *data and multiple applications*. *e*PATA uses a central database as the permanent repository for data and keeps track of which tools are being used and which data is being used where. Any change to a data element in a browser client is relayed to other *e*PATA tools and other clients that are using the data. Each client receives notice and processes the data

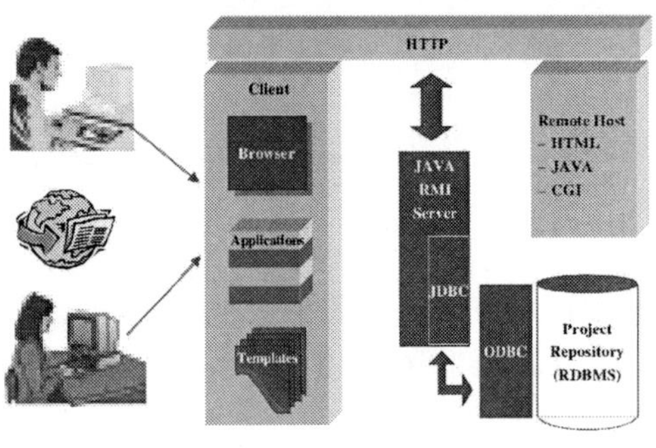

Figure 3. ePATA Architecture

change in its own context. Figure 3 shows the *e*PATA architecture.

For example: A project manager, a customer, and a design engineer are all working in *e*PATA at the same time. The project manager and the customer are working together, although separated physically across the Web. Each is using the Requirements Matrix, Figure 4, and desirability curves, Figure 5, tools. They discuss the relative desirability of values achieved near but not exactly on the target objective. During their exploration of objectives and acceptable variations around the objective (thresholds), each person can change discrete values in the matrix or drag the corresponding set points on the analysis curve to indicate new relationships. Any change in either tool will be reflected to the other users' tools in real time. A change in the matrix can cause the curve to redraw or dragging a set point in the curve can cause a field in the matrix to update.

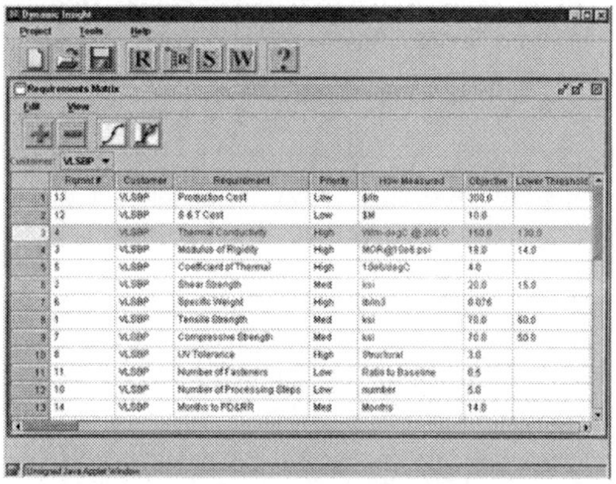

Figure 4. Requirements Matrix and Tree

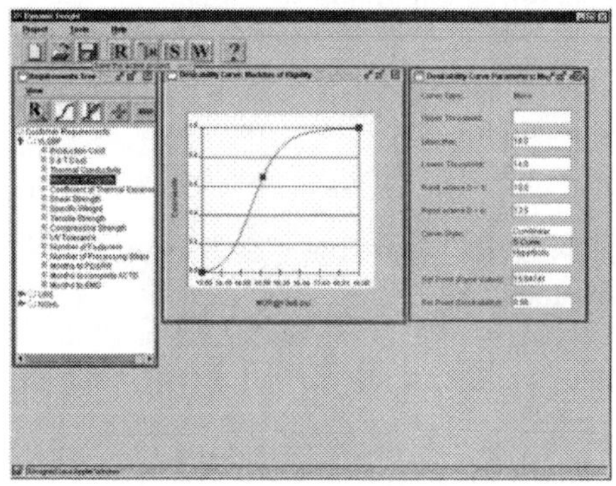

Figure 5. Desirability Curve

While the above is going on, a design engineer has entered the results of preliminary testing for some performance criteria. When the information is entered, specifically, the mean value achieved along with standard deviation, the tool performs a risk analysis using the new data along with the requirements data to indicate the risk of failing to stay within the customers' parameters. When the customer and project manager make changes to a requirement, and while they are in collaborative mode, the change will propagate to the engineer's worksheet, Figure 6. Information and changes made to the matrices or worksheets is propagated to the Value Scorecard, Figure 7.

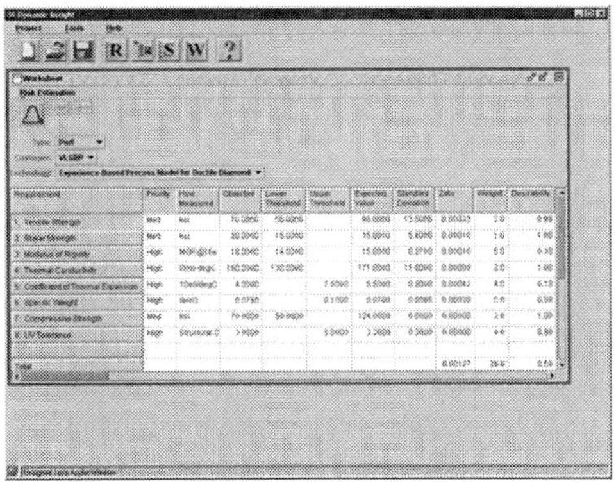

Figure 6. Worksheet

Modes of Collaboration. The *e*PATA tools support multiple modes of usage with respect to collaboration. When the users launch the toolset, they are presented with a menu of collaboration options. Users can choose to run in read-only mode, in which they will be able to see all data, including dynamic

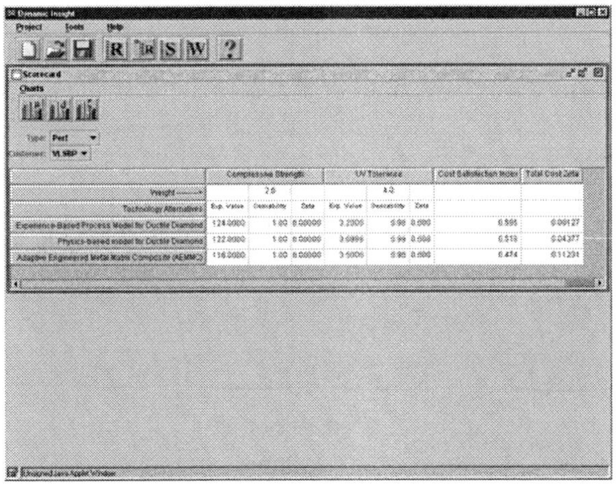

Figure 7. Value Scorecard

changes that are occurring elsewhere, but will not be able to modify anything. They can choose to start in 'sandbox' mode, in which they can run any analysis and change data, but not save any. At the other extreme, a user can choose to launch as the only person who can save changes. Finally, users can start in collaborative mode that allows others to see what they are doing and all have privileges to save changes. The central *e*PATA server keeps track of what modes are already running and presents the current options to new users at login time.

Data Checkin and Checkout. There are always occasions when IPT members may want to work off-line, that is, in local mode using the original PATA Excel tool. Offline mode is made possible via a checkin-checkout mechanism provided for the tools. With the checkin-checkout tool, users can download the *e*PATA central database to their local platforms, run the PATA Excel tool on it, and then upload the database to the central server. When the central database is checked out for local use, the *e*PATA tool will not allow saves to the database, but will allow read-only and sandbox modes.

*e*PATA provides control over the granularity of checkout and locking. An IPPD project is as a set of system/subsystems in which related data can be aggregated into individual units that can be locked for write access while other systems are left free for all other modes of access. In this model, individual subsystems can be checked out for use with the local PATA tool while other distributed IPT members can access the remaining IPPD data through *e*PATA.

Security and Web-based Project Rooms. Because IPTs are composed of multiple companies whose data are managed on a central server, security is a high priority for ensuring trust and cooperation among members and their companies. Security has been addressed at multiple levels to satisfy a wide range of requirements. In addition to the *e*PATA tool and database, IPTs have other data and documents they wish to share securely. Each IPPD project team has its own 'project room' where it can access and manage its own tools and data, separate from other IPTs who may be using the same server. The IPPD project room is a Web-based interface to a secure area behind a firewall, where a unified presentation of tools and data is given to the user. The project rooms provide tools to share data with other team members and provide encrypted transport for uploading and downloading data as well as when running *e*PATA.

Firewalls are part of doing business over the Web, so the *e*PATA architecture is designed to detect the presence of firewalls at either or both the server and client locations and adjust transport protocols to comply with the intended security arrangements.

Web-Based Workflow Coordination. The project management function together with a workflow tool is used to assign task responsibilities to individual users and coordinate the sequence of execution. In this paradigm, the project manager has authority to assign responsibility for units of work or areas of responsibility, to a specific team member. Units of work that require expertise in a particular domain can be given exclusively to the persons who have been brought onto the team for just that reason.

Coupled with the ability to checkout or lock subsystems, the project manager can divide portions of the IPPD project into units of concurrent tasks.

Given the complexity of some projects and the distributed nature of the work, it is often difficult to determine what to do next. To meet this challenge of coordinating the order in which work gets done, as well as assist each individual IPT member in determining what work can or needs to be done, a workflow tool is layered on top of the current tools and database. With a workflow tool, the dependencies between units of work and data are designated and then the tool automatically updates work lists as work is completed. Each team member has an individualized work list that is automatically updated as other team members complete their work.

Architecture. The *e*PATA Architecture uses a combination of advanced Web technologies and new Internet techniques developed at James Gregory Associates to achieve real time collaboration across multiple platform types, Unix, Microsoft Windows and Macintoshes, and multiple firewalls. The software is implemented in Sun Microsystems standard Java. It uses Sun's advanced graphics library, Java Swing, that provides for complex browser-based dynamic rendering of line graphs, bar charts, trees, spreadsheets, and radar charts.

All clients dynamically load the *e*PATA code in the form of Java applets from a central Web server. Sun's Java applet technology implements the highest form of security available over the Web, ensuring that the downloaded code cannot access any system resources outside the browser. This means that the *e*PATA applet cannot read or write to the local user's disk, cannot start any local applications without the permission of the user, and cannot read system variables outside the browser environment. The code and data transmitted between the client browser and remote server is 128 bit encrypted running over an automated https encryption service.

All end users access data from a shared remote central database using the Java Remote Method Invocation (RMI) technology. The Java client running in the browser makes the Java RMI call to a central *e*PATA RMI server running on the Web server's host. The *e*PATA server receives data requests in the form of Java calls and converts them to JDBC/ODBC calls, which then execute against a co-located database server. To date, the *e*PATA server runs against Oracle and Access databases, and is currently being ported to additional databases. See Figure 3. The *e*PATA Architecture.

Enterprisation is achieved architecturally by a reflection mechanism developed by JGA. The Reflection Manager keeps all client platforms synchronized by tracking changes in each client and relaying the event change to all other active clients. Because firewalls set at a high level of security will only allow http calls and will close off Java RMI calls, another unique solution was called for in the *e*PATA architecture. ePATA uses an agent technology to transmit an RMI call in the standard http format. The host sever activates the agent and allows it to execute and return to the client inside the https security protocols.

The Scalability of the *e*PATA architecture is enhanced by the *e*PATA RMI architecture in two ways. First, unlike standard html interfaces which do all application processing and screen formatting at the server end, the *e*PATA client does full application and graphics processing. This greatly reduces the load on the central server and provides much better performance in the browser implemented in a much more extensible and maintainable language.

The second advantage is that data exchanges between the client and remote server are done in Java RMI rather than SQL or ODBC. The actual database access is performed by the *e*PATA server that is co-located with the database at the central host site and large amounts of data requiring many complex fetches are all done locally with the results returned over the Web in a continuous stream from the *e*PATA server.

SUMMARY

The U.S. Air Force-sponsored research into providing a collaborative environment for product development in the S&T arena has produced a suite of tools. Evolving from a stand-alone prototype to a Web-enabled application, *e*PATA offers many benefits and capabilities to the S&T program manager and IPT members. Chief among these benefits is the ability to conduct analyses from any computer platform that has an Internet connection and an appropriate Web browser. *e*PATA is commercially available, and more information can be found at www.epata.com.

REFERENCES

Brink, J.R., G.D. Peisert, and C. Ventresca, Managing Research and Development Projects: A Systems Engineering Approach to the Early Stages of Design. Proceedings of the INCOSE Ninth Annual International Symposium, 1999, Brighton, England.

Brink, J.R. and G.D. Peisert, S&T Affordability Toolkit. Presented at the 1999 Conference of the American Institute of Aeronautics and Astronautics, 27–30 September, 1999, Albuquerque, NM.

Brink, J.R. and G.D. Peisert. IPPD for S&T Quick Reference: Toward More Affordable Defense Technology. James Gregory Associates, 1998.

Schrage, Michael. Shared Minds: The New Technologies of Collaboration. New York: Random House, 1990.

BIOGRAPHIES

Roger D. Moulder, Senior Operations Research Analyst for James Gregory Associates consults with Air Force and Navy Affordability programs, as well as assists industry in their implementation of Integrated Product and Process Development and use of tools for a systems engineering approach to Affordability. Mr. Moulder also serves as an instructor for the JGA training courses: *Affordability: An Introduction* and *Affordable Technology through Integrated Product & Process Development (AT/IPPD) for S&T.*

Mr. Moulder has over 27 years' experience in software development, modeling and simulation, and statistical analysis. Following his 21 years of Air Force active duty, he became a Principal Research Scientist with Battelle Memorial Institute where he managed several R&D efforts in the Air Force's Armstrong Laboratory including investigating tools and methods to support implementation of the Air Force S&T IPPD Processes. He was a Computer Research Simulation Scientist in the Avionics Laboratory where he developed software for such programs as the Cruise Missile Advanced Guidance system and Low Altitude Navigation and Targeting Infrared for Night (LANTIRN). He holds a B.S. in Computer Science from the University of Kentucky and an M.S. in Operations Research from the Air Force Institute of Technology.

Bruce R. Reed, Jr. is James Gregory Associates' vice president for Internet technologies. He leads a team of programmers and systems engineers in developing the software to support systems engineering and collaboration over the World Wide Web with a focus on IPPD to achieve Affordability. He is currently helping users integrate *e*PATA, the Enterprise Process Analysis Toolkit for Affordability.

Formerly at Universal Energy Systems, Mr. Reed was Lead Designer and Programmer for the Internet-enabling KI Shell workflow product. Mr. Reed also was a Principal Research Scientist at Battelle Memorial Institute, where he designed and developed artificial intelligence applications and tools. As a Scientific Programmer/Analyst for Goodyear Aerospace Corp., he developed parallel processing applications of artificial intelligence, was Project Engineer for a contract to demonstrate a military expert system running on a parallel processor, and developed software to cross-compile VAX-based knowledge applications to a parallel architecture. He holds a B.A. in mathematics from the University of Akron and an M.S. in Computer Science from Kent State University.

Progress towards Systems Modelling for the Extended Enterprise

P.F.Sims, A.Epifanie, G.Fitzgerald, J.Lott, D.Miles, I.Plastow, C.Slack
BAE SYSTEMS
New Filton House
Filton
Bristol
BS99 7AR

Abstract. The paper will describe the Airbus Integrated Modelling Environment (AIME) developed at BAE SYSTEMS. The AIME provides the ability to produce a single integrated system simulation using a number of different specialist modelling tools. In an AIME based model for the A340-600 Aircraft, Flowmaster® is used to accurately predict the fluid mechanical behaviour of the fuel system, Simulink® to filter and process fuel probe signals and accurately gauge tank quantities, and Statemate® to simulate the control functionality. The user can interact with all of these tools at any point in time while running a dynamic simulation of overall system behaviour.

The open nature of the AIME is allowing the Airbus extended enterprise to integrate a Parker Aerospace developed model of fluid mechanical behaviour with the British Aerospace developed Control and Indication models. Integration of the models allows the companies to reach a common understanding of the target system's required functionality.

INTRODUCTION

Modelling now plays an important role in the development of complex systems in the aerospace industry. The increasing cost of flight, ground and rig-specific tests means that there is a need for increased confidence in system maturity as early as possible in the development lifecycle. Furthermore, a lack of maturity at the entry into service of an aircraft can have critical implications for the profitability of that project. The fuel systems department at British Aerospace has been developing a modelling capability to contribute to aircraft maturity on a number of related themes including; validation of functional requirements; identification of testing scenrios and strategies; and investigation of different software architectures.

A key factor in the move to increased modelling capability to support maturity was the requirement to create and manipulate models which integrated domains (e.g. fluid mechanics and control and indication) that have been modelled separately up to that point. This integration should also be achievable using the "best in class" commercially available tools for each of the sub-models.

A survey of commercially available products revealed that most "integration facilities" offered within existing tools were (understandably) geared towards an application programming interface for other tools to use in order to communicate input to that particular, "lead" tool. More complete interfaces involving a mutual exchange of information between tools was available but these were geared to specific pairwise interactions. One product which did aim towards a more open environment couldn't achieve the basic performance requirements at that time. Hence the decsion was taken to generate an in-house capability under the auspices of the United Kingdom Department of Trade and Industry's **P**latform **A**pplications for **C**ommercial Aircraft **T**ransportation **S**ystems for the **21**st Century (PACTS21) Fuel System Studies project. The AIME is one result from work carried out on that project.

INFLUENCE OF STANDARDS ON AIME

Three key technologies affected the development of the AIME:

Distributed Simulation Architectures – Distributed simulation architecture standards propose means of inter-connecting a number of sub-models to form a complete model that may be simulated. Data exchange between the simulation models, during a simulation execution, consists of simulated events and/or associated data and control events necessary to co-ordinate the sub-models. The standards may additionally specify off-line data exchanges that are necessary for configuration and similar purposes. Standards considered for the AIME included:

- DIS (Distributed Simulation Architecture) the mature DOD standard for real time simulation (DIS, 1999)
- ALSP (Aggregate Level Simulation Protocol) the mature DOD standard to link analytical and training simulations (ALSP, 2000)
- HLA (High Level Architecture) a DOD standard using the best ideas from DIS and ALSP (HLA, 1999)
- OMF (Open Modelling Forum) developed to complex digital IC models (OMF, 1999).

Design Data Representation - Standards in this category are concerned with representation of design data, i.e. products of the systems development process, in standard format. This has many benefits such as data portability and other improved quality factors.

- SEDRES (Systems Engineering Data Representation and Exchange Standardisation) The SEDRES project is working to provide a Systems Engineering meta-model based on the STEP standard (SEDRES, 1997)
- CDIF (CASE Data Exchange Format) a standard information meta-model for design data transfers between CASE (Computer Aided Software Engineering) tools (CDIF,
- Modelica is a general purpose language for representing models of systems (Modelica, 1999)

Client Sever Development – These standards provide the supporting infrastructure upon which the other categories of standards are used.

- ToolTalk provides information exchange between applications from different developers but is limited to UNIX applications (Tooltalk, 1995).
- CORBA (Common Object Request Broker Architecture) a standard for distributed applications over a client-server networks through an object request broker (ORB) (CORBA, 2000).

Of the types of standards considered the distributed simulation architectures were most appropriate for consideration in the development of AIME. The project developed its own, simplified design data representation, but it is believed that the standards mentioned above will eventually provide meta-models for the application of AIME once developed. The current implementation of AIME works only on UNIX and uses sockets for communication.

AIME ARCHITECTURE

The Airbus Integrated Modelling Environment (AIME) allows the linking a number of individual sub-models to form a unified model.

The architecture of the AIME is based around the concept of a central server that receives from and distributes packets of information to a number of modelling packages (Figure 1). The server forms the hub through which all data must pass. Each package runs as a separate process and communicates with the

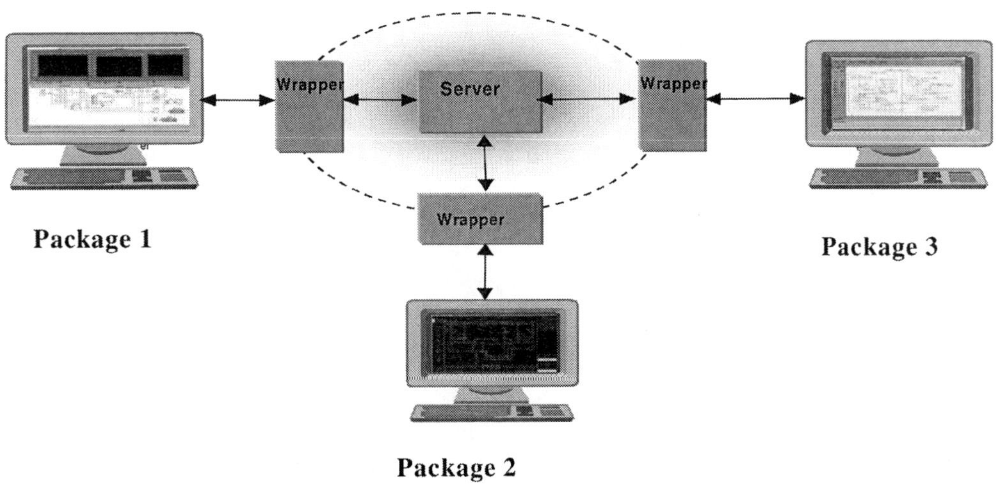

Figure 1. AIME Conceptual Architecture

server via a "wrapper". The server is the central core of the interface, it controls the wrappers, packages and data flows during each simulation. It interpolates data (when necessary) from each package, and it also manages the overall control of the process with respect to a central simulation clock. The wrappers control the individual packages which make up the intergated model. This primarily involves starting and ending the packages in line with instructions from the server, and sending to and receiving input data from the server as required. This central server only routes messages and knows nothing about the modelling data being transmitted. Since the AIME system is made up of a number of communicating processes, it is possible to distribute the processing load over a number of computers using a standard Ethernet as the physical connection medium.

Fundamental performance requirements meant that the AIME could not run with all its associated models on a single processing platform. It has been developed to run on a network of UNIX workstations using TCP/IP as the communication protocol between machines. UNIX sockets have then been used on top of this basic architecture to effect point-to-point communications between processes running on different machines. An application specific protocol has then been designed to communicate across the stream-based sockets to control the behaviour of the individual modelling packages via a defined interface. This interface is known as the AIME Internal interface and is implemented as a set of C language function calls; this defines the syntax of the interface. The "wrapper" for an individual package is then responsible for implementing the semantics of the interface by interacting with that package. The way this is achieved varies from package to package depending on the capabilities and programmability of the package.

A simulation that is required to interact with an external system (be it man or machine) needs to be capable of processing various inputs and outputting the required results in a time frame that does not interfere with the expected operation of that system. As long as this premise is adhered to, the simulation can perform its various functions asynchronous to any other external influences.

The speed of and ability to time synchronise a simulation depends to a great extent on the environment in which it is running. There are other factors that influence these properties, such as processing speed and algorithmic efficiency. However these are constraints on the environment rather than designed-in features.

For each variation of application, the concept of time within the simulation was required to be handled in different ways. These differing requirements can be grouped into three separate categories; Batch Mode, Man in the Loop and Hardware in the Loop. Each of these represents increasing demands on the timing requirements of the model.

Batch Mode. The only timing requirement for batch mode is that the order in which the various sub-systems should execute is set in a predefined and predetermined sequential fashion. The simulation time in the computer program (as it is running) is not related to the real world time.

Man in the Loop. Man-in-the-loop simulations are used for many applications including system design, validating system requirements, operator training. The simulation includes various interface panels that may be exercised by a human operator. The user may try out different test scenarios and experience and respond to the resultant outputs. The real-time aspects of such applications are more stringent than that for Batch Processing, but not as restrictive as for hardware-in-the-loop simulations. Human action is not precisely defined, and is not deterministic. As long as the simulation provides outputs and responds to stimuli in a time frame that is broadly acceptable to the operator, further precision or accuracy is not required. This may allow for a higher accuracy of calculated results as the integration algorithms used are allowed to stretch the base time frame (within reason).

Hardware-in-the-Loop. When a simulation is designed to interact with an external piece of hardware, it is imperative that there should be no time frame jitter. The simulation should provide an environment such that the hardware that is being exercised acts and reacts as if it was installed in the system it was designed for. The only way to ensure this is for the simulation algorithms to utilise fixed step integration methods. This may decrease the accuracy of the simulation, and great care must be taken to ensure that the fixed time frame that is used are faster than the system dynamics of the hardware.

In order that the AIME achieves these three different timing categories, and that a real-time simulation is able to run in a deterministic and repeatable fashion, the simulation and algorithmic processing must be guaranteed to complete in each time frame. The individual components of the AIME run with fixed time step integration algorithms. The fixed time frame can also be set to be compatible with the time frame of any hardware it is interfaced to. The various simulations that comprise an implementation under the AIME run synchronously under the control of a real-time executive that does not rely on operating system functionality. In addition, system flexibility is significantly increased through use of dynamic binding

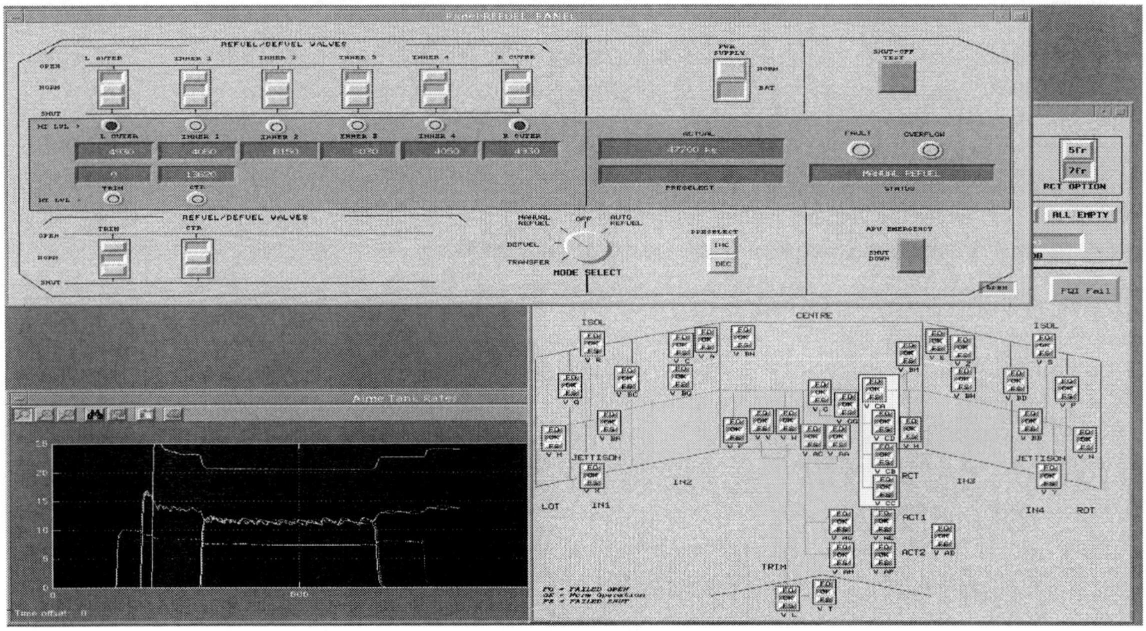

Figure 2. Example of the AIME running an A340-600 Refuel Model

between the executive and the simulation software modules. It should be noted that as the link from each tool to the server is a discrete, scheduled data transfer, then none of the interfaces between the sub-models can model continuous behaviour (e.g. the simulation may have to wait whilst a particular sub-model achieves convergence). As a consequence, the simulation parameters which are set by the server and transferred to the tools must specify a discrete solver.

AN IMPLEMENTATION FOR AIRCRAFT REFUEL

The AIME has been used to construct an integrated model of an A340-600 type fuel system with at least seven fuel tanks and including refuel, defuel and ground transfer capability. A fluid model has been constructed using Flowmaster, including pressure source and the functions of all of the components which transmit the fluid. A model of the fuel management system using Simulink filters and processes fuel probe signals and accurately gauges tank quantities. It also controls all the pumps and valves in accordance with the required functionality set by the Human Computer Interface (HCI). The HCI has been modelled using Statemate to reflect the expected look and feel of the on-aircraft system. The AIME allows some 112 different inputs and outputs to be communicated between the different sub-models at each simulation time step. None of the fidelity or functionality of the individual models is compromised by including them in AIME and so features such as the data display offered by Simulink can be used to provide additional debugging and system monitoring functionality. Figure 2 shows a typical example of the screen when the model is running. The Refuel Panel at the top is used for setting valves and overall functional targets, a environment panel to the right is used for setting failure cases, the fuel density and other parameters, and an example of a Simulink generated graph of flow rates is shown in the bottom left. The integrated model has been shown to customer focus groups allowing them to contribute directly to system design in a timely manner and before detailed design has been completed

As indicated above, Hardware in the loop was a key consideration when developing the AIME and Figure 3 shows how the AIME was interfaced to a Hardware set up to allow combined Simulation/Hardware in the loop capability with a Remote Data Concentrator (RDC) providing input data such as the Fuel Quantity in one or more tanks. The collection of the data from the ARINC bus was treated as a uni-directional application with a wrapper sending the data on to the AIME Server for subsequent use.

MODELLING IN THE EXTENDED ENTERPRISE

The most recent use of the AIME has been to replace the Flowmaster fluid model with one generated by BAE

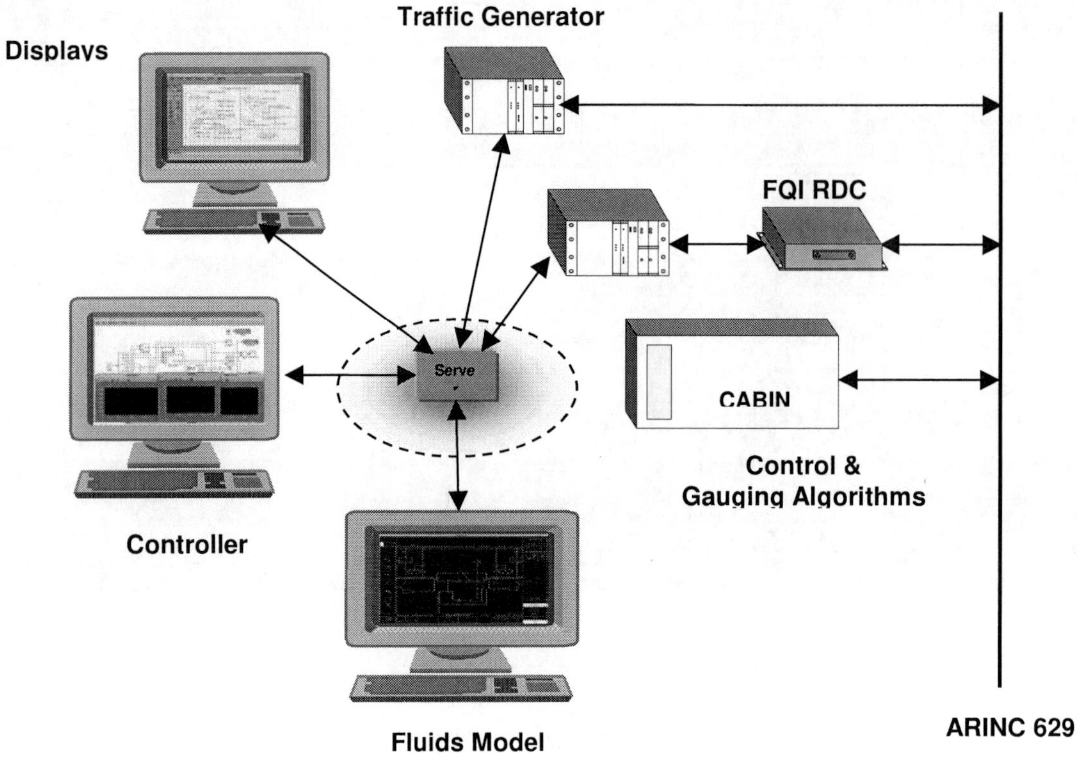

Figure 3. AIME with Hardware in the Loop

SYSTEMS' partner Parker Aerospace as part of developing the Fuel system for the A340-600. This is providing several further business benefits for the partnership. Using AIME has meant that the Parker model has been developed according to Parker's own local requirements for low level system design and implementation. Once it had reached a sufficient level of maturity then its integration with the independently developed BAE SYSTEMS Control and Indication models could then be considered. The only additional cost incurred at this stage is of developing a wrapper for the Parker fluid model to achieve this integration. Once achieved under AIME then the partnership can conduct testing to confirm that Parker has a clear understanding of the requirements that BAe has placed on it for sub-system design. It can implement and validate the interactions between different sub-systems, including the exchange of data to and from the components that each of the partners have separate responsibilities for.

DISCUSSION

The AIME is by no means original in concept. There have been, and are, a number of integrated environments developed to support systems modelling . However, its current strength lies in its simplicity and the aim of maintaining independence from any individual tool/package. The issue of different models representing the same data to different levels of fidelity has not yet been an issue. Each input wrapper tests the data for the format required by a model and translates the input accordingly, a process which allow makes it straightforward to experiment accordingly.

All integration to date has taken place through transferring models to a common Local Area Network at one of the sites, and work in the near future will include ensuring that the AIME can coordinate tools working across a heterogeneous processing environment However the nature of the applications carried out to date are such that the communications overhead is low, and the nature of the data being transferred is (in itself) relatively meaningless. This does suggest that an Internet based architecture could be used to assist model development and combination.

The AIME has shown real benefit in implementing

intergated models of the fuel system, both within BAE SYSTEMS, and across the extended enterprise.

REFERENCES

ALSP, www.alsp.ie.org/alsp, 2000

CDIF, www.eigroup.org/cdif/online.html, 1997

CORBA, www.omg.org, 2000.

DIS, www.arpa.mil, 2000

HLA, http://www.dmso.mil, 1999.

Modelica, "*Modelica – A unified OO Language for Physical Systems Modelling*", www.dynasim.se/modelica.html, 1999.

OMF, http://www.dmso.mil

SEDRES, "*Systems Engineering Application Protocol*", ISO New work Item Proposal, 1997

Tooltalk, www.unix.digial.com/faqs/publications/base_doc/DOCUMENTATION/V40D_HTML/TT_UGD , 1995

BIOGRAPHY

All of the authors are currently employed in BAE SYSTEMS working on the specification modelling and test of Fuel Systems for a range of aircraft.

System Design and Validation Through Modeling and Simulation

Dr. D.G. Garrett
Mr. Jeffrey Wolff
Mr. T.F. Johnson
Lockheed Martin Naval Electronics & Surveillance Systems-Eagan
3333 Pilot Knob Rd.
Eagan, MN 55121

ABSTRACT

This paper will discuss the methods and techniques required to successfully model and simulate modern avionics systems. Emphasis is placed on techniques to separate hardware and software models. The use of system model and simulations throughout the life cycle of a system is discussed. Several examples from the S-3B Ada program are cited.

INTRODUCTION

The use of modeling and simulation techniques is commonplace in many fields. The concept of model construction to describe natural phenomena is at least a century old—if not much older. The history of modeling and simulation applied to system design is much shorter—perhaps beginning in the 1960s with the introduction of such tools as Simula and Simscript. These event queue modeling tools, and their successors, have been very successfully applied to a wide range of problems. Any queuing theory student of the 1970s can attest to the application of these tools to the operation of McDonald's and Burger King. However, the inherent complexity and clumsiness of these tools have, until recently, limited the scope of their use. Complete system simulation models of complex computer-based systems such as modern avionics have been difficult to create or have been limited in scope.

Recent advances in computer power and particularly in event queue modeling tools have made it possible to apply these techniques to large complex systems. In this paper we describe recent advances in modeling techniques that enable us to model modern avionics systems in support of the system engineering effort. These techniques allow us to separate the specification of the software model from the hardware model, which greatly increases the flexibility of the system model. With this increased flexibility we are able to incorporate the use of the model in all phases of the system engineering process.

The emphasis of this paper is entirely on system performance modeling. System performance is all to often ignored in software and hardware design of modern system, particularly where hardware (computer) are off-the-shelf. There are many reasons for this state of affairs, including difficulty of timing and performance predictions in large complex computer based systems. This work attempts to address this issue.

The body of this paper roughly follows the form of a case study of the S-3B Ada program. In addition, we will relate our experience on several other similar projects. Emphasis will be placed on the new techniques developed to separate the specification of the software and the hardware models. Also the roll of the simulation models in the overall system engineering process will be described and discussed in some detail.

DEFINING THE MODELING REQUIREMENTS

Before embarking on the construction of a system model, the expectations for modeling effort should be well understood. In other words the model requirements should be defined. In the context of large avionics systems, the system model development should be driven by system engineering questions. The overall goals of a well-executed system engineering program are to answer fundamental engineering questions about the system, and to use these answers to guide the system design and development. To ensure that a system modeling effort is a mainstream portion system engineering effort it must be directed towards the fundamental system engineering problems.

The goal of S-3B Ada project was to replace the existing mission avionics on the S-3B aircraft with new computing hardware and software. The overall purpose of the replacement program was to extend the life of the aircraft and provide sufficient platform capability to incorporate new sensors and weapons. Much of the hardware design in this program was dictated by existing systems components in the aircraft. The modeling and system engineering effort therefore was directed at the processing engines and the software. The major questions the modeling and simulation effort needed to answer are shown in Table 1.

The questions in Table 1 are typical of those asked in the early stages of a system engineering effort.

1	Can three 68030 processors provide sufficient processing power to handle the computing load?
2	How should the software be distributed among the processor to handle the demand load (i.e., operator entry driven load)?
3	How much will 68060 processors improve system performance?
4	Can two 68060s provide sufficient processing power to handle the computing load?

Table 1: Sample of Modeling Questions from the S-3B Ada Program

Although the questions communicate the system engineering problems, they must be refined at least one more level before they can be used as a basis for developing the modeling requirements. The refinement process essentially combines the global questions asked in Table 1 with system requirements. Essentially the qualitative questions in Table 1 are transformed into quantitative questions as shown in Table 2. This is the usual system engineering methodology and leads to a set of answerable questions that reflect the program or project requirements.

In a more traditional system engineering process, i.e., one not using modeling and simulation, the questions in Table 2 would be answered using some other form of analysis. Modeling and simulation are not a replacement for these techniques: rather they are intended to supplement and extend the analysis, particularly in cases where the system is either too large or too complex to easily apply more traditional methodologies. The general system engineering process uses the answers to these questions to guide the system design process. This process of course leads to yet another level of questions, which are used to further refine the system design. The introduction of modeling and simulation into this process should not change the fundamental process. Rather, the modeling and simulation capability should improve the accuracy of the analysis and extend the details of the analysis to a level beyond that which can be reached with more traditional techniques.

An important consideration when incorporating a modeling process into the overall system engineering process is: "Who is going to construct the model, run the simulations and analyze the results?" Often the modeling and simulation effort is "added onto" the system engineering effort. That is, the modeling effort is handed over to a separate individual within the system engineering team or, even more often, to a specialized department. Given that the modeling and simulation effort is intended to provide information and analysis results to guide the system engineering team, it is very important that the system engineering team be intimately involved in the construction of the models as well as the analysis of the simulation results. Equally critical is that the models are sufficiently flexible and that the simulation is sufficiently efficient so that the results can be obtained within the time frame needed by the system engineering team. Highly accurate results from a model are of no value or use if it is too late to affect design decisions made by the system engineering team.

1. Can three 68030 processors provide sufficient processing power to handle the computing load?	Is the processor loading less than 50%?
	Is the worst case response time for a sonobuoy launch less than X msec?
	What is the system response times when one processor has failed?
2. How should software be distributed among the processor to handle demand load (i.e., operator entry driven load)?	Where are the performance bottlenecks?
	What is the best allocation of software and hardware?
	What is the effect of the "demand" (operator driven) software?
3. How much will 68060 processors improve system performance?	What is the system response time with 68060 processors (versus 68030s)?
4. Can two 68060 provide sufficient processing powers to handle the computing load?	Is the processor loading less than 50%?
	Is the worst case response time for a sonobuoy launch less than X msec?
	What is the system response time when one processor has failed?
	What is the difference in the best allocation of software to the hardware with 2 versus 3 processors?

Table 2: Sample of the Refined Modeling Questions from the S-3B Ada Program

DESIGNING THE MODEL

Once the system engineering team has developed modeling requirements, a system model can be designed. This step is perhaps one of the more critical in the overall process. Simulations often fail simply because the model was not designed to answer the expected or required questions. Simply put, the model fails if it does not meet the requirements of the system engineering effort. There are perhaps two mistakes that are often made at the outset of this phase of the modeling effort. First and foremost is the creation of a model that is inconsistent in its resolution or detail. Often, hardware models will contain tremendous detail, whereas the software portion of the model will be glossed over, or vice versa. Similarly, a model is often constructed with either too much or too little time resolution to answer the system engineering questions for which it is being developed. Therefore, the first and most important step in model design is determining the model's resolution. In the S-3B system, response time questions require answers with resolutions that are on the order of 2 to 4 milliseconds. This is driven by the system's requirements of response times on the order of 40 to 60 milliseconds for several critical functions (see Table 2). If the model is going to answer questions regarding these critical system response times, it is necessary to use a model resolution at least an order of magnitude smaller. Previous generation modeling and simulation tools often led to a model which could not be constructed within the time frame required. However, the latest generation modeling tools provide a sufficiently rich and useable environment. This makes it quite possible to develop very detailed models, with very small time resolution, and within a very short schedule period.

The issue of model flexibility is almost as important as the resolution issues. In order for a model to be useful in the system engineering process, it also must be sufficiently flexible to support system trade studies. This means that the model must be sufficiently flexible to support trade-off studies of both the hardware and software architectures. This is clear in the S-3B example. Here it is necessary to examine the issues of the number of processors, the performance of processors, and the allocation or distribution of the software within those processors. In this particular example the range of the hardware architecture trade-offs is very much limited by the particular nature of this program. However, in general it is necessary to have almost equal flexibility in changing the hardware as it is for the software architecture.

The key to providing this flexibility in a system model lies in the ability to separate the specification of the hardware model from that of the software model. Virtually all of the modern event queue simulation tools provide a combination of block diagram and finite state machine representations of the model. This view of a system lends itself particular well to modeling the hardware functionality of the system. It is also possible to construct models of the software using these paradigms. This approach leads to a system model, which in a single set of hierarchical block diagrams and finite state machines represents the entire functionality of the hardware and software system. If it is necessary to change the hardware model to explore multiple architectures, it also might be necessary to modify the software model. This is true because the hardware and software models become intertwined when combined into a single block diagram.

A desirable solution to this problem is to separate the hardware and software model specifications. Figure 1 depicts an example of how the authors have accomplished this separation. The hardware is specified in a BONeS block diagram using traditional event queue simulation techniques. The system functional flow, specified separately, really determines the functionality of the system. It includes the software functionality and both sequencing and initiation of the hardware activities dictated or specified by the software. In Figure 1 the system consists of two peripheral devices (a radar and a display screen) connected through I/O boards to a general-purpose computer. A portion of the functional flow for this small system is also shown in the form of a flowchart in Figure 1. In this example the radar initiates a message every 50 milliseconds. When the processor receives a message it will initiate a processing task (in the computer). Therefore, the radar message timing and generation falls into the functional flow of the system and not into the hardware specification. The sequence events shown in the flowchart are those required to conduct the message from the radar into the CPU.

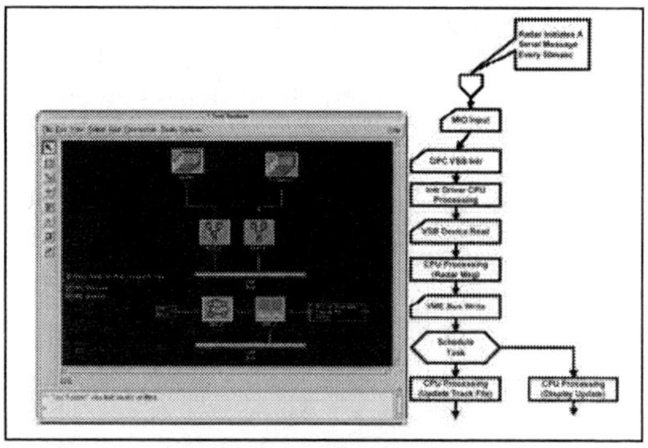

Figure 1: Illustration of Separate Software Hardware Models

The process steps in Figure 1 are shown with rectangles to indicate CPU processing. Those steps depicted by rectangles with clipped corners represent hardware activities necessary to accomplish the flow. The diamond-shaped steps represent a task in the software of the system. After the radar messages are received and "pre-processed" two software tasks are scheduled (one representing updating of a track file, and the other representing a display update). The example discussed here reveals a small portion of the scripting capability of this model. Additional functions are included to model a wide range of modern software functionality, including rendezvous, blocking semaphores, and many others.

This separation of hardware and software models is accomplished by building onto the existing scripting capability of the BONeS event queue simulation tool. Similar capabilities exist in many event queue simulation tools. BONeS was chosen largely because of its rich built-in hardware library as well as its ease-of-use and flexibility. Essentially, the scripting capability allows a simulation model to read a file at simulation initialization time. The scripting file contains the definition of the specific model operations to be performed during simulation. This includes such information as system resource loading and timing. In the S-3B example, this is represented by the flowchart to the right side of Figure 1. The process to incorporate the scripting information into the simulation is detailed in Figure 2.

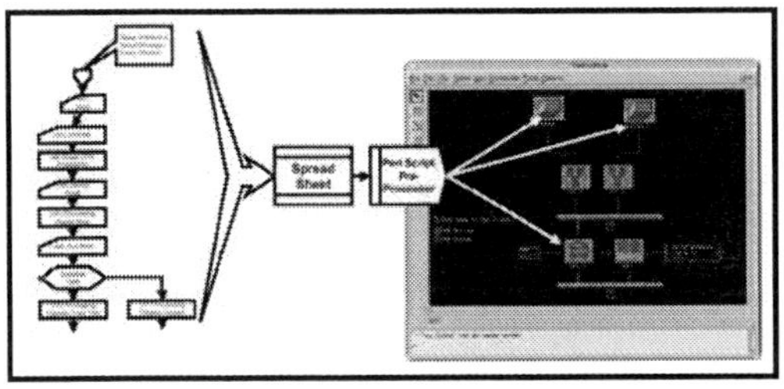

Figure 2: Modeling Process Diagram

The functional flow is captured in a spreadsheet. A Perl script converts them into files that can be read by the hardware model separately defined as a BONeS block diagram.

As depicted in Figure 2, the system's functional flow is captured in a spreadsheet. Thus the spreadsheet is merely a convenient editor that can capture the functional flow information in a tabulated form. This simplifies the process of translating the functional flow from human readable form into a form that can be read by the simulation model. A Perl script was written to translate the spreadsheet file into a series of files known as "traffic generator files." These traffic generator files consist of a list of BONeS data structure specifications that contain all the information necessary to specify each of the functional flows in the system. Each of the devices, i.e., hardware models, that are capable of initiating a functional flow in the system reads a unique traffic generator file. Each of these models interprets the traffic generator file and initiates the appropriate sequence of functional steps within the simulation. All of the hardware models are responsible for handling any resource allocations, blocking, sequencing, and timing required to model the hardware device they represent. In this way essentially all of the software and functional flow of the system is specified in the spreadsheet file; and all of the hardware architecture and organization is specified in the BONeS block diagram.

Although BONeS Designer and several other event queue simulation tools have a scripting capability, generally we have found that they are inadequate to capture the functional flow to a necessary level of detail and accuracy. This problem is solved by the construction of several extensions to the BONeS Designer tool. In particular, a series of C/C++ code primitives were written. The heart of these extensions is a primitive block, which can read the text file specification of any arbitrary data structure and transform it into internal BONeS data structures. These extensions collectively represent approximately 5,000 lines of C/C++ code. These extensions allow us to represent the functional flow of the system, and hence the software architecture, as a series of data structures. The precise interpretation of the data structure depends upon the details of the hardware model being used. The extensions allow the data structures specifying the functional flow to be defined in an external text file and read into the simulation at execution time. This, to a very large extent, separates the software architecture from the hardware model. This also means virtually any text editing tool can be used to specify the functional flow of the system. The authors have used various spreadsheet tools for this role because they provide a simple and easy to read, easy use, and well structured environment for this work. The spreadsheet files are converted into text files and then pre-processed by a Perl script to create the specific required data structure specifications. Also, the Perl script reorganizes the functional flows into separate files—one for each hardware element in the system block diagram. This provides overall a simple method of specifying the software/functional flows of the system.

As discussed earlier, it is important that a consistent time resolution be used throughout the entire model. In the case of the S-3B project, it was determined that a time resolution of approximately 5 milliseconds or less was needed. As indicated in Figure 3, this applies not only to the hardware model, but also to the software or functional flow model. Each of the hardware elements is modeled with an event timing level on the order of 0.01 to 5 milliseconds. Also, the hardware model incorporates all intrinsic blocking and sequencing. In a similar fashion, the functional steps defined in the scripting files are represented in the upper left corner of Figure 3 and have a similar time resolution. Each of the basic steps in the functional flow represents events with a resolution of 5 milliseconds or less. In the present example, this leads to a relatively fine-grained model. Notice that both hardware and software have a similar granularity. One argument against providing this level of resolution is that: "we can't possibly know what the software flow is in any detail until we get done writing it." However, the reverse argument is also true: if during the design process these details are not determined, we can't know if the system will work until after it is built! We argue that spending time to develop and provide necessary details early in the system design phase will repay time spent many times over later in the project by ensuring that the system is likely to work. Based on experience in the S-3B program and others, this argument is clearly true.

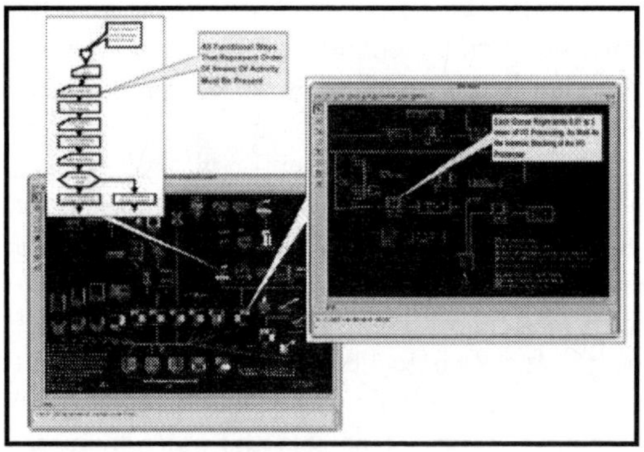

Figure 3: S-3B System Hardware Model (Left) and I/O Processor Sub-System Model (Right)

Although very appropriate for the avionics system described in this paper, this fine grain model is not suitable for every system. We have used a similar but much more coarse grained technique to model large client/server systems. These systems involved over 150 workstations, and five million lines of code. In these particular systems, the system engineering questions required a resolution of approximately 0.1 sec. This meant that much of the detail of the I/O system could be ignored. Certainly this is true for the VME bus interactions that were explicitly represented in the S-3B system. Again this approach leads to a model which has separated the hardware architecture from the software architecture. This client/server model has proven to be flexible and extremely useful in determining various resource loading, timing, and software allocation issues.

BUILDING THE MODEL

Given a model design, the construction model can proceed. Generally this step is considered very straightforward and simple. However, there are several things that can go wrong, which bear some discussion. The model we are trying to construct represents the entire system, both the hardware and the software; hence, there are several new considerations. First is the knowledge base of the people implementing the model. Clearly, the construction of the model will require a functional decomposition of the software, and hence knowledge of the software. In the example S-3B system, the system functional flow includes the software and its interaction with certain critical components of the hardware. Therefore, it is necessary for the engineers performing the functional decomposition of the system to have knowledge of the hardware and software operations. In short they are required to have extensive system operation and application domain knowledge.

One of the difficulties that arises in this approach stems from the fact that simulation models require a functional decomposition of the software. Functional decomposition often appears to be orthogonal to the decomposition techniques used by the software organization to design the software. This is particularly true of object-oriented designs. Thus it is not unusual to find that the functional flow representation of the software bears little or no relationship to the CSCI's, objects, context diagrams and other explicit software representations. This fact often acts as a deterrent to developing a good set of functional software architecture flows. While this is unfortunate, the functional representation of the software is the best and perhaps only representation that supports performance analysis of the system. Despite this conflict a functional decomposition must be done to support any meaningful performance analysis. The best solution to this difficulty is to rely heavily on a combination of domain knowledge of the system engineers and senior software engineers. It is important that the software engineers have a similar depth of domain knowledge.

No software "rock" should go unturned in the development of the system flow diagrams. In other words all of the software is important. This includes a functional decomposition of the operating system, run-time systems and other services used by the application software. After all these services also require CPU resources and hence cannot be ignored. In addition I/O drivers represent significant processing load, especially since these are often blocked by hardware functionality and by various priority schemes within the operating system. Finally, one of the most overlooked system resource hogs in the software is the various protection mechanisms for locking the data. Modern software designs often rely heavily on multiple tasks, heavyweight threads, lightweight threads and other mechanisms to represent potentially parallel software operations. The use of these paradigms requires extensive use of data protection and locking to guarantee the coherency of the data structures within the system. Virtually all systems use a combination of mutex's, semaphores, data interlocks, and flags to implement these protection mechanisms. It is often claimed that these mechanisms require little CPU overhead. In fact in many Unix-based systems these mechanisms can account for most of the operating system overhead. In some systems it has been observed that they represent as much as 20 to 25 percent of the CPU load. Moreover, the overhead required by these mechanisms is sometimes proportional to the system load. In fact, in large client/server systems we have found it necessary to incorporate special models which represent the load dependency of these factors into the hardware model in order to achieve the desired level of accuracy for the overall system model.

Occasionally, in the course of the construction of a simulation model, the model becomes too complex. That is, either the functional flow diagrams or hardware block diagrams or both become complex and unwieldy. Very often this situation is attributed to either too detailed of a model or some other problem with the modeling tool. Such a model is represented in Figure 4. This is a functional flow diagram of a very small piece of an X-window-like video display control unit. The colored boxes in this diagram represent software control semaphores and flags. The small boxes indicate various counting semaphores and other internal data control mechanisms within the software functional blocks. This diagram represents one of over 35 such diagrams required to describe the entire system. In fact the diagram in Figure 4 represents an object-oriented design (and implementation) of what amounts to little more than 5 circular I/O buffers. Much of the complexity in this diagram stems from applying object-oriented design and implementation at the lowest possible level in the system. Initially, the engineering group responsible for the design dismissed the complexity of Figure 4 by saying it was a result of the tool and not the design. In the short-term, this model never really matched the operational system very well. The model predictions seemed to be either overly optimistic or overly pessimistic with respect to the observed system performance during the test and integration phase. In the long-term, however, engineering staff judged the modeling effort to be of value. The functional flow diagrams proved to be very useful in the integration and debugging phase of this system. The message in this story is: believe the modeling results, or at least apply some critical engineering thinking to the results of building and using the model. Clearly, in this case the model construction showed that the design was too complex, and the integration debug phase program proved this to be true. The authors believe that if the engineering group had examined the complexity early on, when the model told them it was too complex, much of the pain, schedule impact, and expense of the integration phase could have been avoided. The rule here is: the functional flow is what the processor does; hence, it determines performance.

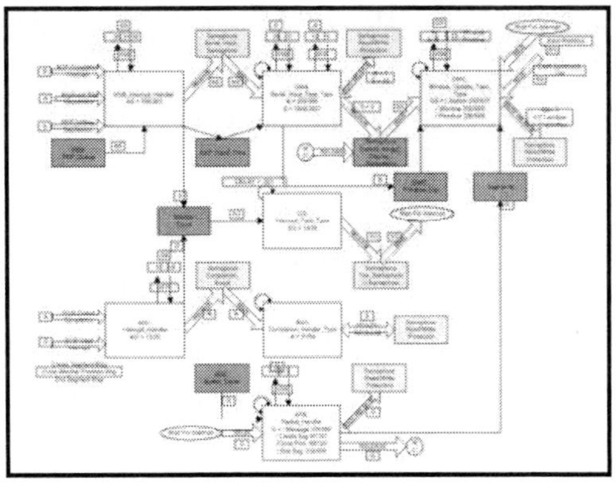

Figure 4: Functional Flow Diagram of the I/O Driver from an "X"-Like Display System

VALIDATING THE MODEL

There are several good ways to validate a model. In this regard the models constructed for the purposes of system engineering are no different from others. A good way to validate a model is to compare it to an existing or similar system. In the case of the S-3B model, the major components of the system were compared with actual benchmark measurements on the CP-2044 system. An important aspect of validating a model is that it is an ongoing effort. Clearly, in the early stages of the system engineering on a new product few if any actual measurements will exist. In this phase, best engineering judgments may have to suffice. One very good approach to improving the situation is to use the initial simulation results to identify critical bottlenecks and/or the processes that drive the performance. Then these processes can be further analyzed and designed. Perhaps a rapid prototype can be built and benchmarked. Either one of these methods can further validate and improve the accuracy of the model. Such benchmarking data can be extended to revise the estimates of the entire model and hence improve overall accuracy. Also during early phases of a program it is important to perform "sanity checks." For example the total software CPU load estimates can be compared with the number of source lines of code bid to complete the program. These two things should be consistent with each other. If they are not, then there is trouble with either the model or the bid. Finally, it is important to back up the simulation results with a certain amount of paper and pencil analysis. For example CPU loading estimates and timing estimates can be compared with their corresponding rate monotonic analysis. Modeling and simulation do not replace paper and pencil analysis, they extend it.

Because a simulation is only as good as the underlying model and is dependent on the accuracy of the provided data, it is often useful to provide detailed event queue simulations such as BONeS simulation with realistic data sources. In recent projects we have incorporated "real-life" scenarios into our modeling efforts. For example, in an effort to study the processor loading and system behavior for an air traffic control system, we have used another simulation tool to first built a realistic air traffic scenario with aircraft arriving and departing from airports and the radar sites feeding into the BONeS simulation. The software tool we chose was originally developed by the US Army Space and Missile Defense Command for Theater High Altitude Air Defense, but has rapidly become the standard tool for a much broader variety of scenarios. This simulation tool, called EADSIM (extended air defense simulation), has the ability to create very realistic models of radar propagation, voice, and data networks, and models the effects of atmospheric and environmental factors (e.g., a mountainous terrain that might obstruct the view of a radar site). By using EADSIM to stimulate the event queue simulation via the distributed interactive simulation protocol, we are able to co-simulate an event queue simulated system with a very high level of fidelity. More accurate benchmark results and realistic system inputs enable the designer to take into account unforeseen events, that could lead to very costly changes if detected later on in the design process. It is often reassuring for the customer to know that the input parameters were derived from realistic data. Further, if the customer wishes to evaluate the system under a different scenario, the system behavior can be changed "on-the-fly" by loading in an alternative scenario. These scenarios do not have to be built by system experts. In fact, it is preferable to have them built by operational experts possessing domain knowledge of the system's eventual deployment. This will guarantee operational accuracy and help to validate the model.

The following diagram (Figure 5) represents an example scenario developed in EADSIM.

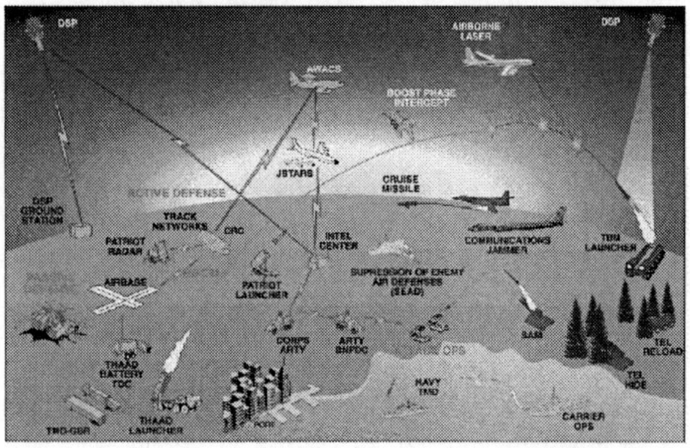

Figure 5: EADSIM Scenario Used to Stimulate a BONeS Event Queue Simulation

Each of the platforms represented in the above scenario can be modeled in detail within the BONeS simulation. The actual scenario events, such as a missile launch, deck-launched interceptors, or airborne reconnaissance INTEL data, which can otherwise only be represented in a very abstract way, can be used in practice to provide real-time data feeds for the various system components. For example, if a missile takes out an air operations center, then the processing load on another system element may drastically increase due to the rerouting of data. Such events can be modeled in minute detail and give the model an even higher level of realism. As the model becomes increasingly refined, system deficiencies can be tracked down and localized during the design process of the project. The results gained from this sort of co-simulation very closely resemble the results we actually find with the deployed systems.

USING THE MODEL

An important question regarding use of the type of models advocated by this paper is whether or not they produce useful results. The answer is resoundingly affirmative in the case of the S-3B. Figure 5 contains a sample of output from the S-3B modeling effort. The time and resources required to obtain these results were as follows:

1. Approximately 2 1/2 man-months to construct the hardware model,
2. Five days of effort by 10 software/system engineers to produce the system functional flow diagrams,
3. Two weeks by two system engineers to complete the simulations and analysis.

In short, the effort represented approximately six man-months. The following information was gleaned from Figure 5. First, the fact that the operator keyboard may cause a heavy processing load is incorrect. Once this was understood a reallocation of engineering resources was made. Engineering resources applied to the demand processing functions were reduced in favor of additional effort on some of the "periodic" functions. Motivation for this was that the periodic functions accounted for most of the system load, and it was necessary to improve their efficiency as much as possible to achieve the goals of the program. Second, several unexpected system bottlenecks were revealed. In particular, several of these related to the use of vendor-supplied I/O drivers, and certain aspects of the Ada run-time system chosen. This allowed the engineering group to begin developing work-arounds, and new I/O drivers before these issues became critical schedule items. In addition to these items represented in Figure 5, several other design changes were made based on model results. These include the choice of two 68060 processors versus the original baseline three 68030 processors. As the program has progressed through most of the integration and factory acceptance testing these early design decisions have proven to be correct and beneficial to the program.

Figure 6 illustrates another important technique in using event queue simulation models. The particular system configuration used in computing the graph in Figure 5 used two 68060 processors. However, notice that the ordinate of this graph is the processor performance. Nominally, the 68060 processor has a 14 MIP performance. A broad range of processing performance benchmarks was used to construct the curves in Figure 6. This allows us determine the sensitivity of the system to small changes in the processor performance. Notice that the curve is relatively flat in the region around 14 MIPS. If the curve had been steep in this region more care in interpreting the results would be required. This is because a large slope would indicate that small changes in a processor performance estimate would have large changes in the overall estimates of CPU loading. This conclusion would indicate that actual system performance is sensitive to the resource loads and processor performance values. Small changes in these factors would have a great effect on the observed performance. Put another way, a large slope would indicate the overall results could be inaccurate. Of course this case can be dealt with by using conservative estimates for processor performance. Up to this point we have concentrated on modeling and simulation as they relate to the early phases of the program and the system engineering process in that phase. However, it is a mistake to simply apply modeling and simulation techniques to this phase. Even though the investment in building models is moderate, using them throughout the program can increase the cost-benefit ratio. In the early phase of the program we have demonstrated how models and simulations can be used to make basic system engineering and architecture decisions. In addition models can be used to derive and refine the next level of subsystem component requirements. In particular on the S-3B project the early simulation results were used to develop performance requirements for certain software elements (particularly for I/O drivers).

During the implementation and integration phases improved estimates for the system resource loads of various functions can be obtained from benchmarks and unit tests. These improved resource load estimates can be compared to the original estimates. When major discrepancies occur, a critical examination of both the model and the component design and implementation can be made to determine where the differences lie. This situation can be very useful in revealing aspects of poor design, poor implementation or poor modeling. If the problem lies in the modeling area, then the new refined estimates can be used to upgrade the model and determine if the system will meet its performance goals. If the trouble lies in the design or implementation of the component, then improvements can be made early in the program before the problem becomes a schedule-critical item. In any case this process allows engineering and program management to take corrective action early in the program when it is still relatively inexpensive compared to late in the integration phases.

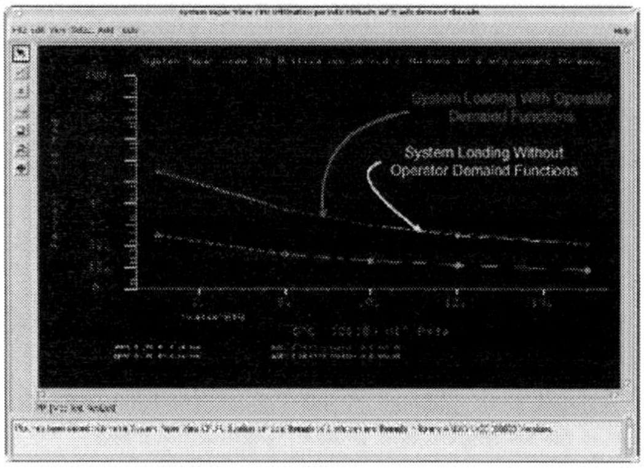

Figure 6: Sample Simulation Results From the S-3B Project

If the model has been continuously updated and validated during the implementation and integration phases we should have a fully validated model when the system test phase of the project is reached. In this phase the fully validated model can provide several important functions. First a fully validated model can be used to determine, i.e., estimate, otherwise difficult-to-measure performance parameters. An example of this might be the system performance and behavior under an unusually heavy message traffic load from a radar. Depending on the test facilities such heavy message traffic from the "radar" might be very difficult to obtain. In contrast, running the simulation with an increased radar message load may be as simple as changing a parameter in the simulation. Thus the model can be used to extrapolate the data collected during the system test phases to situations otherwise not readable with the test procedures. It is also important to note that the model should provide more accurate extrapolation than traditional techniques. This is because a fully validated model should have most of the nonlinear interactions that are present in the real system but otherwise make extrapolation difficult. Another valuable use of a fully validated system model is to predict the performance of site-specific installations and configurations. Often large software systems are installed in various configurations depending on the particular site and other adaptation factors. Further it is too expensive to test the system against all the possible installation configurations. A model and simulation can simulate these specific installation configurations and provide performance predictions, thus greatly reducing the cost, with nearly the same accuracy.

During the system maintenance phase a fully validated model continues to be useful. Such a model can be used to predict the effectiveness of proposed product improvements. By incorporating existing validated modes with new elements to represent the proposed enhancements, solid predictions of proposed changes and improvements can be made. This ability can greatly reduce the resources needed to assess the benefit versus cost of any proposed product improvement. Another important aspect in this phase is using a validated model to predict performances in system configuration changes. No system in the field remains static, as various maintenance functions occur, and the configurations change over time. The use of a model can help predict the effect of such configuration changes on the overall system performance. Avoiding the pitfalls and problems associated with field configuration changes can greatly reduce the life-cycle cost of a system.

SUMMARY

Several conclusions can be drawn from our experience with the S-3B program. First and foremost we emphasize that it is possible to build a quite detailed model of a system even in the early phases of its development. A key factor in using models in the early system engineering efforts is the separation of the hardware from the software model. Although this step generally requires extensions to the modeling tools, the investment is well worth the effort. Models constructed in this way have proven to be sufficiently flexible to explore broad ranges of hardware and software architectural considerations. Overall our experience with the S-3B and other programs demonstrated that the models are useful throughout the entire engineering process. The correct use of a model during the program can alert the engineering management staff to potential problems before they become critical to the program: "an ounce of prevention is worth a pound of cure." Modeling and simulation properly applied early in the program and carried throughout the life-cycle provide this ounce of prevention.

ACKNOWLEDGMENTS

BONeS and BONeS Designer are registered trademarks of ALTA-Group of Cadence Design Inc.

EADSIM is a registered trademark of Teledyne Brown Engineering Inc.

BIOGRAPHY

Dr. David Garrett received his B.S. in Physics and Mathematics form Iowa State University in 1971 and his Ph.D. in Physics from Indiana University in 1979. Dr. Garrett has 25+ years of experience in aerospace systems design and engineering. His work experience includes operations analysis, acoustic signal processing systems design, networked computer systems engineering, air traffic management system design, and command control communications systems engineering.

Mr. Jeffery Wolff received his B.S. in aviation computer science from Embry-Riddle Aeronautical University in 1998. He is currently pursuing a M.S. in computer science at University of Minnesota. His current work includes modeling and simulation design support for both avionics and ground based computing system.

Mr. Terry Johnson is the System Architect for the S-3B Ada Program. Terry's previous assignments include Integration Test Lead, Systems Engineer, Lead Engineer, and Operator Machine Interface Design Expert. Terry joined Lockheed Martin in 1984 after leaving the U.S. Navy where he was a crewmember in the carrier based S-3A/B aircraft.

The Use of an Information Model to Describe the SIRTF Spacecraft

Jeffrey A. Harrison
Lockheed Martin Space Systems Company – Missiles & Space Operations
P.O. Box 3504; O/L1-50, B/107
Sunnyvale, CA 94088-3504
jeff.harrison@lmco.com

ABSTRACT

A space system information model (SSIM) was developed to guide the identification of the contents for a document which describes the spacecraft system of the NASA/JPL Space InfraRed Telescope Facility (SIRTF) program. The model was adapted from a general model presented by Dr. David Oliver in his tutorial, *Engineering Complex Systems with Models and Objects*. The contents of the description document are summarized. Additional benefits from using the SSIM for this and other space systems are identified. A range of further applications which can evolve from the SSIM are also discussed.

BACKGROUND

The Space InfraRed Telescope Facility (SIRTF) - the fourth of NASA's Great Observatories - is tailored specifically to observe in the infrared region of the spectrum. The overall SIRTF consists of the Observatory and the Ground System. The spaceborne Observatory consists of the following systems: the Spacecraft (S/C), the three Science Instruments (SIs), and the Cryo-Telescope Assembly (CTA). The launch of the SIRTF Observatory is planned for December 2001. The configuration of the S/C before being integrated with the SIs and the CTA is shown in Figure 1. The Spacecraft (S/C) consists of eight subsystems: structural and mechanical, thermal control, power generation and distribution, pointing control, command and data handling, reaction control, telecommunications, and flight software. Acronyms are defined in the acronym list at the end of the paper.

THE CHALLENGE

When I accepted the assignment to develop the SIRTF Spacecraft System Description Document (SSDD), I had no prior knowledge about the program and no prior experience developing this specific type of document. This meant that I would have to solicit inputs and gather information from other program personnel who were already very busy working on the design of the

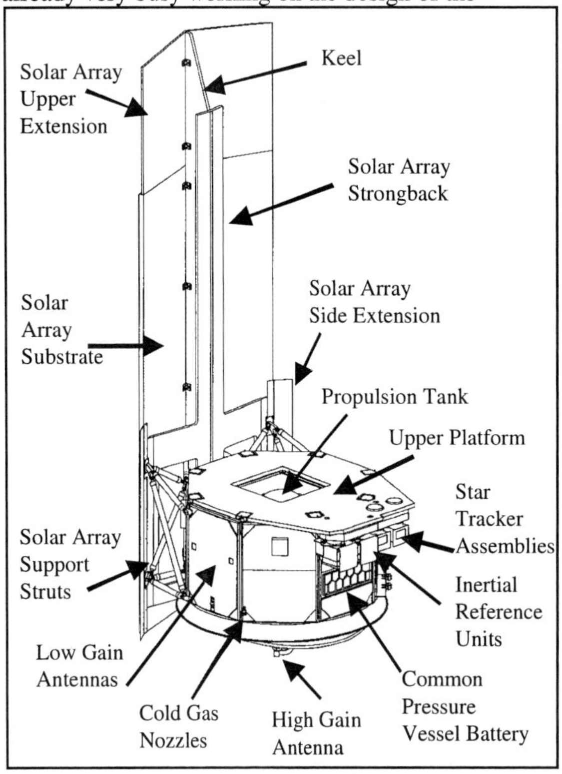

Figure 1. SIRTF Observatory's Spacecraft System

S/C subsystems at the time in the program inbetween PDR and CDR. Various PDR briefings were also available as information sources. Because of the busy schedule, I needed to be efficient about what I asked for to keep the disruption of the other engineers to a minimum. But there was no one to go to for a writeup on the overall spacecraft. That would be up to me.

Direction as to how the document should be organized and what it should contain was minimal. There was only a paragraph in the Program Documentation Plan to explain the purpose of the document and its expected contents. There was no established data item description (DID). The JPL customer was primarily relying on the contractor's judgment to determine what information was to be included and how it was to be presented. Other systems within the Observatory had already written a description document but none of them were usable as a guide for the S/C. There were also plenty of examples of description-type documents from my own library and from various websites. However, there was no way for me to know if they were complete or had taken the right approach.

So before I really started the task, I needed to determine how to describe the spacecraft, especially the one for SIRTF. However, as it turns out, the question ended up being more basic than that. It ended up being how do I describe any object. With the answer to that question in hand, I would then have to determine how to apply it to the spacecraft domain so that I could describe an object like a spacecraft in a methodical and deliberate manner as opposed to a haphazard, off-the-top-of-the-head kind of manner.

Considering the wise words of Albert Einstein that "all models are wrong...but some are useful", I determined that I needed a useful model that could be used as a checklist to identify what information I needed to gather. What I needed was what I would call a Space System Information Model (SSIM) which I could use for the SIRTF S/C.

THE SOLUTION

As it turned out, this challenge provided me with my first on-the-job opportunity to put into practice what I had learned from one of the San Francisco Bay Area Chapter INCOSE tutorials that I had attended about a year earlier. The tutorial was presented by Dr. David W. Oliver and was entitled *Engineering Complex Systems with Models and Objects*. I also subsequently read the book by the same title which he co-authored with Timothy P. Kelliher and James G. Keegan (Oliver, Kelliher, and Keegan 1997). The main item that was directly applicable to this task came from one of the information models which Dr. Oliver presented during his tutorial. Figure 2 shows his Basic Modeling Abstractions or, what I call, the Universal Information Model (UIM) because it starts with the ultimate system, namely the Universe. Because I was starting at a much lower level in the Universe's hierarchy, I adapted the UIM by placing the spacecraft level in the top box and adding Context to the rest of the applicable universe (i.e., the supersystem) and moved external interfaces from the "Role" to the Context. Figure 3 shows how I adapted the UIM to create the first level of a SSIM.

According to the SSIM, the SIRTF S/C is made up of a number of objects. The first level of which are its subsystems. Each of these subsystems are built from a number of smaller objects of hardware, software, or both. This aggregation of the S/C can continue until the smallest piece part is identified. Each of these objects, at whatever level, can be classified as being either passive or active objects. The difference between

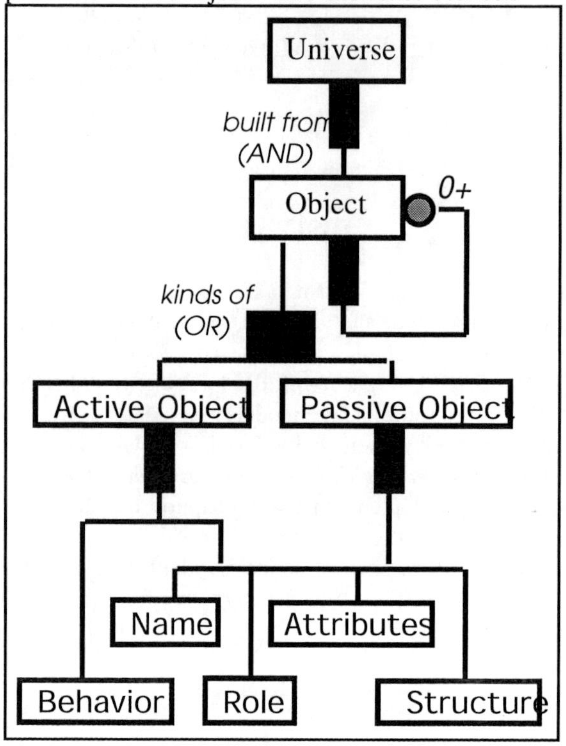

Figure 2. Oliver Universal Information Model

passive and active objects is that the active ones have a power source (e.g., electrical, mechanical, chemical, nuclear) while passive objects do not. For the SIRTF S/C, examples of passive objects include the S/C bus structure, thermal control heat pipes, and thermal blankets. The passive objects can be described by identifying their name, their role within the system, their structure, and their attributes. The active objects can be described in the same way as the passive objects with the addition of a description of their behavior.

Structure. The structure is a description of all of the items that comprise the spacecraft and the relationships among these items. A description of the structure is satisfied by identifying the parts breakdown within the object, the different types of similar parts that are used, how many of each type of part is used in the design, how and in what order the different parts are interconnected or assembled, and where the different parts are located within the structure with respect to each other. Since no one view can sufficiently satisfy a complete description of the structure, the structure needs to be represented by a variety of views such as a hierarchy tree, a hardware and software list, a block diagram, schematic drawings, interface drawings, or 3-D modeling displays as shown in Figure 1. For the SIRTF S/C, the SSDD identified the different objects which make up the S/C in a system hierarchy, their locations within the S/C bus in a layout diagram, and their interconnections using block diagrams.

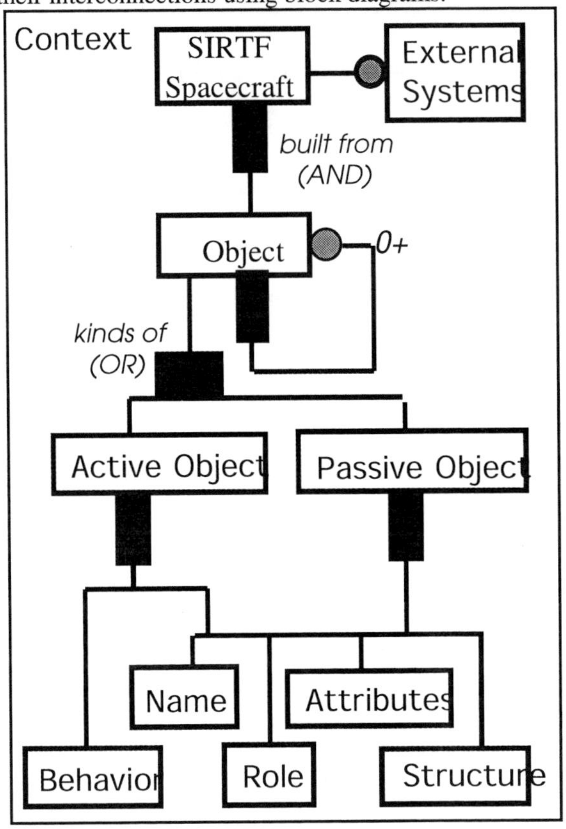

Figure 3. SIRTF S/C Information Model

Attributes. The attributes (aka characteristics) are the properties shared by each similar item. These include all properties needed for the engineering problem at hand. The various SIRTF S/C characteristics that were discussed in the SSDD were the coordinate system, mass properties, dimensions, heritage, thermal, power, grounding and isolation, and safety concerns.

Role. The description of each S/C object should include an identification of the role that it and each of the lower level objects plays within the S/C. These roles are depicted in Figure 4. In this case, the SIRTF S/C is the subject system. The lower level objects can be a subsystem, component (e.g., box) , subcomponent (e.g., circuit cards, backplanes), or part (e.g., chips) or their software equivalent depending on where they fall within the spacecraft hierarchy. Cables and wiring would have the role as an interface between any two or more component objects.

In addition, inputs from and outputs to the system can be characterized as objects. For the SIRTF S/C, examples of inputs include the gaseous nitrogen pumped into the propellant tank and photons hitting a solar array while outputs include outgassing vapors and exhaust from the thruster nozzles.

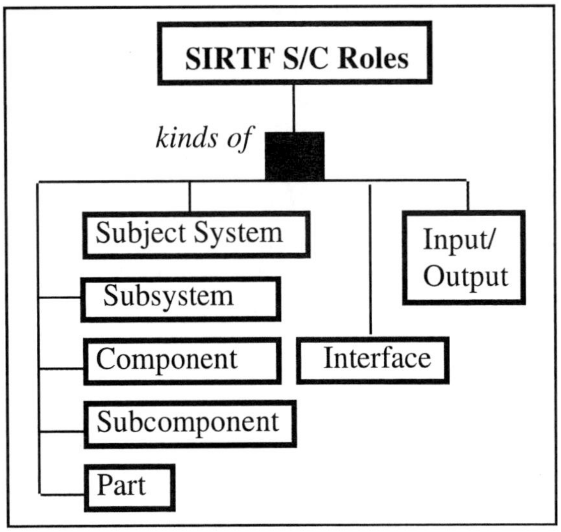

Figure 4. SIRTF S/C Information Model for Role

Behavior. The SIRTF S/C behavior (aka operations) is governed by a set of unique modes within which the S/C can operate during the mission. The S/C operates in only one mode at a time. Within each mode, the S/C can perform all or a subset of its functions as ordered by one or more control operations. Each function generates and consumes at least one output and one input, respectively. These inputs and outputs can be categorized based on whether they turn functions on or off (i.e., their effect) or they provide the criteria by which the S/C decides to initiate a control operation (i.e., their condition). Figure 5 represents the SIRTF S/C application of the Oliver information model for behavior.

In the SSDD, the S/C behavior was discussed primarily using statecharts for each S/C mode to define the states that the various subsystems could be in and mode transition diagrams to show what other modes the S/C could transition to or from. The mode descriptions also identifed the entry and exit criteria that would cause the S/C to enter or leave a particular mode. The description also covered the functions that the subsystems could support and the transition criteria that would cause the subsystems to change modes while in a particular S/C mode. Narrative discussions of each of the S/C functions were also included. Other techniques that could have been used to describe S/C behavior include functional flow diagrams, behavior diagrams, timeline diagrams, command and telemetry listings, and N^2 charts.

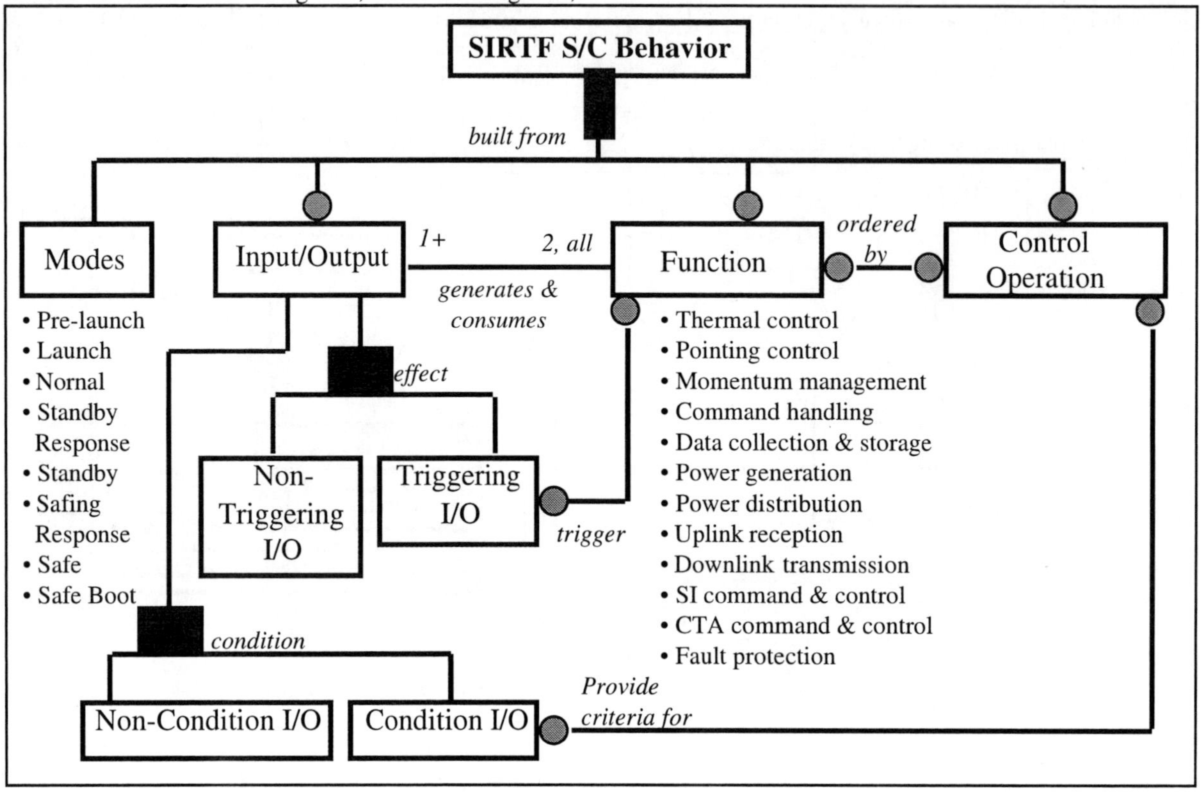

Figure 5. SIRTF S/C Information Model for Behavior

Context. In addition, the S/C design is influenced by the context in which it is to be developed, built, integrated, tested, launched, and operated. As shown in Figure 6, elements of this context include the mission, its external interfaces with other items outside of the system, the environments (i.e., both man-made and natural) that the S/C will encounter, available program resources, and other program constraints within which the S/C design has to conform. The Mission context identifies mission objectives, mission phases, and mission profile. S/C external interfaces include the science instruments' warm electronics, the CTA, the Delta II launch vehicle, ground support equipment for transporting and positioning the S/C, the Deep Space Network for communications, and the facilities for manufacturing, test, and launch. The S/C will need to survive the on-orbit environment where it is exposed to solar flux, solar pressure, radiation, and meteoroids. The man-made environments include the electromagnetic radiation that the S/C is exposed to at the launch base and the vibrations, acceleration loads, pressure changes, and shock during launch and ascent to orbit. The available program resources include the schedule, financial budget, people, tools, and facilities. The other program constraints on the design include the hardware and software that the program chose to reuse from other programs and the governmental standards and regulations (e.g., EWR 127-1) that the program had to adhere to.

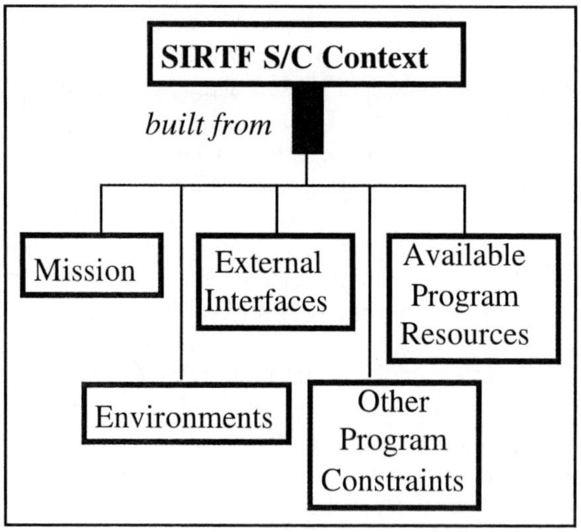

Figure 6. SIRTF S/C Information Model for Context

THE RESULT

The SSDD was developed and arranged using the SSIM as much as possible. A high level version of the SSDD's table of contents is listed in Table 1. Section 1 provided an introduction for the document which included a brief discussion of the SSIM. Section 2 applied the SSIM to describe the spacecraft as a whole by addressing the mission context within which the S/C is being designed, its architectures, its characteristics, and its operations. Fault Protection was broken out as a separate section because it includes both structural and behavioral features. Using the same model, Section 3 included an overall description of each of the subsystems and a description of their next lower level components.

1.0 INTRODUCTION
1.1 Purpose and Scope
1.2 Document Control
1.3 References

2.0 SPACECRAFT OVERVIEW
2.1 Spacecraft System Context
2.2 Spacecraft Architecture
2.3 Spacecraft Characteristics
2.4 Spacecraft Operations
2.5 Fault Protection

3.0 SPACECRAFT SUBSYSTEMS
3.1 Structural and Mechanical Subsystem
3.2 Thermal Control Subsystem
3.3 Power Generation & Distribution Subsystem
3.4 Telecommunications Subsystem
3.5 Command and Data Handling Subsystem
3.6 Pointing Control Subsystem
3.7 Reaction Control Subsystem
3.8 Flight Software

Appendix A - Acronyms
Appendix B - Glossary

Table 1. SSDD Table of Contents

LESSONS LEARNED

Various lessons were learned from the application of the SSIM to the SSDD development activity. On the positive side, using the SSIM helped to focus on what information was needed to be included in the document. It also provided a measure against which to status the quality of the document.

Even though the SSIM adopted the UIM's use of Object Model Notation (OMT) which was originally designed for use with software, I found the notation easy to apply to higher level objects which contain both hardware and software. The OMT notation is especially applicable to the definition of the S/C's behavior since the SIRTF S/C's behavior is driven primarily by its Flight Software.

On the negative side, I should have communicated the SSIM concept to the other authors earlier in the process. This could have helped to make the subsystem sections more consistent and complete. Developing the document with the aid of the model also helped identify holes in the available information which correlated to deficiencies in the design description especially with respect to the S/C behavior.

OTHER BENEFITS

Besides being useful to develop a description document, I believe the SSIM can also be used for a variety of other activities. The SSIM can be a key tool to identify what information you need to know about a product domain (e.g., space systems). A SSIM can be used as a checklist to determine completeness for requirements databases, specifications, and design review packages. Additional SSIM uses could include the identification of evaluation criteria for trade studies, the development of a metric to measure product quality, the comparison of different product designs across the domain, and the identification of traceability across hierarchy levels when multi-levels of a SSIM are linked. In addition, proposal teams may want to use SSIMs to compare their design with previous competitor designs, with previous in-house designs, or with all historical designs within the domain or mission category. If SSIMs are available from other space system programs, they can be evaluated to determine their applicability for a current development program, to learn how others solved a similar design problem, or to perform a theirs-to-yours design comparison (e.g., weight, cost).

The SSIM could be an important tool to support a company's knowledge mangement activities. It can be used as a communications tool to share the knowledge of lessons learned and development experiences with not only others currently employed but also future generations of employees who have yet to enter the workforce. A SSIM can be used to help capture all knowledge about a product domain from across the enterprise so that it is not dependent on the experiences and the memories of those experiences of only the people on a current project. The SSIM could also be instrumental when bringing new employees or new transfers from other domains up to speed quickly to ensure their productivity. By documenting the knowledge, the SSIM can keep it from being highly volatile; that is to keep it from evaporating when someone who solely held that knowledge leaves the company, retires, or even dies unexpectedly.

RANGE OF APPLICATIONS

The basic SSIM and its more advanced derivatives offer the potential to provide some of the above benefits over a wide range of applications as depicted in Figure 7.

Basic. I consider the use of a SSIM to develop a document such as the SSDD to be the most basic application of this concept, one that can be easily implemented with widely available word processing tools. For SIRTF, the SSDD was developed as a Microsoft Word file and then later converted also to an Adobe Acrobat Reader "pdf" file. The SSDD was created primarily for an audience interested in only the SIRTF program.

Database. The current state of the art for information models seems to be individual files of information of varying depth from a variety of sources, both electronic and hardcopy. A SSIM database capability would build upon the current availability of space system description data which is available in individual files on the Internet and in numerous publications. Examples of databases of individual files which are accessible over the internet include the following:

- Goddard Space Flight Center's National Space Science Data Center Master Catalog (`http://nssdc.gsfc.nasa.gov/nmc/sc-query.html`)
- JPL's Mission and Spacecraft Library (`http://msl.jpl.nasa.gov/home.html`)

What these databases cannot do is to compare between the files seamlessly (i.e., without copying down or printing out the data and comparing manually). So as part of a database capability, individual SSIMs would be developed from the information that is currently available and then incorporated into a database which would not only allow the display of the individual files but also allow the user to compare the information between the files.

Trying to develop a database of information about a diverse domain such as space systems presents several challenges. One of these challenges was alluded to above and that is the vast multitude of information from which to obtain source data. Due to the immensity of the available data, separate files may be needed to make it easier to use and to minimize retrieval time for individual space system objects as well as separate mission categories of systems (i.e., separate files for spacecraft, instruments, subsystems). With so much data to choose from, it is difficult to decide what data needs to be entered first; that is, which data would provide the most immediate benefit. Another challenge is that all of this data is presented in different formats with similar objects given different names.

One of the strengths that this kind of database can have is to be able to compare like items despite the fact that they may have been named differently. To do this, the database would need to include not only each item's original name but also a common name upon which to search for much like someone would use a keyword to do a search on the internet.

However, the use of a common name brings with it

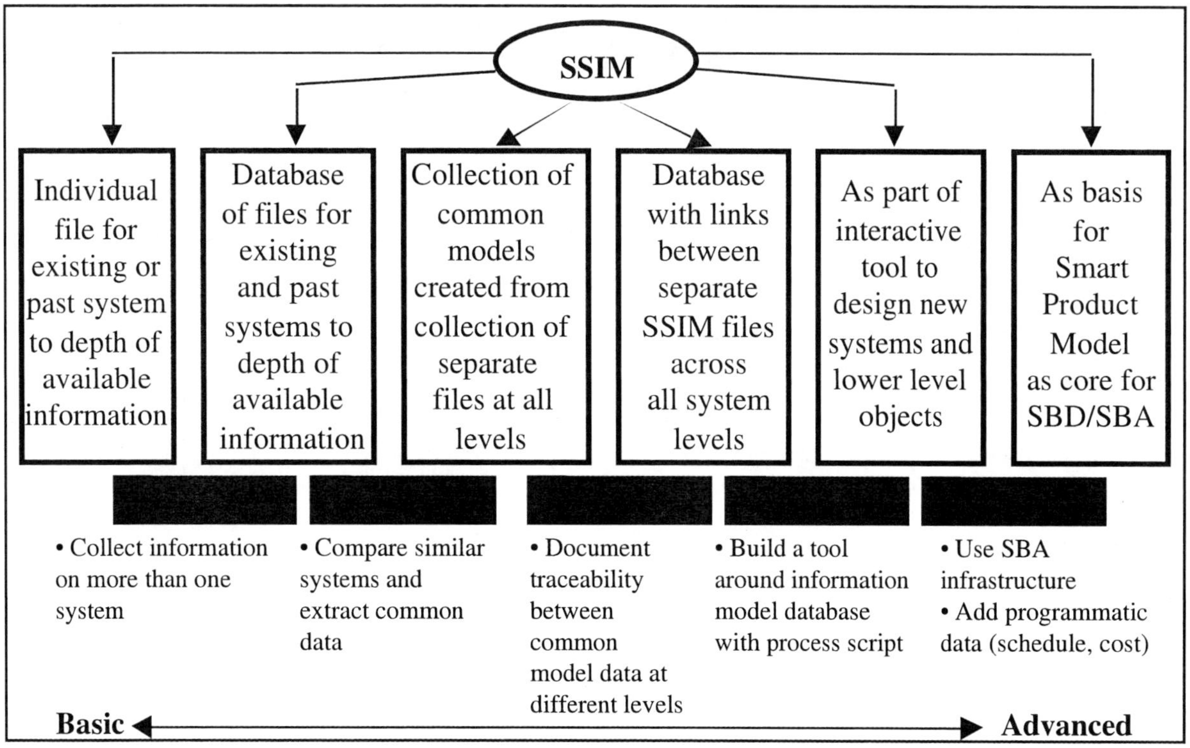

Figure 7. Range of Potential SSIM Applications

a configuration management challenge to use one and only one common name for each like item. To meet this challenge, an entry into some sort of logbook could be used to record the first time that a common name is used. Then the next time that another like item is entered into the database, one could look up in the logbook which common name was previously used.

To allow the database to support information searches and retrievals, it would need to incorporate a data structure that would allow the user to search for information by either single or multiple parameters. My current data structure concept for a SSIM-based database would consist of the following items: program type (e.g., government, international, commercial), mission category (e.g., Earth remote sensing, astronomy), name (e.g., actual name, common name, acronym), role (e.g., system, subsystem, interface), view type (e.g., structure, attribute, behavior), parameters (i.e., unique to each view type), source material (e.g., web site, journal), and privacy level (public, proprietary, copyrighted). To develop the database, a common computer tool such as Filemaker Pro would be a likely candidate.

Common Models. With enough SSIMs from a variety of programs within a certain category of systems (e.g., communications, remote sensing), a more advanced capability could be developed by comparing the separate files from all levels of the basic database, extracting common features to develop common or generic models for a class of space systems and their lower-level objects. A generic SSIM could be used to support requirements development (engineer) and requirements review (peers and managers), to support description/user manual/operations manual development (engineer) and document review (peers and managers), and to help prepare for design reviews (engineer and manager) and assess design review performance (review board members and subcontractor review attendees). The database of common models could be developed in the same manner as the specific space system information models using Filemaker Pro. Consideration should be given to using a relational type of database software if it is desired to eventually evolve to the linked files concept.

Linked Files. Using common models at all levels of the space system hierarchy, the models in the database could be linked or traced from one level to another. This would document the understanding of inter-level relationships between the space system objects. Electronic QFD-like matrices could be used to document the link between the customer needs with the common system-level IM and the system-level IM with the lower level common IMs. These linked files could provide the basis for a traceable common requirements database which could help systems engineers to more quickly flowdown system level requirements to subsystem level and to help them develop a more complete set of requirements when they're done. A relational database would be needed to implement the traceability aspects of the linked common models. Any number of popular requirements management tools could be adapted for this purpose.

Interactive Tool. If incorporated within an interactive computer tool, the SSIM could guide a developer (e.g., requirements engineer, designer) through the specification and development of a new space system and its low-level products. This concept merges all three previous SSIM concepts with a computer interface with an user. With these capabilities brought together in a seamless and supportive manner, the tool could help speed up the development cycle and potentially reduce costs by reducing redesign caused by incomplete or inaccurate requirements development at the front end of the program.

Figure 8 provides an overview of the interactive tool concept. The tool would still allow a user to do data searches and retrievals as with the previous concepts. However, by identifying which mission category (e.g., remote sensing, astronomy) and space system object are of interest, the tool would identify a list of potential external interfaces for that object for the user to select from. Once the user has selected the applicable external interfaces, the tool could provide a requirements database for high-level objects or a spec fill-in guide for lower level objects. By accessing the specific space system database, the tool could suggest values for the blanks in the guide. By accessing the linked files, the tool could identify which pairs of requirements need to be traded and suggest trade alternatives or ranges as well as possibly evaluation criteria. A finished spec or database would result after the user enters the design values. Until all of the design values are entered, the tool could also keep track of any TBDs remaining to be filled-in.

Smart Product Model. The Simulation Based Architecture (SBA) environment for a domain such as a spacecraft requires a tremendous amount of knowledge to model the product. This includes not only knowledge about the product and each of its lower level objects, but also about the relationships between the objects at the same level and across levels. For this reason, I have chosen the most advanced application for a SSIM to be as the technical basis for the development of the Smart Product Model at the core of the SBA. This application would include all of the technical information about a space systems product which may also include some program-related information such as cost, development time, and risk. This application could lead the developer through the design process, allow the developer to run simulations of different design concepts, and support trades in requirements and design. To be incorporated into the SBA, the

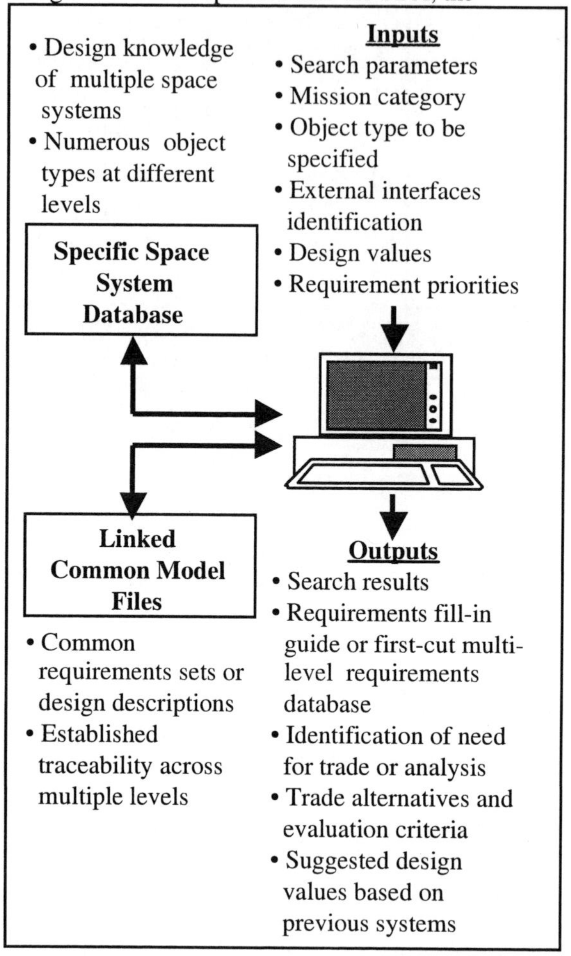

Figure 8. SSIM-Based Interactive Tool Concept

interactive tool or one of the lesser capable SSIM concepts would need to be "wrapped" through the use of a tool such as Netbuilder.

CONCLUSION

In this paper, I have tried to share my experience in working a challenging assignment to develop the Spacecraft System Description Document (SSDD) for the SIRTF program. I have explained why I needed to develop a Space System Information Model (SSIM) to support the development of the SSDD. I also showed how I converted a higher level model provided by Dr. David W. Oliver (*Engineering Complex Systems with Models and Objects*) for a more specific application for the SIRTF S/C. I further described the various elements of the SSIM and how they were applied to describing the SIRTF S/C. I also indicated how the SSIM can be applied over a wide range of applications for basic to advanced concepts to help reduce development cycle time, knowledge management and improvements in product quality. I hope this paper will provide other engineers that find themselves in a similar situation with a methodical approach that they can use to prepare a quality document.

ACRONYM LIST

Acronym	Title
3-D	Three dimensional
CDR	Critical Design Review
CTA	Cryo-Telescope Assembly
DID	Data Item Description
EWR	Eastern Western Range
IM	Information Model
JPL	Jet Propulsion Laboratory
NASA	National Aeronautics and Space Administration
OMT	Object Modeling Technique
PDR	Preliminary Design Review
QFD	Quality Function Deployment
SBA	Simulation Based Architecture
SBD	Simulation Based Design
S/C	Spacecraft
SI	Science Instrument
SIRTF	Space InfraRed Telescope Facility
SSDD	Spacecraft System Description Document
SSIM	Space System Information Model
TBD	To Be Determined
UIM	Universal Information Model

REFERENCE

Oliver, David W., Timothy P. Kelliher, and James G. Keegan Jr., *Engineering Complex Systems with Models and Objects*, McGraw-Hill, New York, 1997.

BIOGRAPHY

Jeff Harrison has been performing as a systems engineer on the SIRTF spacecraft development program at Lockheed Martin Space Systems Company – Missiles & Space Operations (LMSSC-MSO) since March 1998. He is responsible for the development and maintenance of the Spacecraft System Requirements Document, the Spacecraft System Description Document, and the Spacecraft System Verification Plan. Mr. Harrison has over 16 years of systems engineering experience with LMSSC-MSO in support of space systems development involved primarily with environmental remote sensing. He has a MS in Aeronautical Engineering from the Naval Postgraduate School and a BS in Aerospace Engineering from North Carolina State University.

A Toolset for modelbased AOCS-Design

F. Hoecherl[1], M. Wilke[1], O. Quirmbach[2], M. Surauer[2], E. Igenbergs[1]

[1] Institute of Astronautics
Technical University of Munich
Boltzmannstr. 15,
85748 Garching, Germany

[2] Dornier Satellite Systems GmbH
Postfach 80 11 69,
81663 Munich, Germany

Abstract. Due to increasing commercialisation in satellite business modern companies have to create proposals quicker and cheaper than ever before. To cope with those demands a model based design approach is currently implemented at the satellite division of DaimlerChrysler Aerospace.

The attitude and orbit control system (AOCS) is one of the key subsystems within a satellite, as it's heavily interfacing to all other subsystems.

A tool was developed which supports the AOCS-designer in selecting suitable COTS-components based on functional requirements. For each functional requirement (product-function) a set of reference solutions is identified. Based on the designers selection of those reference solutions, a pre-selection of suitable COTS-components is being filtered from a component database.

After the designer has selected the final set of components, the tool provides a compliancy check to the initial requirements.

INTRODUCTION

Increasing commercialisation of the satellite business forces companies to create proposals quicker and cheaper than ever. To meet those challenges, the satellite division of DaimlerChrysler Aerospace (Dornier Satelliten Systeme GmbH) created the "Satellite Design Office" (SDO), a Concept Design Center to support the integrated concurrent engineering of satellites, similar to JPL's Project Design Center. The software tool MuSSat [Wilke et al, 1999] is used as a common basis for data exchange among the different disciplines. Within MuSSat each discipline can create or integrate their own set of models and connect it to those of the other disciplines to create one integrated model of the satellite.

By saving all modelled variants of a satellite proposal and the ability to reuse different building blocks easily MuSSat makes it possible to quickly generate different configurations of the satellite in response to changes in customer's requirements. This accelerates the design work.

Nowadays the design of the AOCS is driven not only by technical requirements but also influenced by strategic or political considerations. Due to both missing product and availability information and misjudgement of the impact of AOCS-design to the rest of the satellite the cheapest or most reliable system is not always identified and selected.

This paper shows an approach to build a model that on the one hand perfectly integrates into MuSSat and on the other hand makes it possible to create different configurations for the AOCS based on technical and economical requirements and to evaluate those configurations objectively using different Measure Of Effectiveness (MOE's).

The model is intended to support the AOCS designer in selecting suitable commercial-off-the-shelf (COTS) components based on the system level requirements and finding the optimum configuration to meet all those requirements.

APPROACH

Three building blocks have been identified that support the design process as key elements:

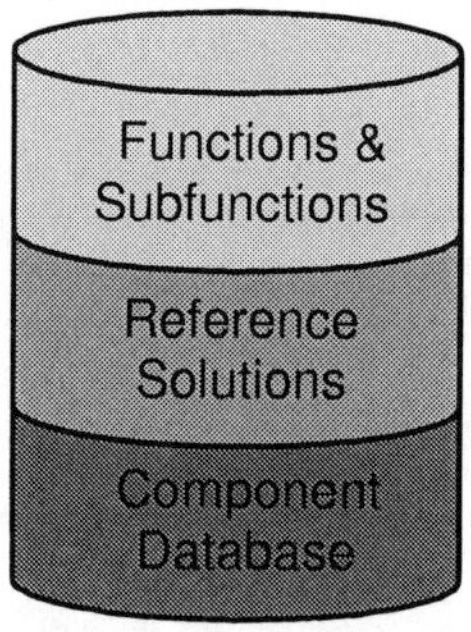

Figure 1: Key Elements

The block *Functions and Subfunctions* collects all functional requirements regarding the AOCS. Those functions are arranged in a hierarchical structure.

In the block *Reference Solutions* the designer's experiences how to realise a certain function are modelled. Basis for those reference solutions may be flown or investigated satellite projects or subsystems modelled in MuSSat, sets of COTS-components or a set of formulas describing the solution.

These two functional blocks are supported by a *product database* that contains data about all commercially available hardware parts (COTS components), as well as company internal products.

These three blocks have to integrate seamlessly. The interfaces between them are modelled as links, that point at informations in the other blocks (see Figure 2).

Thus the functional requirements (Function) of the AOCS refer to either single components (Comp) or to reference solutions (RefSol), which themselves refer to components or sets of components.

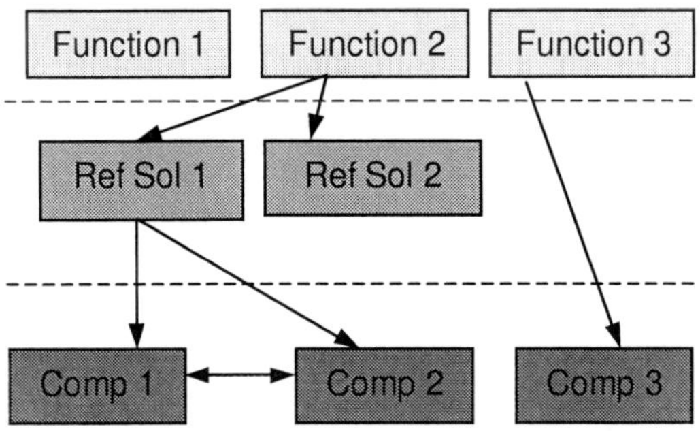

Figure 2: Pointing between the building blocks

Functions. All tasks of an AOCS are structured in a hierarchical tree. This function-breakdown can also be used as a guide for manual design of the system (checklist).

Figure 3 gives an example of a function breakdown. The function *Rate Damping* describes the process of controlled reduction of the rotational rate of the satellite. To accomplish that task sensors are required for measuring the actual rotational rate and actuators are used for generation of torques (in opposite direction to the rate). Thus the function *Rate Damping* is split into two subfunctions (*Sensing* and *Actuation*).

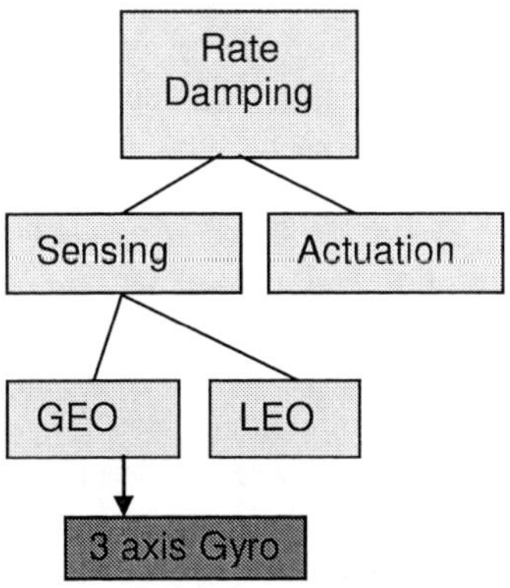

Fig. 3: Function Breakdown

Reference Solutions. In the example shown above there are several options to measure the rotational rate which are described in reference solutions. In this case in a geosynchronous earth orbit the rate can be measured with a 3-axis gyro. Hereby *3 axis gyro* describes a reference solution containing a set of components (in this case just one 3-axis gyro), that is able to fulfil the task of the subfunction.

Each subfunction is being linked to one or more reference solutions. These are standard procedures or specific design experiences and can be of different kinds (Figure 4):

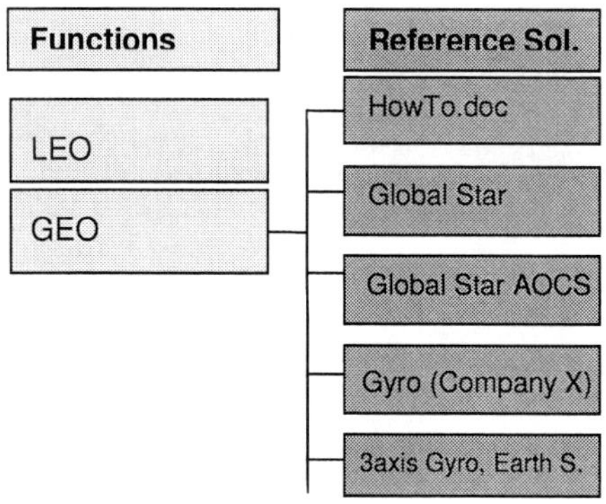

Figure 4: Reference Solutions

- sets of component types
- COTS components
- documents
- links to or descriptions of modelled projects
- parts of modelled projects (e.g. subsystems)

The hierarchy of functions and subfunctions is adaptable to the users needs. So when he continues working within that tool, he can introduce new functions and subfunctions as well as reference solutions for those specific AOCS tasks. By modelling new projects or project variants in MuSSat this "database of experiences" continuously grows.

Component Database. To enable the first two building blocks to easily and efficiently access the contents of the product database, it has to meet the following requirements:

1. *no empty fields*. Those could be interpreted as 0, which would lead to undesired automatic selections (costs = 0). Unknown parameters have to be filled with dummies, such as '?' or '-'.
2. *entries without units*. The units of each property have to be defined in advance, and all entries into the database have to cling to that definition.
3. *use of SI-units*. Thus suitable entries are guaranteed, to be sure not to mix different types of units as that has proved fatal (not only) to Mars Climate Orbiter.
4. *Links to other records*, pictures or documents should be permitted to be able to attach further information.

5. *Clearly understandable and expandable structure.* In this work the database was implemented as a hierarchical class-model. By that components can be grouped together in classes which share certain properties. The properties are attached to a product class and thereby describe each element belonging to the class.

Figure 5 shows one branch of the database. It's structure allows the storage of information concerning AOCS products (like sensors and actuators) as well as propulsion hardware or solar array components (not shown in Fig. 5). There is no limit to the number of hierarchy levels either. Each new partition increases the clarity of the structure.

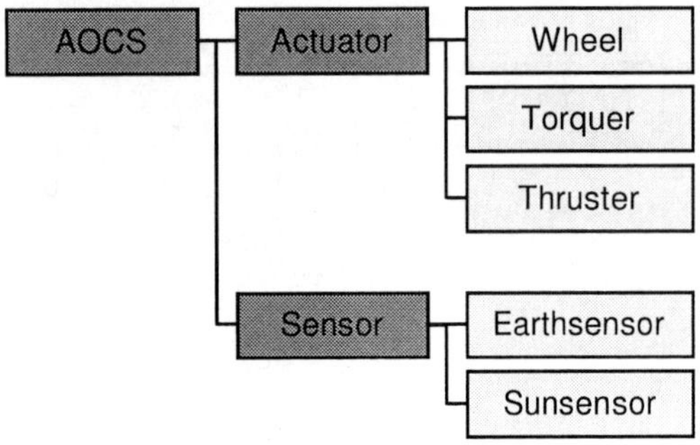

Fig. 5: Database Structure

The dark fields are named classes, the light fields are called elements. The elements represent the lowest level in the database structure and contain the records describing the components. It is not possible to describe components in a class for consistency reasons. If users could attach records to a class, it is no longer possible to identify their exact purpose (to allow a sensor in the class 'sensors' doesn't support automatic preselection and invites users to collect all new component types at a higher level instead of creating a new class or element). If further distinction is necessary, new elements can be appended to an element which thus becomes a class. All records are automatically moved to the new elements.

This structure permits quick and easy generation of new systems as subordinated elements are already described by the properties of their father-classes. It is also possible to create new elements or classes by deriving them from existing ones very easily. The only thing remaining is adding the properties describing the new type of components.

If in the example shown above the property 'Mass [kg]' is attached to the class *Sensors*, it is necessary to give an information about the mass in each record of the subordinated elements *Earth Sensor* and *Sun Sensor*.

The following links have been integrated:

1. links to a any other record
2. links to any documents or URLs

Hence components can be described that fulfil functions of a combination of elements. Their properties are determined in the various elements and the records can afterwards be linked.

The possibility to attach up to four URLs or documents allows the description of components by external references in addition to the record itself.

The database is managed by an authorised administrator in a central position (database server). To allow the description of new components working offline an import-/ export functionality has been integrated which allows generation of a record template, sending it by e-mail and after filling in all necessary information re-importing it easily.

Because of the continuous use of the database by MuSSat and the system designers in the SDO it should not be a problem to keep the information up to date.

THE AOCS DESIGN PROCESS

The process of designing an AOCS is performed in the following steps (see Fig. 6):

1. Selection of functional requirements from the function breakdown
2. Selection of reference solutions
3. Internal generation of a requirements catalogue for the components
4. Internal preselection of components using the key requirements as a filter
5. Final choice of components by the designer using additional filters
6. Performing a compliance check
7. Building and saving of variants (iteration)
8. Evaluation and comparison of system-variants using MuSSat
9. Final decision for a AOCS-variant

1) The designer selects the functional requirements for the AOCS tasks using the functional breakdown as a checklist.

2) For each chosen function or subfunction the designer must decide for one of the reference solutions that are able to meet the function's requirements. To find out the most suitable one he can look up the necessary information in the linked documents that describe the reference solution in more detail. For both functions and reference solutions, the designer can create new entries at any time, he is even wanted to do so. Creating a new reference solution means e.g. identifying a set of components that fulfil the addressed function. He is then expected to describe the source of information in any kind of document, which is automatically 'attached' (i.e. connected by hyperlink) to the function / reference solution.

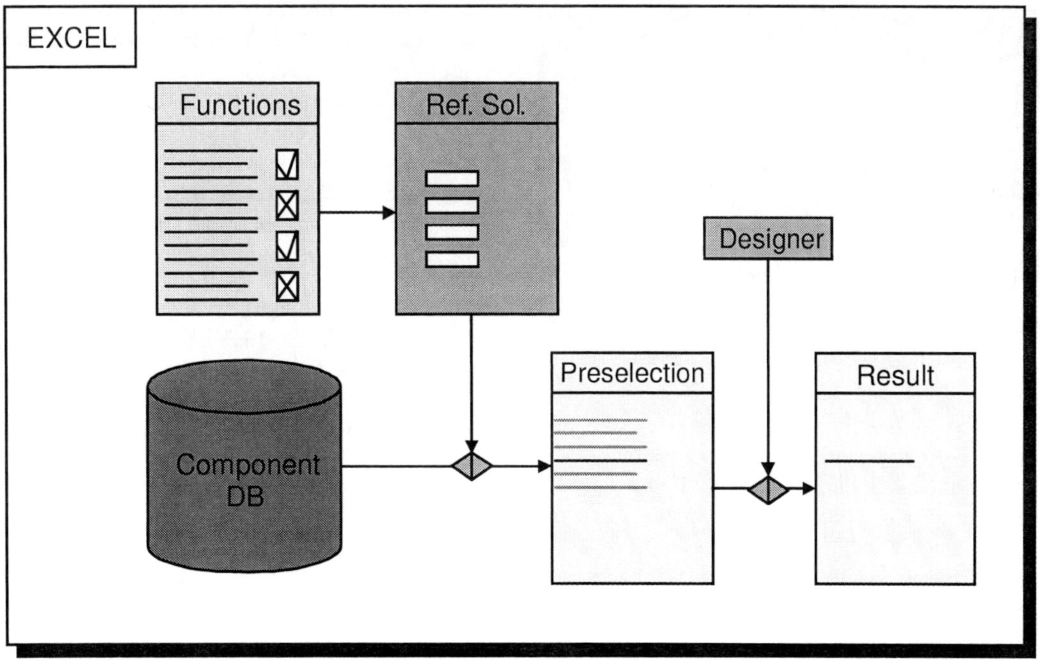

Figure 6: The design process

3) A set of key requirements is computed automatically summarising the dominating demands on the system caused by the selected reference solutions. If this kind of automatic requirement generation is not wanted it is also possible to allow the designer to specify those key requirements on his own.

In the class *Actuators* the two driving requirements (Orbit Control Requirement and Torque Requirement) for the preselection of components are calculated by formulas. In the class *Sensors* the requirements are based upon from the properties describing the selected reference solutions and are used as limitations for the component preselection (for example a defined accuracy).

4) The above specified / computed key requirements are now used to select components out of the component data base. Of course only the properties that have previously been defined can be used for the filtering process.

5) By providing the database structure described above the records can be filtered using all modelled properties of the components such as mass, cost or power consumption. In this way the designer's experience concerning certain parameters can be taken into account. Furthermore some properties of a whole system can hardly be computed automatically (e.g. the reliability) and must be considered by the designer.

6) After having completed the configuration of the AOCS components the designer again needs to check if all requirements have been met. This part of the process is supported by a compliance check table where all functional requirements and the results of the designers selection are listed.

7) The structure of the model allows the definition of several variants without loosing information about earlier ones. By changing only parts of the configuration and taking over parts of other ones it is possible to create those variants very quickly and the results can be improved continuously.

8) With the help of the design tool MuSSat the variants can be compared and evaluated concerning every parameter modelled, even combinations of parameters are possible (e.g. an 80% of mass and 20% of costs optimisation). The AOCS can also be reviewed concerning the whole satellite (sometimes an optimum AOCS as a single system is not the optimum for the whole satellite).

9) By comparing the modelled variants, an objective judgement and decision for one of the variants can be taken.

THE TOOL

The AOCS model in this approach is divided into two main subsystems: sensors and actuators (analogue to the database structure). Furthermore two additional models have been integrated to provide mission data and calculate orbit disturbance torques.

The *mission model* (see Figure 7) allows the static simulation of undisturbed elliptical orbits. Upon this data the *disturbance torque model* (Wertz, 1980)

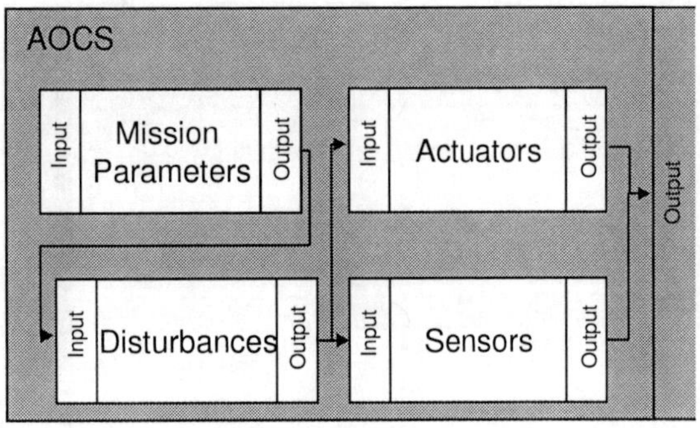

Figure 7: Information Flow

calculates the torques on the satellite over one orbit, caused by gravity gradient, aerodynamics, solar pressure and the earth's magnetic field (Figure 8).

Here the continuos reorientation of the solar array was taken into account as well as the changing Moments of Inertia (MOI) caused by it. Furthermore the changes in the position of the center of gravity caused by fuel sloshing, thruster activity and decreasing propellant mass were considered (Larson, Wertz, 1995).

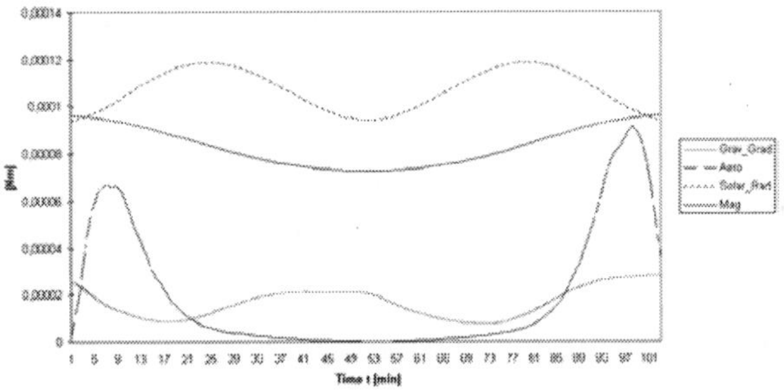

Figure 8: Disturbance Torque Model

The *models for sensor* and *actuator* configuration guide the designer through the above defined process. The worst case torques data is necessary to calculate the torque requirements in the *actuators* model.

The preselection of components from the database is automatically performed by the *sensors* and the *actuators* model. They also contain the functions and subfunctions breakdown (see Figure 9).

For the reason of transparency and the principle of an open architecture MS Excel and MS Access have been used to construct the models and the component database to enable the designer to check formulas used and the relations between the modelled parameters. Besides that the models can be changed easily and adapted to individual needs.

SYSTEM-LEVEL INTEGRATION

The described tools can either be integrated into MuSSat or used as a stand-alone version. When integrated into MuSSat, most of the necessary input information can be supplied from the models of the other disciplines (MOI's from *Configuration*, disturbance torques from M*ission Analysis*, etc.). If the tools are used outside of MuSSat they generate and provide any necessary information for the AOCS configuration themselves.

CONCLUSIONS

The described approach enables the reuse of models or parts of a model by generating new reference solutions during normal design work. Furthermore the time to design the system is reduced. Once modelled, all of the reference solutions are saved and the necessary knowledge can be mapped.

Using the design process defined above and the supporting software tools the AOCS designer can quickly create different variants of the AOC-system to cope with a set of top level requirements.

He is also able to compare and evaluate those variants objectively on both the subsystem and system level. Thus his creativity is not limited but supported. The open architecture of this approach guarantees a steady growth of the functionalities and enables control of the automated steps by its transparency.

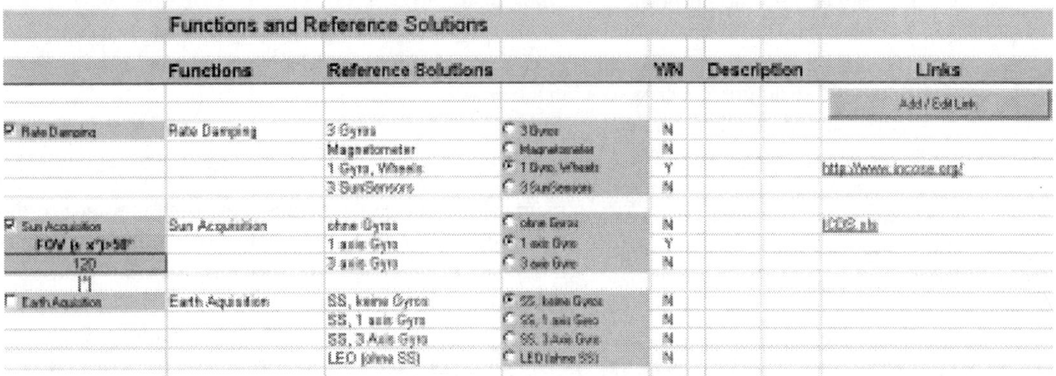

Figure 9: Sensor Model

REFERENCES

[1] M. Wilke, O. Quirmbach, H. Negele, E. Fricke, E. Igenbergs, 1999:
MuSSat – A Tool for Model-Based System Engineering of Commercial Satellite Systems,
Annual International Symposium of INCOSE, Brighton, 1999

[2] E. Igenbergs,1993:
Grundlagen der Systemtechnik
Lecture Notes, Institute of Astronautics, TU München, 1992/93

[3] J. R. Wertz, 1980:
Spacecraft Attitude Determination and Control
2. Edition, D. Reidel Publishing Company Dordrecht, Holland / Boston, USA, 1980

[4] W. Larson, J.R. Wertz, 1995:
Space Mission Analysis and Design
Microcosm Inc.., Torrence, CA

BIOGRAPHY

Florian Hoecherl received his M.S. degree in Aerospace engineering in February 2000. During his studies at the Technical University of Munich he focused on attitude control systems and systems engineering by making a student thesis modelling MIR's attitude stability at the German Aeronautics Research Center (DLR) and his master thesis in the field of systems engineering at Dornier Satellite Systems GmbH (DSS), which is a subsidiary of DaimlerChrysler Aerospace.

Martin Wilke is research assistant at the Institute of Astronautics at the Technical University of Munich. He received his M.S. degree in Aerospace engineering in January, 1998. During his studies he focused on systems engineering by making a student thesis and his master thesis in the field of systems engineering at the Institute of Astronautics. Currently he is working on a project aimed at developing a tool for the model-based systems engineering of satellite systems. The project is a joint effort of the Institute of Astronautics and the Dornier Satellite Systems GmbH, which is a subsidiary of Daimler Chrysler Aerospace. He is a founding member of the German Chapter of INCOSE.

Oliver Quirmbach is research assistant within a co-operation of DaimlerChrysler Aerospace and German Aerospace Research Center. He received his M.S. degree in Aerospace engineering in May, 1997. During his studies he focused on systems engineering and economics. Currently he is working on a project aimed at developing a tool for the model-based systems engineering of satellite systems. The project is a joint effort of the Institute of Astronautics and the Dornier Satellite Systems GmbH, which is a subsidiary of Daimler Chrysler Aerospace.

Michael Surauer has received his master degree in aerospace engineering in 1977. After his studies he joined Dornier Satellite Systems and in 1996 became chief Engineer of the avionics department. He has been working on many satellite projects such as INTELSAT V, TV-SAT, GLOBALSTAR, EUTELSAT-II, SPACEBUS 3000 and others.

Eduard Igenbergs is Professor of Astronautics and Director of the Institute of Astronautics at the Technical University of Munich. He has a Ph.D. and a masters degree in mechanical engineering. He had a dust counter experiment on the Japanese HITEN spacecraft to the moon and a space debris experiment on board the German BREMSAT. Another dust counter experiment is currently flying to mars with the Japanese Planet-B spacecraft. He developed the Munich Space Chair (MSC), a body restraint system on board MIR. He has been teaching and researching in the field of Systems Engineering for more than 15 years.

Emergence : A Challenge for the Systematic

G. R. McConnell
BAE SYSTEMS
Grange Road, Christchurch
Dorset, BH23 4JE
United Kingdom

Abstract. The word emergence is being used with increasing frequency. Emergent properties are recognised as a fundamental distinguisher of systems, but what exactly are these emergent properties?

This paper examines what these terms mean and why these concepts are not just relevant, but extremely important, to the systems engineering community. It represents an introduction for INCOSE to research which is being carried out in this area. It is therefore a 'work in progress' report which will hopefully be followed up at future conferences.

The aim of the research is to determine ways in which emergence could be better modelled so that it is less of a surprise when it occurs. Perhaps most important, from the viewpoint of the systems engineer, is to predict emergence which has a negative impact on the functioning of the system. It is these unpleasant surprises, often the cause of major problems, which must be addressed.

THE PROBLEM CONTEXT

Expecting the Unexpected. This is, of course, one of the problems facing everyone involved in systems engineering. It must be addressed at all stages of every project. In the words of the former Vice-President of the United States of America, J. Danforth Quayle, we must be "ready for any unforeseen event that may or may not occur" (Quayle, 1990). It is not the intention of this paper to address all possible sources of unforeseen events, rather to concentrate on one particular area which is not widely understood and therefore often neglected – so called **emergent behaviour** of systems.

Systems are, of course, crucial to this audience and (Checkland, 1981) suggests that emergent properties are indeed central to the definition of what is a system:

"A model of a whole entity; when applied to human activity, the model is characterized fundamentally in terms of hierarchical structure, ***emergent properties****, communication, and control. .... When applied to natural or man-made entities, the crucial characteristic is the* ***emergent properties*** *of the whole."*

Another definition of a system which emphasises emergence is (Hitchins 1997):

"A set of complementary, interacting parts with ***properties, capabilities and behaviours emerging*** *both from the parts and from their interactions"*

It is easy to get hung up on the terminology of a concept and miss the importance of the basic ideas behind the words. For this reason, the term "emergent behaviour" does present several problems as it means different things to different people – in effect it actually has its own emergent properties.

WHAT IS EMERGENCE

Difficult to Define. The term emergence, at its most straightforward, is an acknowledgement of the fact that when systems interact there are synergies which result in the 'whole being greater than the sum of the parts'. Many have tried to define what is meant by emergence. However, it would seem that (Holland 1998) gets close to the truth when he says:

"It is unlikely that a topic as complicated as emergence will submit meekly to a concise definition"

In terms of trying to understand what is meant by emergence, it is perhaps easier to use general descriptions like 'something out of nothing', although (Goldstein, 1999) does produce a more precise description :

"Emergence ... refers to the arising of novel and coherent structures, patterns, and properties during the process of self-organization in complex systems. Emergent phenomena are conceptualized as occurring on the macro level, in contrast to the micro-level components and processes out of which they arise."

So, when considering the individual parts of a system, it is impossible to assign the property or behaviour to any of those individual parts. This brings out the important point that emergences are not able to be perceived from the viewpoint of the components which comprise the system. Unfortunately, this type of definition allows a very wide range of attributes to be described as emergent – not all of them are useful in this context.

It is therefore useful to describe the different types of 'emergences' which are important or useful within the systems engineering context.

Types of Emergence. Emergent behaviour can be categorised in many ways. For the purposes of this paper there are two basic distinctions to be made:

1. There is a difference between what could be called 'static' (or combinatorial) emergence and 'dynamic' (or evolutionary) emergence. In the former, the emergence results from the interaction between two systems or components. There is an (in)famous example from the defence industry involving the positioning of radar equipment next to the funnel of a ship - no one had considered the effect of the heat of the funnel on the operation of the radar. Dynamic emergence is a result of a system evolving through time to produce different behaviour (the self organisation from Goldstein's definition referred to earlier). This may be as a result of a change in usage caused by a change in the system operator's role or it could be the result of the system being used in a different set of circumstances to that which was originally envisaged.
2. The other distinction is between those emergences which are truly 'unpredictable' and those which are merely oversights. While it is possible to address each of these in the same way – i.e. improve the process – it is useful to distinguish those which result from a defective process – the oversights – and those that require a novel process.

It's Not All Bad. Something which is often forgotten is that not all emergent behaviour is negative. Often the system will exhibit characteristics which are beneficial to its effectiveness and which were not designed for. Of course, it is more important – especially in cases where safety is of prime importance - that the negative emergence is predicted and controlled. Often the control is straightforward - the prediction is always problematical.

In order to address emergence it is necessary to be not just systematic – this will hopefully address those features of the system wich would otherwise be overlooked – but also systemic. We will address the difference between these terms later, but first we must put the need for a 'systems' view into context. Within this paper we will deal, primarily, with systems in which computers play a major part. However, the general principles apply to all types of system.

INCREASING COMPLEXITY

Some History. In the formative years of the computer industry, the systems were – certainly by today's standards – quite straightforward and could certainly be classed as simple systems. This is not to diminish the achievements of those pioneers, but as the technology has advanced, so have the possibilities in terms of just what can be achieved using a computer. Everyone could now own a tiny calculator capable of putting the processing power of the early computers in the shade. While not every system produced today is complex, there is an undeniable trend towards complexity in all systems. Most devices in use today include extra gadgets. How many of us now drive cars with an integral computer. When they fail the car is as stranded as when the engine itself fails.

In parallel with – or rather following more or less closely behind – the advances in what could be done there have been a stream of methods and techniques which have tried to make the engineering process less "hit and miss" and more grounded in good practice. What has always been a problem – and always will be a problem – is ensuring that all possibilities have been catered for - i.e. identifying what has been overlooked by the process.

Again, in the pioneering days it was possible to lay down some strict rules which would avoid most common errors – although these were almost always only drafted after someone had made the mistake. As well as these rules, there were guidelines such as tight coupling and low cohesion which, if followed, improved the chances of the design behaving as expected.

Methods and Methodologies. As systems have become more complex, so have the methods and techniques available to minimise the risk inherent in the process.

Intuitively it is understood that when dealing with complex systems there is a great deal of truth in the old adage that the 'whole is greater than the sum of the parts'. The emergent properties which are exhibited by such systems are crucial to the behaviour and effectiveness of the system. Each individual in a symphony orchestra may be able to make beautiful music, but the sound and emotion generated by the whole orchestra is equal to more than just the simple addition of each player. The way in which each individual's part relates to the others is also critical to the finished sound.

In complex systems, such as Command and Control systems, the interaction and inter-operation of the parts of the system have a similar synergistic effect. This is particularly true where humans or the environment make a significant impact on the system. This synergy is not well understood, nor is it well catered for during the design and creation of such systems. Indeed, the way in which these systems are specified and procured often ignores this critical aspect altogether. The result is often a system which, far from being greater than the sum of its parts, actually falls short of that combined capability.

As computer power increases and the problems being tackled by computer systems become increasingly complex, there is a perception that it is possible to make the solutions more and more intricate. While the software and hardware may be capable of this, often the design and implementation are not.

Indeed, most systems engineering processes are rooted in a worldview in which the systems behave in a linear, stepwise, predictable and causal manner. They do not deal well with behaviour which is non-linear, unpredictable or, essentially, haphazard. Unfortunately, as the systems which are being built become more complex, so their behaviour is tending towards the latter set of descriptions.

SYSTEMIC vs SYSTEMATIC

Systematic Engineering. There is no doubt that great strides have been taken towards making the systems engineering process more systematic. There are now many methods, techniques and methodologies available which will guide you through the life cycle so that, all being well, you come out at the end with a system which meets needs of the users of the system.

This is, of course, laudable and more must be done to ensure that best practices are included within these techniques. However, the nature of systems engineering is such that it is not possible to generate a check list or recipe for a good, robust, effective system. Certainly, the systematic approach helps, but only within the framework of what is known. To a greater or lesser extent such approaches make a number of assumptions.

1. The requirements are known, or at least where they are not known then they will be added in a controlled manner later.
2. The specifiers of the system know what they wants, what is achievable and, even when they change their minds, the new requirement will not contradict existing requirements.
3. It is possible to break the system down into smaller 'chunks' for the development process without losing information.

Unfortunately these three assumptions are never (or very rarely) completely true, but they are the foundations on which many development processes are built. To mix metaphors, they are also the rocks on which many founder.

The Systemic Alternative. Reality demands that a more holistic viewpoint be taken. This is not a new idea. There are many whom the work here uses as 'giant's shoulders'.

Typical of this is the Generic Reference Model (GRM) (Hitchins, 1997). Figure 1 shows the top level of this model, the GRM map.

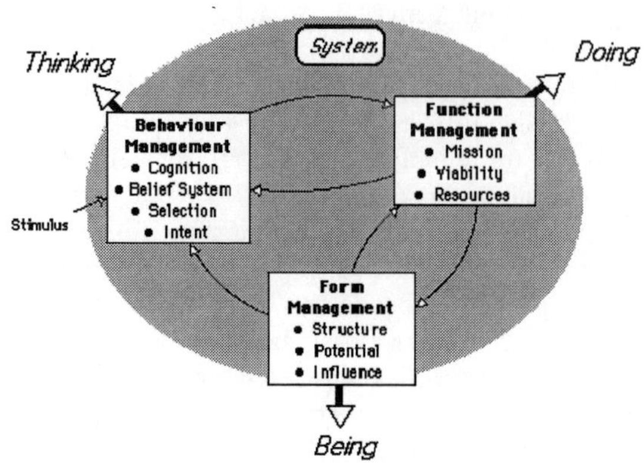

Figure 1. Generic Reference Model Map

The Generic Reference Model offers a number of different perspectives on the system and is representative of the approaches which try to establish a holistic view of the system, often by allowing the modeller to address different facets of the same system within different parts of a single model.

Those who are familiar with systemic modelling, perhaps as popularised by (Senge, 1988), will know that regardless of the type of system being addressed, the method recognises, crucially, that the nature of systems is that they are constantly changing. This acceptance of change as the norm is fundamental when considering emergence. Without change there can be no emergence.

Crucially, these changes are often unpredicted (some would say unpredictable) and lie at the root of many of the problems which arise during system development. What is required is some way of forecasting the changes – or indulging in some sort of systemic crystal ball gazing to see what the future might hold.

PREDICTING THE UNPREDICTABLE

Emergence. What seems to be required is further development of the systems engineering processes to enable the designer to know the unknowable, predict the unpredictable and expect the unexpected. While many have identified emergent properties as integral to the identification of systems, no one has yet established a way of predicting those properties or of using modelling to identify them.

One important point to be made is that the search is not necessarily to find hard and fast predictions of this and that emergent property – rather it is to increase our understanding of the way in which the system will work, both at the point of modelling and in the future, and the way in which the system will interact with other systems. The emphasis has to be on developing a greater awareness of the impact a system will have on its environment.

In many respects this is similar to risk management – we ask the question 'what might happen' and we produce contingencies to cope if and when it does.

It is not sufficient to say that an emergent property is something which we haven't thought about – they are still emergent even after they are 'discovered'. Instead they are properties of the whole which cannot be described using the models of the parts. This assumes that the models of the parts are complete. Something extra is, however, required in order to model the whole.

We described above some categories of emergence and ended up with four categories – static and dynamic, and for each those which are 'unpredictable' and those which were oversights. We can dismiss the oversights, for the present, on the grounds that while the elimination of these is indeed a concern, it is not the primary purpose of this paper.

Modelling Strategies. The static and dynamic types of emergence require different approaches and it is these which will become the focus of the research over the coming months. This is a multi-disciplinary problem and there are a number of techniques and methods that could be employed to address the prediction of this emergence.

The prime requirement of the modelling is to increase, systemically, our understanding of the way in which the system will behave. To this end there are several aspects of modelling which are possible contributors to a solution.

1. Complexity Theory
2. System Dynamics
3. Pattern Theory
4. Perspectivism

Complexity Theory. There are too many different branches of complexity theory to be considered within the space available, but one important concept as far as emergence is concerned is the idea of the self organising system. Many authors have described self organisation and for many commentators it is the main source of emergent phenomena. We have already seen the quote from (Goldstein, 1999) and that is typical of the complexity theorists view of emergence.

Much of the work of that school is in the realm of complex adaptive systems – looking at systems which learn and change their behaviour based on their 'experiences' with the environment. (Holland, 1998) in his book further restricts the type of systems with which he deals to what he calls constrained generating procedures (cgp) . These are systems which have a limited rule set.

Self organisation can be seen in many common situations. One of the commonly cited examples is that of the ant hill (Hofstadter, 1979).

"Somehow the simple laws of the agents (the ants) generate emergent behaviour far beyond their individual capacities." (Holland 1998)

System Dynamics. This is a very well known and widely used technique. The technique dates back to the work of Forrester in the early sixties. It is, perhaps, not something that you would necessarily associate with modelling of emergence having its roots in control theory. However, much of the self organisation (and therefore emergent behaviour) can be attributed to the 'learning' process that is going on within the system. This learning can only result from the reception and understanding of feedback.

It is (Senge, 1988) who has popularised this particular view of system dynamics. He shows how a system – in his case it is an organisation - learns as a result of its behaviour. However, Forrester himself warns of the dangers of taking too populist an approach and stresses the need for the formalism of system dynamics.

"Unquestioning and superficial enthusiasm for systems thinking may lead some people into trouble. Some people attain enough revealing insights from systems thinking that they feel the need for nothing else" (Forrester, 1994)

One of the criticisms of the system dynamics approach is that the type of modelling which is done does not allow for individual parts of the system to have independent strategy. Rather it looks at the effect of the feedback (and feed forward) on the system as a whole. This could be answered by adopting an object or agent based approach, where each individual agent can be invested with the intelligence to change its behaviour in the face of particular information and a system dynamics model used to govern the feedback received by the agents.

Pattern Theory. One of the more recent developments in the software field is the use of pattern languages. These are actually the result of the adoption by the software community of an idea from a completely different domain – that of architecture (real buildings, not systems architecture) (Alexander, 1979). (Barter, 1998) suggested to a previous INCOSE conference that a systems engineering pattern language be created which captured the systems engineering body of knowledge.

Patterns, and pattern languages, capture more than just emergence. The particular view of patterns which may be of interest here is that which (Holland, 1998) describes when he says that :

*"emergence usually involves **patterns of interaction** that persist despite a continual turnover in the constituents of the patterns".*

To illustrate this he uses the example of a standing

wave in front of a rock in a fast flowing river – the wave remains despite the fact that the water which makes it up is continually changing. Holland believes that an emergent phenomena is **recognisable** and **recurrent**. This, of course, does not make it any easier to predict but it does suggest that we will know emergence when we see it!

One recurrent pattern in Command and Control systems is ODA - Observe, Decide, Act. This pattern, together with subtle variations on it, is seen whenever there is a decision making process. First information is gathered; then it is assimilated and a course of action chosen; finally, the action is carried out.

This may seem perhaps a very superficial viewpoint. However, using this pattern and others like it can help to identify what a system is doing and how it is doing it. It is interesting that the Systems Dynamics technique could be seen to incorporate this very pattern as the use of feedback loops is precisely what the ODA pattern embodies when placed in its true real-time, continuous, environment.

A good discussion of modelling the Command and Control decision cycle is contained in (Hughes, 1992). He also points out the dangers of 'one-sided analysis'. Hughes is talking about the impact of the enemy's own Command and Control structures, but we can take from this a warning that when we are modelling our systems some of the emergent properties will come, not from other co-operative systems, but from competitive systems which are actively trying to disrupt our system.

Perspectivism. The final aspect that is considered in this paper is a philosophical one. It is vitally important for systems engineers to realise that their own view of the world is just that. It may coincide in some ways with the view of the customers, the users or the developers but, inevitably, much of their views will be different – and perhaps contradictory. It is essential that we acknowledge, not only that someone else has a different view, but that it is entirely reasonable that two contradictory perspectives can **both** be correct.

It would be asking too much to expect that everyone could have a common perspective – that is neither necessary nor useful. What is required is that the different perspectives are not just acknowledged, but incorporated into the process.

A lack of awareness of other perspectives can easily result in some very undesirable emergent properties. In particular, one man's complex system can be another's simple system (and, of course, vice versa). So, if the systems engineer perceives a simple system, which to the developer is complex, there are inevitably going to be problems. (Klir, 1985) illustrates this well:

"to the neurophysiologist the brain, as a feltwork of fibers and a soup of enzymes, is certainly complex; and equally the transmission of a detailed description of it would require much time. To a butcher the brain is simple, for he has to distinguish it from only about thirty other 'meats'."

As systems engineers we must ensure that the system has the correct perspective of the problem to be effective – not too complex, not too simple – and we must be aware of the perceived complexity of the system from the point of view of all the stakeholders.

LOOKING FORWARD

Putting It All Together. It is (Holland, 1998) who suggests that in the future we will be using models as **guides** – i.e. instead of using them to predict the future, we will instead be attempting to understand the future. Instead of trying to find out whether something is possible, we will be trying to develop ideas about the nature of complex situations.

This change of objective will not come easily, however it is fundamental to the understanding of emergence and the modelling of the ever increasing complexity of our systems. It will require the acknowledgement of the fact that we are creating systems which are so complex that we cannot be completely sure of their behaviour in all circumstances. This is, of course, no different to what we encounter in everyday life in the 'real world', but underpinning the systems engineer's method of working to date has been the assumption that created systems will behave as specified.

The Way Ahead. The ideas stated in this paper are of the nature of setting the scene. There is still no solution available to predict emergence, however, it is hoped that this research will eventually result in some useful insights into the modelling of emergence. This paper has given some insight into the way that this research is developing. More importantly, the paper lays the basis for understanding the later stages of the development of the ideas.

In Summary. It is crucial that we, as systems engineers, continue to adopt a systematic approach to our work. The real worth of systems engineering does not, however, come from the mechanistic 'turning the handle' to produce a system, but from the 'art' of creating systems which are effective within the context in which they are required. The ability to understand the emergent properties of complex systems would be a powerful tool to add to the systems engineer's tool bag. This research will hopefully take us some steps towards that goal.

REFERENCES

Alexander, Christopher, *The Timeless Way of Building*. Oxford University Press, New York, 1979.

Barter, Robert H, "A Systems Engineering Pattern Language", in *Proceedings of the 8th Annual International Symposium of INCOSE*, 1998.

Checkland, Peter, *Systems Thinking, Systems Practice*. John Wiley & Sons Ltd, London, 1981.

Forrester, Jay W, "System Dynamics, Systems Thinking, and Soft OR", in *System Dynamics Review* Vol.10, No.2, 1994

Gharajedaghi, Jashmid, *Systems Thinking: Managing Chaos and Complexity, a Platform for Designing Business Archictecture*. Butterworth-Heinemann, Boston, 1999.

Goldstein, Jeffrey, "Emergence as a Construct: History and Issues". In *Emergence* Vol.1-1, 1999, pp 49-72.

Hitchins, Derek, *Basic Models for System Thinking*, `http://ourworld.compuserve.com/homepages/Prof_Hitchins/`, April, 1997.

Hofstadter, Douglas R, *Gödel, Escher, Bach: An Eternal Golden Braid*. Basic Books, New York, 1979.

Holland, John H. , *Emergence: From Chaos to Order*. Addison Wesley, New York, 1998.

Hughes, Wayne P. Jr, "Command and Control within the Framework of a Theory of Combat". In *Proceedings of the 1992 Symposium on Command and Control Research*, 1992

Klir, Georg, "Complexity: Some General Observations". In *Systems Research* Vol 2-2 pages 131-140; 1985.

Quayle, J. Danforth, Referring to the Middle East situation, 22nd September 1990.

Senge, Peter, *The Fifth Discipline*. John Wiley & Sons Ltd, New York, 1988.

BIOGRAPHY

George McConnell is currently studying towards a PhD with the Open University. He is researching ways in which the challenge of emergent properties can be addressed within the systems engineering process. He has worked for what is now BAE SYSTEMS for over 23 years, the last 12 within Systems Engineering. He is a Fellow of the Fellowship for Operational Research, a Chartered Engineer and EurIng through the British Computer Society and a member of the IEEE.

The Perception-Reaction Simulation Model for Enterprise Control Systems

Ralph D. Gibson
Science Applications International Corporation
22299 Exploration Drive Suite 200
Lexington Park, Maryland 20653

Abstract. Throughout the history of warfare, battle decisions have been made based on the perceptions of both friendly and enemy forces. Perceptions in early history were based on visual sightings and relayed back to the commander through a slow communication system of runners. Technology has changed the methods of information collection and transmission, but the concept of battle has not changed the fact that commanders make decisions based on their perception of the battlefield. What technology has done is to place so much information in front of the commander at an ever increasing pace that misunderstanding or completely missing vital information could drastically affect the outcome of the battle. The purpose of the Joint Force Air Component Commander (JFACC) Project is to revolutionize military command and control, specifically in Joint Aerospace Operations. The Joint Air Operations Enterprise will consist of three major components: a control system, a feedback system, and a plant. This paper discusses the use of a perception-reaction simulation model to perform the physical actions of the plant. The definition and relationship of the three components are described in terms of their contribution to the Joint Air Operation Enterprise. A description of the perception-reaction model and its relationship to the physical actions of the battlespace are given. Examples of current perception-reaction methodology are provided. Finally, the perception-reaction model is integrated into the Joint Air Operations Enterprise, and it is shown how the perception-reaction model can fully support the enterprise.

INTRODUCTION

Throughout history, battlefield commanders have made critical decisions concerning tactics and force deployment based on their understanding of the battlespace. The information they receive, or don't receive, is critical to the outcome of the battle. The information that is received can be true, inadvertently wrong, or intentionally false. The commander cannot "know" about the enemy with absolute certainty. Had General Custer known the true size of the forces against him, the Battle of the Little Bighorn may not have occurred. It was the use of deception, that is the sending false of perceptions, that caused the German Army to be held back during the invasion of Normandy in World War II. Using information received, the U.S. Navy was able to know the actions of the Japanese forces and defend Midway Island instead of move their forces toward the wrong avenue of perceived attack. Therefore, it is not knowledge but perception that determines the commander's decisions.

To simulate the battlespace best, the simulation must be based on the perception-reaction model. First, perception-reaction warfare and how the perceptions are derived are discussed. Next, the perception-reaction simulation model is introduced, and it is shown how it is applicable to the Enterprise Control System being developed for the Joint Force Air Component Commander (JFACC) Project. Descriptions of the concept of perception-reaction warfare, the particulars of the JFACC project, the Joint Aerospace Operations Enterprise model are presented. The design process for the JFACC project system design is then given. Finally, a perception-reaction simulation model currently in use are presented.

PERCEPTION-REACTION WARFARE

Warfare, as it has been fought over time, is not based on facts about the enemy, even though there may be considerable information about those forces, but is based on what is perceived about the enemy. Through the use of perceivers, commanders obtain information about the opposing force. Some of the information may be accurate, some may be old and useless, while some of the information may be intentionally false, sent out by the enemy to trick the commander into making a wrong decision. That decision could be either to withdraw when facing a weaker force, or to attack when the opposing force is stronger and conceivably able to defeat the commander's forces.

Historical Perspective. Perceptions about one's adversary are the basis of many historic great wins and spectacular losses. They can take many forms: accurate perceptions (I know what they are doing), unknown perceptions (I have no clue what is going on), mistakenly inaccurate perceptions (this is what I think is happening, but I'm wrong), and intentionally inaccurate perceptions (these are the signals I am receiving from them, and they are wrong).

The history of warfare has many instances where missing, inaccurate, or misleading information received from sources has dramatically changed the outcome of battles. As stated earlier, missing information about the strength of the combined Indian forces led General Custer to believe he could easily defeat the 'small' Indian force when he led the 7th Cavalry at the Little Bighorn. It was this misconception that led to his defeat. The Trojan Horse can also illustrate the concept of misunderstanding a perception. When the Greeks left their gift at the gate of Troy, the Trojans figured that the Greeks were giving up the fight and wanted to leave a gift as a sign of surrender. This misperception cost the Trojans their city.

Understanding an enemy's plans, without giving away that those plans are known, has greatly aided commanders in making decisions concerning the placement of forces. The perceptions provided by radar during the Battle of Britain greatly assisted the British Air Force in finding and destroying German aircraft. Breaking the Enigma code used by the Germans allowed the Allied forces to hunt and destroy the U-boats, saving valuable supplies and personnel.

Intentionally false information can cause what was hidden to become known or cause a misdirection of effort. During World War II, the Americans knew through intelligence data that the Japanese were preparing for an attack. The question was 'where?' By intentionally transmitting false information about the water situation on Midway Island, the Americans were able to discover the attack location and rally their forces in defense of the island, turning the tide of the war in the Pacific Theater.

Modern Perceivers. The various methods used by the commander to obtain perceptions have changed over the centuries. Initially, perceptions were obtained by observation, either by the commander surveying the battlefield or by scouts assigned to the commander who went out and looked at the enemy's strength, location, direction of movement and types of arms. Today's commanders use many different methods, but the concept is still the same, find out as much as possible about your enemy. Perceptions are obtained by using either passive or active perceivers.

Passive perceivers (Figure 1) can best be described as receivers only. They receive a signal or other information but do not send out any energy or leave behind any traces. Examples of passive perceivers are radio receivers, infrared and heat detectors, sonar and other listening devices, and optical receivers. These types of perceivers are difficult to counter unless their location is known.

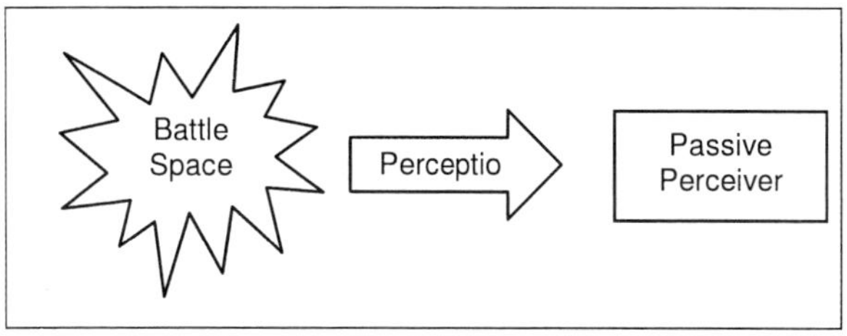

Figure 1. Passive Perceptions

Active perceivers (Figure 2) are those that emit energy as part of their perception action. Radar and radio transmitters are the best examples of this type of perceiver in that they emit an electromagnetic signal that can be received by other forces, and the transmission source can be located or the signal countered.

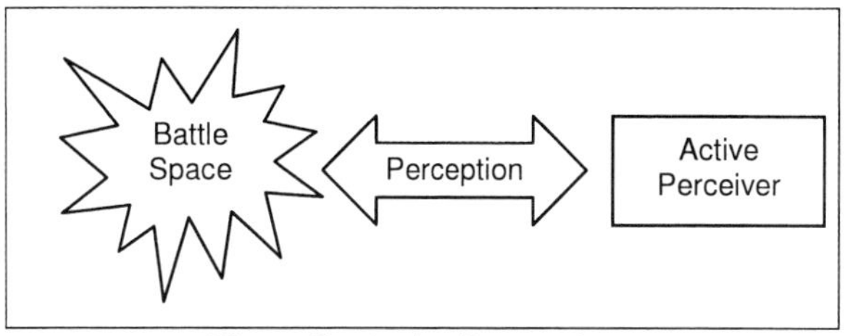

Figure 2. Active Perceptions

Problems of Modern Warfare Perceptions. Modern technology has done many things to assist the commander in understanding the enemy. High speed electronics, more sensitive devices and remote capability has made information faster and easier to obtain. It has also caused some difficulties for the commander.

These difficulties include:

Types of Perceivers. In the past, the only type of perceiver was personal observation, either by the commander or a forward lookout. Today, perceptions can be gained by numerous means, including personal observation, remote sound, thermal, infrared and motion sensors, aircraft and satellite reconnaissance. The differing types available may make determining the best perception difficult.

Number of Perceivers. When perceptions were gained by personal observation, the number of perceivers was less than or equal to the number of personnel sent out to observe the enemy. With the modern perceivers and remote access to the information, the amount of information gained has grown significantly to the point where the number of perceivers can outnumber the communication links available.

Relay Speed of Perceptions. Personal observation perceptions were first relayed to the commander at the speed of the human runner. As new methods were found to relay the information, the speed became faster, but the amount of information was still limited. With modern communications through radio transmissions and satellite links, the information can get to the commander nearly instantaneously and present an immediate picture of the current situation. By combining the number of perceivers with the relay speed of the perceptions, a commander can be overwhelmed by the information received.

To increase the effectiveness of a commander, systems must be able to (re)act in a more autonomous and more anticipative way, and must include advanced user interfaces that allow interaction at several levels of abstraction. The discrete character of future functional extensions, the extended timescales and the expected massive amount of information that must be handled, call for the use of advanced representation, search, and reasoning techniques. It will be a real challenge to identify and formulate expert knowledge and to evaluate it for relevance, consistency and completeness. In addition, this expertise will have to be incorporated in a system in such a way that operators can effectively use it. [Boasson]

JOINT FORCE AIR COMPONENT COMMANDER (JFACC) PROJECT

The JFACC project aims to catalyze a revolutionary change in the military command and control (C^2) of the future by tackling one of its toughest problems – the agile and stable control of distributed and dynamic military operations conducted in an uncertain and rapidly changing environment. [JFACC] Command and control is the exercise of authority and direction by a properly designated commander over assigned and attached forces in the accomplishment of the mission. Command and control functions are performed through an arrangement of personnel, equipment, communications, facilities, and procedures employed by a commander in planning, directing, coordinating, and controlling forces and operations in the accomplishment of the mission. [AFDD2]

If there is to be a revolutionary change in the military command and control systems of the future, there must be scientific study, exploration, and experimentation with the agile and stable control of distributed and dynamic military operations. This revolutionary C^2 system must be able to overcome operational gaps in the current systems, while providing agile control of dynamic military operations.

Operational Gaps. Today's command and control systems for operations have evolved through a number of important stages. They have undergone profound enhancements over the years based on practical experiences and technical analyses. However, to make a quantitative and qualitative leap in the direction of dramatically increased agility, today's systems must overcome a number of critical gaps including: [JFACC]

Limited Agility. The ability to rapidly and effectively respond to varying time constraints, changeable resources, erratic hostile responses, asymmetric threats and unpredictable anomalies is an unsolved challenge. Today's C^2 systems necessitate fairly long response times and are limited in their ability to react or act proactively, consistently and efficiently to rapid changes in environment, in opportunities, in effects of execution, or in higher-command objectives.

Constrained Flexibility. Today's C^2 systems are poorly adapted to the wide spectrum of military conflicts and activities that they are called upon to support. Air Operations can run the gamut from humanitarian relief through enforcement of no-fly zones and surgical strikes to full scale war, but the tools (software applications) and processes currently in-place are based on bombs-on-target warfare and cannot provide the scalability and the extensibility needed.

Ad Hoc Stability. Humans are the stabilizing elements of current military operations. Management of destabilizing events, such as time critical targets, changes in guidance, or windows of opportunity are only processed by humans with little, or no, help from decision support systems. Their C^2 systems do not offer the ability to perform rapid, efficient changes in current operations, while simultaneously taking into account the long-term effects and requirements.

Ineffective Feedback. Many decisions are made without the benefit of the disciplined incorporation of feedback on operations. The feedback does not support the commander and staff in a reliable, timely, consistent, or relevant fashion, nor at the level of abstraction and integration that allows decision makers to make effective decisions.

Expansive Personnel and Facility Requirements. Today's C^2 systems rely on large numbers of highly trained personnel, making C^2 operations expensive and difficult to deploy, while necessitating large physical and informational footprints, which expose such organizations and their facilities to asymmetric threats.

Ineffective Use of Assets and Resources. To increase their flexibility and responsiveness, today's systems rely on the multiple use of resources, ready availability of large quantities of assets in theater, and redundancy. When a rapid change is executed, inadequate coordination between various functional activities often leads to a relatively high percentage of incorrectly planned and executed missions.

Project Objectives. The purpose of the JFACC project is to develop a C^2 system that will assist the commander in making timely decisions that will use the proper forces and send those forces to the target with the least amount of danger. The JFACC responsibilities include planning, coordination, allocation, and tasking of joint air operations based on the concept of operations and air appointment decisions. [JP3-56] A commander must have the ability to use all the information available to complete assigned responsibilities.

To meet the project objectives, the following areas of emphasis need to be covered [JFACC]:

Agile Control of Dynamic Military Operations. As observation, orientation, decision, and execution times are driven toward progressively shorter timelines, the control of dynamic phenomena within real-time operations becomes the key challenge to practical implementation of any new generation of C^2 systems. This key insight is the reason why the emphasis is on theories, models, technologies, and concepts that manage the dynamic effects of large scale, highly agile command and control systems.

Intended End-State of the Project. To achieve this kind of agile control, experimental studies, technical insight, theoretical underpinnings, and technology development in the arena of dynamic behavior of the control mechanisms that will underlie future agile and stable military C^2 structures are needed. Even though any individual process within the current C^2 systems can be made more efficient, effective and responsive using available resources of the information revolution, the overall systemic effects are expected to present formidable, complex challenges characteristic of large scale, dynamic control systems. The products and results of the JFACC project will address these challenges.

Preliminary System Design. A fixed architecture and system design specification will enable rapid and focused development of the experimental "breadboard" system in the Prototype Phase of the JFACC project.

Theoretical Techniques and Tools. In general, there is very limited understanding of the potential effects of automation on the dynamics of an enterprise control system as complex as military C^2. History offers many examples where the introduction of automation, and particularly the introduction of a feedback loop, has caused complex, counterintuitive and unexpected dynamic phenomena. There is anecdotal evidence that recent attempts to shorten the military decision cycle via computerization can cause undesirable dynamic effects, such as uncontrolled oscillations. [JFACC]

JOINT AIR OPERATIONS ENTERPRISE MODEL

The intent of the Joint Air Operations Enterprise Model is to enable, conduct, and analyze experiments that provide insights into possible dynamic phenomena; verify the value or contribution of various theoretical techniques and tools that are developed; and identify the qualitative and quantitative characteristics of required functional component technologies. Enterprise models are useful tools in the re-engineering or improvement of an enterprise. [Whitman] The Joint Air Operations Enterprise model is not the solution to creating a revolution in military C^2, but it will be an important tool for generating and testing the overall system. [JFACC]

The enterprise model requires an intelligent simulation of the battlespace. The strategy of the intelligent simulation of the battlefield is to integrate other systems, both existing and planned, as subsystems into an overall framework using artificial intelligence to bind them together. [Gerber] This capability is difficult, as there is not yet a C^2 system standard. The Joint Air Operations Enterprise model is an initial project to look at the use of intelligent simulation for C^2.

The Joint Air Operations Enterprise Model (Figure 3) is comprised of three major components; the control system, enterprise plant, and feedback. The control system contains the Air Operations Plans with the objectives, tasks, activities and missions. The inputs to the control system (1), and the primary drivers in command and control decisions, are the guidance from higher echelons, the observations of the current situation, and the resources available to carry out the objective. The outputs of the control system (2) are the Executive Orders that contain the commander's guidance for execution of the mission.

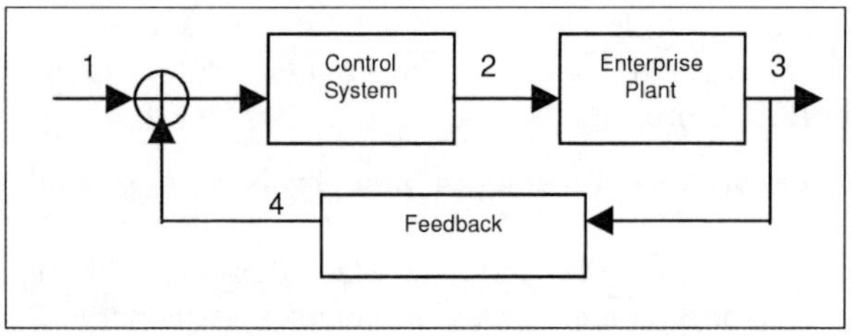

Figure 3. Joint Air Operations Enterprise Model

The enterprise plant contains the operational assets available to carry out the mission as directed by the control system. This is the component where all the physical actions of the battle space take place. Execution orders are received from the control system, and the players perform those commands as best as possible. There are three directly controlled plant elements: the air forces, which provide the war fighters; the battle managers, which provide real-time control of the forces; and the aerospace systems. Indirectly controlled by the plant are the enemy forces, noncombatants, and physical phenomena such as the weather. For simulation and analysis purposes, the distributed virtual environment must provide an accurate portrayal of threat, phenomenology, environmental, and allied activities that is also structured, controlled, and amenable to analysis. [Stytz] The outputs from the plant (3) are the air operations. This is the simulation of the interaction of the various forces, status of all the controlled forces and current tasking and availability. This is what an omniscient observer would see happening from outside the battlespace.

The requirement to provide the current state as well as changes from a previous state implies a need to maintain access to that information on demand. To make the information available one must first determine how to transform the data available from the simulations to match the data model for the C^2 network. [Paola] Thus, the feedback portion of the model takes in the results of the air operations, the current situation for the blue, red, and neutral forces, and the current status of operations, and returns the information in a form usable by the control system. All of the actions taking place are then assessed for compliance and outcome of the various actions. Predictions of future movements of all forces, evaluation of the outcome of the actions and identifications of future points of contention and opportunities for advances are produced by the feedback block and sent to the control system (4).

JFACC PROJECT SYSTEM DESIGN

The JFACC Air Operations Enterprise Model is using the systems engineering process for development. This development will be done concurrently, with other components of the JFACC project, particularly the development of the control system. Concurrent engineering is the process whereby a number of distinct aspects of a product are engineered simultaneously. [Kott92] This allows those that specialize in control systems and their application to command and control and scheduling, to work independently of the teams providing the plant/feedback simulation model.

The development process for the JFACC Air Operations Enterprise Model is best explained using the system development life-cycle model (Figure 4).

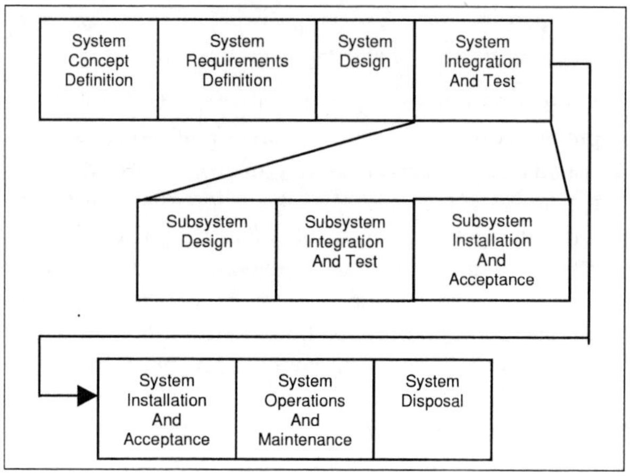

Figure 4. System Development Life-Cycle Model [SEAS]

The system concept definition and system requirements definition were prepared by the Defense Advanced Research Projects Agency (DARPA) in the proposal document. [JFACC] The system requirements definitions for the enterprise model were intentionally stated in such a way as not to drive the entire system design. The intention is to provide sufficient information to allow the developers of the control system (a subsystem in the life-cycle model) enough leeway to develop several different instantiations of the system. This way, the various control system models can be integrated into the final control subsystem design. At the same time, the plant/feedback subsystem is undergoing requirements definition, design, integration and test at different location to provide several different instantiations of that subsystem. This is the current phase in the development life-cycle.

The next step will be to bring all the different subsystems together. This will be a two part process. First, the several different control system subsystems will be compared and evaluated to determine which one(s) will be used for the enterprise model system. For the plant/feedback subsystem, the same selection process will be used. DARPA will use its selection criteria to select the components that it feels will provide the best components for the enterprise model. One or more of each subsystem will be chosen, and the components will be integrated into a complete control system or plant/feedback subsystem. Then, the subsystem components will be selected. Further development, integration and testing will take place to finalize the subsystem designs. Once the subsystems are finalized, they will undergo integration and testing as a system. Prior to testing, a comprehensive test plan will be developed to ensure all requirements are met based on the criteria selected by DARPA.

The system installation and acceptance, operations and maintenance, and disposal domains of the life-cycle model follow system integration and testing. At this time, the procedures for these domains are not known and will be determined at a later date.

PERCEPTION-REACTION SIMULATION MODEL

Perception-reaction simulation models are in use today by all the branches of the Department of Defense. Each has its own special ability to handle various missions and simulation scenarios. One simulation model that will fit the requirements of the JFACC project is the Joint Interim Mission Model used by the Joint Strike Fighter Project Office [JIMM].

Joint Interim Mission Model. The Joint Interim Mission Model (JIMM) is a general purpose, event driven, conflict simulation. This means that one can describe conflicts across a broad range of issues, detail, geography and time, with a balanced approach, or equal treatment to physical and mental aspects of the conflict. The strong point for JIMM is that it is an environment generator. This is an important function for the JFACC project in that it provides a realistic backdrop for other simulations, stimulations, or man-in-the-loop activities. The architecture of JIMM allows for easy integration with other simulations and simulators. This architecture will allow JIMM to be easily connected to the JFACC Air Operations Enterprise Model through a network, and run independent of the model. JIMM can fulfill all the functions of the plant and the feedback segments.

The mental aspects of JIMM are associated with the gathering, assimilation, processing, and dissemination of information, and all decision-making processes. The physical aspects include the environment, communications, information gathering, physical influences, disruption, and movement. As an environment generator, JIMM does not emphasis mental activities over physical activities, or vice versa. This allows the model to simulate a variety of conflict types, political, economic, limited combat, or major conflict. The user determines the type of conflict and the depth to which the simulation will model the mental and physical aspects of the conflict. The more detailed the model, the more interaction that can occur between the commander and the modeled players.

JIMM can be used for many applications. In the past, the predecessors of JIMM have been used in conjunction with studies to analyze different hardware and software components. As capabilities have been added to JIMM, the applications have expanded to include test and evaluation, training, mission planning and rehearsal, force-mix analysis, tactics and procedures development, and cost and operational effectiveness analysis. This versatility will provide a variety of mission scenarios for the enterprise model to test its ability to use the perceptions it receives and provide the commander with the options he needs to make a correct decision.

"In a planning problem the solver is given a description of the current state of the problem world and a set of goals to achieve. The task is to find a plan – a sequence (or more generally – a network) of activities that will lead to the desired goals". [Kott96] The desire of the Air Operations Enterprise Model is to automate some of the activities required to make a force implimentation decision. JIMM can support these activities by providing the appropriate information based on the current state of the simulation and continuous inputs by the commander. With minimal changes, the same begin state of the simulation can result in different outcomes during the simulation, thus providing varying situations to the commander. Different situations require different actions by the commander, thus providing a learning tool. By using this capability of JIMM, the commander can implement various decisions and see the results.

The Joint Interim Mission Model is a proven perception-reaction model capable of simulating a variety of conflict situations. The size and depth of the simulation is set by the user and easily changed. The Joint Interim Mission Model can easily be connected through a network interface to the enterprise model and simulate the components of the plant and the feedback systems.

CONCLUSION

The need for increased capability to assist the force commander in utilizing the vast amount of perception information available to properly direct his forces is becoming of major importance. With the increased number and types of perception receivers available to the commander, the amount of information available to the commander is fast overtaking his ability to assimilate and use the information presented. Through the development of the Joint Force Air Component Commander Air Operations Enterprise Model, assimilating and coordinating the perceptions will be automated. By presenting the information to the commander in an easier to understand format, the commander will be able to direct his forces to those areas that require the most attention and with the best response for the situation.

REFERENCES

[AFDD2] Air Force Doctrine Document 2, "Organization and Employment of Aerospace Power." 28 Sep 1998

[Boasson] M. Boasson, "Simulation in Operational Systems," *Simulation Interoperability Workshop*, Spring 1998.

[Gerber] W. Gerber, A. Henninger, and G. Stone, "Intelligent Extraction, Filtering and Reporting of Critical Decision Information from a Simulation," *Simulation Interoperability Workshop*, Spring 1999.

[JFACC] JFACC Project, BAA 99-18, Agile Control of Military Operations, Proposers Information Package. Defense Advanced Research Projects Agency, Arlington, VA. March 31, 1999.

[JIMM] Joint Interim Mission Model User's Guide, Volume I, Version 1.2, 1999

[JP3-56] Joint Publication 3-56.1, "Command and Control for Joint Air Operations." 14 Nov 1994

[Kott92] A. Kott, C. Kollar, and A. Cederquist (1992). "The Role of Product Modeling in Concurrent Engineering Environments." [Online at **www.cgi.com/web2/govt/product.html**]

[Kott96] A. Kott and V. Saks (1996). "Continuity-Guided Regeneration: an Approach to Reactive Replanning and Rescheduling." [Online at **www.cgi.com/web2/govt/ks-cgrl.html**]

[Paola] A. Paola and R. Ressler, "Stimulating the Army Tactical Command and Control System Using the Run Time Manager: Concepts and Implications," *Simulation Interoperability Workshop*, Spring 1999.

[SEAS] Computer Sciences Corporation, "SEAS Training Program: An Overview of Systems Engineering."

[Stytz] M. Stytz and S. Banks, "Requirements for the Next Generation of Air Force Models," *Simulation Interoperability Workshop*, Fall 1998.

[Whitman] L. Whitman and B. Huff (1997). "A Living Enterprise Model." *Proceedings of the Sixth Industrial Engineering Research Conference*

BIOGRAPHY

Ralph Gibson is currently a Systems Analyst for Science Applications International Corporation working at Air Combat Environment Test and Evaluation Facility, Naval Air Warfare Center – Aircraft Division, Patuxent River Naval Air Station, Maryland. He is a member of the Model Development Team tasked with enhancing and maintaining the mission model to meet the requirements of the facility. Ralph Gibson is a graduate of the United States Air Force Academy with a degree in Astronautical Engineering. He is currently working on a Master of Software Engineering degree at the University of Maryland.

COST ENGINEERING WITHIN A MODEL-BASED DESIGN PROCESS FOR SATELLITE SYSTEMS

O. Quirmbach[1], M. Wilke[2], E. Igenbergs[2]

[1] Dornier Satellite Systems GmbH
Postfach 80 11 69
81663 Munich, Germany

[2] Institute of Astronautics
Technical University of Munich
Boltzmannstr. 15
85748 Garching, Germany

Abstract. This paper describes a method to integrate cost analysis, cost planning, accounting and systems engineering within one integrated system model. It is called **I**ntegrated **S**ystem **Co**st **M**odel — ISCOM. This model has been implemented in a tool supporting the important early phase of satellite design. The tool is called MuSSat – Modelling and Simulation of Satellite Systems – provides the user with the means to easily and quickly model all aspects – and the various interdependencies between them – of a satellite system and to compare various alternative designs (Wilke, Quirmbach et al. 1999*)*. Basis of the software tool is a modelling methodology developed at the Institute of Astronautics at the Technical University of Munich, which allows an integrated way of product, process and cost planning.

MuSSat supports Target Costing process by allocating Target Costs to functions, objects and processes. Therefore it provides creation of cost tables for all kind of system elements in order to get element specific and actual cost estimation relationships. Thus MuSSat enables a company to improve its performance in the new market segment of commercial satellite applications by supporting integrated concurrent engineering.

INTRODUCTION

Global Situation. In the commercial satellite market the aerospace industry has to be in a position to recognise the changing demands of its customers. This requires active decision making which takes into account customers needs and his willingness to pay for these needs. The systems life cycle costs (LCC) are the most important design parameter. They are strongly influenced by the early phases of product development. More than 70 percent of the LCC are fixed in the design phase while most of the actual expenses occur during the later phases (Production and Launch). But the design process is strongly dominated by engineering departments where cost knowledge is traditionally low. One of the most critical points in the commercial satellite market is the necessity of offering firm fixed price proposals in the early phase of product design process. To reduce the risk resulting of this insecurity a Target Costing process and a high level of cost knowledge is needed. Problems in the traditional way of product planning are (Quirmbach, Wilke et al. 1999):

1. Complex systems have many interacting requirements, design parameter and cost drivers

2. Product- and cost planning are not yet one integrated process. Different disciplines have different data models and tools. Accounting uses ERP (Enterprise Resource Planning) software while engineering needs requirement engineering and modelling tools. Information flow between these tools is complicated.

3. Availability and consistency of design parameters to analyse cost influence. For example the engineers of the solar array subsystem calculate more than ten different power parameters. For cost analysing these different values are often a source of error. But it is important to compare equal product properties.

4. The accounting system allows to allocate cost for

product elements (e.g. components) but not to allocate them to the cost driving product functions or requirements. Value engineering is a way of function cost analysis and is strongly separated from the accounting process. ERP software allows to create a work breakdown structure (WBS) but there is no link to product functions or requirements.

5. Creating and especially maintaining cost tables in order to analyse costs is difficult.

As the customer's requirements are not yet fixed while a prime contractor for a new programme is selected, customers are frequently changing their requirements to asses the design flexibility of different supplier's with regard to cost and efficiency. Thus the possibility to compare many design variants quickly in order to optimise customers cost-benefit ratio will become more and more important. In addition the required cost reduction for commercial satellites systems exceeds 50% of traditional satellites cost. The system costs (SC) are a multivariable function (Wildemann 1982):

SC = f (system performance, configuration, project organisation, schedule and price factors)

Studies have shown that the influence of system performance is about 40% of SC, configuration is about 15%, schedule and project organisation is about 10% each and factor prices are about 5%. 20% of system costs are determined by system environment (e.g. laws, exchange rates,...). Traditional accounting and engineering processes are not sufficient for todays business environment. Rather the necessity of an integrated and interdisciplinary system and cost engineering approach is obvious.

GOALS

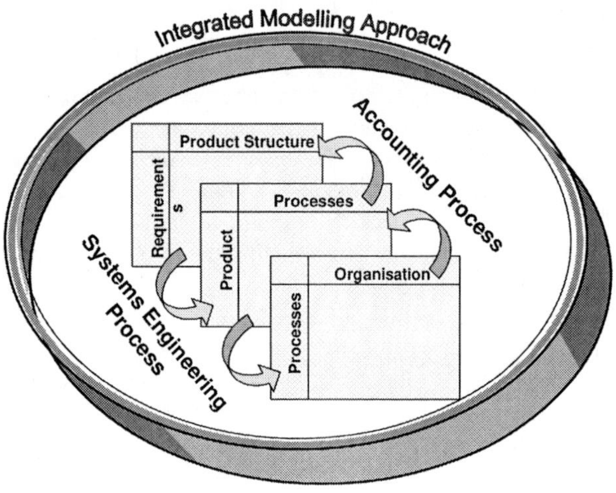

Figure 1. Integrated Modelling Approach

This paper describes a method to integrate cost analysis, cost planning, accounting and systems engineering within one integrated system model. It is called ISCOM— **I**ntegrated **S**ystem and **Co**st **M**odel — and its goal is to support an interdisciplinary design process of satellite systems.

Therefore the model

- shall support the user to determine the cost driver of all system elements like requirements, functions, product tree and processes on any hierarchical level.
- shall support the Target Costing process and allocation of Target Costs to functions, product tree and processes.
- shall enable to create cost tables and cost functions for all of these system aspects.
- must be applicable for technical models as well as for accounting objects. The modelling approach has to include all kind of technical and economic parameters and their relations.
- shall support the evaluation of alternative design solutions to become more objective.
- shall allow to save all kind of project data and ensure the data consistence out of the working process. This shall enable the creation of key indicators and cost estimation relationships for all aspects of the satellite system.
- shall be applicable in the software tool MuSSat.

APPROACH

Modelling Basics. To be able to model any complex system there has to be a set of formal components to describe a system. To keep those components applicable regardless of the system they are applied to, they have to describe a system on a very abstract level. All definitions refer to Figure 2:

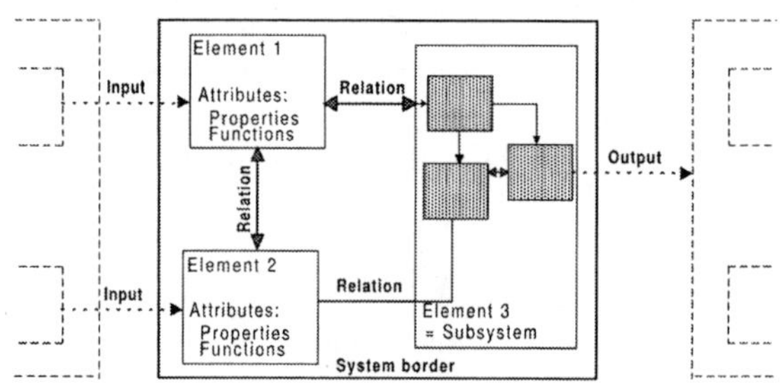

Figure 2. System Definition (IGENBERGS 1993)

(Igenbergs 1993) defines a system as follows:

- a system consists of elements
- elements are described by their attributes, i.e. properties and functions
- elements can interact via relations
- an element can be a system, i.e. it can be a subsystem

A system is any object that can (mentally) be separated from its environment. The system border represents the separation between the system and its environment. Where the bounding has to be drawn is determined by the actual problem statement. Thus the borderline has to be adaptable to a changed problem definition. It is the primary purpose of the system boundary to reduce the complexity of any real system to a manageable level.

Within the last years a couple of applications have been developed based on this global definition (Kreichgauer 1994 and Walter 1994).

(Negele 1998 & 1999) developed a systemic approach to the modelling of product development systems — ZOPH. He distinguishes between four major systems within the product development:

- Zielsystem (requirements, customer needs etc.)
- Objektsystem (all aspects of the deliverable items)
- Prozeßsystem (processes, activities etc.)
- Handlungs(-träger)system (resources, organisation structures, equipment etc.)

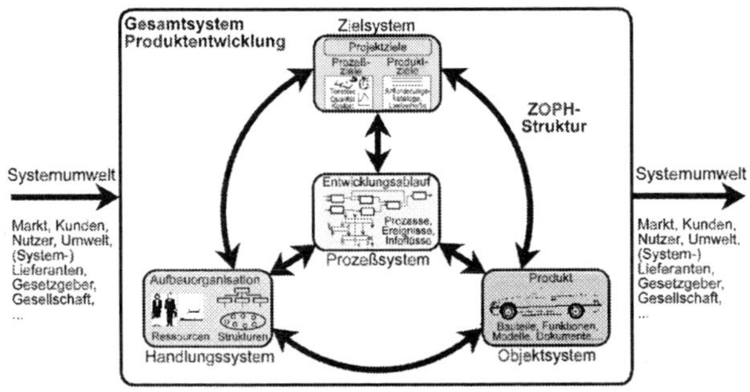

Figure 3. ZOPH-Model (NEGELE)

Because of its homogeneous coverage of all product and process data this modelling approach provides the generic basis of ISCOM.

Target Costing. Target Costing is a japanese approach of cost management and planning which has been developed at Toyota. (Sakurai 1989) defines:

"Target Costing can be defined as a cost management tool for reducing the overall cost of a product over its entire life cycle with the help of the production, engineering, R&D, marketing, and accounting departments."

The Target Costing process can be separated in three phases:

1. Setting Target Costs
2. Allocating Target Costs
3. Realising Target Costs

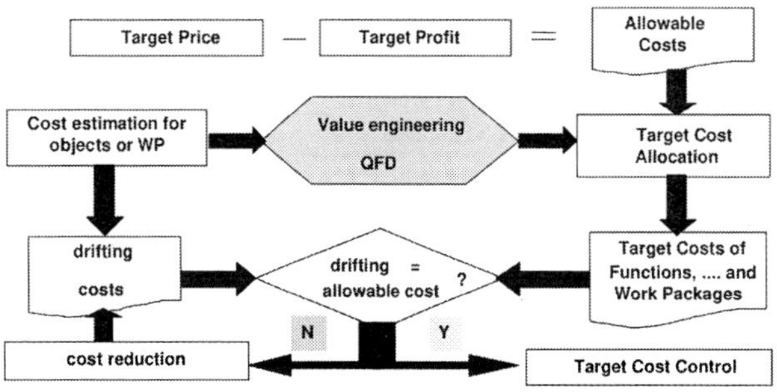

Figure 4. Target Costing Process

The process as shown in Figure 4 is based on a market driven target price. The target costs are the difference of Target Price and Target Profit. The allocation of Target Costs onto the product components is the critcal task in this process. The Engineering data to be used within the Target Costing Process is not clearly defined in the relevant literature. Methods like Quality Function Deployment (QFD) can be used to allocate customers needs to product functions and then to system components (Seidenschwarz 1993). But Systems Engineering provides different levels of abstraction (e.g. function tree, product tree and matrices). The methodology discussed above enables to describe all these system structures. In so far systems engineering and Target Costing shall be part of an integrated and interdisciplinary design process. This process including cost allocation, cost analysis and cost estimation should formally be supported within the integrated model.

Model requirements. Analysing the satellite business and the target costing process, the following requirements for an integrated system cost model have been identified:

- The model has to include all different types of elements (e.g. product functions, object structure, work breakdown structure (WBS), activity network, organisation structure and resources)
- The model shall include different types of properties and relations
- It must be able to allocate costs for each system element and include all cost sources
- Each element has directly allocated cost, total

direct and indirect cost as well as cost inputs from their children and output to their parents

- All kind of elements are reusable for different projects and variants

To further improve user acceptance all models existing in the various departments of the company are transferred step by step to MuSSat to enable the users to work with exactly the models they used before. If the models can not be transferred to MuSSat (special programmes or dynamic simulation tools) interfaces are to be implemented to access those models and programmes from MuSSat.

MODELLING STRUCTURE

The goal of this modelling approach is to allocate cost to all kind of elements from the resources, cost centres, processes, product elements and functions up to the requirements. Especially the influence of requirements and product functions to system costs is important within the early phase of product design. Therefore it must be able to analyse characteristic cost drivers for all kind of elements and to compare elements by their common properties.

Object Oriented Model. The reusability of elements for different projects is an important advantage of the modelling method. It is possible to copy elements and to change, add or delete properties and functions. They have their own evolution and mutation. But elements are defined by their properties and functions (see above). To keep elements manageable and comparable the following principles of the object oriented analysis (OOA) and design (OOD) are used for the modelling method (Quirmbach, Wilke et al. 1999):

- Each element is an object (instant) of a class
- Objects inherit properties and functions of their classes

This approach is useful to manage the evolution of the different elements and classes and allows to compare different elements by their common class properties. Different types of solar arrays (flexible or rigid panels) can be compared by their cell area, number of cells, mass, reliability and so on.

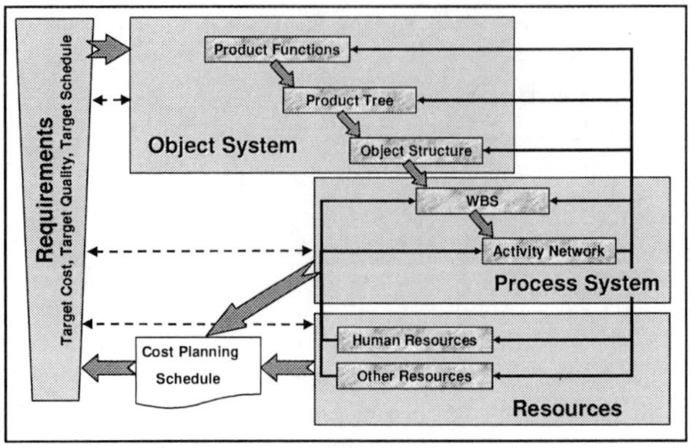

Figure 5. Model structure

Figure 5 shows the model structure and the modelling process. The most important classes of the model are:

- Requirement elements
- Product function elements
- Object elements (incl. Product Elements)
- WBS Elements
- Activity Elements
- Organisation Elements
- Resource Elements

Each object of these elements can be a cost accounting element and has one property type which includes all cost categories and cost sources of the enterprise accounting system. All Elements have directly allocated cost (DAC) and total direct cost (TDC). TDC of an element are calculated as the sum of all DAC of this element plus the TDC of all its children. E.g. Solar Array (product element) has DAC form WBS Elements (e.g. integration, acoustic test etc.) and TDC from its children (e.g. Solar Cell Assembly). Costs originated by higher level elements can be distributed to lower level elements. These costs are called indirect cost (IDC). This theory derived from traditional accounting theory is applicable to all kind of system elements identified above.

PROGRAM CONCEPT

MuSSat is an integrated tool for an interdisciplinary proposal team. A relational Database has been chosen to realise the program and the database design is defined by the modelling methodology. The use of MuSSat within a proposal process is shown in Figure 6:

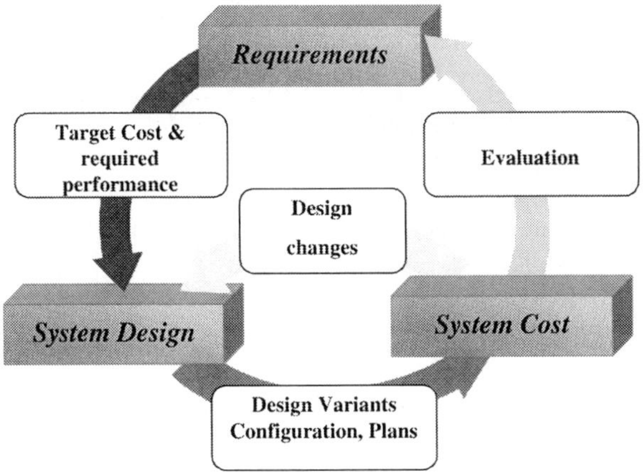

Figure 6. Proposal Process in MuSSat

The tool has an import and export interface to R3 ERP software of SAP™. Thus cost analysis, CER's and key indicators are also based on actual cost. Work Breakdown Structures and their planning data can be transferred to and from SAP's Project System (PS).

MuSSat allows to generate cost estimation relationships (CER) for any level of the different system elements; for a solar cell as well as for a complete solar array. Therefore the user is able to analyse all kinds off technical and economic parameters of different projects and variants within cost tables (c.f. Figure 7). This approach allows to get actual CER's based on the latest data of other projects and variants. For example the user is able to determine learning curves for all kind off objects and work packages. The tool enables top down cost estimates as well as bottom up cost planning for alternative variants. The less product and process experience is available the more detailed the cost estimation will be performed. Procurement costs can be taken from an integrated component database. A WBS can be generated quickly or imported by SAP™. Cost splitting is not only provided between recurring and non-recurring cost, but the user has also the possibility to differentiate between any cost breakdown he needs. The quality of the generated cost functions can be determined by different factors, standard deviation, Person's correlation squared, and others. The most critical point concerning risk of the cost estimation is development of new technology. For example the use of new solar cells can lead to higher production losses.

Budgeting over schedule includes escalation factors. In combination with management of milestones this allows an detailed cash flow analysis and calculation of project's expected internal rate of return.

Figure 7. Program concept of MuSSat

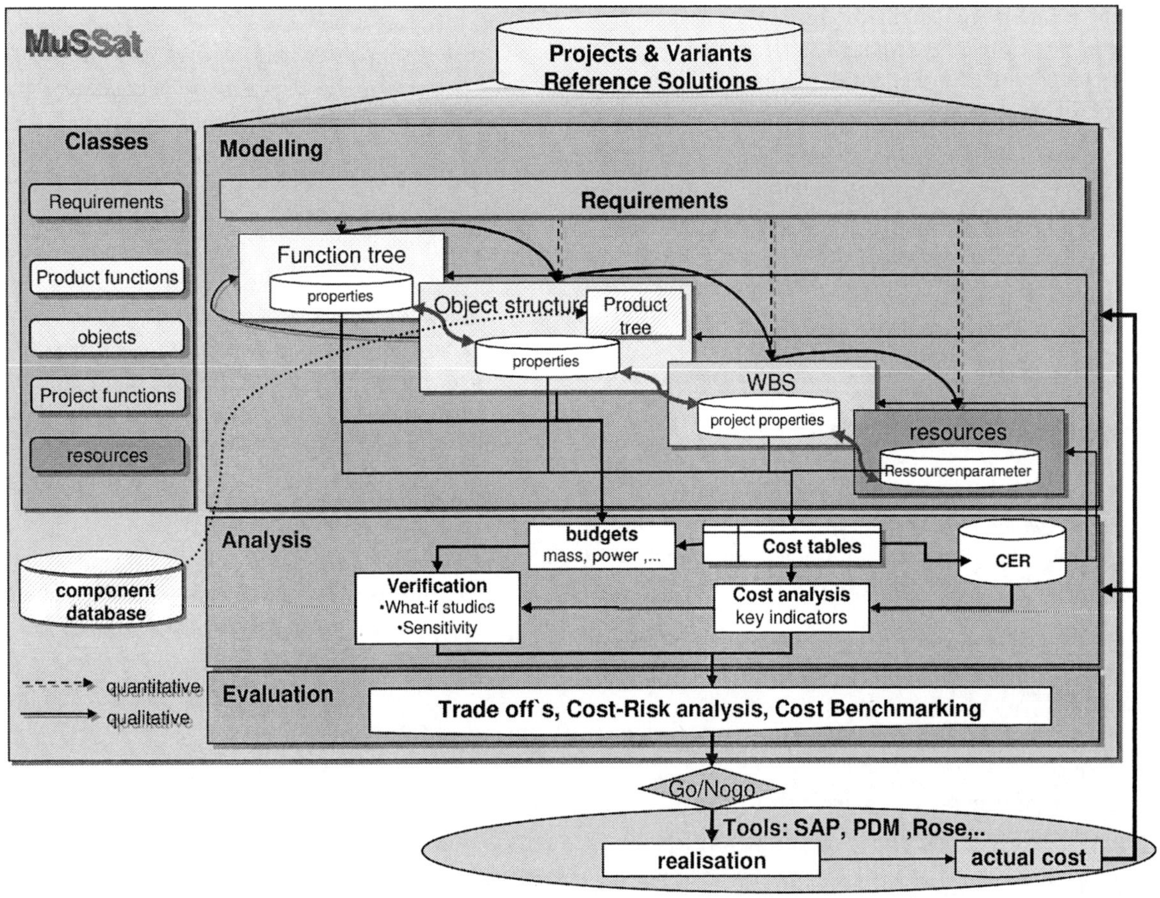

CONCLUSION

The Integrated System and Cost Model which has been presented in this article is useful and applicable for modelling complex systems. MuSSat is designed to be used by an integrated and interdisciplinary design team to quickly develop proposals for commercial satellite applications. The proper environment to use MuSSat is Dornier's Satellite Design Office (SDO) similar to the Project Design Centre at NASA's Jet Propulsion Laboratory (Shisko 1997).

The tool is being developed since February, 1998. The tool was put in use by Dornier Satellite Systems GmbH in October 1999. The first projects have been evaluated. This experience has shown that the approach described above enables to compare a lot of design solutions from a technical and economic point of view. This increases the quality of a proposal. Yet the most important factor within this kind of process is the team and its experience. Because of the better design transparency for all disciplines due to MuSSat, the tool supports better team integration and system understanding.

So far MuSSat can cover all expactations. This due to an effictive cooperation of Institute Astronautics of Technical University Munich and Dornier Satellite Systems GmbH. Further steps will be the adapting to users wishes.

REFERENCES

M. Wilke, O. Quirmbach, H. Negele, E. Fricke, E. Igenbergs, 1999:
"*MuSSat – A Tool for Model-Based System Engineering of Commercial Satellite Systems.*"
Annual International Symposium of INCOSE, Brighton, 1999

O. Quirmbach, M. Wilke, E. Igenbergs, 1999:
"Kostenmodellierung in einer integrierten Entwicklungsumgebung für Satellitensysteme."
In Jahrbuch der DGLR, Berlin 1999

H. Wildemann, 1982:
"Kostenprognosen für Großprojekte."
University Passau, 1982

E. Igenbergs, 1993:
"*Grundlagen der Systemtechnik.*"
Lecture Notes, Institute of Astronautics, TU München, 1992/93

K. Ehrlenspiel, A. Kiewert, U. Lindemann, 1998:
" Kostengünstig Entwickeln und Konstruieren."
Berlin, Heidelberg, New York: Springer-Verlag 1998

H. Negele, 1998:
"Systemtechnische Methodik zur ganzheitlichen Modellierung am Beispiel der Produktentwicklung."
PhD Thesis, Technische Universität München, 1998

H. Negele, E. Fricke, E. Igenbergs, 1998:
"ZOPH – A Systemic Approach to the Modeling of Product Development Systems."
published in: Proceedings of the 7th Annual Sympossium of INCOSE, LA,1997

C. Walther, 1994:
"Systemtechnisches Verfahren zur Bestimmung der Zusammenhänge zwischen Eigenschaften und Funktionsstruktur technischer Systeme."
PhD Thesis, TU München 1994

O. Kreichgauer, 1994:
"Quantitatives dynamisches Modell zur Simulation von Systembelastungen in Luftverkehrsabläufen."
Dissertation TU München, 1994

W. Seidenschwarz, 1993:
"*Target Costing*"
München: Vahlen-Verlag 1993

M. Sakurai M, 1987:
"*The Concept of Target Costing and it`s Effective Utilization*"
Cost Management Systems Phase2 Research, CAM*I CMS Program Report, Arlington/TX 1987

Shishko, R. 1997:
„Integrated Design Environments for Mars Exploration (The JPL Project Design Center)„
Presentation at the Institute of Astronautics, Technische Universität München, 20.11.1997

BIOGRAPHY

Oliver Quirmbach is research assistant within a cooperation of Daimler Crysler Aerospace and German Aerospace Research Center. He recieved his M.S. degree in Aerospace engineering in May, 1997. During his studies he focused on systems engineering and economics. Currently he is working on a project aimed at developing a tool for integrated systems and cost engineering within a model-based design process for satellite systems. The project is a joint effort of the Institute of Astronautics and the Dornier Satellite Systems GmbH, which is a subsidiary of Daimler Chrysler Aerospace.

Martin Wilke is research assistant at the Institute of Astronautics at the Technical University of Munich. He received his M.S. degree in Aerospace engineering in January, 1998. During his studies he focused on systems engineering by making a student thesis and his master thesis in the field of systems engineering at the Institute of Astronautics. Currently he is working on a project aimed at developing a tool for the model-based systems engineering of satellite systems. The project is a joint effort of the Institute of Astronautics and the Dornier Satellite Systems GmbH, which is a subsidiary of Daimler Chrysler Aerospace. He is a founding member of the German Chapter of INCOSE.

Eduard Igenbergs is Professor of Astronautics and Director of the Institute of Astronautics at the Technical University of Munich. He has a Ph.D. and a masters degree in mechanical engineering. He had a dust counter experiment on the japanese HITEN spacecraft to the moon and a space debris experiment on board the german BREMSAT. Another dust counter experiment is currently flying to mars with the japanese Planet-B spacecraft. He developed the Munich Space Chair (MSC), a body restraint system on board MIR. He has been teaching and researching in the field of Systems Engineering for more than 15 Jears.

Guiding Principles for Next Generation Computer-Aided Systems Engineering Tools

Mark E. Sampson
SLATE Solutions Group, SDRC
2425 N. Central Exp. Suite 200
Richardson, TX 75002

Abstract: The Standish Group recently made major waves when it reported a disturbing 50%+ failure rate among software development projects. It places the blame squarely on a number of factors including; failure to understand and deliver customer requirements to design personnel, lack of real time decision support in concert with requirements, as well as delivery mechanism to feed requirements to downstream development tools--all of which falls in CAD/CAE poor purview of systems architects. This was brought closer to home at the 1999 INCOSE International Symposium, when Gerard Le Lann[1] in his "Reality Check" paper threw the focus of blame from software to systems.."like blaming the transmission for engine problems". This paper attempts to define some high level guiding principles for tools needed to support "systems thinking" and describes the features of these next-generation systems development CAD/CAE environments needed to counter these alarming trends.

What is this System's Perspective…

Because the definition of Systems Engineering is still the subject of heated argument INCOSE, most Systems Engineer will agree "it" requires that you define the problem before you solve it. As such the reader will forgive a brief discussion on defining systems engineering and setting it's context. In this case several high profile systems engineering failures…

- *Denver's international airport opening is delayed 25 months (at a rate of $1.1 million/day) while problems with the hardware and software to control the automated baggage handling for the airport are worked. Eventually a traditional manual baggage handling system is put in place since no one can predict when the software and hardware problems will be worked out. "Software's Chronic Crisis", Scientific American, Sept. 1994*

- *The Central Artery project or "big dig" in Boston to move the main surface artery underground and add a third tunnel to connect Boston to Logan International Airport was one of the nation's largest public works projects (with a budget of $7 billion). The work was halted at a cost of several million dollars per day as they decided what to do with the sludge being dug up from the bottom of Boston harbor which is considered a hazardous material (nobody had considered the fact that maybe the sludge being dredged up from the bottom of Boston Harbor might be considered polluted material and require special handling).*

- *Hanford Washington's Liquid Nuclear Waste disposal problem consists of 177 tanks with 55 million gallons of high-level radioactive Plutonium by-products of nuclear bomb manufacturing since W.W.II. The tanks are leaking and produce explosive gases that could result in catastrophic environmental problems--especially since the tank farms sit near the Columbia River. (Web reference: www.hanford.gov/twrs/twrs.html)*

...each of these represent a class of problems that is typical of our modern, industrial age. These types of problems have grown beyond the boundaries of any single engineering discipline to demand many different disciplines be involved in their resolution--including environmental, electrical, software, and mechanical to name a few. These multi-disciplinary problems require integrated thinking to solve—what we call "systems-thinking." This systems perspective is typically held by the project visionary, architect, or project engineer. This is the person(s) who is responsible for overseeing and directing the various disciplines towards a common goal (just as a building architect is responsible for integrating all the different systems of a building to achieve a desired result--customer needs, heating, aesthetics, cost, schedule, security, etc.). The project architects understand that "no decision is an island;" that all perspectives--environmental, ergonomics, reliability, cost, safety, performance, maintenance, plus the myriad other issues need to be considered as a whole before a design or implementation decision is made (cost vs. performance, safety vs. reliability, maintainability vs. reliability,...) to achieve a balanced solution to the problem. The consequences of not taking all the issues into consideration can be embarrassing...

> *Upon completion of his first automobile in his workshop, Henry Ford was amazed to discover it didn't fit through the door (Henry Ford, p. 30, Alfred A. Knopf, 1966)*

…or even dangerous.

In March 1986 a patient in Tyler Texas complained of a burning sensation while undergoing what was supposed to be a painless radiation therapy treatment. A similar incident occurred the following month. Both patients died within a few months from what coroners said was massive overdoses of radiation. Investigations found similar incidents in Washington, Georgia, and Ontario and an additional two deaths that resulted from an extremely unlikely, but possible sequence of operator commands in the control software that bypassed safety limits and subjected the patient to massive overdoses of radiation. (Jacky Jonathan, "Inside Risks", Communications of the ACM, Dec. 1990, p. 138)

Tools that support a systems perspective…

The really big mistakes on a project are made the first day. Dr. Eberhardt Rechtin USC

Looking back on these problems, we wonder why the designers/developers like Ford couldn't see them coming until it was too late…thus one of the benefits of this systems perspective (downstream problem avoidance/risk reduction) and one of its drawbacks (non-tangible development effort that's hard to see the benefits of--especially if the downstream problems are avoided!). For example, most systems architects are familiar with the 70%-80% rule-- that is 70%-80% of the downstream production design and manufacturing costs are committed by systems architects early in the project, but only 3%-5% of the traditional accounting costs are carried in engineering.[2] Figure 1 shows how engineering cast the biggest shadow by committing costs while being the smallest cost according to traditional accounting measures.

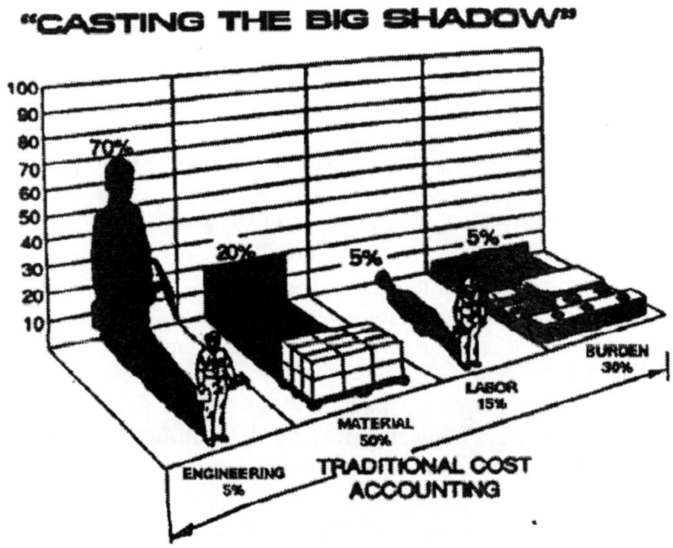

So looking at where the money is being spent (and thus saved), most of our cost reduction efforts such as automation have been spent at the back end of the process (automated warehouses, robotics, process simplification, factory automation, etc.). However, looking upstream we can see that the downstream costs are determined/committed long before the material is purchased and machined. As a result, if we want to really to affect downstream costs, we must get the engineering design and in particular the systems architecting done right--where the commitments are made, not where the costs show up.

We can see this cost-oriented development priority by looking back at CAD development history, where one notices the back-to-front end slant of the development effort--CAM systems, to CAD systems, on to CAE systems. To pick an example from the electrical engineering (EE) domain, EE's have been driven to new levels of productivity and complexity by market forces (for example the average disk drive has a product launch window of opportunity of 2-3 months with a product life expectancy of less than 18 months, imagine the impact of being 6 months late to market).[3] These market forces have continually driven EE designers to reduce cycle time, increased reliability, more accurate documentation, and greater capabilities. The result has been dramatic productivity improvements by moving the design process further upstream as represented in the following table and timeline:

	Engineering Design Approach	Cycle Time	Complexity	# of iterations
1 pre 80's	engineer defines logic with template on paper, netlist/logic is typed up and handed to a technician for manual taping of etches on film, which is reduced and used as manufacturing tooling	~200's of days	low	few (not enough time to do it again)
2 80's	engineer defines logic with template on computer, netlist automatically generated and imported to CAD software which allows for computerized taping (routing) of etches, computers drive film plotters that create manufacturing tooling	~100's of days	medium	more(easy to make changes & regenerate tooling)
3 early 90's	engineer using standard component libraries captures schematic, simulates/verifies design, since schematic and layout are in the same database, layout directly accesses schematic which automatically tracks the logic of the schematic, computer drives direct-write on silicon to create product	~10's of days	high	many (updating schematic updates manufacturing databases)

These trends have continued as EE's have moved into behavioral modeling (using VHDL, etc.) to describe chips and "compile" them into hardware. This has enabled them to continue to compete by packing more systems into fewer chips, which in turn has begun to surface architectural issues (or lack of system architecture). For example, Texas Instruments (TI) recently undertook a study into ASIC (Application Specific Integrated Circuit) design cycle time and the largest contributors to ASIC cycle time problems.[4] The study gathered information from a number of ASIC design efforts across TI's Defense Systems Group and compared these efforts looking for common contributors to cycle time successes/failures. The following two bar charts in figures 2 and 3 show the comparisons.

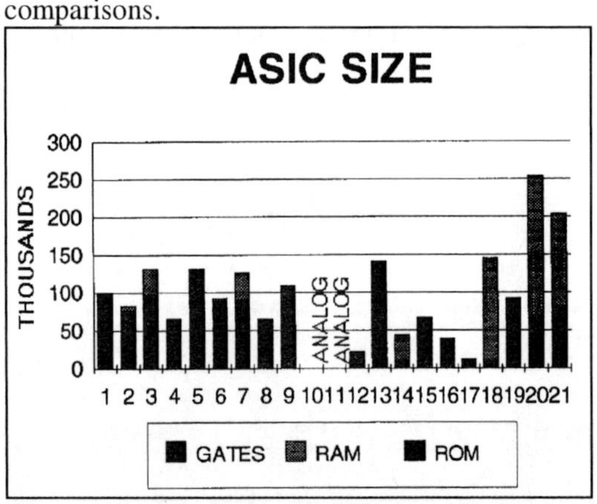

Figure 2&3: Compares ASIC size with Design Effort

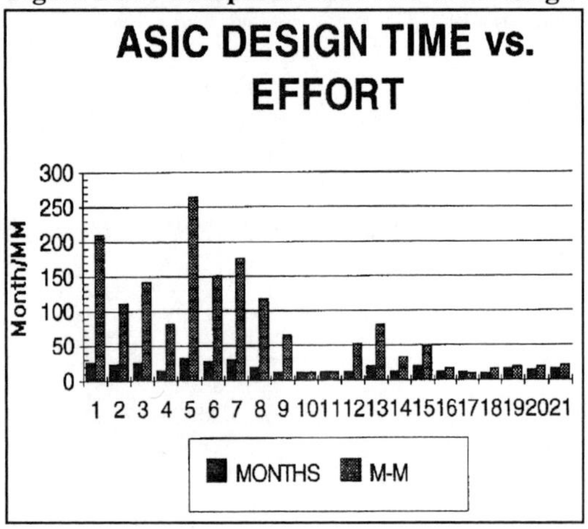

Although comparisons between ASIC's on different projects are not exactly "apples to apples", we can roughly compare ASIC sizes (in gates) from ASIC's 18-21 against ASIC's 1-9. Comparing the Man Month (MM) design effort between two of the ASIC's (say 1 and 19), the reader can see a substantial difference in the labor involved to the complete the ASIC designs. For example, ASIC 1 took 200+ MM to complete while ASIC 19 took ~20 MM--an order of magnitude difference in design effort! If we used a $5000/MM running rate to figure the labor effort involved with each ASIC design--ASIC 1 cost $1,000,000+ while ASIC 19 cost $100,000 despite comparable complexity. Although there were many reasons for these cost differences, the ASIC Cycle Time Report places the majority blame on:

1. Missing, inadequate, incomplete or excessive specifications
2. Lack of planning and clear direction
3. Poorly defined interfaces

...all the job of systems architects (Systems Architecting was done on ASIC 19; Systems Architecting was not done/or done as an after thought on ASIC 1).

With the growing recognition of the importance of systems architecting, tools, technologies, and management practices have been developed to handle the mind-boggling complexity of these problems that defy comprehension. Operations Research, Critical Path Analysis/Gannt Charts, and Failure Modes Effects Analysis (FMEA), and Quality Function Deployment (QFD) to name a few all had their origins in search for tools to deal with complexity.

Many of these methods/practices have been captured in a variety of Computer-Aided Design/Engineering and Project Management tools--but have yet to present an integrated environment where the many different views of the problem can be seen in a cohesive manner (i.e. what is the impact of a requirement change on the schedule; or if this component changes what is the impact on reliability of the product...). Interdisciplinary problems like those described above require interdisciplinary tools—tools that understand the relationships among the various discipline specific views (in Ford's case a facilities layout tool and his automotive design tool). Systems Design tools of the future will need to understand these complex interrelationships among the different discipline views.

A typical systems problem/example from the automotive world will help tie the rest of our discussion together…

In preparation for production on a new car model, purchasing had ordered several million brake pedal connecting rods. Too late they found out that a mistake had been made…somewhere along the line someone had dropped a decimal point meaning all the connecting rods were a ½ inch too short. Rather than send them all back and eat the cost, production engineering decided to move the brake pedal a ¼ inch so they could use the short connecting rods. This meant the brake pedal slot in the firewall must be enlarged, which required the tooling to be modified (which was taken care of with a welding job). There began to be a rash of cut accidents in the carpet installation area—they needed to cut the hole in the carpet larger to accommodate the change in the brake pedal. The interior noise analysts were also disturbed to find that noise levels had mysteriously risen and suspected the elongated brake pedal hole was the culprit…

These domino-effect problems are typical of almost any complex development problem--with almost no industry or product immune (I recently received notice that my home thermostat is Y2K compliant!). Looking "down at the problem" (where systems architects live) is the only vantage point that makes sense to manage complex product development since that is the only place high enough to see global impacts of decisions such as moving the brake pedal. This is made worse by the default situation where just letting decisions sit around causes other decisions to be made around it (i.e. not making a decision is a decision). Either way, it creates a sort of concrete that keeps getting deeper the longer into the project the problem created by it goes unresolved—thus, putting off hard decisions by default cost real time and real money.

So what features do these systems tools need to have? Here are a few high-level requirements.

Systems tools care more about interrelationships among the data, not just the data itself.

Water, water every where, Ne any drop to drink. "The Rime of the Ancyent Marinere" William Wordsworth

Put another way--data, data everywhere, but what can I do with it? Our ability to produce data has far outstripped our ability to know what it means. Ask any modern manager, they will tell you that information is not their problem--they have too much information. It's what all the information means that he/she wants to know. This flood of data has spawned the data management industries with Product Data Management (PDM) and Configuration Management (CM) tools that do a good job keeping up with CAD and other data. PDM tools typically manage files. Their file level-granularity does not support the fine-granularity, interactive response needed to understand the impacts among the data at the conceptual level--this means that systems tools should work hand-in-hand with data management tools.[5]

Using our brake pedal example above, the systems tool would understand the relationship between the interior noise level of the car and the brake pedal hole in the firewall. The firewall design database, tooling files, and the noise models are managed by data management tools.

Figure 4: Differences between systems tools and data management tools. At the risk of over simplifying the development process as a cylinder (above left) starting with concept moving to the back dock through the development cycle. The reader can see that the systems (front end) and the data management (backend) deal with different aspects of the design process. With systems architecting characterized as highly dynamic "what if'ing" and data management characterized by "nailing things down". Early in the design process, dynamics holds sway, late in the process, stability is king. Slicing the development process cylinder creates the interface between the two worlds with requirements, design documents, etc. flowing from the systems world into the data management world and feedback, structures, etc. flowing back to the systems design world where in development trade-off decisions can be made. The intersection between the two worlds in this case is an ellipse with the area of the intersection representing the amount/type of interactions between conceptual design and data management.

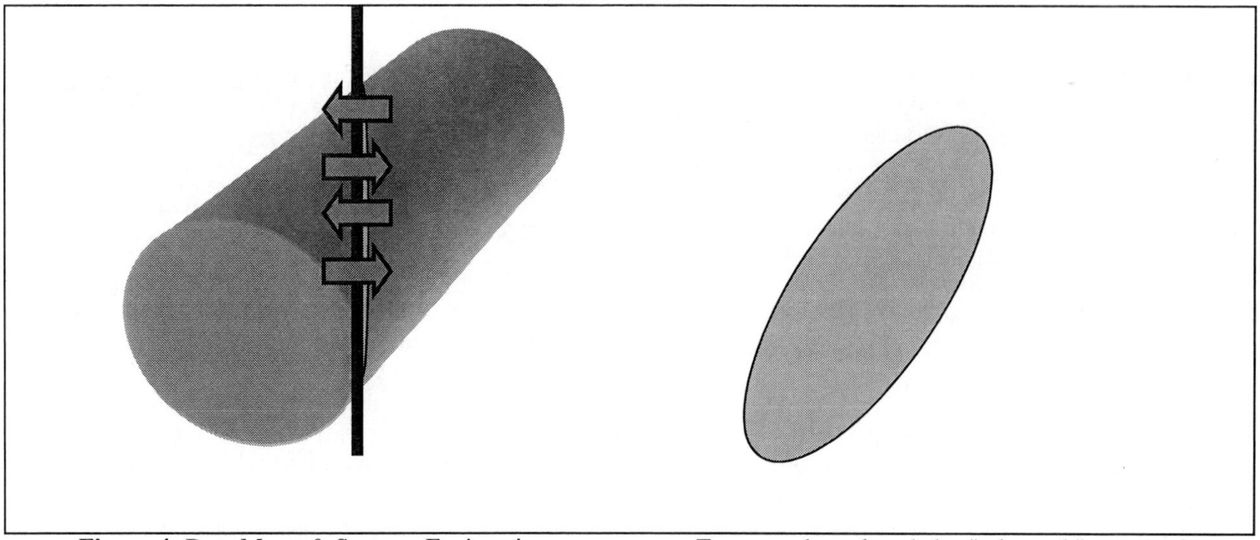

Figure 4: Data Mgmt & Systems Engineering

<u>System Tools need to understand requirements and how they flow among the relationships.</u>

> *"The customer can have any color he wants as long as it's black". Henry Ford*

Since the days of dictating to customers what they will buy is gone we need to build what the customer wants. This means we have to define the problem before we solve it--typically done by gathering requirements. Every system has many different perspectives and views--cost, safety, maintenance, suppliers, distribution, organizations, functions, manufacturing,...to name a few. Each of these perspectives needs to be addressed and balanced against the other views to enable global product optimization. The only common denominator among the many perspectives and views of the system is the customer's requirements. As such system's oriented tools need to:

1. understand requirements (what they are, how they apply, who's responsible,...)
2. relate requirements into the design (this component is driven by these requirements) and across the interrelationships (this component manufactured in this facility means that the machine tool used to cut the part is helping to fulfill the customer's requirements)

Using our car with the brake pedal problem, a requirement for noise level limits could be linked into all elements that contribute to the noise level. As shown in this example, failing to manage customer requirements effectively creates an open-loop development process that runs the risk of building something the customer does not want (and thus won't buy), lead's to runaway projects, and lot's of rework.

Everyone has played the "telegraph" game where you whisper something in the first person's ear who then whispers it to the next person and so on and then laughed at how much its changed between the start and the finish. This is the same game going on at the corporate level--only it's the customer's wants that get lost along the way. A recent report by the Standish Group estimates that Fortune 1000 companies spent more that $275 billion on development projects in 1996, with over half of these becoming some form of runaway or failed project. At the core of these project failures is a consistent lack of understanding of the customer's goals for the product[6] --the "telegraph effect".

Looking down at the spiral of the product development life cycle with each part of the organization fitted into it, we see that marketing is supposed to understand the customer wants and translate those wants into feature specs that accurately describe those wants. These are typically "thrown over the wall" to design who continues to translate those wants into designs that can be thrown over to the manufacturing organization...with each person/organization along the way adding their interpretation of the customer wants...resulting is we're building something the customer doesn't want.

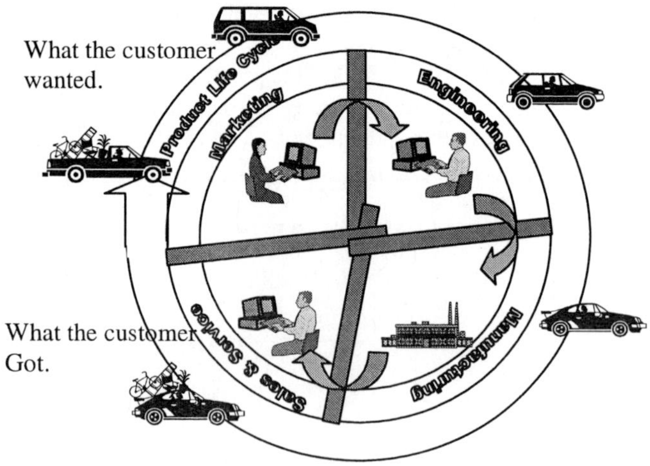

...we're suggesting an integrated requirement management database that bridges the gaps between these views so all can see the interrelationships of requirements to the design along each step of the process. The result is a consistent view of customer wants across the entire organization--giving you a better chance of keeping your eye on the ball and delivering what the customer really wants.

Figure 5: Spiral development process without/with integrated RM environment.

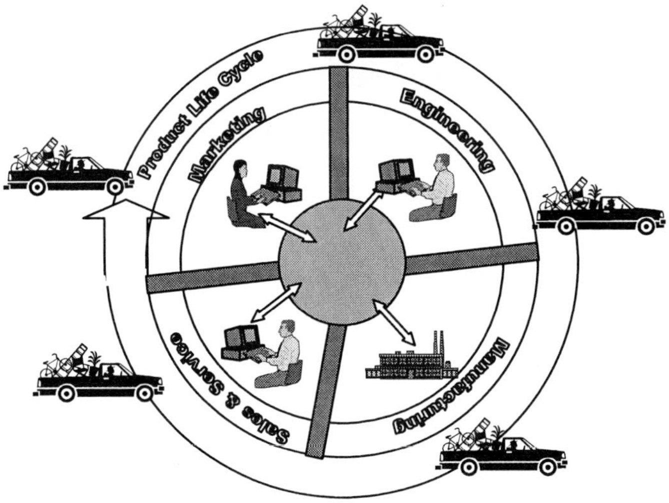

How else will you know when your finished? How else will you know you have a quality product? Since according to Phillip Crosby, Quality is conformance to requirements.[7]

These requirements can come from many places other than customers. For example regulations and standards produce many requirements that constrain designs--even to the point of driving some products in some highly regulated industries such as pharmaceuticals. It is safe to predict that given our increasingly litigious society, that regulatory and standards compliance will become increasingly important to the bottom line. Environment Today puts it at 5%-8% of a product's revenues are chewed up by regulatory and standards compliance efforts.[8] To give the reader a sense of size of this regulatory burden problem, let's just look at environmental regulations.

> *In the U.S. alone there are 12 new/revised environmental regulatory documents/month and 15 emerging standards documents per month in 191 subject areas (each containing hundreds of requirements). That's 2,700 requirements or regulations to be monitored, with 2,000+ documents already in effects (and all subject to change). Doing the math, that's 200,000+ requirements that need to be kept up with.*[9]

To produce compliant products demands that regulatory requirements are with the design from the get-go rather than an after-thought or monitored by a project-external function. These requirements, along with customer wants, need to be pervasive throughout the project--tied into both the product under development and the process used in the development so they are "built-in" to the product rather than patched later.

System Tools need to understand the development process and context

> *"A process can not be understood by stopping it."*
> *Frank Herbert, The Dune Chronicles*

No product is developed in a vacuum (even no development process or an ad-hoc development process is a process). Since the development process (or lack of one) contributes to the product development the development can only be understood (and improved) in the context of the development process. This means that systems tools need to understand the development process in addition to understanding the product so opportunities for optimization in the product and the process can be found. This gives us the benefit of:

1. Monitoring and improving the development process since we can see how parts of the process contribute to the developing product
2. Once captured, we can look backwards to the genesis of the problems--traced back to decisions, trade-offs, mistakes, process steps, etc. This enables us to focus on the source of the problems rather than constantly deal with band-aiding the symptoms.
3. Creates a balanced view where we can see who contributes what towards the meeting of customer needs. This leads to balanced approaches and avoids sub-optimization (this also finally gives us real ammunition and metrics in deciding what parts of organizations are the most important to meeting customer needs and rewarding people based on their direct contributions to the bottom-line--meeting customer wants).

This process-orientation is being driven from several sources. For example, there is an expanding emphasis on process understanding driven in part by the emerging capability maturity models (EIA/IS 731--see www.geia.org for details)--with the idea being that improved processes will result in improved productivity, repeatability, global optimization, and a better bottom-line. With measurements of 0 (ad hoc/initial) up to 5 (optimizing--ala Software Maturity Models from Software Engineering Institute at Carnegie Mellon University)--with higher scores corresponding to more competence, thus giving contracting organizations a metric for source selection. In addition, understanding the development process is the only way everyone can agree upon what they do, how they fit into the product development effort, and how interfaces among the disciplines work. For example, TI recently undertook a "Landmark study" to identify tools to support these Systems Architects. Part of the problem was deciding exactly what these architects/systems engineers did, what did they need as inputs, what they produced. As a result, they spent a lot of time working through the development process to understand how architects participated in that process. Once that was understood, they could than identify which tools were needed, how/what they communicated to other tools around them, and what aspects of the tools were most important.[10] Figure 7 shows a summary of Systems Architect/Systems Engineer (SE) involvement in various DOD-oriented project phases (concept exploration, , demonstration/validation, and engineering development). Of the overall task set, SE's need these types of tools:

90% will require some type of documentation tool
70% will need a requirements management/traceability tool
15% require a simulation tool of some type
7% require a tool to aid in partitioning of the design
2% involve the electronic capture of documents
9% needed no tool support

Reading from the chart below, for example, 95% of the 242 Dem/Val tasks have Systems Architecting involvement. Of those tasks that have systems involvement:

The reader can draw their own conclusions from the above data, but several important points stand out:

1) Systems Architects spend about half their time dealing with documents--in particular using word processors to capture and manipulate documents as it is their primary communication mechanism (the Landmark study concludes that this time is of dubious value since nobody reads the documents and they are obsolete by the time they are printed)
2) Systems Architects should be "front loaded" in the project where most of their tasks are. Typical projects ramp up engineering as the projects move forward, systems people need to be front loaded and then ramp down (see Figure 4 for a discussion on front end conceptual design).
3) Systems tools to this point have been focused on system simulations/trade-off analysis. This data would suggest simulation is only a small portion of the development problem with few specialized engineers needing these types of tools.

To get back to our car with the brake pedal problem, the development process would be managed by the systems environment ensuring that impacts were analyzed, appropriate approvals, reviews, and notifications were made.

Systems tools need to be viewed by everyone and be methodology independent

> *"Two people can design a computer in 4 months, three can do it in 6 months, four can do it in 9 months, and five or more can't do it." Pope's Postulate of Computer Design*

Very few products can be designed/built with one or two individuals any more, with most requiring hundreds or thousands of people involved. The Systems tool needs to deliver requirements to the entire development crew (including management, accounting, manufacturing, etc. even in geographically dispersed organizations) so that all decisions can be made within the context of the customer requirements. This means this systems environment needs to be realtime, groupware, with a web component where everyone can participate in the development process. This ensures that:

- ✓ Everyone is working off of current information--no more decisions based on stale data
- ✓ Everyone is monitored by the development process
- ✓ Management has insight into the product development process
- ✓ Customers have insight into the product development

It is important to point out that we are after removing as many barriers to users using this environment as possible--this means:

1. Zero-learning curve, web-oriented approaches
2. Methodology independence is critical--many people are aware of tools which have been purchased and put on a shelf, never to be used again (sometimes referred to as shelfware). Tools which espouse/enforce methodologies do not work on the "general public" of the project and will go unused. Methodology independence is a must.[11]
3. Seamless integration with other desktop environments--including office suites, word

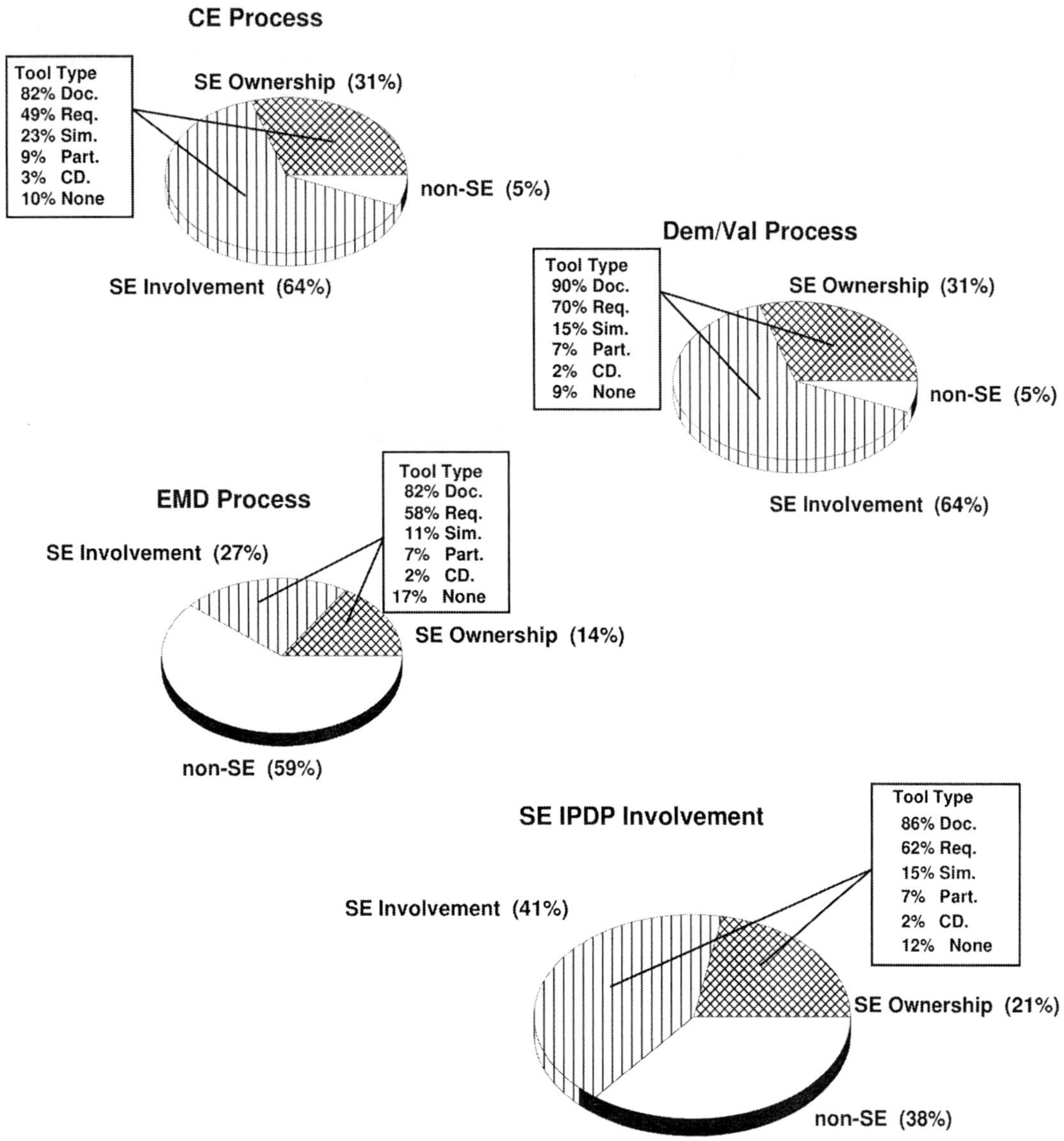

Figure 7: Shows Systems Architect/Engineering involvement in various project phases.

4. processors, spreadsheets, email, etc. are all required for the quick adaptation to using/participating in the development environment.

In the case of our car example with the brake pedal problem, the environment itself can be accessed from the web to input approvals, make comments, review status, etc.

Conclusion… We started this paper by pointing out several high profile "runaway projects" that are infamous only by their notoriety. Closer to home, each of us knows of projects that are out of control within our own organizations. If we could compare all of these projects (given sufficient altitude and omniscience) we would find among other things…

A poor understanding of customer needs, combined with an inadequate delivery system that understands how the requirements relate to the product under design. This critical missing environment combined with the systems perspective to provide context is what is needed to deal with the relentless trends ahead us…

- ✓ More software intensive systems
- ✓ More complexity
- ✓ More regulation/litigation around product failures (even perceived failures)

✓ Shorter time schedules due to increased competition along with ongoing shortages of development talent

A "real time" systems perspective is needed to deal with these trends.

We've described several features of a systems-oriented environment that can counter these trends by:

1. Capture of the interrelationships among system elements, enabling global optimization (this is much more than just exchanging data among discipline specific tools this is understanding relationships among the system elements).
2. Driving requirements through the development process and design--requirements everywhere--including regulatory/standards oriented requirements so regulatory compliance and litigation resistance can be built in to the product.
3. Providing everyone participating in the development process access through a comfortable user interface to the requirement information needed to support real-time decision making

...laid on top of an integrated (i.e. understood by the tool environment) development process that is measured and improved.

This is much different than discipline-specific tools exchanging information (i.e. thermal analysis tools exchanging information with circuit board layout tools for example). Exchanging data does not address the interdisciplinary trade-off issues. If we are going to deal with these trends, we need to stop reinventing, understand our requirements, make sure lessons get passed on to the next generation, and do it all in an improving development process. This will have the effect of raising everyone's sites from tree level, up to the forest level. Thus giving the entire project opportunities for global optimization they were never able to see before, reuse on a "chunk-of-project" basis, and bringing the lessons learned from the back end of projects up front to where they started--which is where the real productivity lift is at.

Biography Mark Sampson received his BS in Design Engineering from BYU and his MS in Systems Analysis/MIS from USC. His education and work experience at GE and TI exposed him to CAD system development and support where he quickly realized the need for a system-level CAD/CAE environment described in this paper. Mark began working with developers at Texas Instruments in 1990 developing a number of patented, systems-oriented CAE features in what they called the SLATE (System Level Automation Tool for Engineers) environment, which went public in 1994. He is currently at TD Technologies/SDRC where he works in the ongoing development and marketing of TD's system-level CAD/CAE products. You can reach him at sampson@tdtech.com.

---

[1] Le Lann, Gerard, "Models, Proofs and the Engineering of Computer-Based Systems: A Reality Check", International Council on Systems Engineering, 1999 Annual International Symposium.
[2] Percivall, George S., "Systems Engineering in the Automotive Industry", National Council on Systems Engineering 2nd Annual International Symposium--Systems Engineering for the 21st Century, Seattle, WA., July 1992
[3] Smith, Preston G., and Donald G. Reinertsen, Developing Products in Half the Time, Van Nostrand Reinhold, 1991 pp. 29-41 See also Clark, Kim B., and Steven C. Wheelwright, Managing New Product and Process Development, Text and Cases Free Press, 1993, pp. 552-574
[4] Cline, Jim, et. al., "ASIC Cycle Time--a first look, A study in ASIC cycle time contributors", January 1994. Texas Instruments, Defense Systems & Electronics Group.
[5] Burdick, D. "VPDM: A New PDM Application Vision", Gartner Group Research Note, Apr. 29 1997
[6] Berryman, A. "Requirements Management Tools, A Special Compass Report", The Standish Group International, Inc. Jan. 1998
[7] Crosby, P., Quality is Free, The Art of Making Quality Certain, Mentor Books, Aug. 1992
[8] As referenced in EMAX and Environment Today's joint survey located online at www.emax.com/sur_int.htm
[9] Tominey, K., LaTorre, R. & M. Sampson, "Enterprise-Level Regulatory Analysis and Requirements Management" presented at the 1996 International Symposium of the International Council on Systems Engineering, Los Angeles, CA, USA. July 1996.
[10] Sampson, M., et. al., Systems Engineering Design Automation Landmark Study, Texas Instruments, Inc. Volume 1. The Systems Engineering Process. April 1993.
[11] INCOSE (International Council On Systems Engineering) Tools Database Working Group in concert with the Systems Architecting Working Group has produced a survey of Systems Architecting Tools--which includes among its requirements "Methodology Independence". Requirements and results can be seen at http://www.incose.org/tools/tooltaxs.html July 1998.

A Data Structure Approach to Systems Engineering

D. J. Battersby
BAE SYSTEMS
Kings Meadow Road,
Nottingham,
England.

ABSTRACT

A fundamental aspect concerning the implementation of an efficient systems engineering process is the management and control of the data arising from the systems engineering process itself. This paper concentrates on defining the overall co-ordination of the disparate processes needed to define information flows within an extended organisation.

The problems of data control with respect to current data configurations are addressed and a concept for the future engineering environment developed. Discussion is presented in terms of the configuration management requirements of an organisation with semi-integrated, large-scale software solutions implemented across its business, design, development and manufacturing operations. A data structure concept is developed by matching the requirements of the organisation to the trends seen in the wider business environment.

In this context the systems engineering process is seen to be that by which a number of related databases evolve into a structure fitting the practical objectives of a project. The potential difficulties in achieving this are discussed in Section 2. One result that emerges from this view of systems engineering is the importance of collaboration in developing compatible data structures between organisations throughout the supply chain. The potential benefits arising from collaborative working and the associated control measures are discussed.

INTRODUCTION

BAE SYSTEMS recognises the importance of effective systems engineering upon all its products but the precise implementation of processes, tools, and techniques will be appropriate to its component businesses. Dependent upon the type and complexity of application the systems engineering approach may be highly structured, using defined tools in a predetermined way or may be more flexibly implemented at least to ensure that good practice systems engineering principles are applied. The latter case, where there has been perhaps more limited investment in systems engineering software tools, provides the context for this paper. From this latter position are analysed future business requirements for systems engineering - as one would for other projects needing investments for business development. Through the results of such an analysis implementation of systems engineering technologies fits into a strategic framework, arising from a vision of how the business will operate in the future.

Section 1 of this paper describes the process followed to determine the requirements placed upon the systems engineering activity in the areas of project and product development. The systems engineering activity is governed by the need to control business data and the development of a structure by which to manage data flows through the software tools utilised within its environment.

The stated requirements are matched against trends affecting the business and various actions are identified to prepare the business to be in the strongest position to match these trends, thus developing a concept of operation. The importance of collaborative working through computational tools, in a number of specific business areas involving partnership scenarios, is also highlighted as a key success criterion.

Section 2 presents some of the practical issues that are likely to arise in the implementation of such a concept. A statement of some of the key issues for development in terms of the concept identified in Section 1 is made, along with a list of potential barriers. The manner in which progress can be made is suggested to be evolutionary rather than revolutionary.

SECTION 1. CONTEXT AND CONCEPT GENERATION

CONTEXT

This paper is developed from the position of a medium sized business within the BAE SYSTEMS company with experience of implementing large-scale software solutions. At the heart of this capability is a highly developed Enterprise Resource Planning tool (SAP), and an information management tool (IMAN). Throughout the business, other functionally implemented tools also exist. Wide use is made of the BAE SYSTEMS Intranet for internal communication with other business units within the company. In addition to these wide scale tools, local use is also made of CAD Modelling/Rapid Prototyping tools (Unigraphics), Requirements Capture, Operations Analysis, Systems Assessment Modelling, Cost Modelling, Design Analysis and Performance Simulation tools.

Requirements of Systems Engineering Concept

The process of systems engineering is fundamentally one of processing diverse information from a number of sources into a coherent solution. The tools and methodologies for processing this information may be under continuous development but it is the data underlying a company's operation, which are rapidly becoming a most valued asset. The computer tools used to control these data should be seen as a key issue for systems engineering to address. Hence as the dependence on these specific to purpose tools increases the need to examine how an optimised solution to the control of data may be reached is also highlighted.

To address these requirements a concept based upon the existing data structure of the business is developed. The concept is based upon an understanding of the data flow through the present computational tool set used in product design, development and production. The links that exist to facilitate data transfer are at present a mixture of structured compatibility, for example links between SAP and IMAN and conceptual links, which are often in the form of tool-user-tool interfaces. A diagrammatic representation of this model is shown in Figure 1.

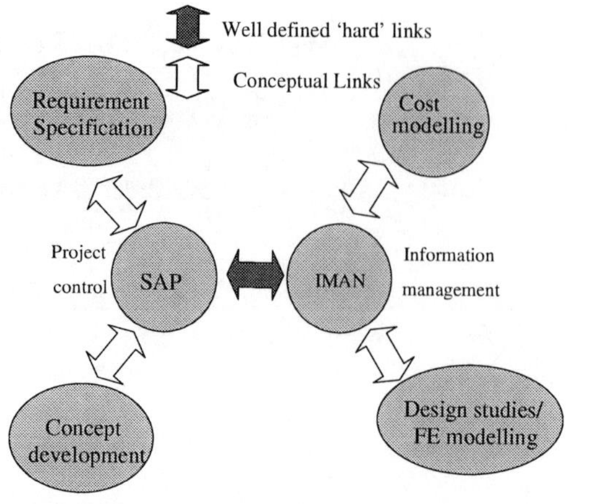

Figure 1 Current Data Structure

At present the controlling influence over the business operations is through the SAP Enterprise Resource Planning tool with the data control handled through IMAN. In considering the data that contribute to control of product requirements the focus is on capabilities rather than on specific tools available within the present data structure.

As contributors develop specific tools to provide different capabilities the context diagram of Figure 1 will change to that of the

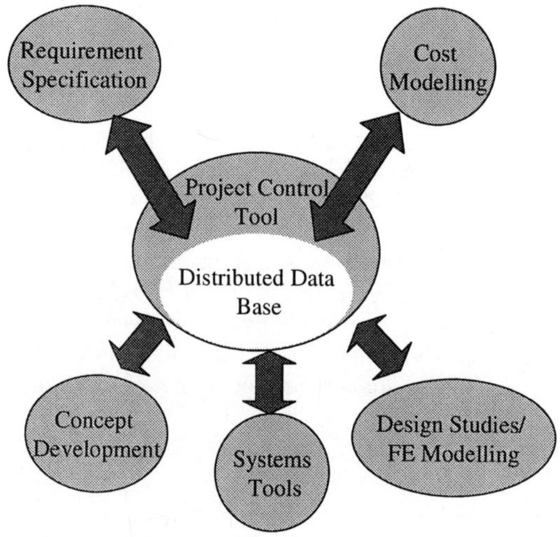

Figure 2. Capability-focused Data Structure with tangible data links

Figure 2. What becomes important to the business is the ability to select tools on the basis of high performance in a specific capability, whilst maintaining compatibility with the main business systems. This compatibility will be more easily maintained by considering the capability provided via the software tools and through combining information management and project control capabilities. By considering capability rather than project tools the acceptance of open data transfer standards will be more easily encouraged.

Relation of Primary Requirements to the wider Business Environment

To develop the concept of operation into a model for the future we have reviewed the external factors that will impact on how the business develops its operations. Some examples of major trends affecting defence industry are shown in Figure 3. These trends can be linked through to the business requirements for systems engineering as shown in the central circle in the Figure.

communication amongst partners, as they can share project information. Benefits will be apparent: one example is in the collaborative establishment of requirements between customer and supplier helping to ensure customer expectations are not overlooked. Another benefit will be through enabling manufacture to be performed more efficiently by providing visualisation of prevailing issues: for example, finance for a project or readiness to supply of linked organisations. Such communications would avoid mismatches caused by local updates or cultural incompatibilities. Throughout a collaborative project a compatible structure would also lead to reduction in administration costs and other overheads.

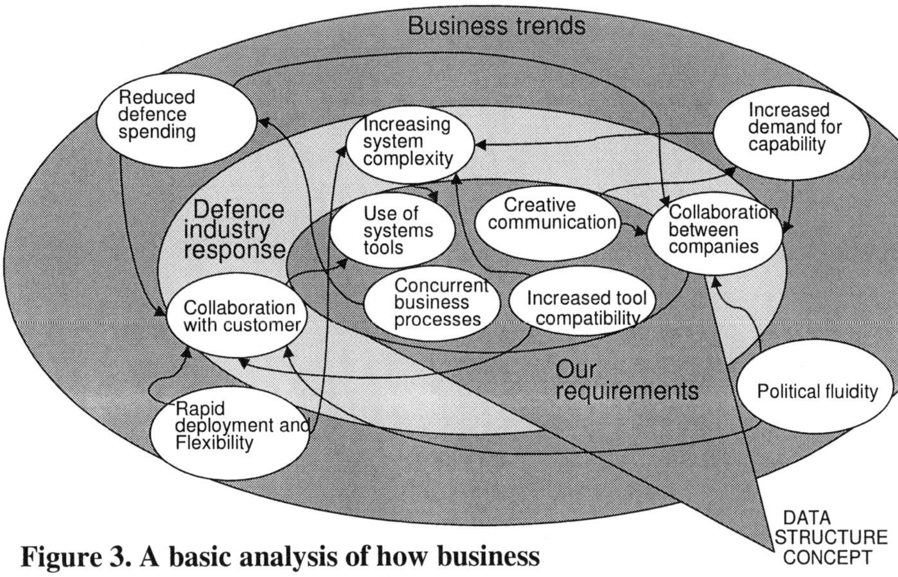

Figure 3. A basic analysis of how business trends map to company requirements.

It is apparent from Figure 3 that there are a number of links driving collaboration, both with business partners and with customers. This in turn implies that collaboration will be an area of considerable importance for computational tool providers to address when developing and supporting their products. Industry needs to see the benefits of a workable, well-defined collaborative interface between the capabilities used in their projects. When achieved such a concept of operation will reduce significantly some of the practical problems inherent in implementing partnerships.

The benefits of collaborative interfaces between companies may be numerous but primarily the approach will enable direct

For customers and suppliers, satisfying multiple requirements is of paramount importance, and a collaborative interface with customers would need to focus on this issue. An example of how the interface would work would be if a customer was able to enter requirements into a common interface shared with the prime contractor. As the supplier develops concepts the customer is able to see the extent to which requirements are being satisfied. From the supplier viewpoint this has the particular advantage that the customer can see and feed into trade-offs that occur during requirement analysis. This type of relationship may be particularly relevant in the UK with the advent of the MOD Smart Procurement Initiative.

Implementation of a collaborative communications framework based around systems tools may have many important benefits but these will not be realised without wide scale use of compatible systems. The full benefits will only become apparent if a large scale approach to compatible standards and to systems engineering is adopted.

Compatibility between system based tools

For any technical industry it is beneficial to make essential knowledge held by its personnel an inherent property of its concurrent business processes. This requirement suggests it is important that business systems are configured to allow long-term traceability of project history. Effective maintenance of such knowledge should enable streamlining of the business without drastic reduction of capability, as repetition and misunderstandings are avoided.

The need for long-term traceability demonstrates the importance of including all business tools within a systems engineering based approach, as many of the non-functional constraints placed on the development of a product, and much of the knowledge gained about the project as it reaches maturity will be held within the Business Process and Data Management tools. As time progresses and systems tools increase in capability it will become increasingly important to design systems tools and processes capable of using data held within the business tools. This is likely to be an issue as dependence upon computational modelling to define and verify products increases.

The medium by which access to a project is granted is via the business process tools, and hence compatibility amongst business partners' business process tools, regardless of the tool provider, is essential. Combining a collaborative approach with the need to maintain and control data within business partnerships develops into a vision of a distributed project database. Through this database work performed using systems tools can be monitored and results and rationales recorded.

The shared working environment, controlled via business tools allows us to envisage the role of systems engineering as a powerful tool with strategic influence.

Statement of Concept

The concept developed is represented in Figure 4. Part A of this diagram shows the configuration whereby a joint database, its control structure and related business tools could develop. This representation shows a core comprising an Enterprise Resource Planning (ERP) tool and an information management database extruded through multiple projects. The link to "Our partners database" might represent multiple links to a number of different partners.

Initially the data structure may be perceived by those working with it in terms of its physical form, which may be similar to Part A, with

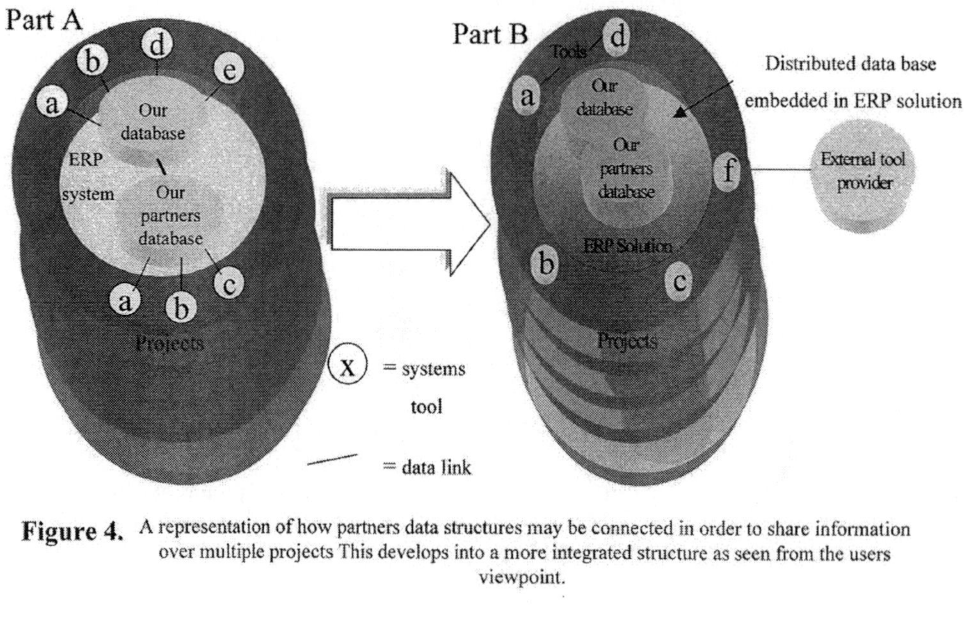

Figure 4. A representation of how partners data structures may be connected in order to share information over multiple projects This develops into a more integrated structure as seen from the users viewpoint.

separation between databases but with a high level of integration in the business planning tools. As the distributed database develops into an integrated working environment it will only really be successful when perceived by those working within the structure in terms of the more seamless diagram as in Part B. What the user then sees is a common data structure for a given project and truly shared systems tools. If a partnership is perceived to be working in the seamless manner of Part B there is a high likelihood that the partnership is operating close to the optimum efficiency.

When a partnership over a domain of multiple companies is being run in this way the focus will be upon working to exploit each company's strategic strengths. This focus may aid smaller companies who instead of being regarded only as sub-contractors can become strategic partners on a project. One concept presented to aid such collaboration is that of an external tool provider, as shown in Figure 4B. This would enable companies to gain access to a specific tool for a limited duration during the collaborative stages of the partnership. This concept leads us to understand the way in which a flexible approach to developing software might lead to further opportunities for tool providers in the future.

SECTION 2.
PRACTICAL CONSIDERATIONS IN THE IMPLEMENTATION OF THE COMPLETE DATA STRUCTURE APPROACH.

Even if a company aims towards the concept of Figure 4 many practical issues will remain. There may be high costs and penalties, both in terms of tool development and in the impact upon the business, should the approach fail. Development should be evolutionary, proceeding in small, safe steps. This approach might be regarded as selective breeding in that we are working towards the capability we need to be developed.

Figure 5 shows how from the view of the user we might expect the concept to develop as it passes through each conceptual stage. It highlights the principal stumbling blocks for the concept, shown via the interfaces representing change. How to maintain the vision of shared tools whilst maintaining data integrity within our organisation? Many of the stages needed to fulfil the vision of shared systems tools are currently being implemented, for example, in many companies the necessary concurrent processes are already in place. However, further understanding of the importance of data processes must be developed as this will be the key to further progress. It will also be important to develop business processes flexibly to ensure alignment with partners.

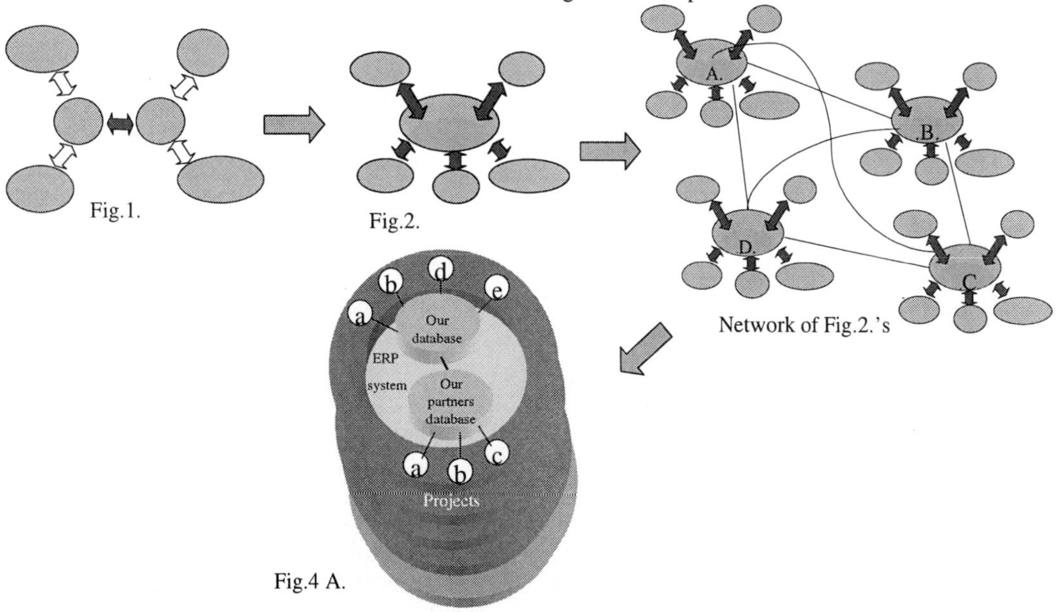

Figure 5. The Evolutionary/ Selectively Bred Development Process

Standardisation for provision of compatible interfaces and data transfer protocols is one of the central aspects of the approach, and presents a fundamental area to be addressed if the concept is to be realised fully. Work on data interfaces for systems modelling is being undertaken by the systems engineering community, and the work will be of great value to the development of the concept.

In building up capability one of the main issues will be the fact that each step taken will have to have an identifiable benefit to the business in its own right. Only if this is the case are organisations likely to invest in the tools which provide the components of the concept. This places even more emphasis on the need to develop data transfer standards now, to avoid the cost of rework or replacement later.

Successful implementation of the data structure concept will be dependant upon companies (of all sizes) recognising the benefits to be gained in collaborative working through these tools and demanding such functionality from vendors: vendors must then respond!

Practical Barriers to the Implementation of the Complete Data Structure Concept

In promoting the concept a scope of argument has been developed from that of a single business's investment in systems engineering technologies to that of championing cross-company solutions. The problems in implementing the concept should not be underrated and many problems will only become apparent as further work is undertaken. Some basic problems facing the concept fit broadly into the following categories.

Technological

From an engineer's viewpoint the first issue to arise is technological and can be divided into hardware and software aspects. In terms of hardware, advances in server based technology mean that the physical infrastructure is unlikely to be a barrier to the concept. Software presents more of a problem. With current and developing data transfer standards it is likely that an integrated approach to systems modelling will be widespread within a few years. Unless standards do remain flexible there will be the chance of obsolescence as greater functionality and compatibility with non-modelling tools is demanded. There are also many challenges present in software implementation and it is likely problems will occur if vendors are over ambitious or provide inflexible applications.

Security

Security is a key issue in the sharing and transfer of data amongst partners. Some security issues will be technically soluble, via developments in web based security technologies and via newer methods of encryption. The issue of preventing access to commercial and other sensitive information must also be addressed.

Timing Problems

If the concept is implemented too quickly it may well fail. This may happen because the cost of implementing a system of this type is likely to be high both to develop and to operate. However, if the concept is developed collaboratively in stages the advantages will become clear. Using an evolutionary or selectively bred approach with agreed standards set amongst the collaborating companies is considered essential.

Attitude of users

The concept presented here defines a mode of working which is likely to be increasingly important throughout industry. Whenever changes to the way people work are proposed resistance will be encountered in terms of the attitude of some of the people working within the system. This issue will need to be addressed to ensure a strategy is developed for managing successfully the impact on people.

CONCLUSIONS

A concept has been presented which places emphasis on collaborative working through computational tools using compatible interfaces. The advantage of the concept is that it allows companies to develop systems capabilities in a way that is matched to the business need for collaboration. If improving data transfer protocols exist amongst systems tools they are likely to be working towards the ideal of an integrated system. The evolutionary approach suggested has the advantage that it is also applicable to smaller companies.

At present the data structure concept is focused onto the engineering function, but in future it may develop into a medium of control for operation of business itself. The information needed to manage any design or manufacturing process, as part of a highly developed holistic system, may also be used to indicate critical performance measures for the business.

REFERENCES

Bracket, Michael H, Data Sharing using a common data architecture, John Wiley & Sons Inc 1994.

Brown, Philip J and Lavender Jack K Jr, Exploiting Web-Based Technology to Foster IPDT Productivity, INCOSE Proceedings, 1999.

INCOSE, Report of the tools Integration interest group, 1996 "Tools Integration Work Group Report: Scenarios Leading towards a concept of operations for an integrated Systems Engineering Environment" International Council on Systems Engineering 1996

Johnson et al The Future Systems Engineering Data Exchange Standard STEP AP-233: Sharing the results of the SEDRES Project, INCOSE Proceedings 1999.

Martin, James N, Systems Engineering Guidebook "a process for developing systems and products" CRC Press Incorporated. 1997.

The Ministry of Defence Smart Procurement Implementation Team, The Acquisition Handbook "A guide to smart procurement" 1999.

Reilly, Norman B, Successful Systems Engineering for engineers and managers, Van Nostrand Reinhold, 1993.

Sage, Andrew P. Systems Engineering, John Wiley & Sons Inc, 1992.

Tagg, Rodger and Freyberg, Chris. Designing distributed and co-operative information systems. International Thompson computer press, 1997.

BIOGRAPHY

Since graduating from Loughborough University, England with a BSc in Engineering Physics in 1998, David Battersby has been working as a Graduate Systems Engineer for BAE SYSTEMS RO Defence. He has had involvement in the use and implementation of wide scale computational business tools in addition to applying Systems Engineering practice in his working environment. He is currently involved in a technical programme for which he is the focus for the integration of project information within the data structure of the business.

Selection of a Requirement Management Tool for a Semi-Custom Design Company

Dale Glyn Langston an Mary Lynne Hansen
Litton Denro
9318 Gaither Road
Gaithersburg, MD 20877

Abstract. The purpose of this paper is to define how a requirements management tool might fit into a semi-custom design company. The paper identifies why this selection is more complex for a semi-custom design company than either a project-based company or a pure product-based company. The paper finally identifies a minimum set of requirements that must be satisfied by the requirements management tool.

INTRODUCTION

As engineering begins looking for a tool to assist in the management of requirements, the question arises as to what does a semi-custom design company need or want out of a requirement management tool? How does such a tool fit into the semi-custom design company's organization and culture? These questions appear very simple to individuals answering them and are simple from their individual point of view. From an overall corporate point of view, these issues are extremely complex. The purpose of this paper is to clarify the issues involved in the selection of a requirement management tool and to provide some insights into the high-level requirements that any tool being considered must satisfy. This paper uses LEBA Industries, a fictitious company, as a representative example of semi-custom design companies. The collective experience of the author's was used in the paper. LEBA Industries is not intended to describe a particular company, but rather to represent the situation faced by every semi-custom design companies.

WHY DOES LEBA INDUSTRIES NEED A REQUIREMENT MANAGEMENT TOOL?

LEBA Industries' market requires the delivery of systems that meet a specific customer's needs and thus a perceived set of requirements. The ability to manage a project to deliver a system that meets those perceived requirements is paramount to the continued success of the organization. In the early days, LEBA Industries designed and delivered products that met a single customer's needs – the United States Government. As commercial and international contracts were won, LEBA Industries has seen a massive increase in the number of requirements that must be met by its products. Looking over the projects that have seemed overly difficult to manage and execute, the evidence clearly points to difficulty with understanding and managing requirements. This difficulty is found throughout the life cycle of the projects.

The difficulty with requirements begins early in a project's life cycle, in the proposal phase. In this phase, a customer's requirements are examined to determine if LEBA Industries' products satisfy each requirement. For each requirement not currently satisfied, a decision is made as to whether the proposal will contain a bid to satisfy that requirement or whether the proposal will be submitted with LEBA Industries non-compliant to that requirement. If LEBA Industries is to comply with that requirement, a bid is made against the requirement. Though all this is done in the initial phase, the information is seldom used after the initial proposal is submitted. Frequently, it is lost or simply not used by organizations after the contract is signed. This lack of availability or use affects the execution of a project. For example, the proposal itself denotes that the proposed solution is non-compliant on a requirement, but engineering has to make a design change to satisfy the requirement because it was not removed from the statement of work or specification. Another example occurs when marketing examines the product baseline and believes LEBA Industries' product complies with a particular requirement, but it does not actually comply with the requirement. Unplanned work must then be performed to bring the system into compliance. In both cases, LEBA Industries loses profit because the requirements were not managed.

During the design phase, engineering makes design changes to meet LEBA Industries' understanding of the requirements, but this understanding may not match the customer's understanding or the customer's need or desire. This lack of understanding can be in the form of a technical requirement that was not understood or a statement of work activity that was misunderstood. For example, a customer requested that LEBA Industries deliver a system that turned on and off a feature of a particular communication device. LEBA Industries agreed to do this by supplying a contact closure for changing the mode of operation. Unfortunately for the customer and LEBA Industries, changing the operational mode of the communication device did not work in this manner; thus both sides ended up being dissatisfied. An example involving a statement of work activity occurred when a customer wanted LEBA Industries to execute a MIL-STD-499 and MIL-STD-2167A program. LEBA Industries stated that the company's standard process would meet the needs of the customer and thus would be used. However, the customer proceeded to manage the program as if the military standards were being used. In these two cases, LEBA Industries ends up losing money and making the customer dissatisfied with its performance.

The improper handling of requirements shows up in LEBA Industries testing to sell off a project. In many cases, LEBA Industries has been asked to satisfy requirements that can not be tested or that are just not tested. In one program, the customer placed a requirement concerning noise that was improperly specified. During the execution of the FAT procedures, LEBA Industries and the customer discovered that the requirement was not clear and that there was no real method for testing the requirement. Though a solution was agreed upon, the FAT experienced a delay because this was not addressed at the proper time. There are other examples where requirements were not verified because they were either vague or were contained in referenced documents that were not available. This lack of understanding of the requirements has led to the sell-off of systems in factory acceptance testing that did not work as needed when installed in the customer's facility. LEBA Industries was required to make changes to a fielded system which was very expensive to both LEBA Industries and the customer.

These problems would have been eliminated or at least identified with a disciplined handling of the requirements. Though requirements can be managed outside of a tool, the process is one that is prone to errors if done manually. A tool provides the capability to track the compliance throughout the life cycle of a project. A tool provides the means that can be used to ensure a common understanding of the requirements between the customer and LEBA Industries. Finally, a tool provides an easy means to determine that all requirements are verified.

WHAT MAKES THE SELECTION OF A REQUIREMENTS TOOL COMPLEX?

The selection of a requirement management tool at LEBA Industries faces three complications. The first complication is the business model that is used at LEBA Industries. The second complication is that requirements are both technical and non-technical. The third complication is that the users of the requirements come from many different areas of the organization.

From the beginning, LEBA Industries established its reputation as the leading deliverer of semi-custom products. As a supplier of semi-custom systems, LEBA Industries modifies or adds features to its core products to meet the requirements of individual customers. These new or enhanced features in turn become available to other customers. In addition, when new development work is being performed, design engineers look at requirements historically, over all current and past projects, to determine what behavior a particular function should perform or have the option of performing. Using this business model, requirements have two distinctly different views: a project view and a product view. From the project view, requirements are managed only for the length of the project. From the product view, requirements, particularly functional requirements, have a lifetime far greater than the duration of the project. This product view of requirements is usually not supported by requirement management tools in general and especially by tools that originated in the software realm.

As a commercial supplier of products to numerous customers throughout the world, LEBA Industries receives contracts that do not cleanly separate statement of work activities or requirements from technical requirements. In addition, many contracts awarded to LEBA Industries are for the delivery of multiple systems to a customer. On these contracts, the system may have a slightly different set of either technical or non-technical requirements for each system or site. These requirements must be managed both from a contract basis and from a system or site basis, which is difficult in many requirement management tools.

On most US government contracting efforts, requirements are managed by systems engineering with other technical disciplines only dealing with the few requirements allocated to them. In many cases, only the "system level" requirements are managed in the requirement management tool. In LEBA Industries, requirements must be managed as a group from the first receipt of a requirement until the requirement has been superceded. Requirements are used and must be managed by many different groups throughout the company. These groups include marketing, systems engineering, hardware engineering, software engineering, program management, test engineering, system integration, customer service, logistics, training, and quality. In companies that have only a project orientation, most of these individuals are users of the requirements and do not require management or tracking capability. In a product-based company, these groups all require management and tracking capability. At some point in the process, the groups listed above generate, use, verify, and track requirements. Most requirement management tools support multiple users of requirements, but these multiple users over several different organizational boundaries complicate any attempt to define a requirement management philosophy.

HOW SHOULD A REQUIREMENT MANAGEMENT TOOL BE USED IN LEBA INDUSTRIES?

As shown in the previous section, many different organizations at LEBA Industries need access to the requirement management tool. The use by each group is substantially different from other groups. An optimal requirement management tool cannot be selected without an understanding of how each group will use such a tool.

Marketing

The first place requirements typically arrive at LEBA Industries is in marketing. These requirements take many forms and come from a variety of sources. The requirements may come from customers in the form of a request for a budgetary estimate, a rough order of magnitude estimate, or a proposal. Marketing uses these requirements to make bid/no bid decisions, generate compliance matrices, and communicate with engineering concerning the potential work. These requirements need to be entered into the requirements database and tracked over the life of the proposal process. In generating the compliance matrix for a set of requirements, marketing needs to search a master requirement database to determine if current products are compliant to this set of requirements. This information is necessary in making the bid/no bid decision.

In addition to explicit requirements from current customers, marketing also identifies requirements resulting from competitive analysis of the marketplace. These requirements may be features that are provided by competitors' products but not by LEBA Industries' products. The requirements may be from a market that its products do not currently address but which the company wants to enter. In either case, these requirements must be managed in the same manner as an explicit requirement from a customer.

Systems Engineering

From the perspective of industry and government standards such as MIL-STD-499, EIA-632, SE-CMM, SECAM, and SECM, requirements analysis and management is predominantly the realm of the systems engineer. The systems engineer is responsible for taking the requirements received from marketing and developing or identifying the architecture that should be used to satisfy the customer's needs. This architecture selection process may identify new requirements after conversations with the customer. These requirements must be entered into the database and managed like any other requirement.

When developing new system architectures, internal requirements – functional, behavioral, performance, or physical – are identified that must be added to the requirement database and managed with the other requirements. Once again, this process may identify additional interface requirements that must be addressed.

In most requirement documents, numerous government and industry standards are identified as being applicable to the project. These requirements need to be entered into the database and managed as if they were explicit requirements from a customer's specification. Since LEBA Industries is in a well-defined market, the same industry specifications are identified by multiple contracts. As a product house, LEBA Industries wants to satisfy these requirements in the same manner every time, thereby requiring a single master requirements database.

Having identified the high-level requirements, the systems engineer's next involvement with requirements is allocating those requirements to the subsystems. The allocation process requires the derivation of new requirements that are linked to the parent requirement. Having allocated all the requirements to the appropriate subsystem, the systems engineer allocates the requirements to individual configuration items. After allocating the requirements for a project to a CI, the systems engineer collects the requirements for the particular CI together from all projects and then allocates the group to the individual processor for software (CSCI) or card/ASIC for hardware (HWCI). The allocation to CI, HWCI, and CSCI is performed using the same process as used to allocate to subsystems.

Having allocated the requirements to the lowest level, the systems engineer verifies that the implementation satisfies the subsystem- and system-level requirements. This verification comes in the form of analysis and testing. The systems engineer uses the analysis generated at the HWCI and the CSCI level to verify the requirements allocated to the CI level. This analysis must then be linked to the requirements at the CI level for use in the future. The same process of performing an analysis and linking the results to the appropriate requirement is performed at the subsystem and the system level. Verification of a requirement by test is discussed in the hardware engineering, software engineering, system integration and test, and quality test engineering sections.

Hardware Engineering

To hardware engineering, requirements are inputs to the design process. Typically, the requirements allocated to the HWCI are at such a detail level of definition that no additional allocation is necessary. If, however, additional allocation becomes necessary, the requirement management process is the same as at the CI level for systems engineering

Since hardware engineering is typically answering requirements, hardware engineering needs a requirement management tool that allows them to link the results of their activities to the individual requirements. Hardware engineering needs to link the parts of the design to the requirement that it satisfies. The hardware engineer needs to link analyses results, test procedures, and test results to the requirements as evidence that the design meets requirements. These results may not be textural in nature, but whatever the format they must be linked to the requirement.

Software Engineering

To software engineering, requirements are both inputs to the design process and results of the design process. Typically, the requirements allocated to the CSCI are not at sufficient level of definition, making additional levels of allocation necessary. Software engineering typically will further allocate the CSCI requirements to individual modules using the same process as was used by systems engineering.

In addition to supporting further allocation, software engineering needs a requirement management tool that allows them to link the results of their activities to the individual requirements. Software engineering needs to link modules or parts of modules to the individual requirement that they satisfy. The software engineer needs to link analyses results, test procedures, and test results to the requirements as evidence that the design meets requirements. These results may not be textural in nature, but whatever the format they must be linked to the requirement.

System Integration Engineering

System integration activities begin early in the project where the integration engineer determines how the subsystems and the configuration items are going to be integrated prior to delivery to system test. The systems integrator examines each requirement and determines how it can be verified by test during the integration process. To ensure that all subsystem and configuration requirements are verified during integration, the integration engineer links each requirement with the appropriate integration procedure and steps. After completing the integration activities, the results of the integration tests are linked to the appropriate requirements.

System Test Engineering

System test activities begin early in the requirements analysis process when the system test engineer determines how each requirement is going to be verified prior to shipment to the customer. The system test engineer links each requirement with the appropriate test procedure and steps. After completing the test activities, the results of the system tests are linked to the appropriate requirements.

Site Survey & Installation

Early in each project, an installation technician is sent to each site to gather information concerning how the system is to be installed. The information gathered includes length of cable runs between pieces of equipment and the location of power inputs. The information that is gathered during these site surveys is in fact requirements that are equal to those specified in the requirement document. These requirements have to be tracked and managed in the same manner as any other requirement.

Product Engineer / Product Support

The product engineer deals with problems found in the field with a LEBA Industries system. When either a customer or customer service reports a problem experienced in the field, the problem is tied to a requirement that the system is failing. After determining the source of the failure, the product engineer ties the solution to the problem. The product engineer then searches the requirements database to determine which systems on other projects will experience the same problem. The requirements that will be violated in those systems are also linked the problem to enable product support to know which systems need to be updated.

Research & Development

In a product based company, R&D activities are tied to the needs of the market that are currently not being met by LEBA Industries equipment. To establish these needs, the research engineers examine the requirements database focusing on the requirements that prevented LEBA Industries from bidding on a program or caused it to lose a program. In addition, the research engineer looks across the programs that have been won to determine the requirements to which LEBA Industries stated non-comply. This list of requirements becomes the basis of future development work.

Logistics (Pubs & Training)

Logistics engineers responsible for publications, training, and reliability also require access to the requirements database. The logistics engineers use the requirements database in two ways. First, they track the non-technical requirements in the same manner as the systems engineer tracks the technical requirements. Second, they use the architecture links to assist them in the development of training courses, writing manuals, and performing reliability analysis.

Program Management

The last group using the requirements database is the program managers. During the proposal phase, the appropriate groups bid against each technical and non-technical requirement. These bids are linked to the requirement in the database. When changes to the requirements occur during the negotiation phase, the program manager can identify the financial effect of the change.

During a project, the program manager uses the requirements database to track and manage non-technical requirements. Frequently, a PM receives ECPs that affect the requirements baseline of the program. The program manager can use the database to identify what parts of the system would change as a result of the ECP. The PM could then track the bid from each area against that change.

The PM can also use the tool to assist in tracking program activities. The PM can search the database to determine to what level requirements have been allocated. He or she can also determine the status of design activities, analysis activities, and test activities. This ability aids the PM in ensuring that the program is executed properly and that the system is designed, built, and tested correctly.

WHAT ARE THE REQUIREMENTS FOR A REQUIREMENT MANAGEMENT TOOL?

Having determined why selection of a requirement management tool for LEBA Industries is difficult, this paper established the operational concept as to how such a tool could be used to improve the performance of LEBA Industries. These operational concepts provide an insight into a minimum set of requirements that a requirement management tool should meet if it is to be accepted as the standard for LEBA Industries. These requirements are listed below with a short explanation of their importance. These requirements do not represent an exhaustive list, but rather an initial set of considerations. The requirements are listed in no particular order.

1. *The tool shall utilize a database for storage of data that supports user-defined searches.*

   This tool needs to support the numerous searches made that are not on a project basis. These searches include looking across all projects for requirements relating to a particular function and looking across all projects to view requirements to which its products non-comply.

2. *The tool shall allow multiple users simultaneous read and write access to the requirement database.*

   Since LEBA Industries is a semi-custom design company, a master database must be maintained that contains the requirements of all projects in the company. With multiple projects going on, the tool used must be capable of allowing engineers from each of the projects to access and update the database simultaneously.

3. *The tool shall provide an automated means for parsing specifications into the database.*

   Marketing receives numerous statements of work, requests for proposals, and specifications on a weekly basis. Most of these proposals reference many industry specifications. The requirements from each of these documents need to be entered into the tool. If the documents must be entered manually, the drain on marketing (or engineering) resources will be such that there will be time and resources to enter only a subset of these documents, or, worse, the tool will not be used because of the effort involved. Therefore, to provide the benefits required by LEBA Industries, the tool must provide the capability to parse documents into the tool automatically.

4. *The tool shall support management of both technical and non-technical requirements.*

   Most contracts contain requirements in the statement of work that are not technical in nature but that do need to be allocated and tracked. The tool must provide this capability since these non-technical requirements frequently affect the technical effort.

5. *The tool shall support viewing requirements on a project basis and on a product basis.*

   As a semi-custom design company, LEBA Industries view requirements from both a project and a product view. To allow program managers to manage a project, the tool must allow them to view all the requirements for a project. To allow engineering to add a new function to the product baseline, the tool must allow them to view the requirements from all projects that affect that function.

6. *The tool shall support storage of non-textural objects in the database.*

   LEBA Industries is required to satisfy specifications that are not in a textural format. For networked systems, the interconnection requirements between sites are frequently presented in the form of drawings or tables. Most specifications for analog interfaces contain requirements that are shown in graph format, particularly relative to frequency response, noise, and testing. Though not common, LEBA Industries has been required to satisfy shock and vibration requirements that are specified in graphical format.

7. *The tool shall support linking requirements to multiple projects simultaneously.*

   Most system specifications reference industry or government standards. Though each system specification references a different set of industry standards, any single standard will be referenced by multiple specifications. LEBA Industries needs to track the requirements from the industry standards only once. Therefore, these industry and government standards must be referenced by multiple projects.

8. *The tool database shall support allocation and derivation of lower level requirements.*

   A major task in managing requirements is the allocation of system requirements to subsystems (and hence to configuration items) and the derivation of requirements resulting from the allocation. For requirements that are allocated completely to a lower level in the system, the tool must track to what subsystem or configuration item the particular requirement is allocated. For requirements that are allocated partially to several subsystems or configuration items, the tool must support the derivation of new requirements resulting from the allocation. The tool must provide the capability to track these derived requirements to the original requirement.

9. *The tool shall support the addition of company-specific fields to the database.*

   To support the product view of the systems, the tool must support marking to what functional area each requirement belongs. To support marketing and program management needs, the tool must support adding fields linked to the requirement such as compliance and bids.

   Additionally, LEBA Industries' product addresses a specialized market. When dealing with specialized products, it is often the case that commercial tools either do not contain all needed information or require information that is not appropriate for the particular market being addressed. Without some customization capability, there is no assurance that the product will fit LEBA Industries' current needs or continue to meet its needs in the future.

10. *The tool shall support management of functional, behavioral, performance, and physical requirements.*

    Technical requirements placed on the LEBA Industries products take the form of functional, behavioral, performance, and physical requirements. Each requirement type takes a different form and is allocated in a different manner. The tool must support requirements of all types.

11. *The tool shall support m-to-n hierarchical decomposition.*

In many cases, especially in a distributive-processing environment, single requirements cannot be allocated individually, but must be allocated with other requirements. This set of requirements is then allocated to a set of lower levels. Since the LEBA Industries product line is a distributive architecture, the tool must be based on a hierarchical structure that allows m-to-n allocations. Note, however, that the structure is still hierarchical.

12. *The tool shall support automatic generation of documents, including but not limited to specifications, verification matrices, and test procedures.*

The tool required by LEBA Industries contains all allocated requirements as well as the verification method for those requirements and links to the procedures that will be used to verify those requirements. The tool must support generating verification matrices and specifications and should support the generation of test procedures. This not only prevents duplication of effort, but also assures accuracy and consistency between departments and products.

13. *The tool shall support documentation of the system architecture.*

Requirements cannot be separated from the system architecture nor can architectures exist without requirements. Given this relationship, the tool should provide the means to document and model the system architecture. In documenting the architecture, the tool must support documenting the behavioral view, physical view, and the user view of the architecture. The system should support modeling the behavior of the system and performing performance analysis of the architecture.

14. *The tool shall ensure integrity of the requirements database at all times.*

When a single tool controls the entire collection of requirements for both the products and the projects, the tool must guarantee the integrity of the requirements database. This integrity includes supporting baselining requirements, identifying all the requirements that are affected by a single change, and identifying who changed the requirements and when they were changed.

15. *The tool shall support electrical, mechanical, environmental, and software requirements.*

LEBA Industries products must satisfy electrical, mechanical, environmental, and software requirements. All four types of requirements are of equal importance to LEBA Industries. The tool must support all types of requirements naturally without requiring a certain type of requirements to be maintained in files outside the tool's database.

16. *The tool shall not enforce a particular design methodology.*

Because of the product view, LEBA Industries must be able to use the requirement tool to track historical data. As many of these products are already in existence, or at least currently under development or bidding, the problem arises of it being nearly impossible to retrofit a design methodology onto a project. Also, there is no methodology that has been accepted as standard or required by LEBA Industries, and it would be difficult to determine one methodology that works well for all product areas. It would be wrong to base design on what is required by a tool rather than on what works best for the product and people.

HOW SHOULD A REQUIREMENT MANAGEMENT TOOL BE SELECTED?

Selection of a requirement management tool requires a small team that selects five or six tools that appear to meet the needs of LEBA Industries. These venders should be brought in to present and demonstrate their tools. After viewing all venders, the team should select the three tools that appear to be best suited for LEBA Industries' environment. The venders should be given this white paper and asked to describe or preferably demonstrate how their tool satisfies the requirements. After reviewing the three venders' answers, the team should determine which tool that meets all requirements is best suited for LEBA Industries.

If no team meets the requirements, the team should work with all groups to determine if the requirements are too stringent. If the requirements are not too stringent, the team should report that no requirement management tool is currently available that meets LEBA Industries' needs. A trade-off then would need to be performed to determine if some requirements should be removed or if LEBA Industries would be better served by developing its own requirement management tool in house. It also may be possible to have a vender modify a tool to meet the requirements, and this should be investigated.

SUMMARY

This white paper has provided a brief study on the need for a requirement tool at LEBA Industries. This paper has established that the lack of requirements management has had detrimental effect on LEBA Industries both on its reputation in the market and financially. The paper explained that a requirement tool is needed, but selection of the right tool for LEBA Industries would be difficult. The paper then described the operational concept of how the tool would be used through the eyes of the groups that would need access to the tool. This paper then defined a set of requirements that a tool must meet if it is to be capable of meeting the needs of LEBA Industries. Finally the paper provided a brief overview of a recommended selection process. This paper should ease the selection process for a requirement management tool.

BIOGRAPHY

Dale Glyn Langston is a senior systems engineer for Litton Denro with over 19 years experience in the design of complex systems. Mr. Langston worked as a system designer specializing in RISC processor design for IBM in Poughkeepsie, NY. He has also worked as a system engineer in the area of radiation hardened processors for Loral Federal Systems- Manassas and a systems architect in the area of information technology for Electronic Data Systems. Mr. Langston is currently serving as the system architect for Air Defense C^4I applications at Litton Denro. Mr. Langston received a Bachelors of Science in Electrical Engineering and a Masters of Electrical Engineering from Mississippi State University. He has done post-graduate studies in systems engineering at George Mason University. His research interests are in fault tolerant systems, where he holds a patent and numerous technical disclosures.

Mary Lynne Hansen is a senior software engineer for Litton Denro with over 13 years experience in software design and development. Ms. Hansen worked as a consultant for Coopers & Lybrand in Washington, DC. She has also worked independently as a consultant in the Washington, DC, area. Ms. Hansen is currently serving as a lead software engineer at Litton Denro. Ms. Hansen received a Bachelors of Arts in Comparative Literature at the Pennsylvania State University. She has a Masters of Arts in Comparative Literature from the State University of New York at Binghamton.

A generic approach to implement information-based system development

Ernst Fricke[1], Armin Schulz[1], Pamela Wehlitz[2], Herbert Negele[1]
[1]Division of Astronautics
Technische Universität München
Boltzmannstrasse 15, 85748 Munich
Germany
E.Fricke@Lrt.mw.tum.de, http:\\www.lrt.mw.tum.de
[2]BMW AG
Munich
Germany

ABSTRACT

The idea of information-based system development is to analyze, capture and model information flows within a company's processes related to system development. Building on those information flows an appropriate development process can be implemented. This has to be done throughout the entire life-cycle, that is from first ideas and concepts to after-sales service and field support.

This paper introduces a generic approach to set-up and implement information-based system development. A high level process as well as an appropriate modeling method to approach and capture information-based system development is addressed. Typical results, insights and benefits gained from an implementation of information-based system development are highlighted.

BACKGROUND

The increasing complexity of technical systems and the necessity to shorten the time to market, coupled with a fast changing technology base, leads to the consequences to improve the system view in product development process as well as focusing on information flows in product development.

Today there is an ongoing discussion about information-based system development. Gartz (1997) showed an implementation at Boeing for the development of the 777. This paper is based on theoretical research and practical experience on implementing an information-based system development. The practical experience is derived from a wide range of projects within automotive and space industry, whereas one specific implementation example at one project partner. Building on that, a generic approach to set-up and implement information-based system development was developed.

The right information at the right time to the right person means that those person who needs an information receives it instantly after the information is generated or changed in the form and granularity as needed. That includes fuzzy information or unfinished designs. After a product focus and then a process focus in system development, an information-based focus is necessary to integrate all the different views as product, process, functional or organizational views. As it was said in Gartz (1997) the product development process has to be structured around the necessary information flows and shouldn't be developed independent from these. The idea of information-based system development is to analyze, capture and model information flows within a company's processes related to system development and building around it and implementing appropriate development process. It is important here, to plan the information flow and exchange independent from its type of documentation. This has to be done throughout the entire life-cycle, that is from first ideas and concepts to after-sales service and field support. Therefore, consistent and mandatory processes have to be implemented, which are accepted and obeyed by all people involved within the product development.

Additionally, it incorporates transparency within the entire development process (documents, components, in-/outputs, information systems and involved organizational functions/departments), in order to facilitate a mapping of all information flows and all identified information objects, as well as their interrelations in a generic process, as a basis for a following implementation in a set of information systems, e.g. product data management (PDM) system.

INFORMATION-BASED PROCESS MODELING AND ANALYSIS APPROACH

The knowledge of information and information flows[1] over the entire life-cycle is a necessary

[1] Information-focused process view, i.e. the processes are viewed by identification of the input and output information of each process step

prerequisite, to improve the development process as well as to support the development process by IT-toolsets. The capturing of the information flows between identified processes as well as the related information objects to be exchanged enables a necessary transparence of the entire life-cycle process with its process chains, subprocesses, In-/Outputs, IT-Systems, organizational owner etc.

The proposed and used approach to implement information-based system development is structured into three steps. The fields of activity and the relevant questions can be addressed systematically and regarding their causal-logical sequence.

The three steps can be described as:

1. Analysis and determination of the scope of processes to be addressed, including relevant information objects and the different high-level process chains
2. Modeling detailed development processes by capturing the information flows within these processes and their mapping on a process model over the entire life-cycle
3. Process optimization and implementation Identification of improvement potential in the information and the process model. Implementation of an optimized and well-defined, but flexible information-based process model.

Consequently, the main question behind building up an information-based system development is:

Who requires or delivers When from Whom or to Whom Which kind of information in What kind of format ?

MODELING METHOD

In Fricke et al. (1998) a detailed market study was conducted, in which about 30 tools for business process modeling (e.g. ARIS, Bonapart, IDEF, Facets, etc.) were analyzed and evaluated by a variety of criteria. None of these tools met the requirements of information-based process modeling as understood by the authors, not only concerning the method, but also concerning supporting factors like easy and fast input of data, multi-user and database support. Another important factor was the fact, that the process model also should be the basis for project planning and scheduling. Hence, a smooth data flow from process mapping to project planning and scheduling should be possible. One reason for this result may be that these tools and the underlying methods were developed for and used in projcts whose focus was the reengineering of business process in preparation for the introduction of new information systems (Lullies et al., 1998). Therefore, the development of methods tools was driven by IT specialists and their needs, thus leading to results that didn't meet the requirements of the engineers very well. These methods support very good the implementation of processes in IT systems, but do not support a realistic modeling of the development processes.

One widely used and accepted method to model development processes is the Design Structure Matrix (DSM), which supports very good analyzing and visualizing the structure and dependencies of development processes (Stewart, 1981; Eppinger et al., 1994; Browning, 1998). But it seems to lack in describing the content of the information flows between the processes, which is not ideal for an implementation of the modeled processes into an IT system.

Therefore, the IPO-method (Fricke et al., 1998; Negele et al., 1999) is used in this approach to model and implement an information-based system development, as this method is focusing on the information flow between the processes.

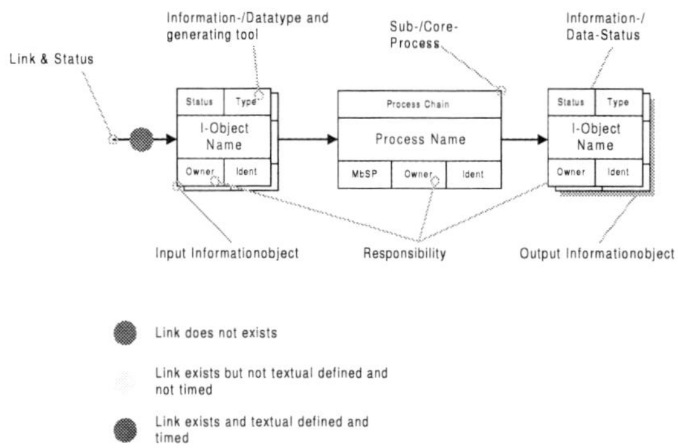

FIGURE 1: MODELING METHODOLOGY

Based on these kind of process models, the information objects and related workflows that are needed for an IT implementation can be identified.

ANALYZED INFORMATION OBJECTS

For a transparent presentation of the scope of the information objects to be analyzed for an information-based system development, a distinction has to be made between

- Primary and
- Secondary information objects.

The primary information objects are all those, that finally get into the product, e.g. SW-code that will be implemented in an electronic control unit inside a car.

Secondary information objects are those, that are produced as a means of communication inside the development process and do not represent components that will be implemented in the product, e.g. documents, simulation models.

Areas		Questions
Analysis of information objects	⇨	Which kind of information objects have to be analyzed and modeled?
	⇨	Which information objects finally get into the product and which I-objects are a means of communication?
	⇨	Which modeling approach is useful for a later implementation in a supporting IT infrastructure?
Analysis of Product Development Process	⇨	Which process chains and sub-processes do exist in the Product Development Process?
	⇨	What are the information flows in the Product Development Process?
	⇨	What are the links and information flows between the processes?

Table 1:Relevant Areas and Questions for Information-Flow Analysis

For an analysis of the software life-cycle in an automotive company, i.e. from the car concepts from market perspective to requirements, to coding and implementation to sales and service, this was modeled with the IPO method. Especially in the electric/electronic environment it is necessary to get a detailed understanding of the specific problems of data management. The most known approaches in the PDM area are from the mechanical engineering and CAD area. These are only partial applicable and efficient for electric/electronic and software development. Different requirements regarding information structures (hierarchical, network, layered, hybrid) from HW- and SW-parts, integrated components and partially abstract components and behavior, as well as fast change loops with short technology cycles, make new, specific approaches for these highly-interrelated and integrated systems necessary.

TYPICAL RESULTS FROM INFORMATION-BASED PROCESS MODELING AND ANALYSIS

Results from conducting information-based analysis of product development processes typically clearly indicate, that there is much more information exchanged among the processes, than requested or delivered in defined information containers (e.g. documents, data files, plans) or available in defined information channels (i.e. information retrieval system). Often it is unclear who is the supplier or receiver of information is, and how this information is or has to be provided (i.e., in what form, when, by which means, in which quality/maturity).

In the second step this information-based process models have to be used to talk with the relevant process owners about interfaces and information exchange, to stepwise clarify the above mentioned open questions.

The results from such an approach can be structured into four categories:

- A modeled development process with all its information links
- A list/summary of all information objects and its attributes (e.g. format) being used within the development process
- Analysis and evaluation of the development process based on the information flow network
- Implementation strategies for the information-based development process and recommendations for optimization

As mentioned above, results of such an information-based process analysis are the basis to implement and establish consistent processes primarily based on the information flow network. Knowing which kind of information has to be provided and used by whom at what time in the process is elementary to implement such a process in a supporting IT-structure, e.g. a product data management (PDM) system or in a model-based tool environment. Also, as pointed out by Negele et al. (1999) such an information-based process model can be used to implement it into a scheduling tool, by adding distinct dates for information delivery. Additionally, results can be used as a basis for a continuous evaluation and optimization of the development process, e.g. using elements of capability maturity models.

APPROACHES FOR FURTHER ANALYSIS

Some of the major analyzing approaches after having modeled the development process are related to the information objects and the processes:

- Changes in format of information objects inside and between single processes

- Clear ownership of content and changes of information objects
- Clear ownership of the single processes
- Check of existence and status of information links, meaning coordination regarding time and content of outputs and related inputs between two processes.

Typical problem areas to be looked at. Based on the experience of some of the authors (from university), there are in general typical problem areas in product development processes that can be analyzed easily with an information-based process model. Therefore after the modeling, the process model should be analyzed and improved regarding the following four categories and its typical problems:

1. Availability and State of Input-Information

Due to mostly proprietary/locally oriented, redundant and even frequently still paper based data capture and storage, as well as inappropriate and incomprehensive revision schemes, availability and actuality of information can be intransparent. Distribution of information and data in terms of content, scope, timing, receiver may be not controlled which can result in either lack or overflow of information and data of all process participants. These deficiencies would be in particular severe consequences in a context of changes and their impact about which process participants learn only too late, in an insufficient matter, or even worse not at all. Linking among primary and their related secondary information objects accompanied by a complete and consistent lifecycle may not be existing.

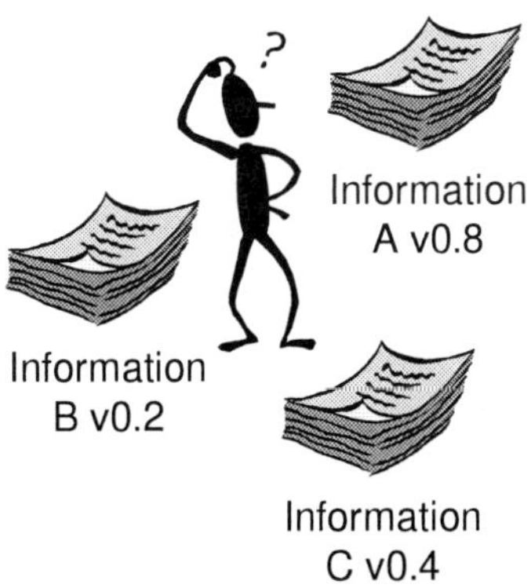

Figure 1. Possible Uncertainty about quality of available information in terms of correctness, maturity, and actuality

2. Ambiguous Responsibility and Ownership

Responsibilities for information objects and processes related to those information objects may be only insufficiently defined. Thus contributions of various process participants to content, quality/maturity, or schedule of specific information objects can be unclear and unnecessarily decomposed. Moreover contributions of process participants to interfaces, scope and responsibility of processes and their tasks may be unclear and unnecessarily decomposed, which partially can result from or may even enhanced by the before mentioned distributed responsibility for information objects. Sufficient 'process discipline' in a sense of process participants actually performing their tasks according to defined processes could therefore not be established in a comprehensive and appropriate manner.

In environments shifting more and more towards extended enterprise, that is distributed development with suppliers located worldwide, a definition, planning, and control of processes as well as their results is becoming even more difficult.

Figure 2. Uncertainty about information and Process respronsibility and Schedule Requirements

3. Open process chains and unclosed loops

A check of the information generated in sub-processes regarding its original values is often only being performed insufficiently. That means the verification if results are meeting the original requirements may be often poorly done. This seems to be related to an insufficient definition of the degree of information necessary regarding the different versions or levels of maturity of information, meaning generated information can not be linked to unambiguous states of information. Additionally, open processes, or loose ends, in different process chains could be identified, showing information that are generated in one process, but not used in any other process (Negele et al., 1999). Sometimes for example test results may be generated, that are actually not being used in other processes, but could be very helpful in some design processes. A systematic back-feeding of this information in other processes may not been done.

4. Grown process structures

Due to the rapid evolution of sub-systems and the emergence of new technology being delivered from suppliers the entire development processes in some companies show a process structure that is very heterogeneous grown and less than sub-optimal. That may lead to a partially weak definition of single important process chains and no consistent tool chains as support. Consistent standards for content and structure of information or interfaces, and the scope of process chains may be sometimes poorly defined and implemented. It has also to be looked at if clear process ownership and related responsibilities are missing or unclear.

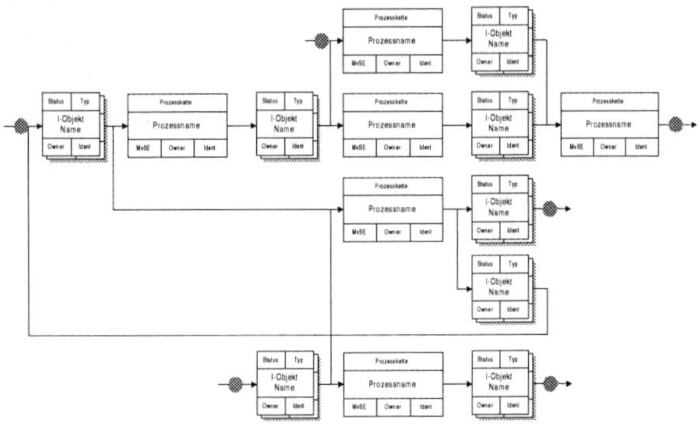

Figure 3. Section of Information Flow Chart as typical Result of Analysis

IMPLEMENTATION APPROACH

After having modeled and analyzed the processes and its information flows, a selected status of those can be implemented into a supporting IT infrastructure, with the objective of improving the "operation" of the product development processes, especially enhancing the information flow and network.

Recommendations for field of actions have to be done depending on each individual development process. Some more or less generic recommendations to implement the information-based system development and make it really operational are given now. One tool that may help to implement information-based system development is to use a modern and highly flexible product data management (PDM) system into which the analyzed information network, the processes, and the information objects can be mapped. It can help to solve some of the above mentioned problem areas.

The actuality, consistency as well as the controlled distribution of information can be realized by the implementation of the beforehand analysis and definition of the information-based system development into the PDM system. The supply of the PDM toolset as a data highway is to be seen as prerequisite to establish closed process chains or cycles, as by this central and consistent interface the feedback of information in any process gets possible. An intensive involvement of the employees as later user of the system when analyzing, defining and implementing the information-based process structure makes it possible to realize "lived" processes. But as said in the beginning of the paper, first the information network and model has to be analyzed and defined, that results into an information-based process structure, which then can be implemented.

Application example. In general a selection among three different approaches to implement the derived information-based process structure has to be made (Ploenzke, 1999):

1. Integration of application systems along the process structure, being responsible for generating or absorbing the identified information objects.
2. Integration of organizational units along the process structure, being responsible for generating or absorbing the identified information objects.
3. Integration of information objects along the process structure.

All three strategies are highly interrelated, since an integration of a specific information object also request for an integration of the corresponding process section and subsequently of the corresponding application system. However there are some distinguishing features of these strategies making those more or less eligible for the situation at the outset.

In particular the last two approaches are appropriate for large and complex development processes, characterized by a large number of different information objects and organizational units. A focus is put onto specific organizational units playing a key role within the overall development process (i.e. generating basic information necessary for a large number of subsequent process steps) and thus having strong requirements for an information management across several process section. A stepwise integration oriented along specific information objects moreover offers the opportunity to respond to specific requirements within single process steps, like for example availability of information objects for a subsequent process step depending on a specific state of that information object (i.e. pre-released, released, etc.).

Within the selected strategy four stages of an integration are to be taken. Within the first stage ('integration of information objects') the most important information objects and their referenced objects are to be implemented into the information management system. The identified information objects have to be checked-in manually and are subsequently controlled by the information management system.

For example, in the automotive industry it could be found that in the case of Electronic Control Units (ECUs) local data management solutions are insufficient, information objects associated with one ECU are manifold and generated within various processes. During an analysis in one automotive company 16 different subprocesses were identified, each contributing to a different degree to information objects associated with ECUs.

Thus specific sub-processes incorporating information objects rated highly important are selected and implemented in a stepwise approach.

The selection of sub-processes and information objects to be implemented is to be based on a variety of criteria. First, the significance of each sub-process for the entire process has to considered. An evaluation of this criterion is derived from considering aspects like the degree of interrelation of the sub-process within the entire process, or a classification of the sub-process in terms of time sequence.

Additional criteria are i.e. quality and availability of local data management solution within the sub-process or robustness resp. stability of the sub-process in terms of its definition, but also boundary conditions like available resources supporting an implementation. Within those sub-processes, appropriate information-objects are selected, whereas their significance for the overall process is the focus.

Subsequently the selected sub-processes and the handling of the associated information objects is summarized in use cases, which form the baseline for defining a data model. These use cases incorporate a detailed and comprehensive description of user (inter-)actions (i.e. procedures to check-in a data file), necessary and form the user (inter-)actions resulting in-coming or out-going information objects (i.e. necessary data files to generate a new data file), interfaces to other use cases or external applications, a definition of systems states before and after each user (inter-)action, rules applying to each user (inter-)action, and general rules and prerequisites.

From these use cases a number of functional (i.e. automated check-in of multiple date files) and non-functional requirements (i.e. layout of a user dialog window) for the information management system are derived, which have to be implemented not being part of the standard functionality.

Besides the use cases specific information concerning the selected information objects has to be gathered. These information result in the definition of the corresponding section of the data model, incorporating a definition of types of necessary objects, their attributes, and their relations.

The definition of the data model is a central task during the implementation of an information management system. Usually one central or baseline data model is defined first, on which all subsequent modeling activities are based. A new baseline has to be derived from time to time, that is configuration management principles apply also to such systems.

Moreover workflows and lifecycles for each selected information object are determined and implemented. While workflows typically represent narrow section of the information flow within the overall process in terms of a specific information object, lifecycles describe all different states an information object might adopt during its entire lifecycle, that is from its generation to its deletion. In general an appropriate workflow is directly derived form the selected sub-process. However, careful consideration has to be taken on the implementation of existing processes without any optimization. Even though the information management system may well work as a driver of reengineering badly or even not at all defined processes, enough flexibility has to be incorporated to adapt process towards users needs during the prototyping and operational phase.

During the analysis and definition of workflows and lifecycles a user and role model/concept is to be determined. Usually this incorporates the definition of levels of access to information and an assignment of roles or groups granted these privileges. Thus the privileges of individual users are separated from he user itself and transferred to a role or group a user belongs to within a specific context.

After having analyzed, defined, and implemented all of the fore-mentioned aspects for each selected sub-process and associated information object, prototyping runs with pilot users are performed, ensuring that requirements have been understood properly and appropriate functionality has been implemented. Several iterations are conducted in order to enhance functionality, user interface and data model. After successful completion of this task information access to a wide range of users may be admitted. For sure, in an evolutionary process more development process models will be implemented and existing will be improved. The risk of implementing product development processes into an IT infrastructure, e.g. PDM, is to get a rigid, non-flexible process. Due to the focus on the information flows and a recurring analysis of the development process this risk can be minimized.

SUMMARY

The idea of information-based system development is to analyze, capture and model information flows within a company's processes related to system development. Building on those information flows an appropriate development process can be implemented into a IT structure. This has to be done throughout the entire life-cycle, that is from first ideas and concepts to after-sales service and field support.

This paper introduced a generic approach to set-up and implement information-based system development. The application of the IPO method to model an information based development process was successful and such modeled process models gain important insights into how a company runs the product development process. It could be used as a basis to improve the development process and eliminate typical problems in the area of information generation and distribution. The implementation of such information-based models can be done with an acceptable effort, though the role of the later user of such a system is a very important subject to be looked at in more detail. It also came out, that it is important to understand the different existing views on a product, that result in the requirement of having a flexible information structure. The experience from the presented approach was very positive and this approach may also be used in start-up companies or absolutely new projects, where it's all about communication and information before coming to a structured process. With this approach the transfer from a previous exploratory environment to a structured product development process seems to be possible.

REFERENCES

Browning, T.R., 'Modeling and Analyzing Cost, Schedule and Performance in Complex System Product Development', Ph.D. Thesis, Massachsuetts Institute of Technology, December 1998.

CSC Ploenzke (Eds.), Tagungsband des 8. Internationalen Life Cycel Management Kongresses, Mainz, Mai 1999

Eppinger, S.D., Whitney, D.E., Smith, R.P., Gebala, D.A., 'A Model-Based Method for Organizing Tasks in Product Development', Research in Engineering Design, Vol. 6, p. 1-13, 1994.

Fricke, E.; Negele, H.; Schrepfer, L.; Dick, A.; Gebhard, B.; Härtlein, N.: „Modeling of Concurrent Engineering Processes for Integrated Systems Development.“ Proceedings of the 17th Digital Avionics Systems Conference (17th DASC) „Electronics in Motion“, IEEE, Bellevue, WA, 31 October - 6 November 1998.

Gartz, P.E., 'Commercial Systems Development in a Changed World', IEEE Transactions on Aerospace and Electronic Systems **33/2**, 1997.

Lullies, V., Pastowsky, M., Grandke, S., 'Geschäftsprozesse optimieren - ohne Diktat der Technik'. Harvard Business Manager, S. 65-72, 1998.

Negele, H., Fricke, E., Schrepfer, L., Härtlein, N., 'Modeling of Integrated Product Development Processes.' Proceedings of the 9th International Symposium of INCOSE, Brighton, 1999.

Stewart, D.V., 'The Design Structure System – A Method for Managing the Design of Complex Systems', IEEE Transactions on Engineering Management, Vol. 28/3, p. 71-74, 1981.

AUTHOR'S BIOGRAPHIES

Ernst Fricke is Assistant Professor at the Division of Astronautics at the Technical University of Munich. He received his master's degree in aerospace engineering from the Technical University of Munich in 1994 and his Ph.D. in Systems Engineering from the Technical University of Munich in January 1999. His research focuses on managing changes and evolution in product development. He is a co-founder and active member of the German Chapter of INCOSE and Technical-Co Chair of the 2nd European Systems Engineering Conference. He is also a graduate of the International Space University SSP.

Armin P. Schulz is Research Assistant and PhD candidate at the Division of Astronautics at the Technical University of Munich. He received his master's degree in aerospace engineering from the Technical University of Munich in 1998, after completing his master's thesis at the Center for Innovation in Product Development at MIT. His research focuses on technology development processes, systems design and architecting. He is a co-founder and currently secretary of the German Chapter of INCOSE.

Pamela Wehlitz, is Project Lead for Product Data Management implementation within Electric/Electronics department of BMW AG, Munich. She received her masters degree in aerospace engineering from the Technische Universität Berlin in 1985. From1985 until 1993 she has been working as an design engineer within aerospace and automotive industry. Until 1998 she worked in the area of vehicle project management, organization, and process consulting within the engineering division at BMW. She is an active member of the German Chapter of INCOSE.

Herbert Negele recently started working for BMW AG. He received his master's degree in aerospace engineering from the Technical University of Munich in 1993 and his Ph.D. in systems engineering from the Technical University of Munich in 1998. Until November 1999 he worked as an Assistant Professor at the Division of Astronautics in the field of systems engineering with special focus on systems modeling and simulation, integrated product and process development, and management. He is a co-founder, former vice-president and active member of the German Chapter of INCOSE and Technical-Co Chair of the 2nd European Systems Engineering Conference..

Discovering The Value of Systems Engineering

Jack Ring
Kennen, Inc.
32712 N. 70th St.
Scottsdale, AZ

Abstract: Question: What could systems engineering do for my product, project, and organization? Answer: The practice of systems engineering could yield the best return on any investment you have ever made. Question: How much systems engineering is appropriate? Answer: It depends on your unique situation, and this paper outlines a way to find your answer.

INTRODUCTION

The value to a given product, project, and organization of the practice of systems engineering (SE) has been a chronic question. Many have tried SE and liked it but others have been disappointed. Others are waiting on sufficient rationale and justification for adopting the practice. The majority of those who could benefit are not yet aware that the practice of SE exists.

In the midst of this opportunity, SE practitioners have not been able to produce a convincing case for their own worth and have received little help from their professional associations. Meanwhile, international standards organizations are preparing prescriptions for SE that, although permitting customization, may turn out to be bitter medicine for those who do not know **how much** of **what kind** of SE to apply in each situation.

Accordingly, the purpose of the is paper is to suggest a way to discern the ideal amount and kind of SE for any project. This is done in two parts. First we seek clarity regarding the factors that influence the value-add that SE can achieve in a given situation. Second, we outline a self-adaptive technique for arriving at the best amount and kind of SE for each situation. Interestingly, the technique allows decision makers to use different styles of self-adaptation depending on how quickly and accurately they want to pursue improved value and the requisite investment they are willing to make.

SYSTEM VALUE CYCLE

For context this section summarizes the System Value Cycle, described in (Ring 1998). Starting at the top of Figure 1, a Community Situation triggers a need to address a gap between a situation that exists in the community and what the community prefers.

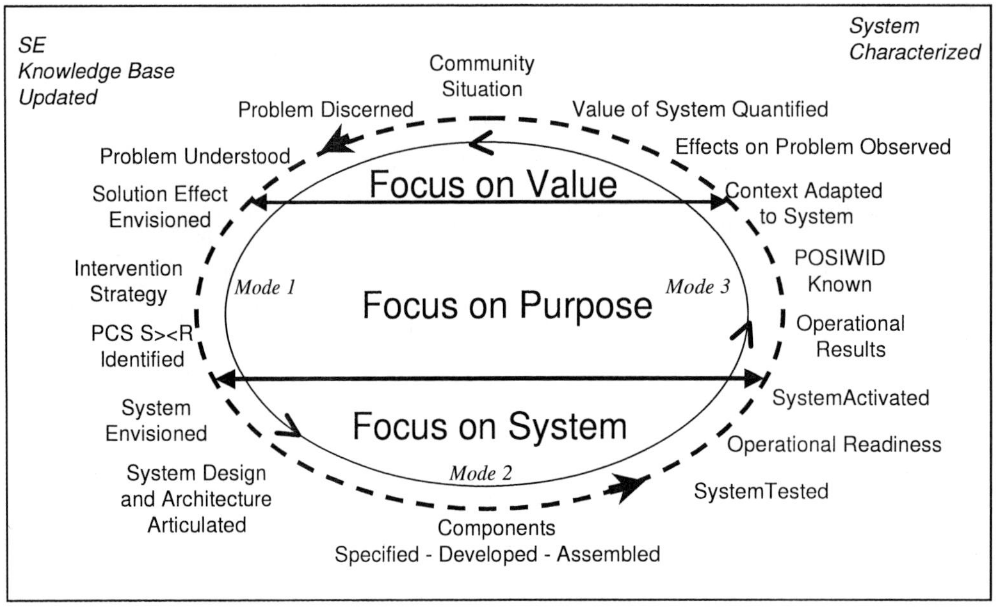

Figure 1. System Value Cycle

SE practitioners can discern, understand and describe such Problem System (PS), even though the preference may not be clear nor consistent across the community, by modeling the interrelations among drivers and outcomes and elucidating the content, structure and processes of the problem space. Simulation can reveal the likely range of behaviors of the problem system. The better the SE Team is able to describe the PS and clarify which of its behaviors the Sponsors do not like, the more intelligently the SE Team can enlist component engineers to create a solution system that will help cope with the problem. To do so the SE Team first forms a solution vision that highlights alternative, and perhaps conflicting, solution effects that may be desired by various segments of the sponsoring community. The envisioned solution gives rise to a problem intervention strategy. For larger, more complex and dynamic problems a single intervention is rarely adequate. Instead, an intervention strategy may call for a series of distinctly different actions over time. Such treatment scenario demands a problem control system that can generate the treatment

The purpose of the problem control system (PCS) is to mitigate the problem system (PS), according to the intervention strategy. The value of a PCS is determined by how well it fits its intended purpose. The relationship between the PS and PCS can be clearly defined by a set of Stimulus><Response scenarios that connect the two systems. The PCS must be able to honor each stimulus from the PS and must generate an appropriate response. Typically, large, complex problems have numerous points of intervention, thus Stimulus><Response scenarios. However less than 10% of the scenarios will determine more than 90% of the problem. Discovering this minimal set is a key contribution of systems engineering. Otherwise the project gets bogged down in details and loses sight of the objective.

With a clear, firm understanding of the problem intervention to be mechanized the project can confidently transition to a focus on the system to be built. Until this body of knowledge is produced a focus on the system to be built would be premature.

With the ability to explain both the problem and the intervention strategy to those who have innovative ideas and pragmatic successes with problem control systems, the expanded SE team proceeds to envision the PCS and articulate its design and architecture to the point of being able to specify the components that are intended to comprise an operationally acceptable system. This includes the articulation of System Design and Architecture aided by SE principles and practices. System envisioning (Hodgson 1997) is helped by writing a Concept of Operations document which may include a simulation of the system's intended behavior during interactions with the problem space.

At the bottom of Figure 1, note that components are materialized to comprise the physical system. For example approximately 8,000 components comprise an automobile, over 80,000 components comprise a commercial airliner and and about eight million components comprise a current microprocessor.

Component specification, design, development and assembly is fundamental to the engineering of systems but are the province of discipline engineers, not of SE. However, SE does contribute by ensuring that the numerous individual design ideas and decisions actually converge to an harmonious whole.

Successfully integrated, the gaggle of components undergoes system test in a pseudo-operational environment. When sufficient problems have been detected and resolved the gaggle earns the label, "system," and is declared to be ready for operation.

Proceeding around the cycle, we see that a system undergoes an activation phase and the cycle transitions from a focus on the System to a focus on the Purpose for which the system was created. At this point users and sponsors begin to see how well the system does what is needed. Usually they find that the real operational environmen differs considerably from the pseudo-operational environment that was represented in the system test scenarios and differs even moreso from the earlier presumptions of the system sponsors, requirements engineers and designers.

As operational results start occurring, users and sponsors react with a spectrum of behaviors possibly including joy, dismay and anger. Their interaction with the original project team, if the original team is still inolved, may get intense. Such surprises are not accidental. They stem from the systems principle known as POSIWID, the Purpose of a System Is What It Does (regardless of what the designers intended it to do). Accordingly, the balance of the systems engineering work can only be done from this point forward because it must be conducted *in situ*.

This situation does not imply that the foregoing SE, and related, work was sloppy. Even if the work is done perfectly, the compound likelihood of misunderstanding and of changes in either PS or intervention strategy during the system development time period means that problems will be found in the operational phase. Additionally, because all solution systems impact the situation into which they are introduced, the project team must be prepared to purposefully adapt the interfacing systems and the users to the solution system. The adaptation is rarely painless but the pain is considerably less if the system was designed for ease of change. Still, however, the project team must design, prioritize and implement the changes. With hard work, convergent decisions regarding hundreds of changes and a good deal of luck, the project team can nudge the system around to the point where its purpose aligns reasonably well with the users needs.

As the system stabilizes and the operational results become repeatable the engineers, users and sponsors can observe the effects of the solution system on the original problem. Finally, this leads to assessing the Value of the solution system by ascertaining the goodness or effectiveness of the system from the vantage point of its contribution to the beneficiaries in the community that sponsored the system.

WHERE SE ADDS VALUE

Illustrated inside the dashed lines that denote the system value cycle in Figure 1 is a solid line that denotes the "Project System" which is the system that accomplishes the engineering of the operational PCS system. The Project System goal is to deliver value to the sponsor but the Project System cannot create value directly. Instead, it creates the PCS which is a carrier that actually delivers the value.

The three phases on the inner circle in Figure 1 indicate the three modalities of SE contribution. Mode 1 focuses on the PS and Conceptual PCS and produces an adequate, accurate and timely description of the components and the acceptance criteria for the contemplated PCS. Mode 2 focuses on ensuring that all the other project participants are converging on a set of components that, when interconnected, will behave in a way that will be found acceptable. Mode 3 focuses on observing the PCS in real world operations and identifying and adjudicating modifications to the system and adaptations in the system context in order to increase system effectiveness.

Because the user value criteria cannot be presumed stationary over time the Project System must be a pursuit-type (goal-seeking) system. Further, the project produces, prudently, a PCS that is also sufficiently agile as to be easily morphed to match the dynamic value vector as the real needs are discovered during operations.

How well a Project System can pursue its goal is limited by its sensitivity to disturbance and its stability lmits. These, in turn are affected by: degree of alignment with context (how well the Project System matches the challenges inherent in the PS, intervention strategy and PCS). Also affecting goal achievement are; project member communications style, the number of elements or loops in the actual project processes, and the team competence decrement due to stress. Consequently, these are four more clues to maximizing the degree to which SE can add value to a project.

Due to space limitations the amount and kind of SE appropriate for modes 2 and 3 are not further discussed herein. However, it is important to note briefly that if Mode 1 is performed with inadequate SE the value-add may become so negative that even if excellent SE is performed during Mode 2 the cumulative add may be only modest. Further, the value of the system at Acceptance may be as low as 50% of its inherent or potential value. Thus the value-add of SE can be very high during mode 3 even though this mode of SE is rarely mentioned in SE literature.

SE VALUE-ADD CONTRIBUTIONS

The value-add of SE is best modeled by noting the contribution of the practitioners of SE (PSE's) to the project, the system and the organization. All other factors should be related through the PSE's who manifest the outcomes. Outcomes, of course, are fundamental to determining Value from the viewpoint of the beneficiaries. -- the Value of the contribution made by the right kind and amount of SE, the relative value of one PSE vs another PSE or the expected value from immersing an PSE in another cycle of learning in order to get the "new and improved" model of that PSE. Accordingly, any measure of PSE and SE that does not quantify relative outcome is potentially toxic waste.

In light of the foregoing section the top three contributions of SE in general and PSE's in particular are; a) languages the project, b) imagines and structures both the problem system and the solution system and c) converges risk and creativity to closure. Each is described as follows.

"Languages the Project" - wherein a common language is installed in (actually adopted by) all project participants as eloquently described and demonstrated by Fernando Flores in (Rubin 1999). A common language enables participants to dialog about a systems life cycle, systems terminology, work products, methods and tools for analysis and synthesis and numerous other topics (McDavid 1996). Usually a generic language is installed followed by specific terms and names for each system that is the subject of a project. The contribution of SE is the generic language while the contribution of PSE's in a specific project is the naming of phenomena regarding the problem space, the conceptual representation of the solution system and the logical representation of the same system. MOE's, Risks and Critical Success Factors are also discerned and named by PSE's who also elucidate their network of interrelationships and respective significances.

"Imagines and structures both the problem system and the solution system" - wherein the artifacts of SE are produced. In (Evans and Patterson 1998) we are reminded that the eventual solution system evolves from a conceptual understanding of the problem to a model and simulation of the problem symptoms and problem suppression strategy. Then an initial, nearly inexplicable thought occurs regarding the solution system. It is followed by a conceptual diagram or story followed by a model and simulation followed by a set of abstractions that are interrelated in an architecture. To preclude this evolving model from becoming incomprehensible the few key determinants of system behavior and cost are identified. System development progresses to specifying and creating physical manifestations (aka components) and on to interconnected sets that finally qualify as a deliverable system. The balance of a PSE's contribution occurs subsequent to delivery. Having confirmed that the set of components exhibited acceptable behavior in the pseudo-reality of the development project, PSE's next confirm that the web of components produce acceptable behaviors in the real operational environment. Also, PSE's help discern the inevitable adaptations to interfacing systems that will further benefit the users.

"Converges risk and creativity to closure" - In this contribution the key (hopefully few) determinants of system success are used to guide all trade-offs and judge all design proposals and design change proposals. Clearly, the "ilities" must be decided in step with design progress, not separately from "over the wall." Also, PSE's deal with numerous new ideas and suggested shortcuts by other project members as well as employers and sponsors. And the PSE's must adjudicate all within the "heartbeat" of the project. Only those persons having understanding of the systems theoretic view of the design -- typically the PSEs' -- are qualified to specify the allowable sequence of design reviews and baseline reconciliations.

VALUE MODEL

In most cases the value of an item, be it product, service or advice, is determined primarily by what someone is willing to pay. What they are willing to pay depends, in turn, on how much value they assign to having it or to how much loss they expect if they have to proceed without it. Value is not an absolute, inherent property of an entity. Value is an emergent characteristic that depends on both the entity and the user/usage situation.

The unit of measure of value is money. As quality guru, Phil Crosby, counseled the best way to talk with management about quality is in terms of money. His Price Of Non-Conformance, PONC™ metric has proven applicable to a variety of quality situations whether in manufacturing, banking or janitorial services to name a few examples. Similarly, this paper presumes that the best way to talk with propective managers about the practice of SE is in terms of money – money they can save and money they can gain that would never have been available to them otherwise.

The value proposition for SE is in the degree to which an increment of SE enhances system, project and organization. In most cases "more SE" is not the goal. An ideal level of SE produces the best value and more SE is simply more expense without adding value. The value of SE is maximized when the amount and kind of SE maximizes the generic measures of effectiveness (MOE's) of system, project and organization respectively.

The generic MOE's for a System are;

- Fitness For Purpose (FfP): which quantifies the match between what the beneficiaries need and what the system actually does.
- TBO/TCO (TBO/TCO): Total Benefit of Ownership quantifies the return enjoyed by having the system as contrasted to not having the system. TCO denotes Total Cost of Ownership including both the development cost and the on-going cost of sustaining system operation. The TBO/TCO ratio is, of course, the investment leverage that accrues to the beneficiaries.
- Agility (Ag): According to (Dove, http://www.parshift.com) "agility is the capability to thrive in an environment of unpredictable change." The inverse of agility is rapid obsolesence. A syno-meme is reusability.

The generic MOE's for a Project are; Quality (Q), Cycle Time (CT) and Return on Resources (RoR).

The generic MOE's for an Organization are the same as for System, even for an organization of extent = 1.

Accordingly, we are interested in maximizing the implicit function d(FfP(S), TBO/TCO(S), Ag(S), Q, CT, RoR, FfP(O), TBO/TCO(O), Ag(O))/d(SE).

The S factors are amplified by the Scope, Span, and Complicatedness of the problem system and the

Size, Complexity, and Order or Intelligence of the problem control system. The Project factors are amplified by readiness, urgency and style. The O factors are amplified by technologies, work climate and culture.

All is implicit because the relationships are not a "given" but can only be discovered. Ironically, these are discovered more quickly and accurately by SE than by other means. Accordingly, the vaue of SE is maximized when the amount and kind of SE is sufficient to reveal, accurately, the amount of kind of SE yet needed.

Implicit relationships can be maddening but we need not despair because there are interative techniques for finding the roots of such relationships. The balance of this paper indicates how this can be done.

MAXIMIZING SE VALUE

The possible outcomes of SE value-add are indicated in Figure 2.

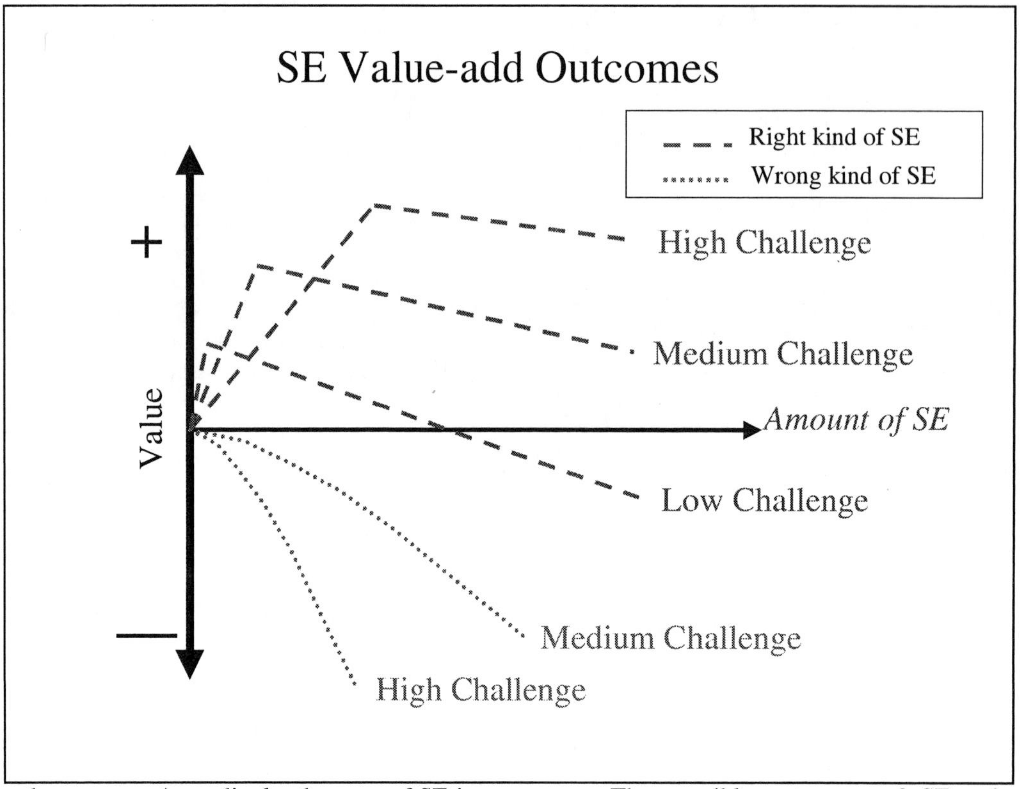

Figure 2. SE Value-Add Outcomes

The Value of SE is the Y axis and the amount of SE is the X axis. The amount of SE is essentially the number of PSE's, their respective competancies and proficiency levels, the amount of time alloted for their work all multiplied by the productivity leverage realized from their tools and the avoidance of rework stemming from their quality ethic.

Curves for both the right kind of SE and the wrong kind of SE are shown. The kind of SE is concerned with three factors inherent in the system value cycle; the degree of ambiguity faced by the PSE's, the degree to which the chosen or customized SE method adequately covers modes 1, 2 and 3, and the degree of rigor exercised in the convergence activity. The principle of requisite variety drives the selection or customization of method. The method of SE must match the variety inherent in each mode else the method is the wrong kind.

SE contributes the most value in High Risk situations but more SE is required than in other situations. The penalty gradient for too much SE is slight, less than 10% of gradient for too little SE. Conversely, if the wrong kind of SE is niavely applied (e.g. using a "ballistic" SE process in a high-order system situation or a project situation involving contested sponsors) then the more SE the greater the negative cost to the project. This is because the wrong kind of SE will drive the PCS design materials to being inadequate and internally conflicting even though the ramifications may not show up until the system test phase. On lower risk projects SE value-add peaks at lower levels of value but with lower amounts of SE. The penalty gradient for too much SE on a medium risk situation is steeper than on the high risk situation but still lower than the penalty gradient for not enough SE.

These value curves highlight the issue of SE scope. INCOSE and others have defined SE as having a broad role. But as Lanchester's Law points out a broader role invites more ways of losing or leaking value-add. Making the SE role broader means having PSE's perform lower value-add tasks which could be done by others. This creates lower Return on Resources for the project not to mention masking the uniqueness of the SE contribution.

DISCOVERING YOUR UNIQUE ANSWER

Because of the high degree of implicitness in the value proposition the correct amount and kind of SE can only be guessed in advance and then "dialed-in" during a project. The initial decision regarding the amount and kind of SE should be taken by the consensus of staff and consultants. The manager's job is to direct subsequent iterations. The goal is to interate fast enough so that there is still time to adjust as the findings surface. These cycles of observation, evaluation, decision and implementation may be implemented in three alternative ways; oversight, embedded and systemic. (Ring 2000) describes these and discusses the tradeoff considerations. Oversight is exemplified by the CMM™ procedure. Embedded is exemplified by a process improvement activity within the project. Systemic is achieved when every participant has internalized a quality ethic, a SE life cycle model and a collaborative work style. The systemic way is required in order to reach the higher levels of SE value.

The Role of SE Artifacts. The value frame of reference is the customer. In this case the customers are the other downstream project participants as well as the system's intended beneficiaries. SE artifacts are the SE value carriers that add value to subsequent activities and, eventually, the system. SE skill/participation adds value only through the SE artifacts.

The scope and content of SE can be defined not by descriptions of activities or processes that are performed but by descriptions of artifacts and their interrelationships. A focus on process rather than results masks the good from the bad. For example, all football teams have the same roles and largely the same plays but not all end up going to the Superbowl. Process is not a predictor of value. Neither is People. And neither is Competency. Only when all these are mixed in a project and an artifact emerges is latent value created and available to the customer. Even then, only when the user perceives the usefulness of the artifact and the value it has in his situation do we know the magnitude of the reward we have earned.

The role view (Sheard) may be useful in relatively immature SE organizations but, in the limit, is antithetical to goal-seeking workgroups because roles have no goals. In a value oriented model PSE activities are orchestrated by the artifacts to which they contribute, not by titles of roles they play.

Example SE artifacts include:

1. PS Model (called a mission model document or a market target description).
2. ConOps (PS mitigation scenario).
3. Acceptance Criteria and Specification.
4. PCS Model – Concept (content, structure and behavior) and Constraints.
5. PCS Acceptance Risk Assessment and Mitigation Alternatives – Feasibility view.
6. PCS Model – Architecture (function, feature, performance and TCO).
7. PCS Acceptance Risk Assessment and Mitigation Alternatives – Effectiveness view.
8. PCS Model – Component view.
9. PCS Acceptance Risk Assessment and Mitigation Alternatives– Implementation view.
10. Design Review and Baseline Reconciliation Scenario
11. Change Proposal Assessments
12. Updates to each of the above as necessary.

Three key iterations: Set SE management checkpoints at 5%, 10% and 20% of the expected elapsed time for the Mode 1 phase of the project. At each checkpoint have reviews of the Indicators as described in Table 1.

Indicator 1 = Community – the % of current project staff who understand the terminology of SE, a generic process for performing SE and the specific process for performing SE on this project. This can be revealed by a simple survey.

Ideally your professional organization can provide an SE lexicon and a variety of system life cycle process templates. At least three templates are preferred, one of which should encompass modes 1, 2, and 3 as illustrated in Figure 1. If your professional organization cannot supply such information you should find one that can. Meanwhile, try one or more consultants, the "SEwebring" on the internet or challenge your staff of PSE's to evolve your own three versions.

Indicator 2 = System Views – Artifacts

scheduled to be completed by the checkpoint event. For the 5% checkpoint these should include as a minimum artifacts 1 – 3 above. For the 10% checkpoint these should include artifacts 1, 3, 4, and 6. For the 20% checkpoint these should include artifacts 8, 10, 11, 12, and 13.

Indicator 3 = Drivers – Artifacts 5, 7, and 9 document the system risks foreseen in achieving system acceptance and their respective scores relative to their probability of occurance and magnitude of impact. Also, the relationship map of these to underlying technologies, economics, and availability factors. Finally, a precedence network that shows the "order of battle" for resolving the risks in order to converge on a consistent progression of design baselines (note: only system risks are included, not project risks).

Indicator 4 = PSE Collaboration Index – the degree to which PSE's on this project are in alignment regarding the system problem. The various viewpoints may range from Groupthink to Inquiry to Anarchy. The Spreadthink technique (Warfield 1995) is appropriate for revealing the Collaboration Index.

Indicator 5 = SE Cost – the project expense incurred to date by the PSE's.

Diagnoses: Space limitations preclude a detailed diagnoses map but the following illustrates how the indicators can inform SE managagement decisions.

If Indicator 1, Community, shows less than 10%, 20% and 40% of project participants (at first, second and third checkpoint respectively) understand the SE process and terminology then the Languaging contribution is insufficient. At the first two checkpoints this is likely due to inadequate amount of SE. If it persists to the third checkpoint it is likely due to wrong kind of SE.

If Indicator 2, System Views are not available then the Imagining contribution is inadequate. This is due to wrong kind of SE. If the artifacts are available but with internal conflicts and gaps then the Right Amount of SE is suspect.

If Indicator 3, Drivers, is lacking then the Converging contribution is inadequate and the wrong kind of SE is suspect. If the acceptance risk index is not declining by the 10% checkpoint then the right amount of SE is suspect.

If Indicator 4, Collaboration, shows either anarchy or group think then the competencies of the PSE's are suspect. If this persists in the second checkpoint the project is in trouble. If it persists at the third checkpoint the project should be cancelled.

SUMMARY

Value is situation dependent. Factors affecting Value are implicitly related. Accordingly a discover and adapt approach is indicated for maximizing the value of SE.

The value add of SE is manifested through PSE's to the degree they a) language the project, b) imagine and structure both the problem system and the solution system and c) converge risk and creativity to closure.

Both amount and kind of SE are important decisions. The penalty gradient for too much SE is not nearly as severe as for too little. However, the penalty for wrong kind can be very severe.

Value is in the eye of the beneficary and is assignable only to artifacts. A preoccupation with process can mask the real situation.

The System Value Cycle, thus the span of opportunity for SE to add value is far greater than most SE literature, including international standards, acknowledges.

REFERENCES

Evans and Patterson, *"Perfecting the Image System Development as a Continuum of Design Decisions."* IEEE-SMC Conf. Proc., 1998.

Hodgson, R., "*Envisioning Systems.*" OOPSLA 1998 Annual Conference Workshop Reports

McDavid, D., "*Business Language Analysis for Object-oriented Information Systems.*" IBM Systems Journal, Spring 1996

Ring, J., "*Engineering Value-seeking Systems.*" IEEE-SMC Conference Proceedings, 1998

Ring, J., *Effective Control in Peopled Systems*, INCOSE 2000 Annual Conference Proceedings.

Rubin, H. *The Power of Words,* Fast Company, Issue 24, pg 142, 1999

Sheard, S. *Twelve Systems Engineering Roles*, verson 2.3, 1996

Warfield, J., "*Spreadthink: Explaining Ineffective Groups.*" Systems Research, Vol.12, No. 1, pp. 5-14, John Wiley & Sons, 1995

Design-to-Market - From Product Development to Market Potential

Andreas Vollerthun, Eduard Igenbergs

Division of Astronautics, Technical University of Munich
Boltzmannstr. 15, 85748 Garching, Germany
Phone: +49 (0)89 289 16018
Fax: +49 (0)89 289 16004
Email: A.Vollerthun@lrt.mw.tum.de
Internet: http://www.lrt.mw.tum.de

Abstract. This paper presents a continuous information based model and process that integrates traditionally separated activities of marketing/market forecasting, determining requirements, and creating first conceptual designs. The process focuses on the very early systems engineering activities and aims at establishing a link between the economic and technical world of today's product development. This link is realized by mapping characteristic design parameters on market volume and thus evaluating different design alternatives. A general process of market, requirements, and concepts is proposed. Within this paper the focus is on the initial phase of market forecasting and establishes the link to the requirements phase. Using the development of the European satellite navigation system and the German market as an example, the initial process steps are demonstrated.

INTRODUCTION

The motivation for this paper are the common problems companies across all industries have, when trying to place new products in a commercial market. Common problems can be a too long time-to market, a too high price, but most of all products do not meet essential customer requirements of the targeted market segment. Success factors for product placement therefore are in-time introduction, meeting customer requirements, while possibly generating an added value compared to competitors products.

The importance of these interrelations becomes more and more obvious also to space industry as the failure of Iridium painfully revealed. Product development in space industry has gone from initially performing Design-to-Performance, now practicing Design-to-Cost (especially for scientific space missions), but the approach that should be applied (concerning commercial business) is Design-to-Market.

The objective of the research project initiated at our institute therefore is to build an integrated model for the early systems engineering process, representing the interrelationships between market volume, requirements and design (Figure 1). The integrated model shall help to derive characteristics for good product development by mapping current design alternatives on their potential market success and thus support companies at a more effective and efficient design.

This paper is the first in a row, giving a general overview over the integrated model, and discussing in one more level of detail what the model will look like concerning the determination of market volume, and deriving customer requirements. As an example for the determination of market volume the planned European satellite navigation system will be investigated. The results presented are the findings of a market forecast (for navigation equipment and services in Germany) performed by our institute under contract with the German Aerospace Center (DLR). Throughout succeeding papers the satellite navigation system will be used as an example, enabling a verification of the proposed process.

Figure 1: „Market in the Loop"

MARKET - REQUIREMENTS - CONCEPTS

The idea to integrate the voice of the customer is not new to product development. Many methods (e.g. QFD) have been developed and also implemented to align the design with customer requirements. For traditional space missions this meant to have a prime contractor

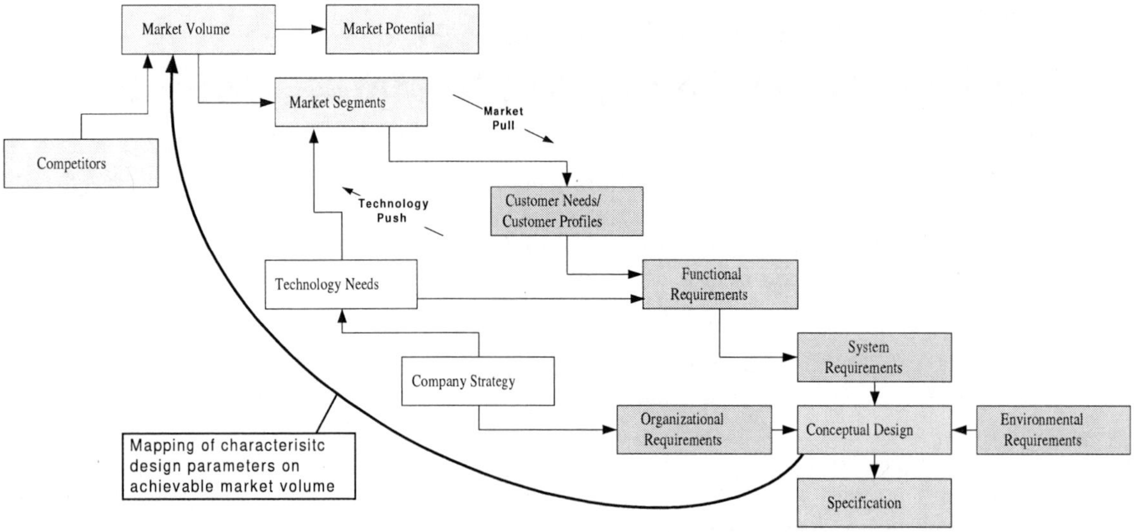

Figure 2: Elements of the 'Market-Requirements-Concept' - model

who precisely defined what requirements had to be met. Now facing the challenge to develop a space system for a wide use of commercial applications makes the identification of requirements a lot harder, especially concerning the rapidly changing market conditions. Suddenly there is no precise mandate from a certain customer. The problem therefore is twofold: First the right set of requirements has to be identified, and second the engineers have to be "taught" the sensitivities of the market in order to understand the effects (on market volume) of changes in their design. Only with this understanding will they be able to provide a flexible design in order to react flexible to changing market requirements. This results in the primary question the developed model has to answer: **What are crucial performance criteria and what are the monetary effects** (in the term of achievable market volume/share) **in changes among them**.

The model developed contains the following elements/steps (refer to Figure 2): In an initial step the existing **market volume** (=overall sales on the market, realistic demand) is determined to calculate the available market potential (=maximum saturation of the market, theoretically possible demand). The market volume is the basis to determine the probability of success for a new product an it is divided into **segments** in the next step. These segments are identified using criteria such as user groups, regional, or economical criteria. For every market segment an individual set of **customer needs** is identified. If a company aims at more than one market segment, the design of the product has to fulfill an optimum choice of requirements of those segments. The targeted market segments extremely influence the design. Anticipating the example of the European satellite navigation system already the selection of the right market segment is a delicate task. The applications that can be thought of are so manifold that certain application-profiles have to be developed that cover a certain set of applications. Continuing in the process, identified customer needs are satisfied by certain **functional requirements** that in turn are the basis for system requirements. Still, for a conceptual design there is more requirements, such as environmental (regulations, laws, ecological, ...) and organizational (resources: Money, manpower, ...). Organizational requirements are very much dependent on a companies policies and strategies. **Conceptual design** has not to be understood as feasibility studies, but as a preliminary design, defining the major subsystems of a system for a detailed design in later phases.

The presented process from one element of the process to the next is not necessarily only market driven (market-pull). It may also be stimulated by a company wanting to implement a new technology into an existing product and thus creating an added value compared to competitive products (technology-push). This value-added obviously influences customer behavior and therefore market segments through available market volume.

The process as it is presented in Figure 2 is similar to existing approaches, such as the waterfall model (e.g. Sage, 1992) or also QFD concerning the mapping of user needs on design (Cohen, 1995). What is new, is the validation of the design not only against initially stated requirements but more importantly against currently and in future achievable market volume. This validation path is represented by the curved arrow in Figure 2.

Taking the 'Market-Requirements-Concept'-model as a basis the next part of the paper will now concentrate on the market part (upper left boxes in Figure 2).

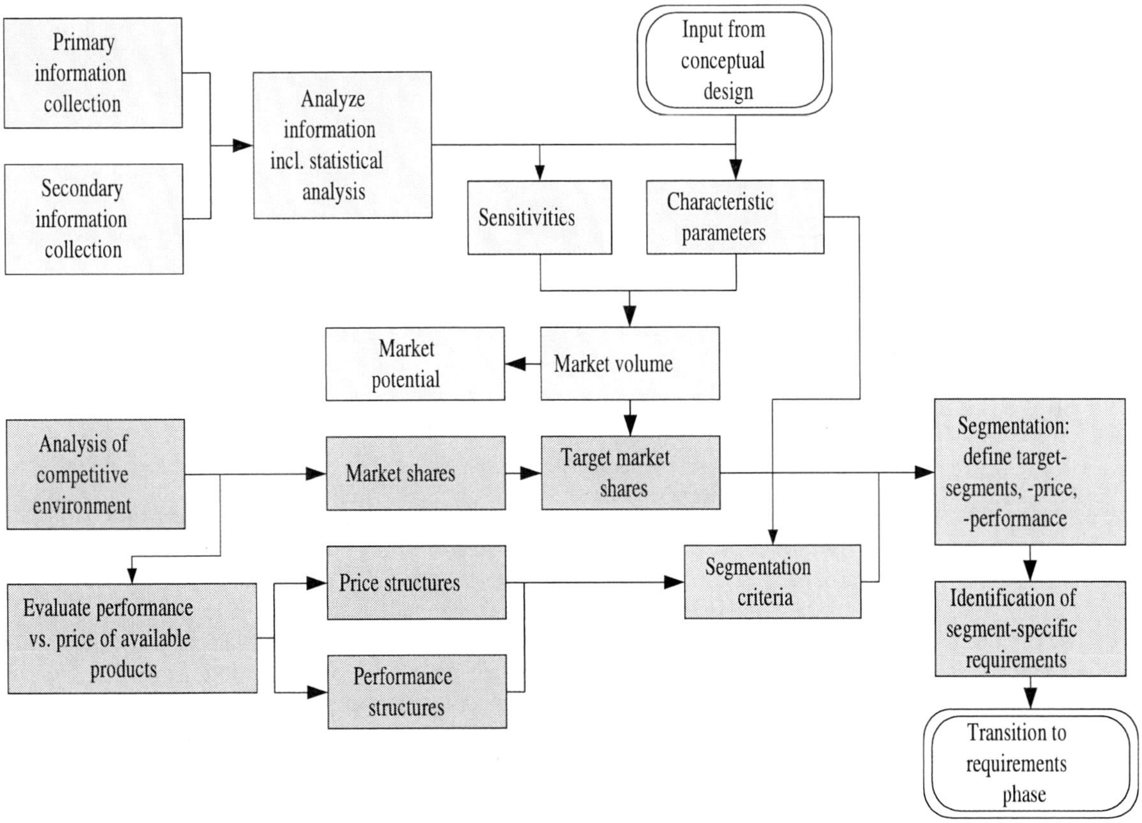

Figure 3: Process to determine market volume and market segments and derive customer requirements

MARKET FORECAST - VOLUME, POTENTIAL, AND SEGMENTS

Market forecast involves the systematic collection and objective recording of information from individuals and organizations and includes social, qualitative, quantitative, or survey research. Information is aggregated and analyzed to investigate the behavior, needs, and requirements to derive the market volume for a certain product (Hüttner, 1997).

The basic task of market forecast thereby is to satisfy a current or future need of information concerning the situation and development of certain markets. This information is a fundamental need for decision making in companies in order to decide, which product to develop, at which quality, to which cost, and in what time. The process that is necessary to prepare this decision making consists of the general steps of information collection, information analysis, and information synthesis (Meffert, 1986). These shall be explained in more detail now (refer to Figure 3).

Concerning **information collection**, two possible approaches have to be distinguished: Primary and secondary information collection. Primary information collection is defined as collection analysis of already available data. Methods used to collect this information include oral, written, and computer form.

To **analyze the collected information** it may be necessary to reduce the amount of data without, of course, losing important information. A factor-analysis method (an economical matrix method) supports this step. On the other side it may be required to build clusters of similarity to on one hand classify data and on the other hand to form certain requirement-profiles (compare to Figure 10). This cluster-building in combination with the factor-analysis is an important input for **market segmentation**. This market segmentation will be the basis for a decision, which market segment/s is/are the

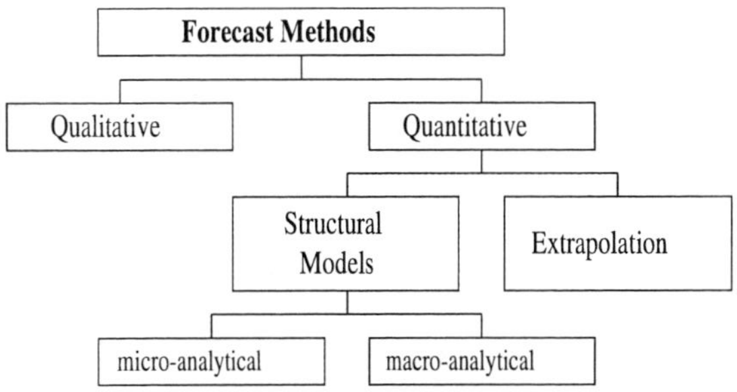

Figure 4: Forecast Methods

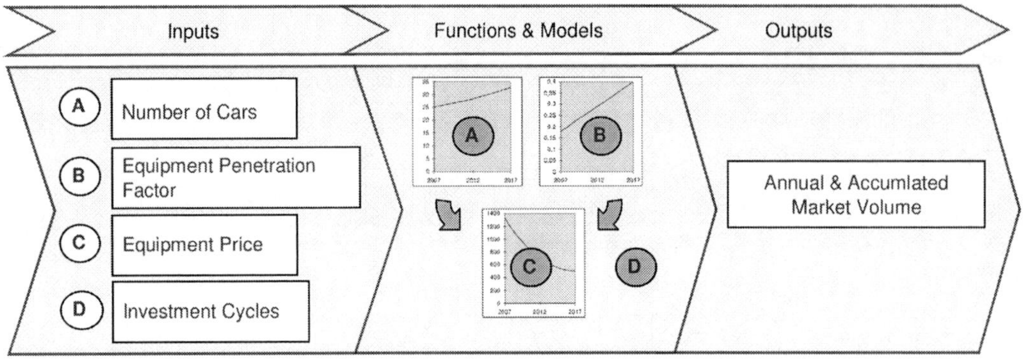

Figure 5: Generic element structure for the market model - exemplary parameters for 'Galileo'-market

most promising in terms of benefit for the company.

Another output of the information analysis is the knowledge of **characteristic parameters** (product performance, customer groups, prices, ...) that influence the future market volume. In later design phases this is where the validation loop of Figure 2 delivers the current design characteristics as an input to the market model to continue with the next process step.

Based on these parameters the most common approach to forecast **market volume** is to analyze the past and current demand and to extrapolate for the future. Other quantitative forecast methods (see Figure 4; Hammann and Erichson, 1994) use structural models. These may use generalized/aggregated demand data (macro-analytical) or information about individual (micro-analytical) demand. From the determined market volume the market potential can be derived. As mentioned before, market potential is a not observable parameter. It is that market volume that can be theoretically reached by a certain product, assuming the demand would be infinite. Since the market potential is not required for the next process steps its determination is not discussed here.

Parallel to the determination of market volume the market model investigates the **competitive environment** to estimate what market shares the company has and also wants to have in the future. The result of analyzing the competitive environment is the knowledge of **performance- and price-structures**. Combining the identified characteristic parameters and price- and performance structures the market as a whole can be divided into segments. For each segment a target performance and target price are defined, while also the **requirements** (with respect to the determined characteristic parameters) that have to be fulfilled in each segment are defined. These requirements are the basis for the transition to the requirements phase that will be presented in a future paper.

All elements that only appear as „black boxes" in Figure 3 have the same conceptual interior: For each element, inputs and outputs are defined, and within the element certain functions apply (see Figure 5). These functions can be either (existing or newly developed) mathematical models or other methods.

Having introduced this 'idealized' process, the first steps that have been applied within a market forecast performed by our institute shall be presented in the following section.

EUROPEAN SATELLITE NAVIGATION - GERMAN MARKET

The objective of this market forecast was to establish a sound basis for a decision of the German government for whether or not it was economically reasonable to participate in the development of a European satellite navigation system ('Galileo').

The approach for the market forecast is visualized in Figure 6 (Vollerthun and Wieser, 1999). Simultaneously to the evaluation of previous market forecasts (Frost & Sullivan, 1998; Intex Management Services, 1998) (secondary information collection), new data was collected (primary information collection, where required) with a focus on the German market. A software tool was developed based on EXCEL™, to be able to quickly change the input parameters of the market model, in order to perform sensitivity analyses. Based on the results for the market volume the forecast also involved the investigation of the Value-Adding-Chain (employment effects and tax revenues for the state).

To collect information on the different market segments, questionnaires, personal and telephone interviews, and workshops were used. Analyzing the collected information the following set of **characteristic parameters** (see also idealized process in Figure 3) was identified as a basis for the determination of the market volume:

- A distinction between satellite navigation

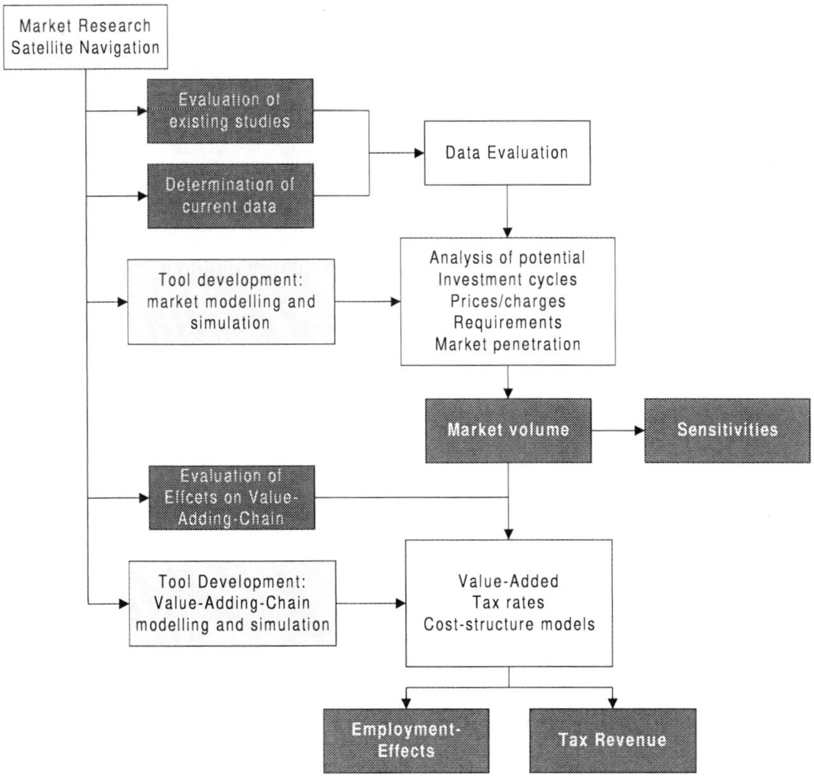

Figure 6: Study Logic

equipment and related services was required due to big differences in the quality of information

- Number of equipment (e.g. number of new cars) and services including a linear/quadratic trend model
- Equipment penetration factor (percentage of e.g. new cars equipped with a satellite navigation system) including a linear/quadratic trend model
- Prices/Charges including a linear/quadratic trend model
- Investment cycles
- Sales taxes, value of production, industrial cost breakdown structures
- Sensitivity analysis based on best-/worst-case scenarios

To ensure a robust market forecast, the volume for satellite navigation equipment and services was determined separately. The relevant period of time for the market forecast was 2007 through 2017. This period was chosen, since 2007 is the estimated operational start (with full capability) of the planned 'Galileo' system. The identified volume is not necessarily that available for 'Galileo', but available for all operational systems at that time. An analysis of the competitive environment (basically only the US-American Global Positioning System (GPS)) is required to determine what conditions/requirements have to be considered. The basic question that has to be answered within this competitive analysis is: What is a guaranteed and more precise 'Galileo'-signal worth for a customer in comparison to a not guaranteed but free GPS-signal.

To forecast the market volume, the market was broken down into the following **application areas**: Road traffic, other terrestrial, recreational, civil aviation, rail road, maritime applications, military, and space (Airbus Industries, 1997; Ocean Shipping Consultants, 1998). These application areas are not necessarily identical to previously mentioned market segments (Figure 3), since they are just used to structure the applications by topic. To identify distinguishable market segments and derive requirements clusters, an analysis of requirements that are common to several applications was performed. This analysis is not part of the paper.

The market forecast was performed separately in every application area. Within the application areas different user groups were identified and analyzed. Within each user group six to seven applications were identified. For each application the number of sold equipment/sold services, the equipment penetration factor, prices/charges, and investment cycles were determined. This data was the basis for the forecasted

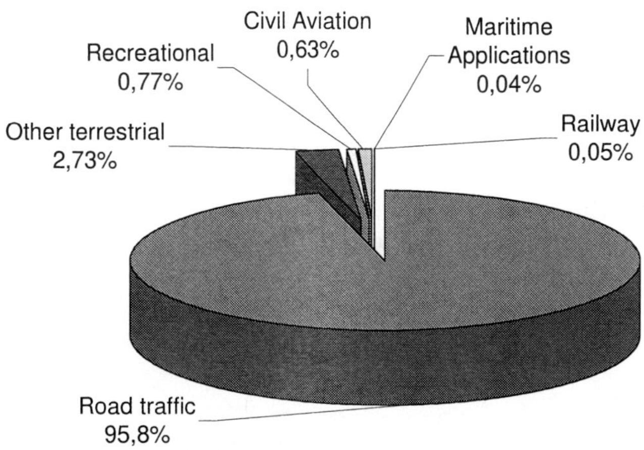

Figure 7: Market Volume for Navigation Equipment

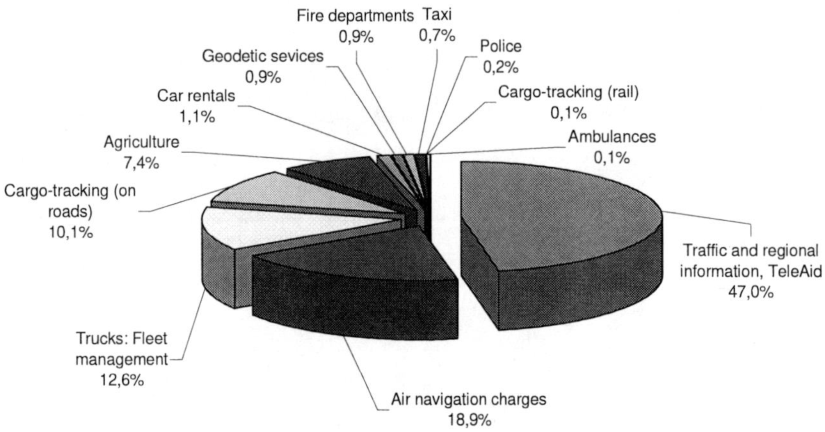

Figure 8: Market Volume for Navigation Services

market volume.

For the mentioned period of time a **market volume** of DM 83 billion was determined, which is equivalent to a yearly volume of DM 7,5 billion. This almost constant yearly volume turned out, even though the assumption was made that for example the prices for in-car satellite navigation systems would drop more than 65%. This decrease in prices is more than compensated by the increasing number of cars that will be equipped with satellite navigation systems.

With regard to the differentiation of equipment and services the volume of DM 83 billion is divided into two almost equal parts. The volume for satellite navigation equipment is estimated to be DM 39,8 billion, whereas it is DM 43,2 billion for related services.

Market Volume - User Equipment. A robust analysis for the volume for satellite navigation equipment was possible, since a forecast can be made, based on statistical data. As mentioned before the volume amounts to DM 39,8 billion. The major part of this volume (almost 96%) is contributed by the 'Road traffic' area (see Figure 7). It was often argued that a European satellite navigation system is needed especially for the big market of civil aviation applications. Figure 7 reveals that the 'Civil Aviation' area only makes up about 0,63% (i.e. DM 249,1 million). If the intention of Europe is to build a commercial satellite navigation system the aviation area is not decisive. Concerning political arguments and especially the increasing load of air traffic over Europe, the special requirements of the aviation area will have to be considered adequately.

Market Volume - Services. Determining the volume for satellite navigation services proved to be delicate, since, with the exception of the aeronautical segment, not very many services exist today and it is especially difficult to predict what charges can be raised. Nevertheless, it seems certain that the volume for services is higher than that for navigation equipment. Already the (conservative) assessment of the services volume performed here, predicts a volume of DM 43,2 billion. It has to mentioned that only a comparatively small number of services was analyzed. The list of services could have been extended by far, but to ensure a robust market forecast, only a limited number (those services that are being designed today) was investigated.

Similar to the market volume for navigation equipment the largest part in services is again the 'Road traffic' segment with DM 31,4 billion (Figure 8). Within that emergency systems represent the largest amount (DM 18,2 billion). The readiness of an individual to invest into a security-related service seems to be much higher, than the interest in information-providing services. This has mainly two reasons: First an increasing interest in security, and secondly insurances may offer discounts, when the individuals use satellite navigation services for special applications. Today the most significant part in services is 'Fleet management'. The determined market volume amounts to DM 11,1 billion. This includes cargo business, police, fire department, ambulances, car rentals, and taxis. The volume for civil aviation equipment is very limited: Within services it is the second largest segment with DM 8,2 billion. The assumption was made, that charges in this segment would be similar to those existing today with a decreasing tendency.

In order to cope with the already mentioned uncertainty in the prediction of the services volume sensitivity analyses were performed within this market research. The analysis of these best/worst-case scenarios results in an expected volume for satellite navigation services in a range from DM 34,0 billion to DM 52,5 billion.

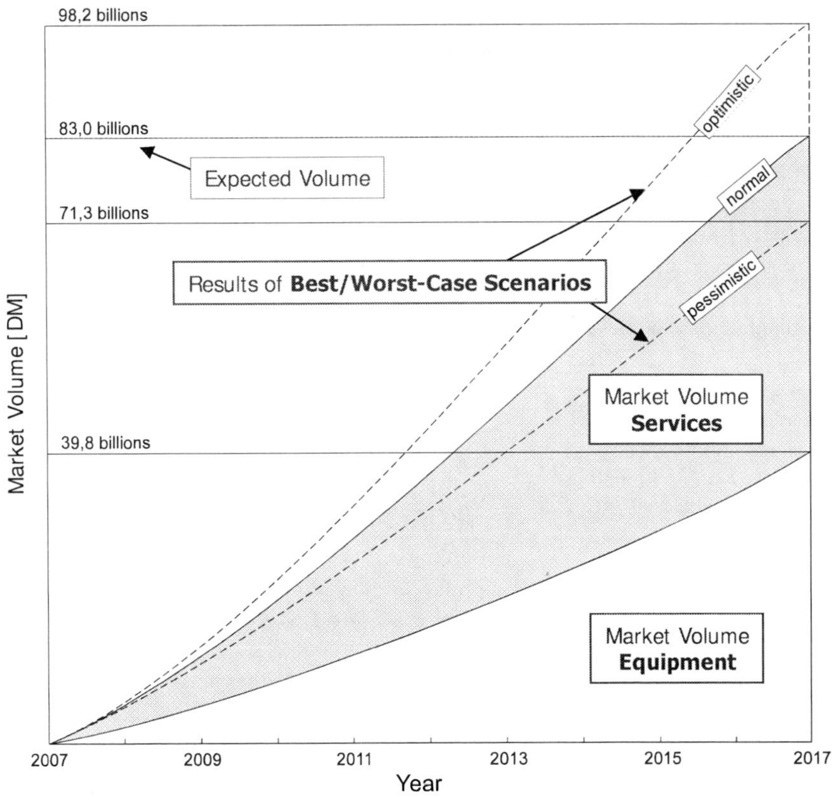

Figure 9: Overall Market Volume for Satellite Navigation Equipment & Services

Overall Market Volume. Figure 9 summarizes the previously determined numbers for the market volume of satellite navigation and services. For the market volume related to services the best/worst-case scenarios are also visualized revealing sensitivities related to the pessimistic and optimistic market forecast.

CONCLUSIONS

Starting with the example of the European satellite navigation system it has to be said, that in general it is very hard to predict a market volume for a product not existing yet. Especially the long period of time that was investigated and the late full operational capability of the satellite navigation system is a handicap, since most companies that were interviewed do not have a planning-horizon that is aiming that far. On the other hand, the market will create products and services that are not conceivable today, and therefore these effects can hardly be accounted for.

Concerning the proposed process and its application it turned out that its transparency and methodical approach impressed our customer/contractor (DLR) very positively, since we not only presented an unexplained number for the market volume, but were able to make clear what parameters influenced it and how it was determined. This transparency highly contributed to the acceptance of our forecast and was the basis for corresponding political decisions.

The objective of the research project is to build an integrated model for the very early systems engineering phases, representing the interrelationships between market volume, requirements, and design. It is thereby extremely important to map the design on achievable market volume instead of only validating the fulfillment of a previously defined set of requirements. Otherwise any commercial space project is going to encounter the same problems Iridium had.

Having in mind design centers that have been implemented at NASA's Jet Propulsion Laboratory (Project Design Center; Shishko, 1997) or DaimlerChrysler Aerospace (Satellite Design Office; Wilke et al., 1999) and equipped with integrated multidisciplinary teams it becomes obvious that one important team discipline, marketing, has been neglected. Especially for commercial space project (with a long time to realization) this may turn out to be a real disadvantage. From our point of view it is therefore absolutely necessary to integrate the marketing function into these design teams, in order to reveal real design sensitivities with respect to market trends. The insight that it is necessary to create integrated teams in order to make clear to every subsystem engineer what effect he/she has on the system level has, has been won. It is therefore only consistent to do the same for the marketing function to enable engineers to understand what effects their design changes have on commercial success of the entire project. Figure 10 visualizes this understanding: The achievable price is displayed versus one design parameter (here resolution of 'Galileo'). The bubbles indicate certain requirement profiles (market segments), while the diameter is a measure for the market volume. The current design is displayed as a square and it turns out that this particular design covers two market segments. Taking this diagram as a starting point engineers can now see to where to shift the design in order to penetrate other market segments and thus increase the available market volume. Assuming dynamic markets the bubbles will tend to move: Prices will sink while performance requirements will increase. The distance between a bubbles center and the border of the current design is a measure for its robustness.

Generating these insights into the current design enables a more market oriented design. The integrated market model functions as a communication channel for engineers and marketing specialist.

The proposed process integrating marketing, requirements, and concepts to one model will have to be completed in the areas of requirements and concepts in order to really create a design process that can be called „Design-to-Market". Concerning the 'Galileo' project meanwhile a set of twelve requirement profiles has been established. The next step in our project is to evaluate the baseline design of the 'Galileo'-constellation against these requirements profiles to determine the market volume this design is capable to achieve.

As our research project continuous the process and results will be presented in future papers.

REFERENCES

Airbus Industries, *Global Market Forecast 1997-2016*, Blagnac Cedex (France), March 1997

Cohen, L., *Quality Function Deployment–Making QFD Work for You*, Addison-Wesley, 1995

Frost & Sullivan, *European Electronic Navigation Equipment Markets*, Mountain View, CA (USA), June 1998

Hammann P., Erichson B., Marktforschung, Gustav Fischer Verlag, Stuttgart, 1994

Hüttner, M., *Grundzüge der Marktforschung*, München, Oldenbourg Verlag, 1997

Intex Management Services, *The Worldwide Market for Navigation and Tracking Systems*, Wellingborough (England), May 1998

Meffert, H., *Marktforschung*, Wiesbaden, Gabler, 1986

Ocean Shipping Consultants, *World Shipbuilding to 2010*, Chertsey/Surrey, 1998

Sage, A. P., *Systems Engineering*, John Wiley & Sons, New York, 1992

Shishko, R. 1997: *Integrated Design Environments for Mars Exploration (The JPL Project Design Center)*„ Presentation at the Division of Astronautics, Technische Universität München, 20.11.1997

Vollerthun A., Wieser M., *A European Global Navigation Satellite System – The German Market & Value Adding Chain Effects*, Published: 50th International Astronautical Congress, 4-8 October 1999, Amsterdam, The Netherlands

Wilke, M., Quirmbach, O., Negele, H., Fricke, H., Igenbergs, E., *MuSSaT – A Tool for Model-based System Engineering of commercial Satellite Systems*, Published in: Proceedings of the 9th Annual Symposium of INCOSE, Brighton, 1999

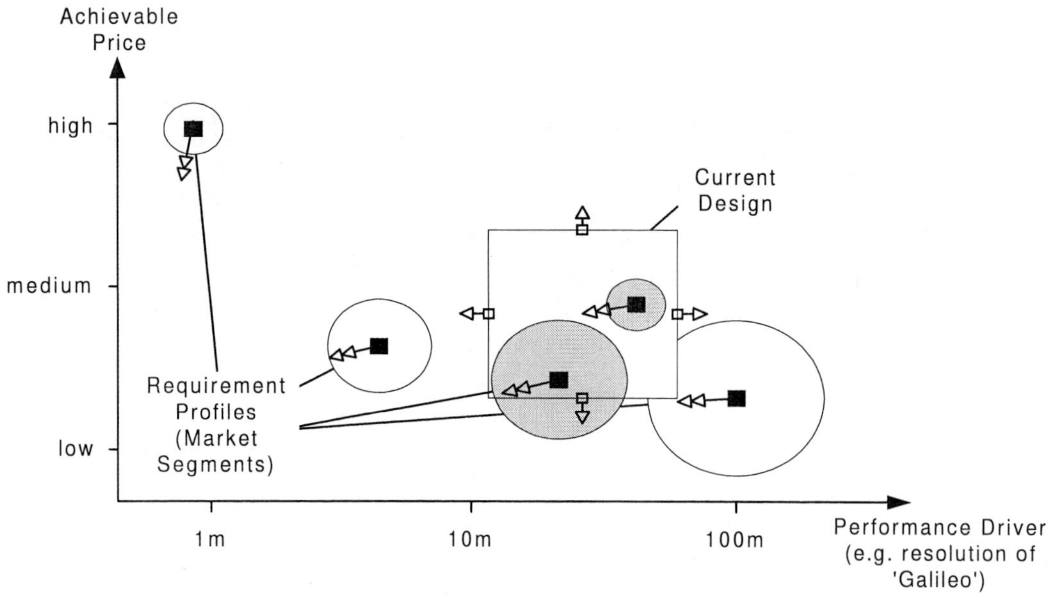

Figure 10: Current design and identified market segments

BIOGRAPHY

Andreas Vollerthun is Ph.D. candidate and research scientist at the Division of Astronautics at the Technical University of Munich. He received his master's degree in aerospace engineering in 1997 after completing his master thesis at NASA's Jet Propulsion Laboratory (Pasadena, Ca., USA). His Research focuses on the model driven design process and the significance of economical aspects in early design phases.

Eduard Igenbergs is Professor of Astronautics and Director of the Division of Astronautics at the Technical University of Munich. He holds a Ph.D. and a masters degree in mechanical engineering. He developed several dust counter experiments for different spacecrafts, including the Japanese Nozomi spacecraft currently on its way to Mars. He developed the Munich Space Chair, a body restraint system on board the Russian space station MIR. He has been teaching and researching in the field of Systems Engineering for more than 20 years.

Towards a Common Management Process for Projects, Systems Engineering and Software Development?

John K Davies
BAE SYSTEMS
Grange Road, Christchurch, Dorset, BH23 4JE, UK
john.k.davies@bae.co.uk

Abstract. In harmonising Systems Engineering, Project Management and Software Development Processes, the aim is to provide each project with a single source of best-practice process definition for the activities it needs to carry out. In this paper, several methods of harmonisation are considered: producing a combined Project Management and Systems Engineering Process, closely integrating the processes, and having loosely coupled engineering and management processes. Drivers for each option are discussed and their advantages and draw-backs explored.

The major issues that emerge are 'Should Engineering Management be part of the Systems Engineering Process or part of the Project Management Process?' and 'Can Engineering Management be considered in a separate process to the Engineering itself?' In considering these issues, methods and tool issues to support process harmonisation are discussed. The optimum solution to these issues probably depends on the structure of the project and the organisations involved, but it is argued that for Integrated Project Teams, a common management process offers many advantages.

BACKGROUND

Several authors have studied the correspondence between Systems Engineering and Project Management by analysing the content of standards and guides. (Kauffman 98) and (Bottomley et al. 98) have presented detailed comparisons basing their work on a wide range of standards and looked into where Systems Engineering and Project Management appear to overlap and complement, in terms of the activities that need to be carried out. Similar comparisons could be made with Software Development standards (for example ISO 12207). These analyses show that there is considerable overlap between standards for Project Management, Systems Engineering and Software Development. A similar situation also exists for other engineering disciplines. This overlap is not really surprising from two points of view.

1. Any major enterprise needs management. The techniques for managing a whole project or programme, the engineering within the project, and the development aspects are likely to be similar although they may be managing at a different level of the overall enterprise.

2. The management of the programme is of interest to the project manager and the engineering manager, even though they may have different roles and responsibilities with regard to particular activities. The planning of the project involves the project manager but is largely determined by the engineering activities.

(Kauffman 98) and (Bottomley et al. 98) refer to many sources in making their comparisons. From the practising systems engineer point-of-view, the most pertinent sources are Systems Engineering process standards such as IEEE 1220, EIA 632 and ISO/IEC 15288. In addition many companies are now looking at their capability maturity using standards such as SE CMM, SECAM, EIA 731 and in the future CMMI. All of these deal with the management of engineering as well as the performance of engineering. In fact, many focus on the management of engineering activities and products rather than the 'what you do' and 'how you do it'.

Within our business, the need to improve our Software Engineering was recognised about four years ago and a Software Process Improvement programme launched. This work has developed following the guidance of the Software Capability Maturity Model and Assessment SEI CM. Software CMM standards are aimed at 'software companies' - companies whose aim is to develop software products, rather than at companies in which software is developed as part of a larger system. In order to improve the software capability in a 'systems company' it is necessary not just to improve the way we produce software, but also our business process, our Project Management and our Systems Engineering.

The initial work on software improvement was followed by an initiative to improve all our business processes. This included definition of process and best practice for Project Management, Systems Engineering, Software Engineering and Hardware Engineering, Procurement, In Service Support etc. This resulted in a number of separate processes for defining the way different aspects of a project should be carried out. (Davies 99) described the way the engineering processes could be integrated using an 'Overarching Systems Engineering Process' in which all engineering disciplines contributed. This provided a means by which the various engineering processes could be harmonised, brought together and understood as a single process.

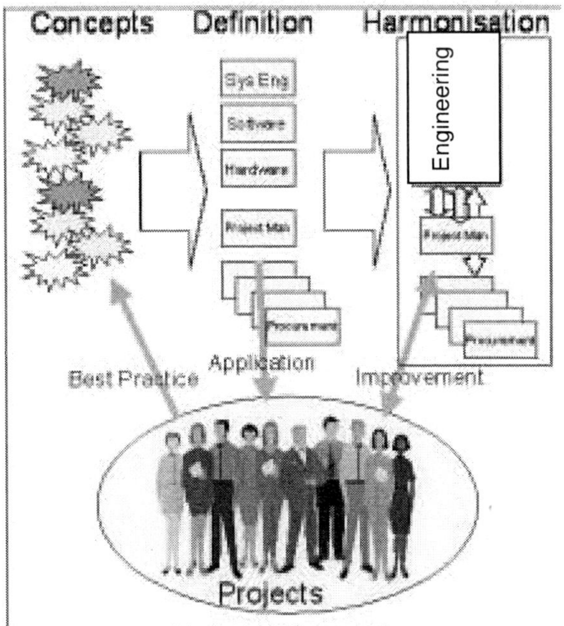

Figure 1: Process Definition and Harmonisation

What needs to be addressed is not just the harmonisation of engineering processes but also their harmonisation with other processes, in particular project management.

WHERE IS THE PROBLEM? WHAT IS THE PAIN?

Systems Engineering, and indeed all engineering does not exist in isolation. It is part of the business and needs to inter-operate with many other business processes. One issue is how should this inter-operation take place, and at what level of the process?

If we consider a 'traditional' organisation that has a programme management department, a systems engineering department, software development and similar departments, then each can operate its own processes and the interfaces between departments could be defined. What is needed are well-defined processes within each department and well-defined interfaces at each boundary. But just like any system its not just the interfaces that need to be well defined, the interoperation between the departments needs to be efficient, not just the operation of the process within each department. If a business carries out most of its work in the same way, then such an organisation can be effective.

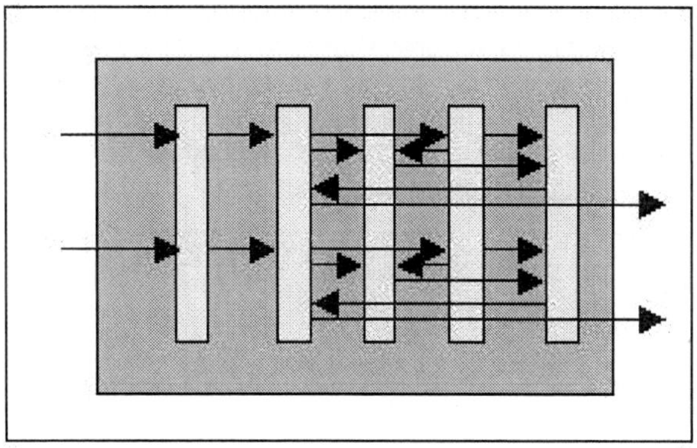

Figure 2: Project Route in a Department-based Organisation

However, for more innovative programmes where processes and interfaces need to be flexible, such organisations become inefficient. Integrated Project Teams (IPTs), as reported by (Thornton et.al. 98) and (Dawson 99) appear more suited to such innovative programmes. With IPTs the organisation is project-based and programme management, systems engineers and developers are all part of the same project team. In principle, all of the team works together, contributing to forming the plans, and working to achieve the milestones.

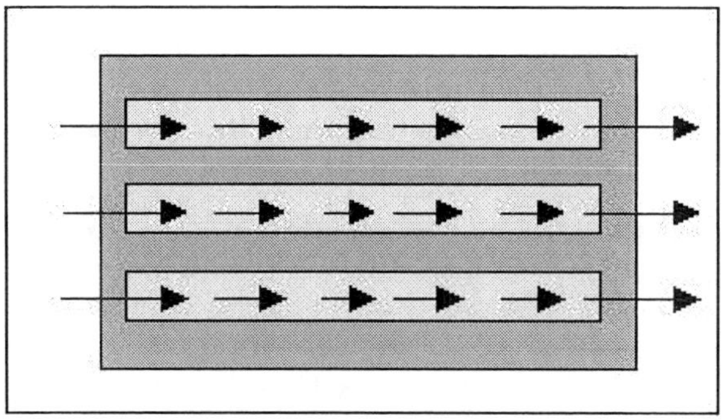

Figure 3: Project Rout in a IPT-based Organisation

So where are the problems with having separate multiple processes in either departmental-based or IPT-based organisations? What goes wrong? It all works, doesn't it? We all know what we are doing, don't we?

Well the Project Manager thinks he knows what's happening, and the Systems Engineers think they know what's happening, the Software Developers would often like to know what's happening, but are they seeing different sides of the same picture or two or even three different pictures?

1. We have multiple plans - on any project we can have a Project Management Plan, a Systems Engineering Management Plan, SEMP, and a Software Development Plan. In some areas they cover different aspects of the project, but in others they cover the same aspects. Which is right? We only want to do one project and that's hard enough.

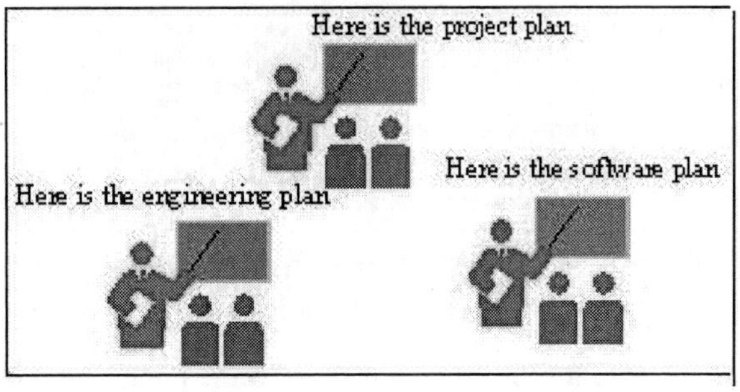

Figure 4: One project, or three?

2. We do estimates - the project manager does his estimate, systems engineers do their estimates, development do their estimates, you add them all up to get some overall estimate, but have the developers estimated to develop the items the engineers are going to design? Has the project manager used the engineering estimates, multiplied by some factor, or taken the customer's expected time-scale and cost and used those?

3. We all report on how things are going - We all report against 'the plan' but if we have three different sets of plans, does anyone know how we are doing overall?

4. Fortunately we have experts to help us - We have Project Management Gurus, Systems Engineering Gurus and Software Gurus. We can get consultants in to tell us how to do our Project Management better, our Systems Engineering better and our Software Development better. There are over 100 books a year written on project management. Many of the 'new' methods are re-worked combinations of previous methods with new buzz-words. New methods, or re-badged methods are being developed for Software Engineering. Fortunately Systems Engineering does not seem to be attracting such rapid apparent change.

5. We have assessments of our Software Development and Systems Engineering Capabilities. Software CMM and Systems CMM (such as EIA 731) provide the mechanisms, but what do they really assess?

They focus on the management of the engineering, rather than the activities and methods used. EIA 731 splits the assessment into categories, seven are technical, eight are management, three are environmental. Of the eight management processes, three have clear overlap with project management: Plan and Organise, Manage and Control and Co-ordinate Suppliers. Software CMM has similar categories.

It appears that there is little difference in the processes and methods needed for managing Projects, managing Systems Engineering and managing Software Development. What differs are the activities and products that needs to be managed and this causes different application of the management processes in different areas.

So, why have two (or three, or four) processes for managing plans, staff, costs, timescales, effort, deliverables? Why not just have one generic process or set of processes that can be applied when and where needed?

BACK TO BASICS, BACK TO REALITY

At the lowest level, an engineering project carries out its work through a number of activities, which using IDEF0 terminology have Inputs, Outputs, Resources and Controls as in Figure 5. One way of thinking about this is the Inputs, Activity, and Outputs are 'Engineering Axis', and the Control and the provision of Resources are the 'Management Axis'.

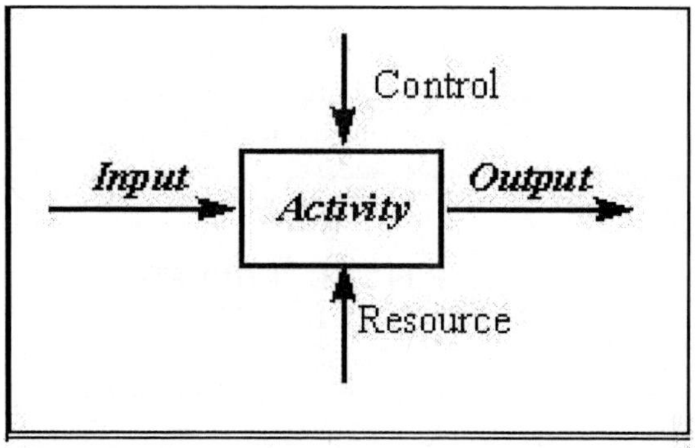

Figure 5: IDEFO representation of an Activity

In this picture, Management includes Planning Tasking, Reporting, Reviewing: where reviews can be targeted on progress, technical areas or quality of the process activity. The outputs can be various products: which have content, quality, may include changes to other products.

What can we use to distinguish Engineering Management from Project Management in this simple case?

Consider the methods and tools we use for Engineering Management. We use planning tools such as GANNT and PERT, we use estimating methods, we use Risk Management and Issues Logs and we use reporting, both qualitatively and through metrics. These same tools are used for Project Management as well as for Engineering Management.

At the conceptual and practical level, management of the project, systems and software development serve the same general purpose and may use the same tools.

WHAT IS DIFFERENT?

So where does Engineering differ from Project Management? Systems Engineering covers User Operations, Analysis, Requirements, Design, Development, Integration, Support, Verification, System Performance etc.

Software development covers planning and managing the software effort, software requirements, design, development, integration and test, together with the processes, methods and tools to support these activities.

Project Management needs to encompass finance, resource, contract management, customer management as well as 'management' activities that are common to both Systems Engineering and Project Management.

The way the engineering is managed is similar to the way other activities are managed. In simple terms, it is the engineering that is different, not the management aspect of that engineering.

A MANAGEMENT PROCESS AND ENGINEERING PROCESS

If we consider 'Engineering' and 'Management' as two separate but interacting processes, can we identify what the interactions are? To what degree is engineering governed by management? Where does the engineering determine what needs to be managed? Can management decide everything? (Would we engineer without management?)

If we take a simple design and development project, we might think we could define the plan at the start and manage all the activities according to that plan - determine all the milestones, products, activities, effort needed, duration, costs etc. before we do any engineering. So what's wrong with that?

The real situation is that we start the engineering according to 'the plan', get the customer's requirements and start analysing them, determine the system requirements and design the system. It is then that we know what the system is, what parts of the system we are going to need to buy or develop, what the integration, proving, installation and hand-over activities are going to involve. It is not until the Software Requirements are identified that software plans can be quantified. The initial plan produced to manage the project can identify these activities in a generic way, but it is not until the system is designed that we can properly define them and quantify the duration, effort etc. The plan for the project cannot be determined until the system design is in place. You can plan some of the development activities at a general level, but until you know what you need in the system, you cannot define them.

Management of the Project, the Systems Engineering and the Software Development have many common features and are often regarded as the same thing by organisations such as CMM assessors. Having a common management process or set of processes overcomes differences of understanding and conflicts that may arise from having different generic processes.

The issue is then how such a management process should be defined and how it should interact with the systems engineering and software development processes.

OPTIONS FOR PROCESS HARMONISATION

There are several ways of defining engineering and project management processes and their interactions. IEE 1220 and EIA 632 define the interactions between the various parts of the engineering and management processes to some extent. ISO/IEC 15288 identifies Enterprise, Project and Technical processes, but not the interactions between them. ISO 12207 defines Enterprise, Project and Technical processes for developing 'Software Systems', it has major overlaps and some differences with ISO/IEC 15288 for developing 'Systems'. If the software developers insist that the company processes and standards are developed to fully meet ISO 12207 and systems engineers insist they should meet ISO/IEC 15288, this could cause major problems.

All these standards provide requirements for a business' own engineering process, they are not at a level of defining such a process themselves. In principle, a company could use a disparate set of processes that met all the requirements of ISO/IEC 15288 but which do not work together and would be a disaster for that company. What is needed is an integrated process, or set of interoperating processes with effective interfaces, that meets the particular company's needs. Several ways of achieving this are considered below in Table 1. They range from a single process that specifically defines the management of every activity – to separate processes for engineering and management without defined interactions.

Option	Benefits	Drawbacks
Single Systems Engineering and Project Management Process	Seamless Only one place to look	Too complicated Management of each engineering activity is similar Harder to update/maintain Harder to distinguish roles
Fully integrated Engineering and Project Management Processes	Clear distinction of roles Defined interfaces	Can be inflexible Difficult to change one aspect and not the other Difficult to apply to some projects Can lead to 'them and us', who is in charge?
Interoperating Engineering and Project Management Process	Easier to maintain/update Distinct roles Flexible	Interfaces not as well defined Can be gaps/conflicts/overlap issues Needs effort to make it work in practice
Separate Engineering and Project Management Process	Easy to produce Distinct Roles	Real 'Them and Us' Tendency for disconnects and insularity
Common Management Process, Engineering Process as the 'how to' process not the 'how to manage' process.	Flexible Maintainable Obviates many interface problems Clarity of purpose Supports 'one-team' approach	Needs wider 'buy-in' Needs specific tailoring/application in different areas

Table 1: Options for harmonising Systems Engineering and Project Management processes

NEEDS FOR A GENERIC MANAGEMENT PROCESS

Why define processes anyway? Why not just let it happen?

We define processes to capture best practice, save time and effort, and make us more efficient. To make the widest use of processes, we need a 'superset' of processes that can be tailored to each project and be able to insert appropriate methods and tool support.

The tailored processes for the project needs to cover the life-cycle, milestones, activities, the engineering within each activity and its management.

The process definitions need to be flexible enough to cover different contractual regimes such as formal customer/supplier relationships, Integrated Project Teams and working with partner companies. We need to cover different life-cycles such as classic waterfall, incremental, recursive or phased development. We need to work with different customer domains: military and civilian; land, sea, air, strategic and tactical. We work with different technologies: sensors, communications, CIS, weapon systems, using different platforms: land, sea, air, hand-held, vehicle mounted, aircraft, ships, cabin and office.

We want processes that are maintainable, a 'future proof' structure to allow improvements and changes.

We want to facilitate transfer of information and control: plans, estimates, activities, reporting, products, metrics, between the management of activities and the engineering processes they are managing.

Management activities basically manage three sorts of things:

1. activities, such as project, engineering, development, production,
2. assets, such as information, products, materiel, people, resources
3. unknowns, such as risks.

Examples of these are shown in Table 2 for Project, Systems and Software Managers. Management is very similar, what is changing is what is managed.

Management Activity	Project Manager	Systems Manager	Software Manager
Plan	Project Activities	Engineering Activities, Development and Engineering Changes	Software Development Activities
Estimate	Overall Project Effort, Timescales and Costs	Systems Engineering Effort, Timescales and Costs	Software Development Effort, Timescales and Costs
Resource	Project Activities	Systems Activities	Software Development Activities
Report	Progress against project milestones and deliverables	Progress against Engineering Milestones	Progress against Software Milestones
Review	Progress and costs	Progress, engineering quality	Progress, software quality
Manage Assets	Project Information, Contract, Deliverables, People	Engineering Information, Configuration, Engineering Changes, People	Software Specifications, Designs, Code, Builds, People
Manage Risks	Project Risks	Technical Risks	Technical Risks

Table 2 Application of Generic Management Activities to Project, Systems and Software

ADVANTAGES OF A GENERIC MANAGEMENT PROCESS

The main advantage of a generic process is to ensure cohesive management across the whole project. Particular advantages can be seen when considering IPTs and CMMs.

Advantages for Integrated Project Teams: In IPTs the team works together to achieve the project's objectives. The project needs management and engineering. Having a single generic management process that can be applied at all levels of the project obviates complex interfaces that would otherwise have to be created between the different disciplines working in the team and increases the team's effectiveness.

Advantages for Capability Maturity: Having a generic management process enables assessment of the business against Software, Systems, Project Management and Integrated Capability Maturity Models. uncertainty and conflicts caused by having separate management processes addressing each area are obviated. Process improvements can be defined and applied across all disciplines and the effort going into different areas reduced.

WHICH WAY IN THE FUTURE?

Up to now in large organisations management of projects, Systems Engineering and development have been considered as separate activities needing their own management processes. Process improvement activities have highlighted the need for all processes to work together efficiently and effectively. The particular need to harmonise the Project Management and Systems Engineering processes has revealed overlaps and conflicts, misunderstandings and inefficiencies that could be overcome by the definition and adoption of a generic Management Process.

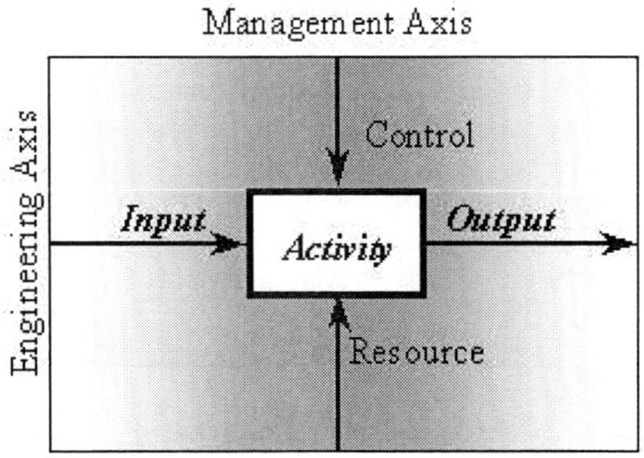

Figure 6: Systems Engineering as an Engineering Process and a Generic Management Process

This application of two processes to Systems Engineering may be regarded as providing orthogonal axes for the management and engineering aspects of the project as a whole and for every activity, as shown in Figure 6. Such a process could be applied across all the project, to the programme, systems engineering, software and other development areas. A generic Management Process would provide major benefits to Integrated Project Teams and in terms of improving capability maturity, across all disciplines. However, it is not a panacea and would need to be applied as needed within each area.

REFERENCES

Bottomley. P.C., Brook. P., Morris. P., and Stevens. R. "A Study of the Relationship of Systems Engineering and Project Management" Systems *Engineering: a Matter of Choice. Proceedings of the INCOSE-UK 4th Annual Symposium 1998.*

Davies. J.K. "Developing an Over-Arching Systems Engineering Process" Systems *Engineering; Sharing the Future. Proceedings of the INCOSE '99 Symposium, Brighton.*

Dawson. A.J. "Engineering in Integrated Project Teams" Systems *Engineering; Sharing the Future. Proceedings of the INCOSE '99 Symposium, Brighton.*

EIA 632 Processes for Engineering a System

EIA 731 Systems Engineering Capability Model

IEEE 1220 Standard for Application and Management of the Systems Engineering Process.

ISO 12207 Information Technology – Software life cycle processes

ISO/IEC 15288 Life Cycle Management – System Lifecycle Processes

Kauffman. D.C. "Project Management and Systems Engineering: Where the Professions Intersect – Generate Synergy Not Conflict" *People, Teams and Systems. Proceedings of the INCOSE '98 Symposium, Vancouver.*

SE CMM EPIC Capability Maturity Model for Systems Engineering

SECAM INCOSE Systems Engineering Capability Assessment Model

Thornton. J.A., Hutcheson. R.T., Luczak. M.A., Castor. R.A. "Implementation of a Government – Contractor Leadership Team in an Integrated Product Team Environment" *People, Teams and Systems. Proceedings of the INCOSE '98 Symposium, Vancouver.*

Biography: Dr John Davies works with projects at BAE SYSTEMS across several sites, on the engineering process, standards and support tools. John is currently supporting the design integration activities for the Sampson Multi-Function Radar. He has worked on the integration of the Engineering Process across all engineering disciplines and has recently completed work on the interoperation of the engineering process with the project management and business management processes.

After studying physics at Bristol University and University College London, John worked in high-energy physics, at Geneva and Oxford, before joining Plessey in 1981. He has since worked as a software and systems engineer and manager on a series of varied projects.

Are Formal Methods Ready for Prime Time?

The Use of Formal Methods in Development Large Software Systems

T. Scott Ankrum
University of Maryland University College
Adelphi, Maryland 20783

Abstract. Formal Methods is a term used to describe the use of a formal language for the specification of a software product at some level. The use of a formal language allows requirements to be specified more crisply and less ambiguously than a textual document. It can also allow the developers to formally prove that an implementation meets the specified requirements. Some formal languages can even be transformed into executable code. The use of formal methods is explored for large software projects in commercial enterprises, government, and the military. A comparison is made of the attributes and results of these projects. A table at the end supports the conclusion that formal methods can be successful on a large scale.

INTRODUCTION

A useful definition of formal methods from one of the papers studied is: "The application of mathematical synthesis and analysis techniques to the development of computer controlled systems." (Craigen et al. 1995)

Can formal methods can be scaled up effectively and efficiently from academic research and pilot projects to large-scale software development projects? Several large projects are investigated. Information is gathered from reports on projects that have been completed or are well under way, written by people involved with or close to the project. Each project is investigated for: its size, the formal language used, the fraction of the software effort subjected to the formal method, other aspects of the formal method, whether formal or informal proofs were done on the specifications and conclusions reached on that project's use of the formal method.

The number of project reports found for this survey is surprisingly large. Reports were selected for this survey if the project involved a real system or design. In all, 24 projects were selected from 16 papers. Most of the papers reported on an actual development effort or verification of a specification for an actual development effort. Four papers reported on an academic exercise to formally specify an existing informal specification. These were chosen because they demonstrate as well as the others that formal methods can be scaled up to an industrial size project.

CASES SURVEYED

IBM CICS Transaction Processor. IBM's transaction processor, Customer Information Control System (CICS) was an existing product with a well-established development process when its Hursley, U.K. development laboratory began a joint project with the Oxford University Programming Research Group. IBM was planning to restructure a large part of CICS for version 3 of the product. The collaboration involved the use of the Z formal language (pronounced "zed", as the British do) to specify requirements and high level design for what became 37,000 lines of code, about 14 percent of the effort. An additional 11,000 lines of code were partially specified in Z. Low level designs were specified using Dijkstra's guarded command language within Z. (Collins et al. 1987), (Hayes 1993), (King 1993), (Nix & Collins 1989)

The efforts of the project produced 2,000 pages of Z specifications and designs. Including all verifications and tests, the code coming from Z specifications had two and a half times fewer errors than the non-Z code. More errors were found in the Z specification, than in the other specifications, but fewer errors were found in the Z specified code during Function Verification Test and System Test than in the non-Z code. So, for the formally specified functions, the errors were caught earlier in the development process than for traditionally specified functions. Training in Z added about three months to the project, but IBM estimated that it saved about nine percent on the development cost because of rework that formal specification avoided. The project was clearly a success and IBM is continuing to use formal methods on the succeeding versions of CICS. (Collins et al. 1987), (King 1993), (Nix & Collins 1989)

COBOL Reverse Engineering. This is one of only two projects surveyed that was stated to be a failure. Lloyd's register wanted a tool to help reverse engineer COBOL programs. The Z language was used to design 23,320 lines of C code, 43 percent of the total project. This required about 100 person-days of effort to produce 250 pages of Z design. The problem was that Z was used for low level design and the detail was such that the Z to code ratio was only 1 to 2. Because Z was used at such a low level and no proofs or automatic checking were done, the syntax was poor and a high error rate occurred in the Z design: 25 percent attributable to errors in the Z specification and 13 percent to misunderstandings. The fact that Z was used in a procedural manner also contributed to the problems. The project was declared a failure and the product was not delivered. (Neil et al. 1998)

SSADM CASE Tools In this project, the British firm Praxis used Z to develop a Computer-Assisted Systems Engineering tool set to support the use of the UK's Systems Analysis and Design Method (SSADM) development process. The team found Z easier to use than they had expected and the path from Z to Object Oriented programming seemed direct and natural. Test cases were built from the Z specification. This team found the collection of metrics from formal methods different and/or difficult enough not to make the effort. Subjectively, the product was found to be of good quality with few errors. It is not known, however, if that is due to the formal Z specification, object-oriented programming or just good people. Their biggest problem was a lack of Z tools. The project was deemed a success, although, for unrelated reasons, the product was never released. (Groote at al. 1994)

Multi-net Gateway System A group that was then Ford Aerospace (subsequently sold to Loral, now part of Lockheed Martin), developed an Internet device called a Multi-net Gateway System (MGS), which provides secure data-gram delivery. It was submitted to the U.S. Trusted Computer System Evaluation criteria process with the hope for A1 certification. That level of certification requires a formal specification. The Gypsy Verification Environment was used to produce 10 pages for the security model, and another 80 pages to specify the MGS, representing 6,000 lines of code. This was a post-project certification effort, so nothing can be said about its affect on the project. The hoped for A1 certification was not achieved, only a "developmental certification", but the specification effort was successful and it achieved its purpose. (Craigen et al. 1995)

Kermit FTP No development effort was involved in this project. The well-known communications protocol, Kermit File Transfer Protocol was formally specified using what the author calls an evolving algebra approach. This paper is one of several that serve to demonstrate that an existing, functional design can be formally specified and proven successfully. The entire specification, with the proof imbedded takes 40 pages. The author's purpose was to present the proof, so he provides no effort estimate and there is no lines of code estimate. (Huggins 1995)

Tektronix Oscilloscope Software Tektronix of Oregon was creating a new line of oscilloscopes and wanted a precise design notation to maximize software reuse among the different oscilloscopes in the line. They chose Z over LOTOS, CSD and VDM because it is easier for engineers to learn. (The acronyms are not expanded in the source paper. VDM is probably Vienna Development Method.) Z was new to the developers and it was taught in one and a half week classes over a six week period. The intent was to use Z to design non-executable prototypes, not for specifying requirements. (Craigen et al. 1995)

A total of 30 pages of Z were written, half of that to specify the user interface. This represented about 200,000 lines of developed code. Tektronix did not have an established development process, so they could not report on how the use of Z affected productivity, other than that there were no Z related delays in the project. They did report that the Z designs did not fit well into object oriented development, although Z could capture some design specifications that Object oriented design could not. This report on Z and Object Oriented methods contradicts what was said above in the SSADM CASE Tools project. It was also reported that issues of concurrency and timing were not handled well by Z. Once the design questions that the Z prototypes were written for were answered, the Z designs were not kept up. The development team relied on program code as their only documentation. (Craigen et al. 1995)

No post-development errors were found in the software and the project was rated a success. Post project interviews suggest that any future project with similar reusability needs will employ Z for designs. (Craigen et al. 1995)

Hewlett-Packard Medical Instruments Hewlett-Packard used its own formal language, Hewlett-Packard Specification Language (HP-SL) to specify the Analytical Information Base portion of a Component Monitoring System. Although this was part of a line of patient monitoring devices, it was not considered a health or safety critical component. This was a case of a research organization trying to transfer its formal methods technology to a product development organization in the same company. The HP-SL language is derived from VDM and is used for making abstract machine specifications. The language was used for requirements and design of the new product. The report states that no automatic proofs were attempted. It is difficult to infer from that statement whether manual proofs or consistency checks were done. (Craigen et al. 1995)

A total of 1,290 lines of HP-SL specification and design were produced, equaling 55 pages. 4,390 lines of defect-free code were delivered and another 4,580 lines of support code were written. Productivity was reported at 150 lines of code a day. The only code errors found were in support code that was later designated for delivery. The report hedged on the reasons for few defects, saying that high quality is normal for small systems where the developers have good domain knowledge. That hedging was probably because the development organization rejected the use of formal methods for later projects, saying that HP-SL was too costly for their teams to learn. Thus, the project was reported as a failure. (Craigen et al. 1995)

SACEM Railway Signaling System This project developed a new railway signaling and monitoring system for a Paris, France passenger subway line. The project involved GEC Alsthom, Matra Transport and CSEE (Compagnie de Signaux et Entreprises Electriques). The objective was to reduce the interval between trains from two minutes and 30 seconds, to two minutes, while increasing safety. SACEM is an acronym that, when translated from the French means Driving, Operation and Maintenance Aid System. Specification was done in a combination of Hoare's Proof of Program method and the B method, and expended 120,000 person-hours to check 600 scenarios. This compares to a total of 31,500 person-hours spent on the prototype and final systems combined. That resulted in 9,000 lines of verified code. The entire system was not verified, but the main functions were formally proved. The proof methodology is interesting. The Hoare method was used to progress from the code level up in proofs, and the B method was used to start with the specification and proceed down with the proofs. Both used a state machine model so the proofs could "meet" in the middle. The line is now operational and the project is an obvious success. (Craigen et al. 1995)

Hoorn-Kersenboogerd Rail Yard An existing system for maintaining safe operation in a railway yard was subjected to formal specification and verification in this academic project. The railway is located in Amsterdam, the Netherlands, as are the people who did the formal specification. The purpose of this non-development project was to establish that formal methods could be used to prove the correct and safe operation of this full-size system. The formal representation used was the Micro Common Representation Language (μCRL). Automated proofs were done or attempted using a variety of tools, since the object of the study was to find ways to prove as many aspects of the system as possible. No metrics for the existing system code, specifications or proofs were given. The authors of the study concluded it was a qualified success. Although some of their proofs were confounded by the size of some formulas and/or lack of computing power, the authors end with an optimistic view for the future of formal proofs. (Groote et al. 1994)

Météor Metro Line In this project, a new line, #14 of the Paris Metro was being installed. The dependability and safety of the line were critical aspects of the project, and were the responsibility of Matra Transport. There was already a system called Vital Coded Processor (VCP) in use which is intended to protect against hardware errors or errors in compiling the code. The B method was chosen to formally specify and design the new system. The development process had to accommodate B and the existing VCP system. Some adjustments were made. (Behm et al. 1999)

The system requirements had been written in natural language prose. These were formalized into B. The B specification was transformed, in successive steps, into a concrete design. The concrete design was written in a subset of B called B0. The B0 design was then automatically transformed into Ada program code. The B specification was verified against the informal specification using invariants and substitutions. Similarly, the interfaces to informally specified external systems were verified. A combination of automatic and interactive proofs was used to verify the B0 design against the B specification. An interactive proof is used when the automatic proof cannot be completed. It allows the user to supply missing rules to complete the proof. As part of this project, a corporate guidebook on the B method was written and enriched as the project progressed. A B Validation Book was also written and enriched throughout the project. (Behm et al. 1999)

The size of this project is well documented. Of the 27,800 lemmas, 81 percent were automatically proved without other aids. By adding common rules and proof tactics, the percentage came to 92. The remaining 2,254 lemmas were proved interactively. Of the total number of lemmas, 6,200 make up the abstract B specification and 21,600 make up the concrete B0 design. The generated code consists of 630 Ada packages for a total of 86,000 lines of Ada code. (Behm et al. 1999)

In addition to the specifications, the added rules were verified and only proof errors were found; no code errors were caused by the added rules. Function tests were performed, even though the team felt the proofs made that step unnecessary. System integration testing on the target computer and then on-site testing were performed. None of these tests revealed any defects in the software. The new metro line went into public service on October 15, 1998 and no defects were reported in the four-month time before the project's paper was written. (Behm et al. 1999)

Algebraic Specification of Traffic Regulation This is another specification of an existing system to show that formal methods can be applied to industrial size systems. In this study, Process Specification Formalism

(PSF) was used to specify a dynamic traffic light system. The traffic light system is generalized software that can be installed anywhere that the timing of the traffic lights must react, dynamically to changing traffic patterns. PSF, which creates a data oriented model, was applied to safety critical parts of the system with some simplifying assumptions made. The complete specification in PSF is presented in the paper and consumes 26 pages. No other metric is given. The study was limited to formally specifying the system, and no proofs were attempted. The authors consider the study a success, but qualify that by saying PSF, being data-oriented, did not handle the real time aspects of the software well. (vanVlijmen & van Waveren 1999)

μCRL Specification of Traffic Regulation The previous study invited a follow-up study with a process-oriented approach. This is another academic study that takes up that challenge. The same dynamic traffic light system was modeled with μCRL. Again, important parts of the system were modeled and some simplifying assumptions were made. The authors of this study emphasized the advice not to attempt optimization during formal specification, because of the risk of producing a less readable, complex and redundant specification. This paper also presented the entire specification, consuming only nine pages this time. Assuming that approximately the same fraction of the system was chosen, the smaller size of this specification (the other was 26 pages) provides evidence that a process oriented model is more appropriate. No other metrics are provided. No mention is made of verifying the specification for consistency and completeness, or against any informal requirements. (Keons & Oei 1999)

Darlington Nuclear Shutdown An important system for any nuclear power plant is the emergency shutdown system. Ontario Hydro had two independent shutdown systems built into the Darlington plant. The first drops the familiar neutron-absorbing rods into the core, and the other injects a liquid poison into the moderator. The Atomic Energy Control Board of Canada (AECB) rightly considered these shutdown systems safety-critical and wanted to be sure they would operate correctly before issuing an operating license to Ontario Hydro. AECB's first choice was to have Ontario Hydro rewrite the systems using information hiding, but formal methods verification was allowed as a compromise. The Software Cost Reduction System (SCR) was chosen to formally specify and verify the shutdown systems. (Craigen et al. 1995)

The first shutdown system consists of 7,000 lines of FORTRAN and some Assembler language. The second consists of 13,000 lines of Pascal and some Assembler. There are 6,000 lines of Assembler between the two systems. The formal specifications were written from informal specifications written as English prose and pseudo-code. No metric for the size of the specification was given, but the manual proofs required 35 person-years to complete. No tools were available for automated proofs. From another perspective, out of the $16 million for the hardware and software of the shutdown systems, 25 percent went to verification. The cost of this verification was considered high, but it was successful in that the operating license was issued. (Craigen et al. 1995)

NATO Air Command and Control As part of specifying NATO's Air Command and Control System (ACCS), the security policy for it was formally modeled in Z. The model was created with two views. A state-based view modeled the static security properties, and an operation-based view modeled the dynamic security constraints. Diagrams were used in the early stages, but were not kept as part of the specification. The formal specification consists of 65 schemas, mostly in the range of 11 to 20 lines each. Some large schemas are over 20 lines. (Boswell 1995)

The schemas were first syntax checked and verified with a type checker. Then, informal proofs were performed. This process generated 30 changes, mostly minor. This project observed some tension between achieving abstraction and completeness in the specification. A wish for a more object-oriented notation was also expressed. The author declared this effort a success but warned that manually proving the 65 schemas was approaching the limit of formal methods. (Boswell 1995)

Traffic Alert and Collision Avoidance The Federal Aviation Authority (FAA) requires that all aircraft over a certain size use the Traffic Alert and Collision Avoidance System (TCAS II). The official specification for this device is maintained and published by RTCA, Inc. (formerly called the Radio Technical Commission for Aeronautics). RTCA commissioned Nancy Leveson of the University of California at Irvine to formalize the specifications for TCAS II. Dr. Leveson and a team of graduate students started with the existing specification, which was a combination of English prose and pseudo-code. That informal specification totaled about 7,000 lines. The formal specification was written using mostly a modified version of Statecharts. Augmenting the Statecharts, transition conditions are represented in a tabular "disjunctive normal form." The entire formal specification is about as long as the original, informal specification. Independent verification of the formal Statecharts specification to the informal prose and pseudo-code was underway at the writing of the source paper. (Craigen et al. 1995)

Flight Guidance System A well-defined subset of a

civil aviation flight guidance system was subjected to formal specification in this project. This effort shadowed a real development project so real requirements were used, but there was no feedback of the formal specification into design. The effort was defined as the mode logic of the system, the software that selects which flight control laws are applicable. Several simplifying assumptions were also made, including the assumption that only normal flight behavior would be modeled. (Miller & Hoech 1997)

The formal method used was the Consortium Requirements Engineering (CoRE) method, developed by the Software productivity Consortium. CoRE is actually not fully formal and because it does not have a formal syntax and semantics, the team had difficulty creating some necessary extensions to it. CoRE is a behavior model based on finite-state machines and an object-oriented approach, and it presents a system level view and a software level view. A major extension made to CoRE for this project was providing multiple levels of abstraction with Hierarchical Finite-State Machines. (Miller & Hoech 1997)

The source paper presents the entire specification in 65 pages. This took 560 person-hours to produce from the informal specification, 35 person-hours of which went to informal verification in the form of inspections. A total of 35 defects in various categories were reported. The authors conclude that with some extensions and the addition of tools they wish they had, CoRE can be used successfully in the future. (Miller & Hoech 1997)

UK Civil Aviation Praxis built an air traffic control system for the U.K. Civil Aviation Authority. This project concerns formalizing the specifications for the Central Control Function Display Information System of that air traffic control system. The original specifications were in a combination of forms: Entity-Relationship diagrams, Yourdon-Constantine Structured Analysis and a formal specification language to define the data and operations. Crucial portions were respecified using Vienna Development Method (VDM). The major formal methods application was to designs. Each of four development groups applied a different design method, the first three being formal: VDM, finite state machines, Milner's Calculus of Communicating Sequential processes, and pseudo-code. (Pfleeger & Hatton 1997)

No metrics for specification or design size were provided in the source paper, but it goes to great lengths in reporting defect metrics. The project delivered about 200,000 lines of C code. Because only some of the specification was formal, and different methods were used to design the system, the authors attempted to draw conclusions about code quality and formal methods, based on where and when the 3,000 faults were found. No mention was made of formally verifying the specification or designs. Their efforts were partially successful. The data were somewhat contradictory, but far fewer post-delivery faults were found in the formally designed software, a rate of 0.81 per KLOC (thousand lines of code) was reported. They also reported that a source code analyzer tool found the formally specified code, regardless of design method, was made of simpler components, with lower coupling. It was also easier to understand and test. (Pfleeger & Hatton 1997)

Space Shuttle GPS This is the first of three Space Shuttle projects reported on by the same paper. This project used SRI's Prototype verification System (PVS) to create concrete functional specifications for the Space Shuttle's navigation system based on the Global Positioning System (GPS). The original, informal requirements were 110 pages of prose, pseudo-code and tables. These were converted into PVS functions, which take the form of: inputs plus previous state, lead to outputs plus next state. (Crow & DeVito 1998)

The formal, PVS specification is of two principal GPS functions, divided into 11 PVS theories and 3,300 lines of PVS. This required two person-months over a four-month period. Type checking was done for consistency, but no theorem proving was done. The hardest part was inferring the state variables from the informal requirements. The process of formalizing the requirements revealed 86 issues of various types and severity. Most of the problems were found just by writing the PVS, not by type checking. (Crow & DeVito 1998)

Space Shuttle HAC This Shuttle project involved the formal specification of a part of the Jet Selection software. The Vernier/Alt. function handles rotation of the Space Shuttle and has 31 of the 38 jets, or 11 of the 14 groups at its disposal. The algorithms for selecting the combinations of jets to accomplish the desired rotation were expressed, in the informal documentation, as 70 pages of low level diagrams and tables. (Crow & DeVito 1998)

The formal specifications were expressed in PVS as functions of input sequences to outputs. Any state information was implicitly defined as a finite sequence of inputs or as traces. The main problem in this project was that the informal specification diagrams were at a code level. Formal specification was more a matter of reverse engineering. The formal PVS consists of 500 lines written as eight theories. This took one person-month over three calendar months. Verification involved proving 12 property lemmas. Six problems were found by the formalizing process, including one failed proof. The resulting formal specification is simpler than the original diagrams might have indicated. (Crow & DeVito 1998)

Space Shuttle HAC The Space Shuttle Heading Alignment Cylinder (HAC) defines the proper position and trajectory for atmospheric re-entry. The original specifications for this system were in 20 pages of tables and prose. The formal specifications were copied, almost verbatim, using the PVS Table feature. PVS provides type correctness conditions, which include proofs of coverage and disjointness for the conditions in the PVS Tables. Two tables were constructed, comprising about 200 lines and taking two weeks through revision. (Crow & DeVito 1998)

Formalizing was fairly easy because of the small size, but the authors expressed concern about scaling this method to larger systems. Problems encountered include unstable assumptions, under-specified conditions, and assumptions that depended on domain knowledge. All of these are good reasons to formalize a specification. (Crow & DeVito 1998)

Space Shuttle 3E/O The last of the four Space Shuttle projects being reported used Stanford's Murϕ (pronounced like "murphy") finite state verification system. Three Engines Out (3E/O) is a fault handling system that deals with mode switching and exception handling, and has little algorithmic complexity. It determines the abort contingency during ascent if three of the main engines fail. Its input and state spaces lack an easily recognized structure, so type checking and theorem proving were not expected to be effective methods. Murϕ uses a brute force method of enumerating the entire input and state space, then checking the sequencing constraints, transitions, and invariants (from crucial properties) for all reachable states. (Crow & DeVito 1998)

The informal specifications consisted of 70 pages of prose, pseudo-code, flowcharts and tables. Initial experiments with Murϕ resulted in models too large to compile. Some abstraction of the state machines was done and the result was two main functions of 1,200 lines, including 12 invariants. The Murϕ specification and analysis took one and a half person-months. Of the 18 errors found, only one logic error was found and that was also revealed by traditional analysis. The other errors, undocumented assumptions, inconsistencies, imprecise terminology, redundancies and the like, were newly discovered through the formal specification process. (Crow & DeVito 1998)

Space Station High Level Fault Detection In this project for the International space station, a subsystem called Fault Detection Isolation and Recovery (FDIR) was specified at a high level in PVS. This is a system that involves many on-board computers. It detects faults, isolates them to the smallest component it can, and attempts recovery by restarting or switching to a redundant component. (Esterbrook et al. 1998)

The 18 pages of PVS took two person-months to write. It was automatically type checked and for syntax and parameter consistency. The PVS Proof Assistant was used for a variety of proofs and some 15 issues were identified. (Esterbrook et al. 1998)

Space Station Communications Bus Fault Detection The same FDIR mechanism as in the previous project was specified at a lower level, and only for the communications bus controller. The original specifications were in natural language with supporting flow charts. As part of independent verification, the requirements were coded into tabular form using SCR (not expanded in the source paper, probably the Software Cost Reduction System). (Esterbrook et al. 1998)

The 15-page specification required one and a half person-months over four calendar months. (It is unclear whether the 15 pages refers to the original or the formal specification.) This was type checked and properties tested with the SCR Checker. Dynamic properties were tested by translating to PROMELA and using the SPIN model checker. Each of the formalizing stages: tabularizing, static checking and dynamic checking found errors. (Esterbrook et al. 1998)

Cassini Deep Space Probe This is the third of three projects in a report on fault detection and recovery systems on spacecraft. Fault tolerance is important for Cassini because it is expected to operate far away, for a long time and without human intervention. The original requirements were 85 pages long. (Esterbrook et al. 1998)

The formal specifications were coded in 15 pages of OMT (an object-oriented modeling tool) diagrams, and 25 pages of PVS. Verification included proving 24 PVS lemmas. The specification and verification took 12 person-months and identified 37 issues. (Esterbrook et al. 1998)

CONCLUSIONS

A table in the appendix summarizes information from all 24 projects surveyed. It is difficult and dangerous to draw conclusions from a research survey like this because the results are not statistically valid, but some trends can be seen.

Most of the projects surveyed were safety critical, but these are clearly not the only projects to which formal methods are being applied. In the Unites States, the majority of formal methods projects have been for NASA or to answer government aviation standards, but U. S. private industry is represented in this survey, and for non-safety critical systems. Europe seems to be the only area that has found formal methods useful for ground transportation systems. While the industries represented are few, considering the size of the survey, the representation is broad enough to show that formal methods are not the exclusive domain any one industry, or any one group of related industries.

The variety of formal methods chosen by the different projects shows that no one or two are dominant, and the detailed comments indicate that different formal languages are chosen based on how well they fit the project. Despite the diversity, Z and PVS seem clear front-runners, being used on five projects each. SCR and μCRL are the only other formal languages that show up in more than one project. The fact that Z was used in the CICS project, the earliest reported, and in very recent projects, might say something about its pervasiveness.

This survey attempted to report on the sizes of the projects chosen, but the diversity in the way specification size is stated in the papers and the lack of code size metrics for so many projects, makes comparison impossible. The specification effort, where reported, could be converted to a common unit, but it is probably not valid to compare an effort that was part of the development cycle, like that for CICS, to validation for licensing, like the Darlington effort. Even some of the specification efforts that were part of development were really part of independent verification, which makes comparison difficult. All that can really be said about size is to point out the largest success stories: CICS, Tektronix, Météor, Darlington Nuclear, U. K. Civil Aviation, and say that they surely demonstrate that formal methods can be scaled up to industrial size projects. Two of those large projects provided evidence of more than just scalability, by formalizing as part of the development cycle. For the CICS project, IBM reported a saving of effort, not a cost due to formal methods, and the Météor project remarkably found zero defects in its testing. (King 1993), (Behm et al. 1999)

Formal verification was inconsistently applied in the projects surveyed. Only a few projects had the tools for automated proofs. It is not clear why automated proving tools are not as widely available as the specification languages and tools. That seems to be the greatest impediment to wide acceptance of formal methods.

Even so, this survey makes clear that formal methods, when properly applied, can be a valuable and cost effective asset to almost any software development project.

REFERENCES

Behm, P., Benoit, P., Faivre, A. & Meynadier, J-M. (1999 February). Météor: "A Successful Application of B in a Large Project". [Postscript file], 19 pages. By private E-mail from: Jean-Marc.Meynadier@matra-transport.fr [1999 March].

Boswell, A. (1995). "NATO Air Command and Control System Security Policy in Z". IEEE Transactions on Software Engineering, 21(2), 63-68.

Collins, B.P., Nicholls, J.E. & Sorensen, I.H. (December 1987). "Introducing Formal Methods: The CICS Experience With Z". 11 pages. IBM Technical Report TR12.260.

Craigen, D., Gerhart, S. & Ralston, T. (1995, January). "An International Survey of Industrial Applications of Formal Methods". [2 Postscript files], 118 & 188 pages. Available: http://www.ora.on.ca/ personnel/craigen.html [1999 March].

Crow, J. & DeVito, B. (1998). "Formalizing Space Shuttle Software Requirements". ACM Transactions on Software Engineering and Methodologies, 7(3), 296-326.

Esterbrook, S., Lutz, R., Covington, R., Keyy, J., Ampo, Y. & Hamilton, D. (1998). "Experiences Using Lightweight Formal methods for Requirements Modeling". IEEE Transactions on Software Engineering, 24(1), 4-13.

Groote, J.F., van Vlijmen, S.F.M. & Koorn, J.W.C. (1994 October). "The Safety Guaranteeing System at Station Hoorn-Kersenboorgerd". [Postscript file], 46 pages. Available: http://www.phil.uu.nl/ preprints.html [1999 March].

Hayes, I. (1993) "Applying Formal Specification to the Development of Software in Industry". Hayes, I. (Ed.), Specification Case Studies (pp. 181-201). New York: Prentice Hall.

Huggins, J.K. (1995 July 13). "Kermit: Specification and Validation". [Postscript file], 40 pages. Available: http://www.eecs.umich.edu/gasm/ [1999 March].

Keons, M.J. & Oei, L.H. "A Real Time μCRL Specification of a System for Traffic Regulation at Signalized Intersections". [Postscript file], 23 pages. Available: http://www.wins.uva.nl/research/prog/ reports/reports.html [1999 March].

King, S. (1993) "The Use of Z in the Restructure of IBM CICS". Hayes, I. (Ed.), Specification Case Studies (pp. 202-213). New York: Prentice Hall.

Miller, S.P. & Hoech, K.F. (1997 November 19). "Specifying the Mode Logic of a Flight Guidance System in CoRE". [Postscript file], 124 pages. By private E-mail from: spmiller@cca.rockwell.com [1999 March].

Neil, M., Ostrolenk, G., Tobin, M. & Southworth, M. (1998). "Lessons From Using Z to Specify a Software Tool". IEEE Transactions on Software Engineering, 24(1), 15-23.

Nix, C.J. & Collins, B.P., (May 1989). "The Use of Software Engineering, Including the Z Notation In the Development of CICS". 26 pages. IBM Technical Report.

Pfleeger, S.L. & Hatton, L. (1997). "Investigating the

Influence of Formal Methods". IEEE Computer, Feb, 33-43.

van Vlijmen, S.F.M. & van Waveren, A. "Algebraic Specification of a System for Traffic Regulation at Signalized Intersections". [Postscript file], 67 pages. Available: http://www.wins.uva.nl/ research/prog/reports/reports.html [1999 March].

BIOGRAPHY

T. Scott Ankrum is a software designer, project manager and developer with over 22 years of experience in many aspects of computing, from mainframe systems to Graphical User Interface development and client/server design. He has managed projects and led development teams, and has been personally involved in software development from requirements definition to final testing. He has worked mostly in information systems development and maintenance. Mr. Ankrum holds a B.S. degree in Computer Science from American University and is currently pursuing a Master of Software Engineering degree at the University of Maryland. He is a member of the Association for Computing Machinery (ACM).

APPENDIX

This table summarizes the projects, categories and statistics. Information not available is indicated by "n/a." Specification Effort is in person-months.

Project Name	Loca-tion	Sector	Industry	Safety or Security	Part of Project	Relation to Devel.	Language	Verify	Spec. Size	Code Size	Spec. Effort	Suc-cess
CICS	U.K.	private	software	neither	part	develop	Z	no	2,000 pages	48 kloc	9% saved	yes
COBOL reverse eng.	U.K.	private	software	neither	part	develop	Z	no	250 pages	23,320 loc	5	no
SSADM	U.K.	private	software	neither	whole	develop	Z	no	n/a	n/a	n/a	yes
Multinet Gateway	U.S.A.	private	commun-ications	security	whole	verify to certify	Gypsy Ver.Env.	yes	80 pages	n/a	108	yes
Kermit FTP	U.S.A.	academic	commun-ications	neither	whole	academ. exercise	Evol-ving Algebra	yes	40 pages	n/a	n/a	yes
Tektronix	U.S.A.	private	electronic equip.	neither	whole	develop	Z	no	30 pages	200 kloc	n/a	yes
H-P Medi-cal	U.S.A.	private	electronic equip.	neither	whole	develop	HP-SL	no	55 pages	4390 loc	150 loc/day	no
SACEM	France	private	railroad	safety	whole	develop	Hoare & B	yes	n/a	9kloc	20	yes
Hoorn-K rail yard	Nether-lands	private	railroad	safety	part	academ. exercise	μCRL	yes	n/a	n/a	n/a	yes
Météor	France	private	railroad	safety	whole	develop	B	yes	27,800 lemmas	86 Kloc	n/a	yes
Algebraic Traffic Reg.	Nether-lands	academic	traffic	safety	part	academ. exercise	PSF	no	26 pages	n/a	n/a	yes
μCRL Traffic Reg.	Nether-lands	academic	traffic	safety	part	academ. exercise	μCRL	no	9 pages	n/a	n/a	yes
Darlington Nuclear	Canada	private	nuclear power	safety	whole	verify to license	SCR	yes	n/a	26 kloc	420	yes
NATO Cmd & Cntl	U.K.	military	command & control	security	part	develop	Z	yes	11-20 lines, 65 schemas	n/a	n/a	yes
Traffic Alert Avoid	U.S.A.	gov't	aviation	safety	whole	maintain standard	State charts	not yet	7,000 lines	n/a	n/a	yes
Flight Guidance	U.S.A.	private	aviation	safety	part	shadow develop	CoRE	no	75 pages	n/a	0.933	yes
UK Civil Aviation	U.K.	gov't	aviation	safety	part	develop	VDM CCS state mach	no	n/a	200,000 loc	n/a	yes
Space Shuttle GPS	U.S.A.	gov't	space	safety	whole	develop	PVS	no	110 pages, 3300 lines	n/a	2	yes
Space Shuttle JS	U.S.A.	gov't	space	safety	part	develop	PVS	yes	8 theories, 500 lines	n/a	1	yes
Shuttle HAC	U.S.A.	gov't	space	safety	whole	develop	PVS	yes	200 lines	n/a	2 weeks	yes
Shuttle 3E/O	U.S.A.	gov't	space	safety	whole	develop	Murφ	yes	1,200 lines	n/a	1.5	yes
Space Sta. FDIR	U.S.A.	gov't	space	safety	part	develop	PVS	yes	18 pages	n/a	2	yes
Space Sta. FDIR Bus	U.S.A.	gov't	space	safety	part	develop	SCR	yes	15 pages	n/a	1.5	yes
Cassini	U.S.A.	gov't	space	safety	part	develop	PVS OMT	yes	40 pages	n/a	12	yes

Three Types of Systems Engineering Implementation

Sarah A. Sheard
Software Productivity Consortium
2214 Rock Hill Rd. Herndon, Virginia 21070
sheard@software.org

Abstract. INCOSE has been bedeviled by arguments about the definition of systems engineering. Many definitions have appeared, but the only one that is widely accepted is so broad as to be almost a tautology. As a result, INCOSE has been unable to answer many questions in a way that most members can accept.

This paper claims that systems engineering can be defined in a way that leads to clean answers to many questions. This definition claims that what people have been calling "systems engineering" can be split into three basic implementations or types of systems engineering: ***Discovery***, a discipline or specialist type that involves significant analysis, particularly of the problem space; ***Program Systems Engineering***, a coordination or generalist type that emphasizes the solution space and technical and human interfaces; and ***Approach***, a process type that can (and should) be performed by any engineer. Such a breakout resolves controversies and has implications on systems engineering training, research, processes, standards, and promulgation.

INTRODUCTION: THE PROBLEM

"But that's not systems engineering!" This phrase has been stated frequently on the INCOSE discussion list server. One member mentions what he or she clearly thinks is systems engineering, usually an aspect of coordination that has little to do with analysis. Another member then retorts that what is described may be program controls, but it is not systems engineering. Could it be that INCOSE members do not share a common definition of systems engineering?

"Why can't we impose systems engineering on the commercial world?" "How can we justify the expense of performing systems engineering?" These issues, too, arise periodically on the discussion list.

Other questions that are often raised but not yet answered fall into the following categories:

Definition. Isn't systems engineering just solving problems according to the scientific method? Isn't systems engineering turning a complex problem into a statement of objective function? Isn't concurrent engineering just good systems engineering? How does systems engineering relate to integrated product teams? Can you do systems engineering outside the field of systems engineering (for example, in law, education, or social science)? How does systems engineering fit with program management or disciplines such as software? Is it a discipline, a process, an approach, a program phase?

People. Who are systems engineers? Is systems engineering a job title, or does it describe anyone who wants to think about the larger system that a product fits into, or only people with "Systems Engineering" degrees, or something certifiable by Texas?

Value. What is the value of performing systems engineering? What are the benefits of systems engineering? How do you convince a manager to fund systems engineering?

Training. How should a systems engineer be educated? What on-the-job training is important?

Tools. What tools do systems engineers use? What tools can provide support for everything systems engineering does, in an integrated manner?

Measurement and assessment. How do you measure systems engineering? How do you assess a research and development organization, a maintenance organization, or an order fulfillment organization against a systems engineering model?

Standards. Who should use systems engineering standards, and how should they use them? Do the various standards apply differently to different implementations of systems engineering? How do systems engineering standards apply to a small company making piece parts or consumer goods?

Research. What kind of research is needed to make systems engineering a discipline on par with electrical or mechanical engineering?

Future. How is systems engineering going to change in the future?

These questions, when answered, will define systems

engineering in a manner that will help INCOSE turn systems engineering into more of a science—predictable, repeatable, trainable, and usable for improvements to the products of the world.

Many books and papers have attempted to define systems engineering (Kasser 1996, Bahill 1996, Blanchard 1998, Lake 1996, Senglaub 1996, Harwell 1996, Sheard 1996a, and many others). But they have not provided answers to these questions.

INCOSE needs a broad yet detailed description of systems engineering. This description should apply to most implementations and encompass most of what has been claimed about systems engineering, without being confusing or chaotic. It should also suggest a way to define products and directions for INCOSE. A definition meeting these criteria is suggested here, in the form of three types of implementations: ***Discovery***, ***Program Systems Engineering***, and ***Approach***.

THREE TYPES

Type 1. *Discovery*. This is a specialist-type implementation of systems engineering in the form of (large) groups of "systems engineers" performing primarily systems analysis. This kind of systems engineering was one of the first recognized kind types. Several cases are very well characterized in (Hughes 1998), which describes the SAGE computer project, Intercontinental Ballistic Missile development, the Boston Central Artery/Tunnel project, and Arpanet/Internet. Air traffic control is another example. In this type of implementation, the problem space is incredibly complex. Modeling the problem space, and really understanding it, is most of the goal in ***Discovery*** implementations.

An unambiguous and unarguable statement of objective function, along with the models and analyses behind it, provides most of the value of Type 1 systems engineering.

The models and analyses created in ***Discovery*** implementations include requirements modeling, system behavior modeling, environmental and system simulation, reliability or survivability analysis, orbital analyses (for space systems), and contingency scenarios, to name a few. The output of ***Discovery*** systems engineering includes relationships between functionality and design implementation, cost and risk to achieve performance, technical feasibility, and new ways to allocate functionality. Analysis results include models from which a solution can be designed in a subsequent phase.

Type 2. *Program Systems Engineering*. The Defense Systems Management Guide (DSMC 1990) describes a generalist type of systems engineering in a way that sounds a lot like program management. A check of recent INCOSE proceedings books showed about two thirds of the papers were talking about ***Program Systems Engineering***. In this implementation, specific people are designated "the systems engineers" and made responsible for the top-level design of the system, including system budgets, for specification of the pieces, and for coordinating the build and integration of the pieces. Large programs using ***Program Systems Engineering*** tend to designate a group of people as "systems engineers," while smaller programs often call out a "chief engineer" or a sole "systems engineer."

Program Systems Engineering contains less emphasis on systems analysis than ***Discovery*** because the problem space is more precedented (commercial communication satellites, for example), and the unprecedented aspect is how the pieces fit together to provide a new variation on a type of service (new communication frequency, higher power, different stabilization mechanisms, etc.) The systems engineering types called "discovery" and "reduction to practice" in (Dahlberg 1999) match these first two types.

In some cases, ***Program Systems Engineering*** is the follow-on to ***Discovery***, which defined the overall problem and showed that a solution is feasible. ***Program Systems Engineering*** then creates that system.

The emphasis in ***Program Systems Engineering*** is on producing cost-effective solutions that meet quality and schedule criteria. Organizational processes can be defined and improved to standardize this type of systems engineering. Process standards and assessment models such as EIA 632 and EIA/IS 731, while they may apply somewhat to the other two implementations of systems engineering, apply particularly to ***Program Systems Engineering***.

Type 3. *Approach*. The previous two types of systems engineering apply to large, complex systems. Can it truly be said that "systems engineering" is performed on smaller or less complex systems, such as the subsystems that are integrated by the "systems engineers" of ***Program Systems Engineering***? Yes, and in this case (***Approach***), systems engineering is implemented as a process or approach.

Approach is the systems engineering that every engineer must perform on the product, including understanding risks, understanding the operational need, clarifying requirements before jumping to a solution, doing at least informal trade studies to make decisions, and so on through the process or focus areas of the chosen capability model. This is the kind of systems engineering that translates to toasters and cell phones. It is different from coordination or management as in ***Program Systems Engineering—Approach*** is what the individual engineer does. ***Approach*** is the set of lifecycle roles as applied on a small project or as implemented on a small, commercial development project.

Although systems engineering capability models were created with ***Program Systems Engineering*** in mind, all their process areas can be used also in a much smaller way by an individual engineer, whether writing a symposium paper or building a receiver power supply. Systems life cycles can be adapted to apply to any type of engineering that is performed using a systems engineering approach.

This type of systems engineering is most readily implemented in the commercial arena, although large commercial endeavors might implement ***Program Systems Engineering*** as well. This is also the type that you can first convince subsystems engineers, such as software engineers, to start using. Eventually, when this type proves meritorious (by increasing communication with customers and customer satisfaction and decreasing interface problems, for example), some of the larger software engineering efforts may institutionalize the implementation of systems engineering for software as ***Program Systems Engineering***. See also (Roe 1996).

Many people call much of ***Approach*** just good management or just good engineering. But the systems engineering community is beginning to develop a body of knowledge to help with managing or engineering well, and this body of knowledge goes by the name of "systems engineering."

Table 1 summarizes these three types and also notes how they affect many of the aspects of systems engineering implied in the questions in the introduction. Note that what seemed insoluble three pages ago can now be scoped out in a few words.

Table 1. Three Types of Systems Engineering Implementation

	Type 1	Type 2	Type 3
Name	***Discovery***	***Program Systems Engineering***	***Approach***
Also known as	Specialist systems engineering Concept exploration "SYSTEMS engineering" "The engineering discipline applied to the science of complexity" (Senglaub 1996) A discipline	Coordinator or generalist systems engineering Technical side of program management "systems ENGINEERING" "Reduction to practice" (Dahlberg 1999) Concurrent engineering	The systems engineering process Just good common sense Problem solving using the scientific method What every engineer should do
Main goal	Verifying that the problem can be solved and finding a feasible solution to the problem. Very high complexity in **problem space.**	Maintaining focus on customer need, trading off solutions, providing a cost-effective solution on time and under budget. Complexity in **solution space** and possibly organizational.	Not jumping to a solution, functions before objects, maintaining focus on what customer really wants, ensuring integration. Complexity in the **variation of applications,** and possibly product lines.
Timing	Can be the initial phase of creating a large system	Can follow ***Discovery*** in building a large system	Cradle to grave
Consists of	Systems analysis and modeling; mission analysis, threat analysis. Unprecedented problems.	Unprecedented ways of putting together largely precedented components to meet a new variation of a known need.	A method or process for performing any kind of engineering
Examples	Postwar large projects like Atlas, SAGE, even Boston Central Artery/Tunnel, air traffic control, space missions, war fighting capability	Realization of satellites, airplanes, avionics systems, control systems, large information systems, especially those including hardware	Elevators, consumer goods, software, subsystems and components of larger systems, and many applications outside engineering
References	(Hughes 1998, McClinton 1994, Shishko 1999)	(Jeffroy et al. 1999, Kasser 1994 and 1996, Sheard 1992)	(Harwell 1996, Bahill 1996)

	Discovery	*Program Systems Engineering*	*Approach*
Customers	Generally government, including military	Government, or sometimes commercial	Usually commercial
Precedence	Unprecedented problems, completely new solutions	Precedented problems, largely precedented subsystems, new solutions	Precedented problems and solutions, with innovation here and there
How measured	Progress toward technical problem. Somewhat research-like, so process measures are not very common or very predictive.	Precedented project measures such as in the combined Practical Systems/Software Measurement guidebook.	Typical engineering measures with a bit more in the up-front, validation, and customer satisfaction areas.
How assessed	No capability models address complex analysis well	EIA/IS 731 and predecessor models assume this as the typical type of systems engineering	Must be tailored. Rarely assessed to date.
Standards	None apply well	EIA 632 and IEEE 1220 (Velman 1999)	IEEE 1220
Benefits and Value	Solve problems not otherwise solvable. Generate innovations and revolutionary approaches. (Schoening 2000)	Prevents problems with interfaces and customer dissatisfaction downstream. Prevents test problems and rework. Helps organize work.	Same as ***Program Systems Engineering*** but on a smaller scale. To get benefits, teach software engineers and other subsystem engineers to do this type.
Funding	Systems engineering constitutes the bulk of the program	Often level of effort, sometimes overhead, but increasingly activity-based	Nothing specific, just do your job a different way – better and maybe cheaper (reduce test time or rework).
Training	Directly relevant education is critical. Mathematics, electrical engineering, computer science, systems analysis, general engineering, astrophysics (for space systems), domain areas, training in the analysis tools. "System Technology" (Grange 1999) How to make sense out of uncertainty, give form to the formless, and create organizational structures that help promote understanding (Schoening 2000).	Broad variety of engineering courses as well as others (statistics, business, chemistry or physics, even liberal arts with technical minor), organizational dynamics, domain areas. Formerly specialist engineers (especially controls or software) who have broadened their expertise. Much on-the-job training. Organizational processes (budgeting process, change requests, marketing and business, engineering courses outside employee's specialty), systems engineering processes and process assessment, process improvement. Project and program management and measurement. "Primary systems" (Grange	Training in the engineering discipline used to make the product, plus additional training in the systems engineering process. Lower-level systems (Grange 1999)

		1999). Also (Plowman 1999).	

	Discovery	*Program Systems Engineering*	*Approach*
Tools/Methods	Systems analysis and modeling tools and methods, such as behavior diagrams (Alford 1994), dynamic simulators, and complex nests of models. Simple models showing relationships rather than details, including analogies (Schoening 2000).	Office tools (word processing, spreadsheets, briefing tools, etc.) Particularly, those tools called out by the program processes (templates). Meeting tools (especially if development is geographically distributed).	None in particular, although requirements management tools are becoming more popular.
Primary Roles (Sheard 1996)	System Analyst, Requirements Owner, Information Manager, Technical Manager	System Designer, Coordinator, Technical Manager, Customer Interface, Glue, Validation and Verification, Requirements Owner	Requirements Owner, System Designer, Validation and Verification, Logistics and Operations, also Customer Interface and Technical Manager
Evolution	Decreasing numbers of huge programs are available. Needs to evolve to more civilian work, but then a major aspect is politics (less important in aerospace/defense programs of the past). As software builds up its store of reusable objects and becomes "object oriented" (as hardware systems have been at least since Henry Ford's assembly lines), then many of the current ***Discovery*** software system projects will become more like ***Program Systems Engineering***.	Pyramids to present day. Probably the need will never change. However, when money gets tight, this type of systems engineering tends to be targeted as "non-value-added" and cut. Need to evolve clear statement of return on investment of systems engineering activities under given conditions.	Should be taught to all engineers. This type is "below the radar" of many managers, so practitioners can suffer lack of recognition. Very bottom-up, so it can be hard to institutionalize. Eventually, when this type proves its worth in new fields (by increasing communication with customer and customer satisfaction and decreasing engineering interface and test problems and rework), the systems engineering effort in some of these may become larger and more formalized, like ***Program Systems Engineering***.
Research needed	Methods for improving analysis quality and applicability to the real world. Easier and faster simulations. Lessons learned in understanding problem spaces and demonstrating feasibility.	Cost-effectiveness of processes and organizational structures (return on investment). Coordination with program management, system test, software and other associated disciplines—best practices.	How to implement "systems engineering in the small" where not used before. Benefits of implementation. How to tailor systems engineering standards and assessments for small implementations.

Table 1. Three Types of Systems Engineering Implementation (continued)

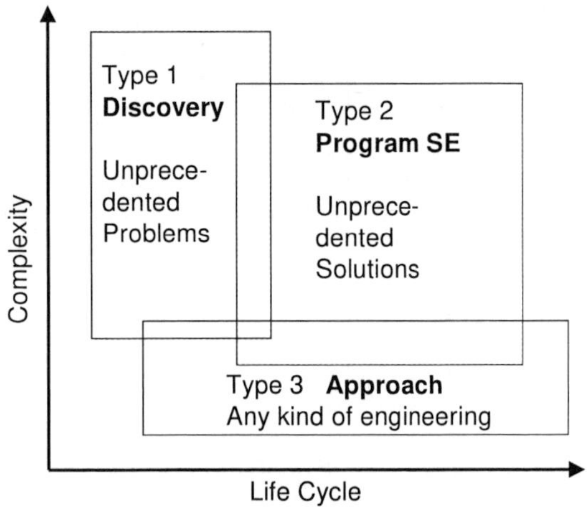

Figure 1. Three Types of Implementation

INTERFACES AMONG TYPES OF IMPLEMENTATION

All three types. Figure 1 shows how the three types overlap. ***Approach*** can be used with any kind of engineering and addresses the full life cycle, but when the complexity increases, people tend to split off a separate group called "systems engineers" or "systems engineering." Two main types of complex situations stand out, the type where the complexity is due to unprecedented problems (***Discovery***) and the type when the problems are fairly well known but the solutions are very complex (***Program Systems Engineering***).

Example. (Cook, Lawson, and Allison 1999) show a hierarchy of military systems. Many of these "Systems of Systems" (military task forces, "Defence Organisations") would require ***Discovery*** systems engineering, whereas the "Primary Systems" (man-in-the-loop weapon systems, communications networks) would probably require ***Program Systems Engineering.*** Lower level systems (buildings, rifles, thermostats) would use ***Approach*** systems engineering.

Example. (Grange 1999) also shows three types of systems engineering as a continuum.

Type 1—Type 2. Clearly ***Discovery*** and ***Program Systems Engineering*** overlap. The difference is primarily that the focus in the first type is on analysis and problem space, and the focus in the second type is on solution space and getting a product out. However, note that even ***Discovery*** implementations eventually end up creating a realized system. It is often obvious to the practitioners when the focus of the program shifts from analyzing the problem to getting something built. This is the boundary between ***Discovery*** and ***Program Systems Engineering*** in time. Additionally, ***Program Systems Engineering*** implementations also have a short ***Discovery*** phase when deciding what to propose. Sometimes an organization has "trappers" who specialize in this concept exploration phase and "skinners" who take over to get the system built.

Example. In one government agency, a group called Systems Engineering performs analysis-intensive, future-oriented, and big-picture-oriented (***Discovery***) tasks. ***Program Systems Engineering*** is not recognized as such, and is performed by integrated product teams (IPTs) for the various products. However, the engineers on IPTs recognize that they are performing systems engineering and wish the Systems Engineering group would be a bit more helpful to them.

Example. (Carlok et al. 1999) describes top level systems-of-systems as requiring political, economic, operational, and technical considerations, in that order. These are ***Discovery*** systems. For more typical ***Program Systems Engineering*** developments, the order is reversed. This paper also shows three levels of "systems-of-systems" engineering, of which the first two can be mapped to ***Discovery*** and the third can be mapped to ***Program Systems Engineering***. The difference between the first two levels is that the first level is primarily political and economic, and the second level is primarily analysis that verifies the technical and operational characteristics.

Type 2—Type 3. ***Program Systems Engineering*** and ***Approach*** both concentrate on the realization of systems. Both types exist on most large programs. Figure 2 shows a typical large-program structure that has a ***Program Systems Engineering*** organization at the system level, and systems engineering tasks that are performed in an ***Approach*** manner at subsystem and element levels. (Adamsen 1996) shows similar tiers of integrated product teams.

Example. Most people who want to apply systems engineering to commercial companies or to software development are thinking ***Program Systems Engineering***, but they would probably be better off starting

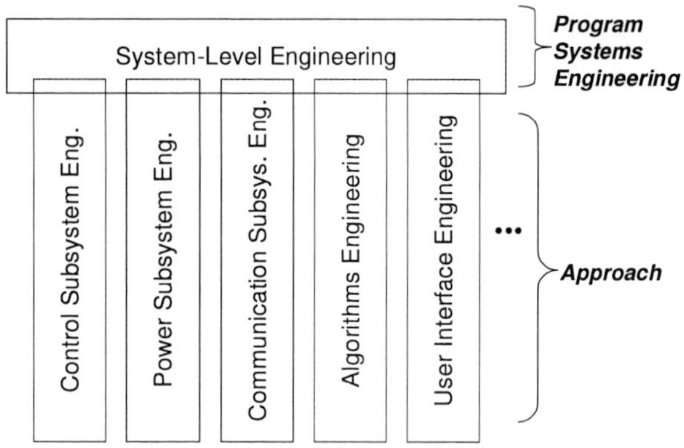

Figure 2. Program Systems Engineering and Approach

with *Approach*. See (Jackson 1996).

Type 2—Program management. ***Program Systems Engineering*** and program management are closely related. (Kasser 1996) concludes that systems engineering is just management with an extra emphasis on requirements. In addition, the systems engineering capability models disagree whether "integration of disciplines" is in the Engineering (SE-CMM) or Management (EIA/IS 731) category. INCOSE and the Project Management Institute intend to get together and work out the definitions and interfaces between these two disciplines. The author suspects that the overlap is great and both are solutions to the same need: solid management of interfaces among technical groups.

CONCLUSION

Many questions can be answered and problems can be resolved when systems engineering is viewed as consisting of more than one basic thing. Consider the three types discussed in this paper when you talk about the kind of systems engineering you do or should do. INCOSE technical working groups should address these three types separately, e.g., measurement of ***Discovery*** systems engineering, measurement of ***Program Systems Engineering***, measurement of the systems engineering ***Approach***, or assessment of the three types. All work products of INCOSE should address one or more types explicitly. For example, the Systems Engineering Handbook might specify it is for ***Program Systems Engineering***, and/or include tailoring guidance for ***Approach*** and perhaps ***Discovery*** implementations.

If INCOSE adopts this definition, the future direction will be clarified, as will its relationship to other disciplines such as program management and software.

REFERENCES

Adamsen, Paul B. Jr. "Controlling the Chaos: An Integrated Approach to Managing a System Development Project." *Proceedings of INCOSE*, 1996.

Alford, Mack. "Issue Driven Design: Planning and Managing Design Iterations." *Proceedings of NCOSE*, 1994.

Bahill, Terry. "The Design Methods Comparison Project" web site: http://www.sie.arizona.edu/sysengr /methods2/

Bahill, A. Terry and Frank F. Dean. "What is Systems Engineering? A Consensus of Senior Systems Engineers." *Proceedings of INCOSE*, 1996.

Blanchard, Benjamin S. *System Engineering Management*, 2nd Ed., Wiley, NY, 1998.

Carlock, Paul G., Steven C. Decker, John A. Scardina, Robert E. Fenton, and Charles W. Pate. "Agency-level Systems Engineering for Systems of Systems," *Proceedings of INCOSE*, 1999.

Cook, S. C., E. Lawson, and J. S. Allison. "Towards a Unified Systems Methodology for Australian Defence Systems-of-Systems." *Proceedings of INCOSE*, 1999.

Dahlberg, Sten, Message posted to INCOSE list server, October 1999.

Defense Systems Management College. *Systems Engineering Management Guide*, January 1990.

Frantz, W. Forrest. "The Impact of Systems Engineering on Quality and Schedule, Empirical Evidence." *Proceedings of INCOSE* 1995.

Grange, Gordon W. "Systems Engineering Education – Academic or Vocational?" *Proceedings of INCOSE* 1999.

Harwell, Richard. "Systems Engineering Is More Than Just a Process." *Proceedings of INCOSE*, 1996.

Hughes, Thomas P. *Rescuing Prometheus*, 1998, Pantheon Books, NY, ISBN 0-679-41151-8.

Hyer, Scott A. "An Integrated Approach to Systems Engineering Training." *Proceedings of NCOSE*, 1994.

Jackson, Scott. "Introducing systems engineering into a traditionally commercial organization." *Proceedings of INCOSE*, 1996.

Jeffroy, Alain, Jean-Michel Nouge, M. Cambet, Ron Ashpole, Jesus Gonzalez, P. Heller, and T. Nevelling. "Airbus Systems Engineering Policy," Proceedings *of INCOSE* 1999.

Kasser, Joe. Systems Engineering, Myth or Reality? *Proceedings of INCOSE* 1996.

Kasser, Joe. "Gaining the Competitive Edge through Effective Systems Engineering." *Proceedings of NCOSE* 1994.

Lake, Dr. Jerome G. (Jerry). "Unraveling the SE Lexicon," *Proceedings of INCOSE* 1996.

McClinton, David F. "Driving the First Stake in the Ground." *Proceedings of INCOSE* 1994.

Plowman, Catherine. "Systems Engineering Training Architecture for the US Department of Energy," *Proceedings of INCOSE* 1999.

Roe, Charles L. "Project Management and Systems Engineering in an IPD Environment." *Proceedings of INCOSE*, 1996.

Schoening, William W. Personal communication, 2000.

Senglaub, Michael. "Systems Engineering: A problem of perception." *Proceedings of INCOSE*, 1996.

Sheard, Sarah A. "Capturing the Systems Engineering Process," *Proceedings of NCOSE*, 1992.

Sheard, Sarah A. "Twelve Systems Engineering Roles," *Proceedings of INCOSE*, 1996.

Shishko, Robert, Jacob R. Matijevic. "Summary of Results from the Risk Management Program for the Mars Microrover Flight Experiment," *Proceedings of INCOSE*, 1999.

Velman, John R., E. R. Widmann, and G. J. Hudak. "Standards: A perspective and some future directions for the systems engineering community."

Proceedings of INCOSE, 1999.

BIOGRAPHY

Sarah A. Sheard has twenty years' experience in systems engineering, including hardware systems such as satellites and software systems such as air traffic control. Currently at the Software Productivity Consortium, Ms. Sheard helps companies activate systems engineering process improvement efforts and integrate the software and systems engineering aspects of both development work and process improvement efforts.

Ms. Sheard's previous INCOSE papers attempting to define systems engineering include "Twelve Systems Engineering Roles" in 1996 "The Frameworks Quagmire, A Brief Look" in 1997, and "Systems Engineering Standards Compared" in 1998.

Ms. Sheard is currently the chair of INCOSE's Measurement Technical Committee and in the past has served INCOSE as chair of the Communications Committee and as Programs Chair of the Washington Metropolitan Area Chapter. Ms. Sheard received a bachelor's degree in chemistry from the University of Rochester and a master's degree in chemistry from the California Institute of Technology.

Examining the Necessity and Benefits of Systems Engineering in the Trenches

Gregory G. Chapin
The MITRE Corporation
HQ USEUCOM/ ECJ25-S
Geb. 2302, Zi. 109
Patch Kaserne
70569 Stuttgart

Abstract. This paper examines the necessity and benefits of systems engineering in the trenches[1]. Planner, orchestrator, negotiator, relationship builder, and communicator are key roles for a systems engineer to take in the trenches. The systems engineering approaches used and roles taken to provide technical and business process engineering solutions required to implement collaboration[2] that operators used successfully to coordinate and approve fixed targets during the Operation Allied Force air campaign are documented. System objectives were: modify the existing process, leveraging collaboration to improve the effectiveness of information processes; improve product quality; and benefit federated efforts by geographically separated partners. This systems engineering effort took place at the United States European Command (USEUCOM) from February 1998 to June 1999 and continues as of this publication. USEUCOM targets community representatives estimate that using collaboration decreased target approval time from 2-4 days to 2-3 hours. Participants indicated collaboration improved process efficiencies, product quality, and synchronization. The success increased interest in and expansion of collaboration within the intelligence and operations communities, including expansion to the North Atlantic Treaty Organization (NATO). Clearly, the results and impact on mission effectiveness indicate systems engineering in the trenches is both necessary and beneficial.

INTRODUCTION

"The command, control, communications, and computer (C4) support to Operation Allied Force was highly successful. Several important communications capabilities saw their first significant combat application: use of Web-based technologies for coordination and information sharing; video teleconferencing for command, control, and coordination; and e-mail for coordination and tasking."[3] This paper describes the system engineering approaches used and roles taken to provide collaboration at the United States European Command (USEUCOM) to support portions of the targeting process during Operation Allied Force. The main points presented are:

1. System need, objectives, and requirements
2. System components
3. Challenges and issues encountered
4. Approach to providing collaborative capabilities: the infrastructure and tools components
5. Approach to applying collaboration to the mission: the people, process, and information components
6. USEUCOM collaborative sessions
7. Results and impact on mission effectiveness
8. Transfer considerations
9. Summary

SYSTEM NEED, OBJECTIVES AND REQUIREMENTS

The system need stemmed from an extended mission that required a continuous and increased production process. The extended air campaign against Serbia lasted 78 days and required an efficient targets development and production process. The USEUCOM Chief of Targets requested that the fixed targets development and nomination process be modified, leveraging collaboration to improve the coordination and approval process. The objective was to improve process efficiencies to increase target availability in support of mission objectives and strike operations.

According to Operation Allied Force participants, it is important to understand the process used prior to

[1] "In the trenches" refers to a systems engineering assignment at an operations or production site with customers and end users.

[2] "Collaboration" is more than just the technological capabilities (e.g. web-based applications, whiteboard, text chat, and audio). For this paper, collaboration includes:

- Technological capabilities
- Collaborative session techniques
- Concept of operations (e.g., process owners, roles and responsibilities, and procedures)
- Standardized product templates

[3] Kosovo/Operation Allied Force After-Action Report to Congress, 31 January, 2000, p.26

applying collaboration in order to fully appreciate the benefits gained after modifying the process to use collaboration. Nine geographically separated organizations coordinated products sequentially. One organization forwarded its initial work as email attachments, message traffic, fax, and/or phone calls to other organizations with different responsibilities. Another organization made product changes and sent the updates to participating organizations. The process continued until the final product was sent to decision-makers for review and approval. Decision-makers either accepted the product information or returned it for further development.

The serial workflow extended the process timeline and provided opportunities to introduce ambiguities and errors. Participants indicated that communicating point-to-point without consensus created confusion, reduced accuracy of product information, and caused duplication of efforts. The organizations involved did not always have a thorough understanding of other organizations' tasks and goals. Therefore, some organizations only understood the purpose, interdependencies, and value of their contributions from a parochial perspective. Process deficiencies made execution and approval too time consuming and difficult due to the following:

- Redundant information flowing to decision-makers
- Sequential coordination and approval by multiple organizations
- Maintaining currency of information and products existing in multiple versions and media types
- Understanding the rationale behind changes to avoid repetitious errors
- Tracking the status of products held for refinement or outstanding action
- Inconsistent quality control and standardization

The systems engineer selected collaboration to address the process deficiencies and inability to meet increased product demand and schedule requirements. The operational objectives and requirements were to:

- Provide collaborative capabilities at multiple geographic sites. The process owner's[4] initial requirement in mid-April 1999 was five geographically dispersed organizations:
  - ➢ Headquarters United States European Command (HQ USEUCOM) Stuttgart, Germany
    - ➢ Targets
    - ➢ Crisis Action Plans
  - ➢ Joint Task Force (JTF) NOBLE ANVIL Naples, Italy: Joint Target cell and Judge Advocate (JA)
  - ➢ United States Air Force Europe (USAFE) Ramstein AB, Germany: 32nd Air Intelligence Squadron (AIS) Targets
  - ➢ Joint Analysis Center (JAC) Royal Air Force (RAF) Molesworth, United Kingdom: JAC Targets

  At the end of Operation Allied Force, four additional organizations participated:
  - ➢ Headquarters United States European Command (HQ USEUCOM) Stuttgart, Germany: Judge Advocate/Operations Law
  - ➢ COMSIXTHFLT Gaeta, Italy: Tomahawk Land Attack Missile (TLAM) Strike Cell, Plans and Targets
  - ➢ Defense Intelligence Agency (DIA)/Joint Staff (JS) J2T Washington DC: Targets
  - ➢ Combined Air Operations Center (CAOC) Vicenza, Italy: CAOC Targets U.S. representatives

  Figure 1 Operation Allied Force Participants depicts the geographic locations of the organizations that participated.

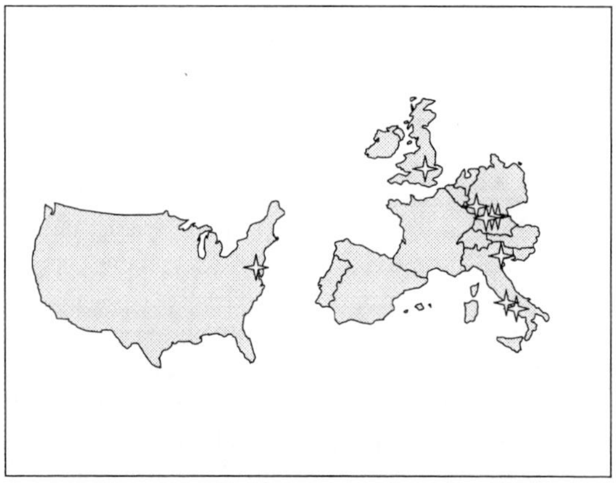

Figure 1 Operation Allied Force Participants

- Engineer a system with acceptable reliability, performance, simplicity, and flexible expansion
- Develop an approach to conduct collaborative sessions to support portions of the overall targeting process
- Modify the business process and apply collaboration to reduce or remove process deficiencies and decrease process timelines

SYSTEM COMPONENTS

The system had the following components:

- People: process owner and participants, the

[4] The process owner is responsible for mission and session focus, participant roles and responsibilities, and results.

USEUCOM Chief of Targets and U.S. targets community representatives from multiple disciplines (e.g., intelligence, operations, legal, and execution)

- Process: current and modified, a portion of the U.S. contribution to the NATO target development and approval process
- Tools: collaborative capabilities (e.g., multi-point text chat, voice audio, and application sharing), briefing slide and web-page software
- Infrastructure: enterprise neT.120 conferencing server and software, Wide Area Network (WAN), site Local Area Networks (LANs), site baseline client workstations and software
- Information: current and accurate targeting information

The systems engineer integrated the system components shown in Figure 2. Planning, orchestration, negotiation, relationship building, and communication skills were necessary to perform this integration.

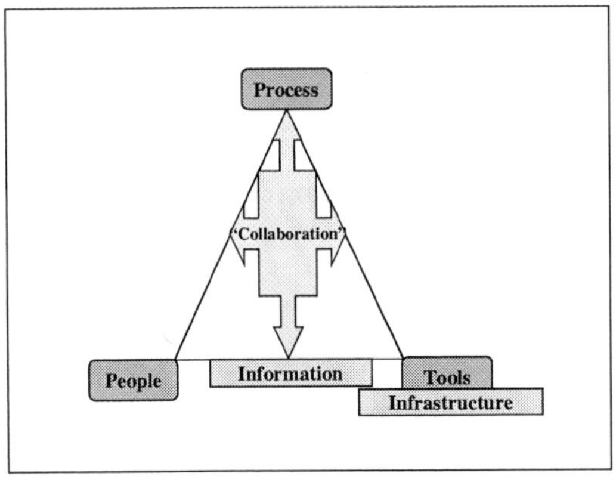

Figure 2 System Components

CHALLENGES AND ISSUES ENCOUNTERED

The systems engineer faced several challenges to meet the system objectives and requirements. Each site had an independent and unique:

- Local Area Network (LAN), hardware and software baseline
- Security accreditation criteria and authority
- Operational user culture and business process

The systems engineer analyzed the Wide Area Network (WAN) and orchestrated the implementation of the enterprise server. The systems engineer did not have authority over personnel. Gaining cooperation required informal influence. Building working relationships between key personnel (e.g., enterprise and site operational, systems/networks, and security) played a key role in asserting informal influence and gaining cooperation.

Environment. USEUCOM has a dynamic Area of Responsibility (AOR). A dynamic AOR requires flexible systems that responsively support expansion to new locations or changing requirements as much as possible. Planning, orchestrating, and communicating with personnel at operational customer sites are subject to spontaneous limited "windows of opportunity". Being prepared for these opportunistic meetings to delegate action, provide or obtain information, and execute actions germane to the systems engineering objective is imperative. Listening to site personnel benefited cooperation. Choosing local solutions improved responsiveness and is a recommended approach as long as the overall system objectives are met.

Systems/Networks. Sites controlled the configuration of their LAN, and software and hardware baseline. Site baselines were unique. The systems engineer looked for system component common denominators across baselines that met the system requirements. The systems engineer orchestrated, negotiated, and coordinated baseline modifications to ensure the availability of necessary capabilities, infrastructure, and interfaces at each site. Relationship building, negotiation, and realistic planning were critical to modifying independently controlled baselines. What may take a few hours to install in a laboratory may take days or months to obtain approval and installation at independent sites within an operational command.

Security Accreditation and Approval to Operate. Each site has an independent security and approval to operate authority. Each authority's criteria varied. As a result, the amount of systems engineering involvement and security requirements varied greatly from site to site. The systems engineer took on the roles of orchestrator and negotiator to ensure security accreditation issues were addressed.

Obtaining accreditation and "approval to operate" for collaboration requires dedicated effort. Cooperatively working with each site's security authority is the recommended approach. Site operational users and systems/network personnel assisted the systems engineer or independently accomplished this task. Security accreditation personnel must be included in the team from the beginning to implement procedural and technical solutions that satisfy *both* collaboration and accreditation requirements.

Operational User Culture and Business Process. Operational personnel had the shortest and fewest "windows of opportunity". The systems engineer gave priority to these "windows of opportunity". Actions taken to build relationships with the operational community included:

- Attending community conferences to meet and get to know users and leadership from multiple organizations
- Learning what tasks users perform by spending time with them during operations in their environment to obtain a feel for the mission objectives, environment, and constraints (e.g., timelines)

This investment yielded significant returns in developing mutual respect and building rapport with the operational community. Nurturing efforts to integrate the process with the appropriate mix of collaboration proved valuable. Moreover, important operational requirements and areas to impact mission effectiveness were highlighted. The intent of system requirements documented in specifications or verbally provided by users may be difficult to understand. Placing systems engineers with users in the operational environment provides a realistic understanding of the intent of individual and aggregate requirements (e.g., how the capability will be used and for what purpose). In addition, the myriad of constraints (e.g., time, footprint, regulations, organizational politics, and funding) with which the system interacts, are more likely to be experienced.

This systems engineering experience clearly demonstrated that *the best technical systems solution may not be the best "systems" solution* because of the numerous constraints and interactions found in an operational environment. According to Operation Allied Force participants, the performance, reliability, and simplicity of the collaborative capabilities were the primary factors that affected acceptance and use. If the important operational requirements are met and mission effectiveness benefits, the system has a higher probability of being sold and used. The key requirements obtained using this systems engineering approach included:

- Capabilities must reside on a baseline workstation. The environment does not allow separate workstations for unique capabilities. Users need access to existing baseline applications, services, and information.
- The capabilities must be *reliable*, tested, and proven in the operational environment (vice a laboratory environment). Operational processes do not allow for reboots or system lockups during sessions. Users defined reliability in terms of system down time to be less than one 15-minute segment per month during crisis operations.
- Capabilities need to be *simple* to allow operators with basic computer skills to participate. Users defined simple collaborative capabilities as someone who has not seen the capability being able to use it after 15-30 minutes of training, supplemented by a two page instruction sheet. Moreover, users can train colleagues after using the capability for 2-3 sessions. A trade off between complex capabilities and keeping the system simple should be made with users. Use of capabilities will probably evolve as the process matures and increased benefits are realized.
- Capabilities must have acceptable *performance* to meet operational timelines
- Capabilities selected should remain in place long enough to resolve technical issues and determine best fit in conjunction with the current/modified processes. *More capabilities are not necessarily better and changing capabilities frequently in search of more productivity will often result in less.*

APPROACH TO PROVIDING COLLABORATIVE CAPABILITIES: THE INFRASTRUCTURE AND TOOLS COMPONENTS

The systems engineer took the role of communicator to obtain capability alternatives from research and development engineers. The system engineer analyzed and determined the best overall systems solution to meet operational, systems/networks, and security requirements within the operational environment and associated constraints at the enterprise and local site levels.

The systems engineer orchestrated and built a systems foundation with systems/networks personnel at the initial organizations requested by the process owner. Obtaining systems/networks and security personnel approval to establish the initial capability at the initial organizations took ten months. Users received insight into the system's potential by using the capability to support a few operational sessions. Users recognized that the system benefited their processes and levied a multi-point audio requirement on 20 January 1999 during a TLAM mission planning session.

The formal multi-point audio requirement proved imperative to meet the operational community's requirement for immediate and daily use during Operation Allied Force. The systems engineer analyzed network topology, performance (e.g., latency, bandwidth) and concept of operations (e.g., roles, responsibilities) to determine the best location for the enterprise conference server. The multi-point requirement and analyses provided operational and systems justification to request systems/networks personnel at HQ USEUCOM install a multi-point server. The systems engineer took on the role of negotiator to obtain cooperation. Negotiations resulted in a planned evaluation between two different conferencing software alternatives that could meet the multi-point audio, standards compliance, and other system requirements. HQ USEUCOM's systems/network staff constraints and competing tasks did not allow this plan to be executed. Three months later, in April 1999, the Chief of Targets requested the capability for immediate use to support Operation Allied Force. However, only one of the conferencing software alternatives was installed and the evaluation had not yet started.

Communication with systems colleagues at other commands uncovered an alternative. Colleagues confirmed the availability of a multi-point conference server approved for use in Hawaii at another command. Operational demands outweighed network latency and reliability concerns from Europe. The system engineer orchestrated and conducted operational tests and demonstrated the viability of this alternative.

The systems engineer used past investments and efforts in conjunction with working relationships developed with enterprise and each site's systems/networks, security, and operational personnel to establish a 3-6 May 1999 initial operational capability. Operational users experienced some audio corruption due to latency during the first hour of each collaborative session. USEUCOM's dependence on a server not under its control also increased mission risk. For this reason, the systems engineer continued to address the need for a local multi-point conference server with HQ USEUCOM's systems/networks personnel.

Successful operational demonstrations of the conference server located in Hawaii allowed the systems engineer to negotiate with HQ USEUCOM's systems/networks personnel and supercede the planned evaluation. The HQ USEUCOM's systems/networks supervisor approved the use of the local multi-point conference server. The May 7 transition to the European based server decreased mission risk as shown by the following results:

- Improved performance
- Resolved latency issues
- Removed dependence on another command's server
- Increased confidence in reliability

The process owner requested the participation of four additional organizations prior to the end of Operation Allied Force. The effort taken to provide a systems solution that supported flexible expansion to new locations allowed the process owner's requests to be satisfied quickly. Figure 3 shows the system infrastructure.

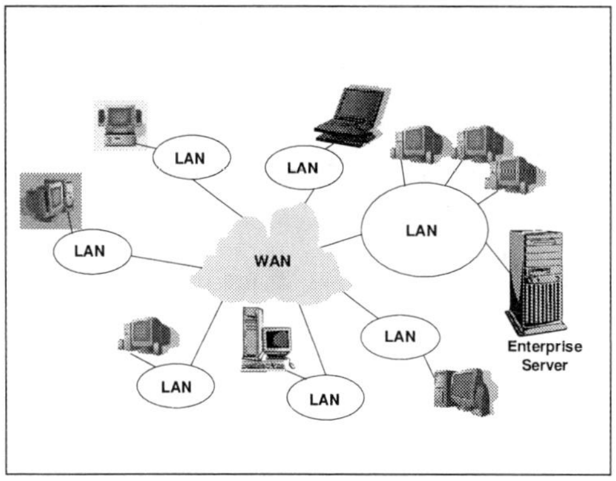

Figure 3 System Infrastructure

Finally, the systems engineer planned for the migration to the intelligence community standard. By communicating with the USEUCOM enterprise architecture planners and operational community directors, the capabilities used during Operation Allied Force are part of the intelligence community standard. This planning and communication eased the potentially turbulent transition and introduction of the new system to the user community.

APPROACH TO APPLYING COLLABORATION TO THE MISSION: THE PEOPLE, PROCESS, AND INFORMATION COMPONENTS

Often in system's development, two of the most critical system components are overlooked and may not even be considered part of "the system". These components are the users and process. Dedicating a significant amount of system engineering resources to understand and integrate the user and process components into the overall system's solution is necessary based on this project's experiences.

The systems engineer requested the command appoint a process owner with existing or delegated authority and responsibility recognized by participating organizations. The command appointed the Chief of Targets as the process owner.

The process owner assigned a veteran user, who had broad operational expertise and professional contacts at participating organizations, to work with the systems engineer. The systems engineer and operational user identified required participant organizations and selected part of the overall targeting process for modification, focusing on coordination and approval by applying collaboration. The user selected a standardized product template with targeting information and imagery as the collaborative session's focus. The systems engineer provided recommendations on how to apply collaboration. The systems engineer and operational user developed a concept of operations and standard operating procedures taking into account process preparation requirements, roles, responsibilities, and system performance. The standard operation procedure used the Keep It Simple Strategy (KISS) since multiple organizations were staffed by three rotating shifts and new temporary users. Collaborative capabilities and techniques selected for application with the modified business process took into account reliability, number of participants, simplicity, performance, business rhythm, timeline constraints, and environment. The three primary capabilities used were text chat, voice audio, and application sharing.

Prior to the first session, the process owner issued a directive to participants. The user representative distributed the concept of operations and standard operating procedure to each participating organization. With the operational user's assistance, the systems engineer orchestrated system testing, a training walk-through of procedures, and a discussion of roles and responsibilities with each organization. The results of the first operational session, compared with the previous process, gave the Chief of Targets confidence to conduct daily sessions.

Defining roles and responsibilities in a Concept of Operations (CONOPs) and preparing for the collaborative sessions is important to achieve success. Session roles (e.g., leader, information coordinator, product developer) and responsibilities assigned took into account the process timeline, experience, control desired, command structure, and number of participating organizations. The interdependent roles and responsibilities required definition for the "before", "during", and "after" phases of the collaborative session. These roles and responsibilities were critical to establish and execute successful sessions. All organizations, except those with the lead role, participated for coordination purposes. Examples of three key roles[5] are described below.

Leader: The leader works with the information coordinator to ensure preparation and execution of collaborative sessions.

Before Session

- Determine what items to review and distribute
- Assign preparation responsibilities
- Identify products to review and revisit during session
- Inform organizations of key personnel and functional skill mix required during session
- Develop agenda and set schedule

During Session

- Run the session and obtain results in a reasonable time frame
- Task development work and issue priorities
- Assign action items and suspenses
- Chair session in close coordination with information coordinator
- Approve or hold information and product release
- Act as final authority on questions and decisions

After Session

- Write and provide summary of session and actions to participants

Information Coordinator: The information coordinator works with the leader to ensure preparation and execution of collaborative sessions. The information coordinator is responsible for information and product management.

Before Session

- Schedule session time and setup conference on server
- Coordinate agenda with session lead organization
- Test participant organizations' systems (e.g., audio checks)
- Gather product information for sessions

During Session

- Manipulate data and share product information with participant organizations
- Make and save final product changes
- Record text log of significant audio discussions, decisions with rationale, actions, due dates, and product hold or approval status

After Session

- Save text chat log and provide to participants
- Post products in proper format for participants, consumers, and next phase of process

Product Developer: The product developer provides product information to the information coordinator before or during sessions.

Before Session

- Perform detailed development, research, and analysis
- Address data and information shortfalls
- Develop product for session review

During Session

- Obtain priorities from lead organization
- Provide rationale or explain product information

After Session

[5] An organization may have multiple roles or role may be shared by multiple organizations.

- Work action items assigned from lead organization and prepare for next session

The systems engineer also planned and orchestrated the necessary product and information management efforts with the information coordinator and user representative. Tasks included:

- Selecting mission application software to use and developing standard product templates to organize information that focused the collaborative session
- Determining information used in session, information structure, and information repository location for products
- Determining product format
- Developing an information flow and structure to transfer and hold product information between various stages in the process
- Developing information change procedures to ensure the currency, accuracy, and integrity of the information. Information change procedures for shared information is critical to provide version control.

The importance of information management to conduct productive collaborative sessions cannot be over emphasized.

USEUCOM COLLABORATIVE SESSIONS

Daily, USEUCOM and US national-targeting agencies held regularly scheduled, collaborative sessions. The standardized template contained specific target information required for approval and aided the communication and coordination process. The template standardized terminology and ensured accurate documentation of required targeting information prior to delivery to executive decision-makers. The collaborative sessions focused on targeting information. Participants used the concept of operations with roles and responsibilities and standard operating procedures to properly prepare for and control sessions.

The Joint Task Force (JTF) targets cell led the sessions. Headquarters USEUCOM targets branch controlled the target information during sessions and monitored quality control. Intelligence product development or other functional personnel (e.g., legal and operations) contributed to or reviewed the product information. Collaboration enabled participants to view imagery products and collate existing intelligence information into a single product. Collaboration allowed the target information to be reviewed, discussed, and modified. Concurrence of JTF decisions and action items was documented. The JTF targets cell approved or held target information for release to operations. Operations forwarded the target information to executive decision-makers for final approval or provided additional requirements during the session. Figure 4 depicts USEUCOM's collaborative sessions during Operation Allied Force.

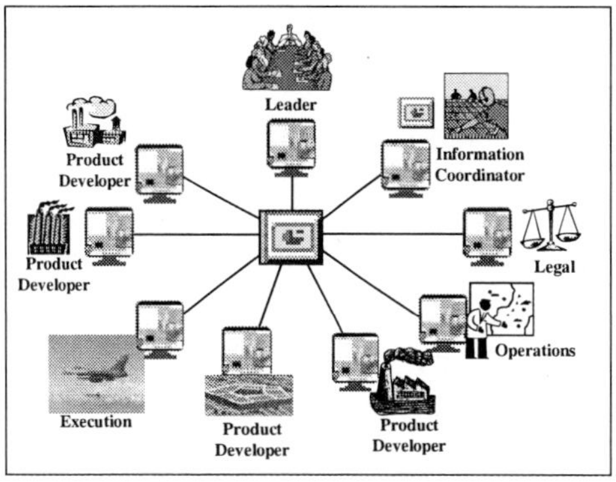

Figure 4 USEUCOM Collaborative Sessions

RESULTS AND IMPACT ON MISSION EFFECTIVENESS

Government systems acquisition and development efforts typically measure success by how well they meet system specification and contractual requirements. This systems engineering experience provided an operational perspective on measuring success. Operation Allied Force participants' responses to and an assessment of the following questions provide an operational perspective on meeting the systems requirements and measuring the success of this effort.

What benefit does the system provide?

- Collaborative sessions successfully facilitated synchronized and consolidated coordination and approval of fixed targets
- Collaboration removed or reduced previous process deficiencies
- Posting synchronized information to web-sites replaced multiple email attachments
- Collaboration drove parallel, not sequential planning and real time, not prearranged, decision-making
- Targets community representatives estimate that the timeline decreased from 2-4 days to 2-3 hours
- Coordination and synchronization benefited, improving process efficiencies and product quality
- Collaboration provided an alternative to video teleconferences that senior leadership dominated
- Estimated daily productivity increased 200%-300%
- Staff effort significantly reduced

Is the system reliable and does the system fit into the operational environment?

- No systems problems reported, other than infrequent workstation-specific issues

- System used daily for more than a month during Operation Allied Force
- System support to operations and contingency planning since Operation Allied Force has reported no problems

Are operators using the system on different missions/task?

- System used approximately 2 hours/day during Operation Allied Force
- System use expanding as necessary to support on-going and new operations and contingency planning. Collaborative sessions are now applied from beginning-to-end for target development, nomination, and production processes. USEUCOM's dynamic Area of Responsibility (AOR) required expansion of participants since Operation Allied Force. As a result, ten new organizations now participate in collaborative sessions.

What is the system impact to the enterprise?

- Due to the positive impact of collaboration on the process, USEUCOM senior leadership is advocating the expansion of collaboration within the intelligence community, including expansion to NATO allies. Senior executives from USEUCOM and other commands have requested and received demonstrations. *Prior to this success, collaboration was regulated to a non-interference basis with operations.*

This effort met the systems requirements and was successful from an operational perspective. According to Operation Allied Force operators, proper application of collaboration improves the effectiveness of information processes, improves product quality, and benefits federated efforts by geographically separated partners. Collaboration allows USEUCOM's geographically separated organizations to work as a team and manage increased battle management complexity by mitigating the effects of information overload, improving team decision-making, and synchronizing situational awareness.

TRANSFER CONSIDERATIONS

Are the systems engineering experiences and lessons learned from this project transferable or applicable to industry? Considering the successful results from this project, this question is worth exploring. Four different transfers or applications come to mind. First, training and placing systems engineers in the trenches will provide opportunities to build key relationships and assist in understanding the intent of systems requirements and objectives. Second, collaboration could be judiciously applied to system engineering processes internally and between partners to improve process efficiencies and quality. Third, global companies with geographically separated partners could substantially benefit product quality, time to market, team decision-making, synchronization, and customer support objectives. Fourth, in the services sector, slow sequential processes may be streamlined with collaboration driving parallel processes and real-time decisions. Collaboration does not replace the need for the right functional combination of well-trained, prepared personnel who have access to current and accurate information.

SUMMARY

Based on the successful results at USEUCOM, it is possible to apply customized systems engineering approaches and take on multiple systems engineering roles successfully in the trenches. Are systems engineering approaches and roles necessary and beneficial in the trenches? One must only examine the results of the systems engineering approaches and roles taken through and operational perspective in meeting system requirements to answer this question. Clearly, the answer is yes to both based on this experience.

REFERENCES

Kosovo/Operation Allied Force After-Action Report to Congress 31 January 2000

BIOGRAPHY

Gregory G. Chapin has been a systems engineer for 13 years. Currently, he is a senior systems engineer for the MITRE Corporation. He is assigned to the European Operations site located at the Headquarters United States European Command in Stuttgart, Germany. His focus the past two years has been the application of collaboration to mission processes. He has a Master of Arts degree in International Relations from St. Mary's University in San Antonio, Texas. He also holds two Bachelor of Science degrees, majoring in Electrical Engineering; and Mathematics and Computer Science from Valparaiso University in Valparaiso, Indiana.

Implementing Systems Engineering

James R. Armstrong
Software Productivity Consortium
2214 Rock Hill Road
Herndon, VA 20170

Abstract. The task of implementing systems engineering is always a challenge. Many times, the task is given to a technical expert with little training in people skills. Further, even the social scientists struggle with getting people to change. Much has been written about change management. However, recent research in this area has developed a process for change that provides more structure to this activity and has application to systems engineering. This paper provides a translation from the social environment to the technical.

INTRODUCTION

Issues in Implementing SE. One common theme among those trying to implement systems engineering is the lack of support from the organization. The resistance may come from management or other disciplines. The barriers seem to go on forever. In one set of discussions, every other item in the list of challenges was "change the culture". Several of the barriers were recorded with possible responses in a paper at the Brighton symposium (Sheard, et al). The demand for return on investment data is primarily due to the need to convince management of the value of a good systems engineering program.

When trying to implement a systems engineering program, organizations frequently create a plan and try to sell management that its actions are needed. Often, these action plans die a painful death in the throes of the approval process. One response is that the plan is approved, but there are no resources provided to implement the actions. Other times they are accepted and then lie dormant as middle managers or the key practitioners take a passive resistance stance.

Even if accepted, there are no guarantees that the new process will be accepted in a manner that cause them to have any meaningful half-life. One recent paper on the implementation of systems engineering on a major program (VG) was more interesting if you realize that it was the third incarnation of systems engineering on that program.

Why is it such a problem? Why do systems engineers have such problems implementing their function? And more importantly, are there

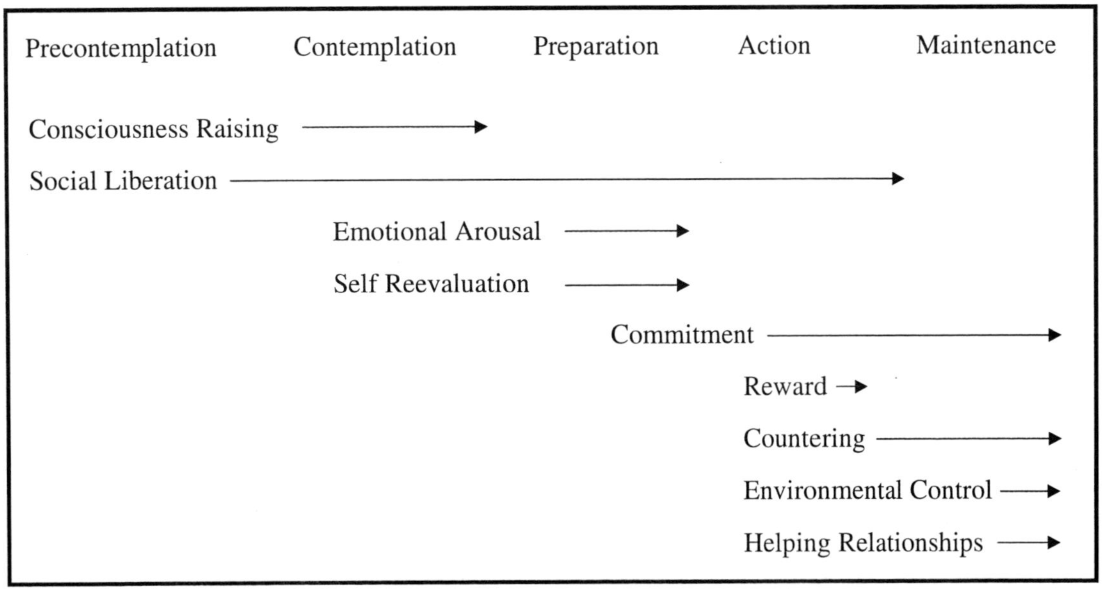

Figure 1. Six Stages and Supporting Processes

solutions? To a great extent, the answers do exist in research done on individual change. The book Changing for Good documents the work the authors performed looking into how individuals successfully make changes in their individual lives. The information, theories and suggestions in this book specifically address problems such as smoking, drugs, diet, etc. However, the discussions, events, and attitudes sound eerily familiar to anyone who has tried to make changes in the way a company performs product development.

A new approach. When trying to change a development approach, the resistance can be at the organizational level or the actions of key individuals that can become insurmountable roadblocks. The lessons in this book have been translated to the technical environment and initially applied to the implementation of systems engineering activities. The easy translation would be to consider corporations or individuals as addicted to the old way of doing business. In part that does work. The more correct translation is to take the basic theories of this work and identify the technical situations, examples and actions that are equivalent. This paper provides an initial effort of that translation and some results of application of the theories to systems engineering and other technical efforts.

The authors have reviewed their clinical experience and performed research sponsored by the National Institute of Health and multiple universities. The have looked at the behaviors of thousands of people who have successfully made a behavioral change in their lives. The purpose was to find out what the successful changers did and how it was different from what didn't work. The principal outcome was the identification of a six-step program and the actions that work at each stage.

Part of the study was the review of various methods used by the counseling community to see which methods worked in successful programs. In this case, the unexpected results were that they all worked. However, they worked at different stages. The result is a mapping of methods to stages. Several of these methods have analogous techniques used in technical areas. The mappings should sound familiar and there are examples provided in this translation of some instances where they have been applied at the wrong stages.

A six stage process. The six stages that successful changes go through are Precontemplation, Contemplation, Preparation, Action, Maintenance, and Termination. The experiences observed in the successful changers indicate that change is strongly dependent on the orderly progression through these stages. This is similar to the need to complete requirements analysis before charging into design. The early stages build up to readiness for successful change.

The problem observed with unsuccessful programs in personal change is that the changer enters the action phase before the proper groundwork has been laid. For instance, many programs to quit smoking start with the application of the change method, be it a patch, gum, filter, or just plain quitting. Failure often occurs when the changer has not bought-in to the program or unanticipated challenges arise.

Similar instances occur when the systems engineering proponent develops a plan for implementation, gets approval and then charges directly into implementation. When the action level personnel are not part of the plan, the change is at high risk to fail.

It is also noted in the book that there is such a thing as relapse. This is true in the technical world also. The important activity in relapse is the understanding of how far back one has slipped, why it happened and the use of that information in the next iteration of change.

The relationship of the six stages and the social processes are mapped in figure 1. and explained in the following sections.

PRECONTEMPLATION

The first stage. The first stage is the stage that is characterized by strong resistance to change. In social change, the person may refuse to recognize the situation or consider the situation their fate. They often refuse to recognize that a problem exists. Similar responses are often observed when lack of a systems engineering practice is identified as a problem. To understand this better, let's look at the defense mechanisms that change candidates apply at this stage.

Denial or minimization. Smokers refuse to believe that there is a health hazard. Engineers and managers fail to believe that inadequate requirements could possibly impact their considerable technical skills.

Rationalization. There are always excuses. The cost or schedule constraints are beyond the program's control and prohibit additional expenditure of time.

Turning outward – projection and displacement. It's always a good defense to put the problem on someone else. After an assessment identifies that an organization is weak in developing concepts of operations or tracing them to the requirements, it's quite common to hear that the customer won't let them do it.

Turning inward. If the problem has been recognized but nothing has happened to change the situation over an extended period, the potential changer may be totally demoralized. The result can be the attitude that "I can't do anything about it."

So what can we do about it? At this stage, whether it's an organization that fails to recognize the need or an individual, it's not the time to propose an action plan. However, you don't have to give up either. The two change processes that apply are consciousness raising and social liberation translated to technical situations as follows.

Defense mechanisms. The basic activities linked to consciousness raising at this stage are related to becoming aware of and responding to defense mechanisms. For each of the mechanisms mentioned there is a response that can turn the tide in that situation. Some of these translate more easily than others. For instance, for projection – blaming the customer, the recommendation is to see the situation through others eyes. It doesn't make a lot of sense to ask people who don't want to do something try to understand why the customer being a roadblock needs understanding. However, I've seen the most success in systems engineering training when the project personnel and the customer take a class together. At the end of the course, they not only have learned the material, but both have a real understanding of what the other is doing with the process.

Don't push action. Another activity deals with the interactions of the change agent with the person or group intended to change. The first rule is don't push into action. This is difficult to do. The temptation is to try to force immediate implementation of the new methods. If the person or organization is really in denial, all that you will get is stronger push back. The next two rules are difficult yet necessary to balance. They are don't nag and don't give up. Somewhere in the middle is the right amount of external pressure to make things progress. The last, and perhaps most important is don't enable. Softening consequences, making excuses or rarely addressing the problem is enabling. One perhaps unintentional enabling act seen frequently is making heroes out of managers who skip early tasks and then have enormous problems to solve at the end. This is usually accompanied by overlooking the manager who does the right things and proceeds easily to success.

Social liberation. The activities related to the term social liberation refer to things such as providing a no-smoking area or low-fat items on a menu. Translation to engineering is a bit more difficult. However, providing easily available tools and training are likely entries in this category. Little things that make the changer feel that there is a ready and welcome environment can stir interest in participation.

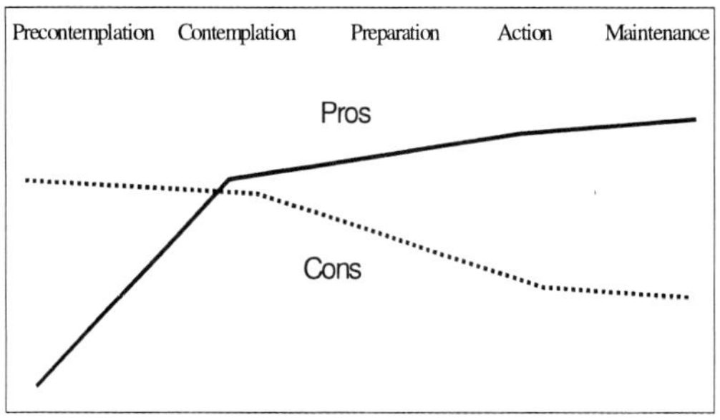

Figure 2. Pro/Con Shift

Where are we? Throughout the book, the authors provide short tests to check whether the client is ready to proceed to the next step. All will not be addressed in this paper; however, one sample is provided here for the shift to contemplation:

"I look for information related to my problem behavior.
I think about information from articles and books on how to overcome my problem.
I read about people who have successfully changed.
I recall information people have personally given me about the benefits of changing my problem."

Each statement is scored from 1 to 5 for never, seldom, occasionally, often or repeatedly. A score of 10 or more generally indicates readiness to move on. If the "problem" is failure to do systems engineering, this test can be applied almost verbatim. It also indicates some action the change agent must take to ensure that information is available to be thought about and benefits have been related personally.

CONTEMPLATION

The second stage. It may start as the gee-maybe-I'll-at-least-listen-to-you stage. It ends with agreement to change – not start of action – just agreement. During this stage the methods to be applied are emotional arousal and self-reevaluation.

Emotional arousal. The first method has the key ingredient of propaganda. In process change this is usually in the form of posters, tee shirts, mugs, assemblies, etc. The key point here is that these are of little value during the pre-contemplation stage. A process group may be down the road in their thinking and feel the time is right for these things. The rest of the organization may find them only amusing or possible offensively pushy of non-relevant. One could conclude that other means should be employed to raise consciousness and the mugs brought out once people at least recognize that there is something worth considering involved.

Self-reevaluation. The second method involves thinking about the intended change and creating a new self-image and making a conscious decision to proceed to make that image a reality. This may be a good place to include informal assessments against standards, introductory training, and other means to help participants understand and analyze where they are and what could be done. It would probably not be the time for full scale assessments or how-to training that could be rejected and push people back into pre-contemplation.

Indicators. The test questions relating to completion of this stage relate to viewing change as better than the status quo and a feeling of discontent with the thought of not changing. However, higher cumulative scores of 14 or above are needed on the four question test for this transition.

PREPARATION

The third stage. This is one that is frequently shortcut. Once the changer decides to proceed, the end condition is often too irresistible to not charge off unprepared into action. If you're one of those who buy a snow shovel as the flakes start to fall, this stage could be a problem.

Adding commitment. Of the prior four methods, all but consciousness raising continue. If the changer hasn't gotten enough information about the need for change by now, you're still stuck in contemplation. The one new process that is added at this point is commitment. This is the time to establish charters and funding, sign action plans, etc. All expected to take part in, support, or manage the change need to agree to the plan of action.

Of course, the basic task in this phase is preparation. This is the time to determine what systems engineering activities will be implemented in which programs, what support will be needed, whether additional areas such as proposal processes need to be addressed. This may be a good time to have some form of maturity model appraisal to identify the best places to apply resources in the action stage.

UNDERSTANDING PROS AND CONS

Pros and Cons. This is a good point to address one general concept that applies through the entire process. One of the techniques used to track readiness to proceed is a comparison of the pros and cons the changer perceives in connection with the change. The changer is, at each stage, asked to list the pros and cons of the change. The chart in figure 2 shows a typical graph of responses from 12 different groups addressing issues such as smoking, weight control or exercising. The individual group charts had considerable variation in the shapes of the curves. However, they had two significant characteristics in common.

Pros up first. It is important to note that the Pros always went up between the pre-contemplation stage and contemplation. This indicates that the most important information at this point is the benefits. Good ROI data would be very valuable in this stage. Lacking that, the best information available about problems avoided and increased quality need to be presented. Recognize that you probably will not win by trying to counter the objections at this point. Being positive is more than a slogan with dealing with a naysayer. You are trying to get them to agree to listen to the possibility you have something that will help.

Then cons down. Second, the Cons always went down between the contemplation stage and action. This tells us we will have to address the concerns before we press into action. Forcing the parties into trying something they have serious concerns about is a risky path.

How much? It should also be noted that the Pros went up 1 standard deviation and the Cons went down only ½ standard deviation. This means that we should expect to make a serious dent in the Cons but not expect the changer to give up all concerns. Also, we really need to have a strong set of Pros ready. On the other hand, once the dialog has begun, we must also be able to deal effectively with concerns.

ACTION

Doing it. When the prior stages have been completed, the change is ready for action. At the start of the discussion of this phase, the authors provide a caution about what not to do that have a very familiar ring to those who have tried to implement systems engineering.

First, don't take preparation lightly and jump into a change without laying the groundwork. This is usually seen when management decrees that something big will have to take place within the quarter because the customer is unhappy.

The result may well be the second caution – cheap change. It's not uncommon to have management call for implementation with no budget. Other times, there is budget for a couple of people to do a little preparation, but no training, tools or continuous support. In process improvement efforts of all kinds, it's not unheard of for management to fund an assessment and not budget a dime for corrective action.

A corollary is the search for the "silver bullet". The hope is that one thing can be implemented that will solve the entire problem Often, this is a tool that has promised miracles. One wrong first question at this point is "what tool do you recommend?"

The final warning is to beware of "more of the same", doing more of something that was partially successful in the past. The result is, predictably, partial success again.

Countering. The social behavior methods that are applied to the action phase start with countering. Most of the activities of countering relate to react to avoiding temptation by exercising or relaxing. These are difficult to adapt to systems engineering. It's not useful to ask the entire program to go jogging when the manager orders the premature start of design. It may be useful to ask the manager to take a deep breath and not panic at the first problem or delay.

Another part of countering that does have application is assertiveness. Without being irritating, a new function must be aggressive in finding a place in the corporate culture.

Environmental control. A second method is environmental control. This is where the concept of organizational process standards and support apply. Where there are organizational standards, network support, training and top level interest, the changes have a better chance of survival than when the individual engineer or programs are left to fend for themselves.

Reward. One of the big discussions is always about the existence of a career path in a new discipline. Another is the impact on the bonus structure. These need to be addressed, but even the little things count such as simply letting the practitioners know they are doing a good job.

Helping relationships. The last method is where an INCOSE chapter can help with access to other practitioners who can share their lessons learned. Internal or external experts or consultants can also provide the kind of support this method is calling for. Many companies have benefited from a relationship with a college or university program.

MAINTENANCE

Long term change. The maintenance stage calls for the same kind of long term support that systems need once deployed. The change must be continually watched both to detect and prevent backsliding and to provide continued improvement. There are lots of examples of companies that once did systems engineering well but then lost the capability. One of the activities that holds promise in this area is process quality assurance. This more than looking at the product for quality, it also confirms compliance with the process that was intended.

TERMINATION

If ever. Termination is the sixth stage and refers to the theoretical point where the change has reached the point that it is now the baseline. At this point, systems engineering would be the normal activity unless consciously countered. The book gives this stage little emphasis and leans towards the thought that change never really reaches this point. From the experiences of several major corporations that were at one time recognized as leaders in systems engineering, one would have to agree that this is not a stage to plan on reaching

SUMMARY

The implementation of systems engineering has always been a challenge. Most of the time, the changes are managed by technical people with little training in social sciences. The book

Changing for Good is an excellent source of information for the technical person who has the task of making changes happen. This discussion has provided some of the translation from social to technical language.

The main point is not to charge into the action phase and expect everyone to gleefully join in. The early stages can be applied to the overall organization or to individuals. When a new person becomes involved in an ongoing action and seems to be a new roadblock, the understanding of these stages can help by providing structure to dealing with the reluctance.

These methods are currently being applied in several change situations and provide much improved results than an unplanned approach. They should be useful to anyone tasked with implementing or improving systems engineering.

REFERENCES

Prochaska, J.O., Norcross, J.C. and DiClemente, C.C. *Changing for Good,* Avon Books, New York, New York, 1994

Sheard, S.A, Lykins, H., Armstrong, J.R., "Overcoming Barriers to Systems Engineering Process Improvement." INCOSE, 1989.

BIOGRAPHY

James R. Armstrong has over 30 years experience in systems development. For the last decade, he has been a consultant and trainer in systems engineering and is a lead assessor for systems engineering appraisals. He is a member of the author teams for EIA/IS 731 and other systems engineering standards and has also worked on the IPD-CMM and the CMM Integration project.

Fuzzy Sets as Requirements Antecedents

Ronald S. Carson, Ph.D.
The Boeing Company
P. O. Box 3707 MC 43-19
Seattle, WA 98124-2207

Abstract. Arguments for requirements completeness have relied on the notions of mutually exclusive and universally complete antecedents to ensure complete requirements. The world of hardware tolerances suggests that mutual exclusivity and completeness may not be simultaneously achievable in realistic systems. The discipline of "fuzzy logic" does not require such mutual exclusivity, and the achievement of universally complete antecedents is inherent in the methodology. We show that the use of fuzzy logic methods is more appropriate for design rather than requirements definition.

INTRODUCTION

Set theory models for requirements antecedents (Carson 1995) have relied on the concepts of mutual exclusivity and universality to establish completeness. Hardware tolerances have received a more limited treatment (Carson 1998). Recent work on stimulus-response requirements methodology (Cooper and Ito 1998) emphasizes the need to precisely establish the conditions under which requirements are to be performed. (Carson 1998) attempts to address the consequence of overlapping antecedents using an "either/or" construction (either of two outcomes is equally acceptable for certain ranges), as indicated in figure 1.

Additional thresholds can be added so that the overlapping antecedents are addressed using what is often labeled, "hysterisis". For example, in figure 1, the values indicated as A-D could be interpreted as indicated in table 1.

"Fuzzy logic", as its name implies, addresses the inherent fuzziness in the world around us. This paper attempts to synthesize the requirements completeness methodology with the fuzzy logic formalism.

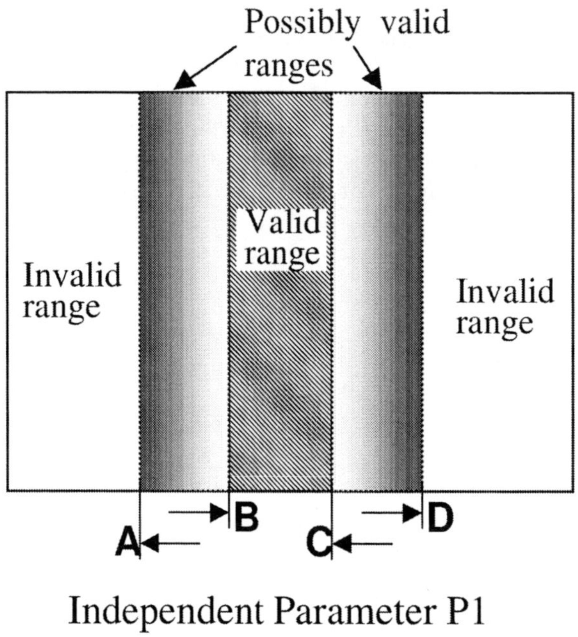

Figure 1. Hardware tolerances are addressed by allowing either of two possible outcomes. Additional thresholds can be added as indicated to accommodate possible dependence on the sign of the parameter change (hysterisis).

	Required Action at threshold			
Direction of parameter change	**A**	**B**	**C**	**D**
Increasing	May change	Must change	May change	Must change
Decreasing	Must change	May change	Must change	May change

Table 1. The direction of the parameter change can be used to more precisely control the system behavior when P1 is in a range where either behavior may be acceptable.

REVIEW OF REQUIREMENTS COMPLETENESS

(Carson 1995) developed the notion of complementary sets to ensure completeness of requirements antecedents. The sets took the form of mutually exclusive sets whose intersections were (by definition) the null set, ∅, and whose union is the universal set, *U*, of all possible condition. Using this model it was proved that there are no antecedent conditions not definable in a requirements set. Figure 2 displays a parameter set composed of several mutually exclusive and collectively universal conditions, of which two are valid ("low" and "high") with desired, defined behaviors, and three are invalid (low, medium and high), with potentially ill-defined behaviors. The value of the membership function in any set is either 1 or 0 (definition of "crisp" in "fuzzy" terminology).

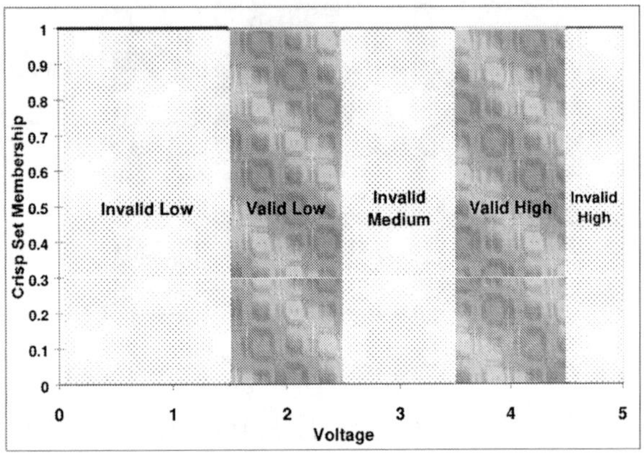

Figure 2. Mutually exclusive and universally complete input conditions for a single parameter (the lowest and highest ranges formally extend to ± ∞).

Two factors exacerbate this situation. First, conditions may appear to overlap (non-mutual exclusivity) or be disjoint (non-universality) because of real hardware tolerances. There are ways to mitigate the non-universality effect by allowing abutting antecedents with optional outputs as discussed in the introduction. However, for an input at the boundary value of two adjacent ranges, there exists the probability that different behaviors will be exhibited among groups of otherwise identical units due to hardware tolerances, regardless of the precision of the specification. But there is no obvious method for ensuring mutual exclusivity unless one is willing to sacrifice universality (completeness) by widely separating the antecedents. In figures 1 and 2 this would be accomplished by failing to define those regions labeled, "invalid", defeating universality.

Second, the execution of any function is dependent on the interpretation of conditions by the end-item to which is allocated the requirement, regardless of what any other observer determines the state of the condition. Any hardware interface will respond to an input condition based on its conception of that condition, even if it disagrees with what the test conductor or adjacent subsystem believes is being presented to the unit. Aside from obvious failure to satisfy requirements for "valid" input conditions, one is left with tolerance issues due to disagreements in the measurement of the input conditions. In other words, there is no absolutely correct standard of any parameter unless we are going to insist that the measurement of such parameters be traceable to the National Institute of Standards and Testing (NIST). Again, there is no solution which will satisfy all observers that is based on sharp-boundary requirements.

MOTIVATION FOR FUZZY LOGIC

The major impetus for considering fuzzy logic is that it addresses the problems identified above by explicitly accounting for the inherent fuzziness all around us, rather than assuming sharp boundaries where none exist. (Rechtin 1991) notes that fuzzy logic can be effective when boundaries and boundary conditions are not well defined.

For example, in electronics we typically consider states of digital logic circuits by specifying "1s" and "0s". For the software designer, these mean nothing less than that which is stated, *i.e.*, software will interpret a bit as either a "1" or a "0". However, the software must interpret hardware states. Here we define our binary logic states as given in figure 3 for TTL logic.

For voltages less than 0.7V, we have logic "0". Voltages greater than 2.0V give a logic "1". In "normal" requirements analysis we would specify the function and performance requirement for each condition, such as the following for a simple lighting controller:

Rule 1. If input is 0, turn light off.
Rule 2. If input is 1, turn light on.

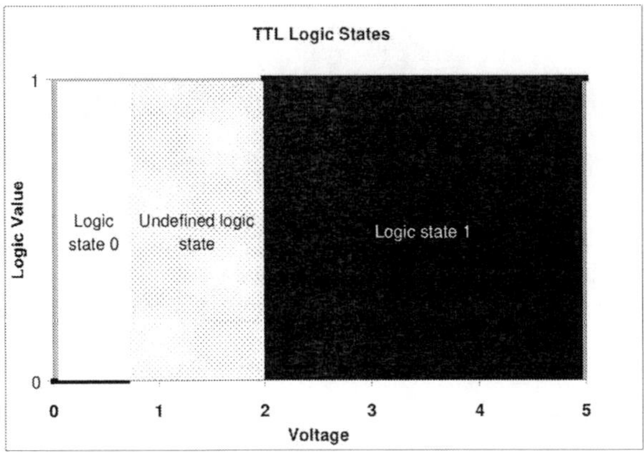

Figure 3. TTL logic states, "0" and "1". Any value between 0.7 and 2V is undefined.

What happens to in-between voltages (between 0.7 and 2.0V)? The hardware will determine a "state" which will be interpreted by software as either a "1" or a "0"; there is no "in-between" for software, since a "crisp" decision must be made (software is intolerant of digital ambiguity). So, the system will "respond" to the condition (the light will either be on or off), but the system designer may not correctly anticipate the response(s). Worse, there may, indeed, be some valid in-between voltage state which is recognizable by the hardware and software, and which leads to a unique, possibly undesired response. Either of these conditions may eventually lead to rework. Some may lead to disaster if not recognized and corrected in time. For example, the loss of the initial Arianne V launch was due to an ill-defined (out-of-range) horizontal velocity. (Le Lann 1997). Anytime the system response to a parameter is not defined over some physically possible range then an undesirable system behavior is possible.

Fuzzy logic treats such ambiguous conditions by first recognizing that they exist, then constructing a formalism to enable further analysis. Using fuzzy logic in this example the system designer defines two "membership functions", ordered pairs whose first element is the input voltage, and whose second element is a number between 0 and 1, inclusive, and is called the "grade" of the input voltage in either the state "0" or the state '1". Two possible membership functions are shown in figure 4.

The curves of figure 4 are "membership functions", μ_i, i=0,1, defining fuzzy sets for the states "0" and "1", for input voltage in the range 0 to 5.5V. Stated another way, we "map" the input voltage onto the fuzzy states 0 or 1 by these membership functions. In contrast to figure 2, there is no sharp boundary between ranges. The membership function, μ_i, can be any number between 0 and 1, inclusive. The sum of all values for a given voltage does not have to equal 1 (as it does in this example). This "degree of membership" value, μ_i, is used in calculating results of rules. The functions span the previous "no-man's land" of figure 3, and, when extended to $\pm\infty$, span the range of physical possibility, ensuring antecedent completeness (Carson 1996, 1998).

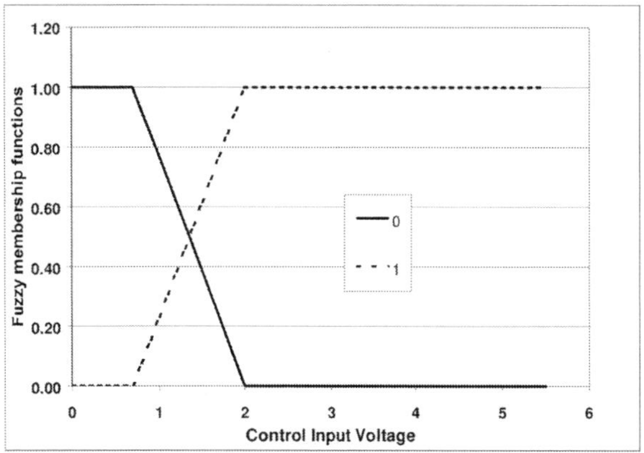

Figure 4. Membership functions for "0" and "1" vs. voltage.

The real strength of the fuzzy logic is that it is not generally necessary to precisely quantify definitions. Adverbs such as "very", "more", and "less", and adjectives such as "large" and "small" are part of the "natural language" of fuzzy logic. This supports the continued use of natural language specifications (Cooper and Ito 1998) if the fuzzy logic methodology is otherwise applicable.

FUZZY OPERATIONS

Some additional fuzzy set theory algebra is required. Given the *intersection C* of two fuzzy sets *A* and *B* the degree of membership of *C* can be defined as[1]:

$$\mu_C(x) = \text{minimum}\{\mu_A(x), \mu_B(x)\},$$

for all x between 0 and 5 (the universal set for this problem). This function would trace the lower of the two curves of figure 4 at every voltage.

The membership function of the *union, D,* of two fuzzy sets is likewise given by:

$$\mu_D(x) = \text{maximum}\{\mu_A(x), \mu_B(x)\}.$$

This function would trace the higher of the two curves of figure 4 at every voltage.

Finally, the membership function of the *complement, ~A*, of the set A is given by:

[1] Definitions follow Zimmerman, 1991, but are not absolute; other definitions are available in the literature on fuzzy logic.

$\mu_{\sim A}(x) = 1 - \mu_A(x)$.

It is known that fuzzy logic is not the same as probability. Whereas probability models random uncertainty, fuzzy logic models deterministic uncertainty in conditions and consequent parts of requirements. In fact, outputs generated by fuzzy logic-based systems are no less deterministic than crisp logic, since every antecedent has a provable consequence, according to the rules (requirements).

When we apply fuzzy logic to stimulus-response systems we are prescribing rules of behavior which recognize the ambiguity of input states and output states.

The processing of "real-world" or fuzzy inputs proceeds according to a standard description:

1. Convert the input conditions into fuzzy sets (partition the parameter space for each input into several overlapping regions). This is known as, "fuzzification" (figure 4 in our example).
2. Execute processing rules for each element of each fuzzy set.
3. Convert calculated outputs back into non-fuzzy parameters. This is known as, "defuzzification".

FUZZY LIGHTING CONTROLLER

In the example above, any reference to digital logic requires that inputs be converted *from* binary states, and outputs be converted *to* binary states. How do we do this?

Fuzzy controllers process inputs according to rules (read, "requirements") based on syllogisms of the form, $A \rightarrow C$. In the example above, we take figure 4 as our set of input conditions (voltage between 0 and 5), and rules 1 & 2 as the processing rules.

In fuzzy logic, we process inputs using all rules concurrently; the membership function of the antecedent of the rule is the weighting to be applied to the result of the rule (Zimmerman 1991, Zadeh 1984). For any input voltage between 0 and 5V we determine the result using both rules described above.

To obtain the conditions "off" and "on", we must define relationships between some output voltage level and the states of "off" and "on". We can use the same membership functions as indicated in figure 4, where we replace "0" with "off" and "1" with "on", respectively. For any output voltage, we take the output state which has the *maximum* membership function for any input voltage. This is the "defuzzification" process for discrete outputs (Klir and Folger, 1998), the results of which are indicated in figure 5. (Other defuzzification processes may be appropriate when the output is analog rather than binary.)

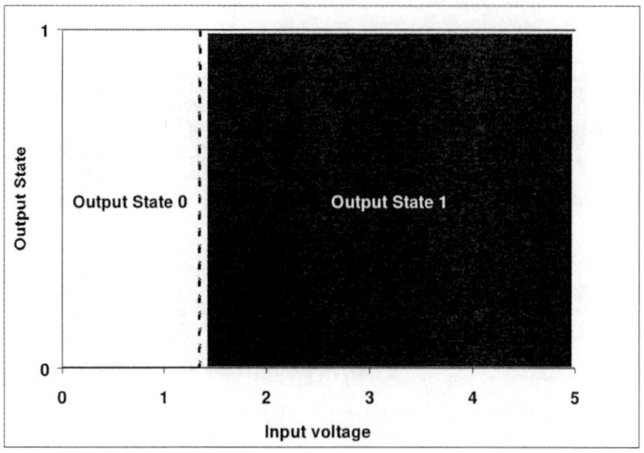

Figure 5. On-off states vs. input voltage for a simple lighting controller. The "gap" of figure 3 has been replaced by complete coverage so that every input voltage has a defined, unique output state.

Figure 5 indicates that, for any positive voltage (as measured by the controller) less than or equal to 1.35, the required output state is "off". Similarly, for input voltages above 1.35V and less than or equal to 5V, the required output state is "on". This result removes the ambiguity of the TTL logic which is defined only for certain voltages as indicated in figure 3. Regardless of whether or not voltages between 0.7 and 2.0V are ever experienced, the requirements are complete in the interval 0 to 5V.

We can also extend the result to all possible voltages in keeping with the requirements of (Carson 1996) to cover all possible physical space. In this case, we would need to declare rules for all negative voltages and all voltages above 5V.

In this example we have essentially converted a "fuzzy" input voltage into a "crisp" output state, by the use of the defuzzification rule that allows exactly one of two possible outcomes. Rather than tolerating ambiguity in the interval between 0.7 and 2.0 volts we have *required* explicit behavior by the introduction of the fuzzy computing machinery (membership functions and rules). The implications of this will be discussed later.

COMBINATIONAL ANTECEDENTS

Normal requirements processing rules will generally operate on more than a single condition. Let us broaden our processing rules to include an additional parameter so that the full methodology of fuzzy logic can be examined.

We take as our next independent variable the input voltage which powers the lighting controller. For the sake of variety we define three states, "off", "normal", and "emergency", where the desired operation is a combination of the digital control inputs and the input power. We form the following rules (requirements) consistent with the possible conditions of the two independent input parameters (we ignore state transitions in this example):

Rule 1. If input power is "off", then the light shall be "off".
Rule 2. If input power is "on" and the light control is "off", then the light shall be "off".
Rule 3. If input power is "on" and the light control is "on", then the light shall be "on".
Rule 4. If input power is "emergency", then the light shall be "on".

Notice that in rules 1 & 4 we ignore the state of the light control and dictate the output based solely on the state of the input power. We have also neglected to define the "else" condition which may introduce additional issues (Carson 1995).

We can construct a table which shows the combinations of the two input parameters and the results according to the rules.

	Lighting Control Input	
Input power	0	1
Off	Off	Off
On	Off	On
Emergency	On	On

Table 2. Tabular form of rules 1-4.

The lighting control states have already been defined in figure 4. Figure 6 indicates the membership functions for the 3 possible states of input power.

Given figures 4 and 6 and the rules of table 2 we have a complete description of the interpretation of the response to any voltage pair provided to the lighting controller hardware. Let us describe such pairs using the notation (*Input power voltage, lighting control voltage*). Thus, the pair, (10, 1.5), yields membership functions as follows:

- Input voltage "off": 0.33
- Input voltage "on": 0.67
- Input voltage "emergency": 0.8
- Lighting control voltage "off": 0.38
- Lighting control voltage "on": 0.62

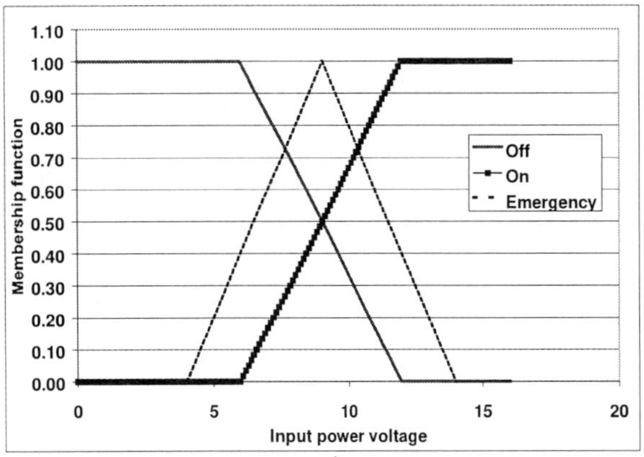

Figure 6. Membership functions vs. input power voltage.

Forming the combinational antecedents using the definitions above yields the following truth values for each rule for the input state (10, 1.5):

Rule #	Rule	Truth Value
1	If input power is "off" [0.33], then the light shall be "off". [=0.33]	0.33
2	If input power is "on" [0.67] and the light control is "off" [0.38], then the light shall be "off". [min(0.67,0.38)=0.38]	0.38
3	If input power is "on" [0.67] and the light control is "on" [0.62], then the light shall be "on". [min(0.67,0.62)=0.62]	0.62
4	If input power is "emergency" [0.8], then the light control is "on". [=0.8]	0.8

Table 3. Evaluation of rule truth.

In table 3 we have formed the "and" condition using the "min" function as indicated above. The "else" condition would be formed by using the "complement" rule above.

Taking the maximum "truth" of all rules yields 0.8 for rule #4. Therefore, the correct state of the lighting controller for the input condition (10, 1.5) is "on". This process can be applied for any pair of voltages in the defined range (and the ranges can be extended from $-\infty$ to $+\infty$ to achieve physical space completeness).

To assess the sensitivity of the result to hardware interpretations of the input voltage, we examine the results for two neighboring points: (9.5, 1.3) and (10.5, 1.7). Table 4 indicates the truth value of each rule:

	Voltage Pair (Power, Control)	
Rule	(9.5, 1.3)	(10.5, 1.7)
1	0.42	0.25
2	Min(0.58,0.54)=0.54	min(0.75,0.23)=0.23
3	Min(0.58,0.46)=0.46	min(0.75,0.77)=**0.75**
4	**0.9**	0.7

Table 4. Rule truth for neighboring points.

For (9.5, 1.3) the maximum truth value still corresponds with rule 4. For (10.5, 1.7), however, the maximum truth value corresponds to rule 3. In both cases, however, the correct output state is still, "lights on".

ANALOG PROCESSING RULES

The historic application of fuzzy logic has been for continuous variables (*cf.*, Zadeh 1984). Extending the above discussion to continuous variables requires a slight modification of our rule application and defuzzification.

We modify rules 1-4 for the dual-input lighting controller so that the consequence is a voltage given by the following "target" states:

1. "off" = 0V
2. "on" = 14V
3. "emergency" = 8V.

Using these values with table 3 yields the output voltages indicated in table 5. The "correct" analog output voltage would then be 7.1V (see table 5). (For the sake of brevity we have used "crisp" rather than "fuzzy" output conditions. One would normally assign membership function curves to each of these conditions and then form a weighting of the "truth" of each output in order to determine the output voltage).

RELATIONS TO REGULAR ANTECEDENTS AND REQUIREMENTS

In contrast to the 3-step process for fuzzy sets, our "normal" deterministic logic approach executes a transfer function on inputs to produce outputs without any conversion into fuzzy sets. Both input and output parameters as well as the transfer function operate using values which require no further transformation.

The benefit of the fuzzy methodology is that we have explicitly accounted for whatever ambiguity may exist in the measurement of the input and output values at the interface between hardware and software.

How would such a set of fuzzy requirements appear compared to a "normal" set? The latter would simply be expressed as rules 1 and 2. What modified or additional requirements would be needed to enforce a fuzzy methodology?

Rule #	Rule	Output Voltage
1	If input power is "off" [0.33], then the light shall be "off". [=0.33]	0.33*0
2	If input power is "on" [0.67] and the light control is "off" [0.38], then the light shall be "off". [min(0.67,0.38)=0.38]	0.38*0
3	If input power is "on" [0.67] and the light control is "on" [0.62], then the light shall be "on". [min(0.67,0.62)=0.62]	0.62*14
4	If input power is "emergency" [0.8], then the light control is "on". [=0.8]	0.8*8
Weighted sum voltage		**7.1V**

Table 5. Analog output voltage using fuzzy logic processing rules.

If we recall the 3-step fuzzy methodology above, we must address (1) the conversion of inputs into parameters suitable for rule-based processing, (2) concurrent operation of all rules, and (3) determination of the (discrete) output based on the maximum value of all outputs as processed by the rules (or the weighted sum of the outputs of all rules for continuous functions).

Given this process, the first change would be to add graphs of the membership functions for the possible states used as rule inputs based on the measurable hardware voltages. This would be implemented with a requirement such as: "The "truth value" of any input condition shall be established using the membership functions of figure 6."

The second change would be a requirement to calculate the relative "truth" of all related rules based on the degree of truth of the antecedent, and form a weighted sum of the results of all rules. In addition to the rules themselves, additional requirements would be: "The *end-item* shall determine the truth value of any output (outcome) as the truth value of the antecedent of the associated rule." Where multiple conditions make up the antecedent (see combinational antecedents above) the fuzzy operational rules above for "intersection", "union" and "complement" are used to calculate the truth value of "and", "or", and "not" conditions, respectively.

The final change would be to form a weighted sum of the product of the truth value of each rule and the value of its associated consequence. This would be expressed in a general requirement as: "The *end-item* shall determine the output state for any function based on a weighted sum of the product of the truth value of each rule and its associated output value." Mathematically this could be expressed as:

$$Output = \frac{\sum_{i}^{all\ rules} (Output_i) * (Truth_i)}{\sum_{i}^{all\ rules} (Truth_i)}$$

For "discrete" outputs, these last two steps could be simply combined into a single step: operate only the rule with the highest antecedent "truth" value.

PROBLEMS

The difficulty with this approach is that we have now crossed the threshold from specifying the *requirements* into specifying the *implementation*. Such words as "shall determine", "using", and "based on" indicate that the specification has now become a *design* rather than a requirements document.

So, what have we gained? In the first example (binary state lighting controller), we have applied the fuzzy computation machinery and given ourselves sharp-boundary results where none previously existed (a *required* output state change at 1.35V input voltage, rather than allowing either state to exist in the range of 0.7 to 2.0V). And in all examples we have invoked "how to" requirements in addition to the "what" and "under what conditions" of the operating rules.

Fuzzy logic is attractive an attractive methodology because some ambiguity is inherent in fuzzy logic through the use of natural language in the processing rules. Such ambiguity, however, may leave the system design unknown until the detail designer has defined the thresholds and membership functions. The only way to remove the ambiguity from the requirements would be for the system designer (requirements engineer) to quantify the membership functions *as requirements*, effectively removing the allowable fuzziness from the process, and more tightly linking the "requirements" and design implementation (generally resulting in requirements rework). In any case, the added complexity of the fuzzy machinery would appear to be negative value added, and alternate methods discussed in the introduction would appear to be more straightforward (*e.g.*, either/or constructs and hysterisis).

SUMMARY

We have shown how one can use the methodology of "fuzzy logic" to address the tolerances inherent in the measurement of any parameter used as an element of a requirement antecedent. While fuzzy logic inherently supports the use of "natural language" specifications by apparently reducing the necessity of precisely defining every parameter, the resulting requirements will either be ambiguous (unquantified and unverifiable input states) or overly restrictive. The use of fuzzy logic also inappropriately forces implementation into the requirements. Because of these features other approaches should be used for dealing with tolerances.

ACKNOWLEDGMENT

The author gratefully acknowledges his introduction to fuzzy logic and review of this paper by Mr. Suray Bhatia of The Boeing Company.

REFERENCES

Carson, Ronald S., "A Set Theory Model for Anomaly Handling in System Requirements Analysis", *Proceedings of NCOSE 1995* (St. Louis, MO), pp. 515-522.

Carson, Ronald S., "Designing for Failure: Anomaly Identification and Treatment in System Requirements Analysis", *Proceedings of INCOSE 1996* (Boston, MA), pp. 771-778.

Carson, Ronald S., "Requirements Completeness: A Deterministic Approach", *Proceedings of INCOSE 1998*, (Vancouver, BC, Canada), pp. 739-746.

Cooper, Kendra, and Ito, Mabo, "Advantages of Stimulus Response Requirement Specification Techniques for System Testing", *Proceedings of INCOSE 1998*, (Vancouver, BC, Canada), pp. 141-147.

Klir, George J., and Folger, Tina A., *Fuzzy Sets, Uncertainty, and Information,* Prentice Hall, Englewood Cliffs, NJ, 1998, page 257.

Le Lann, Gerard, "Analysis of the Ariane 5 Flight 501 Failure - A System Engineering Perspective", *IEEE Intl. Conference on the Engineering of Computer-Based Systems*, (March 1997), pp. 339-346.

Rechtin, Eberhardt, *Systems Architecting: Creating and Building Complex Systems,* Englewood Cliffs, NJ: Prentice Hall PTR, 1991, p. 37.

Zadeh, Lotfi A., "Making computers think like people", *IEEE Spectrum*, August, 1984, pp. 26-32.

Zimmerman, H.-J., *Fuzzy Set Theory and Its Applications.* Kluwer Academic Publishers, Boston, 1991, 2nd Edition, p. 17.

BIOGRAPHY

Dr. Carson is a Systems Engineer on the Joint Strike Fighter program at Boeing, analyzing effects of subsystem failures. He received "Best Paper" Award at the 1995 INCOSE Symposium for his work on "A Set Theory Model for Anomaly Handling in System Requirements".

Five Realities for Systems Engineering in Commercial Enterprises

V.A. Lentz
Otis Elevator, a United Technologies Company
Five Farm Springs Road
Farmington, Connecticut 06032 USA

Abstract. System engineering has its origins in the complexity business,. The legacy is in the large unprecedented systems built primarily in support of telecommunications, defense, and space applications. As the products provided by other segments of industry become more complex, smarter, systems engineering by what ever name is probably a good idea. There are several parallel initiatives which do some of the same things - but systems takes the most holistic view. This is important to the profitability of a company over time - the decades that it takes to discover, mature and incorporate disruptive technologies. It is also important to companies that support many similar products over a life span dictated by the customer rather than the producer.

INCOSE has asserted that the methods and tools of systems engineering do apply. Several outreach programs have been initiated with mixed results. The experiences of companies that are having successes in the holistic approach might be useful to others trying to adapt systems engineering to their product development process. This paper describes some realities based on the experiences of some of the companies working this issue over the last decade. If we are careful to learn from history, we may be able to address new problems in the coming decades.

BACKGROUND

Origins. As we all know, systems engineering has origins in the complexity business. It was not until folks wanted to connect those telephones over longer and longer distances and needed more phones connected at each end of the line that AT&T and the telecommunications industry started codifying the methods of systems engineering. The Departments / Ministries of Defence got involved when the battalions were no longer independent units with an occasional communiqué from headquarters - but rather air and ground fighting had to be coordinated. The space industries got involved because they needed it too - and on and on and on. The transition of systems engineering out of the very complex, highly regulated industries where the product was built to a customer's specification has been rocky at best and stalls frequently.

Current state. Acquisitions and Mergers over the last two decades have brought together some strange bedfellows. There was the diversify-out-of-the-cyclic-aerospace/defense business - add commercial industries to the portfolio!!! cycle. That brought together some natural places for systems engineering to leak into the commercial side of the house - but it didn't ! Now we are back to consolidate to our strengths and form mega-aerospace / defense companies.

Does everybody need Systems Engineering according to EIA 632 and 731? What in commercial industry is similar enough to the INCOSE Legacy companies such that some one might be convinced that systems engineering as a discipline is a value add - and how might it get institutionalized in those organizations. What are some of the barriers to be overcome?

Improvement Initiatives. There are some diehard pioneers and transplants in commercial organizations - they are fighting from within, using all the fodder INCOSE provides them to make the case for systems engineering. Parallel activities include business process reengineering (BPR), enterprise productivity and quality improvement. Different folks are making the same argument. The support from upper management is mixed. The good news to engineering regarding BPR and Quality improvement initiatives is that if we wait long enough they will go away, and perhaps be replaced with something else that will also go away.

Systems engineering is focused first on the product and secondly on the processes used to produce and support the product. The pendulum swings from 'the only system is the universe and everything else is a subsystem→ the thing we shall call a system is something that provides an operational capability in the field → anything is a system (that is a part of a bigger system and somewhere along the line contributes to producing an operational capability in the field). Commercial industry looking at systems engineering for the first time typically adopts the 'anything is a system' definition. This is politically driven by strong Chief Engineers. If 'Systems' has been adopted by the executives as the solution to improving profit and everything else, good leaders follow along, adopt it as well - and keep on with business as usual.

THE REALITIES

1. This is a culture change. Culture changes take time: 5 to 7 years at a minimum, more than the typical executive champion's tenure. The evolution of a systems engineering organization within the enterprise is not for the faint hearted.
2. Legacy Exists! The clean sheet of paper method, 'all-new-starts' doesn't work for commercial industries. There is a great deal of reuse from product to product.
3. Yes, all the activities in the SyE process need to be done. They won't necessarily be done in the same order and with the same focus. When getting started, only a few of the myriad of methods and tools will get used. There may or may not be a systems engineering organization doing these things. They may or may not be accomplished under a systems engineering banner. The biggest problem in this area is the terminology, the vocabulary, and the lexicon.
4. The INCOSE Legacy Systems Engineer doesn't know enough about the commercial application and the commercial organization to go in and be productive without a couple of close associates that do understand the application and the organization. This is not a job for consultants, it is a job for insiders: folks who are there day after day, with the luxury of watching and suggesting.
5. Not everybody needs everything in the INCOSE medicine bag - the lag between available technology, the product cycle, increasing complexity and the product life are factors to be understood, The transient nature of the engineering population and the multiplicity of the competition are other factors. If the apprentice ← mentor ← village wise man system works for your business, maybe you don't need systems engineering (Yet!).

So where might INCOSE and systems engineering have a chance - and what would the systems elephant look like if it did? Commercial industries with large amounts of external regulation (external rigidities (Clausing 1999)) are interested. Even other government agencies with large amounts of external regulation are interested . The external regulations amount to large quantities of requirements that have to be tracked, traced and verified. Global companies, (and who can afford not to be these days?) have multipliers on the regulations. The age of the product has a direct correlation to the quantity of external regulation. Yes governing bodies are working toward harmonization of the regulations and toward performance regulations instead of prescribing regulations but that change happens slowly and filters into the market place even more slowly.

The knowledge management industry, and the related intellectual capital industry are eager to 'let us help you understand your key information, who has it, how it might be shared and how much does it contribute to the bottom line'....whether by story telling or information technology doesn't matter. They help you make your knowledge work for you. Enter another set of consultants. How do we work with them to incorporate the best of all in the solution to the ever increasing request for better faster cheaper? Are they some of the keys to systems engineering in some commercial enterprises?

Reality 1: Culture change. We need to recognize this as a culture change. Culture changes take time: 5 to 7 years at a minimum, more than the typical executive champion's tenure. The evolution of a systems engineering organization within the enterprise is not for the faint hearted. We need to map the insertion at commercial organizations. We need that map to reflect the reality of the champion changes, we need guidance on the impact of the champion changes and how to get the Systems initiative restarted or reinvigorated. We need to be flexible on the terminology - there is a product development terminology in most companies (yes of course it differs in each). We have long been the universal translators for the various engineering disciplines, let us also become the universal translators for the product development communities.

(Senge, et al 1999) describes the 3 major participants of change and sustained learning as the Executive Leader, the Local Line Leader and the Network Leader (a.k.a. the subject matter expert). The line leader and the SME is the core of a generally small team of folks trying to implement product and related process improvements via systems thinking. The Organization's perspective of this small team changes over time along the line of team formation: forming, storming, norming, performing (Tuckman, 1965). Prior to the 'arrival' of systems within an organization - the lack of systems is to blame for every problem, if we only had a system's perspective...This is the Joe Befstek phase. You remember Joe from the Lil Abner cartoon - he always had a black cloud over his head. Then the 'Systems folks arrive' lots of fanfare, loud music (think Lone Ranger Theme and how we need those silver bullets). Not even Systems Engineering is a silver bullet, SOOOOO next comes the Rodney (I don't get no respect) Dangerfield phase. This can either be ***the end*** - or a transition to the Junkyard Dog Phase (Systems will do all that stuff nobody else wants to do. The next step and the start up the norming curve is the Dudley Do Right phase. The Systems team is making some headway, only occasionally tying themselves to the railroad tracks (and the PM or the Champion has to rescue them). Pilot programs are proving the value of requirements and verification according to a plan, trade studies are consistently used to make decisions. Things are looking up. We then move on in the norming phase: whatever will work for the organization and start performing, adding more and more of the systems methods and tools until the systems team is performing a role similar to the orchestra conductor. Then it all gets internalized, and we don't need the focus anymore, and we need to downsize (but everybody has to deal with the cyclic size of the SyE team). Reality, this is a culture change - the same as other culture changes. Face it, deal with it, and overcome it. There is lots of help out there. Use it. Data from the early nineteen nineties relative to the adoption Concurrent Engineering tell us that there is value in the home port alignment of the functional organization. The value is to expedite the insertion of processes and consistent application of the processes across an organization - it also provides the spot for the improvement of the organization's systems processes. Find a way to be a process driver.

Reality 2: Legacy Exists. We need to recognize that Legacy Exists! The components that comprise today's offerings were the heart of the business and will continue to be. They and the innovations associated with the components will continue to be the basis for new product offerings. This is a regenerative business. For many, the product of yesterday provides the same function as the product of today - today's product is just more complex (those previously little computers are creeping in to provide 'smart', more robust products). The clean sheet of paper method, 'all-new-starts' doesn't work in commercial industry. Not even under very special conditions where disruptive technologies come together in more than 50% of the components. The legacy in the product line is reflected in the legacy in the organization. These legacies are interrelated. Both are driven by the need to be constantly introducing improved products to stay ahead of the competition, to maintain the market leadership within an industry segment. The same people build multiple physical versions to meet essentially the same functional need. They internalize the functions to the point that they think the physical stuff is the function. They internalize the performance measures, superceding the driving measures the customer is looking for. It is not until innovation upsets the status quo (whether in the company or by the competition doesn't matter!!), that somebody has to apply the systems engineering processes of functional analysis and allocation and synthesis to optimize the engineering of the next generation product. The interfaces, lost in the Sheard's Twelve roles inside the Glue Role become one of the most important roles for commercial systems engineers (Sheard 1996). In commercial, the need for a modernization plan for both old and new products is key to the growth of the company, and is one of the paths to better, faster, cheaper. Again it is focused on the modernization of parts to be incorporated in the existing system. The technological life of the component drives the change rate. The product and component form factor is critical to manufacturing, installation and support productivity. The System is engineered at the level of a Product Line, and the system integrity is maintained across many generations.

The regenerative nature of the commercial business, provides the opportunity to join with the Knowledge Management folks and position the companies for reuse of information: the functional requirements, the architectures, the interface specifications, the test plans, and drawing trees. These are just for starters. Write 'em once, store 'em - and use the information innumerable times for decades. The tools, once very cumbersome and autocratic are just getting better and better.

For others, the technology and the product are evolving so quickly that even if they wanted to worry about systems engineering by the time they followed the EIA 632 process, (much as in the aerospace, computer based systems business), the product would be obsolete. For global enterprises, the legacy of engineering and production facilities and supplier base also is also a key part of the legacy. In these industries, the entrepreneur is the SyE and the Intellectual Capital of the Company.

Reality 3: SyE Process and Methods. While all the activities in the SyE process need to be done, they won't necessarily be applied in the same order and with the same focus. When getting started, only a few of the myriad of methods and tools will get used. There may or may not be a systems engineering organization doing these things. The processes and methods may or may not be applied under a systems engineering banner. We need to stop thinking of EIA632 as a cookbook and think of it as a doctor's medicine bag. And yes there is a significant difference in the training and skill of the user of a cookbook and the Doctor. There is no right place to start and no right path to follow. The dynamics of the organization define the place to start. The path to follow will be discovered, and cleared as the systems organization forms, storms, and norms. Just as a doctor is helped by a conscious patient, any core systems group needs the participation of the other parts of the organization to be successful.

The methods generally grouped under the label 'Systems Analysis and Control' have the greatest likelihood of being valued by the organization. Trade studies in some form have been around for a while. Modeling and simulation is also in place for the components. The other methods for technical reviews and managing change are also in place - a legacy of the stage gate reviews that were implemented when Integrated Product Teams / Development was adopted by the organization.

The other easy to accept SyE process is requirements analysis / engineering / management - whatever the organization is going to call it. The Total Quality Management initiative a few years ago gained recognition of the need for capturing, understanding and prioritizing requirements from a variety of perspectives. The follow through into requirements management and then verification and validation that the resulting product met the original set of requirements is a harder sell. The latter aspects of the requirements process take a little longer.

At the beginning Verification / Validation is demonstration that the product works in a manner consistent with the practices of the business. What you see is what you get. For fast technology turn product this is often as good as it gets.

The legacy basis for the product line makes synthesis and functional analysis and allocation two processes that have long been internalized within the organization. The founder of the company, the inventor of the product is probably the last person to perform an extensive functional analysis and allocation leading to the synthesis into a physical implementation. The functions and the performance parameters have been internalized by the organization for so long, they have become the functions and the performance measures. Understanding the functions and the architectures behind the solution is key to moving into verification. These two are also key to introducing innovation across the product not simply in a component or two. The barrier to recreating the functional analysis and the architecture is that everybody knows what it is (there are however several variations in the minds of the engineers,) so why do we have to take the time to write it down. The driving customer requirements need to be traced to the engineering parameters. Who has the time, the corporate memory or the corporate commitment to recreate the driving customer requirements and trace them to the requirements. We again have internalized the functions of the product - we know what it has to do - and it will. Who has time to do other than document and trace the performance and physical requirements?

The answer is to employ the principles of knowledge management so that generating the requirements and the plans for the next generation is a matter of tailoring the last one rather than creating a new one. This needs to be a parallel activity, not on the critical path for a specific product. It also helps to wait until a couple of projects have taken the recreation path. It helps the knowledge manager to understand the commonalties, and it helps in the calculation and sale of the expected savings. This provides a better appreciation for the value of the tools, for tracability and for providing views of data that can then be written once, and 'viewed' many times for a wide variety of projects. This is another change - to an organization that recently (within current employee's memory) reduced the number of administrative assistants and put Word ™ and PowerPoint™ on the desktop. The resistance to rigorous application of process, method and tools is often manifested by the question: 'Do you want product or paper?' closely followed by 'do you want product or reviews?'

In spite of the resistance, the organization recognizes the need for a new approach. There are several methods an organization might employ to facilitate the introduction of a systems approach: train an existing employee (hereafter called 'the scout'); hire an experienced systems engineering practitioner; hire a consultant; or bring in training. None of these approaches alone will provide immediate results. What is required is a knowledge of the organization, the product, and systems engineering principles and practices. The scout understands the organization and the product. It will take even the broadest minded scout time to learn and adapt the systems processes to the immediate needs of the enterprise. The imported systems engineering practitioner needs time to understand the organization and the product The trainer will bring the training and stories from their experience - and for most commercial enterprises, the experience is not readily applicable. The consultant will have many of the same problems as the trainer - and will seldom be in attendance for the adhoc discoveries that will be crucial to the adoption of the systems by the organization. Which leads us to ...

Reality 4: INCOSE Legacy Systems Engineers. We need to recognize that systems engineers are not interchangeable. The INCOSE Legacy Systems Engineer doesn't know enough about the commercial application and the commercial organization to go in and be productive without a couple of close associates that do understand the application and the organization. One of those freed up to work with the Systems subject matter expert (SSME), needs to be the Scout. The Scout provides the history and the pot holes. There should also be a Systems network that is outside the core team and yet includes the folks that will be integral to the adoption of the systems by the organization. For a distributed organization, this network needs to include committed folks in all of the distributed locations. One of their roles is to keep the core team pragmatic, another of their roles is to spread the use of systems methods and tools as appropriate in their local organization. The SSME also needs to learn the product and business of the adopted enterprise - and does not have the luxury of the fifteen to thirty years that were spent really understanding the last application.

Without previous systems experience, the Scout, while well intentioned will not have the intuition to skip parts of the systems engineering process for the near term. There is always the risk that the organization will not come back to that process step, thus the need for the experienced inside practitioner. The somewhat cookbook approach often taken by the Scout is manifested by the decision to include a tool to 'help' with the requirements management The requirements tool vendors appear on request. Demonstrations are provided. Other parts of the organization are included in the demonstrations, and suddenly there is a need for a requirements study for the to-be-selected tool and consensus among the anticipated users. There is a need to decide with which existing enterprise tools this one needs to interface, and how many licenses of these typically more expensive than word processing tools we need and where will they be? And what about sharing data? All of a sudden we are into tool architectural studies and three more products have been released before we get the requirements tool decision made.

Reality is that this is not a job for consultants, it is a job for insiders. Folks who are there day after day, with the luxury of watching and suggesting working with multiple folks with a range of skills and knowledge.

Reality 5: Not every Enterprise <u>needs</u> Systems Engineering. Before you have heart failure, go back and read the section title and the underlined "needs". The cost benefit analysis is simply not there. We cannot even articulate the cost benefit to the INCOSE Legacy companies. Yes, any enterprise can be improved by a holistic view of products and processes. But what are the levers that drive a company to invest in the culture change(s), to invest in the training and the tools? To deal with the organizational trauma? Which enterprises are most likely to make the investment? Will the others follow? (NOTE: We are at the point where my personal experience over the last decade doesn't have answers. I do have suggestions.) Figure 1 presents a timeline of product development and product life for a variety of industries, starting with the INCOSE legacy of the DoD / Space industry.

Figure 1. PRODUCT LIFE & EVOLUTION

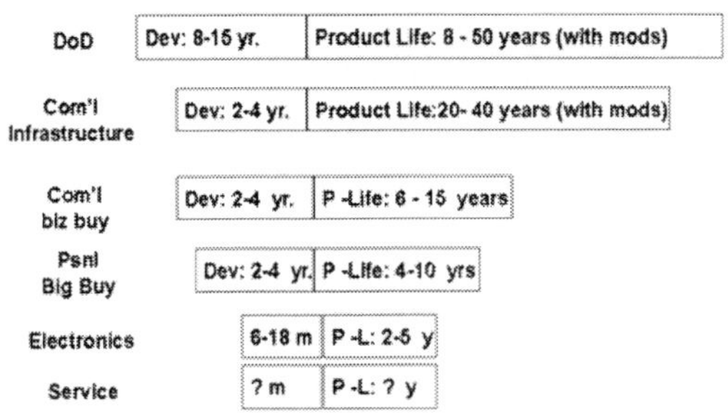

I have not addressed technology turn in Figure 1, but I know it plays a part as well. The faster the technology turn, the less <u>routine</u> the need for systems. Particularly when dealing with what I am beginning to call enabler products: those that establish new markets, are invisible to the end user, and are generally tossed with the next technology insertion. Depending on product life and cost, the products which incorporate those enabling technologies, do need a systems approach. the incorporation of disruptive technology in these products requires systems thinking and engineering. This is particularly important when the form factor changes. Until the form factor changes again, the SyE is managing interfaces and product integrity. Does anyone replace more than the carafe on the coffee maker? An automobile has many 'replaceable parts'. Does Krups™ do its own electronics research and manufacture? Most likely, it applies electronic technology to coffee makers et al. Military and space systems have planned improvement programs for the shorter lived subsystems. (Gillis 1999) provides a summary that compares the DoD Major Systems Development time of 8-15 years to the commercial market place that has new technology 4 to 8 times faster. He further lists technology cycle times for Electronics at 18 months, Avionics at 6 years, Aircraft Engines at 14 years, and Airframes at 25 years. The supporting technology for both the military and commercial systems is constantly evolving. One difference is that the commercial products are incorporating the technology at a faster rate with a smaller performance delta between products.

Another key difference is that the Military / Space industry is based on a 'build-to-specification' model vs. the 'build-on-speculation' model of commercial industry. It will be interesting to watch the results as the former 'specified' satellite companies move into the 'speculation' satellite business. The 'financial analysts' might be ready to choose a winner, I'm not. And what do we really know about the methods employed? Who moved the principles and practices of systems to the speculation side and who simply moved the best of the chief engineers? Just a space segment does not a system make. De-facto interface specifications do contribute to making a system.

Let's consider Clausing's external rigidities. More and more companies are being driven by external regulation to formally manage requirements in some form. They are also required to validate for the regulating body that the regulations have been met. Requirements traceability tools are a wonderful solution. Does every organization that needs requirements tracability need systems engineering? For the profit making product or for the information systems infrastructure that supports the product? The information technology /software community understand well the need for systems engineering. That is a part of the Legacy.

If you are manufacturing a throwaway product, maybe you don't need systems engineering. You don't need it until your competition starts using it, until you have eked all the possible improvements out of the business process reengineering, the quality initiatives, and it is time to integrate the improvements in the product and the process across the life cycle of your product. If you get to the Joe Befstek stage of needing the holistic approach that systems thinking and systems engineering can provide it is too late.

In the commercial environment, a couple years are a long time. Some Web startups don't last that long….do they need Systems Engineering a la INCOSE? Will they ever realize it? Do they have their own version (are the good entrepreneurs basically systems engineers)?

Does the distribution of the enterprise contribute to the need for systems engineering with some rigor? Probably yes, the governments use it at the program level to manage distributed contractors building parts of the same product. They use the same terminology, and the same training, so that all parts of the program organization are applying systems engineering in a similar manner, and as appropriate for the part of the system each is producing. The life cycle focus of systems engineering can also improve the efficiency of globally distributed, manufacturing, installation, and service organizations. Yes that is infrastructure, but it crosses many functions and is there because there is a product to be produced, distributed, installed and maintained.

The electronics community has recognized the need for a new type of engineer to support the development of systems on a chip. Or since many of our members are in the Electronics business do we have an inside path??? For whatever reason the INCOSE folks representing electronics companies represent primarily the federal support side of the house - What access and influence do they have to the commercial parts of the enterprise? The Hewlett Packards and IBMs have not been large players in INCOSE. When I was at IBM Federal Systems the future systems on a chip folks were not interested - the Systems Integration Outreach parts of the enterprise were interested. They took what we had, let us help them adapt it and are now in a separate consulting business. The Systems Integration enterprises run the gamut of Complex systems built with commercial parts, to pack and ship of individual configurations of standard components. The former is in the INCOSE Membership base - what do we have to offer to the latter?

The transient nature of the engineering population and the multiplicity of the competition are other factors. If the apprentice ← mentor ← village wise man 'system' works for your business, maybe you don't need systems engineering. If you are defining or enabling a market, maybe you don't need systems engineering.
Figure 2 is an initial presentation of the various methods for managing knowledge in industry today. The group that has recognized the need for some processes and procedures, and tools is a candidate for systems engineering. The craftsman whose product is increasing in complexity to the point that a computer literate apprentice can't handle the whole job is a candidate for systems engineering. The area within the oval should be INCOSE 's target commercial market.

Figure 2. KNOWLEDGE MANAGEMENT STYLE

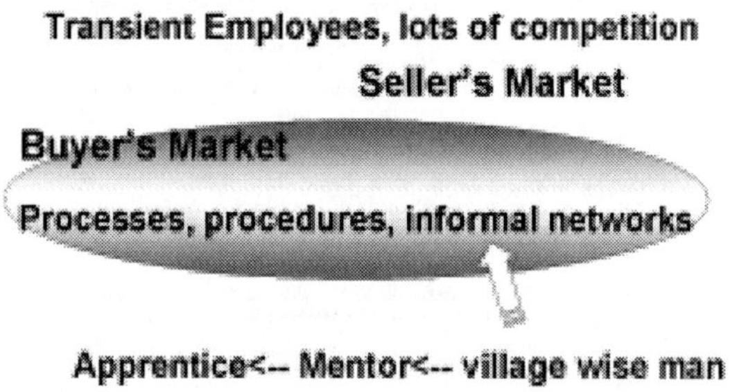

SUMMARY

The Big 5 of the Systems Engineering Process: Requirements Management; Functional Analysis; Synthesis; Systems Analysis and Control and Verification fit in the commercial enterprise. Requirements analysis, verification and parts of systems analysis and control seem to be the most used in the regenerative product business. The automobile or the elevator provides the same functions from generation to generation of the product line, the differences in technology and design modify the physical manifestation of those functions. There is significant opportunity for reuse of information across all three of those processes in the regenerative business. While safety and reliability are critical to all complex systems, they become significant business drivers for commercial product lines. The Design - fors (assembly, installation, maintenance …safety) become key drivers as they are reflected in the bottom line. One of the new initiatives is design for sustainment / modernization. This applies to segments of industry that produce long lived products. Long lived products require the original equipment manufacturer to 'support and supply' that old equipment until it is taken out of service….that can be a drag on the business performance numbers. Commercial performance improvements are more incremental than in the aerospace and Defence business. The cycle times are shorter. These are the elements of the Product Design initiatives in academia and industry. They already exist. They are well funded and endowed in the US by the Manufacturing giants. The related industry associations tend to be focused on the business side of product development.

Systems Engineering tools are more complex and expensive than the Microsoft Office Suite. They require lots of bandwidth to support global development. And we really need a common vocabulary to minimize the confusion relative to what the requirement means. For US headquartered companies, that common language is generally the American version of English. A common vocabulary is still required - to be used regardless of the language being spoken.

INCOSE arrogance and focus on the 632 / 731 / CMMI will not gain members from the commercial segments. Any of the improvements made to accommodate aspects of the commercial environment will improve the efficiency of the INCOSE legacy organizations. INCOSE needs to listen carefully to the few members of commercial enterprises that are remaining members. INCOSE has a lot to learn.

REFERENCES

Axelband, Elliot and Clausing, Donald. 'Commercial Systems Engineering'. Briefing to the INCOSE Board of Directors. January 1999.

Gillis, Matt, "Open Systems Joint Task Force Gets the Word Out." *Program Manager,* July - August 1999.

Senge, Peter et al, *The Dance of Change The Challenges of Sustaining Momentum in Learning Organizations.* Doubleday, 1999 .

Sheard, Sarah, "Twelve Systems Engineering Roles." *Proceedings of the Sixth Annual International Symposium of INCOSE*, pp 481-488, July 1996.

Tuckman, B.W. "Developmental Sequences in Small Groups". *Psychological Bulletin* 63, pp 384-399. 1965

ACKNOWLEGMENT

The author would like to acknowledge the contirbutions of the members of the INCOSE Constitution chapter for an early review of this material.

BIOGRAPHY

V. A. Lentz is a Past President of INCOSE and a recipient of the Founders Award. She was a practicing Systems Engineer for at least 23 of her 30 years at IBM Federal Systems, Loral, Lockheed Martin where she worked large, unprecedented, computer based systems such as Global Positioning System. In 1996 she joined United Techologies Research Center to gain insight to Systems Engineering in a more commercial area. She is currently with Otis Elevator, a United Technologies Company, working to continue the cultural change of making systems engineering an integral part of a global commercial organization.

Acquisition Strategies for the Management of Multinational Cooperative Research and Development Programs

Charles L. Roe
The Johns Hopkins University Applied Physics Laboratory
Johns Hopkins Rd.
Laurel, MD 20723-6099

Abstract. Collaborative efforts allow nations to pursue common-interest programs too expensive for any one nation to attempt. The difficulties of these multinational developments are formidable. Program Managers must devise an acquisition strategy that allows them to control the direction and goals of the program by mobilizing programmatic, technology, management, and contracting processes. Several alternatives are available to these managers, and their choice of acquisition strategy can have a major impact on their ability to guide the program to a successful conclusion.

INTRODUCTION

U.S. participation in multinational cooperative research and development programs has grown rapidly in recent years. These collaborative efforts are a way for nations to pursue common-interest programs too expensive for any one country to attempt by itself. Sharing developments is a way to initiate programs that would otherwise be unaffordable. A number of Congressional and DoD directives are aimed at encouraging these cooperative endeavors.

Such programs are often initiated to meet a strategic requirement that is common to all the nations. A Memorandum of Understanding (MOU) is usually negotiated which sets forth the conditions for each country's participation in terms of its contribution to and expected return from the program with respect to "workshare" and products.

A program office is then set up in any one of several structures, as discussed later, and a program manager (PM) is assigned to lead the acquisition effort. A program office often has a multinational staff. Thus, each staff member may come with a different policy and procedural approach to the acquisition process. To give the staff, as well as the signatory countries of the MOU, a common understanding of the acquisition objectives and environment, one of the PM's first tasks is to devise and document an acquisition strategy.

The strategy will encompass program objectives, direction, and control. It is based on the integration of all the acquisition processes, including programmatic considerations, technology issues, management alternatives, and contracting vehicles. The strategy essentially outlines the plan that both the government and contractor PMs will follow in executing the program. Often the strategy is prepared in parallel with the MOU and serves to further define the relationships among the participants' technical and business communities.

This paper examines some of the factors essential to formulating an acquisition strategy for a multinational cooperative research and development program. It further offers some thoughts on the acquisition process itself and how to make it more supportive of these international efforts.

FACTORS INFLUENCING ACQUISITION STRATEGY

In formulating an acquisition strategy that captures the intent of an international MOU, the PM first must establish a managerial approach to control and direct all elements of the acquisition process, including performance, cost, schedule, and risk management. The strategy must also consider the acquisition environment in terms of competition, DoD rules and directives, and opportunities for tailoring or streamlining the process (INSTR 5000.2A 1992). On the basis of this environment, the PM can then detail the programmatic, technology, management, and contracting methodologies to attain the program objectives (Figure 1).

The foremost **programmatic** issue in a multinational cooperative research and development program is to establish agreement on requirements among the participating nations. It is the task of the PM to coordinate the requirements to meet each nation's needs within the constraints of the overall program and the agreements of the Development MOU. Early in the development process alternative approaches will be assessed. Each must be evaluated in terms of meeting the

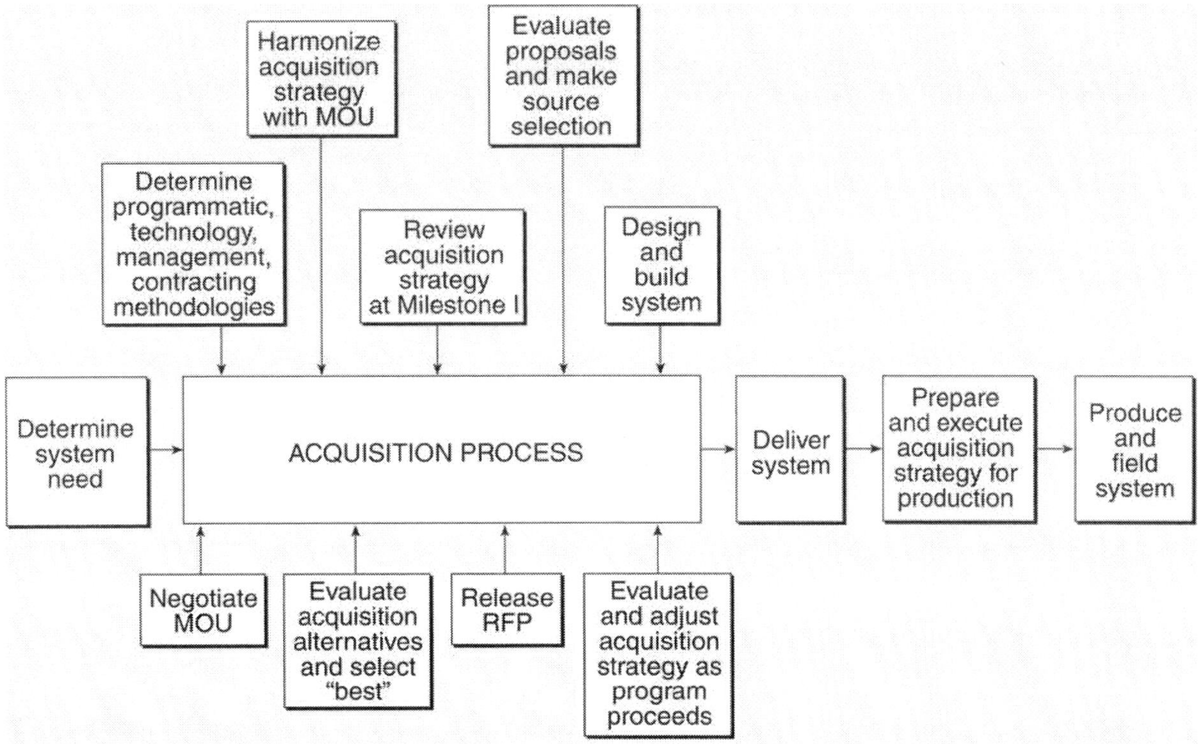

Figure 1. The process to formulate and execute the program acquisition strategy includes programmatic, technology, management, and contracting aspects.

requirements and must be balanced against budgetary and schedule constraints. Those alternatives that satisfy the needs of the participants should be advanced, and those that tend to favor one country's parochial interests to the general detriment of others should be discarded.

The PM must follow the guidance of the MOU in determining the fair and equitable sharing of costs and responsibilities among the cooperating nations. In addition, the PM must see that offsets maximize the efficient use of each nation's resources in terms of its contribution to the overall product, while taking into account the overall economic repercussions.

Technology issues concern approaches to the acquisition strategy for meeting program goals regarding system design, performance, and reliability/maintainability/availability. Since industrial participation from several countries may be involved, systems engineers may have to determine how the technology will be shared and also how to integrate the technology into the product. Participating governments may require that specific technical approaches be used so that their own industries can better participate. Technology transfer issues must also be dealt with.

The acquisition strategy will usually identify the kinds and amount of product testing to be done and where it will be performed, since this too may be part of the workshare considerations. Elements or components of the system that are developed overseas may need to be transported and integrated with other subassemblies before system-level testing. Logistics planning and ways to maintain and support the fielded system are also addressed in the acquisition strategy plan.

To lessen risk, alternative technical concepts to meet program goals will be explored. Before award of the development contract, it is often useful to provide small fixed-price contracts to selected industry or government laboratories to help evaluate the approaches being considered. After feasibility studies are completed, a government concept is documented and requests for proposals (RFPs) are solicited from international teams of contractors. These teams are usually led by one company designated as the prime contractor and through whom the government program office contracts for the work.

There are various alternatives for setting up a program office for the **management** of the acquisition effort. The program may be managed from an office with a multinational staff representing each participating country. This arrangement gives each country an added insight into programmatic activities. Participating nations can also gain some assurance that their industry will be treated fairly and that the accountability of each country is maintained. Alternatively, the nation through which the acquisition is being made can assume full responsibility for staffing the office and managing the program. The policies and procedures of the lead country will obviously dominate the program under this arrangement. Another scheme is to set up an office in each participating country and let each one manage its own part of the development effort. This requires a tremendous amount of coordination. It also requires that a steering committee made up of representatives from each nation must remain active in the program. Whichever government program office structure is chosen, the contractor must mirror that same structure to effectively work with the participants and interface with the customer (Roe 1997).

The **contracting** process is an important consideration in formulating the acquisition strategy. Particularly in a multinational research and development effort, the approach must accommodate the involvement of overseas participants and take into account constraints imposed by national laws and regulatory practices. A number of other factors may also impact the contracting process, including expiring terms on funding, differences in exchange rates, rules on how money can be spent, and timing on when the funds must be available to be applied to the contract.

Customarily, the contracting rules of the country in which the contract is being written will prevail. Thus, if separate program offices are set up in each country and the contract is between the office and industry in that country, then the laws and procedures of that country will apply. More typical, however, one company will be designated as the lead or prime and will contract on behalf of all the industrial partners with the government.

In making the source selection, the RFP must clearly communicate the requirements. It must precisely define the program objectives, the relative importance of the goals, acceptable design trade-offs, the legal basis for evaluation, and data disclosure requirements. The RFP must be drafted with attention to differences in language, business approaches, and the conceptual understanding of potential participants. The contract type being sought by the government should be specified.

The RFP will explain what non-U.S. input to the source selection process is expected and how it will be integrated into the evaluation. This may further include an explanation of how technical competence, capability, and price realism will be evaluated from a non-U.S. perspective. Potential bidders must be given a sense of an appropriate evaluation/decision schedule based on proposal complexity.

CHOOSING AND EXECUTING THE "BEST" ACQUISITION STRATEGY

Several alternatives exist for the acquisition of systems using multinational cooperative development approaches. For example, the system may be developed by a consortium of nations without U.S. participation; co-developed among U.S., European, and other nations; or developed by a multinational consortium in which the United States is asked to take a leading role (i.e., use U.S. contracting offices, program management, and acquisition rules). The range of possibilities varies from those in which the United States is merely an interested observer (e.g., when a system is developed outside the United States and is sold to potential adversaries), to those in which U.S. military forces may have a "need to know" since the system may be used by our allies, to those in which the United States is the primary player, i.e., pays the greatest share, provides program oversight, and contributes the greater number of personnel.

When several non-U.S. countries are participating, their options on competition may be limited and they may have to look to subsystem or component development for their workshare. Competition may also be limited because of offset requirements. Other conditions incorporated in the MOU may affect the ability to compete as well. Contractor source selection by European governments is typically limited to a few well-known firms for major system development. This contrasts with U.S. policy and presents a major issue for collaborative programs that must select contractors for joint acquisition. Typically, one of the parties will be designated to contract with the selected sources on behalf of all the governments.

The goal of the PM is to obtain the best trade-off among cost, performance, supportability, and schedule. There are two generic forms of competition: design competition, where two or more contractors develop individual design approaches, and production competition, where two or more companies bid to secure all or part of a production contract. Competition can be enhanced by teaming, second-sourcing, leader-follower, and breakouts (DSMC Guide 1987). U.S. firms may decide to team with overseas firms to gain a competitive advantage. Each approach to competition requires the PM to possess an adequate database, a knowledgeable in-house team, and a detailed definition of the objectives of the contracting strategy.

Sole-source contracts are permitted where a knowledge base for development of the system is found to reside only with a single prospective contractor. Justification for such an acquisition strategy must be provided. The contractor's level of experience, manufacturing, and resources necessary to perform the effort can provide this justification. Special tooling, test equipment, and facilities can also be cited if these would represent a significant start-up cost by a competitor and add risk to the schedule.

The acquisition strategy will be tailored to match the character of the program and will enable program requirements to be met most effectively, consistent with the degree of risk involved. The PM may maintain multiple alternatives, e.g., competitive prototyping of critical items, a strategy that combines developmental and operational test and evaluation, dual-sourcing, and multi-year procurement. The benefits and risks associated with reducing lead time through concurrency will be specifically addressed in tailoring the acquisition strategy. The use of integrated product and process development (IPPD) is a consideration and may be mandated (Roe 1996). Streamlining the process will encourage the use of "contractor format" for specifications and other deliverables as well as overall minimization of documentation. (A contractor format allows the developing agency to use its own format for specifications and other documents rather than following rigid government guidelines set forth in DoD or military specs. The move toward contractor format is part of acquisition reform in the United States that is aimed at substantial savings of development costs.) Pre-planned product improvement (P3I) may be considered for systems if refinements to the requirements are anticipated or where technology risk discourages immediate implementation of a capability.

Often when the system transitions to the production phase, another MOU must be negotiated to address its manufacture, assembly, and sale. Again, nations may use the leverage they have in purchasing systems to ensure that their own industries can participate in building some or parts of all the systems. An acquisition strategy for production is also required, and here too several options are available, based on the structure established by the participating nations. The system may be produced by a number of nations without U.S. involvement (assuming the development has resulted in successful test and demonstration and the complete data package is available). Or the United States may be involved, but U.S. industry does not choose to participate. The system could also be developed entirely by the United States while production is licensed out of country. Conversely, a system may be developed without U.S. participation, but a U.S. company can be licensed to produce it. Likewise, the system could be produced just as it was developed, with the U.S. acting as an equal partner in the production or taking the lead and subcontracting certain subassemblies or piece parts to overseas subcontractors.

The acquisition strategy presents and justifies an approach that meets the stated desires of the participants as expressed in the MOU. It may spell out the terms of a prime contractor/subcontractor structure, the terms of a cooperative or teaming structure among all the contractors qualified to develop the system or its components, or the contractual terms between an individual country and the component developers.

At appropriate milestones the acquisition strategy is reviewed to ensure that controls are in place to identify and retire risks and to provide flexibility for implementing U.S. and allied workshare agreements. The strategy will hold certain contractors responsible for delivery of an integrated and tested system that is ready for production. After a further MOU negotiation for production of the system, the acquisition strategy developed for production is implemented and a workshare negotiated by the partners results in

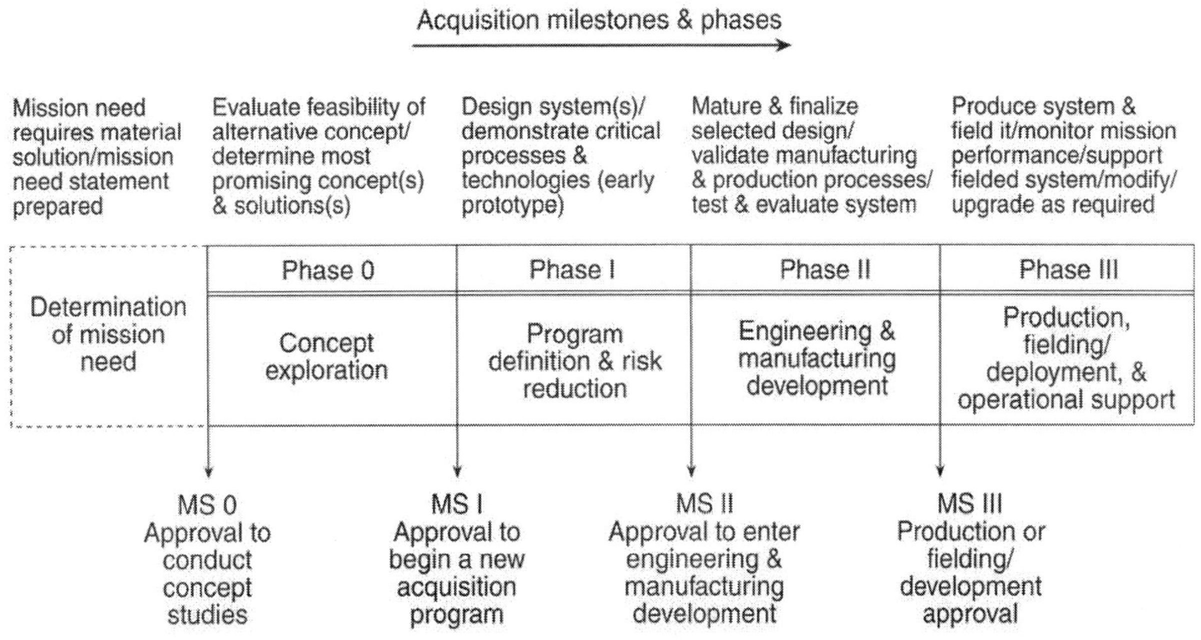

Figure 2. The acquisition process. At Milestones I, II, and III the acquisition strategy must be reviewed and approved. Shown is the U.S. process; European nations have similar, but slightly different processes/phases.

production and delivery of the system to the nations, first through a low-rate initial production, and then full-rate production.

The U.S. acquisition process is shown in Figure 2. Other countries have similar phases for major system developments. These generally proceed from identifying the requirement, through exploration of alternative approaches, to performing feasibility studies and selecting a contractor(s), to developing and fielding the system. The acquisition strategy guides these efforts and provides direction for dealing with risks and uncertainties about cost, schedule, performance, and supportability.

IMPROVING THE ACQUISITION PROCESS

Continued cooperation with international partners in defense acquisitions requires that acquisition managers learn from past efforts, continue to educate themselves in the nuances of collaborative efforts, and stand ready to take fresh, creative approaches to devising acquisition strategies that will see the programs past the numerous pitfalls that await the unwary. As more and more of these programs are initiated and successfully pursued, more trust will be built between ourselves and our allies. Dispelling the perception that an effort will become a U.S.-dominated DoD program is a real hurdle that the PM cannot ignore. Overseas partners must be consulted on all matters and their concerns and viewpoints considered equitably to maintain this trust.

The acquisition PM for an international program must continuously seek advocates for the program, both from among the overseas partners and within the U.S. defense establishment. There will always be domestic opponents who will attack a program with arguments that U.S. requirements are being subordinated to other nations' interests or that U.S. costs are excessive relative to those being paid by its partners. Opponents in other nations may express similar doubts.

The PM also must be on guard to avoid MOU negotiations that result in watered-down requirements such that the need that propelled the joint effort in the first place is not met. The requirements must be identified early, well before the MOU process begins, so that negotiators can concentrate on nontechnical issues. In setting these requirements the needs of the allied nations must be considered equitably. Although the PM may be assigned by the United States, he or she is responsible for looking out for the interests of all participants.

Again, various acquisition alternatives are available to the PM that may be used to advantage. The PM may link program decisions to the contractor's demonstrated accomplishments in development progress or in early production efforts; use competitive prototyping or second-sourcing to foster a competitive environment that spurs development; force concurrency to speed development; or influence the systems engineering of the product by requiring that the contractor provide a rationale for its architecture and component breakout, since this affects subcontracting and worksharing with the international partners. In short, the PM should not be deterred by apparent barriers to the program. He or she must be given the tools and the responsibility to see the program through to a successful conclusion.

Clearly, program office personnel will need preparation in these types of procurement. Training can be provided by various Defense Systems Management College courses (DSMC Guide 1987). However, efforts must be made to retain those professionals who gain experience on these types of programs and encourage them to stay in the field to act in mentoring roles on new programs. Countries that do not have such training programs need to take steps to either send their acquisition professionals to training centers or establish programs of their own.

CONCLUSIONS

The keys to a successful collaborative program are a recognized multilateral need, an acquisition strategy that makes good business sense, management commitment via the MOU to include financial management considerations (e.g., funding stability), and program follow-through by the participants. Delivery of a product within cost and schedule limitations that fulfills the participants' expectations occurs only after a complex and often adventurous development effort.

The PM has a wide range of options available in putting together the acquisition strategy, but these are often reduced in number by the vagaries of the particular program. Thus, options on competition may be limited, participants from some nations may specify specific industries that they want involved, and U.S. firms may want to team with overseas companies that may offer them competitive advantages. The strategy that was first decided upon may have to be modified during the course of the development effort. In the U.S. acquisition process the acquisition strategy must be reviewed and approved at Milestones I, II, and III (Figure 2).

With the experience of past collaborative efforts, a body of lessons learned is starting to accumulate. Chief among these is the need to build trust among the participants. The integrity of the PM in pursuing the development on behalf of all the nations must be above reproach and he or she must continuously be sensitive to all viewpoints and concerns. DoD offers training courses for acquisition professionals involved in these multinational cooperative efforts. A dedicated PM with an experienced multinational staff has a good chance to succeed.

REFERENCES

Guide for the Management of Multinational Programs, Defense Systems Management College (DSMC), Fort Belvoir, VA, 1987.

Roe, C.L., "Project Management and Systems Engineering in an IPD Environment," *Proc. Sixth Annual INCOSE Symp.*, pp. 1049–1054, 1996.

Roe, C.L., "Systems Engineering and Management of Multinational Cooperative Development Programs," *Proc. Seventh Annual INCOSE Symp.*, pp. 561–567, 1997.

Secretary of the Navy Instruction 5000.2A, Enclosure 5, Part 5, *Acquisition Planning and Risk Management, Section A, Acquisition Strategy*, 9 December 1992.

BIOGRAPHY

Charles L. Roe is a member of the APL Surface Combat Systems Program Office, where he manages projects related to ship self-defense for U.S. and NATO navies. These tasks emphasize combat system analyses, upgrades and integration of new developments with existing Fleet equipment. Mr. Roe received a B.S. in computer science from the University of Maryland and an M.S. in technical management from JHU. He joined INCOSE in 1994 and is active in the Chesapeake Chapter.

Assessing the relevance of systems engineering for electrical commercial product development

Olivier Parrot
MGE UPS Systems
140 av. Jean Kuntzmann
38334 St Ismier - Cedex
France
olivier.parrot@mgeups.com

Alain Rouge
Q-Labs
Villa Baudran
F-94742 Arcueil - Cedex
France
rouge@objectif.fr

Claude De Paoli
MGE UPS Systems
140 av. Jean Kuntzmann
38334 St Ismier - Cedex
France
claude.de-paoli@mgeups.com

Catherine Dutey
Schneider Electric
36 Rue Henri Tarze
38050 Grenoble - Cedex 9
France
catherine_dutey@mail.schneider.fr

Abstract. Traditionally, MGE UPS Systems, like most commercial product suppliers, was used to rely on stamped-commercial product development practices to manage time-to-market. But practices like concurrent engineering, project-based and steering committee-driven organization, system life-cycle, are not anymore sufficient to answer always growing global market constraints. New practices as well as the solving of concurrent engineering side effects are becoming unavoidable.

This concerns in particular the introduction of global systems optimization Vs. Component optimization, which traditionally drives product commercial product development.

Systems engineering offers potential solutions to solve that issue although it was used so far for types of development and types of system which correspond to features that are almost opposite to ours (large vs. small systems, long vs. fast development, mono-customer vs. market).

Time is a very precious resource for companies like ours, it is very difficult to find some time and motivation to set new practices in use; and especially practices that somehow tell that "you should waste a bit of your time at the beginning of the project to save more later on".

Not an idea to be easily accepted by a product developer or manager ! This is why we carried out the SYRENA experiment, to address both in technical, managerial and cultural terms, the adoption of some systems engineering practices to develop faster small electrical systems.

This paper gives a bird's-eye-view of the findings of the SYRENA project w.r.t. to the technical, managerial and cultural acceptance of systems engineering.

From a technical standpoint, the experiment focused more specifically on the interface between marketing and engineering and addressed the interface of the system-level requirements engineering process.

THE CONTEXT OF THE SYRENA EXPERIMENT

Who are we ? MGE UPS SYSTEMS is a world-wide company of 2200 employees, with 4 production sites in Europe, USA and Asia, and 150 sales and after sales offices. The worldwide UPS market in 99 was of USD 4.7 Billion. The MGE UPS SYSTEMS turnover was of USD 450 Million, which represents 10% of the global UPS marketplace. The MGE UPS SYSTEMS catalogue offers a full product range from 200 to 4800 kVA (http://www.mgeups.com).

The rationale of the Syrena experiment. The global aim of Syrena is to improve the Time-To-Market[1]

[1] TTM will be used as an acronym for Time-To-Market

capability of MGE projects. Developing a system quicker means either **(goal 1)** to shorten one or several phases of the product life-cycle, and **(goal 2)** to avoid that later phases are made longer because of errors introduced in earlier phases.

The major and starting point to shorten a phase of the life-cycle is to make the corresponding process more systematic and accepted by their users. This is an unavoidable prerequisite, which, if it is not fulfilled, closes the door to efficient time reduction of the corresponding process.

Avoiding late impacts of earlier introduced errors requires first to set in place techniques that can help to detect and avoid errors in earlier phases. It also requires to set in place a change management process that allows to track changes over the life-cycle and to identify their origin.

Setting new objectives for MGE TTM reduction. Reducing development time is not a new issue at MGE and conducted to past implementations of goals 1 and 2. The past TTM capability improvements at MGE first resulted in the systematization of the downstream part of the product life-cycle, precisely between R1[2] and R5, thus opening the door to shortening this phase. It also led to the deployment of a change management process in this part of the life-cycle, thus, preparing the work to avoid reworking due to earlier introduced errors.

New market factors and the spreading of software in our solutions required yet a new TTM improvement step to be made and this is why the Syrena initiative was launched.

This experiment had to build on top of previously achieved results and to further implement goals 1 and 2. First, since process systematization was achieved for the downstream part of the product life-cycle, but was not for its upstream part. It was therefore decided to address the process systematization of the R0-R1 part of the product life-cycle. This made our first Syrena Objective: *Objective 1- Implement a process covering the R0-R1 part of the MGE product life-cycle, that is systematic and that is well accepted by practitioners.*

Secondly, since a change management process was now in place in the later phases of the life-cycle, it was possible to see whether better practices introduced in earlier phases (R0-R1) would avoid rework during the later phases. Such rework is often detected during the test integration and therefore analyzing rework avoidance of R0-R1 outcomes accounts to identifying whether late-identified rework finds its origin in elements that are built during the R0-R1 phase. This made our second Syrena objective: *Objective 2 - Introduce practices in R0-R1 in order to decrease rework in the R1-R5 phases.*

[2] The MGE Life cycle is depicted in figure 1.

A quantitative expression of the goals. Regarding objective 1, we intended to reach an average acceptance of 80% of the queried MGE population sample

Regarding objective 2, the new targeted improvement intended to show that by better working in phase R0-R1 on one of the various activities to be carried out, namely requirements engineering, it is possible to reduce the global project duration by 10%. A typical MGE project duration is 24 months. Therefore, in the context of the experiment, we considered that we had to see whether a 2.4 months rework over R1-R5 could have been avoided due to better requirements engineering practice in R0-R1.

ACCEPTANCE ASSESSMENT OF SYSTEMS ENGINEERING FOR SMALL COMMERCIAL PRODUCT DEVELOPMENT

In parallel to a technical acceptance (i.e. making a technical experiment to assess the suitability of systems-level requirements engineering for commercial product development) and to managerial acceptance (i.e. cost and time assessment of requirements engineering introduction), we carried out a cultural assessment of the potential of systems engineering to improve the time-to-market capability of a product- developing organization.

Cultural assessment: systems engineering Vs. traditional concurrent engineering practices. From the very beginning of the experiment we felt concerned with the potential cultural reluctance to adopt Syrena results. Product developing companies, although they have to deal with fast evolving business and technical conditions, are rarely inclined to improve their capabilities in a formal way.

Acceptance is a common issue when attempting to evolve practices. But in the context of time-to-market, this is even worse, especially with the introduction of systems engineering. Indeed, with time pressure people naturally have a tendency to hurry up by for instance starting to build the solution as soon as possible , and without a sufficient understanding of the problem the system is expected to address. There is also a tendency to jump on the details very quickly and to avoid or makc major and global decisions implicitly, sometimes leading to breakable solutions and which breaks might be discovered very late.

These are for instance typical side-effects that are experienced with concurrent engineering. Concurrent engineering also introduces more technical and managerial complexity due to the need to manage technical and managerial interfaces between components and organizations.

Furthermore, with the introduction of systems engineering, which adds one or several layers on top of engineering disciplines (SW, HW, mechanics, etc.), many people share the belief, and this is human, that adding more work will in fact contribute to augment the global development duration and not decrease it.

The cultural assessment was achieved via an interview program and a questionnaire survey.

Main results of the interviews. Interviews were used as a media to formally install a communication with the MGE practitioners and to avoid they have the feeling that the proposed approach was enforced. It also helped us to customize the requirements engineering process from a technical point of view (see figures 2 and 3).

The main tracks of improvement identified by the interviews can be synthesized in the following way:

1. Enlarge the vision of the client : improve the knowledge of the client and of customer environments,
2. Balance time-to-market with cost and performance points of view. Although time-to-market was identified as the major objective of the experiment. The interviews made clear that in practice each decision-making is not made along one dimension only but is a trade-off of several dimensions like cost, performance, time-to-market, and revenues for the company,
3. Consolidate the marketing vision with internal needs ; involve all disciplines earlier in order to collect their needs and confront their point of views to other needs,
4. Consolidate the requirements at the system level, to establish a system requirements baseline, around which discussions and agreements can take place,
5. Capitalize and improve the reusability of requirements since it was generally assumed that at least 80 % of requirements can be reused from a product line to another one,
6. Include useful information in the baseline to be able to analyze the impact of a requested evolution and decide objectively,
7. Make top-to-bottom information traceability in order, the steering committee can embrace very quickly the impacts of a change whatever the level it occurs at,
8. Establish a suitable documentation structure to improve the efficiency of the access to the information,
9. Improve the communication and coordination between the different disciplines to accelerate the integration phase of the system and optimize the solution globally,
10. Increase efficiency of risk management while making the approach lighter,
11. Coordinate Configuration management at system level, and not only at component or discipline level,
12. Enlarge the validation scope and work earlier on validation.

Analysis of the questionnaire survey. Table 1 and Figure 4 give an idea of the level of relevance rating , according the interviewees, of selected practices to increase the time-to-market capability of MGE. The sum of the relevance rates gives an average acceptance of 82%; which satisfies our expected target of 80%.

Theme of practice	Relevance rate in %
Define System Requirements	
Collect stakeholder needs	100
Consolidate and formalize all stakeholder needs and constraints	100
Problem refinement	91
Define the Technical problem	
Requirements analysis	82
Requirements quality	100
Requirements evolution and maintenance	100
Requirements feedback and evolution	82
Validate system	
Validation strategy	100
Requirements validation	91
Manage risks	
Identify risks…	100
Risk quantification	73
Risk analysis	55
Developing a risk mitigation strategy	55
Monitoring risk mitigation activities	73
Communicating, coordinating risk status …	73
Manage configurations	
Identification	64
Change management	55
Status communication	27
Integrate disciplines	
Involvement of impacted individuals	82
Understanding, communication and coordination	91
Average acceptance	**82%**

Table 1: Percentage of practice relevance to time-to-market

Common and specific concerns of the different stakeholders. During the Syrena experiment, we did not face in fact direct cultural reluctance barriers. But nevertheless, several leitmotiv hints made during interviews of MGE practitioners make us still believe this problem was anyway a concern. This manifested itself in particular in statements like "Even if you have systems layers, documents and information, data must anyway be easy to use, access and find" or "we don't need a heaviness culture at MGE".

There was a fairly good understanding of the need to trace from system-level decisions. The interviews confirmed that system-level decisions are major choices which impact in terms of cost and time the remainder of the development. And it was also well-understood that late engineering changes, which affect these decisions, imply growing resource consumption as you proceed throughout the life cycle.

Compared to sectors where systems engineering is traditionally deployed, we felt that the decision-making-related process had a much greater importance and particularly for managerial stakeholders of the engineering effort.

Technical stakeholders were more concerned with an another aspect. They often claimed that people forget the importance of the global engineering picture (e.g. global system optimization vs. System part local optimization), and that all individual functional areas have forgotten to communicate efficiently. It turned out that the problem was to ensure that all stakeholders understand the viewpoint of other actors as well as they should exchange viewpoints.

Organizational impact of systems-level requirements engineering adoption. The main organizational change to manage is finally not the introduction of a formal requirements engineering process but the need to better and earlier communicate requirements and viewpoints on these requirements between all concerned stakeholders, and even those who will be impacted late in the product life-cycle.

The difficulty to involve the marketing people in the Syrena experiment was particularly representative of that issue.

People are in generally fully committed on projects that are in the development phase and therefore have few or even no availability for projects on the start. More generally due to time pressure, people will concentrate their efforts on the activities they are responsible of, and will give up with activities where they should be involved but for which they have not the direct responsibility. We therefore designed a requirements engineering process that enforces an early communication on requirements of all concerned stakeholders. Figures 2 and 3 give an idea, respectively of the global systems engineering process and of the system-level requirements engineering process we introduced.

While addressing the assignment of the systems engineering role to project actors, we also discovered a difference with traditional systems engineering. The systems engineering role is not fulfilled full time by individuals. It is generally fulfilled part time by global system and subsystem Project Managers.

BUSINESS IMPACT OF SYSTEMS-LEVEL REQUIREMENT ENGINEERING FOR COMMERCIAL PRODUCT DEVELOPMENT

The main targeted business impact was a time reduction in phase R1-R5 due to better requirement practices in phase R0-R1 that would avoid later rework and save 10% of development time.

To perform this assessment, we fully developed the system with the old approach and redeveloped it partly with the new approach. And we took the errors identified by the old one to see whether they could have been avoided with the new one. We then estimated the cost of rework of these defects.

In reality, we did not apply strictly the old approach but an evolved version taking into account some results of the new approach and on a paper basis. The reason for this was because of the impatience of the practitioners to adopt the first results of the new approach ("Yes chaps, it may happen !").This also means that this bias must be dealt with and that an adjustment had to be done to really compare the new and old approaches in a sound way.

Type of defects	N°
Requirements-related defects	**15**
• False requirements	2
• Missing requirements	5
• Incomplete requirements	1
• Non-developed requirements	1
• Changes requirements	6
Other defects	**45**

Table 2: list of defects by categories that were detected between R1 and R5

The rough analysis of table 2 shows that 15/60 = 25% of errors are linked to requirements But in fact an adjustment must be applied. The adjustment can only be applied on the sort of defects that introduced practices can help to avoid, namely false, incomplete and non-developed requirements. We made the hypothesis that it could not help avoid requirements changes and missing requirements. Furthermore, we considered there was an equal distribution of types of defects. And we used as calculation basis the types of requirements that were not solved by the experimented practices a reference, reaching therefore an average number of 5.5 requirements per type of requirement-related errors. This helped us to adjust the number of found defects. Then the percentage of defects becomes 28/60=46.5%. This figure is not very far of some existing figures for software development that state that in average 50% of errors come from requirements-related errors.

Type of defect	Adjustment need	Original value	Adjusted value
False requirements	Yes	2	6
Missing requirements	No	5	5
Incomplete requirements	Yes	1	5
Non-developed requirements	Yes	1	6
Changes requirements	No	6	6
Total number of defects		**15**	**28**

Table3: Readjustment of detected errors during R1 and R5

Time reduction due to better requirements engineering. Regarding the cost of reworked requirements, we reached a global person load of 8,5 person.months. We made realistic, optimistic and pessimistic scenarios of people allocation to perform these reworks. The most optimistic scenario (and probably over-optimistic) would be to have 1/3 of the team available to rework the product, that is 3.66 people out of the 11 technical people assigned to the project. The corresponding delay is then of 8.5/3.66= 2.32; which is a bit lower than the target of 2.4 for our optimistic scenario. But roughly speaking, we can agree that the planned target of 10% is satisfied.

The literature reports a global 50% time reduction for an improvement covering all impacted processes (Cooper 86). Due to our experiment which was limited to a single process, we believe that such a value is not over-ambitious.

Benefit analysis of the approach. We also made a cost benefit analysis of the improvement. The price to pay this time reduction is 17 K and corresponds in average to a ½ day a week of requirements engineering during R0-R1 (± 6 months) and ½ days every two weeks during R1-R5 (± 18 months). This cost is to be compared with the market loss which is avoided due to late market commercialization and which was estimated 245 K . This gives a return of investment of 14. Although this return calculation does not integrate the tooling and training costs, it clearly shows the financial potential of the experimented approach.

Systematic requirements engineering Vs. Informal and expertise-driven analysis. The usefulness of the systematic application of requirements was also evaluated. As reported by table 3, it turned out that in the experiment, the use of a systematic approach by a single domain expert gave almost as many errors detected than with the numerous experts involved in traditional reviews of requirements – 15 out of 35 defects = 45% of totally detected errors during the requirements engineering activity. Therefore systematic analysis seems to be an as efficient technique as classical peer review.

Profile of expert	Defect number	New/old approach
Validation expert	10	Old
Development expert	9	Old
After sales	1	Old
Systematic analysis	15	New
Total	**35**	

Table 4: found errors per category of experts

We also investigated other rules about requirements, that would need however further validation on other experiments. Let's quote our major finding on the number of changed requirements that can be detected during requirements engineering. In Syrena, we reached the rate of 1 evolution for 1 initial requirement (i.e. input requirements before they are analyzed and transformed).

CONCLUSION

The Syrena experiment validated in our context the suitability of system-level requirements engineering for the fast development of small commercial electrical products.

At the moment, a user package is under completion to well manage the transfer from the experiment to the rest of the company. It includes a methodological and usage training, a methodological guide and a tooling user manual based on Requisite Pro from Rational.

The main change is probably of organizational nature since it requires the early involvement of many of the stakeholders; period at which they are generally busy with other ongoing and finishing projects.

ACKNOWLEDGEMENT

Our thanks to the ESSI program of the European Commission, a program that was devoted to the support of software and system improvement actions.

Also our thanks to our American colleague Jason Selvidge from Q-Labs Germany for his useful review of the paper and to make it understandable to English-native speakers.

REFERENCES

De Paoli, Claude, "Initial lessons of model-based systems engineering for small commercial product development in the electrical domain (for Uninterruptible Power Supply System)", INCOSE'99, Vol. 2, Pioneering Applications 7.3.3.

Robert G. Cooper, Winning at new products, Addison Wesley, 1986.

Claude de Paoli et al, "How do time-to-market and a market approach impact the development process ? The experience of MGE UPS System in the electrical domain". Proceedings of the 12th International Conference of Software and System Engineering and their Applications, ICSSEA'99, Paris, Dec. 99.

Claude de Paoli et al, l'impact des contraintes du marché sur le processus de développement : un retour d'expérience de MGE UPS Systems dans le domaine de l'industrie électrique, Revue Génie Logiciel et Système, Décembre 99.

BIOGRAPHY

O. Parrot has been working for MGE since 1987. He began as an electronic design engineer. He has designed different kinds of UPS. Now as a project manager, he is in charge of system projects.

C. De Paoli has been working for MGE since 1986. He began as a software designer. He has designed different kinds of UPS. Now as a project manager, he is in charge of system projects.

A. Rouge is in charge of systems engineering business at Q-Labs, formerly Objectif Technologie. As a consultant, he worked for several large and small internationally-based French companies of defense Electronics, railways, telecommunication and energy sectors. He is now supporting Bosch Automotive to deploy requirements engineering in Germany. He is also a trainer in systems engineering, requirements engineering and time-to-market, and an assessor for the SE-CMM and SECM maturity models.

Catherine Dutey is in charge of systems engineering studies at Schneider Electric. As a researcher, she works for different Strategic Business Units in Schneider Electric Group.

Figure 1: MGE Product Life-cycle

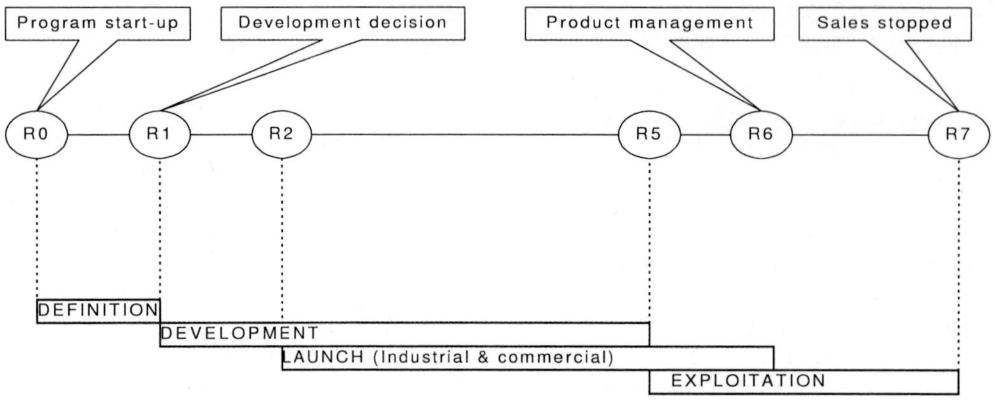

Figure 2: Experimented Systems Engineering Process

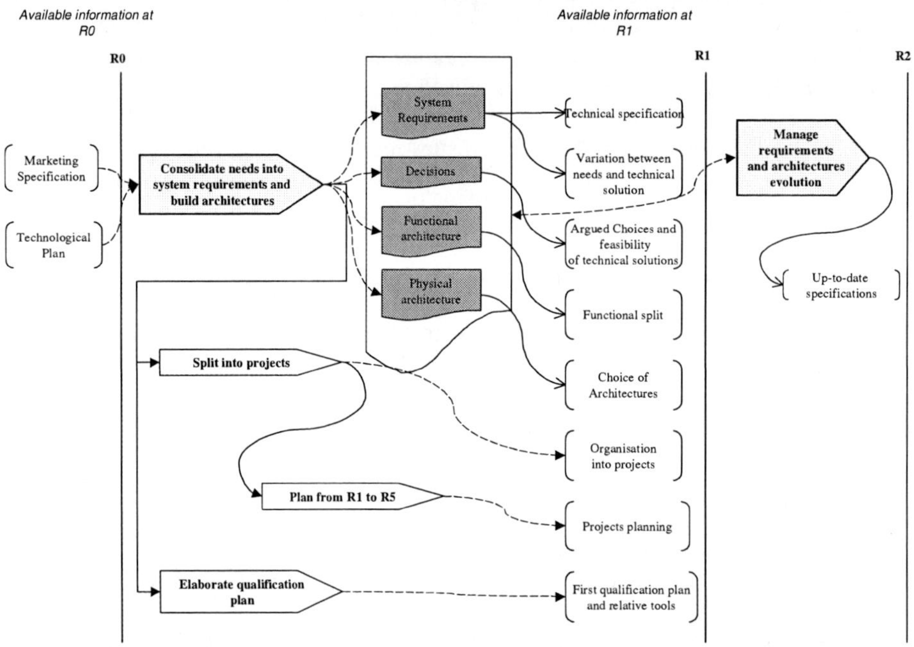

Figure 3. Experimented system-level requirements engineering process

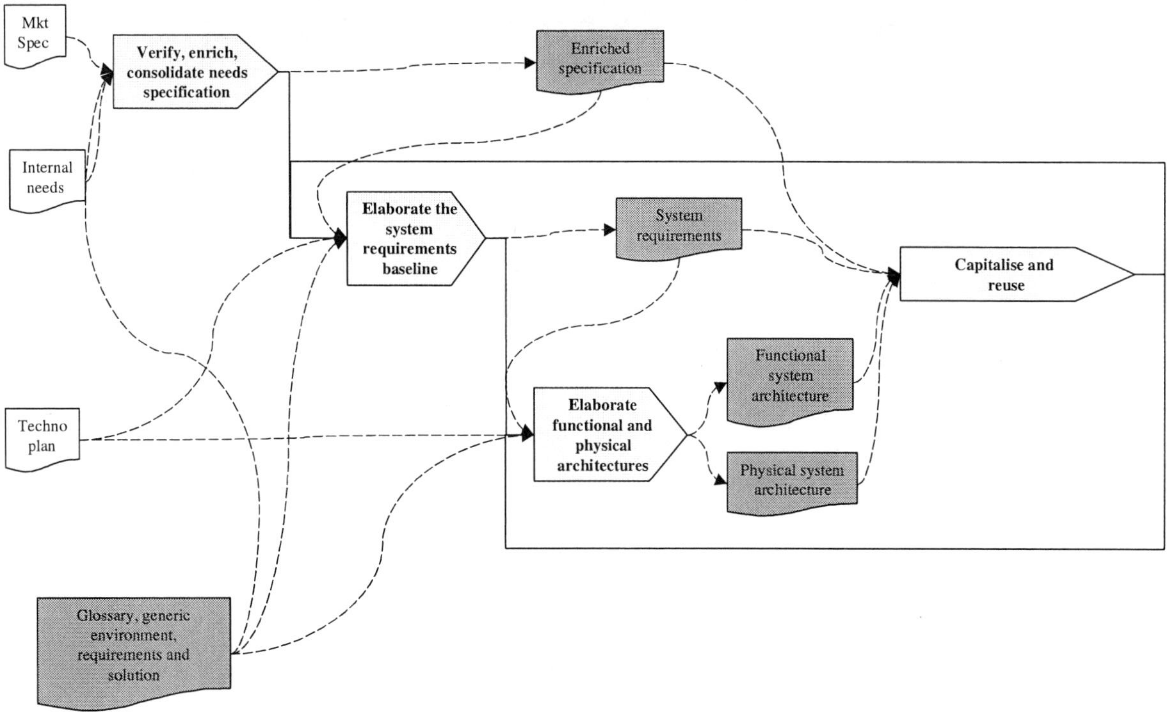

Figure 4. Distribution spectrum of activities over the system life-cycle activities

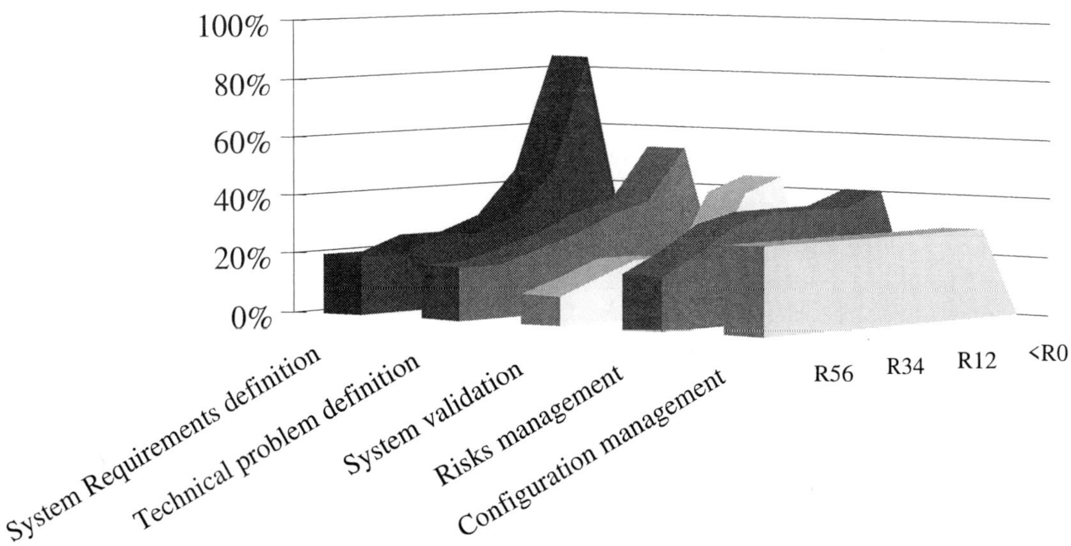

Exploring Concepts during Pre-System Definition

William W. Schoening
The Boeing Company
schoening@incose.org

Abstract. Despite the fact that Pre-System Definition (PSD) is a precursor to the later life-cycle phases, organizations continue to perform this phase poorly. PSD projects (also called Concept Exploration or Feasibility Studies) can be characterized as being of relatively short duration with rapid transitions in focus. Since PSD is before design, the issues and approaches are different from the later design phases. This paper describes many of the causes for poor PSD execution and discusses techniques for helping a poorly executing PSD project recover. Brief diagnostic questions are posed to help readers implement the approaches proposed in this paper.

INTRODUCTION

Exploring new concepts for products and services during Pre-System Definition (PSD) is the "basic research" for the practicing systems engineers who specialize in developing innovative and unprecedented systems. EIA-632 calls the life-cycle phase Pre-System Definition; US Department of Defense documents and the INCOSE Systems Engineering Handbook call it Concept Exploration; commercial businesses sometimes use the term Feasibility Study. Regardless of what you call it, primary activities are outlined in Figure 1.

- Requirements are gathered from stakeholders and explored
- Requirements are validated
- Alternative system concepts are examined for feasibility, cost, and risk

Figure 1: Primary Activities during PSD

There is a life-cycle phase called pre-Concept Exploration or pre-Milestone 1 in which the stakeholder requirements are barely defined. The topics and issues that appear in this paper apply to this earlier life-cycle phase equally as well.

The relatively new term of Pre-System Definition (PSD for short in this paper) certainly captures the timing of the life-cycle phase and suggests that system definition is not being performed, but it lacks the energy and imagination evoked by the word "exploration." Developers explore and discover during PSD instead of designing the product or service.

It is surprising how little is said about PSD in EIA-632 or in ISO 15288 (draft) – less than one page. EIA-632 has strong roots in MIL-STD-499, and US military standards are intended (Snoderly and Lake) for what we now call the System Definition life-cycle phase. While material in those standards might be applicable to other life-cycle phases, such applicability is a byproduct rather than a primary product of the standards.

The INCOSE Systems Engineering Handbook gives considerable insight into PSD, but does not address PSD as a single topic. EIA/IS-731 addresses some of the issues at a very top level in the Systems Engineering Technical focus areas called Define Stakeholder and System Level Requirements, Define the Technical Problem, Define Solution, and Integrate System. However, EIA/IS-731 is about process improvement, and processes are just one part of a successful PSD project.

Characteristic	PSD	System Definition
No. of Projects	Many	Few
No. of People	Few	Many
Project Duration	Short Term	Long Term
Company Profits	Future	Sustaining
Staffing and Skills Stability	Rapidly Changing	Fairly Constant

Figure 2: Characteristics of PSD and System Definition

Figure 2 shows how PSD fits into the business base of companies and how management often perceives this life-cycle phase. Despite the larger number of PSD projects, System Definition projects dominate management attention because more people are involved, the projects last longer, and they are the most likely source of sustained income and profit. In contrast, PSC projects are numerous, risky, of short duration, require rapid and continuing changes in staffing. In short, they demand a lot of attention. However, well-conducted PSD projects help management separate the winners from the losers – the ones that should be pursued and the ones that should be cancelled. At the very least, PSD helps management understand the consequences of pursuing a project beyond PSD. PSD projects, at least some of them, are the future of the company. Despite the apparent importance of PSD projects, companies for which PSD projects are not a primary business sometimes pay little attention to how such projects should really be performed Instead, they opt to view them as short term versions of System Definition.

In the remainder of this paper, a series of diagnostic questions are provided to help you determine whether your PSD project is suffering from a particular problem. Solutions are almost always situation dependent, but approaches are at least implied in the paragraphs that precede each diagnostic.

WHAT IS PRE-SYSTEM DEFINITION?

PSD is about exploration and discovery. In some ways it is a big trade study that examines the broad spectrum of the design space where one is looking for revolutionary, rather than simply evolutionary, improvements in products and services. Typically, the needs of direct customers and other stakeholders are not well understood at the beginning of PSD. During what the US DoD (Department of Defense) calls pre-Milestone 0 or pre-PSD, the requirements are barely recognizable, just recognition that a need must be filled. Gathering and gaining an understanding of those needs becomes one of the important early tasks during PSD. The more surprises there are in the stakeholder needs, the more likely that PSD is needed.

Governments sometimes conduct PSD in-house, but often out of house. The contractors for the PSD and even pre-PSD may not even be the contractors who will be called upon for the System Definition and later life-cycle phases.

The technical feasibility of a product or service is one of the major issues during PSD. However, PSD is not technology development; rather it addresses whether technologies are sufficiently mature for successful integration into the product or service.

PSD Products -The products that one expects out of PSD provide additional insight into what this phase is all about. There are many stakeholders and many expectations for the products of PSD, but let's begin with what the US Defense Systems Management College teaches as the three primary questions (first three items in Figure 3) that government program managers must answer at the end of PSD.

1. Is the program technically feasible?
2. Are the costs within acceptable bounds?
3. Are the risks within acceptable bounds?
4. Is the potential profitability sufficient?

Figure 3: Key Questions for PSD

When the buyer of the development is the same as, or acts for, the ultimate user (as in government procurements or in-house procurements in commercial businesses) the first three questions are not only necessary, but also sufficient for making a decision about going ahead with the project. If the product or service under consideration is for outside sale, then a fourth question (Figure 3) about potential profitability is of major importance.

These questions must be answered before proceeding to the next life-cycle phase – System Definition. PSD is about concepts and answering the key questions; design comes later. That does not mean that design concepts developed during PSD are inconsequential; they form the link between the answers to the questions and the needs of the stakeholders. Design concepts provide the mechanism for understanding which combinations of needs are driving technical feasibility, cost, risk, or potential profitability. Faced with the realities of implementation, stakeholders may modify their needs leaving the PSD designs as poor solutions to the new requirements.

Stakeholders have other needs beyond the answers to the questions in Figure 3. Some want detailed design concepts they can use to keep the program sold. Others want detailed cost estimates for budgeting, detailed weights, insight into how the project is managed, and documentation. Responses to these needs might require detail that exceeds what is available in PSD designs. The challenge for the systems engineer is to establish the relative importance of theses various demands and manage the expectations of the stakeholders.

PLANNING PSD

Planning a PSD project is somewhat like planning any other life-cycle phase, but there are important differences. Imagine that there are three separate key stages during PSD, as shown in Figure 4. In reality, the three key stages overlap significantly, but it helps to think of them as separate and in sequence.

1. Requirements gathering, analysis, and validation
2. Alternative design exploration
3. Preferred design development

Figure 4: Three Key Stages for PSD

Requirements gathering and validation come first. Analysis and validation should be mostly completed before beginning any design work, otherwise it is difficult to keep the designers from performing design studies based on substantially incomplete or incorrect conceptual requirements. Significant derived requirements should be formulated as part of the analysis. For example, if a ship must maneuver around mines, the derived operational requirements for stopping, turning and backing should be developed. The operational requirements provide the framework for the questions addressed while exploring design concepts.

Exploration of alternative designs should be mostly completed before developing a preferred concept. Jumping to a preferred concept too quickly usually stifles the discovery and exploration that are the purpose of PSD.

Diagnostic 1: Are the three key stages planned and fairly separate?

STAFFING

A direct result of the three separate stages is a staffing plan than emphasizes certain skills early on and changes over time. Planners like to have constant staffing by skill because it is easier, but that does not make it appropriate. It should be clear from the three PSD stages that the early staffing should be dominated by those who gather, analyze, and validate the requirements. These are usually operations analysts plus a few designers who can provide top-level design concepts to support the analysis.

In military applications operations analysts explore the interactions and contradictions inherent in the stated needs. A typical issue might be a need masquerading as a design requirement, such as "the aircraft shall be supersonic." How fast, and under what circumstances? The skeleton design staff can explain the consequences of trying to fly a long way with a supersonic planform, while the analysts are trying to find out from the users just how fast they want to fly. (In one such case, the analysts discovered that the users wanted very good acceleration at subsonic speeds, but the users had observed such performance only in supersonic aircraft.)

Once a reasonable set of candidate requirements is available, the design engineers begin to dominate the project. In a well-planned project this middle activity consumes most of the elapsed time and staffing resources of the entire PSD effort. The design staff that develops the alternative concepts should be phased in toward the end of the examination of the operational needs. Just when to phase them in is more art than science. Too soon and the designers will design things barely related to the requirements; too late and the project will stall. A strong indication that it is time to bring more designers onto the project is that questions being asked by the analysts require additional design support. Unfortunately, the timing of such circumstances is hard to predict in advance.

As the analysts switch from examining the requirements themselves to examining how well the conceptual designs meet the requirements, cost analysts and risk analysts begin to join the project. Just as with the designers, too soon and the project will bog down with questions that are too detailed for the state of the project; too late and the project will stall.

Diagnostic 2: Does the staffing plan match the three key stages? Are there too many designers before they are useful?

Execution of a PSD project, particularly when the project has already gone awry, depends heavily on the people, their skills, their experience, and their ability to deal with uncertainty. Since the level of uncertainty is extremely high during PSD, it is essential that the people be comfortable in dealing with uncertainty and know how to resolve it.

Some engineers and managers are extremely rule based; they apply the existing engineering and management rules to the letter. Any deviation from the rules is anathema. Uncertainty is very disorienting to this group. When faced with new technologies with different rules, rules that have not been well defined, people at this end of the spectrum keep applying the old rules or simply freeze and make little progress. An identifying characteristic of very rule-based people is their tendency to demand detailed explanations so as to minimize the level of uncertainty.

At the other end of the spectrum are the non-rule-based people for whom uncertainty is an opportunity instead of a constraint. These are the true explorers who thrive in the PSD phase. They tend to be starters rather than finishers of projects, although they often carry their unusual concepts to a surprising level of detail, particularly if adding the detail involves further investigation into uncharted territory. The non-rule-based people are very uncomfortable on projects that are well into System Definition; they want to change and improve the product long after design freeze are counterproductive during detailed design. Projects in preliminary and detailed design are often not happy to have them.

My personal experience with troubled PSD projects is that many of the people staffing the project are very rule based. Many of those with rule-based behavior can be taught to deal with uncertainty and begin exploring; they have never been given an opportunity. For others their personalities are so ingrained with rule-based thinking that the best approach is to get them off the project. Otherwise, they tend to be disruptive as they waste the time of the explorers with demands for detail that will not be available for months or years. (Michael Jordan was a great basketball player, but he could not hit a curve ball. PSD is just not the right sport for rule-based thinkers.) There is certainly a place on PSD projects for those who challenge new ideas as well as the old; just be sure the project has the right mix.

If the project is successful during PSD and the decision is to proceed into System Definition, many of those rule-based people will be needed when it comes time to put the meat on the bones of the PSD concepts. Making them aware of the future need for their services is an important step in the winnowing process when helping a troubled PSD project recover. Telling people, "I want you back when we get to such and such a point." is not only good for their ego but also good for the future of your program.

A long prevalent theory holds that managers (and engineers) should follow a project throughout its life cycle. In reality the necessary skills and personalities of the people change with the project. Corporate cultures need to accept preplanned replacement of managers and engineers as projects matures.

Diagnostic 3: Are the people on the project suitable for the kind of discovery expected of them during PSD? Can they handle uncertainty?

Training the Retained Staff - Purging the staff of those who will never fit into PSD is just half the battle; most of those retained are going to need some training about how to deal with uncertainty.

During your schooling how often were you confronted with a problem for which, within the bounds of the implied design space, there was no solution? When I asked this question over the last several years, 98% of the time the response is "Never." Yet many of the problems during PSD do not have solutions within the implied design space. Note that the operative word here is implied. There are two problems at work here.

First, since technical feasibility has usually been addressed during PSD, engineers whose experience is limited to preliminary and detailed design tend to ignore the feasibility issue. Picking the right people is the part of the solution to this problem.

Second, there does not seem to be a general approach to showing how to establish that something is not feasible. Domain-specific examples do exist. For example, suppose the issue is whether a conceptual design of a fighter aircraft will be light enough to land on an aircraft carrier. If the most optimistic weights are assumed, then adding fidelity to the design and real weights will only make the fighter heavier – it is infeasible. Teaching this skill probably best handled with examples and on-the-job training with supervisors and peers who do have experience.

This kind of thinking is important to successful exploration during PSD. Blind alleys can be identified early. The approach cited above seldom works with rule-based thinkers – it is too uncertain. One manager who was so focused on producing detailed weight descriptions (because the customer had asked for details) that he missed that they wanted such detail only for feasible conceptual designs. The net result was that weeks were spent developing detailed data on irrelevant design concepts instead of looking for candidates that would be light enough to land on a carrier. A corollary of this experience is that rule-based managers can undo even the best approaches of their not-so-rule-based workers.

In addition, people working on PSD projects should be proficient at looking outside the implied design space; they should be able to visualize and understand the bigger system. They have to be able and willing to think out of the box.

Diagnostic 4: Are the people on the project adequately trained in PSD skills?

Explaining – Explaining a concept in concise and understandable terms is virtually a lost art, or maybe it never was. A good friend from Oklahoma once told me, "The work ain't done 'til the report's writ." Nothing could be truer for PSD. The more unprecedented the work, the more important is the ability to explain it. Major innovations remain unknown and unused because the people who developed them cannot adequately explain them and their use.

Notoriously bad explainers just do not belong on PSD projects. A chart with 96 pieces of data has little value without some guidance as to what is important. Saying, "Those are the results!" does not do the job. One must discover and then explain the messages contained in the data.

Diagnostic 5: Can the engineers who are performing the exploration and discovery explain complex and unfamiliar ideas?

PROCESSES

The distinctly different nature of the three key stages should be a strong hint that process implementation for a PSD project is not straightforward. Part of the problem is that the processes for most organizations are designed to work during System Definition instead of PSD. The assumptions behind the processes are geared to a very different set of conditions: e.g., less uncertainty, a single design in progress, requirements defined. The organization's processes are imposed with little thought about whether tailoring would be appropriate. This seems to be particularly true in organizations that have made a substantial effort at process improvement for the System Definition life-cycle phase. It is akin to the "We have a hammer for a tool and will apply it every time" syndrome.

Risk management, configuration management, and requirements management are three process areas that are often misapplied. In addition, formal decision making is often side stepped as inappropriate with the high level of uncertainty.

Risk – Risk management, one of the major topics of PSD, must address both execution risk and technology roadmap risk – risks associated with technology that must be developed or demonstrated in later life-cycle pahses. One project manager held regular risk review meetings attempting to make risk a high profile topic. However, only one of the top twenty identified risks was an execution risk. Risk mitigation plans for the technology roadmap risks could be planned during PSD, but carrying out those plans would have to wait for the next life-cycle phase. Number 38 on the list was something that needed immediate attention (improving the cost estimating techniques during PSD), but is was beyond the cut off and the project manager was unaware of this critical risk. The lesson learned is that simply ordering the risks in importance is insufficient; the consequences of the risk must be taken into account.

Configuration Management -- Configuration management is an example of how processes must be planned to change over the course of PSD. CM managers tend to think in terms deliverables to customers; however, there are many products for purely internal use that require some form of configuration management. Consider the descriptions of the alternative concepts. Should they be under configuration management from the beginning, never, or somewhere in between? What about the preferred concept? The answer depends on the number of people on a project, geographically dispersion, complexity of the problem, and other considerations unique to a particular project. Not only should the PSD project have a list of what belongs under configuration management, but an indication of when or under what circumstances configuration management is initiated for the item.

During the fast moving part of PSD when alternative concepts are being developed and changed daily, configuration management of the description may be inappropriate. However, if the team is geographically dispersed, establishing some sort of configuration management of the description may be necessary for everyone to have a common reference.

Requirements Management – Projects in PSD for the US Defense Department often start out with a document called the Operational Requirements Document (ORD.) The task is to examine these requirements in light of the key questions for PSD listed in Figure 3. The job is to examine the requirements, challenge some, and recommend a few derived requirements. Consequently, the requirements management task is often very limited. When requirements management is given too much emphasis, the staff of the PSD project, particularly if their experience is heavily oriented toward System Definition may begin writing and submitting requirements. In the absence of guidance, they do what they know how to do. The challenge is to restrict requirements management and associated activities to the level appropriate for the exploration and discovery stages in PSD, and plan the transition as the project progresses toward a preferred concept near the end of PSD.

Decision-Making – The transition to making formal decisions (criteria rooted in the business and technical objectives, alternatives for consideration, and formal evaluation against the criteria) is often difficult for PSD projects. In the beginning, changes come so rapidly and are so self-evident that formal decision making seems a waste of time. By the time formal decision making is imposed, chaos has set in.

This issue is closely coupled with when to begin configuration management of alternative concepts and the preferred concept. Feeling the need to control the descriptions of the alternative and preferred concepts is a sure sign that too many cooks have their hands in the pot. It is time to not only control changes but to make the associated decisions in a formal manner.

Trade studies should be reviewed and approved, disapproved, or returned for more work as part of the formal decision-making process. In one project, results of trade studies were incorporated into the design concepts without formal review. Six months after a trade was completed the project manager was pushed into being briefing. Much to his surprise, key business assumptions were totally backwards in the evaluation criteria. Even worse, once that first decision was reassessed and reversed, many later decisions were overturned. Recovery was painful.

The INCOSE Systems Engineering Handbook contains an excellent discussion about conducting trades studies.

Tailoring the Processes – Tailoring processes is a lot like developing a new design. In many ways, process engineers are the ultimate in rule-based behavior. They are likely to tailor processes according to "rules," and they are likely to spend considerable effort solving the problems they encountered on previous projects instead of paying attention to the current context. The INCOSE Systems Engineering Handbook has a very good discussion about tailoring processes.

One of the most common problems associated with tailoring processes is over-specifying. Having failed to get users to perform the steps the way they intended, process engineers try to increase the detail of the process steps. The authors of one trade study process stressed pushing down in design detail until a cost differential could be identified, even though the associated level of detail was much greater than appropriate for the trade. Unfortunately, design details at levels inconsistent with the overall project are often built on a house of cards.

Limited by their own experience, process engineers often fail to recognize and address multiple contexts. Should resources be spent on detailed cost analyses or risk assessments if an alternative is known to be technically infeasible? Should resources be spent on detailed design studies if an alternative is known to be way over cost? That same trade study process answered yes to these questions.

Diagnostic 6: Are the processes tailored to PSD, and do they change appropriately as the project progresses through the three key stages?

OBJECTIVES

The importance of explicitly identifying, interpreting, and making clear the technical and business objectives to the entire team cannot be understated. On more than one occasion I have observed technical decisions that were backwards because the business issues were not deployed. In one such case, the technical decision-maker assumed that the cards in an electronics box would be procured rather than developed in-house when, in fact, a significant business issue was to consider in-house development.

Explicitly stating project objectives is, as always, the first step in planning. Having observed project planning for PSD in several companies over a long time, stating the objectives is often treated as a punishment for planners rather than an essential ingredient of a good plan. In poorly performing PSD projects, the technical objectives degenerate into focusing on a design solution instead of understanding the consequences of alternative solutions on the key questions for PSD in Figure 3 The business objectives are frequently ignored. Part of a PSD effort, particularly an internal PSD effort, might be to determine whether the company should pursue a particular line of work. If the engineers do not firmly understand that business issue, they are likely to assume that the decision has already been made favorably, else the project exist would not exist. With that mind set, they are not likely to address the truly critical questions.

Diagnostic 7: Are the business objectives as well as the technical objectives articulated and deployed throughout the project, with particular attention to the criteria for decision making?

EXECUTION

"Cookbooks do not bake cakes." – Dave Hamilton

Despite having a well-developed project approach and plan with lots of processes, there is no assurance that the project will execute properly. Simply having people, a plan, and processes does not lead to success. The people will execute, but not necessarily in a way that breeds success for a PSD project. The people must invest intellectual capital in the project. They must think, they must question, and, above all, they must explore. It is during this life-cycle phase that the unknown should be discovered and examined.

Given the difficulties that one encounters with rule-based people during execution of a PSD project, a plan that incorporates guidance and "rules" that foster desired behavior is a major factor for successful recovery. The plan, or the revised plan, should include events, activities, and guidance that focus the efforts in the desired direction and away from the undesired. A plan that simply lists products, without providing an understanding of what is really needed, is not useful. The systems engineers may have to define the alternatives and write the questions that need answers.

A major part of exploring is sharing what you learn. Frequent show-and-tell sessions with customers present works very well. The explorers have a chance to show what they have and learn from each other. Clear and concise explanations not only help understanding, but also help the speakers better understand their own results. I try to live by the credo that if the audience does not understand, then the problem lies with the presenter. PSD is filled with new and unusual problems. Most people will not understand explanations that are put together too quickly or are too complicated. As Mark Twain said, "Sorry this letter is so long, I didn't have time to write a shorter one." He could just as well have said "made it easier to understand." It takes time and effort to develop an easily understood explanation.

Questions – Do the engineers know what questions they are trying to answer? Or are they simply performing tasks? Since PSD is about discovery, questions would seem to be a natural part of the inquiry. "Questions? What questions?" was the response of one presenter during a briefing. He had a large amount of data, but little idea about what data was relevant because he had not formulated his work in terms of questions. If the engineers cannot state the questions they are trying to answer, you have almost certainly uncovered one of the reasons the project is in trouble. The use of questions is intimately connected with good explaining. Presenting the questions will help an audience understand the rest of the briefing.

Diagnostic 8: Do the engineers know what questions they are trying to answer?

Alternative Concepts – Alternative concepts are the core of a good PSD project. A common problem with troubled PSD projects is they focus on either a single design or a very narrow set of design concepts. The project needs to be planned to force exploration of alternative concepts. Alternative concepts should help the team explore the design space by asking questions that develop understanding of relationships between the major components. Detail and internal consistency of the alternatives is not a prerequisite during PSD; alternatives are simply vehicles for answering the key questions in Figure 3. I try to help engineers understand the role of the alternative concepts by explaining that whatever design detail they develop for a particular alternative must be used to decide one of the key concerns or be applicable to most of the alternatives. Otherwise the information will be thrown away. The prospect of wasted effort usually gets their attention.

A big step toward recovery is defining alternatives, even if late in the project. Since the project staff has considerable effort invested in what is usually a single concept, gaining acceptance for new alternatives hinges on explaining what key questions need to be addressed.

Diagnostic 9: Are alternative concepts being investigated as a means of discovery?

Over Planning – Lack of planning is disastrous, but over planning can be equally disastrous. Defining 100 design trade studies during the planning of PSD is counterproductive; PSD is for exploring, not designing. Troubled PSD projects often have too many predetermined trades studies that are not appropriate for the issues that need to be addressed during PSD. One of the first steps toward recovery of the project's PSD health is to defer most of the trades until their relevance to PSD can be determined.

In one project that I had just joined, I discovered that engineers were still doing trade studies on issues that had been already decided. A subsystem had been deleted, but they were examining whether we should use an existing version or develop a new one. They were aware of the decision to delete, but had been told that the trades studies in the Integrated Master Schedule (IMS) had to be performed. The effort for changing the formal schedule and the contracted deliverables was so onerous that it was almost easier to perform useless tasks. Excessive detail in the IMS was at the root of the problem. The original planners of the PSD project were so uncomfortable with the uncertainties of execution that they had demanded tightly defined work packages as a solution to their discomfort. A much better approach for exploration is to use monitoring and controlling techniques, appropriate for PSD, to manage the pace and direction of the project in real time.

Diagnostic 10: Is there sufficient flexibility in the plans to permit going where the exploration takes you?

MONITOR AND CONTROL

PSD projects can be controlled effectively by managing the implementation of the processes, keeping sight of the key questions for PSD, selecting alternative concepts that help answer those questions, and controlling the level of detail of the work performed.

Engineers experienced in System Definition are used to working all the way down to the lowest, most detailed levels. In contrast, PSD is about concepts rather than details. There is nothing more disheartening than hearing on the first day of PSD that selection of the sensor for the hydraulic system is one of the most important trades. Has someone already decided between aircraft, ships and satellites as the primary platform? Does the design concept even have a hydraulic system? Equally frustrating is discovering "requirements" for the font size on displays during PSD for a new Navy destroyer. These examples are clear indications that some people are not grasping the objectives of PSD; they need to be trained or removed from the project.

Two tools for effectively controlling the level of detail during PSD, and thus the overall flow of the project, are the functional flow decomposition and the product decomposition. By describing the level of detail in terms of the levels in the two decompositions, a systems engineer can usually communicate the common desired level to all members of the team. A good PSD project plan includes a description of what level of detail is appropriate throughout the PSD. Not surprisingly, failure to do so is a characteristic of troubled PSD projects.

At what points should the level of detail shift from the whole ship, to the radar, to the boxes within the radar, to the chips on the cards inside the radar? Without such guidance, engineers tend to work on the unsolved problems from their last project. (The hydraulic sensor cited above was one such unsolved problem.) By planning and deploying an understanding of the level of detail, the problems associated with people inexperienced with PSD, the execution of PSD, and issues with processes can all be helped.

Diagnostic 11: Are the monitoring and control mechanisms being employed appropriate for PSD?

SOFTWARE DEVELOPMENT

When I first started working with software and hardware engineers on the concurrent development of a computer and its software in a PSD project, I had considerable difficulty communicating the notion of concept exploration to the software engineers. What a strange project it is when the hardware engineers think of themselves as being in PSD and the software engineers think of themselves as past PSD! At this point in the project there was an open question as to whether a new style of coding for military computers would really work with hardware that depended heavily on commercial-off-the-shelf components. The only method the software engineers seemed to have for examining many of the questions was to write a large amount of code to prove or disprove the assertions. This code writing was taking months for each situation. Once a chunk of code was written, it was not to be thrown away, at least in the minds of the writers.

Upon reflection, software code writing is the ultimate realization of rule-based engineering. There exist software engineers who understand and work well in PSD, but they seem to be in even shorter supply than for hardware development. Personal experience suggests that letting more than very few software engineers on a PSD project is tantamount to failing before you start. They will start coding right away. Don't worry about not having a design concept in hand; they will start coding something.

Software design explorers have my highest regard. Methods for estimating technical feasibility seem obscure and immature compared to similar activities for hardware. With an incomplete tool set they most invent techniques as they go. Furthermore, other software engineers seem to have little understanding of exploring concept.

There are, of course, many software engineers who can grasp the fundamentals of PSD; they just lack the opportunities. Nonetheless, I find it more difficult to teach communicate the elements of PSD to software developers than to hardware developers. Part of the difficulty may lie with the much heavier emphasis on formal processes in software than in hardware. A number of process areas that Systems Engineers see as important to systems development in EIA/IS-731 do not even appear in the SW-CMM™ except possibly in passing. Requirements are seen as rigidly fixed on stone tablets instead of objects to be challenged to their very core in an attempt to find cheaper, better performing solutions.

DIAGNOSIS AND RECOVERY

After a PSD project has been executing for some time, someone finally notices it is wandering aimlessly and is in trouble. With the patient ill and possibly terminal, it is time to bring in the doctor – the systems engineer specializing in PSD. Successful recovery depends on how much time is left, the willingness of the patient to take strong medicine, and the ability of the doctor to diagnose the causes of the malaise.

What are the keys to helping a struggling PSD project recover? The high leverage issues have been captured in the diagnostics identified throughout this paper:

1. Recognition of the three key stages of PSD
2. Staffing that matches the stages
3. People who can deal with the uncertainty
4. People trained in PSD skills
5. Good explainers
6. Processes tailored to PSD
7. Business and technical objectives articulated and explained to all participants
8. Engineers with questions that need answers
9. Alternative concepts
10. Sufficient flexibility in the plan
11. Mechanism for monitor and control appropriate to PSD

This discussion has touched on some of the common problems with PSD projects. There are many other problems, some of which seem to defy resolution. The approaches cited here have, however, been field tested by the author.

It would be a mistake to presume that any single solution will turn a troubled PSD project into one that is healthy. These problems almost always come in groups, so you will have to address several at once if you are to see improvement.

REFERENCES

EIA/IS-731, Systems Engineering Capability Model, 1999.

EIA-632, Processes for Engineering a System, 1999

INCOSE, *Systems Engineering Handbook,* 1998

ISO 15288, Life Cycle Management - System Life Cycle Processes (Draft), 1999

Snoderly, Dr. John, and Lake, Dr. Jerry, Conversations with

BIOGRAPHY

Bill Schoening has spent 33 years as a Systems Engineer and Operations Analyst working mostly on PSD projects for Boeing. Those PSD projects include radar, aircraft, system-of-systems weapons, naval destroyers, software, and aviation electronics with concurrent development of software and hardware.

Bill continues to support PSD projects at Boeing, lectures on systems engineering at the University of Missouri-Rolla, is a member of the product development team for CMMI, co-chairs the INCOSE Capability Assessment Working Group, is a Director by Appointment for INCOSE, and is a past president of INCOSE.

Role of Design, Design Validation, and Verification Activities in Development of Software Systems

David Kaslow
Lockheed Martin
Management & Data Systems
P.O. Box 8048
Philadelphia, PA 19101

ABSTRACT

Often on a large program, the management structure focuses on the management of the work and monitors the development and approval of the program baseline but does not provide the day-to-day design direction. At best, program management has knowledge of the high-level portion of the baseline. Integrated Process and Product Teams (IPPTs) are one mechanism for providing day-to-day direction. This paper recommends establishing Design, Design Validation, and Verification Activities for the day-to-day coodination of the design. These Activities can be used very effectively in the traditional management structure or as an integrating force among IPPTs.

INTRODUCTION

System development can be generalized into phases: definition of the system concepts and requirements, design and implementation of the system elements, followed by the test and verification of the elements and system.

Successful system development is contingent on the system functional capability being defined and elements designed to satisfy the functional and performance requirements. One factor that contributes to inadequate system development is too much focus on the functional design and too little emphasis on the validation that the implemented design will satisfy requirements, particularly the performance requirements.

The engineers design the system and the developers implement the elements according to what they think the design will deliver rather than validate that the design will achieve the required performance. This results in a test and verification phase punctuated with questions like: What does that requirement mean? How should it be verified? Where does the test data come from? What are the loading conditions for that performance requirement?

This paper recommends that a System Design Validation Activity and System Verification Activity be emphasized early on in system development and that the activities be closely coordinated with the System Design Activity, as shown in Figure 1. The paper identifies the interactions between the activities that will result in unambiguous and verifiable requirements and in a system that has been modeled and designed to meet performance requirements.

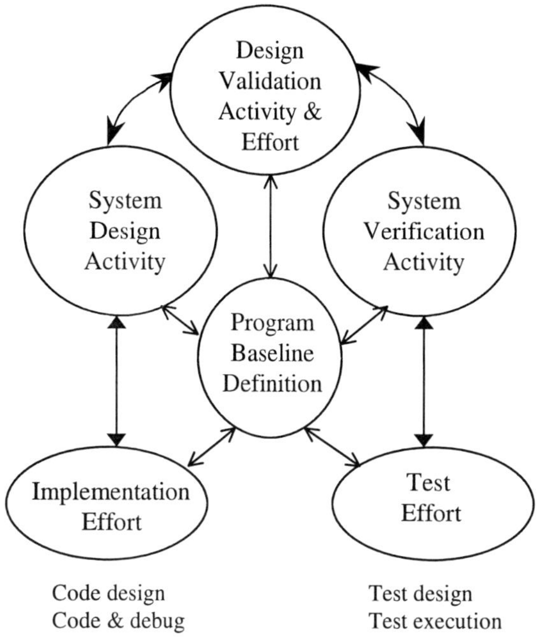

Figure 1. The synergetic inteactions of the System Design, Design Validation, and Verification Activities are instrumental to the successful develoment of software systems.

There is a subtle but important distinction between an activity and an effort. The activity encompasses planning and guidance. Effort is the actual execution of the tasks specified by an activity. This distinction is important because hard work alone may not be sufficient to assure a successful design. The catch phrases "Doing the right thing is not the same as doing things right" and "You don't know enough to know what you don't know" have great meaning to those who have toiled for years in developing large systems.

These activities can be implemented by the traditional management structure or by an Integrated Product and Process Team. These activities provide robust support for proving, reviewing and approving the design:

- System Design Activity has responsibility for directing investigation of and for assuring closure of design issues.
- System Design Validation Activity has responsibility for directing the investigation of and for assuring closure of performance issues.
- System Verification Activity has responsibility for directing and assuring success of verification of the functional and performance requirements.

OVERVIEW

These activities work in concert to lead the design effort. These activities provide the focus for success of the design effort through their daily interaction with each other and with the individual engineers and developers. Additionally, their role is to provide design evaluation and approval criteria to the Engineering Review Board (ERB) related to their expert areas. There should be specific approval criteria for each phase of development with the criteria becoming more detailed and demanding as the development matures.

The three activities work together to assure completeness and closure of the design in the following three areas. The first is the design to satisfy the functional portion of the mission - this is providing the functionality for "what" the system is to do, i.e., image stars or collect data on ozone depletion.

The second is the design to satisfy the performance portion of the mission design, i.e., the accuracy of satellite pointing, the resolution of a sensor or the timeline to generate a mission plan.

The third is the design of the hardware and software support architecture. Examples of software support architecture are operating systems, database engines, and messaging services. Examples of hardware support architecture are the compute servers, data servers and network infrastructure. Particularly important is the performance of the support architecture. The performance requirements are critically important in systems that have critical timing or timeline requirements.

The oversight of these three activities is key to the success of a program. The Design, Design Validation and Verification Activities work together to assure that from program inception through system delivery that the system is being designed, implemented and verified with the functional and performance requirements in the mission and support architecture well in mind.

Figure 1 shows the overall interaction of the three activities. Also shown in Figure 1 is a Program Baseline Defintion which also includes the ERB. The program baseline is that set of products that establishes the concepts, requirements, and design of a program. The baseline is truth at any point in time and truth changes as the program matures. The embodiment of the baseline can range from hardcopy and softcopy documentation to softcopy models to executable models of processes. There must be one repository of the baseline that is well known and easy to navigate. Establishing and maintaining a program baseline is important in any size program but it is especially important in large programs.

The discussion begins with the Design Validation Activity since the development of the design must result in a system that satisfies performance requirements.

SYSTEM DESIGN VALIDATION ACTIVITY

Figure 2 shows the interaction of the System Design Validation Activity with the other elements of the program.

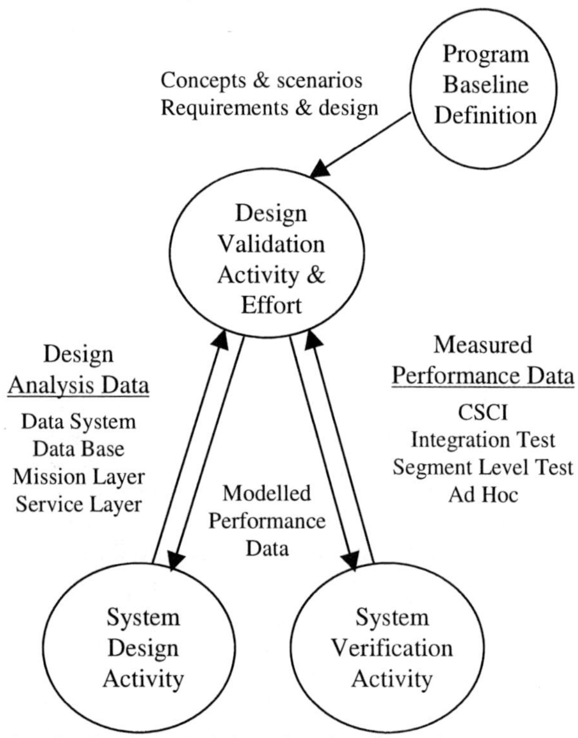

Figure 2. The Design Validation Activity initially models system peformance based on design analysis of the critical details of the proposed design and their performance characteristics.

The Design Validation Activity and Effort should have a very visible and responsible role on large software programs that have critical and challenging performance requirements that cannot be directly measured and evaluated until all the code is integrated onto the operational computer configurations and integrated with the end-use environment.

Mission plan optimization, mission scheduling timelines, command timing, spacecraft modeling and control system reliability are examples of critical performance requirements in a remote sensing satellite system. It is easily seen that a problem with one of these critical performance requirements may not show up until the code is integrated in final testing, or later, and the problem can be very difficult to track down. For example a problem with a timeline requirement can reside in the mission layer or service layer of code, in the contention for processor, database or messaging resource, or in an unexpected amount or frequency of input.

The design and verification emphasis is usually on the mission functional and mission performance requirements since they express the desires of the customer. The performance of the support architecture usually has to be derived from the mission performance requirements. Thus the Design Validation Activity must play an active role in the specification of these derived requirements and the associated verification scenarios.

The Design Validation Activity develops and matures the models used to estimate and evaluate system performance. The size of this effort ranges from modest for a small system to major for a large system. The effort itself ranges from "best guesses" and "spread-sheet analysis" at pre-acquisition phase to detailed and a finely tuned model during the implementation phase.

The Design Validation Activity evaluates system performance initially on design analysis and ultimately on measures from the verification effort. The Design Validation Activity receives the design analysis data from the Design Activity and reciprocates by supplying the performance modeling results back to the Design Activity. For example, design analysis data crucial to timing and timeline requirements includes how the mission layer of design uses the service layer and the processor, database and messaging resources.

The results of the modeling will be used by the Design Activity to evaluate the strengths and weaknesses of the design and to develop design modifications as necessary. The Design Validation Activity receives measured performance data from the Verification Activity and uses this data to calibrate and drive the performance models. Results of the modeling are sent back to the Verification Activity to support the analysis of the verification results.

The role of the Design Validation Activity in the ERB process is to make sure that requirements and design are being developed and documented in detail sufficient to support the evolution of the performance modeling effort. This includes requesting that the system concepts and scenarios address the interaction and loading of all the mission and support architecture. It should also be made certain that the ERB approves the scenarios used for performance requirements undergoing design validation, such as the Mission Planner timeline and optimization requirements discussed in the next section.

SYSTEM DESIGN ACTIVITY

Figure 3 shows the interaction of the System Design Activity with other elements of the program.

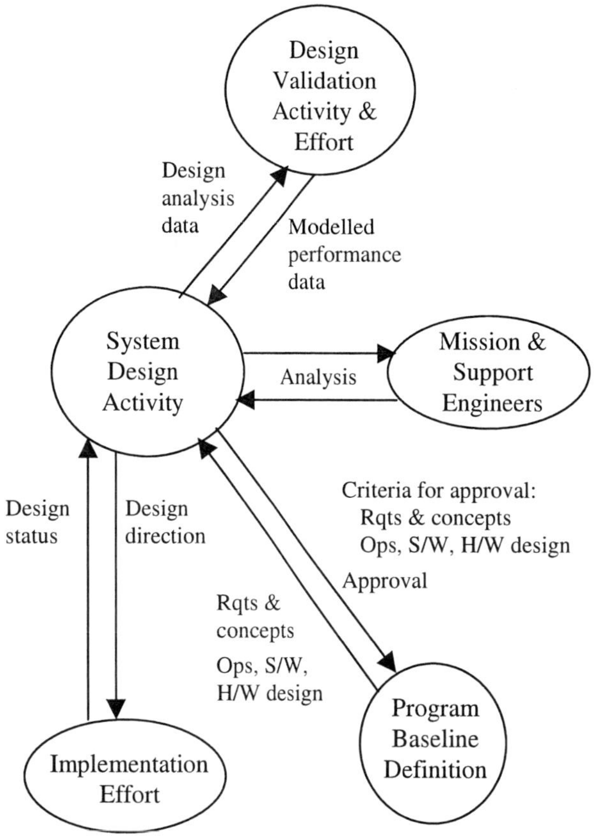

Figure 3. The Design Activity assures that the mission and support architecuture are well integrated and satisfy performance requirements

The Design Activity has responsibility for the integration of the mission and the support architecture. The Design Activity focuses on translating the Mission and Support System Engineering requirements/architecture into the design implementation produced by the System Implementation Effort. Mission Engineers, Support System Engineers, and Implementers have different, and usually non-overlapping, areas of expertise. Yet the function and performance of the mission architecture is often directly reliant on the function and performance of the support architecture. Furthermore, the success of both the mission and support architecture depends on the soundness of the implementation.

The Design Activity interacts with the Mission and Support Engineers by assessing the ability of the architectures to be implemented and by assuring that this implementation is meeting the intent of the architecture.

The Design Activity interacts with the System Implementation Effort by assessing design maturity and providing design direction. The assessment is made through formal and informal meetings and through one-on-one consulting with individual implementers. Design direction is provided through a well-known and controlled forum.

The Design Activity supports the Design Validation Activity by supplying design analysis data and using performance modeling results in design analysis and modification.

The Design Activity provides design approval criteria to the ERB. For example, the Design Activity should specify the required level of design detail at each phase of development. This includes not only the design produced immediately prior to production but the initial design as specified in requirements and operations concepts. These requirements and concepts should cover both the mission aspect of a design and the support layer of the design, such as messaging, data storage, and process control.

SYSTEM VERIFICATION ACTIVITY

Figure 4 shows the interaction of System Verification Activity with other program elements.

The Verification Activity's role in the ERB process is to make sure that the design is being developed with verification in mind. For example, there must be the capability to stop and restart processes and to save and restore data. The Verification Activity makes sure that requirements are stated in verifiable language and that performance requirements have appropriate verification scenarios.

The Verification Activity supports the Design Validation Activity by supplying measured performance data and can use performance modeling results to verify requirements.

On a small to medium sized program the Verification Activity and the Verification Effort can be one element. Large and complex systems with challenging requirements may require separation of these element so that proper focus can be maintained on the technical aspects of verification.

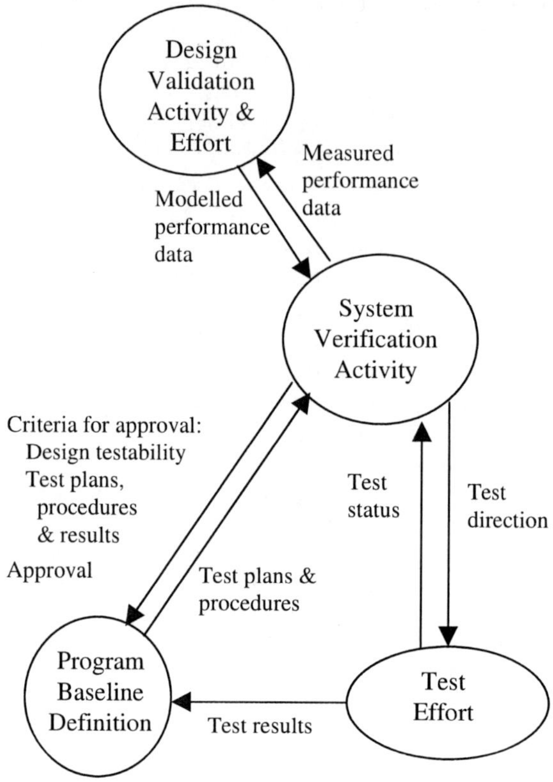

Figure 4. The role of the Verification Activity begins with assuring requirements are verifiable and verification scenarios are defined.

DESIGN, DESIGN VALIDATION, AND VERIFICATION ACTIVITIES IN DEVELOPMENT OF A MISSION PLANNER

Figure 5 illustrates how requirements should be analyzed relative to the design, verification and performance issues. The requirements are representative of those needed for a remote sensing satellite planner. Although they are the highest level, they are illustrative of how requirements should be worked in a coordinated manner between Mission Engineering, System Design, Design Validation, and System Verification Activities.

The first two requirement groups are inputs to and the outputs from the Planner. All static and dynamic inputs and outputs must be described in detail, including the source, destinations, media, format and timing. At the beginning of design effort, the inputs and outputs are described at a data group level. As the design matures, they are described at the individual data item level.

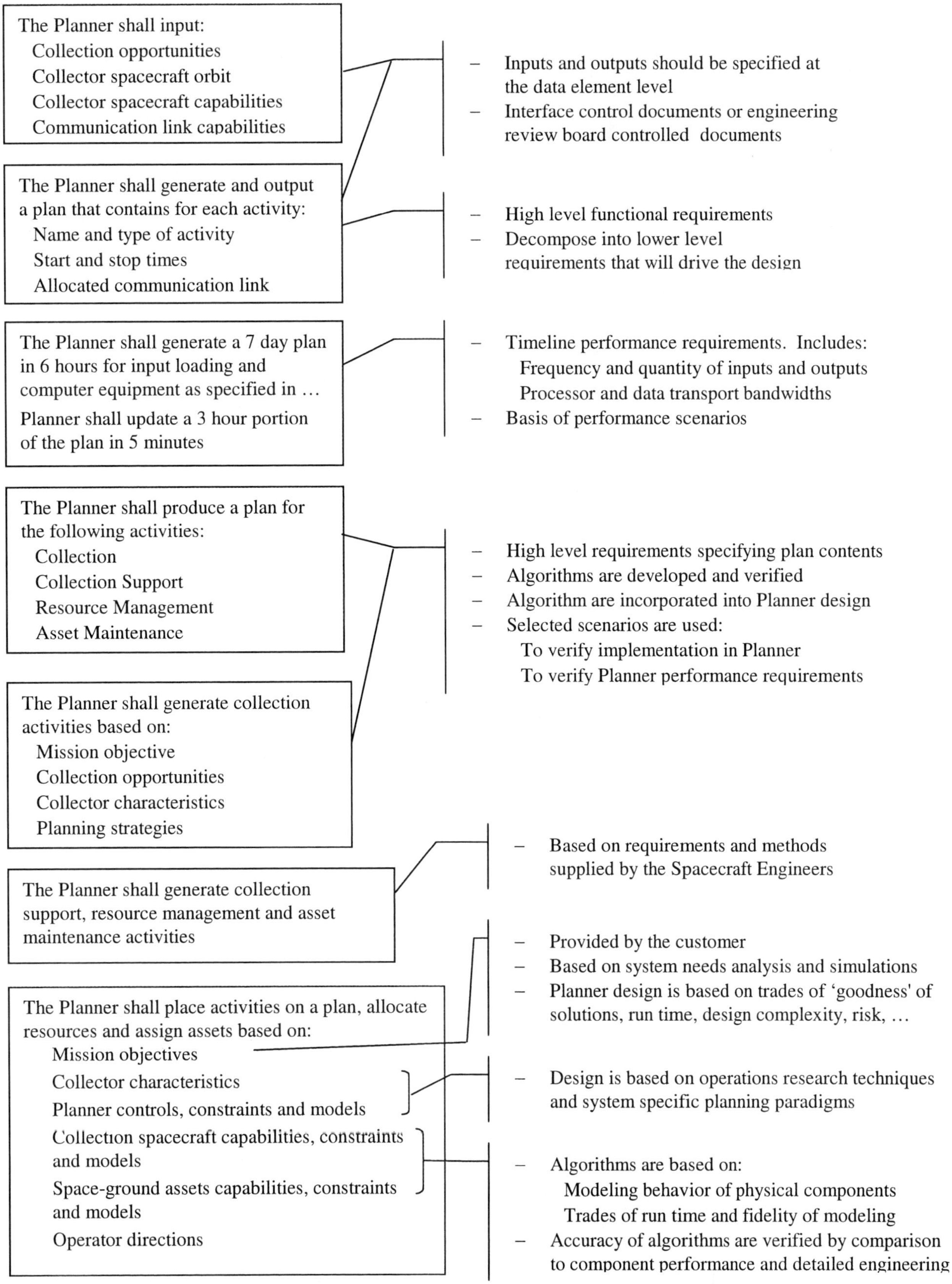

Figure 5. Planning requirements are designed to and verified by a number of different techniques

The third group of requirements are the timeline specifications. In particular, how long it takes to generate an entire plan or to update a section of the plan. The timeline specification must include system loading factors such as frequency and quantity of inputs and outputs. The timeline specification should also identify the computer configuration including factors such as processor and data transport bandwidths.

The System Design, Validation and Verification Activities must work together to make certain that all the critical input and output timeline requirements are clearly stated. If the system loading and computer configurations are not specified by customer requirements, then they must be derived, documented and approved by program management. These timeline requirements coupled with system loading factors are key to defining the performance scenarios discussed below.

The next requirement group specifies the type of activities that a plan must contain. These are very high level requirements that can only be verified by demo. That is, the planning software executes without error to produce a plan. However, there is nothing in the requirement statements that can be used to judge the correctness of the plan. These requirements have to be decomposed into the lower level requirement groups discussed below.

The next two requirement groups state how each of the collection, collection support, resource management and asset maintenance activities are to be generated. In this remote sensing system, the collection activity is to image a specific set of objects - targets - on the Earth. A collection support activity could be an uplink to the satellite or a calibration of a satellite payload. Solar power gathering is an example of a resource management activity and battery reconditioning is an example of an asset maintenance activity.

The requirements for the collection support, resource management and asset maintenance activities are generally straightforward. They are supplied by the Spacecraft Engineers and should be specified in interface control documents and accompanied with methods when needed. This gives the System Design and System Verification Activities all the detail needed to implement and test the requirements.

The requirements for stating how a collection activity is to be generated can be specified by four sub-groups of requirements: mission objectives, collection opportunities, collector characteristics and planning strategies.

The next group of requirements covers placing activities on a plan while allocating resources and assigning assets. These requirements can be categorized into six sub-groups ranging from the satisfaction of mission objectives to meeting spacecraft capabilities to following operator directions.

The requirements for satisfying mission objectives and for accommodating collector characteristics when generating and placing collection activities on a plan while meeting timelines are the most difficult to address in the Planner. The System Design, Validation and Verification Activities must work together to make sure that these requirements are defined so that they have the details needed to begin, mature and complete the design and implementation.

Satisfaction of mission objective usually means to plan the collection activities to maximize collection priority and worth. In this paradigm, each collection opportunity has priority and worth and there are more collection opportunities than collection capability. Thus the Planner selects the subset of collection opportunities based on maximizing the collective priority and worth.

Use of the words 'maximize' or 'optimize' in a requirement should be avoided. Those words can be subjective and open-ended. It is difficult to show that a specific collection activity maximizes priority and worth of the contained collection opportunities. To do this, you would have to show that all other combination of collection opportunities have lower collective priority and worth - and you would have to do this for all possible input scenarios.

Correspondingly, it is impossible to show that the many collection activities on a seven-day plan have been generated and placed to maximize the collection priority and worth over those seven days. Scenarios with defined system loading condition agreed to by the customer and developer are a way to demonstrate compliance with these complex requirements.

Accommodating collector characteristics means having rules and models of the collector spacecraft and payloads that can be used when allocating collection opportunities to a particular collector. More detailed rules and models result in a more accurate allocation, at the expense more of code to develop and maintain, and the possibility of increasing the runtime.

PERFORMANCE MODELS AND SCENARIOS FOR MISSION PLANNER DEVELOPMENT

The development of a Planner that successfully addresses the mission objectives, collector characteristics and timeline requirements is carried out in basically three steps involving the interaction of the Mission Engineers, System Design Activity, Design Validation Activity, and System Verification Activity. The first step is the design and verification of the individual planning algorithms. This is followed by the implementation of the algorithms into the Planner design. Finally the Planner is exercised against a robust set of test scenarios.

Algorithm design and verification by Mission Engineering is separate from the Planner software design and verification. The algorithms from Mission Engineering are usually developed in a prototype test bed in a manner that supports extensive analysis and modification of the algorithms. Individual algorithms can undergo functional and performance testing within the prototype test bed. But, the System Design Activity and Design Validation Activity are needed to project the performance of a group of individual prototypes into the timeline performance of a suite of algorithms in an operational environment. This is especially true in very large software system consisting of scores of algorithms and hundreds of thousands of lines of code.

The System Design Activity develops the architecture and design for the Planner software. This includes determining how the algorithms should be integrated into software modules and how the modules should be distributed across a suite of computer processors, with all the necessary services from the database, messaging, and operating sub-modules.

The System Design Activity and Design Validation Activity work together to develop a performance model of the Planner. During the initial stages of design, a very simple performance model can be used - a static model based on the amount of input and output data and steady state processing capabilities. This static model is replaced by a dynamic model as the design matures. This dynamic model is based on the flow of data and time triggering different processes within the Planner. The processing times can be derived from the prototyping results or from the estimated number of lines of code, any looping schemes within the design, and the lines-of-code execution rate for the specified processors. The dynamic model should also account for the interaction of the mission software with the service layer software, including data access and messaging times. This modeling effort is used to providing insight into problems with the integrated design during the design and initial test phases, not the final verification of the timeline requirements.

The Mission Engineers and System Verification Activity work together to develop test scenarios that are used to verify that the Planner satisfies the mission objectives, collector characteristics and timeline requirements. The test cases are scenarios that are defined in great detail and thoroughly analyzed by Mission Engineering. These scenarios have their origins in the simulations or in the real data the customer may have from their system needs analysis or from the algorithm prototyping. In any event, the scenarios are reviewed by, and approved by, program and customer management.

DESIGN VALIDATION & VERIFICATION ACTIVITIES AND ABD VIEWS

A companion paper (Kaslow 2000) discusses how Architecture Based Design (ABD) was applied to the preliminary architecture of a Mission Planner for a remote sensing satellite system. The ABD process provides a mechanism and a series of repositories for evolving and documenting an architecture and design. An architecture view is a description, from one cohesive aspect, of what a system does and how it is put together. The collection of views, the relationships between the views and the implementing models define the architecture and design to the level needed to efficiently and effectively build the system.

The ABD mission scenario views coupled with the mission application, hardware and infrastructure views provide the basis for the development of the performance model. The mission scenario views are also a foundation for the test cases carried out by the Verification Activity.

CONCLUSION

On very large programs, the day-to-day design is best served by using a collaborative effort of Design, Design Validation, and Verification Activities. Program management plans should incorporate the role of these Activities by defining their individual charters, including their role in providing design direction and ERB approval.

The ABD mission scenario views coupled with the mission application, hardware and infrastructure views provide the basis for the development of the performance model. The mission scenario views are also a foundation for the test cases carried out by the Verification Activity.

BIOGRAPHY

Dr. Kaslow is a Senior Staff Engineer with Lockheed Martin Management and Data Systems. He has twenty-six years of experience in both the technical and management aspects of developing a ground mission element. He has co-authored two chapters in *Cost Effective Mission Operations*. The chapters are "Defining and Developing the Mission Operations Element" and "Activity Planning". He has been a standing member of a Hubble Space Telescope Vision 2000 external review panel. David E. Kaslow.

REFERENCES

Kaslow, David, “Architecture Based Design Applied to a Remote Sensing Satellite Planner”, INCOSE, 2000.

Properties of a High Quality Informal Requirements Document

Richard E. Schneider
ITAC
6301 Union Mill Road
Clifton, VA 20124

Dr. Dennis M. Buede
Department of Systems Engineering and Operations Research
George Mason University
4400 University Drive
Fairfax, VA 22030

Abstract. One way to improve the quality of a system level informal requirements document is to check it for goodness properties and fix any checking errors. Several lists of goodness properties are available but they differ by author. And a sound basis for selecting goodness properties is seldom provided. We propose a set of goodness properties which were developed from a larger list of properties using selection criteria as this sound basis.

In previous work we established a set of criteria for selecting which properties represent high quality in an informal requirements document. This paper extends that work by applying the selection criteria to a large set of candidate properties. Through a process of refining, combining, splitting, and discarding of candidate properties using the selection criteria, we arrived at the limited set of high quality properties. This paper describes that process.

INTRODUCTION

General. Requirements engineering is one of the earliest phases in the life cycle of a system. During this phase requirements are elicited, documented, and analyzed, as described in (Buede, 2000). One objective of this phase is to develop and document a set of high quality system level requirements representing the needs of the StakeHolders (SH). Every document has properties and an Informal Requirements Document (IRD) must have specific properties to serve this purpose. Analysis can improve the quality of this document through inspections by reviewing it for certain properties representative of high quality and fixing any defects found. The focus of this paper is on the process for identifying those properties which represent high quality in a system level IRD. These goodness properties are called High Quality Properties (HQPs) in this paper.

An IRD is a set of requirements, usually written in English, using some SH terminology. In contrast, a formal requirements document is written in a formal specification language. Following the notation of (Buede, 2000), the IRD is the same as his ORD (Operating Requirements Document or Originating Requirements Document). Preceding the ORD are the MENS (Mission Element Need Statement), SEMP (Systems Engineering Management Plan), and CONOP (Concept of Operation). Following the ORD is the SRD (System Requirements Document).

In the next section we provide some background information. In the following three sections we describe the process used to define the HQPs. This includes an ordering for applying the selection criteria, results of applying the selection criteria, and how the HQPs were refined to form the final set of HQPs. The last two sections of this paper compare our HQP list to other lists of such properties and describe our plans for future work.

BACKGROUND

The Problem. Systems are still being built that do not meet SH needs. Systems are built to IRDs but the IRDs are flawed. Significant unresolved errors exist in final IRDs. This means that despite analysis focused on making sure an IRD has high quality, errors still get through. Current analysis processes are not uncovering many errors in an IRD. Although inspections using goodness properties are very helpful in finding errors in IRDs, they are not fully effective. More of the IRD errors need to be found early.

We think one reason more IRD errors are not found during inspection using goodness criteria involves the goodness criteria itself. IRD inspections using goodness criteria are very labor intensive because they are done manually, driven by the informal nature of an

IRD. But they are seldom done the same way twice. One reason reviews differ so much is there is no standard list of properties for a high quality IRD. If a list is missing some key properties (insufficient), some errors in the IRD will not be found. If some properties on the list do not contribute to the quality of the IRD (unnecessary), then valuable review time is wasted. Wasted review time means checking time runs out with some key properties not checked. For these reasons it is important to have just the right properties.

Although lists of properties abound in the literature, little information is provided on which list to use or how such lists were developed. No methods are provided and no criteria are mentioned. Without knowing how lists are built, how would one know which list is the most effective?

Basic Approach. Clearly the focus is on uncovering more of the significant errors in IRDs. Our approach is to develop a better set of goodness properties (called HQPs) which focus more on uncovering these significant errors. We began by establishing criteria for selecting which properties meet this focus. This was called selection criteria, was previously reported in (Schneider & Buede 2000), and is described in Table 1.

Criteria	Definitions
Relevant	Property applies to system level informal requirements
Quality impact	Property impacts IRD quality if check fails
Universal use	Property can be applied to every IRD
Disjoint	No two properties have any checks in common
Coverage	All properties collectively uncover all errors
Supportive	Improvement of a property does not degrade another
Measurable	A property can be checked for pass/fail or quantitatively defined

Table 1. Property Selection Criteria

In this work we apply the selection criteria to a large set of Candidate Properties (CPs) collected from the literature, to get the HQPs. Table 2 shows statistics on how a very large body of related literature was scoped down to 117 relevant papers and 108 CPs and then narrowed to the 15 final HQPs.

117	relevant papers (64 from periodicals, 44 from conferences, and 9 books)
108	candidate properties (CPs) from 117 papers
11	high quality properties (HQPs) from 108 candidate properties (CPs)
15	final HQPs (increase due to spliting)

Table 2. Process Statistics

Overall, the goal is a high quality system. A high quality system is one that meets SH needs. SH needs are expressed through the IRD, which the SH approve. System testing verifies that the system meets the requirements (IRD). Theoretically, if the system meets the IRD, it meets SH needs. But it is possible for the IRD to have errors in it that are not picked up when the SH review it. One way to prevent such oversight is to evaluate the IRD using other methods which are more abstract (less subjective). One abstract approach is to look at properties that a good IRD should have in order to develop a good system, which is where this paper is headed.

So, if an IRD is of low quality (i.e. fails property checks) a system built to this IRD will be of low quality. Since a system is built to the IRD, we want the IRD to be of high quality. We claim that if all the HQPs hold for an IRD, the IRD will be of high quality. We claim that the result of applying the selection criteria to the CPs is an effective set of properties for high quality IRDs, which we call HQPs.

SELECTION CRITERIA ORDERING

Ordering. Review of the selection criteria in Table 1 revealed that some ordering of the selection criteria would reduce the effort in checking the CPs. Table 3 below shows the order we used when checking a CP against the selection criteria. Discussion of the application of the selection criteria is covered in this order in the next section.

Relevant
Universal use
Measurable
Quality impact
Disjoint
Supportive
Coverage

Table 3. Selection Criteria Order

For instance, it seemed reasonable to check a CP for relevance first. If it was not even related to our work on manually reviewing an IRD then why check any other criteria? Universal use is somewhat like relevance and is easy to check, so it was placed second. As for the coverage criteria, it applies to the whole set of final HQPs, is perhaps the most difficult, and is last.

The disjoint and supportive criteria perform pairwise comparisons manually. To keep such comparisons to a minimum, these will be done near the end, just before coverage. Disjoint will be done before supportive because it is easier to perform. Quality impact can not be checked unless it is fairly well understood, which implied being measurable. So measurable was placed ahead of quality impact. Both should be checked before disjoint to make disjoint comparisons easier.

SELECTION CRITERIA APPLICATION

General. The heart of our process is checking whether each of the 108 CPs passes the check for the 7 selection criteria. If a CP failed any selection criteria, its disposition was either to discard it or merge it into a surviving CP. A CP could fail more than one selection criteria, but one failure was enough to force disposition.

A major problem with IRDs is the use of English and the ambiguity it tends to introduce. Unfortunately, all of the definition related information of CPs is written in English, also with much ambiguity. Often this made selection criteria checking more subjective and difficult. Other standard problems occurred such as overlapping definitions, different terms for somewhat the same concept, and the same term with different definitions. All combined to make the application of selection criteria a less than perfect process. Several instances are indicated below, under the descriptions of the selection criteria. After all the discarding and merging was complete, a resulting set of 11 HQPs, before refinement, emerged and is listed in Table 4. Refinement is addressed in the next section.

Annotated	Design independent	Testable
Complete		Traceable
Consistent	Feasible	Unambiguous
Correct	Organized	Understand

Table 4. HQPs Before Refinement

Actually this checking process was even more involved. Checking whether a CP met a selection criteria was based on the definition of the CP. Nearly every CP had several definitions, depending on the authors. So each check looked at one CP definition against one selection criteria. If a check passed, then that CP definition was checked against another criteria. This continued until either a check failed or all the checks passed.

Relevant. A CP is relevant if its definition is clear, if it applies to requirements, if it applies at the system level, and if it applies to requirements informally written. A CP is relevant/clr if it is defined well enough to be understood. Some CP names had insufficient definition information to determine their meaning, such as desirable, constant, well defined, and reuseable. They were discarded.

A CP is relevant/req if it applies to statements written as requirements. For instance, a CP that only holds for SH needs statements or designers specification statements would not be relevant. Let us say that SH needs may be stated such that phrases are acceptable, a phrase may contain more than one need, and not all needs must be clearly identified. Properties for such a needs document would include the CP phrase (permits phrases as well as sentences), the CP multiple (permits more than a single need per phrase), and the CP incomplete (omissions are permitted). Phrase, multiple, and incomplete run contrary to the purpose of an IRD, do not apply to statements written to be requirements, and were discarded.

A CP is relevant/sys if it applies to requirements at the system level. Many CPs came from the software area and apply equally well to a systems level IRD. Some CPs, such as cohesion, coupling, modularity (a section of requirements should map to a software module), readability (based on regularity such as the Halstead Purity Ratio), understandability (based on the number of lines of comments), and several complexity measures, apply at the software level but lacked sufficient development for application at the system level. They were discarded.

A CP is relevant/inf if it applies to requirements written informally (usually in English with some SH terminology). Formal requirements are written using a formal specification language. The CPs executable, reachable, and formal apply to formally written requirements so they were discarded. It made sense to check these four forms of relevance in the order described above.

Universal Use. A CP has universal use if it applies to every IRD. This eliminates properties that might apply to some domains or applications but would give false indications where it does not apply. For instance, if the CP readable implied the use of aircraft terminology, readable would not be a universal property and would be discarded. The CP re-useable, which fails other selection criteria checks, would pass the check for universal use. Even though a particular IRD may not need to be re-useable the property could be applied to every IRD.

Measurable. A CP is measurable if there is a way to determine whether the property holds each place it applies in an IRD. Consider the CPs vague and rigor. Vague is defined as being general and rigor as the opposite of vague. We use these terms a lot but real measurement is so subjective it eludes us. Clear, concise, complex, simple, and sufficient are other CPs which lacked sufficient detail to not be measurable. Non-measurable properties were discarded.

Quality Impact. A CP has quality impact if improving the property for an IRD improves the quality of the IRD. We have assumed that an IRD is of high quality if a system built to it meets the expectations of the SH. Let us say that a property could be checked 100 places in some IRD, that the property fails in only 10 of those places, and passes in the other 90. If the 10 failures are fixed, the quality of the IRD should improve. If improving the property (by fixing failures) has no effect on the quality of the IRD then why check for the property?

Consider the CP unique, which says the IRD is to have no duplicate requirements. If an IRD failed the unique check, would the IRD have low quality? A system built to an IRD with two copies of a requirement is not any different than the system built to that same IRD with one copy of the requirement. Duplicate does not impact IRD quality so it is discarded. For the same reason discard the CPs index, cross reference, table of contents, and single (one requirement per sentence).

Disjoint. Two CPs are disjoint if there is no overlap in the checks they make. No overlap is important to keep the number of checks to a minimum. Given two CPs, let us look at the cases of no overlap (desirable), and the three undesirable cases of full overlap, partial overlap, and contained overlap.

Given two CPs X and Y with no overlap then N is the no overlap (not part of) relation signifying $X \cap Y = \varnothing$ and $(X,Y) \in N$. Consider the CPs X = complete and Y = unambiguous, which do not overlap, so (complete, unambiguous) $\in$ N. But we wish to check the cases of not being disjoint, as described below.

If X and Y have full overlap then F is the full overlap (is equivalent to) relation signifying $X = Y$, $(X,Y) \in F$, and $(Y,X) \in F$. Consider the CPs X = achievable and Y = feasible. Definitions indicate they refer to the same property so (achievable, feasible) $\in$ F. That is, checking an IRD all the places the property achievable applies is the same set of checks one would make for feasible. Discard one or the other. We chose to retain feasible because it is a more widely used term. Communicable and understandable, no implementation bias and design independence, plausible and feasible, were three other pairs of instances of relation F. Understandable, design independence, and feasible were retained. There were several such instances of equivalent terms.

A simple extension handles opposites where $X = \neg Y$ and $(X, \neg Y) \in F$. Consider the CPs X = ambiguous and Y = unambiguous. Clearly (ambiguous, ¬unambiguous) $\in$ F. Since ambiguous is the same as not unambiguous, checks for the two properties would be identical. We discarded ambiguous based on retaining positive property names (unambiguous). There were several other instances such as complex and simple, clear and vague, duplicate (copies of a requirement) and unique.

If X and Y have partial overlap then P is the partial overlap (is related to) relation signifying $X \cap Y \neq \varnothing$ and $X \neq Y$ so $(X,Y) \in P$. Consider the CPs X = complete and Y = consistent. Some definitions have preciseness as part of complete and others part of consistent so (complete, consistent) $\in$ P. Checking an IRD for completeness would include some checks for preciseness, which would also be made when checking the property consistent. This is duplication (overlap) of checks. The rest of the checks for complete are different from those of consistent. Disposition includes removing the precise part from one and assigning it to the other, and no other changes.

If X and Y have contained overlap then C is the contained overlap (is a subset of) relation signifying $X \subset Y$ and $(X,Y) \in C$. Consider the CPs X = relative necessity and Y = annotated. Most definitions of annotation include relative necessity so (relative necessity, annotated) $\in$ C. All the checks made for annotated include those for relative necessity. Relative necessity was discarded. Other pairs were (precise, correct), (closure, complete), and (traced, traceable). There were several such pairs.

Supportive. Two CPs are supportive if improvement in one property does not cause degradation in the other.

All properties must be pairwise supportive. Two properties should not work at cross purposes to each other. Certainly the simplest example of two CPs which are not supportive are opposite CPs. For instance, for CPs clear and vague, improve one and the other degrades.

Consider the CPs design independent (requirements do not unnecessarily restrict the solution space) and granularity (requirements have several levels of detail). In order to define a problem fully, requirements must be decomposed down to some level of detail, its granularity. Without that much detail, the problem is not fully defined. Decomposing below that level (the problem level) goes beyond the problem, results in over specifying, reduces the problem space, and degrades design independence. If granularity is defined with no bounds in its definition, increasing granularity (beyond the problem level) decreases design independence.

Intuitively it seems that properties would support each other. Yet the literature often cites cases of properties that work at cross purposes. Two such cases are discussed to bring out the subtleties of our selection criteria. The first subtlety shows how introducing errors during change might look like degradation. The second subtlety shows how a before and after view might look like degradation.

One case involves the CPs readability and consistency. One approach to improving readability may be to duplicate a requirement several places in the IRD. But the more copies that are made, the greater the chance of overlooking one copy when making a change to the requirement. Overlook leads to contradiction between the changed and unchanged copies, called inconsistency. Improve readability and consistency degrades.

First of all, if the change was made properly, all copies of the requirement would be the same. Readability improves and consistency is not degraded. But if the change was not made properly and inconsistency results, it is not because the properties are defined at cross purposes. Inconsistency resulted from a mistake in the change process, not from improving readability. Inconsistency is not inherent in improving readability through duplication. It is inherent in the change process. A solution is to improve the change process to prevent such inconsistencies.

A second case involves the CPs correct and testable. Assume a requirement is testable. Then an incorrect part is found and fixed, but the requirement now is less testable. Are the CPs correct and testable nonsupportive? It appears that improving correctness of the requirement has degraded its testability. In fact this means that the prior approach to testing was for an incorrect requirement. Testing may have been simple but it was the wrong test. Testing before and after are not comparable and this is not degradation.

In the previous subsections checks of selection criteria significantly reduced the list of CPs. Checking each pair of CPs at this point resulted in all properties being supportive.

Coverage. A set of CPs has coverage if they are able to identify all IRD errors that have an impact on the quality of an IRD. One then assumes that if a set of CPs has coverage, and if an IRD passes all checks for these properties, then the IRD has high quality. Errors that do not have an impact on the quality of the IRD are assumed to have no impact on the quality of the system built to the IRD. If all checks pass, it is still possible to have an error in the IRD, but it has no impact on the quality of the IRD. If a check fails, it may or may not have detected a quality impact error.

In other words, if a particular type of error exists in an IRD which does impact quality, and a system is built to match the IRD, the system would not be what the SH wanted. It would have a defect in it. Some function would not work the way SH had anticipated. We are not considering whether the SH would live with the flawed system. We are trying to define the ideal case. What someone might accept as less than ideal is outside the scope of this paper.

We claim that the final set of HQPs cover all the meaningful errors, based on the assumption that the original set of 108 CPs could be used to uncover all the meaningful errors. Through the reduction process of applying selection criteria, only the properties which expose meaningful errors are retained. In this sense, the final set of HQPs cover all the meaningful errors.

HQP REFINEMENT

Refinement. The purpose of this section is to better define the HQPs found through the process of the previous section, and stated in Table 4. Through the process of refinement, and based on issues which surfaced during the application of the selection criteria, the final set of HQPs emerged, as defined in Table 5.

High Quality Properties	Definitions
Annotated/nec	All requirements annotated for

	relative necessity (must have, desirable, optional)
Complete	For each requirement, all requirement parts are necessary & sufficient (exactly the right parts are there, no missing or extra)
Consistent/req	No 2 requirements are in conflict with each other
Consistent/part	For each requirement, there is no conflict between any of its parts
Consistent/need	No requirement is in conflict with a SH needs statement
Correct	For each requirement, all requirement parts have just the right information (accurate to the appropriate level)
Design independent	Requirements do not unnecessarily constrain the design
Feasible	At least one system could be built to meet the requirements
Organized/form	Requirements are organized according to a document standard
Organized/sto	Requirements are electronically stored to allow basic modification
Testable	For each requirement, a procedure can be found to verify that the system meets the requirement
Traceable/need	For each basic requirements, there is a link to its SH needs statement
Traceable/req	Each requirement has a link to its parent in the IRD
Unambiguous	Each requirement has exactly one interpretation to all reviewers
Understand	Each requirement can be comprehended by its reviewers

Table 5. Final Set of HQPs

For instance, one "finalist" that did not make the cut was the CP modifiable. A requirement is modifiable if the IRD is stored on a processor with word processing capabilities. We assumed that any IRD being built today would have access to such technology. The CP organized included this access to technology so modifiable was discarded. The CP maintainable depends on modifiable, which is part of organized, so maintainable was discarded. The CP useable depends on being maintainable so it was discarded. The CP useable (the IRD is useable throughout the system life cycle) implies that the IRD is maintainable (modifiable), so useable was discarded.

The CP robust means that a requirement has built into it extra measures of system protection beyond what was requested by the SH. Robust is a form of over specification, which is part of incompleteness. Since the CP complete is an HQP, robust was discarded.

This brutal process of qualifying the original list of 108 CPs, especially discarding, did not result in the loss of information. The list of names was reduced but insights from their information base were merged into surviving CPs. But then the surviving CPs (HQPs now) needed to be refined. Several of the HQPs were made up of smaller quality attributes. When this occurred, each such HQP was split into smaller HQPs and checked against the selection criteria again. Any part that passed became a separate HQP. Table 5 reflects this final set of HQPs.

To explain splitting, consider the HQP consistency. Consistency is checked between the parts of a requirement (consistency/part), between pairs of requirements (consistency/req), and between a requirement and a SH need (consistency/need). So it was split into three parts. HQP organized was split into a part that includes following a standard format for readability (organized/form) and a part addressing electronic storage with edit capability for modification (organized/sto). HQP traceability (forward and backward) must link a requirement to its parent (traceable/req) and to a SH need if applicable (traceable/need).

COMPARISON TO OTHER WORK

Comparison. A search of the literature has revealed over 20 lists of goodness properties. Many more partial lists, not well defined, were also found. Four of the more prominent lists were selected to compare to our final list of HQPs in Table 5. Results are summarized in Table 6. Discussion of these results follows the table. We looked for four features; property definitions, overlap, extra properties, and missing properties. Overlap is two properties doing some of the same checking or definitions were sufficiently general that repetition of checks could be interpreted. The first two rows are a subjective indication of just the lists. The second two rows compare these lists to our HQPs.

Features	IEEE 1233	IEEE 830	Davis	Buede
Property definitions	fair	good	good	good
Overlapping	many	many	few	few

properties				
Extra properties	several	2	7	1
Missing properties	3	1	0	1

Table 6. HQPs VS Other Property Lists

One source of a properties list is the IEEE Standard for developing a system requirements specification (IEEE Std 1233, 1998). Actually it contains 3 short lists and several other properties subtly implied throughout, making it difficult to compile a list. Several properties lacked good definitions. This could lead to a fair amount of overlap. If a list were compiled of the obvious properties, CPs correct, feasible, and understand would be missing. These properties are absolutely essential to any list. Many properties are included in their list that add nothing to the quality of an IRD, such as static (requirements change), validation (not done until system is built), abstract (how do you measure it), and unique (no duplicate requirements).

A second source is the IEEE Standard for developing a software system specification (IEEE Std 830, 1998). There is a list of 8 properties, along with several properties woven throughout the text. Many properties are stated more than once and defined slightly different, resulting in overlap. Still the definitions are fairly good. The only property missing is feasibility. Some properties are included in their list that add nothing to the quality of an IRD, such as relative stability and cross referencing.

A third source is the Davis list of 24 properties (Davis, 1998). All definitions are fairly clear and there is little overlap. All of our HQPs are included in this list. The weak part of this list is several properties that contribute little to the quality of an IRD, such as concise, executable (applies to formal requirements), relative stability, version, not redundant (no duplicate requirements), precise (overlaps with correct), and reuseable (not a well defined area yet).

A fourth source is the Buede list of 14 properties (Buede, 2000). Definitions are fairly clear and a couple of cases of overlap exist. All of our HQPs are included in this list except organized/form. One property, unique, contributes little to the quality of an IRD.

Property definition for the four references in Table 6 was adequate to allow us to roughly correlate properties in one list to those in another. They did not provide enough detail to determine more exactly what subproperties were involved. One thing the use of selection criteria did was to force us to define HQPs in detail. More detail than the summaries in Table 5. As a result, we were able to compare our HQPs to the other properties in detail. So although Table 6 shows some degree of agreement with our HQPs, at another level of detail we can not be sure how comprehensive these properties would be in practice. Also note that all four references had overlapping properties which can increase the amount of property checking with no return.

We would like to have compared our method of generating our list of HQPs to other such methods. Within the literature there are many lists of properties but none came with a method to compare to. Many lists of properties have simply evolved over the years based on past inspections. When errors were found in an IRD, they became the source of adding another property check to the list. Our work provides a reason for the properties in our HQP list.

FUTURE WORK

Future. Our next task is to provide tighter definitions for each of the HQPs and then determine more subjective measurement criteria for each HQP. Preliminary work indicates that the order in which properties are checked is important. Is there a natural ordering? Another area in need of further research is defining when a property check failure is an error to be fixed. Given an error, how is correction performed and rechecked? With these improvements to the analysis process, we move closer to an objective process for improving the quality of an IRD.

REFERENCES

Buede, Dennis, *The Engineering Design of Systems: Models and Methods*, Wiley, 2000.

Davis, Alan et al, "Identifying and Measuring Quality in a Software Requirements Specification." Software Requirements Engineering, Thayer & Dorfman, IEEE, 1998, 194-205.

IEEE Std 1233, "IEEE Guide for Developing System Requirements Specifications." Software Requirements Engineering, Thayer & Dorfman, IEEE, 1998, 245-284.

IEEE Std 830, "IEEE Recommended Practice for Software Requirements Specifications." Software Requirements Engineering, Thayer & Dorfman, IEEE, 1998, 207-244.

Schneider, Richard, Dennis Buede, "Criteria for Selecting Properties for a High Quality Informal Requirements Document." INCOSE-MARC 2000.

BIOGRAPHY

Richard Schneider has been an engineer in industry for 35 years in all phases of system development. He has been with Information Technology & Applications Corporation (ITAC) since 1988 as a senior engineer. His work involves many facets of defining and testing requirements. He is a member of ACM and IEEE. He has done adjunct teaching for over 25 years in formal language theory, sequential machine theory, computability, and software engineering. He has a BSEE from Villanova University, an MSEE from Rochester Institute of Technology, and is currently pursuing a doctorate in information technology at George Mason University.
e-mail: 2schneids@msn.com

Dr. Dennis M. Buede is an Associate Professor of Systems Engineering at George Mason University. He teaches courses in systems engineering design and integration and decision/risk analysis. He conducts research for the Center of Excellence in Command, Control, Communications and Intelligence. His Ph.D. and M.S. are in Engineering-Economic Systems from Stanford University. He has a B.S. in Aerospace Engineering from the University of Cincinnati. Dr. Buede has had experience in the consulting industry, including starting and operating a consulting company that specializes in applications and research of decision analysis to systems engineering problems, decision support systems, and multisensor data fusion.
e-mail: dbuede@gmu.edu

End User Involvement in Establishing Software Requirements for Aerospace Software Systems

Mr. Brian Ippolito
Professor Earll Murman
Massachusetts Institute of Technology
Lean Aerospace Initiative
Room 41-205
77 Massachusetts Avenue
Cambridge, MA 02139-4307 USA

ABSTRACT

Requirement practitioners often cite end user involvement as an important element of an effective requirement derivation process. The research reported in this paper provides quantitative data of end user involvement in the software requirement derivation process. The paper includes information on the identity of the end user versus the customer, end user involvement, frequency of end user and customer changes, value added by the end user, enablers, and end user satisfaction. The findings presented were part of a larger two-year research effort involving over one hundred and seventy requirement practitioners from the Aerospace industry, United States Air Force, and MIT. The goal of the research effort was to identify effective practices for deriving software requirements.

INTRODUCTION

The MIT Lean Aerospace Initiative (LAI) is focused on understanding the applicability of the "Lean" concepts to the aerospace industry. Lean originated in the automotive industry and is grounded in the manufacturing domain [Womack, Jones, and Roos, 1990]. The basic philosophy of "Lean" is to eliminate all non value-added activities and be responsive to customer or market needs in order to reduce the product development cycle time, increase product quality, and reduce overall cost [Weiss, Murman, and Roos, 1996].

The information presented in this paper is a product of a two-year LAI research effort focused on applying the Lean principles to the process used to derive aerospace software requirements. As a result of this research effort, major findings were identified in six areas: the software upgrade value stream, enterprise metrics, requirements training, software development process effectiveness, end user involvement, and responsibilities for making sure requirements are cost effective and meet the end users needs [Ippolito and Murman, 2000]. This paper highlights the finding associated with *End User Involvement in Establishing Software Requirements for Aerospace Software Systems.*

During the study, numerous requirement practitioners expressed a need to involve the end user in the software development process. The specific value added contribution of the end user(s) to the requirement derivation process was not well understood or well defined by all of the stakeholders. The definition of the end user and the value added contribution of their involvement is the subject of this paper. After a brief description of the data collected during the study, the paper addresses the identity of the end user versus the customer, end user involvement, frequency of end user and customer changes, value added by the end user, enablers, and end user satisfaction.

DATA COLLECTION

Data presented in this paper were collected from over 45 two hour case study interviews and 125 stakeholder surveys. Case study interviews provided a detailed understanding of the software requirement derivation process for three different aerospace software upgrade efforts (Commercial Auto-pilot, Military Avionics, and Military Space Ground Terminal). To complement these three case studies, survey data from them plus seven additional programs were obtained from the program and process leadership (Program Management, Chief Systems Engineer, End Users, Customers, Software Managers, Software and System Engineering, System Test, etc..).

The LAI industry participants identified the ten systems used in the research believing that each system represented a "successful" program where an "effective" requirement derivation process was used. Figure 1 illustrates some of the characteristics of the ten systems studied.

	Application Domain	Software Development Cycle Time (months)	Case Study	Survey Responses	Development Model
System 1	Commercial Aircraft	32	Yes	13	Incremental
System 2	Military Fighter Aircraft	62	Yes	14	Waterfall/ Incremental
System 3	Military Fighter Aircraft	49	No	12	Waterfall/ Incremental
System 4	Military Bomber Aircraft	46	No	15	Waterfall/ Incremental
System 5	Military Missile/ Munition	Unknown	No	7	Waterfall/ Incremental
System 6	Military Missile/ Munition	84	No	11	Waterfall/ Incremental
System 7	Military Missile/ Munition	29	No	14	Waterfall
System 8	Military Missile/ Munition	Unknown	No	13	Incremental
System 9	Military Space Ground Terminal	7	Yes	18	Spiral
System 10	Military Fighter Aircraft	36	No	11	Waterfall

Figure 1: Discriminatory Characteristics of the Ten Aerospace Software Upgrades Used in the Research

The application domain of the systems fall into four general areas: Commercial Aircraft (System 1), Military Avionics (Systems 2, 3, 4, 10), Military Space Ground Terminal (System 9) and Missile/Munitions (Systems 5, 6, 7, 8). The software development cycle time, defined as concept definition to delivery of the product to the customer, ranged from seven months to eighty-four months. The number of survey responses ranged from seven to eighteen with an average of twelve responses per system. Half of the systems adopted a combination of the waterfall and incremental software development model. One utilized a spiral software development model and two others a waterfall model. The remaining two systems adopted an incremental model for software development. Despite the diverse nature of the products, all of the systems were real-time, mission critical, embedded software systems. This common characteristic forms the basis for a comparison of the findings.

END USER VERSUS THE CUSTOMER

During the case studies, the interviewees repeatedly expressed that their software requirement process was focused on the customer to achieve high levels of customer satisfaction. To clarify their definitions of "customer" and "end user" the program and process leadership were asked the following:

"Assuming that the 'Customer' is defined as the organization/person to whom you deliver your product and 'End User' is defined as the person who operates the system. For your project, which of the following categories best fits the terms Customer and End User."

- Prime Contractor
- Government System Program Office
- Another unit within you organization
- Airline Pilot
- Warfighter
- Other

Survey responses, shown in Figure 2, indicated the definition of the end user was clear to most of the survey respondents and did not show a significant variation between systems or application domains. The commercial auto-pilot defined the end user as the airline pilot. The military avionics upgrades, the missile/munitions upgrades, and the military space ground terminal upgrades defined the end user as the warfighter.

The term warfighter is common among the military technology development community and is intended to represent the operational combat units. For the military aircraft and missile/munitions programs the warfighter is interpreted as the pilots. The military space ground terminal respondents interpreted the warfighter as the operational ground terminal operator.

Assuming that the "Customer" is defined as the organization/person to whom you deliver your product and "End User" is defined as the person who operates the system. For your project which of the following categories best fits the terms "Customer" and "End User". (End User Responses Only)

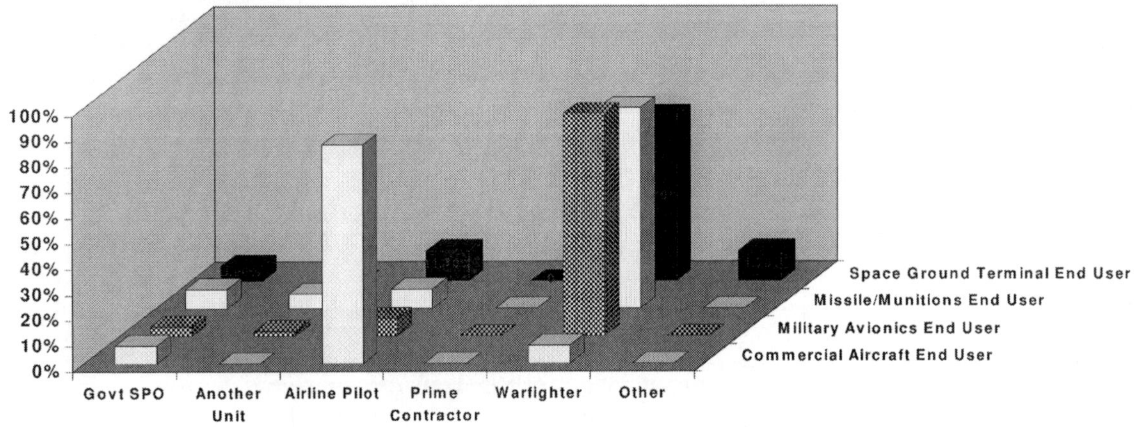

Figure 2: Defining the End User

Unlike the definition of the end user, the term customer had multiple definitions. While some dominant categories did exist, Figure 3 illustrates a majority of the interpretations of the tem customer were not the same as the end user.

Assuming that the "Customer" is defined as the organization/person to whom you deliver your product and "End User" is defined as the person who operates the system. For your project which of the following categories best fits the terms "Customer" and "End User". (Customer Responses only)

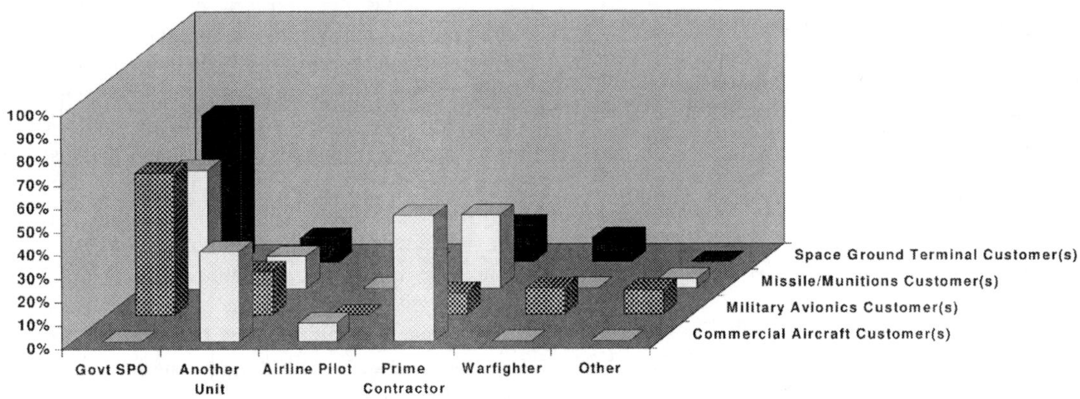

Figure 3: Defining the Customer

Case study interviewees offered two explanations for the lack of a uniform customer definition across all systems. First, the respondents felt the term "customer" represents the next organization or person in the software development process. Software developers repeatedly mention the system test organization as their customer because the code was delivered to test and their involvement in the development effort subsided. As a result, some responses indicated "another unit within your organization" as their customer.

A second explanation offered by the interviewees suggests the multiple organizations and companies involved in the development effort create artificial barriers in the product flow. Once the product was delivered to the next company or the government, the development process was complete. In the case of the military avionics program, delivery of the software to the government system program office is not equivalent to delivering the product to the pilots. The government system program office notifies the United States Air Force Operational Test and Evaluation (OT&E) organization the software has met the contractual requirements and is ready for operational testing. The OT&E organization is responsible for the process to evaluate and examine the product prior to delivery of the software to the operational pilots.

The multiple definitions of "customer" indicates that one must be cautious in using this term. On the other hand, "end user" has a clearer identify. If one uses "customer" when meaning "end user", communication could be imperfect.

END USER INVOLVEMENT

Case study interviews identified a common belief that end user involvement in the requirement derivation process was a valuable enabler for the program and process leadership to focus the organization and their activities on increasing end user satisfaction.

The program and process leadership were asked to estimate the level of involvement of the end user in the phases of the software requirements phases. The responses, shown in Figure 4, indicate the level of end user involvement varied significantly across the systems and across the major requirement derivation activities. The four missile/munitions systems and the commercial auto-pilot system had the lowest level of end user involvement in all phases of the requirement derivation process. The military avionics and space ground terminal systems had the highest level of end user involvement. In these systems, the case study interviews indicated the concept definition phase of the requirement derivation process was heavily influenced by the military end users. In all cases, end users involvement was highest during concept definition than any other phases of the process.

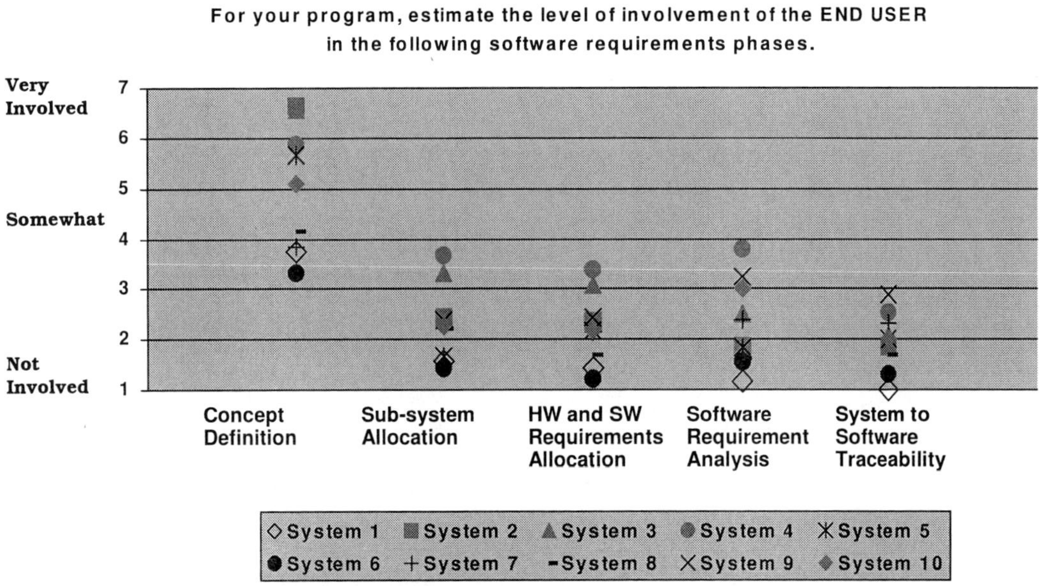

Figure 4: Estimated Level of End User Involvement in the Software Requirement Derivation Process

FREQUENCY OF END USER AND CUSTOMER CHANGES IN NEEDS AND EXPECTATIONS

Case study interviews indicated requirement stability was important to requirement practitioners. To better understand the frequency of changes associated with the end user, the program and process leadership were asked the following:

"For your program estimate the frequency in which the following factors contribute to unplanned changes (additions, modifications, deletions) to the derived software requirements."

- Changes in End User Needs
- Changes in End User Expectations
- Changes in Customer Needs
- Changes in Customer Expectations
- Software Unable to Meet Requirements

The responses, shown in Figure 5, indicate most of the processes experienced varying levels of changes in customer and end user needs, and changes in customer and end user expectations. Despite the large distribution of average responses across the systems, no system experienced the changes "very often".

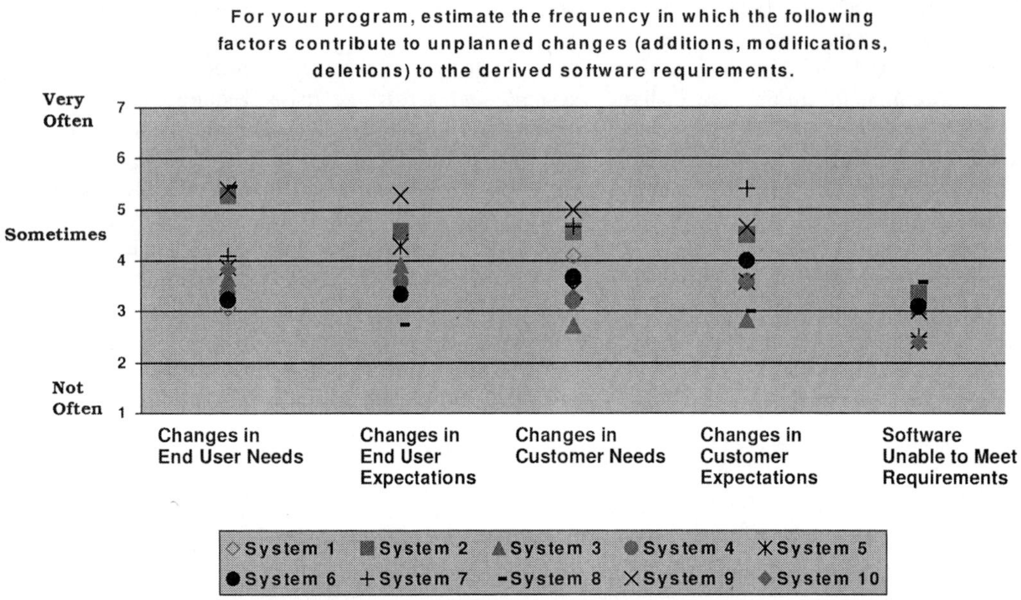

Figure 5: Average Estimation of Frequency of Unplanned Changes to Derived Software Requirements

VALUE ADDED END USER CONTRIBUTION

The value added contribution of the end user appears to be a function of the ability of the process to effectively capture the critical end user information. To better understand what end user information was critical, the program and process leadership were asked the following:

"How important are the following aspects of End User involvement in the software requirements process?"

- Agreement between end user and developer on performance expectations.
- Give developers an understanding of the operational environment of the system.
- Give developers an understanding of how the system will be used.
- Build trust between developers and end users.
- Clarify validation/verification expectations.
- Develop new business opportunities.

The six areas were defined based on feedback from industry practitioners and prior research done by the Software Engineering Institute (SEI) at Carnegie Mellon University [Bracket, 1991].

The responses for all ten systems are shown in Figure 6. As a whole, the most important aspects of end user involvement were: the agreement between the end user and developers on performance expectations, giving developers and understanding of the operation environment of the system, and providing an understanding of how the system will be used. Clarifying validation and verification criteria was considered very important by seven of the ten systems. Developing new business opportunities was considered somewhat important by all 10 systems.

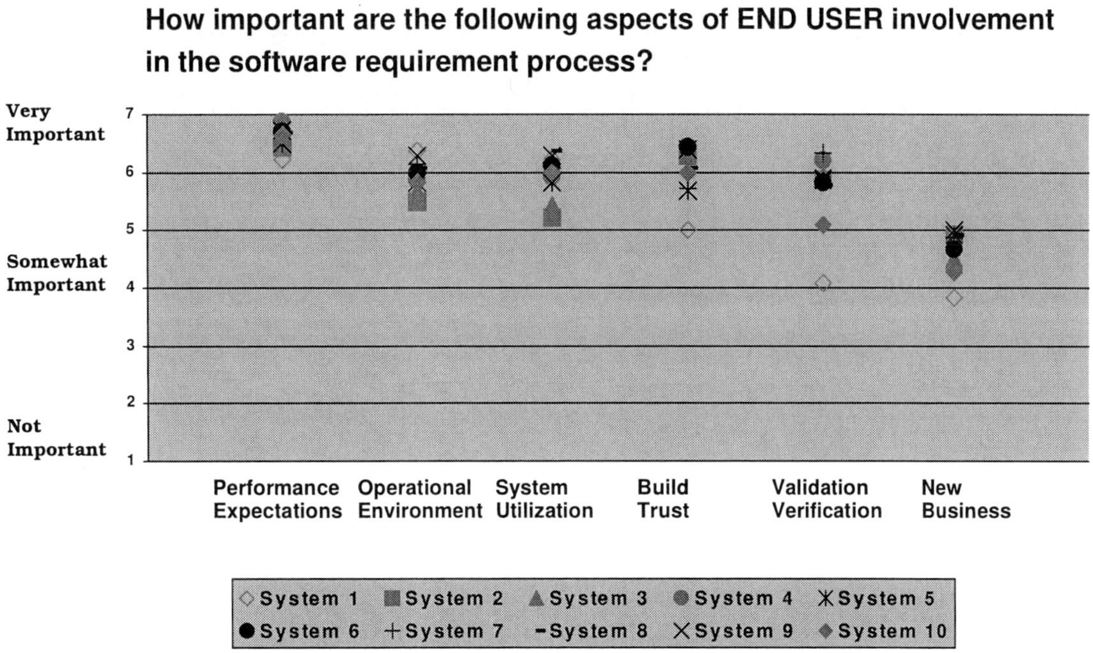

Figure 6: Average Response for all 10 Systems

ENABLERS

Three key enablers were observed to increase the value added contribution of the end user involvement during the requirement derivation process. First, regular reviews with the end users allowed the developers to focus on the effective and efficient capture of critical end user information. Most of the military systems studied as part of this research had development cycle times in excess of 36 months so early definition of critical information was difficult. Case study interviews identified numerous examples of situations where the military end user(s) did not want to provide critical information to the software developers in a level of detail the developers desired. Interviews with military end user requirement practitioners identified that the long software development cycle times made many end users uncomfortable providing some of the critical information early in the development process. End users wanted to "keep their options open" and not commit to performance expectations or how the system will be used. However, the use of regularly scheduled review board meetings with end user throughout this period correlated with the effective capture of end user input.

Second, when end user information is provided, organizations can increase its value by effectively capturing and making available this information. The military avionics case study developed a centralized electronic database to capture the end user information for the avionics software developers to reference during the code generation process. The database connected requirement documents to end user needs that were expressed during the concept definition phase [Ippolito and Murman, 1999]. Case study interviews identified this as an important enabler for their software development process to be effective.

Third, "successful" software requirement derivation processes studied in this research allowed for some unplanned end user and customer changes in needs and expectations. However the frequency of these changes were not large. In one case study, the military space ground terminal program, a continuous requirement evaluation process was initiated to rapidly evaluate evolving end user needs and clarify end user performance expectations.

END USER SATISFACTION

The research approach was designed to include only programs the LAI industry and government participants believed utilized an effective requirement derivation process. Despite this focus on successful programs, quantitative measures of end user satisfaction were not observed. Interviews on all three case studies indicated anomaly reports of field discrepancies were considered indicators of end user satisfaction but no metric was used to measure satisfaction on a consistent basis.

On the survey, the program and process leadership were asked to estimate the level of end user satisfaction. Responses shown in Figure 7 indicate end user satisfaction varied across systems. Interestingly, the number of end user responses did not appear to adversely impact the data. Systems 2, 3, 4, and 10 had the highest level of end user input with varying degrees of end user satisfaction. One possible explanation of this is the manner in which the data were collected. Surveys were mailed directly to MIT and kept confidential. Survey respondents did not appear to fear any form of retribution within their organization. Case study interviews offered insight into the possible causes of varying levels of satisfaction. First, developing software requirements and subsequently the coded software for aerospace systems can be very challenging. Success is viewed by some as a relative experience. During the case study interviews, many practitioners shared experiences of failed software programs and ineffective requirement processes. For these individuals success may have simply been the delivery a software system within the budget available, the time required, and the performance that pleased the end user.

A second explanation relates to the lack of firm requirement effectiveness measures with respect to the end user. The lack of any clear and quantitative measure makes evaluating requirement process effectiveness difficult. Further research is needed to identify effective metrics to measure end user satisfaction.

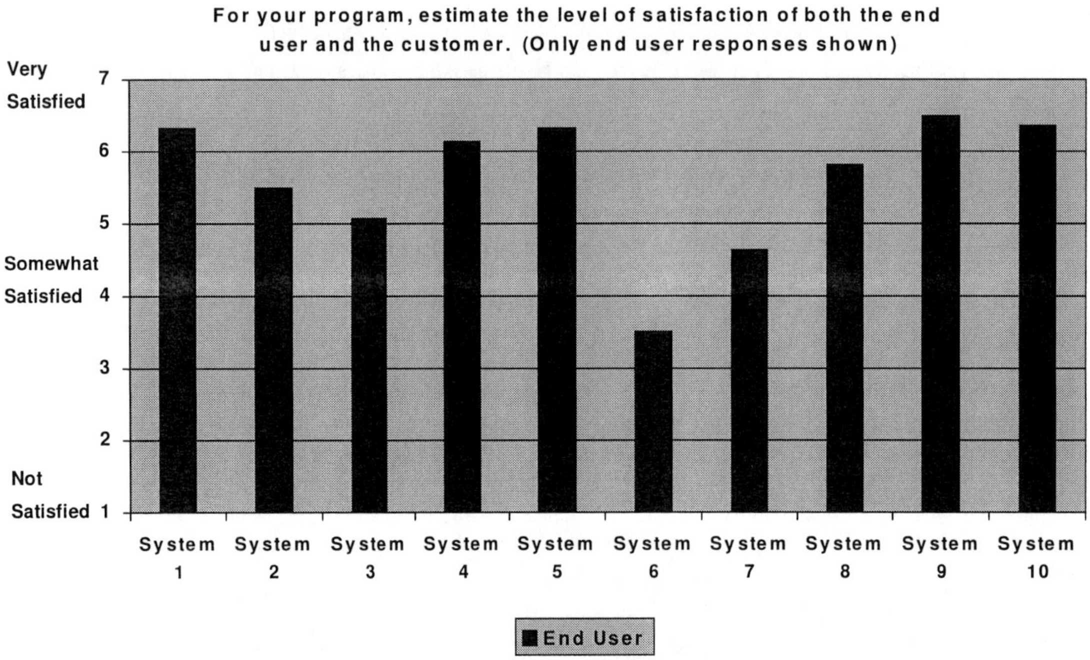

Figure 7: Estimated Level of End User Satisfaction

SUMMARY

Characterizing the value added contribution of the end user(s) during the requirement derivation process can be a challenge. The lack of quantitative end user satisfaction measures makes this task more difficult. Case study interviews and survey data reported in this paper provided insight into some of the factors contributing to successful value added end user involvement.

Effective processes for deriving software requirements studied as part of this research all included the end user in establishing requirements. Involvement was greatest early in the software development process, during concept development.

Feedback from requirement practitioners suggests certain information provided by the end user is "critical" to the requirement derivation process. This information includes an agreement between the end user and developers on performance expectations, the operational environment of the system, an understanding of how the system will be used, and clarifying validation and verification criteria.

Three enablers were identified as part of the research. First, the use of regular reviews with end users during the concept definition phase was observed. The reviews helped process practitioners capture the "critical" end user information. Including the end user in the process does not guarantee success. The quality of the end user input appears to be more of a deciding factor.

Second, the efficient capture and distribution of critical end user information is an important enabler to increase the effectiveness of the software requirement derivation process. One example, provided by the military avionics case study, found electronic databases in use to help facilitate the distribution of end user information to the developers.

Third, a successful requirement derivation process can withstand some changes to end user and customer changes to needs and expectations.

REFERENCES

Brackett, John W., Software Requirements, *SEI Curriculum Module SEI-CM-19-1.2,* Carnegie Mellon University, January 1990,

Ippolito, B. and Murman, E., "Establishing Requirements: A Step in the Software Development Value Stream", *Technical Proceedings of the Thirteenth International Conference on Systems Engineering August 9-12,* 1999, SE-151

Ippolito, B. and Murman, E., *Improving the Software Upgrade Value Stream: Findings, Recommendations, and the Identification of Lean Practices for Deriving Software Requirements*, Massachusetts Institute of Technology, April 2000

Weiss, S.I., Murman, E.M. and Roos. D., "The Air Force and Industry Think Lean", *Aerospace America*, May 1996, pp 32-38

Womack, James P., Jones, Daniel. T., and Roos, Daniel, *The Machine That Changed The World*, Rawson, 1990

BIOGRAPHY

Brian Ippolito is a former United States Air Force officer with over seven years of experience in aerospace software development. He received a B.S. in Aerospace Engineering from Illinois Institute of Technology in 1992 and a S.M. in Engineering and Management from Massachusetts Institute of Technology in 2000. He is currently an employee of Northrop Grumman Electronic Sensors & Systems Sector in Baltimore, MD.

Earll Murman is the Ford Professor of Engineering and Co-Director of the Lean Aerospace Initiative at MIT. He previously served as head of the Department of Aeronautics and Astronautics and the Director of Project Athena at MIT. In addition to his 20 years in academia, his career in aerospace engineering includes 10 years in industry and three years at NASA's Ames Research Center. Dr. Murman is a member of INCOSE, the National Academy of Engineering, and a Fellow of the American Institute of Aeronautics and Astronautics. His professional interests include aerodynamics, systems engineering, product development, lean enterprise issues, and engineering education.

Commercial System Development Models

Tim Cathcart
Program Coordinator, Lean Sustainment Initiative
Massachusetts Institute of Technology
Cambridge, MA 02139

Ravi Jain
Staff Systems Engineer
Beckman Coulter
Brea, California

Jeffrey O. Grady
JOG System Engineering, Inc.
6015 Charae Street
San Diego, California 92122

Dan Surber
System Integration Manager
CNH Global (NV)
Burr Ridge, Illinois

Abstract. The authors believe that system engineers commonly fail to include the full sweep of program possibilities in their view. Their views do not always encompass the full programmatic scope of marketing, system development, and programmatic life cycle issues. As a result they are not able to contribute to their full capacity in the evolution of maximally effective strategies for their enterprise. This paper does two things of value to this engineer so constrained: (1) attempts to expand the readers model of the development environment to the ultimate and (2) offers, in the process, a general model that includes within it several commercial models as well as the fairly traditional aerospace/defense development model. The authors maintain that essentially the same system engineering process will be effective within any of these particular applications of the general model, though the practitioner will have to make choices among alternative techniques.

INTRODUCTION

For several years there has been a reluctance in many commercial firms to apply the full power of systems engineering techniques because these techniques have been somewhat unfairly associated with high cost military and aerospace products to the extent that they are thought by many to be inseparable from this industry sector. At the same time, there has been a reluctance among practicing system engineers to expand the horizons of our profession to firmly include the commercial market place and the marketing strategy component of the commercial development process. The authors maintain that the techniques of systems engineering are appropriate in any industry sector, product line, and customer base provided that they are applied within context of valid program needs. It is possible to apply them inappropriately increasing program cost unnecessarily.

The principal hurdle the commercial practitioner must overcome is the notion that system engineering is only appropriate in context with the one-time-through waterfall development model. Yes, it can and has been used very effectively in this model on many military programs but the techniques will work in any case where the development team is confronted by complexity of product and process in combination with challenging cost, schedule, and performance requirements. To make this point, the authors have constructed a process model embracing several viable commercial marketing and development strategies without eliminating the one-time-through model. We hope to show that a sound systems engineering approach is compatible with these several development models and thus encourage a more common appeal to the power of these techniques in commercial practice. It is also hoped that professional system engineers will look beyond their own horizons to take in a much richer set of possibilities. We will assume that the reader will accept that there is an effective system engineering process for use in the one-time-through model.`

MODEL OVERVIEW

Product and process systems can be developed, manufactured, delivered, and used over their useful life in a single straight through fashion as shown in Figure 1 without appeal to cyclical development or in service modification. This pattern may work for some products but it is not an ideal mental or physical framework for most commercial products. Generally, we wish to maintain a stream of product deliveries (and therefore a profitable revenue stream) over a considerable period of time. In the absence of competing firms and changing customer attitudes, the one-time-through model with a life long manufacturing period may be realized but these are realistic constraints in few, if any, real commercial market situations today.

No matter the product line or customer base, the product must be developed (F41), manufactured (F42), verified to comply with requirements and design (F44), delivered in some fashion to the ultimate users (F46), and finally used by that person or organization (F7). Most readers will relate without open hostility to the other life cycle process steps included on Figure 1.

The authors have, however, overlaid three different cyclical patterns that are of interest to both aerospace and commercial producers in addition to this one-time-through model to form a comprehensive suite of strategies to cover most commercial (and aerospace) development situations. Three strategic policy subsets have been identified called the short, medium, and long cycles based on the nature of development cycling during the product life cycle.

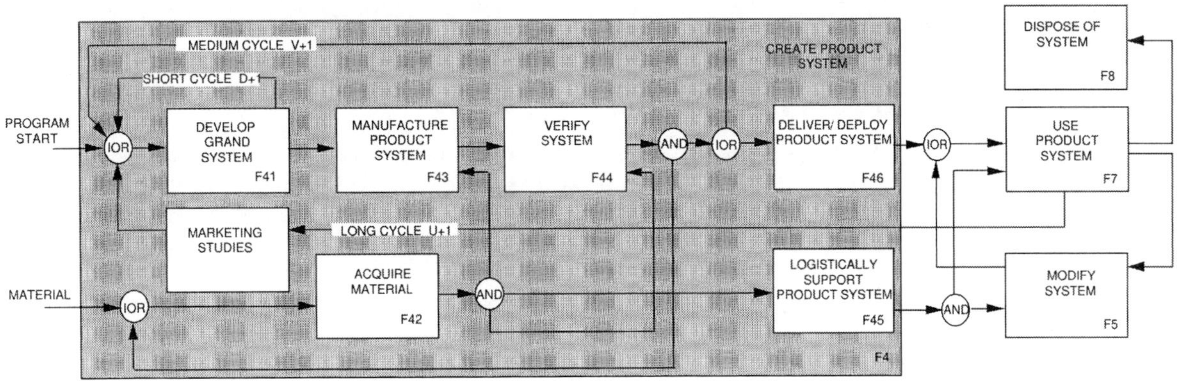

Figure 1 Development Cycles

The short cycle has two expressions in the form of the one-time through model also called the waterfall, exposed in Figure 1, the V model which is simply the waterfall bent in two at the design stage, and the spiral model. In the spiral development model the developer passes quickly through the several development steps, including building laboratory samples and testing them, and folds the results of each development cycle into the next version with no real intent to deliver any product but the one exiting the final spiral. The spiral simply increases the repetition rate of the waterfall model leading up to product delivery.

The medium cycle involves production of major elements of the system and subjecting them to verification in two or more cycles before delivery of the final product to customers. These cycles may correspond, for example, to prototyping that many companies apply. The long cycle depends on feedback from users/ customers of the system to identify areas where improvements can be made.

SHORT CYCLE STRATEGIES

One-Time-Through. One common approach in past military and aerospace programs has entailed a single pass through the development process using either the waterfall or the V development sequence model. In these programs, there is no long term intent to develop the system throughout its life cycle. Rather, there is an intent to complete a contract in one effort delivering a product that satisfies the requirements in a specification.

In most successful programs, the reality is that these product systems survive their initially intended application exposing additional opportunities to the user that require an enabling modification of the product. An example of this reality is the USAF/Boeing B-52 bomber which has long survived its initial application and may still be flying a century after its initial development. However meritorious the result, this was not the intent at the time the B-52 was first developed.

Spiral Development. In this paper, the authors have accepted that the spiral model is normally intended to evolve a single product design for delivery or deployment rather than act as a long term continued evolution of the product system. In this application, the developer simply repeats the waterfall model at a higher repetition rate than in the waterfall case. The developer defines requirements, develops a design, builds a product version, and subjects it to testing. In the process, the developer comes to a better understanding of the needed features (requirements) and goes through another cycle with changed requirements and new concept ideas. This may be repeated as needed hopefully with rapidly decreasing change magnitude in subsequent cycles. The spiral model is especially effective where it is very difficult to pre-define the requirements as in the case of the man-machine interaction necessary in computer software development as well as the requirements associated with fighter pilot control of a combat aircraft. The interface between men and machines is very simple involving the senses and physical actions but the stimulus-response relationships are determined by the internal operation of the person's mind – not an easy thing to predict where many different people will have to complete that interface. Criticism being less costly than creativity, it often is possible to develop an effective and affordable system through several spiral rotations rather than one straight through process where this kind of interface is involved. Almost all software is interactive with a human using the keyboard, mouse, and screen windows so is a good candidate for this development model.

MEDIUM CYCLE STRATEGIES

Poly-prototyping. The product development process used at JI Case Corporation is illustrated in Figure 2. It exemplifies a concurrent engineering process using integrated product development teams to establish or build on a platform baseline design. The material discussed in this section summarizes the copyrighted manual from the former Case Corporation, now merged with Ford-New Holland to form the Case-New Holland (CNH) Global (NV) sector of the Fiat Group. In addition, the process embodies many of the concepts put forth by the following researchers in the field of product development: Dan Clausing, Kim B. Clark, Steven C. Wheelwright, James Lacy and Ben

Blanchard. The Case Integrated Product Development Process (CIPDP) is undergoing a further revisions at this time as it incorporates material from the merging companies, and from the ideas of Genichi Taguchi, Jeffrey O. Grady, Peter Senge, Bill Eureka and W. Edwards Deming. This present discussion will focus on the CIPDP as it was being applied over the last 5 years (1995-2000).

The basic intent of CIPDP was to enable identification, scoping, planning and execution of four kinds of product development projects: research/development, breakthrough, platform or derivative designs (Wheelwright and Clark, 1992, p. 49)[1]. Some product development groups had slightly different time line and change content (new or revised engineering) "targets", but in general the following "rules of thumb" were desired:

- Research: sufficient to ensure user-ready
- Breakthrough: 36 months & > 50% change
- Platform: 24 months & 20-50% change
- Derivative: 6-12 months & 5-15% change

A set of these projects in a vehicle or model line would be collected into an "Aggregate Project Plan" for the director and management team of the product development group (Wheelwright & Clark, 1992, p. 34). This plan formed the basis for budget and manpower planning and execution for multi-year projects. The product development process allowed for several prototype builds, if needed, to support the product development stages. Each development group had its own "style" of implementing the guidance in the process documentation and training material provided by a functional engineering department. The research and development component that created the "technology stream" of innovations that were "user-ready" was also managed in part by the groups, and in part by the functional engineering department. (Wheelwright & Clark, 1992, p. 117-120) The rest of this section will discuss the INTENT of the CIPDP, not the execution and results that were obtained.

The company's strategic goals and its CIPDP employment were intended to define the design and its (manufacturing) processes concurrently with the integrated involvement of all the members of the value chain (Clausing, 1994, p. 27)[2]. The project team was meant to behave like the "heavy-weight" teams described by Clausing, Wheelwright and Clark. (Clausing, 1994, p. 27) (Wheelwright & Clark, 1992, p. 194).

Disciplined process execution is expected to provide the leadership (Product Development Director, Program Manager, Team Leaders and Senior Executives) with program phases and review opportunities to ensure the business rationale, cost profile and the technical content/quality were progressing adequately so that program risks could be understood and managed. This expectation creates a sort of "contract" between the executives and the product development group to deliver a product that would satisfy the marketing and sales objectives used to establish the initial business case for the project, including its scope, target cost, technical content and market regions. The core team planned and executed the project, while functional groups provided expertise and support as planned and requested. Executive reviews are strategically scheduled to facilitate funding approvals in accordance with corporate policy and procedures.

The major phases of the process are intended to provide for swift, concurrent development because technology development is NOT on the project's critical path. Therefore, the sequence of prototypes serves to study and confirm the technical content of the developing design to its requirements. The prototypes named in Figure 2 serve the following purposes:

- Alpha: Functional feasibility
- Beta: Functional verification & durability
- Gamma: Reliability Growth & Integration
- Delta: Production Quality

Both the platform and breakthrough type of project would develop all four prototypes, while the derivative would only develop the Gamma and Delta in most cases.

Maturation of analytical tools and modeling that are validated by lab or field test results helped reduce this dependency on "hardware" prototyping and testing. However, due to the dynamic behavior of customers as they used the machines, and their desire to "innovate" and adapt the design for new uses, there does not seem to be any way to eliminate all field testing of the functional (Beta) or production-intent (Gamma) prototypes. The stages, or development phases, of the product development process are illustrated in Figure 3. Each of the prototypes nominally fits into those phases as follows:

- Alpha: Product Definition (after SDR)
- Beta: Product & Process Development (PDR)
- Gamma: Development for Production (post-CDR)
- Delta: Mfg. & Production Confirmation (post-PRR)

The Program Definition phase was recently added to account for the fact that projects were going through the phase, but each team had highly variable success and no process guidance was available. The Executive reviews are held at the end of each phase to review the business and financial merits of the project. The program cost, schedule and technical progress is covered by the Development reviews, and General Design Reviews are held by the team(s) in between the Development Reviews to facilitate the day-to-day work of product development.

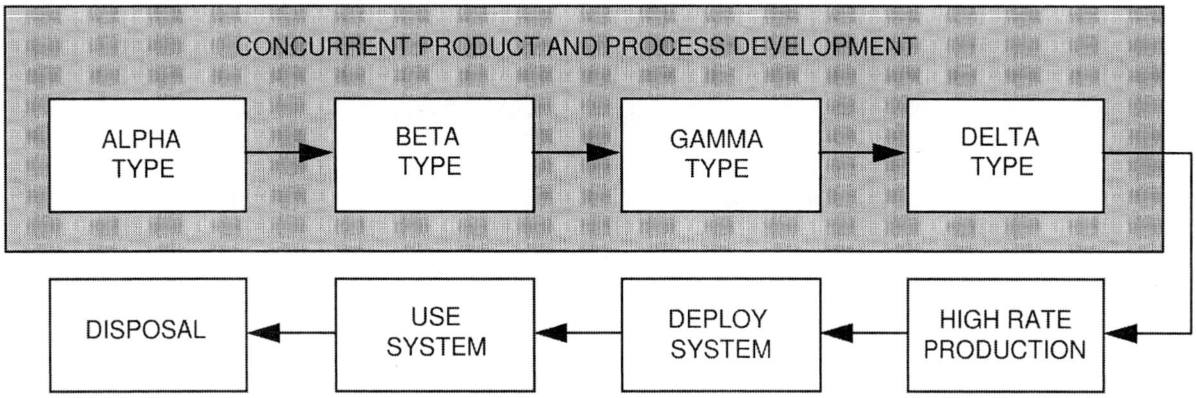

Figure 2 Poly-Prototyping Product Life Cycle

PHASE	PROGRAM DEFINITION	PRODUCT DEFINITION	PRODUCT & PROCSS DEVELOPMENT	DEVELOPMENT FOR PRODUCTION	MANUFACTURING & PRODUCTION CONFIRMATION
DEVELOPMENT REVIEWS(2)	FOR TFR	SRR SDR	PDR CDR	TRR PRR	SRA PRR
EXECUTIVE REVIEWS	EPR-0	EPR-1	EPR-2	EPR-3	EPR-4

Figure 3 Program Phases and Development Reviews

The names of development reviews identified by acronyms in Figure 3 are given below:

POR – Program Objectives Review
TFR – Team Formation Review
SRR – System Requirements Review
SDR – System Development Review
PDR – Preliminary Design Review
CDR – Critical Design Review
TRR – Test Readiness Review
PRR – Production/Support Readiness Review
SAR – Shipping Authorization Review
PPR – Product Performance Review

The development reviews within each phase serve three essential needs:

(1) To be working reviews that the team has developed the essential information from each business function area needed to evidence completion of the project plan.

(2) To confirm the system's baseline is continuing toward convergence on a design solution; that the team has a definite understanding of the risks (cost, schedule and technical) (Grady, 1993, p.18)[3].

(3) To show there is a clear plan ensuring they can reach the next milestone.

These General Design Reviews (GDR) are meant to include the suppliers, functional support elements and test engineering in order to ensure the technical characteristics of the design and manufacturing process are compatible and closing on complete satisfaction of their respective requirements. A chief feature of this concurrent development process is the use of several preventative/proactive quality-engineering tools. These tools include: quality function deployment (QFD) matrices, failure mode effects analysis (FMEA) and robust design engineering to ensure the quality of the system solution is not sacrificed while satisfying the aggressive cost and schedule objectives the teams are challenged to meet (Clausing, 1994, p. 57, 73, 96).

It is important to remember that no process, no matter how well it is flow charted, described or taught is a substitute for disciplined, focused execution. Dr. Clausing sums it up quite well,

"*Total quality development* brings a much better decision style, the best that we know how to practice. After making each decision by using the best approach, we can have confidence in the result...Our commitment to the decisions provides a firm foundation for the ongoing work." (p. 97)

Approaches to Certification of Reconfigurable IMA Systems

Paul Hollow[1], John McDermid, Mark Nicholson
Department of Computer Science, University of York, York, YO10 5DD, UK
Email: paulh | jam | mark @cs.york.ac.uk
Tel: (+44) 1904 432789

Abstract. *The aerospace industry has been investigating integrated modular avionics (IMA) for some years. IMA offers greater flexibility in the use of computing resources by reconfiguring the software to employ different processors and communications, in order to recover from failure and to redistribute workload. Such reconfiguration offers benefits, but poses difficulties for certification since current certification practice requires assessment of each configuration.*

The approach we have adopted is to seek means of clearing a configuration of a system and to identify a number of "equivalent" configurations. This requires us to establish "safe" reconfigurations for the IMA system. Technically, we have formulated the search for a set of "equivalent" configurations as a multi-objective optimisation problem. Pragmatically, the search produces configuration tables which could be used by the IMA operating system to make a "safe" change to an "equivalent" configuration, when necessary.

INTRODUCTION

Conventional aircraft systems are *federated*, with each major function, or application, in a separate hardware unit. These units may be interconnected, but each is considered independently from the point of view of certification. This type of federated system can be seen in most current aircraft, with those of the A320's generation having perhaps 40-50 systems, and about 100 computers. These federated systems are expensive to develop and certify. They are also relatively inflexible, and give relatively poor resource utilisation. These limitations, amongst others, have led to research into an alternative approach known as *Integrated Modular Avionics (IMA).*

The aim of IMA is to bring the flexibility of distributed architectures, such as networks of PCs, to aircraft applications. With IMA a number of functions or application run on a processor, communicating via services provided by an operating system. At any time, a function will be allocated to a particular processor, but reconfiguration allows applications to employ different processors, and communications to use different media, e.g. buses, to respond to system load, failures or battle damage. IMA has many potential benefits including simplifying software upgrades, making it feasible to add new applications without changing the hardware, and assisting in meeting requirements for maintenance free operating periods (MFOPs).

The use of IMA changes systems in a number of ways. For example, there may be no physical boundaries between applications, and sensors and actuators may be interfaced to buses, rather than linked directly to the hardware unit where they are used. However, in this paper, our main focus is on the impact that the introduction of such IMA systems has on *safety certification*.

Under current certification procedures each system is assessed in isolation, and the certification process assumes that the software behaves in a deterministic manner. Applying this philosophy to IMA, it is likely that each possible architectural configuration would need to be analysed and certified separately. Applying IMA to an aircraft of the complexity of an A320 is likely to yield many millions of valid configurations. Thus, unless it is possible to find an alternative to the classical certification process, the cost of certifying different system configurations is likely to outweigh the benefits of IMA.

The objective of the work described here is to find ways of identifying a "family" of different IMA configurations which can be shown to be "equivalent", and which can be certified by analysing only one representative member of the family. To achieve this we employ off-line analysis of different possible configurations, producing tables of "safe"

[1] Paul Hollow is a Research Student within the DCSC at York funded by EPSRC with a CASE award from BAE SYSTEMS.

reconfigurations. This supports reconfiguration under failure based on the tables produced during the off-line analysis. This basic approach should also provide pointers for certification of more advanced reconfiguration techniques.

In Section 2 we set the scene by considering the issues surrounding the certification of IMA systems and scope the problem addressed by this paper. In Section 3 we propose a process for identifying and analysing a group of equivalent architectures. In Section 4 we outline our heuristic search based approach to determining the group, provide details on the scoring of different proposed architectures and give some preliminary results. In Section 5 we return to the issue of the value of the approach to certifying IMA systems.

CERTIFICATION OF AVIONICS SYSTEMS

Accepted practices in the aerospace industry are to assess systems independently, for the purpose of certification. Recent international standards such as ARP-4754 (SAE 1996) and the accompanying ARP-4761 are intended to deal with "complex and integrated systems" for commercial aircraft. However they do not explicitly deal with issues such as IMA and, implicitly, they still reflect the "system at a time" approach to certification. Military standards such as DS 00-55 (MoD 1996a) and DS 00-56 (MoD 1996b) in the UK, and MilStd 882C (DoD 1993) in the USA are similarly mute on the subject of certification of IMA systems. Thus the standards do not help us when considering IMA, and we need to go back to more basic principles. However, it is first worth identifying in more detail the challenges posed by IMA.

For computer-based systems, certification currently relies on two main assumptions:

- system can be viewed, and assessed, as a single entity
- the behaviour of the system is *deterministic*

Neither of these assumptions is likely to hold for IMA systems due to their ability to reconfigure following failure. Even if reconfiguration occurs on the ground, the behaviour of the system isn't determined through its life. In fact the situation is even more complicated than this. Bradley (Bradley et al. 1998) lists seven areas of avionics system certification which are affected significantly by the use of IMA principles and technology:

- Isolation can no longer purely be provided by physically separating the system functions.
- Priority based scheduling (Burns 1995) will be required to support varying workload (this is non-deterministic, although it is predictable).
- Common cause failures may be introduced by means of the management units employed to provide isolation and reconfiguration.
- Safety critical application functions will be placed on standard commercial processors.
- Hardware modules will need to be interchangeable for ease of maintenance.
- Reconfiguration can affect system safety analyses, e.g. zonal analyses, as well as just properties local to a "system".
- If systems are reconfigured, or are to be allowed to evolve, then it must be possible to re-use certification evidence for those parts of a system that have not changed – even though the old and the new functions may share resources – otherwise certification will be prohibitively expensive.

Space doesn't allow us to investigate all these issues fully. In this paper we assume priority based scheduling will be employed. We concentrate on the issues of reconfiguration with the aim of allowing re-use of safety evidence. Note is taken of the other aspects so far as practical.

CERTIFICATION OF RECONFIGURABLE IMA

As we have seen the issues surrounding IMA are numerous and complex. We have focused on one particular aspect, reconfiguration, that we believe is amenable to systematic analysis via heuristic search techniques. We suggest that analysis of a reconfigurable IMA architecture, sufficient to support certification, can be achieved the following steps:

1. Model the system and allocate the software components to the given IMA hardware components to produce a "baseline" system. This "baseline" model must be shown to meet all performance and safety requirements[1].
2. Produce a list of systems that would result from any single hardware failure. That is, list every hardware architecture resulting from a single module, processor or link failure. Identify those systems that no longer meet their performance or safety requirements.
3. For those systems that no longer meet their performance or safety requirements after failure, reallocate the software components to produce a new hardware-software mapping which does meet the requirements (these are "equivalent" configurations). Produce a "reconfiguration table" of allocations for each new configuration[2].

---

[1] We assume that the architecture includes a level of redundancy. For example, if we required 30 triplex systems, we might employ 100 processors, giving the ability to lose 10 processors without degradation (assuming that communication is still available).

[2] The IMA operating system would use these tables at run-time to identify an appropriate change, to an equivalent configuration, in the event of failure.

4. If there remain failed systems for which there are no allocations that meet all performance or safety requirements then revisit step 1 to produce a new baseline model. Repeat steps 1 to 4 until an acceptable set of "equivalent" systems are found or a stopping criterion[3] is met.
5. Investigate the *mode change* problem for each new configuration (see below).
6. Repeat steps 2 to 5 for larger numbers of hardware failures, up to the planned limit. Note that, beyond this limit, it may be possible to use configurations with degraded performance, e.g. by discarding non-essential functions.
7. Produce safety evidence for the baseline configuration, and evidence from the reconfiguration process that each "equivalent" configuration meets its requirements.

To be useful, this approach must be acceptable to the certification authorities. Whilst we have not discussed the approach in detail with the authorities it seems to us to be the smallest practical shift from current practice, whilst dealing with the complexities of IMA. We now discuss the means of realising this process, then return to the issue of acceptance by the authorities in the conclusions.

There is a choice between carrying out reconfigurations and mode changes in the air, or on the ground at the end of the flight. In the latter case, the exposure to further failures is relatively high, but there is no need to show that the mode change is safe. In the former case, which is more likely to be appropriate for military systems suffering battle damage, it is necessary to investigate the mode change time, and the risk of further failures or damage in this time. The models we develop below include mode change, but it would be simple to remove it to consider reconfiguration on the ground.

TECHNICAL APPROACH

For the purposes of showing the basic elements of our approach to reconfiguration we have produced a model of a simple IMA architecture. The aim is to extend and improve this model as work progresses to be more representative of industrial scale architectures. The model (Figure 1) consists of one IMA cabinet containing three line replaceable modules (LRMs). One LRM contains four processors, one contains three processors and the third two. All processors are fully connected using ADPM network links within the LRM. LRMs are fully interconnected within the cabinet via ATM point-to-point network links. Each LRM has a "system" processor residing on the LRM and the network links external to each LRM.

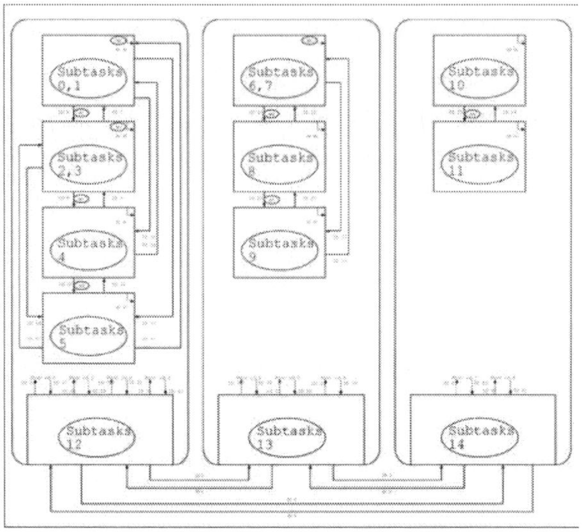

Figure 1: IMA Architecture Model

Three abstract tasks are defined to execute on the architecture. Each task is composed of a number of sub-tasks (processes). Each sub-task may generate one or more messages. The majority of the information contained within this architectural model remains constant under failure conditions, such as the memory capacity of processors and the requirements on the system. Some of the elements of the architecture however are amenable to change under failure conditions such as which processors are linked, the allocation of processes to processors and of messages to communication media. Thus we have an allocation problem; to allocate processes to processors and messages to communication media such that all performance and safety related requirements are met.

Extensions to this architecture can be easily envisaged such as multiple cabinets, heterogeneous processors within modules and restrictions on placement of software elements due to zonal issues, battle damage and failure. We are confident that the approach presented here can be adapted to incorporate such elements.

Determining an "Equivalent" IMA Architecture

Two IMA architectures can be said to be acceptable and equivalent if they both meet all the performance and safety requirements on the system. If a reconfiguration between two such architectures is to be acceptable then the *mode change* problem must also be addressed. Thus we define two IMA architectures to be equivalent under configuration if they meet all their requirements and a safe mode change path exists from

[3] This may be a suitably low fitness value of the "baseline" system, or time spent on analysis.

one configuration to the other.

A safe mode change (done in the air) is one whereby the application code can be reloaded on the new processor, and data brought into step with other replicas of the application in a sufficiently short time that the likelihood of further failures giving rise to a hazard is acceptably low (Blackwell et al. 1999). In practice, the length of time needed for a safe mode change will depend on the characteristics of the application. Some applications may be virtually stateless, so the mode change time reduces to the code re-load time. In other cases there may be a large state, but it is fairly static, e.g. flight plan data. The worst systems will be those with large, dynamically varying, data where the new application will have to "play catch up" with a changing data set, e.g. information from sensors which deliver data at high rates.

In general, we can represent the notion of equivalence as a fitness value (function) which indicates how close to being equivalent two proposed configurations are. In fact, such a fitness function can be used directly to guide heuristic searches. At this stage in our work, we use a simple fitness function with four main elements:

- Resource usage - hardware and software constraints placed on the system.
- Timing properties - each task must be shown to meet its worst case response time (WCRT) deadlines.
- Time to Failure - each task must be shown to have an acceptable failure probability, expressed as the mean time to failure (MTTF) of the task.
- Costs of reconfiguration - cost of moving from one configuration to another must be within acceptable bounds.

If two IMA architectures are equivalent then their fitness values will be the same. In practice it is convenient to represent fitness by "penalties" for allocations (hardware-software mappings) which do not meet the requirements. A "basic" fitness function is:

$$P(s) = k_1\, \textit{net} + k_2\, \textit{proc} + k_3\, \textit{task} + k_4\, \textit{subtask} + k_5\, \textit{mes}$$

where

k_i = weighting factor for the element

net = penalty for too many messages on a communication medium, plus penalty for too many bytes of data, plus penalty for number of messages that should not be placed on the same communication media, for fault tolerance reasons, but are.

proc = penalty for processors with too many processes allocated, plus penalty for too much memory being used by resident processes, plus penalty for inappropriate placement of system processes, plus penalty for number of processes that should not be placed on the same processor, for fault tolerance, but are.

task = penalty for number of tasks that fail to meet timing deadlines plus penalty for tasks that fail to meet MTTF requirements

subtask = penalty for subtasks allocated to inappropriate processor (including failed processors), plus penalty for subtasks that do not meet their deadlines

mes = penalty for messages using a failed link, plus penalty for messages routed so that they cannot reach their destination process, plus penalties for any message that fails to meet its delivery deadline.

As can be seen, even this "basic" fitness function is quite complex, due to the need to represent elements for each major aspect of the system resources of the IMA architecture.

The primary reason for determining a set of equivalent architectures is to allow reconfiguration under failure. Suppose that the system is working in its baseline configuration and a processor fails. Suppose further that four processes reside on this processor. A new system configuration is required such that these processes arc placed on different, working, processors. This new configuration must be "equivalent" in that it meets all the system requirements. Extensive changes may be required to facilitate this, such as changing priorities of processes, reallocating messages to different communication media and moving processes other than the four directly affected. In Figure 2 we show two reconfigurations under failure for the example presented in Figure 1; the first reconfiguration is optimal the second is not.

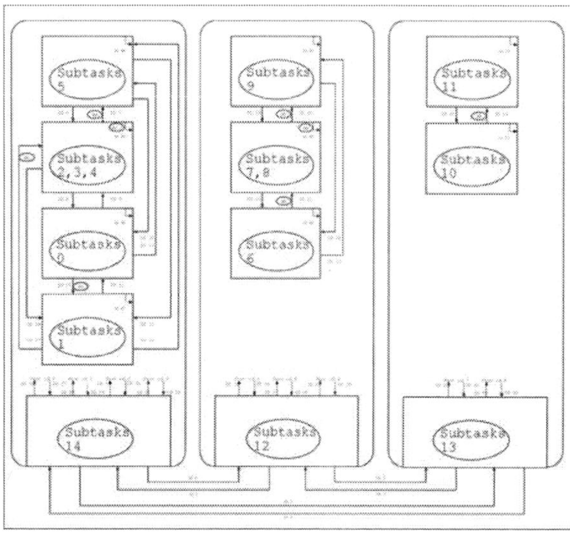

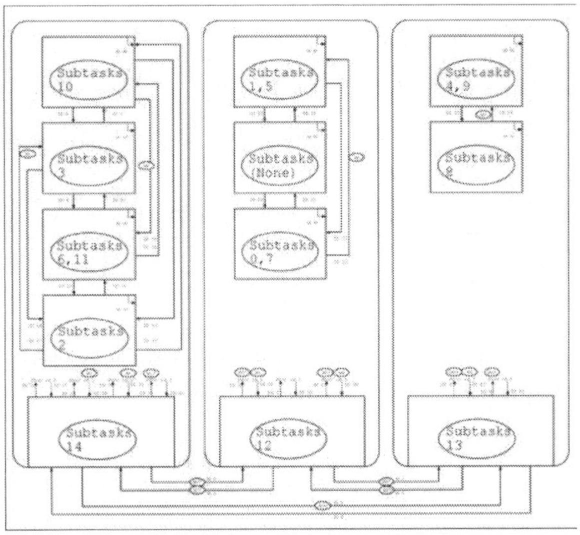

Figure 2: Two equivalent Architectures under Failure for Example Architecture

To include the elements of system reconfiguration and reliability and also the worst case response time, the fitness function is extended as follows:

$$P(s)' = P(s) + k_6\, \textit{reconfig} + k_7\, \textit{reliability} + k_8\, \textit{WCRT}$$

where
reconfig = penalty for time taken to reconfigure the system (minimise mode change time).
reliability = penalty for MTTF of tasks in the system (maximise overall MTTF).
WCRT = penalty for gap between WCRT and deadline (maximise to indicate timing flexibility in the system).

This extended fitness function is adequate for identifying "equivalent" configurations which meet basic performance and safety requirements, assuming that functionality is assessed independently, and is not impaired so long as the software has sufficient resources to execute.

In order to evaluate these parameters we require a number of systems and software engineering models. For example, we use standard reliability models, specifically reliability block diagrams (Sahner et al. 1995) derived from the hardware-software mapping, to evaluate reliability. As we are ultimately interested in safety, we will need to model the rate of occurrence or probability of hazardous failure conditions. At this stage, out concern is more with establishing a basic framework, so we have not employed fault trees or Markov models. (We have previously used Markov analysis in such applications (Nicholson 1998) so we are confident that we will be able to extend the approach, in due course.) Worst case response time requires models of the worst case execution time (WCET) of the individual processes, and a global scheduling model (Burns 1995).

Searching for Good "Equivalent" IMA

In some circumstances it may be easy to define an acceptable equivalent architecture when a system failure has occurred. However, in general this will not be the case. For certification purposes we need to show that no single point of failure can lead to the system not meeting its requirements. Thus, we have to find n+m+1 equivalent architectures, where n is the number of processors and m is the number of communication media, if we are to show that no single hardware failure can lead to the loss of the critical services provided by the IMA system. Clearly, the greater number of failures we consider, the larger the space of possible configurations we have to analyse – however the problem is much worse than just finding a set of valid hardware configurations.

Only a proportion of the attributes of an IMA architecture are amenable to change under reconfiguration. These are the:

- processor a process resides on
- communication medium a message travels on
- priority of processes and messages

Setting the values of these attributes for a given IMA architecture is known as the Allocation Problem. We thus have to solve at least m+n+1 allocation problems. Each allocation problem can be formulated as an assignment type problem (ATP) (Chern 1992). The important features of an ATP problem, with respect to producing a solution for non-trivial sized problems, are:

1. checking whether a proposed solution is "acceptable"' with respect to a given set of criteria can be undertaken in polynomial time.
2. finding the optimal solution, with respect to a given set of criteria, is non-polynomial (NP). That is, calculation and enumerative searches cannot in general be guaranteed to find an optimal solution in polynomial time.

Ribeiro (Ribeiro et al. 1994), indicates that an implicit enumerative (guided) search, or some other form of problem specific heuristic, is required in order to find good solutions for such problems within a "usable" time period. At this stage of our work, Simulated Annealing (SA) (Chern 1992; Kirkpatrick et al. 1983) has been chosen to address the problem of finding a group of equivalent allocations, although we anticipate that it may prove appropriate to use other heuristics at a later stage.

Simulated Annealing (SA) has been applied to a wide range of practical problems (Dowsland 1994). As its name implies, it models the behaviour of cooling substances, e.g. metals, that go through an annealing process. Consequently the algorithm is controlled by setting an initial temperature and a cooling rate. A simple sequential SA algorithm for a minimisation problem, is presented in Figure 3. Tools exist to implement this search algorithm. We use the X-Samson tool developed at the University of East Anglia (Mann 1997). The initial solution, s_0, is chosen randomly, and therefore may or may not be a legal solution. The value P(s) for each proposed IMA architecture is calculated using the fitness function presented in Section 4.1. The initial temperature, t_0, is chosen automatically by the algorithm so that virtually all proposed moves to other possible solutions are taken. The temperature is reduced by a factor α each iteration, thereby reducing the number of moves that are accepted. As the temperature reduces, the set of solutions considered reduces, and the algorithm terminates with the result being the closest approach to a solution which meets the systems requirements, or an "optimised" solution if more than one is found which meets the requirements.

Problem: minimise P(s) such that s ∈ S

```
Select an initial Solution s0;
Select an initial temperature t0> 0;
Select a temperature reduction function α
Repeat
  Repeat
      Randomly select s∈N(s0);
      δ=P(s)-P(s0);
      if (δ>s0) then
          s0=s;
      else
          generate random x in range (0,1);
          if (x < exp(-δt)) then s0 =s;
      Until iteration_count = nrep;
      Set t = α(t);
  Until stopping condition = true;
S0 is the approximation to optimal solution
```

Figure 3: SA Minimisation Algorithm

Each proposed solution represents a possible IMA architecture and is coded as an integer string of three sections; one representing the allocation of processes to processors, one representing the allocation of messages to communication media and one representing the priorities allocated to processes and messages. Thus the length of the integer string is dependent on the number of defined processes and messages between these processes.

Once a baseline architecture has been produced by running this search algorithm for the scenario where all hardware items are working we can investigate reconfiguration under failure. We do this by making a single hardware component unavailable. We then rerun the search algorithm to find the best equivalent architecture that does not employ the failed component. To facilitate this we restrict the set of admissible allocations so that no software component can use this piece of hardware and we employ a minimum change metric in the form of a measure of the time it takes for a reconfiguration to complete. We then repeat this procedure for each single hardware point of failure. Clearly this approach can be extended to deal with multiple failures which can still be accommodated within the levels of redundancy provided by the IMA system.

If we find that there is no reconfiguration available for some failures, especially for single failures, then a more extensive redesign may be required. However, it is also possible that we failed to employ an appropriate baseline architecture. We may wish to revisit this architecture in the light of this new evidence. It is hoped that eventually we may be able to co-evolve the baseline and configurations under failure.

The results of this analysis are a baseline architecture and a set of reconfiguration tables that can be used by an IMA operating system to reconfigure a running system in the event of failure, knowing that the resultant configuration still meets performance and safety requirements. Figure 2 illustrates the results that can be achieved by this form of search[4]. It is our contention that the certification evidence for the baseline configuration and evidence that all the allowed reconfigurations are "equivalent" should be viewed as sufficient to clear the system.

Results to Date and Current Activities

We have analysed a number of simple example systems to develop the ideas and the analysis testbed.

[p1]By doing this, we have gained confidence in the soundness of the approach, as we have produced configurations which are amenable to manual checking. This gives us a suitable base for investigating industrial scale problems, which can't be assessed manually.

[4] Note that in this run the "minimum change" metric is not employed.

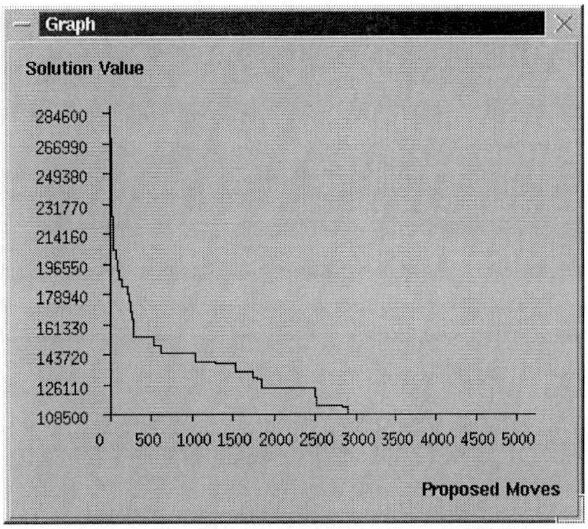

Figure 4: Solution Evolution Graph

Figure 4 shows the results obtained from a particular X-SAmson search using the simple architecture presented in Figure 1. The initial solution was initialised with random values which had a fitness value of 284600. As the guided search progressed, the solution evolved towards better (lower scoring) architectures in an asymptotic fashion. After 395 seconds a solution score of 108500 had been obtained. This score was improved to 108000 after 863 seconds and later lowered further to 103000, but only after 1794 seconds. This demonstrates the computational complexity of the guided search and solution evaluation algorithms used within the search tool. The values quoted above were obtained using an AMD K6-2 400MHz processor running Linux. Another search using a Pentium 200 MHz processor had an initial architecture score of 233000, but took 517 seconds to evolve the solution to a score of 118000. It is obvious that computational power is a necessity with even the simplest of architecture models.

Our current target is to be able to analyse (a system based on) an industrial technology demonstrator, which is being used to demonstrate integration of flight and engine control functionality, on an IMA platform.

Integrity of the Heuristic and Future Aims

The Simulated Annealing search algorithm is non-deterministic and as such cannot be guaranteed to find an optimal solution. However, it can be set up to be innately pessimistic; that is if it indicates there is a solution there is one. The trade-off for this is that it may fail to find a solution that exists. Thus there is a safety-performance trade-off for the algorithm. However, it is possible to undertake extra analysis on the equivalent architectures and their accompanying reconfiguration tables after the algorithm has run to show their validity. In practice, we expect to have to use this sort of additional off-line analysis to provide evidence that configurations really are “equivalent”, due to the difficulty of showing the soundness of the heuristics.

We plan to extend this work in a number of ways. For instance, we can investigate architectures under more extensive multiple failures. In this case we would need to extend our approach to consider degradation scenarios. That is, situations where we remove less vital functionality from the system. Three levels of importance would appear reasonable; essential, desirable and optional[5]. Restrictions on the set of admissible allocations can be introduced, for example preventing more than one replica of a process being executed on a processor in a particular physical zone of the aircraft.

There are many other issues which could be addressed, e.g. refining the model of failures to deal with safety more explicitly, or to investigate the utility of other heuristics such as genetic algorithms (Beasley et al. 1993). Our intention is to direct our approach to try to produce the simplest analysis framework which will scale to industrial problems, whilst giving credible and useful results.

CONCLUSIONS

The work outlined in this paper is, we believe, a novel approach to the problem of safety analysis and certification of dynamically reconfigurable IMA systems. By modelling and analysing the system off-line a static and deterministic table of legal reconfigurations in the presence of specific failures can be generated. Since these reconfigurations are known before runtime, each can be verified and certified. More importantly, by verifying the baseline system, and arguing that the rest are equivalent, it should be possible to certify a set of possible configurations at little more than the cost of demonstrating the acceptability of the baseline system.

Technically, the usefulness of this approach depends on the detail of the system model used and the criteria employed within the value (fitness) function used to score the model under analysis. External verification can be employed on the results to provide evidence for their validity. If the model detail and the fitness function criteria are sufficient, then we believe that this technique will provide a partial solution to a very difficult problem in the safety analysis and certification of the next generation of avionics systems.

Commercially, the usefulness of the approach is that it may offer the ability to certify IMA applications

[5] Different segments of the industry use different terminology, but these concepts are quite widely used.

at a cost proportional to the scale of the application, not the number of legal configurations. However, in order to realise this benefit, it is necessary to get "buy in" from the certification authorities. We are presenting our preliminary results in the hope of getting feedback on the acceptability of the approach to the authorities, and to see how likely it is to satisfy its commercial as well as technical objectives.

REFERENCES

Beasley, D., Bull, D., and R. Martin. (1993). "An Overview of Genetic Algorithms: Part 1, Fundamentals." *University Computing*, 15(2), 58-69.

Blackwell, N., Leinster-Evans, S., and Dawkins, S. K. (1999). "Developing Safety Cases for Integrated Flight Systems." *IEEE Aerospace Conference*, 2408 Palm Avenue, Manhattan Beach, CA 90266 USA.

Bradley, J., Fletcher, M., Miller, P., Moxon, P., and Wake, A. (1996). "Integrated Modular Avionics & Certification - An IMA Design Team's View." *IEE Seminar: Certification of Ground/Air Systems*, Savoy Place, London, WC2R 0BL.

Burns, A. (1995). "A Preemptive Priority-Based Scheduling: An Appropriate Engineering Approach." *Advances in Real-Time Systems*, Prentice-Hall, 239.

Chern. (1992). "On the Computational Complexity of Reliability Redundancy Allocation in a Series System." *Operations Research Letters*, 11, 309-315.

DoD. (1993). "Military Standard 882c: System Safety Program Requirements.", US Department of Defence.

Dowsland, K. "Variants of Simulated Annealing for Practical Problem Solving." *Adaptive Computing & Information Processing*, 115-133.

Kirkpatrick, S., Gelatt, C. D., and Vecchi, M. P. (1983). "Optimisation by Simulated Annealing." *Science*, 220, 671-680.

Mann, J. (1997). "SAmson v1.6 User Manual." , School of Information Systems, University of East Anglia.

MoD. (1996a). "Defence Standard 00-55: Requirements for Safety Related Software in Defence Equipment." , UK Ministry of Defence.

MoD. (1996b). "Defence Standard 00-56: Safety Management Requirements for Defence Systems." , UK Ministry of Defence.

Nicholson, M. (1998). "Selecting a Topology for Safety-Critical Real-Time Control Systems," , University of York, York.

Ribeiro, C., Treleavan, P., and Alippi, C. (1994). "Genetic Algorithm Programming Environments." *Computer*, 27(6), 27-45.

SAE. (1996). "ARP 4754: Certification Considerations for Highly-integrated or Complex Aircraft Systems." , SAE.

Sahner, R., Trivedi, K., and Puliafito, A. (1995). *Performance and Reliability Analysis of Computer Systems. An Example-based Approach using the SHARPE Software Package*, Kluwer Academic Press.

BIOGRAPHIES

Paul Hollow graduated from the University of York in 1997 with a degree in Computer Systems and Software Engineering (Meng). Since then he has worked as a Research Student in the Dependable Computing Systems Centre (DCSC) sponsored by BAE SYSTEMS at the University of York.

John McDermid is Professor of Software Engineering at the University of York. He directs the High Integrity Systems Engineering group at the University which is a recognised centre of excellence in safety critical computing for the UK Aerospace industry. He directs the Rolls-Royce University Technology Centre (UTC) in Systems and Software Engineering and the DCSC. He has published 6 books and over 200 papers.

Dr Mark Nicholson is a research and teaching fellow in the High Integrity Systems Engineering group at York. He graduated in 1986 and was awarded his DPhil in 1998. He teaches on the MSc course in Safety Critical Systems at the University of York and on-site safety courses for numerous industrial clients. His research interests relate to the use of quantitative methods in safety critical systems design and the certification of IMA. He is currently part of PAMELA, a European Union funded project, looking at the introduction of IMA into future commercial aircraft.

An instrument for establishing the operational need for the Dutch Defense

M.W. Ludema
Delft University of Technology
Jaffalaan 5
2600 GA Delft
The Netherlands

Abstract The information process towards the Dutch parliament on the acquisition of defence material has improved considerable. Though several aspects are not or not to the appropriate detail addressed during the acquisition process, as was shown in an other research on the Dutch Defense System Acquisition Process. The same kinds of research was performed on the information process of the "Establishment of the Operation Need" of the Dutch Defense System Planning Process. This process lacks the structure and contents to adequately inform the Dutch Parliament on the transition from the planning via the operational need toward the actual acquisition process. Part of the problem is found in the way the Defense organization comprehends the actual need, and is a result of inadequate systems thinking. For the structuring problem a solution was proposed in rewriting the procedure and including an aspect list as a check list for writing appropriate documents.

THE DUTCH DEFENSE SYSTEM ACQUISITION PROCESS

Introduction The Netherlands have a total different position compared with the United States of America concerning the development and/or acquisition of new weapon systems. The Netherlands do not have a defense industry of any real significance. For the acquisition of its weapon systems the Netherlands have to rely on weapon systems, like fighter planes, helicopters and armoured tanks that have been developed in foreign countries.

If marine ships are to be acquired and developed the Netherlands do have their share of industry. Besides the marine ship industry, there is some defense industry that focuses on electronics and sensors, and other specialized sub-systems. In the larger NATO programs for the development of innovative weapon systems the Dutch industry often fulfills the role for an important sub-contractor.

DMP-procedure In the year 1984 the current Defense System Acquisition Process (DMP-procedure) was introduced to guide the Dutch defense material acquisition processes. The main goal of this DMP-procedure was to enhance the political control on the processes for the acquisition of weapon systems for the Royal Navy, the Royal Army, and the Royal Airforce, mainly in the case of large capital investments. The DMP-procedure was intended to provide the Dutch parliament with the necessary information to make go-and-no-go decisions concerning the funding of the investments in weapon systems related to the intended role of these weapon systems in politically agreed and essential defense tasks. The DMP-procedure makes it possible for the Dutch parliament to intervene in the Defense System Acquisition Process if necessary.

The Defense System Acquistion Process "(DMP 1990)" starts with a letter indicated as "DMP-Document-A" which marks the start of the actual Defense System Acquisition Process. The DMP-procedure consists the following phases, each phase is completed by a document:

- Pre-study phase, from "DMP-document-A" towards "DMP-document-B", indicating possible defense material solutions for a in "DMP-document-A" indicated Operational Need;
- Study phase, from "DMP-document-B" towards "DMP-document-C", indicating feasable defense material solutions and requesting detailed proposels for two or more defense material alternatives for fulfilling the operational need;
- Pre-Acquisition Phase, from "DMP-document-C" towards DMP-document-D", which consists out of the analysis, testing and comparison of the the defense material alternatives and advising the best choice for the actual acquisition of a weapon system;
- Evaluation phase, from "DMP-document-D" towards "DMP-document-E", evaluating the actual acquisition of achoosen weapon system.

Informing the Dutch Parliament During all phases of the life cycle of defense material starting from the establishment of the operational need till the evaluation of the actual use of the defense material DMP-documents written by the Department inistry of Defense inform the Parliament. Only if the Parliament approves the continuation of the Defense System Acquisition Process the Department of Defense may proceed towards the next phase in the Dutch Defense System Acquisition Process and eventually concluding in the next DMP-document send to the Dutch parliament. These members of the parliament have access to the DMP-documents, though normally only an extended abstract of a DMP-document is provided to the parliament for approval.

DMP-procedures are obliged for all projects larger than 25 million Dutch guilders (approximately 12 million dollars). During the Study Phase and the Pre-Acquisition Phase several alternative weapon systems are assessed and described in the accompanied DMP-documents. In the course of Pre Acquisition Phase tests on sub-systems and/or prototypes of defense material are performed if necessary. A detailled material-situational report based on the DMP-document is send to the parliament in those cases the project will lead to a capital investment larger or as large as 100 million Dutch guilders or if there are important political reasons to do so. In the DMP-document several aspects should be addressed. Important aspects are the fulfillment of the operational need of the Department of Defense, the political context and possible orders for the local industry, the military effectiveness, the (life cycle) costs and many others aspects.

In the case of international NATO programs instead of the normal DMP-procedure, the Phased Armaments Programming System (PAPS) is used. PAPS consists out of seven phases, each phase marked by a mile-stone document. The first phase of PAPS is the "Mission Need Document" (MND), where de tasks based on the military concept of the NATO-countries and the specific situation is addressed), in this phase the current and future threats are evaluated and related to the military capabilities of the current military capacity. The phases of the PAPS System are related to the DMP-procedure. The PAPS-documents are in the DMP-procedures includes as annexes.

INTEGRATED DEFENSE PLANNING PROCESS

After the introduction of the current Defense Acquisition Process (DMP-procedure) the material acquisition became much more transparant for the parliament and the results of the defense policies. From 1984, the initial year of the DMP-procedure the procedure as been evaluated several times. One of the most important changes was established in 1989, when there became a cut between the establishment of the operational need (formerly indicated as the analysis phase), and the fulfilment of this need.

IDDP and operational need In the same period one started to integrate the current DMP-procedure with the Integrated Defense Planning Process (IDPP). The IDPP has a two year policy cycle to establish the Defense Plan. One of the detailed plans of the Defense Plan is the material plan. In this material plan the operational needs are defined. The IDPP is closely related with the NATO-planning process where the input for this process are the military and economic evaluation of the international situation. Because the parliament still wants to be consulted concerning the establishment of the operational need the results of the analysis phase are summarized in the directive "Establishment of the Operational Need". In this directive like the DMP-procedure several aspects are addressed in the document called "Establishment of the Operational Need" for every separate acquisition project. If the parliament approves the contents, it sends a letter to the Minister of Defense. From this moment on the DMP-procedure starts.

On the basis of the Defense Policy developed by the Dutch government, this procedures regulates the long term planning of the Royal Dutch Navy, the Royal Dutch Army and the Royal Dutch Airforce. Long term plans or current shortcomings in the defense material lead to short term plans that will eventually leads to the start of the DMP-procedure that regulates the system acquisition process. Before the system acquisition process can start, the operational need must be accredited by the Parliament. To gather the necessary data to inform the Parliament a document called "CDS-directive no. 101 "Establishment of the Operational Need " provides the necessary guidance for the Secretary of Defense for informing the Dutch Parliament. This document (DMP-document-A) if approved by the Parliament eventually leads to the start of the Dutch Acquisition System that is accompanied by a procedure called the "DMP-procedure". This DMP-procedure consists out of sequential documents (document B, document C, and document D) marking milestones in the acquisition process.

The way the Integral Defense Planning Proces, the Establihment of the Operational Need, and the Defense System Acquisition Process and its document are related is described in figure 1.

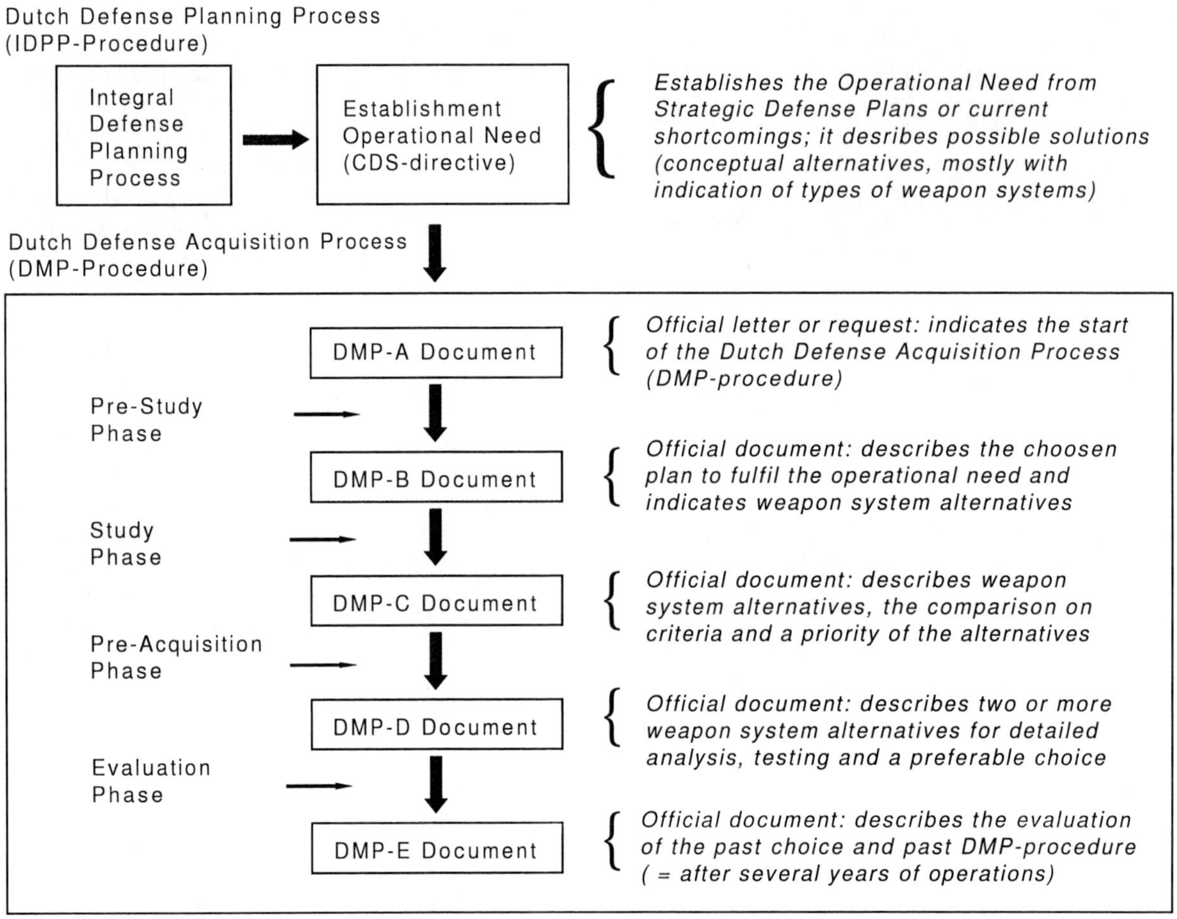

Figure 1: IDDP, Operational Need & DMP

DEFENSE ACQUISITION PROCESS EVALUATION AND PROPOSED SOLUTIONS

Addressing aspects A previous study done by the author of this paper "(Ludema 1994)", aimed at the integration of performing life cycle cost analysis as a part of the DMP-procedure during all phases of the Dutch Defense Acquisition Procedure. A list of aspects was extracted from several texts and models of the DMP-procedure providing a kind of check-list that can be used as a don't-forget list during the information gathering process that is necessary before a DMP-document can be actually written. A large number of aspects is being emphasized during the Dutch Defence System Acquisition Processes (DMP). Processes that can lead to the choice and acquisition of certain types of defence systems. The most important aspects for these processes have been deduced form old (Defence System Acquisition Process)-documents and put into an aspect list. During this research it became clear that during the information gathering process not all aspects were addressed or were only adressed on a very shallow manner. If some aspects were not addressed at all, it was indicated why the missing information was not included. Result of this research was a proposal for a Document Information System (DIS) that would make it impossible to skip an aspect. Until today this DIS still is not implemented for the total procedure. Eventually only the aspect life cycle costing of defense material was formalized in the DMP-procedure, by means of prescribing the use of a procedure called FELSALDO, see "(Bhola, et.al. 1994)" that gives guidance concerning life cycle costs and analysis of the defense material in all phases of the DMP-procedure.

The aspect list The main idea for the analysis of the CDS-directive (Establisment of the Operational Need) was to use the same approach as was used in the analysis of the DMP-procedure. So first from the CDS-directive "Establishment of the Operational Need", a list of aspects that should be addressed during the process was extracted. This aspect list was used to evaluated some 'Operational Need' documents of real projects with an operational need that was already stated in a long term plan op the

Integrated Defense Planning Process (IDPP). Using the aspect list gave the researcher an idea about the manner the aspects were (if they were) addressed in the document, how consistent this was done and to what level of detail this was done. Because it was already planned to rewrite the CDS-directive "Establishment of the Operational Need" in the future, the results of this study can be used as recommendation for the rewriting process.

DEVELOPING AN OPERATIONAL NEED INSTRUMENT

Extented aspect list On the basis of the list of aspects and the ideas that where found usefull during the analysis performed with the aspect list an Operation Need Instrument was developed as an improvement of the current available CDS-directive: "Establishment of the Operational Need". In essence the instrument consists out of a very detailed list of aspects, guidelines for using the list, and additional schematic information that can be used in the case the user of the instrument is not an expert concerning some of the adressed aspects. All alternatives that are proposed in the process can be entered into the list in such a way that they can easily be represented and compared.

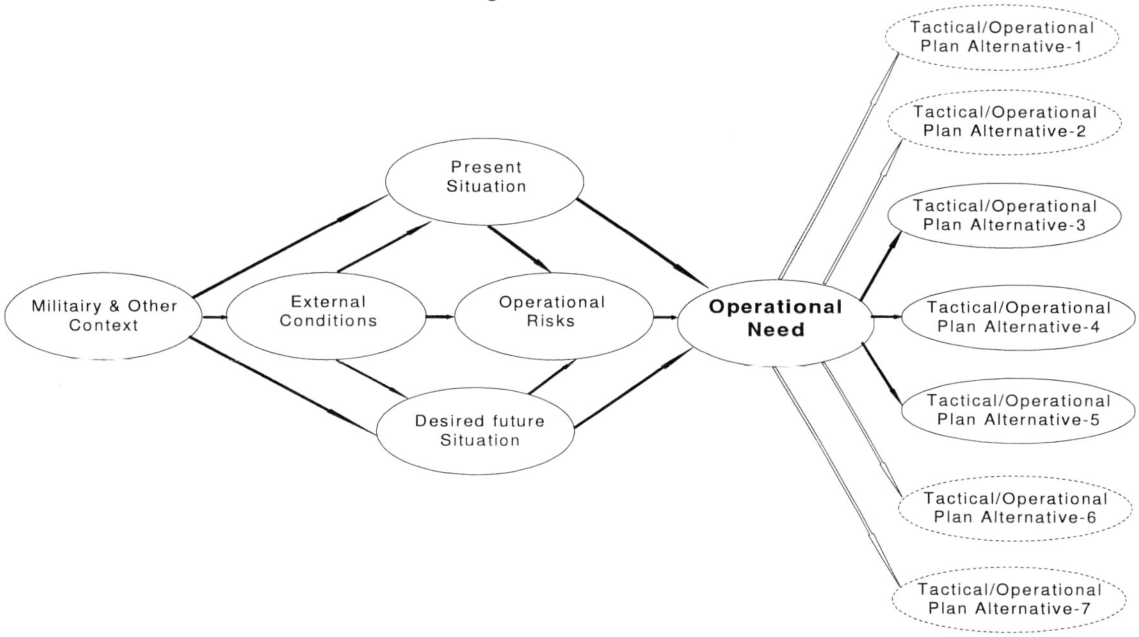

Figure 2: Relationships between aspects

Below the main chapters (contents) of the developed aspect list are indicated:

I	General
II	Context
III	External criteria
IV	Description of the establishment of the Operational Need
IVa	Description of the current situation ('AS-IS-situation')
IVb	Description of the desired situation ('SHOULD–BE-situation')
IVc	Description of the operation risks if the operational need in not fulfilled and the current situation is prolonged
IVd	Description of the developed or yet to develop operational need
V	Description of the operational and tactical plan-alternatives that will fulfill the operational need
VI	Description of the consequences of the acquisition and implementation of the selected operational and tactical plan-alternatives
VII	Description of the acquisition processes
VIII	Decision process and anticipated plan-alternatives
IX	Description the aspects and developments that should be addressed in the DMP-B document
X	Conclusions and recommendations
XI	Decision process and additional directives of the military command

Figure 2 gives an indication about the relation of some apects to be addressed during the gathering of information and the writting of the document Operational Need. Off course the writing process will be non-sequential, only at the end the larger part of the information will be available.

SATCOM-project The instrument is used in the rewriting of the documents of the SATCOM-project (the operational need for a militaru satelite communication system). The SATCOM-document "Establisment of the Operational Need" for this project was already written, but was not accepted due to the way it was structured and because of its poor contents. So the reason for using this certain project was two-fold, first to test the instrument and second to perform an evaluation of the operational need for a SATCOM system. This research does not elaborate on the improvement that were found enhancing the description of the operational need of the SATCOM-system. It will focus on the idea of the functional feasibility of the developed instrument. In the next section, some remarks will be made, that were deduced by using the instrument in the operational need phase of the SATCOM-project. The main goal of this functional feasibilty was to make the necessary design improvement to the instrument. The required next steps in the improvement process of the instrument will also be discussed briefly.

OPERATIONAL NEED QUICK SCAN AND SOME SUGGESTIONS FOR IMPROVEMENTS OF THE INSTRUMENT

Impresions towards the contents of the instrument
The instrument was used during the Quick-Scan of the operational need document that was already written for the SATCOM-project. The instrument, or detailled aspect list was used to collect the data necessary to write a document "Establisment of the Operational Need" based on the contents of the old document. It gave the author an idea of what data was mission or poorly adressed following the rules of the Operational Need Instrument. After the quick scan the following remarks and related suggestions for solutions or improvement could be made:

1 If the operational need document was read in a shallow way, the text was very readable and clear, it looked more like summary of the project than the actual project description.
A good and readable summary was not available in the document. The instrument will be changed to include the presciption of an extended summary.

2 After reading the text to the detail it became obvious that the text was really not so readable and clear.
Statements should be controlable at al times. It would be advisable to separate the general text and the text that relates to the aspects that should be addressed in the instrument.

3 Some aspects were only very globally addressed in the document.
The instrument must indicate the level an aspect needs to be covered in de document. Suggestion towards the detail each individual aspect should be given.

4 Some aspects were more or less related to each other. To what level aspects were related did not became clear after the first time the document was read. After a detailled study of the document one could find these relations, but this became still not very clear concerning the researcher.
In the explanations of the aspects the relations between other aspect must be clearly indicated. When the same tables are used for gatherig data and writing the operational need document the relations between aspects can be made clear from the structure of the tables.

5 Aspects that were addressed in the SATCOM-document seldom were explaned with the relevant date or proper reasoning structure.
The way aspects should be addressed, what kind of data should be include and the kind of reasoning structure that should be followed must be written in the explanations of each aspect.

6 The level of complexity of the text differed considerable. Sometimes one must be an expert to comprehend the text and some times the text is very common. Inclusion of explanation by means of footnotes at the bottom of the page or at in and of the document would be very usefull.
All common definitions concerning the operational need should be inluded in a special annex.

7 The text started with a lengthly description of all the tasks of the defence organisation. At the first time this looked unnecessary. We found that a clear structure concerning the tasks is operational need is related to would greatly improve the insight from what context the operational need did evolve. The interrelationship and dependability of the tasks could also be improved after addressing this subject.
A standard task/activity decomposition of the defense organisation should be included into the context section of the instrument. If such a decomposition does not exist at the moment it would be very beneficial to design such a decomposition.

8 All aspects were included in the instrument and not in the CDS-directive/model were not easy to fill-in, though with a litte effort it was not impossible. They clearly helped to explain the operational need. All aspects should be

enhanced in one or more additional evaluations.

Advancing insight Another aspect that was not addressed in the above analysis is the advancing insight that evolves during the acquisition process, and will have an effect of the requirement at the beginning of each phase of the process and the anticiptated results for that phase, but also all other phases of the project. Figure 2 gives an impression of the advancing insight phenomenon. Basically it states, that expectations are always set back into the earlier established requirements for a phase, because decision makers will have a better view about the possible solutions, and this might change their ideas about the 'real' operational needs. Advancing Insight is probably larger in projects with a long troughput time. Without elaborating on this issue in this study, the author finds this aspect certainly wortwhile to investigate in detail, in another study.

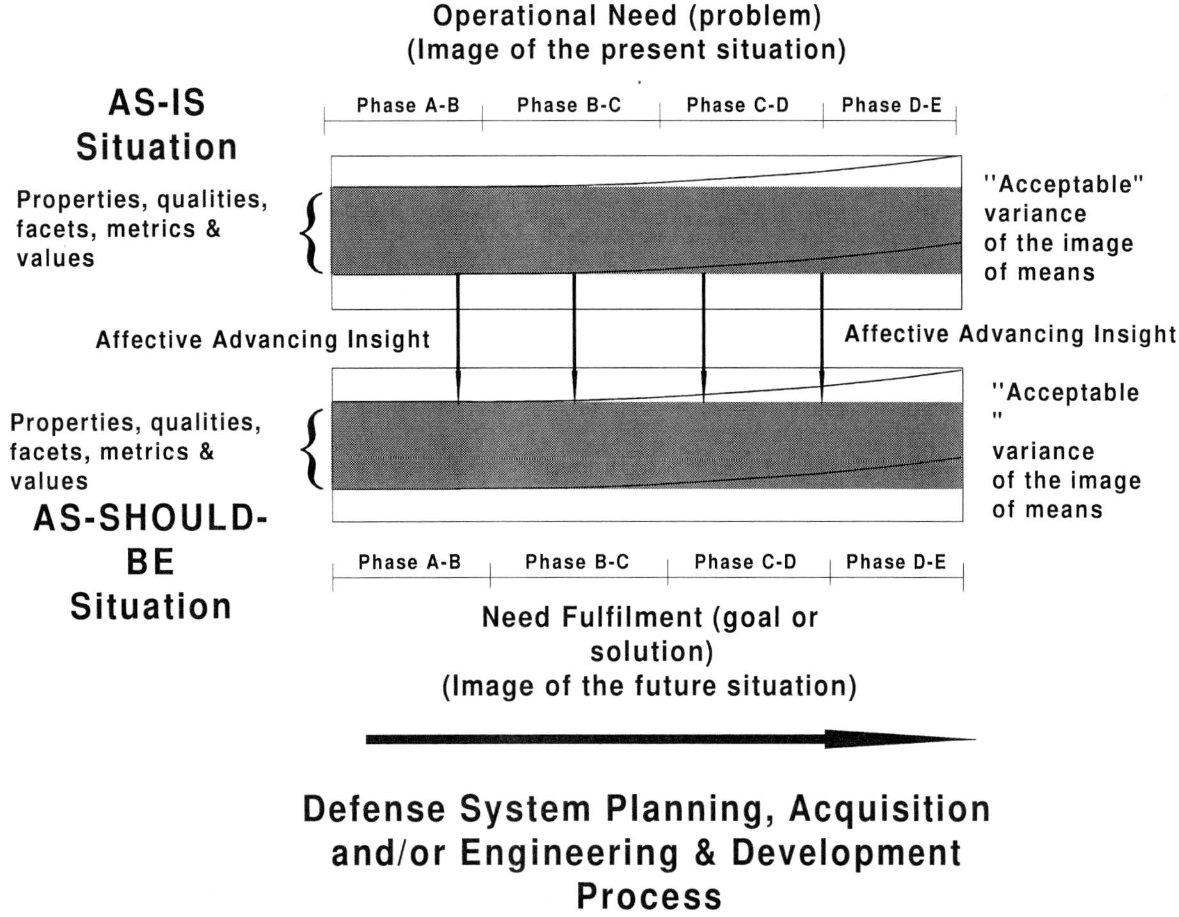

Figure 3: Affective Advancing insight

SUGGESTIONS FOR NEXT STEPS CONCERNING THE OPERATIONAL NEED OF THE SATCOM SYSTEM

The next suggestions for rewriting the document "Establisment of the Operational Need for a SATCOM System" on the bases of the old CDS-directive were made. Though they were not really part of this reseach they are certainly worth mentioning.

1 Rewrite the document including some of the new aspects now included in the instrument.

2 Test the relevancy of the operational need of the SATCOM system on a future date with the improved instrument.

3 Temporarily stop the operational need phase of the SATCOM-project and rewrite this phase with the improved aspect-instrument.

THE DEVELOPMENT OF AN OPERATIONAL NEED INSTRUMENT

Important impressions The evaluation of the instrument has provided some usefull recommendations for the development of a more operational instrument to be used by the Dutch Defense. The used terminology and descriptions of the aspects do need some explaining. The next emphasis should be on the implementation of the instrument into the defense organisation, and the way the instrument should actually be used, who will be responsible for what? A large amount of flows, drawing, figures, and graphs should be included to increase the level of comprehension for the user, and how may these improve the learning effects.

Next steps Recommended is to develop the instrument on the learned lessons of the Quick-Scan. All ideas that are or might be included in de instrument should be tested on its functional feasibility. Evaluation of the instrument, when developed to enough detail, can be done by testsing all included aspects with several existing operatioanl need documents of older Defense Material Acquisition Processes. Every aspects should be adressed at least ones in a document. The roles of the personnel in using the instrument should be analysed and the results should be included in designing the process management aspect of using he instrument.

CLARIFY (OPERATIONALS) NEED VERSUS WANT

Van Gaasbeek "(1999)" states, that is important to distinguish between needs and wants. As an example he mentions the difference between "A need for shelter to keep someone out of the weather and to provide some security" with, "I want a 6000 square foot home at the beach)". He continues, that government and industrial customers will tend to buy, or contract development, based on needs. Customers buy buy based on need, but can also be induced to make purchases based on wants. He also refers to he OMB Circular A-109 "(OMD 1976)", that applies the Department of Defense and for all executive departments in the United States. The statement he refers to is:

"Determination of mission need should be based on an analysis of an agency's mission reconciled with overall capabilities, priorities, and resources. When analysis of an agency's mission shows that a need for a new major system exists, such a need should be defined in terms of the mission, purpose, cabability, agency components involved, schedule and cost objectives, and operating constaints. A mission need may result from a deficiency in existing capabilities or the decision to establish new capabilities in response to a technologically feasible opportunity. Mission needs are independent of any particular system or technological solution"

This sums up more or less the problem the aspect list or instument for the Establisment of the Operational Need was development for. The analysis part of the Establisment of the Operational Need should be based on the mission need and suggested alternatives schould only be descibed in needs not wants. To often decision makers jump to solution and the How's without emphasing enough on the What's. This process kills the creativity and the synthesis in the acqusition process. This process as every systems engineering process should look more closely to the work of the architect they refer to when they speak about an integrated approach.

CONCLUSIONS

An Operational Need Instrument is a functional feasible option as a model for the new CDS-directive concerning the operational need. The procedures concerning the way the instrument is going to be used and by whom should be designed together with the already proposed enhancements The way the operational need is established can be made clear with the developed instrument was possible than with the old CDS-directive. The operational feasibility of the instrument should be proved in one or more tests. If adjustment is necessary due to these tests the instrument should be improved.

REFERENCES

Bhola, B., FELSALDO, FEL-TNO, 1994, Den Haag (in Dutch)

Blanchard, B.S., *Logistics Engineering and Management,* 3rd edition, Prentice Hall, New Jersey, 1986.

DMP; Defensie Materieelkeuze Proces, Brief aan de Tweede Kamer der Staten-Generaal, SDU, Den Haag (in Dutch).

Gaasbeek, J.R. van, Incose Insight, winter 1999-2000, vol 2, issue 4, 1999, p.11-14.

IDPP; Integraal Defensie Planning Proces, handleiding, Ministerie van Defensie, Den Haag, 1991 (in Dutch).

Ludema, M.W., *Defensie Materieelkeuze Proces Formulier*, FEL-94-B020, Den Haag, 1994 (in Dutch).

Ludema, M.W., *Planning, acquisitie en materieellogistieke processen*, FEL-94-B016, Den Haag, 1994 (in Dutch).

OMD; Office of Management and Budget, Major System Acquisitions, Circular A-109, Executive Office of the President, 5 april, 1997.

BIOGRAPHY

Marcel W. Ludema (1963) studied architecture at the Delft University of Technology. In 1989 he graduated on the development of an expert and decision support system for housing and facility management decisions for the Dutch Government. After his military service he joined the TNO Laboratory of Electronics and Physics and developed a life cycle management procurement procedure for the Dutch Ministry of Defense. Form 1993 to 1997 he joined the Faculty of Economics of the Erasmus University of Rotterdam and gave lectures on logistics management. He participated in several commercial research projects of a broad variety of logistics subjects. In preparation of his Doctoral thesis he wrote several research papers At the moment he hold an educational position at the Faculty of System Engineering & Policy Analysis of the Delft University of Technology, and is performing several commercial research activities.

Risk Reduction Through Changing Success Criteria

Dorothy McKinney
Lockheed Martin Missiles and Space
1111 Lockheed Martin Way
B/102 O/L7-01
Sunnyvale, California 94086

Abstract. In the 1990's the big challenge was how to streamline processes to produce systems better, faster and cheaper. In this new decade, the big challenge looming before us is how to dynamically adjust the success criteria for a project to increase its chances for success. Dynamic adjustment of success criteria is one of the most cost-effective ways to minimize project risk in the dimensions which are most critical to our customers and our companies, such as: cost, time-to-market, product features, system stability and evolvability. Precisely targeting system development processes for the level of acceptable risk, while using metrics effectively to ensure that results match intentions, is a challenge best met jointly by program managers and systems engineers. This paper describes this challenge, and offers some approaches for collaboration which might make both program management and system engineering jobs more doable, while improving chances of successful program completion.

BACKGROUND

The Last Decade. The 1990's brought many challenges as well as lessons learned from our attempts to meet these challenges. It became clear that incremental improvement in engineering and other program processes was not enough to enable a company to remain competitive, much less to outstrip their competition in the marketplace. Many companies started programs aimed at achieving breakthrough levels of improvements. Some of these programs included are shown in Table 1, together with the name(s) of one or more organizations who have used each approach. In addition to organizations who have started initiatives such as these targeting breakthroughs in system and product development cycle times and costs, many additional organizations tried to use incremental improvement approaches. Some of the most common of these incremental improvement approaches included improving process maturity (especially in areas such as system engineering and software engineering which have industry-accepted maturity models), and tailoring processes more strongly, to eliminate steps which may add little or no value for a specific project.

Approach	Org(s) Using Approach
Six Sigma	Motorola, General Electric
Faster, Better, Cheaper	NASA
Order of Magnitude Cost Reduction Targets	Hewlett Packard
Eliminating Constraints	Ford Electronics, General Motors
Lean Processes	Toyota, Boeing, General Electric

Table 1: Some Breakthrough Improvement Approaches

Lessons Learned. Many attempts were made by many organizations to implement approaches to achieve the benefits of breakthrough improvements in system and product development. Some of these attempts succeeded despite the skepticism of many seasoned professionals who judged the risks to be unmanageably high. Others failed, and were judged in hindsight by almost all concerned to have been overambitious. The surprising successes taught us that breakthroughs are possible, and even when we take significant risks we can sometimes succeed. Many of the failures illuminated dimensions in which risk-taking was unintentional for some stakeholders. But probably the most interesting lessons were learned from the projects which were neither total succeses nor total failures. Their results often fell into the grey area between success and failure because the system which was produced was not perfect, but it met at least some of the user needs, and it was produced within an at least marginally acceptable cost and schedule envelope.

Programs Examined. This author has examined over thirty programs which were completed in the mid to late 1990's, including both commercial products and government contracts. All of these programs were responding to an improvement challenge, from "better faster cheaper" and other breakthroughs challenges, to just "do it for less". Some of these programs were complete successes – that is, the system specified was delivered within approximately the agreed-upon schedule. A few were failures, in which the program was cancelled outright, or the system was not adopted or fully deployed by the intended end user. The remaining programs were partial successes. Due to proprietary restrictions, names and specific details of individual programs cannot be made available in this paper. It can be noted, however, that these programs include both ones about which the author has first-hand knowledge, and programs for which the source of information has been people in other companies who have been willing to share information on products and programs, as long as their products and companies are not named. In general, companies are very reluctant to release information on programs which are less than full successes. For the purposes of this paper, the successful programs are not the ones of primary interest.

SUCCESS CRITERIA

Definition of Program Success. If we consider the definition of success for a program, it can be characterized either in the large or in the small. In the small, success means that a program was executed in such a way as to produce the result the customer requested and/or contracted to obtain. If the product is a commercial one, this customer is often the marketing department which defines the characteristics of the product, and the market opportunity window within which it is needed. If the system is developed for a single customer who requests it, especially using a competitive bidding process, the customer's contractual acceptance of the delivered system means success in the small. Success criteria for success in the small are therefore easy to identify, since they are reflected in the customer's acceptance criteria, and usually expressed in writing, often in great detail, in documents such as statements of work and requirements specifications.

Success in the large means that the intended result is obtained by the consumer/user with the aid of the system. Success criteria for success in the large are much more difficult to determine. For a commercial product, success in the large usually means not only that a product is developed with the characteristics specified by marketing, within the market window specified, but also that the product meet enough needs of the end user that it generates sales and follow-on business for the company. Mere sales alone are often insufficient, since high sales of a product which turns out to have a latent defect critical to users can have a very deleterious effect on follow-on business.

For a contracted system, the procurer of the system is often somewhat different than the end user of the system (for instance, in many government and military procurements, some offices or commands procure systems for other offices or commands to use). Occasionally, a system accepted by the procuring agency or command turns out to be unsuitable for the purposes of the using agency or command – meaning that a success in the small can still fail to achieve success in the large even when there is a formal contract between buyer and seller which is fully satisfied.

Lessons Learned and Success Criteria. Some of the most interesting lessons learned in the last decade were on programs which did not totally succeed (that is, did not have the requested/specified characteristics working within the specified schedule), but were still accepted by the customer and used by the end user. A look at these programs, both commercial and government-contracting, showed that the common denominator was that customers and users thought that accepting and using the system was the best alternative they had available. This is in contrast to several systems and products which failed outright, and never produced a system or product which was used, or were cancelled before completion. It is very interesting to note that the magnitude of the gap between product/system specifications and program requirements was not highly correlated to whether the program failed; some of the partially successful programs had very major discrepancies between requirements and delivered capabilities. There was more correlation between schedule overruns and program failures. In general, programs which ran more than a single digit number of months past the original schedule were cancelled significantly more often than ones which were closer to their committed schedule. It was not clear that schedule slips of under four to six months made a significant difference, even on commercial products.

CHANGING SUCCESS CRITERIA

Mechanisms for Changing Success Criteria. For each of the programs which was partially successful, the success criteria had to be changed in order for the system to be accepted. For commercial products, this mechanism might be as informal as the marketing department giving grudging acceptance to a product which had only some of the desired features, but was available in time to meet the market window of opportunity. For a system developed under contract for a single customer, mechanisms used ranged from formal waivers of specific provisions of contractual documents (typically the statement or work and/or the system requirements specification), to an overall rebaselining of the contract, with appropriate changes in the contract documentation.

Motivations for Changing Success Criteria. Perhaps

of more interest than the mechanisms used for changing success criteria were the characteristics of the developer, the customer, and the interface between them for the systems which were partial successes -- successes in the large, although they failed to meet the initial criteria for success in the small. Table 2 contrasts some of these key characteristics between programs which were partial successes and programs which were failures. Note that the programs which were examined which were complete successes had much greater variability, with some to many characteristics from the second column of this table. This may suggest that producing a product or system as initially agreed can overcome a great many of the potential problems in the customer/developer interface.

However, it should be noted that none of the fully successful programs examined were judged to be high risk or very high risk at program inception by the developer's organization. Many, but not all, of the failures and partial successes were judged to be high risk by the developer at the start of the program. (To be completely honest, it should also be noted that on programs where risk levels were reflected in formal risk assessments delivered to the customer, the formal risk assessment was almost never above medium, even if the system engineers in key roles on the program privately assessed the risk as high. This may reflect a program management judgment that the engineers were unnecessarily conservative, or it may reflect the political reality that high risk is unacceptable to higher management – on either the customer or developer side – at the start of a program.)

Partial Successes	Failures
Mutual goodwill and trust	Arms length relationship
Vision on both sides of benefits from future follow-on work together	View of this program as a stand-alone procurement or product
Aggressive opportunity management	Risk management, but little/no opportunity mgt
Extensive interaction between key decision-makers on both sides, so information on trade-offs could be shared on a continuing basis	Information on trade-offs shared at intervals, mostly at formal meetings, such as design reviews and technical interchange meetings

Table 2: Characteristics of Customer/ Developer Interface for Partially Successful versus Failed Programs

Frequency of Changing Success Criteria. An interesting characteristic of the changes in success criteria is that they tended to happen much more frequently on the partially successful programs than on the failures, although there were changes in requirements over the duration of both types of program. The fully successful programs showed a wide variation in the frequency of changes, spanning the frequencies of both the partially successful programs and the failures. On all types of programs, formal changes in success criteria tended to be rare in the first six months of a program (or in the first half of the program, for those – mostly commercial – product development programs which were less than a year long). On many of the partially successful programs, changes starting after six months into the program came asynchronously with major program milestones, apparently a result of the continuing dialog between develop and customer personnel on trade-offs and opportunities. On most of the failed programs, the changes came grouped in time. A group of changes would typically come a few weeks to a month or two after major design reviews, apparently in response to issues or problems raised at the design reviews which the developer was unable to address satisfactorily. Other groups of changes would come after major integration or test milestones, in response to problems identified which the program could not afford to fully fix.

Nature of Changing Success Criteria. A brief description of the nature of the changes observed in the success criteria is also of interest. Many times, the changes involved reductions in the capabilities of the system. But on partially successful systems, it was notable that some of the changes involved adding new capabilities, or enhancing the capability in very narrowly selected areas. Most often, these increased requirements were added to reflect the capabilities of new elements which had been added to the system design after the initial (concept) design stage. One frequent example came from the incorporation of a new commercial off-the-shelf technology or product into the system design. In fact, in a few partially successful programs, wholesale changes in system requirements followed developer discovery of an alternate implementation approach which made much more extensive use of commercial off-the-shelf products, even though 10 to 20 per cent of the original set of requirements became infeasible with the adoption of the new commercial products. In these programs, the costs went down sharply after the change to significantly increase the use of commercial products – sometimes resulting in an overall cost reduction for the entire program, but more often reducing the size of a projected cost overrun to acceptable levels.

The fact that added capabilities were found much more often on the partially successful programs than on the failed programs correlates well with the aggressive opportunity management observed on many of the partially successful programs. In other words, identification of opportunities, and their explicit management by both developer and customer, seems to provide the upside that helps the customer accept the downside of decreased capabilities in some areas. Note that on very few of these programs was there any formal opportunity management program. However, opportunity management was included informally on a working basis by the systems engineers and program managers of most of the partially successful programs, as part of their way of working. Customer demand for opportunity management seemed to play a very minor role on any of these programs – it was very uncommon (only a few programs had any customer request for opportunity management), and confined almost exclusively to experimental and science-oriented programs. Perhaps customers who understand that the systems they want may not be technically feasible are the only ones who have had sufficient incentive to pursue opportunity management in any systematic fashion.

Another interesting characteristic of the nature of the changes in the success criteria was that partially successful programs were much more likely than failed programs to have multiple simultaneous baselines for the system. Many partially successful programs had periods of time when the engineering team was working to a baseline which differed from the formal requirements baseline. Sometimes these other baselines were what-if exercises, initiated because lead engineers could see no feasible way of meeting all of the requirements in the baseline, and explicitly wanted to explore alternatives. Sometimes, however, the engineering team seemed to just get technical myopia, and focus on a subset of the requirements rather than all of the requirements. If there had been enough interaction with the customer and the end user for the engineers to have a good understanding of the customer's values and priorities, this technical myopia often led to the identification of an alternate solution approach which the customer found acceptable, followed by a corresponding change in the success criteria which deleted the requirements the engineering team was ignoring. Although formal methods, such as Quality Function Diagrams (QFDs), were not used on the vast majority of these programs, the process being used seemed to have been very much along the lines of the prioritization of customer requirements, and the examination of the relationships among potential solution elements which QFDs entail. It is possible that deliberate introduction of QFDs, and their on-going use to support opportunity management, might enable programs which are more formally managed to obtain some of the advantages of these myopic engineering teams without having to give their engineers even tacit permission to ignore requirements.

Conclusions on Changing Success Criteria. This information on the mechanisms, motivations, frequency and nature of changes in success criteria for partially successful and failed programs suggests several conclusions. The first, and perhaps most startling conclusion is that more frequent changes in program success criteria made a program more likely to achieve partial success than failure. This suggests that holding a program to infrequent changes in success criteria is a high risk strategy – it can certainly lead to full program success (although it does not make full program success any more likely), but it can also lead to program failure. This is in contrast to conventional wisdom in systems engineering, which says that requirements changes should be held to a minimum, and made in a very orderly fashion. (One can certainly argue that the groups of changes following a design review reflect an orderly systems engineering process on behalf of both the customer and the developer). This conclusion equates requirements with success criteria; a reader could quibble that they are different. In hindsight, for a partially successful program, the final success criteria were clearly different from the requirements. However, at the time changes in requirements are considered by developers, the requirements are viewed as the success criteria for the program.

The second conclusion about changing success criteria is that at least partial program success seems more likely if both developer and customer actively look for opportunities to add capabilities to the system. In other words, to the normal discovery process it is constructive to add the discovery of opportunities. The normal discovery process which happens on most programs is the process through which all stakeholders discover more about mission needs, technology, and details and implications of possible design solutions. This normal discovery process results in refinements of requirements, including derived requirements, but only rarely results in significant additions to requirements. But on partially successful programs, the significant additions to requirements appear necessary to reconcile all of the stakeholders to the decreases in other system capabilities and requirements necessary to complete the program within an acceptable cost and schedule envelope.

THE DIMENSIONS OF RISK

The Challenge of the New Decade. The focus of the 1990's was on managing programs to pre-defined success criteria. The challenge for the next decade will be to dynamically optimize on different dimensions on which success can be measured, such as:

- cost (of system/product development, of deployment, of support, of modification, of disposal)
- time-to-market (of the first model, of refined models, of other members of a product family)
- product features (known user needs, experimental new features, usability improvements, and so on)
- system stability
- system/product evolvability

Dynamic optimization will require metrics which reflect real system development progress, not just milestones met. Metrics will be needed to provide additional insight into consequences and implications of progress, as well as new opportunities for optimizing results.

Effective cooperation between program managers and systems engineers will be required to identify the multiple alternative ways in which success can be achieved. The traditional command-and-control approach to program management will need to be augmented by key systems engineering value added, including:

- refining requirements, and identifying areas in which requirements should be discovered or evolved
- managing risks through engineering trade-offs
- balancing different engineering disciplines, and in-house versus commercial off-the-shelf sources

The criteria which define success at the start of a program might be very different from those success criteria which will enable a program to reach success in the large – a functional capability which is actually used by the system's intended users to help accomplish their mission objectives. Managing the evolution of these success criteria offers a new focus for risk management.

STRATEGIES FOR MANAGING RISK

Dynamic Adjustment of Success Criteria. Several of the programs examined for this paper showed clear examples of the evolution of success criteria. Some patterns of success criteria evolution which were observed are shown in Table 3 below. The first pattern is one in which incremental changes are made in success criteria, mostly downward, as cost drivers are discovered and addressed. This approach is sometimes called Cost As An Independent Variable, which reflects its users willingness to examine any alternatives which will contribute to significant cost reductions (or even reductions in potential cost increases). The second pattern is one in which unexpected increases in capability in some areas, together with significant cost decreases, makes the reduction of requirements in many areas acceptable. The third pattern is one of limiting costs and risks in each program phase by throttling back on requirements.

Incremental Pattern	Step Function Pattern	Phased Change Pattern
Ambitious functional requirements	Ambitious functional requirements	Ambitious functional requirements
Cost drivers are identified, and these requirements are scaled back	Discovery of low cost off-the-shelf (OTS) elements which can handle 60 – 80% of requirements	Rising costs and/or risks in the design phase drive decrease in requirements
Discoveries about technical feasibility of capabilities drives addition of feasible capabilities which are desired	Requirements are changed to reflect capabilities of OTS elements, plus what can easily and cost-effectively be added	Rising costs and/or risks in the implementation phase drive decrease in requirements
Discoveries of limitations in technical feasibility or in the chosen design approach drive reductions in requirements	Limitations in OTS elements discovered during system integration may drive a second step-function change in success criteria	Rising costs and/or risks in the integration and test phase drive decrease in requirements

Table 3: Patterns Observed in Changing Success Criteria

All of the partially successful programs examined exhibited one of these three patterns, or minor variations of these patterns. Note that only a few of these programs had explicit management activity directed toward causing changes in requirements or success criteria. On many of the programs, rather than being deliberate, changes in requirements and success criteria were measures taken in desperation, by developers (and occasionally other stakeholders) who feared that failure was imminent without immediate and drastic changes.

Specific Examples of Changes in Success Criteria. Obviously, an extreme relaxation in success criteria could enable any program to be declared a success. However, practical as well as political reality precludes the people involved in a program from declaring a success any system which is really not usable. None of the partially successful programs described in this paper had their success criteria reduced to trivial requirements. Instead, the changes in success criteria involved trade-offs in key requirements, sometimes against each other, and other times against capabilities which had not originally been part of the requirements at all.

One example of a change in success criteria was a communication system which did not meet the original requirement for coverage (geographical range at which the signal-to-noise ratio was high enough to guarantee successful communications connections). Instead, the system provided higher bandwidth connections than originally required, and also provided a wider range of connection types, including light-weight mobile communication stations which were not originally envisioned to be possible, and so were not in the original requirements. In this case, the systems engineering insights into customer mission needs enabled the developer to suggest consideration of a different communications technology which would support both mobile stations and higher bandwidth. This proved to be of such great value to the customer that they were able to persuade all of their stakeholders that the lower coverage was a small price to pay. In this case, the customer used a system Measure of Effectiveness which included the number of users who could use this communication system to enhance their mission effectiveness. The dramatic increase in the number of users who could be served, even with the reduced geographical coverage, and the small delta cost of communication stations for these users, was an effective tool for persuading all of the stakeholders that the change in success criteria was a net benefit. This was one example of a program which used an improvement in one or more Technical Performance Measures to show the value of the change in success criteria.

Another example of a change in success criteria was a commercial software program which shipped a major upgrade that deleted several major features which had been in previous releases. Although these features were used by a minority of the software program's users, the developers convinced their company's marketing executives that the smaller feature set would allow the software to be more stable and reliable, and be ported much more quickly to multiple platforms and evolving versions of operating systems. In this case, the commercial software company had to deal with the short-term storm of complaints of the customers who were using the features which were discontinued. Since some of these customers were ones which had complained most vehemently about the lack of robustness of earlier versions of the software, company management was able to persuade most of these customers of the virtues of having the software become more reliable. And in the long run, over the two years after this feature-reducing release, the company gained significantly more customer for this software product because they were able to bring it quickly to new hardware platforms. In this case, system problem reports and the rework time needed to correct them were used to identify the areas in the product which were inordinately expensive to support. Although this set of metrics was very effective at persuading executives within the company to support the decrease in the product feature set, executives of the company did not choose to use these metrics in persuading customers to accept the changes.

A last example of a change in success criteria was a logistics support system which was originally supposed to interface with over thirty existing systems. The customer identified a need to have the system fielded over a year ahead of the original schedule. The developer could not find a way to deliver all of the orignally planned functionality that quickly, but developed an alternative approach which allowed users to input data into the system using a web-based front end. This allowed the user to skip existing steps in their process, which had been supported by existing systems. Since the user could skip process steps they had previsouly used, and enter data directly into the new system, the system could be fielded without many of the originally planned interfaces to existing data entry systems. In addition, the web front end allowed a much wider array of users to interact with the system, allowing the users to have many more of their people to have insight into logistics order status, with minimal training. This allowed the user to change their task allocations, and rather than having a system usable only by logistics personnel, they ended up with a system usable by a much wider range of their personnel, thus at least potentially eliminating bottlenecks in their own organizational procedures. Note that this web front end did not satisfy any of the original system requirements, but it very effectively addressed user needs. This focus on customer needs – whether or not they are well reflected in system requirements – was characteristic of many of the partially successful programs. The discovery of this new possibility in response to a change in the customer's needs (the need to field a system over a year early) also happened on quite a few of the other partially successful programs. This opporunity management can be a very powerful tool to help a program become a success in the large, serving the user's mission needs, even when success in the small cannot be achieved within the desired schedule or cost. It is worth noting that this program had no formal opportunity management process, but the lead system engineer was a very effective practitioner of opportunity management, on this program and on others.

Political Acceptability of Changes in Success Criteria. In almost all of the partially successful programs, there were factors which made the changes in the success criteria politically acceptable to key stakeholders in the customer community. These factors generally fell into two areas: previously unplanned benefits to the customer, and measures which strengthened the relationship between the developer and the customer, increasing the chances of success of future programs in which both parties had a strong interest. Table 4 shows some examples of each of these kinds of factors, and possible approaches which could be used to identify opportunities to use this factor to provide additional value to the customer.

Factor	Approach for Value ID
Unplanned Benefits	
Faster system delivery to users	Users identify cost savings or better mission achievement from early system use
New system capability	Developer identifies new capability which can be provided at low (or even reduced) cost; user identifies ways this new capability will improve mission performance significantly
Reduced system cost (or, sometimes, reduced cost overruns)	Customer identifies uses for the saved money (or political value of smaller overrun)
Relationship Improvements	
Building components reusable in future systems	Customer and developer jointly identify ways to decrease cost and development time in future programs
Declaration of victory makes both developer and customer look good	Customer and developer jointly identify system features which can be postponed to later system releases, while still allowing the system to be declared fully operational

Table 4: Examples of Factors Supporting Acceptance of Changes in Success Criteria

These factors alone were not sufficient to make changes in success criteria politically acceptable, because in a few of the programs which were failures, one or more of these factors were present. The additional element whih was present in all of the partially successful programs was one or more advocates in each of the key customer (and sometimes user) stakeholder groups, who persuaded the stakeholders of the enefits to them. In some cases, these advocates were literally politicians, who had an interest in both the developer's success and the customer's success. More often, these advocates were influential executives in the customer organization who saw win-win opportunities, and persuaded their colleagues that taking advantage of these win-win opportunities was more important than holding the developer to the letter of the original agreement.

CONCLUSIONS

Learning From The Past. It is really important for the survival and competitive ability of all of our organizations that we learn the right lessons from the last decade. The push for breakthrough improvements in program costs resulted in some failed programs, and many programs which were only partially successful. If one examined all of the failures and partial successes, one could conclude that success could have been achieved on these programs using classical systems engineering approaches, supported by the appropriate resources. This is undoubtedly correct. However, this would have driven program costs up drastically. And this conclusion ignores the finding that partially successful programs have achieved success in the large – that is, they provide useful capabilities to end users who have no better alternative. This examination of over thirty programs completed in the second half of the decade of the 1990s strongly suggests that better value to customers was achieved by partial success of many of these programs than would have been achieved by either program cancellations (resulting from failed efforts to meet all requirements within the cost and schedule available), or from customers who would not have undertaken a program at all had the price been significantly higher.

What Needs Change For The Future. Partial program success clearly serves the needs of all stakeholders, including developers and users of the system, better than program failure. Arguably, partial success is better than a program not being begun at all because costs were too high. So it makes sense to take steps which will increase the prospects of at least partial program success, without driving the costs of the program very high by implementing all of the classical systems engineering processes which have been proven to keep risks low. One promising technique for this is the dynamic adjustment of program success criteria.

REFERENCES

Reference list

Chase, Nancy, "Lose the waste...Get Lean!", Quality Online, March, 1999, found at http://www.qualitymag.com/articles/1999/mar99/0399f2.html

Dettmer, H. William, "Theory of Constraints: A System-Level Approach to Continuous Improvement" found at http://www.rogo.com/cac/dettmer1.html

Liker, Jeffrey K, "Engineering for lean manufacturing: A cross-functional process", Best Manufacturing processes, found at http://www.bmpcoe.org/news/leanmanufacturing.html

Patrick, Francis S., "Program Management -- Turning Many Projects into Few Priorities with TOC" presented at the national Project Managment Institute Symposium in Philadelphia, October, 1999; found at http://www.focusedperformance.com/articles/multipm.html

Pyzdek, Thomas, "Motorola's Six Sigma Program", Quality Digest, December 1997, found at http://www.qualitydigest.com/dec97/html/motsix.html

Spaceviews, "Pathfinder: The Success of Better-Faster-Cheaper" found at http://www.seds.org/spaceviews/pathfinder/better.html

Walmsley, Ann, "Six Sigma Enigma", The Globe and Mail Report On Business magazine, October, 1997, found at http://www.ge.com/investor/article/index.html

BIOGRAPHY OF DOROTHY MCKINNEY

Dorothy McKinney is currently employed by the Lockheed Martin Space Systems Company -- Missiles & Space Operation, where she helps to apply best practices and lessons learned to meet immediate program needs and reduce risks. Dorothy started in 1979 with a Lockheed Martin heritage company as a lead systems engineer, and rose through a variety of management positions. Dorothy spent nine of these years an Adjunct Professor in the Graduate Engineering program at San Jose State University. Other industry experience included three years at ARGOSystems (a Boeing subsidiary), and nine years at SRI International. Graduate degrees include a M.S. in Computer Engineering from Stanford and an M.B.A. from Pepperdine. Dorothy has been active in INCOSE since 1992, is currently on the Board of Directors, and was 1999 President of the San Francisco Bay Area chapter.

Risk Management for the NASA/JPL Genesis Mission: A Case Study

Barney B. Roberts
Futron Corporation
1120 NASA Road-1, Suite 310, Houston, TX 77058
Richard B. Bennett
Jet Propulsion Laboratory, California Institute of Technology
4800 Oak Grove Ave, Pasadena, CA, 91109

Abstract. Processes, just like any product, are designed to meet a set of requirements. The Risk Management Process for the Genesis Project began with the basic requirement to meet NASA and JPL policies and standards. Meeting these basic requirements was not as challenging as trying to avoid process execution flaws observed in the practice in other applications similar to the JPL environment. In addition, there were new issues and changing emphases that required the process to continuously evolve as the project matured.

The process was designed to avoid pitfalls encountered by others as they have tried to implement Risk Management. A set of lessons-learned which covered the experiences of others, specific inputs from the project's Risk Manager, and the evolving needs of Genesis Project management guided the development of the process. This led to the necessity of a facilitated approach. The facilitated approach took advantage of the knowledge of the team members directly involved with the at-risk elements and supplemented them with the specialized skills and tools required for Risk Analysis.

The resulting process was successful in managing the risks to the project. Results varied as the process and project matured. In general, the results indicate a good return-on-investment for the risk management activity. In addition, new lessons-learned are being collected.

LESSON'S LEARNED

Previous Applications. Previous applications of Risk Management have generated the following Lessons-learned (Roberts, 1999).

1. The greatest risk driver is often overlooked.
2. Inappropriate attention may be given to one risk driver over others.
3. Often a risk driver will impact all facets of risk (cost, schedule, technical, etc.,) and the integrated result will be improperly estimated.
4. Often risks are managed by lists that are ranked by subjective qualitative measures resulting in excessive expenditure of risk management resources.
5. Risk Identification is the most critical step in risk management, yet is poorly done.
6. "*Faster, Better, Cheaper*", or other competitive initiatives, exacerbate risks.

Genesis Process. The application to Genesis was designed to eliminate or mitigate the kinds of problems that have been previously observed. In order to fully understand the process, it is important to summarize the project environment in which it was implemented. Genesis is part of NASA's Discovery Program and is executed as a team partnership. Team members include the California Institute of Technology, Lockheed Martin Astronautics, Los Alamos National Laboratory, NASA's Lyndon B. Johnson Space Center, and the Jet Propulsion Laboratory. The challenge of risk management in the Genesis environment is to implement the process across physically separated organizations whose culture and internal processes varied. In the following, we present solutions intended to reduce or eliminate these observed problems.

SOLUTIONS

Devolved. Devolved means the actions, ***and*** the responsibility, accountability and authority are delegated downward as a matched, inseparable set. We use the term "devolved" rather than delegated, deployed, or allocated because the definition of devolved is much more restricted. The intent is to increase our confidence that we have done the best we can do to identify and manage risks by placing the responsibility at the appropriate level.

Other approaches such as oversight by an external organization are generally inefficient and ineffective – they don't "own" the risk. Requiring the person who must experience the consequence of the risk to be the risk owner is the best assurance that the risk will be managed. This places ownership and risk mitigation actions at the place in the project organization where the greatest knowledge of the risk lies.

This, of course, complicates the resolution of other risk lessons-learned such as trying to understand the total integrated effect across the project. It is not uncommon for one person's "few-days" at-risk schedule impact to become an integrated "few-weeks" total schedule impact. Thus, we needed to supplement with integration concepts.

Integrated. The process developed for Genesis recognizes the interactions between risk areas such as cost, schedule, and technical. That is, technical issues can drive schedule and then schedule drives cost. Also, what may appear to be a small schedule problem in one task area may be greatly exaggerated through the interaction with all the other tasks in the integrated network. Therefore, we integrated across risk areas as well as across project activities.

Integration was performed by the Project's Risk Manager who maintained the risk database, consolidated the risks, and integrated the risk impacts using various analysis tools.

Trained. There must be a consistent application and understanding of the processes and procedures from top to bottom. We also needed "buy-in" from all involved in the process. We needed to be sure that risk aversion was normalized across the project, that is, one person's "high" risk was equivalent to another person's "high" risk. This was accomplished through training. As a part of that training, we used expert facilitation, in a brainstorming environment, for the initial risk inputs.

Tailored to Project. Always, the first and foremost question to be addressed in any risk management process is: "What is to be Risk-Managed in this project?" Here, we are using the term "Project" to identify the complete set of activities necessary to produce a product. In this case, the product is a set of material samples obtained during exposure to the solar environment as it streams from the Sun and prior to interaction with the Earth's magnetosphere. This includes the science instruments, the Spacecraft Bus, the Sample Return Capsule, the launch vehicle, all aspects of space flight operations, and the recovery of the samples.

The very specific need to return the samples undamaged and contamination free, is a major requirement to the risk management process.

A second, and more important "risk to be managed", for the near-term, is the cost containment risk. NASA's new requirements for project management improvements as specified in NASA Program Guideline (NPG) 7120.5A require cancellation if a project exceeds its cost authorization by 15%. Missing the launch window would incur extensive costs. Thus, being ready to launch within the schedule target window is a primary driver.

Tailored to Organization. The organization has specific requirements and standards on the execution of risk management within the project. The Genesis Risk Management Plan was written to be fully compliant to both NASA and JPL standards.

The organization is also responsible for providing tools and other support to the project. The process must integrate these tools and supplement where needed. The Genesis web-based Risk Management Application was tailored to fit within the pre-existing web-based Risk Management System. The web based application allowed the various partners to easily input and update risks from their remote organizations into a common database.

Quantification. Quantification is absolutely necessary in order to manage the mitigation investments. We did this by building a Triage Procedure. The objective of the Triage Procedure is to sort out those risks that should be subjected to quantification. Our process first uses a qualitative procedure to evaluate risks and assigns them qualitative values of Likelihood and Consequence. The risks are tested against the Triage rules that filter out the ones that we need to subject to quantitative analysis. The purpose of the quantitative analysis was to improve the likelihood and consequence values of the significant risks and calculate project impact in terms of dollars or days. This information was used to manage the risk mitigation planning as well as to rank order the risks.

One of the most useful tools built into the analysis process was the Double Pareto box. This tool is a matrix of Risk versus Risk-Impacted activity. The individual risks are listed across the top of the atrix and each impacted WBS item is listed down the left side of the matrix. Each cell is filled with at-risk days or at-risk dollars. Then the matrix is sorted to collect the 20% of the risks that are causing 80% of the impact to the WBS items. It allows quick prioritization of which risks are the major drivers and which project activities are most impacted by those risks. The Double Pareto box provides focus for management attention.

Skill Mix. We were careful to manage the skill mix throughout the project. Project team members were responsible for risk identification, qualitative assessments and the risk handling approach because they would have the greatest knowledge and skill for these parts of the process. However, the integrated risk environment and the quantitative analysis was accomplished by experts having substantial experience with the risk management tools.

GENESIS TAILORED PROCESS

All of these considerations were carefully thought out and integrated into the risk management process for the project. A top-level description of the process is provided in Figure 1. The process has three fundamentally unique steps not generally found elsewhere. (1) The collection of confidence levels on the qualitative assessments for likelihood and consequence and the use of a Triage Procedure that used those confidence levels to make decisions on which risks were significant enough for detailed, quantitative analysis. (2) The use of analogous results from prior similar projects. This was very helpful early in the project prior to the availability of mature project estimates. (3) The use of a Double Pareto Box to focus risk actions on those tasks and risks contributing to 80% of the integrated risk impacts.

GENESIS RESULTS: RISK MANAGEMENT PROCESS PERFORMANCE

This section will discuss the individual steps in the process and present the lessons-learned against each.

Planning. The approach was developed to be fully compliant with NASA NPG 7120.5A. We believe that we did have some problems with understanding and buy-in from the project elements that could have been overcome with more attention given to the planning activity. Greater emphasis from the project and cooperation through collaborative development might have helped.

The training was effective for those who participated. However, there were some who were unable to attend because costs for training had not been included in the development plan. Those elements of the project did not have sufficient reserve to accommodate the loss of work. In some areas, only a few personnel were trained to keep costs within the plan. This is of concern due to the great leverage that risk management can have. We were very disappointed in the attendance and believe that we may have missed some risks and know that some risks were identified late due to a limited knowledge of the process, how to use it, and its value.

Lesson-Learned: To include sufficient resources in the planning activity to adequately provide for training.

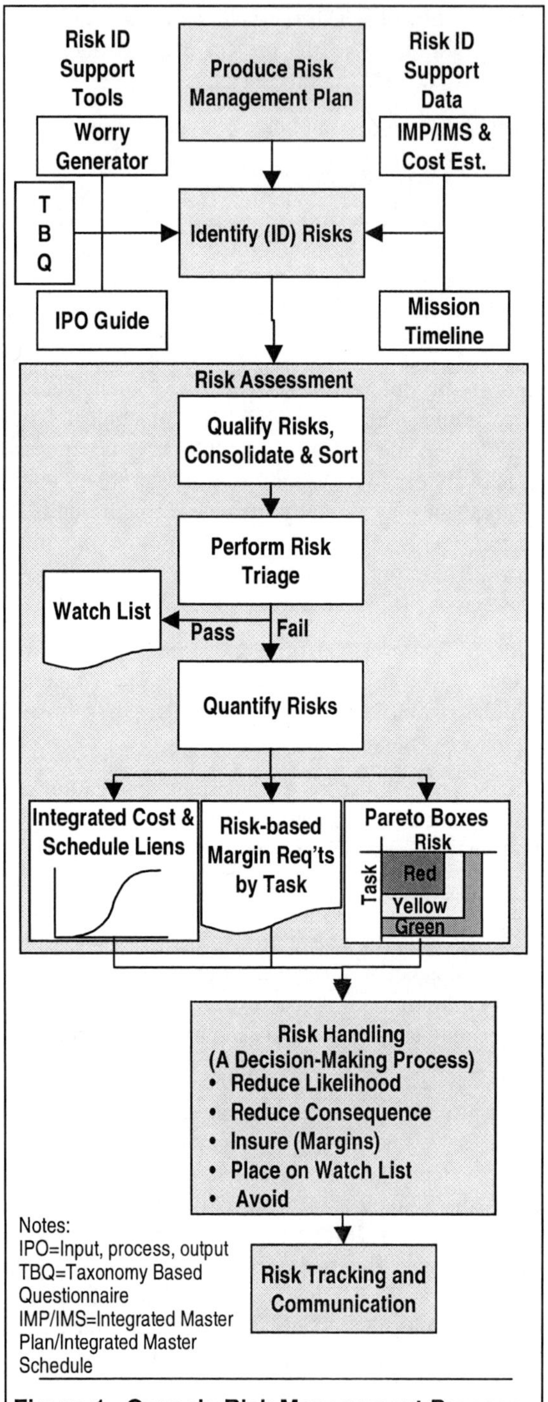

Figure 1 . Genesis Risk Management Process

Identification. Risk identification worked very well in the facilitated brainstorming exercises that were a part of the training, but fell short because of the limited attendance. The Project Risk Manager did the majority of the risk identification activity that occurred after the training. This was done by review, analysis, and constant interrogation to discover the risk items.

One element of the project maintained their own risk tracking system separately from the Project's system. The reports, although sometimes useful, were not reporting risks as much as problems and issues. It was more reactive than proactive. Thus, it lacked the maturity of the mainline Genesis Risk Management process and caused concern as to whether all risks were being identified in a timely manner to implement cost effective risk mitigation plans.

This deficiency became apparent during the Subsystem and System CDRs. New risks were found during the reviews and old ones needed reassessment. Unfortunately, some rather significant problems were also found that should have been identified much earlier as "risks" if the proper maturity had been instilled into that element of the project. For example, a new development for a complex electronic card was beginning to experience schedule delays and cost overruns. This should have been predicted and identified earlier. As it turned out, the card was delivered late and impacted the critical path.

What is the lesson-learned? First of all, this reinforces the lesson regarding buy-in and training. There is also a lesson in the value of striving for early identification. The real value of risk management is the proactive effort to find potential risks early and deal with them before they become "Problems".

Lesson-learned. A strong position must to be taken by project management to enforce participation in the process. Also, the Risk Identification Form did not turn out as simple as planned. It was very detailed and we received complaints about its complexity. We need to presume that some folks were put off by the complexity of the form and that may have caused some risks to not be entered.

Lesson-learned. Keep the input form SIMPLE! If more data is needed, collect it in an interview session.

Assessment. The assessment consisted of two parts, (1) the qualitative risk assessment which assigned ordinal values of High/Medium/Low to the likelihood and consequence, and (2) the quantitative risk analysis which assigned actual probability distributions to the likelihood and consequence. The process included a Triage step. This step sorted the high risks and the medium risks having anything other than "high" confidence in the estimates for the ordinal values. This sorted set was subjected to quantitative analysis. Figure 2. Early in the project, when data was immature or non-existent, we used an analogy model to predict the risk probabilities for likelihood and consequence. As the project matured, we switched to collection of expert opinion for the analysis inputs. Prior to switching to project expert opinion, the analogy model was subject to challenge.

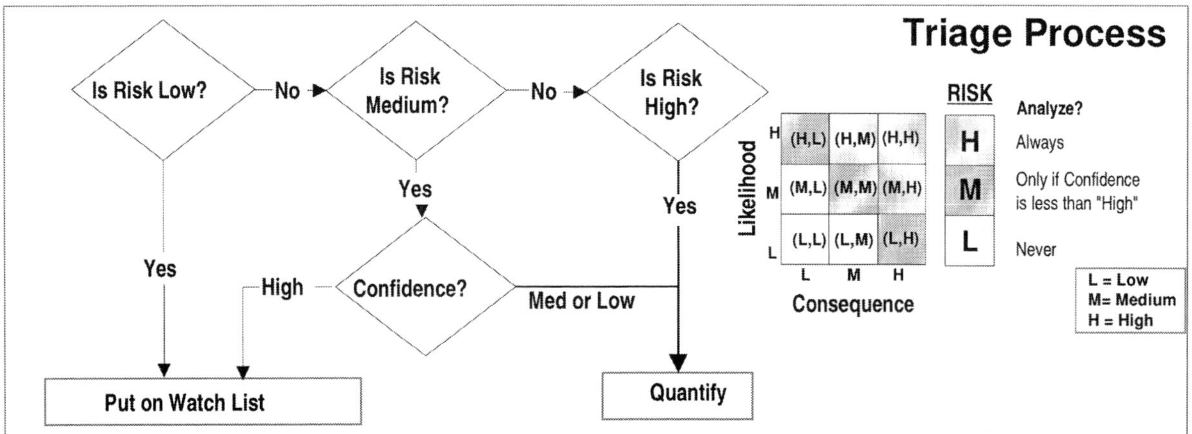

Figure 2 . The Risk Triage Process selects risks for the detailed analysis.

The actual assessment went very well. Four different tools were used: @-Risk Decision Suite©, @-Risk for Project©, Microsoft Project©, and Mainstay's STAR©. The problem we faced was the project's understanding and acceptance of the tools as capable of predicting the probable outcomes. In addition, the tools use project data as input and the quality of the output is obviously driven by the quality of the input. So we had three project acceptance issues to address.

1. Verify the capability and applicability of the tools
2. Validate the project's input data
3. Validate the use of the analogy model.

We did this validation at about the CDR point in the project. It was done via peer review. The review went very well and it did improve the process and improve the project's understanding and acceptance of the results. In hindsight, we should have done this early in the project. Quantitative risk analysis is not generally accepted because of distrust of the quality of the inputs and generally limited understanding of the analytical tools that are used.

Lesson-learned. Validation of the tools and input data needs to be done early in the life cycle of the project.

Handling. The risk handling was uneventful. It appears as though good decisions were made by the project as will be demonstrated in the section "Genesis Results: Project Benefits From Risk Management Execution". Having analytical data, models, and actual quantitative information on the risk impacts in days and dollars along with confidence intervals greatly facilitated decision-making. Decisions were very appropriate and timely, allowing early actions to be made to reduce risk impacts.

Lesson-learned. A proactive approach is extremely valuable. The analysis presented data and information to make timely decisions allowing the project to be proactive rather than reactive in risk management.

Communication and Tracking. One of greatest problems that we encountered was the development and presentation of information in a way that was useful for project management. The type of analysis and the data products are atypical of what most projects normally see. It took a number of attempts to get the pertinent data condensed into useful information for project decision-making and actions.

Lesson-learned. Devote more effort to develop and tailor the process and the information that it produces to match the project and its management culture and styles, and do it early.

GENESIS RESULTS: PROJECT BENEFITS FROM RISK MANAGEMENT EXECUTION

Direct Benefits. Direct benefits are those benefits that result from the direct application of risk management techniques to tasks or process steps. Indirect benefits, discussed in the next section, are those that result from the need to support the quantitative assessments.

The direct benefits are substantial reduction of risks at minimal investment. This was possible by being proactive and catching many risks before they became problems. As Figure 3 displays, the first risk assessment was accomplished at the project Preliminary Design Review (PDR). Almost half the high risks were reduced to mediums and lows within a few months by proactive actions designed to reduce likelihood of occurrence. The "jump" in risks in the May-June 1999 time frame is due to the influx of maturing data that occurs during a project's major design reviews. In this case, the project's Critical Design Review.

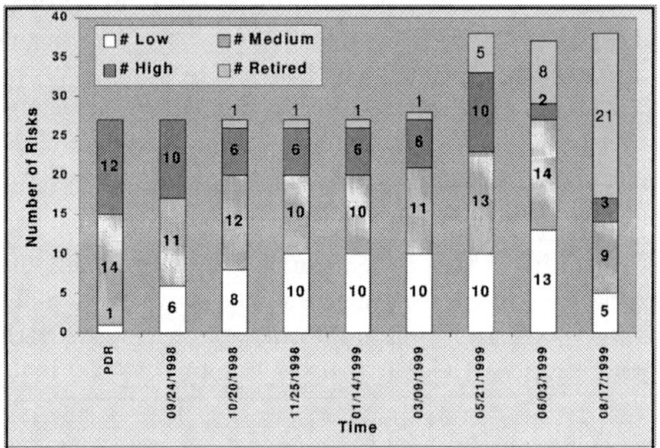

Figure 3. The shrinking High risks demonstrate effectiveness of the process.

While Figure 3 demonstrates the effectiveness of the risk management process in a qualitative sense, we also have quantitative results. The risk management process that was employed used a Triage Procedure to segregate out risks to be subjected to a more rigorous analysis process. As we collected the qualitative risk inputs, we also collected confidence values for each likelihood and consequence estimate. All high risks, regardless of the confidence of the likelihood and consequence estimates, were passed to the analysis step. All medium risks whose confidence estimates for likelihood and consequence were less than "high" were also subjected to analysis based on the assumption that because of the less than perfect knowledge of the risk estimates, these "mediums" may, in reality, be "high".

The risks that passed Triage for analysis were input into the Mainstay STAR Risk Analysis Tool. The resulting schedule calculation was plotted to show the probable threat to the launch date if no action was taken to mitigate it. Figure 3 shows the substantial impact of the risk abatement actions taken over time.

How to Read Figure 4. The vertical axis is the probable launch date. The horizontal axis is the date of analysis. The "Ready Early" band, indicated by gray crosshatching in figure 4, is bounded at the top by the initial planned project date when all elements are stacked and ready to launch. The "Launch Ready" band, the clear band in the figure, is the Launch Window. The "Missed Launch Window" band, the lower band in the figure that begins at launch window closure, means significant project delay and associated cost increases. The two plotted lines represent the continuously updated plan (the upper one) and the stochastic results from the quantitative risk analysis (the lower one). The plan date starts at the top of the Ready-Early (gray crosshatch) band at project start and is an output of the actual project plan. It will change as problems or risks manifest themselves and things need to be re-planned.

The risk result is the lower line that starts deep down in the Missed-Launch-Window band. The bars around the plotted point show the 20th and 80th percentiles where the plotted point is the 50th percentile. As the plot shows, early and proactive risk management has had significant impact on being able to meet the launch window.

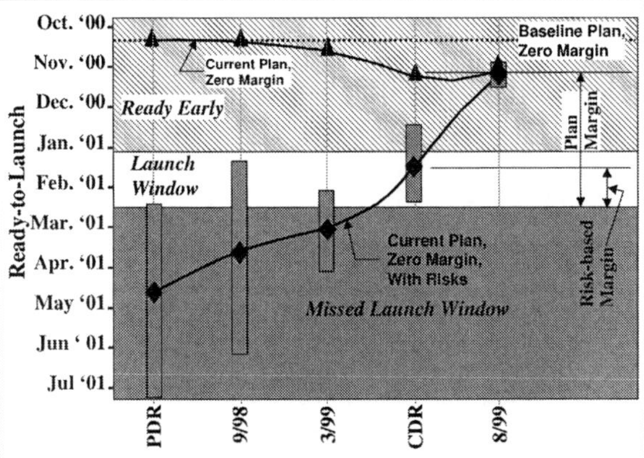

Figure 4 . The quantitative risk analysis clearly demonstrates the project's success in managing risk. The risk threat of 6 months has been successfully mitigated.

Indirect Benefits. The preceding paragraphs discussed the direct benefits of the Genesis Risk Management process. However, there were substantial indirect benefits as well. These benefits resulted from the demand for quality project data to support the quantitative risk analyses. We had made the decision in the beginning that we were going to use quantitative analysis in all cases where it was justified. This was important in order to improve the quality of our decisions. Quantitative risk analysis requires quality inputs such as an integrated schedule with accurate representations of the task constraints and relationships. When we started, various networks and schedules existed in "pockets" of the project and required integration. The project built the integrated schedule that was necessary for risk analysis. In addition, the risk analysis, itself, provided significant and important understanding of the integrated schedule that was not available otherwise. This non-risk insight proved to be beneficial to the project.

Lesson-learned. The indirect benefits of quantitative risk analysis due to the demand for quality project management data are as valuable as the direct benefits.

EVOLVING RISK MANAGEMENT

In the March to June 1999 time frame, the project was performing its subsystem and system Critical Design Reviews (CDRs). The "continuous" nature of the risk management process took advantage of the wealth of data available during these reviews. New risks were identified, some were retired and some were lowered in value. A substantial number of the new risks were in-flight risks that were identified as mission operation plans became available. (Refer back to Figure 3.) With the availability of the flight operations data available at CDR, we were able to hold brainstorming sessions and discussions on what can happen in each stage of the mission; thus yielding new risks. Also, it provided the opportunity to take some very effective mitigation actions as demonstrated by the sharp drop in high risks.

Subsequent to the CDR, our risk management activity was shifted to focus on the Assembly, Test and Launch Operations (ATLO) activities. In addition to "real" risks we began to accumulate some "*problems*" in the project. The difference between a problem and a risk is the likelihood. Things that are certain or near certain are "problems" and generally we did not want to encumber the risk management process with problems. However, some problems have uncertain outcomes and thus are very suitable for analysis by the same tools and techniques used for risk analysis. In the most recent risk assessment, we included all risks and all problems having uncertain outcomes. This provided information that is useful in mitigating all possible consequences.

The point that needs to be made from the preceding paragraph is that the risk management activity is more than just "continuous", it also "evolves" with the project. It changed with changing project foci and maturing project data. The types of changes experienced were: changing risk procedures, alternative risk analyses, and different tools. Figure 5 is intended to illustrate the evolutionary nature of the process. We expected evolution to occur and were prepared, but were not sure from the onset just how this would manifest itself. The results are a very useful lesson-learned.

Lesson-learned. Expect the risk management process to grow with the project and its ever-maturing needs.

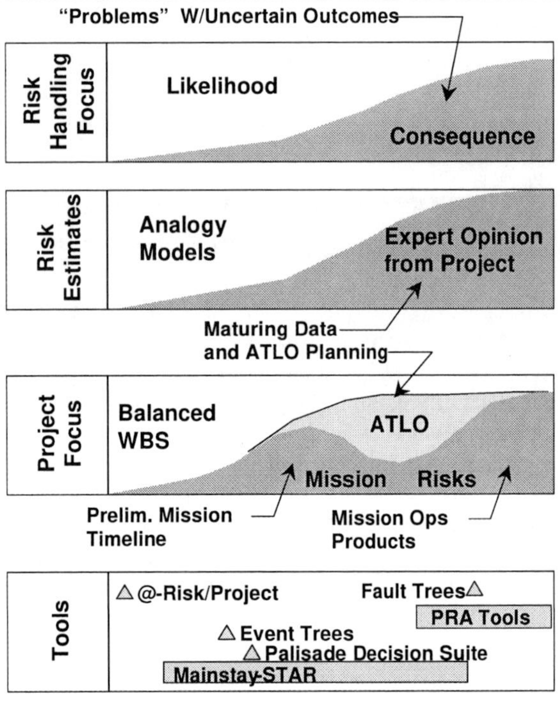

Figure 5. The risk assessment processes evolved through the project cycle as project needs and project data maturity evolved.

Risk Handling Focus. In the beginning, most of our focus in risk handling is to reduce likelihood. Early on there is great leverage in small expenditures to ensure that the likelihood of occurrence is reduced. An example was the lack of recent experience of the team on spin-stabilized spacecraft. The possible risks due to design errors rippled throughout the entire system, including software. The expense to hire and staff the team with seasoned spin-stabilized design experience was very small as compared to the probable outcome otherwise. Later on, as new risks were identified, managing likelihood became more and more of a challenge because of the ever shrinking time-to-respond. There was then a shift to mitigating consequence. An example is that for a number of the mission risks, we had to develop "operational work-arounds"

Risk Estimates. When we first began, we used analogous experience to generate the risk likelihood and consequence values. This involved using a database comprised of 354 NASA flight experiments and space missions. As the project matured, the validity of those analogies was challenged as to whether or not they were better risk estimators than the maturing data within the project. The risk analyses, subsequent to the CDR, were developed using expert data supplied by project personnel.

Project Focus. Prior to CDR, we examined all areas equally for risk and took mitigation actions as appropriate. As CDR passed, we had just about done all that we could for the tasks underway so we focused-in on the next major activity, ATLO. The fabrication of the hardware elements were well under way, so we had a lot of mature knowledge about them and we also had greatly improved planning data for ATLO. Thus, we concentrated our efforts at a close look into ATLO and reduced our attention to the other project elements. When we have finished "wringing-out" ATLO, greatly improved data will be available for mission operations and we will shift focus again.

Tools. In the beginning, we used simplified tools for project cost-schedule-technical risk analysis such as Palisade's @-Risk for Project. As the project matured, we switched to more sophisticated tools such as Mainstay Software's STAR. And, likewise, as we moved into mission risks we began using spreadsheet tools with Palisade's Decision Suite. As more project data is available for mission operations, we will switch to probabilistic risk assessment tools. Sapphire is a typical candidate.

SUMMARY

In summary, we collect and restate the new lessons-learned:

1. To limit risk management training because of the training cost, is a false economy.
2. A very strong position needs to be taken by the project management staff to enforce participation in the process.
3. Keep the input form SIMPLE! If more data is needed, collect it in an interview session.
4. Validation of the tools and input data needs to be done early in the project.
5. Being proactive is extremely valuable The analysis presented data and information to make timely decisions allowing the project to be proactive rather than reactive in risk management.

6. Devote more effort to develop and tailor the process and the information that it produces to match the project and its management culture and styles, and do it early.
7. The indirect benefits of quantitative risk analysis due to the demand for quality project management data are as valuable as the direct benefits.
8. Expect the risk management process to grow with the project and it's ever maturing-needs.

REFERENCES

Roberts, Barney B., "Integrated Risk Assessment: Results and Lessons-learned", *Proceedings, Risk Management Symposium,* USAF/SMC and The Aerospace Corporation, February 1999.

BIOGRAPHIES

Barney B. Roberts. Mr. Roberts is the Director for the Futron Risk Management Center of Excellence. His role in that position is to formalize the risk management practices, procedures and tools that he has successfully developed and utilized in assisting customers in understanding and managing risk for the past 4 years. He has developed advanced techniques for cost-technical-schedule risk management assessments. He assists clients in managing and mitigating risks.

Prior to coming to Futron he was the Manager of the Planet Surface Systems Office, at the Johnson Space Center (JSC). During his last 10 years at JSC, he coordinated the strategic planning and development of concepts and operational strategies for human outposts on the Moon and Mars. He participated in, and led, several international studies for advanced missions.

Mr. Roberts was a significant contributor to the development of the Space Shuttle. He was on the engineering staff of JSC since 1962, involved in such diverse areas as project management, system engineering, hardware and software development and certification, crew training, aerodynamic test and analysis, flight mechanics, flight control design and analysis, rocket engine analysis and test, computational fluid mechanics.

Mr. Roberts has pushed the state-of-the-art in many technical areas and is well published in the professional literature. He has many awards including a patent for an aerobraking orbital transfer vehicle.

Richard B. Bennett. Mr. Bennett is the Risk Manager and Mission System Engineer for the Genesis Project. He manages the mission engineering team and performs global system engineering optimization across the entire project. Prior to the Genesis assignment, he was Team Leader of the Advanced Projects Design Team (Team-X) where he provided daily management and guidance for a seventeen-member space mission conceptual design organization

Prior to joining JPL, Mr. Bennett was the satellite system integration, test, and Launch Operations Manager for Hughes Aircraft Company's three-axis stabilized communications satellites (HS-601), AUSSAT B contract. He also served as assistant Department Manager of 80 scientists, engineers and technicians involved in the design and development of satellite and space shuttle avionics control electronics.

The Relationship of Technology Change Management to Risk Management

S. P. Mosier
S. A. Guenterberg
R. R. Raphael
Litton PRC
1500 PRC Drive
McLean, Virginia 22102

Abstract. As the rate of technology change accelerates, technology change management and the risks associated with technology change grow increasingly important to every systems engineering endeavor. This paper provides an overview of both risk management and technology change management so the similarities of these processes can be highlighted. Further, this paper describes the interactions and synergies between risk management and technology change management, and between the specific elements of these two critical processes.

INTRODUCTION

Background. Technology change management (TCM) is the systematic identification, monitoring, evaluation and selection, planning, application or development, and insertion of technology into an organization, system, process, or product line. In addition, TCM includes the diffusion of effective technologies across organizations, systems, or product lines. Risk management (RM) is the identification, analysis, prioritization, mitigation planning, and monitoring and control "of events which have a potential of causing unwanted change" [DSMC 1989]. There are different categories of risk, including cost, schedule, programmatic, and technical. As Figure 1 shows, both Technology Change Management and Risk Management address technical risk, and in that regard have many elements in common (e.g., identification, planning, and monitoring). This paper describes how using TCM can be used as an integral part of technical risk management. In 1996, Litton PRC embarked on a formal program for technology change management. This paper presents how we have increasingly realized the importance of integrating risk management components in the management of technological change.

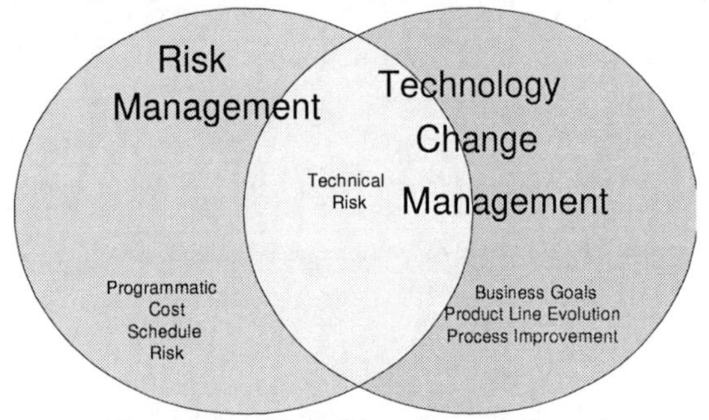

Figure 1. Risk Management and Technology Change Management

RISK MANAGEMENT

Risk Management Overview. A brief look at the key elements of a risk management program is necessary in order to establish the RM-TCM link. There are a number of classic works on risk management. Some, like the Defense Systems Management College work cited above, take a broad system perspective. Others, like the approach recommended by Dr. Robert Charette, are heavily oriented toward statistical analysis to determine the magnitude of risks. Other authors, including Pressman, Gilb, and Boehm, focus more on the risks associated with software development projects. Risk management is addressed in the *Capability Maturity Model for Software* [SEI 1993] in the areas of Software Project Planning, Software Project Tracking, and Integrated Software Management. In addition, Risk Management resides in the *Systems Engineering Capability Model* [EIA 1998] as a focus area in the Engineering Management category.

A common theme of most works on risk management is the classification of risk into categories. These typically include cost, schedule, technical (sometimes called performance), programmatic, and support. It is the technical category that is of interest here, although the nature of risk is such that a risk is often related to more than one category. For example, a technical problem could cause a schedule to slip or cost to increase.

Risks are future events that have a probability of occurrence and a potential for loss. They are not predictable and are caused by a wide range of technical and programmatic issues. Because of the inability to readily anticipate when a risk will occur and what it will consist of, a defined risk management process is used.

Elements of Risk Management. Most RM approaches follow a sequence of steps that include:

- Identification
- Analysis
- Prioritization
- Mitigation Planning
- Monitoring and Control

Identification is the act of determining and describing events that could impact a program. Risk identification techniques to baseline existing risks include the use of a risk taxonomy such as described in *Taxonomy-Based Risk Identification* [Carr et al. 1993], interviews with experts in the field, brainstorming, and analysis of similar programs. Special techniques must be established to accept new risks that are identified after the baseline has been established; this includes setting up email addresses or risk folders where potential new risks are identified.

Analysis includes performing affinity diagramming of identified risks to associate and combine similar risks into individual risks, and assigning a probability of occurrence and impact rating to each risk.

Prioritization involves comparing each risk to the other and establishing a ranking of which risks must be actively mitigated first and which risks can be monitored (i.e., placed on a risk "watch" list). Risk priority is normally based on calculating a risk exposure value, $\mathbf{R_E}$, and sorting the risks in descending $\mathbf{R_E}$ value. However, there are instances when a risk's priority can be "artificially" assigned for political or managerial reasons.

Mitigation Planning is the study of each risk to determine cause and effect relationships and possible mitigation plans and work-around strategies. Its objective is to reduce the likelihood of an identified risk manifesting itself as an actual problem. At a minimum, those risks whose $\mathbf{R_E}$ is greater than an established threshold value are the ones that must be mitigated. Risk mitigation planning involves selecting from four strategies. These strategies are **reduction** (reducing the risk's impact or probability, shifting the risk's timeframe, or changing the risk's consequence); **investigation** (conducting research until a decision on a mitigation approach can be made); **acceptance** of the risk by doing nothing (with the anticipation that the risk may be managed by problem resolution techniques in the future); and **watching** the risk by monitoring the risk and its attributes for early warning signs of critical changes. For risks that use a "reduce" or an "investigate" strategy, a risk mitigation plan is developed. This plan involves defining detailed activities to be accomplished by specific individuals within an established schedule. It also includes identified contingencies and associated triggers (which cause a contingency plan to be initiated).

Monitoring and Control involves watching the identified risk elements and mitigation results both internal and external to a project. Monitoring is the early warning system that triggers a revised mitigation plan, initiates a work-around, or possibly identifies a new risk. Control is managing the risk mitigation plans and being prepared to react to changes in the performance of risk mitigation activities.

A comprehensive risk management effort on a project will involve management, technical staff, planners, and cost analysts, as well as customers and suppliers. A successful organization will not be satisfied with a risk management approach that is focused on a single project. In order to survive and grow, an enterprise-wide effort is needed to develop new products and evolve existing product lines in response to changing market environments and technological developments. To remain competitive, the enterprise must also continuously improve its business and technical processes in response to these same forces. In the following sections, we will explore how a technology change management program can synergistically relate to risk management.

TECHNOLOGY CHANGE MANAGEMENT

Technology Change Management Overview. The objective of TCM, as described in the *Capability Maturity Model for Software* [SEI 1993] is, "...to identify, evaluate, and select new technologies (i.e., tools, methods, and processes) and track them into the organization in an orderly manner." That model advocates a systematic approach to monitoring and evaluating software-related technology changes and innovations, selecting for application those that will improve quality and productivity. This approach is more organizational in nature but also applies to the project level.

Another view of technology management is presented in the EIA's Systems Engineering Capability Model [EIA 1998]: "Manage Technology involves identifying technologies applied to current products and processes; monitoring the progression of currently used technologies through their life cycle; identifying, selecting, evaluating, and investing in new technologies, and incorporating the appropriate technologies into the organization's products and processes to achieve competitive advantage." Yet another perspective of technology change management is presented in the Manage Product Line Evolution Process Area of the Systems Engineering CMM [SEI 1995]. This perspective challenges us to identify the products we plan to offer and evolve these products over time through the insertion of new technology.

These three models are not incompatible, and, in fact, we have developed a single process which satisfies all three, while providing a sound approach for the strategic management of technology to meet business goals and the management of technical risk at both the project and the enterprise level.

Elements of Technology Change Management. The elements of TCM include: Technology Identification, Technology Monitoring, Technology Evaluation and Selection, Technology Planning, Technology Application or Development and Insertion, and Technology Diffusion. Each of the subsections that follow describe our TCM process and how this process benefits from use of risk management elements.

Technology Identification is the act of discerning those technologies that are already in use as well as those emerging technologies that could be beneficial for our customers and to our business. The identified technology base, technology trends and forecasts, "disruptive" or discontinuous technologies, customer requirements, customer plans, and our business base all serve as inputs to this process. The technology base is defined as the set of technologies currently in use. Using our technology base as a starting point, we have devised a functional (customer requirements) and technology area (technology requirements) taxonomy. We refer to the technology area portion of the taxonomy as our critical technology areas. Optimal placement of a technology on our technology area taxonomy has proved to be a challenge as there are many technologies which cut across other critical technology areas (e.g., information security and assurance cuts across Web technologies, database engineering, networking and communications, and other technology areas).

Risk plays a key role in technology identification. Until the technologies in use or planned to be used are known, we can't identify risks associated with these technologies. Technology identification also deals with how to approach disruptive or revolutionary technologies which are likely to forever change the way systems are developed or business is conducted. The basis for this is identifying the function to be performed along with the technology applied to that function today. For example, the use of the Internet would be a disruptive technology from the perspective of telephone touch-tone data entry systems. This risk requires a new level of technology monitoring—not only tracking and watching incremental technology advances but also being cognizant of innovations which are occurring in the relevant critical technology areas.

Technology Monitoring is an ongoing effort, able to provide data on critical developments to support risk management decisions. Having identified the technology base and potential disruptive technologies for monitoring, we then perform a self-assessment of our competency with a particular technology. This assessment provides some of the information needed by the analysis activity of Risk Management by indicating strengths or weaknesses. Following this self-assessment, we then propose initial candidates for technology evaluation and selection. The level of a particular technology's maturation is a key factor in selecting initial technology candidates for further technology evaluation and selection.

Monitoring is conducted in many different ways: active participation in standards bodies and committees, regular attendance at conferences, literature research, communication with vendors, and through tracking developments in universities, research labs, start-up companies, and mainstream vendors. Monitoring is supported by subscriptions to on-line technology research databases; several are used, to provide us a more objective view of technology developments without the bias of one particular subscription service. We are also experimenting with a prototype technology monitoring tool called Tek*Aware*, which uses intelligent agents and Web filtering technology to pull the latest technology trends in a particular technology area to a user's desktop. This reduces our risk in this arena by the use of a more systematic and automated method of technology monitoring. **Technology Evaluation and Selection** explicitly balances technology risk and reward to ensure that we select the best technology candidate for either our investment or for application to particular projects. Since 1989, we have used a formal process to evaluate and select technologies. We also strive to ensure that our customers are able to benefit from all our previous analyses through our on-line Trade Study Repository. Here we store analyses which have been conducted in the past in areas such as database engineering, Web technologies, middleware, security, systems engineering, help desk, and hardware. To jump-start the process, we include access to a research database of over 97,000 products worldwide that includes industry research on technology areas, leading vendors, and industry evaluations of particular products. Because technological advances continue to accelerate, the shelf life of these analyses for complete reuse is limited. We have still found, however, that previous analyses are very useful to our employees for determining relevant evaluation criteria and formats for conducting these analyses.

For our technology evaluation and selection process, we explicitly use our risk identification, risk analysis, and risk prioritization processes to ensure that the impact of risk associated with a particular technology and the associated mitigation costs are commensurate with the interests of a particular customer.

Technology Planning is performed to guide the development and insertion efforts after technology candidates have been evaluated and selected. At the enterprise level, we develop a Strategic Technology Plan which supports business goals. We also develop Technology Insertion and Diffusion Plans for Independent Research and Development (IR&D) projects; these guide the transition of IR&D from a lab environment into operational use. Individual projects typically develop a Technology Evolution Plan. This is required on many contracts, and is sometimes called a Technology Refreshment or Technology Insertion plan. The emphasis here is on maintaining systems operation and supportability over a defined useful-life period. In this plan, risk could be associated with product obsolescence, vendor merger or acquisition, or a number of other issues.

In development of these plans, risk management is of paramount importance. In this portion of the technology change management process, we identify the risk associated with the planned use of a particular technology and devise mitigation strategies to reduce the overall risk. Most of the risks we encounter in the planning phase deal with areas we determine to be "technology gaps" and our strategies for narrowing these gaps. We look closely at the experience of those who will be tasked with development as well as those who will be the end users or receptors of the technology. Customer involvement in each of the steps of the technology change management process through Integrated Product Teams is another effective way of mitigating the risks associated with technological change.

Technology Development or Application and Insertion is the critical step of moving technology development through the lab environment and into production. Although we develop some technology through our Research and Development (R&D) programs, the application and fusion of existing technologies (either developed previously in-house or commercially available) is applicable to the majority of our programs. We define technology insertion as the first instance of transitioning or inserting a particular technology from R&D or from a vendor's development efforts into a deliverable product or service. Our process for technology insertion defines the specific roles to be played by all the major stakeholders to ensure the transition is successful. We have adopted Moore's [Moore 1991] whole product wheel concept to assist in planning for successful technology transition. This concept ensures that the elements present in a technology transition "kit" are adequate for the intended technology receptor(s).

Technology application or fusion of technology into an existing system poses special risks. By using an off-the-shelf product, we often constrain ourselves to a particular development approach. Another constraint is the interfaces imposed by introducing an off-the-shelf product into the existing architecture. These constraints cause risk, namely the compatibility of the off-the-shelf technology with the other architectural components. Innovative approaches to mitigating this type of risk must be found. As an example, we have been able to provide a "wrapper" around components to make them compliant with the Common Object Request Broker Architecture (CORBA). This mitigation approach allows low-risk application of non-CORBA-compliant products, and provides an evolution path into the future as newer, more supportable technology becomes available. This approach to technology application and insertion has proven to be successful on one of our major health care records management programs.

TECHNOLOGY CHANGE MANAGEMENT – RISK MANAGEMENT SYNERGIES

TCM and RM each have unique roles in program and enterprise management. Although many organizations practice both RM and TCM in some fashion, they do not usually think about the two as a complementary set of processes. Table 1 (depicting the benefits that RM can derive from TCM) and Table 2 (showing TCM's benefits from RM) provide some examples of how both processes complement one another.

SUMMARY

Summary. In this paper, we have provided a brief look at both Risk Management and Technology Change Management and how risk processes can be invoked while managing technological change. Both processes have a synergistic relationship as they each contribute to the objectives of the other.

It has been shown that risk management processes contribute to technology change management. Similarly, technology change management is a powerful resource for risk mangers. Having resources handy on technological advancements, risk mitigation planners can more quickly select a risk reduction strategy while minimizing the time needed to investigate risk mitigation approaches.

We believe both these processes are essential for any systems engineering endeavor and simply make good business sense. By utilizing both of these processes, any endeavor can become more strategic in nature and better able to meet current contractual requirements. We also conclude that while the application of new technology is risky, invoking elements of the risk management process as part of the overall technology change management process can reduce this risk. In this way, the special risks associated with a particular technology can be managed.

RM ELEMENTS	TCM CONTRIBUTES BY....
Risk Identification	▪ Helping identify unproven ("risky") technology ▪ Identifying needed infrastructure support (staff, resources) in dealing with new and emerging technologies
Risk Analysis	▪ Providing background information leading to determining risk impact and risk probability values ▪ Suggesting possible risk impact horizons for the advent of emerging technology
Risk Prioritization	▪ Assisting with ranking risks by providing critical characteristics of new technologies (e.g., availability, relation to other technologies, infrastructure needs, etc.)
Risk Mitigation Planning	▪ Providing information that predicts the availability and maturity of emerging technologies ▪ Reducing the length of time needed to research risk mitigation tactics by having technology research databases and information readily available
Risk Monitoring and Control	▪ Providing up-to-date information regarding emerging technologies and supporting infrastructure so risk mitigation plans can be more expeditiously adjusted as the technologies mature (or change focus) ▪ Identifying new technologies that might further improve the risk mitigation effort by adjusting risk mitigation plans

Table 1 – How Risk Management Benefits from Technology Change Management

TCM ELEMENTS	RM CONTRIBUTES BY....
Technology Identification	• Serving as a completeness check of identified technologies • Verifying the accuracy of forecasted discontinuous technologies
Technology Monitoring	• Raising awareness of technologies that may be too risky given target environment • Raising awareness of the position of a particular technology relative to the technology life cycle
Technology Evaluation and Selection	• Assisting in evaluating each candidate technology in terms of programmatic, technical, cost, or schedule risks
Technology Planning	• Assisting in the development of risk mitigation plans for previously identified risks associated with a particular technology insertion or transition activity
Technology Development and Insertion	• Assisting in the execution of risk mitigation plans for a technology development or insertion activity • Assisting by continuously monitoring and re-analyzing the risks associated with a particular technology

Table 2 – How Technology Change Management Benefits from Risk Management

REFERENCES

Boehm, Barry, *Software Risk Management,* IEEE Computer Society, 1989.

Carr, M.J., et al., *Taxonomy-Based Risk Identification,* Software Engineering Institute, Carnegie Mellon University, 1993.

Charette, Robert, *Software Engineering Risk Analysis and Management*, McGraw Hill, New York, 1989.

DSMC, *Risk Management Concepts and Guidance,* Defense Systems Management College, Ft. Belvoir, Virginia, 1989.

EIA, *EIA/IS 731-1, Systems Engineering Capability Model*, Electronic Industries Association, Arlington, Virginia, 1998.

Gilb, Tom, *Principles of Software Engineering Management*, Addison-Wesley, New York, 1998.

Guenterberg, Sharon, *Litton PRC's Technology Change Management Program: The Continuing Quest for Aligning People, Technology, and Strategy*, SEI/Litton PRC TCM Workshop, Hidden Valley, PA, June 1999.

Moore, Geoffrey, *Crossing the Chasm: Marketing and Selling High Technology Products to Mainstream Customers*, New York: Harper Collins Publishers, 1991.

Pressman, Roger S., *A Manager's Guide to Software Engineering,* McGraw-Hill, New York, 1993.

SEI, *Capability Maturity Model for Software, V. 1.1*, Software Engineering Institute, Carnegie Mellon University, 1993.

SEI, *A Systems Engineering Capability Maturity Model, V.1.1*, Software Engineering Institute, Carnegie Mellon University, 1995.

BIOGRAPHIES

Steve Mosier is Director of Systems Engineering in the Systems and Process Engineering Department, Defense Systems, of Litton PRC in McLean, Virginia. He also is a Senior Technical Fellow of Litton PRC. Mr. Mosier earned a Master of Science Degree in Electrical Engineering at Penn State and a Bachelor of Science degree from Case Western Reserve University. He also has an MBA from Penn State.

Sharon Guenterberg is Director of the Technology Change Management program for Litton PRC in McLean, Virginia. Ms. Guenterberg has over 13 years' experience in large-scale systems and software engineering, process improvement, and technology management. She joined Litton PRC in 1986. She holds a Bachelor of Science degree.

Richard Raphael is the "process owner" for Litton PRC's systems and software engineering Risk Management program and chairs Litton PRC's Risk Management User's Group (RMUG). He has over 25 years of experience in systems and software engineering, risk management, and process improvement. He holds a Master of Science in Technology Management from American University in Washington, D. C.

A Development Guide of Robust System Architecture

Il Sang Yoo, Jae Chul Kim, Young Won Park
Department of Systems Engineering
Ajou University
YONGIN P.O. BOX 25, KYONGGI-DO, 449-860, KOREA

Abstract. The term Systems Architecting (SA) is widely used in systems engineering area, but the explicit meaning of the term varies considerably from person to person, depending on his expertise and viewpoints. In this paper, we surveyed the range of variations in definitions and presented the summary. Additionally, the definition of robust systems architecting is suggested along with the associated systems architecture guides that can be followed during architecture development. These guides are written from the viewpoints of art side, requirement specification, system view, principle, tool and environment.

INTRODUCTION

Technologies have developed rapidly since The Industrial Revolution in the 1760s and technologically complex systems flourish in the market place more than ever. For example, the Boeing 777 is composed of about one hundred thirty thousands of parts while a LSI microprocessor is very small, it is very complex enough to have hundred thousands of circuits. Such systems cannot be constructed using only several disciplines because of their complex nature.

Today's engineers are confronted with R&D environment changes such as diverse customers' needs, reduced system development cycle, and improved quality requirement at the same time. Systems engineering emerged to develop a complex defense and aerospace systems to meet government customers' requirements. It became more widespread now because almost all systems including commercial products grow increasingly more complex. It has been demonstrated that systems engineering approach reduces the development period by 60%, design changes by 50% and production cost by 40% when a concurrent involvement by design, production, deployment, logistics and specialty engineers work well applying the front loading design effort (Martin 1997).

The term Systems Architecting has been widely used in the systems engineering community for at least thirty years. It is well understood that the systems architecture provides an important framework for system development. However, the use of this term often elicits more confusion than understanding because authors of existing literatures present different definitions and bounds on it depending on their experiences, views and academic fields (Steiner 1998). Therefore, it is necessary that systems architecting be clearly defined to help new comers into this field.

It was also observed that the more technological complexity of a system is, the more difficult to reduce the discrepancies between the system desired by requirements of stakeholders and the system implemented to meet them. The goal of systems architecting is to reduce this gap in the presence of complexity and uncertainty. Therefore, it is necessary to investigate the systems architecting methods for a robust architecture development.

The objective of this paper is to present definition, roles, and importance of systems architecting through literature survey and to propose a concept of a robust system architecture. Additionally, we present the current best practice guides for system architects.

OVERVIEW OF SYSTEMS ARCHITECTING

Results of literature survey demonstrate that there are diverse views, experiences, and academic opinions on the subject of the relationship between the systems engineering and the systems architecting. These are summarized in the following.

Definitions. Definitions presented by INCOSE SAWG (System Architecting Working Group) are as follows (SAWG 1996);

- System Architecture: The fundamental and unifying system structure defined in terms of system elements, interfaces, processes, constraints, and behaviors.
- Systems Architecting: The Activities of defining, maintaining, improving, and certifying proper implementation of the system architecture.

- Systems Architect: The person, team, or organization responsible for the systems architecting.
- System Design: An Assemblage of realizable system elements and sub-elements and their interfaces.

Roles of System Architecture. System architecture as a framework to show all views of a system to be developed from stakeholders' requirements plays important roles as follow;

- It is used as a comprehensive specification for the subsequent design phase and construction phase after eliciting stakeholders' requirements in the first stage of system development.
- It is used as a communication media between stakeholders and developers.
- It is used to reduce risk by identifying the problems and by trading off various alternative solutions in the early stage of system development.
- It is used to estimate cost, reliability, availability and maintenance of system and WBS for system development.

Importance of Systems Architecting. A study shows that 90% of Function attributes, 80% of schedule related information, 70% of quality attributes and 60% of manufacturing cost are already fixed once a system requirement specification is complete. Good systems architecting in the early development stage, therefore, has the casting vote in achieving system development success. This is expected so since the developed system architecture primarily determines the major functions, the associated performance requirements of a system, schedule, and the cost information.

Systems Engineering and Systems Architecting. In the general systems engineering process, systems architecting begins with an analysis of stakeholders' requirements in the concept phase. James N. Martin (1997) suggests the process shown in Figure 1 where systems architecting is performed during the requirement and architecture definition subprocess. Problems are defined and a solution is obtained through this orderly and iterative subprocess. And also this subprocess includes concept design activities that converts stakeholders' requirements into technical requirements and system architecture (Martin 1997).

A DEVELOPMENT GUIDE FOR ROBUST SYSTEM ARCHITECTURE

Systems architecting is an abstraction or representation of a system under development to forecast and analyze performance, cost, schedule of it and provide guides for research, development, production and management. Especially, the system architecture should precisely reflect stakeholders' requirements. If wrong requirements were reflected in it, the development program would fail. Thus, the success of the program depends on the development of a robust system architecture in the early stage of the program. In this section, a concept of a robust system architecture and some guidelines that system architects must consider are discussed.

Robust System Architecture. In the case of a simple

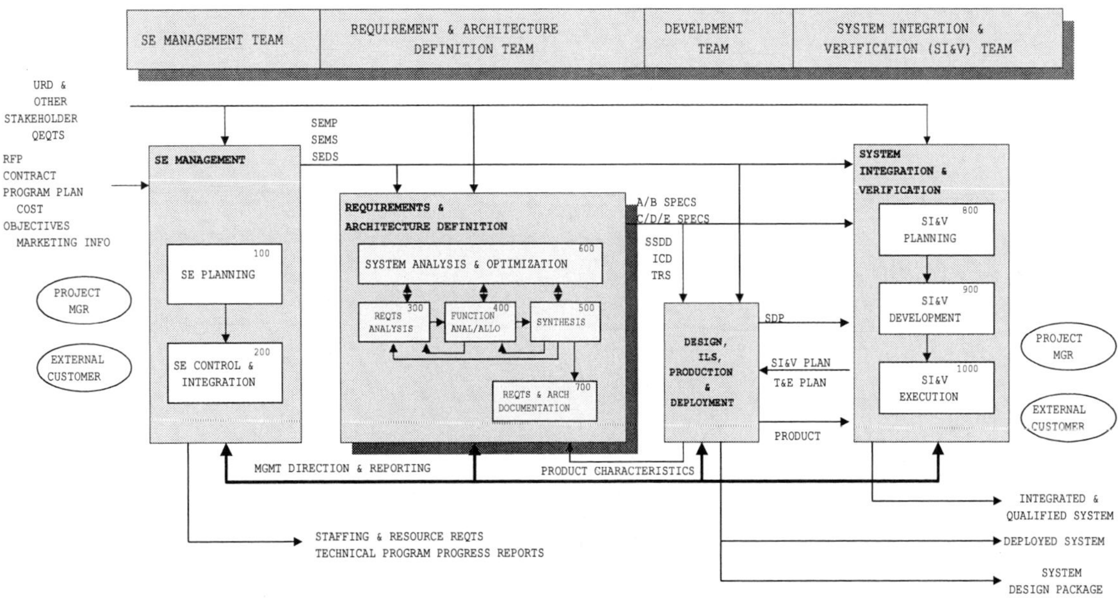

Figure 1. System Engineering Process

system development, physical prototypes are used as communication media between stakeholders and developers. In the case of a complex system development, however, it becomes difficult to build prototypes so that conceptual system architectures should be built to help the communication between them. We suggest a concept of robust system architecture, figure 2, that is defined as an alternative structure of system to minimize the deviation between the system desired by stakeholders and the system developed with insensitivity to noise such as risk and uncertainty. To do so, control factors such as requirement, function and component should be adjusted through requirement analysis, function analysis and synthesis process while communicating with customers. In this paper we discuss it in detail. But we suggest some guidelines to help develop a robust system architecture here.

Understanding of Art Side. Key problems in systems architecting are to identify all complicated system requirements and represent them accurately using abstraction and decomposition based on experience, insight and creativity. In such a systems architecting situation, it should be kept in mind that art aspect is more important than scientific aspect. It is said that, from a practical point of view, the art side of the engineering problem is often the most important. The most severe problems in development and enhancing complex systems originate from this art side; that is, problems that arise later in the development process derive from early judgement decisions on the decomposition of the system (Newbern 1998).

Especially, in the case of an unprecedented system development, the art aspect is most essential. The art aspect can also play an important role in supporting the scientific and engineering side. Art side of systems architecting, therefore, should be understood to develop robust system architecture in addition to scientific aspect. The following problems should be considered to do so;

1 Unquantifiable perception such as value, safety, price, political factor, environmental effect, etc should be accepted from system level model to lower level model.

2 System architects should understand the correct ground of assumption and decomposition at the earliest stage.

3 Heuristics should be used to do concept development, problem solving and decision making during architecting of complex systems. Especially, when uncertainly defined or unquantifiable requirements are handled, they are more useful.

4 Automated tools should be used to overcome human's limit of the power to understand.

Correct Requirement Specification. As expected, the robust systems architecture comes from good requirement specification. Therefore, to develop robust

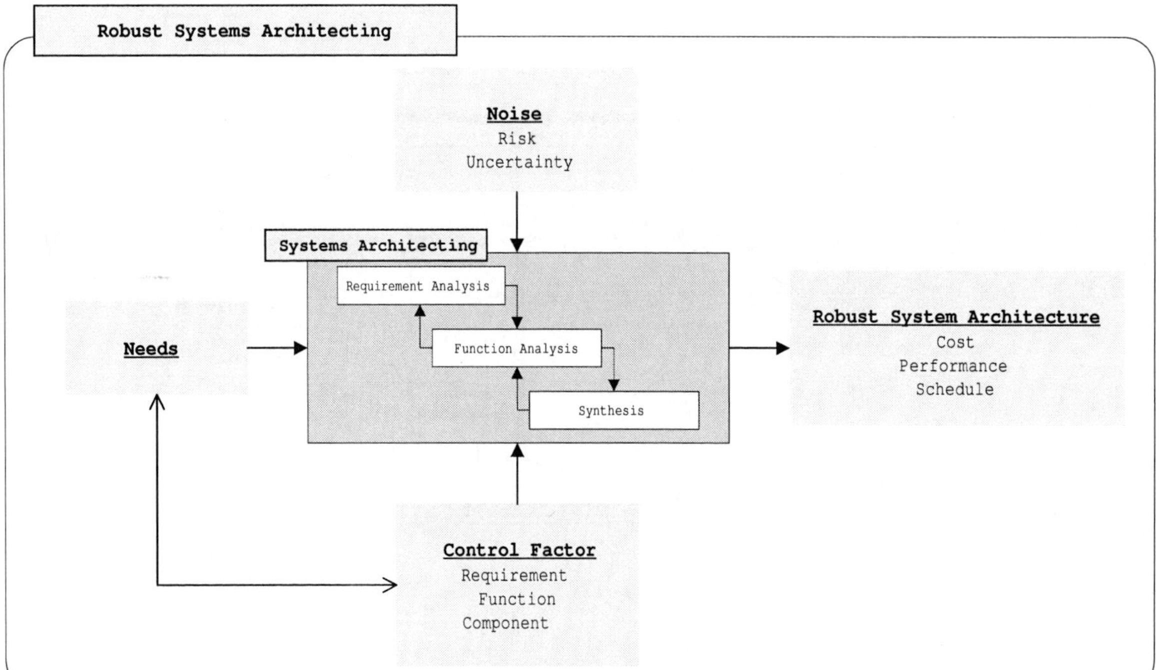

Figure 2. Robust Systems Architecting

systems architecture, requirement specification should have the following principles (Blaauw 1972).

1 Consistency: Good architecture is consistent. That is, with partial knowledge of the system the remainder of the system can be predicted.

2 Orthogonality: This principle requires that those functions that are independent from each other are kept separate in their specification.

3 Propriety: Only function that is poor to the essential requirements of the system should be accepted; in other words, good architecture does not contain any unnecessary functions.

4 Parsimony: No function in the architectural description should be repeated in different forms.

5 Transparency: Functions introduced in the process in the implementation should not be imposed upon the user.

6 Generality: If a function has to be introduced, it should be introduced in such a way that it can be used for as many purposes as possible.

7 Open-endedness: Freedom should be provided for the use of a function in other ways than those envisioned during the design.

8 Completeness: The introduced functions should satisfy the needs and desires of the user as completely as possible within the technological and economic constraints.

Proper System View. An architecture view is a depiction of a particular aspect of the system. Each aspect represents either what the system is or how the system works. The architecture views that have been suggested until now are shown in Table 1 (Maier 1996). These views are not important equally. Views that are important to the architect may play only a supporting role in full development. After systems architect selects one of views, he begins with systems architecting. To develop the systems architecture, he selects the proper view that best models the characteristics of the system.

Relationships among views, analysis, model, architecture, and tools are as shown in Figure 2. Depiction of architecture by a set of architecture views directly supports analysis of a system as a whole. A system analysis determines how well a system satisfies an overall need or meets a system goal.

Each architecture view and system analysis is depicted using one or more models. A model depicts the system using various views through methods as physical model, data model, text, and mathematical equations. For example, the Haltey-Pirbhai(H/P) method is fairly widely used on real-time avionics systems. Object Modeling Technique(OMT) is an object-oriented method target primarily at data intensive software systems. Quantitative Quality Function Development (Q^2FD) is the method for integrating performance modeling with other behaviorally and design oriented methods. Architects can design the robust system by integrated model with multi-views (Maier 1998).

Table 1. Major System View

View	Description
Form	What the system is, its realization
Objective/ Purpose	What the client/user wants the system to do
Function	What the system is
Data	The information retained in the system and its inter-relationships
Managerial	The process by which the system is constructed and managed
Application	All executing elements in a system
Scenario	A set of system critical and common scenarios
Hardware	Inter-element connectivity, physical location of devices, device capabilities and device identification
User	Everything to do with humans
State/Mode	System conditions of state and mode
Infrastructure	Layers of functionality between the mission application and the hardware
Facility	A depiction of the rooms and supporting systems need for development of the system

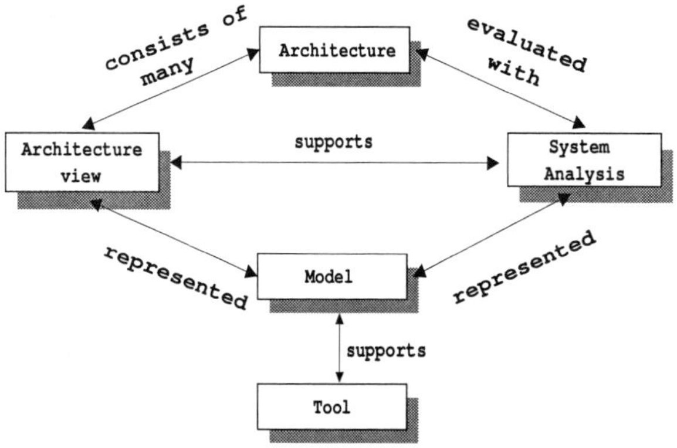

Figure 3. Architecture Relationship

Observation of Principles. There are following principles for robust systems architecting. We should observe these principles in the process of complex systems architecting (Maier 1996).

1 Follow the systems engineering approach. System architects are concerned with systems and with system behaviors. Systems architecting

emphasizes the integrated consideration of function and form to formulate a feasible and satisfactory system concept.

2 Set up the purposes. Clarify the vision and the mission through frequent validation with customer. Systems architecting is driven by client's purposes rather than by technical innovation or builder priorities.

3 Make ultraquality modeling. Ultraquality is the quality too high to be measured. It means specifying a failure rate for a complex system that, if achieved, can never be measured for lack of enough trials.

4 Observe heuristics for insightful judgment. Heuristics are brief statements of distilled wisdom-descriptive lessons learned, prescriptive problem solving guidelines, and warning.

5 Certify by frequent validation with stakeholders and IPPT (Integrated Product Process Team). Certification is the final exam by which the client agrees to accept the system from the builder as fit for use.

Using Heuristics. Heuristics are simple statements that architects accumulate through education, experience, and examples. They can be used when there are no other reasonable approach to problems. So far many scholars have made heuristics according to their need, ability, and experience. The more succinct and even humorous the heuristics, the more easily it is remembered. Heuristics generally come in two forms. The first is descriptive (what is the situation) and the second one is prescriptive (what to do about it). A well-known descriptive heuristic is Murphy's law, "if anything can go wrong it will". A prescriptive heuristic example is "Keep It Simple, Stupid". Heuristics help define the territory ahead and offer some guidelines on how to proceed. Therefore, using the heuristics, system architect can develop the system very effectively and efficiently (Rechtin 1997).

Selection of Proper Tools. The system architect has the challenging job to conceive a concept that will meet clients' needs and then to maintain the vision of that concept until it becomes a reality. To do this a great deal of information must be gathered, manipulated, and communicated. A good systems architecting tool should enable the system architect to capture the highest-level system views to document the system interfaces and performance relative to all external systems. A good tool should enable the system architect to quickly understand the system architecture, including its constraints, from many different views, including user, functional, resource, data flow, and others representing stakeholder perspectives. Therefore, system architects should observe following tool selection process to support the robust systems architecture (Hyer 1997).

1 Define the project mission and purpose

2 Decide what tool capabilities are needed

3 Define practical considerations and constrains

4 Develop comprehensive requirements list (CRL)

5 Collect information on existing tools and vendors

6 Assess tool compliance to CRL

7 Make recommendation

Systems Architecting Environments.

Building the knowledge Database. We made a statement about the art side of systems architecting. That is, it is the architect's experience and knowledge that remains for a long time. These experience and knowledge can be reused in architecting the future new system. We, therefore, have the need to manage the knowledge in art side as well as science side of systems architecting. To do this, we have to build the knowledge database. To build knowledge database tacit knowledge has to be converted into explicit knowledge. More knowledge will be recreated in an applicable organization or team through it.

Integration with PDM/ERP system. There is Island of automation as the result of partial automation in current product development process. To overcome it, it is necessary that systems architecting tools that elicit and analyze the stakeholders' requirements in concept design stage be integrated with PDM/ERP system that support detail design, production and operation. It gives us the consistency of product development.

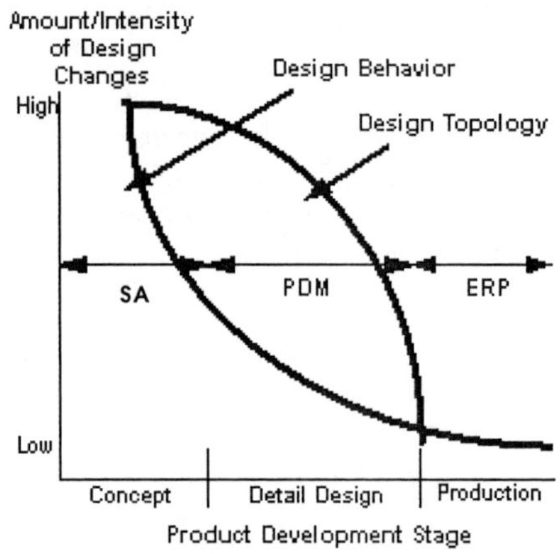

Figure 4. Integration with PDM/ERP

Network environment. It cannot be accomplished without network to investigate the requirements of dispersed customer and market over the world, to analyze requirements by systems architecting, to send specifications to development team, and to manufacture products according to the design. The network makes it possible to develop the products concurrently between contractor and government, to decrease the trial and error, and to optimize the development process. Therefore, the network as the systems architecting environment is very essential.

CONCLUSIONS

The systems architecting in developing complex system plays a role as depiction or abstraction of the system in order to estimate and analyze the performance, cost and schedule of it, and to provide the guidelines for research, development, manufacturing, and management of system. The success of system development project is influenced by analysis of the system in the early concept design stage. Namely, it is necessary to develop a robust system architecture. In this paper we suggested a concept of a robust system architecture that is defined as a structure of system to minimize the deviation between the expected system and the system developed with insensitivity to noise such as risk and uncertainty. To develop it, it is the most important that the system architects have to investigate the customer's requirements correctly and make the correct requirements specification. According to foundation of correct requirement specification, system architects should select the proper view and perform systems architecting through systematic process. They should understand the art side of systems architecting and follow the principles of proper heuristics. They also should choose the tool to support iterative process beforehand and build the systems architecting environments to do it. System architects can develop a robust system architecture as he considers and follows the principles outlined in this paper.

REFERENCES

Frank, Rodger F., "System Architecture - A View Perspective", *Proceedings of 8th INCOSE Symposium*, 1998

Hyer, S. A. and et al, "A Guide to CASE Tools in Support of System Architecting: Background, Capabilities, and Selection", *Proceedings of 7th INCOSE Symposium*,1997

Maier, Mark W., "Systems Architecting; An Emergent Discipline?", *Proceedings of 6th INCOSE Symposium*, 1996

Maier, Mark W., "Architecting Principles for Systems-of-Systems", *The Journal of System Engineering*, 1998

Maier, Mark W., "Reconciling Systems and Software Architecture", *Proceedings of 8th INCOSE Symposium*, 1998

Martin, James N., *System Engineering Guidebook: A Process for Developing Systems and Products*, CRC Press, U.S.A.,1997

Newbern D. and Nolte J., "Engineering of Complex Systems: Understanding the Art Side", *Proceedings of 8th INCOSE Symposium*, 1998

Rechtin, E. and Maier, M. W., *The Art of Systems Architecting*, CRC Press, U.S.A., 1997

SAWG Definitions, *Proceedings of 6th INCOSE Symposium*, 1996

Smith, Timothy B., "Systems Architecting During the Clint Interaction Cycle", *Proceedings of 5th INCOSE Symposium*, 1995

Steiner, Rick, "System Structures and Evolvability: Definitions and Perspective", *Proceedings of 8th INCOSE Symposium*, 1998

BIOGRAPHY

Il Sang Yoo is a Ph.D. student in the department of Systems Engineering, Ajou University, KOREA. He majored in Industrial Engineering as undergraduate in Hanyang University, CAD/CAM and Rapid Prototyping as graduate in Mechatronics department, Kwangju Institute of Science and Technology and then worked on CAD/CAM, PDM, CALS at Hyundai Information Technology Inc. Currently, he focuses on systems architecting and system complexity.

Jae Chul Kim is a graduate student for M.S. in the department of Systems Engineering, Ajou University, KOREA. He holds a B.A. in electrical engineering from Yonsei University. He is interested in Intelligent Building System, and systems architecting. He works at Daesung Engineering and Construction Company as researcher since 1998

Young Won Park is a professor of Systems Engineering at Ajou University in Korea since 1998. Prior to coming to AU, he was a research director at Institute for Advanced Engineering for two years. He worked at McDonnell Douglas Aerospace for twenty years in the area of space system avionics. He received an MS and Ph.D. in Electrical Engineering from Oklahoma State University. His areas of interest include software systems, systems architecting, and transportation systems.

Global System Architecture Optimization: Quantifying System Complexity

Ronald S. Carson, Ph.D.
The Boeing Company
P. O. Box 3707 MC 43-19
Seattle, WA 98124-2207

Abstract. Mathematical optimization techniques are applied to the problem of selecting an optimized system architecture. Using complexity criteria we seek the allocation of functions which globally minimizes coupling and fan-out and maximizes cohesion. The technique requires detailed functional analysis at the next lower level of indenture prior to completing the architecture at the current level. This aspect raises issues regarding the decomposition process, since the "answer" for the prior level is not completed until the functional analysis is at least begun at the next lower level. It is found that a globally optimum architecture probably cannot be defined based solely on the analysis and allocation of functions. However, the attempt to quantify complexity can yield useful data for analyzing architecture alternatives.

INTRODUCTION

Systems architecting has emerged as an important element of the systems engineering discipline. One aspect of the practice is the assignment of functions to end-items. The manner of assignment has been subject to several guiding rules (heuristics). (McCabe 1976) quantified a measure of software complexity, providing a quantitative basis for the evolving practice of structured programming. (Rechtin 1991, and Rechtin and Maier 1997) develop many heuristics for the selection of a system architecture, few of which (by design) are strictly quantitative.

In this work we attempt to apply quantitative techniques to the problem of selecting an optimized system architecture. The goal is to provide a quantitative basis for making an architecture selection among all possible functional allocations.

WHAT ARE WE OPTIMIZING?

In optimization we seek to maximize (or minimize) some objective function for a given problem, subject to certain constraints. (McCabe 1976) defines a "complexity measure" based on the structure of software code (primarily FORTRAN at the time), where the objective is to minimize complexity. Similarly, (Thomas and Mog 1997) define a complexity metric for system development which focuses mainly on system development risk. (Becker et al. 2000) focus on interface reduction using N^2 charts.

For system architecture, the general rules of "maximize functional cohesion" and "minimize coupling and fan-out" (Rechtin and Maier, 1997) are easy to apply in simple comparisons of a few alternatives. But selecting a global optimum that is provably an optimum has not yet arisen in the literature.

It is rather easy to maximize cohesion if we simply allocate all functions to a single end-item. This suggests that there must be some relative cost that increases in proportion to the number of functions within a given end-item

Similarly, coupling and fan-out are likewise minimized if the only interfaces are those external interfaces defined in the problem statement or context diagram. Again, this is easily related to the trivial solution of a single end-item. The relative cost of functional cohesion vs. the cost of internal interfaces will therefore be the only function that actually drives the solution to more than one end-item without prior design constraints.

(McCabe 1976) defines the complexity of a software module as follows:

$$\text{Complexity} = e - n + p,$$

Where e is the number of interface interactions ("edges"), n is the number of nodes ("vertices"), and p is "the number of connected components".

To minimize complexity we would attempt to reduce the number of interface interactions (e) by reducing the number of components (p) for a given number of functional nodes (n). Therefore, less is better, but no specific cost is assigned for increasing the complexity as a way to trade different possible solutions. How do we apply these ideas to the problem of optimizing system architectures?

THE COST OF FUNCTIONAL COHESION

It is evident that placing the implementation of all functionality within a single end-item maximizes functional cohesion (p-n) and minimizes coupling and fan-out (e). The penalty to be paid will be in the form of internal complexity and such potentially practical constraints as size, weight, power, memory, throughput, and any explicit constraint to separate functionality. A cost function which increases with the number of functions allocated to a single end-item clearly has the correct gradient.

A large and complex system may also have such physical constraints as requiring that certain elements be mobile while others remain fixed. This might appear in a cost analysis as a different scaling factor or cost model for those functions requiring such different treatments. One would expect that a valid optimization technique would produce such a "natural" functional allocation if provided the "correct" cost objective function.

For the purposes of this analysis we can postulate several cost models. In the first, we assume a linear cost model, where the cost of functional cohesion increases linearly with the number of functions allocated to the same end-item.

A second model might assume that the cost increases as a polynomial power of the number of functions allocated to a single end-item, such as quadratic or cubic.

A third model might take a more severe approach, and postulate that the coallocation of functions to an end-item increases exponentially with the number of functions (with some suitable scaling parameter). This allows the cost of "a few" coallocated functions to be relatively benign, but the cost of many coallocated functions to increase very rapidly, an apparently reasonable objective function.

THE COST OF MINIMIZING COUPLING AND FAN-OUT

Similarly, we need to establish a method for assessing the cost of interfaces. In electronics, any interface between two end-items will be comprised of two parts: the physical signal connection (*e.g.*, a wire), and a collection of wires into a connector. The cost function is then in two parts. The first part establishes a baseline cost for the presence of an interface (like the connector); the second establishes the per-signal or per-function cost of the interface (like a wire or a specific message on a databus). Multiple functions which are eventually allocated to a single wire may reduce the scaling of the physical interface cost, but the multiple functional interfaces must still be integrated.

ESTABLISHING FUNCTIONAL INTERACTION

If the key to assessing cost is the degree of functional cohesion and interface interaction, how do we establish such interactions in a tradable manner? Put another way, by what functional analysis technique are the functional interactions apparent and available for such assessments?

(Bahill *et al.*, 1998) provides a compendium of several system design techniques that can be reviewed for applicability. The key criteria are that (1) we maintain our focus on functions, and (2) the interactions between functions are explicit so that they can be quantified and priced. Such techniques as functional flow block diagrams satisfy the first criterion, but fail the second because there is no explicit rendering of the interactions between separated functions unless established by a sequential link. Data products of one function, for example, would not appear as interactions with another function unless used by the next function in sequence.

The behavior diagram model appears suited to this task. While focused on functional behavior, every function is related to explicit inputs and outputs. Relationships between functions can be easily established by a common input or product (one function's output is another function's input, no matter where they are scattered on the overall behavior diagram). Similarly, the IDEF0 model explicitly links functions with other functions (activities) via inputs, outputs, controls, and mechanisms. Figure 1 indicates the symbology of an IDEF0 model "activity". "Outputs" of one activity are frequently "controls" for another activity. Caution should be used however, since "mechanisms" are frequently elements of the system architecture we are attempting to define, and we must be careful about assuming the solution!

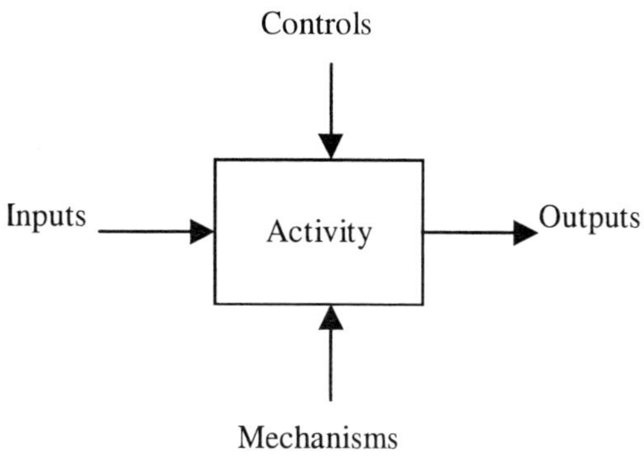

Figure 1. IDEF0 model element.

EXAMPLE

To give some basis for our discussion, let us assume 9 functions interacting as indicated in figure 2. The only consistent element in this example is that every function interacts with the next function in numerical sequence, a typical occurrence in functional analysis.

These functional interactions can be reduced to an upper-triangular matrix which indicates the interactions between functions. This matrix is a slight variation on that proposed by (Alexander 1964). At this stage we don't worry about the direction of the interaction, merely the presence thereof. Hence, only the upper triangle is required. This interaction is indicated in table 1. Total interactions are indicated in the last column. Multiple varieties of interactions between functions could be represented by numbers other than "1" in the table intersections. However, such multiple interactions may indicate a need for additional functional decomposition so that no *function* interacts with another by more than one data item or product.

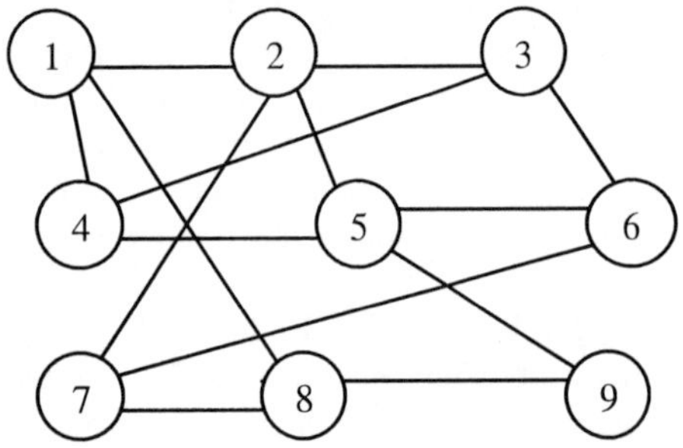

Figure 2. Example interactions among 9 functions. The connectors between bubbles indicate the functional interactions (e.g., function 1 interacts directly with functions 2, 4, and 8, etc.).

	1	2	3	4	5	6	7	8	9	
1		1		1				1		3
2			1		1		1			3
3				1		1				2
4					1					1
5						1			1	2
6							1			1
7								1		1
8									1	1
9										0

Table 1. Functional interaction matrix.

The problem to be solved is to allocate each of the nine functions to a single end-item element, the exact number of which is yet to be determined. We create a second table, table 2, which indicates the allocation of functions to elements. The rules for allocation are that the sum of each row must equal 1 (every function must be allocated to exactly one end-item). Also, the value of any intersection is either 0 or 1 (a function can be allocated to exactly 1 end-item). The number of columns (end-items) is to be determined by the optimization algorithm.

The requirement to allocate each function to exactly one end-item presumes a level of functional analysis that is potentially more detailed than might be available when the architecture is being established. We discuss this in more detail in the last section.

		END ITEMS								
		1	2	3	4	5	6	7	8	9
F	1	X								
U	2		X							
N	3			X						
C	4				X					
T	5					X				
I	6						X			
O	7							X		
N	8								X	
S	9									X

Table 2. Functional allocation to end-items for figure 2.

OPTIMIZING THE ALLOCATIONS

Objective function. The cost of functional cohesion and coupling is optimized when functions are coallocated in such a way that the relative costs between cohesion and coupling are balanced such that the sum is minimized. This requires a degree of normalization between the cost functions for cohesion and coupling.

Our objective function is to minimize the cost. The objective function is written as the sum of the costs of the functional cohesion plus the costs of the coupling:

$$Cost = \sum_i F_i + \sum_{i,j>i} C_{i,j} \text{ ,}$$

where the interaction cost, C_{ij} is summed over all i and $j > i$.

Every element, i, has a cost function which depends on the number of unique functions assigned to it. Assuming an exponential scaling (the most severe case postulated above), the cost function for each element, F_i, has the form,

$$F_i = a_i e^{n_i} \text{ ,}$$

where a_i is the scaling coefficient for element, i, and n_i is the number of functions assigned to element i. It may be desirable to have different coefficients for the n_i to allow different costs for functions that don't follow each other directly in the flow.

The interface costs are broken into two parts to reflect (1) the "base" cost of the fact of an interface, and (2) the cost of the extent of the interface (more functional interaction yields a higher interface cost). For electronics, this can be thought of as the cost of a connector and wire between two electronics boxes (the "base" cost), plus the cost of the number of discretes or databus messages (functions) carried on those wires.

The cost of the interface between elements i and j is then:

$$C_{i,j} = b_{ij} B_{ij} + c_{ij} m_{ij} ,$$

where B_{ij} comes from the functional interaction matrix and indicates whether or not elements i and j have an external interface, m_{ij} is the number of interactions between elements i and j (table 1), and b_{ij} and c_{ij} are the respective cost coefficients.

Constraints. The constraints are that the functions must be allocated to exactly one end-item. Using ordered pair notation, each (function, end-item) pair must be characterized by a value of 0 or 1, so that

$$\sum_j B_{ij} = 1$$

(the sum over all end-items j must be ≡1).

Armed with the objective function and constraints on the solution space, we could attempt to perform the allocation using a generalized, non-linear, constrained optimization algorithm.

TRIAL SOLUTIONS

Using the cost functions above and the example interaction we develop several trial solutions. Let us assume that all coefficients (a, b, and c) are constant for all i and j. The allocation between functions and interfaces suggests that we normalize the cost functions so that we can see the effect of the optimization routine.

The total cost is expressed as,

$$Cost = \sum_i ae^{n_i} + \sum_{i,j>i} (bB_{ij} + cm_{ij}) . \qquad (1)$$

We wish to minimize this cost function subject to the constraints and functional interactions as defined above.

Prior to searching for a global optimum it is useful to analyze and manually calculate the relative costs of three trial architectures. In the first case we assign each function to a unique end-item. In this case, each end-item has exactly one function and the specific interactions are shown in figure 2.

Examining table 1 suggests that functions 1 and 2, which each interact with 3 other functions, should be grouped with their respective interface partners. Possible groupings are indicated in figure 3 and table 3.

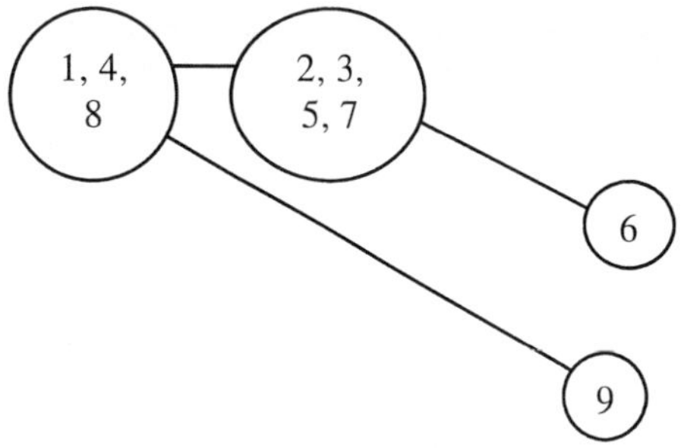

Figure 3. 1st trial grouping to increase cohesion and reduce coupling.

		END ITEMS								
		1	2	3	4	5	6	7	8	9
F	1	X								
U	2		X							
N	3		X							
C	4	X								
T	5		X							
I	6			X						
O	7		X							
N	8	X								
S	9				X					

Table 3. Functional allocation to end-items for figure 3.

We also see that function 6 now has 3 interactions with the functional combination [2, 3, 5, 7]. Therefore, another potential grouping would add function 6 to this group. This renders figure 4 and table 4.

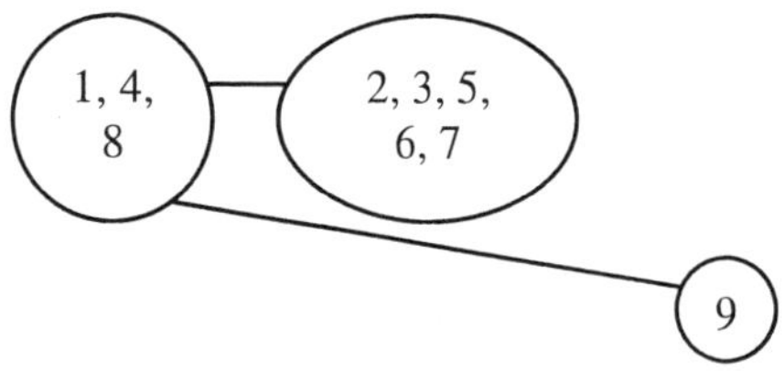

Figure 4. 2nd trial grouping to increase cohesion and reduce coupling.

Using equation (1) we calculate the relative cost of these three functional allocations. We set $b=c=1$, and vary a between 0.1 and 0.3 to show its effect on the relative cost. These results are shown in figure 5.

FUNCTIONS	END ITEMS 1	2	3	4	5	6	7	8	9
1	X								
2		X							
3		X							
4	X								
5		X							
6		X							
7		X							
8	X								
9			X						

Table 4. Functional allocation to end-items for figure 4.

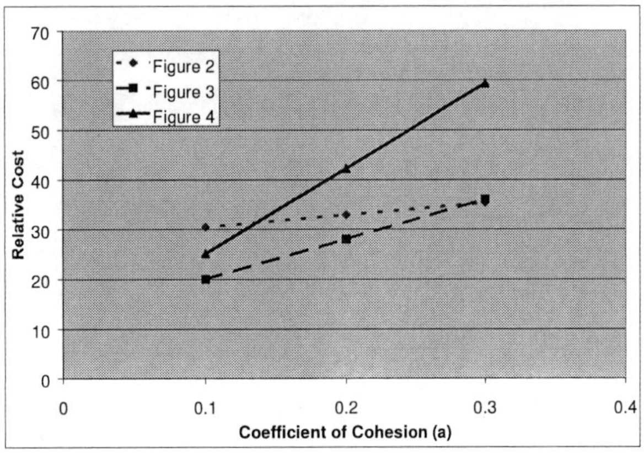

Figure 5. Relative cost for the architectures of figures 2, 3, and 4 as a function of the cohesion coefficient.

The more tightly integrated allocation (figure 4) produces the lowest cost only for the smallest coefficient of cohesion, *a*. The exponential cohesion function makes the allocation very sensitive to the cohesion coefficient.

Figure 6 displays the sensitivity of the relative cost to the coupling coefficient, *c*, with a=0.2. In this case, the lowest cost for the highest level of integration (figure 4) occurs only when the coefficient of coupling, *c*, is above approximately 6.

These quantitative analyses can be useful in understanding the sensitivity of the relative costs to the degree of cohesion and/or coupling represented by various architectural alternatives. Such sensitivity suggests that defining a global maximum would be very difficult because of the difficulty in coming to agreement on the values of the functions and constants in the cost model.

But there is another, more fundamental issue that must be addressed.

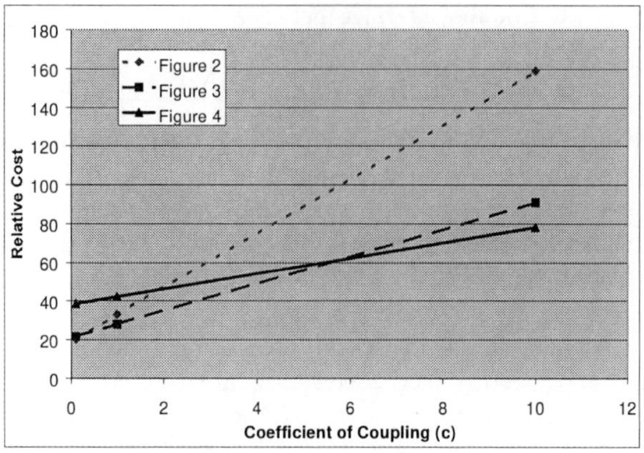

Figure 6. Relative cost for the architectures of figures 2, 3, and 4 as a function of the coupling coefficient, *c*, with cohesion coefficient, *a*=0.2.

WHAT ABOUT FRAT?

(Mar 1992) has consistently stressed the idea that no functional analysis is truly complete at a given level of hierarchical decomposition unless four views are concurrently available. These are the Function, Requirement, Answer (or Architecture) and Test views (FRAT). He argues that one cannot begin work on the next level of decomposition until each of these four views is expressed at the current level.

If we apply this idea to the subject at hand we immediately recognize the potential difficulty. For we are attempting to define functions (F) at the *next-lower* level of the decomposition prior to completing the answer (or architecture, A) at the current level.

Similarly, our approach to functional decomposition necessarily depends on the architecture of the current level. If we truly desire to represent each element with functional analyses and requirements and not design detail, then we must limit our functional analysis to those functions manifested at interfaces. The idea is that any function not manifested at an external interface for a given level of decomposition is not a requirement but an element of design detail. Therefore, the functions to be identified at the next lower level of decomposition necessarily depend on the architecture of the next higher level, because it is the architecture which establishes the interfaces between elements.

So we arrive at something of a quandary. If we wish to globally optimize the allocation of functions at the next-lower level, we must identify all such functions and their interactions at that level. But, to satisfy FRAT and maintain a black-box view of our system elements we must refrain from any further functional decomposition until completing the architecture at the current level. This implies that the completion of the architecture and quantification of the interfaces is a necessary condition for proceeding with the next level of functional decomposition (Carson 1996). And for this conflict there is no obvious answer.

In fact, this conflict appears to suggest that achieving a global optimum cannot depend solely on the analysis and allocation of functions. For the definition of functions suitable for allocation necessarily depends on the *a priori* definition of end-items (and their associated interfaces) to which the functions are to be allocated. Hence we are caught in a trap of circular activity with nowhere to start and no real way to assess completion.

If this is true, then, what becomes of the attempt to find a "global optimum"? Such an entity may not be obtainable by examining functional allocations. For, as we have discussed above, it is difficult if not impossible to define the function primitives at the next level of the architecture without first defining the architecture, in which case we have assumed the solution, optimized or not! (Wymore 1997) makes the point that a system can be optimized when the system allocations are optimized and the subsystem implementations are optimized. But he also suggests that an optimum architecture for both performance and cost may not even exist.

These factors appear to reduce the utility of such analysis techniques to that of analyzing defined alternatives (*i.e.*, trade studies) rather than seeking global optima.

SUMMARY

We have examined the utility of mathematical techniques for defining global optima for system architecture based on minimizing coupling. While it is theoretically possible to do so, such techniques invariably raise two distinct and important issues.

The first is that the objective functions may be very difficult to define and substantiate. The costs of implementing functions are not necessarily obtainable *a priori*, and the cost may well be a function of the end-item to which the function is allocated, regardless of any other functionality allocated to the same item. In other words, it may not be possible to predict the cost of a function without regard to its implementation.

The second and more fundamentally serious is that the process required to determine an optimum architecture must assume some architectural description (the answer we seek!) to be able to define the required functionality which is to be optimally allocated to some to-be-defined architecture. There seems to be no way around this fundamental problem.

We have also suggested methods for decomposing cost functions so that the relative costs of different architectures can at least be discussed. The use of an interaction matrix can be an effective graphical tool for highlighting undesirable complexity in a system design. Even if such complexity cannot be removed, such a tool can be used in risk management and system integration planning so that a program is well prepared when it comes time to begin putting the pieces together.

REFERENCES

Alexander, Christopher, *Notes on the Synthesis of Form*, Cambridge, MA: Harvard University Press, 1964, p.111.

Bahill, A. T., et al., "The Design-Methods Comparison Project," *IEEE Transactions on Systems, Man, and Cybernetics, Part C: Applications and Reviews,* Vol. 28, Number 1, February 1998, pp. 80-103.

Becker, Ofri, Ben-Asher, Joseph, and Ackerman, Ilya, "A Method for System Interface Reduction Using N^2 Charts," *Systems Engineering, 3* (February 2000), 27-37.

Carson, Ronald S., "Designing for Failure: Anomaly Identification and Treatment in System Requirements Analysis", *Proceedings of INCOSE 1996* (Boston, MA), pp. 771-778.

Mar, Brian W., "Back to Basics", *Proceedings of NCOSE 1992* (Seattle, WA).

McCabe, Thomas J., "A Complexity Measure", *IEEE Transactions on Software Engineering,* Vol. SE-2, No. 4, December 1976, pp. 308-320.

Rechtin, Eberhardt, *Systems Architecting: Creating and Building Complex Systems,* Englewood Cliffs, NJ: Prentice Hall PTR, 1991.

Rechtin, Eberhardt, and Maier, Mark W., *The Art of Systems Architecting,* Boca Raton, FL: CRC Press, 1997, pp. 160-161.

Thomas, L. Dale, and Mog, Robert A., "A Quantitative Metric of System Development Complexity", *Proceedings of INCOSE 1997*, (Los Angeles, CA), pp.205-212.

Wymore, A. Wayne, "Subsystem Optimization Implies System Suboptimization: Not!, http://www.sie.arizona.edu/sysengr/wymore/index.html (March 1997).

BIOGRAPHY

Dr. Carson is a Systems Engineer on the Joint Strike Fighter program at Boeing, analyzing effects of subsystem failures. He received "Best Paper" Award at the 1995 INCOSE Symposium for his work on "A Set Theory Model for Anomaly Handling in System Requirements".

Safety assessment of system architectures

John Murdoch, Peter Kirkham,
John A. McDermid
High Integrity Systems Engineering Group
University of York, York, YO10 5DD UK

Philip Wilkinson
Rolls Royce plc, PO Box 31, Derby,
DE24 8BJ

Abstract. Emerging standards and guidelines in the safety engineering field call for the application of safety assessment techniques throughout the development cycle of systems. Since much early work on design projects falls within the discipline of *systems engineering*, questions arise about the applicability of safety assessment techniques to system architectural descriptions and about the role of such analyses. A safety assessment technique applicable to system architectures is proposed, based on the classic concept of *interfaces* and derived from the HAZOP techique widely used in the process industries. The role of the technique in the wider integration of safety and design processes is discussed. A prototype tool to support the analysis is described and a trial of its use in an industrial application is reported. A concluding discussion considers the integration of safety and design processes.

INTRODUCTION

Emerging standards and guidelines in the safety engineering field call for the application of safety assessment techniques throughout the development cycle of systems. For example ARP 4754 (SAE, 1994), applicable to civil airborne electronic equipment, recommends conducting a Functional Hazard Assessment during early design activity, followed by Preliminary System Safety Assessment (PSSA) in subsequent design phases (Figure 1). Since much early work in design projects falls within the discipline of *systems engineering*, questions arise about the applicability of safety assessment techniques to system architectural descriptions and about the role of such analyses.

Work originating in the nuclear industry by Modarres and co-workers (Modarres, 1999) has addressed the use of functional models of systems in safety assessment. Others have also used function block models (van Passen et al, 1999) including developing formal models that are amenable to simulation and automated analysis (Lind, 1994; Garrett & Apostolakis, 1999). The benefits offered by automated tools are substantial but their use does not remove the need for human understanding of systems nor for the creative search for hazardous conditions. In earlier work (Murdoch et al, 1997), we have taken a similar function-centred approach to the core safety problem of hazard assessment. The HAZOP technique, reviewed below, has been applied to functional models in the aeroengine domain (Murdoch et al, 1998). In the following, this work is generalised by proposing a safety assessment technique applicable to system architectures, based on the assessment of *interfaces*. The technique is seen as complementing more formal modelling approaches, because it emphasises the development of human understanding of designs. A prototype tool to support the analysis is described and a trial of its use in an aeroengine control application is reported. The paper concludes with a general discussion of the integration of safety and design processes.

HAZOP

HAZOP stands for *HAZard and OPerability study* and is a safety assessment technique developed in ICI during the 1960s for application to chemical and similar process plant. It seeks to uncover hazardous states which the plant could conceivably enter, thereby providing a basis on which to develop a safety strategy for the plant design and operation. The technique involves a team of people systematically examining design drawings, traditionally *Piping & Instrumentation Diagrams*, and investigating postulated departures from design intent. As such, the technique is best characterised as one of *creative search,* relying on the interaction between knowledgeable people within the team and on the use of guide words (*no*, *more*, *less* etc) applied to attributes of the components in the design, particularly flows, to identify plausible anomalous conditions. Publications in the U.K. by the Chemical Process Industries Association (CIA, 1977) and (Kletz, 1992) have popularised the technique in these industries.

In earlier work (McDermid et al, 1994), we adapted HAZOP to software systems, evolving a technique which was called SHARD. Other independent work in the U.K. includes that of Redmill, Chudleigh and Catmur who have applied HAZOP to computer-based systems, human-centred systems and systems with changing environments (Redmill et al, 1999). They were key contributors to a standardisation effort in the U.K. (MOD, 1996) addressing the application of HAZOP to programmable electronic systems. Although guide word interpretations for several

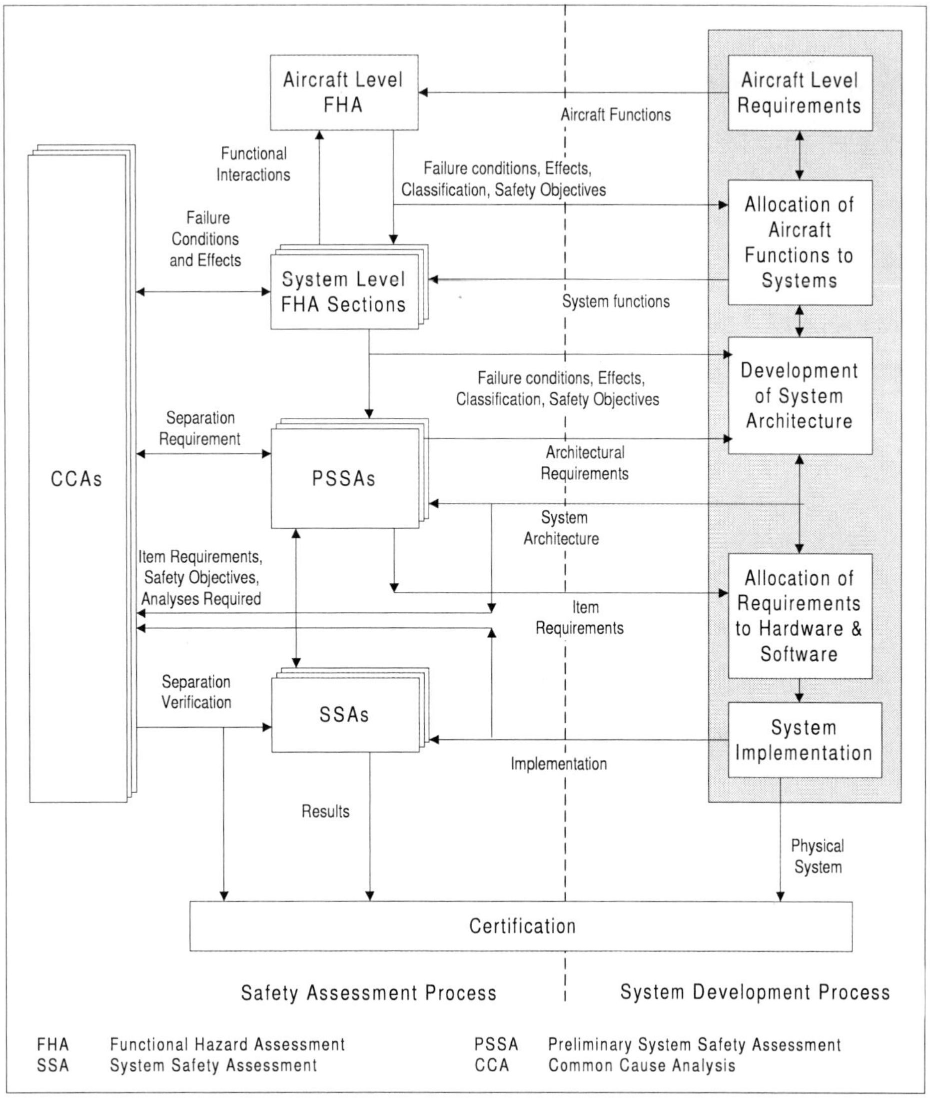

Figure 1. Safety assessment process defined in ARP 4754 (SAE, 1994)

domains (software development, digital hardware, communication systems and electro-mechanical systems) have been developed, there remains a need for a link with systems engineering principles.

SYSTEM ARCHITECTURE

System architecture plays a central role in systems engineering across all application domains and features heavily in standards (EIA 632, IEEE 1220, ISO 15288) and process descriptions in the field (Martin, 1997; Stevens et al, 1998). Architecture is also increasingly recognised as an important factor in the economics and management of design processes and in product development more generally (Rechtin, 1996; Reinersten, 1997). In seeking to generalise the application of a safety assessment technique to systems in any domain, we need to establish links with the foundational principles of systems engineering. We seek to position the HAZOP technique with respect to the decomposition and allocation of functions to physical components, the recursive decomposition of systems into subsystems and the interfaces thereby introduced.

Of particular interest are computer-based systems which exhibit the feature of having a complex subsystem (the processor plus software system) acting as a shared resource, usually providing support to several functional areas of a total system. A topic of concern is the high re-validation and re-certification cost associated with changes in a design, arising from the higher levels of system integration present in such systems. The Evolutionary Design of Complex Software programme (EDCS, 1999), recently completed, has been examining this issue from a software development perspective. Part of the motivation for the work reported here is to progress compatible work at the systems design level,

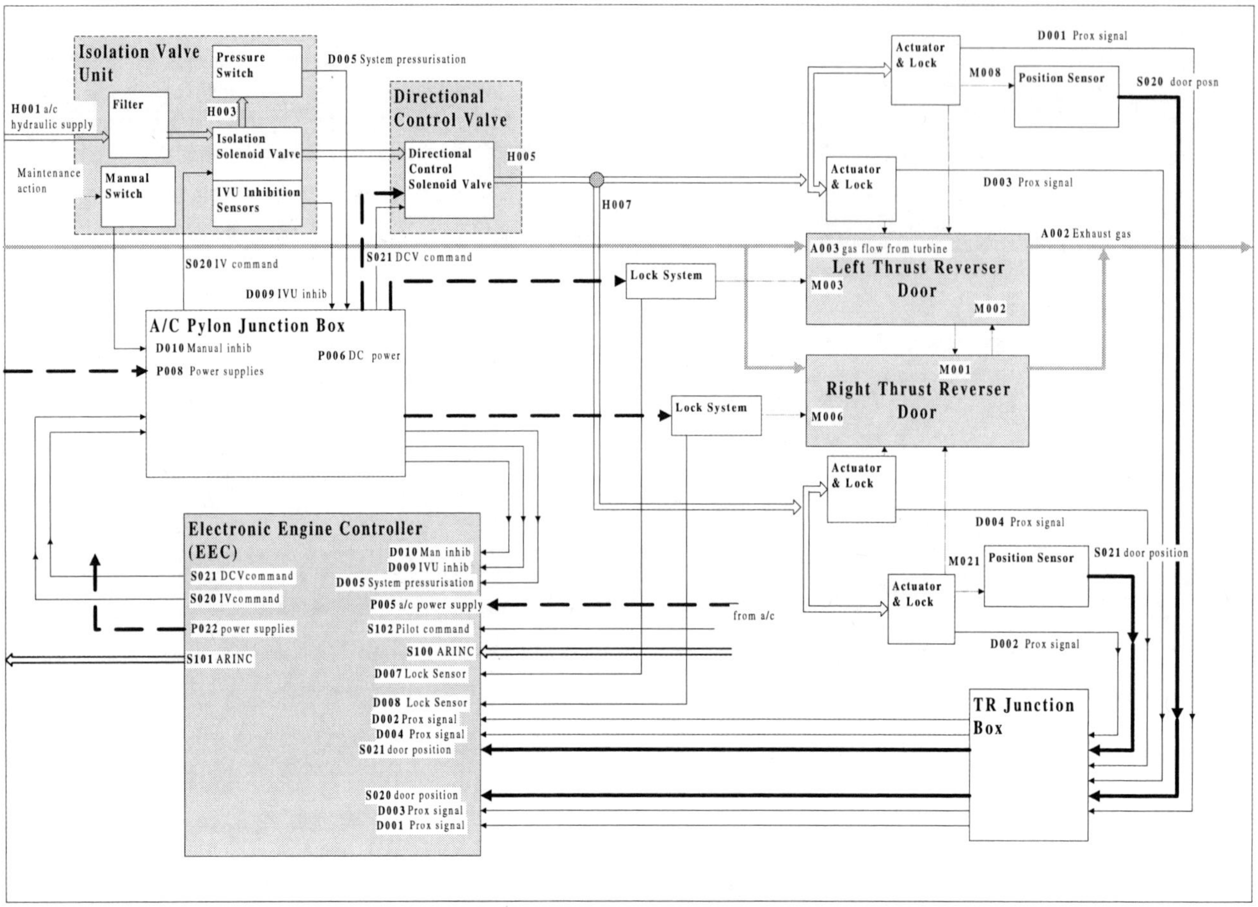

Figure 2. Part of a Full Authority Digital Engine Controller (Thrust Reverser function)

where the functional requirements placed on software components are generated.

SAFETY ASSESSMENT OF INTERFACES

A distinguishing feature of the HAZOP technique (compared with other techniques such as functional hazard assessment and FMEA) is that the *flows* in a design model are investigated as a basis for exploring possible departures from design intent. Traditionally, such flows are physical transmissions of chemicals through pipes, for example. It is a natural step to associate such flows with the interfaces between the components of a system. During the architectural design phase, interfaces will usually be abstract, where the implementation is undetermined or where one or both sides of the interface are described only in functional terms. The application of guide words to flows then translates to their application to components of an interface. For example, we might take an Interface Definition Document and subject each element of it to a HAZOP-style assessment. We would be exploring the causes and consequences for safety of departures from compliance with the interface specification.

A disadvantage of the HAZOP technique is its cost. A "full" HAZOP assessment (Redmill et al, 1999) calls for a systematic consideration of every component of a design model and the step-by-step application and interpretation of a set of guide words. The volume of work is considerable and can consume considerable amounts of staff time. In ealier work on SHARD (McDermid et al, 1995), we recommended the use of simple team structures to control analysis cost. This structure involved a team of two (designer plus one other) doing the bulk of the HAZOP, before undertaking a full team review. In the work reported here, we explore the use of on-line design models and a prototype collaborative computer-based tool to provide a virtual HAZOP meeting. The tool development has the objective of supporting systems engineering work early in a development project and is intended to be low-cost. It is assumed that, later in a project, full product data management systems will be used to manage and store the larger volumes of data produced and to provide the necessary configuration control.

EXAMPLE APPLICATION

The Electronic Engine Controller (EEC) of a jet engine is a computer-based system responsible for providing safety-critical control functions to several different parts of the engine, including fuel flow control, thrust reverser control, surge control (via bleed valves and variable inlet guide vanes) and start-up. Figure 2 shows a functional block diagram in which physical components of the thrust reverser are interconnected via various signal flow paths to the EEC, viewed as a functional block. Feedback control system diagrams, in which causal paths are tracked through the controller and the plant, influenced the layout of these charts. Layered control architectures, involving supervisory and embedded automatic control loops can be treated systematically. A similar approach has been discussed by Leveson (Leveson, 1995). A range of different kinds of flow are used, for example mechanical links, hydraulic flows, power supplies, data busses etc., representing the different attributes of an interface. A particular Interface Definition, for example between the EEC and the hydraulic actuation units (DCV, IVU) of Figure 2, would contain a particular set of flows.

In supporting a HAZOP-style assessment of an interface, we have found it beneficial to work from functional flow charts like Figure 2, since they provide an understanding of the inter-working across the interface. A team of people collaboratively examine these charts; the graphical representation is used to stimulate the creative search for hazardous conditions. At high levels of system design, there will be relatively few committed-to system blocks. At detailed levels, the charts contain more structural information, with functions decomposed and allocated to smaller committed-to physical components.

The function block charts are regarded as providing a core, reference, view of the evolving system design, but do not represent physical and behavioural aspects of an

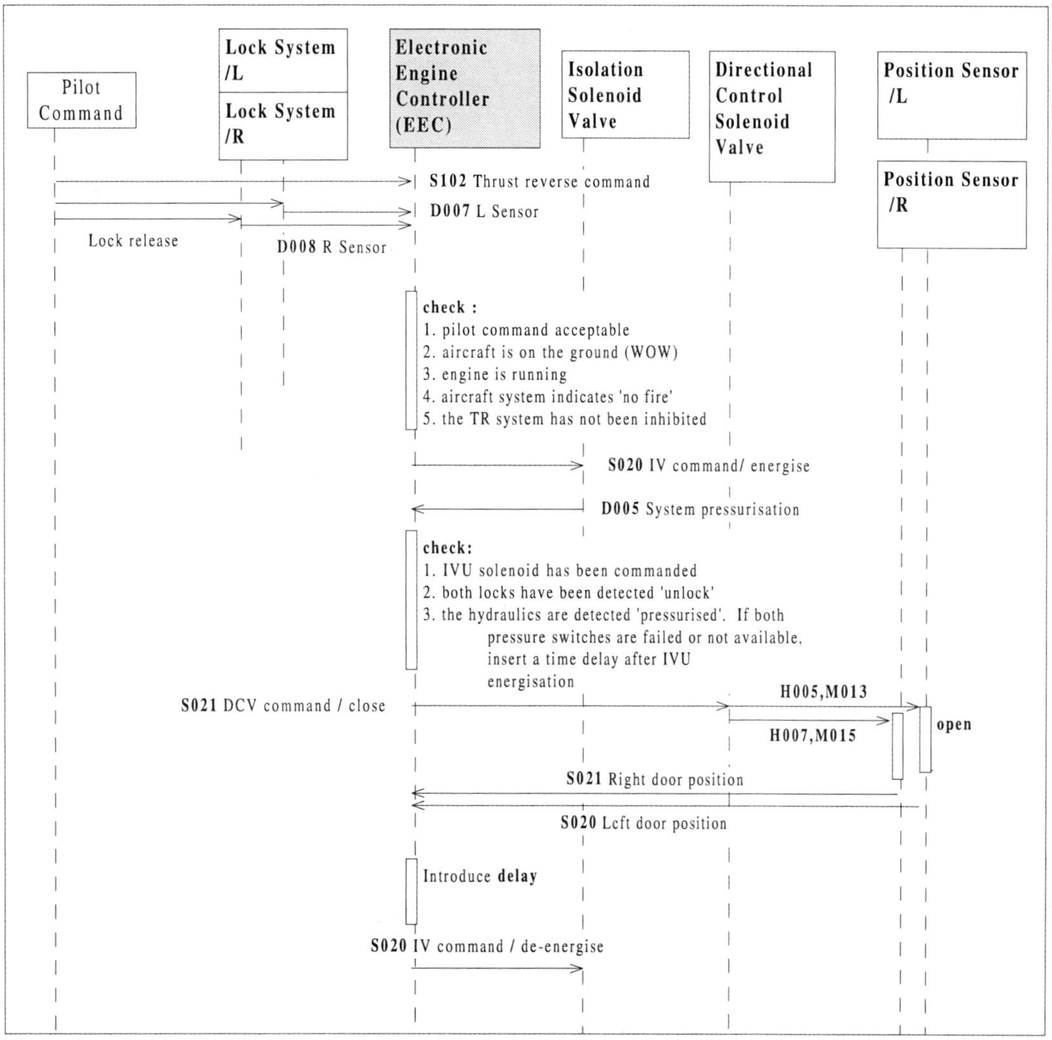

Figure 3 Interaction Chart showing Thrust Reverser deploy sequence

interface. In computer-based systems, information flows dominate. A range of concerns includes read/ write relationships and mode/ state and timing behaviour. Other representations are used to express such interface properties and to support safety assessment. Figure 3 shows an example of an interaction chart used for exploring mode and sequence anomalies. These charts are based on UML (Fowler, 1997), but where we distinguish between signals and the channels over which they are transmitted and where physical (e.g. mechanical, hydraulic etc.) channels are included. There is a similarity here with *use cases* in object-oriented development at higher levels of system aggregation, where human interaction is important.

TOOL SUPPPORT

A prototype tool has been developed to support the computer-based storage, communication and display of function-block system models, and to allow users to interact with them across an HTTP connection (e.g. Intranet). This requires a server with utilities to manage the interactions between models, collaborative authoring and group work on analyses (HAZOP being considered here).

The current support for models is based on a functional view of the system using a similar data model to that developed in the SEDRES project (Johnson, 1999) and in related ISO standardisation work. In this representation, a function is represented as having input and output ports, and internal structure consisting of flows from these ports into sub-function blocks. These models can be linked hierarchically by defining the decomposition of a sub-function in a separate model. Models can be imported from block diagram drawings created in the Visio commercial drawing package, using a custom stencil. It would be straightforward to extend the approach to include interaction charts and other models of an interface.

As an example application of group-based analysis, a HAZOP tool which uses function models has been developed. This tool enables a group of users to create a HAZOP session on the server for a given model, and to generate a HAZOP table with causes and consequences. Users may interact with each other while assessing a model and make use of a shared file of guide words and interpretations. The Extensible Mark-up Language, XML, developed for sharing data on the WWW, is used to store the data for the models and the interrelations between them (XML 1999). XML was chosen because it allows data to be stored in a human readable format that is easily extended and can be parsed and manipulated by any XML compliant application. Compliance with evolving systems engineering data exchange standards should be straightforward.

The following listing shows an example functional model expressed in XML using a custom document type definition.

```
<?xml version="1.0"?>
<Model type="function"
factory="uk.ac.york.cs.ipdm.funcmodel.Function
Model"
source="self"
author="petek">
<flowport bounds="20 52 64 16" id="port1"
shape="2 14 0 2 0"/>
<flowport bounds="20 16 64 16" id="port2"
shape="2 13 0 2 0"/>
<flowport bounds="24 132 64 16" id="port3"
shape="2 7 0 2 0"/>
<flowport bounds="428 32 64 16" id="port4"
shape="2 13 0 2 0"/>
<flowport bounds="428 128 64 16" id="port5"
shape="2 7 0 2 0"/>
<function bounds="128 8 92 80" id="fnF"
shape="1 7 0 2 0">
<Description>Precombustion</Description>
</function>
<function bounds="272 8 100 80" id="fnG"
shape="1 7 0 2 0">
<Description>Combustion</Description></functio
n>
<flow path="84 28 84 28 128 24" src="port2"
id="f1" snk="fnF" line="13 0 2 0"/>
<flow path="372 40 428 40 " src="fnG" id="f2"
snk="port4" line="13 0 2 0"/>
<flow path="296 136 376 136 428 132 "
type="signal" src="fnA" id="f3" snk="port5"
line="7 0 1 0"/>
<flow path="84 60 128 60 " src="port1" id="f4"
snk="fnF" line="14 0 2 0"/>
<flow path="300 88 301 108 260 124 "
type="signal" src="fnG" id="f6" snk="fnA"
line="7 0 1 0"/>
<flow path="220 36 276 36 " src="fnF" id="f7"
snk="fnG" line="13 0 2 0"/>
<flow path="240 124 242 108 193 88 "
type="signal" src="fnA" id="f5" snk="fnF"
line="7 0 1 0"/>
<function bounds="208 124 80 40" id="fnA"
shape="0 7 0 2 0">
<Description>Control</Description>
</function>
<flow path="88 140 88 140 208 140"
type="signal" src="port3" id="f10" line="7 0 1
0" snk="fnA"/>
</Model>
```

The `<Model>` element contains the functional model and includes the name of the Java class the application uses to determine the rules for constructing the model. The `source` attribute of the model indicates whether the model was generated by the tool directly, or would contain the URL of the file it was generated from in the case of an import utility from a different tool. The `author` is the user name of the author of the model.

The model contains `<flowport>`, `<function>` and `<flow>` elements, each containing data for the corresponding parts of the model. The `id` attribute is used to identify the elements uniquely in each resource location. XML provides a linking standard XLink (XML, 1999) for specifying elements from resources based on `id` value, so by using this simple mechanism the links in and between models could be regenerated by any XML-compliant application. Textual description data are placed in separate elements to allow all descriptions of things to be treated in the same way, and allow for context based query mechanisms (for example, where in a given set of system models does 'high pressure' occur in a description).

In this example, none of the functions is decomposed, so the ports to which the flows attach are undefined, and only source, sink and flow types are defined. Figure 4 shows a screen shot of a HAZOP session based on this model. In the top left frame is a graphical depiction of the model. Clicking on a flow here will show the HAZOP table segment for that flow in the bottom left frame. The HAZOP table shows summary information for the causes and consequences for the guide words for this flow. Clicking on the plus signs corresponding to the guide words allows the user to add new causes or consequences. The bottom right frame shows the form to add a new cause for the selected guide word. The upper right frame shows the current set of users logged on to the server and their current activity.

TRIAL USE OF TOOL

The HAZOP support tool has been demonstrated on a representative industrial application in the aero-engine control domain, but in a research setting. A model similar to Figure 2 was constructed, based on project documentation. This is a critical step in the method because it determines the subject of the safety assessment. The model was then stored on the HAZOP server, enabling two engineers, working at PCs in different offices, to conduct a collaborative HAZOP assessment. A common file of guide words and interpretations (also in XML form and stored on the server) was used to support the assessment. Each engineer worked independently on the model, communicating results to the other by *committing to* changes i.e. updating the shared files. Each was kept aware of the general activity of the other in terms of the model and flow currently being investigated.

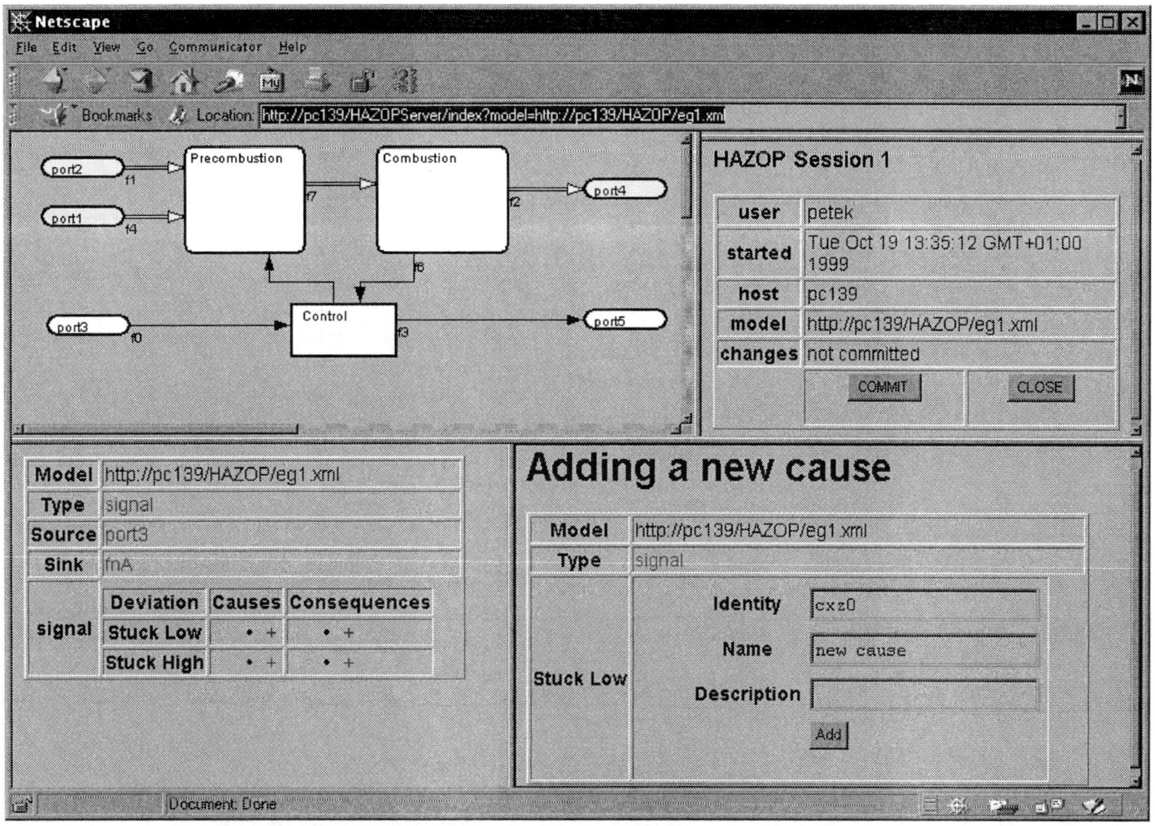

Figure 4 Screen shot of HAZOP support tool

This limited trial established the practicality of the tool for two participants. The trial involved a pre-arranged collaboration, mimicking the conventional HAZOP meeting. A full industrial trial has not been achieved at the time of writing and is needed to assess usability with realistic numbers of participants and to determine the most effective style of use. For example, there is interest in supporting analyses conducted over extended periods. This would involve engineers recording queries in the HAZOP Table results file which others would respond to at a later time.

It is judged that a HAZOP assessment conducted with the tool will deliver most of the benefit of a conventional face-to-face meeting, and at reduced cost. The HAZOP technique benefits from creative interaction between analysts meeting together and some of this is lost with distributed working. Combining tool-supported assessments with brief conventional meetings might provide the optimum approach.

SAFETY - DESIGN INTEGRATION

Safety assessment has been viewed traditionally as comprising a certification activity to be conducted late in the development process. Current trends towards through-life-cycle safety assessment are driven by the high cost of discovering safety problems late in development and by the difficulties associated with software-rich systems. In the terminology of (Reinertsen, 1996) we are moving towards developing indicators of system safety (including hazards) which *lead*, rather than *lag*, design commitment.

The keys to integrating design and safety processes are the availability and information content of the design representations of the system. Interface definitions reflect most of the design commitments made during conceptual and architectural design phases. In principle, associating safety assessment with interfaces, both functional and physical, enables the integration of safety concerns with other design attributes, facilitating trade studies. Safety-related issues include the tightness of coupling (linked to fault tolerance levels), failure detection, annunciation and accommodation and the control of failure effect propagation. Where product families are being developed, interfaces provide the natural basis for assessment of commonality and variability between products.

It is proposed that associating safety assessment with interfaces provides a route to developing a safety certification asset, in which recorded safety data is re-usable across the members of a product family. We speculate that this will assist in the reduction of re-validation and re-certification costs following design change. The effects of a change will be traceable to safety assessment data at an appropriate level of abstraction, enabling estimation and control of the implied re-working of the safety case.

CONCLUSIONS

An approach to the integration of safety assessment and architectural design has been discussed based on the safety assessment of interfaces and making use of standard modelling approaches from systems engineering. The flow-based approach of the HAZOP technique has been exploited. Such an approach involves teams undertaking the creative search for hazardous states. This is viewed as a necessary context within which more formal modelling approaches (automated analysis techniques developed for fault diagnosis, for example) can be developed.

Conduct of the full HAZOP techique is costly; an attempt to reduce analysis costs using a simplified process and a web-based collaborative tool has been described. A preliminary trial of the tool indicates that use of HAZOP in a virtual environment can give substantial benefit at reasonable process cost.

Systematic recording and cross-referencing of safety assessment data with system design data should help to reduce the high re-validation and re-certification costs experienced with complex systems today. Future work will link the above approach to the development of computer-based environments to support system design and to wider developments in model-based systems engineering and product families.

REFERENCES

CIA, *A Guide to Hazard and Operability Studies*, Chemical Industries Association Ltd., U.K., 1977.

Evolutionary Design of Complex Software (EDCS) Programme, DARPA, www.darpa.mil/ito/research/edcs, 1999.

Fowler M. and Scott K., *UML Distilled: Applying the standard object modeling language*, Addison-Wesley, 1997.

Garrett C., Apostolakis G., "Context in the Risk Assessment of Digital Systems", *Risk Analysis*, **19**, 1, pp 23-32, 1999.

Johnson J., "The Future Systems Engineering Data Exchange Standard STEP AP-223: sharing the results of the SEDRES Project", Proc 9th International Symposium of the International Council on Systems Engineering, Brighton U.K., June 1999.

Kletz T. A., *HAZOP and HAZAN*, Institute of Chemical Engineers U.K., 1992.

Leveson N.G., *Safeware: system safety and computers*, Addison Wesley, 1995.

Lind M., "Modeling goals and functions of complex industrial plants, Applied Artificial Intelligence, **8**, pp. 259-283, 1994.

Martin J.N., *Systems Engineering Guidebook: A process for developing systems and products*, CRC Press, 1997.

McDermid J. A., Pumfrey D. J., "A development of Hazard Analysis to aid software design", Proc. 9th Annual Conference on Computer Assurance, (COMPASS'94), Gaithersburg, MD, pp. 17-25, July 1994.

McDermid J. A., Nicholson M., Pumfrey D. J., Fenelon P., "Experience with Applicatioon of HAZOP to Computer Based Systems", Proc 10th Annual Conference on Computer Assurance, (COMPASS'95), Gaithersburg, MD, IEEE, June 1995.

Modarres M., Se Woo Cheon, "Function-centred modeling of engineering systems using the goal tree-success tree technique and functional primitives", Reliability Engineering and System Safety, **64**, 2, pp 181-200, May 1999.

MOD(UK), Interim Defence Standard 00-58 - *HAZOP Studies on Systems Containing Programmable Electronics*, 1996.

Murdoch J., McDermid J.A., Wilkinson P., Reid S., "System modelling for concurrent safety analysis", Proc. First Joint ESA/ INCOSE Conference on System Engineering – The Future, Noordwijk, 11 – 13 November 1997.

Murdoch J., McDermid J.A., Astley K., Reid S., Wilkinson P., "Applying HAZOP to Functional System Models", Proc 16th International Systems Safety Conference, Seattle, 14th-19th September 1998.

Van Passen M.M., Wieringa P.A., "Reasoning with multi-level flow models", Reliability Engineering and System Safety, **64**, 2, pp 151-165, May 1999.

Rechtin E., Mailer M., *The Art of System Architecting*, CRC Press, 1996.

Redmill F., Chudleigh M., Catmur J., "System Safety: HAZOP and Software HAZOP", John Wiley and Sons, Ltd, Chichester, ISBN: 0-471-98280-6, 1999.

Reinertsen D.G., *Managing the Design Factory: a product developer's toolkit*, The Free Press, New York, ISBN 0-684-83991-1, 1997.

SAE, "Certification considerations for highly-integrated or complex aircraft systems", ARP 4754, Systems Integration Requirements Task Group AS-1c, ASD, Society of Automotive Engineers Inc., December 1994

Stevens R., Jackson K., Brook P., Arnold S., *Systems Engineering: coping with complexity*, Prentice Hall Europe, 1998.

XML, XLink: these standards are available from www.w3c.org, 1999.

BIOGRAPHIES

Dr John Murdoch, High Integrity Systems Engineering Group, Dept. Computer Science, University of York, York YO10 5DD UK, telephone - (44) 190 443-4728, facsimile - (44) 190 443 2708, e-mail - murdoch@cs.york.ac.uk John Murdoch has worked for over fifteen years in the aerospace industry, in a variety of specialist, systems engineering and R&D roles. Currently, he is with the Rolls-Royce University Technology Centre, University of York UK.

Peter Kirkham High Integrity Systems Engineering Group, Dept. Computer Science, University of York, York YO10 5DD UK, telephone - (44) 190 443-3375, facsimile - (44) 190 443 2708, email- pete.kirkham@cs.york.ac.uk. Pete Kirkham has worked in the field of tool support for industrial control and aerospace industries for ten years, with particular interests in using hypertext to aid engineering understanding. He is currently working on WWW based tools to support system design, reuse and analysis.

Professor John A McDermid, High Integrity Systems Engineering Group, Dept. Computer Science, University of York, York YO10 5DD UK, telephone - (44) 190 443-2726, facsimile - (44) 190 443 2708, e-mail - John.McDermid@cs.york.ac.uk John McDermid is Professor of Software Engineering and Head of the High Integrity Systems Group within the Computer Science Department of the University of York, UK. He also heads the Rolls-Royce Systems and Software University Technology Centre at York. His research interests are in safety critical systems and software, especially in aerospace applications.

Philip Wilkinson, PCS Department, Rolls Royce plc, PO Box 31, Derby DE24 8BJ UK, telephone - (44) 133 224-7935, facsimile - (44) 133 224-4225, e-mail - philip.wilkinson@rolls-royce.com Phil Wilkinson has been with Rolls Royce for 13 years. He has worked in a range of specialist safety, design and management roles in the systems and engine controls field.

Rapid Architecting Based on Systems Engineering Principles

Florian Harzenetter [♣♠], Bernhard Thomé [♣], Eduard Igenbergs [♠]

[♣] Siemens AG
ZT SE 3
81 730 Munich
Germany

[♠] Fachgebiet Raumfahrttechnik
Technische Universität München
85 747 Garching
Germany

Abstract. This paper provides an approach to Rapid Architecting based on systems engineering principles. After an introduction to the problem area, the notion of "Rapid Architecting" is explained: First a description of a generic process model for Rapid Architecting is proposed. This description is not tied to any specific method for architecting. Then we describe a method that implements this generic process model as well as the models needed for carrying out the process. While explaining the process and the models, we outline the underlying systems engineering principles that have been the basis for the definition of the process and the method.

INTRODUCTION

The first step of system design is to determine an architecture. This step follows requirements analysis and is the basis for subsystem specification and realization. Thus all stages of the system lifecycle, such as preliminary and detailed design, integration, assembly and testing, production and customer support (IEEE, 1999) rely on the initially specified system architecture.

The notion of architecture as we use it in this paper does not encompass all the aspects that are usually tied to the term "architecture". For the rapid architecting process, architecture is the decomposition of the system functionality into several subsystems. In our opinion this is the first step of defining an architecture. This is the basis for the development of other aspects of system architecting, e.g. the definition of system processes, development plans or - for software - physical architectures, compare (Kruchten, 1995)

In the early phases of product development the system architect has little support for identifying an appropriate architecture: technical constraints that could help in finding a partitioning of the required functionality are not yet available since they are a result of the subsystem realization that will be carried out much later. Usually system architects rely on their experience, e.g. known architectures of similar systems, or documented experience such as architecture patterns or heuristics.

Verification of architectures always incorporates implementation considerations, resulting in an intensive study of implementation alternatives for each architectural alternative. Since this is a very time consuming step, architecture definition and optimization is expensive. To ease this problem, the goal of Rapid Architecting is to quickly provide an initial functional decomposition of the system that is a good candidate for a functional system architecture. To this end, Rapid Architecting uses information for the optimization that is already available in early phases of system development.

The first part of this paper introduces a generic Rapid Architecting process. It incorporates some basic systems engineering principles. Then, based on this generic process model, a method is presented that uses this approach for automated architecture definition.

WHAT IS RAPID ARCHITECTING?

In our notion of the term, "Rapid Architecting" is the fast derivation of an initial architecture for a system under development. An "initial" architecture means an architecture that still needs further refinements and typically localized changes due to development considerations that could not be included in the Rapid Architecting process.

This understanding has a strong similarity to the prototyping approach of system development. Accordingly, we can think of initial architectures as "throw away architecture prototypes" or as "evolutionary architecture prototypes".

Throw away prototypes are built to validate one possible alternative realization of a system concept. Having done the validation, the prototype is discarded and a new realization is built, based on the results of the validation. When rejecting an alternative, reasons for the rejection are used as criteria for the definition of a better alternative. This procedure assures that the design process is able to reuse the experience gained while realizing and testing the prototype for a fast convergence of the design process. Evolutionary prototypes are used for validation as well, but instead of being discarded after validation they are improved based on the validation results. The goal is to build the system as an evolution of prototypes.

In both cases the whole process of re-engineering an initial architecture may be regarded as an optimization process. Using architecture prototypes applies an optimization mechanism to system architecting.

Fast determination of near optimal system architectures will help to shorten and clarify the first steps during product development. The evolutionary process of evolving architectures with respect to implementation considerations will be much shorter, since the initial architectural solution is a good candidate already. With Rapid Architecting, the starting point of the optimization process is already near optimum.

Hence an architectural prototype shows an explicit functional decomposition of the product and therefore uncovers design decisions early in the development process. Identifying decision-points early in product development enables the engineer to manage decisions: he can collect criteria and data for systematic decision making and he is free to defer the decision to the optimal point in time in the process. This explicit early preparation for decisions is a systems engineering principle known as "Front Loading" (Fricke et al., 1997) which is applied in Rapid Architecting:

Front Loading. Inadequate decisions made early in system development result in higher rework cost, the later they are corrected. Therefore, techniques should be applied in the early phases of system development that can make effective use of the information available. This will shorten and clarify the development process, since they help to drive the design process by explicit and managed decisions rather than by implicit decisions.

SE Principle 1: "Front Loading"

The result of the Rapid Architecting process is a decomposition of the system functionality into several functional subsystems which guide the designers to find possible implementations that satisfy the stakeholder needs. This functional architecture provides a working baseline for identifying components that apply to the stakeholder needs and to the technology available.

The following sections outline a generic process and the inputs and outputs of a Rapid Architecting process.

HOW RAPID ARCHITECTING CAN BE DONE

Based on customer and other stakeholder requirements, a good functional architecture for the system under development has to be derived. The basic process steps of architecture derivation are synthesis and evaluation steps which must be done iteratively to drive the process towards an architecture fit for the system's purpose. In the Rapid Architecting approach, the goal is to streamline and automate these steps as much as possible.

The Rapid Architecting Process is based on a generic optimization process, which generates various concepts, analyses and evaluates them and finally selects the best concept found as the optimal one, compare Fig 1.

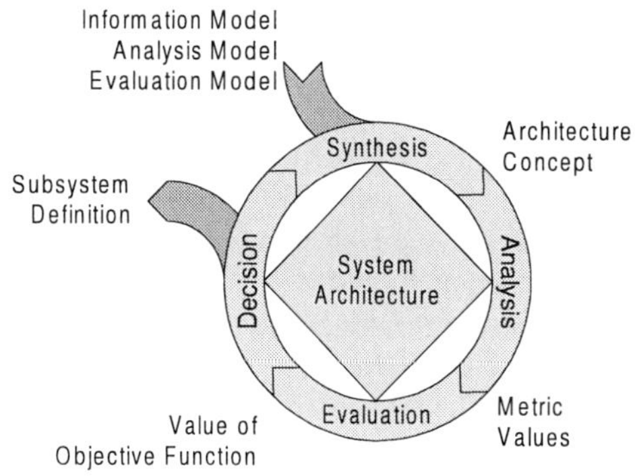

Figure 1: The Rapid Architecting Process

As input into such a process, information of different types has to be provided. We have to draw upon information that is available in these early design steps. Basically, the system architect needs three models or concepts for deriving an initial architecture: First, the architect needs a model describing the properties of the system to build; it will be used for the synthesis of an architecture concept. Moreover he needs a model to determine relevant system properties (analysis) and a model that contains guidelines for the evaluation of these properties (evaluation).

Synthesis & Information Model. Before starting the Rapid Architecting process, the initial input information has to be modeled. The resulting Information Model needs to contain the elements from which the architecture is synthesized. Furthermore, this model has to be able to represent all aspects that are subject to the evaluation (possibly after a transformation in the synthesis step). In case of a functional system architecture, the system "elements" are functions the system is supposed to have. During the whole optimization process the Information Model will be the basis for modeling different alternatives during the architecting process: Synthesis allows to generate alternative system architecture concepts based on the Information Model.

This procedure of generating different Solution Concepts is based on the systems engineering principle of considering alternative solutions.

> **Consideration of Alternatives.** A basic activity in a systematic design approach is to compare alternative solutions. The goal of this activity is to determine (all) possible alternatives, from which then the best one can be selected.
>
> **SE Principle 2: "Consideration of Alternatives"**

Analysis & Analysis Model. In analysis, properties of the system – as developed so far – have to be determined. For measuring the properties of a system, a set of metrics is necessary. Typical analysis metrics are performance or cost measures, either based on a technical or financial Information Model.

In Rapid Architecting, our goal is to optimize architectural fitness for purpose. This relates to the system's quality over its whole lifecycle. Accordingly, our metrics have to be measures of system quality as related to the whole life cycle.

This metrics set maps properties we can analyze in the Information Model to an analysis procedure, therefore we call it the Analysis Model. This metrics set is directly applied to the Information Model which has been enriched with information from the synthesis step. Its application provides quantified properties of the system model synthesized before. These quantified properties alone usually do not allow to rank several architecture concepts, but they provide the basic information for the evaluation of the system.

Evaluation & Evaluation Model. The Evaluation Model contains the means needed to make use of the analysis. The results of the metrics applied to the Information Model have to be processed in a meaningful way to provide a basis for decisions. E.g., when comparing cars, their cost, power and design have to be combined by an evaluation procedure so that these orthogonal properties aid the decision which car to buy.

The Evaluation Model captures the value system (e.g. relative priorities) of the decision maker as it relates the decision problem of selecting one alternative concept as the best one. It can be, for example, a relative weighting of the properties that were measured in the analysis step, resulting in a linear objective function. If we think of the Rapid Architecture process as an optimization, the evaluation step computes the value of such an objective function that has to be maximized or minimized.

Decision. The results of the evaluation step are the basis for rejection or acceptance of an alternative architecture concept provided by system synthesis. In case an architecture concept is considered to not yet be of sufficient quality, synthesis generates a new architecture, e.g. based on the rejected ones and on principles for optimizing architectures.

Underlying Principles. The models introduced here reflect other basic systems engineering principles:

Instead of simply realizing a system architecture that seems to be appropriate, first the relevant information is modeled (Principle "Modeling of the System"), second an analysis method is identified that covers the relevant aspects and then, third, a procedure for establishing comparability between alternative system configurations is selected (Principle "Comparability").

> **Modeling of the System.** A basic activity during measurement of system properties is to create a model that represents the aspects to be measured. Therefore a method evaluating an architecture needs such a model. As a consequence of the principles of User Centricity and of Technology Independence, this cannot be a technical model but must be a model from the customer's viewpoint. (Confer to SE Principles 5 and 6.)
>
> **SE Principle 3: "Modeling of the System"**

> **Comparability.** Selecting the best alternative suggests the existence of goals for the optimization process and the ability to measure to which extent these goals are achieved. In general, more than one system property has to be assessed to measure the required system qualities. Subsequently, a mechanism to realize comparability is required for the selection of alternative concepts.
>
> **SE Principle 4: "Comparability"**

The following sections describe an instance of this general Rapid Architecting approach. Both, the process and the models are discussed in more detail.

A RAPID ARCHITECTING METHOD

The process specified has been applied using the method QuESt (**Qu**ality **E**valuation and **S**ynthesis of **St**ructures), (Harzenetter, 2000). This section will explain the steps of the Rapid Architecting process as carried out using the method QuESt.

We claim that especially the Rapid Architecting process has to be anchored rather in (customer and other stakeholder) requirements than in technical considerations. This allows a solution independent architecture generation and drives the architecture process towards a good architecture from the customers' and the stakeholders' point of view. Again, these assumptions are derived from basic systems engineering principles:

User Centricity. User centric development is an essential factor for product success. Early involvement of customers and other stakeholders ensures that the product meets the purpose it has been designed for (Standish Group, 1999). Hence the system architecture as well should reflect the customers' and stakeholders' viewpoint.

SE Principle 5: "User Centricity"

Technology Independence. According to the principle of user centric development, the system architecture should be designed according to the users demands, and should not be driven by technical considerations.

This principle is only partially realizable, especially for the design of hardware systems, but nevertheless it should be given proper consideration.

SE Principle 6: "Technology Independence"

The method QuESt aims to assess and to optimise quality aspects of an early functional structuring of the product based on the information available at that point in development. The application of the method will provide a good candidate for a product architecture in the early phases of product development and can therefore help shorten the iterations necessary for the definition of a product architecture, (Harzenetter, 2000). The goal of the method is to provide an architecture that realizes the functionalities required by the customers and that meets the non functional requirements at the same time.

Figure 2 shows the products of each step in the Rapid Architecting process applied to QuESt. The next sections describe the models used within QuESt.

The Problem Structure. The Information Model specified in the previous section is realized by the Problem Structure in the method QuESt. It models the information about the design problem that is available for determining the system architecture. It is based on the customer and other stakeholder requirements. Since these requirements are (i.e. should be) solution independent the architect has no valuable information about implementation possibilities for the system architecture. But the architect knows about the intended usage of the system and the purpose for the system. Furthermore, the operational environment of the system is known, e.g. by means of use cases.

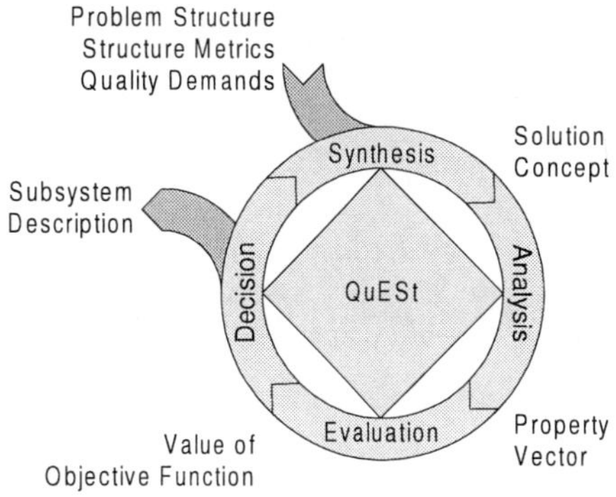

Figure 2: The Process within QuESt

According to (INCOSE, 1998) "A system is an integrated set of elements to accomplish a defined objective". Therefore the Information Model, describing the system to be built, has to comprise a notion of the purpose of the system, the elements of the system that will be part of the architecture, and some model of the operational environment that will enable these elements to realize the purpose of the system.

The notion of an operational environment is necessary for describing objectives: Using a system in an operational environment it has not been designed for often results in accomplishing a different objective. For example, a screw driver is designed for fastening one object to another one using screws. In case the screw driver is used for opening a pail of paint, none of the elements of the intended operational scenario are available, consequently another purpose is realized.

The model used in QuESt therefore comprises three categories of information, (Harzenetter 1999), comp. Fig. 3:

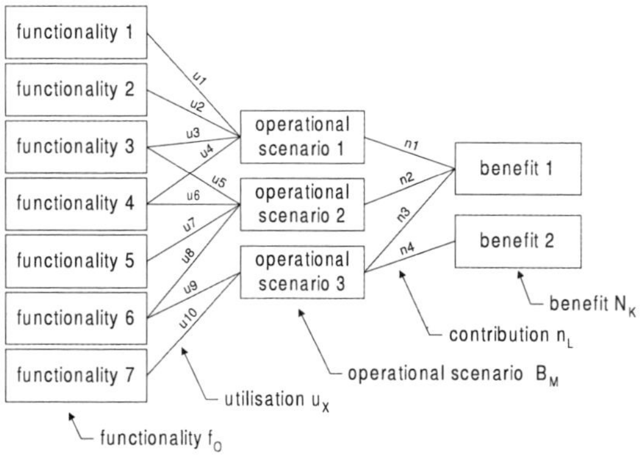

Figure 3: The Problem Structure

The functional requirements are modeled as "functionalities". They describe the behavior the system is expected to realize. The situations in which the system uses these functionalities are modeled by the "operational scenarios" which are comparable to use cases. The "benefits" model the objective the system has to accomplish. The realization of the benefits results from the use of the product in the operational scenarios

The "Problem Structure" embodies a user or customer centric view of the system functionality. Thus, the metrics that will be applied to this model by the Analysis Model will evaluate this system view. Subsequently, the architecture of the system will be evaluated from the customers' viewpoint, realizing the systems engineering principle of a user centric system development, (Fricke, 1999).

One of the first activities in establishing such an Information Model is to define system boundaries:

Definition of System Boundaries. When starting to model a system, first the boundaries have to be clarified. In case of the Information Model proposed, this incorporates not only the functional boundaries, but the operational boundaries as well (How is the system supposed to be used?) and the boundaries of purpose (Which benefits shall be realized?).

SE Principle 7: "Definition of System Boundaries"

Synthesis will use this Information Model to generate system architecture concepts which are allocations of the functional requirements onto a system architecture.

Architecture Synthesis. The first step in optimizing a system architecture concept is to create a first "Solution Concept". This Solution Concept will then be compared to a second one generated in another synthesis step, allowing to select the better concept.

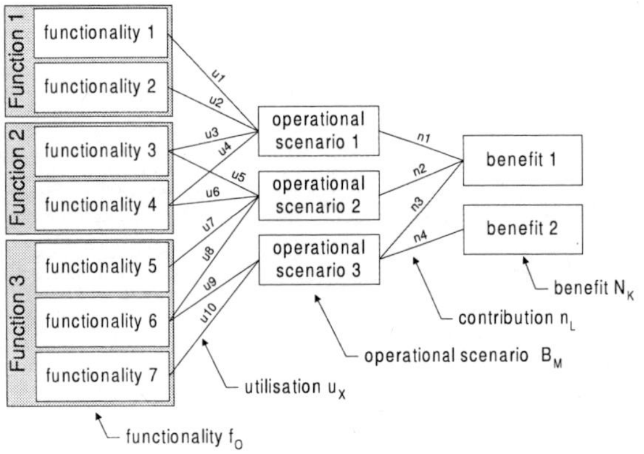

Figure 4: Solution Concept

Basically, a Solution Concept represents one possible functional decomposition of the design problem specified. It consists of the allocation of the functionalities to "functions", comp. Fig. 4. Each of the functions represents a subsystem of the design problem at hand. The functional subsystems are specified by the functionalities within the subsystem.

This mechanism allows to automatically generate possible functional decompositions and to manipulate them.

The task of architecture synthesis is to derive new architectures for the optimization process. The architectures may be determined more or less randomly for a mathematical optimization to be proposed later in this paper, or using heuristics, patterns, or design guidelines that apply to the problem domain.

Depending on the configuration chosen, the Solution Concepts generated have different properties, which are now subject to an analysis.

Analysis & The Analysis Model. The method QuESt proposed here suggests that there are a number of structural properties of system architectures that support quality aspects. The goal of the method is to define an architecture that supports a set of quality aspects , and where these aspects depend on the product's lifecycle.

The structural properties of an architecture are measured by a set of metrics that are applied to each Solution Concept derived. This measurement uses the information model. We use a set of metrics that allows to calculate values for structural architecture properties based on the Solution Concept (more details on this set of metrics can be found in (Harzenetter et al., 1999)). Structural properties are, for example, redundancy, coupling and cohesion, complexity, modularity, fault-tolerance and efficiency. The findings of this analysis constitute a vector containing the metrics results.

Although the realization of the quality aspects mentioned above does not depend on these structural properties alone, the structure of a system supports the ability of a system to meet such properties. For example, redundant structures enhance the reliability of a system. But if there are shortcomings in the implementation of the redundant structures, obviously the system still is not reliable.

For evaluating these architectures, an Evaluation Model has to be defined that processes the analysis results.

Evaluation & The Evaluation Model. The Evaluation Model is used to determine whether the system architecture is appropriate fulfills all requirements placed on it during the full lifecycle.

The functional requirements, mostly resulting from the use of the system during the usage stage of the system lifecycle, will be realized by the architecture concept defined during system synthesis. The requirements resulting from other stages of the system lifecycle mostly address the quality aspects of the system, concerning specific operations on the system during these stages, see Table 1 ('+' indicates a strong, 'o' a medium and '-' a weak relationship).

Quality Aspect	System Lifecycle					
	Concept Stage	Product Dev.	Manufacturing	Customer Supp.	Usage	Disposal
Usability					+	
Modifiability		+	-	o		-
Maintainability			-	+		-
Testability	o	+	o	+		
Portability				+	o	
Integrity					o	
Ease of Creation	+	+				
Performance					+	
Reusability	+	+				+
Reliability				+	+	

Table 1: Quality Demands in the System Lifecycle

These aspects of system development are not subject to the functionality specified by the customer but are properties that are inherent to the architecture of the system, compare for example (Alexander, 1968), (Boehm, 1978), (Huff, 1979), (Kazmann, 1994) or (McCall, 1994).

For example, thc following are important aspects: during system development it is ease of creation and modifiability, during maintenance it is maintainability, during usage it is reliability, performance and usability.

The Evaluation Model assesses the architecture of the system according to these aspects and judges the suitability of the architecture for the intended system lifecycle: In a first step the quality aspects are weighted among each other. Then, using the interdependencies between the structural properties measured by the Analysis Model and the weighted quality aspects, a weighting of the structural properties is derived. These interdependencies are summarized in Table 2.

Since for each structural property we have a metric, this results in weighted metrics. The sum of these weighted metrics constitutes an objective function, i.e. our evaluation model.

The evaluation of the Solution Concept is done by applying the objective function to the analysis results. The result is the degree of fitness for the system in terms of the quality demands of the system lifecycle. Architectures are now comparable in terms of their degree of fitness. Optimization is done by optimizing the degree of fitness.

The evaluation method used within QuESt realizes the systems engineering principle of incorporating systems lifecycle aspects into system development.

Product Lifecycle. An important aspect for measuring the suitability of an architecture of a system is the consideration of the product lifecycle. The stakeholders of the lifecycle processes have different demands regarding the system properties, and these demands are orthogonal to the functional user requirements. A system architecture must meet both, functional and quality requirements.

SE Principle 8: "Incorporating System Lifecycle Aspects"

Decision. For each cycle of the optimization of the system, the decision has to be taken whether the architecture should be optimized further. The stopping criteria for this optimization are strongly dependent on the underlying algorithm.

We have chosen a simulated annealing algorithm to

Strctural properties (measured by metrics)	*Quality aspects*									
	Usability	Modifiability	Maintainability	Testability	Portability	Integrity	Ease of Creation	Performance	Reusability	Reliability
Complexity										
Complexity of a benefit	min.	min.	-	-	-	-	min.	-	-	-
Complexity of an operation scenario	min.	min.	min.	min.	-	-	min.	min.	-	-
Modularity										
Modularity of a benefit	-	max.	-	-	-	max(x)	max.	-	-	-
Modularity of an operation scenario	-	max.	max.	max.	-	max(x)	max.	-	max.	-
Redundancy										
Function Redundancy	-	-	-	-	-	-	-	-	-	max.
Fault-Tolerance										
Function Fault-Tolerance	-	-	-	-	max(x)	max(x)	-	-	-	max.
Participation										
Function Participation	-	-	-	-	min(x)	min(x)	-	-	-	min.
Coupling and Cohesion										
Cohesion	-	max.	max.	max.	-	-	max.	-	max.	-
Coupling	-	min.	min.	min.	-	-	min.	-	min.	-
Efficiency										
Function Efficiency	-	-	-	-	-	-	-	max	-	-

x ... with respect to external resources

Table 2: Analysis metrics and aspects of quality, (Harzenetter 1999)

automatically manipulate the architecture, analyze and evaluate it. The stopping criterion for this stochastic optimization algorithm is a user defined number of consecutive non-improving perturbations of the architecture. The optimization might as well be based on another optimization algorithm that is capable of dealing with such a problem, e.g. a genetic algorithm or a neural net.

The mathematical part of this method can also be replaced by a team process. The team members would probably be able to quickly identify useful architectural alternatives. A team based analysis and evaluation of the architecture might take more detailed aspects into account. But the optimization of the architecture would require more effort, resulting in a slower process.

Subsystem Definition. The chosen Solution Concept finally is the basis for the derivation of the Subsystem Description. It contains the architecture blocks identified by the architecture concept. The functionalities in an architecture block describe the function provided by the block. Furthermore, the interfaces between the architecture blocks may be determined based on the Solution Concept: In case a functionality requires an external input into the system, there is an external interface of the subsystem this functionality has been allocated to. In case two of the functions are used by the same operational scenario, there is a potential interface – which at least triggers a sequential or parallel activation of the subsystem, but might be more complicated as well, e.g. a communication interface.

Figure 5 shows a graphical representation of such a Subsystem Description.

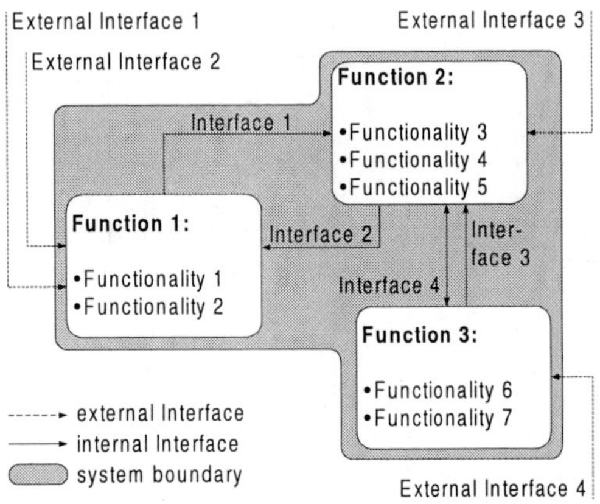

Figure 5: Subsystem Description

Sensitivity Analysis. In defining the Information Model and the objective function of the Evaluation Model, weightings have to be assigned to relationships and to quality factors. Such weightings are, by nature, somewhat imprecise. If we want to nevertheless get trustworthy results from the Rapid Architecting process, we need to determine to what degree its results depend on the margins of imprecision.

Therefore, to complement the Rapid Architecting approach, we have implemented a sensitivity analysis. The result of our sensitivity analysis is a system representation that allows to identify functions that are robust against these uncertainties. If they are not robust, the representation allows to identify which alternative architectures are more likely to be robust and of similar quality.

Application. This method has been applied to a large scale design problem at the Siemens Medical Group. An Information Model containing about 100 functionalities has been derived out of approx. 750 customer requirements. We determined a functional system architecture comprising 32 architectural blocks and their interfaces. The results helped to translate the non-technical customer requirements into a first architecture specification. This specification was subject to further refinement due to considerations that were yet considered. The Rapid Architecting approach provided an effective way to achieve such a preliminary functional structuring, which is still inherent in the current architecture.

FURTHER WORK

Further work in this area will be occupied with the definition of system architectures for product lines. A process and a method will be identified to distinguish architectural elements that belong to the basic system of the product family and those to be implemented only in some or one system that is part of the product family. The goal is to quickly identify architecture relevant information and use it to determine such architectures.

CONCLUSIONS

The proposed Rapid Architecting process is a generic approach to the definition of system architectures. Based on systems engineering principles, a method has been described to derive architectural prototypes based on user and other stakeholder requirements. The architectural prototypes will help to quickly identify a realizable system architecture that complies to the requirements.

Furthermore, the underlying principles of this method are supposed to support the development of similar methods and an extension of this method, providing a methodological framework for architectural evaluation and optimization in early phases of system development. (Most of these principles are taken from (Daenzer, Huber, 1994) and (Negele, 1999).) Every method evaluating and optimizing system architectures should incorporate these aspects as far as possible.

REFERENCES

Alexander, Christopher, *Notes on the Synthesis of Form*, Harvard University Press, Cambridge, MA, 4th printing 1968

Boehm, B.W., et al., *Characteristics of Software Quality*, North Holland Publishing Company, Amsterdam, 1978

Daenzer, W.F., Huber, F. (ed.) *"Systems Engineering, Methodik und Praxis"*, Verlag Industrielle Organisation, Zürich, 1994

Fricke, E., Gebhard, B., Negele, H., Igenbergs, E., 1997, No Innovation Process Without Changes, But ..., in: *Proceedings of the 7th International Conference of INCOSE*, Los Angeles, 1997

Fricke, Ernst, Der Änderungsprozess als Grundlage einer nutzerzentrierten Systementwicklung, PhD-Thesis, Fachgebiet Raumfahrttechnik, Technische Universität München, 1999.

Harzenetter, Florian, "Synthese von Systemstrukturen auf Basis funktionaler Anforderungen und Wiederverwendungstechniken", Ph.D. thesis in preparation, Techn. Universität München, 2000

Harzenetter, F., Thomé, B., Igenbergs, E., "A Framework For Early Evaluation of Functional Product Structures", *Proceedings of the 9th International Conference of INCOSE*, Brighton, 1999

Huff, S. L., Madnick, S. E., "A Systematic Methodology for Designing the Architecture of Complex Software Systems", Sloan School of Management, Massachusetts Institute of Technology, Cambridge, MA, September 1979

IEEE, "IEEE Standard for Application and Management of the Systems Engineering Process", IEEE-Std. 1220-1998, in: *IEEE Standards Software Engineering, Volume 1, Customer and terminology standards* IEEE, 1999

INCOSE, 1998, "Systems Engineering Handbook – A "HOW TO" Guide For All Engineers", Release 1.0, January, 1998

Kazman, R., Bass, L., "Toward deriving Software Architectures From Quality Attributes", 1994, `http://www.cgl.uwaterloo.ca/rnkazman/SE-Papers.html`, 06-18-98

Kruchten, Phillipe, "Architectural Blueprints – The 4+1 View Model of Software Architecture", *IEEE Software*, 12 (6), pp. 42 – 50, November 1995

McCall, James A., "Quality Factors", in: Marciniak, John J. (ed.), *Encyclopedia of Software Engineering*, Mc-Graw-Hill, pp. 958-969, 1994

Negele, H., "Systemtechnische Methodik zur ganzheitlichen Modellierung am Beispiel der integrierten Produktentwicklung", PhD-Thesis, Fachgebiet Raumfahrttechnik, Technische Universität München, 1999

Standish Group, "The CHAOS Report", `http://www.standishgroup.com/chaos.html`, 30.07.1999

BIOGRAPHIES

Florian Harzenetter studied mechanical engineering with special focus on design at the Technical University of Munich and received his master's degree in 1997. In May 1997 he started to work on his Ph.D. thesis at the Fachgebiet Raumfahrttechnik (Institute of Astronautics) under scholarship of Siemens AG. He is a founding member of the German Chapter of INCOSE. Recently he has joined Siemens Corporate Technology.
Email: Florian.Harzenetter@mchp.siemens.de

Bernhard Thomé is Project Manager in the Department Systems Engineering of Siemens Corporate Technology. He is conducting research in the fields of requirements engineering, decision support, and process modeling and improvement. He is a member of the IEEE Technical Committee ECBS (Engineering of Computer-Based Systems) and served as Program Chair for the IEEE international conference ECBS'96. Furthermore, he is a member of INCOSE and served as the founding President of the German Chapter of INCOSE.

Eduard Igenbergs is professor of Astronautics and director of the Fachgebiet Raumfahrttechnik (Institute of Astronautics) at the Technische Universität München. He has a Ph.D. and a master degree in mechanical engineering. He had experiments for the investigation of cosmic dust and space debris in earth and lunar orbit, presently on the way to and orbit around Mars. His systems engineering activities started around 1980, presently he leads courses in basic and applied systems engineering at the Technische Universität München. The team at his institute has various industrial contracts with aerospace and other industrial companies.

Systems Engineering Meta-Tools for Complex Product Development

Herbert Negele
BMW Group
80788 München, Germany
Herbert.Negele@bmw.de

Stefan Wenzel
Institute of Astronautics
Technische Universität München
Boltzmannstr. 15, 85748 Garching
S.Wenzel@lrt.mw.tum.de

Abstract. In order to successfully deal with increasingly complex product development systems, adequate methods can help to structure and classify the numerous relevant aspects in a clear, transparent manner. In this paper, several generic methods for structuring these aspects are presented which provide different useful perspectives. Since the methods presented try to give an integrative, comprehensive grasp of complex product development systems, they are proposed as meta-tools for systems engineering.

INTRODUCTION

Our world is becoming more and more complex in almost every aspect. This particularly holds true for modern product development systems. Adequate processes, methods and tools can help us significantly in coping with these kind of systems. One very important aspect in dealing with large, strongly interrelated systems is to find the right structures, classifications and/or patterns that help to bring order to a seemingly chaotic and intransparent situation. As said by Egon Friedell: "A simple consideration shows that all classifications humans ever made are arbitrary, artificial and wrong. However, a equally simple consideration also shows that these classifications are useful and indispensable and above all inevitable, since they originate from an innate tendency of our thinking (translated from German)."

So, even if it's very difficult or impossible to come up with *perfect* classifications and structures for situations, problems, and things we have to deal with, *good* classifications seem to be helpful, especially when it comes to solving complex problems, e.g., the new product development of an automobile or an airplane. Therefore, it is particularly important for systems engineering and project management – i.e., the functions acting on the systems/project level – to keep a clear overview of the aspects and contents of the product development system. Typically it's the task of systems engineers and project managers to find the right structures for their programs from different perspectives, such as system, business, process, product, organization, cost, time, etc. Useful structures and classifications can serve as systems engineering meta-tools providing the systems engineer with "mental hooks" he or she can use for any project to further understanding and transparency of the given problem situation(s). In order to get a comprehensive view of a product development system, different aspects have to be taken into account (e.g., customer and user needs, requirements and goals, products, processes, people, resources, organizations).

In this paper several systems engineering meta-tools are discussed that can be applied to classify and structure complex product development systems from different, complementary perspectives. Moreover, most of the tools presented are generic and proved to be useful for coping with various kinds of complex problem situations. The SE-metatools suggested and described in the following are:

- ZOPH Model – Systems view
- CE+ Model – Business view
- Cycle Model – Process views (1&2)
- House of IPD – Integrative view

STRUCTURING PRODUCT DEVELOPMENT SYSTEMS — SYSTEMS VIEW: THE ZOPH MODEL

ZOPH Structure Derivation. For evolving a comprehensive structure for product development systems from a systems perspective, first we have to answer: What information is relevant and has to be structured? Leaving aside information that is not necessary for the solution of our problem is crucial, thus enabling concentration on the essence and recognition of links and connections that otherwise would be beyond one's grasp.

Figure 1 shows a collection of different kinds of information that appear to be essential to get a comprehensive view or model of product development systems. Models always represent an abstraction of reality as we try to capture in the model information that is relevant to certain questions or problems we want to solve with the model's help. To avoid a confusing chaos of model elements and (inter)relationships, the so-called *ZOPH Model* structure was developed (Negele et al. 1997, Negele 1998). It provides the prerequisites for a structured arrangement and linking within a product development system model.

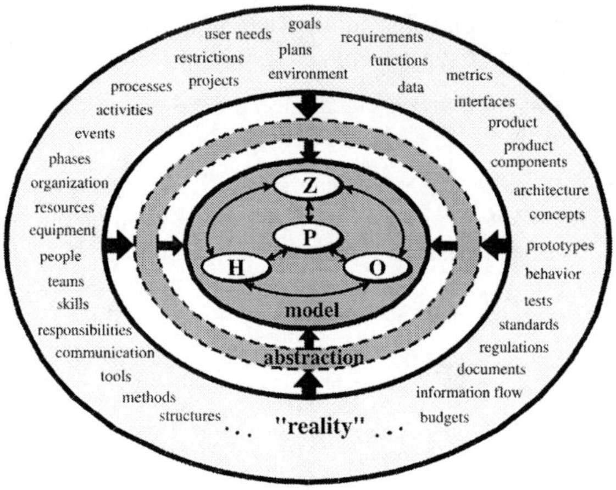

Figure 1. Model Derivation

Structure of the ZOPH Model. From a systems engineering point of view four different system types can be distinguished within the product development system (following Patzak, 1982). These types form the abbreviation "**ZOPH**", which is derived from the first characters of the German terms:

- development system (project system)
  - "**Z**ielsystem" (**goal system**),
  - "**O**bjektsystem" (**product system**),
  - "**P**rozeßsystem" (**process system**), and
  - "**H**andlungs(träger)system" (**agent system**)
- system environment.

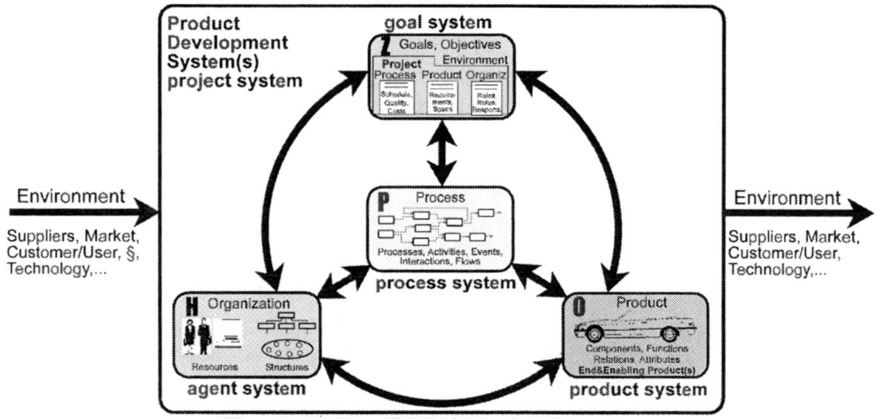

Figure 2. The ZOPH Model Structure

The model structures all the information relevant to the development system by using these four different system types (Figure 2). Influences across the system boundary also can be taken into consideration by modeling elements of the environment system(s) (e.g., suppliers, users, market, legal regulations, social and political environment). In the following, a short description of each ZOPH system type is given.

"Z" – Goal System. The goal system describes the desired outcome, and the conditions for its realization. This can include user/customer needs and expectations, requirements, specifications, plans and schedules, goals and objectives of the different stakeholders/individuals involved, in addition to the legal regulations, standards, constraints, ecological restrictions, etc. The goal system itself can be structured, for example, in goals concerning project, product, process, organization, and environment (fractal application of the ZOPH "pattern").

"O" – Product System. In the product system, the product to be developed is described with its components, functions, properties, (technical) structure, and all the elements/artefacts that are prerequisite for, object or result of the activities of the development system. Also, all the supporting elements and enabling products necessary for developing, producing, operating, or servicing the actual end product can be included.

"P" – Process System. The process system describes the processes, activities and events that have to be carried out in order to attain the objectives specified in the goal system. Also, the connections (e.g., temporal, logical, causal) and flows (e.g., information, material) between the process elements have to be considered here.

"H" – Agent System. The agent system describes the company's organization, its structures and resources that are carrying out all the tasks as agents. This includes all the individuals and organizational units (e.g., departments, teams, employees) as well as important resources such as installations, machinery, equipment or tools, methods, software, specific know-how, and others.

The arrows in Figure 2 illustrate the manifold interrelations between the elements of the ZOPH system types (e.g., which function or component contributes to a certain goal?; who is responsible for a certain process?).

The application of this structure to several industrial projects has shown that the use of the ZOPH Model as a *mental model* is of great benefit. It promotes a structure for systematically analysing a given problem or system. Urging the (systems) engineer to thoroughly think about the system, its boundary, its structure, its elements, and their interrelations supports a better grasp and handling of the problem. A computer-aided realization of the ZOPH Model additional benefits (Negele 1998).

STRUCTURING PRODUCT DEVELOPMENT SYSTEMS — BUSINESS VIEW: THE CE+ MODEL

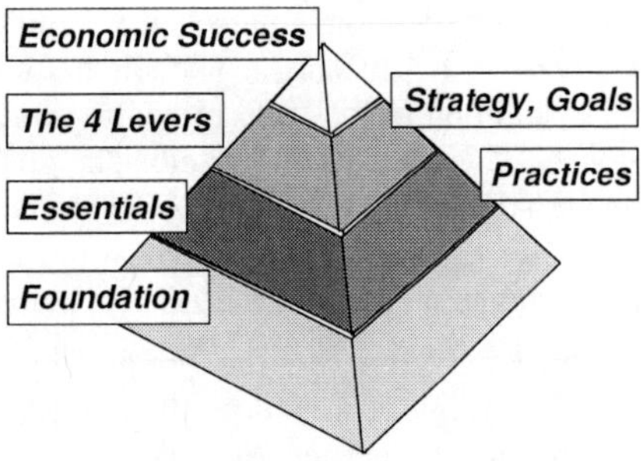

Figure 3. The CE+ Model

Another useful way to structure development systems is provided by the CE+ (Concurrent Engineering and more…) Model. Its purpose is to establish a perspective that focuses on business and organizational aspects (Wenzel et al. 1997).

The pyramid depicted in Figure 3 shows how the major levels/elements of the CE+ Model fit together:

- ***Economic Success*** is placed at the top of the pyramid as it constitutes the most important goal of an enterprise: "Survive and grow by being successful." In a long-term view a company not reaching this objective cannot exist.
- In order to achieve economic success the next level of the pyramid offers ***The Four Levers***: Quality and Cost to market, Effectiveness and Efficiency, Time to Market and Flexibility. The enterprise's ***strategy*** and ***goals*** have to be developed in a way that optimize these criteria for the given business situation.
- In order to engage the four levers, the next level contains both ***Essentials*** and selected ***Practices, Methods and Tools*** for a successful product development. Whereas the Essentials mainly supply an answer to "What to do?", the Practices, Methods and Tools describe "How to do it".
- The ***Foundation*** represents the lowest level of the pyramid and highlights those items that belong to the basis a successful company needs to build on. All tools and methods are just means used by human beings. These tools need a foundation based on trust and the company's culture in order to deal and develop its most flexible resource, the people.

Four Levers. Considering the market is the playing field where the judgment on a company's capability is passed (Tikart, 1994), competitiveness can be defined in four dimensions (Figure 4):

- *Quality and Cost to market:* Offering the customer a high value product or service with an appropriate price, which is the basis for calculating the target costs.
- *Effectivity and Efficiency:* Reducing the aggregated costs of the product or service offered by analyzing the processes over the life cycle, eliminating non value adding steps and determining points of synergism.
- *Time to market*: Speeding up the development cycle for an early market introduction.
- *Flexibility*: Developing flexibility for seizing new market opportunities. As the market is dynamic, a company needs to continuously aligning its processes, organization, people's skills, tools, etc. with the moving target.

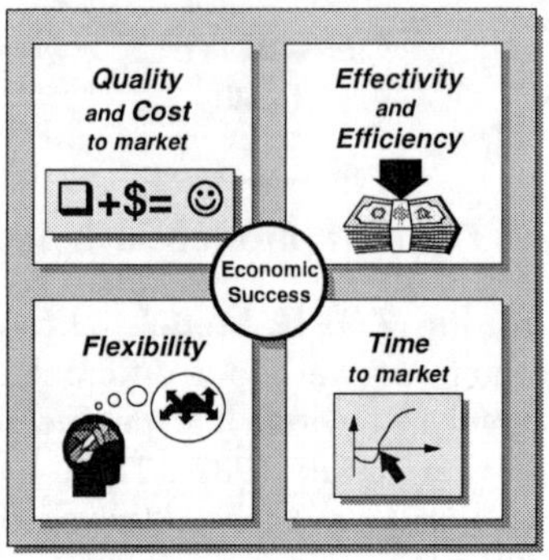

Figure 4. The Four Levers

Essentials for Successful Product Development. In order to reach economic success and to enable the Four Levers, a set of 17 **essentials** has been defined that describe basic success factors (**WHATs**) for new product development (Wenzel & Bauch 1996). The essentials are quite neutral and they should guide the user rather independently from the product, company or environment. The essentials are an "answer" to the goals and problems typically found in today's product development environments (Clark & Fujimoto 1991, Wheelright&Clark 1992, Clausing 1994, Negele & Fricke 1997).

STRUCTURING PRODUCT DEVELOPMENT SYSTEMS — PROCESS VIEW 1: 5 KEY DEVELOPMENT PROCESSES

In a product development system it's not just the product itself that has to be developed. Each new product (generation) is the result of a product development *process*, which is intertwined with the development of new and robust technologies and is conducted by a particular organization using specific tools and methods. It is also crucial to "develop" the adequate organization (e.g., right team or functional structures, roles) and resources (e.g., skills, methods, tools). These four aspects – product development, technology development, methods & tools, and organization – are usually embedded in the company's strategy and the specific project goals and requirements, which also have to be developed effectively (Figure 5). Compared to the ZOPH model (systems view: what are the relevant elements/aspects of a development system and how do they interact with each other and the system environment?) Figure 5 gives a more process-oriented view (what are the main development processes?). Still, the ZOPH structure can easily be mapped to the five key processes (the product is symbolized by the cube in the center of Figure 5, the goal system is represented by the surrounding circle, the process system by the horizontal arrows, the agent system by the vertical arrows).

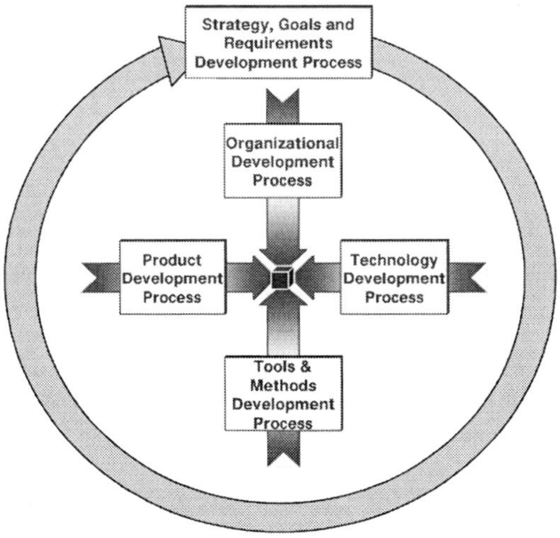

Figure 5. Five key development processes

STRUCTURING PRODUCT DEVELOPMENT PROCESSES – PROCESS VIEW 2: THE CYCLE MODEL

In order to structure the product development process, a wide variety of system development models are in use today. The ones most frequently used are, for example:

- Waterfall Model,
- Prototyping Model,
- Spiral Model,
- All-At-Once Models, and the
- "Vee"-Lifecycle Development Model.

But these system development lifecycle models are unable to consistently develop complex, large scale systems that meet time, budget, and technical constraints imposed by either the end-user or the market place (Scotti et al, 1996). They are also very often characterized by a framework of sequential process steps instead of highly interconnected activities. The *Product Development Cycle Model* (PDCM) brings the customer into the loop and provides a generic approach for all development systems, still considering the manifold interactions.

The Generic PDCM – Product Development Cycle Model. The Cycle Model for development processes consists of six distinguishable subcycles (Figures 6&7): The Core Cycle, the Verification Cycle(s), the Technology/(external) Resources Development Cycle, the Controlling Cycle, the Strategic Check Cycle and the Supply Chain Cycle.

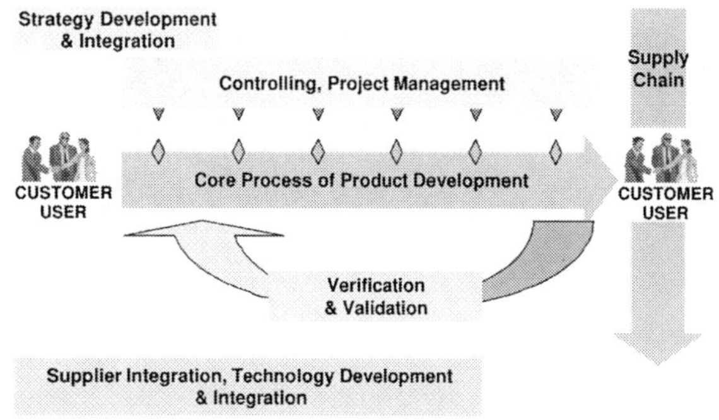

Figure 6: Cycle Model (Overview)

The Cycle-Model (Figure 7) conveys a neutral depiction of a product development process. The steps separating the processes only describe activities and tasks. Thus, they are independent from organizational structures. The arrows (relations) between the activities show the logical connections and sequences of the tasks. In order to avoid reduced insight and prejudged interdependencies it is important to detach at first from familiar organizational structures such as Marketing or Engineering departments. For example, the connections of some processes may appear as sequential work-flow from department to department, but actually the cycles show the logical arrangement of activities that are alternating iteratively between preliminary and detailed planning or execution.

The Core Cycle ① The Core Cycle shows the process of realizing market opportunities. It is a closed cycle from the customer to the customer. It starts with the determination of customer expectations and needs. This can be done by market research, customer surveys, warranty claims, great ideas of engineers, new technologies, and so on.

The definition of a market opportunity is an iterative process. Profitability and feasibility have to be assessed and evaluated step by step. Benefits, efforts, and risks have to be weighed up and the capabilities have to be compared with the expectations defined. The specification (assessment) of a market opportunity concerns product, business, and project issues. A rough product definition, done in early stages, considers market requirements, customer expectations, competitive products and environmental requirements. The definition of the business issues takes into account the benefits, efforts, and risks of realizing the opportunity. The project definition considers time aspects and resource requirements during the execution of the project. All these aspects result in a functional structure of the product and system/product specifications.

Based on the functional structure and the specifications, design solutions are generated. Product and component design are the basis for the development of the production processes.

After the introduction of a new product and

manufacturing process into the current supply chain, the organization starts with (ongoing) realization (manufacturing, assembly, and testing). The number of units produced depends on forecasts, programs and customer order entry. Distribution channels and after-sales services have to be developed and be in place with the product launch. The products are shipped to the customers and revenues flow back into the company. The core cycle is closed.

Verification Cycles ② The purpose of test or verification cycles is the confirmation of anticipated product performance and reduction of uncertainty. Verification cycles start already with the day-to-day communication of ideas and concepts, and continue with calculations, simulations of product characteristics and sample design/creation. The Cycle Model illustrates this through different cycles with varying diameters. As the product matures, the verification cycle expands to incorporate more of the development process. Thus, the verification (validation) is getting closer to the customer.

Technology Development and External Knowledge Integration ③ New technologies, capabilities, and production know how now have to be developed either by internal resources (technology carrier) or be sourced from external suppliers (outsourcing). The proportion of internal technology development or the involvement of external knowledge depends on strategic aspects, the degree of innovation, core competencies, and other company aspects. The external resources have to be coordinated and evaluated early enough to ensure adequate results in terms of time, cost and quality. Materials management has to be established and supplied products have to be integrated into the logistics and order processes.

Controlling Cycle④ The controlling cycle starts after the market opportunity is defined under the aspects of business (e.g., profitability and costs), product (e.g., feasibility) and project (e.g., effort and resources) issues. These definitions are then documented in "control" documents, which follow the core cycle around. Changes in product, project, or market during the core process have to be updated and visualized within the control documents. The controlling cycle provides cost, resource, quality, and time visibility during the whole project in correspondence with the objectives defined.

Strategic Check Cycle ⑤ Development projects should fit into the corporate strategy and project portfolio. Typically projects are reviewed and approved by a higher controlling board. Such a controlling board usually consists of senior management and functional leaders. The initial approval is based on a profitability and risk check. During the development process, strategic checks are done at defined checkpoints (milestones) or just when unforeseen problems occur that jeopardize the project's success.

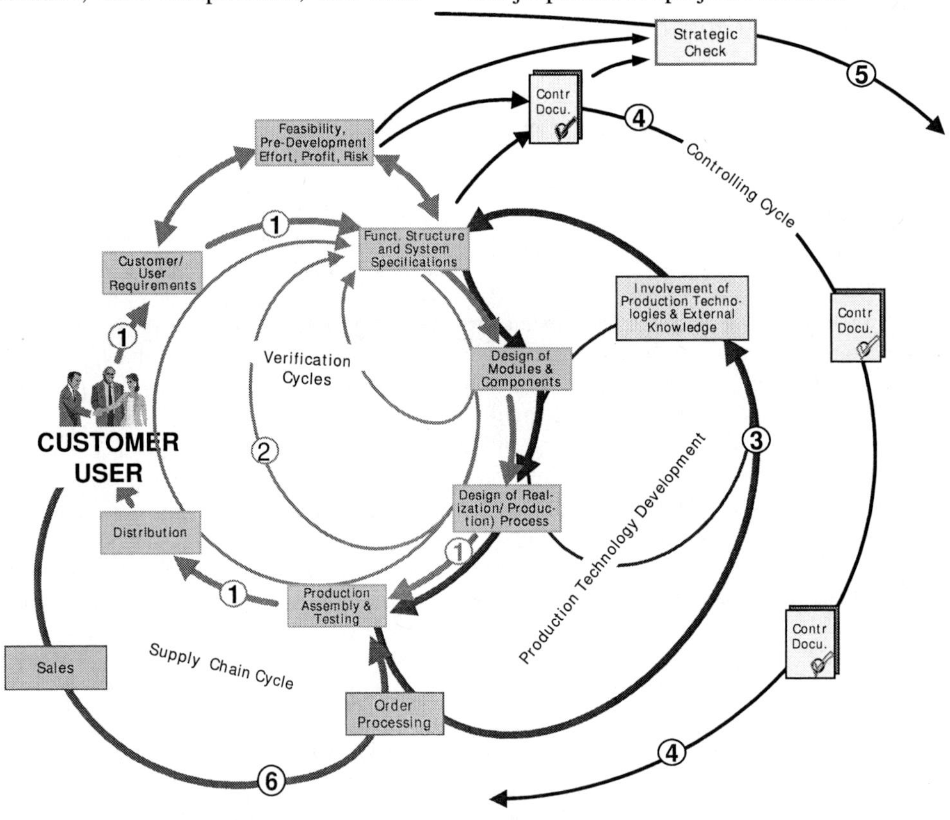

Figure 7. The Product Development Cycle Model

The Supply Chain Cycle ⑥ Customer orders enter the supply chain on a continuous basis. "Order processing" manages the current business, but has also to be set up for the new products. Similar is the situation in manufacturing and assembly where new processes have to be implemented, although the ongoing business must continue to be processed. Distribution and sales have to adjust the current channels, while new (after) sales services have to be set up and trained for a new product. The interfaces and synchronization between "off-line" product development and "on-line" (current) order processing are crucial issues within development systems.

STRUCTURING PRODUCT DEVELOPMENT SYSTEMS — INTEGRATIVE VIEW: THE HOUSE OF IPD

The *House of IPD* (Integrated Product Development) was developed as a methodical approach to structure the interdependencies and relations between goals, problems, essentials, methods, and tools for the specific use in practice (Wenzel et al. 1997, Negele et al. 1998). Therefore, it provides an integrative view on product development systems, bringing together and interlinking several aspects of such systems in one method. Actually, the House of IPD structures the two medium levels of the CE+ Model (cp. Figure 3) into a workable WHY-WHAT-HOW logic.

In analogy to the House of Quality (Hauser & Clausing 1988), a matrix is used to visualize how and to what extent practices, methods, and tools (HOWs) contribute to the realization of certain essentials (WHATs) and which essentials are related to certain goals or problems (WHYs). Figure 8 provides an impression of how this matrix looks in principle and gives examples for possible relations. In the matrix, HOWs are connected with WHATs by a small spanner symbol, whereas WHYs and WHATs are interrelated with dots.

Depending on industry or line of business, adequate essentials or processes can be defined and assigned a relative importance for the realization of the goals set, or the elimination of given problems. After the definition of the most important essentials, proactive or corrective action can be initiated by the implementation of selected practices. These practices enable the essentials and should be "hands-on" methods or tools for the use in day-to-day development work. Also, the specific environment in which practices are to be implemented and the associated constraints have to be regarded (e.g., tools already used, available resources, software and hardware issues, skills of concerned people).

In order to assess and visualize how essentials/practices affect another (positive/negative, high–medium–low), they should also be related among themselves. This aspect is exemplarily shown in the roof of the house and in the triangle on the left. In a similar way this can be done for problems (problem net), goals (goal net), or problems versus goals in the "basement". It is important to carry out these steps, as the combination of certain essentials or practices can promote or sometimes hinder the impact expected. Thus, a specific mix of the "right" practices can be put together for each project. In order to improve the development system continuously, its performance can be measured along with the fulfillment of the most important essentials (Negele et al. 1997). This benchmark is placed on the right side of the house.

WHYs – Problems and Goals. Several field studies revealed many typical problems that hinder an effective and efficient transformation of ideas into successful products (Negele & Fricke 1997). On the other hand, since each gap indicates potential improvement, the problems at the same time are fields or opportunities for corrective action in order to accomplish projects faster, better, and cheaper.

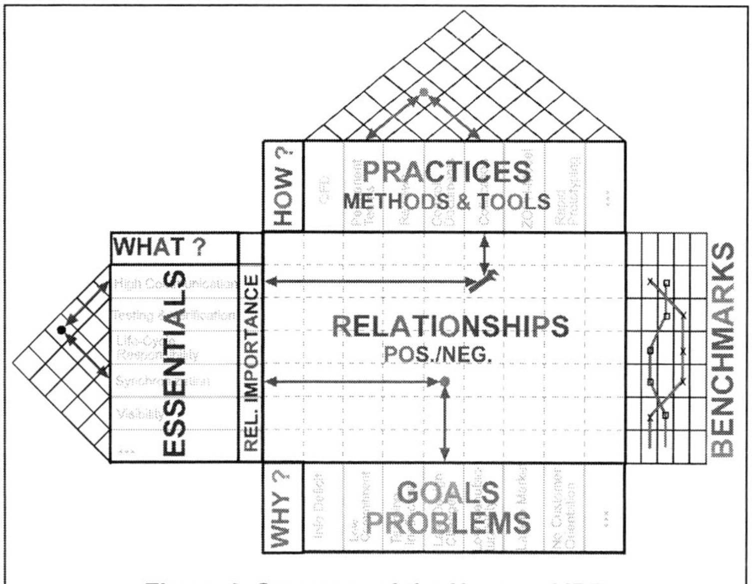

Figure 8. Structure of the House of IPD

WHATs – Essentials for Successful Product Development. With the realization of the essentials, the crucial aspects of Integrated Product Development are taken into account. The essentials are listed below. A short description of each essential is given in Wenzel et al. (1997) or Negele et al. (1997):

- **High Communication Density**
- **Life Cycle Responsibility**
- **2D-Integration (organization: horizontal and vertical)**
- **Synchronization**

- **Clear Goals, Rules and Roles**
- **Testing & Verification**
- **Big Loops: "Lessons learned"**
- **Early and Fast Check of Profitability and Risk**
- **Cost, Time and Resource Visibility**
- **Metrics in the Loop**
- **Balancing Technology and Product Development**
- **Clear Supplier and Partner Strategy**
- **Robust Design and Customization**
- **Customer Focus and Stakeholder Integration**
- **Integration of MIT (methods, information, tools)**
- **Education and Training**
- **Capable Systems Engineering Environment**

The essentials listed above are one attempt to describe the WHATs for successful product development. But, the generic structure of the House of IPD can be applied to varying fields, such as business processes other than product development, like production or maintenance, and at different levels, including company-level, project-level, or subproject-level. With adjusted essentials (processes), the expansible framework also can be employed for the "big picture" Systems Engineering or Project Management ("House of SE" or "House of PM") as well as for a more focused view of specific aspects, e.g. Change Management. For a "House of SE", the 19 different focus areas of the Systems Engineering Capability Model SECM (EIA/IS 731-1 SECM) could be used as WHATs, as an example.

HOWs – Practices, Methods and Tools for Successful Product Development. Practices and methods describe **HOW** we should do what we are doing, and tools are instruments (often, but not necessarily, computer-based) that should help us to accomplish the HOWs faster, better, and cheaper.

The following extract of a collection of more than 50 methods and (best) practices (Wenzel & Bauch 1996) show the variety of possible solutions. Depending on the specific problems, constraints, goals, essentials, processes, and environment, the right mix of these (and other) methods (and supporting tools) has to be chosen und implemented.

- Agreeable Environment
- Common Data Base
- Computer Aided "X" (CAX)
- Collocation (physical or virtual)
- Customer-Satisfaction-Index
- Design for "X" (DFX)
- Failure Mode and Effects Analysis
- Metrics
- Multi-Project Resource Plan
- Process Modeling and Simulation
- Product Value matrix
- Quality Function Deployment
- Rapid Prototyping
- Taguchi Methods
- Target Costing
- ZOPH Model

EXAMPLE FOR PRACTICAL APPLICATION

Due to the limited space, the practical application of the presented SE meta-tools can only be illustrated partly and by means of a simplified example. An automotive company starts an initiative to improve the management of product data within new product development. One project within this product data management (PDM) effort is to develop a consistent PDM data model.

As an example, we want to show the application of process view 1 (five key develoment processes) to this problem (Figure 9). This meta-tool helps to structure the main development activities that have to be carried out within the project. First, requirements and goals have to be elicited and aligned with the overall PDM strategy. An adequate organization (e.g., one or several teams) with the right persons has to be set up; roles, rules and interfaces to other projects have to be defined; and resources have to planned and allocated. The team members have to agree on the vocabulary, methods and tools they want to use to create the data model. When analysing the present processes, data objects and tools, the need for a more comprehensive process description gets clear. Therefore, an adequate method and tool for process modeling has to be developed and agreed upon. Perhaps a new team has to be established that will take care of the process model, and so on.

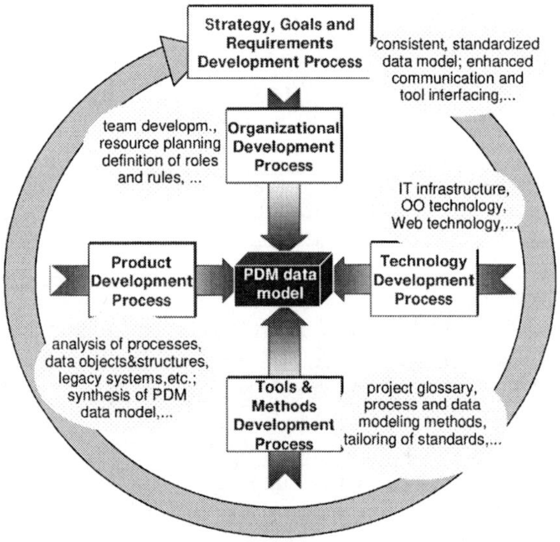

Figure 9. Application of the 5 key development processes

Let's show how the other SE meta-tools described in this paper can be applied to the example project: The ZOPH model could be used to *structure* and *interrelate* the contents and results of the five core processes, e.g., who is responsible for which activities and which activities are supported by which methods/tools, etc. The Product Development Cycle Model (in an adjusted, more generic form) can be used as a guideline of how goal, product and technology development cycles look like in more detail and how they interact. After defining the specific essentials for the PDM data model development, the House of IPD can be used to evaluate the best method/tool mix for achieving the project goals set. For sure, the use of the presented meta-tools in this simplified example may look like overkill. But, when dealing with a large, complex project, e.g., the development of a new car, these compatible tools can further the understanding and structuring of all the elements and aspects that have to be taken into account (Figure 10).

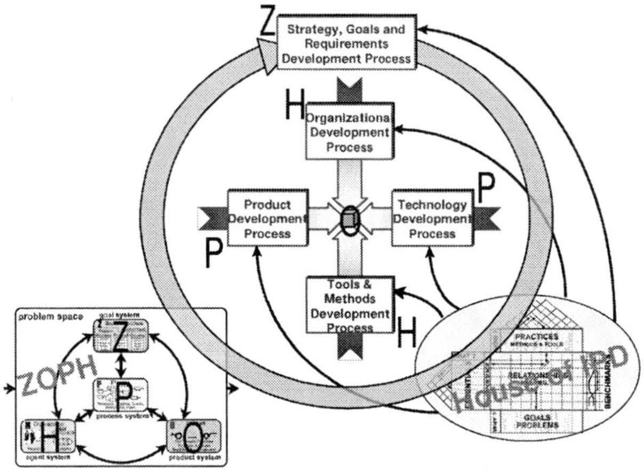

Figure 10. SE Meta-Tools Interaction

CONCLUSIONS

In this paper, different approaches for looking at complex product development systems in a structured way have been presented. For sure, there exist many other approaches, methods and tools for this purpose not described here. The methods discussed above should help building useful structures from linked, complementary views. Thus, the SE meta-tools can form a kind of a SE toolbox, with different, but compatible instruments. These have been derived from case studies within different industrial areas and have been successfully applied in several projects.

ACKNOWLEDGEMENT

We would like to thank Valerie Gundrum for proofreading and her very valuable comments.

REFERENCES

Clark, K.B. and Fujimoto, T., "Product Development Performance. Strategy, Organization and Management in the World Auto Industries." Harvard Business School. Boston, 1991.

Clausing, D., "Total Quality Development," ASME Press, New York, 1994

Hauser, J.R., Clausing, D.: *The House of Quality*, Harvard Business Review 66, No. 3, pp. 63-73., 1988

Negele, H., Fricke, E., Igenbergs, E.: "ZOPH - A Systemic Approach to the Modeling of Product Development Systems." Proceedings of the 7th International Symposium of INCOSE, 1997.

Negele, H., Fricke, E.: "Interrelating WHYs, WHATs, and HOWs for Successful Systems Engineering." Proceedings of the 1st Joint ESA/ INCOSE Conference on Systems Engineering, 11-13 November 1997, ESTEC, The Netherlands.

Negele, H.: "Systemtechnische Methodik zur ganzheitlichen Modellierung am Beispiel der integrierten Produktentwicklung," (A Systems Engineering Methodology for Comprehensive Modeling Applied to Integrated Product Development), Ph.D. Thesis, Institute of Astronautics, Technische Universität München, December 1998.

Wenzel, S., Bauch, T.: "Concurrent Engineering and More – Essentials for Successful Product Development from International Case Studies," Masters Thesis. Fachgebiet Raumfahrttechnik. Techn. Universität München., 1996

Wenzel, S., Bauch, Th., Fricke, E., Negele, H., "Concurrent Engineering and More – A Systematic Approach to Successful Product Development," Proceedings of the 7th International Symposium of INCOSE, 1997.

Wheelwright, S., Clark, K.: Revolutionizing Product Development – Quantum Leaps in Speed, Efficiency, and Quality, New York, 1992

BIOGRAPHIES

Herbert Negele recently started working for BMW AG. He received his master's degree in aerospace engineering in 1993 and his Ph.D. in systems engineering in 1998 from the Technische Universität München. Until November 1999 he worked as an Assistant Professor at the Institute of Astronautics in the field of systems engineering, with special focus on systems modeling and simulation, integrated product and process development, and management. Herbert was a founding member of the German Chapter of INCOSE and serving as its Vice President in 1997 and 1998.

Stefan Wenzel is Research Assistant and Ph.D. candidate at the Institute of Astronautics at the Technische Universität München. He received his master's degree in mechanical engineering from the Technische Universität München in 1996. He has been working in the Systems Engineering field for several years, with special focus on concurrent engineering, integrated product development, and process modeling. From 1997 to 1998 he participated in a 15-month management trainee program at "Energie Baden-Wuerttemberg (EnBW)" and the "Executive Development of the State of Baden-Wuerttemberg."

Improving Systems Integrity by Using Thread Analysis for Design Validation

Rob Collins
Entelecheia Ltd.
Turing House
Queen Mary Avenue
Bournemouth
BH9 1TS, UK
Entelechei@aol.com

Peter Pearson
ACSL
PO BOX 118
Hedge End
S030 2XW, UK
PearsonP@acsl.com

Peter Chattaway
Sentient Systems Ltd
1 Church Street
Wimborne
Dorset
chattawayP@Sentient-Systems.co.uk

Abstract

The techniques described in this paper have been developed and applied on a series of major systems engineering projects, most recently including the BOWMAN programme. BOWMAN will encompass the design, development, manufacture, conversion (rollout) and support of the new communications systems for the British Army. The BOWMAN contract will be valued in excess of £1.5 Billion and be delivered and installed over a period of 6 years.

Thread Analysis is a technique that enables systems design to be systematically inspected with respect to a number of desirable properties. Threads analysis finds application in domains including safety critical systems; security critical systems; concurrent, real-time systems and systems with complex and diverse behaviour.

Thread Analysis is concerned with 'unravelling' and documenting sequences of dependent events within complex systems. The consideration of the way in which one event leads to one or more other events in the system and the consequent changes in that systems state can provide deep insight into its functioning and integrity.

This paper shows how the essentially simple technique of inspecting dependent sequences of system events can be applied in a surprising variety of ways to yield useful and powerful results.

Introduction: The Structure of this Paper

The first section of this paper defines some basic terms that are useful in the following discussion. The second section describes why we believe threads analysis is so powerful for inspecting, and thus improving, system integrity.

The third section provides outline procedures and methods for performing threads analysis and outlines their application in critical systems development. The fourth section describes some of the problems of large scale analysis and introduces a method of describing threads as dependent series of logical facts. The final section refers to the threads based design.

What are Events and Threads?

Events are things that happen. In the domain of systems engineering it is normally considered that an event leads to, or causes a change in system state. Events may trigger behaviour. In older systems analysis techniques (including Yourdon) triggering or initiating events were seen as distinct from the processes or behaviour that were caused by those events (Yourdon 1998). In more modern, object-oriented schemes, dynamic behaviour may be regarded as synonymous with the set of events and the changes of object state that are caused by those events (Douglass 1998; Shlaer and Mellor 1992). It is this latter model that is adopted here. Behaviours are changes of state mediated by events.

Threads are sequences of dependent events. Our formal definition of a thread is that they are sequences of causatively related events. Cause is important in this context. We are not concerned with events that simply happen to have a time-like relationship. Just because two events happen one after the other does not mean that one causes the other. Threads are linked chains of causes.

A message may be considered as a generalisation of an event. Messages pass between system objects and result in state changes. In addition to these essential characteristics for an event, they carry message data. The subsequent sequence of state changes of a system may depend on the information carried in the message. Message data may be used in decision logic that controls future life-cycles.

Threads Analysis is the process of tracing sequences of related events (a thread) and inspecting states, processes, functions and interfaces on that thread's trajectory.

Why is Threads Analysis Effective?

Systems with complex, concurrent, dynamic behaviour are, by definition, difficult to 'understand', analyse and validate. Tracing threads through a system provides an effective method of systematically inspecting a system. There appears to be an underlying mechanism that causes threads analysis to be an effective and powerful technique: structural spanning, which we shall now describe in some depth.

Threads Analysis Spans Functional and Architectural Boundaries

Threads analysis tends to operate 'orthogonally' to system design and analysis. We use the term 'orthogonal' metaphorically to convey the notion that this analysis 'cuts across the grain' or 'intersects the flow' of design structures at right angles.

Whereas analysis and design activities are typically decompositional with respect to system function, threads analysis tends to be 'function spanning'. That is, because system analysis and design considers progressively more detailed components of a system, defects may be introduced due to the interaction of those components. Whilst each of the components might 'work' the system as a whole exhibits some pathology[1]. Threads analysis tends to treat 'end to end' or global functionality of a system and thus seems to be complimentary to functional decomposition.

TA almost invariably spans structural groupings in the system analysis, system realisation and design and analysis process. For example, threads frequently span external system interfaces and inter-subsystem interfaces[2]. Such interfaces are recognised sources of errors and thus warrant some effort during the design validation process (Lutz 1993).

In addition to spanning interfaces, TA tends to span architectural structuring of complex systems. System architectural structures are of increasing importance as systems become more complex (Shaw and Garlan 1996; Bass et al 1997). Not only do architectures provide a decompositional mechanism, they also provide important patterns and metaphors within which systems may be considered (Saunders 1998). TA frequently spans architectural structures and thus tests those structures in a manner that is both realistic and yet potentially counterexpectational.

This important notion of inspecting to detect the unexpected is discussed more fully in the next section.

Threads Analysis Spans Language and Cognitive Boundaries

We have said above that system architectures provide systems engineers with ways of thinking about a system. However, this great strength of system architectures poses its own threat. Analysts and designers may be predisposed to certain types of cognitive error that arise specifically as a result of fixed mental models. In short, knowing very well how a system should work can be an insurmountable barrier to seeing that is does not (Collins and Leathley 1995).

It is not simply the case that threads themselves span architecture. Analysts engaged in threads analysis appear less prone to a mental set dominated by an architecture and thus seem more able to detect weaknesses in it. The language we use to describe systems organises and structures our thinking about them (Whorf 1936). If engineering activities are dominated by a decompositional (that is architectural, sub-system or component-based) vocabulary, then it is likely that thinking will also be so dominated.

In this context our 'vocabulary' includes not just the spoken language of systems engineering but the centrally important language of diagrams and formal symbolisms we employ. Whilst structured analysis and Object Oriented analysis are different in many ways, what they share is a common foundation of decompositional language.

TA provides an orthogonal vocabulary that can be applied to a system and thus provides an escape route from a corporate mind-set concerning that system. The thinking of threads analysts is not dominated by decomposition since it is structured on an entirely different 'vocabulary' - the vocabulary of end-to-end functionality, of initial causes and final goals.

Threads Analysis Spans Organisational Boundaries

In our experience Conway's law (that systems architecture mirrors organisational structure) always appears to be true (Coplien 1998). Consequently a significant barrier to effective interworking of subsystem components is that different groups of experts are responsible for each of them. Knowledge and expertise is commonly clustered within groups of engineers who may be physically, as well as organisationally distributed. Whilst the archetypal systems engineer will have tried to minimise intercomponent pathologies in the architecture it seems to us important that the integrity of the system is validated by inspection across organisational boundaries.

The role of the threads analyst is thus an important one, because it forms a bridge between teams of people. If the analysis and design teams are the analogue of a systems architectural components then the thread analyst is the analogue of its intra-component functionality. Threads analysts are good inspectors precisely because their inspection applies pressure orthogonally to the organisational structures.

Methods of Threads Analysis

This section describes a series of methods for threads analysis. Each of these is built on the same underlying model. That is, they all involve the systematic inspection of causally related events and the changes of system states that result. They involve the inspection of state changes that result from a series of events and the interfaces that threads intersect.

This section is organised so that the methods become progressively more formal. That should not be taken to mean, however, that they become

[1] Such pathologies at the system level have been termed 'Systemic Failure Modes' (SFM). See Collins and Thompson (1995)

[2] What might be termed 'intrafaces'

progressively 'better'. We believe that each of these methods has value when applied appropriately. For a method to be successful it must be ecologically valid: it must match the needs of the organisation that applies it. It is common in our experience that an informal analysis performed early can be more effective at improving system integrity than an exhaustive, formal analysis performed late.

These methods may be used sequentially. Early analysis can be completed using the less formal methods. The results of these analyses can be used as a basis for later, more formal analysis.

Graphical Styles for Informal Threads Analysis

We have found it useful to elicit and document threads at an early stage of architectural design. In this context we have not attempted to tie analysis to design by establishing formal traceability. Rather, the analysis in intended to be a 'quick win'. It is designed to test an overall architectural design against key end-to-end functional requirements.

A second important benefit of this level of analysis is that it provides an explanation of how the system is intended to work at the system level. This technique may be usefully applied by systems architects to communicate to component designers the way in which the system as a whole is intended to function. This is an useful opportunity for two-way information exchange. Architects can communicate their concept of overall system function. Sub-system and component designers can provide useful feedback on likely problems or issues that may emerge at lower levels of abstraction.

Threads analysis at this level is normally captured pictorially rather than as a textual description. This is partly because drawings seem to be a natural method for eliciting and communicating threads within teams. However, we shall return later to another important issue; threads tend to bifurcate. In complex systems events often lead not to a single further event, but to a set of events, each of which may be important in the analysis. It is quite difficult to represent such splitting in linear text without recourse to some special syntax and this quickly becomes more effort than is warranted by the benefit.

We have employed four diagrammatic forms for threads analysis:

- Message Sequence Charts
- Collaboration Diagrams
- Directed, labelled graphs
- Graphics that mimic system architecture

Message Sequence Charts (MSCs) have been popular in communication system design for some time and are becoming more popular for requirements elicitation and analysis in real-time object-oriented software design (Douglass 1998). An example MSC is shown in Figure 1. In this figure, time runs down the page. System objects are shown as labelled boxes at the top of the diagram. The 'life-lines' of objects are drawn as vertical lines, with time increasing down the

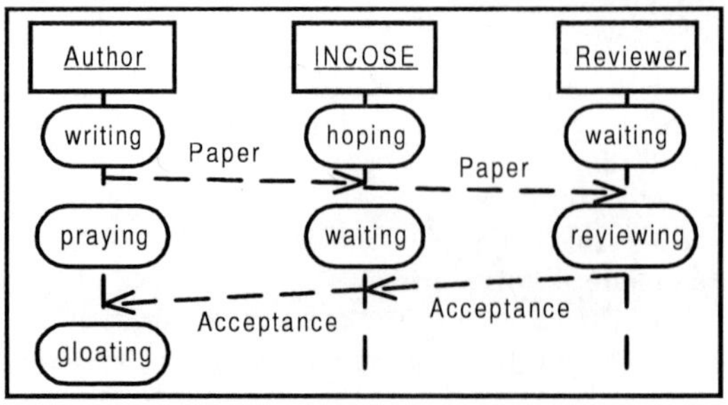

Figure 1: Message Sequence Chart

page. Events (or messages) are shown as labelled arrows running from source object to sink object.

Collaboration Diagrams (CDs) are semantically equivalent to MSCs but are graphically laid out to emphasise component structure rather than 'time-lines'. Figure 2 provides an example of a simple collaboration diagram.

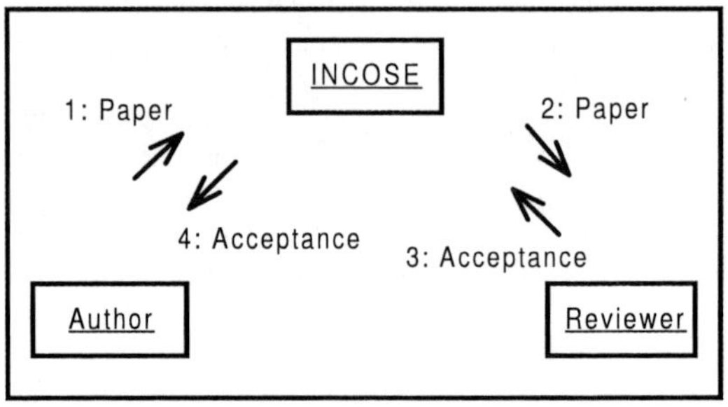

Figure 2: Collaboration Diagram

Notice that in CDs the sequence of events is indicated by numbering the event labels. CDs provide no obvious method recording state changes in objects and are thus slightly less expressive than MSCs.

Both MSCs and CDs are clear and efficient when the events under consideration are 'clustered' within a relatively small group of system components. It is common however, for threads to traverse many components in a more or less linear (although possible bifurcated) sequence. It is clear that in this case the graphical lay-out of MSCs in particular is not very efficient (one wastes a lot of paper). In this case a more linear, connected graph has proven to be a better representation.

Directed, Labelled Graphs (DLGs) are essentially equivalent to CDs and MSCs but differ in their graphical style. The format is not easily illustrated here, since DLGs only become useful when the threads are both long and distributed between many components. Figure 3 is a graphic representation of a DLG that might, in practice, represent a drawing 30cm high and 5m wide.

We have found it convenient in this representation of threads for objects to appear more than once in the diagram. This is unambiguous if objects are clearly labelled and enables drawings to progress in a single direction. If objects do appear more than once they can be labelled with state-information and this provides greater scope for checking against other design representations (for example Statecharts).

Drawings may employ off-page markers for publication within reports. However, we have found considerable benefit in printing long paper copies of such graphics and displaying them in public areas (often in corridors, for obvious reasons).

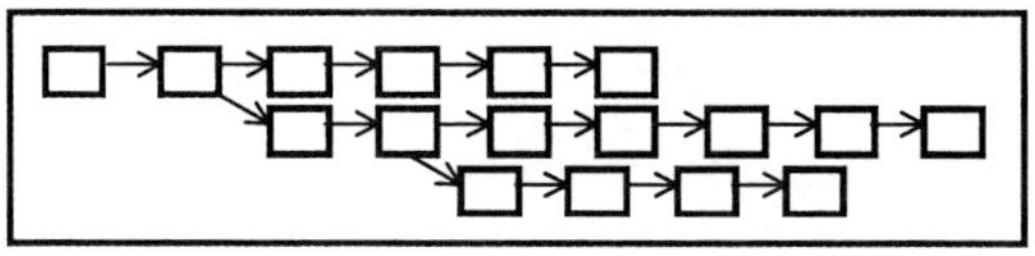

Figure 3: Very small-scale graphic representing a Directed Labeled Graph

Such graphs are usefully annotated with object names, event labels, explanatory notes and the names of interfaces if they are available.

Graphics that mimic system architecture are useful when the system under consideration adopts a recognizable architectural pattern. For example, the BOWMAN system employs a four-layer, communication protocol stack. The way in which layers interact is crucial to system function. Assuring that one layer provides the correct services in the correct manner, whilst avoiding undesirable side-effects is critical when developing a system with a high degree of design integrity.

For the BOWMAN system, drawings of threads that graphically mimic the layered communications architecture have been elicited and documented within the System Architecture Document (SAD). Figure 4 provides an illustrative example of this.

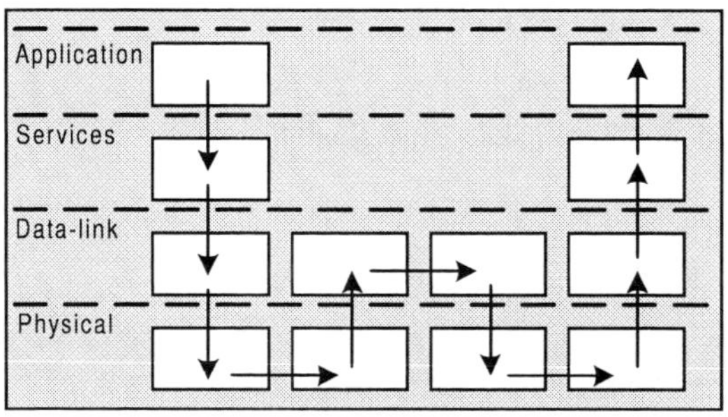

Figure 4: Thread Representation that Mimics Architectural Layering

Notice that Figure 4 represents a system that is distributed. Each of the vertical columns represents functionality that is associated with different items of equipment.

In practice such diagrams would contain a significant level of detail. As in previous notations objects, events and interfaces are labeled. The diagram is typically annotated with comments and notes. The BOWMAN SAD also contains textual descriptions of the overall thread and the implied functionality within each system component.

Formal Traceability

The analysis methods documented thus far are useful for eliciting and documenting intended system functions. They are useful as a sanity check and to improve communication between design groups.

These methods are not, however, sufficiently rigorous to provide a high degree of assurance that particular design aims have been achieved. In order to achieve that aim it is important that the threads analysis be formally linked to design representations and subsystem requirements. For example, if an item in the analysis implies a specific requirement on the design, then there needs to be a demonstrable (traceable, reviewable) link between that analysis item and the design documentation that supports it.

Such traceability can be established in a paper-based design environment but it is very laborious. A more efficient mechanism is afforded by the application of a Systems Engineering Database (SED) that acts as the repository for design information, sub-system requirement information and threads analysis documentation. The use of a SED facilitates direct, traceable links to be established from design representation to analysis documentation. Such repositories are in any case a significant asset to large scale Systems Engineering projects (Collins and North 1999, Collins, Dent and Bennett 1994).

Thread Based Inspection

Formal traceability is a necessary but not sufficient condition for rigor in thread analysis. Additionally, the systematic review of events and state changes should represent stringent tests of integrity. In short the analysis should be the basis of systematic inspection, rather than open-ended review.

Our procedures involves defining a series of inspection questions that must be answered for each:

- event
- state change
- interface that is traversed, and
- function or process that takes part in the thread.

Inspection questions are more likely to reveal weaknesses in the design than open-ended reviews (Gilb and Graham 1993). We employ a variety of inspection questions that are selected in appropriate circumstances. Typical questions might include:

- Where is the functionality implied by the response to this event documented in the system design documentation?
- Have performance issues associated with response to this event been documented?
- Is the design required to handle multiple, concurrent instances of this event?
- etc.

For each of these questions a textual response and a formal link to design data is required.

Threads Based Inspection in the Domain of Critical Systems

Inspection based threads analysis becomes particularly relevant when dealing with security or safety critical systems. In these cases there will be special integrity requirements for the system as a whole. These will have implications for requirements on specific threads, and 'entities' on the trajectory of that thread (system objects, states, required functions, interfaces etc.).

Threads analysis can make a contribution to system integrity in critical systems by basing inspection questions on specific, 'hazard' related integrity requirements. For example a failure based analysis might question the implication of a loss of a message or an error in a state for each event in a thread.

Large Scale Analysis

Common Sub-Threads

We have found the methods described thus far to be very effective at communicating intended system function and detecting design defects at an early stage in the system design life-cycle. However, these methods do suffer from a scaling problem. Whilst single, well identified threads are relatively straightforward to analyze and document there appears to be a great deal of redundant effort associated with documenting a large number of threads. This may be an artifact specific to communications systems but we see no reason to believe that it would not be true of other complex systems.

The problem is this. Consider a set of high-level functions of a communications system that present as different user applications (for example e-mail, HTML browsing, file transfer etc.). These are represented as the lettered boxes Figure 5. Each of these applications should be the source of one or more threads. This is true because we want to investigate the system with respect to each of the high level functions offered by these applications.

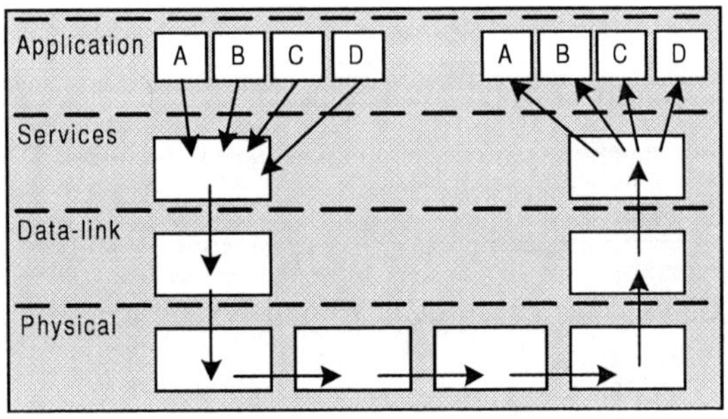

Figure 5: Occurrence of Common Sub-threads

However, in the case of Figure 5 the threads merge at the service layer within one equipment, are identical as they traverse 2 more equipments at the physical layer and only separate again at the service layer on the equipment represented by the right-hand column.

There would clearly be redundant effort associated with analyzing the full path of each of the four threads. It would be desirable to optimize our effort so as to provide the most stringent test for the system, whilst minimizing effort.

Combinatorial Explosion

Another practical problem associated with threads analysis of large complex systems is that of combinatorial explosions. We have already shown how several high-level functions can exercise common sub-functions (possibly with unique constraints and side-effects). The converse of this situation is also possible and is indeed present in the BOWMAN system.

It is possible for a high-level function to be achieved using a selection of low-level functionality. In the case of a communication system this might be because there are a variety of transport mechanisms or bearer technologies available for communications data, for example:

- Radio
- ATM based fibre-optic links
- Local area networks (E.g. Ethernet)
- Public Switched Telephone Networks
- Infra-red optical links

This situation is illustrated in Figure 6.

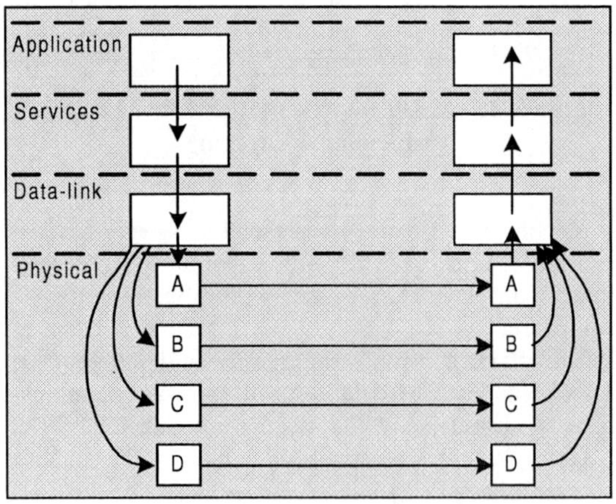

Figure 6: Choice of Sub-threads

In order to reasonably investigate the integrity of the system, each of the potential sub-threads must be explored with respect to the high-level intended functionality. Any constraints specific to the sub-thread need to be investigated with respect to the high-level end-to-end requirement. For example, whilst each of these bearers might be able to transport data, they may not all:

- have the required bandwidth for a specific high-level function
- be reliable enough
- have the required level of integrity with respect to security or safety requirements.

The issue here is the very large number of combinations that needs to be considered if analysis is to be sufficiently complete. The situations described in the last section and the one described in this one may be present at the same time. Indeed there may be optional sub-threads in each layer or architectural component in a system. It is clear that the number of combinations to be analyzed can rise rapidly.

A Flawed Solution

There is an obvious, but flawed solution to the problems described in the previous two sections: giving a name or label to common or optional sub-threads enables them to be referenced repeatedly in the analysis. This is the analogue of a function of procedure call in a high-level computer language or "write once use many".

However there is a problem with this solution. In practice one frequently discovers that both common and optional sub-threads align with architectural boundaries in the system. For example, in a layered communication architecture a typical sub-thread would begin at the invocation of a layer's function and terminate as control was passed to lower levels. This is exactly the case illustrated in Figures 5 and 6.

This solution undermines the foundation of threads analysis as we have argued it. It is not compatible with most of the arguments for threads analysis presented in the early part of this paper.

As we have argued, a key feature of threads analysis is that it cuts across architectural boundaries and thus it is not desirable to employ a mechanism that circumvents that feature. For this reason we believe that it is better to select a series of distinct threads with a small number of shared sub-threads than to dissect the analysis into many small sub-sections.

Using named references to sub-threads should only be employed if there is a reasonable expectation that the thread as a whole (including sub-threads) can be considered. Constructing the thread must not simply become an exercise in documentation. Threads must be viewed as a coherent whole.

If a large number of alternative threads with many shared sub-threads must be analyzed then we would suggest the application of the threads modeling technique described in the next section.

Logical Models of Threads

On the BOWMAN project we first completed an informal threads analysis during architectural design. We then applied some effort to rigorous, traceable inspection based threads analysis during detailed design. However, we wished to complete a much more exhaustive threads analysis effort to investigate design integrity and to de-risk systems integration.

We were confronted with the two problem cases we have described in earlier sections:

- Common sub-threads
- Optional sub-threads

It was clear that given the size of the system and the breadth of functionality being investigated this would cause us significant problems of scale.

These issues lead us to reconsider our approach to threads analysis. The essential feature of thread analysis appears to be that it tests compatibility between a high level end-to-end function (which might be a requirement) and a low-level step-by-step realization of that functionality (which is intimately bound up in the design). Not only must each step (event, message or interface navigation) be compatible with the high-level functional requirement, each of those steps must be compatible with each other. For example none of the steps must cause side-effects that prevent later steps from occurring correctly.

It was clear that the mass of information that this analysis would represent would not be manageable by purely human means. It was thus decided to develop software based 'models' of the threads in the system and to use this to systematically and exhaustively check the threads.

Our solution was to code each of the threads and component sub-threads as a series of 'facts' or 'rules' in a logic programming language. We chose Prolog to model the threads because of the high level of clarity and the explicitness with which it is able to express facts and rules of the type we needed. The use of a logic programming language can be most easily understood by way of a simple example.

The reader should note that the following examples are <u>not</u> drawn from the analysis of the BOWMAN system. These examples have been constructed purely for explanatory purposes.

Consider the case of a named high-level system function (e.g. 'send_a_message') that requires several sub-functions to operate successfully for it to work:

```
send_a_message if
   set_up_network and
   get_message_from_user and
   find_address_of_recipient and
   transport_mess_to_recipient and
   show_message_to_user.
```

The above is a rule. Each of the component parts may be simple facts, or they in themselves be rules. The above rule says that for the high-level function 'send_a_message' to operate successfully, five other functions must operate successfully.

The analysis could continue by adding some trivial facts. For example, the simple fact that there is functionality intended to get a message from a user might be coded:

```
get_message_from_user.
```

This line simply says that 'get_message_from _user' is a true 'fact'. In our model this would be equivalent to saying that we had verified that the functionality offered by this function is available.

Consider the later rule 'transport_message_to_ recipient'. It may be that this can be achieved in a number of ways, for example by using different bearers. This information may be coded as follows:

```
transport_mess_to_recipient if
  transport_message_by_lan.

transport_mess_to_recipient if
  transport_message_by_wan.
```

That is, we can transport a message if we can transport it by a Local Areas Network (LAN) or if we can transport it by a Wide Area Network (WAN).

The logic engine in the Prolog programming language allows options such as this to be investigated exhaustively. With some minor manipulation the engine can be set to investigate all combinations. Whilst the combinatorial explosion problem still exists, the effort is now applied by the logic engine rather than the human analyst.

Expressing Pre-Conditions

The above example encodes only the simple existence of a class of functionality required by the thread. We also need to check compatibility of functions within the thread. For example if our thread had been 'send_secure_message' then it may be that the transportation of data should only be achieved by using a local network, not via the Internet. This can be modeled using a parameter to express the security requirement:

```
send_secure_message if
  Secure = true,
  set_up_network and
  get_mess_from_user(Secure) and
  find_address(Secure) and
  transport_mess(Secure) and
  show_message_to_user(Secure).

get_mess_from_user(_).

transport_mess(_)if
  transport_message_by_lan

transport_mess(Secure)if
  Secure = false and
  transport_message_by_wan
```

In this case the underscore in the parameter lists of 'transport_mess' and 'get_mess_from_user' means 'don't care'. That is, the functionality is independent of the security of the message. The first 'transport_mess' rule states that the LAN can transport messages regardless of their security classification (maybe because we can guarantee physical security of the network).

The second 'transport_mess' rule concerns the use of a WAN. This rule is only TRUE, if the value of the 'secure' parameter is FALSE. In other words it is only possible to transport a message by a WAN if the message is not secure.

An advantage of this scheme is that the necessary constraints and pre-conditions for a thread to be valid are explicitly recorded in the logical statements

The above logic programme would normally be extended to include annotations so that as the logic was explored by the Prolog logic engine suitable messages would be produced. For example, each rule or fact prints its own name to a log file along with any feedback on the success or application of the rule.

Making Assertions About Pre-Conditions

It is sometimes the case that a sub-thread depends on the successful completion of an earlier sub-thread. This may be true if some pre-condition needs to be set up in order for the thread to operate successfully. An example might be that messages can only be sent via a LAN if names and IP addresses have already been defined and distributed.

In Prolog rules and facts can not only be defined explicitly but may also be set dynamically. For example if we consider the elaboration of the rule 'set_up_lan' and the effect it has on the rule concerning the use of the LAN.

```
set_up_lan if
  assert( names_and_ip_set ).

transport_message_by_lan if
  names_and_ip_set.
```

The use of such assertions to model pre-conditions allow isolated parts of the thread to effect each other. Long-range compatibility in threads can be modeled and validated using this technique.

Threads Based Design

This paper has concentrated on threads analysis for design validation. However, there is a growing interest in using this class of technique for design itself.

A deficiency of most validation models is that they may diverge from the emerging design implementation. In our experience there is always a level of effort associated with maintaining a good correspondence between the representations used for analysis and those which exist for design. Clearly it would be useful to be able to integrate design validation models with design models.

Tools such as ObjecTime and Rose-RT support MSCs directly. Vendors have proposed that MSCs be used early in the problem domain analysis in order to capture and represent the required real-time behaviour of systems. In these tools MSCs can be model checked against state-charts of system components. Both tools provide simulation engines that allow state machines to be exercised and their behaviour recorded and observed in the form of MSCs.

Conclusion

In this paper we have described threads analysis and stated why we believe it can make a contribution to improved integrity of system designs. We have argued that threads analysis provides a systematic inspection of the system that is 'orthogonal' to the systems architectural and functional decomposition.

We have presented a selection of informal notations for threads analysis and argued that these are most effective in early architectural system design. We believe that threads analysis can make a contribution to inter-team working because threads tend to cut-across architectural and thus team boundaries.

We have shown how threads analysis can be made more rigorous by adding formal traceability to system design material and sub-system requirements. Rigour may also be improved by using formal inspection questions rather than informal review.

We have described a scaling problem with threads analysis that may arise from a combinatorial explosion due to optional sub-threads.

Finally, we have presented a formal and rigorous method for representing and inspecting threads based on logical rules and facts concerning the function of the system. Our method allows many combinations of thread to be checked for compatibility for example to inspect for necessary pre-conditions and undesirable side-effects.

We would additionally like to pose the following questions for further investigation: How can we obtain a measure of goodness of the threads analysis we perform? We would like to know how many threads should be analysed for a system with a given measure of complexity (number of functions, number of interfaces etc). How many threads would need to be analysed to gain a given level of certainty that omissions in sub-system functionality have been detected? How can we be reasonably sure that the threads we choose are well distributed as opposed to 'clustered' around a specific group of functions?

We believe that threads analysis will become increasingly important and would encourage others to build on the methods described here and to answer the questions posed above.

References

Bass, L., Clements, P. and Kazman, R. (1998) "*Software Architecture in Practice*" Addison-Wesley: Reading. MA ISBN 0-201-19930-0

Collins, R.J., Dent, J. and Bennett, A. (1994) "A Practical Case Study of the Management of Reliability, Safety and other Concurrent Engineering Information" in R.F. Cox (Ed) *Risk Management and Critical Protective Systems* : Safety and Reliability Society

Collins and Leathley (1995) "Psychological Predispositions to Errors in Safety and Reliability Analysis" *Safety and Reliability* 14:3, 6-42.

Collins and North (1999) "The Design, Implementation and Management of a Systems Engineering Database" in *INCOSE 99, Systems Engineering: Sharing the Future*

Collins, R.J. and Thompson, R (1997) "Systemic Failure Modes: A Model for Perrow's Normal Accidents in Complex, Safety Critical Systems" In C.Guedes Soares (Ed) *Advances in Safety and Reliability. Proceedings of the ESREL '97 International Conference on Safety and Reliability, 17-20 June 1997* Elsevier Science: Oxford

Coplien, J.O. (1998) "A Generative Development Process Pattern Language" in L. Rising (Ed.), *The Patterns Handbook: Techniques, Strategies and Applications* Cambridge University Press:Cambridge ISBN 0-521-64818-1

Douglass, B.P. (1998) "*Real-Time UML. Developing Efficient Objects for Embedded Systems*" Addison Wesley.

Gilb. T. and Graham, D. (1993) "*Software Inspection*" Addison-Wesley : Harlow, England ISBN 0-201-63181-4

Lutz, R.R. (1993). "Analyzing Software Requirements Errors in Safety-Critical Embedded Systems". in *Proceedings of the IEEE Int. Symp. on Requirements Engineering* 126-33

Saunders, D. (1998) "Patterns: The new Building Blocks for Reusable Software Architectures." in L. Rising (Ed.), *The Patterns Handbook: Techniques, Strategies and Applications* Cambridge University Press:Cambridge ISBN 0-521-64818-1

Shaw. M. and Garlan, D. (1996) "*Software Architecture: Perspective on an*

Emerging Discipline"
Prentice Hall: New Jersey
ISBN 0-13-182957-2

Shlaer and Mellor (1992)
"*Object Lifecycles: Modelling the World in States*"
Yourdon Press: Englewood Cliffs
ISBN 0-13-629940-7

Whorf, B. (1936)
"A Linguistic Consideration of Thinking in Primitive Communities" in J.B.Carroll (Ed)
Language Thought and Reality: Selected Writings of Benjamin Lee Whorf.
MIT Press : Massachusetts.
ISBN 0-262-73006-5

Yourdon, E (1998)
"*Modern Structured Analysis*"
Prentice Hall International
ISBN: 013598632X

Author Biographies

Rob Collins holds a PhD in the area of Software Engineering and Training. He is the managing director of Entelecheia Ltd, a company that provides consultancy and training in the fields of Systems Engineering and Safety Critical Systems.

Rob lectures regularly both nationally and internationally and is a regular contributor to INCOSE events. Rob teaches the Critical Systems course as part of the MSc in Computation at the University of Oxford in the UK.

Peter Chattaway holds an honours degree in Electronic Systems Engineering. He is a consultant for Sentient Systems Ltd and specialises in software, safety critical systems, requirements engineering. Has spent considerable effort over the last year applying Rose Real Time to a large scale Systems Engineering project, including the development of model checking tools. His model checking activity included application on the Prolog modelling technique described in this paper.

Peter Pearson is employed by Archer Communications Systems Ltd, where he provides support on Systems Engineering tools and methodologies. He has performed a significant amount of threads analysis on the BOWMAN system and has produced procedures and standards for this work.

AUTHOR INDEX

AUTHOR INDEX

AUTHOR INDEX

International Council on System Engineering 2000

Minneapolis, Minnesota, USA
16 - 20 July 2000

Volume 2 of 2

ISBN: 978-1-5108-6245-6

Printed from e-media with permission by:

Curran Associates, Inc.
57 Morehouse Lane
Red Hook, NY 12571

Some format issues inherent in the e-media version may also appear in this print version.

Printed by Curran Associates, Inc. (2018)

For permission requests, please contact John Wiley & Sons
at the address below.

John Wiley & Sons
111 River Street
Hoboken, NJ 07030-5774

Phone: (201) 748-6000
Fax: (201) 748-6088

info@wiley.com

Additional copies of this publication are available from:

Curran Associates, Inc.
57 Morehouse Lane
Red Hook, NY 12571 USA
Phone: 845-758-0400
Fax: 845-758-2633
Email: curran@proceedings.com
Web: www.proceedings.com

TABLE OF CONTENTS

VOLUME 1

SECTION I: SYSTEM ENGINEERING APPLICATIONS

HEALTH CARE APPLICATIONS 3

VEHICLES/TRANSPORTATION 2

INFRASTRUCTURE SYSTEMS ENGINEERING APPLICATIONS

ENVIRONMENTAL SYSTEMS

LEGAL AND PUBLIC INTEREST

SECTION II: MODELING AND SIMULATION

TOOLS

MODELING 2

MODELING 3

SYSTEMS

SECION III: SYSTEM ENGINEERING MANAGEMENT

MANAGEMENT 1

MANAGEMENT 2

MANAGEMENT 4

REQUIREMENTS

RISK 2

SECTION IV: SYSTEM ANALYSIS/PROCESS

ARCHITECTURE

METHODS 2

VOLUME 2

METHODS 3

METHODS 4

LIFE CYCLE 1

LIFE CYCLE 2

SECTION V: MEASUREMENT

CAPABILITY ASSESSMENT 1

CAPABILITY ASSESSMENT 2

ANALYSIS 2

PROCESS 1

SECTION VI: EDUCATION/STANDARDS

EDUCATION AND RESEARCH 1

EDUCATION AND RESEARCH 2

STANDARDS 2

Architecture Based Design Applied to a Remote Sensing Satellite Planner

David Kaslow
Lockheed Martin
Management & Data Systems
P.O. Box 8048
Philadelphia, PA 19101

ABSTRACT

The Architcture Based Design (ABD) process provides a mechanism and a series of repositories for evolving and documenting an architecture and design. It was first introduced at the INCOSE 1998 Symposium and is beginning to be applied to a variety of architecture and design efforts. The application of ABD to the initial architecture and design of a Planner for a remote sensing system provides insight as how to introduce and implement ABD and the ABD tool set on a project.

INTRODUCTION

This paper describes the application of Architecture Based Design (ABD) to the initial design of a Planner for a remote sensing satellite system. The work was carried out as part of an independent research and development (IR&D) project to create a planning and scheduling architecture that could be applied to a variety of satellite remote sensing systems.

The first set of papers (Frank 98 and Frank 99) introduced ABD as a key engineering process and provided the motivation and methodology. The IR&D project provided an opportunity to explore the implementation of ABD from the viewpoint of establishing an initial architecture and design.

Issues examined include how the process should be initiated, in what order the views be should developed, and how an ABD team should operate.

ARCHITECTURE BASED DESIGN

The ABD process provides a mechanism and a series of repositories for evolving and documenting an architecture and design. Figure 1 lists the complete set of ABD views. An architecture view is a description, from one cohesive aspect, of what a system does and how it is put together. The collection of views, the relationships between the views and the implementing models define the architecture and design to the level needed to efficiently and effectively build the system.

ABD views provide a methodology for the depiction, communication and validation of the overall system design. The scope of each view is defined to allow a thorough examination of a unique aspect to the system design. The views are presented by models and the views are related to each other by the information they share.

Architecture Based Design Views	
Mission Application	Hierarchical depiction of the executing elements of the system and connectivity through message traffic and data structures
Mission Scenario	Hierarchical depiction of the scenarios as a sequence of events and actions taken by mission applications to satisfy a system function
Data	Defines all persistent data structures and messages
User	Description of operators and end-users interacting with the system
Object	Depicts construction of the system in terms of objects and classes
Hardware	Description of processing, communication, data server and special purpose computing elements
Facility	Rooms and supporting systems need for deployment
Infrastructure	The layers of functionality between the mission applications and the hardware
State/Mode	System conditions and mission conditions of operations

Figure 1. Each Architecture Base Design View defines the system from one cohesive aspect.

One of the major benefits of applying ABD is that it facilitates complete and thorough reviews since all aspects of the design should be matured in unison. This allows iteration through the views until there is sufficient detail to demonstrate design closure at a given level of architecture and design maturity. This iteration through the views provides the additional benefits of focusing on the design information needed by to implement and manage the scope of system design information.

ABD was implemented on an IR&D project to develop a preliminary architecture and design of a Mission Planner for a remote sensing satellite system. This author has considerable experience in developing several generations of mission planning and scheduling systems using the traditional requirement decomposition and structured analysis methodologies. The IR&D project provided an opportunity to compare ABD to the more traditional architecture and design methodologies.

Because the IR&D project focused on the preliminary architecture and design of a remote sensing planner with a further concentration on the planning methods and algorithms, only a sub-set of the ABD views was used. Figure 2 shows both the ABD views employed and the initiation and iteration of the views.

PLANNING PROBLEM STATEMENT

The first questions asked when applying ABD were: What are the source materials and how do we get started? The answers were the same as for the traditional methodologies. The source materials are the standard high-level mission statement, concepts and requirements defining the Mission Planner. A number of projects were reviewed to extract an essential list of source materials covering a generic Mission Planner. These materials were thoroughly analyzed and a planning problem statement was written.

The planning problem statement was used to initiate the ABD process. It was a text-based document containing both a broad, but concise, discussion that establishes the role of planning within the greater system and the basic planning paradigms. The planning problem statement was developed from knowledge of the high-level concepts, requirements and functionality that make up a Planner.

The problem statement defined the activities, resources and constraints that must be addressed in the remote sensing spacecraft planning process as well as the relationship between planning and the external interfaces.

MISSION APPLICATION VIEW

The Mission Application View is a depiction of all executing elements in the system and their connectivity through message traffic or data structures. The executing elements include software, hardware and operators. The Mission Application View, as well as the Mission Scenario View, as implemented with a design tool, would have all data sources defined in a library and would be navigable to lower levels of the design.

The planning problem statement provided the focus for reviews, discussions and negotiations that resulted in the ABD Mission Application View. Figure 3 is the first level Mission Application View for the Planner. Functional and data descriptions have been omitted for clarity in presenting the diagram.

It was found that the first level Mission Application View is necessarily at such a high level that the view by itself did nothing more than provide a starting point for introducing the architecture. Supplementary textual material was needed if the view were to be provided to someone outside the ABD team.

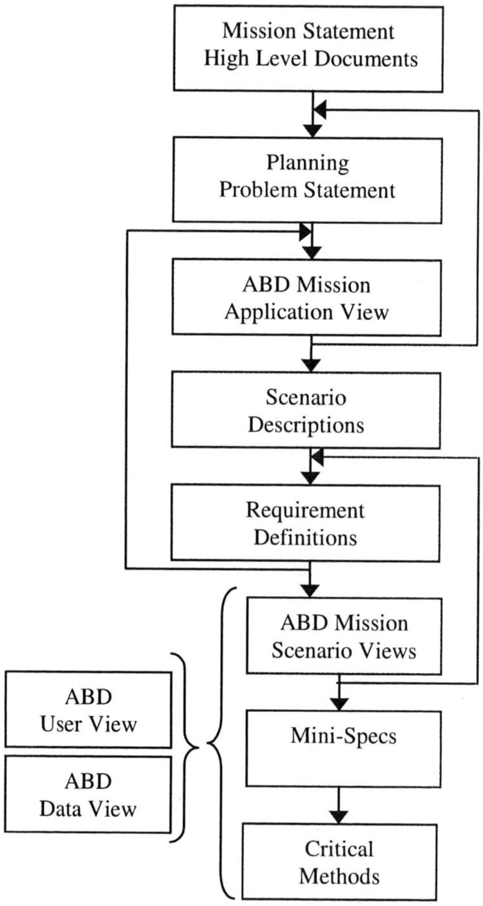

Figure 2. Application of the ABD principles to the prelimary design of a satellite mission planning system.

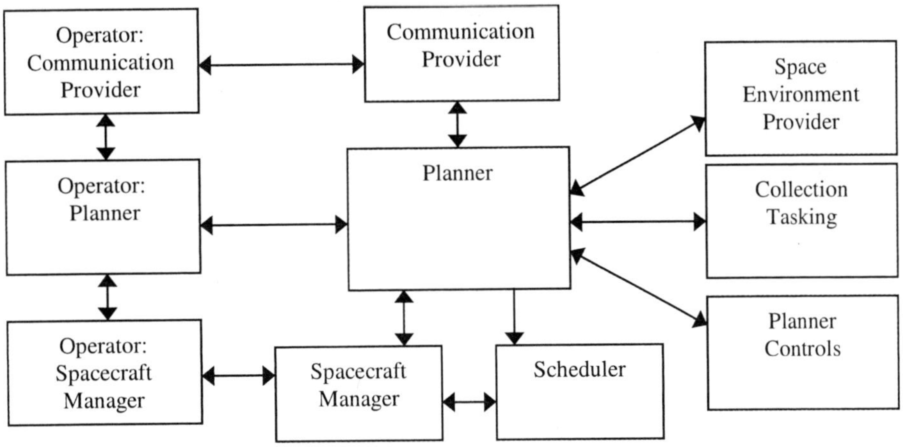

Figure 3. The Mission Application View provides the relationship of the Planner to the other elements. Descriptions of elements and data flow can be attached to the view.

The focus of the Mission Application View was on the relationship of the Planner to the external elements. The relationships between external elements that did not relate to the Planner were not included.

The Mission Application View was a program baseline document that is maintained and controlled. The planning problem statement was not a controlled document. It existed only to initiate the creation of the Mission Application View and the Mission Scenario Views.

MISSION SCENARIO VIEW

It was found that the functional and data descriptions within the Mission Application View were at a high level and thus inadequate for developing the design details. The design details were based on the ABD Mission Scenario Views.

Each Mission Scenario View is a depiction of a sequence of events and actions taken by the mission applications executing elements to satisfy a system function. Scenarios are triggered by a system stimulus such as the arrival of a system message.

Four Mission Scenarios Views were developed for the Planner. Figure 4 shows a portion of the Plan Extension scenario, which is the addition of a seventh day on the plan. The back planes in Figure 4 show the titles of the other three scenarios. Each scenario shows the data and message flow between the entities identified in the Mission Application View.

These initial scenarios were documented as figures in a text-based document and were later transferred to the design tool upon completion of the tool selection and installation process.

The Mission Scenario View was linked, as shown by the number within the ovals, to Mini-Specs and Critical Methods.

It was found that the scenario views were instrumental in establishing a baseline of data flow to and from the Planner. The graphical time flow of data groups forced early-on discussions as to the triggering events that must invoke a Planner response as well as the functionality that provides the response.

SCENARIO DESCRIPTIONS AND REQUIREMENT DEFINITIONS

The Mission Scenario Views were initially based on scenario descriptions and requirement definitions. These were text-based documents that addressed the driving functional and performance aspects of the Planner.

The scenario and requirements matured quickly in the initial architecture and in an iterative manner as illustrated in Figure 2. Clarity in requirements specification and interpretation were key in establishing a sound baseline for a system. Scenario descriptions and requirements definitions were reviewed, discussed and negotiated until program management signed-off on a documented baseline.

Requirements interpretation included assumptions and scope. The scope included stating what was not a requirement but might be inferred to be a requirement by someone else. The requirements were traced to higher level documents and to the functionality within the scenarios.

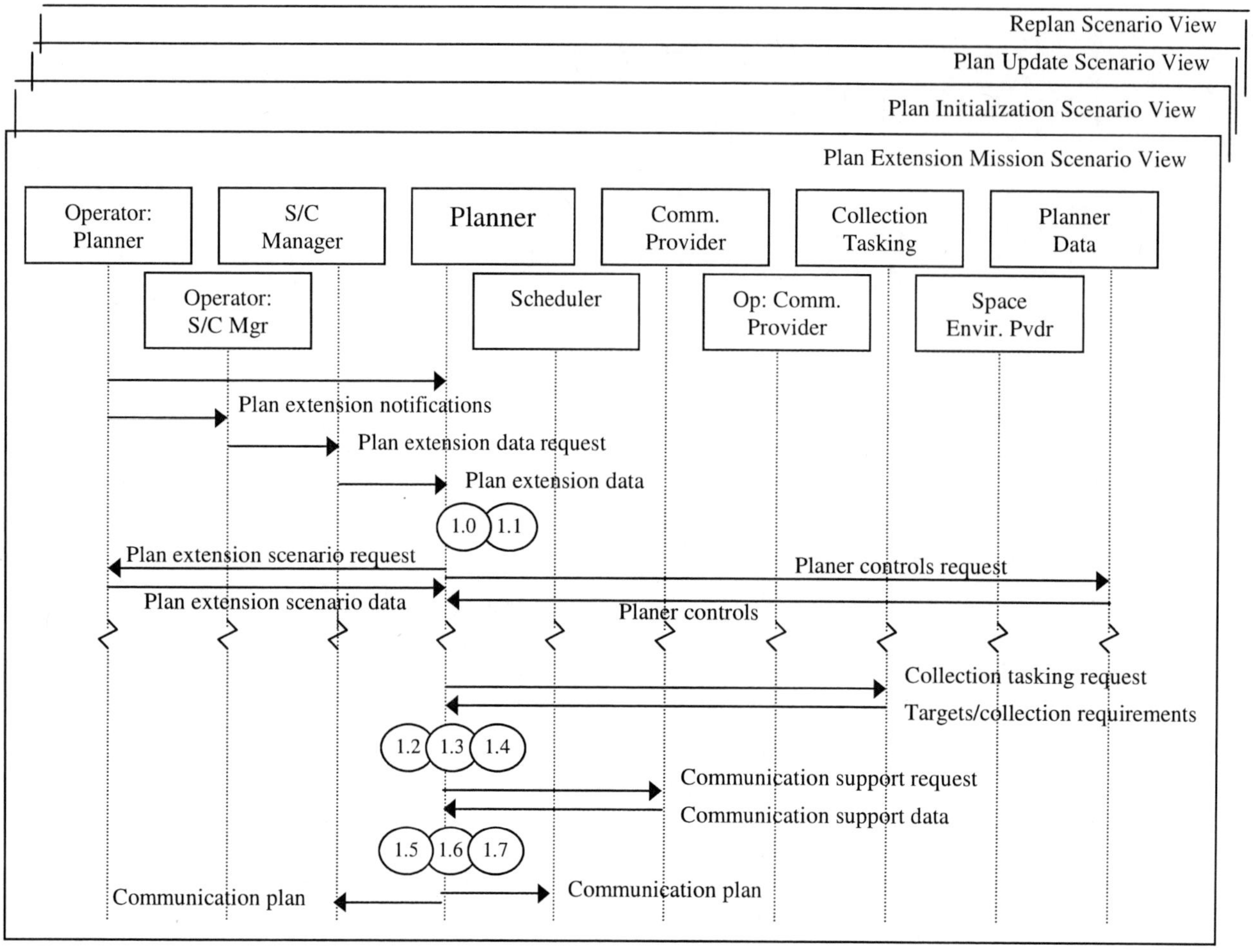

Figure 4. The Mission Scenario Views are hierarchical diagrams that provide the design detail related to specific system functions.

MINI-SPEC AND CRITICAL METHODS

The mini-specs contain requirements and other design information for each executing element. Each scenario contributes its own unique requirements and design information to the mini-specs. The mini-specs can be implemented as a repository within the design tool.

The mini-specs associated with a design tool can be limited in the amount and type of information that they contain. This would be the case for a design that is primarily specified by large numbers of critical methods.

Critical methods are complex and compute intensive algorithms that are best specified with sets of detailed mathematical equations. The preliminary critical methods documentation identifies the input and output data element and describes the process flow and algorithms at a high level. As the design matures, these critical methods become more detailed and eventually contain all the methods and algorithms needed for the design. The final version of the critical methods contains the methods validation results. This is not a validation of the operational code but rather the engineering analysis that demonstrates that the methods satisfy the requirements.

The majority of the Planner architecture and design was driven by the critical methods, which were text-based documents. Figure 5 shows the structure of the Planner critical methods with the paragraph numbering providing a link to the Mission Scenario Views.

ABD VIEWS AND DESIGN VALIDATION & VERIFICATION ACTIVITIES

A companion paper (Kaslow, 2000) presents the role of the Design, Design Validation and Verification Activities in the development of a software system. This includes the definition of performance models and scenarios to ensure that the design will achieve performance requirements. Mission plan optimization and mission scheduling timelines are examples of critical performance requirements. The Design

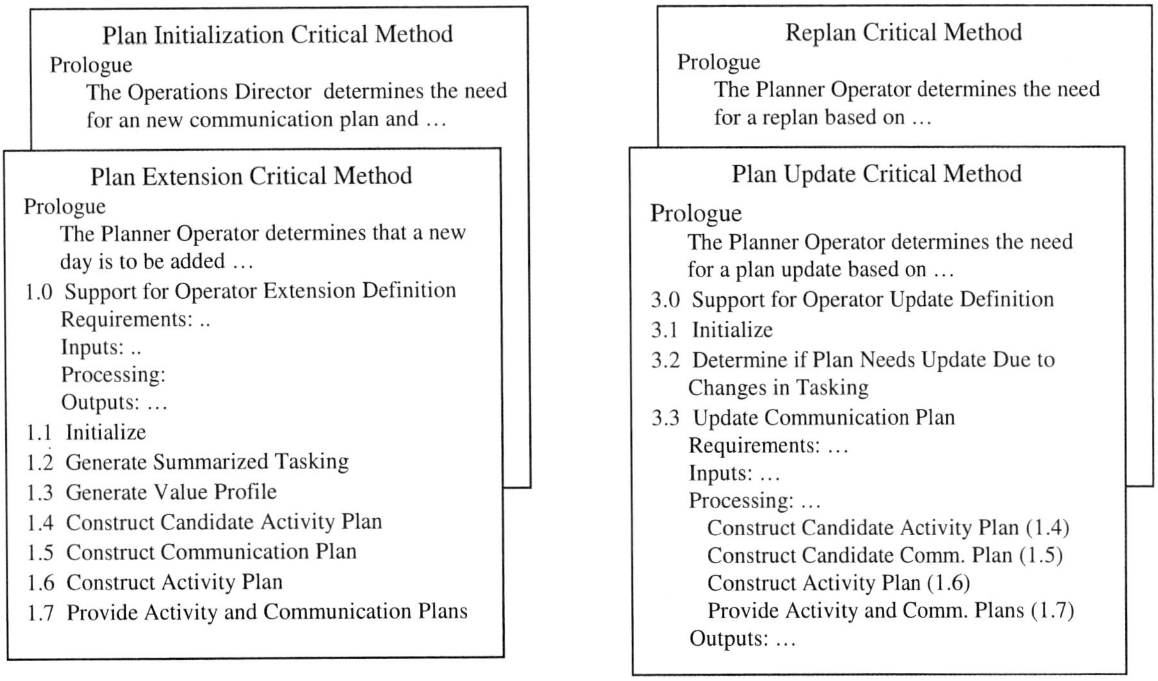

Figure 5. The critical methods provide the detailed algorithms for the software executing elements associated with each scenario.

Validation Activity develops and maintains the models used to estimate and evaluate system performance requirements. The ABD mission scenario views coupled with the mission application, hardware and infrastructure views provide the basis for the development of the performance model. The mission scenario views are also a foundation for the test cases carried out by the Verification Activity.

USER VIEW

The User View presents the system as it relates to human interaction. This includes the operator staffing plan, operator loading analysis, and a description of operator graphical and textual interfaces.

DATA VIEW

The Data View defines all the persistent data structures and messages. It provides the consistency between many ABD entities, particularly the Mission Scenario View, mini-specs and critical methods. It is also used to establish the system data management concepts and design.

It was found that thc data view forced an early-on definition of data element within data groups, which in turn added to the detail provided in the critical methods.

OTHER VIEWS

The object view is not needed for the development of the preliminary architecture and design. It is used when developing the detailed software design. The state/mode view was not used since the focus in the IR&D project was on the single state/mode of normal operations.

The facility view was certainly not needed for the design of the Planner, although it would be critical for coordinating the design of large software and hardware systems within a new or existing facility.

REVIEWS AND CONSISTENCY CHECKS

It was found that the most detailed and effective reviews occurred within the ABD group of engineers and developers. Reviews by program management and other stakeholders were used to establish the completion of milestones and baselines. The internal reviews were carried out with just a few experts and with one person having the final decision authority.

A thorough level of consistency was achieved by referencing critical method IDs within the Scenario View as well as referencing Data View data groups within the Scenario View and data elements within the Critical Methods. The identification of individual critical methods and data elements forced the engineers and developers to organize the flow and structure of the data and the functionality and relationship of the methods.

Just one person was ultimately responsible for checking and verifying all aspects of consistency. Although the checks were tedious and time consuming they were well within the capabilities of one person for the level of detail present in the preliminary architecture and design.

IMPLEMENTATION OF ABD AND THE TOOL SET

The application of ABD on a project that does not have a tradition of using requirement and design tools should begin with one set of engineers and developers laying out the initial architecture and design using just text-based documents and figures. Another set of engineers and developers evaluate and select the requirements and design tool set. Then these two groups work together transferring the initial design to the tool set.

This parallel effort approach on a program without much experience with ABD and tool sets will insure that the initial architecture and design tasks stays focused on how to apply ABD and not become distracted by how to use the tool set.

CONCLUSIONS

The ABD process does not produce concepts and requirements out of thin air. Engineers and developers still begin with a source and good understanding of the concepts and requirements.

The application of ABD does not magically result in an architecture and design. Engineers and developers still need to draw on their knowledge of the system and their years of experience in order to produce an effective system architecture and design.

The breadth of the ABD view, as well as the relationships and consistency checks between the views are what sets ABD apart from other architecture and design methodologies.

ACKNOWLEDGMENTS

James Fretz and Tricia Keller, both of Lockheed Martin Management and Data Systems were members of the IR&D Mission Planning project. They provided insight into the application of ABD and implemented the conversion of the Planner architecture and design into the ABD tool set.

BIOGRAPHY

Dr. Kaslow is a Senior Staff Engineer with Lockheed Martin Management and Data Systems. He has twenty-six years of experience in both the technical and management aspects of developing a ground mission element. He has co-authored two chapters in *Cost Effective Mission Operations*. The chapters are "Defining and Developing the Mission Operations Element" and "Activity Planning". He has been a standing member of a Hubble Space Telescope Vision 2000 external review panel. David E. Kaslow.

REFERENCES

Frank, Rodger, "System Architecture – A View Perspective", INCOSE, 1998.

Frank, Rodger, "A Solution to the Software Design/Architecture Bind – The Mission Object View", INCOSE, 1999.

Kaslow, David, "Role of Design, Design Validation and Design Verification Activities in Development of Software Systems", INCOSE 2000.

A Systematic Method for Development of Reactive Real-Time Systems

Alan Grigg,
British Aerospace Dependable Computing Systems Centre,
Department of Computer Science,
University of York,
York, UK

Neil Henderson
British Aerospace Dependable Computing Systems Centre,
Department of Computer Science,
University of Newcastle Upon Tyne,
Newcastle Upon Tyne, UK

Abstract. In this paper, we identify the need for a more systematic method to support the specification and analysis of reactive real-time systems and propose such an approach based on *real-time transactions*. Firstly, a graphical notation is outlined that can be used to specify the timing properties of real-time transactions. Secondly, a rigorous formal notation is proposed to support the expression of transaction functionality. Finally, a timing analysis method is described that can be used to predict the timing behaviour of the system at any stage of refinement of the formal model. The use of the approach is illustrated via a case study. We suggest that the application of a more systematic approach to the development of real-time systems can provide major cost benefits when considered over the life-cycle of the system.

INTRODUCTION

This paper describes the current results of an ongoing British Aerospace funded research activity within the Dependable Computing Systems Centre (DCSC) at the Universities of Newcastle and York. The research is focussed on providing a more systematic method for the development of reactive[1] real-time systems, from the specification of functionality and timing properties through to an implementation, by continual refinement of system properties. In order to achieve this objective, a real-time transaction model has been developed, consisting of :

- A graphical notation that can be used to specify the timing properties of a system and a rigorous formal notation to express its functionality. We advocate the use of a rigorous formal notation for the specification of system functionality, although the model can be adapted to use a less rigorous notation if the user wishes.
- A timing analysis method that can be performed at any stage of refinement of the system timing properties to predict the overall timing behaviour of the system.

It is often the case that errors in a system's specification, due to the relative timing of computations, are not identified until they manifest themselves as bugs during the testing stage. A considerable amount of costly rework is then required, to correct the code, and modify the specification and design documentation to reflect the changes that have been made. The formal notations have been developed as a useful abstraction to enable the recording and analysis of functional and timing properties of the system in the early to mid stages of the development cycle. The use of these rigorous notations will help to identify more of the errors early in the development process, before the coding stage, to reduce the amount of such rework.

[1] A reactive system is one which is constantly interacting with its environment, and where the behavior of the system is influenced by its speed relative to changes in the environment.

Graphical notations are used to specify a partial ordering of actions within the system, but it is important that this specification is kept sufficiently abstract so that event orderings are specified only where they are essential - for example, to ensure that an input is read before a related computation is carried out. This ensures that the final real-time scheduling solution for the system is not unnecessarily constrained, and the potential for maximal concurrency is retained. It is left up to the run-time scheduling solution to control the actual allocation of hardware resources and appropriate techniques can be used from the real-time systems domain that are both flexible and predictable.

Timing analysis is performed by constructing an abstract (implementation-independent) model of the system, including the perceived target hardware. The abstract model is successively refined to capture the timing properties of the system, so that at each stage of development, the abstract model represents a set of timing obligations on the subsequent stages of development. The technique is known as *reservation-based timing analysis*, as originally published in (Grigg 1999). This model has since been extended and integrated with the formal RTT model described below to give a process for top-down specification and analysis of timing properties for real-time sytsems.

In this paper, we describe the approach and illustrate its use via a case study – an Attitude Guidance Autopilot system, which is a simplified version of a missile system.

WHY DEVELOP A NEW FORMAL APPROACH?

Existing formal specification languages which are capable of specifying the behaviour of reactive systems, such as Petri-nets (ISO 1997), process algebras (for example CSP (Roscoe 1997)) and temporal logics, such as RTL (Jahanian 1986, Jahanian 1988), usually only refer to the ordering of input and output events, not the relationship between those inputs and outputs. Our aim is to characterise the behaviour of reactive systems more fully and this is not possible if the event based reactivity is separated from the functionality of the system.

The approach of Statecharts (Harel 1987) also has severe limitations and does not seem appropriate for systems with internal concurrency for the following reasons :

- States are an inaccurate abstraction of many concurrent and distributed systems. Engineers tend to refer to the mode of a system rather than its state, and while the two concepts are similar there are fundamental differences. For example, particularly with distributed systems, it can take some time for an entire system to respond to a change of mode. This can result in different parts of the same system being in different modes at the same time.
- The *synchrony hypothesis* inherent in the approach means that a statechart must finish responding to one set of inputs before the next set arrives. This requires systems to become "blind" to changes in their inputs once they have started a computation. While this may be true for small systems (although even then only usually only for sequential systems) at a higher level of abstraction a specification may be referring to a complete system, or sub system, and it is unlikely that this property will hold.
- Concurrent and distributed systems which are constructed to obey the synchrony hypothesis tend to be both inefficient and inflexible. Inefficiency arises because they require a fixed schedule that is constructed around the assumption of consistent worst-case behaviour - for example, the period of all the computations is driven by the algorithm that takes longest to execute. In turn, this is not flexible enough to support more reactive behaviour at run-time. Moreover, the resultant lack of flexibility can be a major contributor to development-time and in-service upgrade costs associated with the system.

SPECIFICATION OF REAL-TIME TRANSACTIONS

The real-time transaction (RTT) model (Haveman 1997) has been developed to provide a method to formally specify and reason about the functionality and timing of reactive distributed real-time systems using a new formal notation known as the transaction description language (TDL). The computational model has been kept sufficiently abstract to be applicable to systems that contain internal concurrency or distributed parallelism and so that it can be :

- reasoned about without reference to the underlying implementation;
- adapted to be used with different design methodologies and processes.

A RTT is a computation that is triggered either periodically by a clock or sporadically by one of its inputs, which then reads all of its inputs and produces a (potentially empty or complete) subset of its outputs. The functionality and relative timing of the inputs and outputs are specified using a graphical transaction state machine (TSM) notation.

We will first illustrate the AGA system using UML 'use cases' and then show the specification of part of the system using the RTT notations. Later, we will show how these notations can be used to support a timing analysis of the system.

The AGA system receives data from sensors, which it uses to calculate the attitude of the missile. This information is then passed to an Information Processing System (IPS), and is used together with information about the target, such as infra red image to provide an aim point for the missile which is input back to the AGA system. This aim point is then used together with the attitude of the missile to calculate guidance information for the missile. A UML 'use case' description of the AGA system is shown in Figure 1. This identifies two RTTs, the Attitude Guidance and the Autopilot.

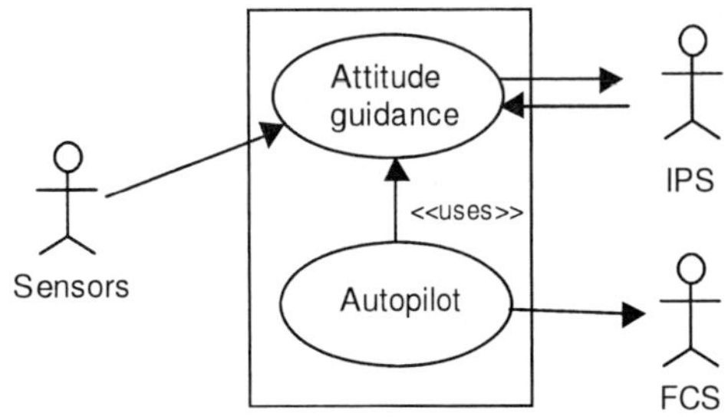

Figure 1. The AGA System

Figure 2 illustrates the TSM graphical notation applied to the AGA Autopilot RTT.

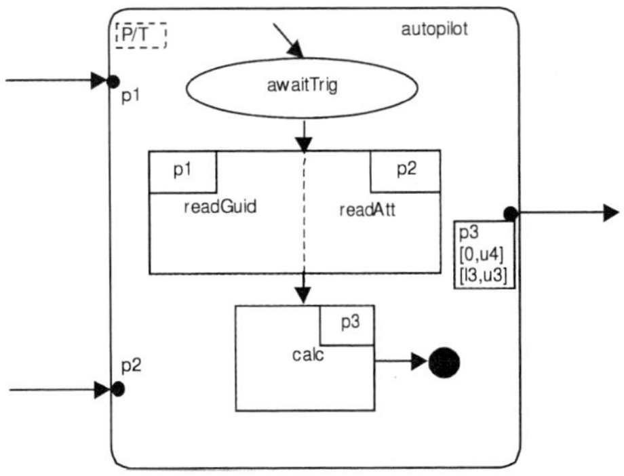

Figure 2. The AGA Autopilot RTT State Machine

The TSM notation is comprised of the following objects :

- Ports, where inputs are received from, and outputs are made to, either other RTTs or the environment.
- Static states, which represent potential blocking/descheduling points such as where it is necessary to wait for data to become available in a buffer.
- Dynamic states, each comprising a single computation that reads its inputs once and writes its outputs on completion.
- Hierarchical states, which themselves contain a RTT, and therefore make it possible to refine the specification of a RTT in a recursive hierarchical manner.
- Composite states, which are comprised of a number of dynamic states, or hierarchical states, which must be non interfering and can be executed in any order, or concurrently. Non interference means that the operations in each state within a composite state must read from and write to

different ports and use different sub-sets of the local state of a RTT.

- Transitions, which lead from one state to another.
- Termination states, which a RTT enters when it has finished its computation. That instance of the RTT then ceases to exist.

We now illustrate this terminology with reference to Figure 2. The RTT is represented by a rectangle with rounded corners, the ports by solid spots on its perimeter, and dataflows by arrows to or from the respective ports. The initial state is indicated by a transition with no source. Timing constraints are shown alongside the port in the TSM, for instance there may be upper and lower bounds for data to be read from or written to a port. For example, the output at port p8 must take place within l3 and u3 after the RTT is triggered and there is a deadline of u4 on the calculation of the output. There is a lower bound of 0 shown with the deadline and it is possible to show a non zero lower bound on the completion of the calculation.

A new instance of the autopilot RTT is created on receipt of the trigger every T time units (shown in the diagram in the dashed box at the top left of the TSM – where P stands for periodic). A RTT may be triggered sporadically by the arrival of data at one of its inputs in which case the minimum separation time of the triggers is shown. It then reads the inputs at ports p1 and p2 (these actions can be executed concurrently) and stores them as part of its local state, and enters state 'calc' where the data to be output is calculated and output at port p3. Finally it enters its termination state and ceases to exist. Each of the dynamic states in the RTT has a VDM (ISO 1993) operation associated with it, with pre and post conditions used to express the computation that is carried out in the state.

All of the information about a RTT is recorded in a tabular format which contains the following information :

- The names and brief descriptions of inputs, outputs and local state variables, together with details of any timing constraints, such as deadlines for outputs or windows during which inputs must be read and outputs written.
- Functionality - this section would contain the TSM description of the RTT, details of any types imported from other RTTs, a description of the operations carried out in the dynamic states of the RTT and any auxillary functions called.
- Guard - a RTT can have a guard which is a boolean condition over its inputs and local state variables and is evaluated when it is triggered. The RTT only executes if the guard evaluates to true.
- Invariants, condition(s) evaluated over the local state of a RTT which must hold when it is executed.

Information is extracted from this table to support analysis under the reservation-based timing analysis model, as described below.

TIMING ANALYSIS OF REAL-TIME TRANSACTIONS

Since the original development of the reservation-based timing analysis (RBA) model and its publication in (Grigg 1999), the model has been extended and applied alongside the RTT formal method described above. Below, the latest version of the RBA model is summarised in the context of the RTT formal method and the AGA case study.

The RBA model supports the notion of continual refinement of system timing properties through the provision of *nested* transactions. At any level of nesting, a transaction is described in terms of *activities* which capture its detailed timing and resource usage requirements. Activities are analogous to the dynamic states referred to above in the description of the formal RTT model. Activities can themselves be refined (alongside the formal model) to produce further levels of nesting in the RBA model. Hence, at any stage of refinement, a 'precedence graph' of activities or dynamic states can be extracted from the TSM and the RBA timing analysis applied.

The following additional information is associated with each activity or dynamic state to describe the resource usage characteristics of a transaction :

- A reservation budget, V, to define the *rate* at which resource is consumed; V is a real number in the interval (0,1].
- A best-case and worst-case total resource requirement, $[c, C]$.

The RBA model can then determine the local delays (and delay variations, *ie.* jitter) associated with each dynamic state and consequently the end-to-end timing behaviour for the RTT in question. RBA incorporates an abstract (technology-independent) model of the run-time operation of each physical resource in the system, typically processing and communication resources. Run-time scheduling policies must, in turn, reflect the assumptions made in the abstract model for the off-line timing analysis results to remain applicable. The RBA method is applied to the case study below.

Figure 3 illustrates the precedence graph of dynamic states for the AGA Autopilot RTT.

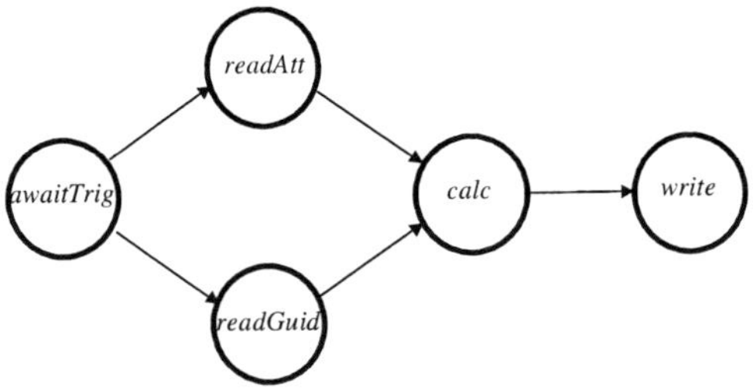

Figure 3. The AGA Autopilot RTT Precedence Graph

Table 1gives some example local delays calculated by the RBA model from a given set of resource usage requirements and reservation budgets. The minimum and maximum predicted delays are denoted by r and R, respectively. These local delays then form the input to an overall end-to-end delay calculation.

	$c_{i,j}$	$C_{i,j}$	$V_{i,j}$	$r_{i,j}$	$R_{i,j}$
awaitTrig	1	3	0.1	10	30
readAtt	1	2	0.2	5	10
readGuide	2	3	0.2	10	15
calc	3	8	0.4	8	20
write	2	3	0.2	10	15

Table 1. The AGA Autopilot RTT Timing Analysis (Local Delays)

The end-to-end delay calculation may be performed manually to give a best-case of 38 and a worst-case of 80. More recently, however, the RBA method can be applied more conveniently with tool assistance. This has been enabled by a MATLAB/Simulink formulation of the RBA model. This tool has been developed to allow engineers to rapidly construct and analyse end-to-end transactions under RBA conditions. The tool allows the engineer to apply the RBA method without detailed knowledge of the underlying analytial model. The RBA tool has been used to construct and analyse the example AGA Autopilot transaction. Figure 4 shows a plot of the predicted end-to-end response time for one hundred simulated executions of the example transaction. During simulation, the execution time of each activity is allowed to vary randomly between user-defined limits, $[c, C]$.

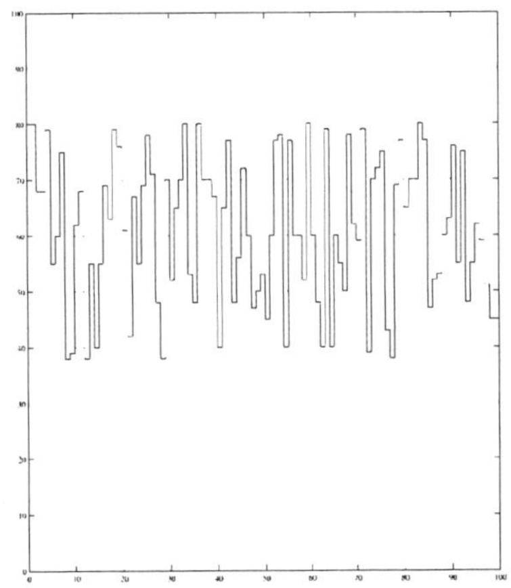

Figure 4. The AGA Autopilot RTT Timing Analysis (End-to-End Delays)

SUMMARY

The paper has described a systematic method for specification and analysis of reactive, real-time systems. We believe that the application of our approach to the development of reactive real-time systems can provide major cost benefits when considered over the life-cycle of the system.

REFERENCES

(Grigg 1999) A Grigg,, NC Audsley, MA Fletcher, AS Wake, "A Method for Design and Analysis of Next Generation Aircraft Computer Systems", Proc. of INCOSE Conference on Systems Engineering, 1999.

(Harel 1987) D Harel, "Statecharts: A visual formalism for complex systems", Science of Computer Programming", 1987.

(Haveman 1997) J Haveman, S E Paynter, J M Armstrong, "A transaction model for real-time systems", Technical Report No 607, University of Newcastle, 1997.

(ISO 1993) The ISO/VDM-SL Committee, "VDM Specification Language", 1993 (Draft).

(ISO 1997) ISO/IEC JTC 1 on Information Technology, "Petri Nets Standard – Project 7.19.3 (Petri Nets), Version 3.4 (Draft)", 1997.

(Jahanian 1986) F Jahanian, A K Mok, "Safety analysis of timing properties in real-time systems", IEEE Transactions on Software Engineering, SE-12(9):890-904, 1986.

(Jahanian 1988) F Jahanian, A K Mok, D A Stuart, "Formal specification of real-time systems", Technical Report TR-88-25, The University of Texas at Austin, 1988.

(Roscoe 1997) A W Roscoe, "The Theory and Practice of Concurrency", ISBN 0-13-674409-5, Prentice-Hall, 1997.

BIOGRAPHY

Alan Grigg received an honours degree in Mathematics at Thames Polytechnic (now University of Greenwich) in 1985. He subsequently joined British Aerospace; eventually working on the specification and design of a software architecture for military IMA systems. He was a British Aerospace representative for the multi-national, military IMA programme ASAAC. In 1996, he joined the British Aerospace Dependable Computing Systems Centre at the University of York to pursue research into real-time system design and timing analysis.

Neil Henderson worked in a leading British Clearing Bank from 1975 to 1994. He subsequently obtained an honours degree in Computing Science at the University of Newcastle upon Tyne in 1998, after which he joined the British Aerospace Dependable Computing Systems Centre at the University of Newcastle upon Tyne to pursue research into the formal specification of safety critical reactive real-time distributed computing systems.

A Collaborative Systems Engineering Approach For Achieving Early Landing Gear Systems Maturity

Aymen Mussad
Airbus UK Limited.
New Filton House
Filton, Bristol
BS99 7AR United Kingdom

Abstract. This paper describes the systems methodology created to exploit in-service aircraft experience to influence the design of a new landing gear system.

The paper opens with an overview of systems requirements, evolution of the design loop, followed by the tools and techniques developed to ensure early product maturity at Entry Into Service (EIS).

Key concepts such as the philosophy of approach, 'why & how', process drivers to implement experiential knowledge into the design and the relationship between maturity and reliability will be discussed.

INTRODUCTION

Need for Maturity. Since the advent of the first modern commercial passenger jet, ever-increasing demands in performance has led to an expansion in the number and complexity of landing gear systems. Next generation landing gear systems have evolved into a network of elements and coercive relationships that intersect to form a highly complex system.

Modern day airline customers expect and demand that the latest commercial airliners have mature design solutions at entry-into-service (EIS). High expectations in terms of reliability and dispatchability are the norm from day one.

CONCEPT OF MATURITY

What is Maturity? Maturity is a developed process used to review and reconfirm stakeholder requirements and that the supplier is following and complying with the Purchaser Technical Specification (PTS) and Airbus Directives (ABDs).

Figure 1, illustrates where mature system thinking lies in the design development process. Simply, it is a process that enables known system requirements and *'influential parameters'* derived from Continued Product Development (CPD) knowledge (as unspecified or undefined requirements) that effect the design, to be linked.

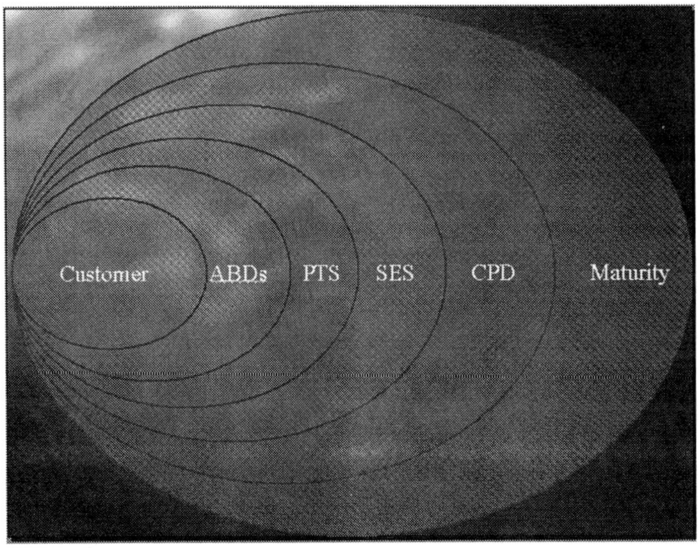

Figure 1. Maturity in relation to project planning.

THE SYSTEM DEVELOPMENT PROCESS

Concept Generation. Over time, Landing Gear (L/G) design in the Airbus aircraft family has become more complex. This can be attributed to demands of increased functionality, performance, more prominence in airline expectation and the economic considerations that place limits on cost. New L/G design methodology demands a new approach that is not wholly dependent on an experience-based approach, since this past approach cannot be reasonably expected to fulfil future design demands. Ever complex L/G systems, limits in human capability & capacity and tighter design/project margins all enervate this methods effectiveness.

Mature systems thinking has been developed to complement and enhance the experience-based approach through the provision of a sound foundation of system engineering principles and process.

Reduction of Uncertainty In designing the A340-

500/-600 L/G system a rational approach was taken whereby the focus was on building on good design practice to reduce the risk of uncertainty on the new system. This philosophy of approach became a dedicated subject of system development. In this phase the first activity involved the compilation and capture of a set list of requirements – usually addressed by the Purchaser Technical Specification.

Purchaser Technical Specification (PTS)[1]. This is a document produced by Systems Engineering to formally notify the vendor of the technical and management requirements for an item of equipment or a package of items of equipment to form a system.

In producing the PTS, guidance and requirements should be considered for any items of equipment that contribute as a subsystem to the overall 'package' of system equipment.

The PTS is written so that the requirements and objectives are unambiguous to allow the vendor to accurately respond. However, this places a larger onus on the knowledge and expertise of the systems engineer in ensuring that all the requirements have been covered. That is, the PTS must be comprehensive and include all the technical and management requirements as identified by the author(s). It should be objective in that each requirement should be identifiable and traceable to aid verification.

The equipment suppliers response to the PTS is submitted in the form of a Supplier Equipment Specification (SES).

The Airbus Directives (ABDs)[2] On the latest commercial aircraft, systems engineers currently work toward a set of documents called Airbus Directives ("ABDs") that have been amalgamated from different policies, processes and methods developed over several years by the consortium's partners. These comprehensive documents guide the systems engineer and equipment manufactures in developing landing gear (and other) systems.

The Airbus systems engineering policy has been developed into two main ABDs.

- ABD0100 – Primarily concentrates on the equipment suppliers.
- ABD0200 – Primarily concerned with Airbus system engineers and/or designers.

ABD0200 in particular fits this paper's theme of 'collaborative working' as it proposes "Right First Time" philosophy, an objective during the early phase of any system design process. The first activity in this phase, is a set list of requirements that apply to the system to be developed:-

- Function requirements.
- Safety Requirements.
- Interface requirements.
- Environmental requirements.
- Maintainability requirements.
- Reliability requirements.

As soon as sufficient requirement information has been gathered, system design can begin. Although not listed as a specific requirement, but in itself giving a 'barometric' indication of success in terms of the past/ previous design, is the area of 'lessons learned.'

OPTIMISATION & CONCEPTS COUPLING

Airbus, is a relatively young company in the aerospace industry (the A300's first flight was on 28-Oct-1972). It cannot therefore allow approaches and processes which would limit or stifle its growth in the market place. The European dimension to the company lays the foundation from which it can pool in and develop a truly unique set of ideas and strategies. However, where knowledge is held by an employee (or employees) of only one of the four partners, the departure of that employee (or employees) could result in a loss of knowledge, experience and hence competitiveness from the business as a whole. To overcome, this 'knowledge entrapment' required Airbus UK Limited to develop a process that enabled an eclectic pursuit of requirement capture. Having the ability to form an all-encompassing set of 'complete' requirements required a process where the use and access of information was not hindered by the departure of an employee.

Airbus in being a four-nation consortium has the necessary *raison d'être* to develop a process whereby loss of knowledge is not detrimental to one or the whole of the partnership. This process needed to be indifferent to the consortium's international culture and multitude of languages. In being able to transcend these barriers, the author had to develop a process that would form a 'translucent model' to enable both internal (e.g. fuel, brakes and steering) and external (e.g flight controls) systems to Airbus UK Ltd to map and follow.

In this phase, the first activity was to list all the areas that the partners use and source, to form requirements.

As stated by "(J. N. Martin, 1998)[3] requirements act as a kind of 'decoupling mechanism' between building blocks - the blocks here being requirements from a customer's 'wish list'.

User Requirements. User requirements are often non-technical in nature and usually conflict with each other. These need to be translated into "technical requirements" that are specific to the domain of the technology to be used in the system.

Customer requirements. Customers will often translate their perceived user requirements into a set of requirements to be given to a development project. These, also like user requirements, are often not of sufficient technical nature and conflict with each other. Moreover, aircraft projects in particular have more than one customer for their product.

Stakeholder requirements. In defining the technical requirements for the system, one must consider that there are other stakeholders for that system. For example, the manufacturing organisation within the company may desire utilisation of existing processes, tool, facilities etc. There are constraints with these 'enabling products', hence the stakeholder requirements that drive the development must be identified.

Requirements Decomposition. Once the system's technical requirements are defined, further requirements are often 'derived' by analysing both the logical and physical aspects of the system. Some of these derived requirements, plus whatever system technical requirements are relevant are "specified" for the system, its end products, and possible subsystems of those end products are described below."

New requirements arise as a result of the selected system architecture and equipment or those components as part of a in-service system not meeting specific requirements. Thus issues pertaining to lessons Learned need to be assessed and included in the validation process since original designs may have had consequences not foreseen by the author of the original set of requirements.

The foundation of mature systems thinking is the conscious use of 'experience wholeness', that is using experiential knowledge gained from airline operations. Mature system thinking provides a framework through which the rationale, design or development philosophy and engineering effectiveness regarding a component can be questioned. Secondly, it provides the medium through which full capability in terms of product sustainment and preparedness can be ensured, so operational performance may be realised.

In order to apply mature system thinking successfully to the sphere of landing gear design, a significant number of influences that shape the system had to be considered. However, it is unrealistic for a systems engineer to fully understand all the constituent landing gear design disciplines, architecture and methodologies, therefore focusing is essential. The first process requirement is 'filtering' to determine discipline of interest i.e. mechanical, electrical, pneumatic and/or hydraulic. This allows the framework to be adapted by other disciplines as required and allow emergent properties/issues of each discipline to be studied.

Mature system thinking emphasises and requires proactive learning and control rather than mere adaptability, with a focus on information processing, viability and pertinence. The collection, transfer and processing of information and subsequent arising actions are paramount in developing systems maturity. Following several maturity iterations, aims and objectives can be accepted thereby giving the process the capability to self-question rather than be solely self-regulating.

L/G SYSTEM MATURITY PLAN

In developing, evolving and operating a mature systems plan, a three pronged approach of ideas had to be developed, namely **Technique perception, Framework identification** and **Mitigation of risk.**

TECHNIQUE PERCEPTION

This arises from a comprehensive catalogued information archive, based on in-service experience – otherwise known as lessons learned.

The underpinning strength of an effective maturity plan, stems from having the capacity and capability to tap into experiential material. To develop and exploit this information effectively requires possessing a 'pool of knowledge'. The list below shows some of the possible source areas that may be explored:-

- Previous twin aisle experience.
- Reflection on single aisle experiences.
- Government / Fedral aviation authorities.
- Airline and customer support feedback.
- Supplier & Vendor experiences.
- Untried and untested risks to the new design.
- New design features.

Figure 2 overleaf, showing the areas deemed to affect maturity and how they influence the landing gear product development life cycle will now be discussed.

In-service Environment. Knowledge of the aircraft's systems environment adds a historical dimension to the robustness of the design, by assisting the engineer to define specific difficulties that may not be prescribed in current standards, such as:

- Vibration induced fatigue.
- Environment moisture and humidity.
- Use of corrosive or abrasive cleaning methods and procedures.
- Particle intrusion into connectors and equipment.
- Electromagnetic compatibility of adjacent equipment.
- High temperature extremes and variation rates.

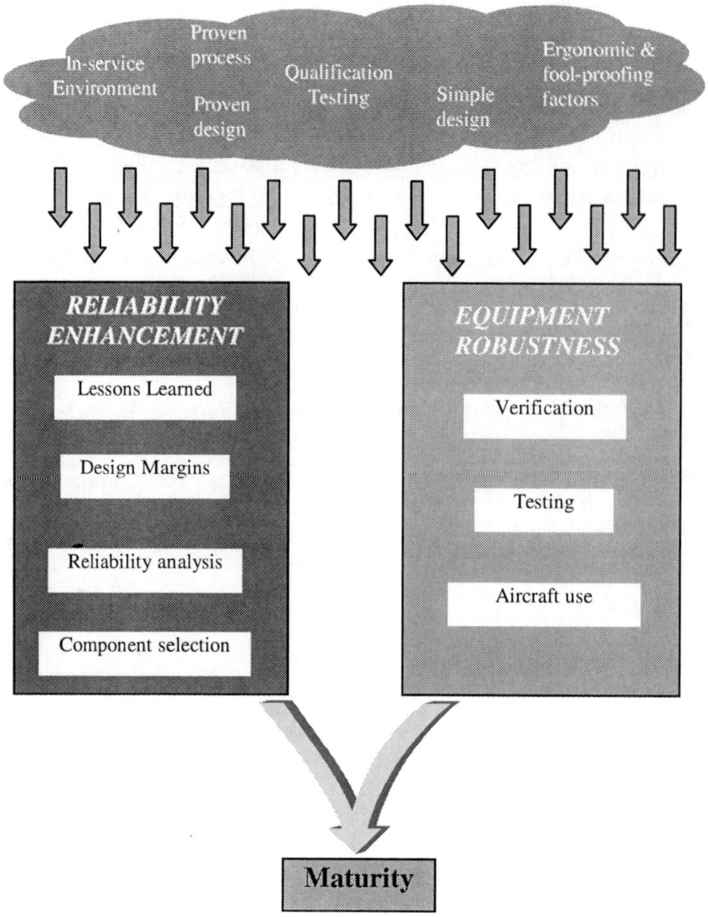

Figure 2. Source areas used to establish a maturity 'Knowledge-Pool'.

Proven Design. This involves locating evidence of best practice / engineering excellence to ensure:

- Maturity by use of proven & tested design.
- Modification on proven design – minimised.

Proven Process. As in proven design, the system engineer should seek evidence of best practice / engineering excellence to ensure:

- Maturity level is enhanced by use of proven & tested process.
- Modification of proven process is minimised.
- Extensive use of best practice.

Qualification. This is used to verify the system / equipment complies with the specified requirements. Furthermore product qualification permits verification not only against safety and airworthiness requirements, but also production processes and procedures.

Simple design. Figure 3, schematically shows the steps of a mature iterated designed:

Ergonomics & Fool-proofing. The design should take into account human factors from all perspectives i.e. crew, passengers and maintenance engineers by:-

- Quality and ease of maintenance procedures.
- Use of customer focus groups.
- Evaluation of the probability of human error.
- Minimisation of crew workload and stress.
- Preparation of efficient training.

A relatively simple example of systems maturity thinking was in refining a maintainability requirement.

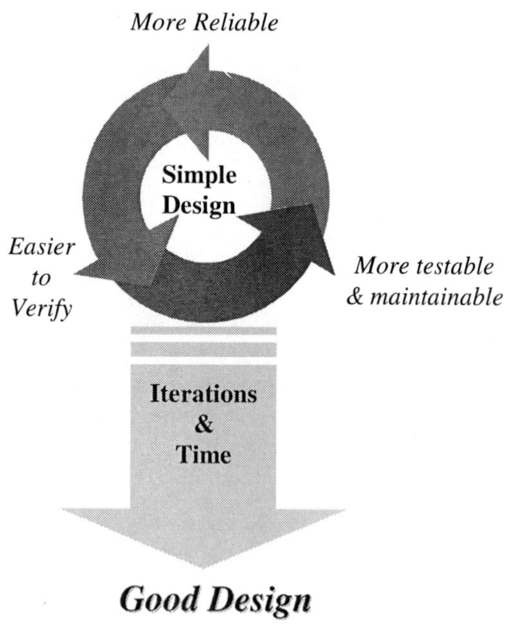

Figure 3. Benefit of simple design to Maturity.

The procedure of L/G shock absorber charging had developed into area of concern with some customers. In exploring these concerns it became clear that source of the problem was not the actual process but the *comprehension* of the instructions. Re-writing the procedure was the straightforward answer, but this merely touched upon the problem. Customer Focus Group inputs revealed that the majority of problems were reported from customers who had small business operations, remote support & infrastructure and resource constraints. Further investigation, revealed that these operators resource were disadvantaged by their limited knowledge of the English language, consequently not being able to fully understand instructions and *labels* used on the landing gears. A specially organised small airline focused workshop led to *simplified English* being used in the instructions and a departure from a graphical to tabular charging table. Normal maintainability requirements capture would miss the fact that approximately 90% of Airbus customers do not speak English as a first language.

Lessons Learned. This involves the exploiting previous program experience into the new design, by:

- Keeping design simple.
- Using customer's comments.
- Complying with specification and standards.
- Making full use of traceability.
- Aiming for a reliable and nuisance free design.
- Selecting suppliers on quality and knowledge.
- Account for environment in design (hermeticity, robustness and fatigue).

Design Margins. Margins must be ensured to manage ensure product robustness and to minimise:

- Component usage outside the specified limits.
- Environments outside the specification.
- Margins for mechanical stresses and fatigue.

Reliability Analysis. The use of Failure Mode Effects Analysis (FMEA), and Functional Hazard Analysis (FHA) ensures in trade-off studies:-

- Potential failure modes, causes, performance degradation and means of detection are identified.
- Fault tolerance is demonstrated.

Component selection. Selecting components according to past experience and basing selection criteria on:-

- Component characteristics meeting environment requirements.
- Components selected on Mean Time Between Failures (MTBF) requirements and useful life.
- Using components already used on past programs.

Verification. Verification provides confidence that the system requirements are met, for all in-service conditions. System verification can be done against:-

- System requirements.
- Line Replacement Unit (LRU) requirements.
- Function and performance.
- Growth capacity.
- Mechanical and Physical characteristics.
- Maintainability, reliability and safety.

Testing. This requires the system to be tested as extensively as possible to simulate conditions that would be faced in operation.

- To increase the level of confidence in equipment with a subsequent reduction in the rejection rate.
- Conduct a range of tests that will represent different flight profiles.

FRAMEWORKS

Framework identification – Evolves from an iterative process of identification and categorisation of issues based on recurring occurrences, which can be grouped into 'maturity themes'. This opens the way for methods, practices and studies employed in achieving the solution to be challenged. At this level, a degree of of 'questioning' or critiquing can be applied to the issue.

This level achieves the goal of providing a point of convergence to the themed issues. Further subsequent subdivisions of the 'maturity themes' into 'maturity petals' gives focus to the contributory or root causes of the theme i.e. specifically derives the details. This process is illustrated in Figure 4(a) & (b).

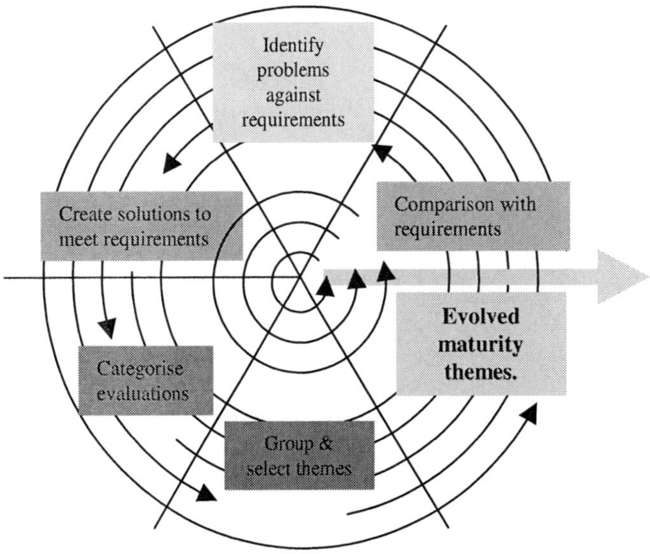

Figure 4a. Iterative process followed to develop maturity themes.

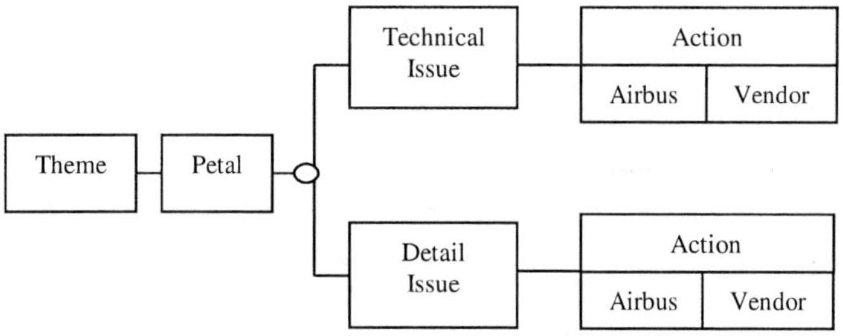

Figure 4b – Flow Chart of Maturity Process.

RISK

Risk Mitigation – Once the specifics have been accurately recorded, a hierarchical selecting procedure can be used to decide the order of importance of the themes and petals, based on occurrences. Consequently, solutions can be prioritised and actioned. In retrospect, by securing and developing a structured process, actions required to ensure maturity can progressed and tackled in a manner that is realistic and achievable in the available time scale.

RELIABILITY & REDUNDANCY

Redundancy. The development of ever technically superior engineering solutions plus the increased used of digital design equipment has led to a dramatic improvement in the levels of redundancy. The increasingly competitive airline market with high frequency and ever shorter turn-around times has led to a requirement for ever-improving dispatch reliability. To achieve this level of redundancy requires a two tier approach:

1. Improve the reliability of system's sub-components.
2. Increasing the levels of redundancy of these components.

This results in a system having the capability of being able to back-up failed units. Mature systems thinking led to improving the level of redundancy of L/G shock absorber by testing the system's components – the gland seals – to as high a level of capability as would be seen in-service. An example of this was testing the seals under multi-axis test loading conditions to simulate a more representative in-service environment. A secondary gland seal for example is carried on the component and is not required during take-off or landing. However, if the primary seal were to fail, this additional seal can be energised to provide back-up, allowing continued operation of the aircraft until such time as the operator locates a suitable repair station. This secondary seal carried on the shock absorber increases the fidelity of the L/G as a whole.

A spare unit is carried aboard aircraft for components that are a vital part of the operating system. These spares can either:

1. Be directly designed into the components, ready to be operational in the event of a component failure.
2. Require engineering assistance to bring it on-line, this usually has to be a swift operation to minimise occurrence of Aircraft On the Ground (A.O.G) or aircraft downtime.

As discussed earlier, this increase in redundancy is part of mature system thinking on components that may lend themselves to areas were engineering infrastructure is less developed. This is outside the general scope of L/G design and includes consideration of airport remoteness, inexperienced maintenance staff, operator reluctance for increased maintenance at turn-around checks and the financial implications of maintaining a support facility.

Mature system thinking provides a vehicle through which these problems and their outcomes can be channelled back onto the component in question. Capturing these problems will prompt the development of a potential necessity, which may later evolve to influence the component's design as a fully-fledged requirement.

Reliability "(Moir I. and Seabridge A.)[4] 1992 Equipment reliability has received considerable attention by the airlines over recent years and is frequently used as a marketing tool by businesses to maintain a competitive edge. Improvements in capability of system design have been impressive but without reliable components, the benefits are of little consequence. Previously the concept of redundancy in L/G systems was discussed, here the question is of reducing failure repetitions is addressed.

Two measures of equipment reliability are generally used:-

- Mean Time Between Failures (MTBF).
- Mean Time Between Unscheduled Replacements (MTBUR).

The former (MTBF) is most often used and is a statistical analysis of component failure and is assumed for the whole device as far as an airline is concerned. The second (MTBUR) refers to the number of times a component is removed irrespective of whether it has been subsequently proved to have failed (if a component is removed as part of the trouble shooting process, MTBUR figure is altered).

Equipment guarantees are generally written around MTBF figures, although airlines favour MTBUR, as there are clearly more removals under this doctrine. Mature system thinking again draws on the experience of an item or component to aid the manufacturer who has little or no control over an airlines maintenance policy, allows feedback on component removal which aids problem finding and future designs.

REFERENCES

1. Airbus Industries, Airbus Directives (ABD) 200.1.2 Part 1 – Product. Requirements and Guidelines for the System designer.
2. Airbus Industries, Purchaser Technical Specification (PTS)
3. Martin, J.N. "Overview of the EIA 632 Standard: Processes for Engineering a System", INCOSE 1998.
4. Moir I. And Seabrdidge, *Aircraft Systems*, Longman Scientific & Technical, U.K., 1992

CONCLUSION

Mature systems thinking is achieved by the reasoning and examination of two key fundamental enablers:-

1. Hierarchy of the problem.
2. Data:
   - Review and Analysis.
   - Filtration and Selection.
   - Abstraction and Aggregation.
   - Prediction (via test) of the emerging properties of the component and later the 'system assembly'.

By exercising these enablers against verified requirements, tailoring basic enablers and principles for a component / system can be developed easily.

Developing these capabilities requires the interface and subsequent overlap of three crucial areas:-

1. The Product – in this case the landing gear composed as assembly and subsystems, together with its respective parts or components.
2. The process – (mature system thinking activities) the phases and corresponding tasks that need to be performed to ensure extensive requirements capture.
3. Organisation or framework – The vehicle used to execute the processes and manage the divisions, teams and individuals that make-up the Airbus consortium.

To address these three areas simultaneously requires the cultivation of awareness and understanding that in addressing design improvements, the contributory cause of a design deficiency is an integrated and not just an isolated problem.

Experiential knowledge to support requirement generation is instrumental in the endeavour. Mature systems thinking processes, requires the power and use of computer databases to be exploited to reduce complexity of requirement analysis. It also allows real data to be used to develop models, perform simulations, and conduct experiments. Thereby understanding and enhancing components, through allowing developers to clearly perceive future in-service issues, patterns and connections, and link these to present best practice or solutions.

The system maturity process secures maturity by ensuring:-

- Appropriate requirements have been allocated to the system or component.
- That the requirements placed upon the component are satisfied not only its design but also by its implementation i.e. testing.
- That the design process is fit for purpose rather than adequate.
- The component fulfils the requirements of performance placed upon it.

Mature systems thinking provides Airbus partners and suppliers with a logical process and tool needed to initiate requirement capture activities in order to achieve early landing gear systems maturity.

ACKNOWLEDGEMENTS

The author would like to thank the friends & colleagues of the Systems Centre at Airbus UK Ltd. for their support and guidance. In particular a special thanks to P. Badman, S. Sharma, B. Stirling and the -600 Landing Gear Team.

BIOGRAPHY

Aymen Mussad is a professional systems engineer at Airbus U.K. Ltd. in Bristol working on mechanical landing systems. He holds an Aerospace Engineering degree from Kingston University and is a member of the IMechE, RAeS and AIAA. He has instigated and developed a maturity process to achieve early "service readiness" for the new Airbus A340-500/600. Previously, he worked at Shell International Ltd. on analytical exploration studies and at IBM UK Ltd. on developing user requirements.

Risk and Performance

Frank J. Snyder
Captain, Signal Corps
United Sates Army
7375 Hidden Knolls Court
Springfield, VA 22153-1910
Phone: (703) 913-8314
EMAIL: flsnyder@erols.com

Dennis M. Buede, Ph.D.
Prof of SEOR
George Mason University
Fairfax, VA 22030-4444
Phone: (703) 993-1727
Fax: (703) 993-1706
EMAIL: dbuede@gmu.edu

Abstract. Risk is constantly present in the engineering design of systems. It influences all lifecycle phases of every system and manifests itself through a system's cost, schedule, and performance attributes. These attributes are expressed through a system's design requirements and therefore provide a measure of how successful a system is. Design requirements are stated by means of a design threshold and a design goal. The distance between the threshold and the goal, known as the design space, provides not only a measure of system performance, but also an understanding of system risk and risk management. Risk management is the sum of activities undertaken to understand, identify, classify, measure, and mitigate risk in the engineering design of systems. This paper presents an output-oriented view of risk and risk management. It provides a taxonomy of risks that exploits the relationship between risk and performance and then discusses several hedging strategies that serve to manage risk in the engineering design of systems.

UNDERSTANDING RISK

Definition of Risk. Understanding risk is essential to the successful engineering design of systems. Further, it forms the basis of risk management and mitigation. Risk has been well described in existing literature as the intersection of two properties: uncertainty and consequences (Browning, 1999), chance and result (Forsberg and Mooz, 1998), or probability and loss amount (Sage, 1995). This paper takes a similar view of risk and adopts the terms *probability* and *consequence* as the two components of risk. A bad outcome (or consequence) includes such things as running over *budget* or *schedule*, suffering a labor union strike that affects the labor *inputs*, and building a car that has a stopping distance of 150 feet (*output*) while the requirement stipulates a threshold of 135 feet. The ideas of budget (costs), schedule, inputs, and outputs will be further developed in later sections of this paper as part of a taxonomy of risks. The taxonomy on risks will further demonstrate the natural relationship that exists between risk and performance.

Figure 1 illustrates the concepts of risk management.

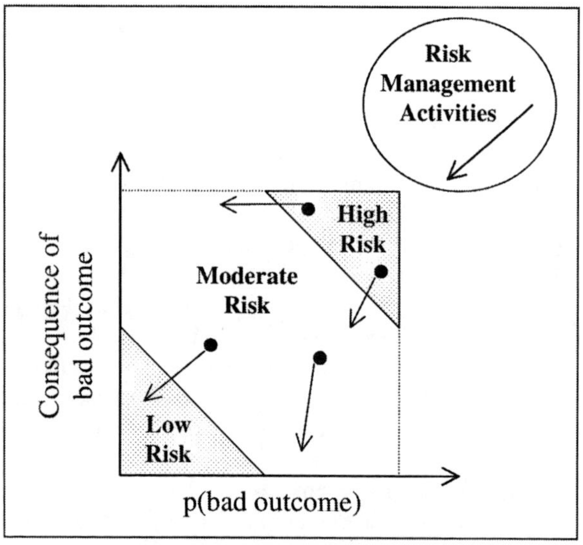

Figure 1. Risk and Risk Management

The x-axis of Figure 1 shows the probability of observing a bad outcome in the engineering design of a system. The y-axis shows the consequence associated with that bad outcome; the larger the negative consequence, the higher the point on the y-axis. The shaded region labeled *low risk* represents an area of acceptable risk in system design that requires less risk management than the rest of the quadrant shown. The shaded region labeled *high risk* represents an area of unacceptable risk that requires different forms of management than the rest of the quadrant shown. Of greatest interest is the unshaded region in Figure 1 labeled *moderate risk* because of the high degree of uncertainty surrounding the probabilities and consequences of bad outcomes. The upper right corner of Figure 1 shows a circle and an arrow. The arrow represents *risk management activities*. This circle represents the goal of risk management which is to move the level of risk associated with a project, down and to the left as represented in the plot. Shown in Figure 1 are four potential risks (represented by dots). The arrows represent risk mitigation efforts to move down and to the left in the plot, or specifically to reduce the consequence or the probability associated with a risk. Note that certain risk management activities can focus principly on reducing uncertainty, others can focus primarily on lessening consequences, and others can be a blend of both.

Risk can be extremely difficult to understand because of its probability component, its consequence component, or both. In fact, the complexity of risks varies greatly from one situation to the next. For example, consider two risky situations that will demonstrate the difficulty in understanding risk. The first situation is playing a casino-style game such as *Keno*. In *Keno,* 20 numbers are drawn each game from a possible pool of 80 numbers, 1 through 80. The player has the option of selecting 2 to 10 numbers and hopes to match his selected numbers to the 20 drawn. This is a very risky venture, however, its parameters are well defined and controlled by the player. In terms of the consequence component of the game, the player controls the amount of the wager and, therefore, has total knowledge of what is at stake. In terms of the probability component of the game, it is a trivial exercise to calculate the odds of winning based on the quantity of numbers played. In fact, the odds of winning are published with the game, so potential gamblers have total knowledge. The gambler then has full autonomy in choosing to play the game or not. Most importantly, the risks are completely defined.

The second situation is building a new airport. When building an airport there are hundreds and perhaps thousands or even millions of consequences of the project. These consequences include the obvious issues of passenger safety and convenience as well as environmental and socio-economic factors that are not as easily identified. Further, if the consequences even can be identified, assigning a probability to the consequence is an estimate, based on expert judgment, at best. Unless serious systematic systems engineering is applied, the potential consequences may go unknown and many probabilities of the consequences may remain sketchy.

Risk is therefore difficult to understand because its parameters may be fully defined, partially defined, or not defined at all. Because of the potential of this uncertainty, it is critical to add as much structure as possible to the venture at hand. This paper advocates the use of the natural relationship between risk and system performance to aid in identifying and structuring consequences and their associated probabilities.

Lifecycle Phases of a System. To understand *all* of the risks associated with the engineering design of systems, it is imperative to identify completely the places where risk resides. Each engineered system has a lifecycle. That lifecycle can be partitioned into seven distinct phases that encompass *all* design activities for that system. Each lifecycle phase, therefore has an associated system with potential risks. These seven lifecycle phases in logical order are (Buede, 2000):

1) development,
2) manufacturing and production,
3) deployment,
4) training,
5) operations and maintenance,
6) refinement, and
7) retirement.

The associated systems are, therefore, the development system, the manufacturing and production system, the deployment system, and so on. There are many potential risks for each phase of the lifecycle. Despite the logical order and numbering, in practice, several of these phases are active concurrently. For example, Buede (2000) has postulated that there are four major periods in the life of a system. These four periods are shown in Figure 2.

In the matrix, notice that during th*e retirement phase*, the deployment, operations, and retirement phases are concurrently active. Additionally, testing systems within each system should also be considered as part of the lifecycle. Each testing system is in fact a risk mitigation activity and contains its own risks.

Lifecycle Phases	Development Only	Pre-initial Operational Capability Development and Testing	Operational Use and Refinement	Retirement
	Periods			
Development	X	X		
Manufacturing/ Production		X	X	
Deployment		X	X	X
Training		X	X	
Operations/ Maintenance			X	X
Refinement			X	
Retirement				X

Figure 2. Lifecycle Phases and Systems Engineering Periods Matrix

Design Requirements. Risk has been established as both the probability of a bad outcome and the consequence of that outcome. The later implies a range on possible observations of system performance. As such, risk can be understood through the sum of design or performance requirements imposed upon a system. The phrase "design requirements" is used interchangeably with "performance requirements," but is intended to highlight that design requirements include all observable system characteristics (outputs) such as cost, schedule, and performance. A performance requirement is characterized by two components: a *minimum acceptable threshold* and a *design goal*. A minimum acceptable threshold is a lower-limit on performance that must be attained to ensure that the system at hand achieves at least a basic capability for which it is being designed. A design goal is an upper-limit on performance that may not be attained; however, a goal marks a most desirable level of performance. The difference between the threshold and the goal is known as the *design space* and defines the maximum possible consequence space for risk in successful engineering projects. Figure 3 illustrates these concepts.

The purpose of Figure 3 is to demonstrate that risk management can not be properly discussed for requirements on which only a point requirement is specified, as illustrated by the left hand side. Risk management is conducted for situations in which there is some uncertainty about how well the system will ultimately perform on some parameters of concern. For these parameters we suggest that a design space be specified with a minimum threshold and a design goal; see the right side of Figure 3. The minimum threshold is such that it can certainly be achieved by all feasible designs and is acceptable (though undesired) by the stakeholders. The design goal is the desired outcome but may be difficult to achieve. Therefore, all designs will result in observed performance levels in this design space. Risk management attempts to increase the probability of getting farther from the minimum threshold and closer to the design goal.

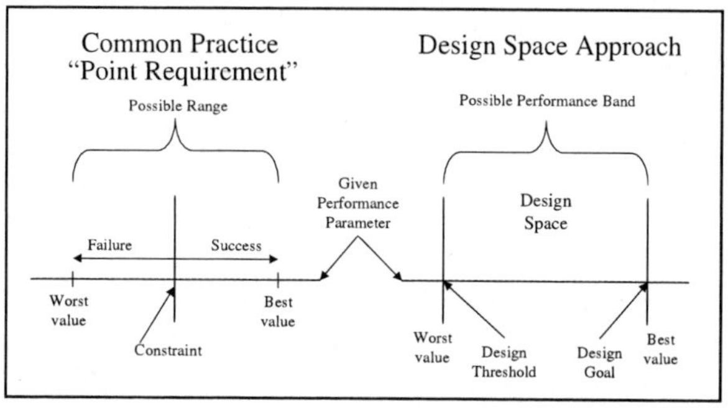

Figure 3. Risk and Requirements: Common Practice vs. the Design Space Approach

In common practice, systems are evaluated through the statement of *constraints* or *point requirements*. In those cases where risk consists of meeting a point requirement, the often unacceptable possibility of failing to meet a requirement without giving sufficient discussion to whether or not this failure is by a small or large margin is addressed. By recasting the discussion in terms of the design space between a minimum threshold and a design goal, the magnitude of change in the probability for specific performance levels can be tackled. In the case of point requirements, a system either fails or succeeds according to the given criteria. No distinction is made between degrees of failure or success as the design space has been eliminated.

Design Space. In the design space approach, shown in Figure 3, the constraint from the common practice graph has been replaced by a design threshold and a design goal. This has created a design space rich with outcomes and consequences. While values of the evaluation criteria are more preferred as they approach the design goal, they are adequate and foster system success to the right of the design threshold. The value of the design space approach, then, is partially in its problem formulation guidelines.

For example, consider the braking system of an automobile as a company designs a new automobile to sell. One measurable performance output of the system that is likely to be used in evaluating system success is the evaluation criteria *stopping distance*. For a given class of cars, a published transportation standard may declare that the maximum allowable stopping distance from 60 to 0 miles per hour is 190 feet. However, among the cars in the given class, the mean stopping distance may be 160 feet and the best stopping distance 140 feet. Often in common practice, systems designers or stakeholders adopt the 160 feet average as a constraint and declare that, "My braking system must be better than the class's average!" Additionally, no additional value is assessed for reducing stopping distances beyond the constraint. This lack of design space eliminates any chance for making design tradeoffs among this criterion and others that might lead to a better overall braking system or automobile. This paper advocates the design space approach and asserts that, in this case, the design threshold should be set at 190 feet and the design goal should be set at least to 140 feet. This approach leaves 50 feet of design space under this criterion. Moreover, this approach rewards design alternatives for each increment of improvement. While this approach allows lower levels of performance to be acceptable for this criterion, it provides a mechanism for analyzing all performance output and trade-off data together (Buede, 2000). It also aids in preventing system failure as a result of performance risk.

Assessing the Design Space Approach. In addition to problem formulation, a method that distinguishes among degrees of success and failure also provides an assessment baseline to determine what value can be expected from a design alternative. Figure 4 demonstrates the value of risk management.

ASSESSING THE DESIGN SPACE APPROACH

Introduction. Once the expected value of a system's performance is ascertained through the design space approach, its expected value with the introduction of various risk management strategies can be determined. The leftmost distribution represents a possible set of expected values under the given evaluation criteria. The rightmost, overlapping distribution represents the changed probability distribution based upon the resulting risk management. The purpose of risk management, therefore, is to undertake activities that increase the expected value of performance of a system under its criteria. Although demonstrated for performance, these principles hold equally true for both cost and schedule outputs. The benefit of risk management is demonstrated as a function of the movement of the expected value of performance output away from the design threshold toward the design goal. The overall value of a risk management activity, then, is a comparison of the derived benefit relative to the increase in expected value to the cost of the activity.

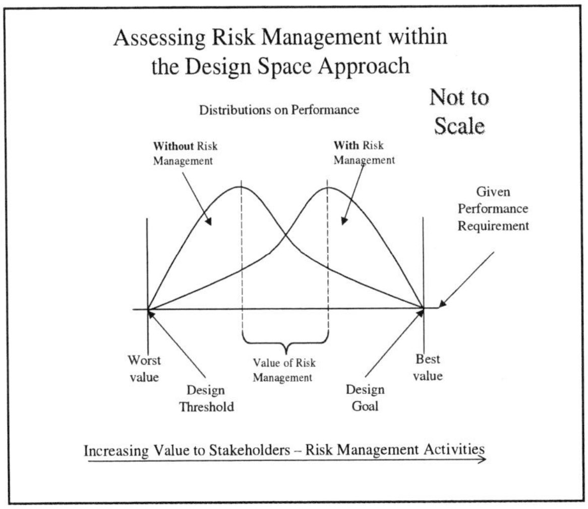

Figure 4. Risk and Requirements

A Taxonomy of Risks. A taxonomy that captures all risks in a collectively exhaustive fashion is critical for a complete understanding of risks and risk management options. This paper provides such a taxonomy in general form. In this taxonomy, five major categories of risk are suggested. These five categories can be partitioned into as specific a level of detail as needed or desired. They are organized from the perspective of system outputs or from the perspective of those who have a stake in the system's performance and risks: the stakeholders. These five categories of risk are represented by the leaves of the tree in Figure 5.

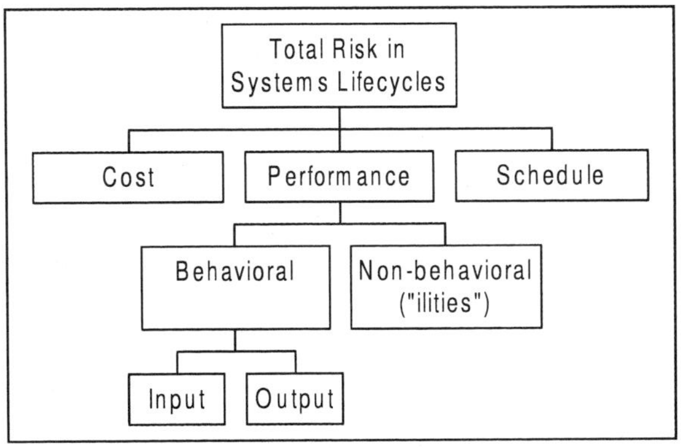

Figure 5 Risk Categories: A Stakeholder's Per spective of System Outputs

Referring to Figure 5, *cost* pertains to all those potential sources of risk that affect the monetary resources of a project. This includes financing, loans, bond issues, interest rates, exchange rates, and others. *Schedule* pertains to all those potential sources of risk that affect the time resources of a project. These issues pertain mostly to completion time of various projects, phases, and milestones, but may include other time resources such as worker-hours or worker-years, depending on how the project is structured. *Performance* captures the greatest number and least tangible potential sources of risk in systems. This category can be partitioned into two sub-categories: *behavioral* and *non-behavioral* risks (Davis, 1993). Behavioral risks are further sub-divided into *input* and *output* risks. *Input* risks include risks to items that are consumed by systems or that govern how systems operate. Examples of such items include labor, raw materials, electricity, laws, and safety regulations. *Output* risks include risks to measurable products of a system that indicate how well the system satisfies the purpose for which it was intended. Examples of such measurable products or outputs are response time in seconds, stopping distance in feet, and gaseous emissions in parts per million. Non-behavioral risks include the "ilities": maintainability, reliability, portability, modifiability, and others. (Davis, 1993).

The taxonomy shown in Figure 5 is important because it aggregates the total performance parameters from which a system is judged and indicates where the sources of risk lie. Further, as the characteristics of a system's performance are developed in depth, so too are its risks.

The structure and type of problem greatly affect how risk factors are classified. For instance, examine the operation and maintenance phase of a passenger railway system. Is the risk to number of trips made by a train each day a function of schedule, cost, or performance? An argument can be made for schedule because of the impact of the frequency and duration of trips scheduled. However, a better argument can be made for performance in terms of train speed or passenger capacity. Yet in another view, almost any risk can be expressed in terms of a "cost" whether it is dollars or some other unit. Why draw attention to the structure of risks? Although some classifications make better sense then others, the point of this discussion is not to advocate one structure over another. The goal is rather two-fold. First, regardless of how risks are classified and organized, it is important to ensure that risks are not duplicated. That is, the listed risks should be mutually exclusive when classified. Risk mitigation is expensive, so stakeholders and engineers are well advised not to adopt any superfluous measures. Second, when in doubt about how to organize and classify risks based on problem structure, it is completely appropriate to consider several risk mitigation strategies associated with the risk classifications. This way, the identified risks might be better mitigated.

Performance, Cost, Schedule, and Risk. Several taxonomies of risk can be compiled from the existing literature. Some suggest that risk is an entity separate from cost, schedule, and performance and that, therefore, it deserves to be a fourth category of consideration in the engineering design of systems. As demonstrated earlier, risk is inextricably imbedded in cost, schedule, and performance and is not an independent category. Risk can best be thought of as a function of the three. It is characterized by the difference between the desired or intended consequences and any realized unintended consequences. Figure 6 illustrates this concept.

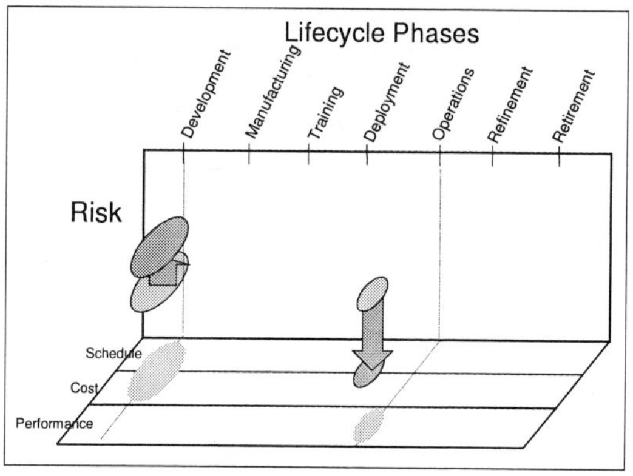

Figure 6. Mapping Risk to Life Cycle Phases

In Figure 6, the vertical plane is the risk associated with each phase of the lifecycle. The horizontal direction represents the various phases of the lifecycle. This risk as shown can be mapped to cost, schedule, or performance (which are shown as a third dimension). Any risk mitigation activity undertaken as part of the development system to decrease risk in the operational system (or any other lifecycle phase system) increases risk for the development system. This risk usually manifests itself through cost or schedule. What should be evident from Figure 6 is that risk is indeed a function of cost, schedule, and performance and not a separate category.

Bear in mind that the strength and purpose of risk classification is to aid in understanding risks and in choosing risk mitigation strategies. The process is not as clean as a mathematical function in that for each risk factor, there is not just one risk mitigation technique. The process has a relational foundation in that many risk mitigation strategies might be appropriate. The classification of risks, however, should provide some insights into how best to mitigate risks.

RISK MITIGATION AND HEDGING STRATEGIES

Introduction. *Hedging strategies* form the basis of risk mitigation. Hedging strategies involve the maintenance of fallback strategies or additional approaches in case a riskier option or approach fails (Buede, 2000).

Risk mitigation begins with assessing the classified risks. While both qualitative and quantitative approaches have a role in this process, the tools of decision analysis coupled with the natural relationship between performance and risk facilitate quantitative risk assessments. Quantitative approaches include applying the tools of decision analysis to measure the effectiveness of a system (Buede, 2000). Qualitative methods depend on knowledge of both systems engineering and the domain in which the engineered system resides. The prudent application of both approaches is useful in mitigating risks.

While there are many ways to categorize risk mitigation activities, the one advocated in this paper after much searching is (1) performing intelligent, comprehensive design, (2) using and increasing redundancy, and (3) increasing and integrating queries of the design. A thorough, but not exhaustive, listing of risk mitigation strategies or *hedging strategies* can be organized according to their relation to the three overarching risk categories, as shown in Table 1. Several are discussed in the ensuing paragraphs.

- Performing intelligent, comprehensive design
  - Maximize the space of feasible designs
  - Use prototypes
  - Review historical results
  - Design an adaptive qualification system
  - Design and integrate concurrently
- Using and increasing redundancy
  - Consider multiple concepts/designs
  - Employ multiple resources
- Increasing and integrating queries of the design
  - Integrate modeling and simulation with qualification
  - Manage/shorten rework cycles
  - Increase "what-if" analyses
  - Increase adaptive qualification activities

Table 1. Risk Mitigation Taxonomy

Design and Conduct Adaptive Qualification Activities. The state of the art in engineering is constantly changing. Because of the dynamic character of modern engineering projects, especially those with a great deal of technological (performance) risk, it is imperative that testing procedures keep pace with designed systems. Testing systems must be suitable for evaluating that "thing" for which they were designed. Adaptive testing means that the testing plans, procedures, and equipment are varied as a function of the previous test results. In cutting edge projects, the maintenance of adaptive testing systems is key to identifying performance shortfalls, and thus the related risks, in a cost-effective manner.

Use Prototypes. Arguably the best hedging strategy against performance risk is the building of prototypes. These can be physical, electronic, or paper representations. If the prototype is built properly, it can provide a great deal of insight into a subset of behavioral performance risks.

Manage the Rework Cycle. One suggested approach to managing performance risk recognizes the complexity of engineering projects. This approach highlights the impacts of such things as cost constraints, supply-chain complexity, project duration, inexperienced staff, project size, socio-economics, product complexity, schedule pressure, changes, and innovation (Mawby, 1999). This hedging strategy is reactive in nature and suggests that to manage performance risk, the rework cycle should be managed because it follows some testing and perhaps the operation phase in the system's lifecycle. This is the time when most (if not all) of the consequences of performance risks have been identified (through realization) and can be best mitigated. It often can be hard or impossible to predict all or even most of a system's potential risks.

Design & Integrate Concurrently. This hedging strategy applies to all three categories of risk. If systems are designed and integrated simultaneously as opposed to sequentially, there is a greater likelihood of finding performance risks that have come to fruition. Moreover, this early discovery makes these consequences cheaper and quicker to fix (Blanchard, 1998). Take for example a nut and bolt that are designed to function as part of a deck fastening system. If the two are designed and integrated before being added to the overall fastening system, then any errors can be found early and corrected before the production line wastes money and time by making one million units, or, God forbid, shipping the system to distributors. It is easier and more sensible to conduct integration testing, especially at the system level, before deploying a system.

Integrate Modeling and Simulation with Qualification. While mostly geared toward mitigating performance risk, this hedging strategy could be stretched to address cost and schedule issues. Simulations are extremely useful in observing system performance and testing is a crucial part of all engineering design. Using simulation results to design testing and then feeding the testing results back into the simulation models both improves the process and develops synergy after several cycles.

Conduct What-if Analyses. The quality application of this hedging strategy increases with knowledge of the domain in which the system under design resides. What-if analyses are conducted through a series of interrogatives in which possible side effects, consequences, actions, or responses occur [Turban]. For example, questions such as: "What if there is a cost overrun?" or "What if there is a hazardous material spill?" are asked. These questions, and others like them, lead to more questions and a respectable idea of what risks exist.

Maximize the Space of Feasible Designs. Referring back to the earlier section on risk and performance, one of the easiest and often ignored hedging strategies is to maximize design space. This mitigation technique also applies to all three categories of risk. Often in the engineering design of systems, artificial and unnecessarily rigid design thresholds or design goals are imposed. Even worse, point requirements or constraints, which are composed of only a threshold, are specified. Since risk and performance are inversely related, a simple risk mitigation strategy involves the prudent choice of design requirements. For example, if a system must be completed 3-5 weeks from now, do not stipulate 3-4 weeks or, worse, just 3 weeks. Design space provides options, trade-offs, and an effective medicine against risk.

Review Historical Results. If not studied and understood, history is doomed to repeat itself. Whenever possible, past similar engineering design efforts should be reviewed to determine what risks to cost, schedule, and performance existed. This is not as useful a strategy in dealing with new technologies or unique projects, but some similarity to other projects is bound to exist.

CONCLUSIONS

Whether referring to the measurable performance outputs of a system or its cost or schedule, it is evident that as performance increases, risk decreases, and vice versa. Though risk is hard to quantify directly, performance can be quantified through the use of design or performance requirements. Risk can then be specified through the design space as the difference between the design goal or threshold and the actual level of performance realized. Further, the relationship of risk and performance can be exploited to create a taxonomy to assist in risk management efforts. These risk management efforts are embodied through an understanding of the intersection of risk and performance and are practiced through hedging strategies.

The hedging strategies presented here are by no means comprehensive, but they are thorough enough to demonstrate the fiber of risk management and to hint toward other strategies. The model of risk management presented in this paper effectively combines the relationship between risk and performance and the sum of risk management activities in mitigating risk.

Understanding risk is critical for understanding the process of risk management. The components of risk, probability and consequence, vary widely in character and are inseparably linked to the systems lifecycle through performance requirements. The design space approach promises to improve design problem formulation, understanding of the expected levels of performance of a system, understanding of the components of risk, measurement of the magnitude of risk, and measurement of the benefit derived from risk mitigation strategies.

REFERENCES

Blanchard, Benjamin S. *System Engineering Management*, Wiley-Interscience, New York, 1998.

Browning, Tyson R. "Sources of Performance Risk in Complex System Development." in the 9th Annual Proceedings of the International Council on Systems Engineering (INCOSE), 1999.

Browning, Tyson R., "Sources of Schedule Risk in Complex System Development," *The Journal of The International Council on Systems Engineering, Volume 2, Number 3, Wiley Interscience*, New York, 1999.

Buede, Dennis M., *The Engineering Design of Systems: Models and Methods*, Wiley-Interscience, New York, 2000.

Davis, Alan M., *Software Requirements: Objects, Functions, and States*, Prentice Hall PTR, New Jersey, 1993.

Forsberg, Kevin and Mooz, Harold. "Risk and Opportunity Management," *The 8th Annual Proceedings of the International Council on Systems Engineering (INCOSE)*, 1998.

Mawby, Dave. "Managing the Rework Cycle not the Schedule – A Project Management Paradigm for the Future?" in the 9th Annual Proceedings of the International Council on Systems Engineering (INCOSE), 1999.

Sage, Andrew P. "Risk Management Systems

Engineering," *IEEE Transactions of Systems, Man, and Cybernetics*, January 1995.

Turban, Efraim. *Decision Support Systems and Intelligent Systems*. Prentice Hall PTR, New Jersey, 1998.

BIOGRAPHIES

Dennis M. Buede received the B.S. degree in aerospace engineering from the University of Cincinnati and the M.S. and Ph.D. degrees from the Engineering-Economic Systems Department of Stanford University. He currently serves as a Professor of Systems Engineering and Operations Research at George Mason University. He is also the Chair of the Education and Research Technical Committee of INCOSE.

Frank J. Snyder received the B.S. degree in systems engineering from the University of Virginia. He is currently enrolled at George Mason University and is pursuing master's degrees in both systems engineering and urban systems engineering. Captain Snyder will report to the United States Military Academy at West Point, NY in May of 2000 where he will serve as a faculty member in the Department of Systems Engineering.will serve as a faculty member in the Department of Systems Engineering.

Using A System Object Methodology in Software Intensive Systems

Richard B. Wray
330-796-9931, richard.wray@lmco.com
Lockheed Martin Corporation, Akron, Ohio
19 March 2000

ABSTRACT

Systems Engineering typically relies upon functionally oriented system definition. However, for software intensive systems that rely upon object-oriented development, functionally oriented system definition provides insufficient input to software development. Development of object-oriented software can be improved by providing input to the software process using an object-oriented system methodology that merges precepts from the Fusion Methodology and the Unified Modeling Language. A hybrid system object methodology must establish at least the user/system context and the models of the key elements of a system design (including the system object model, life cycle model and operations model). Relationships between these models in the methodology include definition of the system boundary, classes and attributes of objects, events and system operations. This paper summarizes underlying object modeling precepts important to systems engineering and describes this hybrid system object methodology.

1. INTRODUCTION

Systems engineering typically is based upon a functionally oriented process of system definition. However modern software development frequently relies on object-oriented software development. Systems engineering must follow compatible approaches to facilitate effective software system design which is using object development approaches.

The typical systems engineering functional approach causes problems in object-oriented design of software due to the difficulties it creates in defining requirements in areas such as run-time operations and concurrent or sequential system behavior, i.e., which functionality is performed or processes execute and with what relationships. The typical functional approach identifies activities (e.g., "*what*" functions) that have to be performed and their outputs-to-inputs dependency relationships. There are difficulties with this approach in identifying, defining and laying out requirements for the system behavior (e.g., "*how*" functions) of software intensive systems, especially for their run-time operations, and in describing concurrent and/or sequential processes. Use of incompatible methodologies creates a strong pressure on software engineering to independently redo the system requirements analysis using their own approach. Such a re-analysis invariably leads to slightly different results, which creates difficulties in system integration, test and customer acceptance.

To effectively support object-oriented, software intensive systems, it is essential that systems engineering follow an object-oriented process providing input to the software process. This does not suggest that system functional analysis is not needed, just that it must be supplemented with object-oriented techniques. There is no commonly accepted system object methodology -- the purpose of this paper is to describe an object-oriented system methodology based on a mixture of the precepts of key software methodologies which better enables systems engineering to support effective startup of the software engineering process. This methodology can improve the transition from the systems to the software development process. Real-time developers can use these methods to model systems better than methods which inherently conflict.

2. KEY ELEMENTS OF THE METHODOLOGY

Key elements needed for the system object methodology are assembled from the Unified Modeling Language (UML) and Fusion Methodology (FM) software methodology. These elements are one set of essential mechanisms for capturing snapshots of the dynamic behavior of a system and its operations over its life cycle.

This paper focuses on describing these object-oriented system methodology key elements (see Figure 1) and their origin:

- models of the user context
- system object model
- life cycle model
- operations behavior model

A set of user context models is needed to fully describe how the users interact with the system (usually with its software components) to perform their tasks and accomplish their goals. A system object model is needed to describe the object classes and behaviors in the system. The life cycle model is needed to describe the allowable operations and interactions over the life cycle of the system's development and operation. The operations model is needed to describe the individual system operations and behaviors, which will lead to the software engineering data dictionary. The life cycle and operations models comprise the interface model, which is an essential element needed early in the systems engineering process.

These system object methodology models are based on third generation object-oriented methodologies used in modern object-oriented software system design. Effective object-oriented software system development requires definition of system requirements with an effective allocation to software object elements, and an object-oriented system architecture which can be efficiently implemented by software engineering. The complexity of modern software requires close cooperation in the methodologies in use by systems and software. Lockheed Martin Naval Electronics and Surveillance Systems has produced initial results on an advanced system implementation of key software system technologies. Two key third generation approaches to software object modeling considered for this initiative are the UML [1, 2,4,5] and the FM [3].

The UML is promulgated by Rational Software Corporation, see *http://www.rational.com*. It adapts and extends the published works of Grady Booch, Jim Rumbaugh, Ivar Jacobson and dozens of others. It supports real-time systems by providing classes, objects, many kinds of associations and use cases, that describe effective systems development. Use cases capture detailed descriptions of required system and subsystem behavior and enable effective modeling of scenarios, including both timing and process synchronization behavior. Objects are defined to

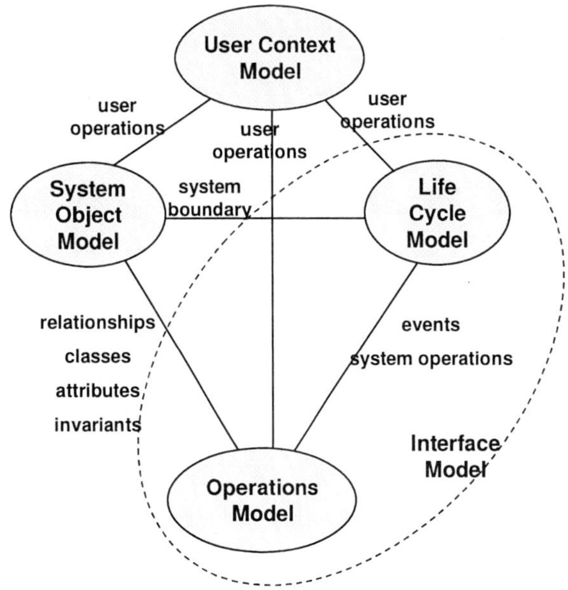

Figure 1. Key Elements of the Object-Oriented System Methodology

capture both data and the functions that operate on them.

The object model is the key to the UML approach. A class can be considered to be a set of object structures characterized by common properties. *Class diagrams* are used to show the important sets of objects and their relationships in the system. The small diamond or triangle at one end of a connecting line indicates ownership (parts-of) or aggregation (subclasses). As the UML notes, "a *uses* association implies that a client class uses some facilities of a server class. An *aggregation* association means that one object is composed, at least in part, of another. An *inheritance* relationship means that one class inherits behavior and structure from the other; that is, one class is a specialization or extension of the other. An *instantiates* association exists between a parameterized class and the class that is created as a result of instantiation. Parameterized classes are specialized as to the type of information they work on.[1]" A subclass inherits data and behaviors of its super-class, and may extend them with new data and operations. Associations are implemented in class diagrams by passing messages from one object to another, which abstracts the interface design details, enabling concentration on control dependencies among objects.

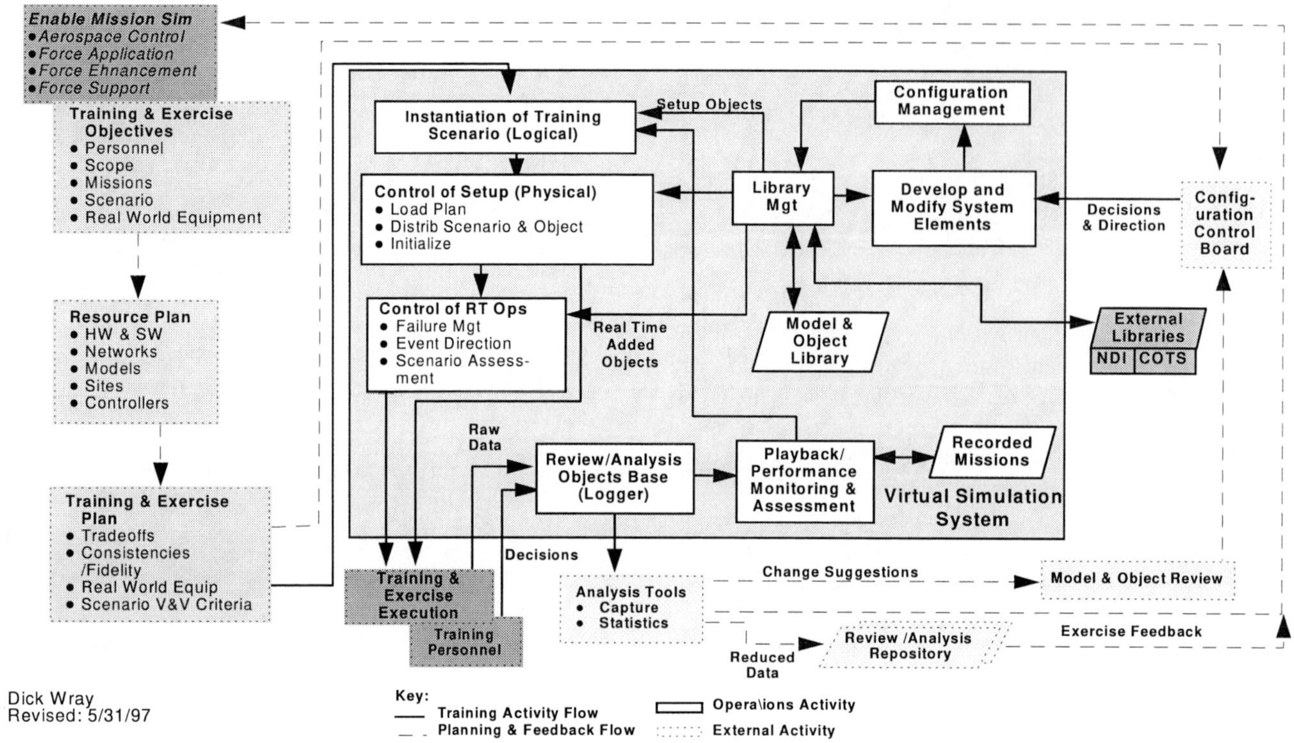

Figure 2. User Context Model

Use cases are especially key to systems engineering since they describe broad behaviors the users need the software to offer, and which are key to successful software implementation. Use cases are the system object context diagrams, system behavior patterns and operating strategies, which offer a high-level view of the system's functionality. This is critical for achieving understanding and agreement on software capabilities by users and engineers. Within a use case there are many threads of interaction that the system may execute. Each of these specific threads is called a *scenario*, i.e., a specific instance of the system behavior. For real-time systems, it is important to capture scenarios defining processes that can be concurrent and must be synchronized.

The FM described in reference 3 encompasses the analysis, design and implementation phases using object-oriented approaches consistently. The key is defining the classes of objects, their relationships, operations to be performed and allowable sequences of operations during the analysis phase -- which is exactly the focus of systems engineering. The FM calls for definition of an object model and an interface model during analysis. The object model captures the concepts of the problem to be solved, their relationships and thus can be used to start defining the system requirements. An important element of the object model is the system object model created by excluding all classes and relationships in the environment. The system object model describes system structure, not behavior. While the FM uses a diamond notation to indicate relationships, for this paper all relationships are identified by notation on the line connecting classes or objects.

The interface model in the FM is used to describe system behavior in terms of events (inputs or outputs) and the changes they cause. The environment is the set of entities the system communicates with. An event causes a change in the system state. An input and its effect are a system operation. The interface model consists of a life cycle model and an operations model.

The author is not aware of any generally accepted computer based tools that can accomplish all the system tasks needed to implement these methodologies.

3. USER CONTEXT MODELS

The user context model is the critical element is describing system behavior (see Figure 2). It identifies the external environment and how it interacts with the system. For example, in a training simulation/exercise operations context, it shows how a system fits into a larger training system picture. For an object-oriented

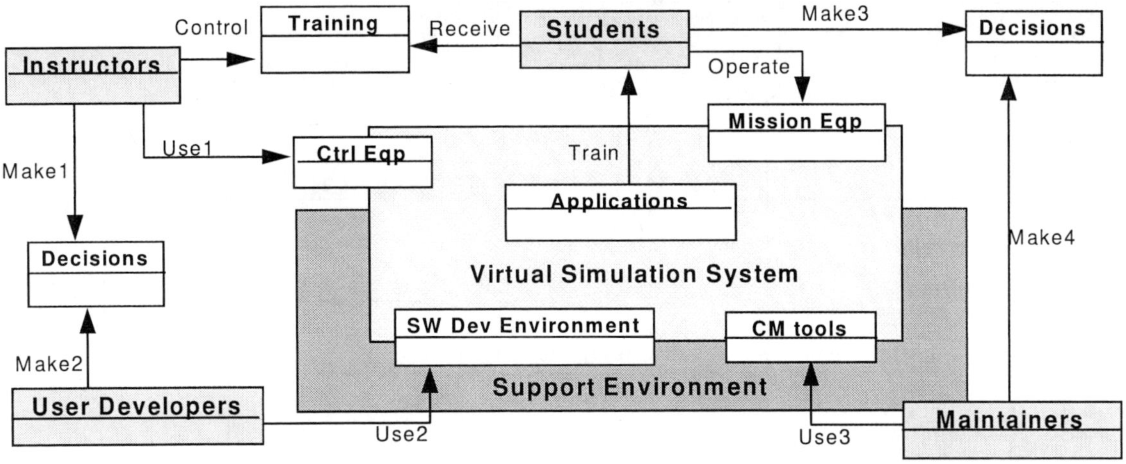

Figure 3. System Users Operating Context Shows Relationships

training simulation, this means the user context model must be developed for the behavior of the distributed software in training operations and exercises. Systems engineering must describe the external elements, their roles and behavior (especially as it potentially impacts the system) and their interfaces to the system.

The first element in the system behavior context model describes the external entities and their interfaces to the system. The user context model identifies the key operations inside and external to the software to be used for training in flight missions. Key elements to the users are the missions in which training is needed and the exercises to conduct this training, as represented in the blue boxes. The user operational missions are converted into training and exercises through the use of outside mechanisms, analysis tools, repositories, and external libraries of objects and models to be drawn upon. If software has the capability to add additional models and objects, then both internal configuration management and external configuration control are needed.

These external entities establish the interfaces that must be defined for the software objects to be required. Within the software, classes are needed to enable logical instantiation representing the scenario to be trained and to enable its physical setup. Additional classes are needed (as shown) to enable a software to be run and results captured for later assessment or revision. The focus is on the external elements and how they interface to system elements.

The system operating context model identifies another key context element: people and how they may or must interact with the resulting system. The model focuses attention on the types (i.e., classes) of people using the system, and how each behaves with the system elements (see Figure 3). The object-oriented system methodology defines the users (classes) of the system. This enables software engineering to accurately understand the scope of classes and behaviors which must be enabled for the system. Then this methodology requires the definition of (sub)system elements (classes) that are needed to enable these people classes to interact with the system and each other. The relationships between people and the key system classes must be defined using a simplified operating context of the system for its users.

In this example, four sets of users have been identified: instructors, students, user developers and maintainers. An effective system operating context model must show how each of these users interact with the system. Such external classes represent elements important to using the system, such as decisions made by people, which have to be handled by the software. Note that the class "decisions" is shown twice to minimize confusion from overlapping of lines.

Only those system classes which interface with user classes are shown inside the system: the control equipment, mission equipment, applications, development environments and configuration management (CM) tools used for development and control. System engineering defines the requirements for the classes in sufficient detail to enable software developers to perform the software engineering of the system and its behavior. A major point of the user context model is to force clearer thinking and more

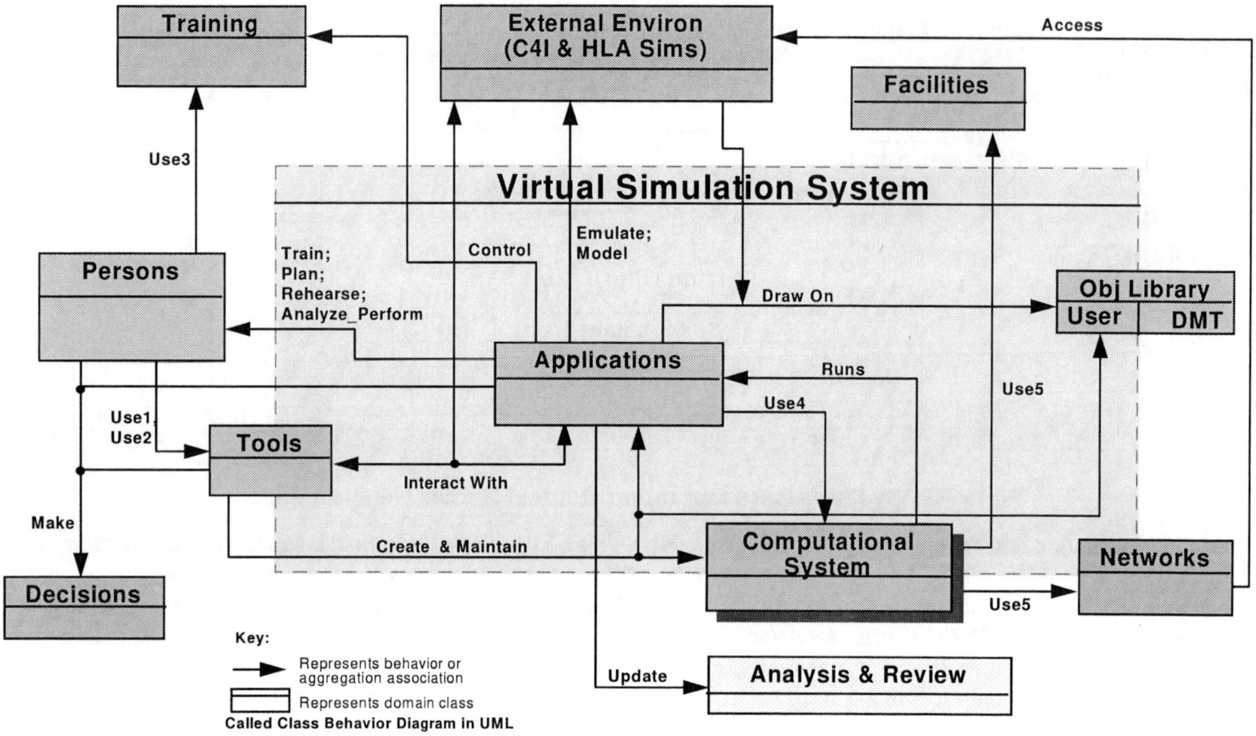

Figure 4. Training/Exercise Software System Object Model

effective examination of all potential interactions involving all potential external entities.

4. SYSTEM OBJECT MODEL

The system object model is used to organize the development of the system elements and their relationships which software needs to prototype and implement the system. The system object model must identify the support environment if it is closely coupled with the system's operation, and the external elements with which it interacts.

The system object model (see Figure 4) captures all (sub)system classes and relationships. The emphasis is on identifying the key system classes for which behavior requirements are needed to effectively describe how the software interacts with its complete environment. Note that the previous set of users has been aggregated into the superclass "persons" and the software development environment and CM tools have been aggregated into the superclass "tools". This enables more complete systems object analysis of all people who might interact with the system and the tools needed. This more complete analysis thus would need to be fed back into the user context models for completeness and consistency.

The system object model provides more high level detail into internal interfaces and behaviors of the system to facilitate early discussions with all stakeholders to ensure that all required capabilities are captured in the user and system models. For instance, note that an "Analysis & Review" class has been added to this model (Figure 4). During discussions, this class and its object would be further defined to provide a better understanding early in the development process of its interactions with users and the software. This enables definition of better requirements and elicitation of more complete requirements. It also enables determination and agreement that all applications classes have been defined, interface relationships have been identified, and requirements allocation criteria are correctly understood and applied.

Associations need to be identified to describe the relationships across interfaces for system relationships or behavior in terms of events and the changes in state they cause. A system operation is an input event **and** the effect it has. Examples of events and effects are shown in Figure 5.

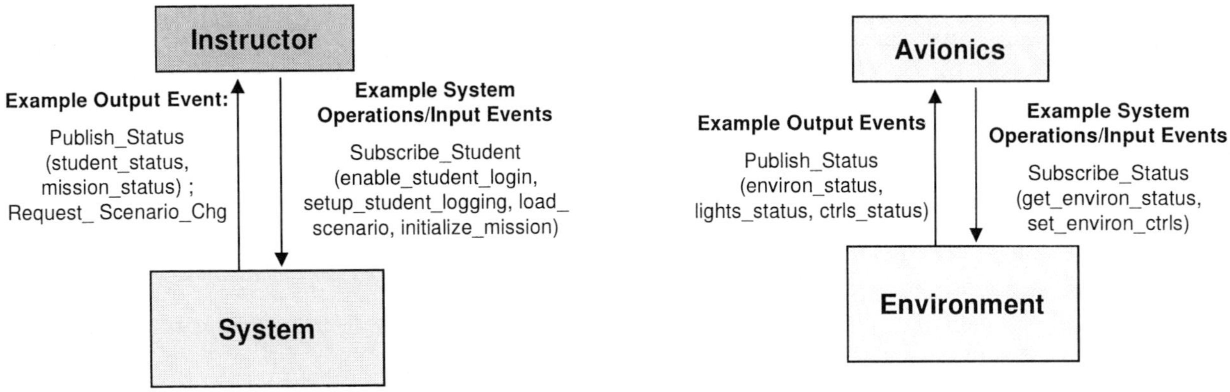

Figure 5. Object Associations and Interface Behavior

5. LIFE CYCLE MODEL AND SCHEMA

The life cycle model is one of two key elements of the interface model. It identifies and describes the allowable operations and sequences of interactions over the system's life cycle that the software must implement.

The life cycle model (see Figure 6) of a system is defined as a series of expressions which capture the behaviors of the system over its entire life cycle. This ensures all operations are effectively developed and executed. An example of a schema for the life cycle model is shown below. In this example, the PROJECT is implemented by the series of expressions shown in bold. These expressions may be operations, such as "develop" or "plan_execution". The "develop" operation provides output "objects," or "models," or "scenarios". Each of these operations is expanded on following lines in more detail until a primitive executable operation is reached.

Life Cycle Model Schema

Name = life-cycle-expression

Identifies allowable operations and sequences of interactions over the system's life cycle.

Figure 6. Life Cycle Model Definition

PROJECT= [**Develop**. (# Objects | # Models | # Scenarios). **Test**. (# Validated_Objects | # Validated_Models | # Validated_Scenarios)]. **Plan_Execution**. (# Instantiation. # Mission). **Setup. Execute**|| (Checkpoint | Observe | Tag | Direct)* . **Stop**. # Record. [**Review_&_Analyze**].**Support.Retire**

where:

- PROJECT is a 'name' for a life cycle element, = is 'implemented by', followed by a 'life cycle expression'
- The life cycle expression can consist of operations or more life cycle expressions:
- **Develop** is an operation
  - Description: Perform knowledge acquisition, engineering analysis, design, implementation, and V&V of models and object for inclusion in the Object_Library.
  - Reads: —
  - Changes: Object_Library (or that + Model_Lib, Scenario_Lib, Mission_Lib)
  - Sends: —
  - Assumes: —
  - Result: the verified and validated models are added to the library
- # **models** is a product or output
- **Plan_Execution** is an expression
  - Plan_Execution = Ident_Scenario. Ident_Classes. Ident_Resources. and Ident_Scenario is an operation

and where: an element is a process, = is 'implemented by', . is separator 'and' or 'then', [ ] is 'optional', # is 'output' or 'produce', || is 'while', ( ) is 'doing', | is 'or', e* is zero or more repetitions of expression e, and e+ is one or more repetitions of e.

6. OPERATIONS MODEL AND SCHEMA

The operations model is the second of two key elements of the interface model. It describes the specific operations named in the life cycle model and identifies key elements needed in the schema.

The operations model (see Figure 7) of a system is defined by the terms identified. An operations schema is analogous to the software data dictionary, except it addresses system operations. Examples of two system operations are shown below: distribute_sim_objects and ident_scenario.

Operations Model Schema

(for individual system operations)

Operation:	Name
Description:	Text
Reads:	Items
Changes:	Items
Sends:	AgentAndEvent
Assumes:	Condition
Result:	Condition

Figure 7. Operations Model Definition

Discussions of the system operations clarify the operations required and thus are more understandable to all developers and stakeholders. Discussions can also identify operations disallowed by implication since they are not shown in the operations model schema. For instance, the potential operation "delete_object" might be disallowed implicitly if not shown in the schema at all (depending on rules setup for using the schema), or explicitly under defined conditions if shown and noted under the description (as shown below) that object deletion can only be accomplished during certain phases of the software. When systems engineering establishes all operations (with the assistance of software), then unclear requirements for executing operations are reduced.

- **Distribute_Sim_Objects**
  - Description: Load models, objects, and data structures into hosts and networks following a Load_Plan.
  - Reads: Load_Plan, Model_Object_Library
  - Changes: Distributed_Computing_Environment
  - Sends:
  - Assumes: a valid Load_Plan exists
  - Result: the Distributed_Computing_Environment is ready for Initialization
- **Ident_Scenario**
  - Description: Identify the Area_Of_Operations, real-world equipment, and Forces that will be used for a particular software instantiation.
  - Reads: Model_Object_Library
  - Changes: Instantiation
  - Sends:
  - Assumes: —
  - Result: a new Instantiation object is created with a consistent set of classes and methods

NOTE: in order to ensure system consistency throughout an exercise, control events such as the creation of a crater on an airfield or the removal of an aircraft from the software are handled using Insert_Sim_Object to insert an event onto the software event cue. There is no direct means of removing or modifying an object in a software execution.

7. SUMMARY

There are four key models needed for effective system modeling: the User Context Model, System Object Model, Life Cycle Model, and Operations Model. Their implementation should follow the precepts of the Unified Modeling Language and the Fusion Method.

The advantages of object-oriented approaches typically include data abstraction, compatibility, flexibility, reusability, extensibility, and ease of maintenance. These are as valid for systems engineering as for software engineering. If software engineering wants to take advantage of object development, then systems engineering should accommodate this approach to facilitate the design of the software. The functional approach will cause problems in object-oriented design of the software due to the difficulties it creates in defining requirements in areas such as run-time operations and concurrent or sequential system behavior. There are also problems with the notations and process detailed elements. Use of incompatible methodologies creates a strong pressure on software engineering to independently redo the system requirements analysis using their own approach. Such a re-analysis invariably leads to slightly different results, which creates difficulties in system integration, test and customer acceptance.

The object-oriented systems methodology presented in this paper establishes an initial framework which should be used by systems engineering to organize their analysis efforts. That would significantly improve the transition of requirements to software engineering and the design of the subsequent software. Unfortunately, there are (as yet) no generally acceptable tools that could implement this process on computers and support transition from the systems to the software domains.

REFERENCES

1. Booch, Grady; Rumbaugh, Jim; Jacobson, Ivar; et al.; Unified Modeling Language (UML), Rational Software Corporation, *http://www.rational.com*,

2. Lyons, Andrew; "UML for Real-Time Overview," Rational Rose Corp: http://www.rational.com; April 1998

3. Coleman, Derek; et al; "Object-oriented Development: The Fusion Method", Prentice Hall Inc: Englewood Cliffs, NJ; 1994

4. Douglass, Bruce Powell; "The UML for Systems Engineering", i-Logix, 8 Dec 1998

5. Rumbaugh, Jim; Selic, Bran; "Using UML for Modeling Complex Real-Time Systems", Rational Software Corporation and ObjecTime Limited, http://www.rational; March 11, 1998

PRINCIPAL AUTHOR BIOGRAPHY

RICHARD B. WRAY has a dual MS/MBA in Systems Management, Acquisition, and Contracting; a MBA With Distinction Honors in General Management; a MS in Systems Engineering and a BS in Mathematics. He is the Chairman of the INCOSE Process and Methods Technical Committee and the Systems Engineering Handbook Working Group. Mr. Wray is a Senior Engineering Specialist with Lockheed Martin Corporation, responsible for developing and implementing software plans, performing software requirements and systems analyses, and implementing software systems. He is leading the development of product team processes and standards. He is leading the assessment of systems engineering capability maturity in his company. He has also led development of generic architecture standards and software using advanced computer aided systems engineering tools. He has performed and led analyses of system operational concepts, functional and performance requirements, hardware/software tradeoffs, system top level design and specialty integration; and strategic system planning for advanced avionics.

Adapting UML for an Object Oriented Systems Engineering Method (OOSEM)

Howard Lykins
Software Productivity Consortium
2214 Rock Hill Road
Herndon, Virginia 20170-4227
lykins@software.org

Sanford Friedenthal
Lockheed Martin Management & Data Systems
3201 Jermantown Road
Fairfax, Virginia 22030
sanford.friedenthal@lmco.com

Abraham Meilich, Ph.D., C.C.P.
Lockheed Martin Mission Systems
700 N. Frederick Ave
Gaithersburg, MD 20879
abraham.w.meilich@lmco.com

Abstract. Object-oriented (OO) techniques have been used predominately by software engineers. Why would systems engineers want to add OO techniques to their existing practices? How should such techniques be adapted to be useful to systems engineers? This paper will show how an Object-Oriented Systems Engineering Method (OOSEM) addresses these questions and how the use of the Unified Modeling Language (UML) at the systems engineering (SE) level can facilitate capture of system requirements and design information and ease communication between systems and software engineers. The techniques overviewed in this paper have been applied to information systems and have allowed engineers to model system needs, requirements, architectural design, and their allocation to hardware, software, databases, and manual procedures. The authors believe that OOSEM is applicable to engineering of other types of systems as well.

BACKGROUND

Motivation for OOSEM. OO techniques have been applied successfully by software engineers to software development for years. However, systems engineering, for the most part, continues to apply classical structured analysis techniques to define the system-level requirements and design artifacts. The use of different modeling techniques can result in incompatibilities and communication problems between systems and software engineering. OOSEM is motivated in part by the need to mitigate these incompatibilities.

This is not the only motivation for OOSEM. As evidenced by several recent books and articles, systems engineers are increasingly interested in the use of OO modeling to more effectively capture, analyze, and communicate system requirements and design information. However, it is the opinion of the authors that software-level OO techniques will require adaptation if they are to fully benefit systems engineers.

Related work. OOSEM has evolved from several initiatives at the Software Productivity Consortium (the Consortium) and Lockheed Martin Corporation. The Consortium developed the Integrated Systems and Software Engineering Process (ISSEP) (Rose et. al 1996; Rose and Scott 1997; Rose 1997), which provides a process framework for integration of systems and software engineering methods. Lockheed Martin Management & Data Systems (M&DS) used ISSEP as the process framework for the initial development of OOSEM (Friedenthal 1998). Key elements of OOSEM were successfully applied to a development increment for the army global command and control system (Meilich and Rickels 1999).

Using OOSEM and other OO methods as inputs, the Consortium is developing an integrated systems and software engineering method. This method, tentatively named Object-Oriented Approach to Software-Intensive Systems (OOASIS), will provide UML-based modeling at the systems and software engineering level.

Integration of non-OO model-based SE and OO software engineering is discussed by Ali (1998).

The SE community also has indicated interest in OO techniques independent of integration with software-level OO. A recent book by Oliver, Kelliher, and Keegan (1997) uses an OO modeling technique to describe both the SE process and the results of the process. An approach for deriving an OO system design from functionally-oriented customer requirements (Hopkins and Rhoads 1998) was presented at the 1998 Symposium of the International Council on Systems Engineering (INCOSE). The need for animating object oriented models (Dockerill 1999) was discussed at the 1999 Symposium, along with some cautionary notes about using OO models for SE (Cocks 1999).

Schoening (1996) discusses use of object-based[1] software to simulate complex systems.

OOSEM APPROACH

The OOSEM approach is characterized as follows:

- It implements a well-defined SE process that encompasses the activities from needs analysis through verification based on the ISSEP process model.
- It adapts UML Version 1.3 (Object Management Group 1999) to capture system requirements and design information. UML was selected because of the rigor of its syntax and semantics and because it has become the de facto industry standard for OO software development.
- It maintains well-defined relationships between its models and components to ensure requirements traceability and system design integrity.
- It addresses the total system, including allocation of requirements to hardware, software, databases (in data-intensive projects), and manual procedures.

It should be emphasized that OOSEM does not advocate replacing specialty engineering models with UML. Rather, it encourages use of OO models to capture system and component behavioral, performance, and physical characteristics that provide the basis for integrating other specialty engineering models. Other traditional techniques and models are required to fully capture the system requirements and design information, such as performance timelines and physical layouts.

UML CONSTRUCTS USED BY OOSEM

This section summarizes the UML constructs most commonly used by OOSEM. Some constructs are used without significant change; others must be adapted for use in the systems context.

Classes, attributes, and operations. A UML class is a template from which one or more objects is derived. OOSEM uses objects to represent input/output (I/O) entities and abstract physical components that can:

- Store items such as data, energy, mass, or parts
- Perform sets of operations on inputs or stored entities in response to a stimulus.

The class from which an object is derived specifies a set of attributes and operations associated with the object. OOSEM uses UML operations to capture functional behavior associated with the system, its components, or external systems. Attributes are used to model system state, transient and persistent data, and performance characteristics, such as response time, size, weight, and cost.

The automated teller machine (ATM) example in Figure 1 illustrates the OOSEM adaptation of UML classes, attributes, and operations. Stereotypes are used to categorize these artifacts by what they represent. For example, a class with the stereotype <<System>> represents the system under development, and <<IO>> designates an input/output entity that captures interface information (described below). OOSEM uses attributes of the <<System>> class to represent system state variables, transient and persistent data stores, and system performance parameters.

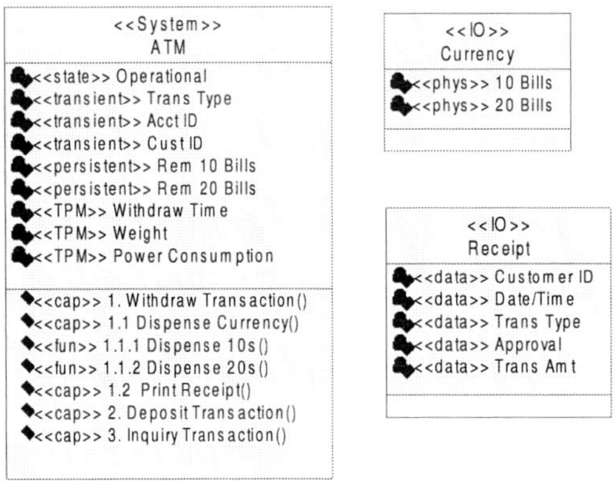

Figure 1. Classes and I/O Entities

Various component types and subtypes, such as hardware, software, and data components, also can be represented as class stereotypes.

Numbering indicates the hierarchy of system capabilities (<<cap>> stereotype) and functions (<<fun>> stereotype). In Figure 1, Dispense Currency and Print Receipt are subcapabilities of Withdraw Transaction. Dispense 10s and Dispense 20s are functions of Dispense Currency. The distinction between capabilities and functions is explained below.

Input/output entities, illustrated in Figure 1, are a special type of class that are used to capture inputs and outputs of the system and its components. The I/O entities have no operations but are characterized in terms of attributes. These attributes include data content and their associated data type, frequency, size, and data transfer method (e.g., File Transfer Protocol [FTP] and database transactions). The data content attributes represent input and output parameters to system functions. These attributes can represent inputs and outputs other than data, such as physical inputs for mass, energy, or parts. Interface control documents and interface requirements specifications are generally used to capture this information. Data attributes are identified by the <<data>> stereotype—physical items such as

[1] Defined to mean "object oriented without inheritance"

$10 and $20 bills dispensed by the ATM are identified by the stereotype <<phys>>.

OOSEM defines system capabilities as operations that produce or consume I/O entities. System functions operate on individual attributes of I/O entities.

Use case diagrams, illustrated in Figure 2, are used by OOSEM to conceptualize system capabilities for both the as-is system and the to-be system and provide the basis for defining detailed scenarios. They are initially defined at the system black-box level and further elaborated to capture system functionality and interaction between system components.

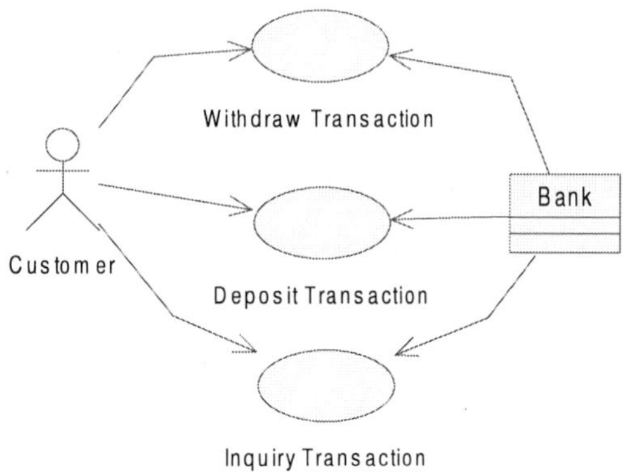

Figure 2. Use Cases

Inheritance is used to capture commonality in OOSEM as in other OO techniques. OOSEM also uses inheritance to capture potential requirements and design variations. For example, in Figure 3, a variant of the ATM system adds a funds transfer capability.

Aggregation is used by OOSEM to decompose the system into components and to decomposed I/O entities into lower-level entities.

Deployment view. OOSEM uses class diagrams or deployment diagrams to represent allocation of software and data components to hardware components and allocation of manual procedures to people or organizational components.

OOSEM ACTIVITIES AND MODELS

OOSEM includes the following development activities:

- Analyze Needs
- Define System Requirements
- Define Logical Architecture
- Synthesize Candidate Allocated Architectures
- Optimize and Evaluate Alternatives
- Validate and Verify the System

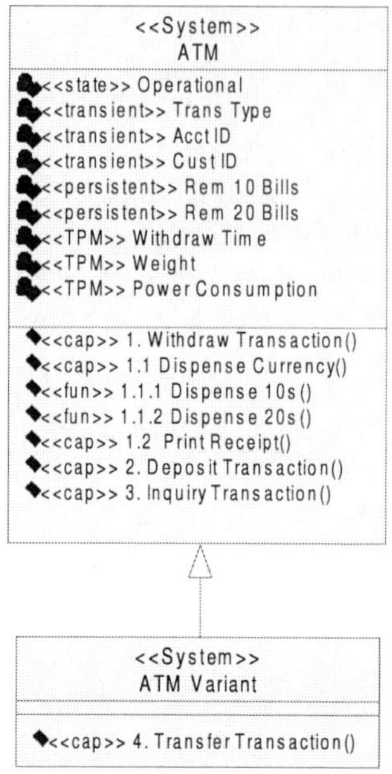

Figure 3. Inheritance

Analyze Needs. This activity characterizes the problem space by defining as-is system operation, current deficiencies, mission/enterprise-level measures of effectiveness, and required capabilities.

This activity applies use cases, scenarios, and other OOSEM models to describe the current system and its processes. Various types of system users are characterized by UML actors and the use of inheritance. The general-purpose actor User, illustrated in Figure 4, captures characteristics common to all users. Specific types of user are modeled as subclasses that add their own unique characteristics. The use cases and scenarios capture the key functionality of the current system.

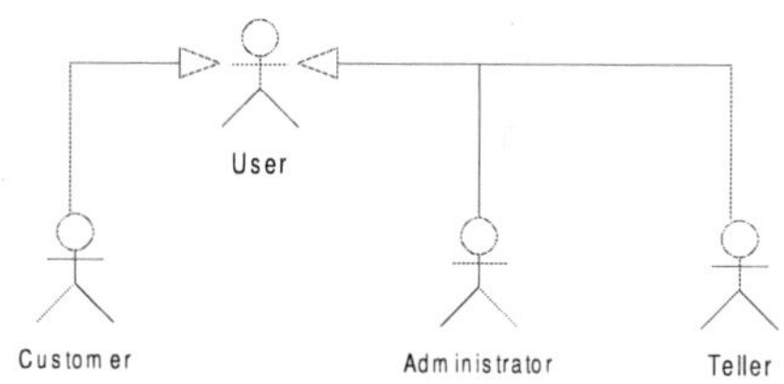

Figure 4. User Classification

Analysis of as-is use cases is used to identify deficiencies of the current enterprise (that the new system will correct) and preliminary measures of effectiveness. A root cause analysis of these deficiencies provides the basis for establishing the needs for the improved system.

An Enterprise Model, illustrated in Figure 5, uses

classes and aggregation relationships to describe how an enterprise is constructed from the system to be developed and other, external systems. In the Enterprise Model, the <<System>> class is shown as a component of the <<Enterprise>> class. Additional classes denote elements external to the system with which the system collaborates to accomplish its mission. Operations on the <<Enterprise>> class denote enterprise-level capabilities (e.g., to withdraw money from the bank), which are allocated to both the system (e.g., ATM) and to the external systems (e.g., bank). Operations on the <<System>> class (shown in Figure 1), on the other hand, will describe system capabilities. Detailed elaboration of these capabilities will be captured in the Define System Requirements activity. Performance attributes of the <<Enterprise>> class (e.g., amount of time to make a withdrawal) are effectiveness measures (<<moe>> stereotype), which are allocated to the system (ATM) and external systems (e.g., bank, user).

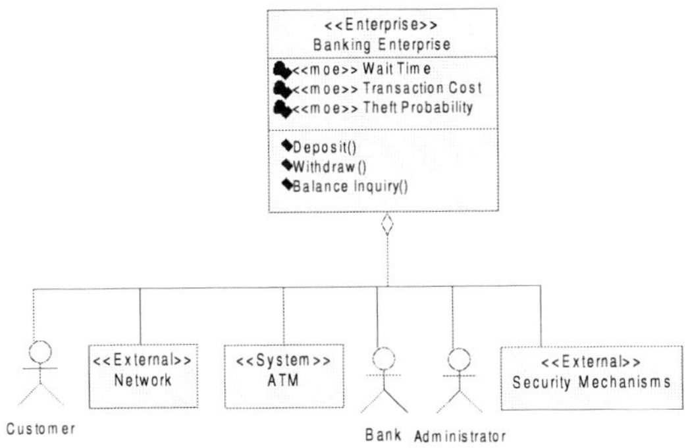

Figure 5. Enterprise Model

Define System Requirements. This activity treats the system as a black box to characterize system stimulus-response behavior and performance requirements. The system, external systems, and users are defined as individual classes as previously described in the enterprise model. The system operational concept defines a set of system-level use cases and scenarios based on the needs analysis. This operational concept is used to derive the system functional, interface, data, and performance requirements. The functional requirements are grouped into system capabilities. System states/modes and related system control information are also defined (e.g., using state machines). The resulting system requirements information is captured in an elaborated system context diagram, as illustrated in Figure 6. In the elaborated context diagram and elsewhere in OOSEM, the <<Actor>> stereotype is used to denote human users. To distinguish humans from external systems, the <<External>> stereotype is used for the latter.

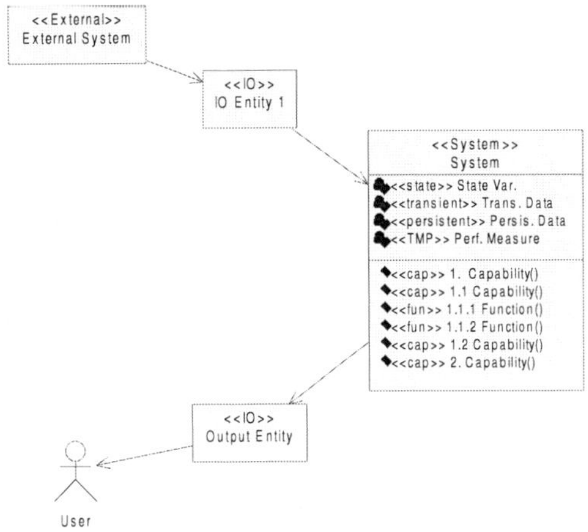

Figure 6. Elaborated System Context Diagram

This activity also identifies system design constraints, which limit the solution space. Examples are pre-identified hardware and software commercial off-the-shelf (COTS) products and legacy databases. The constraints are captured in a constraints list (external to the UML models) and used as an input to the system architecture activities. Requirements variation is also captured and quantified in terms of a probability of change. A typical examples is a system interface that is likely to change because the other side of the interface is still under development. The requirements and verification traceability (RVT) database is initiated during this activity, and traces each system functional, interface, and performance requirement to a system-level use case.

Scenarios are captured using UML sequence, collaboration, or activity diagrams. The purpose of these scenarios is to illustrate how the system will interact with actors and external systems on the context diagram. The scenarios show only the system, actors, and external systems that produce or consume I/O entities and attributes, thus providing the foundation for defining the detailed functional, interface, performance, and storage requirements. Interactions among system components are described in the next two activities.

Define Logical Architecture. This activity decomposes the system into its logical components, defines their interactions, and allocates system requirements to each logical component. OOSEM guidelines for decomposing the <<System>> class into logical components are different from traditional functional decomposition guidelines, emphasizing, among other concerns, planning for change. The interaction between logical components is captured in data flows (represented using associations and I/O entities) and logical system threads. Partitioning criteria are established and used as a basis for partitioning the logical components to address component cohesiveness, design for change, performance, and other design considerations. System functional, interface, data, and performance requirements are allocated to logical components and captured in the RVT database.

The Define Logical Architecture activity uses aggregation relationships to describe a hierarchical view of the system logical architecture, as illustrated in Figure 7. The system is decomposed into logical components, which may be further decomposed into lower-level logical components. Each logical component is an abstraction of a set of possible system components (e.g., hardware, software, databases, manual procedures), any one of which will meet the requirements allocated to the logical component. An example of a logical component is a user interface. The potential corresponding elements in the allocated architecture (developed in the next activity) may be a Web browser with associated screen representations on a PC client. In the ATM example, a money dispenser may be a logical component that could be implemented in the allocated architecture in many different ways. Sequence, collaboration, and activity and state diagrams are used to describe interactions among logical components.

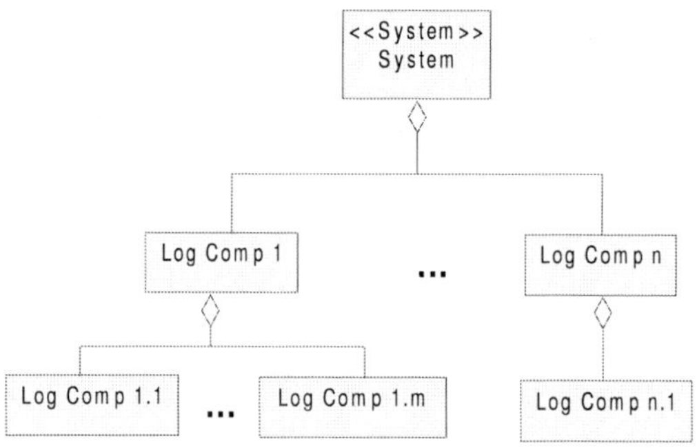

Figure 7. Hierarchical Decomposition Example

The partitioning heuristics in this activity take the following into consideration:

- Design for changes in needs, requirements, and design decisions
- Encapsulation of detailed component behavior and performance characteristics
- Reuse considerations, including use of COTS items
- Timing and other performance considerations
- Reliability and maintainability
- Environmental considerations
- Allocation of development work to subcontractors

Synthesize Candidate Allocated Architecture. This activity maps each logical component to hardware, software, data, and/or manual procedures. The resulting allocated components form the basis for a multilayer system architecture, which typically includes layers for the mission application, a services layer (i.e., functions common to multiple mission applications), and operating system and resources. The allocated components are used to derive the corresponding hardware, software, and data architectures. The software architecture is captured using the full range of UML diagrams and features. The hardware architecture uses UML class diagrams for defining hardware hierarchy; the architecture also uses interconnection and traditional hardware depictions such as physical layouts. The data architecture uses class diagrams to capture data hierarchy and relationships, along with table specifications and other traditional data architecture depictions. Figure 8 illustrates the OOSEM deployment view, using a class diagram to depict the allocation of software and data components to hardware components.

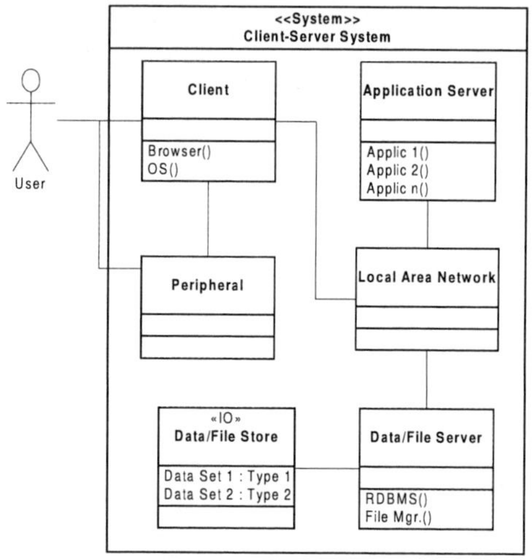

Figure 8. Allocated Architecture

Functional, interface, and performance requirements are allocated to component classes of hardware, software, data, and manual procedures. All system requirements are allocated to system components in this activity. Traceability is maintained between the logical and allocated components and captured in the RVT database.

Process engineers and software, database, and hardware developers use the allocated architecture and associated component requirements as an input to their development activities. Alternatively, components in the allocated architecture can be procured off the shelf. Continued feedback to the system designers is provided to ensure traceability between the system requirements, system architecture, and component design. Traceability is maintained between the allocated architecture and the component design in the RVT database.

Optimize and Evaluate Alternatives. This activity is invoked throughout the other OOSEM activities to optimize the candidate architectures and conduct trade studies to select the preferred architecture. Parametric models for characteristics such as performance, reliability, availability, and life-cycle cost are used to analyze and optimize each candidate architecture to the level needed to compare the alternatives. The parametric models use architectural components defined in the logical and allocated architectures and their associated performance parameters. Trade studies are used to evaluate each alternative architecture based on defined criteria and weighting, which are traceable to the system requirements and measures of effectiveness.

The parametric models tend to use their own unique syntax and descriptions. OOSEM architectural models provide a common definition of the components, performance and physical attributes, and their interfaces, which is used by the parametric models.

Validate and Verify the System. This activity includes the development of verification plans, procedures, methods (e.g., inspection, demonstration), and analysis of verification data. System-level use cases, scenarios, and associated requirements are key inputs to the development of the test cases and associated procedures. A powerful verification technique is for the systems engineer to include the definition of the test/verification systems that implement the verification methods. As illustrated in Figure 9, the test/verification system can be represented in terms of the OOSEM artifacts, beginning with a high-level context diagram for the test/verification system. The RVT database is further elaborated during this activity to trace the system requirements and design information to the system verification methods, test cases, and results.

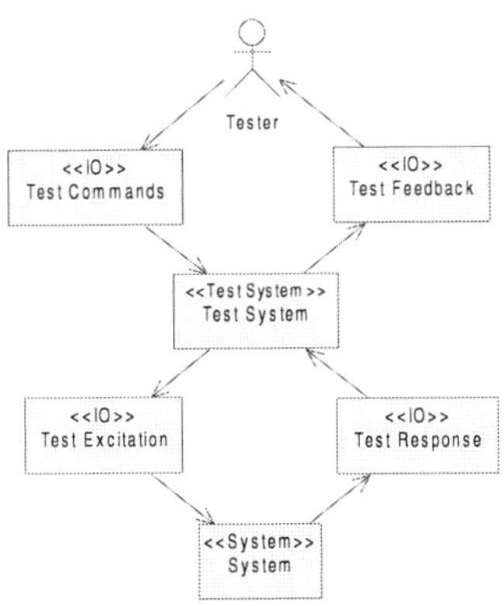

Figure 9. Test System Context Diagram

SOFTWARE OO LIMITATIONS AND OOSEM RESPONSES

This section summarizes some key limitations of software-level OO techniques for use at the system level and discusses how OOSEM addresses each limitation.

OO Limitation. "Flat" (i.e., nonhierarchical) models, such as class, collaboration, and sequence diagrams, inhibit the systems engineer from capturing the decomposition and traceability of a complete system among heterogeneous architectural components.

OOSEM Response: hierarchical decomposition. A key feature of OOSEM is that it decomposes the system into logical components then decomposes the logical components into subcomponents, continuing the decomposition until each logical component can be allocated as a whole to an element of the allocated architecture. This is in contrast to some existing OO techniques that do not take advantage of hierarchical decomposition. The fragment of a logical architecture in Figure 7 is an example of hierarchical decomposition.

OO Limitation. Lack of comprehensive definition of interfaces between the system and its external environment.

OOSEM Response: elaborated context diagram. This is the OO equivalent of the context diagram in classical structured analysis. It replaces the system transformation with a system object characterized in terms of multiple types of attributes and operations that denote system capabilities, functions, and other characteristics. Data flows are replaced by I/O entities, and terminators are replaced by UML actors and <<external>> classes that represent external interfaces. Two lessons learned apply here: First, the context diagram is just as indispensable in OO analysis as in structured analysis. Second, a context diagram can be captured effectively in an OO notation.

OO Limitation. Inability to characterize performance and other non-behavioral characteristics

OOSEM Response: multiple attribute categories. As shown in Figures 1 and 6, OOSEM uses attributes to capture required performance characteristics and requirements for transient data and persistent data. Attributes in software-level OO models tend to be items that will appear directly in the implementation. OOSEM uses attributes in this manner but also uses them to characterize key requirements and implementation characteristics. The effect is to make performance requirements explicit and to facilitate trade studies by specialty engineering.

OO Limitation. Inability to integrate systems and specialty engineering models.

OOSEM Response: application of OO models as a

common framework for integrating engineering models. According to accepted SE maturity models such as EIA/IS 731 (EIA 1999), it is the responsibility of SE to integrate engineering and specialty disciplines. OOSEM facilitates this by using OO modeling to capture behavioral, performance and physical characteristics, and interfaces, which are common to other engineering models. OOSEM can be used to communicate key information among many disciplines.

OTHER UNIQUE FEATURES OF OOSEM

System-level use cases and scenarios. UML use cases are used to capture system-level capabilities and to develop scenario-based requirements, which include functional, interface, and performance requirements. System-level use cases are the basis for system scenarios, which show sequences of events and actions performed by the system, external systems, and users. These scenarios are further decomposed and allocated during logical architecture design to illustrate interactions among logical components of the system. These scenarios also provide the basis for the interactions among the physical components in the allocated architecture and are used as a basis for test cases in the validation and verification (V&V) process.

I/O entities. OOSEM explicitly captures inputs and outputs in terms of I/O entities and their attributes. OOSEM models captured in computer-aided systems/software engineering (CASE) tools use the stereotype <<IO>> to distinguish I/O entities from other types of classes. Use of I/O entities is a marked improvement over OO methods that do not make inputs and outputs explicit (or easy to find) in the model.

Disciplined use of classes. OOSEM uses a systematic approach for identifying classes and objects and their relationships. Classes can represent the system, users, external systems, I/O entities, logical components, and the hardware, software, data, and procedural components in the allocated architecture. Rules for creating classes and objects are well-defined in the method. This explicitness is in marked contrast to guidelines in other methods such as "Look for the nouns in the problem statement to identify your classes."

Disciplined use of associations. A key feature of OOSEM is that it constrains the use of UML associations (relationships between classes) to a well-defined set. The most commonly used associations are inheritance and aggregation. Certain other associations, such as those on the context diagram connecting I/O entities to the system and external actors, are also allowed. However, the constraints on OOSEM associations are intended to ensure that every association is implementable and traceable.

Allocated architecture. OOSEM uses a combination of OO concepts and multilayer architectures to capture allocation of system requirements and design decisions to hardware, software, databases, and manual procedures.

SUMMARY

OOSEM incorporates OO concepts and modeling approaches using UML with classical, top-down SE. The method is intended to facilitate communication among system, software, and other engineering disciplines. . In addition, the method provides an effective means to capture system requirements and design information.

OOSEM encompasses the broad scope of SE activities for defining system requirements and design and allocating the requirements to system components. OOSEM includes activities for needs analysis, requirements analysis, logical and allocated architecture design, alternative evaluation, validation, and verification.

OOSEM adapts UML and, by extension, similar OO modeling notations. The adaptations include defining an elaborated, system-level class with additional attributes representing performance characteristics and defining I/O classes to capture critical interface information. Logical decomposition of the <<System>> class provides the basis for a logical architecture. OOSEM also addresses various component types, including hardware, software, data, and procedural components, which provide the basis for the allocated architecture and allocated requirements.

Future work includes refining and formalizing OOSEM guidelines, refining and improving adaptations of UML, integrating the method with a UML-based method for software engineering, and evaluating tool support for the method.

REFERENCES

Ali, Michael, "Model-Based Systems Engineering and Object-Oriented Software Engineering: An Integrated Approach," in *Proc. Eighth Int. Symp. INCOSE,* 1998.

Cocks, Dan, "The Suitability of Using Objects for Modeling at the Systems Level" in *Proc. Ninth Int. Symp. INCOSE,* 1999.

Dockerill, Kevin, "The Importance of Animation witgh UML" *Proc. Ninth Int. Symp. INCOSE,* 1999.

Electronic Industries Alliance (EIA), Systems engineering capability EIA/IS 731, http://www.geia.org/eoc/G47/731dwnld.htm, 1999.

Friedenthal, Sanford, "Object Oriented Systems Engineering," in *Process Integration for 2000 and Beyond: Systems Engineering and Software Symposium.* New Orleans LA: Lockheed Martin

Corporation 1998.

Hopkins, Frank W. and Rhoads, Russel P., "Object Oriented Systems Engineering—An Approach" in *Proc. Eighth Int. Symp. INCOSE,* 1998.

Meilich, Abe and Rickels, Michael, "An Application of Object Oriented Systems Engineering to an Army Command and Control System: A New Approach to Integration of Systems and Software Requirements and Design," in *Proc. Ninth Int. Symp. INCOSE,* 1999

Object Management Group, *OMG Unified Modeling Language Specification.* Version 1.3, June 1999. http://www.rational.com/uml/index.jtmpl

Oliver, David, Kelliher, Timothy P. and Keegan, James G., Jr., *Engineering Complex Systems with Models and Objects*. McGraw-Hill, New York, 1997.

Rose, Susan and Scott, Peter, "Integrated Development for Computer-Based Systems" in *Proceedings of the IEEE Technical Committee on Engineering Computer Based Systems*, 1997.

Rose, Susan, "Engineering Harmony Between Systems and Software" in *Proc. Seventh Int. Symp. INCOSE,* 1997.

Rose, Susan, Finneran, Lisa, Friedenthal, Sanford, Lykins, Howard and Scott, Peter, *Integrated Systems and Software Engineering Process.* SPC-96001-CMC, version 01.00.04. Herndon, Virginia: Software Productivity Consortium, 1996. (Available to the general public)

Schoening, William, "Using Object-Based Simulations for Exploring and Testing Complex Systems," in *Proc. Sixth Int. Symp. INCOSE,* 1996.

BIOGRAPHIES

Sanford Friedenthal. Mr. Friedenthal has over 25 years of experience in SE and related engineering areas. His experience includes the full life cycle, from conceptual design through development and production, on a broad range of systems, including missile systems, electro-optical navigation and targeting systems, and information systems. Most recently, Mr. Friedenthal was a functional manager for SE at Lockheed Martin M&DS, responsible for ensuring that SE processes were implemented on the programs, and enhancing overall SE capability. He has also been involved in developing advanced SE processes and methods, including the Lockheed Martin Systems Engineering Process (LM-SEP) and the Lockheed Martin Integrated Engineering Process (LM-IEP).

Abraham Meilich. Dr. Abe Meilich is employed as a Certified System Architect at Lockheed Martin Mission Systems. He has a B.S. in Engineering from UCLA, an M.S.M.E. from Stanford, an M.S. in Systems Management from USC, a Ph.D. in Systems Management from Walden University, and a Certified Computing Professional (C.C.P.) Certification. His career spans 30 years in the mechanical, electrical, computer, aerospace, and information SE domains. He is an adjunct professor at the University of Maryland Graduate Program in Technology Management, Systems Acquisition, and Information Systems. He is past Secretary and Newsletter Editor and past Director of the Washington Metropolitan Area Chapter of INCOSE. His current focus is on the application of SE principles and best practices in systems architecture development to the design of command and control systems for the U.S. Army and government information systems.

Howard Lykins. Howard Lykins is a senior member of the technical staff at the Software Productivity Consortium and has over twenty-five years of experience. Since joining the Consortium in 1991, Mr. Lykins has developed or contributed to a number of software engineering and SE processes and methods. His recent accomplishments include adapting the Object Modeling Technique for development of embedded real-time control software and tailoring ISSEP for component-based development. He holds a B.A. from Transylvania University and an M.S. in Computer Science from Washington University in St. Louis. Mr. Lykins is Co-Chair of the INCOSE Model-Driven System Design Working Group.

ACKNOWLEDGMENT

Rational Software provided a gratis copy of Rational Rose 2000 Enterprise Edition to the Consortium for research and development use. This tool was used to generate all figures in this paper except for Figure 8. The authors and the Consortium gratefully acknowledge their support.

Systems Engineering Process Implementation in the Real World (Or Where the Theory Gets Tested)

David Newbern and Jerome Nolte
Litton TASC
4801 Stonecroft Blvd
Chantilly, VA 22151

BACKGROUND

In the past ten years there has been an increasing awareness of the value of formally defined systems engineering processes. Formal engineering processes have been developed and documented in Systems Engineering standards and models [see e.g. Sheard and Lake, 1998]. However, the implementation and application of key systems engineering processes is often not uniform. In fact, implementation often varies markedly even within the same organization. In our individual practice of systems engineering involving different customers and contact with many different systems engineering and development projects, the authors have noted many variations in the way in which new processes are implemented within the organizations. In this paper we present two case studies that illustrate some of the difficulties in implementing systems engineering processes, and provide some lessons learned on techniques that can be useful in identifying and surmounting potential process implementation problems.

The first case study presents an attempt to implement a formal risk management program in an established government program office. This case study emphasizes the difficulties in introducing a new process into an already functioning organization. If the organization does not have a history of process definition and improvement, this can be a difficult endeavor.

The second case study is a discussion of the implementation of systems engineering processes in a new program office. The government selected two major development contractors to design and build different portions of a complex system. The government planned to perform systems integration activities at the system level. Thus key systems engineering processes would be required across the three organizations.

We recommend the idea of measuring engineering process maturity as a means for predicting success in process implementation in a wide variety of circumstances. We suggest that even an informal assessment of the maturity level of an organization can be useful in suggesting the approach to use for instituting systems engineering processes. We also recommend use of an ad hoc estimation of the maturity levels to support the implementation of systems engineering processes involving several different organizations.

CASE STUDY #1 – IMPLEMENTING A SYSTEMS ENGINEERING PROCESS IN AN ESTABLISHED ORGANIZATION

Situation: A joint program office was established a few years ago to focus the development of common systems addressing the interests of two parent organizations. The program office was staffed from the parent organizations, and thus carried a dual cultural heritage. The joint office has evolved into a geographically dispersed organization, with a significant degree of autonomy in acquisition of small systems and upgrades to subsystems. Generally the engineering processes used are not formally documented, with the exception of a strictly enforced configuration management process.

Background: The program office performs acquisition and systems engineering functions for development of data processing systems. In this organization, the systems engineering function includes overall system engineering (definition of requirements, change management, verification planning), general engineering and architecture development for significant subsets of the overall system, which we will call functional segments, and detailed support to the acquisition of the segments. The program office is very technical, including both the government and its contractors (development contractors and SE support contractors). The program office has been characterized as "an organization of heroes" – emphasizing the atmosphere of a continuing stream of high-priority, short fuse tasks being worked as they arrive. The primary relevant aspect of the program office organizational structure is the traditional, intentional allocation of schedule and technical responsibilities to separate acquisition and systems engineering organizations.

Within this organization, risk management was being done to some extent, but not in a formal, structured process. Specifically, the process was not documented, or applied in a consistent manner. Also, there was no senior management emphasis on risk management, so the organization-wide benefits of a risk management program were not being realized.

Risk Management Implementation: Recognizing the opportunity for organizational improvement, several systems engineers supporting the government Systems Engineering organization have made two major attempts to define and implement a risk management program over the past two years. The first of these attempts began with a "bottoms-up" development of a candidate risk management process. The second attempt began with the active support of the government chief of systems engineering within the program office. These two attempts, and the current implementation of risk management are the subject of the remainder of this section.

The initial "bottoms-up" attempt was initiated by several of the Systems Engineering contractors supporting the program office. They defined a risk management process based on the EIA/IS 731.1, Systems Engineering Capability Model (SECM), tailored for the program office. Along with the process, a short briefing outlining the benefits of a formal risk management program was developed. They obtained approval from government systems engineers, but were unable to convince the chief of systems engineering, who controlled the systems engineering budgets, to allocate resources during a period when the total program office engineering support was being reduced. Therefore, this activity never really got off the ground; implementation did not even start.

About a year later, with a new chief of systems engineering, a "top down" attempt to implement risk management was initiated. The "top down" approach got off to a good start when approval was obtained from the government chief of systems engineering to implement a formal risk management program. The program as defined was intended to make the implementation as easy as possible for the key technical segment leads who would be the major information providers. The focus of the program was on identifying risks. There was no major attempt to document a formal process, and obtain full concurrence before beginning. Rather, the process was kept simple, so a few technical personnel could ensure the appropriate execution with minimal effort. Each key technical segment lead was to report on risks at the weekly systems engineering staff meeting. Prior to the meeting, the technical personnel met with the key technical segment leads to discuss and summarize current risks.

For each identified risk, the technical segment lead decided the next step to take. This could be to drop the risk from the tracking system, to continue to work it within the technical segment activity, or to bring it to the next level by presentation to the chief of systems engineering. If brought to the chief of systems engineering, he would decide whether to drop it from his risk program (essentially returning it to the technical segment lead for resolution), to place it on a watch list, or to begin active risk planning for mitigation, abatement, or avoidance.

Even though the chief of systems engineering was supportive of the effort, the program met unexpected resistance from the technical segment leads. A specific issue was raised that risk management was already being done, as stated by one person, along with belief that "how could a segment lead not be working risks?"

Thus, the proposed risk management process was perceived as significant additional overhead: i.e, the paperwork of identifying risks, defining mitigation activities, and tracking status was considered burdensome.

It appears that there was hesitation to expose issues to management, especially when funding needed to work the issue was within the individual's immediate control. This concern is, in fact, contrary to one stated major reason for publicizing an issue to senior management, namely, to obtain funding for activities that are out-of-scope. It also turned out that the weekly staff meeting was not an appropriate forum for risk status review. In this organization, the staff meeting was not held regularly, and when the meeting did occur, it was generally for a specific purpose, and risk management was not actively presented.

After less than satisfactory attempts to implement a fairly standard risk management program, efforts have been retrenched to a more scaled down approach. The current risk management program is associated with the monthly Program Manager's Reviews, and is represented by a single summary risk management chart at each review. The chart shows the current assessment of probability of occurrence and potential impact for the highest priority risks for the program office. The risk management program is informally performed by a few systems engineers who work behind the scenes to obtain understanding of the risks presented at the PMR. For each risk, the appropriate segment leads are interviewed to identify who is working each risk area, what the current status is, what changes (if any) are there in the status from the previous month, and what mitigation or avoidance activities are being performed. The segment leads are also asked to identify any new risks to be worked and tracked.

In summary, the ability to implement a risk management process seems to have been limited from the outset. Without a clear benefit to the major participants, and no history of engineering process implementation and improvement, the prospects for implementing a significant new process were rather bleak.

CASE STUDY #2 – STARTING A NEW PROGRAM OFFICE

Situation: A U.S. government organization established a small, integrated management team consisting of government employees and a System Engineering Technical Advisor (SETA) contractor. Members of the SETA contractor were assigned substantial tasks such as writing specifications, performing configuration management, schedules, and operating requirement management activities.

Contracts were awarded for two major development segments of the large, complex system. The systems integration function was retained within the government program office with SETA support. Systems engineering processes involving all three organizations (which we will call the government team, contractor A, and contractor B) were defined for configuration management, requirements management, and schedule management.

General: The government used the occasion of establishing the new project to mandate the use of standardized tools within the team and both contractors. The government team was familiar with a scheduling tool which was already used by contractor A. The use of the tool was extended to contractor B as well.

A requirements management tool was already standard at both contractors. The government team adopted this tool. Contractor A gave team members extensive training.

The use of Microsoft Word was common to all three organizations and the government team elected to implement configuration management functions using Word as the common standard for documentation.

Current Situation: The current activities of the program office and the two contractors are summarized as follows:

Schedules: The government team prepares the master schedules. Input from contractor A is adequate while contractor B has only recently started active use of the scheduling tool within the project. Training has been provided for both contractors. Schedules are updated every two months.

Configuration Management: The process has been kept simple by the government team. Contractor A has provided good inputs to the team. Contractor B has had problems implementing their internal processes and has misplaced key documents internally. An average of three Requests for Change (RFCs) per month have been processed.

Requirements Management (RM): The government team member performing RM has received extensive assistance from Contractor A who has an excellent internal system in place. Contractor B at the corporate level mandates use of the tool, but project personnel elected to use an Excel spreadsheet to track requirements. The RM tool holds about 130 requirements at the program office level. This increases to about 1000 requirements at contractor A; the number of requirements at contractor B is not currently known – although his draft top level specification now is over eighty pages long (in Word format).

In summary, three systems engineering processes have been implemented across the three organizations. The processes are still not operating as effectively as expected, however. Even the selection and use of the same tools for each of the processes has not ensured smooth and consistent transfer of necessary information.

DISCUSSION:

In both of the above cases, an important aspect of the implementation of systems engineering processes was the readiness of the involved organization to accept and perform structured, documented systems engineering processes. Even though the specific circumstances were quite different, from our experience, the authors believe that it should be possible to rapidly determine the potential for implementing systems engineering processes based on the use of "ad hoc" CMM assessments. We are not talking of formal CMM assessments based on EIA/IS 732.1, Systems Engineering Capability Model Appraisal Method, but the use of a "seat-of-the-pants" best engineering guess at the maturity level of an organization or team.

Our "informal" approach to assessment retains the same definitions used in EIA/IS 731.1: 1 = Performed, 2 = Managed, 3 = Defined, etc. We assessed the organizations in four different process areas: Risk Management, Configuration Management, Scheduling, and Requirements Management. Within the scope of the broader focus areas defined in EIA/IS 731.1, the activities we describe fall into FA 3.1, Define and Improve the Systems Engineering Process and to a lesser extent into FA 2.1, Plan and Organize, and FA 2.2, Monitor and Control.

The informal ad hoc process of assigning maturity levels for organizations is based on our professional experience dealing with numerous agencies and organizations practicing systems engineering. A seasoned systems engineer (more than five years experience working with a variety of organizations) should be able to develop a feel for the maturity level of the system engineering practices of his own organization and also for other SE organizations with which he comes in contact. We have used the same definition for maturity level as contained in EIA/IS 731.1, but without the extensive measurement and documentation used by EIA/IS 732.1 in establishing a formal assessment. We used our "ad hoc" assessments with organizations ranging from several hundred engineers to work groups containing as few as ten individuals.

Our "ad hoc" system of assessment has provided some useful insights into explaining the relative ease or difficulty of establishing working systems engineering relationships between organizations with obviously different levels of maturity in the implementation of systems engineering disciplines and practices.

In particular, we have collected a number of anecdotal observations about customers and contractors based on the use of ad hoc maturity level numbers assigned by the authors. These include the following:

a. If a customer has not established a maturity level of at least 2 or higher, the use of system engineering processes by the contractor is hindered or even endangered by the lack of commitment to good systems engineering practices by the customer.

b. If a difference in maturity levels exists between a customer and a contractor of more than "one level" (either the customer or the contractor may be at a higher level) there will be major difficulties in the implementation of good system engineering processes between the two organizations - i.e. acceptance of system engineering processes will be slowed and in some cases abolished or altered arbitrarily due to the differences in the understanding of the SE process.

c. When the use of system engineering processes (at maturity level 3) has been mandated within an organization (either customer or contractor) and a significant number of personnel lack training in SE disciplines, then the implementation of key SE processes is effectively disabled.

Case Study #1 This case study demonstrated some of the real difficulties in implementing a new process in an existing organization. It was not surprising that the "bottoms up" approach did not work without the support of the senior management. However, we were quite surprised at the limited success we were able to attain with the "top down" approach. Even with the strong support of the chief of systems engineering, and acceptance in principle of the idea of the risk management program, the key players did not get actively involved, so the formal risk management program failed to become fully implemented.

In retrospect, the results may not be very surprising. An engineering estimate of the capability maturity level of the subject organization could have been used to predict the outcome. The organization definitely does not have a culture of implementing and improving engineering processes. The sole exception is the configuration management process, which is rather well defined, and is executed quite formally. This process is the responsibility of the configuration management organization, however, so it has a strong promoter within the overall organization, and also has an easily recognized purpose. Even this process is not well received, however. Many of the engineers complain about the overly complex and costly configuration management process.

On balance, we would rate the organization as a level 1 for Focus Area 3.1, Define and Improve the Systems Engineering Process. Documented processes are not used for most of the work. As noted above, the organization has a culture of encouraging heroic action. We now feel that an earlier recognition of the unfamiliarity of this organization with implementing systems engineering processes, as indicated by the maturity level in FA 3.1, could have pointed us towards a less ambitious approach, with a much better chance of success.

For the near term, a few engineers who recognize the potential value of the risk management approach will continue to implement the risk management process. That is, the process will be embodied in the engineers who want it to be executed.

We believe that the current risk management approach is of some value, but could be significantly improved. Where can we go from here? Since neither a "bottoms up" nor a "top down" approach works, we hope to gradually increase the participation in the risk management process, and slowly enhance the formality. We will attempt to demonstrate value to senior management by providing insight into the status of high priority tasks. We expect that this must be done by performing the necessary work, not by defining a formal risk process.

Therefore, to support the monthly PMR, we will define and track metrics to show tangible benefits of risk management to the organization. We also recognize the need to continue to refine the risk management process to support the needs of the technical segment leads, and ultimately expand the risk management program to the full range of program office activities.

Case Study #2 Table 1, Ad hoc Initial Capability Levels, shows the estimated ad hoc maturity level of the government program office and the two contractors in each of three key practice areas at the time of initial program office formation. The initial estimates are based on interviews with both government and contractor personnel at the start of the project. The initial level of capability is based extensively on the stated level of capability claimed by each organization in three system engineering practice areas: Schedules, Configuration Management, and Requirements Management.

Table 1, Ad hoc Initial Capability Levels

Practice Area	Gov't Team	Contractor A	Contractor B
Schedules	4	3	2
CM	3	3	3
RM	2	4	2

After a full year of experience with the project, the Ad hoc capability estimates for each organization were reevaluated as shown in Table 2, Ad hoc One-Year Capability Levels.

Table 2, Ad hoc One Year Capability Levels

Practice Area	Gov't Team	Contractor A	Contractor B
Schedules	4	3	2
CM	3	3	2
RM	3	4	1

These estimates are derived from working directly with the three organizations. These maturity levels represent an assessment of the way the specific project teams are performing their systems engineering work and are not based on the formal maturity capability level of the parent organization.

The differences in estimated CMM levels between the government team and contractor B for schedules and the combination of the government team and contractor A vice Contractor B for RM are striking. The difference of two CMM levels in two key practice areas underscores the continual difficulty Contractor B has had cooperating with organizations with a higher level of SE capability and maturity.

Equally surprising (and frustrating) was the drop in the CM and RM capability for Contractor B. This drop in capability was due to several factors: 1) Assignment of less experienced personnel to the Contractor B team and 2) Lack of commitment by senior personnel within Contractor B to enforce established engineering processes. This translated into additional work for the government team to ensure that CM and RM activities were completed.

A significant question poses itself, "How can you know that an organization is deficient in key process capabilities even when the organization at the corporate level claims a CMM rating of three?" A partial answer to this problem lies in understanding the commitment of key personnel to use good SE practices and enforce systems engineering discipline on all employees.

The relative success in Configuration Management stems from a more uniform level of capability across the three organizations. It might be noted here that Contractor A would like to abolish the use of Word documents and use the RM tool entirely for CM. While this might work within a single organization, the authors have found that written documentation (albeit in softcopy) is still the preferred method of communication with non-systems engineering personnel.

The availability of good tools did not automatically improve the estimated CMM ratings for a contractor who did not enforce good SE practices. On the other hand, the use of good tools improved the estimated rating for the organizations which enforced good SE practices.

CONCLUSIONS:

Getting an engineering process defined and used by an organization is both a cultural issue and a technical issue. The primary technical issue is to get adequate resources allocated. To achieve this objective, clear value must be demonstrated. In many organizations, engineering process definition and process improvement is not yet the normal way of working. To get the people to change the way they work is a cultural challenge. We have had the greatest difficulty getting the culture to change.

The experiences we have discussed show the paramount necessity of paying more attention within organizations to the broad focus area of "Defining and Improving the Systems Engineering Process." Of slightly lesser importance is the need to allocate sufficient resources for the support of defined engineering processes once the systems engineering process is defined.

The use of capability maturity level as a predictor of the success or failure of two systems engineering organizations working effectively with each other has not been formally tested. The use of "ad hoc" capability maturity ratings provides some insight into the future effectiveness of two organizations working together. A large difference in capability maturity ratings indicates that one organization has developed a higher commitment to systems engineering processes than the other organization. In this situation there is a potential for conflict between the organizations over how to conduct systems engineering processes or even whether the systems engineering processes are required. Finally if an organization has declared itself to have a capability maturity rating of three or higher, there is no guarantee that the individuals within the organization are practicing systems engineering with level three processes.

REFERENCES:

EIA/IS 731.1, Systems Engineering Capability Model, Electronic Industries Alliance, Arlington, VA, Dec 1998.

EIA/IS 732.2, Systems Engineering Capability Model Appraisal Method, Electronic Industries Alliance, Arlington, VA, Dec 1998.

Sheard, Sarah A., and Lake, Jerry G., Systems Engineering Standards and Models Compared, Proc. 8th International Symposium of INCOSE, p. 589, Vancouver, BC, July, 1998.

BIOGRAPHY:

Dave Newbern is a systems engineer employed at Litton TASC. He is an electrical engineer by training and became a systems engineer at some point along the way (he is not sure when this occurred). Dave is currently employed on one of those large, complex government projects. He has experience performing systems engineering from military, government, and contractor points-of-view. He is a registered PE in California and Virginia.

Jerry Nolte is a systems engineer employed at Litton TASC. He is a physicist by training, and migrated into systems engineering through computer and database systems research. He has been involved (with some success!) in establishing standard systems engineering methodologies in both government and contractor organizations.

An Advanced Methodology for the Design Process of a Satellite

Professor Heinz Stoewer
SAC Space Associates
Drachenfelsstr. 9, D-53757
St.Augustin/Bonn, Germany

Ralf Hartmann
Dornier Satellite Systems GmbH,
Daimler Chrysler Aerospace
88039 Friedrichshafen, Germany

L.A.J. Baron von Richter
Technical University Delft
Faculty of Aerospace Engineering
Kluyverweg 1, Postbus 5058
2600 GB Delft, The Netherlands
Avonrichter@hotmail.com

Abstract: This paper describes a methodical and logical approach of process design as employed within the Satellite Design Office at Dornier Satellite Systems GmbH. It concerns the concept development phase (Phase A/B). Many papers have been written on the subject of the concept design centers, but nearly none of them describe the intern design process. At last this paper focuses on the method in which way the design process is analyzed as well as on the description of the process itself. All involved disciplines during a design project are described as well as their prime interfaces.

INTRODUCTION

This paper presents the results of a one-year study at Dornier Satellite Systems GmbH in order to receive a Master of Science in Aerospace Engineering of the Technical University of Delft. Prof. H. Stoewer and R. Hartmann acted as mentors during this study.

The described design process is based on the Satellite Design Office (SDO) at Dornier Satellite Systems GmbH, which is a subsidiary of DaimlerChrysler Aerospace. This design office is in its basic concept comparable to a Concept Design Center (CDC). The scope of this study is on the definition of the satellite bus. The other two basic parameters, the payload instruments as well as the ground system interface are usually part of the customer specification.

THE DISCIPLINES

A satellite consists of at least two main elements: the satellite bus and the payload. The satellite bus carriers the payload, which consists of the instruments and the equipment. Fulfilling the following functions (Larson et al. 1996):

- support the payload mass
- point the payload correctly
- keep the payload at the right temperature
- provide electric power
- command the instruments
- collect housekeeping data
- put the payload in the exact orbit
- provide data storage if required and communicate with the ground.

Thus the satellite consists of the following subsystems providing these functions as listed in Table 1 on the next page.

Specific disciplines represent these subsystems within the SDO. In addition to these disciplines, there are a number of team members who are responsible for the following specific viewpoints:

System Engineer: A complex aspect with emphasis on the creation of system models that facilitate assessment of the alternatives in various dimensions such as cost, performance, and risk (Shisko, 1995). This discipline is maintaining control of the developing configuration and overseeing the integration of subsystems. The system discipline is also responsible for the maintenance of all budgets and aspects of the design, which involve many different disciplines. Furthermore he allocates performance by establishing budgets or allocations for propellant, power, weight, and reliability.

Subsystem	Main Functions
Payload	Collection and conveyance of the primary mission data.
Propulsion	Provide thrust for orbit maintenance and orbit control.
Attitude Determination and Orbit Control (AOCS)	Measurement and control of the satellite orientation and orbit.
Communication	Communication with ground stations/other satellites, tracking of the satellite.
Command and Data Handling	Processing, storage and formatting of mainly payload data. Distribution of commands and collection of housekeeping data for payload and subsystems.
Thermal	Temperature control
Power	Generation of the required power for the satellite, including storage, regulation and distribution functions.
Structure	Carriage, support and alignment of the satellite equipment. Interface structure with the launcher.

Table 1: Satellite Subsystems

Customer: The customer is considered as a direct team member.
Mission and Operations: Mission analysis, including orbit analysis, functional analysis, satellite operations and on-board software definition.
Configuration: Definition & control of the overall mechanical configuration of the satellite i.e. equipment accommodation consistent with mechanical/thermal environment.
Electrical System: Definition & control of the overall electrical architecture, consistent with the electromagnetic environment.
Planning & GSE: Planning and ground support equipment (GSE), planning of the design & development & assembly, verification and integration (AIV) efforts as well as planning of the required ground support equipment.
Cost & Risk: Definition of the life cycle cost of the mission and analysis of risk.
Documentation: Assembly, formatting and configuration management of the final study report.
Moderator: Overall responsibility for organising the study, for coordination with the customer, for organising the study in cooperation with the customer and for planning and conducting group activities [Aguilar et al. 1995].

All these disciplines are strongly related to each other as can be seen in Figure 1.

THE METHODOLOGY OF ANALYSIS

1. Direct data flow via input/output lists: Quantitative data
   Main stream information flow between disciplines which is essential for each project and which can be clearly expressed via the following general types of parameters: Mathematical expressions, enumeration, text block, graphics, external reference.
2. Checklist of discussion: Qualitative data, i.e. descriptive text
   This data list concerns issues, questions and constraints to be clarified with other disciplines, which are not always needed and which need explanation or discussion with the other discipline(s).
3. Discussion during the SDO team session.
   Points and issues, which are very, mission specific and cannot be specified in advance.

Type 1 and 2 of information are formally supported by MUSSAT: "Modelling and Simulation of Satellite Systems" the software tool used to support the SDO [Wilke]. At least a discipline needs information of one other discipline. The flow of information between the disciplines is realised by their input/output parameters. The various interrelationships are determined through the analysis of the sources of the required input parameters per discipline and by the definition of the destinations of the output parameters per discipline.
The analysis of these parameters was done

individually by the author via a bottom down approach and via a bottom up approach by each team member. Then the input/output parameter lists of the SDO team members were analyzed. All team lists were written in MS-word format. In order to connect the parameters of each discipline to these lists were formatted from MS-Word™ into Excel™.

Furthermore they were analyzed in detail in order to attain the same level of depth. All disciplines were interviewed because some changes were applied to their lists. Either some parameters were attached which were missing or some were deleted because they were too detailed. Also some input (output) parameters were missing which were defined as output (input) parameters by the other disciplines.

Table 2 gives an example of some input/output parameters for the Attitude Control and Determination discipline.

These tables not only contain input/output parameters but also a list of tasks to be performed by each discipline, see table 3.

Furthermore each file of the discipline within the ExcelTM program includes a list of discussion. These lists (see table 4, for an example) include parameters which can not be defined clearly by numbers but need detailed description, as for example geometrical requirements. Furthermore these lists are strongly interrelated to another discipline. They consist of two parts namely one, which is of concern by the discipline itself (so these are output for discussion parameters), and another which includes points of discussion which are of concern to the other disciplines (input for discussion parameters).

Source	Input
OPS	Mission Phases
ELEC	Electrical system architecture
OPS	Function tree and allocation

Output	Checked with Discipline
Type of attitude stabilization control	COMS; PROP
operating modes and transitions	PROP
Performance req. on thrusters	PROP

Table 2: Example for Input/Output parameters

Checklist of Tasks to be performed
• Define/derive AOCS functional requirements from input requirements.
• Trade different stabilization concepts.

Table 3: Example for a Checklist of Tasks

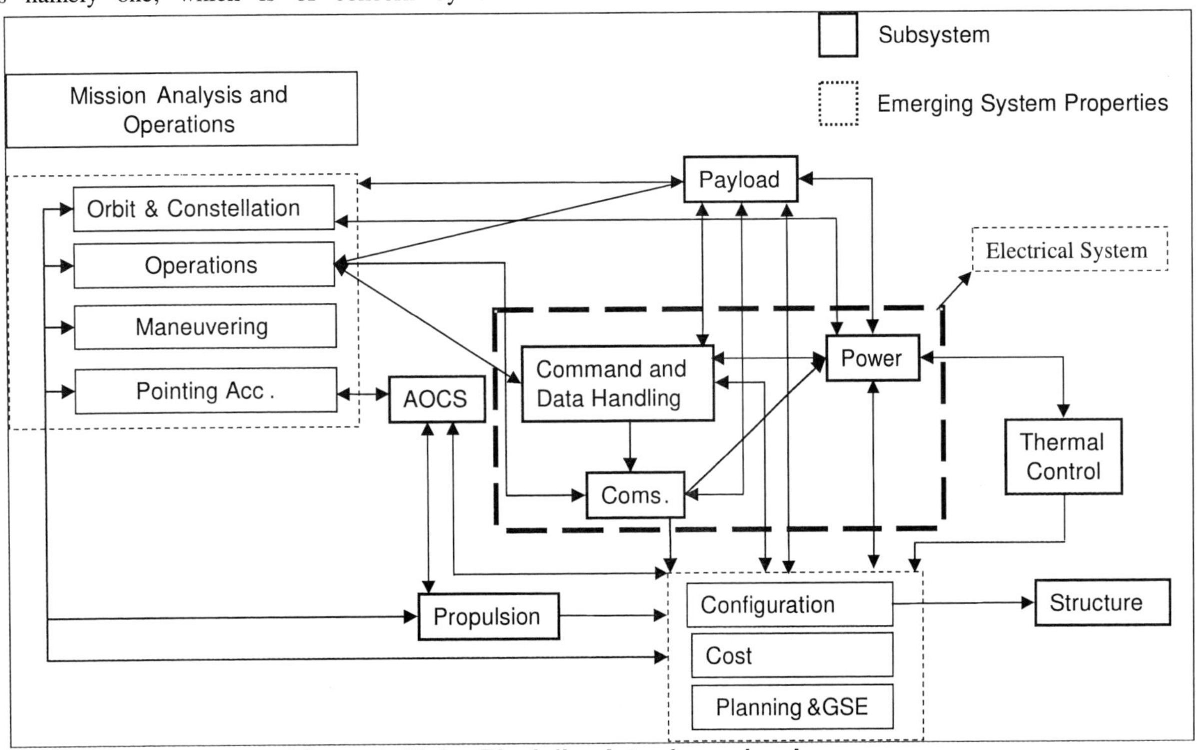

Figure 1: Major Discipline Interdependencies

Output	Checked with Discipline
POW; THER	Solar Array design
DH	Volume/geometry constraints
SYS	Reference axes
THER	(Thermo)elastic requirements
Input	Subject
THER	Thermal geo. Constraints
PL	Geo. Constraints
AOCS	Geo. Constraints
AOCS, PROP	S/C center of pressure
AOCS, PROP	S/C center of gravity
AOCS	Inertia constraints

Table 4: List of discussion

The input/output lists are based on the following assumptions:

- payload (PL) instrument is already defined by the customer,
- only the first iteration is shown. It seems logical that many output parameters need to be refined in the next iteration step but this is not shown in the lists for clarity reasons.

THE PROCESS

The design process is based on the following ground rules:

- main focus of the design study is on the satellite system,
- payload instruments are already chosen by the customer.

For some design sessions more details about the mission are fixed so these can not be changed during the process. Especially in ESA (European Space Agency) missions many parameters are fixed e.g. launcher, ground system and satellite system parameters. A critical analysis of these parameters is recommended.

Before the first SDO session takes place all team members receive available information about the mission, e.g. the invitation to tender by ESA. After having studied this material all disciplines meet together in the SDO.

It is in this meeting that the overall mission objectives are discussed and the overall budgets (weight, power, cost) are defined. If some information is not available, in the first session, the team may need to assume values or use typical values for some parameters. All these assumptions need to be documented and revisited until an acceptable baseline is established.

It is essential that the following aspects be discussed during the first session:

- determination of mission design drivers,
- identification of technical alternatives and solutions,
- determination of system impacts of candidate satellite design options.

After an agreement is reached for a first baseline each discipline develops a conceptual design for its respective subsystem.

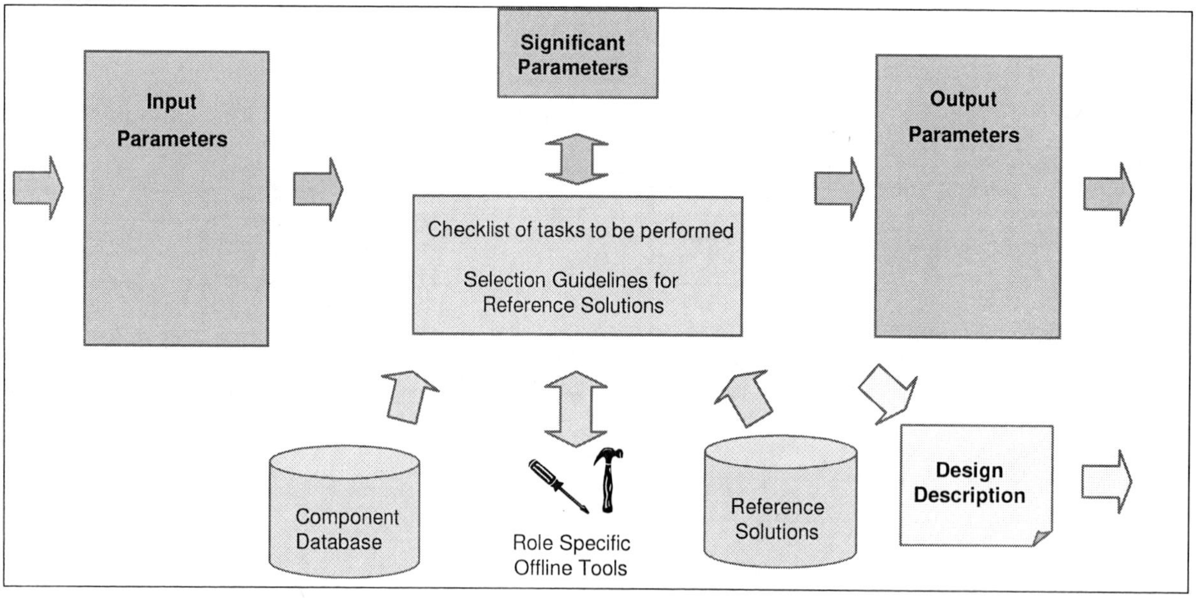

Figure 2: The design process

To design a subsystem, each discipline engineer has to:

- develop and analyze satellite subsystem requirements,
- identify technical alternatives and solutions,
- determine system impacts of candidate satellite design options,
- trade off design features, and size the system iteratively until he arrives at the best concept for a particular mission.

Analyzing requirements includes performance, interfaces, and physical characteristics. Design trades investigate:

- different types of subsystem components and concepts,
- selection criteria,
- and design factors for the specific mission.

For the trade off studies design drivers or key performance requirements are of great importance because they have the greatest impact on the effective operation, weight and cost of the subsystem. All choices must meet design requirements within suitable margins. All output parameters are selected by comparing cost, risk, delivery schedule, weight and size, power consumption, operability, and past history, as well as performance against different mission objectives and in respect to the other subsystems.

Although each design will vary, basically the design process would proceed as follows:

In the beginning rules of thumb and experience is used in order to estimate the spacecraft size (volume and dimensions) and to establish a first baseline for the weight budget and power budget which are also essential for the spacecraft overall configuration. Based on prior experience a product tree is developed which comprises all equipment and components which are essential for the satellite design.

Mission & Operations (OPS) is the first discipline, which starts in the process because it has a significant influence upon the satellite design. A sophisticated analysis of the mission objectives, and consequently the payload operation is required. Orbital aspects are handled via the orbit analysis engineer. The orbit affects mostly propulsion, attitude control, thermal design, and electric power subsystem. Most of these design effects are secondary to the orbit's effect on payload performance.

Selecting a launcher is also of concern in the operations discipline. The launcher selection will affect a spacecraft's linear dimensions and thus its configuration. The ground link and coverage are also analyzed because visibility periods affect the communication and data handling system design. Furthermore the trade off between ground operations and the autonomy level of the spacecraft is a very important issue of operations design.

This discipline is concerned with the operational concept of all satellite subsystems. This includes a functional analysis and the definition of software functions and hardware functions. This is a very interdependent issue. It is very beneficial to develop the mission operations concept in parallel with the spacecraft design because it enables the minimisation of life cycle costs (Wall et al. 1999).

Parallel to the operations engineer the payload discipline (PL) defines his subsystem. The payload is in most cases the single most significant driver of the satellite design because it is for example in most cases the driving source for the orbit selection and the AOCS system. Attitude control requirements are based on those for payload pointing and the satellite bus pointing. Its physical parameters – size, weight and power – dominate the physical parameters of the satellite. Payload operations and support are key requirements for the satellite's subsystems, as well. The payload may also impose significant special requirements that drive the design approach.

Then a basic concept for the AOCS system can be defined because it is strongly dependent on the payload pointing requirements. Furthermore it is tightly coupled to other subsystems on board, especially the propulsion and in some cases the data handling system. The mass properties of a spacecraft are key issues in determining the size of control and disturbance torques. For more detailed design it is essential to know the location of the center of mass or gravity as well as the elements of the inertia matrix: the moments and products of inertia about chosen reference axes.

A first estimate for the design of propulsion (PROP) subsystem can be worked out after the determination of the impulse requirement. This major design driver, the total impulse that the propulsion system must deliver, derives from the total ✤V budget it must impart to the satellite for maneuvers. The allowable offset for center-of-mass affects the number and location of propellant tanks, which usually occupy most of the propulsion system's volume. In order to align its thrusters properly it has specific geometrical layout requirements towards configuration. Configuration requirements include envelope dimensions, thruster locations, and alignment.

On the basis of the concept of the attitude control system and payload concept a first configuration (CONF) can be established. The weight, size and shape of the payload and the launch vehicle diameter normally drive the size and shape of the equipment compartment. The spacecraft's overall size may depend on such payload parameters as antenna size or optical system diameter.

Sensing devices, instruments, antennas, solar arrays, and thermal radiators always require specific field of view and pointing accuracy that must be satisfied by their mounting on the spacecraft and the spacecraft's orientation. The design must match these requirements and provide fields of view appropriate to the payload functions e.g. sensors must be located such that they are unobstructed by antennas or solar arrays. The AOCS system and Propulsion layout also strongly influence the spacecraft's configuration.

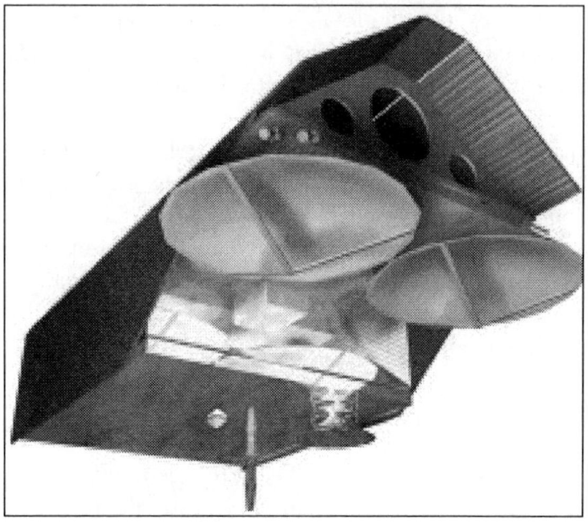

Figure 3: A configuration of a satellite

At the subsystem level, the communications (COMS) subsystem directly interfaces with every subsystem except the one for propulsion. The interface with AOCS deals primarily with antenna pointing (and mounting depends on the sort of AOCS control concept). First of all the data rates need to be established which include: payload command and data, and spacecraft bus commands and telemetry. The data rate sets the communication subsystem's bandwidth, which establishes the received power required detecting signals. Then an antenna can be chosen and a first baseline for the link budget is established.

The first step in baselining the command and data-handling (DH) system is to define the primary functional requirements needed to receive, process and format payload instrument data and to monitor and control the spacecraft. Of critical importance to the system design is the quantity of data and how fast it must be acquired. This discipline interfaces mainly with the payload in order. It is also connected with the communications subsystem from which it receives commands and to which it sends the formatted telemetry stream for the other subsystems.

For the design of the power (POW) subsystem the power budget needs to be estimated by adding the payload's power requirements to power estimates for spacecraft bus subsystems. This budget includes most of the information in order to size the power subsystem: the spacecraft's needs for operating power, storage requirements, and how the power subsystem degrades over the spacecraft's lifetime. The remaining steps to size the power subsystem are selecting a solar array approach, sizing the array, sizing the batteries and the components that control charging, and sizing the equipment for distributing and converting power. The solar array layout depends on the type of attitude control and from the overall spacecraft configuration. Key design issues for solar arrays include spacecraft configuration, required power level (peak and average), operating temperatures, shadowing, radiation environment, illumination or orientation, mission life, mass and area, cost and risk. The operating temperature of the array is a key issue because the solar cell's performance depends on temperature.

Strong interaction exists between the thermal control (THER) subsystem and the other satellite subsystems. In order to design the thermal subsystem, the first step is to identify heat sources and the location of radiating panels to dispose of excess heat. The power subsystem typically has the greatest interaction with the thermal control subsystem because all the dissipated electrical energy within the spacecraft must be radiated to space and batteries generally have a narrow temperature range. Finally, satellite attitude control can have a significant influence on the thermal control subsystem design. The attitude of the spacecraft determines the thermal radiation inputs from the Sun and Earth and these inputs affect radiator performance and spacecraft temperatures.

The following inputs are required from the other subsystems: spacecraft geometry, orientation, surface radiation properties.

The discipline concerned with the structure is strongly related to configuration. It is essential that the overall layout of the satellite is known in order to start the design. Furthermore it requires basic inputs from the system discipline e.g. weight, unit dimensions etc. Also it has to consider the requirements from the thermal control system. In most cases the launch loads drive the structural design of a satellite that's why launcher requirements and the launcher adapter requirements area are of interest.

The satellite systems costs are best defined as early as

possible in the design process so that the best cost-effective solution is found. The cost discipline estimates the mission cost via two basic cost estimating models:

- Detailed bottom-up estimating: Based upon cost per item, cost of materials and labor to develop and produce each element. This approach requires detailed design data which is usually not available in the beginning of the design process
- In parametric estimating an equation (Cost Estimating Relationship, CER) is used, that expresses the cost as a function of design sizing, performance variables or parameters. Furthermore it utilizes complexity factors, such as design difficulty or heritage, to the parameters.

In order to apply one of these approaches all cost elements of the satellite need to be identified and implemented in a cost breakdown structure at the start of the study. If a cost of a unit is not know the cost is estimated via the CER. That's why relevant subsystem characteristics need to be selected. Furthermore the sources of uncertainty need to be identified in order to arrive at a program level cost uncertainty. This process is called risk assessment.

The Planning and GSE discipline is concerned with aspects of assembly, verification, integration (AIV) and with the development of the further schedule for the next design phases. It can only start if some design aspects are already established in order to define a baseline for the AIV concept. The planning of the next phases can also only be accomplished if a mission baseline is already chosen.

CONCLUSION

It has been discovered that there is a basis hierarchic relationship between the various disciplines, which is shown in Figure 4. The figure shows that Configuration and Electrical System have to coordinate respectively the mechanical and electrical design of the satellite. The disciplines Cost & Risk and Planning & GSE can only start to develop cost estimations and further planning if certain design aspects are already known. At the start of the study it is absolutely necessary that each discipline makes certain assumptions in order to start to design their concepts, even the downstream disciplines power, thermal and structure. Team members must determine their most important design drivers quickly and focus on them.

The efficiency of the design process is depends strongly on:

- The interdisciplinary knowledge of each team member
- The cooperation of each team member
- The team leader
- Team experience

Only after the establishment of the first baseline the team members can start to develop a first concept for their subsystems. The design process has been supported by this work by introducing the new input/output parameter definition. These input/output lists serve as a baseline the communication between the disciplines and are used by MuSSat. The implementation and improvement of MuSSat is still in progress at DSS. Even though the design development is an iterative process it is strongly systemised via the input/output lists which have been established by author.

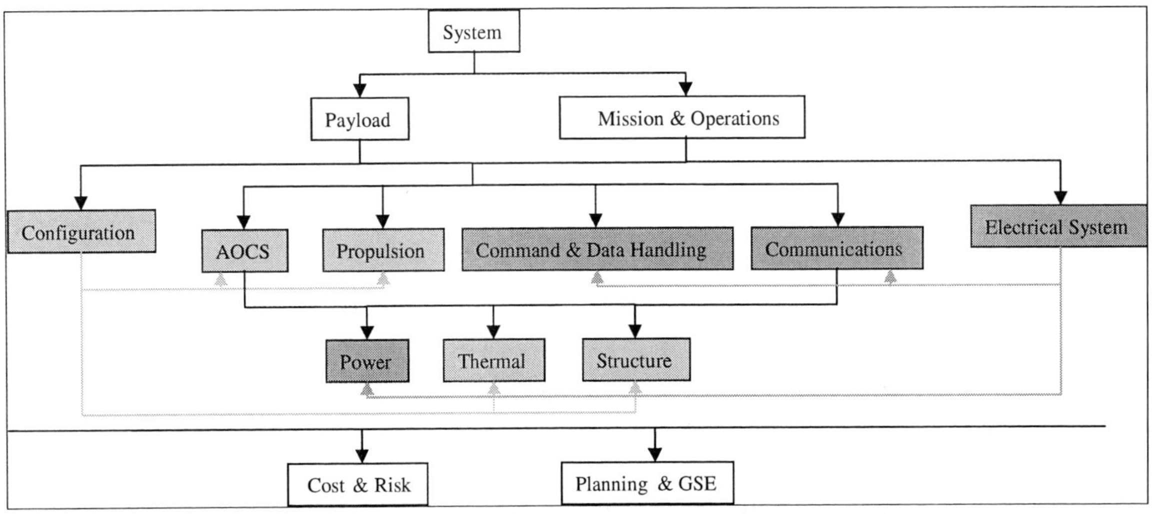

Figure 4: Hierarchical Relationship between the disciplines.

In order to reduce the design time and to improve the quality of the concept development studies the author recommends that the following aspects have to be considered:

- In the SDO process design data has to be open to all disciplines. Consequently the system level implications of design options/trade-off will become visible. This tends to result in more questioning of assumptions and to revelation of subsystem design and costs.
- Team members must determine their most important design drivers quickly and focus on them.

The real time nature of the design studies at the SDO demands that information be processed rapidly. In general it is this limitation that most inhibits the development of real time integrated concurrent engineering processes. Unless information can be processed rapidly into figures of merit upon which design decisions can be based, real-time concurrent/collaborative design is not possible.

REFERENCES

Aguilar, Joseph A., Dawdy, Andrew B. Glenn, Law W., "The Aerospace Corporation's Concept Design Center", Aerospace cooperation, Conference Proceedings of the eighth Annual INCOSE Symposium, Vancouver, Canada, 1998.

Larson, W.J. and Wertz, J.R. (editors), "*Space Mission Analysis and Design*", Second Edition, Space Technology Series, Kluwer Academic Publishers, NL, 1992.

Sishko, R. et al., "*NASA Systems Engineering Handbook*", NASA, USA, 1995.

Wall, S.D. and Smith, D.B., Koenig, L.J., "Team Structure and Processes in the Design of Space Missions", California Institute of Technology, paper presented a the 1999 IEEE Aerospace conference.

BIOGRAPHES

L.A.J. BARON VON RICHTER

In March 1999 Andreas has finished his studies at the Technical University Delft (The Netherlands) with a M. Sc. degree in aerospace engineering. During his last year of his studies he focused on space system engineering. He has followed a stage period at Cost Analysis Division the European Space Agency. He wrote his master thesis: "Definition and Analyses of Integrated Concurrent Engineering Process for a Satellite Design Office" at Dornier Satellite Systems GmbH, DaimlerChrysler Aerospace under the supervision of Professor Heinz Stoewer and Ralf Hartmann.

RALF HARTMANN

Since twelve years Ralf is a System Engineer at Dornier Satellite Systems GmbH, DaimlerChrysler Aerospace in Germany. He is the team leader of Satellite Design Office. For a number of smaller projects he has been project manager and system engineer. He is a member of the ECSS level 2-system engineering working group and of the level 1 engineering working group. He holds a M. Sc. degree in Electrical Engineering from the University of Karlsruhe (Germany) and received a certificate in Project Management from the German Project Management Association (GPOM/RKW). He is the head of the German Chapter of INCOSE.

PROFESSOR HEINZ STOEWER

Prof. Stoewer is well known expert on space system engineering. He is Co-Chairman of the Technical Board of INCOSE.

1990-1995: Member of the board of directors at the German Space Agency.

1987-2000: Professor for Space Systems at the Technical University Delft, The Netherlands.

Since 1995: Director of the Space Associates Consultancy GmbH (SAC) at St.Augustin/Bonn. An international consultancy company for strategical planning and System-techniques.

1995-1999: Director of the Technical University Delft/Top Tech international post graduate SpaceTech program:" Master of Space Systems Engineering".

A Case Study in Modeling Company Policy Documents as a Source of Requirments

Kathleen Marie Crumpton
Department of Computer Science
New Mexico State University
Las Cruces, New Mexico 88003-8001
USA
kcrumpto@cs.nmsu.edu

Regina M. Gonzales
Klipsh School of Electrical and Computer Engineering
New Mexico State University
Las Cruces, New Mexico 88003-8001
USA
regonzal@nmsu.edu

Sharon Trauth
Sandia National Laboratories
Albuquerque, NM 87185-0535 USA
sltraut@sandia.gov

Abstract. This paper describes an approach that was developed to produce structured models that graphically reflect the requirements contained within a text document. The document used in this research is a draft policy document governing business in a research and development environment. In this paper, we present a basic understanding of why this approach is needed, the techniques developed, lessons learned during modeling and analysis, and recommendations for future investigation.

The modeling method applied on the policy document was developed as an extension to entity relationship (ER) diagrams, which built in some structural information typically associated with object oriented techniques. This approach afforded some structure as an analysis tool, while remaining flexible enough to be used with the text document. It provided a visual representation that allowed further analysis and layering of the model to be done.

INTRODUCTION

Determining requirements is a daunting task demanding in-depth knowledge of the environment for the requirements to effectively represent an issue or problem. Loucopoulos and Karakostas (Berry, 1999) describes Requirements Engineering as a "systematic process of developing requirements through an iterative cooperative process of analyzing the problem, documenting the resulting observations in a variety of representation formats, and checking the accuracy of the understanding gained." Dr. Berry points out that the problem in establishing requirements is that requirements always change. As peoples' perceptions change and more information is gathered, requirements need to be adjusted. Generally, people are reluctant to deal with requirements because they simply don't want to deal with the chaos (Berry, 1999).

There are always many sources of requirements, irrespective of the kind of product under development. These can include regulatory requirements, quality requirements, interface requirements for existing systems, technical requirements for functionality, and user requirements -- to name just a few. This information can come in different forms, many of which are textual. Clearly, these various sources of requirements are not written at the same level of abstraction. In fact, a single document can, itself, contain requirements at several abstraction levels. Individuals attempting to enter text into a requirements management tool may discover that several sections of a source document will cover facets of the same topic, necessitating some way of grouping or merging the thought behind the words. It is, therefore, imperative that a consistent method for modeling requirements from such sources be used, especially in critical systems, so that requirements can be analyzed, synthesized, and addressed effectively.

This paper focuses on a particular type of text-based requirements documents. Specifically, we present the approach developed and the results obtained in analyzing requirements in a policy document that was under development and evolving. The methodology in this paper has also been successfully applied to a standards document and to a subset of a collection of user-specified needs. Our experience shows that simply representing requirements' information graphically is not sufficient for adequate human use and interpretation. Although not intentionally complex or ambiguous, human thought transferred to text on paper can lead to documents that are inherently ambiguous and difficult to read. This can be true even when an outline is used prior to writing the full text. This makes it difficult to know for sure that one has met the intended requirements contained in the documents. Representing such information graphically in a layered model can provide a mechanism for semi-formal verification of written requirements. Customers and developers can more readily understand the requirements and the relationships between them by studying the graphical model.

BACKGROUND

This paper covers a portion of the work done using this methodology. Originally, the project task was to develop a modernized engineering process that could be readily used by anyone in the technical community in their daily work. It was desirable to understand the programmatic and regulatory requirements with which the process had to comply.

As the project evolved, it became apparent that, to be used, the process had to be easily implementable in a desktop engineering environment. Further, it was recognized that managerial support and advocacy was essential if we were to realize widespread use of the process. To address the need for management support, an initiative was launched to create the policy behind the process.

By their nature, policy documents are typically at the highest level of abstraction in a comprehensive system of doing business. Further, policy documents typically specify only the "what's" that must be done, leaving the "how's" to the process. Thus, as the policy specification emerged, the process group needed to be sure their process specification would be consistent with the emerging policies. In the spirit of concurrent engineering, both the policy and process development proceeded in parallel, with many of the same individuals working on both projects.

The modeling approach discussed in this paper was intended to provide some specific benefits. First, it was desired to identify specific policy statements related to the process so that the process being developed could be verified for its compliance with the policy statements. Second, it was hoped that by modeling the policy, we could identify any gaps or inconsistencies within the policy structure that would have to be addressed. As discussed below, both these expectations, as well as others, were met.

CASE STUDY

The policy document that was the focus of our attention was under development for Product Realization in the Nuclear Weapons Strategic Business Unit (NW SBU) at Sandia National Laboratories. A small committee developed this document, such that the policy is part of an overall structure. Policy development is an on-going activity as of the writing of this paper.

As noted earlier, preliminary work had already been done in developing an approach to modeling a more static regulatory standards document. We began by applying this ER-based approach to our draft policy and investigated other viable approaches for potential comparison. Many of the other possible approaches were either based on ER diagrams (as ours was) or were more suited to be used during brainstorming sessions prior to creating the document (Robertson, 1999).

Since the majority of the initial effort in our modeling methodology was simply parsing the sentences contained in the document before we could determine abstraction layers, we continued using the modified ER diagrams. We wanted to work with the detailed text in the policy and did not want to draw simply from the headings in the document and fundamentally reproduce the outline structure. We felt it was important to understand the connectivity of the information contained within the document, since we hypothesized that documents have inherent overlaps and inconsistencies when written without modeling first. We expected this to be true for this case, especially since this was an evolving document.

We created an initial raw ER model and analyzed the network of nodes and connections so that structures could be abstracted, synthesized, and suppressed as necessary. In this way, a layered model emerged that was easier to understand and that clarified important entities and interfaces within the document.

FACTORED ER MODELS

In order to create our initial models, we analyzed the policy document sentence by sentence. Nouns, verbs, and adjectives were identified and used to parse each sentence into a graphical entity relationship (ER) model. Within the model, nouns are represented as nodes. Nodes are linked together by verbs. A node may have adjectives listed, attached as attributes, if deemed appropriate. In this particular document, however, there were not many adjectives included in the text to describe a noun.

Two characteristics of this document made modeling activities unique and inherently complex. First, the policy was still under development. Second, we found it necessary to rely on a domain expert for interpretation of the text to fully specify the model. This was necessary given the level of abstraction of the policies and their intended strategies. We had access to a domain expert who could interpret for us the intended meaning whenever the meaning was ambiguous. To illustrate why interpretation became important, consider the following statement from the configuration management portion of a June 1999 version:

Management of issues, lessons learned, and recommendations resulting from support and evaluation activities is required to assure that issues are addressed.

Figure 1 is a representation of the purist approach to modeling from the document. Represented in figure 2 is a model of the same sentence after the domain expert evaluated the purist model. Notice how the concepts of evaluation activities and support activities inter-relate with issues, lessons learned and recommendations. The graph in figure 1 is a directed tree structure, whereas that of figure 2 becomes more of a network structure. Besides the simple relationships that were clarified by the domain expert, some questions were posed like, *who manages* and *what are the support and evaluation activities*. This information is intentionally left obscure to be defined further in the processes that implement the policies.

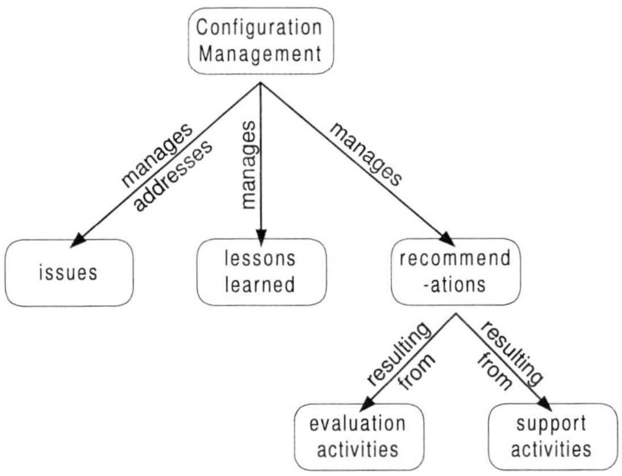

Figure 1. Modeling straight from the text

This is a simple example, but in general the domain expert is able to review the graphs generated by parsing the text and provide feedback regarding the strategic intent, assumptions, and ambiguous phraseology. As part of the interaction with the domain expert during the modeling we added brackets around nouns and verbs to represent the idea that something was inserted in the model that the corresponding document did not specifically include. The domain expert always approved these insertions.

ANALYSIS AND LAYERING PROCESS

The goal of the layering process is to gather clusters of entities that can be suppressed as part of other super-entities, while at the same time, to highlight the significant entities, giving an accurate representation in a synthesized global model. It is here where we borrowed from object oriented approaches (Coad and Yourdon, 1990). We analyzed the connectivity of entities and evaluated graphically the coupling and cohesion of the entities. Part of the process included understanding the significance of certain entities. We replaced clusters of nodes, where possible, with a single 'super' node. Sometimes we absorbed nodes into another entity such that the resulting super-entity was described by a structure of its own.

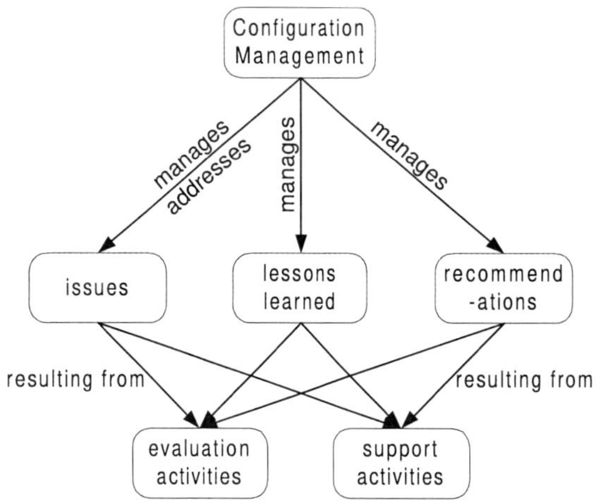

Figure 2. Model with Domain Expert Intervention

During this phase, we looked for structures that represented assemblies and inheritance, focusing on 'part of' and 'is a' relationships. In this way, we iteratively developed a simplified diagram, and a high-level entity relationship diagram, evolved where the relationships were between structures (figure 3). At this point our models were complete, and each structure, as well as the general model, was individually transferred to a single page.

STRATEGIES APPLIED

Orthogonal Entities. We observed that there were two orthogonal sets of entities that had complex relationships to one another. These orthogonal entities were contained in the document as major heading and subheadings. Figure 4 conceptually depicts the complexity between these relationships. We found that in order to accurately model the complex interfaces represented by these entities, we needed to work with the whole of the document. This means that we could not layer the model based on one or the other set of entities shown in figure 4 and then combine, since interrelationships vital to whole would be buried.

Tagging Entities. We also tagged significant nodes

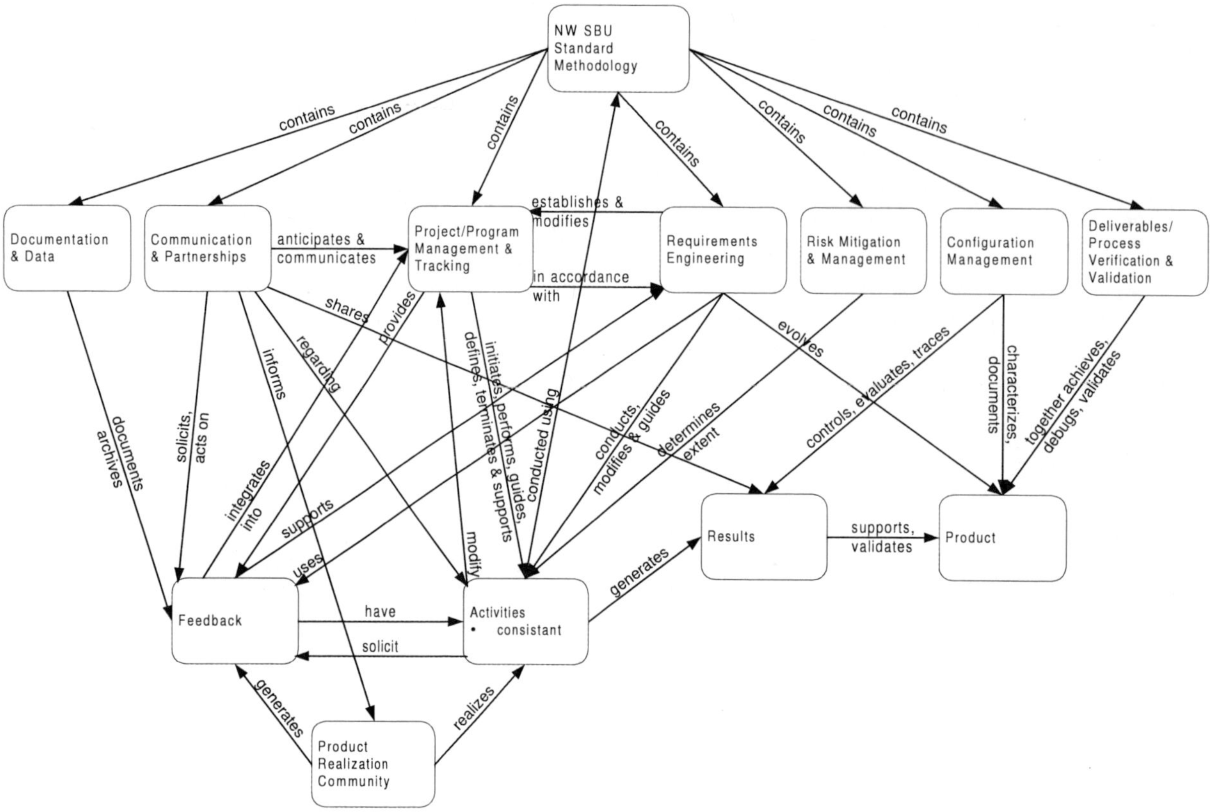

Figure 3. Highest Abstraction Layer of the Final Model

using a hexagonal icon to indicate significance (figure 5). This included the entities along the x-axis of figure 4, referred to by the domain expert as the crosscutting processes. These entities included, Communication & Partnerships, Project/Program Management & Training, Requirements Engineering, Risk Mitigation & Management, Deliverables/Process Verification & Validation, Configuration Management, Documentation & Data. The nodes representing these entities were ones we did not want to become subsumed while we were conducting analysis and layering. Our strategy was to provide a way of moving structures around more freely while minimizing confusion in the graphical representation. Another form of tagging included using color to tag the significant entities that were now being represented as structures or 'super' nodes allowing the attention to be focused on the entities that were singleton entities, those that were on the highest abstraction layer but were not super-entities. These entities were candidates for new structures to be

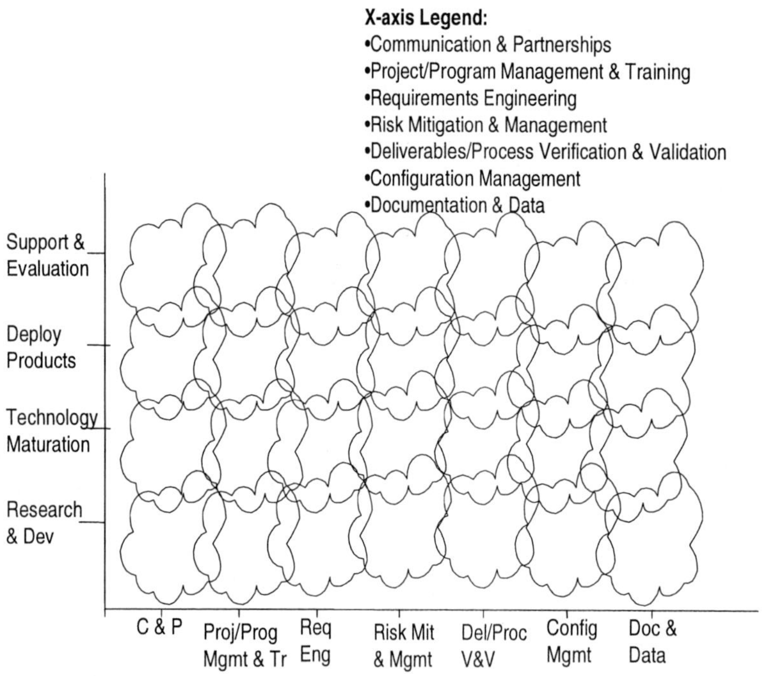

Figure 4. Conceptual Framework for Policy Information

created.

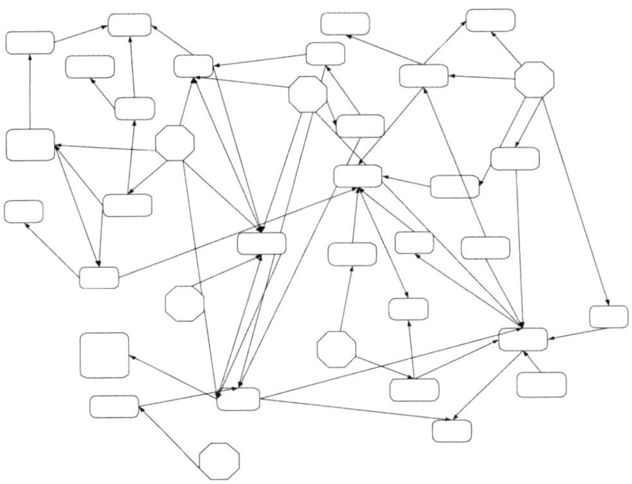

Figure 5. Graph in Development

Incidence Frequency. Another strategy applied to evolve interfaces between the two orthogonal entities was to generate an incidence frequency table for entity nouns (table 1). Those nodes having a relatively high frequency were identified as being possible candidates for consolidation in the graphs.

Noun	Freq	Noun	Freq
requirements	7	Defects	3
cost	4	Review	7
activities	9	Develop.	3
results	5	Research	4
support	3	Form	3
programs	3	Process	5
evaluation	3	Technology	10
system	4	Status	3
product	13	Partner	2
inform.	6	Project	3
risk	6	Plan	4

Table 1. Incidence Frequency

Using the incidence frequency, we repeatedly tagged the entities containing certain nouns. One such entity was 'activity.' Each activity node was colored for initial identification. Subsequently, all such nodes were consolidated to form a new 'activity' structure. Sometimes we had to identify connections and make appropriate substitutions without changing the original meaning of the model. For instance, our analysis revealed a connection between 'ability' and 'results,' so we changed 'ability' to 'usability.' Since 'usability' appeared on several occasions, and making this adjustment preserved the original meaning, this slight adjustment allowed us to make a consolidation in the graph.

Iteration. On occasion it was necessary to back out of the suppression of clusters when it obscured meaning at a higher abstraction level. Examining the words and talking out loud were part of the intense effort to understand and consolidate without taking away meaning.

Nouns were chosen and discarded for several reasons. The primary basis for making a structure was the strength, significance, or ambiguity of the noun. Sometimes it became apparent that the node was weak. Weak nouns are those that can not stand on there own. An example of a weak noun was technology. Even though it appeared ten times in the document, it existed in the outermost parts of relationships and was, therefore, ineffective in simplifying the structure of the model. In some cases, nouns existing only in the extremities of the model were also small quantitatively, so that they were insignificant in the analysis, as well. Other nouns did not form strong relationships and were ambiguous, leading to modifications based on discussions with domain experts.

In making judgements regarding what noun to build a meaningful structure around, we were looking for nodes that would stand out as germane, or terms that would offer some insight into the interface between the orthogonal entities. For example, when we pulled out the structure for activities, we found that there were *Research and Development activities, Technology Maturation activities, Deploy Products activities, and Support and Evaluation activities.* The structure created for 'activities' formed a key interface between the two sets of orthogonal entities.

Initially, the term 'requirements' looked like a candidate because there was a reasonable amount of redundancy, and it suggested a tighter coupling between elements. But further analysis revealed that it was too embedded within the model and, therefore, counterproductive for our goals. In other words, it convoluted the graph while providing little insight about the interaction between the orthogonal entities represented in figure 4.

Once super-entities were created, the links between the super-entities had to be examined for continuity and clarity. Many links represented by verbs could be discarded based on the strength of the other verbs. For example, in a link between 'activities' and 'product life cycle,' we were able to remove the verb 'has' because another existing verb 'integrates early' already had 'has' implied. Many times verbs like 'has' and 'creates' stood out as superfluous verbs and could be absorbed into stronger verbs that connected the same nodes –verbs like 'documents' and 'manages' could provide a more meaningful relationship that also embodied the more simple or implied relationships.

ANALYSIS OF THE FINAL MODEL

Once the synthesized, global model was generated, we examined the model for insights about the policy being generated and the associated programmatic structure. In the final highest layer of the model (figure 3), we observed some clear interconnections between the crosscuts indicated along the x-axis of figure 4. For example, the link between the nodes, Requirements Engineering and Program/Project Management and Tracking shows up heavily and understandably, while the in-depth technical linkage between Requirements Engineering and Product/Process Verification and Validation does not. The same is true regarding the need for stronger interconnections between Configuration Management, Requirements Engineering, and Verification & Validation. For the work in the NW SBU, the activities just mentioned form the heart of a technical approach to assuring that the product is really what is wanted and will meet the customers' needs. The review of the synthesized graph revealed that since Requirements Engineering, Configuration Management, and Product/Process Verification and Validation must work tightly together if they are to be effective, perhaps more explicit links should be addressed within the policy document.

LESSONS LEARNED

Orthogonal Entities. It was clear that there were two orthogonal sets of entities as shown in figure 4 that had complex relationships with one another. We first tried to project one set of entities onto the other set and then combine along one axis of entities. This approach actually resulted in suppression of the critical interfaces between these entities. After exploration and discussion, we abandoned our initial attempts with this approach and used the entire raw model as the basis for analysis and layering.

Changing Documents. At the time analysis was being conducted, the policy document was under frequent review and revision. As a result, progress with the modeling activities was difficult. Our initial efforts were largely directed at keeping up with modifications as opposed to analyzing a static document. This was positive in the sense that we provided feedback into the revision process, but also frustrating, and at times, confused our attempts at modeling and synthesis.

Strategy Considerations. Some surprising and important issues came out in the analysis process. One example is the relationships, similarities, and differences between Technology Maturation and Research and Development. Technology Maturation has a smaller scope than Research and Development, but the two are strongly related. The focus of Technology Maturation is to assure that a given technology should be matured by review against a collection of requirements to determine whether the risk associated with its use is low enough to warrant its incorporation into a product. If the review indicates otherwise, the product, itself, has to mature the technology during the associated development effort. This latter approach can make a difference in an estimated lead-time to turn out the product, and the associated risks to the product can increase dramatically. Initial attempts to synthesize the graphical model of the policy documents included recommendations to merge the Technology Maturation and the Research and Development functions into a single entity. Discussions with the domain experts revealed that such a simplification would loose a significant strategy of the policy structure itself – namely to focus on technology maturation as a separate and distinct process. Further development of the policy is required to delineate the crucial role that Technology Maturation plays so that it is not treated casually.

Roles. The roles that people played in modeling the policy document were another important outcome in this study. It was found that a modeling expert could successfully drive the analysis process. Although our process contained rules and elements conducive to repeatability, modeling as described in this paper is still something of an art that is perfected with experience. The massaging of the data and getting the intuitive feel of how things should go are skills that are not yet taught, but passed on to others through experience over time. In this case study, the modeling expert also had some domain experience and was able to draw from that. But, in general, the modeling expert is one that draws out pertinent data from domain experts and then converts this information into an accurate representation of that data.

As mentioned earlier, of particular note was the role of the domain expert in both analyzing and approving models of the policy document. In contrast is the situation we experienced in modeling a draft of ISO 9001 (a standards document). Although also in draft form, the ISO 9001 document was more structured and stable, and there also was no domain expert available to assist in the analysis.

In a third situation, that of a document listing user interview information, strategy and intent were not present as they were in the policy domain. While this user data was clearly the most flexible, there exists no single domain expert in this situation to represent the underlying intention behind the users' statements. It was desired to obtain a true essence of the users' statements, so that assuring that user requirements were more faithfully represented was an essential objective of the analysis. Thus, based on the type of document being analyzed, the role of the domain expert can provide essential input to the analysis.

Also important to this analysis process was the role of the average engineer – to observe the process that was unfolding, to recommend alternative ideas for the analysis, and to ask questions. In this case study, this person had no prior experience in a project of this nature. This lack of experience was not particularly troublesome; in fact this person was more able to probe and offer an unbiased point of view that sometimes people with experience might not have.

CONCLUSIONS

The work described by this paper not only assisted in identifying requirements specifically associated with the process work under development, it provided policy developers a framework to determine the completeness and sensibility of the policy structure and associated programmatic strategies. Basically in real-time, the development team was able to review text that was particularly problematic or ambiguous, and to determine a more effective way to re-word the text. This resulted in text that could be more easily understood and that would reflect the desired intent.

Additionally, the inclusions of review and discussion with the domain expert enabled the determination of policy strategies that could likely be mistakenly compressed or even edited out of the text, inadvertently.

An additional benefit was also obtained from this process. When the final synthesized graphical model was reviewed, it was clear that interrelationships between policy elements had not been explicitly articulated in the draft document. This insight was available to reviewers at a glance, rather than through many hours of intense document review and discussion, or rather than being overlooked completely. Policy developers were then able to determine whether the interrelationships were better elucidated in the "what's" called out in the policy, or left for the processes to define the specific "how's."

In this particular case study, we observed that the inclusion of the domain expert produced more of a model of intent, as opposed to one that would be 100% true to the written text. While this enabled synthesis of the model, it was somewhat disconcerting to more experienced modelers. This intent versus literal 'war' of sorts may actually be characteristic of this particular type of case study. As was mentioned, the policy effort evolved as an outgrowth of the process development effort that preceded it. The policy development team contained personnel who also participated in the process development effort. The policy development team intentionally included provisions for many of the "how's" that were created in the process effort – namely the crosscutting process functions.

As such, it is certain that the policy effort did not begin at ground zero as if no analysis had ever been conducted. When the policy statements were written, only essential details were included. The details specified were those directly related to a strategy of specifying environmental changes for which a movement along a continuum of outcomes was desired. Thus, the policy was the result of both some pre-analysis and consciously chosen omissions of detail. This type of approach to policy specification may naturally result in the need for a domain expert.

FUTURE RESEARCH

The approach discussed in this paper is an attempt at structuring and establishing a process for the difficult tasks of analyzing, synthesizing, and simplifying requirements statements. The positive results obtained in this and related efforts indicate some natural areas for follow-on research.

Other modeling approaches need to be examined further and compared. Other graphical and natural language approaches to examining text documents should be compared with regard to advantages and disadvantages.

Automation is also a goal. Applying a natural language tagger, used in much of the research in Natural Language Processing (NLP), to the textual document seems very feasible. Once a document has been tagged, a first cut graphical rendering of the document could theoretically be produced automatically. However, synthesis and simplification would probably require interactive intervention by the analyst, perhaps using intelligent agent technology. Once an initial ER rendering of the document is created, another tool could be developed based on graph theory that assists in identifying clusters and entities that could replace several nodes, i.e., part of this automated process could include suggestions for possible structures.

Another area for research is that of alternative approaches to text policy documents or formats for standards documents. It is possible that the graphical representation could be more easily integrated into the human mind through web-based systems, resulting in more readily assimilated documentation. Such graphical representations could assist not only human learning, but also implementation, traceability determination, and audit interpretation.

Realistically, however, the analysis and graphical abstraction process presented in this paper will support such automation and application only as it becomes more formalized. Progress is being made in finding methods that represent data accurately and in a usable, meaningful way. But, as yet, there exist no easy solutions (Berry, 1999). Only further application and study of this promising technique will progress it beyond its current state of being largely an art form.

ACKNOWLEDGEMENT

Sandia is a multiprogram laboratory operated by Sandia Corporation, a Lockheed Martin Company, for the United States Department of Energy under Contract DE-AC04-94AL85000.

BIBLIOGRAPHY

Berry, Daniel M., "Requirements Engineering Requirements Iceberg," Presentation given at New Mexico State University, Computer Science Dept, August 11, 1999.

Coad, P., and E. Yourdon, Object-Oriented Analysis, Prentice-Hall, 1990.

Robertson, Suzanne, The Atlantic Systems Guild, "Requirements Patterns via Events/Use Cases", http://www.atlsysguild.com/GuildSite/SQR/Requirements_Patterns.html, June 1999.

Schvaneveldt, Roger W., "Pathfinder Associative Networks: Studies in Knowledge Organization", Ablex Publishing Corp, New Jersey, 1990.

BIOGRAPHY

Kathleen "Kit" Crumpton is a graduate student at NMSU where she is working on a Masters Degree in Computer Science. She currently holds a Bachelor of Science in Computer Science with a minor in Mathematics from NMSU and a Bachelor of Science in Administration of Justice from American University in Washington, D.C. She has 12 years experience in business software applications and has worked in the manufacturing community, telecommuniations and the banking industry.

Regina M. Gonzales is on the faculty at New Mexico State University. She has over ten years experience working full-time in industry as a Computer Systems Engineer and Project Manager. Regina also consults for several companies including Sandia National Laboratories and Insight Technologies Group. She has a B.S. in Electrical and Computer Engineering form New Mexico State University, an MS in Electrical and Computer Engineering from University of Arizona, an MS in Computer Science from University of Colorado, and is finishing up a PhD in Requirements Engineering from New Mexico State University.

Sharon Trauth has worked at Sandia National Laboratories for over 15 years and is a manager in the Engineering Business Practices and Information Center. She has extensive experience in many aspects of the systems development lifecycle including quality engineering, component design engineering, manufacturing processes, and failure analysis. She has applied this knowledge to her recent assignments of developing a standardized engineering and lifecycle process as well as the associated policy infrastructure. She has a Bachelors degree in Physics and a Masters in Electrical Engineering from Louisiana State University.

An Integrated Information Representation Schema for Complex Human Centric Systems

Dr. Harry E. Crisp
NgocDung T. Hoang
Cuong M. Nguyen
Naval Surface Warfare Center, B05
17320 Dahlgren Road
Dahlgren, Virginia 22448-5100

Nicholas E. Karangelen
David Britton
Trident Systems Incorporated
10201 Lee Highway, Suite 300
Fairfax, Virginia 22030

Abstract. This paper will introduce the development of an information representation schema that can be used to support the development of complex human centric systems. Technology that was adopted to support schema evolution to accommodate new methods and tools or schema tailoring for the need of a specific program will also be addressed.

INTRODUCTION

Major military systems as well as civilian manufacturing, transportation, health care, and information management systems are getting bigger and more complex as we approach the 21st century. The cost and schedule required to develop major systems is rising far faster than anticipated and nearly every large system is delivered over budget with significant performance or functionality shortfalls, not to mention some outright failures (Dalcher 1994).

The development of complex human centric systems is particularly challenging (Bost, et al. 1998). Such systems are a complex mix of hardware, software, and human resources. Human operators and decisionmakers play key roles in enabling the system to achieve overall mission and performance objectives. The requirements to provide user support to humans, habitability resources for long duration missions, operator and maintenance training, and career path considerations are significant factors in total system life cycle costs.

The combination of rapid advancement of computing technology and the desire to reduce system life cycle costs while improving system performance have become a driver for the automation of many system functions normally performed by humans. The automation of such functions must be carefully planned and evaluated throughout the system development cycle. The allocation of functions and tasks between humans and non-humans is a non-trivial procedure and needs to be based on the utilization of an integrated systems engineering and human engineering process. The application of the integrated process will typically be performed by a multi-disciplinary team, supported by a mix of tools.

Within each phase of the system engineering process, methods and tools have been developed and enhanced to support specific engineering activities. Modern computer aided tools have dramatically improved the productivity and quality of computer software (e.g. advanced compilers and debuggers) and hardware development (e.g. VLSI chip design and board level tools) as well as for mechanical system development (e.g. CAD/CAM tools) and other engineering specialties. Likewise, methods and tools to support human workload analysis as well as team performance and organization structure are on the rise. These tools provide development engineers the necessary automation support to address the challenge of developing large complex software programs of a million SLOC or more, to efficiently design and develop the future generations of computer hardware, or to improve human performance through training. A major challenge for system engineers is to synchronize among the various disciplines to achieve a balanced total system development. Although methods and tools for system engineers have been developed, they tend to lack the scope and scaleability to effectively address the rising complexity of system development challenges and provide essentially no interoperability between tools even for data interchange. Technologies to support the design of a total system, of which the human operator is a vital part, are essential for the successful development of future systems.

The focus of this paper is to introduce an

information representation schema to support the development of complex human centric systems. Technology that was adopted to support schema evolution to accommodate new methods and tools or schema tailoring for the need of a specific program will also be addressed.

BACKGROUND

An initial prototype of an integrated engineering environment has been developed under the Science and Technology Manning Affordability Initiative (S&T MAI) Program, sponsored by the Office of Naval Research, to support the development of large-complex human centric systems (Crisp, et al. 1999). The S&T MAI program has recognized the need to inject human user considerations into appropriate activities of the system development process. It is noted that this effort is much more profound than the usual Man-Machine Interface (MMI) consideration. It envisions an integrated human/system engineering process to support the appropriate allocation of functions among operators and system components throughout the development process. The IEEE 1220 standard "Application and Management of the Systems Engineering Process" has been used as the framework by the MAI program for defining such an integrated process. This human engineering process has also been included in the latest version of the IEEE standard (IEEE 1220-1998). The basic human engineering activities are shown in Figure 1. The detailed description and execution of the associated human engineering activities can be found on the S&T MAI web site (www.manningaffordability.com).

A specific tool was selected for each representative activity of the above engineering process for the creation of an initial integrated engineering environment called the Human Center Design Environment (HCDE). Figure 2 depicts the fully developed HCDE which is expected to be completed and validated against a sample Navy design problem by 2001.

Currently HCDE provides both system and human engineering capabilities through COTS and prototype tools including:

- System Requirements Management via Dynamic Object Oriented Requirements System (DOORS)
- System Function Analysis via CORE
- Ship Board Manning Analysis via IMAGE
- Human Performance Modeling via IPME
- Physical Design Analysis via ENVISION/ERGO

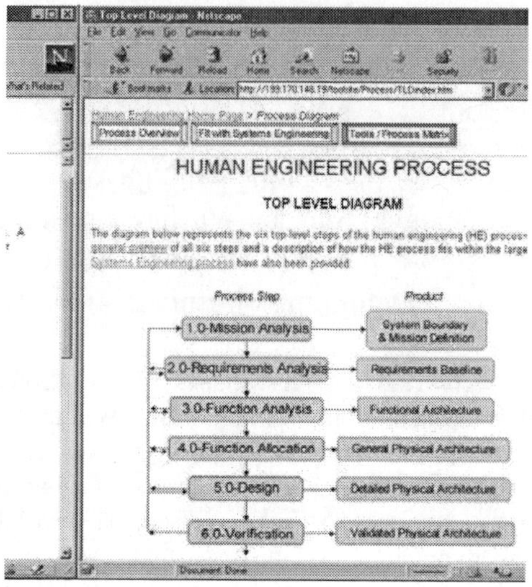

Figure 1. Human Engineering Process

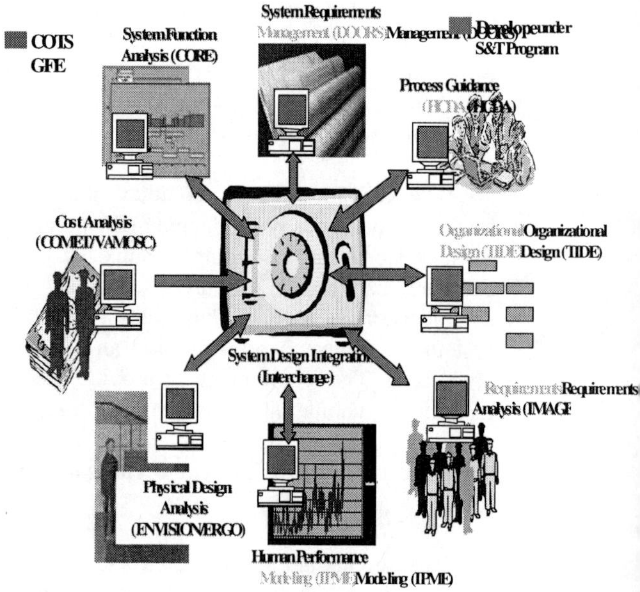

Figure 2. Human Centered Design Environment

INTERCHANGE is used to enable the sharing of information among these tools as well as among all members of the development team. An example of this is, given a set of requirements generated by requirement engineers in DOORS, it can then be imported to the INTERCHANGE repository and made available to the entire project. All project members may then view the most current requirements set via the INTERCHANGE viewer without the need to access via DOORS.

In addition, if tools within HCDE need to share data with one another, they can extract from or update the information within the repository through the appropriate plug-in. This allows users from different engineering disciplines to work from the same design baseline that is under strict management configuration. Significant reductions in development time can be realized by eliminating the need for entering redundant design information from tool to tool. Various types of linkage can be established among repository information to maintain traceability. The individual user may also set up a notification alert on the design object that is pertinent to his or her job such that he or she will be notified everytime the object is changed.

Although INTERCHANGE provides many essential functions for the creation and management of project information, the basis for its tool interoperability capabilities is the data schema underlying the tool.

REPOSITORY SCHEMA

Data must often be interpreted or translated by human operators and re-entered for each tool employed in a typical development process. Inconsistent and incomplete capture and representation of the design across various tools often causes design errors the tools were intended to resolve. The emerging CORBA (CORBA 1995) standards represent a mechanism for data exchange. However, the remaining larger challenge of establishing a common set of data semantics is the largest roadblock to integration of even similar systems engineering tools. An example of the difficulty in establishing common systems engineering tool semantics is illustrated by efforts such as the CASE Data Interchange Format for data flow models (CDIF 1995) which took many years to reach agreement on relatively non-contentious data flow diagram semantics, but which has not been adopted in full by key systems engineering tool vendors.

The ISO 10303 Standard for Technical Exchange of Product (STEP) data is an example of an effort that began in the early 1980's to provide standards for product data interchange within CAD, CAE, and CAM tools. More recently, an ISO 10303 - AP 233 Working Group (Johnson, et al 1999) has been established to develop a new STEP standard for an information model to capture systems engineering information. This is expected to encompass both requirements information and behaviour information.

An integrated system information schema will establish the means for developing a comprehensive multi-domain product model definition with formal data traceability and other inter-relationships. A common data interchange format will allow various design synthesis, capture, analysis and simulation tools to extract system data relevant to a particular analysis from the common data base . This common repository will then facilitate a shared common understanding of the system, will support collaborative distributed engineering, and will promote seamless integration of multiple engineering disciplines. The structured multi-domain representations of system designs in executable format will enable rapid evaluation of multiple design options and electronic exchange of system models instead of large volumes of English language design specifications.

The multi-domain integrated product and process model format is the key for maintaining a consistent and interrelated system data repository which supports extraction of system models in multiple disciplines including requirements, conceptual design, functional design, implementation design, manufacturing, and management. A consistent central design repository means that design data needs to be captured only once. This aspect alone will dramatically reduce the inefficient manual transfer of design information into various forms needed to support the broad spectrum of system engineering tools and activities. These capabilities will empower distributed Integrated Process Teams (IPT's) in the creation and assessment of multiple system baselines through efficient automation and concurrent simulation capabilities.

The common Integrated Process and Product Model (IPPM) schema is central to achieving interoperability among design capture, analysis, and simulation tools by providing a means for diverse tools to access a common data repository. As such a common schema becomes a defacto standard, it provides an incentive for tool vendors to make their existing and future tools compatible. Many examples of how successful standards have driven competing vendors to become compatible in the past include the Rich Text Format in the word processing industry and VHDL in the custom computer chip building industry.

The HCDE schema concept evolved from various standards including CDIF and IEEE 1220. It provides a formal means for capturing system information including top level system requirements, environment considerations, conceptual design, functional design, implementation design, manufacturing, system support, and management aspects. The use of a class hierarchy for defining the data objects takes advantage of inheritance for propagating common attributes across many classes

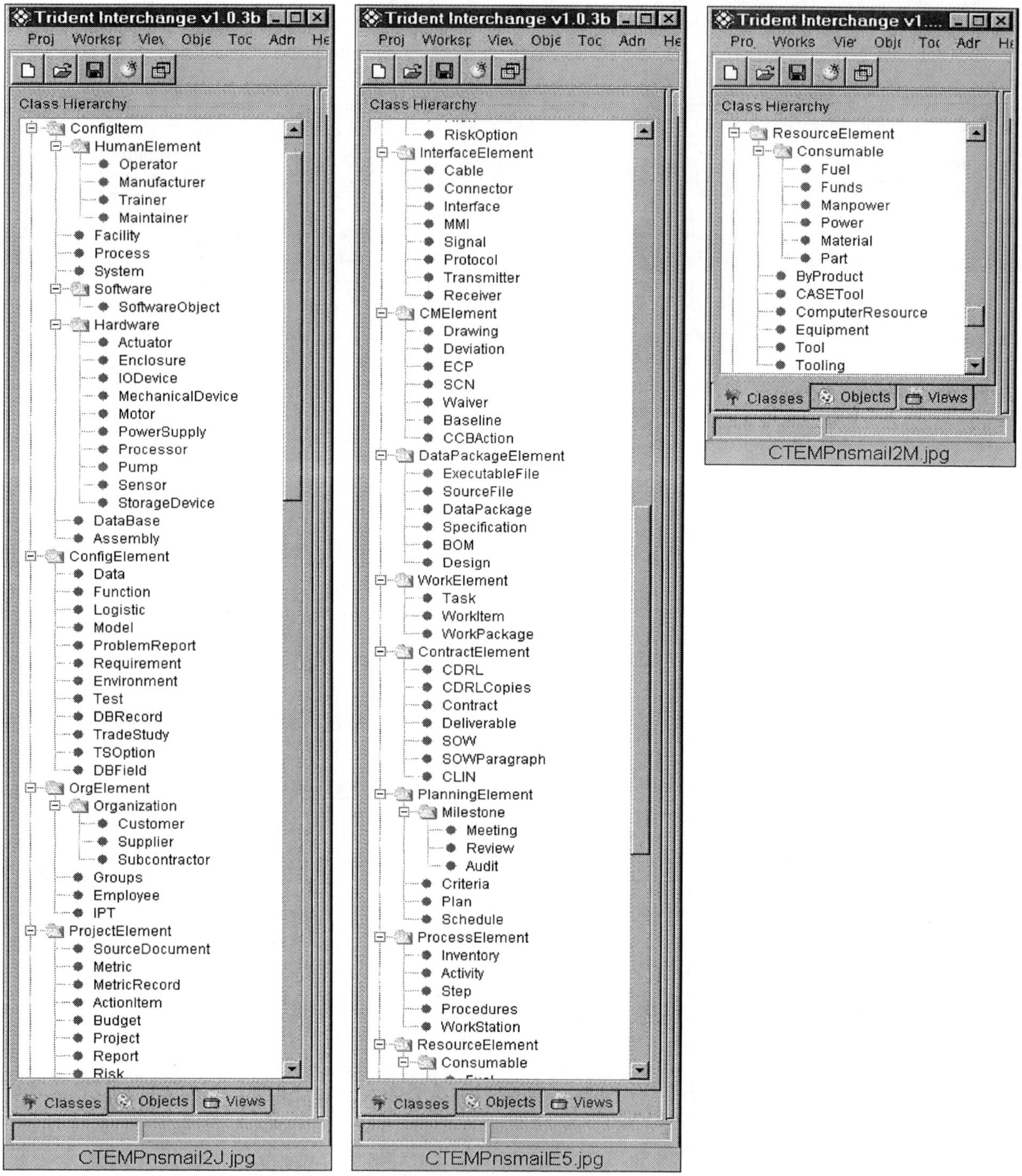

Figure 3 HCDE Data Schema

and provides a structure for formal definition of a common open data representation standard. These classes must be constructed to address the multiple domains and levels of abstraction necessary to represent the system under development. Explicitly defining the attributes and methods associated with each class provide the means for automated manipulation and interpretation of design data. The class hierarchy also provides a means for managing changes to the HCDE schema which will, no doubt, require revision through addition of new object classes, modification of attributes and methods on existing classes, and through creation of relationships and instances. Methods for dynamic schema evolution have recently been demonstrated in advanced object oriented data bases which will provide a means for accommodating emerging data representation needs.

Figure 3 illustrates the current HCDE schema where the object class structure is organized such that it may accommodate products and the associated processes and also, the related project information. For example, while ConfigItem, InterfaceElement and ResourceElement classes are clearly related to type of product under configuration management, ContractElement and ProcessElement classes deal with different types of process. Likewise classes like OrgElement, PlanningElement and ProjectElement tend to support different types of project information.

This initial schema provides a formal structured approach for representing and relating system information across the entire life cycle enabling traceability and consistency analysis across domains and over time. It provides a mechanism for constructing a single consistent system information repository which can serve as a common data base for advanced tool employment.

An integrated system information schema establishes the means for developing a comprehensive multi-domain product model definition with formal data traceability and other inter-relationships. A common data interchange format will allow various design synthesis, capture, analysis and simulation tools to extract system data relevant to a particular analysis from the common data base. It also allows system data to be captured once and then used across many tools. This common repository will promote a shared common understanding of the system, will support collaborative distributed engineering, and will facilitate seamless integration of multiple engineering disciplines. The structured multi-domain representations of system designs in executable format will enable rapid evaluation of multiple design options and electronic exchange of system models.

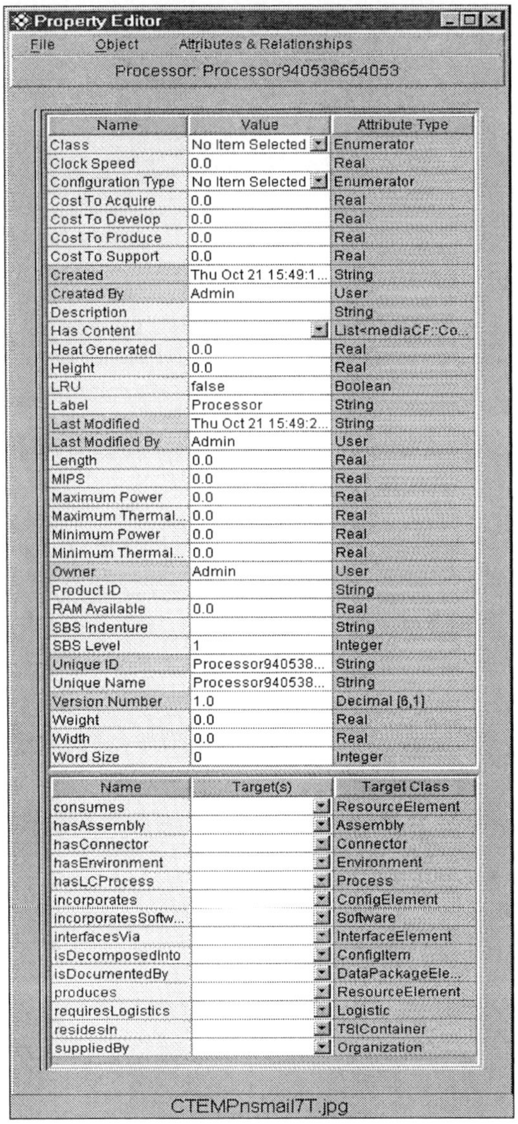

Figure 4 Example of Class Attribute and Relationship

Figure 4 depicts an example of attributes and relationships belong to the Processor class of HCDE. For security purposes, user access can be controlled at the attribute level. The color code of the attribute and relationship names indicates the different accessing levels.

For each class within the HCDE schema, a set of attributes and relationship is defined. A fixed value or a method can be assigned to the content of attributes and relationships. This format can be viewed as a predefined template from which design objects can be created. Hence, from the same class, users can create many type of objects to be utilized during the development. This allows designers to quickly explore various design options as well as to speculate about potential designs based, for example, on projected technology developments.

The list of attributes and relationships for each object may be extensive since it includes all information about that object. It is anticipated that each engineer in a multidisciplinary will populate and maintain a subset of this list and all project members will then be able to utilize the populated information.

As a neutral format for representing design information, this attributes and relationships list also serves as a mean for tools integration. This list includes all information that is required to be shared among tools within the environment. The "plug-in" which is developed for each tool within the environment is the means to pull or push the shared information between it and the repository. Tool specific information is also maintained by the repository for the reconstruction or update of the model within the original tool.

Since many changes typically happen during the lifetime of a project, the repository supports schema evolution and old data may then be migrated to the new schema accordingly. This also allows new design tools to be added as needed and be able to share information with the rest of the project.

CONCLUSION

The current HCDE schema allows information to be shared among the various disciplines involved in engineering human centric systems, including requirements engineers, hardware and software engineers, human engineers and management. Available tool plug-ins to the repository include DOORS, CORE, IMAGE and IPME. Plug-ins to Navy cost databases, VAMOSC and COMET, and a physical design and simulation tool, ENVISION/ERGO, are under development. Although the plug-ins may need to be updated as the new version of each tool is released, the benefits of an integrated tool environment clearly outweigh this investment.

HCDE is not an incremental step beyond the current systems engineering methods and tools employed today, but instead represents a major paradigm shift towards a comprehensive integrated design synthesis, capture and analysis environment which addresses the entire system development life cycle and the spectrum of engineering and management disciplines.

HCDE has demonstrated that development programs can now flexibly construct an environment of choice without being totally dependent on any particular tool vendor. Further, for the typical engineering environment, as the number of tools utlized within the integrated environment increases, tool-to-tool integration is costly and unscaleable. The neutral object model approach developed by the HCDE project is a very feasible solution for cost as well as configuration management.

Nonetheless, the lack of data representation standards remains a significant barrier to near term realization of the full benefits of the neutral object model approach. Considerable effort is required to synthesize, test, and refine a common schema for data representation which can serve as the foundation for interchange of system engineering data and for cross referencing multiple domains. The S&T MAI program has taken an initial step in verifying the object model technology underlying the HCDE infrastructure development. It is anticipated that other programs as well as industry and tool vendors will realize the significant benefits of this approach and advance the development of standards for a common date schema.

REFERENCES

Bost, J. Robert, McKneely, Jennifer A. B., Hamburger, Trish, "Surface Combatants of the Future – Reduced Crew Warships." Proceedings of the Human Factors Ergonomics Society Annual Meeting, October, 1998.

CDIF 1995 Integrated Meta-Model - Data Flow Model Subject Area, Electronic Industry Association CASE Data Interchange Format (CDIF) Technical Committee, March 1995

CORBA 1995 CORBA Common Object Request Broker Architecture and Specification, Object Management Group, December 1995.

Crisp, Harry, Hoang, Ngocdung, Schmidt, Richard, "A Human Centered Design Environment for Complex Systems." Procedings of the International Symposium of the International Council on System Engineering, Brighton, England, June 1999.

Dalcher, D. "Falling down is part of growing up: the study of failure in the software engineering community." Proceedings of the 7th SEI Conference on Software Engineering Education, 1994.

Johnson, Julian, Luise, Federica, et al., "The Future Systems Engineering Data Exchange Standards STEP AT-233: Sharing the Results of the SEDRES Project." Proceedings of the 9th Annual International Symposium of the International Council on Systems Engineering, Brighton, England, June 1999.

BIOGRAPHY

Harry E. Crisp, II is currently serving an assignment as Director of Special Projects in the office of the Chief Engineer for the Assistant Secretary of the Navy for Research, Development, and Acquisition. He holds a B.S. degree in Electrical Engineering from Clemson University and an M.S. and Ph. D. in Electrical Engineering from Auburn University. He has been employed at NSWCDD since September 1971. He is a member of the Institute of Electrical and Electronics Engineers, the American Society of Naval Engineers and the International Council on Systems Engineering. He is currently serving as the Government/Academic Director for INCOSE Region V.

Ngocdung Hoang is the task leader of the HCDE Framework and Infrastructure task within the SC21 Manning Affordability Science and Technology Initiative. She graduated from the University of Maryland in 1987 with a B.S. degree in Electrical Engineering. She has been employed at NSWCDD since July 1987 and has conducted research on methods and tools to support the development of complex systems.

Cuong M. Nguyen is the task leader for the HCDE Test-bed Integration and Application effort which is a part of the SC-21 Manning Affordability Initiative Program. He supports HCDE in term of research and development, networking, tools integration, wide area collaboration, test-bed security, and application of HCDE capabilities in the Land Attack Functional decomposition/analysis group. Mr. Nguyen received his BSEE from the University of Maryland in 1987 and MSEE from the Johns Hopkins University / Applied Physics Laboratory in 1989, He joined the Naval Surface Warfare Center, Dahlgren Division in 1987.

Nick Karangelen is the president of Trident Systems Incorporated and has 16 years experience in the operation, development and analysis of ASW combat systems. He has served as a Naval officer in the Atlantic submarine force and worked as a systems engineer for TRW and IBM. As president of Trident, he has participated in a variety of systems engineering projects including recent R&D efforts in development of advanced systems engineering methods and tools.

David Britton is the Director of Technology Development Division at Trident Systems Incorporated and has 13 years experience in the development and analysis of large complex computer based systems. He has 10 years experience in the research and development of advanced systems engineering methods and tools and is currently leading the development of a commercial product for sharing and managing engineering tool data.

Reuse and COTS Lessons Learned for the Development Process and Team of Surveillance Radars

Kathleen McGuire
Electronic Sensors and Systems Sector
Northrop Grumman Corporation
Box 1693
Baltimore, Maryland 21203

Abstract. Surveillance radars developed in the 1990's have extensively exploited the use of previous developed components and subsystems to significantly reduce development cost and schedule. The wide array of experiences has offered interesting examples and lessons learned. Development of air traffic control and military ground based and airborne surveillance radars using reuse and COTS have saved millions of dollars and years of time.

Tailored Systems Engineering development processes were key to optimize system quality, time and cost savings when using COTS and reuse. Tailored processes helped minimize the amount of "bumps in the road" and team morale issues frequently experienced with previously developed components.

REUSE AND COTS– WHAT IS IT

Terms. Both the terms COTS and Reuse describe an element that has been previously developed. COTS is an acronym for Commercial Off The Shelf. It has been used for elements of hardware, software or combined hardware and software subsystems. The commercial nature implies that the intended users are many, the design information is owned by the developer and is not available to the user (as it potentially can be with a subcontracted or in-house development). The typical commercial uses may not be as stringent as a more complex system. Also, requirements and testing can be much less and varied.

Reuse applies most typically to software, but may be applied to hardware and hardware/software subsystems. Reuse means that the hardware or software element previously exists, but does not infer much else. Its original design application may be very different, its maturity may vary, and its quality may be a wide range. It may or may not have much run-time.

COTS and Reuse Implemented. For one air traffic control (ATC) radar, over 50% of the total 450,000 lines of code were reuse. The sources included the U.S. Government (research study), two previous products from the same company, several commercial companies and a self-employed engineer with an Internet site. The software components included elements for the development environment, operating system components, startup elements, several application functions, database and management functions, and Microsoft Windows NT.

The hardware reuse and COTS elements came from external large commercial companies, very small commercial companies, and previous developed products internally from the same company. The components included Motorola 68000 series processors, ancillary daughter cards for the 68000 processor from various smaller manufacturers, a specialty low volume, high throughput parallel processor from a small company, PC's, and several eighty-inch cabinets making up a secondary radar subsystem and a rotating thirty foot antenna and platform equipment.

The traits, maturity, stability and support varied widely. The table below summarizes the variety of traits of the previously developed components used.

Trait	Variety of Reuse & COTS Used
What was reused or COTS	Commercial processors, existing code, previous developed subsystems, processor support tools, interconnect hardware
Who developed	Large and very small companies, U.S. government, previous employees, present employees
Where developed	Various U.S. locations, Europe, unknown
Why developed originally	Small system use, govt. study, internet global application, variant radar, small company products
How developed	Commercial, military contract, R&D, many unknowns
Present use	None/new, continuous at many sites, discontinued use

Table 1: Reuse and COTS traits widely varied

PROBLEMS ENCOUNTERED

Categories of Problems. The development teams reaped great benefits from numerous cases of COTS and reuse, but in many instances had unexpected problems. Table 2 summarizes some typical problem causes. These categories were true independent of whether it was reuse or COTS, hardware or software. The following paragraphs provide some example uses and problems.

• Brought errors with it
• Unknown limits in previous uses & present design
• Don't understand how to implement
• Your use is breaking new ground
• More run time finds more errors
• "Broke" something when modifying or connecting to it
• Unexpected unknown design "feature" or detail
• See system anomalies but hard to determine if COTS the cause since less BIT, debug hooks
• Multi-purpose COTs item not optimized for any use
• Doesn't work the same in your system

Table 2: Typical Problems encountered

Software. Externally procured COTS software was used in a number of design areas, including the operating and software development system of radar. Implementing the development environment and operating system are complex operations. Several problems were encountered due to not understanding the product at the beginning and having few reference materials. Support for COTS software may not be available or only if it is purchased. This did not progress until a support contract was procured and support personnel were on-site.

The operating system and board support packages had several years of maturity and several customers. However, it was not well understood until several problems consumed significant time that our application was breaking significant new ground in a number of respects. Interprocessor communications in particular had several levels of complexity more than other users.

The applications software obtained from the research study was a major savings of time overall. The research study took the algorithms from an existing product that were not in the "C" software language and converted them. However, more time than expected was invested optimizing it to run in a real time environment. Once running, several functions worked very well in a live operation but one was not performing. Months of integration problem solving were invested before conversation with the original developers uncovered this was the only function that had not really begun, much less passed a verification check. It was also the only function that had been radically modified from the original algorithm. This function was replaced with code that closely emulated the function on the older product.

Several application code modules were ported from an existing product within the same company. Several personnel were available from that product support group for consulting. The product is fielded around the world in continuous operation in over a dozen sites. However, the porting to the new processor real time settings and integrating into the new architecture interfaces consumed much more time than expected. In addition, regression testing experienced several recurring existing problems that had rarely been seen before.

Hardware. The Motorola boards were extremely mature platforms on which to run new untested software. The schedule and complexity reduction compared to developing the processor board at the same time as the software is many magnitudes. However, Motorola boards come with existing functions that can not be optimized for a radar's time-sensitive operations. The extent of commercial built-in-test and monitoring points are much less than boards developed in-house in the 1980's for government developments. Broken boards do occur and may be harder to detect. To address this issue, the cost of boards is so reduced that spare boards and less time for diagnostics may be easier to justify.

A great savings was incurred with procurement of a specialty low volume, high throughput parallel processor. Although the per-board cost was significant, the lack of paying for the full development saved much risk and cost. However, the board development first lot had anomalies when in the system. The vendor factory tools and our off-line software development tool did not experience the problem, forcing all debug activities to be done on the system integration bench. The debug and eventual fix took longer with a vendor two time zones away with a small support staff who could not reproduce the problem there. The first lot of boards experienced higher failure rates due to a commercial (unscreened) part that had a manufacturing problem. This took many months to resolve since all lots of boards were mixed in the system and the problem took months to develop. It was uncovered that our radar application was putting much more run time on these boards than other customers were.

Addressing the Problems. The issue for the development effort and the team was not only that previous developed components had unexpected frustrating problems, but that time and money budgets was not at first fully incorporating the "transition" effort to implement the components. In almost all cases the use of COTS and reuse was the right way to go, but the process and team had to adapt to implementing it in a structured approach.

TAILORING THE PROCESS FOR REUSE - LESSONS LEARNED

Process Phases & Reuse & COTS. Considerations for use of previous designs impact all phases of the System Engineering process, shown in Figure 1. The great benefit of previous designs is that large savings in each step of the process that should be obtained. One may be tempted to skip many or all steps since the element is "finished." But a proper assessment and tailoring did streamline the implementations and reduced unforeseen delays and frustration.

User requirements and functional analysis phase. The user requirements and functional analysis phase should not omit elements that may decided to be a previous design. A flowdown of at least top level requirements and functions are used in assessment decisions, modification needs assessments, and test or regression to ensure compliance. A requirements allocation document or database should be developed.

SYSTEM DEVELOPMENT PHASES

User Requirements and Functional Analysis→

→Concept Architecture & Trade Studies

→Design

→Verification

→Production

→Support/Mods

Figure 1 Reuse & COTS Impact every Phase of the SE Development Process

Decision to Use. The decision to use COTS and reuse is part of the Requirements Analysis and Concept Architecture & Trade Study phases of the process. A thorough assessment at this stage is important even if it is obvious that use of a previous design is preferred to a new development. An assessment questionnaire example is provided in Table 3. The assessment uncovers the true cost, schedule and risk impacts. If there is a trade study between several sources for previous designs, a thorough assessment may uncover a critical difference.

Reuse/COTS Assessment
Subject
Define what is & is not in the "unit" under assessment (tools, licenses, support, ancillaries)
Requirements
What does it do now?
Compare to your requirements?
How does the operating environment compare? - temperature, vibration, real time, run length
Can it be modified ($, sched)?
Design
Can the design be assessed?
How does the architecture & design major features compare (multiple CPU, users, ..)?
Do the interfaces work with yours?
If not, can it be modified ($, sched)?
Is it becoming an industry "standard" (more development, maturity and support)?
Quality
Can the unit quality be assessed?
What is the quality of the design?
What is the quality of the code? To standards?
What is the manufacturing/workmanship quality?
Has there been qualification testing? Any data?
What is the production testing?
What is the change & repair process?
Stability/Maturity- How long has it been in use? How much run time? Tough environment?
Support
If you have problems, what support is available?
Can the source afford to give you support?
What is the documentation available?
What will you need to provide to your customers? Will they find that sufficient?
Business, Legal, Cost, Schedule
What are cost & schedule impacts of above
What is cost of your support of their problems
Can it be shipped internationally if needed?
Are you notified of configuration changes? Are they tracked by you or by them? Will you have to do a system update?
Who "owns" the design (customer, supplier, you)
Does the product have a life cycle? Is there an upgrade path?
What is the full cost of obtaining production oriented quantities, SW licenses, and spares?

Table 3: Assessment Questions in COTS/Reuse Decision

Design. One may be tempted to skip effort in this phase altogether since the design is "done". The focus of this stage is to:

(a) Refine the assessment of requirements and design, especially documenting the differences from the previous use(s) to your application

(b) Define & implement all modifications and interconnections required to integrate the component.

Both of these areas of focus are a cause for potential noncompliance problems and implementation risk. In place of a top-down design document, documentation that describes the top level design, major features, differences for your uses, modifications and interconnects to be made by your team. These may be done in a summary fashion, but are critical for later support and for managing areas of change. Note that major requirements, design differences, and sources of modifications become the "verification matrix" for the integration and test phase.

COTS equipment may not be as rigorously verified or have as much margin as one may be used too. In high temperature runs, one COTS element stopped functioning one to two degrees above the specification, while another continued long term running even several degrees above the design specification. If this is a critical parameter, some level of testing or checkout may be the only way to know.

Another method to assess the design compatibility is akin to the "prototyping" of a new design. Instead of treating the subject of reuse as a low risk area that can be addressed later, consider early bench testing to find the unknowns. Unknown incompatibilities or problems can be debugged before the element is needed.

This was done with code ported from a previously developed radar. The code was "wired in" slightly differently than in its original system. By quickly porting and trying it on the new processor, it was found that several timing settings were also different. Time critical optimizing was required which changed the functional performance. This took two months to achieve satisfactory timing and functional performance balance.

Verification. The focus of verification changes as one moves from low level and unit testing to system verification. At low level testing, focus on areas of change and new interfaces should be done in a detailed fashion. A slight change in format of a very mature ported function caused one of the only customer-on-site problems for one radar. If those managing the process are not aware that such changes are made, then ensuring that the change was verified is impossible. In complex systems, it can be easy to "break" a working function without knowing it.

Major requirements, design differences, and sources of modifications become the "verification matrix" for the integration and test phase. Functions may become "broken" due to a number of causes. Decisions on whether to verify, regress, not test or accept by previous data must be weighed.

Changes that impact system level verification should be assessed in concert with the decision on how much lower level testing is to be done. Using previous designs should motivate one to do less testing. The time and cost savings is a key reason to use COTS and reuse. Problems that exist are still a problem with your system, however. Wise judgment and a decision making process that assesses the risk areas helps tailor testing efforts but still reduce undetected problems.

Debug of problems is not as straightforward with COTS hardware and software. Fewer debug capabilities are typical of these elements. Knowledgeable support is not as accessible. These impacts are balanced with encountering much less problems and by using creative approaches to those encountered. The team established "networks" with those who were also using the previous designs in our company. Multiple benches with different parallel "experiments" helped debug problems. Brainstorming with those who had design experience with similar elements helped if existing support was weak.

The less straightforward debug was balanced by less overall problems and also by more users who found problems. An intermittent noise-like problem that did not occur at the factory was greatly expedited toward a solution when another customer experienced a similar problem. Understanding the characteristics of the customers who did and did not experience the problem was the chief ingredient to solving the problem.

Production. Aspects of this phase to be considered include the business and legal considerations of the previous designed element. To use certain COTS software, including Microsoft NT, licensing arrangements had to be negotiated to support production volumes. Support contracts had to be renegotiated for less support. It was decided in some instances to have no support contract, with the ability to pay for a short-term amount if needed was available. Certain COTS hardware had short life cycles, so potential upgrade paths should be in place if this is the case.

Configuration issues with reuse and COTS must be managed. There are two common problems with COTS configurations, the vendors that don't keep configuration well and those that change without notification. If configuration is not kept well and the vendor house is small, there may be opportunity to improve his process. If it is a larger manufacturer, it may be prudent to develop one's own configuration system for the COTS. This was done in two cases.

Extra identifier tags were attached.

Configuration changes by vendors may be forced on your system. Several vendors do not offer earlier configurations after they update. This may happen in the middle of a lot shipment of hardware or software. This may happen if a unit is sent back for repair. By having a process that ascertains this has happened, a timely decision on whether your system requires an update or regression check can be made before a problem is shipped. We had several instances where it was decided to do nothing and several instances where a regression and update was decided. Vendors encourage staying with the latest revision, since their support of previous configurations is much weaker.

Support/Mods. The reuse or COTS element may not come with much support data. In some instances we generated support data that our customers might require. In general, transitioning to less support data was a process we had to pass on to our customers and field support personnel also. It was very helpful have the "tailored" documentation from the development phase to augment installation and customer support information.

Modifications at a later date are greatly aided by development phase documentation. The requirements and design/modification/support information should be configured for later use if modifications are likely.

Planned reuse. There was very little experience with reuse components that were planned from the beginning to be reused. This made a significant difference in the effort of implementing and problem solving. However, the need to approach elements with a structured methodology still exists even with items made with planned reuse.

TEAM ASPECTS

Team Issues. Just as the types of components of reuse were a wide range, so were the issues among the team members. The team contained some members who were or knew the previous components' designer. It also contained members that were very interested in the latest COTS and commercial offerings. Most members had most previous engineering experience with in-house new designs for a particular product. Table 4 summarizes some typical team problems that recurred intermittently.

Team Lessons Learned. The team issues were addressed on an ongoing basis and were able to be eventually minimized. It must be recognized that not all potential team members work well in a COTS/Reuse oriented development. There is different and less creativity and sense of ownership for some. Others see it as the wave of the future and are motivated to work with it.

The manager of the development effort must recognize the need for coaching and training in terms of process tailoring. In the compressed time to implement the reuse component, there is temptation to skip many steps. Enforcing structured steps and wise decision making is key.

• Members with some ownership of a previous design may be defensive of design
• Members with some ownership of a previous design may be resigned to problems
• Members with no ownership may see every problem as proving reuse is a bad idea
• Members with no ownership may be resigned that problems that need fixing won't be fixed
• Members are frustrated with design or problems
• Less creativity and creation by members may lead to job dissatisfaction
• Members see no need to follow a process – it's done.
• Members frustrated with trying to figure out how to adapt processes to reuse
• Members angry at "surprises" and unknowns

Table 4: Typical Team issues encountered

It is also important to share and emphasize the enterprise and product benefits versus costs of implementing the reuse and COTS components. Encouraging the members to buy in to the benefits and to expect some "costs" of unknowns makes them part owners of the benefits. In the case of one radar development, the extensive use of COTS was the reason the product could be developed at all, and what made it market competitive.

The members must expect to work with and be given a larger support team. When working with distant, tightly staffed vendors it is necessary at time to obtain the involvement of the management, quality or the procurement staff. Engineers need to be encouraged that there are business avenues available to solve larger problems. They must also come to learn that many small problems may not be fixed. This can be a significant transition for some.

The career aspects of working with COTS and reuse may have to be balanced by alternating members between new designs and reuse. Opportunities to learn new skills may also be used to augment career development. This may include cross-disciplinary development of hardware, software and systems engineers for example.

SUMMARY

Reuse and COTS utilization is a very powerful approach to achieve faster time to market, lower risk and cost, fewer problems in integration and being profitable in today's business environment. Experience with a wide variety of previously developed hardware, software, and system elements has shown that a wisely tailored development approach and wise team management minimizes the unexpected cost, schedule and product performance issues as well as team morale.

REFERENCES

McGuire, K., "Optimizing Systems Engineering for a Commercial Product Line: A Case Study in International Air Traffic Control." *Proceedings of the Ninth Annual International Symposium of the International Council of Systems Engineering (INCOSE) (Brighton, England, June 6-11, 1999).*

Reuse-Driven Software Processes Guidebook. SPC-921019-CMC. Version 02.00.03. Herndon, Virginia. Software Productivity Consortium, November, 1993.

Shishko, R. and Matijevic, J.R., "Summary of Results from the Risk Management Program for the Mars Microrover Flight Experiment." *Proceedings of the Ninth Annual International Symposium of the International Council of systems Engineering (INCOSE) (Brighton, England, June 6-11, 1999).*

BIOGRAPHY

Kathleen McGuire has almost 20 years in product development experience. She has had various responsibilities in Systems and Program Development Management of Surveillance Radars. This includes various ground based commercial air traffic control and military surveillance radars as well as an airborne military surveillance radar, the AWACS. Her responsibilities have included management of systems, software, hardware, supportability and systems integration and test. She has a B.S.M.E. from University of Notre Dame, Indiana and an M.A.S. from Johns Hopkins University.

The Systems Engineering Started in the Middle Process

Terry Bahill, Fellow of INCOSE
Systems and Industrial Engineering
University of Arizona
Tucson, AZ 85721-0020
terry@sie.arizona.edu
http://www.sie.arizona.edu/sysengr/

Clark Briggs
Systems Engineering
University of Idaho at Idaho Falls
Idaho Falls, ID 83402-1575
briggs@if.uidaho.edu
http://www.if.uidaho.edu/~briggs/

Abstract. The systems engineering process often begins somewhere in the middle of a project. Naturally, the systems engineering process should be different for a project where systems engineering starts in the middle versus a project where it starts at the beginning of the project. This paper presents a consensus of senior systems engineers at the Idaho National Engineering and Environmental Laboratory about how systems engineering should be done when it starts in the middle.

INTRODUCTION

In the textbooks, the systems engineering process usually starts at the beginning of the project and most of the systems engineering effort occurs during the first two phases of the system life cycle, namely, stating the problem and investigating alternatives (Chapman, Bahill and Wymore, 1992; Sage, 1992; Wymore, 1993; Blanchard & Fabrycky, 1998; Bahill & Gissing, 1998; Bahill & Dean, 1999; Sage & Rouse, 1999, which is probably the most complete description of systems engineering; and Buede, 2000.) However, in the real world, the systems engineering process often begins somewhere in the middle of the project, for example it may start two years into a five-year project. This paper explains the systems engineering process when systems engineering begins in the middle of an ongoing project. We call this the *systems engineering started in the middle process.*

Problem statement. Identify the similarities and differences in the systems engineering processes when the process is started at the beginning of the system life cycle versus a project when it is started in the middle. To solve this problem we interviewed 17 experienced systems engineers at the Idaho National Engineering and Environmental Laboratory. This paper summarizes their experiences. It starts with a synopsis of the systems engineering objects. Then it shows four specific systems engineering started in the middle processes that have been used in the field by these systems engineers. It augments the systems engineering objects. Finally, it closes with generalizations and limitations.

When joining in the middle of a project, the first thing the systems engineer should do is **ask questions** like the following. What are you doing? Why are you doing it? Who is the customer? What does the customer need? What products will be delivered to the customer? What is the existing system? Where are we going? How are we going to get there? What might be the next big problem? Is something broken? Answers to these questions will be used to describe the customer and to choose the systems engineering products, the source documents, the selling points and the particular systems engineering started in the middle process.

The systems engineer's primary **customer** is the project management team, which consists of the project manager, the chief systems engineer, the program controls representative and the technical specialists (leads).

The systems engineer's **products** are a mission statement, a requirements document including verification and validation, a description of functions or objects, a test plan, a drawing of system boundaries, an interface control document, a listing of deliverables, models, a tradeoff study, a risk analysis, a life cycle analysis and a description of the physical architecture.

Source documents that are usually available with greater or lesser quality in various projects include the contract, the statement of work (SoW), work breakdown structures, task statements (from the contract officers), PERT charts, product descriptions, piles of paper, tech memos, design reviews, requirements documents (if you are lucky), a document hierarchy, decision trees, safety analysis reports, tech specs, regulatory agreements, project management plans and monthly management reviews. Of course, a primary source of information is not documents, but conversations with members of the integrated product development team (IPDT).

Selling points are the high value-added systems engineering products or services that should be provided to the project manager early in the process to point out the value of systems engineering. Typically, selling points include a description of interfaces, issues to be resolved, functions not required, requirements not verified and sensitivity analyses. A sensitivity analysis of the set of requirements can highlight the cost drivers. Showing these to the customer often causes the customer to relax a requirement and thereby reduce cost. The selling points should dramatically improve project performance and dramatically reduce cost.

Earlier we stated that the systems engineering products are a mission statement, requirements, functions or objects, a test plan, interfaces, deliverables, models, a tradeoff study, a risk analysis, and the physical architecture. However, this is not necessarily the **sequence** in which the systems engineering products are discovered. This sequence will depend upon the particular systems engineering started in the middle process that is used.

FOUR SYSTEMS ENGINEERING STARTED IN THE MIDDLE PROCESSES

In this section, we will look at four systems engineering started in the middle processes. Only the first one will be elaborated. Here is an abstract of it. Start with the existing work breakdown structure (WBS) and make sure that it is complete and valid. Then decompose it to the lowest level for which data exist. Then from the individual WBS blocks, identify system functions. From the system functions, infer system requirements and then from the requirements write a mission statement, which should then be approved by the customer. Go back to the WBS blocks and find the system deliverables. From these, you can deduce the system interfaces. Finally, use the WBS blocks to find assumptions. These help assess risk.

A WBS is a hierarchical description of work elements that ideally includes start and end dates, a description of the work, customers, inputs, products, interfaces, constraints and staffing. The systems engineer will find information about the WBS in various places. There might be an electronic data system where the WBS is maintained. It might also be in the Project Management Plan or even in the overview of a Design Review. The systems engineer should flesh out the WBS as required. A typical WBS element is shown in Figure 1.

The text in this WBS element is terse, yet the systems engineer must glean several vital elements from it. He or she can use the WBS Title for the Component Title; capture the WBS Element Description in the Component Description; and use the WBS Element identifier as the Component Abbreviation.

The systems engineer should study the WBS elements for implied functions. Particular system functions will be needed to accomplish the work in the WBS Description. In addition, items delivered across interfaces hint at functions. Create functions in the project model at this time, even if the functional hierarchy is not yet evident. References to compliance requirements and other regulatory documents might also provide hints about needed functions.

The systems engineer should list the requirements in the project model and create source elements for the regulatory document. The hierarchy for the requirements may become clear as the systems engineer discerns the structure of the project through the WBS, or the structure may have to be developed later.

The systems engineer can use the WBS Customers and Interfaces fields to create interface elements and note the Customers as the Primary Organization. Use judgement to clean up the nomenclature for organizations so that the model as a whole is consistent. For example, this WBS element identifies "LMITCO" (Lockheed Martin Idaho Technologies Company) but another might simply say "Lockheed Martin." When it is clear from the context "LMITCO" would provide better consistency. The products, the deliverables, are called `DiscreteItems` in Figure 1. When possible each `DiscreteItem` should be linked to an Interface.

WBS elements, as in this example, might not provide sufficient information for the needed connectivity in the project model. For example, the three deliverable products are not associated with either of the two interfaces. Just as this WBS has not listed its inputs, no other WBS element will note accepting these three products as inputs. The project schedule might help, since task interdependencies might indicate that a subsequent WBS element depends on this WBS element for those products. Similarly, products delivered to customers might be represented on the project schedule as delivery milestones.

Many WBS systems have a field for assumptions or issues. In practice, managers tend to document unverified agreements or planned activities of others in such slots to remind everyone to do it later, or to simply cover their bases. This leaves disconnects in the project planning and provides good areas for the systems engineer to investigate. The expectation is that these issues become negotiated and documented so that no one is surprised later. Each of these assumptions should be considered in the risk analysis.

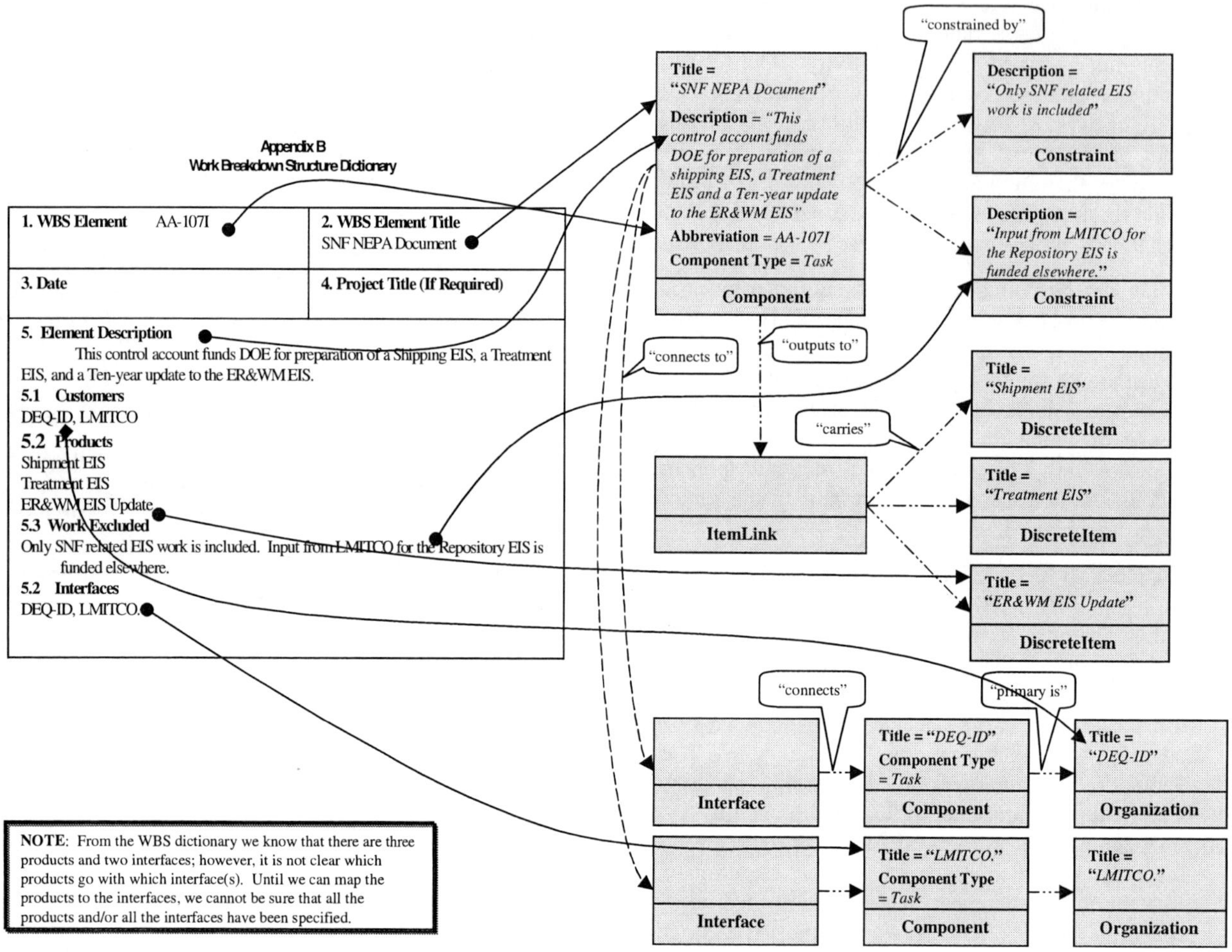

Figure 1. Mapping WBS elements to the project model

In **summary**, our first systems engineering started in the middle process creates a project model from a WBS. From this model the systems engineer can choose the selling points, translate them into project management terms (Kerzner, 1995) and deliver them to the project manager.

Gardner, Nipper and Plowman (1999) created **a second systems engineering started in the middle process,** which is shown in Figure 2. It was designed specifically to help make the legislative process more rational. In their normal systems engineering process, the flow is clockwise. In this reverse process the tasks are performed in a counter-clockwise sequence.

Our **third** systems engineering started in the middle process identifies outstanding issues and decisions, constructs a decision tree, and provides the project manager with guidance for his choices. It uses *Precision Tree*, a spreadsheet add-in, to help the engineer make decision trees. Probabilities and payoffs are associated with decision nodes and the tool calculates outcomes. It also uses *@Risk* to help the engineer perform Monte Carlo simulations and sensitivity analyses for engineering and financial data.

A **fourth** systems engineering started in the middle process starts with a description of the physical architecture. This is decomposed into a hierarchy of components or subsystems. These subsystems become the objects for an object-oriented model or they provide a springboard for discovering the functions for a functional model. The interfaces between the subsystems are then defined. The deliverables that are passed between the subsystems help identify these interfaces. Finally, the subsystem owners are queried to help identify the requirements. Experience has shown that this is a hard task.

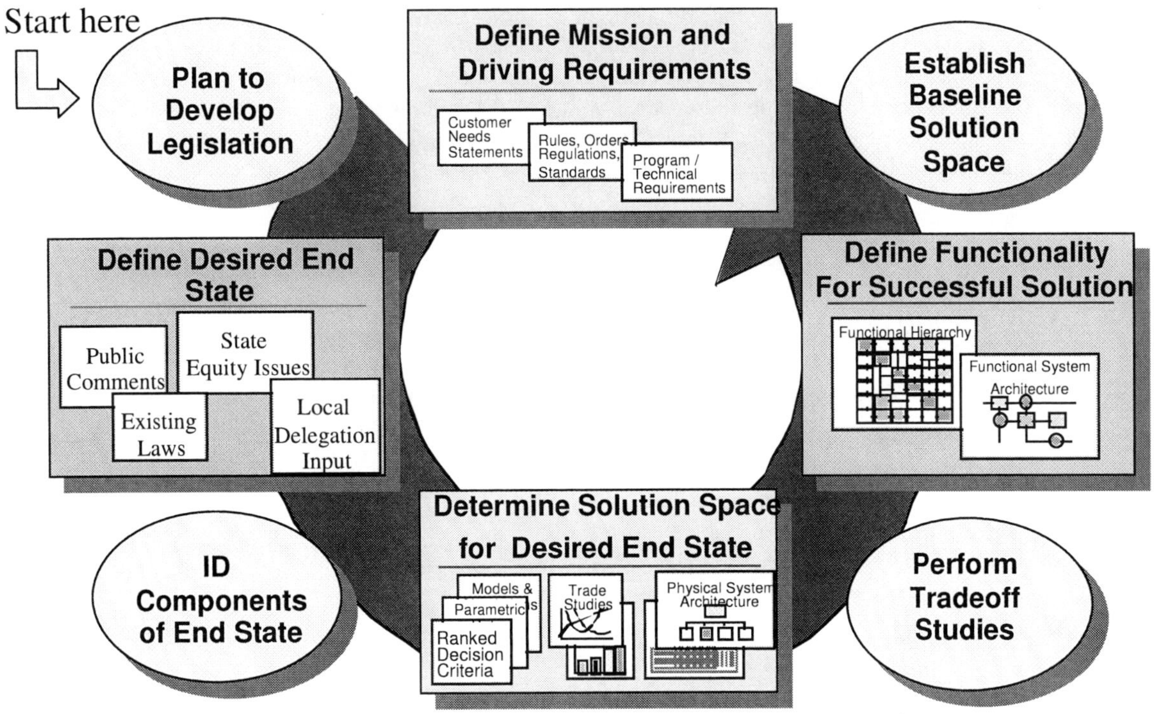

Figure 2. Reverse systems engineering process for developing legislation

AUGMENTATIONS

Augmentation of the customer. As the systems engineer expands his or her realm and becomes more valuable to the project, the systems engineer's customer should evolve through three phases. In the beginning, the systems engineer will be struggling to educate and earn the trust of the project manager. Then, the systems engineer provides leadership for the project management team. And in time, the systems engineer interfaces with the external customer, the sponsor, corporate officers and external oversight boards. The systems engineer often becomes the advocate of the external customer.

Augmentation of the systems engineering products. (1) System functions or objects must be identified. For classically trained systems engineers, it is most appropriate to discover the system functions first. This can be done with functional analysis and decomposition (Wixson, 1999) and functional flow block diagrams. For modern software projects, it is more appropriate to highlight the system objects and only provide functions in the detailed breakdowns. (2) Models will be constructed for the project and for the existing system. *Project* models allow us to study scheduling changes, create dynamic PERT charts and perform sensitivity analyses to show the effects of delaying or accelerating certain subprojects. Running the project models reveals bottlenecks and fragmented activities, reduces cost and exposes duplication of effort. *System* models help explain the system. (3) Tradeoff studies for the system should be simple. It may not be cost-effective to perform extensive *quantitative* tradeoff studies. However, it is important to do at least simple *qualitative* tradeoff studies, because examination of simple alternatives (especially the "do nothing" alternative) is a great way to discover additional system requirements. (4) The requirements should be validated (Are we building the right system?) and verified (Are we building the system right?). (5) The physical architecture of the existing system must be described. This will allow us to discover the system purpose and to map the functions to physical components. The mapping of functions to physical components can be one to one or many to one. But if one function is assigned to two or more physical components, then you probably made a mistake. (6) The three most important care-abouts for a project manager are performance, cost and schedule. Performance should be tracked with figures of merit (metrics) and technical performance measures should be created for high-risk items (Moody, et al., 1997). Important resources such as weight, volume, price, communications bandwidth and power consumption should be managed. Each subsystem is allocated a portion of the total budget and the project manger is allocated a reserve. These resource budgets are managed throughout the system life cycle.

Schedule should be managed with the aid of PERT Charts or Gantt Charts. (7) Often the project specifications (requirements and functions), the project schedule and the project cost estimates are done by three different people. The systems engineer can make a valuable contribution by making these three consistent. Then the systems engineer can help the project team make tradeoffs between performance, cost and schedule. (8) To help reduce cost, the project activities should be analyzed with an activity impact matrix, as shown in the following table.

Table 1. Activity Impact Matrix

<table>
<tr><th></th><th>Adds value</th><th>Does not add value</th></tr>
<tr><td>Mandated</td><td rowspan="2">Adding value is tested by seeing if the mission or its performance measurements are aided by accomplishing the activity</td><td>Test requirements for these activities to see if they can be changed.</td></tr>
<tr><td>Not mandated</td><td>Drop these activities immediately.</td></tr>
</table>

Most, but not all, of the systems engineering products are deliverables for the systems engineer. For example, the mission statement and the requirements document will be delivered to the customer; however, the system model will not be.

Augmentation of the selling points. (1) The existing system might be an integration of many subsystems. The integration plan might provide insight into potential opportunities for improvements in subsystem integration. The interfaces between subsystems must be defined, and defined consistently. Gap analyses and N^2 diagrams help describe interfaces. (2) There may be issues that need to be resolved. The impact of each issue should be assessed. Those that pose the greatest project risk should be highlighted. TBDs (to be determined) are an example of issues that need to be resolved. (3) By linking system functions to system requirements, we can expose activities or functions that are not linked to requirements. Unlinked functions are often the result of system evolution. Either unlinked functions are non-value-added functions that should be eliminated or they are necessary functions that point out missing requirements. This linking of functions to requirements might also expose requirements that have no function performing them. These would also be cause for concern, probably necessitating the creation of more functions. (4) A complete set of system documentation with a mission statement, functions, requirements and validation gives the project manager a defensible position for his or her project and a clearer understanding of it. (5) Providing information and insight, and identifying project omissions should be of value to the project manager, and therefore should help demonstrate the need for using the systems engineering process. (6) The selling points do not include *all* of the traditional systems engineering products, however, just the high value-added ones. Determining which systems engineering products will produce the highest value is done using experience, intuition, knowledge of project management, and customer statements of priority.

GENERALIZATIONS

Words of advice. If systems engineering was not done at the beginning of the project, then management either (1) lacked experience, (2) felt that systems engineering cost too much, (3) believed that their process was sufficient, because it had not failed them in the past, (4) thought that they had done the systems engineering, but just did not write anything down, or (5) did most of the systems engineering tasks, but needed help with some, like tradeoff analyses. If the perceived cost created the lacuna, then the systems engineer should not expect to get approval to do everything that needs to be done. In this case the systems engineer should use euphemisms for systems engineering such as *a systematic, comprehensive approach.*

To map out the best course of action the systems engineer should discover why he or she was assigned to the project. Some possible reasons are (1) the project needs cosmetic enhancements, (2) the project is under control, but the manager wants to keep the house of cards intact and has some extra money to spend, (3) the project needs some help, a fix or two, or a minor course correction, (4) the project is in deep trouble, well past salvation and the manager is grasping at straws, and (5) the sponsor has said that the project is in trouble and needs systems engineering.

When a systems engineer is assigned to a project in the middle of its life cycle, the project manager may hear the message "Someone thinks that I have screwed up and they have sent this outsider to bail me out." The systems engineer's job is to help the project manager without seeming threatening. He or she should not try to sell systems engineering. Rather, create the selling points and let them sell systems engineering. These are difficult tasks and they require a systems engineer with a lot of experience.

The systems engineer also needs to learn the political environment so he or she can know where to push for change and where to back off. He or she must know when to walk away and know when to run.

The systems engineer needs to describe the maximum failing requirement (the best you can do and still fail) and the minimum passing requirement (the worst you can do and still pass). Anything outside of these bounds should be avoided, if one is attempting to fix a project with limited time, money or personnel.

There is a need for continual communication between the systems engineer and the project manager. If the project was not well thought out at the outset, then even the goals might have changed. Do not tell the project manager this, with your help he or she will discover it. We cannot overstress the need for continual communication. After all the Tower of Babel did not fail because of technical deficiencies.

Of course, there are **limitations** to the statements in this paper. There are some projects where nothing applies and there are others where everything applies. One of the obvious differentiators is the size or cost of the project. For example, we have said that a formal large-scale quantitative tradeoff study might not be cost effective. This is probably true for small projects, but for a billion-dollar project it might be necessary, as well as cost-effective. Also, our advice would be different for a product or the process that produces the product.

Another differentiator is the innovativeness of the project, which can be characterized by whether or not a similar system has been designed and built before. Precedented projects, where similar systems have been produced previously, such as bridges and cars, are not high-risk projects. There is more risk with unprecedented projects, which can be decomposed into three categories: (1) projects where the individual components have precedent, but the integration of these components into a large system has never been done before, such as the Apollo program to put a man on the moon, (2) projects where similar large-scale integration has been performed before, but the components are of a new technology, such as making a computer with transistors instead of vacuum tubes, and finally (3) projects where both the component technology and the integration is unprecedented, such as the Manhattan Project of World War II. Projects with unprecedented components and integration have the highest risk. As a topic for future research we would like to determine what type of systems engineering started in the middle process would be best for each of these four types of projects.

Text continues

Table 2. Comparison of Systems Engineering Processes

	When systems engineering starts in the **middle** of the life cycle	When systems engineering starts at the **beginning** of the life cycle
Primary customer	Starts with the *project manager* and grows to a broader group	Starts with the *customer* and grows to a broader group
Role	Archaeologist	Leadership
Sources of information	Documents and physical architecture	Interviews with customers and stakeholders
Products	Limited resources force products to be scaled down and not all are produced or delivered	Complete systems engineering documentation
Selling points	Description of interfaces, Issues to be resolved, Functions not required, Requirements not verified, Sensitivity analysis	Complete systems engineering documentation
Sequence	Varies with the process	Starts with mission statement, requirements and functions or objects
Process	Must be tailored for the particular project	Must be tailored for the particular project

The **consensus** of our senior systems engineers is that a complete systems engineering started in the middle project would cost two to ten times as much as a systems engineering project that started at the beginning of the system life cycle. Therefore, when using a systems engineering started in the middle process, you cannot do a complete job of systems engineering, because it would cost too much. Consequently, you must deliberately decide what portion of the systems engineering process is essential for each project and tailor the process appropriately.

Acknowledgements. We thank Kevin Bailey, George Beitel, Bob Caliva, Jim Close, Bob Harris, A.B. Hubbard, Jerry Jaggers, Jim Johnesee, John Nonte, Cathy Plowman, Mark Powell, Virginia Randall, Don Schilling, Neil Snyder, Rafael Soto, Finis Southworth, Bob Turk and Larry Zirker, all of the Idaho National Engineering and Environmental Laboratory, for the ideas in this paper. This work was supported by the U.S. Department of Energy, Assistant Secretary for Environmental Management, under DOE Idaho Operations Office Contract DE-AC07-94ID13223.

REFERENCES

Bahill, A. T. and Gissing, B, Re-evaluating systems engineering concepts using systems thinking, *IEEE Transaction on Systems, Man and Cybernetics, Part C: Applications and Reviews,* **28**(4), 516-527, 1998.

Bahill, A. T. and Dean, F. F., *What is Systems Engineering?* http://www.sie.arizona.edu/sysengr/whatis/, 1999.

Blanchard, B. S. and Fabrycky, W. J., *Systems Engineering and Analysis,* Prentice Hall, 1998.

Buede, D. M., *The Engineering Design of Systems: Models and Methods*, John Wiley, New York, 2000.

Chapman, W. L., Bahill, A. T. and Wymore, A.W., *Engineering Modeling and Design,* CRC Press, Boca Raton, 1992.

Gardner, B., Nipper, D. and Plowman, C. M., A systematic approach to environmental legislation, INEL-EXT-99-00096, 1999.

Kerzner, H., *Project Management: A Systems Approach to Planning, Scheduling, and Controlling*, Van Nostrand Reinhold, NY, 1995.

Moody, J. A., Chapman, W. L., Van Voorhees, F. D. and Bahill, A. T., *Metrics and Case Studies for Evaluating Engineering Designs,* Prentice Hall PTR, Upper Saddle River, NJ, 1997.

Precision Tree, Palisade Corp., Newfield NY, 1997.

@Risk, Palisade Corp., Newfield NY, 1997.

Sage, A. P., *Systems Engineering,* John Wiley & Sons, 1992.

Sage, A. P. and Rouse, W. B. *Handbook of, Systems Engineering and Management,* John Wiley & Sons, 1999.

Wixson, J. R., Functional analysis and decomposition using function analysis systems technique, *Proceedings of the Ninth Annual Symposium of INCOSE,* Brighton, England, pp. 963-968, June 1999.

Wymore, A. W., *Model-Based Systems Engineering,* CRC Press, Boca Raton, 1993.

Work Breakdown Structures. Many web sites give guidance for work breakdown structures. Here are two: (1) This is a link to the MIL-HDBK-881, which is the DOD document describing how work breakdown structures are to be created by and for the military:
http://www.acq.osd.mil/pm/newpolicy/wbs/mil_hdbk_881/mil_hdbk_881.htm
(2) This is a link to a presentation that was given by Neil Albert of MCR Federal, Inc at the 9th Annual International Cost Schedule Performance Management Conference. It provides another opinion on the preparation of work breakdown structures:
http://www.acq.osd.mil/pm/paperpres/1097conf/albert/index.htm

AUTHOR BIOGRAPHIES

A. Terry Bahill is a Professor of Systems Engineering at the University of Arizona in Tucson. He received his Ph.D. in electrical engineering and computer science from the University of California, Berkeley, in 1975. He holds a U.S. patent for the Bat Chooser™, a system that computes the Ideal Bat Weight™ for individual baseball and softball batters. He is Editor of the CRC Press Series on Systems Engineering. He is a Fellow of the Institute of Electrical and Electronic Engineers (IEEE) and of the INCOSE. He is the chair of the INCOSE Fellows Selection Committee.

Clark Briggs is Associate Professor of Systems Engineering at the University of Idaho at Idaho Falls. He graduated from the U.S. Air Force Academy in 1972 and received his doctorate from Columbia University in 1978. After 13 years in the Air Force, he worked for 12 years as an Avionics Systems Engineer at the NASA Jet Propulsion Laboratory.

Learning and improvement in Product Innovation Processes: Enabling behaviors

José F.B. Gieskes
University of Twente, Faculty of Technology and Management
P.O. Box 217, 7500 AE Enschede,
The Netherlands

Ilse W.H.A. Langenberg
Hollandse Signaalapparaten B.V., Research, Development & Technology Department
P.O. Box 42, NL-7550 GD Hengelo,
The Netherlands

ABSTRACT

This paper describes Product Innovation as a continuous and cross-functional process involving all stages of the product life cycle. This approach gives way to study knowledge transfer and learning in companies from a continuous improvement viewpoint. Based on a model developed in CIMA, a European ESPRIT project, the way in which a company shares and transfers knowledge and learning experiences in its product innovation process are assessed. The results can be used to give focus and direction to improvement actions (such as systems engineering and software development improvement plans).

The model describes learning and knowledge transfer within product innovation processes in terms of a number of interrelated variables: (improvement) performances, behaviors and levers to stimulate improvement, contingencies and learning / innovation capabilities. At the Research & Development Department of SIGNAAL the model was used to assess its current practices with regard to learning and improvement in product innovation. The results validate efforts on current and past improvement actions and provide additional insight into the past, current and future situation. Furthermore, the recommendations provide guidelines on how to continue with improvement.

INTRODUCTION

To survive in a demanding and turbulent environment companies are investing a growing amount of resources and managerial attention to product innovation. They also aim to increase their effectiveness, exploit synergy and learn in product innovation processes. Although these efforts are of a more and more continuous nature and involve partners outside the organizational boundaries on a global basis, most literature is still mainly focused on how product development projects, seen as isolated efforts, are organized and managed.

In this paper an alternative perspective is proposed: New Product Development (NPD) as part of a more general process of product[1] innovation that involves parallel as well as sequential product development projects, including phases of the product life cycle that follow the initial development phases. Evidence from best practice companies, for instance, shows how manufacturing, maintenance and service, though not integral parts of the development itself, can still provide valuable feedback and additional opportunities to innovate products. In this perspective Product Innovation, is a continuous and cross-functional process involving and integrating a growing number of different competencies inside and outside the organizational boundaries.

Mastering the sharing and transfer of knowledge within this process is a powerful competitive weapon, but requires new managerial skills. Rather than generating and driving innovation, management should foster and focus it by giving individuals and groups at all levels of the organization opportunities and tools to learn from their own and others experience and to use this learning to innovate the product according to business priorities.

Based on a model originating from the Euro-Australian[2] research project Continuous Improvement and Product Innovation Management (CIMA) (Boer et al. 1999), ESPRIT 26056, this paper presents how a company can share and transfer knowledge and

---

1 Where in this article the term product is used, it can have the meaning of system, subsystem, product, unit, component, etc.

2 CIMA Consortium partners arc: Politechnico di Milano (I), MIP (I), ETASS (I), Trinity University Dublin (Ire), CORE Chalmers University Gothenburg (S), CENTRIM University of Brighton (UK), Twente University Enschede (NL), INCITE University Western Sydney Macarthur (Aus), Monash University Melbourne (AUS), Edith Cowan University Perth (Aus).

learning experiences in its product innovation process. The required focus and direction of improvement activities (through systems engineering and software development improvement plans) will be discussed as well.

KNOWLEDGE MANAGEMENT IN PRODUCT INNOVATION

Starting from the early 80's, a renewed interest has been placed on product innovation. Under the joint pressure of an increasingly demanding global market and the accelerating pace of technological change, awareness has risen that companies need to compete on quality and speed. One of the main consequences of this focus was the emergence of product innovation models almost totally focused on the management of the NPD process. Integration among different phases of a project, heavyweight project management and autonomy of the project team were considered as synonymous with best practices. Concurrent engineering was thought to represent a long lasting paradigm for product innovation management.

Next, in the early 90's, a new stream of studies emerged which enlarged the perspective. Studies demonstrated how focusing on single projects is not enough to sustain competition. Success depends even more on exploiting synergy among projects, for example by fostering commonality and reuse of design solutions over time (Wheelwright and Clark 1992, De Maio et al. 1994). In this perspective attention progressively shifts from single projects to a project family (Meyer and Utterback 1993, Sanderson and Uzumeri 1995) and to the process of learning and knowledge transfer and reuse (Imai et al. 1988, Bartezzaghi et al. 1997). These streams of literature, however, consider product innovation as occurring only within the boundaries of the product development process. Downstream phases in the product life cycle are still important for innovation but only as long as they represent valuable sources of information or constraints that should be anticipated and considered during development (Clark and Fujimoto 1991). Evidence is emerging, to the contrary, that other phases in the product life cycle may actually represent additional opportunities to innovate products. This is a direct consequence of rapid product development and time to market reduction: several companies, especially in rapidly shifting environments, purposely release to market products that are not fully optimized, followed by a rapid almost continuous stream of enhanced releases (i.e. software industry).

The boundaries and the concept itself of product innovation are therefore changing. Feed backs and opportunities coming in from the field phases are not only stored for feeding next generation product development projects, but can also provide valuable opportunities for product innovation within a product life cycle (Bartezzaghi et al.1997), see figure 1.

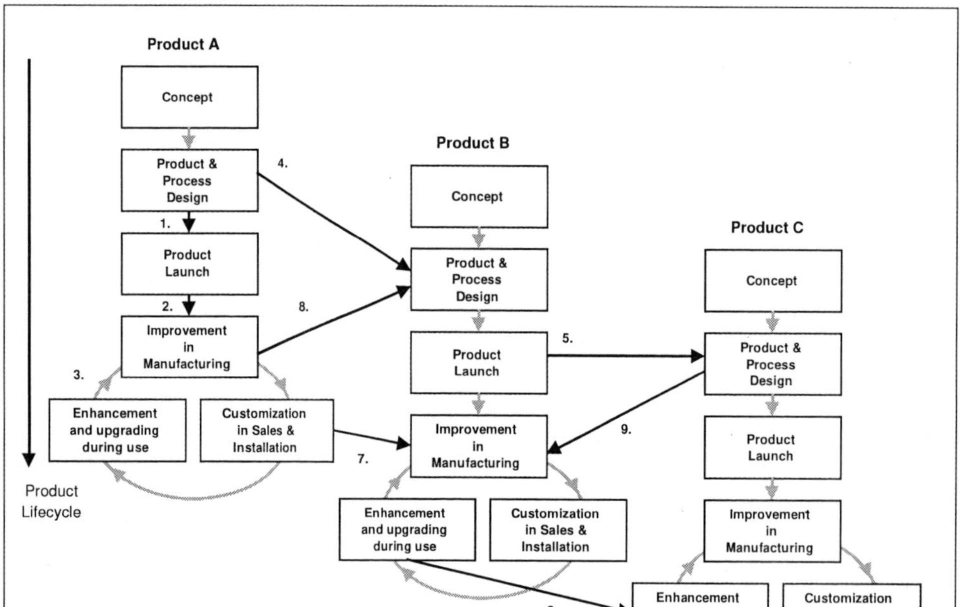

Figure 1. The process of continuous product innovation (source: Barthezagghi et al 1977)

Several examples of knowledge transfers are highlighted in the figure. They encompass the following categories:

- Knowledge transfer between different phases within one product development (1/2/3)
- Knowledge transfer within one phase between different product developments (4/6)
- Knowledge transfer between different phases between different product developments (5/7/8/9)

All knowledge transfers constitute a very strong potential for learning and for innovation which could be exploited by an active effort for designing and implementing adequate mechanisms to enable transfer of knowledge. Every knowledge transfer can be fostered by particular enablers whose successful implementation strongly depends on the actors involved and their influence on the process, and on the typology of knowledge that is transferred (or from a broader viewpoint, knowledge that is managed).

Different dimensions of knowledge transfer [see Henderson and Clark 1990, Barney 1991, Collis and Montgomery 1995, Hedlund 1994, Nonaka, 1991, Bohn 1994) can help interpreting the process of acquiring, transferring, consolidating and applying knowledge in order to design appropriate enablers to foster and sustain it. Such a process can also be labeled as continuous improvement i.e. learning within product innovation.

Based on these considerations the CIMA-research project aimed at developing a methodology to suggest which enabling mechanisms could be used to support continuous improvement learning in product innovation knowledge transfer within and between product innovation processes.

THE CIMA- MODEL

The model underlying the CIMA-methodology was developed through literature study, in-depth case studies and was tested for its validity and reliability in several companies in different countries. The model describes the learning and knowledge transfer within product innovation in terms of a number of interrelated variables:

- ***P:*** Continuous Innovation (CI) Performance;
- ***B:*** Behaviors underpinning continuous innovation and learning within Product Innovation (PI);
- ***L:*** Levers that can foster these behaviors;
- ***E:*** Company contingencies (E = external);
- ***C:*** Continuous learning/innovation Capabilities.

The relationships between these variables are depicted in figure 2.

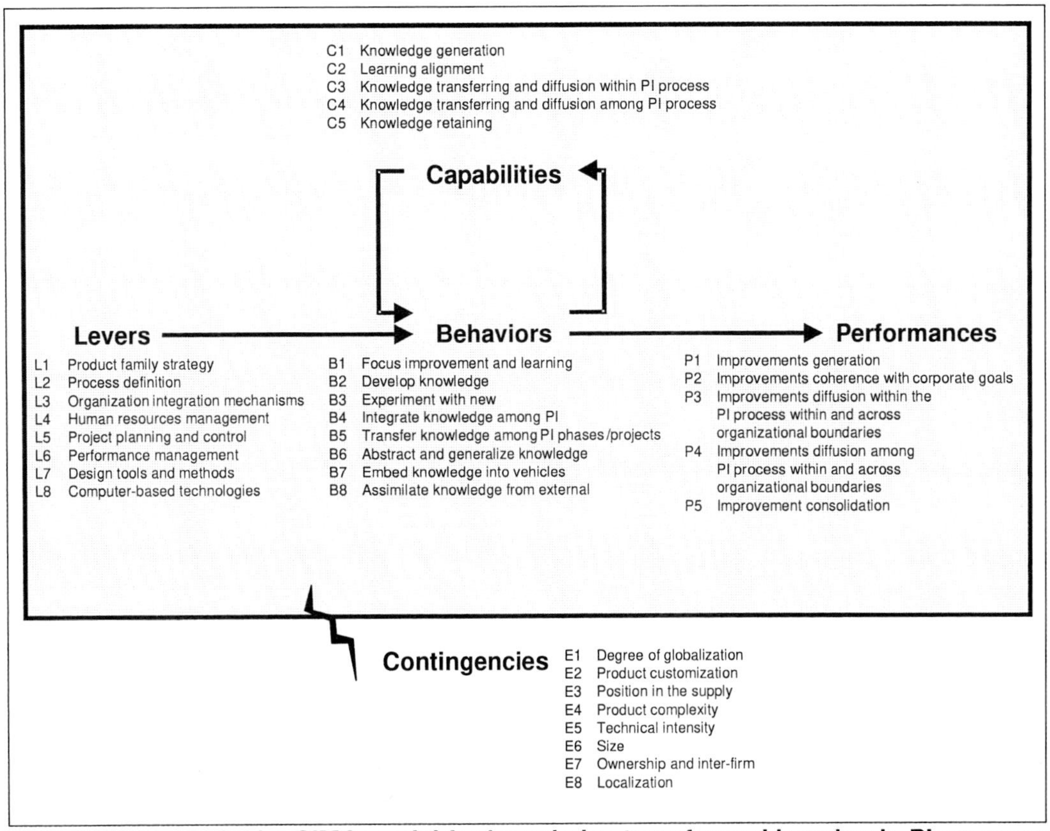

Figure 2. Elements in the CIMA model for knowledge transfer and learning in PI processes

The ***performance*** is the result of improvement activities carried out in the product innovation process. It can be 'measured' by, for instance, looking at the generation of the number of improvements or the diffusion of improvements and learning experiences within and between product innovation processes.

The CI performance is achieved by a set of eight categories of ***behaviors*** enacted by individuals, such as creating, using and transferring knowledge; aligning improvement activities with strategic goals and objectives; and experimenting with new solutions. The behaviors have two dimensions: the frequency with which the behavior is shown and the distribution of the behavior throughout the product innovation process. The implementation and application of certain levers (or enablers) can influence these behaviors.

Levers are mechanisms that managers use when managing the product innovation process, even though they may not be consciously aimed at improvement and stimulating learning. If adequately oriented, however, these decisions can have a substantial influence on a firm's attitudes and practices in creating, storing and transferring knowledge. These behaviors can be influenced by the implementation and application of *levers* such as strategic planning, human resource management policies, project planning and control, performance measurement, design tools and methods, and computer based technologies. Also eight categories of levers are described.

Not all eight levers impact on all eight behaviors. There are strong relationships, but there are also absent relationships between levers and behaviors.

The ***contingencies*** are factors that influence the choice of levers to influence behaviors (for instance the size of the company, the market situation, and product and process complexity).

The ***capabilities*** can be described as integrated stocks of resources that are accumulated over time through learning, or established through deliberate decisions. These stocks of resources include internalized behaviors, technical skills, organizational routines, and corporate assets (i.e. information systems, databases, libraries, tools, and handbooks). The level of a company's CI capabilities determines the efforts that are needed to influence the corresponding behaviors.

The CIMA-model was used at SIGNAAL[3] to assess its current practices with regard to learning and improvement in product innovation, with interesting results.
The following case studies focuses on performances, behaviors and levers.

LEARNING AND IMPROVEMENT IN PRACTICE

SIGNAAL is a 76-year old large Dutch subsidiary of Thomson CSF that specializes in designing and producing integrated defense systems for command & control, sensor and communication purposes. The portfolio of the company is divided into three sections: naval systems, ground based systems and other activities. The company has a high internal product and market complexity due to size, dimension, lead-time and life expectancy of the systems, which are developed by different partners, contractors, and subcontractors and then integrated. There is also a high external complexity due to different goals of partners, i.e. political constraints.

As a manufacturer of high-tech and complex systems the company works together with a large number of suppliers from all over the world. SIGNAAL is focussed on improving processes, both as a result of (ISO) certification and CMM-goals for the software-development and systems engineering processes. Next to this, a number of larger improvement programs are carried out on a company level, such as a Quality Improvement Program and a Configuration Improvement Program. These are larger generic improvement projects trying to force more fundamental improvements in the company's way of working.

The CIMA model was applied within the R&D Department through studying documents and conducting interviews with responsible people. The responsible manager filled in a questionnaire[4] that formed the basis for the case-study. Feedback was provided on the results, which lead to a discussion on improvements.

For the last few years the R&D department has been working on improving their Systems and Software engineering processes using Capability Maturity Models (SE-CMM, SW-CMM). Particularly in the field of Systems Engineering the principles of the SE-CMM, combined with principles

---

3 SIGNAAL = Hollandse Signaalapparaten B.V.

4 For more information on the research methodology and its application, see Boer et al 1999. The questionnaire is available in paper form, but also in computerized form. The latter form allows for fast and company specific feedback because of the availability of a computerized report generator.

of Méthode d'Ingénierie Système Thomson-CSF (MIST), and MIL-STD-499B / EIA / 15-632, have been tailored and complemented according to SIGNAAL practices. Based on these activities systems and software engineering improvement plans were / are developed and implemented (ongoing).

For CIMA two innovation projects A (recently completed) and B (completed before A) were compared on their performances, behaviors shown and applied levers. Without going into the detailed findings, the CIMA results (as shown in figure 3) listed several improvement areas (structured by behaviors and indicated by levers).

Focus improvement and learning (strategy) (B1). Implementation of three categories of levers could facilitate and foster this behavior. The first category (L5) are levers concerned with Project Planning and Control. The formalization and explicit deployment of the (emerging) strategy into specific goals and involving people in the further development of this strategy will improve the alignment of improvement behavior to strategy. A second category can be found in L7, Design Tools and Methods, since the mandatory use of these tools and methods will direct people's behavior. The organization already has begun with implementing a standardized set of tools for the entire PI process. The success of this implementation will to a large extent determine how people's behaviors are directed towards company goals The third category is to be found in defining the process. Within parts of the organization the process has been re-designed and other parts of the organization can benefit from the changes, which calls for communication.

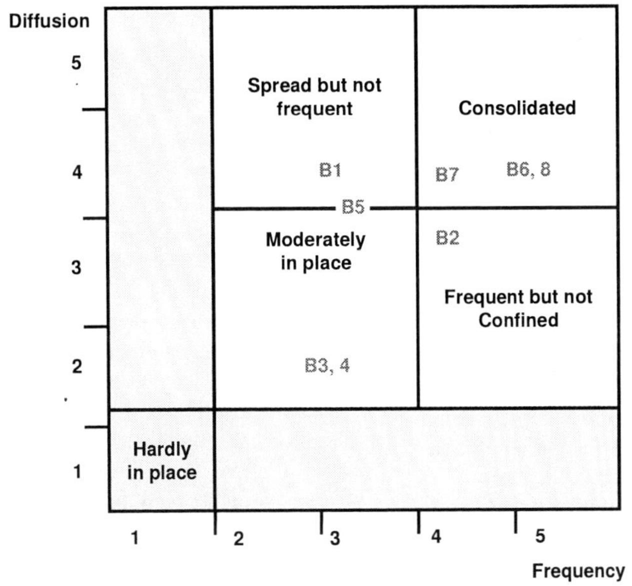

Figure 3 Frequency and Diffusion of Behaviors at SIGNAAL[5]

Although the company already has implemented several levers to influence behaviors, there are also a number of levers that are not yet implemented or applied to their fullest potential (these levers are selected from an explanatory model developed in the CIMA research, based on best practices). The levers that could be of value are discussed in the following text.

Develop knowledge (B2). Levers related to human resources management policies (L4) could improve and strengthen this behavior. As this already is the case for people employed by the company itself, this is not yet the case for "flex-workers". A discussion

5 The relatively low score for B3,4 is due to the choice of projects for the analysis. In general, this behavior is more frequent and more diffused.

on how to stimulate this behavior and consolidate it within the company could be of added value.

Experiment with new solutions (B3) In the current situation there is limited time and budget available to experiment with new solutions, whereby condition is that these experiments are product and project related. There is no formal time / budget available to experiment in a "Greenfield way". Maybe a discussion is in order whether more people should be challenged to experiment more, even outside the limited scope of their assignments. In the recent past the emphasis was on incremental innovation, with the result that the organization heavily emphasizes process improvement at the moment, thereby not giving product innovation the attention, time, etc. that is needed. To stimulate product innovation, experimental time is required for all involved in the PI process. This could be stimulated through Human Resource Management activities (L4) such as the development of specialist skills, departmental assessment and development plans. Also L5 (project planning and Control) contributes to the development of these behaviors, such as project planning and control systems directed at improvement projects. A last lever can be found in L6 (performance measurement) where feedback systems and benchmarking activities can be beneficial, as well as measures for creativity (for instance number of proposed improvements).

Integrate knowledge among PI phases (B4). The effort already put in stimulating (both frequency and distribution of) considering implementation / strengthening of different levers could increase this behavior. First of all, L2 (innovation process definition) can help the knowledge transfer and learning: the current activities in a part of the process on developing a new innovation process and its implementation could be diffused to other parts of the organization. L3 (organizational integration mechanisms) can have effects as well, such as temporary teams and / or liaison roles and cross-disciplinary meetings. Spreading results of the new PI-process is of importance in stimulating, diffusing and increasing the frequency of the behaviors. Human Resource Management activities such as job rotation policies support this.

Transfer knowledge among PI phases / projects (B5). Levers concerned with the definition of the innovation process (L2) could stimulate this behavior. This is already referred to in the previous paragraph.

Abstract knowledge and generalize it (B6), Embed knowledge into vehicles (B7), Assimilate knowledge from external sources (B8). To a large extent, these behaviors already seem to be engrained in daily routine. They require no short-term interference, but awareness is in order to maintain the behaviors on the current level.

RESULTS / CONCLUSIONS

The CIMA-recommendations validated efforts on current and past improvement actions within SIGNAAL and as such the CIMA-tool was considered to reflect the situation very well and its findings were sometimes enlightening. Already filling in the questionnaire of the CIMA-methodology increased insight into the current situation with regard to knowledge transfer and learning. The obtained results added to this insight and provided guidelines on how to continue with improvement.

Current models (like CMM) and methodologies used within SIGNAAL to facilitate systems engineering and software engineering improvements all state *what* should be done or *what* is the end-goal, but give little to no information on *how* this should be accomplished. The CIMA methodology fills this gap. Next to the *what and how* insight is provided into the interrelations between behaviors and their influencing levers. Also does the methodology provide guidance on how future improvement actions can be accomplished and it provides explicit insights as to how and why (implicit or explicit) past improvements were achieved.

The results within SIGNAAL are used to enhance current improvement plans and expand implementation plans.

ACKNOWLEDGEMENT

The authors wish to express their gratitude to the CIMA research team for their support and permission to publish case-study results.

REFERENCES

Barney J.B., 1991, "Organization Resources and Sustained Competitive Advantage"; in *Journal of management*, 1, 99-120

Bartezzaghi, E., Corso, M. and Verganti, R., 1997 "Managing knowledge in Continuous Product Innovation", 5th International Product Development Conference, EIASM, Como

Bartezzaghi, E., Corso, M. and Verganti, R., 1997, "Continuous Improvement and inter-project learning in New Product Development".

International Journal of Technology Management, Vol. 14, No1, 116-138.

Boer, H., Caffyn, S., Chapmna, R., Corso, M., Coughlan, P., Gieskes, Hyland, P.,J., Magnusson, M., Pavesi, S., Ronchi, S., Sundgren, N., "Continuous Innovation and knowledge management: the CIMA supporting methodology". *Proceedings EIASM-conference* Cambridge UK, July 1999.

Bohn, R.E., 1994, "Measuring and Managing Technological Knowledge", *Sloan Management Review,*Fall

De Maio, A., Verganti, R. and Corso, M., 1994, "A Multi-Project Management Framework for New Product Development", *European Journal of Operational Research,* 78, 178-191.

Clark, K. B. and Fujimoto, T., 1991, *Product development performance - Strategy, organization, and management in the world auto industry*" - HBS Press, Boston Meyer M. H.,

Collis, D.J. and Montgomery, C.A., 1995, "Competing on Resources: Strategy in the 1990s", *Harvard Business Review,* 4, 118-128.

Hedlund, G., "A Model of Knowledge Management and the N-Form Corporation". *Strategic management Journal*, Vol.15, 73-90 (1994).

Henderson, R.M. and Clark, K.B., 1990, "Architectural Innovation: the Reconfiguration of Existing Product Technologies and the Failure of Estabilished Firms", *Administrative Science Quarterly*, 35, 9-30

Imai, K., Nonaka, I. and Takeuchi, H., 1988, "Managing the New Product Development Process: How Japanese Companies Learn and Unlearn", in Clark, K.B., Hayes, R.H. & Lorenz, C. (eds), *The Uneasy Alliance: Managing the Productivity-Technology Dilemma*, Boston, MA: Harvard Business School Press, 337-375.

Nonaka, I., 1991, "The Knowledge-Creating Company", *Harvard Business* Review, November-December, 96-104.

Sanderson, S. and Uzumeri, M., 1995, "Managing product families: the case of the Sony walkman", *Research Policy*, Vol. 24, 761-782.

Utterback J.M., 1993, "The Product Family and the Dynamics of Core Capability" in *Sloan Management Review*, Spring, pag. 29-47.

Wheelwright, S.C., Clark, K.B., 1992, "Creating Plan to Focus Product Development", *Harvard Business Review,* 2, 70-92.

Drs. José Gieskes (Public Administration, 1983) worked as a consultant and researcher. Currently she is an Assistant Professor at the Faculty of Technology and Management of the University of Twente. She is teaching in the field of quality management and improvement management.
Her research activities are focussed on issues related to the possibilities of Learning and improvement in New Product Development.

Ir. Ilse Langenberg (Engineering and Management, 1996) worked as a consultant in the area of machine safety in correlation with European Directives (i.e. CE-mark). Currently she is working for Hollandse Signaalapparaten B.V. as a process engineer. She is the leader for process improvement in the field of systems engineering. Her activities are focussed on the development and implementation of improvement actions

Complex System Product Development: Adding Value by Creating Information and Reducing Risk

Tyson R. Browning
Lockheed Martin Aeronautics Company
P.O. Box 748, MZ 2222
Fort Worth, TX 76101
tyson@alum.mit.edu

John J. Deyst, Jr.
Department of Aeronautics & Astronautics
Massachusetts Institute of Technology
Room 33-109, Cambridge, MA 02139
deyst@mit.edu

Steven D. Eppinger
Sloan School of Management
Massachusetts Institute of Technology
Room E53-347, Cambridge, MA 02142
eppinger@mit.edu

Daniel E. Whitney
Center for Technology, Policy, and Industrial Development
Massachusetts Institute of Technology
Room E40-243, Cambridge, MA 02139
dwhitney@mit.edu

Abstract. Many firms expend a great amount of effort to identify and eliminate waste in their processes. Much recent effort has focused on lean manufacturing. Now lean product development has become a goal as well. Yet, in product development, determining how and when value is added is problematic. The goal of a product development process is to produce a product "recipe" that satisfies requirements. Design work is done both to specify the recipe in increasing detail and to verify that it does in fact conform to requirements. As design work proceeds, certainty increases surrounding the ability of the evolving product (and production process) design specifications to be the final product recipe (i.e., performance risk decreases). The goal of this paper is to advance the theory and practice of evaluating progress and added value in complex system product development. The paper proposes that making progress and adding value (to the customer) in complex system product development equate with producing useful information that reduces performance risk. The paper also contributes a methodology—the *risk value method*—that integrates current approaches such as technical performance measure (TPM) tracking charts and risk waterfall charts.

INTRODUCTION

Over the last decade, lean manufacturing has entrenched itself as part of the Western industrial landscape.[1] Many manufacturing firms are expending tremendous efforts in the quest for lean production. Some firms also realize that most of a product's life cycle cost is determined before production, during the *product development* (PD) process. To deliver better products faster and cheaper, some firms are attempting to create lean PD processes.

PD spans the gamut of marketing, design, management, and other activities done between defining a market opportunity and starting production.[2] The goal of the PD process is to create a "recipe" for producing a product (Reinertsen 1999). The recipe must conform to the requirements stemming from customer or market needs. The recipe includes the product, its manufacturing process, and its supply, distribution, and support systems. PD entails a myriad of activities working together to deliver the recipe.

The first step in getting lean is to understand and specify what adds value in a process. According to Womack and Jones, there are three types of activities: (Type 1) those that add value, (Type 2) those that do not but are necessary, and (Type 3) those that do not and are unnecessary. Once found, type 3 activities should be removed. Type 2 activities should be made as efficient as possible. This approach has yielded impressive results in production and business processes (Womack and Jones 1996).

But PD processes are unlike typical business and production processes in several ways. Terms like "iterative" and "creative" apply to PD. Designers may start with one design, find it deficient in several ways, and then change it. Especially with novel products, designers learn much along the way about what will and will not work (Petroski 1985). The desire is to create useful information, which is acted upon by a number of activities and disciplines. The information is valuable if it decreases the risk that the product will be

[1] The book *The Machine that Changed the World* (Womack *et al.* 1990) brought several lean concepts to industry's attention.

[2] There is not necessarily a clean break between development and production: some test and evaluation units may be produced prior to the official start of production, and some development work may continue past production start.

something other than what it is supposed to be—i.e., if it improves confidence in the recipe. Trying, analyzing, evaluating, testing, experimenting, demonstrating, and validating create valuable information (Reinertsen 1998).

When an interdisciplinary group attempts to classify PD activities as one of Womack and Jones' three types, it typically experiences some passionate debate. PD activities can be difficult to classify, and no one wants to see their activity branded as "waste," necessary or not. Fortunately, a lot of this difficulty can be avoided. Think of the PD process as a hierarchy of activities, with large, general activities containing small, specific activities. Actually, most of the non-value-adding activities are small, buried deep inside value-adding activities. In the largest sense, the overall PD process adds value (i.e., is a type 1 activity). Yet, decompose it and type 2 and type 3 activities appear within. Continue to decompose the type 1 activities, and activities of the other two types continue to appear. Decompose *ad infinitum*, and the only thing left adding value (by the "three types" definition) is the product recipe (or the product itself) materializing out of thin air! Thus, debating whether an activity is type 1 or type 2 is not very helpful in practice, since the former contains much of the latter anyway. Just think of the entire process in economic terms: remove type 3 activities and make everything else as productive and efficient as possible. The concept of "necessary waste" can be an unnecessary distraction.

In deciding what adds value, it helps to consider the goal—a product design or recipe that conforms to requirements. What information is needed to complete the recipe? How can one be certain that an acceptable recipe will materialize? What is the risk it will not? Figure 1 depicts risk as a function of the availability of useful information. The goal of PD is approached by producing useful information that reduces uncertainty. The activities that ensure that the right recipe materializes are the ones that add value, and their completion constitutes progress in PD.

This paper contributes a method for evaluating the value added in PD as a function of risk reduction—i.e., as a function of the generation of useful information. The *risk value method* is based on understanding overall product performance risk and its components. The approach integrates several concepts and methods, including: *technical performance measures* (TPMs), risk waterfall charts, customer preferences, and uncertainty. The goal of the paper is to advance the theory and practice of evaluating progress and added value in PD.

ADDING VALUE IN PRODUCT DEVELOPMENT

The goal of PD is to produce a product recipe that conforms to requirements with some certainty. PD is a problem solving process. Progress is made by creating useful information that reduces uncertainty and/or ambiguity (Schrader *et al.* 1993; Sutherland 1977). But it is challenging to produce information at the right time, when it will be most useful.

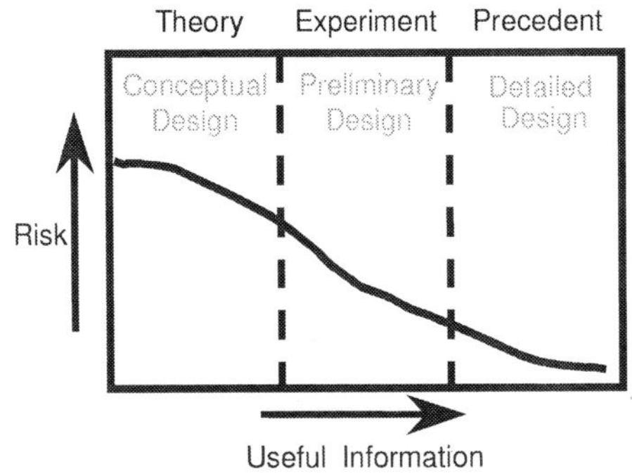

Figure 1: Risk Decreases with Availability of Useful Information[3]

The final product recipe contains a large amount of information, which is based on an enormous amount of supporting data, which in turn rest on still other data, etc. This information structure must be built from the ground up. Certain information must be created before it becomes possible to create other information. The dependencies between PD activities define a necessary sequence in the process of producing useful information. Most of the work done and the decisions made depend on the results of other work and decisions. The value of the information an activity produces is a function of, among other things, the value of the information it receives. In general, then, activities are done to create deliverables, and *the value of an activity depends on the value of the deliverables it uses and creates*. Thus, in many cases, *lack of value stems less from doing unnecessary activities and more from doing necessary activities with the wrong information* (and then having to redo them). Adding value is less a function of doing the right activities than of getting the right information in the right place at the right time. Hence, the focus of lean must turn away from activity "liposuction" and towards addressing the PD process as a system.

It is well known that progress in PD is difficult to gauge. Several authors have noted various reasons contributing to the problem. For example, Goldratt (1997) and others note how, if ten work items must be done, people tend to do the easiest ones first. When eight items are completed, many assume 80% of the work is finished. This is one problem. Rework provides another complication. PD planners often "plan to succeed." Typically, little attention is paid to *process failure modes* and their effects (i.e., rework). Furthermore, actually doing PD work unearths the need

[3] Figure adapted from (Harmon 1999)

for additional information (and additional activities to generate it). Sometimes, these effects and others combine to make "the last 10% of the project take 90% of the time" (implying a schedule overrun, or a cost overrun to prevent one). Thus, one cannot equate value added with progress through an arbitrarily defined statement of work for several reasons: it may contain superfluous activities for which no value is added, its work elements may not be equally valuable, and it may not account for missing activities, rework, or iterations.

Since PD is a discovery process, it is harder to determine what value is added and when. In PD, approaches are proposed, analyzed, evaluated, and advanced or rejected. The effect of one activity changing its approach and outputs can ripple throughout the process, changing other activities' inputs and assumptions and causing rework. A discovery process has lots of change and rework. It is iterative. The values of its activities are not predetermined—they are partly a function of the activities that precede it and those that follow.

When an activity produces some information, the quality of that information is extremely difficult to determine immediately. There is a time lag between the point of value creation and the point of value determination.[4] When does the value actually accrue? Rework can render useless what was previously useful information, because it can negate supposed progress and assumed value. Actually, the desired value was not added in the first place (although perhaps designers learned something). Forecasting which activities will add value and when is problematic in the PD process.

Merely examining the latest performance estimates of the design is also an illusory indicator of progress. When a design baseline is proposed, it is put forward with the expectation that it will be able to satisfy requirements. The collection of performance estimates will look good until a problem is revealed, at which point they may suddenly degrade. Good design performance levels cannot indicate progress unless they include a notion of how much uncertainty remains.

What are the contributions of analysis, measurement, review, test, and prototyping activities to progress and added value in PD? Activities such as these may not change the performance level (read "form, fit, and function") of a design at all (although they may force a decision that may cause another activity to do so). The purpose of these activities is to increase *certainty* about the ability of the design to meet requirements. That is, these activities decrease performance uncertainty. Since risk is the product of uncertainty and consequences, reducing uncertainty usually reduces risk.

[4] As in control systems, time lags contribute to system (in this case, process) instability.

All of these issues point to the need for a way to measure progress that provides a more realistic picture of the state of the project and accounts for how much is known about the product design. This paper proposes tracking the uncertainty surrounding the ability of the design to meet requirements as the way to measure progress and added value in PD. The paper shows how both (1) increasing the performance level and (2) reducing performance risk can be accounted for by a single measure of added value. The approach can help PD managers add value by focusing effort on eliminating the critical sources of risk in their projects.

CONCEPTS AND DEFINITIONS

Technical Performance. Technical performance (sometimes just called performance) refers to a product's technical attributes and entails a product's conformance to its technical requirements. Does the product do everything it is supposed to do, as well as it should? Is there an absence of defects, bugs, and non-conformances? Is there reasonable confidence about these conditions? Generally, technical performance equates to the benefits provided by a product because of its design, capabilities, and functionality. A product performs well if it does everything it should as well as it should.

Technical Performance Measures (TPMs). Designers use metrics to plan and track the level of each technical performance attribute. These metrics are called *technical performance measures* (TPMs), *measures of effectiveness* (MOEs), figures of merit, and other names. TPMs often have the same name as the performance attribute they measure, such as payload, range, etc. TPMs may also measure aggregate defects or nonconformances.

TPMs change as the design progresses. Each TPM may be estimated early in the design process, once a baseline design is established. Initial estimates are very subjective and uncertain. As design work is done, estimates are refined based on data from analyses, simulations, prototypes, demonstrations, etc. Estimates become more and more objective as design work provides TPM verification and uncertainty reduction. When the product recipe is ready, the TPMs specify the level of performance provided by each of the designed product's attributes.

The idea that TPMs become more accurate as the design matures leads to an important concept: the reduction of uncertainty. Information produced by design work is used to reduce the uncertainty surrounding TPMs. Some design work (analyses, evaluations, reviews, experiments, tests) may not change the actual capability of the design (the TPM levels), but these kinds of efforts are crucial for reducing the uncertainty in the design.

Performance Risk (R_{TPM}). Performance risk is uncertainty that a product design will satisfy technical requirements and the consequences thereof (cf., Browning 1999). Thus, the amount of performance risk associated with any TPM depends on two factors: (1) the number of possible outcomes, cases, or situations that fail to meet requirements and (2) the consequence or impact of each.

Uncertainty. The uncertainty component of performance risk can be quantified using the familiar methods of schedule risk assessment. Treating a TPM as a random variable, its possible outcomes can be represented by a *probability density function* (PDF). The PDF in Figure 2 shows the relative likelihood of an aircraft product having various range capabilities. The vertical line at 725 nautical miles (nmiles) signifies the required performance level. The part of the PDF to the left of the requirements line represents the fraction of outcomes that fail to meet requirements—or the probability that the design will not conform to requirements.

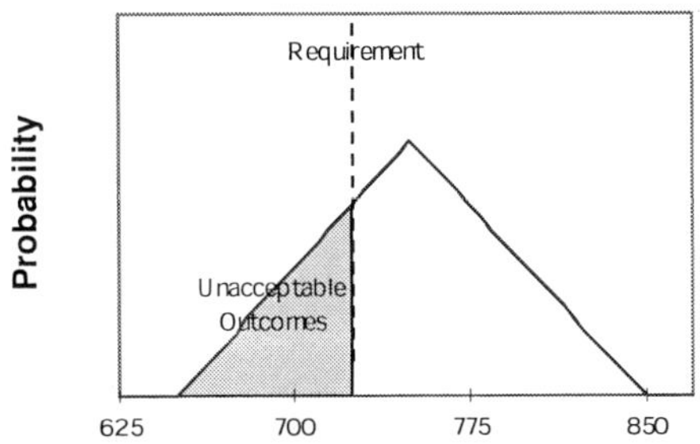

Figure 2: PDF Showing Relative Probability of Various Range TPM Outcomes

How is the shape of the PDF determined? Since the PDF represents possible outcomes and their relative probability, its shape depends on what kinds of outcomes are anticipated and how likely each is thought to be. Usually, one does not have much information about every possible outcome. When information is scarce, it helps to focus on a few important outcomes—the most likely case, the optimistic (best) case, and the pessimistic (worse) case. Estimates of these cases can be used to construct a rough, triangular PDF (triPDF) as in Figure 3. The area under the PDF is usually normalized to one.

Consequences. The consequences of failing to meet a requirement must also be considered. Some requirements are absolute thresholds below which the entire design is unacceptable. Other requirements represent customer preferences, where more is better but less might be acceptable. In the case of aircraft range, would missing the requirement by one mile be as bad as missing it by fifty? Customer needs and preferences data can be used to estimate the impacts of various adverse outcomes. For example, the customer may allow missing the range requirement (as long as this lack of value is compensated for in some other product attribute). However, the customer becomes more displeased the more range falls short. This increasing dissatisfaction might be represented using a quadratic impact function, where dissatisfaction grows as the square of the gap between the TPM and the requirement.[5] Figure 4 exhibits (A) quadratic and (B) linear impact functions. Together, the probability of the adverse outcomes and their impacts determine the level of performance risk for a TPM.

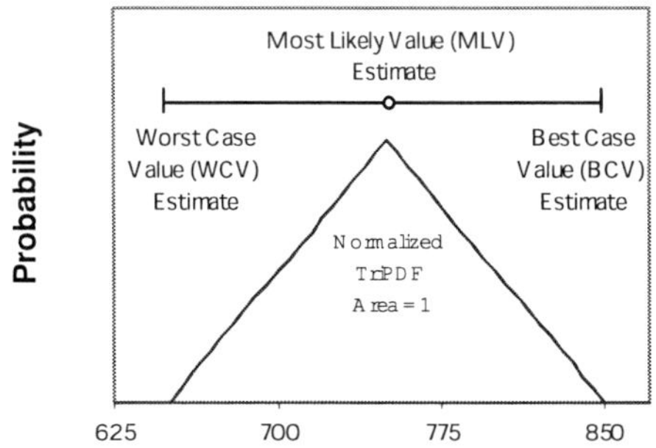

Figure 3: Conversion of Three-Point Estimate to TriPDF

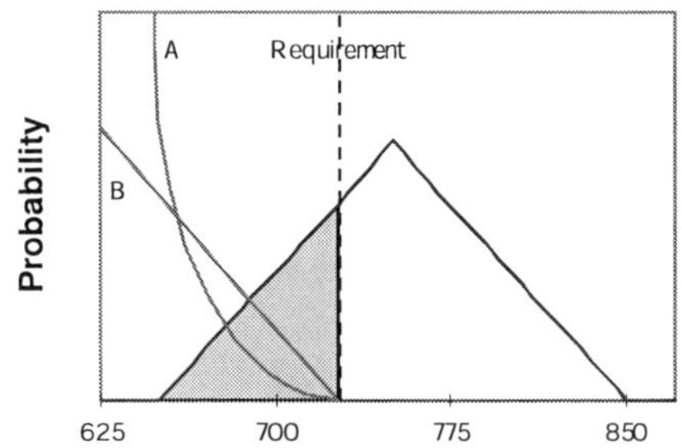

Figure 4: Two Example Impact Functions Overlaid on TriPDF

Utility curves provide a useful approach for documenting customer preferences for various performance levels. Figure 5 shows an example (piecewise linear) utility curve for aircraft range. The length of the *x*-axis is chosen to span the continuum from disgusting to delighting the customer or market. In this example, perhaps the customer wants an aircraft for a particular use that requires a 700 nmile range.

[5] Taguchi (1980) highlighted the usefulness of quadratic quality loss functions.

Nothing less will do. Slightly greater range is of marginally increasing value to the customer, to the point that a range of 1000 nmiles would be delightful. The utility curve can be used to determine the impact of various range TPM outcomes in terms of customer utility or value.[6] The impact is the gap between the utility of the outcome and the utility of the requirement:

$$I_{TPM} = \kappa_{TPM}\left[U(T) - U(x_0)\right] \tag{1}$$

where x_0 is a TPM outcome, T is the target (requirement), $U(\bullet)$ is the utility, and κ_{TPM} is a normalization constant (e.g., for converting units of utility to more intuitive measures of value, such as number of units likely to be purchased). In this case, the shape of the impact function depends on the shape of the aircraft range utility curve and the chosen requirement.

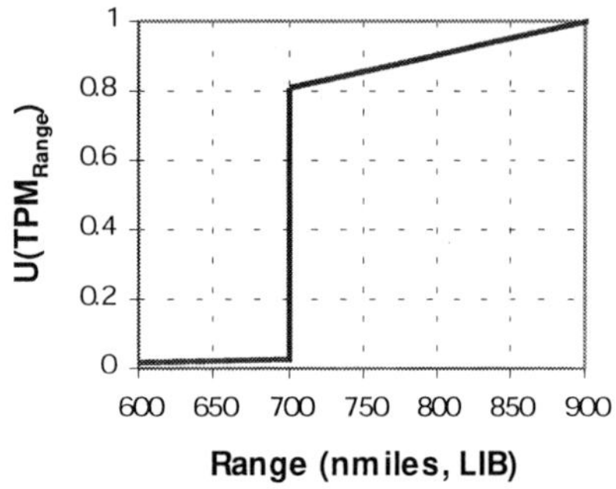

Figure 5: Utility Curve for Aircraft Range

Risk. The performance risk for a "*larger is better*" (LIB) TPM is the sum of the products of probability and impact for each unacceptable outcome, which, for the continuous case, is:

$$\mathrm{R}_{TPM} = \kappa_{TPM} \int_{-\infty}^{T} f_{TPM}(x_0)\left[U(T) - U(x_0)\right]dx_0 \tag{2}$$

where $f_{TPM}(x_0)$ is the PDF of all TPM outcomes. The integral is approximated with a summation for the usual case of a finite number of discrete outcomes.

Product Performance Risk (R).[7] The overall performance risk for a product design, R, is the weighted sum of all the R_{TPM}s:

$$\mathrm{R} = \sum_i w_i \mathrm{R}_{TPM,i} \tag{3}$$

where w_i is the relative importance of TPM$_i$. (It is usually helpful if all the w_is sum to one.)

METHODS FOR PLANNING AND TRACKING TECHNICAL PERFORMANCE

This section reviews two performance planning and surveillance methods, the TPM tracking chart and the risk waterfall chart. Both methods are used in a number of system development projects in industry. The two methods are combined and used in the next section to illustrate the risk value method.

TPM Tracking Chart. A TPM tracking chart forecasts and monitors an evolving TPM relative to its requirement. Initially, experts with applicable project, system, and technology experiences may forecast a "planned profile" for the TPM. The profile is projected based on a number of factors, including technology risk, planned test and validation activities, historical data, experience, and expert opinion. The planned profile integrates information from these sources into a format that helps planners and managers make decisions. As the project unfolds, demonstrated measures are recorded periodically. Ideally, the actual profile will meet or exceed the requirement, and uncertainty will decrease. TPM tracking also enables margin and risk management methods (e.g., NASA 1995, p. 62).

In Figure 6, an example aircraft design project is planned to last eight months. The requirement for effective mission range is set at 725 nautical miles and is shown in the tracking chart as the dashed, horizontal line. The circles represent a point estimate or measure of the most likely level of performance delivered by the design at various times. Each estimate conveys uncertainty with the high-low bars showing the optimistic and pessimistic possibilities. (In practice, however, many projects omit the uncertainty bars.)

Risk Waterfall Chart. Areas requiring risk reduction may be anticipated and tracked using a "risk waterfall" chart. The example in Figure 7 shows an assessed risk level for a particular structural loading case in an aircraft operational scenario. At the outset of the project, it is determined that the risk of unacceptable performance in this case is medium to high. The goal is to plan and track a chain of activities intended to mitigate this risk. As when building a TPM chart, one solicits expert opinion on the appropriate activities to reduce the risk and the amount of reduction anticipated for each, which are indicated in the chart as step functions of risk reduction. In Figure 7, the information produced by activities 1, 2, and 3 directly contributes to reducing the risk that the aircraft will not conform to requirements in this area. The expected, combined effect of the information created by these activities is to decrease the risk to a level deemed acceptable.

[6] For more information on constructing utility curves, see, e.g., (de Neufville 1990).

[7] The methodology in this section was suggested by Hugh McManus.

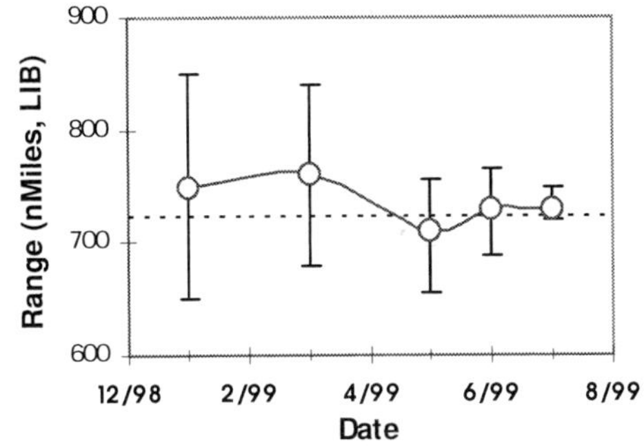

Figure 6: Example TPM Tracking Chart for Aircraft Range

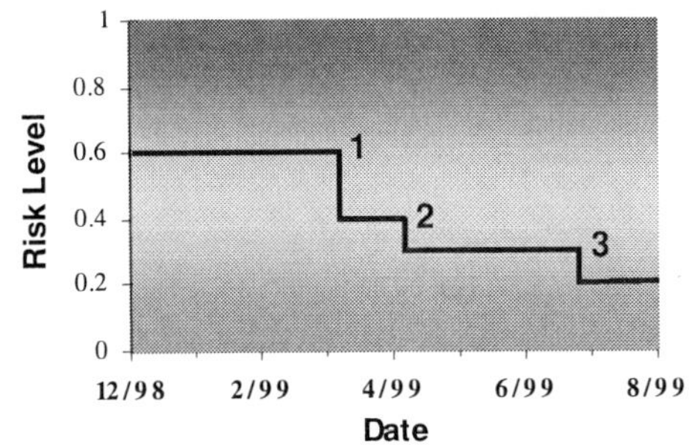

Figure 7: Example Risk Waterfall Chart for Aircraft Structural Loads

Combination Chart. The convenient format of the risk waterfall chart can be applied to the TPM tracking chart to monitor the risk inherent in a TPM level. Figure 8 provides an example, where risk levels (normalized on a zero to one scale) are overlaid on Figure 6. Each risk level is computed using equation (2) and a quadratic impact function.

TPM BEHAVIOR

Over the course of a project, the behavior of the TPMs is difficult to predict. Their starting points depend on the quality of initial estimates. For many TPMs, their change over the interval t_i to t_{i+1} seems random. For example, Cusumano and Selby show defect (bug) TPMs for Microsoft Excel 5.0 and Microsoft Word 4.0 where the overall effect is a gradual decrease but the localized fluctuation seems random (1995, pp. 318, 324). McDaniel (1996) also documents that design quality does not improve monotonically over design time. While progress occurs in one area, other activities discover new problems. There is no guarantee that problems will be solved faster than they are discovered during any given interval. Globally, performance seems to improve more steadily; locally (represented by a TPM), performance seems more random. In many cases, however, the direction and approximate magnitude of a TPM change during a specific interval can be predicted by an experienced person with knowledge of the information created during the interval.[8] If an interval contains a number of design decisions, the expected result may be improved performance. On the other hand, an interval containing many tests and reviews often leads to decreased TPM estimates.

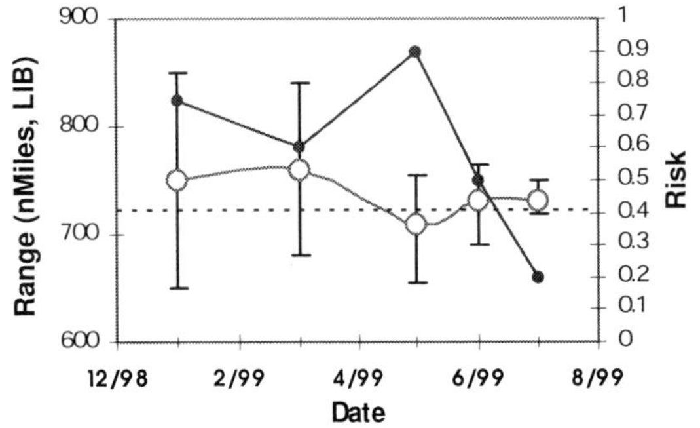

Figure 8: Combination TPM and Risk Tracking Chart

ADDING VALUE BY DECREASING PERFORMANCE RISK

If adding value equates with reducing performance risk, R, how can this effect be measured over specific time intervals? How much value is delivered between t_1 and t_2? Or, how much has R been reduced between t_1 and t_2? Figure 9 shows an example risk reduction profile for a project (cf., Figure 1). During some interval, Δt, information is created that provides some risk reduction, ΔR. The profile in Figure 9 represents Womack and Jones' ideal project—continuously added value. Figure 10 depicts some alternative performance risk reduction profiles. Project A reduces risk quickly and then has diminishing returns. Project B makes slow progress at first but then advances quickly. Project C has periods of risk increase when problems are detected; this profile is probably the most realistic. Project D is never able to reduce performance risk to satisfactory levels.

The profiles are functions of how new information affects the TPMs (including uncertainty) and the impact of falling short of requirements. To illustrate this more specifically, consider the TPM tracking chart in Figure 8. Let t_1 be 1/99 and let t_2 be 7/99, six months later. Figure 11 shows the TPM at these two times with the uncertainties represented by PDFs. At time t_2, useful information has been created that has reigned in the uncertainty that was evident at time t_1. The probability

[8] This assertion has not been verified empirically.

of an unacceptable outcome has decreased, and especially poor outcomes with greater consequences have been eliminated. The combined effect is a reduction in risk (as tracked in Figure 8) for this TPM.

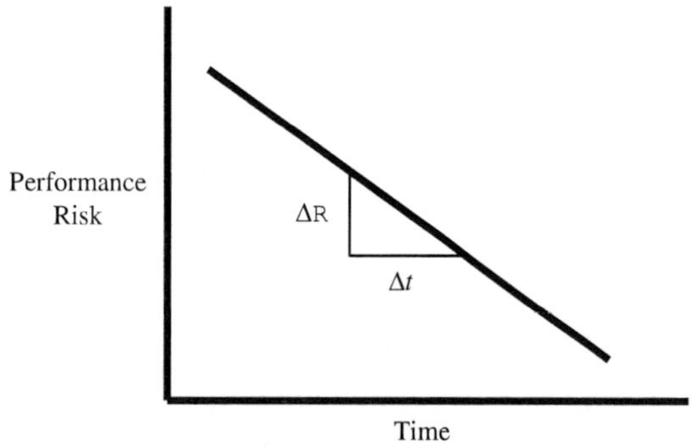

Figure 9: Change in Performance Risk Over Time

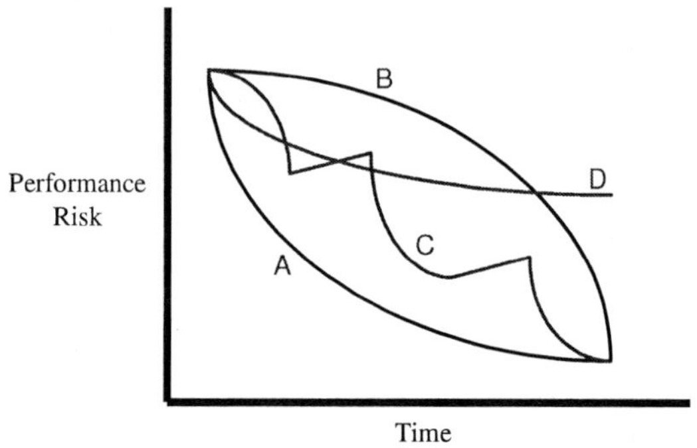

Figure 10: Alternative Performance Risk Reduction Profiles

CONCLUSION

> "To solve our basic problem [of improving the product development process], any methodology that is to be developed must be useful in evaluating the partially-developed product at any time during its development life."
>
> —Sidney Sobelman (1958)

The problems of how to evaluate the status of a product design and how to measure progress or value added in PD are very similar. This paper presented an integrated concept and methodology—the *risk value method*—that addresses these issues. The value of the PD process as a whole (and of every activity within it) is based on the value of its product(s). Many of the products of PD activities serve not only to improve the design but also to confirm it. During PD, activities contribute value by creating information that increases certainty about the ability of the design to satisfy requirements.

Until an actual product is produced and used, its performance level is uncertain. In the early stages of PD, a baseline design is proposed that is supposed to satisfy requirements and deliver desired performance. During PD, new information is created as the design is analyzed and tested. This information may reveal that the design or some portion of it does not suffice. The performance level of the evolving product design will fluctuate over time. The only thing that increases monotonically with time is the amount of useful information available. The value of that information provides an improved way to think about progress and added value in PD.[9] The risk value method really gets more at how value is measured than it does at how value is created. But the measure is what guides decisions about what additional value remains to be added and what the PD project will do about it.

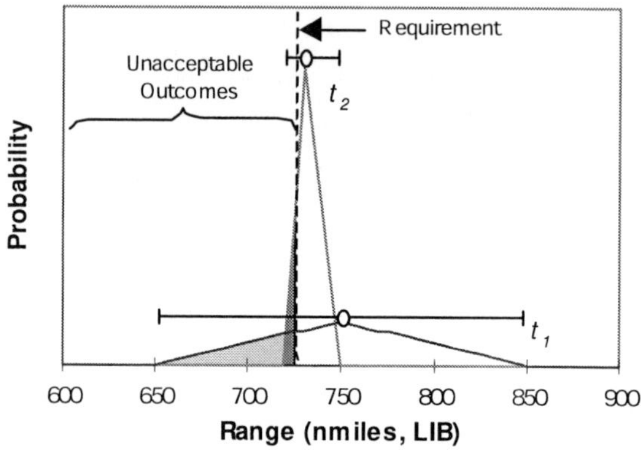

Figure 11: Reduction in Unacceptable Outcomes from t_1 to t_2

Therefore, the risk value method is a useful and helpful technique in PD project planning and control. It has many applications and benefits. It can help in deciding what information should be created (and therefore what activities should be executed) to produce an expected risk reduction profile and ensure a sufficient stream of value creation (Weiss and Warmkessel 1999).[10] When the contributions of each activity are tracked, their cost and cycle time can be used to determine their productivity or efficiency in adding value. (These types of applications require a sufficient process model or description—one that accounts for the information dependencies among activities.[11]) In addition, the approach enables analyses of the effects of iteration, rework, testing, and other types of activities on value. Perhaps the expected value

[9] Note, however, that the value of the information is not guaranteed to increase monotonically, since the value attached to any given portion of the information can change based on new information.

[10] At least one systems engineering text (Oliver *et al.* 1997) lists "Assess Available Information" as an explicit step in the core technical process.

[11] An excellent tool for this purpose is the *design structure matrix* (DSM—Browning 1998; Eppinger *et al.* 1994; Steward 1981)

of additional iterations of design activities can be forecast. The risk value method also facilitates post-project analysis and learning. Planned risk reduction profiles can be compared to actual achievements to evaluate a firm's project planning and control capabilities and to improve the PD process. New activities may be used to create certain information in future projects.

Furthermore, the risk value method emphasizes the importance of making a rough estimate of each TPM and its uncertainty during the first parts of the design process, perhaps as early as when a concept or architecture is seriously considered. Early estimates help ensure that primary TPMs are not overlooked during the initial stages of design.

Finally, paying more attention to the uncertainty connected with each TPM emphasizes the importance of risk reduction and maintained flexibility. Early risk reduction can be achieved by earlier, more directed testing and validation of uncertain aspects of the design and more appropriately timed and postured design reviews. Maintained flexibility is necessary when uncertainty persists. Paying explicit attention to uncertainty can decrease the focus on point solutions and increase the attractiveness of approaches such as set-based design (e.g., Ward *et al.* 1995) and robust design (e.g., Phadke 1989). All of these advantages accrue when using the risk value method in practice. Companies that effectively manage and reduce uncertainty and risk should realize competitive advantages (Levy 1999).

Although the risk value method provides an improved measure of progress and value added, it has some limitations. Certainly, metrics are no better than the data used to construct them. Most of the information addressing uncertainty and risk in a PD project is subjective. Nevertheless, the risk value method integrates the most useful information available in a meaningful way to support decision-making. It facilitates trading off various dimensions of performance to achieve a correctly balanced product. A strong argument for the risk value method, despite its limitations, is that these same, subjective data—used in an *ad hoc*, unsystematic, and unintegrated fashion—constitute the current state of practice.

Another limitation is that measures can be "gamed." The PD organization culture must exhibit proper attitudes towards performance measures and uncertainty if the measures will be meaningful. If process participants merely pad uncertainty estimates to justify more uncertainty reduction activities, the PD process may not be able to clear a business case hurdle. After all, adding value continuously is a means to an effective enterprise, not an end in itself. Value must be delivered as efficiently as possible.

In closing, consider the value of certainty and predictability, both to the PD organization and to the customer. Customers of commercial products usually assume the PD organization is certain about its products. The PD firm has a reputation to maintain. This aspect of certainty is primarily valuable to the PD organization. However, especially in the case of large, novel, complex systems, certainty (termed "low risk") is clearly a criterion of customer preference. At least in these cases, if not more generally, certainty is of direct value to the customer.

It is also helpful to turn the problem around and consider the cost of uncertainty. Uncertainty has many costs during PD—e.g., costs of resource buffers and options—and these costs are passed along to the customer as higher acquisition costs. Whether the customer considers certainty explicitly or not, product costs reflect the costs of uncertainty. Reducing uncertainty in PD can improve affordability and thereby increase value to the customer.

ACKNOWLEDGMENTS

Support for this research from the Lean Aerospace Initiative <http://lean.mit.edu/> at the Massachusetts Institute of Technology and Lockheed Martin Aeronautics Company is gratefully acknowledged. This paper draws on material from (Browning 1998, Ch. 7). Hugh McManus and Joe Dean provided helpful comments that improved the paper.

REFERENCES

Browning, Tyson Rodgers (1998) *Modeling and Analyzing Cost, Schedule, and Performance in Complex System Product Development* Unpublished Ph.D. Thesis (TMP), Massachusetts Institute of Technology, Cambridge, MA.

Browning, Tyson R. (1999) "Sources of Performance Risk in Complex System Development" *Proceedings of the Ninth Annual International Symposium of INCOSE*, Brighton, UK, June 6-11.

Cusumano, Michael A. and Richard W. Selby (1995) *Microsoft Secrets: How the World's Most Powerful Software Company Creates Technology, Shapes Markets, and Manages People*, New York: The Free Press.

de Neufville, Richard (1990) *Applied Systems Analysis: Engineering Planning and Technology Management*, New York: McGraw-Hill.

Eppinger, Steven D., Daniel E. Whitney, Robert P. Smith and David A. Gebala (1994) "A Model-Based Method for Organizing Tasks in Product Development" *Research in Engineering Design* **6**: 1-13.

Goldratt, Eliyahu M. (1997) *Critical Chain*, Great Barrington, MA: The North River Press.

Harmon, Ed (1999) "Anatomy of the Product and Process Design Process" Presentation to the Lean Aerospace Initiative Product Development Focus Team, : Northrop Grumman.

Levy, Nino S. (1999) "Reducing Uncertainty and Innovation Risk in Product Development" in Dorf, Richard C., Ed.

Technology Management Handbook. Boca Raton, FL: Chapman & Hall/CRCnetBASE, 90-96.

McDaniel, Christopher D. (1996) *A Linear Systems Framework for Analyzing the Automotive Appearance Design Process* Unpublished Master's Thesis (Mgmt./EE), MIT, Cambridge, MA.

NASA (1995) *NASA Systems Engineering Handbook*: NASA Headquarters, Code FT, SP-6105.

Oliver, David W., Timothy P. Kelliher and Jr. James G. Keegan (1997) *Engineering Complex Systems with Models and Objects*, New York: McGraw-Hill.

Petroski, Henry (1985) *To Engineer is Human: The Role of Failure in Successful Design*, New York: St. Martin's Press.

Phadke, M.S. (1989) *Quality Engineering Using Robust Design*, New Jersey: Prentice Hall.

Reinertsen, Don (1998) "Testing: Annoyance or Opportunity" *Electronic Design* **46**(26): 64H.

Reinertsen, Don (1999) "Lean Thinking Isn't So Simple" *Electronic Design* **47**(10): 48.

Schrader, Stephen, William M. Riggs and Robert P. Smith (1993) "Choice Over Uncertainty and Ambiguity in Technical Problem Solving" *Journal of Engineering and Technology Management* **10**: 73-99.

Sobelman, Sidney (1958) *A Modern Dynamic Approach to Product Development*, Dover, NJ: Office of Technical Services (OTS).

Steward, Donald V. (1981) *Systems Analysis and Management: Structure, Strategy, and Design*, New York: PBI.

Sutherland, John W. (1977) *Administrative Decision-Making: Extending the Bounds of Rationality*, New York: Van Nostrand Reinhold.

Taguchi, G. and Y. Wu (1980) *Introduction to Off-Line Quality Control*, Nagoya, Japan: Central Japan Quality Association.

Ward, Allen, Jeffrey K. Liker, John J. Cristiano and Durward K. Sobek II (1995) "The Second Toyota Paradox: How Delaying Decisions Can Make Better Cars Faster" *Sloan Management Review* **36**(3): 43-61.

Weiss, Stanley I. and Joyce M. Warmkessel (1999) "Systems Engineering the Product Development Value Stream" *Proceedings of the Ninth Annual International Symposium of INCOSE*, Brighton, UK, June 6-11.

Womack, James P. and Daniel T. Jones (1996) *Lean Thinking: Banish Waste and Create Wealth in Your Corporation*, New York: Simon & Schuster.

Womack, James P., Daniel T. Jones and Daniel Roos (1990) *The Machine That Changed the World*, New York: Rawson Associates, HarperCollins.

AUTHOR BIOGRAPHIES

Dr. Tyson R. Browning conducts applied research and provides internal consulting on engineering process development for Lockheed Martin Aeronautics Company in Fort Worth, Texas, USA. He previously worked with the Product Development Focus Team of the Lean Aerospace Initiative at MIT. He holds a B.S. in Engineering Physics from Abilene Christian University; an S.M. in Aeronautics and Astronautics from MIT; an S.M. in Technology and Policy from MIT; and a Ph.D. in Technology, Management and Policy (interdisciplinary technology management and systems engineering) from MIT.

Dr. John J. Deyst is Professor of Aeronautics and Astronautics at MIT. His research has identified the productivity gains achievable using integrated product teams, design/cost integration, and highly automated processes for developing flight and mission critical software. His current efforts concentrate on quantitative models for evaluating risk and value in product development. In the course of his career has served on numerous government panels and committees concerned with issues of performance and safety of complex systems. He was Chairman of the AIAA Guidance and Control Committee (1980/81), he is currently on the advisory board of the SAE Aerospace Control and Guidance Committee, and he is a Fellow of the AIAA.

Dr. Steven D. Eppinger is Associate Professor of Management Science and holds the General Motors Leaders for Manufacturing Chair at the MIT Sloan School of Management and a joint appointment in MIT's Engineering Systems Division. He received the S.B., S.M., and Sc.D. degrees from MIT's Department of Mechanical Engineering before joining the faculty in 1988. Dr. Eppinger's research creates methods for improving product design and development practices. This work has been applied primarily in the automotive, electronics, aerospace, and equipment industries.

Dr. Daniel E. Whitney is Senior Research Scientist at the MIT Center for Technology, Policy, and Industrial Development. He conducts research on product development, automation, CAD, mechanical assembly, outsourcing strategy, and comparisons of American and Foreign companies. His main activities are in the International Motor Vehicle Program, the Leaders for Manufacturing Program, the Center for Innovation in Product Development, and the Lean Aerospace Initiative. He also teaches mechanical assembly and product development in the MIT Engineering and Business Schools. Prior to joining MIT, Dr Whitney spent 19 years at Draper Laboratory where he conducted research and consulting on robotics, assembly automation, design for assembly, and CAD tools for assembly processes. He is a Senior Member of IEEE, a Fellow of the ASME, and a Charter Member of SME/RIA. He has published over 80 technical articles, co-authored a book on Concurrent Engineering, and holds a number of patents.

One Engineering Process – Integrated!

Barbara Denny and Richard Bennett
Rockwell Collins, Inc.
400 Collins Rd. N.E.
Cedar Rapids, Iowa 52498

Abstract. Process definition is not new at Rockwell Collins. Processes have been documented and repeatedly updated throughout the Rockwell Collins history. Process variations have existed due to the number of disciplines, Business Units, degree of adherence, level of senior management support, customer influence, etc. During the past two years Rockwell Collins has documented an enterprise level standard engineering process framework. The resulting Engineering Technical Consistent Process (ETCP) addresses the disciplines of Systems Engineering, Software Engineering, Hardware Engineering and Application Specific Integrated Circuits (ASIC) Engineering and is one of a suite of enterprise level processes that encompass the full business lifecycle.

BACKGROUND

Discipline Process Definition. During the past decade, as the enterprise evolved, matured and reorganized, the engineering processes were documented starting first at a project level, then department level, then BU level, next the combined commercial BU level and finally, as exists today, at the enterprise level. Historically, senior management support determined which engineering disciplines were documented at the different organizational levels. At the time Rockwell Collins, and subsequently its engineering organization, restructured into its current organizational configuration there were two systems processes (one government & one commercial), two software processes (one government & one commercial), five ASIC processes, and one hardware process (commercial). Each process was developed to focus on the unique needs of the BU customers and as such resulted in processes with differing terminology and definitions. Additionally, these processes did not attempt to integrate the various technical disciplines together so expected inputs/outputs from one process were not always defined as inputs/outputs to other affected disciplines. The level of process maturity and compliance of each process varied considerably within and across the BUs. The visible variation in support of these processes by senior management had a direct affect on the acceptance of and level of adherence to these processes. Over time, as the level of senior management support increased so did the level of influence.

Process Influences. Shortly after Rockwell Collins endorsed the Software Engineering Institute (SEI) Capability Maturity Model for Software (CMM-SW), the software process definition was the first engineering process to be formally documented. Next systems engineering proficiency was developed at Rockwell Collins using EIA-731*:* Systems Engineering Capability. Customers advocating and requiring the use of these models had a strong influence on the level of management support and the subsequent development and documentation of processes.

Business Process Definition. Rockwell Collins is in the process of developing a business management lifecycle process that encompasses the Decision Point Process, Bid and Proposal Process, Management Consistent Process (MCP), and the ETCP (see Figure 1).

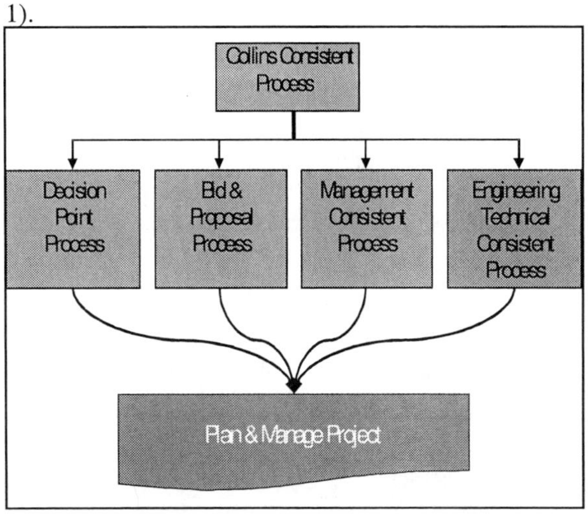

Figure 1. Business Management Lifecycle Process

Organization. Rockwell Collins designs and manufactures state of the art communication and aviation electronic solutions including cockpit electronics, handheld GPS units, communication systems, flight management systems and in-flight entertainment systems. In Rockwell Collins there are four Product/Systems BUs. These BUs are geographically located in California, Iowa, Florida, Texas, Oregon and Illinois. The Engineering Technical Consistent Process applies to all of the Product/Systems Businesses Units. The Consistent Process Department

(CPD), the group that oversees the development, and deployment of the ETCP, was moved under a Lean Electronics organization to better serve all of the engineering process groups and address related process issues at the enterprise level. Lean Electronics is an enterprise-wide staff organization chartered to be the catalyst and champion for application of lean principles and continuous process improvement. CPD as part of the Lean Electronics organizations has a direct and independent reporting chain to senior management. Direct communications to senior management helps keep management better and more uniformly informed. Independent reporting also provides focused opportunity to influence organizational acceptance and implementation of the enterprise wide engineering process.

CATALYST FOR CHANGE

External Need Identification. There were a number of external considerations that caused a need for change:

- The systems development environment was experiencing rapid change. Demands for faster processing, decreased size and weight, and more application flexibility resulted in increased system complexity and increased percentages of software and ASICs in systems.
- Customer demands for open systems architecture (OSA) were increasing. While OSA products allow the customer greater flexibility to easily mix, match and assemble components from a variety of companies, complying with this practice can make retention of market share problematic.
- Shrinking markets, increased competition, decreased brand loyalty and prices were translating missed cost and schedule goals into profit losses. Customers with fewer dollars were demanding more value and shorter lifecycles.
- Demands for critical engineering resources were outpacing supply. A lean, agile, multi-talented workforce was becoming a necessity.
- More customers began requiring use of industry standards, models and best practices as selection criteria for companies to compete for their business. This trend meant that Rockwell Collins would have to adopt these standards and practices to remain competitive. Additionally, non-complying proprietary processes would have to be abandoned or revamped.

Internal Need Identification. Internal environmental changes reinforced the need for change:

- Rockwell Collins was restructured from separate autonomous entities into a single enterprise.
- Analysis of engineering environments uncovered significant inefficiency resulting from maintaining BU unique processes.
- An enterprise resource planning (ERP) system was installed to revamp legacy financial processes and outdated information management systems.
- Management processes were consolidated across the enterprise to optimize benefits of the new ERP and to help institutionalize industry best practices.

These trends and changes identified the need for new processes. The ETCP was one process developed to address these needs.

A SINGLE ENGINEERING PROCESS

Process Endorsement. The Rockwell Collins Chief Engineer's Council (CEC) is a forum, comprised of the Engineering Directors from each BU, that coordinates engineering technical activities across the enterprise. The CEC formed and chartered the Consistent Process (CP) Configuration Control Board (CCB) to develop and deploy the enterprise wide engineering process. The CEC tasked CPD to chair the CP CCB and coordinate process development and improvement (See Figure 2).

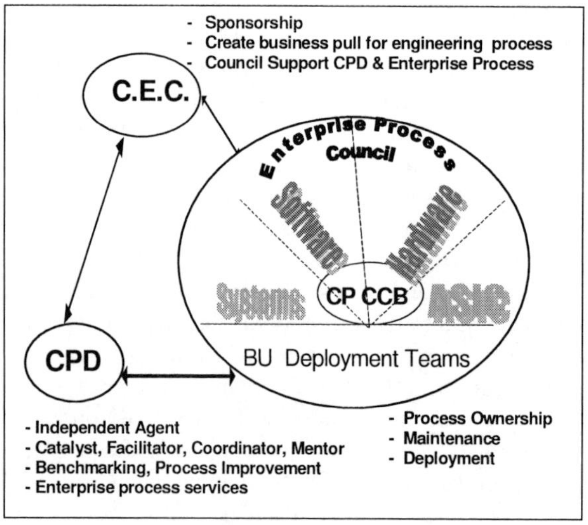

Figure 2. Chief Engineers Council

BU Involvement. The CP CCB has membership from all the BUs, all the key technical engineering disciplines within the BUs, and all the key interfacing functions (i.e. Configuration Management, Quality Assurance, Operations, Program Management, etc.). In support of CP CCB activities there are also cross-BU working groups, one per technical discipline, that meet bi-weekly to address technical and management issues. CPD members facilitate these teams.

One Process Framework. After initial deployment, benefits from one process definition will include:

- More effective development/delivery of training – It will be more effective to develop, maintain and deliver a single, consistent set of process training material than to do so for many different sets of material.

- Rapid redeployment of engineering resources - Rockwell Collins will be able to share critical engineering resources within and cross BUs more effectively and with minimal process retraining.

- Standard enterprise-wide metrics - Standard metrics will be developed and tracked to allow consistent and objective process assessments for programs and projects within and across BUs.

- A single process suite for all customers – Customers who deal with multiple Rockwell BUs will no longer have to learn multiple internal processes and languages. Instead they will learn one comprehensive framework.

- A single common process language – Historically, each BU process developed its unique process terminology and definitions. Usage of an enterprise wide consistent process suite institutionalizes the use of common terms and definitions.

- Consistent interfaces between Systems, Software, Hardware and ASIC Engineering – Integrating the technical disciplines into a single process suite and defining interfaces between these disciplines will foster communication and understanding.

- Cost savings on audits and certifications (ISO, CMM-SW, EIA 731) - Enterprise level process will reduce the need for multiple audits on individual BU unique processes.

- Easier adherence to industry and customer standards – It will be more effective to manage, improve and follow a single process suite than to simultaneously address several unique processes.

Phased Development. The ETCP is being developed and implemented in three phases.

Phase I. Phase I, which is now complete, created and formally baselined the enterprise-level process framework. This framework established the common language used to identify process activities and associated tasks and included a template for future capture of BU and enterprise-level methods, templates, and tools. The activities and tasks included in each version of the framework provided a baseline to trace industry standards and existing Rockwell Collins processes against. Phase I documented "what" process activities were to be performed.

Phase II. Phase II, currently in progress, involves collecting BU methods, templates and tools and making these visible at the enterprise level. The Phase II version of the process will begin to document specific methods, the "how" to do it, as a natural progression to the activities and tasks, the "what" to do, provided in Phase I. Additionally standard enterprise-wide objective metrics will be defined.

Phase III. Phase III will begin to employ analysis techniques utilizing objective metrics defined in Phase II to identify the best common methods, templates and tools so that the variation in process instantiations might be appropriately minimized. The goal of Phase III is to produce a process framework that contains a finite manageable set of methods, templates, and tools based on methodical analysis and evaluation of project data.

Compliance to Industry Standards. Rockwell BUs **have** identified all industry and customer standards to which engineering processes must comply. The CP CCB have performed compliance analyses between the identified requirements and the baselined ETCP and documented the results in a traceability matrix. The gaps and deficiencies identified became the basis for change requests written against the ETCP. The CP CCB has utilized change control principles, methods and tools to evaluate these change requests, improve the ETCP and deliver updated versions. BUs can use the matrix to easily determine what gaps exists and ensure their instantiated process is augmented to cover those gaps.

ENGINEERING PROCESS DEFINED

Systems Approach. The ETCP follows a structured, disciplined systems process that defines and allocates requirements, examines trade-offs, performs studies, implements solutions using best engineering practices, and traces verification processes to ensure the end product satisfies the original requirements. The ETCP uses a systems model called the RFS-IVV. This model has the six following phases: **R**equirements Capture, **F**unctional Analysis & Design, **S**ynthesis, **I**ntegration, **V**erification and **V**alidation (See Figure 3).

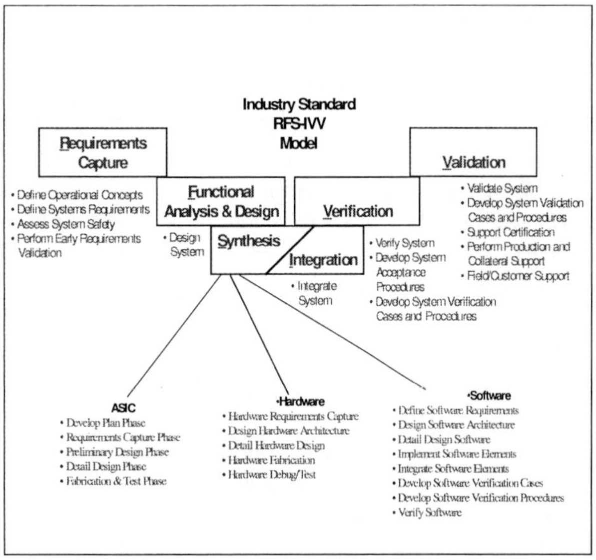

Figure 3. RFS-IVV Model

RFS. The phases comprising RFS identify needs, evaluate solutions, and implement a system solution that satisfies those needs.

- **Requirements Capture.** During this phase customer operational requirements, regulatory requirements, applicable standards, and company quality standards are identified to ensure that requirements are complete, consistent, real and verifiable.
- **Functional Analysis & Design.** During this phase functions and interrelationships are identified that will accomplish the system performance objectives. Also, the system architecture is defined and system requirements are allocated to functional elements (HW, SW, ASIC).
- **Synthesis.** Designing and building system elements is performed during synthesis. Synthesis supplies the "how" that accomplishes the "what" defined during Functional Analysis & Design. Synthesis is an iterative process that coordinates development of the HW, SW and ASIC elements.

IVV. The IVV phases integrate system elements together, verify system performance, and validate that original customer requirements have been satisfied.

- **Integration.** During integration system elements are assembled and tested to ensure that interfaces are compatible, system elements together provide proper functionality and expected performance can be achieved.
- **Verification.** Verification assures the system meets specified architectural and functional requirements
- **Validation.** Validation ensures that the system requirements specify a system that meet customer performance, operational and safety expectations acceptably.

Iterative RFS-IVV. The RFS-IVV model applies equally well and is flowed down to the functional discipline level (see Figure 4). Each discipline has its own requirements and design elements. Synthesis at the system level translates into Fabrication, Build and Implement at the ASIC, Hardware and Software discipline levels, respectively. Each discipline has its own verification element. Validation is usually performed only at the systems level. Each discipline tailors their implementation of the RFS-IVV accordingly.

ETCP. The ETCP is a library of individual processes segmented by technical discipline, each containing activities and tasks, and practiced consistently across all Rockwell Collins BUs (See Figure 4). Information flows between functional disciplines within the ETCP and from disciplines inside the ETCP to sources outside the ETCP (see Figure 5).

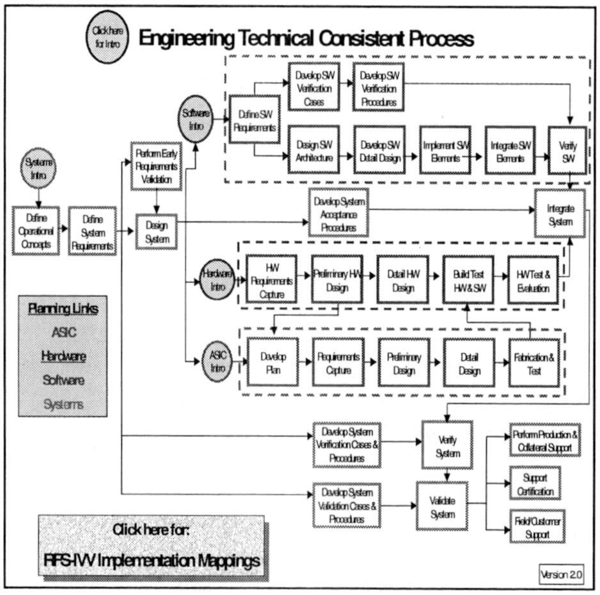

Figure 4. ETCP Model

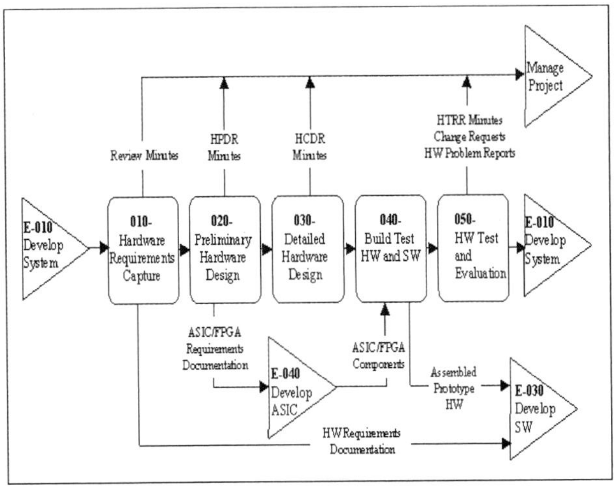

Figure 5. Information Flow Diagram

Lifecycle Model. The ETCP does not prescribe any particular lifecycle model. Execution order of the activities within the ETCP is determined by a project's chosen execution model, such as spiral, evolutionary, or waterfall and is documented in their project plans and schedules. Projects are free to select the lifecycle model that best fits their development strategy and risks. A project can address high risk items in the first cycle while lower risk items are addressed in later cycles (see Figure 6). This allows adjustments to be made to manage uncertainities.

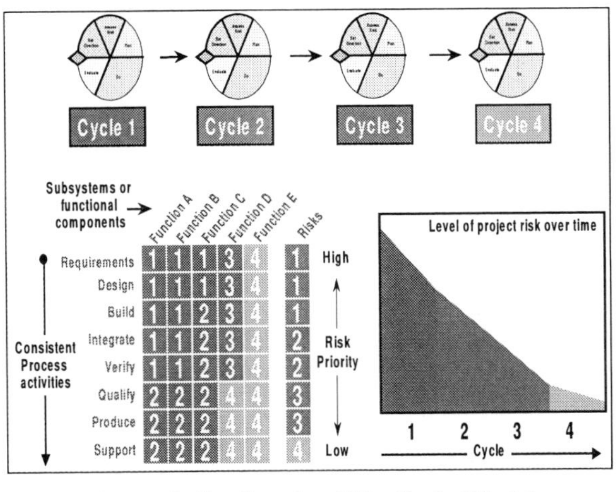

Figure 6. Configuring Life-Cycle Model

Discipline Communication. A single consistent process suite that provides a common understandable language and that addresses and is used by all technical disciplines promotes enhanced communication between these disciplines. Each discipline can easily comprehend the needs and expectations of the others. The included technical disciplines are Systems Engineering, Software Engineering, Hardware Engineering, and ASIC Engineering.

FRAMEWORK

Activity Based Model. The ETCP process descriptions are structured using an entry-task-exit (ETX) format. Each individual activity defines inputs, sources of inputs, entry conditions, technical tasks, outputs, output sources and exit conditions. Inputs specified are used during the activity. The list is not all-inclusive as other documents created by other activities are available for reference. Entry conditions are criteria that the inputs must satisfy before the specific activity can begin. Tasks are the "what" that are performed in order to transform inputs into outputs. Outputs list the successful results of completing the activity and are available as input for other activities. Exit conditions are criteria the outputs must satisfy to determine when an activity is complete. In addition, there is a synopsis of the purpose and description of the activity. (See Figure 7)

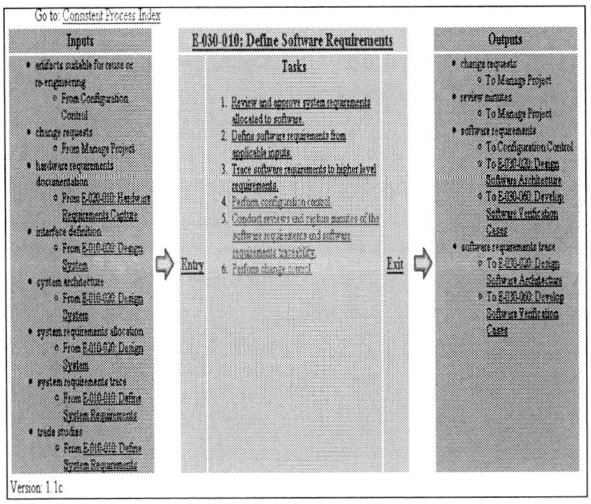

Figure 7. Entry-Task-Exit Model

Methods Implementation. In the web page model of the ETCP, each task within an activity has a linked page that contains a detailed description of the task effort. This page also includes Company and BU methods, templates, and tools identified for accomplishing the task. The Method, Template, and Tool Matrix describes "how" tasks may be accomplished. The framework allows the businesses to identify unique methods, templates and tools to address individual project implementations of process activities and tasks. In this way, customer requirements and industry standards can be addressed. This flexibility effectively addresses development without burdening all projects with non-value added steps not associated with their market focus. The web model developed during Phase II will provide greater visibility into the difference and similarity between BU methods (See Figure 8).

E-030-010 Task 2: Define software requirements from applicable inputs.

	Method/Guideline	Template	Tool
RC	none available	none available	none available
AT	QSS DOORS Tool Users Guide Rational Requisite Pro Tool Users Guide Flight Control Department's Software Development Plan (SDP) Large Format Display System (LFDS) Software Development Plan (SDP)	Communication Navigation Systems Department's Software Development Plan (SDP)	QSS DOORS Rational Requisite Pro
BRS	Software Requirements	Software Requirements	none available
GS	none available	none available	none available
PS	none available	none available	none available

Define derived software requirements which are not directly traceable to higher system level requirements. Categories of requirements to include: functionality, performance, sizing and timing (internal and/or external memory, target CPU processing time), safety requirements, security requirements, design constraints (use of particular processor and/or configuration of processors), software quality factors (from contract - include a method of compliance), human performance and/or human engineering requirements (human information processing capabilities and limitations, foreseeable human errors under both normal and extreme conditions), implications for the total system environment - training, support, and operational environment).

When defining software requirements, consider software documentation from previous programs for potential reuse and consider specifying requirements for future reuse. There are two methods which should be considered: salvaging requirements from a previous program and creating or reusing a product line application

Ensure that each software requirement is uniquely identifiable and verifiable. Collaborate with the systems representative to ensure all system requirements allocated to the computational elements have been accounted for in the software requirements document.

Version: 1.1c

Figure 8. Methods, Templates, and Tools

Web Based Process Definition. The web based process definition allows electronic navigation through the index, activities, tasks, inputs and outputs. The web based process definition provides a single point of reference for methods, templates, and tools and provides access to all employees guaranteeing the latest technical information is always available. It also enhances and facilitates communication between the technical disciplines.

Common generation source. A database was used to store all of the ETCP components and information. Through report generation this information can be formatted into a web page or translated into a Microsoft Word document. This allows two separate representations of the same information to exist while minimizing the maintenance efforts required.

Change Management. Process changes are managed by the CP CCB using the Rockwell Change Tracking System (CTS) process. CPD facilitates the CP CCB and maintains the ETCP model plus related artifacts. The CTS tool allows project team members across the enterprise to submit change requests (CR) against the engineering process. Anyone and everyone are encouraged to submit them. CRs are assigned to the appropriate functional discipline working group for further clarification and resolution. CRs affecting more than one discipline are assigned to the cross-functional working group. This group formulates a recommended solution and provides it to the CCB for acceptance or rejection. Each CR is assigned to an ETCP baseline (i.e. version 1.0, version 1.1) for implementation. Intermediate working builds are used to implement and resolve the CR. CRs are closed with the release of a new ETCP baseline.

Tailoring. ETCP tailoring is accomplished in one of two ways. The first method is through use of project categories and involves tailoring tasks within the activities. The second method involves selecting appropriate methods and tools to be used by the project and establishes the level of rigor and discipline to be followed by the project. Project characteristics such as customer requirements, team size, and criticality level determine the method and tool selection for a project.

Process Implementation. During the program management project planning process the ETCP will be instantiated for the project and a Work Breakdown Structure (WBS) will be constructed. The WBS will follow a deliverable-based architecture that breaks the System deliverable into Subsystems, then Subsystem Line Replacement Units (LRUs), then LRU modules, and finally critical items or modules (See Figure 9). Work will be assigned and managed based on deliverables. Also, parametric and bottoms-up estimates will be developed and tracked based on deliverable entities.

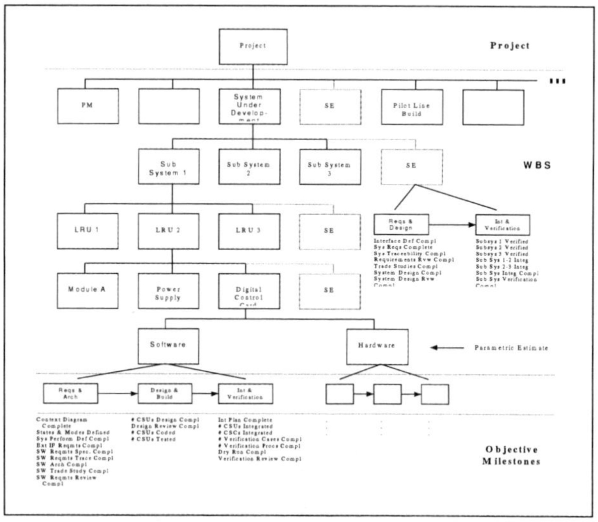

Figure 9. WBS Example

ETCP Alignment. A project's instantiation of the ETCP is documented in the project WBS as "activity networks." The activity network names closely align with the associated ETCP activity names. The activity network, an extension of a WBS leaf, defines individual activity blocks and the sequence in which they will be performed. Inclusion of this information within the WBS element is also the method by which a project's implementation of the chosen lifecycle is incorporated into the schedule. Objective milestones are the mechanism to claim earned value performance on a regular consistent basis. These milestones are the tasks, or work products, identified in the ETCP. When projects are estimated the ETCP provides a framework of the standard activities required for development projects. Historical cost data are captured and evaluated across the enterprise based on the standard WBS model and activity network.

EV Milestones. Objective milestones are essential for effectively managing project plans and accurately tracking earned value. Objective milestones help abolish subjective claiming by identifying specific, quantifiable accomplishments that are measurable. All tasks within the ETCP have quantifiable outputs that are suggested for use as earned value milestones in project plans. Tracking earned value based on objective milestones allows early detection and management of risks and opportunities on a project.

Standard Metrics. Standard metrics are available to projects and are based on the WBS schedule. Metrics can be reported by analyzing project/program change requests stored in databases. A recent enterprise analysis of engineering CRs revealed that a variety of names were being used to describe essentially the same categories of injection/detection points. This variation posed great difficulty in analyzing CRs across the BUs and enterprise. With the advent of the engineering process, the ETCP activity names can be used to consistently identify injection/detection points on CRs for projects throughout the enterprise.

ISSUES WITH AN ENTERPRISE APPROACH

Gaining Consensus. A major hurdle to conquer was creating a process that all BUs would agree they could live with. The diversity between commercial and government BUs posed the challenge of merging two different cultures. BU participation in discipline specific and cross-discipline working groups, and on the CCB provided forums for the BUs to negotiate and reach consensus. Management support demonstrated by continued CEC involvement helped the team stay motivated and break cultural barriers. Facilitation and maintenance efforts provided by CPD has helped the team to stay focused, productive and adhere to delivery schedules.

Process Definition Changes. Rockwell history has set a stage steeped in culture and tradition in terms of process evolution and practice. Prior engineering processes were heavily focused on BU specific markets. Commercial processes addressed certification and other flight safety issues not included in the government processes. Government processes addressed requirements levied by military customers that were not pertinent to the commercial businesses. Because of these differences, as the processes were merged, BU specific requirements were dropped and only the common tasks retained. Instantiation will add back the BU specific requirements. The level of process adherence and process maturity also varied. Through the years some disciplines had matured their definition into highly detailed processes. The ETCP, an enterprise-level common process framework, has met with resistance from disciplines who felt it to be a step backward from their high level of definition.

Process Framework Changes. Process definitions varied based on their focus and ranged from phase-based to activity-based to role-based. The ETCP adopted an activity-based focus to best support desired metrics collection. Successful deployment of the ETCP requires continued attention to cultural strongholds and issues. The enterprise continues to struggle to make the paradigm shift required to adopt the concept of using a single, generic enterprise-level process framework.

Project Management Process Change. Many of the prior process definitions included project management activities. In the Collins Consistent Process suite, the enterprise level business management lifecycle process currently under development, the project management activities have been moved out of the ETCP into the Management Consistent Process (MCP) so that project/program management can be developed as a single cohesive process. The engineering disciplines expressed strong dissention over this seeming loss of ownership and control of the technical project planning/management activities, especially since their current process maturity called for close coupling between management, technical and support activities. The pending release of the MCP combined with closer involvement between the developers of the MCP and CP CCB members have helped to address many of the expressed concerns.

Culture Change. Defining the process at an enterprise level and providing tools to gauge compliance can increase the visibility of project compliance. However to make process use an enterprise-wide reality senior management must be convinced that an integral relationship exists between process performance and company competitiveness. They must also be educated about their active and visible role. Senior and middle management must accept, support and facilitate process use since institutionalization of process into the engineering ranks begins with management.

THE FUTURE

Phase II. This phase, which is currently underway, involves the collection of BU methods, tools, templates and training. An updated version of the framework containing this information will be released in March 2000. Missing BU and discipline information will be identified and targeted for inclusion in a future release.

Report Cards. Work has begun to establish standard

criteria to measure a project's instantiation of the ETCP. This is an initial step toward evaluating a project's level of adherence to the framework. Use of the new ERP tool will provide management with views of cost, schedule and other planning data, including ETCP use, on all projects so that they may be consistently tracked and monitored.

Training. Computer Based Training (CBT) is being developed to respond to ETCP training needs. This will provide a practical solution to address the challenges presented by geographically distributed BUs and limited training resources (instructors and money). CCB members will act as training mentors and CPD will host periodic sessions to provide additional training as needed. The first ETCP CBT addressing the overview and the software process has been completed. Plans are in place to complete CBT material for the remaining discipline processes this year.

Document Tree. Document trees will show the relationships between the documents defined in the ETCP. The document tree will be a tool for project instantiation and a navigation tool for project libraries.

Phase III. This phase will focus on identifying enterprise level common methods based on business cases developed from objective metrics. This will include identification of the similarities, differences and variations between methods. Tailoring guidelines appropriate for methods will also be defined.

CMMI. The SE/SW CMMI is a merging of the systems and software capability models. This model will be used as a benchmark for the ETCP and will help define management and support processes at the enterprise level (i.e., training, formal configuration management, etc).

Historical Metrics. Over time, as data becomes more standardized through use of common language and process, projects will be compared against upper and lower control bounds to determine when a detailed evaluation is necessary. Collection and analysis of parametric data will enable Rockwell to identify lessons learned on projects that perform well and on those that appear to have unique difficulties. These historical data will be used to continuously improve the ETCP, methods, templates and tools.

REFERENCES

1. Software Engineering Institute (SEI) Capability Maturity Model (CMM-SW)
2. Electronic Industry Alliance (EIA) 731: Systems Engineering Capability

BIOGRAPHY

Barb Denny has over 14 years of experience in software development and has been involved in process definition and improvement for more than 9 years. She managed the commercial process group, which facilitated process improvement and historical data collection. Her focus was on software and the company's effort in achieving and maintaining CMM-SW compliance. She participated in the development of CMMI v0.2.

Richard Bennett has 17 years experience with a broad engineering background with government and industry, developing and evaluating systems/software, performing operational test and evaluation, managing projects, and assessing process compliance. He is a Senior Software Process Engineer with Rockwell Collins, Lean Electronics Division, and Consistent Process Department where he is responsible for leading development of hardware and ASIC processes. He has a BSEE from Texas Tech Univ. and MSEE from the Air Force Institute of Technology.

Enabling Changes in Systems throughout the Entire Life-Cycle – Key to Success ?

Armin P. Schulz, Ernst Fricke, Eduard Igenbergs

Division of Astronautics
Technical University of Munich
Boltzmannstrasse 15, 85748 Munich
Germany
A.Schulz@lrt.mw.tum.de, http:\\www.lrt.mw.tum.de

ABSTRACT

In the past decades the world has been changing in almost every aspect. Systems development is facing rapidly changing and increasingly global environments in markets, competition, technology, regulatory and societal systems. Systems to be delivered must be designed not only to meet customer or market needs, but increasingly to meet requirements and constraints of systems sharing its operational context and throughout their entire lifecycle. The design of a system must provide for a continuous evolution of its architecture either by upgrading a system already in service or releasing a new version.

Based on these key challenges imosed on development systems, this paper will evolve the idea of incorporating changeability into a systems architecture. Flexibility, agility, robustness, and adaptability as four key aspects of changeability will be defined and described. Design principles to enable flexibility, agility, robustness, and adaptability within integrated systems are proposed and described. A measurement of a degree of implementation of certain aspects of changeability as well as cost associated with it are addressed with metrics. A basic process outlining and guiding an application of the framework described concludes this paper. Examples from varying industries will illustrate the applicability and implementation of selected principles.

Thus this paper spans a view from **why**, **when** and **where**, **what**, and **how** changeability has to be incorporated into a systems architecture.

INTRODUCTION

During the past decades several global factors tremendously shifted our world to a more complex one in almost every aspect. Based on Wenzel et al. (1997) and Schulz & Fricke (1999), three aspects are major drivers of development systems within the future:

- Dynamic Marketplace
- Technological Evolution
- Variety of Environments

Dynamic Marketplace. A high number of new markets is emerging rapidly , while existing markets are changing. Staying ahead of competition requires high responsiveness in terms of supporting late design decisions of a system architecture to narrow down the time gap between design freeze and system delivery. The ability to address evolving customer and market needs by implementing late changes into a system architecture will affect a systems success throughout its entire lifecycle. That is architectures must not only incorporate the ability to be changed easily and rapidly within late design phases but also when already being in service. Additionally, an increasing trend towards individualization requests for an individualization of mass products. Therefore the degree of variety supported by standard product platforms and their derivatives becomes crucial for commercial success.

Automotive industry provides an example, where luxury car manufacturers statistically produce no car twice due to a high number of variants imposed by a wide range of equipment selected by the individual customer.

Technological Evolution. The fast evolution of all our systems (Ring & Fricke, 1998) driven by a half life of technologies significantly shorter than system life cycles[1] or even system development cycle times leads to further problems for system architectures. Functions of systems are evolving rapidly within a system life cycle, in terms of number and performance of available functions. Or as Iansiti (1998) puts it '*... many business environments no longer have a stable technology base, instead it is novel, changing rapidly and unpredictable ...*'. Therefore, steady insertion of new technologies is necessary to keep a system competitive. Processes, organizational structures, tools or methods also have to

[1] The gap between technology half-life and system lifecycle is in particular driven by an increasing percentage of system functionality being based on electronic and software

be adapted accordingly.

For example the wireless application protocol (WAP) has been recently introduced into the mobile telecommunication market to offer mobile internet access. Older cell phones do not support this protocol, but by installing a software update, short message service (SMS) may be used to achieve mobile internet access.

Variety of Environments. The composition of those systems increasingly relies on components based on rather diverse technologies and origin (i.e. mechanical and electrical hardware, embedded software, etc.). An integration of all those systems results in more complexity and integrity in all systems. Additionally, those complex systems are embedded into a higher system, that is they are part of a system of systems (e.g. a single satellite within a communication constellation, a car within cooperative traffic management, a cellular phone in varying national networks). As pointed out before also these system are subject to a dynamic marketplace and an increasing technological evolution. Since the dynamics of our economy is increasingly ruled by the logic of networks (Kelly, 1998) the elements of the overall system are highly interrelated and affect each other.

Thus each system is affected by changes and the evolution of its embedding system and/or the systems within its operational context. Hence system architectures also need to incorporate the ability to adopt towards changes within its environment.

Key Challenges. Eventually these three drivers of future system development lead to two key challenges which have to be met within the design of system architectures.

(1) system architectures have to incorporate the ability to be **changed easily** and **rapidly**
(2) system architectures have to incorporate the ability **to be insensitive** or **adaptable towards** changing **environments**

It is moreover necessary to reduce the time gap between freezing properties, functions, features and architectures of a product and the product market delivery to a absolute minimum. In a study on Toyota's development system Ward et al. (1995) come to the conclusion that delaying design decisions is a major success factor for Toyota's superior performance in development time and quality. Ward and his co-authors call that the 'Second Toyota Paradox'. However, this approach being recognized within Toyota's development is more related to the implementation of the system architecture design process, incorporating the principles introduced and will be elaborated in future work.

ARCHITECTING FOR SYSTEM EVOLUTION ?

Evolve Idea. The current practice is to prevent and front-load changes, being based on the experience that late changes – and therefore any evolution – of systems are very costly. This is described by the 'Rule of Ten' stating that with each subsequent program phase the implementation of a change becomes ten times more costly and therefore recommends to prevent or front-load changes (e.g. Boehm, 1981, Clark & Fujimoto, 1991). But in today's fast moving business environments this is simply not enough, as preventing change and evolution is a serious obstacle to technological evolution and endangers competitive advantage due to technological leadership. With regard to front-loading Wheelwright & Clark (1992) point out that even the best forecasters and most clever downstream engineers will encounter unexpected changes in design.

Hence, companies have to deliver systems incorporating an architecture which supports changes throughout its entire life-cycle. Being part of higher systems (system of systems), as well as being part of a human response system (markets, customers and their needs), the ability to adapt towards changing environments is a further requirement. This is supported by different other authors (e.g. Adaptive Systems Group 1998, Dove 1999, Iansiti, 1998, Kelly, 1998, Open Systems Joint Task Force, 1998). In particular Kelly (1998) pointed out that instability and imbalance are the norm in today's economy and therefore systems optimized to a single design point will not last very long. But not only delivered systems have to have those abilities. Companies itself need to incorporate these abilities within their entire development system (i.e. development processes, test and verification, manufacturing, etc.).

There is a set of distinguishing characteristics, for which type of system architectures an incorporation of changeability should be considered or should not be considered. Steiner (1998) introduced a set of distinguishing features for enduring architectures, which is in the context of system evolution comparable to the approach the authors have taken. Basically incorporating changeability within a system architecture is required for systems, which

- are subject to a dynamic (that is rapidly and strongly changing) marketplace with varying customer base and strong competition
- have a long lifecycle compared to cycle times of technologies driving major quality attributes (i.e functionality, performance, reliability, etc.)
- are highly interrelated with other systems sharing their operational context

- require high deployment and maintenance cost

SOLUTION APPROACH

Four Aspects of Changeability. As an answer to the challenges imposed on today's development system the approach 'Design for Changeability', which has been first proposed by Fricke (1999) is introduced. Basically four aspects of changeability are distinguished:

- Flexibility
- Agility
- Robustness
- Adaptability

These four aspects describe a systems ability to cope with changes within itself or its environment (Schulz & Fricke, 1999). A set of varying design principles is used to enable each aspect of changeability within architecture design. While some principles only support a single aspect, other principles support several aspects. A different mix of practices supports the implementation of the principles and is partially domain specific. Finally, a set of metrics is needed to evaluate and control the design of a system architecture regarding changeability.

Flexibility and Agility. *Flexibility* represents the property of a system to be changed easily, that is low effort and without undesired effects. *Agility* represents the property of a system to implement necessary changes rapidly. Flexibility is a prerequisite to achieve agility, i.e., agility is an evolutionary level of flexibility (Figure 2).

Robustness and Adaptability *Robustness* characterizes systems, which are not affected by changing environments, that is robust systems deliver their intended functionality under varying operating conditions without being changed. Taguchi (1993) and Clausing (1994) have performed extensive research in the area of robustness within systems. *Adaptability* characterizes a systems ability to adapt itself towards changing environments to deliver its intended functionality. Robustness is a prerequisite to achieve adaptability, i.e. adaptability is an evolutionary level of robustness (Figure 2).

Solution Framework. The Design Principles are enablers for the realization of changeability. Among the principles being identified as characterizing flexible, agile, robust, and adaptive systems, a distinction is made between *Basic Principles,* supporting all four aspects of changeability, and *Extending Principles,* supporting only selected aspects of changeability and also having interrelations (Schulz & Fricke, 1999). The matrix in Figure 2 indicates which principle is contributing to what extent to each aspect of changeability. Although examples presented in this paper are mainly covering product systems, the authors believe the proposed principles to be applicable to any type of system (i.e. processes, organizations, etc.). Whatever type of system is under analysis, the design of its architecture is based on a system's elements, their attributes in terms of functions and properties, and their (inter-) relations. The degree to which a single principle is incorporated within a system architecture may be measured using various types of metrics.

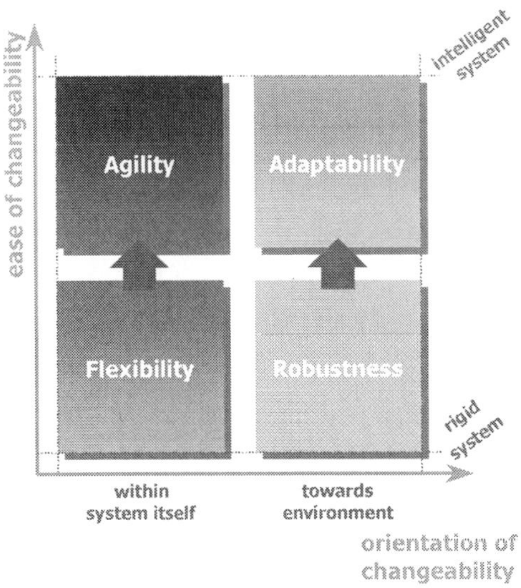

Figure 1 The Four Aspects of Changeability

The principles have been derived of various research projects and a number of sources in literature like Adaptive System Group (1999), Altshuller (1984), Dove (1999), Fey (1998), Fricke (1999), Maier (1998), Negele (1998), Open Systems Joint Task Force (1998), Rechtin (1991), Rechtin and Maier (1997), Suh (1990).

THE BASIC PRINCIPLES

Ideality/Simplicity. This principle is derived from the basic Pattern of Evolution in TRIZ[2], that all system evolve towards increasing ideality. Ideality in this context is defined as the ratio of a systems sum of useful functions against a systems sum of harmful or undesired effects. Based on that principle an ideal system consists of only useful functions, which may be interpreted as establishing small, simple units/elements with a minimized number of interfaces (loose coupling among and strong cohesion within modules) within an architecture. Moreover, an ideal system makes use of already existing resources and applies principles of

[2] comprehensive material on TRIZ and the patterns of evolution is contained in Altshuller (1984), Fey (1998), and Schulz and Clausing (1998)

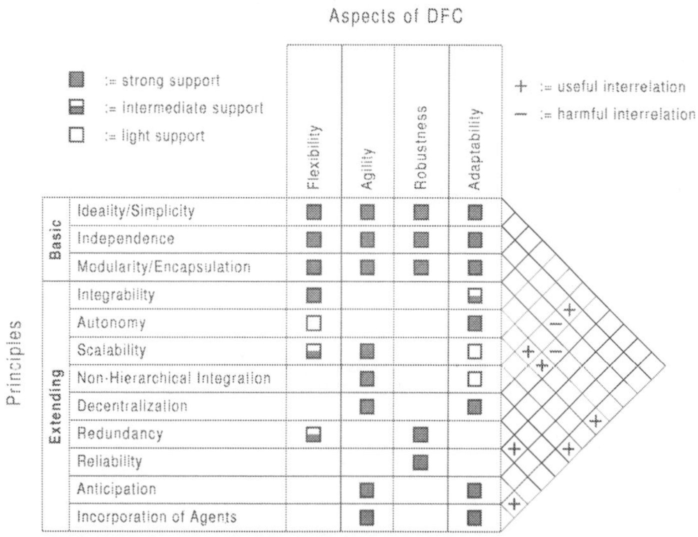

Figure 2. The Aspect-Principle-Correlation Matrix (Schulz & Fricke, 1999)

design streamlining. A similar approach can be found in Function Analysis (Akiyama, 1991), where the number of secondary functions, i.e., functions only supporting primary or main functions is to be minimized.

The principle of ideality/simplicity directly correlates to the information axiom (second axiom) in axiomatic design as introduced by Suh (1990). Suh defines an 'information content' incorporated within each system architecture, which is basically representing the degree of complexity needed to describe the architecture. A system architecture with a low information content is thus less complex, that is 'simpler' and therefore to prefer or to aim at. Suh also provides an approach to measure the information content and thus to evaluate alternative architectures.

Independence. This principle is derived from the axiomatic approach to design as introduced by Suh (1990). According to the first axiom in axiomatic design each system function or functional requirement has to be satisfied by an independent design parameter. A design parameter is representing the physical embodiment of a functions solution, that is i.e. a physical principle, a parameter, a component, etc. Independence of design parameters means, that changing a design parameter does not affect any related design parameters and thus not the proper operation of related functions. Suh (1990) distinguishes three degrees or levels of independence, which are defined as coupled, decoupled, and uncoupled. The relation between system functions and design parameter and their degree or level of coupling is displayed using design matrices. Capturing the properties of an architecture with respect to independence in that type of matrices is basis for evaluating alternative architectures applying metrics.

Modularity/Encapsulation. Building a system architecture that clusters the system's functions into various modules while minimizing the coupling among the modules (loose coupling) and maximizing the cohesion within the modules (strong cohesion) yields great benefits. In general two basic types of modularity may be distinguished, vertical and horizontal modularity. While horizontal modularity represents the clustering of a systems functions in different modules within a common layer, vertical modularity represents a layering of an architecture. According to Tate (1999) three types of modularity[3] may be distinguished, which basically correlate to the different type of architecture under consideration within the various phases of the design phase (e.g. problem architecture, operational architecture, functional architecture, physical architecture, etc.).

Modular architectures support reuse of elements, modules or even entire sections of an architecture with a certain scope of functionality and defined interfaces. Ease of exchanging and adapting modules or layers is facilitated incorporating self-sufficient, distinct, and not intimately integrated units. An implementation of platform concepts is possible as well as the use as a reference architecture for system evolution. Robustness is greatly enhanced since the impact of changes or noises is limited or isolated within the modules or layers.

SELECTED EXTENDING PRINCIPLES

Integrability. This principle is key to achieving flexibility and adaptability. Integrability is characterized by compatibility and inter-operability applying generic, open, or common/consistent interfaces. Compatibility and inter-operability are necessary in a rapidly changing environment built of multiple interrelated systems. These abilities are even enhanced by implementing only mature and robust functions delivering a constant range/degree of functionality and thus ensuring stable interfaces independent of the environment. Concerning the principle of intgrability there is a strong correlation to the work being pursued in the area of open systems which is mainly driven by the DoD and related

[3] Tate (1999) distinguishes between resource (ease of manufacturing), interfacial (independence of system modules), and operational (range of operational variety) modularity

industries (Open Systems Joint Task Force, 1998). The principle of integrability is in particular critical for architectures in the context of system of systems, that is architectures having strong interrelations with systems sharing its operational context. This perspective is also supported by Maier (1998).

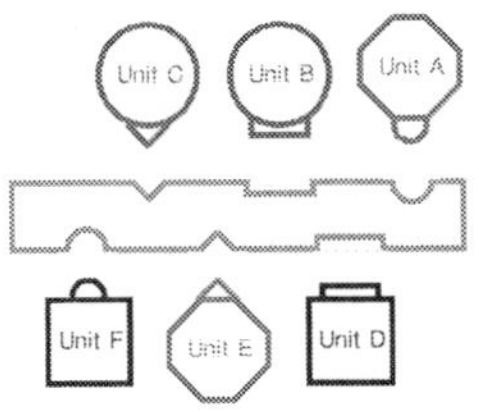

(a) proprietary interfaces
(all units have specific interfaces and are not interchangeable)

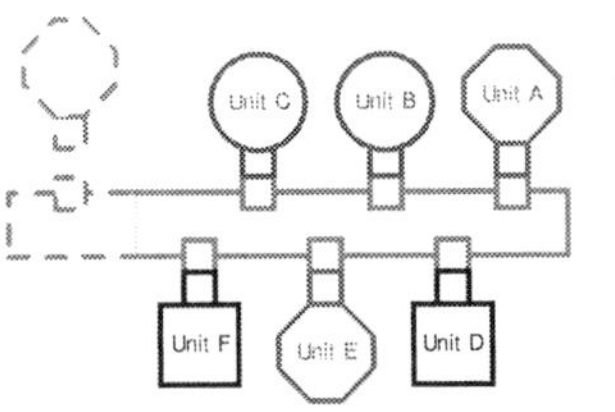

(b) generic and common interfaces
(all units share a common interface and are interchangeable)

Figure 2. Principle of Integrability

As an example for integrability web-clients may be mentioned. These clients serve as a generic interface for information retrieval independent from the hardware platform they are running on. To cope with the dramatically increasing number of Electronic Control Units (ECUs) automotive industry introduced bus communication among the ECUs to provide common interfaces for at least groups of ECUs. A new ECU could be added with regard to the already existing interface. This is also an example for scalability.

Decentralization. This principle is key to agility and adaptability. Based on loose coupling and strong cohesion a decentralized distribution of control (see autonomy), information, resources, attributes, and properties within the system architecture strengthens the capability of the system to rapidly adapt itself towards its environment and to respond autonomously to changing requirements. Thus necessary decisions are made at the point of 'best knowledge and information', while all knowledge and information has to remain accessible throughout the entire system for decisions on system level. This also enables the allocation of attributes or properties to the most appropriate location within the system.

A critical aspect within distributed control is to ensure consistency of objects/units throughout the entire system, that is this principle may have a harmful interaction with the principle of integrability.

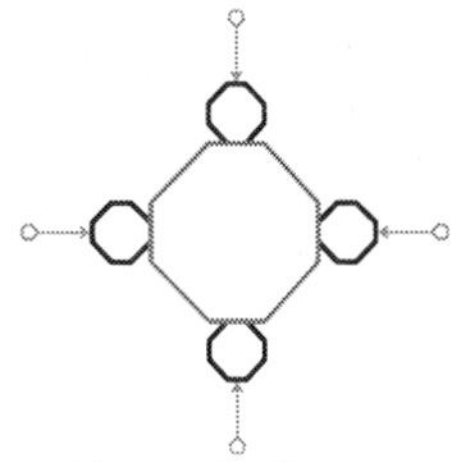

(a) centralized system
(all resources located at a single place)

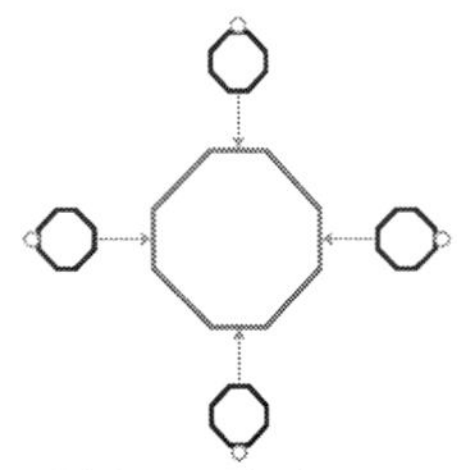

(b) decentralized system
(resources distributed to appropriate locations)

Figure 3. Principle of Decentralization

Within modern fly-by-wire flight control systems elevators, rudders, or spoilers are no longer steered by force of the pilot but by actuators located directly at the elevator, rudder, or spoiler and acting on stimulation by electric signals.

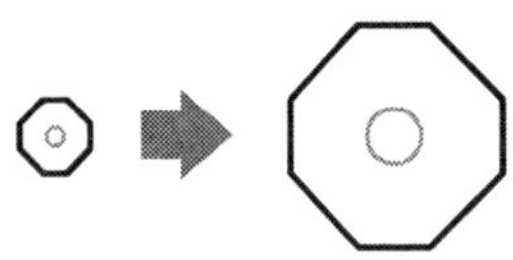

(a) single element scaled by up-/downsizing
its characteristic parameters

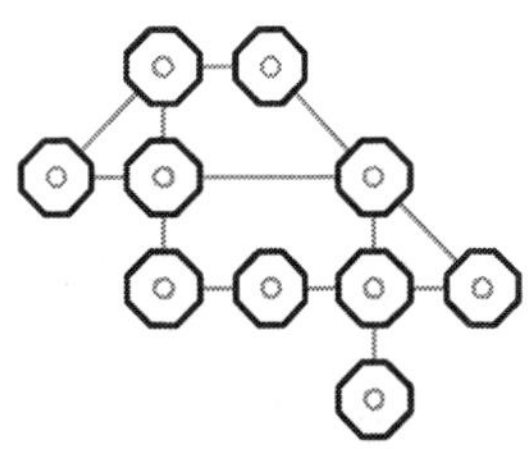

(b) increase/decrease number of multiple identical
elements linked to provide a scaled architecture

Figure 4. Principle of Scalability

Scalability/Self-Similarity. This principle is a key to flexibility, agility and adaptability. Based on elements independent from scale (fractals), architectures may be scaled upwards or downward. Basically there are two different ways of approaching scalability. First several identical elements of the architecture may be linked together to provide scaled performance or functionality. Second a single element of the architecture may be scaled by up-/downsizing its characteristic parameters. As a basis the system architecture has to provide the necessary capability for an unrestricted increase or decrease of total unit population within the system.

Typical examples for scalability besides bus communication in today's cars' on-board networks (see integrability) are expandable launchers using additional boosters for higher payload into orbit (e.g. Ariane 4, Titan IV, etc.).

Non-Hierarchical Integration. This principle is key to agility and adaptability. Non-hierarchical integration is characterized by linking object/units across the total system, that is with no respect to any type of modularity or encapsulation. This ensures a direct, flexible, and fast communication, negotiation, or interaction among objects/units. It also covers the evolution of new and the destruction of obsolete links among objects/units, partially self-organized by objects/units based on autonomy and incorporation of agents.

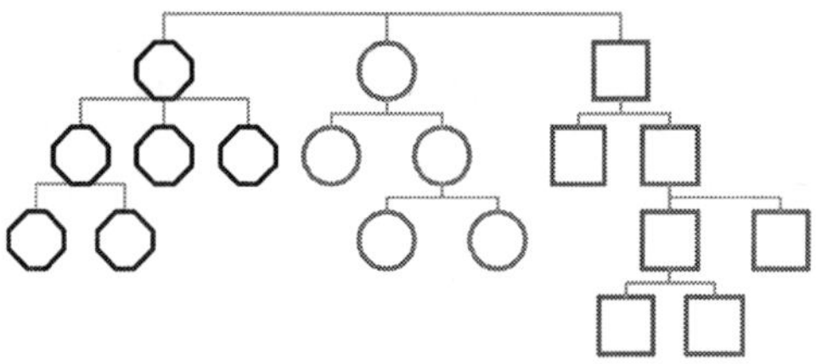

(a) hierarchical integration
(inflexible and slow communication across system)

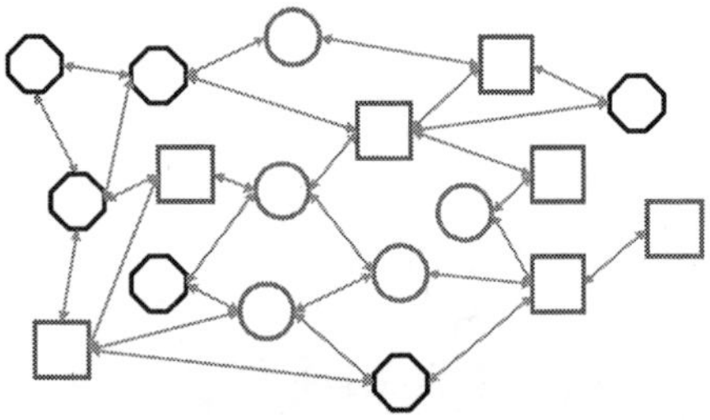

(b) non-hierarchical integration
(interaction interfaces on same level ensure fast and flexible communication across system)

Figure 5. Principle of Non-Hierarchical Integration

A critical aspect within non-hierarchical integration is establishing links among objects/units within different modules or layers of the system architecture, that is this principle might have a harmful interaction with the principle of modularity/ encapsulation.

Any type of cross-functional or integrated product team represents a typical example for non-hierarchical integration. Moreover the world wide web is another example for rapidly changing but direct communication based on standardized and common interfaces (i.e. TCP/IP Protocol).

PRACTICES AND METRICS

Practices. The enabling principles introduced in the paragraph above merely indicate which characteristics system architectures should incorporate in order to be changeable. But are these characteristics actually implemented within the design of a certain architecture? The need to answer this question lead to the definition of a variety of practices supporting the implementation of single principles. Due to the scope of this paper only few simple examples shall outline the general idea.

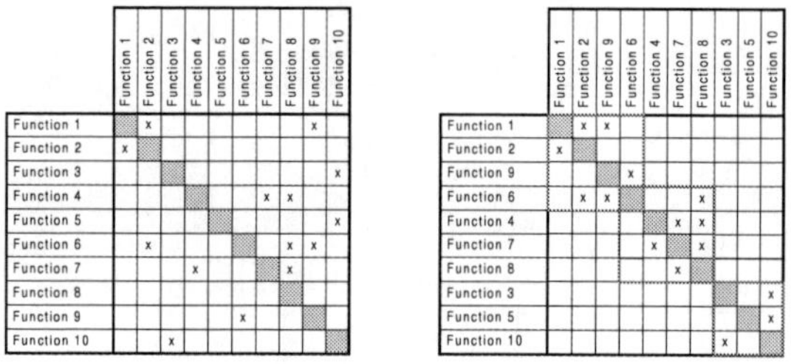

a) Initial Design Structure Matrix

b) Restructured Design Structure Matrix

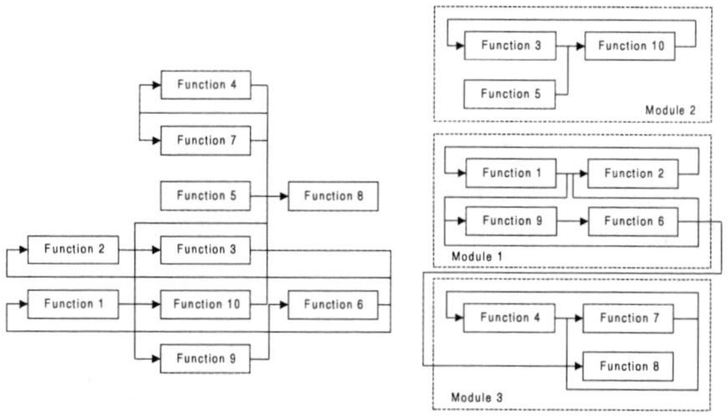

a) Initial Functional Model

b) Restructured System Architecture

Figure 6 Defining Modularity using the Design Structure Matrix

Within the principle of modularity a well-known practice can be introduced. A clustering of system objects/units into modules is supported by the design structure matrix, which has been first introduced by Steward (1981) and is illustrated in Figure 6. Design structure matrices capture the existence and type of interrelations among a system's elements. Various algorithms depending on the objectives are applicable to restructure these matrices in order to achieve a modular/encapsulated architecture (Browning, 1998). Based on the resulting clusters within the architecture platform concepts are applicable to incorporate rather static functions, that is functions not imposed to rapid technological evolution and highly dependent on specific market segments, into a common platform, serving as a basis for a flexible product family. Rather dynamic functions, that is functions imposed to rapid technological evolution and highly dependent on specific market segments, will be incorporated into derivatives of the platform.

Measurement. It is not necessarily useful to implement changeability into a system architecture to its full extent, that is implement all four aspects of changeability throughout the entire system architecture. Basically the architecting process should be guided by the question: **Where** in the system architecture do I need **what type of** and **how much** changeability?

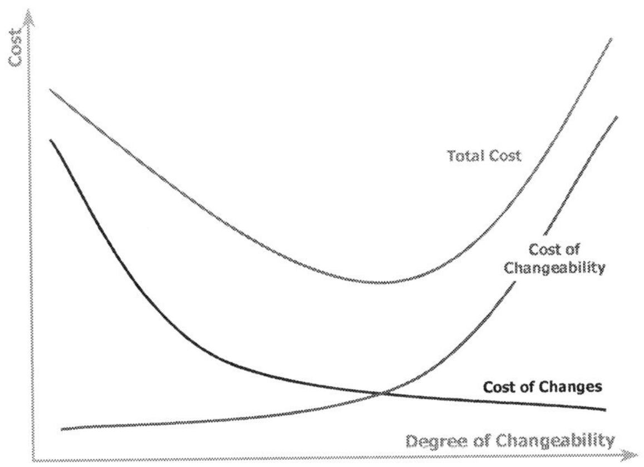

Figure 7 Degree of Changeability vs. Sources of Cost

Further, implementation of changeability might be accompanied by a certain effort in terms of money or time. The trade-off between the right price to pay or the right amount of time to spend to the expected benefit is a critical consideration. Therefore our current research focuses on advancing our knowledge in two critical areas:

First, the measurement of the degree to which certain principles enabling changeability have to be implemented within a system competing in a specific business environment. This area is mainly guided by the following questions:

- How much X (i.e. modularity) is incorporated?
- How much X (i.e. integrability) is required?

Second, the measurement of the impact an implementation of certain principles within a system architecture has. This area is guided by the following questions:

- What is the cost for implementing it ?
- What is the benefit for implementing it ?

A typical relationship between the cost imposed on a system architecture due to incorporating changeability and due to changes expected within its lifecycle is illustrated in Figure 7.

Cost of changeability within an architecture is typically imposed by higher design or manufacturing effort due to **incorporating** changeability, while cost of changes are typically imposed by a higher effort to change a system architecture at any time within its lifecycle due to **not incorporating** changeability. Both curves result in a distribution of the total cost of a system architecture depending on its degree of changeability. A certain range of changeability within the architecture results in minimized total cost. This window of opportunity is what should be aimed at during the design of a specific system architecture.

CONCLUSIONS

Benefits. To stay ahead of competition in dynamic environments it is inevitable to ensure sustaining superior system capabilities, i.e., offering state of the art systems throughout their entire lifecycle. Therefore, systems and their architectures have to offer changeability throughout their lifecycle not only within themselves but also towards their environments. To cope with these challenges a strategy 'Design for Changeability' is proposed, incorporating the following four attributes.

- Flexibility
- Agility
- Robustness
- Adaptability

System architectures characterized by these attributes will yield great enhancements. Technology insertion throughout the entire system life-cycle to ensure superior system capabilities and customized functionality is possible. Upgrade opportunities and the ease of customization leads to high attractiveness to customers or stakeholders. Rapid responsiveness to emerging and changing markets is facilitated by adapting the architectures accordingly based on modular and platform concepts. Reduced life cycle cost result from cross-platform integrability, reuse of units, modules, or architectures, while the impact of changes necessary to adapt the architecture throughout the entire lifecycle is minimized.

Discussion and Outlook. Although a wide range of benefits already has been achieved there are open issues which have not been addressed yet. A consistent framework building from strategies incorporating the four attributes of 'Design for Changeability', principles characterizing the properties of architectures meeting the four attributes, practices supporting the principle's implementation, and metrics measuring and controlling the maturity of implementation has been proposed. The principles introduced are not considered to be comprehensive yet. Moreover case studies have to be performed ensuring applicability of the framework and its elements. The question what principles and practices are to applied in which environment and context is still to be answered. Interrelations, both useful and harmful, among the strategies, principles, practices, and metrics so far have only been identified on a very high level and are a main subject to further research.

REFERENCES

Adaptive Systems Group, The Harlequin Group, http://www.harlequin.com/products/asg, 1998

Akiyama, K.V., Function Analysis – Systematic Improvement of Quality and Performance. Productivity Press, Cambridge, 1991

Altshuller, G., Creativity as an Exact Science. Gordon & Breach Science Publishers, New York, 1984

Boehm, B.W., Software Engineering Economics. Prentice Hall, Englewood Cliffs, 1981

Browning, T.R., Modeling and Analyzing Cost, Schedule and Performance in Complex System Product Development, Ph.D Thesis, Massachusetts Institute of Technology, 1998

Clark, K. and Fujimoto, T., Product Development Performance. Strategy, Organization and Management in the World Auto Industries, Harvard Business School Press, Boston, 1991

Clausing, D., Total Quality Development, ASME Press, New York, 1994

Dove, R.K., Design Principles for Highly Adaptable Business Systems, Paradigm Shift International, Taos County, NM, 1999

Fey, V., Theory of Inventive Problem Solving (TRIZ), The TRIZ Group, 1998

Fricke, E., Der Änderungsprozeß als Grundlage einer nutzerzentrierten Systementwicklung, Ph.D. Thesis. Technical University of Munich, 1999

Fricke, E., Gebhard B., Negele H., Igenbergs E., No Innovation Process without Changes, but... Proceedings of the 7th International Symposium of INCOSE, Los Angeles, 1997

Iansiti, M., Technology Integration, Harvard Business School Press, Boston, 1998.

Kelly, K., New Rules for the New Economy, Viking Penguin, New York, 1998.

Maier, M., Architecting Principles for System of Systems, Systems Engineering, Vol. I, No. 4, 1998, pp. 267-284

Open Systems Joint Task Force, (OSJTF) http://www.acd.osd.mil/osjtf, 1998

Rechtin, E., Systems Architecting - Creating and Building Complex Systems, Prentice Hall, 1991

Rechtin, E. and Maier, M.W., The Art of Systems Architecting. CRC Press, Boca Raton, FL, 1997

Ring, J. and Fricke, E., Rapid Evolution of All Your Systems – Problem or Opportunity?, Proceedings of IEEE 17th DASC, Seattle, October 1998

Schulz, A., Fricke, E., Incorporating Flexibility, Agility, Robustness, and Adaptability within the Design of Integrated Systems – Key to Success?, Proceedings of the IEEE/AIAA 18th Digital Avionics Systems Conference, St. Louis, 1999

Steiner, Rick, Systems Architecture and Evolvability - Definitions and Perspective. Proceedings of 8th Annual Symposium of INCOSE, Vancouver, 1998

Steward, D.V., The Design Structure System – A Method for Managing the Design of Complex Systems, IEEE Transactions on Engineering Management, Vol. 28/3, 1981, p. 71-74

Suh, N.P., The Principles of Design, New York, Oxford University Press, 1990

Taguchi, G., Taguchi on Robust Technology. ASME Press, New York, 1993

Tate, D., A Roadmap for Decomposition: Activities, Theories, and Tools for System Design, Ph.D. Thesis, Massachusetts Institute of Technology, 1999

Ward, Allen, Jeffrey K. Liker, John J. Cristiano and Durward K. Sobek II, The Second Toyota Paradox: How Delaying Decisions Can Make Better Cars Faster, Sloan Management Review 36(3): 43-61, 1995

Wenzel, S., Bauch, T., Fricke, E., Negele, H., Concurrent Engineering and More – A Systematic Approach to Successful Product Development, Proceedings of the 7th International Symposium of INCOSE, Los Angeles, 1997

Wheelwright, S., Clark, K., Revolutionizing Product Development, The Free Press, New York, 1992

AUTHOR'S BIOGRAPHIES

Armin P. Schulz is Research Assistant and PhD candidate at the Division of Astronautics at the Technical University of Munich. He received his master's degree in aerospace engineering from the Technical University of Munich in 1998, after completing his master's thesis at the Center for Innovation in Product Development at MIT. His research focuses on technology development processes, systems design and architecting. He is a co-founder and currently secretary of the German Chapter of INCOSE.

Ernst Fricke is Assistant Professor at the Division of Astronautics at the Technical University of Munich. He received his master's degree in aerospace engineering from the Technical University of Munich in 1994 and his Ph.D. in Systems Engineering from the Technical University of Munich in January 1999. His research focuses on managing changes and evolution in product development. He is a co-founder and active member of the German Chapter of INCOSE.

Eduard Igenbergs is Professor of Astronautics

and Director of the Division of Astronautics at the Technical University of Munich. He has a Ph.D. and a masters degree in mechanical engineering. He had a dust counter experiment on the japanese HITEN spacecraft to the moon and a space debris experiment on board the German BREMSAT. Another dust counter experiment will fly 1998 to mars with the japanese Planet-B spacecraft. He developed the Munich Space Chair (MSC), a body restraint system on board MIR. He has been teaching and researching in the field of Systems Engineering for more than 15 years. He is an active member of the German Chapter of INCOSE.

COTS: What You Get (In Addition to the Potential Development Savings)

James E. Long
Vitech Corporation
2070 Chain Bridge Road, Suite 320
Vienna, Virginia 22182
(703) 883-2270

Abstract. It comes as no surprise that incorporating an existing component into a system means you save in having to develop the component yourself—savings in schedule and development costs. What often is surprising is the impact that incorporating an existing component has on the system engineering process.

This paper reviews the system engineering process and shows where the incorporation of COTS (Commercial-off-the-shelf) and GOTS (Government-off-the-shelf) fits into the process. It discusses the savings you get from a COTS component as well as the cost of these savings. Also described are the issues of interfaces and life cycle maintenance and modification. Once you incorporate a COTS component, how do you handle the upgrades to the COTS? Before jumping in to take advantage of COTS products, take time to consider whether the system and design process are robust enough to handle the additional constraints.

INTRODUCTION

A goal of system engineering a system is to define the set of cooperating components that comprise the system and satisfy the originating requirements, including cost, schedule, and performance. The purpose of this paper is to discuss how the consideration of COTS (Commercial-off-the-shelf) and GOTS (Government-off-the-shelf) system components impact the system engineering process. The emphasis here is on the top-down and middle-out process, since the reverse engineering of an existing system starts with a system consisting of legacy components.

The consideration of COTS has received added emphasis in recent years because of the potential to significantly reduce the time-to-market and cost-to-market of a system under development. However, this approach does not come for free. Since COTS elements already exist independent of your system, they were probably built to satisfy a set of requirements that may vary widely from those you need for a given component of your system. Matching the COTS interfaces, behavior, and life-cycle characteristics to your system may be challenging.

BACKGROUND AND CONTEXT

In order to put the subject in context, let's look at an overview of the system engineering process as shown in Figure 1.

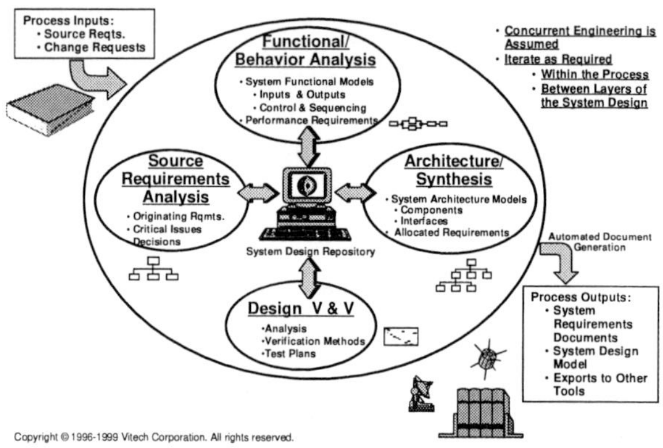

Figure 1. The System Engineering Process: An Overview

The COTS element is involved in the Architecture/Synthesis activity where the physical architecture of the system is defined. The physical architecture is comprised of those hardware, software,

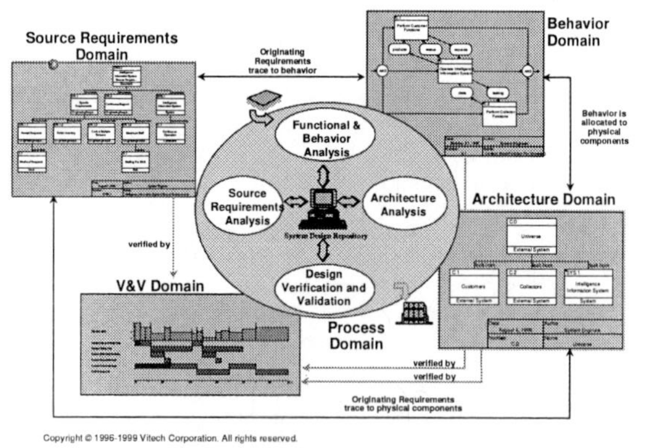

Figure 2. The System Engineering Process: The Domains

and human elements and their interconnectivity that define the deliverable system. Figure 2 shows the results of the activities in each domain.

DECIDING TO USE COTS

The decision to use COTS components can arise in two ways: it can be given as an original requirement from the customer, or it can arise later, as you are adding layers of detail to your physical component hierarchy diagram. In the case where the decision to use COTS is directed from the customer, it may appear to some that the inclusion of the COTS component in the system engineering process requires a major change to the process, but this is not the case. Looking at the system engineering process as shown in Figure 3, this capability has always been provided in *Activity 3, Capture Originating Architecture Constraints*. The requirement to use a specific COTS as a component in the system is viewed as an Originating Constraint from the customer and is handled just like other originating architecture constraints such as a specific printer or specific word processing tool.

Often the decision whether to use COTS isn't an original requirement and doesn't arise until you are adding layers of detail to your physical component hierarchy as represented by *Activity 6, Derive Component Hierarchy* of Figure 3. Each layer of the

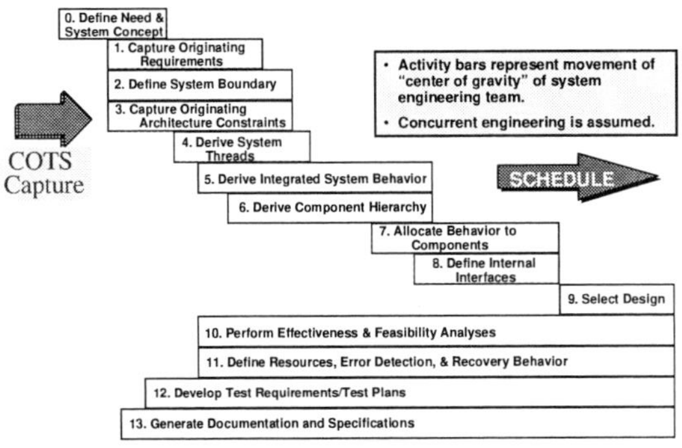

Figure 3. Where a Requirement for COTS Fits On The Road Map

component hierarchy represents concurrent engineering activities. Beginning with Layer 1, as shown in Figure 4, you add detail to each of the four primary activities and you do not go to the next layer until the current layer is completed and verified.

As you add components to each layer of the decomposition, you make a develop-or-buy decision for each component. If there is an existing element that fits the needs (functional, physical, cost, and political) you have the option to use it as a part of your system.

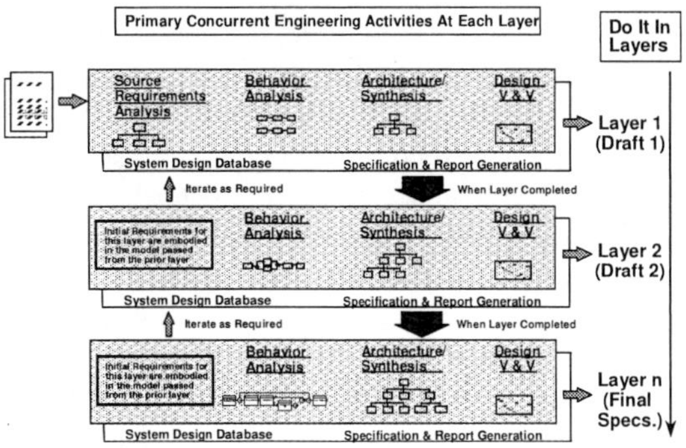

Figure 4. The Onion Model. Do Your System System Engineering in Increments/Layers

Figure 5 shows an example of the physical architecture for one layer of the Automated Personal Assistance System (APAS) system.

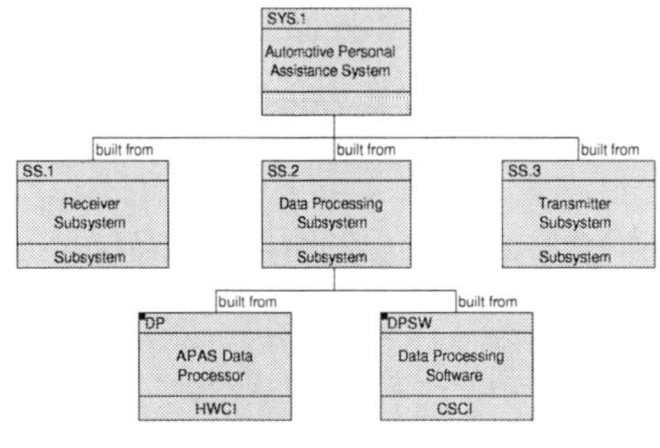

Figure 5. Component Hierarchy For The APAS

As you develop the physical architecture and select or identify those components that could be satisfied by a COTS product, you have the potential to save development schedule and cost by eliminating the need to further specify and develop that element in-house.

WHAT IS PROVIDED?

A commercial product (COTS) or government product (GOTS) comes with two predefined features: the physical interface and the behavior (stimulus-response characteristics).

The physical interface of the COTS has already been defined and implemented, and your system must be designed to integrate with it. Modifying the COTS interface to match your design violates the concept and reason for using the COTS component in the first place.

In addition, the COTS behavior has already been defined. Its response to each stimulus and combination of stimuli is already implemented. Modifying this behavior modifies the COTS product, which would not result in the desired development schedule and cost savings. Although, since the documentation of the COTS may be less than complete, it's possible you may be required to analyze and document this alien component.

You want the COTS product to be just as much an element of your system as if you had designed and developed it. This means that the test plans should be expanded to incorporate COTS and to catch COTS inconsistencies. An ideal system consists of a collection of cooperating components, including any COTS.

LIFE CYCLE PROBLEMS AND OPTIONS

You should expect new releases of the COTS component to occur during the operational life of your system. These updates potentially involve changes to the interface or changes to the COTS behavior. Sometimes these changes are minor, but sometimes they can include a complete overhaul of functionality. You need to be prepared to deal with these changes should they occur.

Your engineering options to handle new releases of COTS components are to:

* Design enough flexibility into the system to absorb these future and unknown changes.
* Decide to not accept any future releases of the COTS. This means that you have an element in your system that does not have supplier support during part of your system's operational life.
* Plan Product Improvement Cycles in your product's life cycle for accepting COTS upgrades.

Whichever option you choose, dealing with new releases of the COTS component means increased Configuration Management and Logistics effort during the Operations and Maintenance phase of your system, especially if multiple copies of the system exist.

DESIGN PROCESS PROBLEMS?

If the COTS decision is made too early in the system design cycle, it may reduce the designer's ability to produce a "balanced" system. This is like earlier days in which the design process was crippled with a "Hardware First" philosophy.

OTHER OBSERVATIONS

As you decide whether to use COTS, keep in mind,

* The COTS documentation is usually not adequate or completely accurate, causing you to test/verify the real COTS interfaces and stimulus/response behavior
* The COTS product you need is often not released yet
* If you spend time and effort to modify COTS, it isn't COTS anymore

The COTS approach often results in shifting problems into future support in order to get reduced time-to-market now

CONCLUSION: SHOULD YOU USE COTS?

Yes, you should take advantage of COTS products, but make sure that the system and the design process are robust enough to handle the additional constraints. COTS alone is not the "silver bullet".

REFERENCES

Reference list.

Baker, Loyd and Long, James E. "Specifying A System Using ERA Information Models," *Proceedings of the Sixth Annual International Symposium of the International Council on Systems Engineering*, Volume 1, 1996, pp. 399-405.

Buede, Dennis M. and Long, James E., "System Engineering – The Complete Process," *A Tutorial for the Washington Metropolitan Area Chapter of the International Council on System Engineering*, (Vienna, VA, March 28, 1998).

BIOGRAPHY

Mr. James Long is the President of Vitech Corporation – the developer of the system engineering support tool CORE®. He has been a performing system engineer and innovator since creating the first behavior diagrams (then called Function Sequence Diagrams) at TRW in late 1967. He played a key technical and management role in the maturing and application of that system engineering process and technology at TRW. Both CORE® and RDD-100® are based on the TRW developments.

He is a member of INCOSE and served as vice-president and then president of the Washington Metropolitan Area Chapter, the largest chapter of INCOSE.

Mr. Long has been selected as an Eminent Engineer by Tau Beta Pi, the honorary engineering scholastic society. The eminent engineering designation is recognition for career achievement in engineering

The Discovery Based Development Approach: A Process Aberration Or A Better Way To Develop Complex Applications?

Jeffrey K. Shupp
Management & Data Systems, Lockheed Martin Corporation
P.O.Box 8048, Philadelphia, PA 19101

ABSTRACT

The world of complex software systems has been marred by a less than stellar track record. These systems have largely been the domain of civil or military government procurement, as opposed to commercial industry, since the former institutions can absorb not only the tremendous initial costs and long development time, but also the intrinsically higher risk of initial failure. However, the commercial world is beginning to move quickly toward much more sophisticated applications, and evidence suggests similar or worse rates of failures as complexity is increased.

One such complex system has been under development for five years at M&DS. In early 1998, it was headed for a classic default of specified capabilities on all major fronts: runtime performance, functional stability and quality. This paper examines the circumstances that led to this state, and the success that has since been achieved. Most important is not the fact that a recovery had been accomplished, but rather how a new approach, called out in this paper as *Discovery Based Development*, was instituted to repair the damage and reputation in weeks instead of months or years. Armed with this technique, and applied earlier in the normal incremental or spiral developments that typify the commercial marketplace, a much higher success rate is quite possible for complex systems.

FIRST A DEFINITION

The technique discussed in this paper is applicable to those systems that are deemed complex. (Jones, 1997) ascribes 20 different types of complexity that can influence a software project and admits that the topic of complexity is a potential Achilles heal of functional metrics used to predict project size, and hence schedule, staff, defect rates, etc. Complexity can create ambiguity in the system's defined behavior. Its presence generally slows down a development effort proportionally to the added functionality involved. From the perspective of this paper, complex systems are also characterized by behaviors that are emergent, wherein the behavior of the whole cannot be inferred by the sum of the behavior of the individual parts, and therefore does not reveal itself until the system is examined that way.

NOT A GOOD TRACK RECORD

Commercial ventures into the development of software systems have been noticeably less successful than comparable ventures for military or systems development projects when more functionality is involved. Over the span of just 10 years (1985-1995) the average size of a commercial software PC based project went from 500 function points to 5000 function points. Interestingly enough, commercial ventures transition from being more successful than both control systems and military projects (9% failure rate compared to 12% for control systems and 15% for military systems) to being dramatically less successful (45% vice 25% and 33% respectively) as the number of function points associated with a project increases from 1000 to 10000 - fully in the range of the average project size in 1995. This situation degrades even more as the size grows to 100,000 function points - fully 70% failure for commercial projects compared to 40% for control systems and 55% military systems (Jones, 1997). As the commercial industry continues to evolve, complex systems will be required in larger numbers to support the industry. If we can better address system complexities, we can develop at higher levels of function point counts with less risk of failure. This paper addresses one such way.

THE PROBLEM

The system in this paper is a complex communication service allocation system. The allocation problem is analogous to the problem faced by a hospital in a growing community scheduling the use of its multiple operating rooms, which are being expanded and refitted to handle the increased needs. Patients have different requirements on the hospital's "assets", which include the facilities, physician and nursing staffs, as well as special support equipment. The same doctors and nurses cannot be conducting surgery on different patients concurrently, and must account for pre- and post-op time between patients. Some operating rooms are better equipped for certain types of operations. The schedule is filled in based on need as time approaches current time, with higher priority patients bumping previously granted elective surgery allocations. And then there is the occasional last minute jockeying in case of emergencies.

The subject planning system deals with a service assignment update capability that preserves the existing allocation wherever possible, but shows significant flexibility in the face of changes to isolated input changes. Turnaround time for incorporating changes is measured in minutes. According to the human overseers of the planning system, the only legitimate reason for a lack of service is when the system resources are max'd out, and just as importantly, the "right requests" are ungranted. Both the number of service requestors and the supporting system resources are expected to expand by a factor of 2 after just a few years in the field. All the while, overall satisfaction is expected to remain high over that entire time period.

Development on this system started in the fall of 1994. The project was developed in C++ and C, with a heavy reliance on a database defined set of allocation rules. The system discussed here is estimated to be 4,000-5,000 function points in size, plus an additional 3,000-4,000 function points added for its intrinsic complexity and the sophistication of its algorithms, putting it in the range of a typical commercial project of the mid- to late-nineties. Indeed, even though the current application of the system is classified, the system has been examined for exactly the kind of commercial applications as the industry is currently facing: optimal airline and rail equipment maintenance scheduling; enterprise level call center staffing management; providing sufficient communication bandwidth in support of cellular calling regions.

Three years later, in the fall of 1997, the planning system went into integrated test along with other components. To be perfectly honest, many things were not working well, but the planning system was having a particularly tough time. By the spring of 1998, it was clear that this new planning component was failing on all fronts: where the response specification was measured in minutes, the actual response experienced was nearing 12 hours. It was unstable, core dumping with unnerving regularity. It was allocating barely 50% of the possible resource time. And this was for the initial size of requesting units. By this time in the program, the original engineering and design team had been largely dispersed to other problems, and the overall program was on a testing "death march" and could not afford to stop and wait for the planning system to get well. A team comprised of systems engineers, software designers and architects most familiar with the system - its mission, concepts, coding practices, and architectural and design decisions - were brought together to find a way to put the product "right" and soon. We needed to know very quickly whether or not we had built a classic *tender ship*[1]. What the program had failed to accomplish over a three year period with its incremental development needed to be to achieved in 6 months; in fact, the first wave of improvements had to be in place in a month. The existing engineering and development process could not guarantee recovery in such short order. We were on new turf.

DISCOVERY BASED DEVELOPMENT (DBD) IS BORN

What the team had were test observations. What it lacked were ***root causes***. Before we could fix anything, we had to know what was wrong. Rather than building the capability increments in a traditional manner, the Performance Team initiated a process that focused on understanding these root causes to develop the path to recovery. The process that was developed, and described in this paper, is known as Discovery Based Development (DBD).

DBD requires more of a Level of Effort staffing profile, with the "four horsemen" of development - analysis, design, implementation, and test - ongoing virtually throughout the entire period. Some issues can move quickly through the four steps, while others might require much more time in one or two steps, thus creating a dynamic of when "fixes" would be ready to re-introduce back into the program. This required the creation of "drops" of capability at regular intervals over the ensuing months.

Figure 1 illustrates the comparison of the DBD approach to the standard waterfall / incremental technique.

[1] This phrase originates from the early shipbuilding industry in Europe, when it referred to a new vessel design that, when built, did not survive even nominal conditions at sea. (Squires, 1986) generalizes this term to include any engineered system that fails during - usually inaugural – operations due to a critical design flaw.

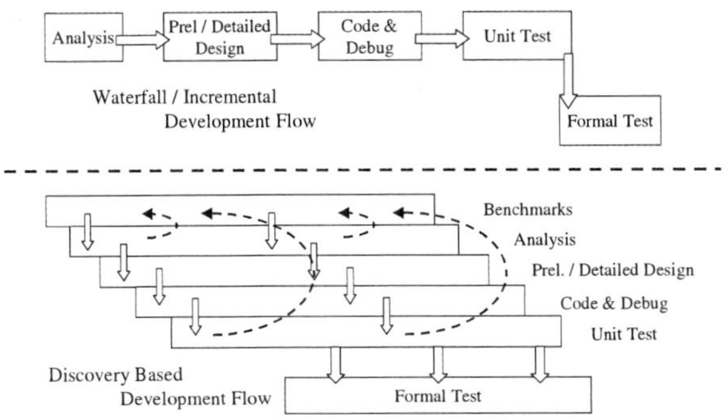

Figure 1: Comparison of Waterfall/Incremental Development to DBD

THE FUNDAMENTALS OF DBD

In brief, Discovery Based Development requires a strong understanding of what the expected behavior of the system is in meeting the mission, and benchmarks to gain understanding of the observed behavior. Once these two components are in place the development centers around closing the gap between the observed and expected behavior. This approach requires a discipline not to "attack anything that moves", instead concentrating the efforts of the team only on those changes that will yield the best position from which to launch additional benchmarks. The following paragraphs illustrate the details of the process.

Don't start too early or too late. The value that DBD brings to a complex system comes from its iterative nature in exposing the "learned" performance of that system's particular feature. Whether it be the aggregate inefficiency of a complex database read, the overhead of in-memory paging, or the search depth and breadth of a branch and bound combinatorial algorithm, there are many examples where the actual behavior of a system capability cannot be predicted with a high degree of accuracy before a given implementation is "complete". These aspects of the system must be learned through proper instrumentation and analysis of the product running with realistic data and then refined through changes to the implementation and even design. That is not to say that we have to be completely finished the development of the operational product before this step can be useful. On the contrary, DBD's intent is to gain as much insight using "intermediate" incremental code output -- even prototype, or proof of concept code -- to avoid being in system level test when these discoveries are made, as long as the system level behaviors can be expressed by these earlier renditions of the final implemented product. The sooner that the performance can be learned and dealt with, the greater chance that the system will meet its expected behavior in the end. However, DBD is a methodology for attacking emergent behavior; trying to glean system performance characteristics from a truly incomplete set of nested or interrelated functions may not yield the necessary improvements.

Identify the problem. In all convergence algorithms, there is an initial condition. The problem is identified when a desired expectation is not realized by the design. In the system discussed here, the problems had been identified by the manner in which the system was being tested. For projects in their formative stages, requirements, ops concept characteristics, even design assumptions can be the source of a DBD initial condition. Before this step can be realized, however, two key ingredients must be present.

An expected behavior must be articulated in detail. Behaviors can be of many forms, including process runtime, an operator's ability to interact with the system, response to fault conditions within or external to the system, throughput, and quality. DBD requires the existence of a concern or challenge about a system's behavior, an area to focus the energy of the process. Challenges to meeting the expected behavior fall into one of two general categories: technology and cost. The more robust a system is, the greater the chance that mathematical, compute, or even HMI technology is beyond the grasp of the implemented system. More and more, in civil and military government, as well as commercial circles, systems are using cost as a design parameter as part of a CAIV (Cost as an Independent Variable) trade. The technology may exist, but has been traded away for a reduced, more uncertain, capability to drive cost out of the program. The inherent risk of exhibiting either a technology or cost challenge is that the system may fall significantly short of the behavior expected by the customer.

One or more benchmarks must be present to demonstrate the system's current behavior in its intended environment. As in the case of the planning system, test program data was available to exercise the operational code, but it had to be "massaged" to drive to a true operational environment. In applying DBD earlier in the development phase, prototyping activities can and should be conducted before the actual implementation gets underway to determine the current system behavior, as long as the prototype is robust enough to capture the system level behavior. Early work in benchmarking can pinpoint those paths of the design in which to spend little to no energy worrying about the mathematically possible, but realistically improbable outcomes.

Determine Success Criteria. For some types of system behavior, success is attained simply when a requirement is met. In real systems, though, there may be several interim rungs on the success ladder that need to be met in succession. As in the case of the planning system, where both runtime and quality had to be met as the request traffic and resource availability grows, interim points were defined to gauge progress. Operator interaction may also exhibit several interim success points in order to get concurrence on an evolving ops concept in which the operator trusts the system to produce the solutions without extensive controls being placed on it.

Sometimes success against a given behavior is not so easily stated or measured. Usually, these behaviors have to do with "ilities" expected of the system, such as maintainability, operability, or quality. In these cases, where each individual encountered has his/her own perspective of the expected behavior, success is achieved when a consensus is agreed among the stakeholders of the system. Wherever possible, tangible metrics need to be defined to address some attribute of the behavior. Goodness, however, is in the eyes of the beholder, and contrarian examples can always be uncovered, no matter how many iterations through the development cycle one takes. It takes a disciplined team to set a goal that conforms to the consensus, and then to stick to that goal when odd cases are presented as proof that more work needs to be done.

Analyze the benchmark results to identify points of attack. Once the benchmarks have been generated, information needs to be gathered and analyzed to determine where the observed behavior had indeed fallen short of expectations. Analysis tools may need to be purchased or developed internally to draw out the information contained in the benchmark. Code may need to be instrumented with additional logging / printout statements that can then be extracted. The earlier these tools can be put in place, the sharper the initial discoveries will be. As each discovery is made, and understanding of the system's behavior becomes clearer, adjustments to these tools may be necessary to key on a new attribute of the design or execution that up to now had not been deemed critical.

With the tools in place, and metrics collected, the DBD team can focus on the root cause of the expectation falloff shown by the benchmark. Ideas are gathered about how to make corrections. At this point any idea has merit, and just because it may perturb the baseline design or implementation significantly doesn't mean it should not be explored. In fact the more revolutionary ideas also have the better chance of making major contributions in closing the gap.

Prioritize options by greatest payoff. Once the ideas are found, analyzed, and shown to close the expectation gap, they must be ranked, with the top ideas getting the nod for implementation. The remaining ideas are not cast out; rather, they are held in reserve. It may very well be that a very valid change is better served to wait until more evidence of the flaw is proven. At this point, new ideas are compared to ideas that were left behind in preceding iterations. It may be that a new discovery negates the need to expend any more effort on a previous idea, or is so dominant that it moves to the top of the stack for implementation. There may also be occasions when the "right" answer has to wait until an intermediary step has been achieved.

The discipline of the team is tested in this step more than any other, because there is a tendency to solve other discoveries in addition to the ones agreed to be analyzed or implemented because its in the same algorithm or section of code. Care must be taken to minimize this, for it puts pressure on the process to not fall behind in the "drop" schedule, and it undermines the agreed to prioritization.

The priority call must also not be a unilateral decision. The team owns the ideas, the schedule, the goals for getting back to the desired expectation. Their input and recommendations make for a harmonious environment for driving the gap closed.

Determine the time to implement. This step is a standard one in project management where tasks are load leveled to accommodate people and equipment constraints. The key to the success of this step lies in the ability for management and the team members to keep distractions to a minimum. Because this approach requires discovery to lend direction, pulling team members away can shut down the pipeline of issues, analysis results, or an implementation that prevents the next set of changes to take place.

Develop the next increment. This step of DBD can be incorporated into the latter stages of a standard incremental development processes provided there are sufficient increments to inculcate understanding gained from early benchmarks and analysis into later benchmarks. A 2 year program with 7-8 increments each lasting less than 3 months could benefit from DBD without any modifications to its process; one with two increments, each lasting a year, would need to augment its development schedule with 3-4 internal drops per external increment. The subject system utilized 7 drops, each 6-8 weeks in duration, within the overall baseline increment moving through system level test.

Because there may be literally dozens of ideas being worked on at any one time, the team may be concurrently working on changes that will go into three different drops. Therefore, care must be taken to implement and manage a check-out / check-in strategy for the code, database, and methods reports, and then retrofit changes from the current drop into the later capabilities as it moves into the baseline. This characteristic of the methodology lends itself very nicely in organizations used to handling multiple baselines associated with an incremental development approach.

Determine the incremental improvement in performance. The benchmark which seeds the discovery of focus areas, which in turn seeds the analysis and generation of ideas to fix the observed behavior has to be used at this point to determine a reality point. Decisions are being made about future ideas under the premise that the current bundle of capability will achieve a certain measure of success. If the improvements are not as substantial as originally thought, other ideas may be bumped higher or lower in priority in the next iteration. Since this is an iterative technique, the benchmark serves in the aggregate to show the progress over time as well as being the source of initial and future discoveries. This in turn is the outward and visible sign that the methodology is yielding results by showing the rate that improvements are being moved into the baseline.

Return to Analyze Benchmark until success criteria are met. This step is what makes DBD so powerful in dealing with development issues of complex systems. The technique actually has a feedback loop built into the process, whereby failure to meet expectations is in fact the expected result, rather than banking on every assumption and decision being perfect and then having to scramble when reality strikes. Because there are planned multiple cycles through the steps above, each individual cycle does not have to be - or want to be - a "home run". Indeed the methodology encourages small steps to allow the discovery process to feed on itself.

By the same token, if a change exceeds its intended progress, the methodology has a built in mechanism to indicate that no more work needs to be done. One of the worst fears facing program management when this methodology was introduced was one of not knowing when to end. After all, this is an LOE staffing for a fixed length of time; they needed some assurance that if a proper success criteria had been met, that the team would in fact stop looking for more things to fix. Again, this requires discipline in managing the discoveries in the benchmark reruns in the preceding step above. Experience with this technique on the planning system proved that this step can be managed very well, in fact it was fairly easy to locate the point of diminishing returns and we exited on this step with all parties well pleased with the results.

A WORD ABOUT MANAGING DBD

While the DBD process provides the necessary mechanisms to know what corrective actions are required, management of the process provides the focus necessary to implement those actions. A separate technical and management authority within the team working cooperatively allows for both aspects of the team leadership to concentrate on key obstacles lying in the path to success. For the subject system, weekly meetings were held by the technical leadership to drive to the "right" technical baseline and priorities. The resultant tasks were then turned into detailed near term schedules, resourced, and statused by the management leadership. Short management meetings were held – at first daily, but slowed later to weekly – to work any problems keeping the analysis, implementation, or benchmarking activities from meeting their objectives (e.g. lack of available database to initialize a new benchmark). On a monthly to quarterly basis, the technical and management leadership supported meetings with senior program management and/or customers to air progress and concerns and raise issues outside the control of the Performance Team (e.g. external interface data traffic characterizations). Therefore, managing the DBD process through the use of this two pronged cooperative leadership approach had as much to do with the success of the project as the process itself.

DBD IN ACTION

What follows are examples from the application of DBD on the planning system described earlier. While each example addresses a separate kind of expected system behavior, the same technique was used and proved to be very powerful, independent of the behavior being examined.

Example 1 -- Controlling RunTime - Initial Operations Sizing. In order to perform rapid plan updates, the design called for the planner engine to be run on independent intervals of the plan in parallel, with a post-processor step running serially to ensure data integrity in the database. Since the engine contained the combinatorics, it was envisioned that the post-processor would run much faster than the engine. A benchmark run was defined with a request traffic profile consistent with the system expectations, but when measured, there wasn't much parallel processing going on at all. Further, the post-processor was not a small contribution as envisioned; it was running slower than the engine, and since it was serial, the engine could not continue until the post-processor had finished the preceding intervals. Timing analysis tools were used extensively to measure specific functions and operations.

Because the post-processing function was I/O bound while the engine was CPU bound, the exploration led to completely different discoveries, but ultimately some of the most significant points of excess ended up in low level operation calls to COTS products within the architecture. Changes were made in how the mission applications called these operations, and a rerun of the benchmark immediately showed a marked improvement. More importantly, the new run exposed new areas that were now using up an inordinate amount of time -- ones that could be readily corrected.

Figure 2 illustrates the improvement profile as DBD was applied over 4 iterations. As can be seen from the "initial discoveries" profile, a standard development cycle lasting 6 months would have missed the performance requirement in formal test – again. With DBD in place, though, we were able to make more significant finds through subsequent iterations on the process and ultimately beat the threshold timeline without any more requirement relief.

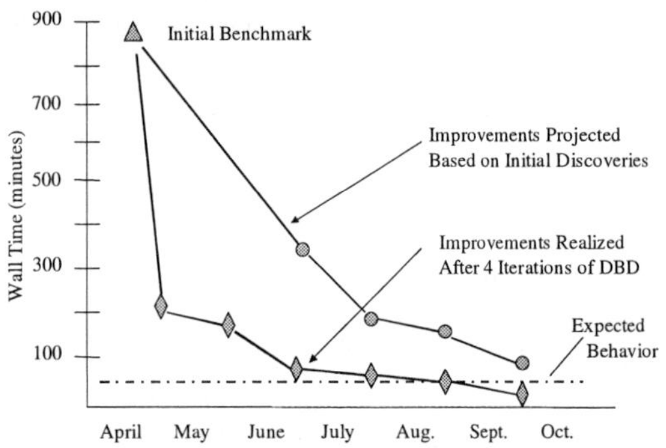

Figure 2: Runtime Improvement after 4 Iteration of DBD

In a matter of weeks, the post-processor's runtime had plummeted from nearly 2 hours per interval to 8 minutes -- it ultimately would reach 40 seconds -- right in line with the original expectations of the design.
We were able to make that first crucial shipment at the end of June, something we could not have achieved with the serial development methodology in place up until this time.

The engine time dropped decisively in this first round, also. But more importantly, with the post-processor running in shorter time, the ability to run multiple intervals returned, thereby gaining much more timeline relief than improving the individual interval runtimes. We knew that the ultimate key to controlling the engine's runtime was to control its combinatorics, but this first step bought the team tremendous breathing room from which to launch additional efforts.

Example 2 -- Improving Resource Allocation Satisfaction and Reducing Ungranted Requests.

In order to meet the expectation of perturbing the plan only in the face of locally modified inputs, a new kind of search technique had to be developed. Its premise centered around the ability to test a candidate assignment addition to the existing plan, draw conflicts among the competing assignments, then using that information, pivot each of the activities in conflict to new assets. It then took the resulting new plans and restacked them by a heuristic rule, extracted the one at the top, and repeated the process until the mission value of the candidate could not be improved any more. In essence, the algorithm was building branches dynamically at the same time it pruned other branches, with the goal of minimizing the total combinatorics explore extensive number of options in a reasonable runtime.

The analysis focused on whether the "right" solution -- one that an operator could produce quickly -- had been created and whether it failed to rise to the top of the stack before the pivot count was exceeded. We found examples of both types, and one very important surprise. Each time a change was identified and built, the benchmark reruns yielded more insight into the remaining losses. From an initial estimate of nearly 70 losses above the threshold at the outset, by the fourth iteration of the DBD process, we had reduced the number to 7 -- only two of which were improveable within the constraints defined, and these two fell into the category of mathematically interesting. Figure 3 shows the comparison of losses existing at the beginning of this behavior correction and after four drops of improvements.

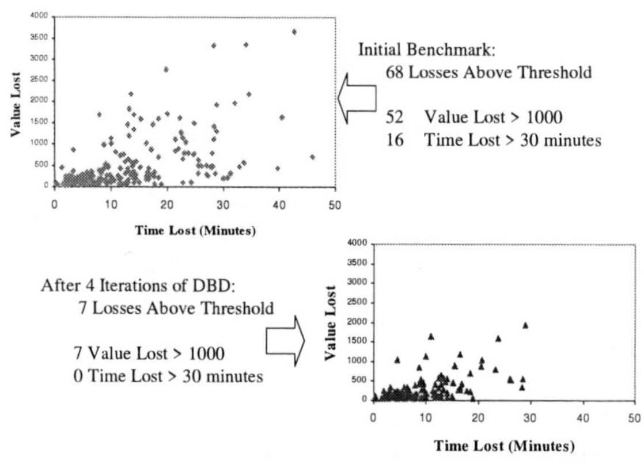

Figure 3: Improvement in Loss Characteristics through DBD

Every time we focused on a new design approach that put upward pressure on the runtime of the engine, the same benchmark tools that solved the problem in the first example yielded places where additional efficiencies in processing could be found. In one iteration, we delayed a quality improvement until a subsequent drop while the runtime improvement was pushed ahead in the current drop. This allowed the baseline to maintain or better its quality, without ever backpedaling on runtime, which had become a highly charged issue.

Figure 4 shows the trend in overall value and time satisfaction over the course of the 4 iterations.

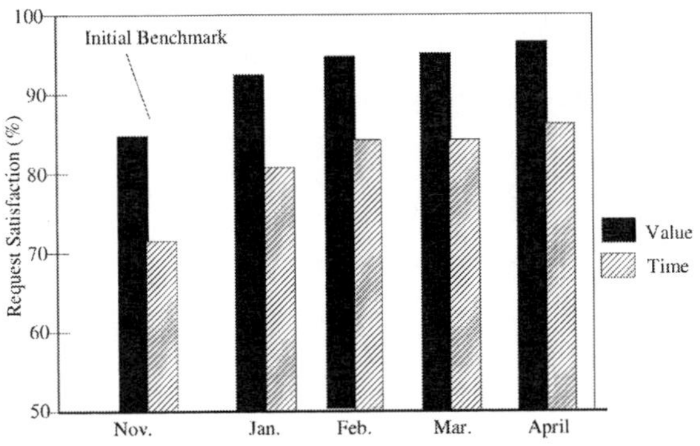

Figure 4: Satisfaction Improvements Based on 4 Iterations of DBD

The figure illustrates how the team was able to wrestle the many possible "fixes" into a cohesive strategy that gained tremendous improvements in the early iterations, quickly picking off the "low hanging fruit". Each improvement subsequent to the initial set was treating a smaller subset of the remaining observations, which allowed the team to terminate the iterations with a greatly enhanced product and concentrate on other issues.

Example 3 – Evolving the Operator Response to Processing Abnormalities. The original concept for the operator's roles and responsibilities focused on the mission -- ensuring that the allocations were appropriate. Dealing with processing abnormalities was considered a secondary issue. Test experience showed that the operator's role was moving away from proactive mission analysis to one ensuring that the processing was proceeding normally. What we found was that we could apply DBD to this most ambiguous behavior very successfully and prove that the planning system was in fact of high quality, as defined in (Prahalad et al, 1999), for it was a product that could evolve with the changing needs of its users.

The planning system was designed with "traps" in its input and database update processing components. These points ensured that both the incoming data and plan updates would not corrupt the internal data characteristics of the plan elements. One of the more critical traps had to do with whether the updated plan contained conflicts that were not resolved, either through human interaction, or an errant software logic path. Early in test, we discovered that the post-processor would sometimes back the operator "into a corner", rejecting the plan save request because of a conflict, but also preventing the operator from editing the solution because of gaps in the method's logic.

The first iteration of DBD entailed giving the operator the tools necessary to save the plan near-in with a conflict; once saved, the operator had additional capabilities available to resolve conflicts. Upon subsequent analysis, we discovered that operators were too quick to utilize the new "back door" feature, because they were receiving conflicts that were benign and superfluous, masking the more serious ones. So the second iteration included a capability for the software to recognize the benign cases and not alert the operator to action if these were the only types of conflicts detected. Finally, it was discovered that some of the benign conflicts were a symptom to another problem – lack of tolerance of small shifts in the requests, something that the design was supposed to handle. Therefore a third iteration redesigned the constraint checking logic to ignore a conflict that really represented nothing more than a compression of a buffer. These changes allowed the operators to monitor the processing progress with the assurance that a trap indicated a significant and real problem that required their immediate attention, and gave them the confidence to get a plan out to the requestors even when the processing was abnormal.

IS DBD REALLY DIFFERENT?

Upon first examination of this methodology, readers are reminded of similarities that DBD seems to share with processes already in existence. Indeed, (Kulich, 2000) describes Technical Performance Measurement (TPM) as "a plan of expected technical achievement to which the actual progress is compared using periodic measurements or tests. The difference ... represents a technical variance of sorts which is either good, bad, or somewhere in between." Whereas TPM is a useful methodology for identifying risk in the technical aspects of the program (Martin, 1996; Pisano, 2000), DBD is a useful methodology for attacking that risk. Further, progress against the risk can be made more rapidly than a traditional waterfall or incremental development cycle allows.

Readers might also conclude that DBD is a methodology that duplicates more pragmatic commercial development practices with regard to debugging and instilling performance improvements. (McConnell, 1993, 1996) discusses several "best practice" development methodologies, including evolutionary prototyping, evolutionary delivery, staged delivery, and spiral. All of these share one underlying theme: to "put working S/W in the customer's hands early". What's important to note however is that the functional instability found in the subject system did not manifest itself until the system was "fully loaded" in an operational perspective, so these techniques may not uncover the issue until the later spirals / deliveries also. Neither is the topic of performance proven with these techniques. In fact, (McConnell, 1993) suggests that performance is an area that is not to be addressed "as you go", that it should be addressed post-hoc in order to address global issues. This puts DBD in concert with and an extension of, not in opposition to, these commercially accepted "rapid" development techniques.

CONCLUSION

While DBD may have been born as a process aberration, it has proved that it is indeed a very powerful methodology for address complexities due to emergent behavior in systems. Armed with a development process that manages the behavioral expectations of products under development, complexity present in the more sophisticated solutions facing commercial or military systems of the future can be much less ominous than it is today.

REFERENCES

Jones, Capers, *Applied Software Measurement*, Second Edition, McGraw-Hill, 1997

Kulick, Kathryn, http://www.acq.osd.mil/tpm/kulick.htm, 2000

Martin, James N., *Systems Engineering Guidebook : A Process for Developing Systems and Products (Systems Engineering Series),* CRC Press, 1996

McConnell, Steve, *Code Complete*, Microsoft Press, 1993

McConnell, Steve, *Rapid Development*, Microsoft Press, 1996

Pisano, Commander N.D., http://www.acq.osd.mil/pm/paperpres/nickp/nickpaso.htm, 2000

Prahalad, C.K. and Krishnan, M.S., *The Meaning of Quality in the Information Age,* Harvard Business Review, Sept.-Oct. 1999

Squires, Arthur, *The Tender Ship: Governmental Management of Technological Change*, Birkhauser, 1986

BIOGRAPHY

Jeffrey K. Shupp is a Principle Systems Engineer with the Technical Operations group at Lockheed Martin's Management and Data Systems operation in Valley Forge, Pennsylvania. He has 21 years experience developing software systems, first in the Nuclear industry with GE's Nuclear Business Group, then in the Aerospace industry with M&DS. Mr. Shupp has been a member of INCOSE since 1996, and is a founding member of the newly formed Delaware Valley local chapter. He co-presented a paper in the 1996 INCOSE Symposium on the topic of System Design drivers and again at the 1998 Symposium on the topic of System Function Points. Mr. Shupp has a B.S. in Engineering from the Pennsylvania State University, and a M.S. in Engineering from the University of California at Berkeley.

Tailoring the EIA/IS-731.2 Questionnaire

Anne Lilly Dustin and Clint J. Graden
Idaho National Engineering & Environmental Laboratory
P.O. Box 1625, Mail Stop 3750
Idaho Falls, ID 83415-3750

Abstract. A tailored EIA/IS-731.2 assessment was performed on an organization responsible for oversight management. This project presented the assessment team with an opportunity to learn more about the EIA/IS-731.2 Systems Engineering Capability Model Appraisal Method while performing an assessment with limited resources. EIA/IS-731.2 emphasises tailoring the appraisal method to meet the objectives of the organization being assessed. However, with regard to tailoring the questionnaire, EIA/IS-731.2 only discusses the selection of the appropriate Focus Areas and the method in which the questionnaire is administered. It is apparent that other types of tailoring could be just as productive to the assessment process. With regard to tailoring the questionnaire, our main objectives were: 1) to make the assessment process more efficient and less cumbersome by decreasing the time spent interpreting questions, and 2) to allow participants to better focus on the real issues by using language familiar to the participants. Tailoring the EIA/IS-731.2 assessment questionnaire proved to be important to the success of this project. We increased customer satisfaction, decreased the time required for the participants to respond to the questions, and enhanced participant focus during the interview phase of the assessment. This paper discusses several areas in which the questionnaire was tailored for this assessment and the affect the modifications had on the questionnaire and the assessment. Additionally, this paper addresses other areas in which the quesitonnaire can be further tailored in order to increase clarity and succinctness.

INTRODUCTION

Introduction. This paper discusses the recent application of the EIA/IS-731.2 Systems Engineering Capability Model Appraisal Method to assessing a small organization. Specifically, it discusses the extensive and, in some instances, innovative means in which the standard questionnaire was tailored. Tailoring included deleting systems engineering terminology, omitting extraneous descriptive words, rewriting several questions, including introductions at the beginning of each Focus Area (FA), and rearranging the order of appearance of the FAs. Furthermore, the questionnaire was administered electronically using a spreadsheet adaptation of the EIA/IS-731.2 questionnaire (Graden and Nipper, 2000). The rationale behind each of the tailoring mechanisms is addressed in this paper, as well as an outline of additional suggestions.

BACKGROUND

The assessment method. The assessment method used was EIA/IS-731, its underlying objective is process improvement with respect to procedures, documentation, communications, operational and/or process metrics. This method uses a facilitated process and focuses on self-improvement instead of audit. The EIA/IS-731.2 provides an introduction to the philosophy of organizational maturity, training on specific tools and techniques for increasing organizational maturity, metrics and a baseline for the organization being assessed, and a path forward for improvement. The questionnaire is one of the tools used. It serves to obtain each participant's unique perspective about his/her work processes, work environment, problem areas, and potential solutions. The questionnaire is the only part of the EIA/IS-731.2 assessment that allows participants to respond anonymously. Additionally, the responses obtained from the questionnaire are not influenced by human interaction as they may be in the interviews. Lastly, the questionnaire establishes a foundation for the interview phase of the assessment.

DOE's Interest in EIA/IS-731.2. Increasingly, organizations are using systems engineering capability models to improve their business practices and increase the efficiency and effectiveness of their processes. Historically, most of these ogranizations reside within the private sector or the Department of Defense (DoD). However, several years ago Department of Energy (DOE) began incorporating systems engineering into their programs. A 1994 report from the Defense Nuclear Facilities Safety Board (DNFSB) stated "the DOE has not consistently taken a formalized systems approach to solving safety, technical, and managerial problems". The DNFSB report also noted that "failure to use a systems approach in planning can lead to greatly increased cost, delays, inferior solutions to problems, and even inability to solve some problems".

In response, the DOE issued an order in 1995

mandating the use of an integrated, systematic approach in all DOE programs. Consequently, the Idaho National Engineering & Environmental Laboratory (INEEL) began to incorporate systems engineering, as described by EIA 632 and EIA/IS-731.1, into their programs and projects. However, the DOE environment is unique and quite unlike that found in the private sector and DoD. Therefore, application of both the standard and the capability model to the DOE requires extensive tailoring. As part of this on-going effort, a tailored EIA/IS-731.2 assessment was performed on a small organization within a DOE field office at the INEEL.

The assessed organization. This assessment was performed on a entity responsible for both planning and operational oversight of projects and programs dealing with disposal and treatment of several categories of radioactive waste. While those within this entity were familiar with the term "systems engineering", they were unfamiliar with most systems engineering terminology, practices, or tools (e.g. systems, technical management plan). Furthermore, initial investigations indicated a Maturity Level of approximately 1 for this particular entity. Therefore, there was a large probability that the assessment participants would experience difficulty with comprehending and answering the questions, as written in EIA/IS-731.2.

TAILORING THE QUESTIONNAIRE FOR THE DOE ENVIRONMENT

Summary. For this assessment, the questionnaire itself was tailored extensively. Where applicable, tailoring included omitting systems engineering terminology and extraneous descriptive words. Several questions were rewritten. Brief introductions were added to the questionnaire at the beginning of each Focus Area (FA) and the arrangement of the FAs within the questionnaire was changed.

Systems engineering terminology. To keep the questionnaire as simple as possible for all of the participants, many of the systems engineering terms were omitted or replaced as suggested by Cusick and Bruce, (1999). All systems engineering terms were deleted from the questions contained in Category 1 (Technical) and Category 2 (Management). These deletions did not effect the essential meaning of the questions; they merely did away with the systems engineering subject matter while retaining the project and management contents. The systems engineering terms were not omitted from Category 3 (Systems Engineering Environment), specifically FAs 3.1 and 3.4, as they directly address systems engineering. FA 3.1 "involves those activities needed to establish, maintain, and improve processes required to accomplish systems engineering" (Electronic Industries Alliance, 1998). Similarly, FA 3.4 includes providing the "infrastructure ...and tools that systems engineers need to perform their jobs effectively" (Electronics Industries Alliance, 1998). Table 1 lists several examples of systems engineering terms that were replaced with generic terms.

SE term	Replacement term
systems engineering	program
technical management plan	program management plan
systems engineering personnel	personnel
captured	documented
system components	program components

Table 1: Systems engineering terms and their corresponding replacements.

Tailoring Questions. The verboseness of many of the questions was expected to decrease the participants ability to fully comprehend the questions posed. These questions were condensed by deleting descriptive words and/or paraphrasing sentences.

Before:

SP 2 5 8 2 a	Is a multi-functional group for risk management involved that spans both technical and business specialties?

After:

SP 2 5 8 2 a	Does the risk management team include both technical and business specialties?

Figure 1. Rephrased question SP 2.5-8-2a; before and after.

Two examples of questions that were rephrased are shown in Figures 1 and 2. The essence of each question remains the same, however, each rephrased question is clearer and more concise than its corresponding original.

Before:

SP 2 4 1 2	Does the organization perform trade studies to determine the trade-vs-buy decisions based on business needs?

After:

SP 2 4 1 2	Are trade-vs-buy decisions based on business needs and trade studies?

Figure 2. Rephrased question SP 2.4-1-2; before and after.

Introductions. Brief introductions were included at the beginning of each FA in order to provide some context for the associated questions. The inclusion of the introductions was based on the fact that some of the participants lacked a formal systems engineering background. It was therefore decided that short introductions would aid the participants in understanding the quesitons. These introductions were extremely condensed versions of the FA descriptions given in EIA/IS-731.1. Figure 3 shows the revised introduction used for FA 2.1.

Plan and Organize involves the identification of needs and constraints at the program level. The results of planning may be classified in terms of technical requirements and program requirements. These requirements define the technical and program structure required to bring a system into being. Planning includes: program requirements definition; identification, integration, and scheduling of all engineering functions and tasks; work breakdown structure development; organizational structure definition; and references to key policies and procedures. Planning is documented in a technical management plan that sometimes references other planning documents.

Figure 3. Introduction for Focus Area 2.1.

Reorganization of Focus Areas. As a reminder to the reader, Category 2 deals with management. FA 3.2 addresses competency management and FA 3.3 addresses technology management. Because the assessed organization was predominantly responsible for planning and operational oversight (i.e. management), Category 2 FAs, FA 3.2, and FA 3.3 were determined to be the most applicable. Therefore, their order of appearance in the questionnaire was rearranged. The new arrangement was as follows: all Category 2 FAs at the beginning; FAs 3.2 and 3.3 followed directly; Category 1 FAs followed next; and FAs 3.1 and 3.4 brought up the rear. The rationale: the participants would be more alert at the beginning of the session as compared to the end (2-3 hours later). Therefore, the chances of getting more thorough and accurate anwers to the applicable FAs increased with this arrangement. This rationale was verified by the number and placement of the comments received from the particpants. Approximately 80% of the comments pertained to Category 2 and FA 3.2.

OUTLOOK

Summary. The main objectives are to make the assessment process more efficient by decreasing the time spent interpreting each question and to allow the participants to better focus on the real issues by eliminating unfamiliar jargon. This would also affect the participants' buy-in to the assessment and improvement process, resulting in less frustration and a more positive attitude. Suggestions for additional questionnaire modification include: 1) tailoring the focus areas, 2) tailoring the themes, 3) further tailoring the questions themselves, 4) condensing the length of the questionnaire, and 5) clarifying the participants' viewpoints.

Tailoring focus areas and themes. EIA/IS-731.2 recommends omitting non-pertinent FAs and themes from the questionnaire. As this was the team's first attempt at an assessment, only one FA was omitted from the questionnaire. The decision to omit this particular FA (3.4) was based on the fact that the responsibilities of the entity being assessed focused on planning and operational oversight. The decision was made that the FA was not within the scope of the mission. In order to enhance our understanding of the entire process, no themes were omitted. Subsequent discussions with the participants indicate that omission of other non-pertinent FAs and themes would greatly increase particpant comprehension and assessment efficiency.

Further tailoring the questions. Because some organizations "use different terminology from that in the maturity model" (Sheard 1999b), further rephrasing of the questions to better reflect the entity being assessed would be beneficial. Therefore, the assessment team should spend more time familiarizing themselves with the entity's mission, work scope, and related terminology. The questions should be rephrased in such a ways as to better "personalize" the questions. Because this activity makes the questionnaire easier for participants to answer, it is given a high priority rating by Sheard (1999a).

Condensing the questionnaire. Sheard (1999a)

recommends condensing the questionnaire such that there is only one page per FA. According to Sheard, this would result in "clearer questions" and a reduction in the number of Generic Practice questions. This would address one of the more widely heard complaints from the participants of our assessment. Most felt that the Generic Practice questions were tiresome, distracting, confusing, and redundant when applied to each FA.

Clarification of viewpoints. During this assessment, there was some confusion as to the viewpoint from which the assessment participants should approach the questions. For example, if risk management was outside their scope of work, yet it was accomplished by their subcontractor, how should the risk management questions be answered? Should they answer "yes" because risk management was done? Should they answer "no" because risk management was not directly done by the participants? Clarification of these types of issues would decrease the time spent on interpretation, enhance the accuracy of the results, and increase the efficiency of the assessment.

CONCLUSIONS

Conclusion. We felt that tailoring the questionnaire was critically important in ensuring the success of our project. We saw an increase in customer satisfaction, a decrease in the time required for the participants to respond to the questions, and enhanced participant focus during the interview phase of the assessment.

The questionnaire is a useful tool for eliciting certain types of information. It serves to obtain each participant's unique perspective about his/her work processes, work environment, problem areas, and potential solutions. The questionnaire is the only part of the EIA/IS-731.2 assessment that allows participants to respond anonymously. Additionally, the responses obtained from the questionnaire are not influenced by human interaction as they may be in the interviews. Lastly, the questionnaire establishes a foundation for the interview phase of the assessment.

With that in mind, in order to succeed in eliciting valuable information and setting the expectations of the participants, tailoring the questionnaire is essential. Our main objectives of tailoring were: 1) to make the assessment process more efficient and less cumbersome by decreasing the time spent interpreting questions, and 2) to allow participants to better focus on the real issues by using language familiar to the participants. Language that clearly applies to their environment gets people thinking insightfully about their work processes. Avoiding vague or inapplicable jargon is essential to help get participants on page with Maturity Modelling philosophies. Essentially, the questionnaire itself defines organizational maturity.

The success of our tailoring was measured qualitatively, not quantitatively. According to the EIA/IS-731.2 itself, the average time for a participant to complete the questionnaire is 4-6 hours. Our average was 2.5 hours. Additionally, our tailoring was reviewed and validated for fidelity to the model by one of the original authors of the standard. In addition, our immediate customer felt that this tailoring was critical to the success of the assessment in this particular environment. Lessons learned from this experience include suggestions for additional questionnaire modifications such as 1) tailoring the focus areas, 2) tailoring the themes, 3) further tailoring the questions themselves, 4) condensing the length of the questionnaire, and 5) clarifying the participants' viewpoints.

REFERENCES

Defense Nuclear Facilities Safety Board, 1994 Annual Report.

Department of Energy, Order 430.1.

Electronics Industries Alliance, *Systems Engineering Capability Model Appraisal Method, EIA/IS-731.2,* 1998.

Sheard, Sarah A., "Fifty Ways to Save Your Budget: Reduced Cost Systems Engineering Process Improvement." *Proceedings of INCOSE*, 1999a.

Sheard, Sarah A., Lykins, Howard, and Armstrong, James R., "Overcoming Barriers to Systems Engineering Process Improvement." *Proceedings of INCOSE,* 1999b.

Cusick, Kerina, and Bruce, Jim, "A CMM For All Disciplines." *Proceedings of INCOSE*, 1999.

BIOGRAPHY

Anne Lilly Dustin is a systems engineer at the Idaho National Engineering & Environmental Laboratory. She has a B.S. in Biological Systems Engineering from the University of Idaho. Prior to obtaining her degree, Ms. Dustin was an electronics technician in the United States Navy for seven years.

Clinton J. Graden has worked at the Idaho National Engineering and Environmental Laboratory as an environmental chemist for over ten years. Prior to that, he worked for the Environmental Protection Agency Environmental Monitoring Systems Laboratory in region IX. He has a BS in chemistry and a BA in modern languages both from Montana State University.

An Innovative Adaptation of the EIA/IS 731.2 Systems Engineering Capability Model Appraisal Method

C. J. Graden and D. W. Nipper
Idaho National Engineering and Environmental Laboratory
2525 North Fremont
Idaho Falls, ID 83415

Abstract. In response to an opportunity to learn EIA/IS 731 appraisal methods while performing a real appraisal with limited resources, an appraisal team has developed an innovative approach to the questionnaire and interview/meeting analysis phases. First, a spreadsheet adaptation of the EIA/IS 731.2 questionnaire was prepared, providing a compact presentation of the preparatory briefing information, the question text, an area for answers, and an expanded area for comments. The net effect was one of combining the questionnaire completion with the data entry. Second, a method of grouping observed comments and questionnaire comments by topic was employed which reduced analysis time. As a result of this first trial, a number of further innovations based on database and Web technologies are discussed.

INTRODUCTION

Introduction. This paper is intended to record an innovative approach to the use of EIA Interim Standard 731 in assessing a small organization. A number of impediments to this effort are discussed. An innovative approach was used to overcome some of these impediments, and this is described in some detail. A direction for further improvements is outlined, and possible benefits discussed.

Background. The assessment method used was EIA/IS-731, its underlying objective is process improvement with respect to procedures, documentation, communications, operational and/or process metrics. This method uses a facilitated process and focuses on self-improvement instead of audit. The EIA/IS-731.2 provides an introduction to the philosophy of organizational maturity, training on specific tools and techniques for increasing organizational maturity, metrics and a baseline for the organization being assessed, and a path forward for improvement. The questionnaire is one of the tools used. It serves to obtain each participant's unique perspective about his/her work processes, work environment, problem areas, and potential solutions. The questionnaire is the only part of the EIA/IS-731.2 assessment that allows participants to respond anonymously. Additionally, the responses obtained from the questionnaire are not influenced by human interaction as they may be in the interviews. Lastly, the questionnaire establishes a foundation for the interview phase of the assessment.

THE ASSIGNMENT

Our Scope. As a part of a management and operation contractor team for a Department of Energy field office, we were asked to participate as facilitators in a self-assessment of a portion of that field office. This effort was undertaken, in part, as a training opportunity. A consultant was obtained to train our assessment team "on the job", and limited funding was agreed to by our sponsors to assist them in their self-assessment. A limited amount of time was allotted (about three weeks), and participation by the target group was readily volunteered.

Target Group. The target group, approximately 14 people, represent a program/project management oriented team with little or no formal Systems Engineering background. Initial investigations resulted in an estimate of Level 1 maturity. Further, the group was not familiar with formal Systems Engineering terminology, practices, or tools. Many Systems Engineering functions were being performed, but the standard questionnaire wording was a source of confusion.

Resources. A review of EIA 731 methods showed that we had somewhat less than enough time and money for the process. The minimum time seemed to be 4-5 weeks, and more seemed to recommended. Allocating the last week for reports and briefings, the middle week for interviews and analysis, and the first week for our training and preparation, we had no time to spare.

Point of attack. With all of the above allocations tied to face-to-face contacts, there was little hope of reducing them. The remaining task, not as yet allocated, was the questionnaire. A review of the questionnaire showed that there were more than 600 questions, and we were asked to minimize tailoring-out in order to enhance understanding of the whole process.

With a dozen questionnaires, the questions of data entry, validation, integrity, and reduction were non-trivial. How could we prepare, administer, transcribe, validate, and chart these results in the time available?

APPROACH

Preparation. Discussions with the consultant led us to understand the possibilities for shortening the questionnaire, but we were only able to justify omitting one focus area, the management section on the Systems Engineering environment. Our target group was in no way involved in that process, and it was eliminated from our questionnaires. Discussions with our target group leadership resulted in an understanding that the language of the questionnaire would cause problems, and this was revised, which is the subject of a paper (found elsewhere in these proceedings) by Anne Dustin. The remaining candidates which we identified for time savings were the administration and data entry phases of the questionnaire. An innovation was proposed that would combine these phases. Time could be saved if we let the target group do the data entry as they completed the questions. A prototype of this was prepared using a spreadsheet to present the questions in a column with a place for the answers beside them. This was given a trial, and was found to be reasonably

	A	B	C	D	E	F	G
27	Theme 1.1-2 Systems Level Requirements		Yes	No	N/A	D/K	Comment
28		Theme questions address the process for defining, describing and maintaining the system level requirements					
29	SP 1.1-2-1 a	Is the functionality required by users analyzed and quantified?					
30	SP 1.1-2-1 b	Are customer/user requirements transformed into a set of system level requirements?					
31	SP 1.1-2-1 c	Is a system requirements baseline defended?					
32	SP 1.1-2-1 d	Is an agreement obtained between acquirer and developer that system level requirements reflect their needs and expectations?					
33	SP 1.1-2-2 a	Are operational concepts and scenarios developed that include functionality, performance, maintenance, support and disposal, as appropriate?					
34	SP 1.1-2-2 b	Is the adequacy of system requirements to meet stakeholder needs reviewed with key stakeholders?					
35	SP 1.1-2-2 c	Are operational concepts and scenarios reviewed to refine and discover requirements?					
36	SP 1.1-2-2 d	Are system requirement decisions that have a significant effect on cost, technical or schedule performance, and the rationale for the decisions recorded?					
37	SP 1.1-2-2 e	Is the environment in which the system will operate, including boundaries and constraints, defined?					
38	SP 1.1-2-3 a	Is an agreement negotiated between stakeholders and developers that system level requirements represent an optimum balance of their needs and expectations?					
39	SP 1.1-2-3 b	Are expansion and growth allowed for in system requirements?					
40	SP 1.1-2-3 c	Is the Functionality indicated by stakeholder requirements analyzed and quantified?					
41	SP 1.1-2-4	Are analyses, simulations or prototypes performed to assure that system requirements will satisfy stakeholder needs and expectations?					
42	Theme 1.1-R Effectiveness and Utility Ratings		Rating		N/A	D/K	Comment
43							
44	GA 1.1-R-0 a	Rate the effectiveness of the Stakeholder and System Level Requirements definition activities: Marginal (M), Adequate (A), Significant (S), Measurably Significant (MS), Optimal (O)					
45	GA 1.1-R-0 b	Rate the value of the Stakeholder and System Level Requirements definition work products: Marginal (M), Adequate (A), Significant (S), Measurably Significant (MS), Optimal (O)					

Identity / 2.1 / 2.2 / 2.3 / 2.4 / 2.5 / 2.6 / 2.7 / 2.8 / 3.2 / 3.3 / 1.1 / 1.2 / 1.3 / 1.4 / 1.5 / 1.6 / 1.7 / 3.1 / End

Figure 1. Row of worksheet tabs

effective, but cumbersome. A revised version provided individual tabbed worksheet pages (Figure 1.) for each

	A	B	C	D	E	F	G
20	Theme 1.4-1 Selection of Appropriate Decision-Making Techniques		Yes	No	N/A	D/K	Comment
21		Theme questions address the process for selecting the decision-making techniques.					
22	SP 1.4-1-1	Are structured decisions making techniques used to resolve technical issues?					
23	SP 1.4-1-2	Are appropriate decision-making techniques selected and the rationale for their choice recorded?					
24	Theme 1.4-2 Consideration of Alternatives		Yes	No	N/A	D/K	Comment
25		Theme questions address the process for considering the alternatives.					
26	SP 1.4-2-1	Are all alternatives that are presented considered when making a decision?					
27	SP 1.4-2-2	Are alternatives identified for consideration in addition to those supplied with the problem statement?					
28	Theme 1.4-3 Evaluation Criteria		Yes	No	N/A	D/K	Comment
29		Theme questions address the process for defining and describing the evaluation criteria.					
30	SP 1.4-3-1	Are established, documented evaluation criteria used?					
31	SP 1.4-3-2 a	Are the reasonableness and validity of assumptions evaluated?					
32	SP 1.4-3-2 b	Is the sensitivity of analysis results considered when establishing evaluation criteria?					
33	SP 1.4-3-3 a	Are technology limitations, environmental impact, and risks included in evaluation criteria?					
34	SP 1.4-3-3 b	Are total ownership and life-cycle costs included in evaluation criteria?					
35	SP 1.4-3-3 c	Are the rationale for the selection and rejection of evaluation criteria captured?					
36	Theme 1.4-4 Selection and Communication of Alternatives		Yes	No	N/A	D/K	Comment
37		Theme questions address the process for selecting and communicating the alternatives.					
38	SP 1.4-4-1 a	Is a balanced solution selected based on established criteria?					
39	SP 1.4-4-1 b	Are affected parties involved in the selection of preferred alternatives?					
40	SP 1.4-4-2	Are decisions and their rationale captured and communicated to affected parties?					
41	SP 1.4-4-3	Are alternative solutions and the rationale for their rejection recorded?					

Figure 2. Comment box before

focus area, all in a spreadsheet workbook. Further refinements provided explanatory material at the head of each page, "stretchable" comment areas (Figures 2. And 3.) that expanded to take variably-sized comments for every question, and color-coding (Figure 4.) to aid navigation. The resulting set of sheets was then supplemented with a hidden "collection" sheet, which

	A	B	C	D	E	F	G
20	Theme 1.4-1 Selection of Appropriate Decision-Making Techniques		Yes	No	N/A	D/K	Comment
21		Theme questions address the process for selecting the decision-making techniques.					
22	SP 1.4-1-1	Are structured decisions making techniques used to resolve technical issues?					
23	SP 1.4-1-2	Are appropriate decision-making techniques selected and the rationale for their choice recorded?					
24	Theme 1.4-2 Consideration of Alternatives		Yes	No	N/A	D/K	Comment
25		Theme questions address the process for considering the alternatives.					
26	SP 1.4-2-1	Are all alternatives that are presented considered when making a decision?					
27	SP 1.4-2-2	Are alternatives identified for consideration in addition to those supplied with the problem statement?					
28	Theme 1.4-3 Evaluation Criteria		Yes	No	N/A	D/K	Comment
29		Theme questions address the process for defining and describing the evaluation criteria.					
30	SP 1.4-3-1	Are established, documented evaluation criteria used?					
31	SP 1.4-3-2 a	Are the reasonableness and validity of assumptions evaluated?					This is a user added comment in an area which can grow to accept even very large comments.
32	SP 1.4-3-2 b	Is the sensitivity of analysis results considered when establishing evaluation criteria?					
33	SP 1.4-3-3 a	Are technology limitations, environmental impact, and risks included in evaluation criteria?					
34	SP 1.4-3-3 b	Are total ownership and life-cycle costs included in evaluation criteria?					
35	SP 1.4-3-3 c	Are the rationale for the selection and rejection of evaluation criteria captured?					
36	Theme 1.4-4 Selection and Communication of Alternatives		Yes	No	N/A	D/K	Comment
37		Theme questions address the process for selecting and communicating the alternatives.					
38	SP 1.4-4-1 a	Is a balanced solution selected based on established criteria?					
39	SP 1.4-4-1 b	Are affected parties involved in the selection of preferred alternatives?					
40	SP 1.4-4-2	Are decisions and their rationale captured and communicated to affected parties?					
41	SP 1.4-4-3	Are alternative solutions and the rationale for their rejection recorded?					

Figure 3. Comment box after

combined all the answers in a single table using references to the entered answers. As a final step, a

	A	B	C	D	E	F	G
1	Category 1 - Technical						
2	Section 1.6 Verify System						
3		Verify System ensures system stakeholders that the incremental and final work products and system conform to requirements. System verification is a stepwise approach to ensuring that each element of a system satisfies its requirements. Verification at each level of the system hierarchy substantially increases the likelihood that the complete, integrated system will satisfy the system-level requirements. Just as requirements are successively developed for each level of system decomposition (i.e., system, segment, subsystem, unit, components, etc.), the system verification process is successively applied to determine, for a given level of development activity, that the implementation satisfies the requirements specified at that level and that interfaces are as defined in the interface control documents. Verification is accomplished via a combination of methods: test, analysis, simulation, demonstration, and inspection.					
4	Theme 1.6-0 Fundamentals		Yes	No	N/A	D/K	Comment
5							
6	GP 1.6-0-2 1	Are recorded and approved plans and processes followed in implementing system verification?					
7	GP 1.6-0-2 2	Is compliance with approved system verification plans and processes verified, and is appropriate action taken when performance deviates from plan or when processes are not followed?					
8	GP 1.6-0-3 1	Is there a well defined, standardized and recorded process for system verification?					
9	GP 1.6-0-3 2	Is the organization's standard process for system verification tailored, using standard guidelines, to meet specific program or organizational needs?					
10	GP 1.6-0-3 3	Are the system verification activities (i.e., tailored process) implemented and improved per established and approved formal procedures?					
11	GP 1.6-0-3 4	Is the organization's standard process for system verification improved using information from work product reviews and process compliance reviews?					
12	GP 1.6-0-4 1	Are metrics collected and analyzed to determine the performance of the tailored system verification activities?					
13	GP 1.6-0-4 2	If the tailored process for system verification is not performing as expected, is appropriate action taken to align tailored system verification performance and expectations?					
14	GP 1.6-0-5 1	Is there a criteria for identifying system verification activities for which it is appropriate, and inappropriate, to quantify process data?					
15	GP 1.6-0-5 2	Are quantitative goals established for improving the effectiveness of the standard process for system verification?					

Figure 4. Intro in Color

database was prepared using a tool which allows direct import from our spreadsheets, and data validation scripts were written to allow identification of data entry, handling, or import errors. After validation, a version of the data suitable for analysis (i.e. with attribution removed) was exported back to our spreadsheet package for charting.

Implementation. It was apparent that administration of the questionnaires would require each participant to be in possession of a suitable computer loaded with the correct software and our spreadsheet in blank form. As the target group were situated in multiple locations, had varying computer assets available, and had to be briefed on the process, we decided to have them meet in one place, and to arrange that place to be one with the required equipment. We were able to rent a classroom at a nearby computer training facility which met our needs.

The briefing and administration were completed in less than four hours, with actual questionnaire completion times from 1.5 – 2.5 hours, averaging 2 hours.

The questionnaire files were collected, logged, backed up, and imported into our database for validation. Then the reduced version was returned to a spreadsheet for analysis. After some refinement, this process was reduced to a few minutes work. Development of the presentation charts, which served to both establish ratings and provide insight about internal differences within the target group, took two days. The charts, as they are spreadsheet based, could be re-used on new data with little additional effort.

The first approximation ratings, along with the areas identified as showing intra-group differences, were used to prepare for the post-questionnaire interviews. A synergistic effect of the electronic questionnaire format was the large number of detailed comments provided. It seems that the paper version of the questionnaire has a small area allotted for each question simply due to the size of the space required to offer a large blank space by each of more than 600 questions. This inhibits expansive comments. The "elastic" nature of the electronic questionnaire encouraged people by growing in size to accept whatever they wished to add. These comments provided a wealth of information, direct from the target team, and which was directed immediately at specific focus areas, themes and questions. The volume of comments exceeded the eventual volume of information produced from the post-questionnaire interviews and meetings. The relative privacy of the electronic questionnaire process seems to have allowed recipients to overcome inhibitions that may have been present in group meetings, while, in turn, the energy of group interaction in meetings seems to have increased understanding for some while stimulating and enabling cooperative responses. On the whole, the combination of the two venues permitted every participant an opportunity to voice their responses.

Data Consolidation and Analysis. Data collected during interviews was consolidated by a small subset of the assessment team. The small size of the group performing this specific task worked well for us because every choice was not debated by committee and the participants were chosen for their ablilty to logically group sets of diverse items and accurately abstract thematic connotations in succinctly worded findings.

The consolidation process used the standard yellow-stickie method of pasting butcher-paper to the wall for each Focus Area in the assessment. Each butcher-paper was titled and divided into Positive and Negative comments. All interview notes were rewritten on stickies that were placed on the appropriate Focus Area and subsequently grouped thematically.

The thematic grouping process was greatly simplified by developing a concise topic statement to place on the grouped stacks. Devising a concise topic statement at the time of data consolidation helped with accuracy and accelerated the process.

In this fashion, we allocated hundreds of interview notes on yellow stickies to each finding. We felt this to be tedious and costly, but there is no substitute for direct excerpts from the interviews when questions arise in the Findings Review meetings.

We cannot over-emphasize the value of being able to reference direct quotes from the interviews during the Findings Review meetings. When we were conducting the review, the customers were constantly asked if the finding, as stated, captured the feelings of those interviewed. Whenever the customers were in doubt, out came the archived butcher paper and the pertinent pile of stickies was detached and read to the customers. The effect was electrifying.

As the interview excerpts were read back to the interviewees and the leaders, they became aware, as if for the first time, of the extent and nature of their own insights into the problems besetting their organisation. They became more animated and began discussing the findings.

The only drawback was that it required making and shuffling large numbers of stickies and having a butcher-paper/yellow-stickie curator at the meeting to assist the meeting presenter. In the Outlook section that follows, we discuss an automated process that could replace piles of stickies with one effective reporting engine to cut cost and retain all the value.

Results. Our sponsors were unable to schedule time for the final briefings within our delivery schedule, but we were finished and ready to brief within the allotted time. Final products were delivered a week later. Costs were below budgeted funds. More importantly, the time impact on the target organization was less than that described in EIA-IS 731.

Effectiveness. Was the process effective? We will only be able to tell when changes result, and another assessment is made. A noteworthy comment from a manager in the target group observed "How is this method any different from the other tools we've used?, your results are the same as the last study, which took two years and cost millions". If no more change results from this process, then the methods are, indeed different only in the amount of wasted resources.

OUTLOOK

Benefits. This first effort yielded great benefits in four areas. First, the time, and associated labor costs for the participants were reduced by one third to one half compared to paper questionnaires. Second, data entry and transcription errors, and the related costs of data validation, were avoided. Third, participants were given a presentation that was less imposing than the paper version, and which included explanatory information. Lastly, the participants were enabled to provide many more comments than was convenient with the paper questionnaires.

Future innovations. Each of these items has prompted thinking anout the potential for more innovation. Here are some of the possibilities we are exploring:

The electronic form of the questionnaire can be converted into a database-driven Web page. This provides several enhancements. First, it can be taken from anywhere that a computer can be connected to the net. Second. It can be tailored electronically by the team by creating a simple selection table for each group of participants. Alternate wordings or languages can likewise be specified for specific users or groups. This may be further enabled by a "pre-questionnaire" to elicit the jargon and terminology of the group to be assessed, then applying this information automatically via a related database of question contents and terms. Third, explanations and help, acronym expansion and word definitions can be made "point-and-click" features.

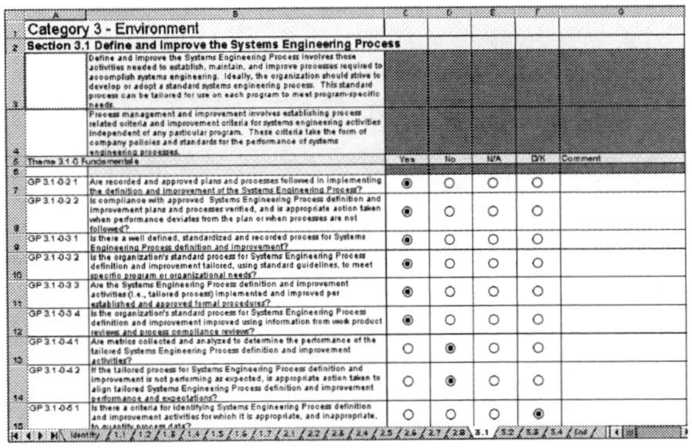

Figure 5. Radio Buttons

Web and database-driven engines allow more thorough data validation at entry time, and can lead the participant to providing better input. This has been demonstrated, in part, by a second version of our spreadsheet questionnaire, which uses "radio button" inputs to limit the possible entries to those which are appropriate (Figure 5.) They also allow the possibility of mixing and merging question pools from other appraisal methods, thus providing the possibility of improved integration with those other methods, with resulting lower costs. We are currently investigating the addition of Integrated Safety Management to our question pool.

Lastly, reduced time investment for participants, rapid turnaround, and the increased utility of direct automated analysis, all combine to make the method more acceptable for repeat measurements. This, in turn, will yield a product which is more likely to be a comparable measurement, and which should engender a higher degree of trust.

Improved Post-interview Analysis Tools. During the data consolidation phase we allocated hundreds of stickies with interview comments to the various Focus Areas. Though very valuable, the process was laborious and costly, so we immediately began looking forward to automation.

For our next assessment we will develop a database of interview comments instead of rewriting interview notes on stickies. We expect the database automated process to have major benefits: (1) able to quickly generate a number of reports that capture all the interview notes in various contexts (e.g. management/leaders/practitioners points of view)., and (2) an electronic version for use by the presenter during the Findings Review meetings to address questions that may arise about the basis of the findings.

CONCLUSIONS

Reduced resource consumption. The innovations developed as a result of this effort were beneficial to our organization and sponsor. There is a potential for wide-spread cost reduction and increase acceptance of appraisals using these methods.

REFERENCES

Ahern, Dennis M, and Dunaway, Donna K, "CMMI Assessments". " *Proceedings of the Ninth Annual International Symposium of the International Council on Systems Engineering* (Brighton, England, June 6-11, 1999)

Cusick, Kerinia and Bruce, Jim, "A CMM For All Disciplines". " *Proceedings of the Ninth Annual International Symposium of the International Council on Systems Engineering* (Brighton, England, June 6-11, 1999)

Electronic Industries Alliance, Systems Engineering

Capability Model Appraisal Method, EIA/IS 731-2, Version 1.0, 1999.

Radke, Neill B., "Managing in an Environment with a Level 1 Customer" *Proceedings of the Ninth Annual International Symposium of the International Council on Systems Engineering* (Brighton, England, June 6-11, 1999)

Sheard, Sarah A, "Fifty Ways to Save Your Budget - Reduced Cost Systems Engineering Process Improvement". " *Proceedings of the Ninth Annual International Symposium of the International Council on Systems Engineering* (Brighton, England, June 6-11, 1999)

Sheard, Sarah A., Lykins, Howard, Armstrong, James R.., "Overcoming Barriers to Systems Engineering Process Improvement". " *Proceedings of the Ninth Annual International Symposium of the International Council on Systems Engineering* (Brighton, England, June 6-11, 1999)

BIOGRAPHIES

Clinton J. Graden has worked at the Idaho National Engineering and Environmental Laboratory as an environmental chemist for over ten years. Prior to that, he worked for the Environmental Protection Agency Environmental Monitoring Systems Laboratory in region IX. He has a BS in chemistry and a BA in modern languages both from Montana State University.

David W. Nipper has been a scientist and engineer for the Idaho National Engineering and Environmental Laboratory for over ten years. He has worked with command and control systems , sensor systems, unique radio antenna designs, database systems, and internet-based information systems. This second career follows a full career as an Air Force officer in the fields of information systems, tactical communications engineering, and research and development test. He has a bachelor's in chemistry from San Diego State, and and a Master's in Public Administration from Golden Gate University.

SCE II™: Comprehensive, Integrated System Measurement During Use

G Philip Rust
TECHMANS
P O Box 39202, Moreleta Park
0044, Pretoria, SOUTH AFRICA
techmans@tn.co.za

Abstract. The paper explores a comprehensive, integrated approach to the measurement of value-for-money during system utilization and highlights the role of systems engineers in the performance of this important activity. The linkage back to designed system cost-effectiveness is illustrated and the transformation of the cost-effectiveness model for application during system utlization is explained. The approach emphasizes the fact that only the total system can deliver total value and therefore the total, business system must be measured. The philosophy, principles, concepts and methodology of the measurement approach is elaborated. The paper concludes by listing the advantages of this new measurement approach.

INTRODUCTION

The measurement and evaluation of large systems during the creation process have received considerable attention from systems engineers and numerous references can be cited. The same cannot be said for measurement during the system utilization process. Apart from their involvement during system upgrades (which in nature often boils down to a mini-acquisition), systems engineers have tended not to play a major role in the operations and support phase of large systems.

For most systems the operations and support phase of the system life cycle is the most expensive and longest in duration of all the life cycle phases. The standard of management during the operations and support phase can eventually result in the system being labelled a failure or a success. The overall system manager (business manager) of the system needs the contribution of systems engineers in order to be successful during this phase. One such challenge to systems engineers is the area of measurement of the business performance of total systems.

This paper explores this area of measurement, and proposes an integrated measurement methodology (called SCE II™) which measures value-for-money comprehensively during system use.

BACKGROUND

Business processes create value for the client (either directly or indirectly). These high-level, overall processes are performed by total systems, i.e. business systems. A business system comprises (as appropriate) all the various system elements, synthesized into a particular configuration to produce the required output. Elements typically included in the business system are:

All equipment, related facilities, supplies and consumables, computer software, documentation, data/information, services, procedures, practices, a management system and personnel required for its operation and support to the degree that it can be considered a self-sufficient unit in its intended operational environment. The management system includes the policies, directives, regulations, organizational structures and business plans as well as the business performance measurement-monitoring-reporting system.

Typical examples of total, business systems are:

Industry	Example
Manufacturing	Car assembly line
Mining	Mineral processing plant
Military	Artillery system
Logistics	Mechanical warehousing system

Business systems/processes relate to the systemic level of a business organization (or not-for-profit organization) as displayed in Figure 1.

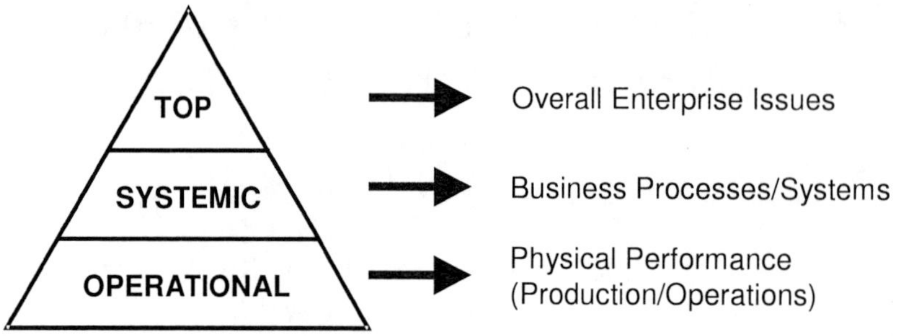

Figure 1: Levels in the Business Enterprise

Measurement at systemic level is vitally important, because the sheer size of medium and large businesses necessitates systemic measurement to avoid not seeing the wood for the trees. Since the measurement system forms the backbone of the control system, which ultimately plays a major role in the management system of a total, business system, it is cardinal in the success of system management during operations and support.

Furthermore, levels of competition today and in future demand continuous improvement, which requires measurement and comparison. This comparison needs to be also at systemic level and not only at the level of physical production/operations.

TRADITIONAL MEASUREMENT APPROACHES

The measurement approach followed by many business organizations may be characterized by the following:

(1) Performance is measured at the operational level (e.g. output quantities, various quality aspects, on-time deliveries, numerous partial and multi-factor productivity metrics, various cost categories) plus overall financial measurements at top level (e.g. profit/loss, return on investment, expenditure against budget, gross sales).

(2) From the multitude of production/operations control data, a large number of so-called management information statistics are calculated.

(3) Only certain categories of system elements are measured (e.g. main equipments and operating personnel).

(4) In worst case scenarios the operations fraternity would identify measures and metrics on their own without input from the systems engineers, who would have gone through a similar exercise during development, resulting in mismatch (e.g. measures of efficiency versus productivity measures).

Unfortunately these measurement approaches often have one or more of the following results:

- A gap in business performance reporting exists between the operational and top levels, with much of the intermediate level reporting nothing more than periodic summaries of operational level reporting
- Certain measures and metrics are difficult (even impossible) to connect mathematically and to integrate into a unified measurement model (i.e. no roll-up possible)
- Certain measures and metrics are difficult to relate mathematically to lower levels (i.e. no drill-down possible)
- The system manager tries to act on too many information signals, which makes purposeful management impossible
- The complete business system is not measured, therefore measurement results do not reflect the complete picture and may be misleading in the medium term
- System managers become fixated on lower level optimizations and do not focus on overall system optimization
- Improvement efforts are sometimes misdirected and degenerate into fruitless cost-cutting exercises, without attempting to achieve a best balance between cost and value created
- No real effort is made to make the system achieve its overall designed business performance
- No universal measurement approach exists for application to the various business systems of a business organization

Some of these problems are described in (Schonberger et al. 1994). It is suggested that the SCE II™ approach overcomes the above-mentioned problems of traditional approaches.

SCE II™

Philosophical Foundation of SCE II™. During the concept and definition phases of system acquisition, systems engineers expend considerable resources to model and analyse system cost-effectiveness, and to select the solution with the highest cost-effectiveness from the alternatives that conform to stated requirements and constraints. (We assume here that all other decision criteria, e.g. timescale, strategic suitability and societal acceptability, were met by the alternative solutions.) The client then accepts this selected solution mainly on the basis of its cost-effectiveness attributes. This is the designed system cost-effectiveness which the client will pay for during development and procurement, and which the acquisition team should achieve (hopefully!).

The philosophy behind SCE II™ is simply that the *client is entitled to the system cost-effectiveness that he/she paid for*. Therefore, measurement during system utilization must be against the same cost-effectiveness attributes (or their direct equivalents). Due to the complexity of large systems, this measurement effort should be performed by systems engineers, in support of the system manager of a total, business system. Figure 2 graphically portrays this life cycle concern of systems engineers for system cost-effectiveness.

Principles and Concepts of SCE II™. The approach acknowledges that cost-effectiveness is the pre-eminent measure at systemic level. Its two constituent measures, cost and effectiveness, provide direct measures of *all expenditure* on inputs and resources committed and *all value* created (added) as output of the business process, respectively. Figure 3 reflects this basic concept of cost-effectivness as process measure.

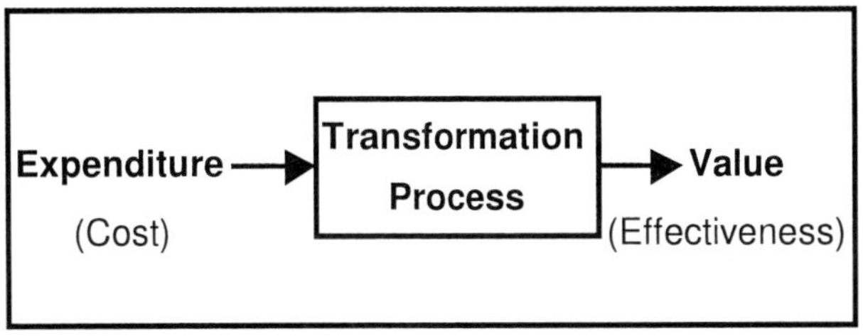

Figure 3: Cost-effectiveness as Process Measure

Cost-effectiveness therefore combines the measurement of effectiveness and efficiency (productivity) for the business process as performed by its business system.

The formulation of effectiveness is well-known. Effectiveness (E) is the product of capability (C), dependability (D) and availability (A) or:

$$E = C \times D \times A$$

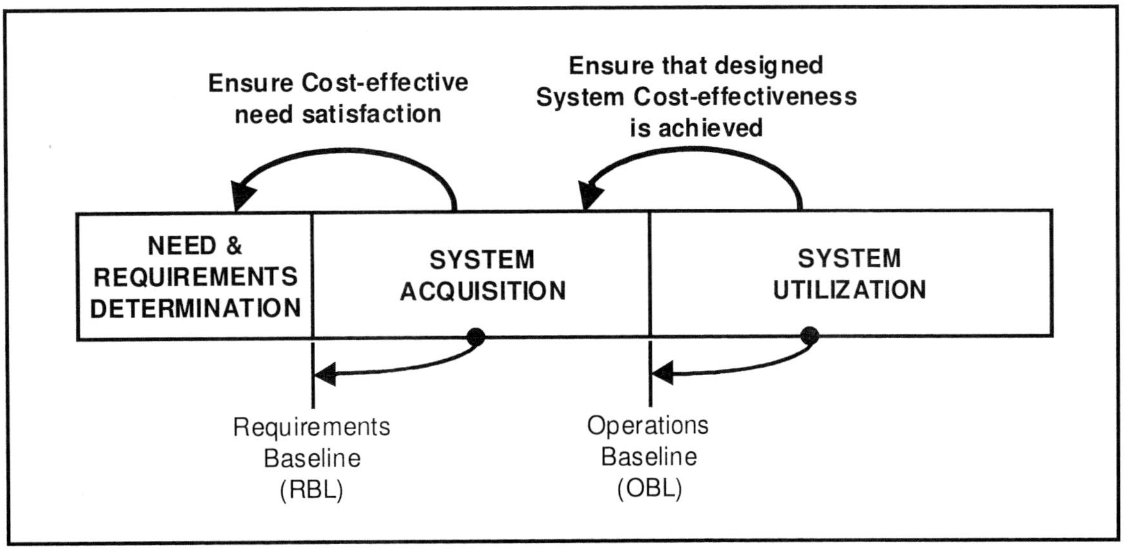

Figure 2: Systems Engineers' Life Cycle Concern for System Cost-effectiveness

This formulation is axiomatically true. Furthermore, it follows logically that effectiveness represents total value delivered by the system, because if the system meets all requirements relating to:

A: It will be ready to start performing required tasks when called upon to do so.

C: It will be able to produce the required output quality levels at the required output delivery speed (rate) and timeliness.

D: It will be able to continue performing required tasks satisfactorily over the specified operational cycle and produce the required output quantities at the required quality levels.

The system thereby renders the total value expected of it.

The formulation of cost-effectiveness (CE) is the equally well-known effectiveness (E) divided by cost (LCC) or:

$$CE = \frac{E}{LCC}$$

This enables us to express value-for-money during system utilization as a single number. (The fact that the units of cost-effectiveness measures are not common, should not prevent us from using them. If we can think through cost-effectiveness analysis during system selection, we are also allowed to express it numerically.)

A few other aspects of SCE II™ are listed briefly:

- All system elements are included in the measurement (e.g. personnel are part of the availability model and not only equipment)
- Both effectiveness and cost are measured concurrently for a clearly demarcated business process/system
- Under normal circumstances and without improvements to the system, the designed system effectiveness cannot be exceeded
- A business system/process maintaining 80% or more of its designed cost-effectiveness (after inflationary correction) is considered to be world class

Methodology of SCE II™. This comprises the following main tenets:

- Transformation of the designed cost-effectiveness model to an equivalent model for application during system utilization
- Providing direct traceability between the process and system dimensions
- Providing for cost correction due to inflationary effects
- Providing for systems/processes with predetermined or random readiness requirements
- Providing for systems/processes delivering tangible or intangible output
- Providing discreet and continuous assessment methods for output quality
- Enabling planning, monitoring and management of value-for-money during system utilization

An example (from the process industries) of the transformation of the cost-effectiveness model to an equivalent measurement model will be described below:

<u>Capability</u>

In the so-called process industries it is too expensive and too time-consuming to measure overall system capability periodically (let alone continuously). Therefore, capability measurement is substituted by the measurement of output quality (Q) and output quantity, denoted as productiveness (P). In the case of many process industries, e.g. a mineral processing system, output quality is not a discreet (go/no-go) issue but covers a range from "required" quality down to some minimum level of "partial" quality. The system will not be stopped for falling below the required quality level, provided it stays above the minimum level of partial quality. The significance of the variation in output quality over this acceptable range, however, warrants measurement. The concept of an attribute utility curve (attribute-value relationship) may be employed in this measurement of quality.

The quality model includes all the quality characteristics and may use weighting as well as attribute utility curves. The quality model may even show a deep hierarchy. (We therefore notice that the quality model is similar to the capability model used during system design.)

<u>Availability</u>

Many process plants operate continuously for months, perhaps only stopping for the annual shut-down or for product change-overs. Availability in the classical sense of readiness, therefore only comes into play at the moment of predetermined start-up time. After start-up the system operates and the dependability factor comes into play. We therefore see that this type of system really does not require the measurement of availability, because it "merges" with dependability measurement.

<u>Dependability</u>

The dependability model includes all system elements from the categories of equipment, personnel, consumables, supplies and, in exceptional cases, also infrastructure. (There is really no need to measure the dependability of something like a building in this type of system.) The dependability model is further based on:

- The process logic of an operational cycle and takes redundancy, stand-by equipment, personnel absenteeism, in-process preventive maintenance, etc. into account
- The life cycle planning for the system (i.e. the designed operations and support) and takes personnel training, annual holiday leave, shut-down maintenance, etc. into account

Figure 4 summarizes the transformation of the system effectiveness factors for the above example.

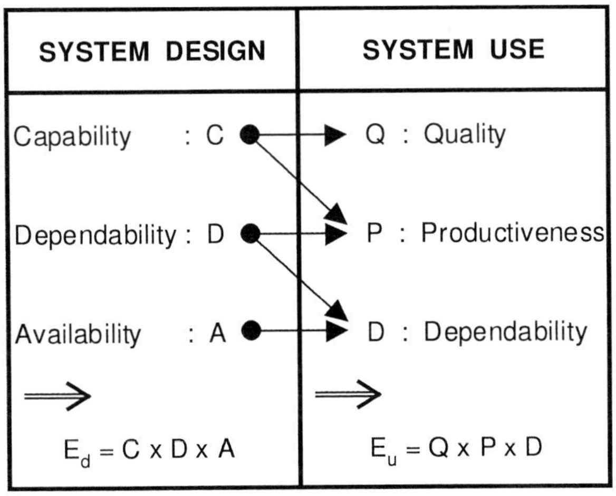

Figure 4: Transformation of System Effectiveness Model

Cost

Many of the typical cost breakdown structures (CBSs) used by systems engineers to model life cycle cost (LCC) during system design are not fully compatible with the cost categories of clients' accounting systems. It is therefore often necessary to translate some LCC cost categories for application during system utilization. The resulting cost model must also carefully split LCC into:

- Acquisition cost (considering whether initial spares and repair parts should rather be included with operations and support cost)
- Operations & Support cost (considering whether phase-out and disposal cost should be a separate category)

Cost-effectiveness

This model follows directly from the above submodels. It is useful to run cost-effectiveness measurement at two strata:

- One where only operations and support cost is considered (used for medium-term measurement)
- The other where full LCC is considered (used for long-term tracking and decisions on upgrading and phase-out of the system)

Note 1: Treatment of the system effectiveness model for services requires additional perspectives to the example discussed above. Most military systems deliver a service as output, and the timeliness factor of the service may then be included as part of the quality model as it is essentially a quality characteristic.

Note 2: Clearly, to be able to measure at the top level of the system/process also necessitates more operations modelling at the level of the total system during system acquisition.

COST-EFFECTIVENESS TRACKING

The tracking of value-for-money during system use is the primary application of SCE II™, with upgrade decisions only a secondary application. Hence the inputs to the system cost-effectiveness model are recorded continuously at the physical production/-operations level. The computation of actual system cost-effectiveness from these inputs is, however performed only periodically.

The measurement cycle for system cost-effectiveness is typically monthly, or 3-monthly in the case of certain types of system that are not frequently operated. System cost-effectiveness measurement is not recommended for cycles shorter than monthly. The factors comprising system cost-effectiveness are influenced by many short-term effects (e.g. seasonality, fluctuation in operational demand, preventive and corrective maintenance), and meaningful trends may only be detected after 3 or 4 months or even longer. System cost-effectiveness measurement is therefore not about short-term (e.g. daily or weekly) operational control. The monthly measurement, however, may be an early indicator of a trend, and must be acted upon if unsatisfactory.

System cost-effectiveness tracking and planned improvement may typically be as reflected in Figure 5, with a 24-month time window of which the first 6-month period shows history.

The following aspects about system cost-effectiveness calculation, tracking and assessment should be noted:

(1) In the case of certain types of system, e.g. a fighter aircraft system which rarely sees actual combat during its life span, it must be remembered that value is delivered also when performing training missions, joint peace-time exercises, peace-keeping missions, etc.

(2) The input Operations Baseline (OBL) is changed and must be updated every time money is spent on the system that was not envisaged (planned) during acquisition of the system. Costs must be

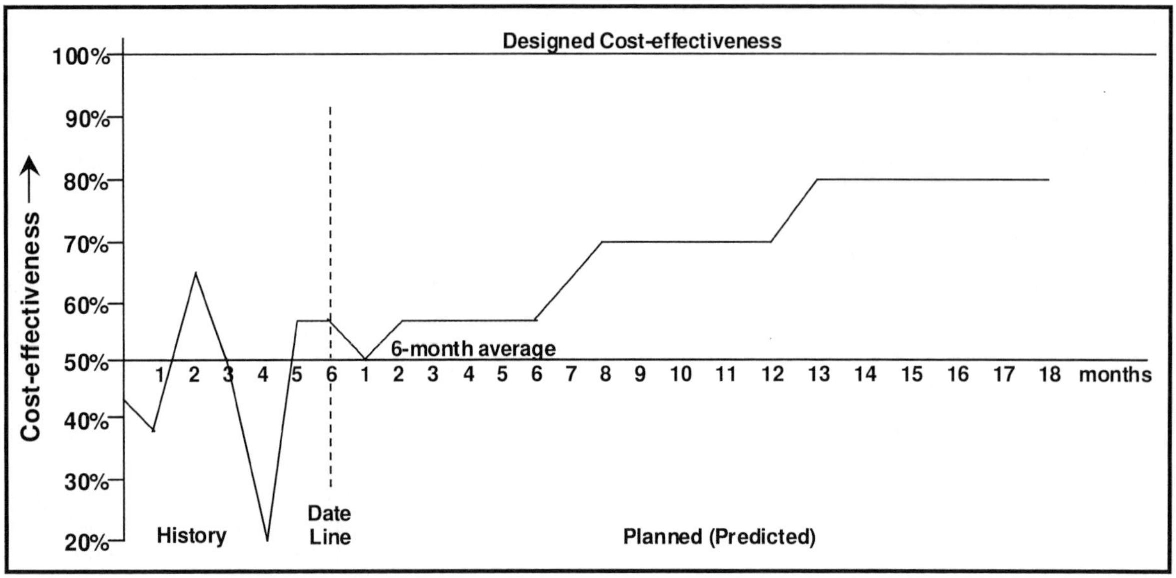

Figure 5: System Cost-effectiveness Management

added to the LCC value established during acquisition, and the system effectiveness model may require updating. This generates an updated baseline for system cost-effectiveness, which must be used in measurement henceforth.

(3) To cater for situations where system/process output is deliberately reduced below the designed output, measurement is made against this new planned system cost-effectiveness value. This situation occurs for instance when market (operational) demand is down for a period. It similarly requires adjustment of the system cost-effectiveness baseline, but now due to external factors.

(4) The world-class standard of 80% may seem low, but it is actually very tough to attain. The first system where SCE II™ was applied in the gold mining industry, measured 26%. A second one in a well-run mineral processing plant achieved 65%. However, it is accepted that certain types of system may have slightly less difficulty in achieving world-class standard.

(5) When assessing overall system performance, the system manager together with the owner/-stakeholders of the system will firstly look at only two results: cost-effectiveness (CE) and productiveness (P). If these two results are OK, then there is actually no need to look any further, except for the improvement trend.

(6) Sound systems engineering analyses should form the foundation for planned improvements as depicted in Figure 5. (Merely urging people on or guessing improvements will not work!) This work is part of the systems engineering imperative for the system utilization phase of the life cycle.

CONCLUSIONS

The fractionated approaches of the traditional measurement approaches, such as the measurement of equipment effectiveness or personnel productivity, have become inadequate. (People or equipment on their own do not create value within industrial context; systems do!) The following advantages of the SCE II™ approach are cited:

- All resources and output of the business process/system are accounted for in an holistic manner
- It connects the production/operations fraternity to the system/process design fraternity
- It can be applied to different types of systems, ranging from systems with tangible output to systems delivering a service
- It provides an absolute, universal measure and offers direct comparison with world-class standard
- It allows drill-down to any required level and enables identification of problem areas
- The perspectives of systemic professionals (staff functionaries) and production/operations managers (line managers) are merged
- It bridges the chasm between the top and operational levels by providing for meaningful reporting higher up the organizational hierarchy

- It provides an integrated approach to the planning, measurement and monitoring of productivity improvement for business processes/systems

Business process/system cost-effectiveness is about the combined effects of all groups involved, e.g. operating, maintenance, purchasing and logistics, which calls for a multi-disciplinary approach such as SCE II™.

SCE II™ is about measurement in the customer (user) domain. It enables measurement-based system management by providing inputs for management decision-making.

REFERENCES

Schonberger, R.J. and Knod, E.M., *OPERATIONS MANAGEMENT: Continuous Improvement*, IRWIN, 1994.

BIOGRAPHY

George Philip Rust has over 20 years experience in the areas of systems engineering, programme/project management, technology management and production/-operations management. He held top positions on three of the largest defence programmes in South Africa between 1984 and 1991. His corporate career culminated in a senior management position. This was followed by a post-graduate lecturing position on an international Master's programme in Engineering Management at a South African university. He founded TECHMANS in 1993, a consulting and training business active in a number of industries. Philip has gained extensive international exposure in his professional and academic capacities.

[SCE II is a trademark of TECHMANS.]

Using an Integrated Capability Maturity Model® – The FAA Experience

Linda Ibrahim
Federal Aviation Administration
800 Independence Avenue SW
Washington, DC USA 20591

Abstract. The Federal Aviation Administration (FAA) developed an integrated Capability Maturity Model (CMM), known as the FAA-iCMM®, that integrates the Systems Engineering CMM, the Software Acquisition CMM and the CMM for Software. The FAA-iCMM was released in 1997 and is the first major integrated CMM in existence. Since 1997, it has been successfully guiding the systematic improvement of FAA-wide processes used to manage, acquire, and engineer systems, products, and services.

This paper describes FAA's pioneering experience pursuing integrated process improvement using the FAA-iCMM. Lessons learned are presented regarding model representation, goal setting, the improvement infrastructure, training, transitioning, and appraisal. Plans to evolve the model and relationships with the government-industry-SEI CMM Integration (CMMI) effort are also discussed.

The paper will be of interest to any organization that seeks enterprise-wide process improvement and that might consider using an integrated capability maturity model to guide that effort.

INTRODUCTION

A current concern among the systems and software engineering communities is the relative isolation of these disciplines, and integrated process improvement guidance has been suggested as a means to remedy this situation (see e.g. Boehm 2000; Bate 1998). In 1997, the FAA developed the first integrated capability maturity model, the FAA Integrated Capability Maturity Model (FAA-iCMM) (Ibrahim et.al. 1997), to help solve this problem. This paper provides a brief overview of the FAA-iCMM and then describes its deployment, experiences in pursuing integrated process improvement, and planned next steps based on these experiences.

BACKGROUND

The Need for Integration. The FAA developed the FAA-iCMM to guide improvement of its engineering, management, and acquisition processes in an integrated, effective, and efficient way. In 1996, three single-discipline CMMs had been being used separately in different FAA directorates: the CMM for Software (SW-CMM v1.1) (Paulk et. al. 1993) the Systems Engineering CMM (SE-CMM v1.1) (Bate et. al. 1995), and the Software Acquisition CMM (SA-CMM v1.01) (Ferguson et. al. 1996) . While some improvements were being made, the single-discipline CMMs were being used in an uncoordinated way and without much success. These CMMs have different architectures, goals, terminology, and appraisal methods; they entail considerable overlap; and none alone covers all FAA system life cycle activities. Thus improvement efforts were suboptimal and the goal of FAA-wide, full life cycle, cross-discipline process improvement remained elusive. In addition, the FAA had moved to using integrated product teams as the implementation arm for its new Acquisition Management System and these teams needed processes that interrelated their disciplines.

The FAA-iCMM. The FAA-iCMM faithfully and robustly captures and integrates all principles, concepts, and practices of the SW-CMM, the SE-CMM, and the SA-CMM. It contains 23 process areas that integrate the 52 process areas and key process areas of its 3 source models. Each process area contains goals and base practices, integrated from the best practice guidance of the source models.

As in a continuous model, generic practices guide the improvement of the capability of the process areas. Additionally, the process areas are grouped or staged into maturity levels to provide guidance regarding what areas to focus on next. The FAA-iCMM representation is known as the continuous representation with recommended staging. It provides a path for improving both process capability and organizational maturity.

In order to measure progress, the FAA developed the FAA-iCMM Appraisal Method (FAM) (Ibrahim et. al. 1999) that integrates a variety of approaches for appraising vs. the integrated model. The model and its appraisal method offer guidance for integrated, systematic improvement of engineering, acquisition, and management processes.

The 23 process areas of the FAA-iCMM, with their maturity level stagings, are shown in Table 1. Table 2 lists the generic practices. Details of mappings of source process areas and practices to the FAA-iCMM are provided in (Ibrahim et.al. 1997) and additional architectural mappings are provided in (Ibrahim 1998).

Staging	FAA-iCMM Process Area
Maturity Level 2	Needs
	Requirements
	Outsourcing
	System Test and Evaluation
	Transition
	Project Management
	Contract Management
	Quality Assurance and Management
	Configuration Management
Maturity Level 3	Architecture
	Alternatives
	Software Development and Maintenance
	Integration
	Risk Management
	Coordination
	Peer Review
	Organization Process Definition
	Training
Maturity Level 4	Product Evolution
	Measurement
Maturity Level 5	Prevention
	Organization Process Improvement
	Innovation

Table 1: Process Areas and their Maturity Level Stagings

Capability Level	FAA-iCMM Generic Practice
Capability Level 1	Perform the process
Capability Level 2	Establish policy
	Allocate adequate resources
	Assign responsibility
	Ensure training
	Document the process
	Plan the process
	Use a repeatable process
	Manage configurations
	Assess process compliance
	Verify work products
	Measure process
	Review status
	Take corrective action
	Coordinate within the project
Capability Level 3	Standardize the process
	Use defined process
	Perform reviews with peers
	Coordinate with affected groups
Capability Level 4	Establish quality objectives for product and process
	Select processes for measurement
	Select measures for the process
	Determine quantitative process capability
	Use quantitative process capability
Capability Level 5	Perform continual process improvement on the organizational standard and tailored processes
	Implement improved processes

Table 2: Generic Practices and their Capability Levels

DEPLOYING THE MODEL

FAA's Integration Era (1997-2000). The FAA-iCMM rapidly became the single framework for CMM-based improvement in the FAA. In 1997, the Associate Administrator for Research and Acquisition (ARA) targeted selected major acquisition programs to achieve maturity level 2 on the FAA-iCMM by December 1999. Soon several additional programs and organizations across the FAA life cycle began applying the FAA-iCMM, including FAA's System Requirements Service organization. In 1999, ARA and the Associate Administrator for Air Traffic Services (ATS) committed to a common FAA-iCMM based process improvement goal to realize *high quality solutions to Agency and user needs, predictable cost and schedule, and increasing productivity*. FAA's operational support organization committed its engineering programs to FAA-iCMM based process improvement, and the office of independent test and evaluation adopted the FAA-iCMM.

Early Results. In 1999, the FAA Technical Center achieved its goal of capability level 2 in four FAA-iCMM process areas. Then in early 2000, an extensive full life cycle appraisal determined that several major FAA acquisition and engineering programs have achieved FAA-iCMM maturity level 2. In addition, capability level 2 in several process areas was uniformly achieved in programs appraised across the FAA life cycle. Early anecdotal data indicate that FAA-iCMM based improvement efforts have led to: better predictability, improved communication, improved teamwork, increased quality, greater consistency, cost savings, cost reductions, time savings, clarity of roles and responsibilities and processes, a more streamlined work effort, easier training of new hires, and more appreciation and attention to the roles of different disciplines and processes. First cost-benefit analyses have convinced the Agency that integrated process improvement provides value. More formalized quantitative measures are being established.

EXPERIENCES AND LESSONS LEARNED

Adopt an Integrated Model. From FAA's experience, the use of single discipline models in a multi-discipline organization leads to inefficiency and ineffectiveness in processes and in process improvement. Without an integrated model, cross-discipline improvement remains elusive, and efforts are suboptimal.

Set Joint Performance Goals. Working with an integrated capability maturity model offers powerful opportunities for enterprise-wide collaboration, and establishing high-level performance goals is the way to make that happen. At the FAA, early performance goals jump-started parts of the Agency on an aggressive path to maturity level 2. As experience was gained, joint performance goals were established across more of the agency reflecting increasing emphasis on integrated improvement across lines of business, functions and life cycle phases. Joint goals across directorates and lines of business are a critical success factor in transitioning to integrated process improvement and in synchronizing efforts of integrated product teams.

Align Process Improvement Goals with Business Objectives. Use the integrated model wisely. The FAA-iCMM's continuous representation with recommended staging enables goal setting aligned with the needs and objectives of different parts of the organization. It facilitates achieving goals that focus on improving (to any desired level) the capability of selected core critical process areas. For example, at the FAA, some executives adopted additional process improvement "stretch goals" in areas critical to their operations.

The model also facilitates establishment of the management and cultural foundations that come through achieving maturity levels. However, especially with an integrated model, not all process areas may be applicable to every part of the organization.

Regardless of the approach, goals should be expressed in terms of business needs. Keeping an eye on value-added diminishes the "check-the-box" mentality that might arise during process improvement efforts. To ensure that process improvement is directly tied to the business, align integrated process improvement with other initiatives, communicate relationships between process improvement and other goals, and provide guidance on priorities.

Think Enterprise. Integrated process improvement will surface many cross-organizational issues for resolution. It heightens cross-organizational understanding, appreciation, and problem solving; it requires cross-organizational cooperation. Implementing the FAA-iCMM brings systems engineers, software engineers, and acquisition managers together to clarify and interrelate what they do. Roles and responsibilities of different parts of the enterprise become clear; gaps become apparent.

Establish an Integrated Infrastructure. Integrated process improvement isn't easy and it requires an integrated infrastructure to make it happen. The FAA process improvement infrastructure includes: sponsors at several levels starting with the Chief Information Officer and Associate Administrators; process groups at several levels starting with the corporate integrated process group; corporate working groups including cross-organizational teams for FAA-iCMM evolution, metrics, training, communication, process asset library, appraisal, and others; plus process action teams.

At the FAA, these groups have evolved over time. It is even more important when pursuing integrated, cross-discipline, cross-line-of-business improvement to secure *top management* sponsorship and commitment An *enterprise-wide* process group is needed to lead, advocate and coordinate the effort. It should be staffed with executives and senior technical people who are widely respected, motivated, "turf-challenged," empowered, and persistent. The practitioners on the process action teams need to have adequate time allocated so they can improve *their own* processes.

Offer Training Continuously. At the FAA, a corporate training group manages FAA-iCMM related training. Training on the model, the appraisal method, how to do process improvement, etc. is provided by in-house staff. Domain or discipline-specific training (for example in requirements engineering, project management, configuration management, quality assurance) is typically outsourced. About 3000 people have received training related to the FAA-iCMM. In response to interests of other organizations, and in view of the fact that the FAA-iCMM is not FAA specific, external FAA-iCMM training has been offered

What's different regarding training when working with an integrated model? For course selection and evaluation, it is advisable to involve subject matter experts from across the organization, and to ensure materials are tailored to the integrated approach. For example, a potential course would not just focus on "software" configuration management, or "systems" configuration management, but should be about "configuration management". Also, there may be ongoing training initiatives in the various disciplines and it is important to integrate process training with other competency-building initiatives. (see e.g. Burke 2000).

Integrated process improvement spreads since several disciplines are involved, and it becomes institutionalized through widespread training and workshops.

Ensure Recognition that Legacy Investments are not Lost. Since several organizations in the FAA had been using the stand-alone CMMs, it was important to prepare for transitioning to the integrated model. Critical aids for this transition have been the extensive mapping tables included in the model. They facilitate transition from any source model to the FAA-iCMM because it is easy to identify where each practice and feature is placed in the integrated model. This reassures practitioners that the work they have done is not lost, but is part of the integrated effort. Also, specific guidance has been prepared (Ibrahim 1999) and workshops have been held to identify what's new, what's different, and what's the same between maturity level 2 on the FAA-iCMM and maturity level 2 on the SW-CMM.

Since the FAA-iCMM is described using a continuous representation with recommended staging, it was also very important to map the terminology, features, and principles from the staged and continuous source models to this new integrated representation. From FAA's experience, it was not difficult for those already familiar with either the staged or the continuous representation to understand the new architecture as long as mappings were explained.

Adopt the Continuous Representation with Recommended Staging. Although the debate continues regarding whether the staged or the continuous representation "is better" (SEPG 2000), and the CMMI effort has decided to issue separate integrated CMMs in both representations (CMMI 1999), FAA's experience has been that the features of both representations, together, are necessary and important. Moreover, neither the staged nor the continuous representation alone serves cross-organizational needs. By developing and implementing the FAA-iCMM using a continuous representation with recommending staging, FAA has found that guidance for enhancing both process capability and organizational maturity can be offered by the same model, using consistent terminology. Since unnecessary confusion, complexity, and divisiveness have resulted from perpetuating both representations, the distinct representations should be eliminated while retaining the important features of both in a single representation. Legacy investments based on models in one or the other representation are not lost, and process improvement practitioners are quick to understand and recognize CMM principles in a single format. From FAA's experience, one integrated architecture is both necessary and sufficient.

Recognize the "three for one" efficiencies and benefits. Improving an integrated process improves all 3 disciplines at once, as applicable, and attaining a maturity level on the FAA-iCMM is comparable to achieving equivalent levels on all 3 source models.

For example, the 9 process areas of the FAA-iCMM that are staged at maturity level 2 (see Table 1) integrate the practices and activities performed of 8 process areas of the SE-CMM, 9 key process areas of the SA-CMM, and 6 key process areas of the SW-CMM (plus selected activities of 2 additional SW-CMM key process areas). Achieving maturity level 2 on the FAA-iCMM is a major accomplishment since it means that those 9 process areas are each being performed at a planned and tracked level 2 capability (e.g. the level 1 and level 2 generic practices shown in Table 2 are being applied to each of those 9 process areas). This is equivalent to achieving maturity level 2 on the SW-CMM *plus* maturity level 2 on the SA-CMM *plus* capability level 2 on the 8 process areas of the SE-CMM that are mapped to the 9 FAA-iCMM maturity level 2 process areas.

Have a Variety of Appraisal Methods. The FAA-iCMM appraisal method actually comprises a set of 6 appraisal methods, 5 of which are structured as variations of the standard full FAM framework. Some of the variations have been adapted and integrated from various assessment and evaluation methods that were used with the source models; others are original to the FAA. Many FAA-iCMM appraisals have been conducted and most methods have been used, including the full internal, interview-based, questionnaire-based, document-intensive, and facilitated discussion appraisal methods. Only the full external method (intended for use in external evaluation) has not be applied.

Each method serves a different purpose and it has been very useful to have a variety of appraisal methods to meet needs for initial, quick-look, interim, and full formal appraisals. All methods are tailored to sponsor needs, and accordingly appraisal scope has varied to include organizational appraisals or project appraisals, selected process areas or full maturity level appraisals, and appraisals up to different capability levels.

Enlist High-level Appraisal Sponsorship and Cross-organizational Appraisal Teams. With an integrated model it is especially important to seek high level appraisal sponsorship for full life cycle, cross-disciplinary coverage. In this way, potential gaps and interface problems possibly uncovered during an appraisal can be fully explored, integrated roles and responsibilities across the sponsor's organizations can be clarified during the appraisal, and interdisciplinary findings can be acted upon as endorsed by the sponsor.

Conducting an appraisal vs an integrated model is a major organizational learning tool for both appraisal participants and appraisers. Establishing cross-organizational, multi-disciplinary appraisal teams spreads the learning opportunity across the disciplines.

Generic Practices Make Sense. The common sense appeal of applying generic practices to any process at all is key to applying CMM-based process improvement across multiple disciplines. The generic practices make sense, and the same concepts are used in improving any process. As one FAA executive put it, "This is Management 101."

Once the generic practice concepts become institutionalized, it becomes quite natural to extend their application to other processes and disciplines. It fosters the desire among practitioners to expand the model to include other processes the organization performs. This has been an important factor leading to FAA's "Enterprise Era."

NEXT STEPS

FAA's Enterprise Era (2001-2005). Experiences so far have laid the foundation for evolving the FAA-iCMM and expanding its application across the FAA. The vision is that the FAA-iCMM becomes the reference model to guide FAA enterprise-wide improvement. Best practice guidance from other widely used and recognized models and standards adopted by government and industry are now being considered for integration into the FAA-iCMM.

The general strategy to achieve the vision is to evolve the FAA-iCMM through a series of phases in order to address broader agency needs, thus providing integrated CMM-based process improvement opportunities across the FAA enterprise. The strategy includes maintenance of current content, expansion in new areas, and piloting.

Maintenance includes updating the model to incorporate improvements based on use and to retain currency (including consideration of CMMI releases and other evolving standards). Expansion includes expanding the model in various business and engineering areas that are critical to the agency such as strategic planning, investment management, security, safety, as well as important technical processes that are regularly performed such as operations, deployment, and field level maintenance. The idea is to include both business and technical process enhancements in the FAA-iCMM. Together they provide a holistic approach towards integrating enterprise-level goal setting and business results processes together with the technical processes to accomplish those goals. This is a means to seek overall enterprise excellence. New disciplines or processes are piloted prior to formal inclusion in the model.

Relationships with CMMI. The development of the FAA-iCMM was completed prior to the launching of the government-industry-SEI CMM Integration (CMMI) project. The fact that the FAA-iCMM was successfully developed has provided proof of concept for the CMMI project that CMM integration is possible. Moreover, the fact that the FAA-iCMM has been successfully implemented over the past 3 years provides demonstration to the engineering and acquisition communities that integrated process improvement using an integrated CMM is possible. Since the FAA has been participating in the CMMI effort via steering group membership and product team contributions, and communicating status of its efforts in numerous public forums, one might take the view that the FAA has been pioneering CMM integration for both the CMMI development project and its potential users.

The FAA-iCMM v1.0 however covers different disciplines than the CMMI project since acquisition is one of the disciplines the FAA chose to integrate with systems engineering and software engineering. Furthermore, as discussed above, additional disciplines are now being considered for integration into next releases of the FAA-iCMM. However, upgrades to FAA-iCMM content will take advantage of any new best practice or validated content that results from the CMMI effort. Similarly, it is expected that the CMMI effort will consider FAA products as input to its efforts as it has in the past.

Continued cooperation between the FAA-iCMM effort and the CMMI effort is anticipated.

Using the Model Outside FAA. The FAA-iCMM is not specific to the FAA. It can benefit any organization where systems engineering, software engineering and acquisition are performed, integration of engineering processes is a goal, and integrated product teams carry out engineering, management and acquisition activities.

Some external organizations have been applying the FAA-iCMM as an available and validated solution to the integration problem. Public courses are offered by the FAA periodically, and external lead appraisers are typically included on FAA appraisal teams so that they can gain and bring back to their organizations experience with the FAA-iCMM and its application.

CONCLUSIONS

FAA replaced 3 separate CMMs with the FAA-iCMM, containing all features of its source CMMs. FAA is successfully applying the FAA-iCMM to achieve integrated process improvement. A key ingredient for success in enterprise-wide, integrated, cross-disciplinary process improvement is organizational adoption of an integrated CMM.

REFERENCES

Bate, Roger et. al., *A Systems Engineering Capability Maturity Model, Version 1.1,* November 1995, SECMM-95-01, CMU/SEI-95-MM-003, Software Engineering Institute, Carnegie Mellon University, Pittsburgh, PA.

Bate, Roger, "Do Systems Engineering? Who, Me?" *IEEE Software*, July/August 1998, pp 65-66.

Boehm, Barry, "Unifying Software Engineering and Systems Engineering." *Computer*, March 2000, pp 114-116.

Burke, Gregory D. et. al. , "An Approach to Develop a Systems Engineering Curriculum for Human Capital and Process Improvement", Proceedings of the Tenth Annual INCOSE Symposium, July 2000.

CMM Integration Project, CMMI-SE/SW Continuous Representation v0.2; CMMI-SE/SW Staged Representation v0.2; August 1999.

Ferguson, Jack et. al., *Software Acquisition Capability Maturity Model (SA-CMM), Version 1.01,* December 1996, CMU/SEI-96-TR-20, Software Engineering Institute, Carnegie Mellon University, Pittsburgh, PA.

Ibrahim, Linda, et. al., *The Federal Aviation Administration Integrated Capability Maturity Model^{sm} (FAA-iCMM®), Version 1.0*, Federal Aviation Administration, November 1997. (available at www.faa.gov/aio)

Ibrahim, Linda, "Smart Buying with the Federal Aviation Administration's Integrated Capability Maturity Model", *CROSSTALK,* November 1998.

Ibrahim, Linda, et. al., *The Federal Aviation Administration Integrated Capability Maturity Model Appraisal Method, Version 1.0*, Federal Aviation Administration, April 1999. (available at www.faa.gov/aio)

Ibrahim, Linda, "Transitioning from the SW-CMM to the FAA-iCMM," Federal Aviation Administration, November 1999.

Paulk, Mark et al, *Capability Maturity Model for Software, Version 1.1*, February 1993, CMU/SEI-93-TR-24 and CMU/SEI-93-TR-25, Software Engineering Institute, Carnegie Mellon University, Pittsburgh, PA.

SEPG2000, "Continuous v. Staged Models: Is There a Winner?", panel, *Software Engineering Process Group Conference SEPG2000,* Seattle, Washington, March 2000.

BIOGRAPHY

Linda Ibrahim joined the FAA in 1996. She is the technical lead for FAA-wide process improvement. She formulated the concept and led the development and implementation of the FAA's integrated Capability Maturity Model and its appraisal method. Linda received the Meritorious Achievement Award of the US Secretary of Transportation for her innovative work in CMM integration.

Linda has been working in software engineering for over 30 years, as practitioner, educator, and researcher; in government, industry, academic, and applied research environments; in the US, Europe, and the Middle East. She is a member of the Steering Group for the CMM Integration (CMMI) project.

Linda holds a BA in Mathematics , MS in Information Science, and Ph.D. in Electrical Engineering. She is a member of INCOSE, ACM, and IEEE.

The Taxonomy of Systems Engineering Competency for the New Millennium

E. R. Widmann
Hughes Space & Communications Co.
PO Box 92919
Los Angeles, CA 90009

G. J. Hudak, PE
Stevens Institute of Technology
Castle on the Hudson
Hoboken, NJ 07030

G. E. Anderson
Honeywell International
PO Box 52199
Phoenix, AZ 85072

T. A. Hudak
Stevens Institute of Technology
Castle on the Hudson
Hoboken, NJ 07030

Abstract. This paper provides notable results of the continued development *The Taxonomy Of Systems Engineering Competency*, which is aligned with the EIA/IS 731.1 *Systems Engineering Capability Model* (SECM). The INCOSE Corporate Advisory Board has set a high priority on the development of this Taxonomy, which complements the use of the standard. For an organization to grow in systems engineering capability when implementing the EIA/ IS 731.1 SECM, individuals within that organization must also grow in increasing levels of competency. Key features of the EIA/IS 731.1 SECM, to which the taxonomy is to be aligned, are summarized. A foundation is presented for the development of the taxonomy's architecture, which is comprised of three highly aligned models. Each model is described in terms of its purpose, functions, inputs, and outputs. The basis of the Systems Engineering Competency Model is described in detail. The Taxonomy is linked closely to elements of the EIA/IS 731.1 SECM. An example demonstrates the application of the taxonomy to the development of a set of enabling skills for the conduct of quality management per the EIA/IS 731.1 SECM. The paper concludes with a description of future activities and a clarification of the relationship of this Taxonomy to the Systems Engineering Body of Knowledge being developed by INCOSE. An appendix at the end of the paper provides a completed example of a set of enabling skills for the conduct of risk management per the EIA/IS 731.1 SECM.

INTRODUCTION

Background. At the INCOSE International Workshop in January 1998, the INCOSE Corporate Advisory Board (CAB) decided that the development of a skills and knowledge taxonomy aligned with the Electronic Industries Alliance Interim Standard (EIA/IS) 731.1 *Systems Engineering Capability Model* (SECM) should be a high priority for INCOSE. The EIA/IS 731.1 SECM is a new industry balloted and formally released standard for assessing and improving systems engineering capability in both industry and Government as we enter the 21st Century. The standard was developed under the auspices of the EIA with participation from INCOSE.

A special team was formed in June 1998 within the INCOSE Technical Board, reporting directly to the Chair of the Board, to develop this needed skills and knowledge taxonomy for systems engineering aligned with the EIA/IS 731.1 SECM. After project planning, the core author team developed an architecture for the taxonomy. Because the architecture transcended the lower level of cognitive skills and knowledge to the higher level of competency, the final work product was designated as *The Taxonomy Of Systems Engineering Competency*, with subtitle *Enabling Growth In Systems Engineering Capability Aligned With The EIA/IS 731.1 Systems Engineering Capability Model*. As used here, competency is: "The quality or state of having marked or sufficient aptitude, knowledge, judgement, strength or skill needed to perform an individual action, or of possessing a range of ability or capability." [1]

Results of the initial effort were presented to the INCOSE CAB at the International Workshop in January 1999. In June 1999, a paper [2] was published that provided a preliminary look at the taxonomy and served as a basis for soliciting feedback on the approach. Based upon positive feedback, the team moved forward with development.

Purpose. This paper provides notable results of the continued development of *The Taxonomy Of Systems Engineering Competency*. This Taxonomy is intended to complement the EIA/IS 731.1 *Systems Engineering Capability Model* by enabling growth in systems engineering capability as defined by the standard. The

INCOSE CAB considers the development of this Taxonomy to be a high priority.

When completed, the Taxonomy will provide a foundation for organizations to improve their systems engineering capability as measured by the EIA/IS 731 SECM. For an organization to grow in systems engineering capability when implementing the EIA/IS 731.1 SECM, individuals within that organization must also grow in increasing levels of competency. The Taxonomy could be used by organizations for the professional development of systems engineering competencies that support organizational goals and program needs. It would serve as an objective basis for developing standard training, education modules, and a curriculum of courses specifically targeted for individuals or groups assigned specific roles or tasks.

Figure 1 presents the organization of the paper.

- Introduction
- Task And Product Descriptions
- Key Features of the EIA/IS 731.1 SECM
- Architecture Development
- Strategic Enterprise Model
- Competency Needs Model
- Systems Engineering Competency Model
- Developing The Systems Engineering Competency Model
- Application of the Taxonomy
- Future Activities
- References
- Biographies
- Appendix: Manage Risk Focus Area

Figure 1. Organization of Paper

TASK AND PRODUCT DESCRIPTIONS

Task. Develop a knowledge and skills taxonomy and framework that may be employed by systems engineering managers and technical practitioners to guide professional development.

- The knowledge and skill elements should be aligned with the practices in the SECM.
- The taxonomy should provide an objective basis for developing standard training, education modules, and a curriculum of courses that could be specifically targeted for individuals or groups assigned specified roles or tasks.

Products. Two products are to be developed:

- A knowledge and skill taxonomy and framework that relates individual knowledge and skills to standard practices or processes specified in the EIA/IS 731. The resulting product should include a process description for applying the taxonomy either at a group (e.g., organization) or individual level.
- A survey of available systems engineering training courses and a mapping of these to the knowledge and skill levels of the taxonomy.

KEY FEATURES OF THE EIA/IS 731.1 SECM

General Description And Benefits. The EIA/IS 731.1 SECM [3] is a model, to be applied to an organization using the EIA/IS 731-2 SECM Appraisal Method [4], for measuring and improving systems engineering capability. It references recognized standards, e.g., EIA 632 *Processes for Engineering a System* and IEEE-1220-1994 *IEEE Trial-Use Standard for Application and Management of the Systems Engineering Process*, as the appropriate processes for performing systems engineering. The reader may refer to [5], [6], and [7] for a more complete understanding of the concepts presented herein as well as a description of some of the relationships between the two source models and the EIA/IS 731.1 SECM.

EIA/IS 731 can be used by all product development organizations independent of size, product complexity, product maturity, and product technology. By implementing EIA/IS 731, organizations can expect to obtain the benefits presented in Figure 2. [3]

a)	Reduce cycle time from concept to deployed system products;
b)	Improve the match of deployed system product capability with stakeholder requirements;
c)	Reduce total ownership costs of system products;
d)	Reduce the number of engineering changes;
e)	Improve system quality;
f)	Improve communications among personnel involved in the engineering of a system;
g)	Improve ability to sustain and upgrade system products after deployment; and
h)	Reduce development risks.

Figure 2. Benefits of Using EIA/IS 731

Organization. The EIA/IS 731.1 SECM is organized into 19 Focus Areas (FAs), which are grouped into three Categories as presented in Figure 3. The names of the 19 FAs and the 3 Categories were chosen to be consistent with the terminology in the EIA 632 *Processes for Engineering a System.*

EIA/IS 731.1 SECM	
1.0 Systems Engineering Technical Category	
FA 1.1	Define Stakeholder & System Level Requirements
FA 1.2	Define Technical Problem
FA 1.3	Define Solution
FA 1.4	Assess and Select
FA 1.5	Integrate System
FA 1.6	Verify System
FA 1.7	Validate System
2.0 Systems Engineering Management Category	
FA 2.1	Plan and Organize
FA 2.2	Monitor and Control
FA 2.3	Integrate Disciplines
FA 2.4	Coordinate with Suppliers
FA 2.5	Manage Risk
FA 2.6	Manage Data
FA 2.7	Manage Configurations
FA 2.8	Ensure Quality
3.0 Systems Engineering Environment Category	
FA 3.1	Define & Improve the Sys. Engineering Process
FA 3.2	Manage Competency
FA 3.3	Manage Technology
FA 3.4	Manage Sys. Engineering Support Environment

Figure 3. Categories and Focus Areas

Capability Levels. The EIA/IS 731.1 SECM has six ascending Capability Levels, Levels 0 through 5, with Level 0 being the default level. Capability levels are plateaus of performance that organizations achieve as they improve both their business and technical processes. The levels can be used as organizational goals in structuring improvement plans. The capability levels are synopsized in Figure 4 with complete information available in [3].

Optimizing (Level 5): The organization establishes quantitative performance goals for both process effectiveness and efficiency based on its business goals. The organization continuously improves both its standard and tailored processes by gathering quantitative data. The activities are effectively balanced and work products effectively provide their intended utility.
Measured (Level 4): Metrics are defined for the organization, programs and projects and mechanisms are in place to track each quantitatively, and when necessary, take corrective action based on these measures. Performance of the tailored process is predictable. The activities are measurably effective and work products are of measurably significant utility.
Defined (Level 3): Activities are planned, performed, and managed according to well defined processes using an approved and tailored version of a standard documented process. The organization's standard process is improved qualitatively using customer (both internal and external) feedback. The activities are significantly effective and work products are of significant utility.
Managed (Level 2): Practices are performed according to approved plans and processes. Activities are planned, tracked, measured and verified. The activities are adequately effective and work products are of adequate utility.
Performed (Level 1): Specific practices are performed, but done on an informal basis. There are no defined processes, with the successful tasks performed by "heroes." The activities are marginally effective and work products are of marginal utility.
Initial (Level 0): Activities are not performed or performed poorly. Activities have little effectiveness and work products have little value.

Figure 4. Capability Level Descriptions

Elements Of Capability. The capability structure in the EIA/IS 731.1 SECM is composed of process elements, called "practices," and non-process elements, called "attributes." The capability structure of each FA contains three classes of capability elements, and potentially a fourth class in future releases:

- Specific Practices (SPs) are process elements unique to a particular FA and, along with GPs, describe how well the process is defined, institutionalized, and followed.
- Generic Practices (GPs) are process elements common to all FAs.
- Generic Attributes (GAs) are non-process elements common to all FAs and describe the appropriateness of the process, e.g., how effective is the process and how valuable are the products of the process. GAs provide a "sanity check" on the level of capability indicated by the process elements. For instance, it would not make much sense for an organization to have a high level of process capability if it produced mediocre products.
- A fourth class of capability elements, comprised of non-process elements specific to a FA, was present in the initial review version of EIA/IS 731.1 SECM (draft Version 0.5), but were removed prior to the final release of Version 1.0. The capability elements were initially structured to incorporate the full range of capability as measured by both source models. Using the nomenclature above, members of this class would be called Specific Attributes (SAs). They are mentioned here for completeness and understanding in anticipation of their future re-incorporation; this is a potential enhancement for future EIA/IS 731.1 SECM releases should that occur.

Population Of Capability Levels And Themes. Each Capability Level, i.e., Levels 1 through 5, can potentially contain elements representative of all classes of capability elements. As a minimum, Levels 2 through 5 contain generic practices (GPs) and Levels 1 through 5 contain generic attributes (GAs). Specific practices (SPs) can generally be found in Levels 1 through 5. Level 0 is a default level that contains no practices or attributes.

Within each FA, the SPs are placed into structures called "themes." As presented pictorially in Figure 5, SPs may be present within a theme in one of two ways:

- As a stand-alone practice(s) at a particular capability level as illustrated on Level 3 in Figure 5.
- As a set of related practices that are present in two or more capability levels. The set of related practices represents a core or kernel idea that shows a different manifestation depending upon the capability level, hence forming a "vertical theme" spanning multiple capability levels. This is illustrated in Figure 5 by the vertical arrow. Vertical themes spanning multiple capability levels are quite common; most FA-specific practices reside within these vertical themes.

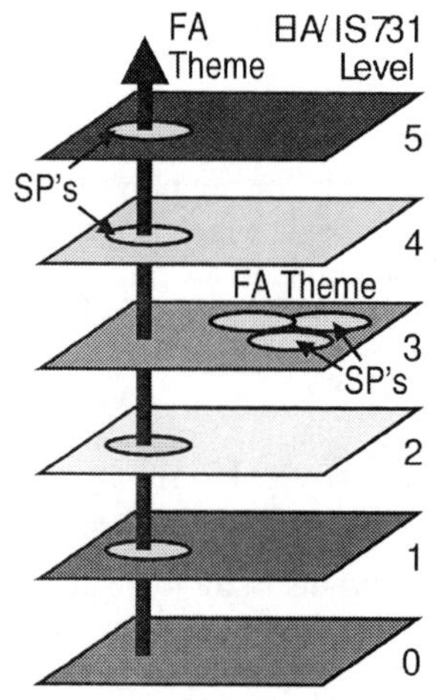

Figure 5. Themes Within EIA/IS 731.1 SECM

The generic elements of the model can also be thought of as forming themes, though they are not specifically addressed as such. For instance, the two GAs are each present in the form of a theme spanning Capability Levels 1 through 5. Among the eleven GPs, several themes span multiple Capability Levels.

ISO SPICE BPG. The GPs are aligned with the International Organization for Standardization (ISO) Software Process Improvement Capability dEtermination

(SPICE) Base Practices Guide (BPG). However, the GPs have been streamlined by significantly reducing their number from those found in both of the source models. The other elements of capability of the EIA/ IS 731.1 SECM were incorporated into the capability levels that are aligned with the ISO SPICE BPG.

ARCHITECTURE DEVELOPMENT

Initial Considerations. As suggested by the INCOSE CAB's task description, Bloom's Taxonomy of Cognitive Skills was initially examined as the basis for *The Taxonomy Of Systems Engineering Competency* aligned with the EIA/IS 731.1 SECM. This examination concluded that, while Bloom's Taxonomy was essential, it had to be considered as part of a more robust architecture in order to be fully aligned with EIA/IS 731.1 SECM.

Architecture Requirements. For *The Taxonomy Of Systems Engineering Competency* to be aligned with EIA/IS 731.1 SECM, it must address both individual and organizational (company, functional, and program) knowledge and skills needs in a product development environment. Bloom's Taxonomy of Cognitive Skills very effectively addresses the needs of individuals in an academic learning environment, but it cannot adequately serve as the sole basis for developing an architecture that must also include organizational needs.

A more encompassing architecture was needed to guide the professional development of systems engineering competency for organizations seeking to achieve the benefits offered by the EIA/IS 731.1 SECM (see Figure 2). In a product development environment, systems engineering takes place within the larger context of an organization, even though individuals apply their expertise on programs. Capabilities associated with the practice of systems engineering are a result of aligning an organization's strategy with its environments, the organization's decision on how to implement systems engineering expertise on programs, and the use of a systematic approach for developing the systems engineers' competencies.

Selected Architecture. The robust, integrated architecture presented in Figure 6 was developed for *The Taxonomy of Systems Engineering Competency.* This architecture, which is comprised of three well-aligned models, addresses both organizational and individual competency development needs in alignment with EIA/IS 731.1 SECM. The hierarchical relationship of the three models requires the downward flow of sufficient needs information to assure that individual systems engineer's competencies support the enterprise goals. Each of the models' processes and their inputs-outputs are described below.

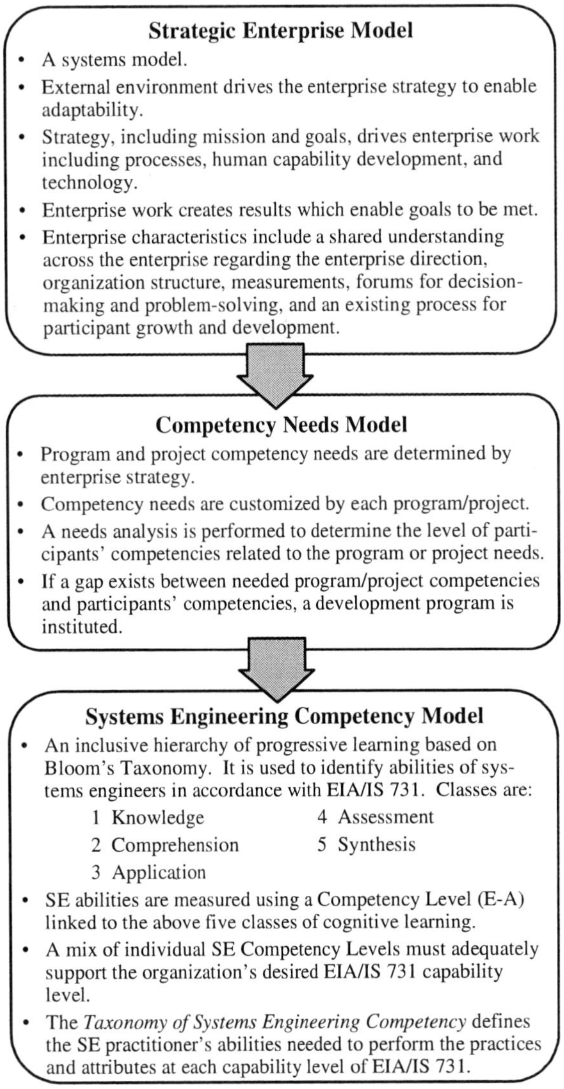

Figure 6. Taxonomy Architecture Consists of Three Aligned Models

STRATEGIC ENTERPRISE MODEL

Purpose. The Strategic Enterprise Model is a conceptual framework for understanding the strategy, environments, and alignment among the major parts of the organization. This theoretical construct has several generic characteristics that can be supported in detail by many currently available business models. *The Taxonomy of Systems Engineering Competency* will not endorse or encourage the use of any specific business model; instead, it is up to the organization using the Taxonomy to decide upon the business model most appropriate for its own application.

Functions. The generic characteristics of the Strategic Enterprise Model are presented in Figure 6. Decisions are made using the Strategic Enterprise Model about the specific processes, technology, and human skills that will be needed, i.e., the organization's work that is addressed by the FAs of EIA/IS 731.1 SECM. After that, the Competency Needs Model can be used to define the curriculum for developing the skills needed to support the necessary organizational processes and technology.

For example, an organization may have as its overall strategy the need to gain more market share for a particular product by reducing costs, and the goals to support that strategy may be to reduce cycle time from concept to deployed system products and to improve system quality. Since the practice of systems engineering should support those goals, it can be said that the work of systems engineering supports the strategy, and is aligned with the strategy. Also, the practice of systems engineering should lead to the goals being attained in the results area.

Inputs. The inputs to the Strategic Enterprise Model include a description of external environmental forces relevant to the enterprise, including needs/demands of consumers, regulations, impact of competitors, and the economy. These external environmental forces form the base from which enterprise managers create a set of assumptions regarding how work will be done to meet the strategic mission and goals of the enterprise. This means assumptions are made about how the enterprise will function within the external environment taking into consideration the resources contained in the internal environment: wealth, human capability, and technological capability.

Outputs. Since the Strategic Enterprise Model is a "systems" model addressing the organization and its programs as a whole, the various outputs from this model address all aspects of the organization's strategies and needs, of which developing competency is one of many.

The top-level outputs of the Strategic Enterprise Model are (1) the results attained from the work accomplished by the programs within the enterprise and (2) an assessment of the results to determine if the organization's goals have been attained. The practice of systems engineering, which is resident within each program, is an integral part of this assessment to determine its contribution to the results and the need for redirection and enhancement, including the development of competency.

If the results of the programs lead to the accomplishment of enterprise level goals, then generally the enterprise's strategy can remain the same as long as the environment doesn't change. However, if program results do not attain the desired enterprise-level goals, then either the strategy must change or the way work is accomplished on the programs must change. If the external environment changes, or if the internal environment changes, the strategy will need to be re-examined. Part of this change process and re-examination will address competency needs.

The outputs of the Strategic Enterprise Model that serve as inputs to the Competency Needs model is a statement of the enterprise's mission and goals, and a description of management's assumptions made explicit concerning resources—human and otherwise. The overall output of the Enterprise Model is derived though information gained in the Competency Needs model—which is if the work that was done as a result of matching competencies to programs, projects was effective.

COMPETENCY NEEDS MODEL

Purpose. The Competency Needs Model is a conceptual framework for assessing and developing systems engineering competency, and developing a curriculum to provide the skills needed to support the practice of systems engineering identified by the Strategic Enterprise Model. *The Taxonomy of Systems Engineering Competency* will not endorse or encourage the use of any specific competency needs model; instead, it is up to the organization using the Taxonomy to decide upon the competency needs model most appropriate for its own application.

Functions. The generic characteristics of the Competency Needs Model are presented in Figure 6. The first action taken in the application of the Competency Needs Model requires the identification and understanding of the organization's strategic goals and business objectives as key information for the identification, analysis, assessment and planning for associate performance improvement needs. This can be provided by input from the Strategic Enterprise Model assessment of organizational alignment with the practice of systems engineering.

In the Competency Needs Model, an organization's strategic goals and business objectives drive the needs for organization and employee competence and performance improvement. A front-end needs analysis is done, with associates learning needs being identified at the macro, rather than micro-level of analysis. Here an in-depth analysis is performed of the characteristics of the learners with respect to the demands of the practice of systems engineering within the organization and project or program. This analysis may include an assessment of the learner's prior and present work experiences, formal academic knowledge, and skills levels. A listing is made of the competencies to be included in learning interventions, and the sequence in which they should be attained. Performance objectives are created, with assessment activities planned to evaluate the learner's performance following instruction.

Inputs. The inputs of the Competency Needs Model include the mission and goals of the enterprise, and assumptions from enterprise management concerning resources contained in the internal environment. Subgoals for individual programs and projects may also constitute input.

Outputs. The outputs of the Competency Needs Model are an assessment of the human capabilities contained in the enterprise related to the capabilities required to meet the enterprise's goals, including any sub-goals for individual programs or projects. Assumptions made by leaders in the enterprise model are tested here. When capabilities match needs, individuals are assigned to appropriate programs and projects. When capabilities do not match needs, a developmental program is instituted.

SYSTEMS ENGINEERING COMPETENCY MODEL

Purpose. The Systems Engineering Competency Model is used for developing the abilities of systems engineers to the levels of individual competency required by the program or product for organizational performance at the enterprise capability level. The Model is based upon a unique relationship between the individual learning classifications of Bloom's Taxonomy of Cognitive Skills and the abilities required to perform the specific practices, generic practices, and generic attributes of the EIA/IS 731.1 SECM.

Functions. The process of the Systems Engineering Competency Model is to first analyze the abilities of each engineer allocated to the project against the Competency Tables in the *Taxonomy of Systems Engineering Competency*. A determination will be made for minimum skill enhancements that can be economically acquired by each engineer to provide an adequate mix of engineers at the appropriate SECLs to support the project. The process will also analyze and determine what abilities cannot be made available from within the organization. This will determine how many new engineers at what SECL must be hired..

Inputs. There are two inputs to the Systems Engineering Competency Model: (1) the Competency Development Requirements created by the Competency Needs Model, and (2) the Taxonomy of Systems Engineering Competency. The first defines the project's systems engineering needs, cxisting abilities within the organization, and those abilities that must be acquired. The second is the solution tool. The input elements include:

- Current EIA/IS 731 assessed capability level.
- Desired/required EIA/IS 731 capability level.
- Estimated labor hours, by Practice and Attribute, to perform all SE tasks through the desired capability level.
- Number of systems engineers needed at each SECL.
- Systems engineers available, listed by their SECL.
- Taxonomy criteria for a systems engineer's abilities to perform each Practice and Attribute.

Outputs. Outputs of The Systems Engineering Competency Model will vary considerably depending on the nature of the organization's needs. The following is a list of typical products:

- Project (or organization) training plan.
- Individual engineer's training development plans.
- Recruitment strategy and plan.
- Requirements for a new hire's resume abilities.
- Training needs assessment and plan.
- Requirements for a course curriculum or class development.
- Assessment evidence for FA 3.2, Manage Competency.
- Input to an organization's training budget planning.
- Input to an organization's product capability marketing.

DEVELOPING THE SYSTEMS ENGINEERING COMPETENCY MODEL

Bloom's Taxonomy. A method of classifying individual learning was developed over a period of years by a group of college examiners. Their work, *Taxonomy of Educational Objectives* [8], was edited by one of the developers, Benjamin S. Bloom, and published in 1956. It became and remains a recognized authority on how people learn in the cognitive domain. Their research determined that learning is hierarchical, i.e., mastery of lower level cognitive skills is necessary before the next higher level skills can be fully mastered. Bloom's Taxonomy, where ability = knowledge + skill [8], is applicable to the systems engineer's hierarchical abilities to perform the Specific Practices, Generic Practices, and Generic Attributes of the increasing, five capability levels of EIA/IS 731. Figure 7 presents the six ascending, hierarchical classifications of cognitive learning in Bloom's Taxonomy, with "Evaluation" being the highest.

Comparing EIA/IS 731 and Bloom's Taxonomy. When comparing the five increasing capability levels of EIA/IS 731 to the six progressive ability classifications of Bloom's taxonomy, it is observed that an individual must increase their competency in some relationship to a maturing organization's increasing capability. Analysis does not reveal a clear mapping or correlation between the two. However, more recent research in the educational community provided the key to a solution.

Creating The Learning Relationship. Although the educational community agrees with the hierarchical premise of Bloom, there are ongoing studies and debates about the number of learning classifications, and their content and sequence. For instance, in the Quellmalz Framework of Thinking Skills [9], Bloom's Knowledge and Comprehension classifications are combined into a single classification, Recall. Similarly, portions of Bloom's Synthesis is merged into the highest classification, Evaluation.

Evaluation: Judgment about the value of material and methods for given purposes. Quantitative and qualitative judgments about the extent to which material and methods satisfy criteria and standards.
Synthesis: The putting together of elements and parts to form a whole. Arranging and combining pieces, parts, elements, etc. in such a way as to constitute a pattern or structure not clearly there before.
Analysis: The breakdown of information into its parts such that the ideas are clear, are organized, and the relationship between ideas are made explicit. Able to understand hypotheses, relate assumptions, see patterns, and recognize hidden elements.
Application: The use of abstractions, information, methods and skills to solve problems in particular and concrete situations. Abstractions may be general ideas, rules of procedures, technical principles and theories that must be remembered and applied.
Comprehension: Comprehension is the lowest level of understanding. The ability to translate, interpret, and extrapolate from a knowledge base without necessarily relating it to other material or seeing its fullest implications.
Knowledge: The recall of specifics and universals, the recall of methods and processes, or the recall of a pattern structure, or setting. Usually a low level of abstraction, and little more than bringing to mind and reorganizing material from previously remembered experiences. Although some alteration of material may be required, it is a small part of the task.

Figure 7. Six Classes of Bloom's Taxonomy

After examining Bloom's two analytical classifications, Analysis and Evaluation, it can be seen that they closely correspond to those abilities needed to perform the Practices of the SECM Level 4, Measured. By adopting Synthesis as the highest cognitive level, and combining Analysis and Evaluation into a new classification, Assessment, this results in five learning classifications that contextually relate one for one to the five capability levels of the EIA/IS 731 SECM. The resulting relationship is illustrated in Figures 8a.

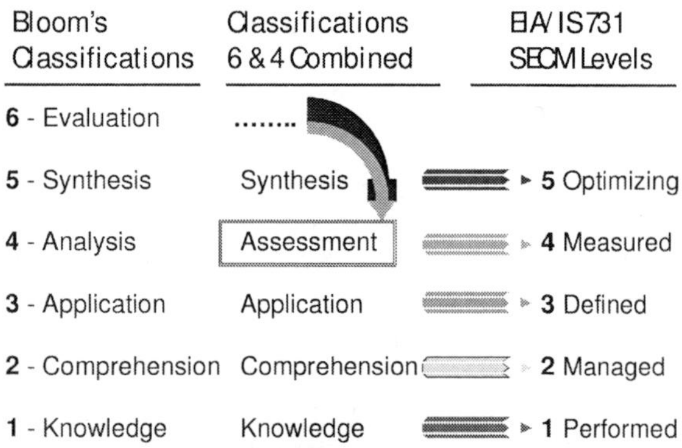

Figure 8a. Relationship Between Bloom's Taxonomy and EIA/IS 731.1 SECM

Defining the Competency Relationship. If the EIA/IS 731 Capability Levels are placed on a vertical axis and this new set of learning classifications are placed on a horizontal axis with intersections plotted you will create the simple relational map shown in Figure 8b.

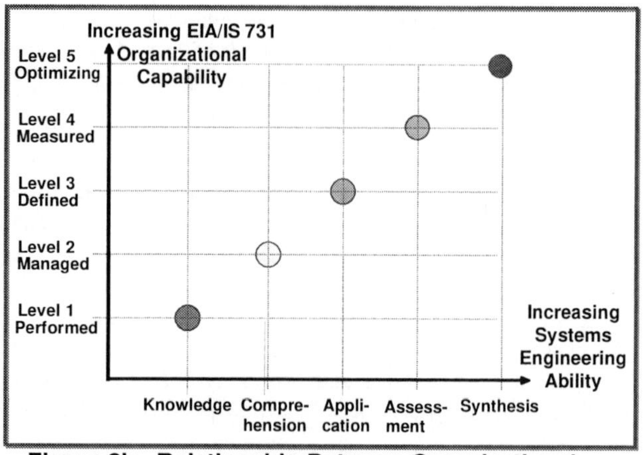

Figure 8b. Relationship Between Organizational Capability and a System Engineer's Ability

By examining the FA Practices in EIA/IS 731 at each Capability level, and the corresponding abilities defined for each learning classification it becomes clear that these are not merely points of intersection, but rather a continuum of areas along the diagonal. Each area represents a level of individual systems engineering competency. This concept is illustrated in Figure 8c as the graphical representation of the Systems Engineering Competency Model showing the five Systems Engineering Competency Levels (SECL), E-A. The letter names were chosen in the academic context where a grade of A is the highest individual achievement.

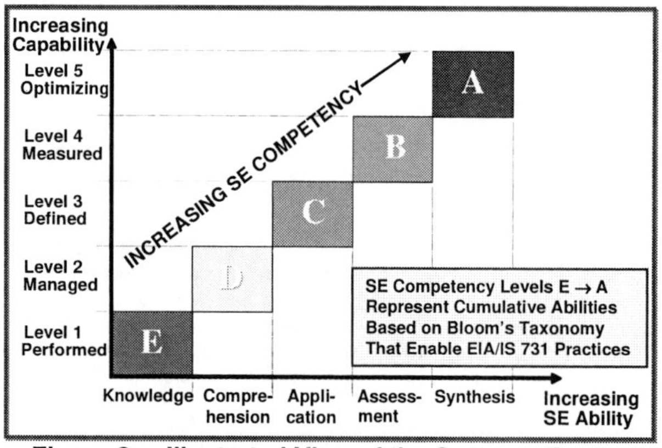

Figure 8c. Illustrated View of the Systems Engineering Competency Model

For a practitioner to adequately function in an organization at a given EIA/IS 731 capability level, he/she must possess a minimum set of knowledge and skills (abilities) to perform the Specific Practices within the Focus Areas (FA) at that capability level along with the Generic Practices and Attributes. Their competency to perform at a given EIA/IS 731 capability level, defined as their Systems Engineering Competency Level (SECL), depends on their learned abilities and experiences. A practitioner's current ability (shown on the horizontal axis) defines him/her to be at a given SECL.

If the SECL's corresponding EIA/IS 731 capability level (vertical axis) is below the organization's assessed (or desired) EIA/IS 731 capability level, the need for skills training is indicated. Note that learned abilities (horizontal axis) are inclusive, all knowledge and skill to the left of a given SECL are a prerequisite for the additional abilities to be performed at that SECL.

The Systems Engineering Competency Model Supports The Architecture of the EIA/IS 731. Figure 9 is an adaptation of Figure 2, Model Architecture, in EIA/IS 731 [3] illustrating how Systems Engineering Competency Levels relate to Categories, Focus Areas, Themes, Practices, and Attributes. For each Focus Area Theme there is a set of Specific Practices that must be performed at each of the five capability levels of EIA/IS 731. Performance of these practices requires corresponding abilities at the five levels of systems engineering competency, E-A, as shown in the bottom row of Figure 9.

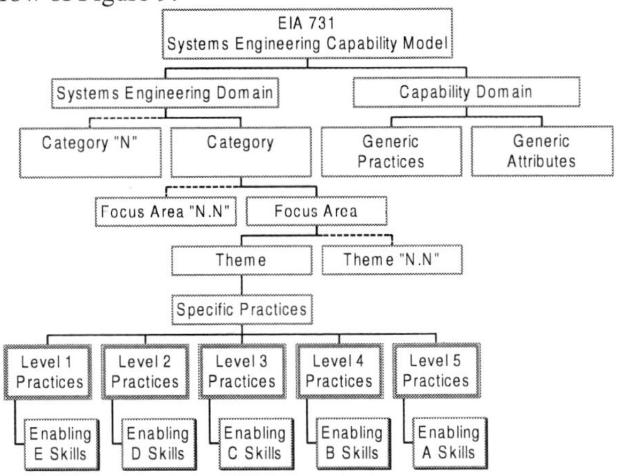

Figure 9. Systems Engineering Competency Related to Architecture of EIA/IS 731

The System Engineer Shall Be Able To ... To effectively function at a given SECL the systems engineer must be skilled in performing the applicable Specific Practices at the corresponding EIA/IS 731 organizational capability level. This may not be the same as the currently assessed level of the organization. It may be higher or lower. Because all lower level Specific Practices up to and including the current assessed level must be performed, a lower skilled engineer at a lower SECL may effectively perform the lower tasks. Likewise, due to process improvement, some higher level Specific Practices may need executing by a higher SECL engineer. One output of the Systems Engineering Competency Model is a training plan that uses a set of training verbs applied to the skills needed to perform each task in every Focus Area of EIA/IS 731. A needed skill for an individual SE may be characterized with a statement beginning, "The systems engineer shall be able to [training verb]......" A sample list of training verbs for each SECL is given in Figure 10. The training verbs articulate the needs prescribed by the organization capabilities and SE abilities at each SECL as shown to the left of the verbs in Figure 10. The *Taxonomy for Systems Engineering Competency* will contain the full population of Specific Practices for each Focus Area linked to one or more required skills, each with a training verb statement. An example of this is give in Figures 11 and 12 for the Ensure Quality Focus Area.

SE CL	Organization's Capabilities EIA/IS 731	SE Abilities (knowledge and skills)	Training Verbs "The SE shall be able to..."
A	OPTIMIZING Practices performed for continuous improvement to meet changing business goals	SYNTHESIS Ability to put together separate ideas to form a new whole with new relationships	adapt, anticipate, formulate, invent, plan, create, design, hypothesize, modify, collaborate, initiate, negotiate, combine
B	MEASURED Practices performed using defined metrics at all organizational levels against measurable criteria	ASSESSMENT Ability to separate information, show relationships, and judge worth against standard criteria	correlate, diagram, analyze, distinguish, categorize, compare, evaluate, critique, judge, appraise, rank, contrast
C	DEFINED Practices performed to tailored procedures that are improved via experience	APPLICATION Ability to use learned information and apply it to new situations	apply, compute, use, instruct, predict, record, solve, demonstrate, show, experiment, utilize, discover, relate
	MANAGED Practices performed to specific procedures with work products of adequate utility	COMPREHENSION Ability to grasp the meaning of information and explain ideas	classify, confirm, convert, describe, discuss, estimate, explain, illustrate, paraphrase, cite, translate, interpret
E	PERFORMED Practices performed informally by learned "heroes" with marginal work product utility	KNOWLEDGE Ability to recall learned information and reapply it to the same or similar situations	define, enumerate, list, describe, draw, identify, label, match, repeat, quote, recognize, select, write, view, recite, memorize, state

Figure 10. Capabilities and Abilities of the Model Define SE Training Verbs at Each SECL

Ensure Quality Example. Figure 11 shows how the three Taxonomy Models are applied to the Ensure Quality Focus Area. Figure 12 presents a detailed illustrative example of enabling skills for the SPs keyed to Figure 11.

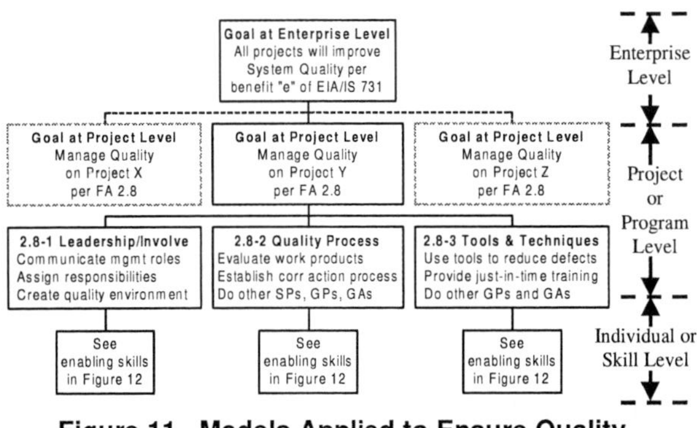

Figure 11. Models Applied to Ensure Quality

FA 2.8 Ensure Quality			
Th 2.8-1	**Leadership and Involvement**		
	SE CL	**Specific Practices**	**Enabling Skills**
	A	None	N/A
	B	None	N/A
	C	None	N/A
SP 2.8-1-2b	D	Create an environment that encourages employee participation in identifying, reporting, and solving quality issues quality issues	Explain problem solving process for solving process quality issues
SP 2.8-1-2a	D	Assign responsibility for product quality activities and improvements to the program team	Describe roles associated with product quality activities and improvements and explain selection of associates for each role
SP 2.8-1-1	E	Communicate management's role in quality improvement activities	Enumerate quality improvement activities and management's role associated with each activity
Th 2.8-2	**Quality Process**		
	SE CL	**Specific Practices**	**Enabling Skills**
	A	None	N/A
SP 2.8-2-4	B	Feed back lessons learned into processes for robustness of future designs	Analyze lessons learned to influence future process designs
SP 2.8-2-3b	C	Perform in-progress or incremental evaluations of work products and system elements against requirements	Demonstrate conformance of work product and system elements against requirements
SP 2.8-2-3a	C	Evaluate processes for adherence to standards and policies throughout the system life cycle	Record standards and policies used throughout system life cycle
SP 2.8-2-2	D	Establish a process to detect the need for corrective actions to products and processes	Describe problems requiring corrective actions to products and process
SP 2.8-2-1	E	Evaluate work products and system elements against requirements	List requirements for products and system elements
Th 2.8-3	**Tools and Techniques**		
	SE CL	**Specific Practices**	**Enabling Skills**
	A	None	N/A
	B	None	N/A
	C	None	N/A
SP 2.8-3-2	D	Provide readily available, just-in-time training on the use of advanced quality improvement tools	Describe readily available training for the use of advanced quality tools
SP 2.8-3-1	E	Use quality improvement tools in a disciplined manner to reduce defects and improve productivity	Select quality tools in the appropriate sequence to initially determine potential root cause problems affecting defects and productivity

Figure 12. Ensure Quality Focus Area

At the Enterprise Level, a goal from the Strategic Enterprise Model of practicing quality management is established based upon the "improve system quality" benefit of EIA/IS 731 (see item "e" in Figure 2). Since this is a corporate goal, every program is obligated to incorporate quality management at some level. Depending upon the type of program and life cycle phase, e.g., concept exploration or full-scale development, different strategies and levels of quality management are developed. The program would then assess using the Competency Needs Model, through a needs analysis, whether the skills exist or whether they need to be acquired at the individual level. If the skills exist, then no further training needs to be accomplished. However, if the skills need to be acquired through training, courses, or hiring, then using the Systems Engineering Competency Model, the objectives are developed and the skills acquired.

FUTURE ACTIVITIES

Near Term Activities. A detailed outline of *The Taxonomy of Systems Engineering Competency* will be finalized. The team plans to complete and prototype several sections of *The Taxonomy of Systems Engineering Competency*. These prototype sections will be given to key reviewers to solicit additional feedback and concurrence.

Mid-Term Activities. An author's guide will be generated and the core team will be expanded; additional sections of *The Taxonomy of Systems Engineering Competency* will be completed. At appropriate times, key reviewers will be asked to provide further feedback and concurrence. The document will be completed using this iterative "generate, review, incorporate comments" process. After the products of the CMMI effort are released, the concepts presented in this paper will be examined for applicability to the CMMI products.

Completion Activities. When *The Taxonomy of Systems Engineering Competency* is close to being completed, per discussions in the INCOSE Technical Board, the author team anticipates receiving a survey of systems engineering courses from the INCOSE Education and Training Technical Committee. This survey will be augmented as needed and mapped to *The Taxonomy of Systems Engineering Competency*. Both of these products requested by the INCOSE CAB will be provided to the INCOSE Technical Board and general INCOSE membership for review, incorporation of comments, and subsequent Technical Board approval.

The Taxonomy of Systems Engineering Competency should not be misconstrued as the Systems Engineering Body of Knowledge (SEBOK) being developed by INCOSE. However, the Taxonomy has the potential of being a significant citation by the SEBOK as a valuable part of the body of knowledge for systems engineering. This would especially be the case if the SEBOK was aligned with the EIA/IS 731 SECM, as is *The Taxonomy of Systems Engineering Competency*.

REFERENCES

[1] Merriam Co.; *Webster's Third New International Dictionary, Unabridged*; Encyclopedia Britannica; Illinois; 1976.

[2] E. R. Widmann, G. J. Hudak, T. A. Hudak, and G. E. Anderson; "Development of a Skills and Knowledge Taxonomy Aligned with the EIA/IS 731.1 Systems Engineering Capability Model";

Proceedings of the Ninth Annual International Symposium of the International Council on Systems Engineering; Brighton, United Kingdom; June 6 – 11, 1999.

[3] EIA Interim Standard 731, *Systems Engineering Capability*, EIA 731.1, Part 1: *Model,* Version 1.0; Electronic Industries Alliance; Arlington, VA; December 1998.

[4] EIA Interim Standard 731, *Systems Engineering Capability*, EIA 731-2, Part 2: *Appraisal Method*; Version 1.0; Electronic Industries Alliance; Arlington, VA; December 1998.

[5] G. J. Hudak; "Using the Capability Maturity Model to Improve Organizations"; *Proceedings of the 5th Conference on Concurrent Engineering and Integrated Product Design*; Hanover, NJ; Sept. 1998.

[6] E. R. Widmann; "Key Features of the 'Merged' EIA/IS 731.1 Systems Engineering Capability Model"; *Proceedings of the Eighth Annual International Symposium of the International Council on Systems Engineering*; Pages 597 – 604; Vancouver, British Columbia, Canada; July 26 – 30, 1998.

[7] "Section 7 Measuring Systems Engineering Capability"; *Systems Engineering Handbook*; International Council on Systems Engineering, Seattle, WA; January 1998.

[8] Bloom, Benjamin S.; *Taxonomy of Educational Objectives*; Longman, New York; 1956, 1984.

[9] R. J. Stiggins; *Measuring Thinking Skills in the Classroom*; National Education Association; 1988

BIOGRAPHIES

E. R. Widmann is in the Satellite Systems Engineering Operation of Hughes Space and Communications Company (HSC). He is currently involved with an effort to improve the management of requirements across several product lines of commercial communications and government satellites in order to achieve increased efficiencies. Previously, at Hughes Aircraft Company (HAC), now Raytheon Systems Company since December 1997, he served as a systems engineering manager on a number of electro-optical product development efforts for both land and airborne applications. He was also a key participant in systems engineering process activities, serving as the: (1) HAC-wide systems engineering representative for improving the HAC-developed, common Product Development Process (PDP) and (2) HAC-wide systems engineering lead responsible for deployment of a common systems engineering process, which was an integral part of the PDP. He also supported process-related activities associated with the transition of Hughes Aircraft Company to the Raytheon Systems Company. Prior to joining HAC, he was an officer in the US Army and spent four years in the Office of the Secretary of the Air Force, Office of Special Projects, and two years at the US Army Satellite Communications Agency. Mr. Widmann is currently a Member of the Technical Board of INCOSE, where he is Chair of a special Technical Board Team to develop *The Taxonomy of Systems Engineering Competency*. He previously served as a Member of the INCOSE Technical Board and Chair of the INCOSE Measurement Technical Committee from 1995 to 1998. He was the Chair of the INCOSE Capability Assessment Working Group from 1992 to 1995, where he organized and significantly contributed to the development of the INCOSE *Systems Engineering Capability Assessment Model.* He was the Associate Chair (US) of the INCOSE Standards Task Force from 1997 to 1998. He was the lead INCOSE representative on the EIA SECM Working Group and a co-author of the EIA/IS 731 *Systems Engineering Capability.* He is currently the HSC representative to the EIA G-47 (Systems Engineering) Committee and the HSC alternate representative to the INCOSE Corporate Advisory Board. Mr. Widmann has published extensively on systems engineering subjects. He has a M.S. Degree in Electrical Engineering from Purdue University and both a B.S. Degree in Electrical Engineering and a B.A. Degree with a concentration in Physics from Rutgers University.

G. E. Anderson is in the Space Systems Division of Honeywell International as the Technical Director for Space Shuttle Multiplexers/Demultiplexers. He chairs Honeywell's corporate Systems Engineering Council and is responsible for developing and deploying systems engineering processes, tools, training and certification guidelines. His 30 years of industry experience spans consumer electronics, urban transportation systems, military cockpit systems, and human space vehicle systems. Mr. Anderson has received many awards for his systems management and technical contributions to the industry. Applied technology experience includes advance research and patents in color television, development of systems for the Washington DC Metro, advanced cockpit display systems on major military aircraft, airborne real time video map optical memory system, and modernized data control & glass cockpit systems aboard the Space Shuttle. He is a recognized mentor and coaches both individuals and groups in developing their domain and process skills. Mr. Anderson represents Honeywell International on the INCOSE Corporate Advisory Board, served as an active member of Working Groups in the Measurement Technical Committee, and presently participates on the Educational Measurement Working Group. He is also on a special Technical Board Team developing The Taxonomy of Systems Engineering Competency, and has served as a Director of the Central Arizona Chapter. He has a BSEE degree from the J. B. Speed Engineering School with advanced studies at Purdue University and Arizona State University.

G. J. Hudak joined the faculty at Stevens Institute of Technology in Hoboken, NJ as a Distinguished Professor and is Director of the Integrated Product Development (IPD) Program. Previously, he was a Senior Member of the Technical Staff at AT&T Laboratories and served as an internal consultant in Project Management. In addition, he was involved in process optimizations at several manufacturing facilities prior to trivestiture at AT&T. At Stevens Institute of Technology, Professor Hudak is a member of the Mechanical Engineering Department and teaches graduate courses in Mechanical Engineering and Concurrent Engineering Programs. He is a registered professional engineer; a Senior Member of American Society for Quality; a member of the International Council on System Engineering and a Senior Member of IEEE. He was one of the co-authors of EIA/IS 731 Systems Engineering Capability and one of the participants in the development of the INCOSE Systems Engineering Capability Assessment Model. He is also on a special Technical Board Team developing The Taxonomy of Systems Engineering Competency. He has a BSEE Degree from Fairleigh Dickinson University, an MS Degree in Technology Management from Stevens Institute of Technology, and is currently in a Doctoral program at Stevens Institute of Technology.

T. A. Hudak is an adjunct professor in the School of Management of Stevens Institute of Technology where she teaches

Organization Behavior to graduate students. Previously she was a member of the Organization Development and Effectiveness Group of Bell Laboratories Advanced Technologies at Lucent Technologies. She is a past Chair of the Princeton Section of the American Society for Quality, and a member of the Association for the Management of Organization Design. She is also on the special INCOSE Technical Board Team Developing The Taxonomy of Systems Engineering Competency. She has an MS Degree in Organization Development from Mankato State University and ABD in Adult Learning from Rutgers University.

APPENDIX: MANAGE RISK FOCUS AREA

In [2] the authors provided an illustrative example consisting of only three themes for the Manage Risk Focus Area. Based upon the positive feedback received and to provide enhanced continuity with the concepts described in this paper and [2], a completed example for all themes within the Manage Risk Focus Area is provided.

FA 2.5 Manage Risk			
Th 2.5-1	**Risk Management (RM) Plan**		
	SE CL	**Specific Practices**	**Enabling Skills**
	A	None	N/A
	B	None	N/A
SP 2.5-1-3	C	Implement RM for key processes within program: design, test, manuf., etc.	Predict risk event impact upon processes.
SP 2.5-1-2	D	Provide an approved RM plan containing risk levels and expected mgmt responses for each level.	Classify risk events to expected management responses.
SP 2.5-1-1	E	Plan RM activities.	Know the elements of a Risk Mgmt Plan.
Th 2.5-2	**Identification of Performance, Cost, and Schedule Risks**		
	SE CL	**Specific Practices**	**Enabling Skills**
	A	None	N/A
	B	None	N/A
SP 2.5-2-3	C	Review all elements of the work breakdown structure as part of the risk identification process in order to help ensure that all program aspects have been considered.	Relate each work breakdown structure element to all other elements to identify all interactions and any high leverage sensitivities.
SP 2.5-2-2	D	Identify cost and schedule risks.	Estimate parametric costs and schedules.
SP 2.5-2-1	E	Identify performance risks.	List performance parameters and tolerances.
Th 2.5-3	**Risk Quantification**		
	SE CL	**Specific Practices**	**Enabling Skills**
	A	None	N/A
	B	None	N/A
	C	None	N/A
SP 2.5-3-2	D	Assess each risk and determine the probability of occurrence and quantified consequence of impact for the program.	Estimate the likelihood of the risk occurring and communicate impact.
SP 2.5-3-1	E	Assess risks qualitatively.	Describe the impact in terms of cost, schedule, and performance to the program.
Th 2.5-4	**Risk Analysis**		
	SE CL	**Specific Practices**	**Enabling Skills**
SP 2.5-4-5	A	None	N/A
SP 2.5-4-4	B	Use collected metrics regarding identified risks and examine them in light of previous risk analyses, and when established thresholds are exceeded, initiate corrective action.	Correlate and analyze data for magnitude and trends against established criteria, and distinguish data threshold values from "noise" in the data.
SP 2.5-4-3a	C	Review the analysis of risks for adequacy and completeness.	Apply standard criteria using a checklist.
SP 2.5-4-3b	C	For each risk, establish cause and effect relationships.	Relate events and outcomes using a decision tool.
SP 2.5-4-3c	C	Analyze each risk for potential coupling to all other identified risks.	Show the relationship between each risk and all other risks using sensitivity analysis.
SP 2.5-4-3d	C	Develop alternative courses of action, workarounds, and fall-back positions with a recommended course of action for each risk.	Apply a decision tree method and impact analysis using a planning tool to minimize negative consequences.
SP 2.5-4-2	D	None	N/A
SP 2.5-4-1	E	None	N/A
Th 2.5-5	**Development of a Risk Mitigation Strategy**		
	SE CL	**Specific Practices**	**Enabling Skills**
SP 2.5-5-5	A	None	N/A
SP 2.5-5-4	B	None	N/A
SP 2.5-5-3a	C	Document risk reduction profiles and re-view them for appropriateness.	Relate risk profile attributes to determine changes and risk triggers.
SP 2.5-5-3b	C	Review risk mitigation (handling) including risk reduction profile for adequacy and completeness.	Record data and apply it to risk mitigation and risk profiles.
SP 2.5-5-2	D	Categorize risk into those that can be avoided, controlled, or accepted.	Classify risks into a risk rating schema.
SP 2.5-5-1	E	None	N/A
Th 2.5-6	**Implementation of the Risk Mitigation Strategy**		
	SE CL	**Specific Practices**	**Enabling Skills**
SP 2.5-6-5	A	None	N/A
SP 2.5-6-4	B	None	N/A
SP 2.5-6-3	C	Document risk analysis results and mitigation plans.	Record data and plans in the prescribed format and location.
SP 2.5-6-2	D	Implement the risk mitigation strategy for the program.	Convert strategic plan wording into implementing actions.
SP 2.5-6-1	E	None	N/A
Th 2.5-7	**Monitoring of Risk Mitigation Action**		
	SE CL	**Specific Practices**	**Enabling Skills**
SP 2.5-7-5	A	None	N/A
SP 2.5-7-4	B	Use collected metrics regarding identified risks and examine them in light of previous risk analyses,	Distinguish new risks based on data analysis and categorize them for needed action.

		and when established thresholds are exceeded, initiate corrective action	
SP 2.5-7-3a	C	Monitor and re-evaluate risks at appropriate milestones.	Record and relate actual vs. predicted outcomes.
SP 2.5-7-3b	C	Provide the results of risk monitoring activities to affected personnel and disciplines.	Apply data sorting, data retrieval, and publication methods based on flag criteria.
SP 2.5-7-3c	C	Provide a mechanism for monitoring corrective actions taken and tracking open risk items to closure.	Utilize a data capture, data organization, data retrieval, and publication process, procedure, and tool.
SP 2.5-7-2	D	None	N/A
SP 2.5-7-1	E	None	N/A

Th 2.5-8	**Communication and Coordination of Risk Status and Risk Mitigation Efforts Across Affected Groups**		
	SE CL	**Specific Practices**	**Enabling Skills**
SP 2.5-8-5	A	None	N/A
SP 2.5-8-4	B	None	N/A
SP 2.5-8-3	C	Include risk management as a part of program formal reviews.	Show the status of risk elements and relate their significance.
SP 2.5-8-2a	D	Involve a multi-functional group for risk management that spans both technical and business specialties.	Describe and illustrate inter-relationships between multi-functional groups.
SP 2.5-8-2b	D	Integrate risk management both vertically and horizontally across the program.	Describe and illustrate inter-relationships between all program elements.
SP 2.5-8-1	E	Establish a communication path between the risk management team and the program management team.	Define a tailored process and describe a step-wise procedure for format, content, distribution, and archiving risk data.

Continuous Appraisal Method (CAM)...
A New Paradigm for Benchmarking Process Maturity

W. Neil Crowder
Lockheed Martin Information Systems
12506 Lake Underhill Road
Orlando, Florida 32825-5002

Marvin J. Carr
Lockheed Martin Mission Systems,
Systems & Software Resource Center
700 North Frederick Ave..
Gaithersburg, Maryland 20879-3328

ABSTRACT

The publication of EIA/IS 731.1 Systems Engineering Capability Model (SECM) establishes a standard against which an organization determines its level of process maturity for systems engineering. EIA/IS 731.2 SECM Appraisal Method provides guidance on the conduct of an appraisal using the SECM. The EIA/IS 731.2 method of derterming the process maturity level is based upon the Software Engineering Institute's (SEI) CMM® (Capability Maturity Model) Based Assessment for Internal Process Improvement (CBA IPI) that has been the engineering process maturity appraisal method of choice since its first use in 1994. This paper presents an alternative method for appraising an orgnaization's engineering maturity level—the Continuous Appraisal Method (CAM). CAM provides a significant advantage over the CBA IPI in three areas. First the cost of using CAM is significantly lower than using CBA IPI. Second, CAM allows considerable felexability in scheduling program time during the appraisal. Third, CAM becomes an integral part an organization's process improvement initiative by providing timely feedback on process improvement opportunities.

INTRODUCTION

The adoption of the Software Engineering Institute's (SEI's) Software Capability Maturity Model (SW-CMM®) as the defacto standard for measuring process maturity has led to more significant process improvement efforts than all previous process improvement initiatives combined. As an adjunct, SEI's CMM® Based Assessment for Internal Process Improvement (CBA IPI) has been the engineering process maturity appraisal method of choice since its first use in 1994. The CBA IPI method has been used to appraise the software engineering process maturity of more than 840 organizations[1].

Although proven effective, the CBA IPI has been the subject of many professional discussions over the past several years as to how the appraisal method might be improved. With the publication of EIA/IS 731.1, "Systems Engineering Capability Model" (SECM) and EIA/IS 731.2, SECM "Appraisal Method", systems engineering is rapidly following software into measuring process maturity.

To date, only a handful of systems engineering organizations have been independently appraised under EIA/IS 731. Lockheed Martin Information Systems Company (LMIS), in Orlando, FL teamed with Lockheed Martin Mission Systems, Systems and Software Resource Center (LMMS-SSRC) in Gaithersburg, MD to conduct an independent SECM based appraisal in 1999. The point of interest of this appraisal was not the maturity level attained but the appraisal method used. The appraisal was conducted over a period of several months using a new EIA/IS 731.2 compliant appraisal method – the Continuous Appraisal Method (CAM).

CAM, developed jointly by LMIS and LMMS-SSRC, represents a significant departure from the CBA IPI method yet maintains the rigor and effectiveness of SEI's proven technique. The intent of this paper is to:

1. Examine the reasons for developing a new approach
2. Describe CAM
3. Report the experiences of the first Lockheed Martin organization appraised using CAM

WHY RE-EXAMINE PROCESS APPRAISAL METHODS?

Continuous Process Improvement (CPI) applies to an appraisal process just as much as it applies to the engineering processes it measures. The CBA IPI assessment method has gone largely unchanged and unchallenged for over five years. There is no doubt the CBA IPI method has proven itself very effective, but it would be unfortunate for the method to be excluded from CPI and CPI's strongest asset, optimization. In addition, since systems engineering is being included in the forthcoming SEI CMM® Integration (CMMI℠), a window of opportunity is open to propose

[1] 840 CBA IPI results have been reported to the SEI as of July 1999

changes/alternatives to the current CBA IPI method.

DEVELOPING A NEW APPROACH

Basic Assumptions. Since LMIS was embarking on the journey of improving and measuring systems engineering processes in somewhat uncharted territory, there was an opportunity to treat the selection of an appraisal process as a process improvement opportunity. This was possible because there was no firmly institutionalized implementation of the "Appraisal Method" requirements outlined in EIA/IS 731.2.

LMIS adopted three basic assumptions for its systems engineering process improvement effort:

1. The Generic Practices (GPs) and Specific Practices (SPs) of EIA 731.1, as tailored for the LMIS business case, would serve as the requirements baseline for the LMIS Systems Engineering standard organizational process.
2. The approach to measuring the compliance to the entire set of SPs could be treated in the same manner as verifying system requirements when building a product.
3. The appraisal process would be conducted by an independent organization with proven credentials in conducting software CBA IPIs.

   LMMS-SSRC was asked to take on the role of independent appraiser. SSRC is a Lockheed Martin corporate resource independent of the operating companies and a recognized leader in process appraisal having conducted over 16 CBA IPIs over the past five years.
4. The appraisal process would fully comply with the requirements of EIA/IS 731.2.

   EIA/IS 731.1 and 731.2 were tailored in one area. LMIS decided not to use the Generic Attributes (GAs), measures of systems engineering work product "value", outlined in EIA/IS 731.1. After considerable discussion the decision was made that the GAs were too subjective and essentially amounted to un-testable requirements. This position was further strengthened when the SEI's CMMI^{SM} draft was published and did not address GAs.

The "Build-a-little-test-a-little" Approach to Process Appraisal. LMIS and LMMS-SSRC agreed to collaborate in developing a plan, which would clearly delineate the appraisal to be conducted. In January 1999, the executives of LMIS and SSRC collectively signed the "1999 LMIS SE Assessment Plan in accordance with EIA Standard 731-2". The basis of this plan was a new approach to be used in conducting both the process improvement and appraisal tasks – "build-a-little-test-a-little" using an incremental testing philosophy.

Both LMIS and SSRC were confident that the new approach was sound, since, although not used in the process improvement appraisal arena to date, the "build-a-little-test-a-little" philosophy had been used quite successfully for years in verifying critical products for the U.S. DoD. In addition, the approach fulfilled the stated requirement for full compliance with EIA/IS 731.2.

Examining the Opportunities for Improvement. The decision to implement an incremental appraisal approach was the result of an analysis of the current CBA IPI appraisal method. The entire process appraisal task was examined to arrive at the opportunities for improvement. The analysis yielded the following areas as candidates for appraisal method improvement:

1. Emphasize proactive process improvement and de-emphasize a pass/fail audit philosophy
2. Create a positive environment by decreasing the fear factor involved in appraisals
3. Accept senior management's (and the customer's) use of maturity level as a process metric
4. Make it less invasive to the product producing projects
5. Make it less expensive...or get more for the money
6. Get more feedback on improvement opportunities from the appraisal
7. Focus on *Continuous Process Improvement* as opposed to a "snap-shot" audit
8. Address the growing DoD perception of "cherry-picking" appraisal target programs
9. Ensure that the independence and rigor of the CBA IPI method is maintained or enhanced

Developing the Appraisal Method Architecture. In developing the appraisal method, LMIS and SSRC first looked to EIA/IS 731.1 & 2. for guidance. A few driving concepts from this review emerged:

> "The scope of the appraisal method is designed specifically to support continuous process improvement."
>
> "The focus and tone of the Appraisal Method is self-improvement versus audit.
>
> "The process described concentrates on a feedback loop that includes multiple levels of the entity being appraised."
>
> "The On-Site phase may occur as several site visits."

This last concept of multiple on-site visits was the

key to deciding upon the incremental (continuous) testing approach of "build-a-little-test-a-little". In addition, EIA/IS 731.2 didnot precluded using the second basic concept of "build-a-little-test-a-little" — regression testing. The bottom line of the EIA/IS 731.2 review was that nowhere in EIA/IS 731.2 was a single event "pass/fail" appraisal mandated. This allowed the LMIS/SSRC team to address all of the improvement opportunities listed above and still be in full compliance with EIA/IS 731.2.

Upon completion of the review of EIA/IS 731.1 & 731.2, the way was clear to develop the basic architecture of the combined process improvement effort and appraisal method as a three-phase approach:

Phase I – Develop the Organizational Standard Process

1. Tailor EIA/IS 731.1 to develop and document an organizational standard process compliant with the GPs and SPs of the target maturity level (SECM Level 3 for LMIS)
2. Form an independent appraisal team
3. Appraise the organizational standard process against the Generic Practices (GPs) and Specific Practices (SPs) for each Focus Area (FA)
4. Identify process deficiencies and recommend improvements
5. Address the identified process deficiencies to improve the process(es)
6. Re-appraise...[repeat 5) though 7 as necessary until the processes in each FA are compliant with EIA/IS 731.1]
7. Re-examine objective evidence after the initial appraisal to ensure process maintenance over time
8. Certify the standard organizational to the target maturity level
9. Prototype the organizational standard process on a LMIS project to "de-bug" the process
10. Roll out the organizational standard process to all projects
11. **Phase II** – Appraise 3 to 4 Target Programs to the target SECM Maturity LevelAppraise the tailored processes for 3 to 4 Programs to the target SECM Maturity Level against the Organizational Standard Process by appraising the Generic Practices (GPs) and Specific Practices (SPs) for each Focus Area (FA)
12. Identify process deficiencies and recommend improvements
13. Address the identified process deficiencies to improve the process(es)
14. Re-appraise...[repeat 11 though 13 as necessary until the processes in each FA are compliant with EIA/IS 731.1]
15. Re-examine objective evidence after the initial appraisal to ensure process maintenance over time
16. Certify the 3 to -4 target programs to the target maturity level

Phase III – Continue to Appraise All Projects to Ensure Institutionalization

17. Continue to independently appraise all other projects in the organization to ensure complete institutionalization of the processes across the organization *[essentially...repeat steps 11 through 15, but for projects only since the Organization Standard Process has already been certified]*

This three-phase method for CPI as used by LMIS and SSRC to develop and appraise Systems Engineering Processes is illustrated in Figures 1 and 2 below. Figure 1 depicts the method's overall flow while Figure 2 depicts the typical schedule for Phase III, continuous appraisal.

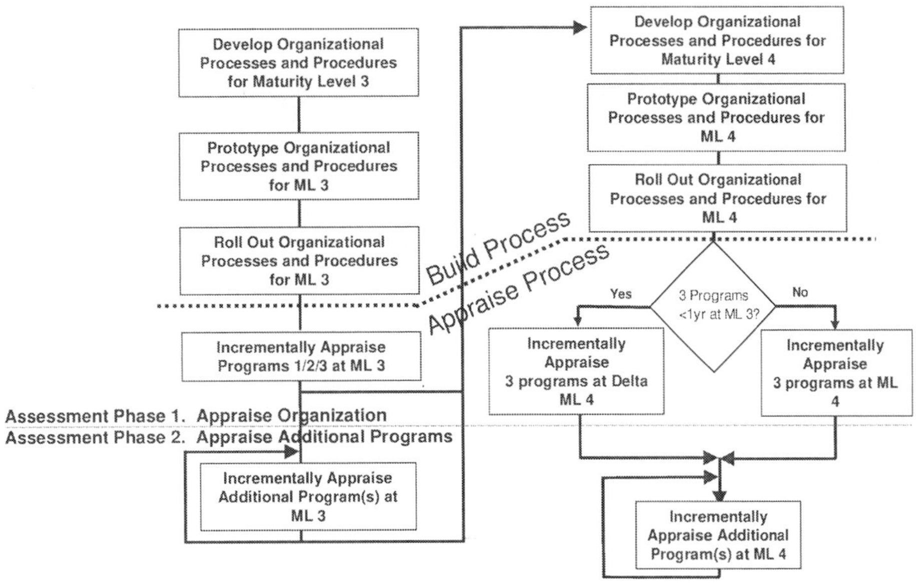

Figure 1. CAM Process Flow

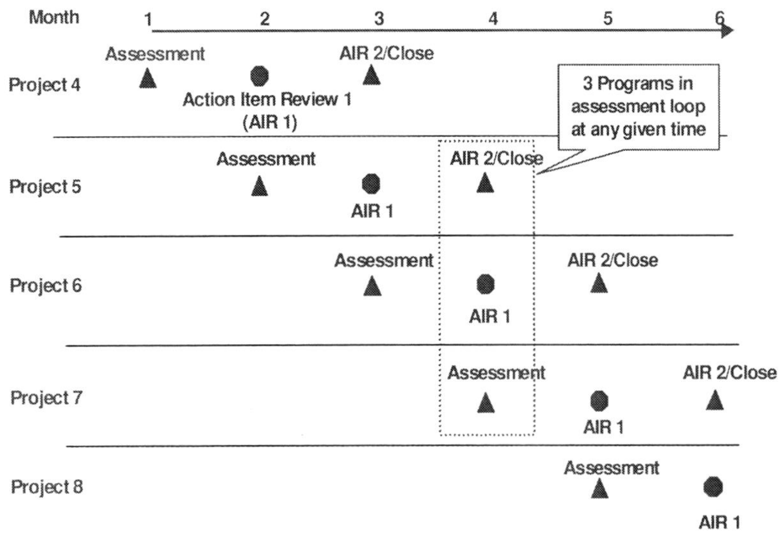

Figure 2. Typical Cam Phase III Schedule

CONDUCT OF THE APPRAISAL USING CAM

Appraisal Team Composition. Because the appraisal is accomplished over an extended period of time, the Appraisal Team for CAM can be quite small. In fact the team can consist of as few as two people:

1. Independent Assessment Team Lead (ATL)
2. Organizations' Systems Engineering Process Owner

   In some companies a VP/Director/Manager is considered the process owner and would be quite impossible to get that person on the team. The "process owner" has to be a person with authority to direct a program to change its process to be compliant with the command media or with the authority to change the command media.

The two-person team is consistent with the common SEI CBA IPI technique of forming "mini-teams" of two people each (one external and one internal) to review specifically assigned SEI SW-CMM® Key Practice Areas (KPAs). In addition, the two-person team is compliant with Lockheed Martin's internal policy of at least a 50/50 mix of external team members to internal team members. In practice, the need for larger teams is driven solely by the amount of information to be appraised over a short period of time. Since the time constraint has been essentially removed in CAM, there is no need for a large appraisal team.

The LMIS Appraisal Team consisted of two people, the SSRC ATL and the LMIS Chief Systems Engineer (process owner) for the detailed SP by SP appraisal. The team was augmented by another independent appraiser from SSRC for the "Maintenance Review" (described in the next section, below).

The LMIS experience demonstrated the effectiveness of an approach, which included the process owner in all appraisal activities. Due to the inherent "pass/fail" characteristic of a CBA IPI coupled with the fact that the organization's process owner is usually the person with the most to lose in the event of failure, having the process owner on the appraisal team has been deemed, and probably correctly, a "conflict-of-interest" (COI) in the past. Certainly if not a true COI, the process owner's basic fear of failure might prove very disruptive to the other team members as well as the appraisal process itself. Since CAM presents little if any fear of failure, the process owner is free to take a full role in the appraisal. This is especially useful, since the process owner usually has the organizational authority to approve various project implementation methods, or, perhaps more importantly, take actions to change the organizational standard process itself if need be. Having the ATL from an independent organization and giving this person "thumbs up/thumbs down" authority thoroughly mitigates any COI.

The fear of failure of this method has been decreased to the point that any organization truly interested in process improvement would welcome any stakeholder, including the customer, on the Appraisal Team as long as the size of the team was kept to a minimum and all team members fully understood the difference between the requirement to appraise for compliance to the practices of EIA/IS 731 as opposed to an opportunity to dictate individual preference.

Appraisal Conduct. The entire appraisal is conducted in an informal manner usually at the workstation of the person who is responsible for either generating or maintaining program artifacts that are objective evidence for the appraisal. There are no interview sessnons that involve several project personnel at one time. Project personnel are not briefed on what to present or to say. The Appraisal Team is free to ask any questions of any person at any time and ask to see any objective evidence at any time. Confidentiality is also of little concern since retaliation for "failure" is no longer a significant factor. The only confidentiality concern is to protect the information gathered for the appraisal in whatever manner thc "owners" of the information (the organization being appraised) desires.

Since the appraisal focuses on improving processes to a level compliant with an industry standard in a largely unspecified time period as opposed to "passing the audit" at a designeated date, fear of the appraisal is for all intents and purposes non-existent. The LMIS experience demonstrated that project personnel were very forthright and participated as critical reviewers, pointing out numerous process improvement opportunities to the Appraisal Team.

An appraisal session, although informal and non-confrontational, can be fairly intensive for the appraisal team, in some cases lasting a full day. Considerable time is required because each FA is reviewed SP by SP. Each systems engineering work product must be thoroughly reviewed by the Appraisal Team, both before the appraisal session as well as during the session with the actual practitioners present. Systematically reviewing 100% of the SPs gives the Appraisal Team a thorough understanding of the organization's systems engineering process as implemented by projects. This is in contrast to a CBA IPI where time constraints imposed on the appraisal team allow only a sampling of the processes.

No hard-copy objective evidence library is required since the Appraisal Team goes to the project and conducts the session in the project area with the appropriate personnel at their workstations, actual work products, such as an on-line Systems Engineering Management Plan (SEMP) or DOORS© requirements database, are used to explain process implementations. Deficiencies against EIA 731.1 GPs or SPs are identified and a detailed action plan is documented for implementation by the project. When the action plan is completed, the deficiency is re-appraised for compliance. If the practice is still deficient, the process is repeated until compliance is reached. CAM can be viewed as a "gap analysis" with action items to fill in the gaps. When the action items have been worked off, the desired maturity level is reached, and CAM is complete. One participant in the LMIS appraisal probably best stated a key concept of CAM:

"...failure appears optional..."

The "Maintenance ReviewMaintenance Review" – Demonstrating Process Maintenance. After the organizational standard process and the 3 to 4 target program implementations have been appraised and deemed fully compliant with the requirements of EIA/IS 731, there is still one issue which must be addressed – process maintenance. It is conceivable that a project could implement an individual FA, get certified, then forget about the process and go on to the next FA. This same concern is the reason for final exams in colleges. To address this concern, the concept of a "Maintenance Review" became an inherent part of the appraisal process. This Maintenance Review has one and only one objective in CAM – demonstrate that the project is performing all the processes previously determined compliant by the Appraisal Team. This review is in no way a re-do of the previous appraisal work. All the organization and target projects must demonstrate that they are performing the processes on a day-to-day basis.

The "Maintenance Review" is executed as a relatively short demonstration of the ongoing execution and maintenance of previously appraised processes. This last appraisal task is based on the objective evidence reviewed during the previous appraisal activities. Essentially, the Appraisal Team will review that objective evidence which has a recurring preparation time. For example, a project demonstrates a process to hold risk meetings once a week with minutes as the objective evidence. It is reasonable to assume that if this process is truly in use, then minutes for numerous risk meetings conducted after the "Manage Risk" FA appraisal was completed should be available. The project will be asked to demonstrate this objective evidence at the "Maintenance Review".

The "Maintenance Review" is conducted on a sample basis as opposed to a census of all SPs. Once the Appraisal Team is satisfied that the target projects are maintaining their processes in the manner previously indicated, Phase II of the appraisal is finished and a documentation of level acheivement is rendered to the organization. In turn, the organization proceeds with appraising new programs. All programs will be appraised at some time in their life cycle for each maturity level.

HOW CAM ADDRESSES THE PROCESS IMPROVEMENT OPPORTUNITIES

As the reader will recall in the previous section, a list of appraisal method process improvement opportunities was presented. If the method described herein is worthwhile, then it certainly should address some if not all of the process improvement opportunities listed. The following demonstrates how CAM addresses these opportunities.

Emphasize Process and De-emphasize Results.

- Creates an on-going, multiple event method (...process oriented...) as opposed to a pass/fail, single event method (...results oriented...)

The goal is truly process improvement instead of "pass the test"

Decrease the Fear Factor Involved in Appraisals.

- Addresses the fear component...the fear of failure...little reward and big risks associated with participation
- Creates a cooperative non-adversarial relationship between the assessors and participants
- Makes failure an "option"
- Fully discusses deficiencies with the project
- Documents deficiencies as action items
- Includes the corrective action plan as part of the AI
- Re-assesses after corrective actions implemented

Accept Process Maturity Level As a Process Metric.

- Accepts the adage "what gets measured gets done"
- Recognizes that SEI CBA IPIs (and SCEs) assessments have fueled more process improvement than almost all other process initiatives combined
- Recognizes that executive management and the customer need (...and are demanding...) a high level process metric
- Accepts this need as a positive requirement and satisfies it

Make It Less Invasive to Projects.

- Goes to the participants and talks to them
- Helps the projects do business better by understanding and discussing their processes fully
- Doesn't create huge "one-use-only" objective evidence libraries
- Doesn't inundate projects all at once
- Doesn't penalize certain projects for participation...all participate equally, just at different times

Make It Less Expensive or Get More for the Money.

- Gets the most process improvement opportunities possible from the assessors...and the participants
- Assessors are given the opportunity to fully understand the processes being assessed
- No time constraints
- Full access to participants...at any time
- No scripts...just in-depth discussions with anyone on the project
- Encourages participants to become self-

assessors...they are also usually subject matter experts

-
- Doesn't reassess an entire organization to correct a few serious discrepancies...Re-test only what's necessary

Get More Feedback.

- Uses the assessors as Subject Matter Experts (SMEs)
- Provides the most effective feedback...direct to the organization/project practitioners
- Opens the discussion of deficiencies to provide full understanding...and more effective correction
- Allows the Organization's process owner (Chief Systems Engineer) to gain detailed knowledge of exactly how each project is implementing the organizational standard process (and to guide projects on tailoring)

The Perception of "Cherry-picking" Assessment Target Programs.

- Three phase continuous process improvement approach
- Certifies the standard organizational process and 3-4 tailored implementations as being compliant at a certain maturity level
- Assesses all other programs as part of an on-going assessment program...no programs are left out
- Assessment reports are open records
- The LMIS Quality Management System (QMS) conducts on-going compliance audits after a project has been independently appraised

RESULTS OF THE APPLICATION OF CAM

CAM was used to appraise two Lockheed Martin Companies in 1999 at an EIA/IS 731 maturity level 3. A comparison of the costs of using CAM to appraise system engineering processes verses the costs to appraise software engineering processes using CBA IPI showed that using CAM was at least 50% less than using CBA IPI to appraise software processes of the same companies. The cost savings came about in the following ways:

- There was no pre-appraisal to ensure the programs had achieved the desired maturity level.
- There was no need to train/coach the program members in the assessment method
- The large hard copy one-shot objective evidence library was eliminated
- The interviews and viewing objective evidence were conducted with the appropriate program personnel at their workstation.

Because the fear of failure was absent, program personnel actively participated in the appraisal by identifying process improvements in the program's processes and providing insight into improving the command media.

LESSONS LEARNED

The following lessons were learned in the applying CAM:

- The process owner must be a recognized expert system engineer.
- If the company's "process owner" leaves the appraisal team, the appraisal is to be re-planned.
- The ATL keeps action item list
- Action items are closed only by concurrence of the ATL and "process owner".
- When an organizational process is verified as being compliant, the process document is placed under configuration management and cannot be changed without notifying the ATL
- It is recommend at least one additional independent appraiser be on the maintenance review team
- At least a 50/50 split of independent appraisers and internal organization members (there can be more independent appraisers than internal organizational members)
- No person who has been on one of the target programs is to be on the final review team. This person brings a definite bias to the table.
- No person who is a member of the Systems Process Group (other than the process owner) is to be a member of the final review team. Members of the process group have a definite ownership in the processes and as such are biased.

SUMMARY

LMIS completed the implementation of Phases I and II of the Continuous Appraisal Method in December 1999 achieving Level 3. The company considers CAM a significant improvement over the CBA IPI. LMIS projects fully support the activity and actually point out improvement opportunities. Independence has been ensured as the LMMS-SSRC ATL is strictly a reviewer/assessor.

A comparative analysis of the 1997 LMIS software Level 3 CBA IPI costs to the costs incurred in the 1999 SECM Level 3 CAM appraisal indicated that the CAM appraisal cost 50% less than the CBA IPI. Care was taken to ensure a like-to-like comparison, however, given the inherent differences of the two disciplines evaluated, further analysis must be conducted. Regardless of the obvious "apples-to-oranges" weakness of the analysis, LMIS is convinced that CAM represents a significant cost savings over the CBA IPI method.

LMIS feels strongly that CAM yielded significant benefits per dollar spent. Fear is almost non-existent, but compliance is exceptional...people recognize that they have total control over "passing the test". Briefings to the customer to date have been very positive and senior management is pleased with the ability to continuously monitor systems engineering processes and compliance.

CAM should be considered a strong alternative to the current CBA IPI method of appraising process maturity.

BIOGRAPHY

W. Neil Crowder. Mr. Crowder is the Chief Systems Engineeer for Lockheed Martin Information Systems in Orlando, Florida. Mr. Crowder graduated in 1973 with a BS from Oklahoma State University. Upon graduation, Mr . Crowder entered the United States Air Force and earned a MS degree in Systems and Logistics from the Air Force Institute of Technology (AFIT) in 1978 and an MBA, concentrating in Operations Research, from the University of Wyoming in 1981. Upon leaving the military in 1981, Mr. Crowder started with Martin Marietta (now Lockheed Martin) in Denver, Colorado and has been with the company since.

Marvin J. Carr. Mr. Carr Joined Lockheed Martin Mission Systems – Systems and Software Resource Center (SSRC) from the Software Engineering Institute (SEI) where he was the Risk Program project leader. In this position, Mr. Carr was the lead and principal developer of the Software Risk Evaluation (SRE) process used to identify risks facing a software-dependent system development. Mr. Carr has led over 25 SREs covering both aerospace and commercial companies. Before joining the SEI, Mr. Carr spent over 32 years developing and delivering real time software systems at McDonnell Douglas, Hughes Aircraft, and TRW. As the senior manager of Software Engineering Technology at the McDonnell Douglas Electronic Systems company, Mr. Carr was responsible for the company's software process improvement initiative.

Mr. Carr received a bachelor's degree in physics from the Michigan Technology University and a master's degree in Organizational development from the University of San Francisco.

Systems Engineering Framework for Deploying eCommerce Websites

Bharat Shah
MASS, Inc.
15008 Eastway Drive
Silver Spring
Maryland - 20905

Abstract. The more recent rise of the World Wide Web (WWW), driven by corporate acceptance and adoption, has revolutionised a new age of doing business. Companies of all types and sizes are faced with doing business via Internet or face the risk of going out of business. This has led to an exponential growth in eCommerce (Electronic Commerce) using integrated communications and electronic data interchange (EDI) technologies.

This paper describes a Systems Engineering Life Cycle framework for the successful implementation of eCommerce application project. A methodology followed is based on systems engineering principles to ensure that eCommerce requirements are understood and designed properly. The highlights in support of this title include:

- Emphasis on eCommerce application needs analysis;
- Understand systems engineering framework to design, implement and maintain eCommerce applications;
- Understand how eCommerce technologies can be applied to achieve competitive advantage by transforming relationships with customers, suppliers and business partners.

ELECTRONIC COMMERCE OVERVIEW

Electronic Commerce (eCommerce) is a platform for selling products and services via Internet. Rather than being a single uniform technology, electronic commerce is characterised by a wide range of business operations and transactions, including:

- Establishment of business-to-business relationship;
- Electronic payment (using electronic funds transfer, credit cards, electronic cheques, electronic cash);
- Electronic distribution of products and services;
- Exchange of information;
- Pre-and post-sales support;
- Customer Relationship management(CRM) and
- Virtual enterprises - groups of independent companies that pool their competencies so that they can offer products or services that would be beyond the capabilities of any of the individual companies.

eCommerce offers companies fundamentally new ways to expand the markets in which they compete, and provides substantial cost savings while simultaneously improving customer service and forging stronger ties with customers. In the past, eCommerce often meant expensive, complicated, and rigid Electronic Data Interchange (EDI) value-added network (VAN) systems for business-to-business transactions. It's no wonder why, in a recent survey of Datamation readers only 6% had installed a VAN-based e-commerce system. Today, however, eCommerce is moving beyond the EDI VAN sphere by leveraging the Internet, either by using Web technology or by extending EDI. According to published report, volumes of goods and services sold via Internet have doubled in the year 1998 to $5+ billion and will reach to 200+ billion by 2002.

eCommerce Technologies. In past two years, there is an unprecedented growth in the number of Internet based technologies on the market. While many technologies can fit within the definition of "electronic commerce," the most important are:

- Electronic Data Interchange (EDI)
- Electronic Mail (e-mail)
- Electronic Forms.

EDI in recent years has become very important technology of eCommerce. It has enabled businesses to extend their enterprise and improve efficiencies for electronic communication between buyers and sellers thereby maximizing the business potential of electronic commerce. Uilizing Internet-based technologies eCommerce platform has protected their EDI investment and business methods. However, each technology needs to be weighed in terms of cost and appropriateness to the specific eCommerce application along with related systems security technologies such as firewalls, encryption, message integrity, and customer and merchant authentication.

eCommerce Applications: eCommerce applications differ from client-server applications in a number of ways, all centered around a core concept: who, when and what:

- ***Who:*** eCommerce is direct to the customer. There are no set users or training classes or manuals.
- ***When:*** eCommerce availability is real-time 24x7 with response time only dependent on network resources. If system is "down" or "slow", customer won't wait, they will use different vendor.
- ***What:*** Traditional client-server applications are directed at cost reduction and labor-savings. eCommerce applications, on the other hand are revenue-oriented applications, where "business partner" is marketing and sales.

This customer driven eCommerce environment, while advantageous for some applications, can be difficult for conducting online applications (identified below) with secure transactions and payment processing.

- Online trading
- Online auctions
- Online publishing
- Online shopping
- Online procurement
- Online billing
- Online payment and
- Many more.

For the purpose of this paper, Systems Engineering approach to successful implementation and disciplines required for implementing **eCommerce based Online Payment Processing** application is described below.

Online Payment. Until recently, bill presentation and payment processing has been traditional client-server based application. With the rapidly evolving electronic marketing channel, for business how small or big, the world of electronic commerce is both alluring and intimidating. According to estimates by Killen & Associates Inc., a Palo Alto, Calif., market research company, if the nation's utility companies switched overnight to delivering bills to customers and receiving payment only in electronic format, the utilities could save $1.2 billion annually. However, for them one of the most confusing issues is how to accept payment. Also adding to the confusion is the wide variety of payment methods available, both in the physical and online world, with everything from payment cards to cash, and Electronic Fund Transfer (EFT) to microtransactions.

However, with the recent development in eCommerce based technologies and tools, today's Online Payment Processing systems feature secure credit card and cash transactions over the Internet, using such protocols as

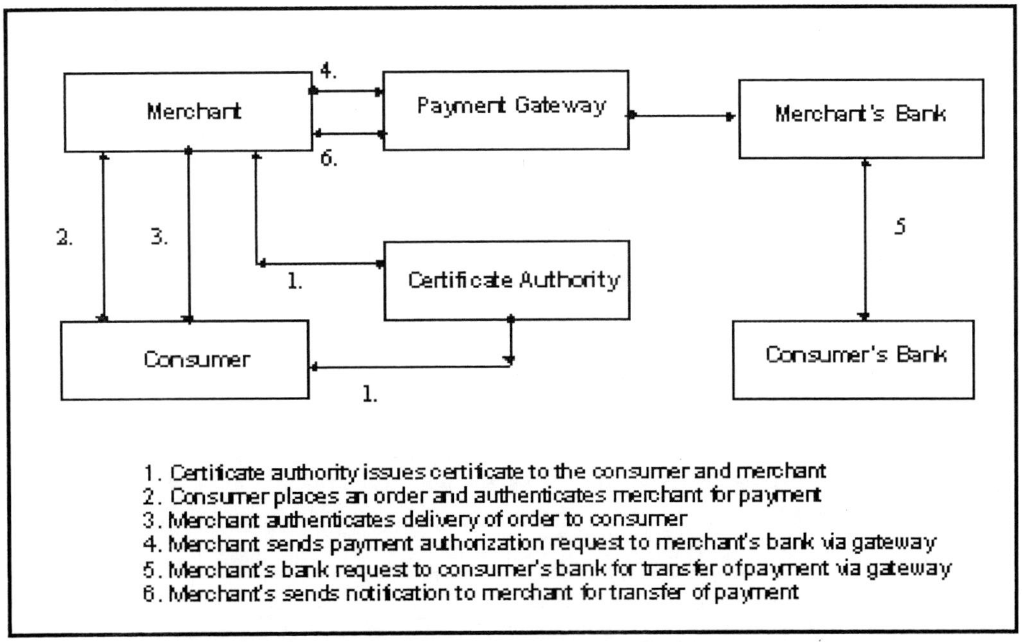

Figure 1: Payment Processing Transaction Flow

digital coins, electronic checks, and SET (Secure Electronic Transaction), defined by Visa/MasterCard. These applications are often turnkey implementations and support the purchase of both digital products (soft goods) and hard goods.

A typical Electronic Payment Processing System Transaction Flow (Figure-1) includes communication between the biller (Merchant), the consumer and the processing banks that handle the transfer of funds. The biller delivers the bill electronically to the consumer for the product or services sold or ordered. The consumers make the payment electronically for the products or services purchased. And the banks provide payment approval to the biller and transfers funds to the billers' bank.

SYSTEMS ENGINEERING FRAMEWORK

Organizations planning to provide such an Online Payment Processing website have to face number of challenges. Many different tools handle some or all of Payment Processing, but these tools provide varying levels of flexibility and require different skill sets for effective development and system implementation. To make such an Online Payment Processing work, the system has to be as reliable and accurate as paper.

This framework model follows the Waterfall systems engineering methodology (Figure-2). Each phase is culminated by either verification or a validation activity to eliminate as many problems as possible before proceeding to the next. Upon completing all the phases listed below for Online Payment Processing, this document can serve as a road map for any eCommerce based project. Some ideas may work as described, but the systems engineers and designers will usually need to creatively adapt an idea to their particular eCommerce requirements:

- Systems Need
- Systems Requirements,
- Systems Design,
- Systems Implementation,
- Systems Integration and Testing,
- Systems Installation and Acceptance,
- Systems Operation and Maintenance,
- Systems Retirement.

A detailed explanation of each phase is described next.

Systems Need

The primary tasks to perform in this phase are to gather information and needs related to the Payment Processing Website deployment. Starting with a well-defined approach helps and provides clarity for the developers. It is also an excellent tool for communicating to other team members and stakeholders on what will be included and what will be left to future releases. Once you have defined the need, prepare the

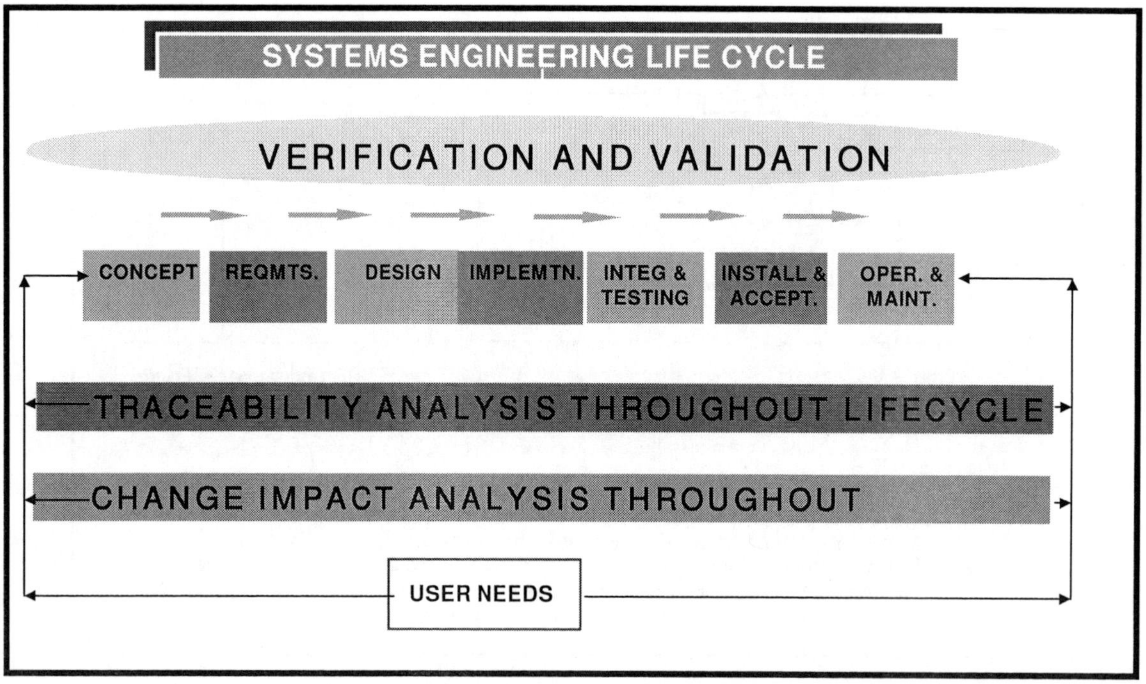

Figure 2: Systems Engineering Life Cycle

website plan that includes answers to the following questions:

1. ***What?:*** What's the need of your site? Understanding your eCommerce needs is an important step to understanding which payment solution is right for you. The right solution is based on your answers to the following questions:

   - Does business currently do selling to consumers, other businesses, or both?
   - Is a business considered as subscription-based business, such as utility company?
   - Does business currently have an existing payment processing mechanism?
   - Does business currently have hardware and software to deploy a website?
   - What volume of business you expect over the next 1,2,5 years?
   - What are the business risks involved in launching an eCommerce website?

2. ***Who?:*** Who are the stakeholders?. Consumer, Cardholder, Issuer, Payment Card, Merchant, Financial Institutions, Certificate Authority and Third Parties. List the stakeholders' background, their interests, skills, values and knowledge.

3. ***When?*** When do you want to start your site? How often do you plan on updating your site - daily, weekly, twice a month, or monthly?

4. ***Where?*** Where is your site going to be hosted? Your existing Internet service provider (ISP), free hosting service or a commercial hosting services?

5. ***How?*** How do you plan to research material for your Website? If you are not sure visit some of the sites on the Internet. Do your research first.

Once you have answered these questions, prepare a mission and objective of the system to be developed.

System Requirements

The purpose of this phase is to document the functional, performance, interface, design, and verification requirements for each system element to be developed. The criteria for defining the general requirements for the Payment Processing system are identified below.

1. The first and most important is the system must be able to present the bill correctly pertaining to a consumer only.
2. The consumer must trust the system with their money transaction security and consumer must be able to authenticate the merchant.
3. The system must support existing payment mechanisms, such as checks and credit cards.
4. The system must be able to integrate with current payment processing and financial systems.
5. The system must be user-friendly.
6. The system must be fast and efficient.

Define all the requirements based on these general criteria to the level of detail necessary to establish the limits of design for the lowest element effected. As part of the system requirement analysis activity examine each function performed in the system from beginning to end. The analysis must involve the entire system and must define requirements for all subsystems for completeness, consistency, testability, traceability, and technical feasibility. The analysis must also include compatibility with project schedule, funding levels, personnel and other project resources such as communication infrastructure and rollout strategy.

The requirement document when completed establishes the system's allocated baseline. In other words, all the systems functions have been allocated to one or more configuration items and the requirements for each function have been defined.

Systems Design

The design of an eCommerce application has become a dynamic process because of the rapidly evolving website development technology tools and methodology. Creating database-driven eCommerce websites isn't at all like writing HTML. It requires more access to the workings of the eCommerce related Internet technologies than what you might be used to.

Proper planning is the key to the success of any eCommerce project design. In Internet based web application, the web browser on a client communicates to a web server who may handle the request or activate a new request on another server. Based on the requirements, you need to consider developing two-tier or three-tier architecture and the host operating system. Until recently, most Internet sites were hosted on UNIX platforms, but the rising speed and power of Intel's Pentium Pro platform, and the accessibility of multi-processor Windows NT machines is enabling rapid migration to this low-cost platform that you may already have on-site.

If you are considering hosting your own site, there is a sequence of operations that must be executed in a predefined order successfully for eCommerce application to work. Hardware, software, telephone service, security, payment approval service, and Internet Service Provider (ISP) all play a significant role and must be managed all the time. Designing for the Web is therefore different from designing traditional software user interfaces. Mainly, the systems engineer has to give up full control and share responsibility for the user interface with users, hardware and software.

There are three approaches to electronic bill presentment and payment processing design:

1. **The Biller Direct Model** where biller presents its bills to customers on its own Web site.
2. **The Bill Consolidator Model** where Consumers go to a single place to view and pay multiple bills.
3. **The Invited Push Model** where Biller E-mails graphically rich electronic bills directly to consumers.

No matter which model your organization chooses, there are three steps for payment processing. First, data from the billing systems (often a mainframe) must be extracted and transformed into a Web-compatible format. Then the data must be pushed into electronic bill templates, which reside on a bill presentment server. Finally, the payments must be collected electronically. Depending on the model chosen, select major components (Figure-3) for your environment including Web Server, Web Application server, Payment Processing Server, Web Browser (Client), Web Programming, Firewalls, Back-end Server and Web Database.

Once you have identified the web components, prepare Systems Design Review (SDR) document outlining 1) System Description 2) System Functions 3) System Hardware and 4) System Software.

System Implementation

System Implementation is one of the toughest challenges for systems engineer. In general, implementing a successful system has a lot to do with defining the right management process, roles, responsibilities and technical feasibility. However, implementing successful eCommerce based payment-processing system involves several critical factors.

1. Outlining the transition from paper based billing to an automated self-service system.
2. Considering the need, both short and long term for dual systems.
3. Reviewing user and security issues.
4. Managing the integration of internal legacy systems with the new web-based payment processing system including links to financial systems.
5. Anticipating technical and cultural barriers and developing a roll-out plan to overcome any objections.
6. Measuring what conditions or actions will determine the implementation process.

System Preliminary Design

The preliminary design activities of the payment processing system design phase has two major goals: 1)

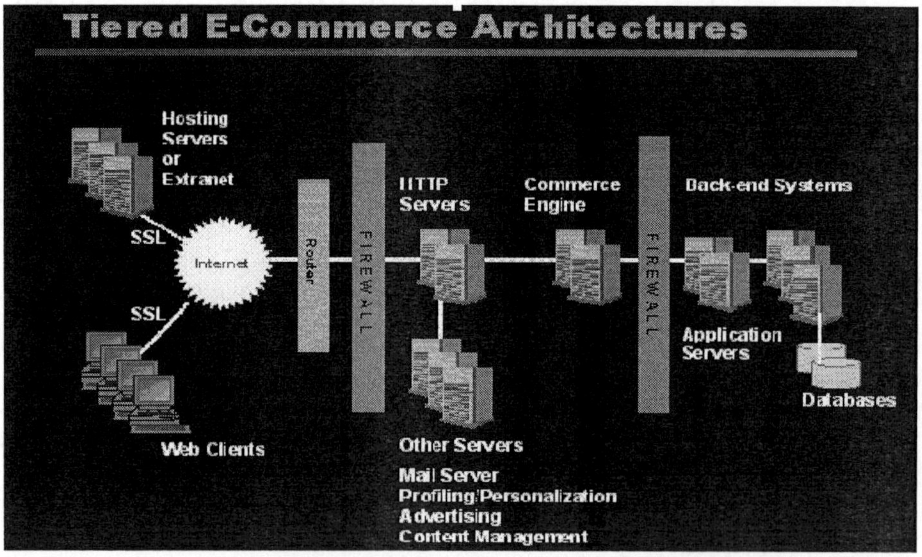

Figure 3: Sun's eCommerce Architecture

defining exactly what payment processing function(s) system must perform and 2) generating a first look at how the new system should be structured to perform the function(s).

Due to the open nature of the Web's architecture and an explosion in the number of payment processing related commercial-off-the-shelf (COTS) products for eCommerce, it is difficult to predict all of the characteristics that the new system will ultimately support. However, it is important that the chosen components share the following characteristics:

- **Availability and Reliability**: The consumer and biller must have an ability to make or receive payments transaction entirely or not at all. This means that the underlying networking services and all major components are sufficiently reliable.
- **Scalability:** The payment server must be able to process single payment or multiple payments with support for multiprocessor and multi-network installations for future growth.
- **Flexibility:** The system must be designed from ground up for enhancements and maintenance.
- **Consistency**: All parties involved for payment processing must agree on currency exchange.
- **Isolation:** Transactions must be independent of each other.
- **Durability:** It must always be possible to recover the last consistent state.
- **Economy:** Conducting a transaction should not be expensive.
- **Interoperability:** It must be possible to move value back and forth between different systems.

Here is a high-level view of the methodology that systems engineer must use:

1. Decompose each function described in SDR into logical services such as user interface, web interface, business rules and data.
2. Identify the workflow and define the interactions between the services.
3. Define the interfaces between the services.
4. Construct the business and data services.
5. Construct the user interface.
6. Build the web services in a way that provides glue between the interface and business services.

With all functions identified, prepare a Preliminary Design Review (PDR) document that includes the hardware and software requirements, function of each system component, its interfaces, operational concepts, databases, and processing sequences that satisfy requirements specified in the systems requirements document.

System Detailed Design

The detail design phase of system engineering is the process of developing a complete design and operational description of each system component down to configurable items and interfaces between them. It uses the modelling techniques to analyze critical design solutions, interface data flow diagrams to ensure compatibility among executable configurable items.

In designing the website you need to identify the best way to present the payment processing system is with friendly user interface and easy site navigation. You need to determine the specific technologies and methods used for payment processing. The core of eCommerce is the exchange of currency, in return for a good or service. You need to consider the payment method you will use for your site. The payment methods for consumer transactions currently used are:

- **Cash:** universally accepted and totally anonymous
- **Checks:** widely accepted but not anonymous
- **Payment Cards:** including credit, debit, and charge, also widely accepted and providing an audit trail, as well as an avenue of recourse for consumers.

There are a growing number of very effective ways to secure financial information transmitted with these payment methods. Analyze and select from the following ways your payment processing website will communicate safely and reliably across the web.

- **Encryption** is simply the process of taking information and encoding it in such a manner as to make it unusable to anyone who may intercept it in transit. By sending encrypted messages across the Web, you make communications secure.
- **Digital Signatures** requires that the payer (consumer) have a secret signing key and a certificate for its corresponding public signature verification key.
- **Secret Keys** requires that the biller (merchant) and the payer (consumer) both have a shared secret key. Password and PIN are examples.

Your payment processing website has many options for accepting payment on the web. For the purposes of this paper, three general categories of options are:

- **Offline Payments** involve no contacts with a payment-processing bank during payment. The payee's payment information is taken and is processed offline by a staff.

- **Online Secure Payments** involve an authorisation server. The payment is not processed and transferred real-time, but the processing bank approves an authorisation for the payment.

- **Online Secure Payments with Real-time Processing** involve an authorisation server and payment-processing bank. The payment if approved, is automatically transferred to the biller bank.

While considering any of the above form of payment acceptance, analyze each for message integrity, authentication, interoperability, and confidentiality Characteristics of secure transaction.

System Integration and Testing

As part of the integration effort, you must recognise payment processing as a new and highly lucrative means of doing business. You must integrate it with the existing business processes and systems such as accounting and customer information. You must plan the level of integration required and its impact on other processes.

The systems engineering testing phase include the activities for testing the system as a whole, its integration with other systems, and verification. The challenges for testing include the extent to which tests can be centrally planned, executed and tracked for maximum efficiency.

For the payment processing system testing, one approach is to develop a pilot website to test its integrity and functionality. Develop test scenarios for the real-world business examples of each electronic-billing process in accordance with the strategic test direction your organization takes. Examples of test scenarios include:

- Present bills available online;
- Perform payment processing;
- Satisfy performance criteria;
- Satisfy platform and browser independence criteria;
- Seamless Integration with other system and
- Customer services.

Prepare a test readiness review document with an overview of testing, the test scenarios, test environment and the detailed step-by-step procedures required to test the system.

Systems Installation and Acceptance

System Installation consists of installing the system in the operational environment to produce the results that were originally defined in the systems specification document. System Acceptance consists of an examination of the detailed design documentation against the "As-built" system configuration. It is conducted to ensure the adequacy, completeness, and accuracy of the technical design documentation.

Installation and acceptance of the payment processing website in a secure manner is a concern to both customers and merchants. Prepare a system installation and acceptance procedures including criteria in sequential order.

Systems Operation and Maintenance

When the system is finally put into operational use, personnel who were not part of the development effort usually exercise it. It is therefore very important to provide operator training and transition support to these personnel before the system is deployed for production. System maintenance involves fixing errors or system component problems that show up during operational use.

The importance of operating and maintaining the payment processing website for ensuring that web information is well managed is very critical as websites grow. Prepare a system operation and maintenance plan document outlining the maintenance team and responsibilities, backup and recovery procedures, up-time objectives, upgrade of hardware and software components, and problem/change management procedures. The planning must address issues related to emergency preparedness and response as well as the restoration of communications and computer systems necessary for normal business operations.

Systems Retirement

We are facing a new evolution and challenges for doing business. Rapid modification to eCommerce based technologies and components will continually improve the deployment time-span and advantages for eCommerce websites. Prepare the strategy for the retirement of system based on following criteria:

- New Internet-2 Technology;
- New hardware and software evolution;
- New products evolution; and
- New requirements.

Conclusion

This paper provides a broad framework of the systems engineering life cycle for eCommerce based payment-processing application. The framework includes phases such as described above and the mechanisms that built in as to how they relate and interact with one another meets the top-down waterfall modelling approach.

In the future, this concept could provide powerful dependent linkages to functional components such as creating of order or service and all the way up to its production for which the payment is made. It can also be integrated to the sales and accounting system of an organization. By orienting the systems engineering components around the business process, the framework presents issues that are not often addressed by development team.

Finally, the paper provides a way of understanding the potential of systems engineering principles that can be applied to successfully deploy eCommerce based systems and fulfil the potential of doing business via internet.

References

1. Creating an E-Comm Architecture, Unix Review, February 1998.
2. Internet-based EDI solutions, InfoWorld, April 6, 1998
3. Many Faces of Electronic Commerce, ENT, August 12, 1998
4. E-Business Work Starts, Information Week, Jan 4, 1999
5. Testing e-commerce, Application Development Trends, July, 1999
6. Orchestrating Today's E-Commerce, Network Computing, September 6, 1999
7. Payment By Electrons, Information Week, July 27, 1998
8. Electronic Commerce, Internet Magazine, February 1997.
9. Systems Engineering Management, Benjamin Blanchard.

BIOGRAPHY

Mr. Shah has over 19 years of information systems development experience across a broad base of application architectures, Internet and information technologies. Mr. Shah is currently involved in developing eCommerce and database driven websites. Mr. Shah can be reached at bharat@massintl.com.

Systems Engineering Capability Model and the Systems Engineering Management Planning Environment

Patricia T. Martin
US Army Aviation and Missile Command
Engineering Directorate
Aviation and Missile Research, Development and Engineering Center
Redstone Arsenal, Al 35898

Terry N. Thomas
Nichols Research Corporation
4090 S. Memorial Parkway
Huntsville, Al 35812-1502

Loyd Baker, Jr.
3SL Incorporated
346 Farmstead Rd.
Huntsville, Al 35806

Fred Knopf
3SL Incorporated
P.O Box 310
Olney, Md 20830

ABSTRACT.

Introduction. Existing Systems Engineering Tool Environments can be used to automate the systems engineering management planning process compliant with the Systems Engineering Capability Model (SECM) contained in EIA-731.1 and other necessary standards and practices. This paper describes how 3SL's Cradle tool is being used to integrate the planning process, using multiple modeling techniques, while maintaining traceability to IEEE-1220-1998, EIA-632-1999, the EIA-731.1 & EIA-731.2 SECM practices and DoD 5000.2. The result is a management plan that is useful for facilitating the processes in an Integrated Product Team (IPT) environment and foster continuous process improvement.

Systems Engineering tool environments are available to create and maintain both the Systems Engineering Management Plan (SEMP) and integrated project databases. Typically, the SEMP and database development activities are disjoint.

Topics. This presentation discusses the dynamics of inserting Systems Engineering Processes into an unstructured IPT environment and how a model-based SE process was embraced to introduce rigor, improve communications, and enforce design consistency. How this integrated SEMP provides traceability into common capability model practices and Government acquisition practices and results is presented.

STATE OF SYSTEM ENGINEERING MANAGEMENT PLANNING INSIDE THE DOD

The cornerstone to any successful project is careful planning. "Planning of technical tasks provides the foundation for cost and schedule planning. It forms the basis for allocating resources, scheduling task elements, assigning authority and responsibility, and integrating all aspects of the technical program" (Electronic Industry Association, December, 1994). Thorough planning of technical tasks also allows the project team to identify the technical processes, and the depth of process implementation, required to accomplish the project's objectives. In Systems Engineering, this planning typically culminates in a SEMP. The SEMP is a plan developed at the project initiation to establish the systems engineering requirements for the project and to ensure effective management of the systems engineering process. It makes visible the project team organization, program direction, tools and methodologies to be used, control mechanisms, and project constraints (Martin, 1998). The SEMP is a living document and as such, is revised to reflect changes in the direction, philosophy, or technical requirements of the project. In other words, the SEMP is a critical, technical management tool.

Traditionally for Department of Defense (DoD) projects, a SEMP was a report generated by the contractor that required Government approval. The SEMP was typically generic and in many cases, simply restated the generic systems engineering processes (i.e. requirements analysis, functional analysis) as the project's technical processes. The SEMP would identify the project organization, schedule, and discuss project milestones. However, little detailed process information was provided. Also, the SEMP was developed totally from the contractor's viewpoint.

The DoD has undergone significant shifts in its technical philosophies in recent years through numerous acquisition streamlining initiatives. The elimination of many Military Specifications and Standards (MIL SPEC/STDs), the use of Integrated Process and Product Development (and Integrated Product Teams), and the reliance on performance specification-based acquisitions has drastically changed how defense projects are technically planned. The DoD technical community can no longer rely on the direction of MIL SPEC/STDs to dictate the technical processes required. Now the project team must develop processes that allow fulfillment of the performance requirements of the system. No longer can the Government project team sit back and critique the contractor through review and approval of numerous delivered data items. We are a joint team, an Integrated Product Team (IPT), with each member of the team responsible for developing the processes, requirements, and critical program events for the project based on the project's objectives.

Communication has been significantly affected by acquisition streamlining initiative implementation. In the past, when someone referred to a MIL SPEC/STD, everyone from project team member to Headquarters personnel knew what was being discussed. If they didn't know, they could simply obtain a copy of the document and read it. Today, each project's language is different based on the contractor's environment and terminology, the project's IPT structure and philosophy, and the project's objectives. This requires a communication bridge that allows full understanding by everyone involved in the program including higher level management.

In the new DoD acquisition environment, the SEMP takes on a new role with substantially increased importance. The SEMP continues to identify critical technical project data and project status as found in traditional DoD SEMPs. Now, however, the SEMP also provides the mechanism that allows the definition of the IPT structure and responsibilities and the systems engineering management and technical processes, procedures, and resources required to successfully accomplish critical program events. The SEMP is now developed from a combined Government and contractor perspective. This combined perspective is important because it addresses the total program requirements including those critical program events that must be accomplished by Government personnel (i.e Milestone Reviews) to ensure a project's success. By fully defining these processes and tailoring them to the individual project, the SEMP then becomes the communication bridge that documents the project's language.

The Utility Helicopter Project Office (UH PO) is responsible for the development, production, fielding, and support of the Army's utility helicopters. As such, the UH PO is responsible for several different helicopter variants. Currently, the UH PO has initiated the UH-60 BlackHawk Modernization program, a major DoD acquisition program. The UH PO also has several modifications and projects underway that will be incorporated into the Modernization program down stream. Given the challenges of integrating these programs, the UH PO recognized the changing technical environment and the need to develop a methodology for defining their currently used systems engineering processes and for improving their system engineering capability. The UH PO decided to use the SEMP development for the Modernization program as the methodology for defining their systems engineering processes and structuring a path for improvement. A Systems Engineering Process Evaluation Team has been established to assess the project's planned Critical Program Events' entrance and exit criteria, the IPT responsibilities for each event, product and outputs from each event, information and documentation requirements, the technical project data to be tracked, and the planned systems engineering management and technical processes against the Systems Engineering Capability Model found in EIA 731-1. The evaluation will be conducted and documented through the project's SEMP. For the Modernization program, this SEMP will provide an integrated management tool for the project team that will consist of detailed project status and process information to assist them in accomplishing their tasks. The SEMP will also provide an assessment of the current state of the systems engineering program and an approach for systems engineering process improvement. For the UH PO, the SEMP will serve as a systems engineering implementation guide for their other product lines.

EMERGING REQUIREMENTS FOR SEMP DEVELOPMENT ENVIRONMENT

Utility of Models in Planning. System Engineers build models to better understand problems, develop candidate solutions, and validate their decisions. Different kinds of models are built to help focus on the appropriate set of questions that need answering in order to find the most reliable and cost effective solution and to qualify the design against its requirements (INCOSE Model Driven System Design Working Group, 1998). In an organization attempting to improve its system engineering activities from initial to defined, a collection of integrated models greatly aids in understanding the problem and focuses the improvement activity.

SEMP Definition. The SEMP will have many meanings to many people in a culture performing system engineering at the initial or informal stages of maturity. The SEMP, which by definition will not exist in a useful way in such a culture, will be hopelessly unbounded and undefined. Its role is likely to be confused with other programmatic documentation if it is the object of discussion at all. It may only exist as a deliverable to "check-the-box" against a higher level requirement. The SEMP must be clearly defined before its development if it is to serve any useful purpose at all.

Object Modeling Technique can be used to graphically represent a logical or physical entity, its structure, and its association with other entities to augment textual descriptions (Oliver et.al. 1997). A SEMP information model can be useful in communicating the SEMP's larger context, i.e., its association with other entities determined to be relevant. Figure 1 depicts a proposed SEMP context for a Government program management office.

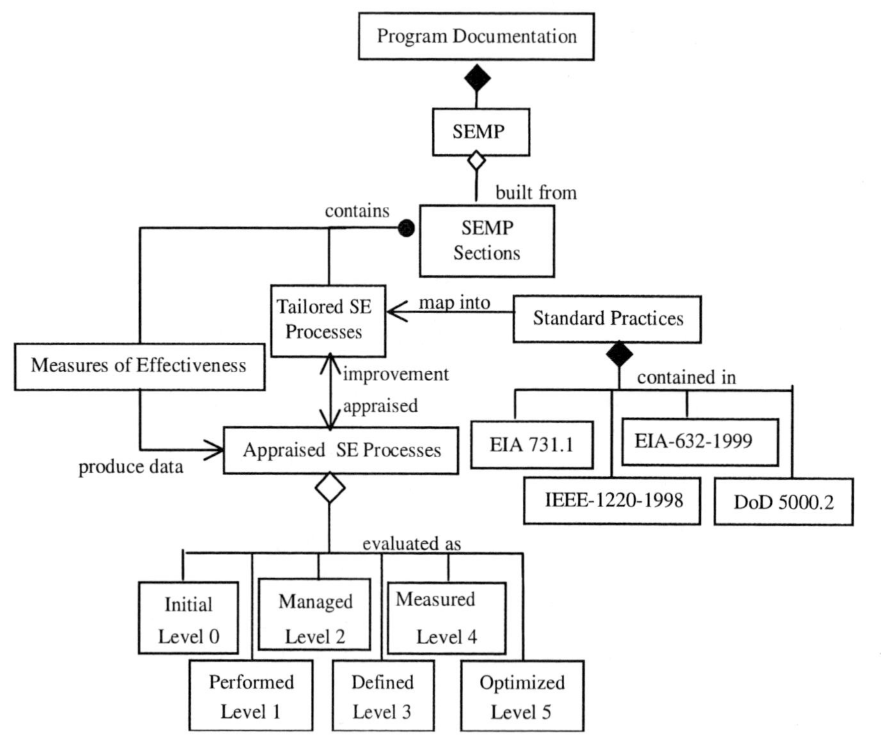

Figure 1. SEMP Definition

This model depicts the SEMP as a structural component of a program's documentation set. The SEMP is built from SEMP sections. SEMP sections contain the program's tailored system engineering practices and processes. *Standard practices* are mapped into the tailored practices and processes to insure completeness. To ensure correlation between the SEMP processes and actual process execution, the tailored processes are appraised and the overall system engineering activity is evaluated at varying maturity levels. Proper evaluation of the tailored processes requires assessment of the effectiveness of the processes in execution, not simply the presence. It is for this reason that SE process measures of effectiveness must be identified and established within each process area contained in the SEMP. These metrics provide data for process evaluation.

It is the intent of this context model to define a SEMP in such a way to insure process completeness and an active feedback mechanism to foster process improvement. It offers the opportunity to define the standard practices, either published or private, that are to be utilized in engineering the system.

SEMP Development [SE Process Documentation & Tailoring]. To suggest that an organization is going to develop and follow a SEMP suggests that the organization is already operating at or very close to a managed level. Initially, the performing organization will likely not have a SEMP. Introducing managed processes into a culture operating at the initial or even the performing level is analogous to the difference of night and day. This presents the system engineer with many problems associated with developing a SEMP that is accepted, thereby proving itself useful.

The System Engineering Capability Model, EIA-731.1, proves very useful in discovering what processes may or may not exist within an organization. Short of a formal appraisal as described in EIA-731.2, the system engineer can assess a program to determine the presence or absence of certain processes. The intent herein is not to discount a formal appraisal at all, but only to say that one can use the stated practices as a methodical guide to discover what processes may or may not exist. The mapping of the SECM practices to the processes contained within the SEMP actually provides a good stimulus for process capture and investigation.

Understanding and conveying the processes, that is, the behaviors, that are determined to exist, easily become complex with an organization made up of teams and sub-teams. Textual descriptions of ordering and timing relationships amongst the teams become very confusing for behaviors of even modest complexity. Since the abstractions needed to convey an organization's tailored SE processes are consistent with the abstractions of behavior, the system engineer can employ one of many diagramming techniques to capture these processes. The organization's time sequence of events, inputs and outputs to the events, including triggers may be presented using Enhanced Function Flow Block Diagrams (EFFBDs). Modeling the organization's tailored processes with EFFBDs provides a method of managing the complexity associated with capturing the processes and sub-processes within an organization and greatly aids the SEMP development process.

The requirements analysis process was the first process captured within the UH PO. Enhanced function flow was utilized to capture the way the process was believed to be executing. The EFFBDs were generated with someone skilled in building EFFBDs facilitating the personnel associated with the process execution. The various interacting functional entities (in this case, elements of Government and business organizations) were identified and easily depicted along the process branches. The information that was passed from one entity to another, to include triggering information, the time sequence of events, and concurrencies were all easily captured. This analysis technique proved to be very useful and easily understood with the personnel associated with the actual execution of the process. All found it easy to read and a very logical, analytical method for representing the interaction of multiple teams and the required information flow. The EFFBD contains much more information than traditional flow diagramming techniques often associated with business process capture. The completed requirements analysis EFFBD represents the first SE process to be documented within this project. The EFFBD now provides the framework for further analysis.

SEMP Improvement [SE Process Improvement]. The previous section dealt primarily with identifying and capturing processes that exist within an organization at the initial or performing level of maturity. This section primarily deals with the omissions discovered as a result of methodically evaluating the organizations processes against the standard practices and improving existing practices as they are discovered to be in place but not effective.

Rigorous traceability from the SEMP into the SECM and other standard practices provide a good mechanism for focusing process improvement efforts whether process areas are in place and immature or omitted and must be created. Within the SECM alone, literally hundreds of practices are associated with an organization's system engineering activities. This compounds greatly with the addition of standard practices derived from other commercial standards, Government regulations, and many other program considerations. By definition, an organization performing at the initial level will not have adequate processes in place to address all the standard practices required. Establishing a comprehensive traceability model between all the standard practices and all sections of the SEMP will bring light to all the areas omitted.

The standard practice themes that do not map to any existing process on-going within the organization must be addressed in the SEMP. The EFFBDs are as useful for the creation and communication of complex behavior requiring implementation within the organization as they are for functional analysis. As process area stakeholders are determined for the new behavior, EFFBDs continue to provide utility for the development of the SEMP.

Analysis of the UH PO's requirements analysis process found the presence of many SECM Level 1 requirements related practices, such as identifying, collecting and baselining stakeholder needs, expectations, and constraints, and partitioning requirements into groups based on established criteria. Other practices were found to be omitted, such as obtaining an agreement between the acquirer and the developer that the system level requirements reflect their needs and expectations, and developing a detailed operational concept.

Executing processes must be assessed for their effectiveness. If the processes are producing products, the products should be assessed for their value to the organization and its overall goals. Herein, the assessment becomes more formalized due to the nature of the discovery needed. More formality and rigor in the appraisal process will continue to bring light to immature process areas. The SEMP must describe the measures of effectiveness that will be used to assess process execution.

The SEMP is a living document, continuously maturing and improving as the system to which it pertains evolves. With rigorous traceability into the SECM and other standard practices, this life is in the context of a capability model. The intent of this traceability is to create a dynamic, almost continuous appraisal environment. Again, the intent is not to discount the value of working through a formal appraisal. Instead, the intent is to maintain the living document in the context of a continuous appraisal where all the process owners are aware of exactly where the current plan falls in maturity and can always be moving the mark up.

Reduced cycle time from concept to deployed system products, reduction in total ownership cost of system products, improved system quality, and reduced development risks are among the benefits listed in the introduction of EIA/IS-731.1, the SECM. These are certainly the attributes of a successful program. It follows that rigorous development of processes using mature modeling techniques and a continuous evaluation process created in context with the SECM will increase the likelihood of program success. If so, integrating the SEMP development and improvement process to the SECM level of maturity provides management the insight needed to know whether or not a program is healthy enough to proceed through any given decision point.

AUTOMATING THE SEMP DEVELOPMENT PROCESS.

Behavior Model of the SEMP. The key concept in automating the project's support environment was the integration of the SEMP behavior model with the project's engineering database. The 3SL's Systems Engineering Support Environment, Cradle, illustrated in Figure 2, was selected to implement the systems engineering management environment because of it's rich set of system modeling capabilities, and its ability to support multi-user, multi-site development activities.

Using Cradle's system modeling capabilities, a Behavior Model of our SEMP showing the project technical processes to be performed by the IPTs (see Figure 3) was developed. This top-level view of the SEMP model, which is basically a view of the system engineering process, shows the technical activities/functions to be performed, the order of execution, and the required input/outputs used/produced by the activities. This model provides the IPTs with a necessary "roadmap" that helps keep the team members focused on the tasks to be performed. This type of model has proven to be a very effective means of improving communication among the team members on the project. Each activity in the model is subsequently expanded into greater detail as required. For example, Figure 4 is an expansion of the Planning and Organization activity shown in the top-level SEMP behavior model. The Planning and Organization Process was expanded into a sequence of activities that includes developing a project schedule, defining a work breakdown structure (WBS), assigning WBS activities to IPTs, designing detailed task sheets, conducting training, and so on. Figure 5 is an expansion of the System Design activity. At this level of decomposition, visibility to the requirements analysis activity is obtained. This modeling approach to SEMP development clearly places the required processes in context with each other and provides a clean structure through which the processes can be managed. All data flows between activities (i.e., project plans and products) are clearly identified for all team members to understand. The Cradle-developed SEMP model integrates multi-disciplined information (text, spreadsheets, drawings, pictures, videos, acceptance & signoffs) for complete

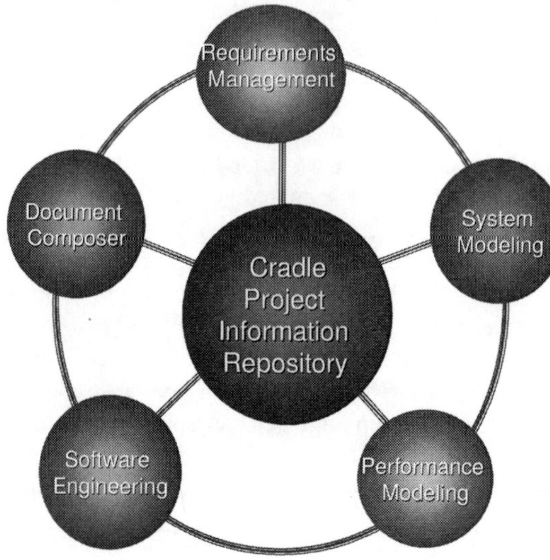

Figure 2. The Cradle Integrated Systems Engineering Environment

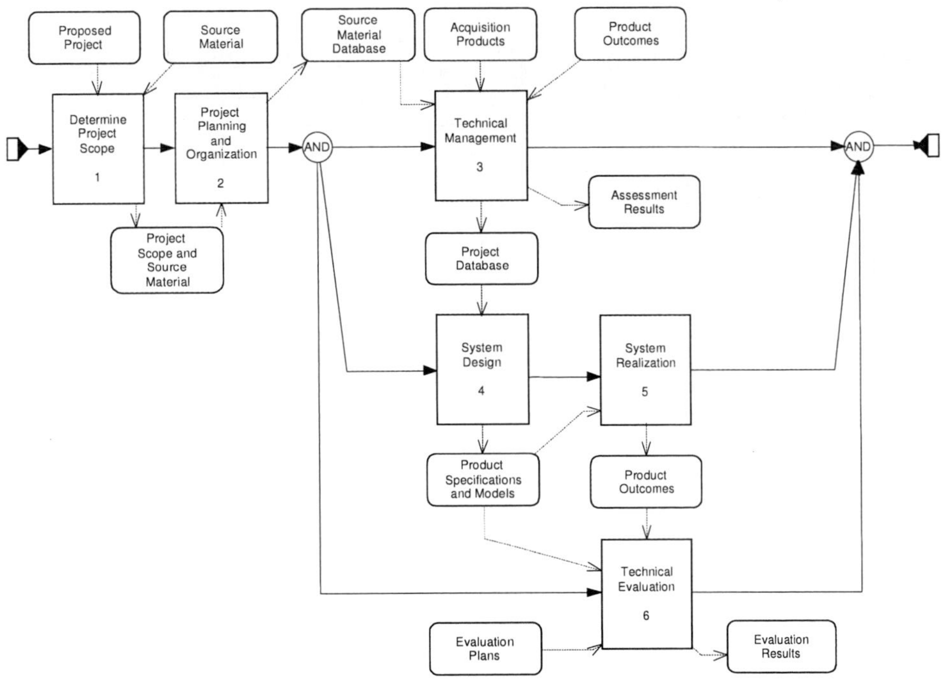

Figure 3. Top-Level SEMP Behavior Model

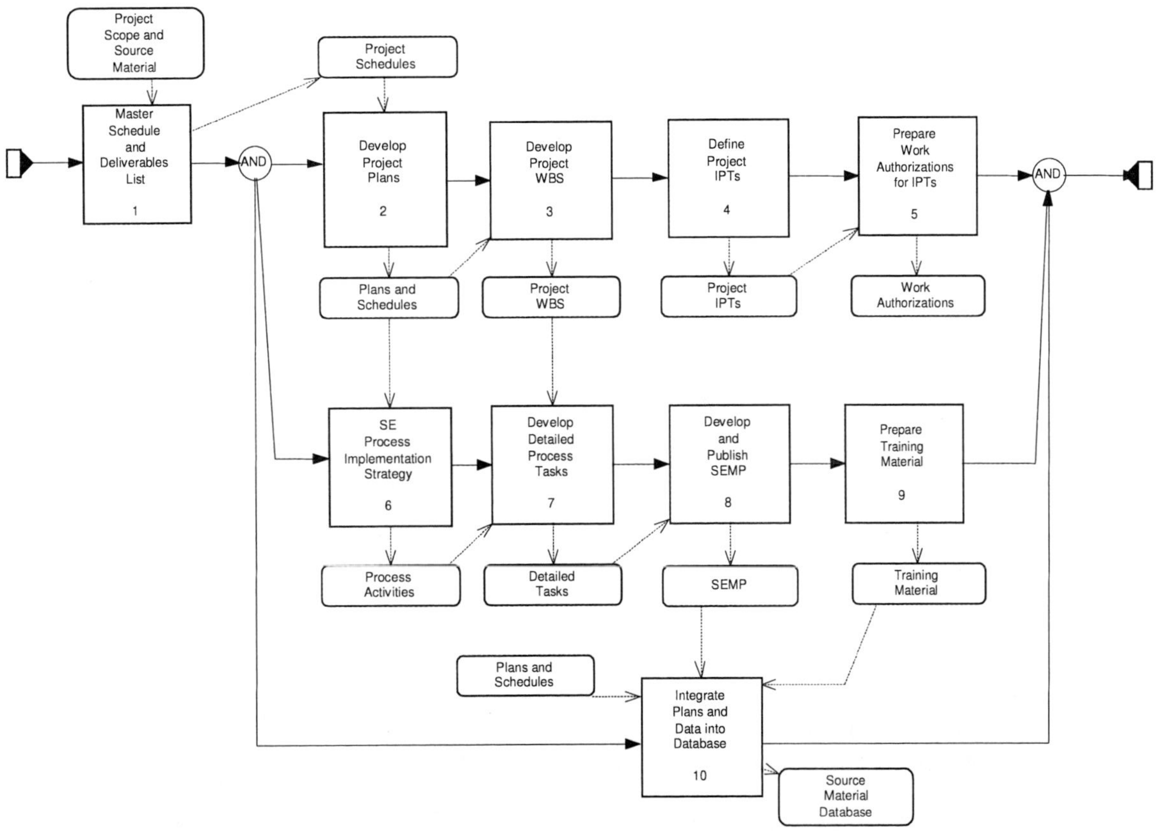

Figure 4. Project Planning and Organization Decomposition

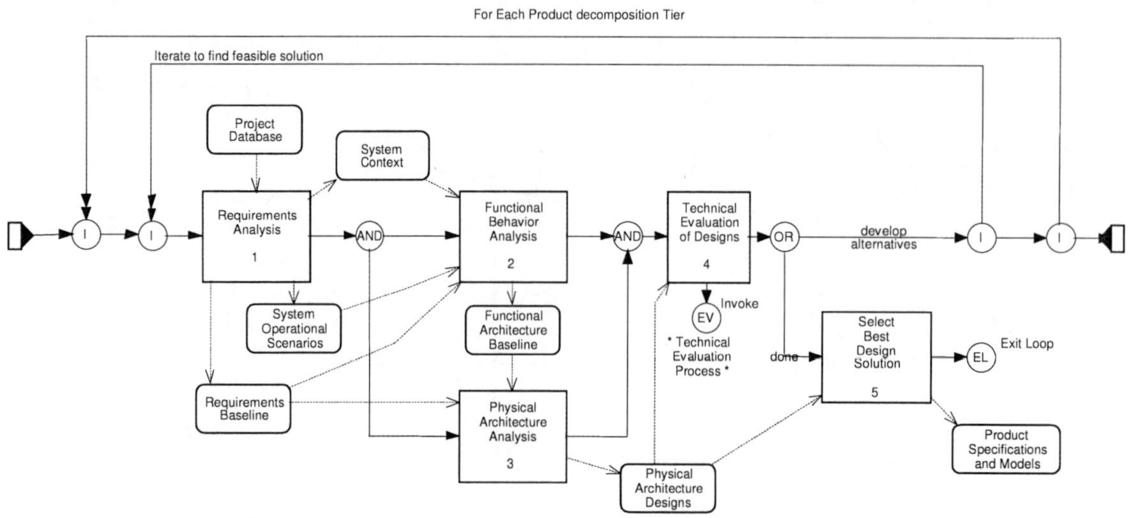

Figure 5. System Design Decomposition.

definition with easy user access.

Traceability. In addition to behavior models, the Cradle support environment manages cross-references (i.e., traceability) between related information in the integrated database. Standard practices are parsed into the database originating from multiple sources such as EIA-731.1 or DoD 5000.2. Cross-references are established between the activities contained in the behaviors and the standard practices providing rationale for the SEMP processes. Figure 6 illustrates traceability between a planned WBS Task and one, or more, Project Activities performed to accomplish the task. For example, key IPT decisions such as the following were captured and documented in the SEMP Integrated Database.

- Basis and rationale for decisions
- Issues, risks, and inherent assumptions
- Alternative solutions considered
- Traceability of the above to the SEMP Behavior Model

Automated Document Generation. The Cradle Document Composer (Figure 2) is used to automatically generate the SEMP document, as well as all project development specifications and review material. We found that having a repeatable, automatic process for the generation of reports, documents, and review packages directly from the engineering database saved time and resources. We discovered that the information, object structure, behavior, and traceability models captured as part of the engineering process could be automatically incorporated into our documents, eliminating the need to manually build these materials outside the SEMP documented engineering process and database.

Conclusions

This model driven approach of developing a SEMP ensures improved visibility into the systems engineering management planning process and project assessment. Behavior models provide the underpinning for any project's systems engineering management planning process. Key advantages of this approach are as follows:

- Improved Program Development
  - ➢ Can associate engineering products with activities
  - ➢ Allows information capture for assessing engineering processes
  - ➢ Promotes consistency and repeatability of processes
- Improved communications
  - ➢ Via better understanding of applied processes and interactions.

Developing the SEMP in an integrated database, such as Cradle, provides an environment for the system engineer to manage the complexity of defining multiple processes and sub-processes accountable to standard practices as determine appropriate. The SEMP and all its associated rationale become a database query.

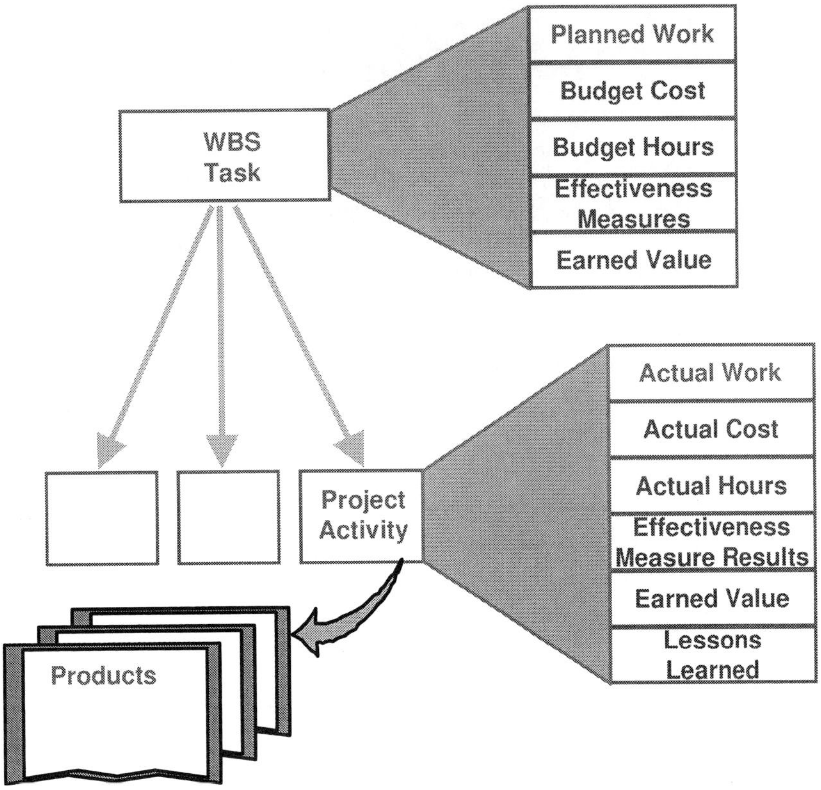

Figure 6. The SEMP Integrated Database Provides Traceability Between Planned Tasks and the Performed Activities

REFERENCE:

Electronic Industry Association, *Systems Engineering, Interim Standard 632*, Washington, D.C., December 1994.

Martin, Patricia T., "A Systems Engineering Management Methodology for Research and Development Projects: Project Leader Handbook," Master's Thesis, 1998.

INCOSE Model Driven System Design Working Group, "Why Program Managers are Adopting a Model-Based Approach to System Engineering",*Insight*, 1998

Oliver, David W., Kelliher, Timothy P., and Keegan Jr., James G., *Engineering Complex System with Models and Objects*, McGraw-Hill, New York, 1997

BIOGRAPHY

Loyd Baker, Jr. is Vice President of Systems Engineering for 3SL Incorporated, Past President of the Huntsville INCOSE Chapter, and serves on the INCOSE, Model Driven System Design, Working Group.

Fred Knopf is Vice President of Operations for 3SL Incorporated, and serves on the INCOSE, Model Driven System Design, Working Group.

Patricia Martin is a Team Leader in the Production Engineering Division, Engineering Directorate, U.S. Army Aviation and Missile Research, Development, and Engineering Center. She is currently serving as the lead Engineering Directorate Systems Engineer to the Utility Helicopter Project Office.

Terry N. Thomas is Manager of the System Definition Directorate for Nichols Research Corporation and serves as the Huntsville INCOSE Chapter Secretary.

The Shangri-La of ROI

Sarah A. Sheard and Christopher L. Miller
Software Productivity Consortium
2214 Rock Hill Rd., Herndon, VA 20170
sheard@software.org; miller@software.org

Abstract. Many INCOSE members are dismayed that there are no hard numbers to justify implementation of systems engineering process improvement. This paper shows that: 1) There are no "hard numbers." 2) There will be no hard numbers in the foreseeable future. 3) If there were hard numbers, there wouldn't be a way to apply them to your situation, and 4) if you did use such numbers, no one would believe you anyway.

We have to get past fantasy and find out how to make the case for implementing systems engineering process improvement without these elusive hard numbers. This paper concludes with suggestions on how to build a case for process improvement that does not rely on hard numbers.

INTRODUCTION

> *When you introduce systems engineering into a traditionally commercial organization, you will have to justify your ideas on the basis of dollars and cents.* (Jackson 1996)

The questions. How can I convince my manager to fund systems engineering? How can I convince my company that improving systems engineering processes by working toward complying with the Systems Engineering Capability Maturity Model (SE-CMM) or the Electronic Industries Affiliates' Interim Standard (EIA/IS) 731 is going to save them money? Where are the hard return-on-investment (ROI) data showing that for every dollar I invest in process improvement, I will get so many dollars back?

Note: This paper considers the implementation of systems engineering to be the same as process improvement of the systems engineering process. The former is equivalent to achieving "Level 1" in a process area in any of the systems engineering capability models.

WHAT I WANT IS HARD NUMBERS

What everyone would like to see is shown in Table 1. There are also many variations on the numbers desired. Many people want "hard numbers," meaning numbers that are statistically proven and incontrovertible, that show the benefit of performing risk management. Some want to prove that completing requirements analysis prior to starting design saves the program time and money, or show the reduction in rework that occurs when requirements and high-level design are reviewed by all affected stakeholders. In general, people want proof that improvements to "do things right" will return enough money to justify the investment.

Parameter	Conditions	Number
Program cost savings for each dollar spent doing systems engineering	All EIA/IS 731 technical focus areas at Level 1	a:1
	Technical and management focus areas at Level 2	b:1
	All focus areas at Level 3	c:1
	"Level 4/5" organization per (Sheard and Roedler 1999)	d:1
Systems engineering productivity	Before SE assessment	x ±20%
	After SE assessment	y ±15%
	After 1 year of improvements amounting to $200 spent per engineer	z ±10%
Required processes to implement to achieve:	Guaranteed "Level 2"	Ref.1*
	Guaranteed "Level 3"	Ref.2
	Guaranteed "Level 4"	Ref.3
	Guaranteed "Level 5'	Ref.4

** Note, these are fictitious. Do not look at the references to this paper. Such processes do not exist.*

Table 1. Desired Systems Engineering ROI Data

Where can we find such numbers? What kind of research should INCOSE do to obtain such numbers? Let us start by looking at what does exist and why it does not provide what we want.

THERE ARE NO "HARD NUMBERS"

Herbsleb report. In 1994, the Software Engineering Institute (SEI) released a report called "Benefits of CMM-Based Process Improvement" (Herbsleb et al. 1994). In this report, information is collected from thirteen companies who published results from process improvement using the CMM® for Software (SW-CMM®[i]) (Paulk 1993). The paper shows returns on investment ranging from 4:1 to 8.8:1 (See Table 2). This means that for every dollar invested in CMM-based process improvement, between $4 and $8.80 was received in productivity gain or other savings.

This is very interesting data, and the authors show it whenever we teach a capability model class. But we bracket it in caveats as follows.

Applicability. First, this relates to the SW-CMM. Can it apply also to systems engineering process improvement? While there are no specific reasons why not, there is a leap of faith required to believe that it does.

Time. Although hundreds to thousands of companies have used the SW-CMM since 1994, updates to this paper have not been released that include more companies or more thorough data. This situation is worrisome because, in the five years since this paper, much has changed in the software development industry, and it is reasonable to believe that studies done now might show different numbers. For example, many companies have already made improvements comparable to those discussed in the Herbsleb report. Is it not possible that early efforts represented "low hanging fruit," and additional process improvement would yield diminishing returns?

Common Definitions.. To determine return on investment, both return values and investment values must be collected. Unfortunately a common definition of return values has not been accepted across industry (Brodman and Johnson 1996). Therefore, the meaning of any published return-on-investment numbers is inherently unclear. What was counted as return? Cost savings are typically included, but what about softer values, like improved morale, reduction in cycle time, and improved predictability? Return parameters are not clearly or consistently defined across the studies that have been publicized

Category	Range
Yearly cost of software process improvement (SPI) activities	$49K - $1,202K
Years engaged in SPI	1 - 9
Cost of SPI per software engineer	$490 - $2,004
Productivity gain per year	9% - 67%
Early detection gain per year *(defects discovered pre-test)*	6% - 25%
Yearly reduction in time to market	15% - 23%
Yearly reduction in post-release defects	10% - 94%
Business value of investment in SPI *(value returned on each $ invested)*	4.0 - 8.8

Table 2. Herbsleb report results

Sample size. Certainly, thirteen companies cannot be representative of the thousands performing process improvement, even if the survey were current. Any study that is truly predictive must use random sampling of far more than thirteen companies.

Bias. Sampling bias is also inherent in this kind of study. Remember, these were actual companies that published their results in the open literature. Let us do a thought experiment here.

Thought experiment #1. Suppose an executive at your company is excited about the promise of process improvement based on the SW-CMM. Suppose the executive is intelligent and implements real improvements that meet the needs of the company. He or she assigns a talented and respected project manager to run the process improvement project, procures knowledge from experienced outsiders as necessary, documents processes that are actually done using up-to-date and efficient tools, and obtains cooperation and buy-in from all affected programs.

Fast forward one year A million dollars has been invested, and the company has reached the next level of process maturity. Now suppose the executive leaves the company. Maybe he or she was offered a better job in another company that wanted to duplicate process improvement success, or perhaps the company was acquired and the executive was offered a severance package. Suppose the executive's replacement is distinctly not a process improvement person. Instead the new executive is a very product- and bottom-line-focused person. To save costs, he or she eliminates all funding for overhead such as process improvement and incentivizes program managers to think tactically and not strategically. Essentially, the CMM-based process improvement effort has been nullified, and the return on the million-dollar investment is approximately zero.

- ***Would your company publish this result in the open literature?***

Readers will recognize that nothing in this thought experiment is unreasonable. Numbers published in the open literature are, at best, examples of what *could* happen in the right circumstances and are not predictive in any sort of general case.

THERE AREN'T GOING TO BE ANY HARD NUMBERS

Data such as productivity, cost to produce systems, process improvement cost, and the like is usually considered highly confidential. Everyone would be more than happy to receive reports on industry trends and data on all the other companies, but no one is willing to provide such data. Even if the data was clearly defined, additional confidential data would be required to verify that the data had the same meaning from company to company. It is hard to imagine ever prying such numbers out of a large number of companies in a manner that has any sort of fidelity.

Therefore, it may be assumed that when any numbers are made public, the publicity is likely to result from motives other than "sharing." Perhaps the company feels that it is ahead of the industry and thus releasing such numbers has marketing value. Other reasons might make one doubt the truth of numbers, but even "we are different from the rest of the industry" makes one doubt their applicability to the general case.

Systems engineering startup. What kind of numbers would help convince program managers to start up a systems engineering effort within a program? The numbers in Table 3 would do. How would you expect to be able to calculate the cost savings? According to (McKinney 1995), systems engineers have been known to estimate risk avoidance at costs exceeding the entire program development cost by several times! Would anyone believe any estimates for these numbers?

Definition of systems engineering. Table 3 also assumes that any two people will agree what is meant by "systems engineering activities." Is systems engineering the creation of software requirements specifications, or is there more? Does it include attending customer technical exchange meetings and subsystem area program reviews, or does your company consider those activities to be project management? Does systems engineering include development of system test procedures, or is "system test" considered a separate activity?

(Sheard 1996a) and (Sheard 2000a) show that definitions vary greatly within INCOSE, from requirements definition and system design to analysis, technical management, coordination, or even configuration management. Definitions vary even within a single company–certainly you cannot expect someone else's numbers to have much meaning for your organization.

Category	Dollars
Yearly cost of systems engineering activities	$x
Cost of rework avoided because systems engineering was done	$y
Costs of risks avoided due to systems engineering	$z
Costs saved because systems engineering came up with better designs	$q
Other cost savings attributed to systems engineering	$r
Return on investment of systems engineering	$(y+z+q+r)/$x

Table 3. Systems Engineering ROI

IF THERE WERE HARD NUMBERS, YOU WOULDN'T BE ABLE TO USE THEM

Comparison to surveyed companies. For a moment, let us suppose that hard ROI numbers do exist for performing process improvement according to any capability model you want, including systems engineering models. Now we must ask whether those numbers can actually be used as desired.

Those who ask for hard ROI numbers want to make a case that process improvement is worth the investment. They want analytical models to tell them how much benefit they will receive from their investment. Any estimation model must be examined to determine whether the numbers can be replicated in a specific situation. Would you be able to find the answers to these questions?

- How much waste was in the baseline process of the companies surveyed? How much waste is in your baseline process?
- How much of their way of doing business depended on "smart people" and how much does yours? Are your people just as smart? Smarter?
- What did the surveyed companies consider "productivity" to be, and how does it compare to your definition?
- How are overtime, overhead, and G&A costs considered in the definition of systems engineering costs?
- How did the surveyed companies calculate return on investment related to a decrease in time-to-market? Would such calculations apply as well in your marketplace?
- Do they follow procurement rules similar to yours, or do you have constraints that would keep you from achieving the same improvements?

Separability of causes. In addition, few companies perform process improvement in a vacuum. Most companies try multiple ways of remaining competitive. Strategies include tweaking executive compensation, making changes in response to financial monitoring and control of operations, implementing quality initiatives, adjusting employee compensation and benefits to obtain the right workforce, entering new markets, and changing bid and proposal strategies or expenditures. These initiatives tend to occur simultaneously, because companies cannot afford to spend a year tweaking each variable to determine its effect on the company bottom line. The environment does not stay constant that long!

Therefore it is difficult to attribute improved bottom line numbers to one cause or the other. Suppose your time-to-market metric decreases. Is this because you implemented improvements leading to Level 3 in the SW-CMM? Or can it be attributed to buying a combined system and software modeling toolset? Or maybe you are now making products that are much closer in content to other products and thus new versions can come out faster? Perhaps the fraction of your company that is building web-based applications is larger, and the fraction serving military customers is smaller. How do you allocate dollar savings among these reasons? And how do you count the cost value of reducing cycle time, anyway?

In addition, there are two questions: one on the value of systems engineering at all, and the other on the return on investment of process improvement, including systems engineering process improvement. How could anyone separate these two activities to produce an ROI number for both implementing process improvement and the value of systems engineering? For this reason, this paper assumes systems engineering and process improvement are inseparable when it comes to calculating ROI.

Thought experiment #2. For extra insight into the problem of separability of causes, imagine that your company's productivity numbers actually *decreased* after a year of process improvement. See how many reasons your process improvement sponsor would come up with for why the process improvement initiative actually made positive changes but other causes combined to make it seem otherwise. Now consider how correct it is to attribute ROI to the process improvement initiative.

Estimation model nonlinearity. The purpose of having hard numbers is to estimate what results investment might bring. These hard numbers then constitute an estimation model, if you will. The concept of ROI used in this way assumes linearity: invest $100,000 and get $400,000 back, invest $100 and get $400 back. Most engineers recognize the limitations of linear models. (Sheard 1999) estimates a full systems engineering assessment as taking 670 hours, which would translate to over $30,000 for just the time of internal people.[1] The cost of external assessors could double that number; remember, that is $60,000 spent just to take the

Trait	Progra m 1	Program 2	Progra m 3
Use of SE	Low	Med	High
Quality	Low	Adequate	High
Relative cycle time Requirements-RFP	2.5	1	1
Relative cycle time Design-Production	n/a	3	2
Test time	16	n/a	10

Table 4. Frantz results

test. No actual improvement has yet been funded! Since your first $60,000 has so far yielded nothing in return, your next dollars need to be very well placed in improvements of clear benefit.

IF YOU DID USE HARD NUMBERS, NOBODY WOULD BELIEVE YOU ANYWAY

How process improvement is done. Thought Experiment #1 provided a hypothetical case in which process improvement was done right (until it was cancelled). In many instances, process improvement is forced from the top down by executives who had no idea what process improvement means or what it will take. These executives may have decided that a certificate stating Level 3 or ISO 9000 registration would be good for business, and took whatever shortcuts they could in order to obtain the desired certificate. The chances of the companies receiving good return on investment from productivity, cycle time, or productivity improvement, though not zero, are quite small, and it is highly unlikely that any such return would be sustained over time. Executives who have a history of taking shortcuts like this should be very suspicious of data promising return on investment, because they have shot magic silver bullets in the past in search of such returns, and the promises were never fulfilled.

Frantz paper. A different approach was taken by W. Forrest Frantz at Boeing (Frantz 1995). The paper analyzed three programs with different levels of systems engineering to determine how well the programs were executed. The results are shown in Table 4. Although the paper concentrated on cycle-time reduction, this was due to improved quality of systems engineering work products and reduction of rework during the test phase.

The Frantz paper may be the closest the industry will get to hard numbers on the value of systems engineering. The analysis compared three programs that ran in parallel in the same company, using approximately the same definition of systems engineering, with the same type of system. Yet the numbers are almost never quoted, and it is widely stated that hard numbers

[1] Assuming salaries of $100,000 a year, including burden.

on the value of systems engineering do not exist. Why is this?

It is because no data, no matter how good, will ever be good enough. There will always be both rational and emotional reasons to decide the data does not apply. Rational reasons include the data consistency issues mentioned above. In addition, almost any executive under extreme cost pressure will not believe that spending more money is good, no matter what numbers are presented.

(Davenport 1998) describes a case where Mobil Oil engineers devised a sophisticated technique for reducing the amount of steam required for most drilling operations. Hard numbers proved that the technique saved significant money. Nevertheless, even with consultants instituting an intensive communications process, including lessons-learned videos, only 30% of the drilling sites were willing to implement the improvement. And these results were for an improvement that had hard numbers showing clear cost savings and insignificant costs to implement! Imagine the difficulty in making people change for reasons that are less clear.

GIVE IT UP

It should be clear by now that we should stop wishing hard numbers existed. We should also stop waiting for them in order to make the case within our organization that systems engineering process improvement would be beneficial. Feel free to use the arguments in this paper to prove that a) hard numbers are not available, b) hard numbers will not become available any time in the near future, c) if there were hard numbers you wouldn't be able to apply them to your company, and d) if you did use them, nobody would believe you anyway.

SO NOW WHAT?

Clearly, the case for process improvement and systems engineering has been made successfully in many instances, because many companies have decided to implement one or both. To the authors' knowledge, none of these decisions has been based on hard numbers. In all cases, the executives made a leap of faith that systems engineering process improvement would pay off. What convinced many was a belief that return would follow the investment. This expected return might be monetary savings, decreased time to market, or an increased degree of manageability and predictability.

Several ways to help convince managers of expected return when there are no believable hard numbers are justification in retrospect, anecdotes, peer pressure, and discussions about the value of systems engineering.

Justification in retrospect using internal measurements. A company that knows its costs because it measures them can make decisions based on meaningful *internal* "hard numbers." Can your company show how much money was spent on systems engineering tasks last year, and which ones? If you can get a baseline, and then perform some improvements with investment funds based on faith, at least those funds can be justified in retrospect when you show improvements in the measurements. In answer to thought experiment #2, you need to be sure that the numbers you are measuring are atomic enough to show the cost reality even in the face of competing initiatives—whereas "systems engineering productivity" may be easy to manipulate, the labor hours required to complete a change request are more concrete.

Anecdotes. Anecdotes are a valuable way to transfer knowledge effectively. Read the literature, including INCOSE proceedings and INSIGHT of course, but also software process improvement literature including the free U.S. Defense Software magazine, *Crosstalk* (STSC 2000). Accept anecdotes as maybe all there is. Talk to people who have participated in process improvement initiatives and ask if they are willing to share their stories with you. Ask consultants to share what they know, but be sure to put on your "what's in it for them?" filter to prevent your company from looking like a nail just because they have a hammer.

Peer pressure. Everybody else may be onto something. Realize that the only way to remain competitive in a fast-moving society is to keep improving. Tie the need for process improvement to bids you have lost recently. Find out from the SEI how many of your competitors have achieved Level 3 (or other levels).[2] Suggest to your management that competitors will "eat your lunch" if you don't do achieve the same levels.[3]

Value of systems engineering. With respect to funding improved systems engineering, first define exactly what you would like to fund. Is it a group, a phase, more time

---

[2] No comparable collection agency currently exists for collecting systems engineering assessment results. Even if there were such an agency, the nature of continuous-view capability models makes comparison difficult. Would you list the number of companies that have achieved Level 2 in all process areas? 80% of process areas? An average of Level 2? And would you list SE-CMM results differently from SECAM or EIA/IS 731 results?

[3] Despair not. While this will not get you commitment to process improvement (it will only get you commitment to getting the certificate), it has happened in a few cases that in the process of attempting to get a certificate, a company "sees the light" and actually decides that this bitter pill has some beneficial effects. It's worth a try, at any rate.

in requirements, more engineers and fewer marketers writing proposals, time for people building different product lines to talk about sharing, IR&D for developing modular products? Use (Sheard 1996a and 1996b) and (Sheard 2000) to help you decide what your company considers systems engineering to be, and determine how it will benefit your company.

Then describe how those kinds of systems engineering can contribute value in your organization. If at all possible try to quantify this value. At a minimum, track the costs of systems engineering activities. Insight into the total effort spent on systems engineering activities in relationship to program performance may provide enough evidence to make your case.

Probably the most overlooked opportunity for building a case for systems engineering process improvement is identifying existing systems engineering activities within the organization. Many organizations assume that if they have not instituted a formal systems engineering process improvement effort, then they are not doing systems engineering. You need to determine if you are already performing activities that should be considered systems engineering process improvement tasks, and build your case from these based on the following three situations.

Not called systems engineering. Some systems engineering is done because you are already under contract to do it. (Or, per (Jackson 1996), you are doing it because you're ISO 9001 registered, or because it is what you need to do to get product out.) For example, creating deliverable documents such as operational concepts, user's manuals, or specifications is often designated a systems engineering task. If you are not calling this systems engineering, just start doing so. Then convince people that an entire professional organization exists to help you do this better.

Program management. There are other systems engineering activities that you are also doing already, but you call them program management (or project management) (Kasser 1996). You have the choice of calling it whatever you like. In either case, both the Project Management Institute and INCOSE have help for you on how to do these activities better. Better program management helps your company reduce cost and schedule overruns and avoid risks.

Not being done. Some systems engineering activities are not getting done. You know you need to do these activities, either instinctually because you have seen problems downstream, or because you learned it from INCOSE or elsewhere. Under-performed activities may include taking time to understand customer needs, identifying and mitigating risks, specifying requirements clearly and rigorously, or coordinating disciplines. Do not insist on calling these activities "systems engineering." Bill them as "reducing rework" or "increasing reusability of components" or "ensuring customer satisfaction." In this way, you avoid triggering any emotional reactions that "systems engineering is too expensive." Later, you can point out that all the good work you did in these areas is called "systems engineering" by some, and you'd like to improve it more using a systems engineering model (and be sure to add) *as tailored to your particular situation* (Sheard, Lykins, and Armstrong, 1999).

REASONS FOR INVESTMENT

Much of the decision to implement process improvement, or any other program, ultimately rests on faith in the minds of executives. What does the executive believe is the best way to a) grow the business and b) maintain stockholder value? Although analysis can show what return on this investment ought to be, it always involves considerable assumptions. Whether the executive believes the assumptions determines whether the investment will be made. Change advocates will be expected to make a case to help the executive believe the assumptions.

Reasons that have been used in the past are grouped in the following categories:

- External reasons
- Resource problems
- Disconnects
- Vicious cycles

In all cases, defining and improving systems engineering processes can provide insight to help answer the problems described below.

External reasons. These reasons relate both to winning bids and to performing on contracts.

"Our competitors have announced a program to reduce their development costs by 20%. If we don't do the same, we'll never get another contract."

"Our customer complains about problems with the delivered product. If we don't improve, and fast, we'll never win another contract from them."

"This proposal requires us to show we have mature systems engineering processes. What processes do we have? Who's in charge of processes around here? What can we write?"

"We're tired of playing 'Guess the requirements' with the customer. We'll build a prototype that meets spec exactly, and they'll run it past their users and it's completely wrong. Why can't they get their requirements right the first time?"

Resource problems. These reasons relate to getting the right people (and other resources) onto programs.

"In this job market we can't hire people fast enough to staff all our programs. We have no choice but to become more efficient."

"We find problems getting larger and more complex, and staffing is more stretched every year. We have to do more with less."

"Software has repeatedly complained that poor requirements are their biggest problem. But our systems engineers don't know enough about software to do it right the first time, and the software people don't want to deal with anything that's physical or mechanical, or in any way indeterminate. They just want the answer and they'll code from there."

Disconnects. When processes are broken, these breakages show up in the form of disconnects.

"Our customer talked to a developer and he agreed to put in a feature they wanted. But the requirements and test people knew nothing about it! This has got to stop!"

"When I ask people for labor estimates for a proposal, they all come in different formats, the mechanical people include system test and no one else does, the software people estimate low and the analysts estimate high, and I have to apply all sorts of fudge factors to get what I think is a good total number. And even so, it ends up being way off sometimes."

"This change request is full of errors, yet everyone signed off on it! How can that be?"

"It looks like both the Radar area and the Test area have requested $200K capital expenses for the same test equipment. Don't these people talk to one another?"

"I'm tired of frustration, tired of running around without getting anywhere, tired of nobody taking responsibility, tired of things being late and not what I wanted anyway."

Vicious cycles. Vicious cycles occur when incentives to continue doing things the current way are strong enough that they prevent sensible change. Management must intervene to reduce the barriers to needed changes.

"We find a lot of problems in test, when it's really expensive to correct them. I sure wish we had found them earlier. But who has time? We have to reserve so much time for test and we have to meet the customer's schedule, that we have to start building before we have all the requirements or we would never meet schedule."

"We have new challenges every year. This year we have a teaming arrangement with multiple contractors. Last year we were bought out and had to figure out how the acquirer did business and try to convince them our way was better (we weren't very successful). The year before that, we had to learn how to deal with the customer on integrated product teams, where they saw all our dirty laundry. The year before that, we had to learn how to do "evolutionary development." How are we supposed to get any engineering done with all these politics?"

"We know our processes are inefficient. We know it takes too long to get signoff on a change request or close out a failure report. But we're all swamped—who has the time to jump over hurdles in the hope that they can get anyone to listen?"

"We need more predictable costs to have half a chance at pushing back on marketing, who always cuts our development funding and time way below what we can handle. And then they wonder why we're late and over budget."

GETTING STARTED

How much is it worth to an executive to solve these problems? According to (Garcia 1996), change is best marketed as a solution to problems: no problem, no investment. The identified problems also need to be those that someone with funding assumes is his or her responsibility to fix.

Phrase problems and opportunities in terms of costs. How much operating cost is wasted when system test takes six weeks when it could take one or two weeks? Can you estimate the cost that can be saved and talk to the person with that budget responsibility? What schedule problems arise when you cannot staff programs? Can you quantify the cost of these slips?

When a systems engineering problem becomes apparent to an executive, the first reaction is sometimes to issue an order that it shall be solved. But the obvious solution is not necessarily the right one. A hotel found that getting room service meals to rooms before the food got cold required buying more towels![4] Try to convince the executive that a) determining the correct solution (the best way to estimate, for example) may take some time, and will require input from a number of people and b) obtaining compliance will be easier if the individuals responsible for following the process are involved in developing it. (Show that previous orders were followed initially but that people went back to the old way after the pressure was off.)

If you know you need to improve your systems engineering processes, consider hiring a consultant to perform an appraisal or mini-appraisal. Initially at least,[5] the purpose of an appraisal is to tell reveal the best places for improvement, according to the people performing the processes. An executive who invests in a formal appraisal is more likely to provide money to

---

[4] Measurements on room service delivery times isolated waiting for the freight elevator as the biggest delay. The freight elevator was overworked because the service staff was frequently going from floor to floor to find enough clean towels to make up rooms.

[5] Once an appraisal has given the organization a set of ratings, subsequent appraisals tend to acquire the purpose of demonstrating that progress has been made. Still, they too produce findings on the next set of steps to take.

address the identified opportunities for improvement.

Begin by implementing process improvement in the small, such as on a program, and measure initial and resulting costs. Plan to have data to present—imagine your program manager showing executives how many engineering staff they needed before and after processes were improved. Measurements produce convincing data that will justify continued investment in improvement.

CONCLUSIONS

A case must be made for implementing systems engineering or other types of process improvement without having magical data that proves such activities will guarantee return on investment. The suggestions in this paper are a good starting point, but you must do the work to demonstrate the benefits of the process improvement approach that you are recommending. A meaningful ROI can be computed only after the resources have been committed and systems engineering process improvement projects have been completed within your own organization using your own definitions of "return" and "investment." Then, when the benefits of process improvement are realized by management, process improvement sells itself without reliance on ROI numbers.

REFERENCES

Brodman, Judith G. and Donna L. Johnson, "Return on Investment from Software Process Improvement as Measured by U.S. Industry." *Crosstalk*, April 1996.

Davenport, Thomas, Larry Prusak, etc. *Working Knowledge*, Harvard Business Press, Boston, 1998.

Frantz, W. Forrest. "The Impact of Systems Engineering on Quality and Schedule, Empirical Evidence." *Proceedings of INCOSE,* 1995.

Garcia, Suzanne M. "How to Survive as a Change Agent in Hostile Territory: Principles of Process Improvement Terrorism." *Proceedings of INCOSE*, 1996.

Herbsleb, J., A. Carleton, J. Rozum, and D. Zubrow. *Benefits of CMM-Based Software Process Improvement: Initial Results,* CMU/SEI-94-TR-13, ESC-TR-94-013. Software Engineering Institute, 1994.

Jackson, Scott. "Introducing Systems Engineering into a Traditionally Commercial Organization." *Proceedings of INCOSE*, 1996.

Kasser, Joe. "Systems Engineering: Myth or Reality?" *Proceedings of INCOSE*, 1996.

McKinney, Dorothy. "The Value That Systems Engineering Can and Should Provide," *INSIGHT*, INCOSE, Dec. 1995.

M. C. Paulk, B. Curtis, M. B. Chrissis, and C. V. Weber, *Capability Maturity Model for Software*, Version 1.1, Software Engineering Institute, CMU/SEI-93-TR-24, February 1993.

Sheard, Sarah A. "Twelve Systems Engineering Roles," *Proceedings of INCOSE*, 1996a.

Sheard, Sarah A. "The Value of Twelve Systems Engineering Roles," *Proceedings of INCOSE*, 1996b.

Sheard, Sarah A., Howard Lykins, and James R. Armstrong. "Overcoming Barriers to Systems Engineering Process Improvement," *Proceedings of INCOSE*, 1999.

Sheard, Sarah A. and Garry J. Roedler, "Interpreting Continuous-View Capability Models for Higher Levels of Maturity," Systems *Engineering* vol. 2 No. 1, April 1999.

Sheard, Sarah A. "Fifty Ways to Save Your Budget," *Proceedings of INCOSE*, 1999.

Sheard, Sarah A. "Types of Systems Engineering Implementations," *Proceedings of INCOSE*, 2000.

STSC (Software Technology Support Center), *Crosstalk*. 2000. Available at http://www.stsc.hill .af.mil/crosstalk/crostalk.asp

BIOGRAPHIES

Sarah A. Sheard has twenty years' experience in systems engineering of hardware and software systems. Currently she is a senior systems engineer and the deputy manager of the systems engineering department at the Software Productivity Consortium. Ms. Sheard chairs INCOSE's Measurement Technical Committee, which encompasses the Measurement and the Capability Assessment working groups. She has participated in the Measurement Working group and is active on the Practical Systems Measurement project. Ms. Sheard also serves as an associate editor of *Systems Engineering*.

Christopher L. Miller is a systems engineer at the Software Productivity Consortium. Mr. Miller has intensive experience in measurement, and process improvement of software and systems engineering processes. He is active in the INCOSE Measurement Working Group and Practical Software and Systems Measurement Technical Working Group. Mr. Miller has a Masters of Engineering Management in Systems Engineering at the George Washington University and is a member of their adjunct faculty.

---

[i] CMM®is a registered trademark of Carnegie Mellon University.

The Effectiveness of Multiple Software Requirements Elicitation Methods – A Case Study

Sara White
Smart LLC
2100 Summit Court
Las Cruces, NM 88011-0535
swhite@ge-smart.com

Regina M. Gonzales and Dr. Eric Johnson
Computer Engineering Laboratory
Klipsh School of Electrical and Computer Engineering
New Mexico State University
Las Cruces, New Mexico 88003-8001
USA
regonzal/ejohnson@nmsu.edu

Abstract. Requirements engineering methods have been developed to assist in requirements specification. Teaching these methods to college engineering students should prepare students to develop a more complete, consistent, and testable requirements specification than they would have developed if they had not used these methods. The "Software Metrics Toolset Software Requirements Specification" was developed using several requirements engineering methods and was completed in Fall 1997 EE590 Software Systems Engineering II class. This report will compare the final set of requirements from the Software Metrics Toolset (SMT) Software Requirements Specification to the developed SMT for completeness and cost impact. The software requirements elicitation methods used in the development of the Software Metric Toolset effectively limited the cost of requirement changes in the actual development and customer delivery stage to less than 3% of the budgeted cost. The results underscore the value of using multiple methodologies that look at different aspects of the requirements.

INTRODUCTION

As engineers, we want to develop products that are a good match to user's needs. We do not want to produce products that are either rejected outright or expensively redeveloped. Not only should the requirements specify the project objectives and required product behavior, but the requirement specifications themselves need to be true, complete, feasible, verifiable (testable) and maintainable. Eliciting requirements may be difficult since requirements often come out in a staggered fashion and there may be conflicting requirements or nebulous, unverifiable requirements. Some requirements may not come out until the user evaluates a prototype or the final product. With complete, consistent, testable requirements, the difficulty and impact of the individual requirements can be calculated. The priority of each requirement and design tradeoffs can be negotiated within project cost, time and resource constraints. The importance of complete requirements is underscored when looking at the impact of requirement changes at different stages of the product life cycle. Pressman (1992) states that for every dollar impact a change would make on the cost if introduced at the definition stage, when introduced at the development stage the costs are 1.6 to 6 times as great, and after release they are 60 to 100 times as great!

CASE STUDY

Project and Methods. The SMT project was initiated at New Mexico State University (NMSU) by the Boeing Corporation to support software process education and to develop a tool to make the collection and use of metrics data as simple and automated as possible. A "Software Metrics Toolset Software Requirements Specification" was developed using several requirements engineering methods and was completed in Fall 1997 EE590 Software Systems Engineering II class. The requirements engineering (elicitation) methods in the order taught and used were:

- Brainstorming (Ad Hoc) from User Supplied Documentation
- Boehm's Theory-W Analysis
- Scenarios
- Structured Analysis (SA)
- Object Oriented Analysis (OOA)
- Usability Analysis

The development process selected for use in the SMT project was based on the spiral model. In the spiral model, various requirement elicitation methods are used to acquire complete system requirements. These requirements are then developed into a conceptual model. That conceptual model is documented in a Software Requirements Specification (SRS) which is reviewed by the customer. Working under the principle "its hard to edit a blank page," the overall goal of the requirements elicitation methods used to create the conceptual model is to provide as complete requirements coverage as possible. The user can correct wrong requirements, and conflicting requirements can be resolved, but completely missed requirements provide little opportunity for customer feedback.

After the conceptual model and SRS are revised using the customer SRS review feedback, a limited prototype of the conceptual model (called an Alpha Model) is developed and provided to the customer for evaluation. An Alpha Model has very limited functionality, but fairly detailed user interface. It models the way the user will interact with the product. The requirements changes that result from the alpha model evaluations are incorporated into another SRS revision. The final goal of these activities is to provide complete, consistent, testable requirements specifications with fine enough granularity to identify risks and aid in risk abatement efforts.

In the actual SMT development, the requirements phase spiral ended with the limited Alpha Model. The Alpha Model was presented to the customer for evaluation. The alpha model was built in Fall 1997 and demonstrated by Sara White to the customer in January, 1998. After reviewing the Alpha Model, the existing requirements were re-prioritized by the customer. The customer requested additional requirements and several existing requirements were re-prioritized as part of the negotiations due to the time and resource constraints of the student developer.

Evaluation Technique. The requirements were evaluated at the conceptual model stage and at the alpha model stage. Since the main goal of conceptual model requirements was to provide as complete requirements coverage as possible, the effectiveness at the conceptual model stage was quantitatively evaluated in the area of requirements completeness. Once the choice of off-the-shelf development environment software was finalized at the alpha model stage, requirement costs could be calculated. The effectiveness was then quantitatively evaluated in the areas of both requirements completeness and potential development cost savings.

The effectiveness of each requirement elicitation method in the area of completeness was measured two ways. First the percentage of verifiable requirements elicited with a particular method over the total conceptual model requirements elicited was calculated. Then once the requirements were finalized and the selection the off-the-shelf database management system software was made, the cost effect of individual requirements was estimated. For each final SRS requirement, a cost (in hours of development time) was made. Costs to open and close forms and "Access wizards" were amortized over all the requirements that were included in that form or wizard. Assigning final requirements to elicitation methods used was not always straightforward. User supplied requirements often contained non-verifiable goals, such as "the system should be easy to learn." More understanding of the system to be developed was needed to help solidify vague or unverifiable requirements into specific, testable requirements. Requirements were assigned to the method where they were first solidified into specific, testable requirements. They were not assigned where the high level, vague general requirement was first introduced (for those not originating in the user requirement documentation).

Then the cost effectiveness of each method with regard to the total budgeted cost was calculated only for the complete SMT. Cost estimates could not realistically be made before this point since the selection of off-the-shelf development environment software package was not made until then

ANALYSIS OF RESULTS

Conceptual Model. Figure 1 shows the percentage of verifiable requirements elicited with each particular method over the total conceptual model requirements elicited. Completeness was very important in acquiring these requirements, since wrong requirements can be found and corrected at this stage much easier than entirely missed requirements. As can be seen in Figure 1, when it comes to requirements elicitation methods, "one size does not fit all". No single requirement elicitation method contributed much more than one third of the final requirements. Yet all together, they presented enough clarity to create a conceptual model that was effective in bringing the developers and customers to agreement on the requirements of the SMT with very few, minor changes occurring during the actual SMT development.

The Theory-W analysis, which seemed to contribute much less than most of the other methods, actually contributed significantly to the completeness of the requirements by introducing 4 high level installation and maintenance requirements. However, these vague requirements needed further clarification, and were assigned to the methods used later where they were solidified.

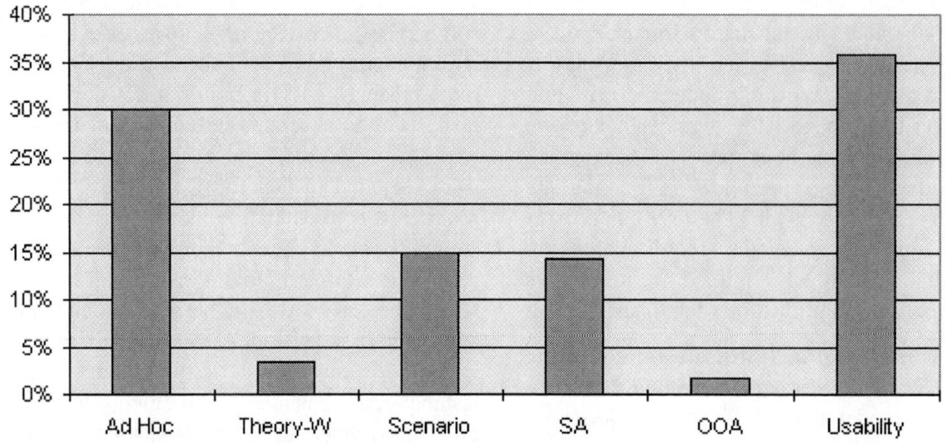

Figure 1. Verifiable Requirement Percentage of Total Conceptual Model by Elicited Method

The Object Oriented Analysis contributed the least to the requirements. This is probably due to the fact that Object Oriented Analysis followed the Structured Analysis. Both methods modularize the system and are strong at defining the "behind the scenes" modular structure and interaction of the system. The Structured Analysis clarified the internal functioning well enough that the Object Oriented Analysis added little. Had they been performed in the reverse order, the results may have also been reversed. Having two functional analysis methods provided important design direction, but does not appear highly necessary to obtain complete requirements.

The selection of requirements methods with strengths in gathering additional life-cycle (Theory-W), user flow requirements (Scenarios), functional data modeling (Structured Analysis, Object Oriented) and user interface issues (Usability methods) worked well in this case. The weakest area was in the area of timing and resource requirements. This was mainly due to the lack of any hard timing or resource requirements. Additional requirement elicitation methods should be added when these issues are present.

Prototype Environment Selection. The Conceptual Model requirements should also aid in the selection of a rapid prototype development environment for the Alpha Model and the final SMT development environment. The chosen software should significantly reduce software development time (cost). Figure 2 shows the number of implemented requirements that were met by

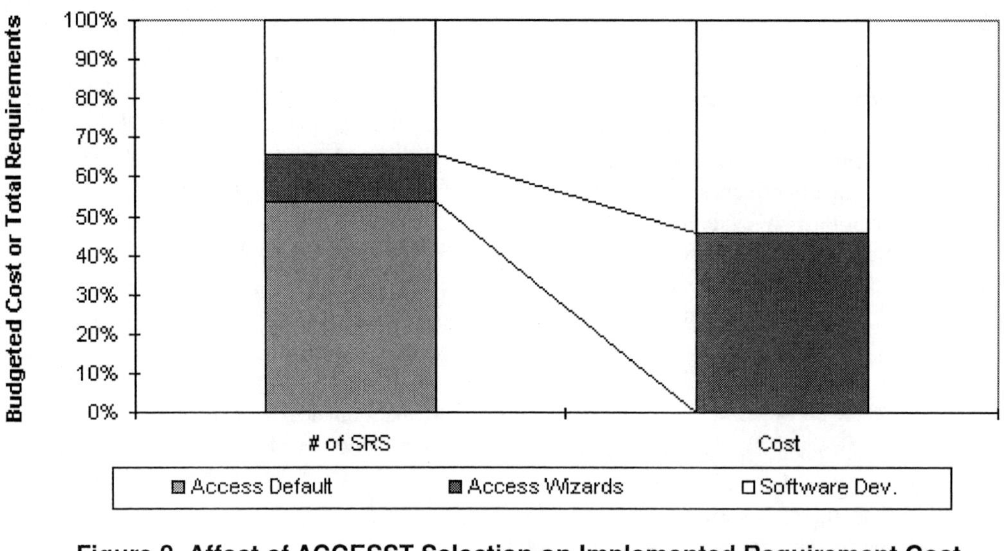

Figure 2. Affect of ACCESST Selection on Implemented Requirement Cost

the environment software chosen (Microsoft Access) by default and through Access Wizards. The remaining requirements required at least some Visual Basic software to be written in order to implement them. It is qualitatively obvious that the Access choice reduced development time by fulfilling requirements by default since over half of the requirements were fulfilled without cost by Access. Since the requirements were used to determine which rapid development package was selected, they are deemed effective for this purpose.

SMT Development Costs. Figure 3 shows the percentage of budgeted costs due to the requirements elicited in each method. No one method clarified more than 34% of the budgeted costs, again showing the effectiveness of using multiple elicitation methods. As before, the Object Oriented Analysis added little to the overall cost. Of interest is the zero cost attributed to the Theory-W Analysis. This is due to the fact that the Theory-W specific verifiable requirements were all met by default by the selection of Access as the development software.

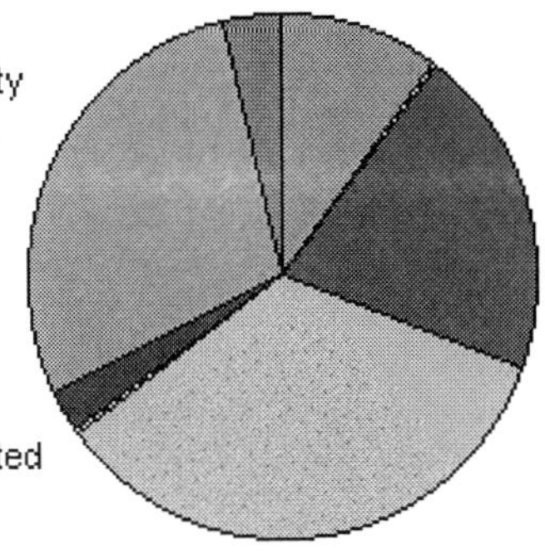

Figure 3. Percentage of Complete SMT Budgeted Costs by Elicitation Method

SMT Initial Version. After reviewing the Alpha Model, the requirements were re-prioritized and the highest priority subset was selected for the initial version, as part of the negotiations due to the time and resource constraints of the student developer.

The cost effectiveness of the methods used is different when looking only at the initial SMT version developed. Many of the most costly requirements were not implemented, since the initial version budgeted cost was less than one fourth of the complete SMT budgeted cost. Figure 4 shows the percentage of initial version (implemented) budgeted costs due to the requirements elicited in each method.

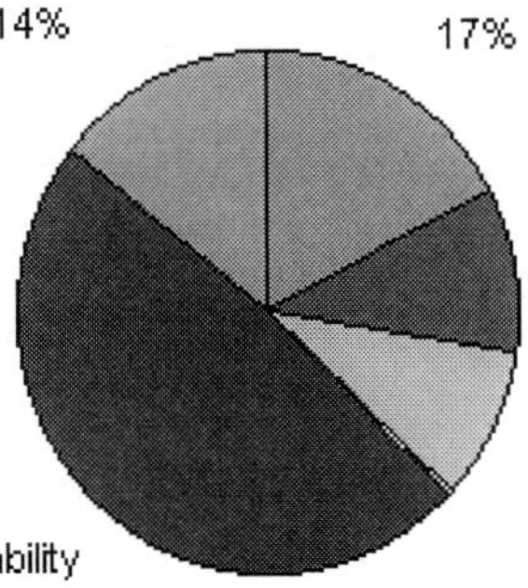

Figure 4. Percentage of Initial Version (Implemented) Budgeted Costs by Elicitation Method

Many requirements clarified in the Structured Analysis and Scenario Analysis were not implemented. Fifty percent of the implemented requirements came from the Usability analysis, many of them implemented by default by Access.

The structured analysis cost impact went from 34% to zero because the remaining requirements not postponed till later versions were all implemented by Access by default at no cost. Effectiveness (completeness) of the final conceptual model compared to the final implemented requirements can be seen in Table 1. The conceptual model provided a fairly complete requirements set with only 7 new requirements being added.

Requirements that were:	SRS Requirements
Implemented as is	58
Modified and implemented	17
Not implemented	26
New requirements	7
Deleted requirements	19

Table 1. Disposition of Conceptual Model Requirement after Alpha Model Changes

The impact of the limitations and constraints due to the Access selection was responsible for 10 of the deletions and 3 modifications and the change to spreadsheet style inputs resulted in 5 more deletions and 6 of the modifications. The 26 requirements were not implemented due to their low priority and high cost. The list of requirements not to be implemented was negotiated with the customer. Any missed requirements would obviously not be negotiated with the customer and could have resulted in the customer assuming that the feature was included in the implementation, causing a development phase requirement change. Late requirements changes result in rework and retrofitting requirements onto the developed system.

Reducing rework and late change costs is an important motivation for having complete requirements. Figure 5 shows the reduction in potential cost of the system (due to a savings in reduced rework) which provides a qualitative effectiveness measurement, since it is impossible to accurately predict the cost of rework or changes necessary if things had been done differently first. As each method further clarifies requirements and adds to the budgeted costs, the potential cost is shown to be reduced. The exceptions were in this case study the Theory-W and Structured analysis, which both had no cost effect because their implementable requirements were fulfilled by Access by default.

The effectiveness of the requirements elicitation methods as a whole can been seen in the actual total development stage cost change of less than 3% of the budgeted cost, and only part of that cost resulted in additional hours (the remainder simply deleted a non-working feature). The results underscore the value of using multiple methodologies that look at different aspects of the requirements

CONCLUSIONS

Did teaching requirements engineering methods to relatively inexperienced college engineering students result in the development of more complete requirement specification than would otherwise be expected? The software requirements elicitation methods used in the development of the Software Metric Toolset effectively limited the cost of requirement changes in the actual development and customer delivery stage to less than 3% of the budgeted cost. Compared to industry data (Pressman, 1992) that indicates that between 50% to 70% of all effort expended on a program will be expended after it is delivered to the customer for the first time, the results of the SMT elicitation methods used by the college engineering students appear to have been very effective.

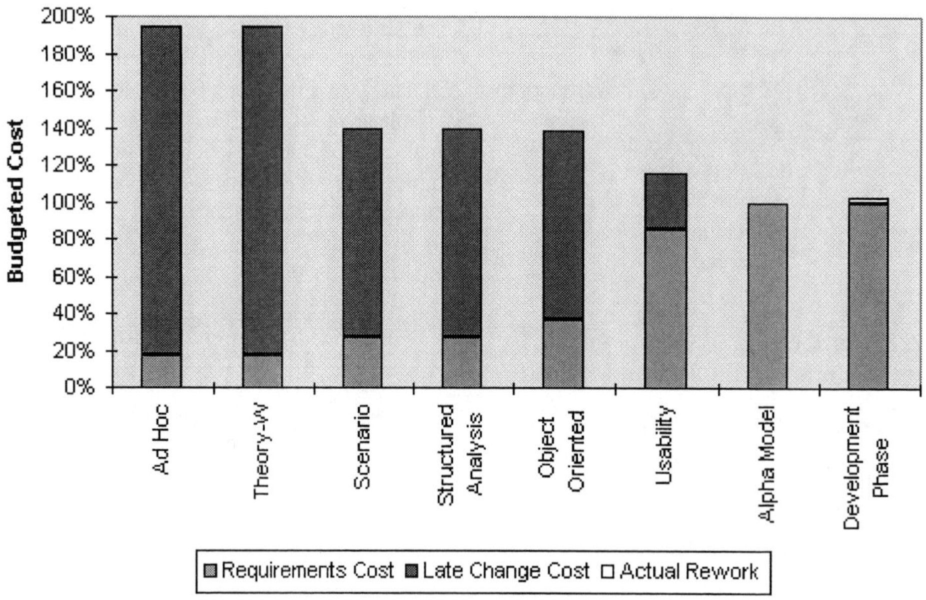

Figure 5. Effect of Methods on the Potential Cost of the Implemented SMT

REFERENCES

ANSI/IEEE Std 1016-1987, "Recommended Practice for Software Design Descriptions", 1987.

Boehm, B., "A Spiral Model of Software Development and Enhancement", TRW Defense Systems Group, 1987.

Boeing Defense & Space Group, "Software Metrics Toolset", Presentation Package, Presented September 18, 1997.

Boeing Defense & Space Group, "Engineering Operating Instruction (EOI) 7-001 Revision A, Software Metrics and Indicators", 1994.

Boeing Defense & Space Group, "Statement of Work - College Project: Software Metrics Toolset", Boeing Defense & Space Group, January 10, 1997.

Boeing Defense & Space Process Group,"S/W Metrics Toolset - Project Overview", Presentation Package, Presented January 23, 1997.

Fagan, M.E., "Design and code inspections to reduce errors in program development", International Business Machines Systems Journal, 1976.

Gonzales, R., "Useability Review Results", January 5, 1999

Humphrey, Watts, "Introduction to the Personal Software Process", Addison-Wesley Publishers, 1997.

IEEE Std 1028-1988, IEEE, "Standard for Software Reviews and Audits", 1988.

IEEE Std 1044-1993, IEEE, "Standard Classification for Software Anomalies", 1993.

IEEE Std 830-1993, "IEEE Recommended Practice for Software Requirements Specifications", 1993.

Mack, Nielson, "Usability Inspection Methods: Executive Summary", John Wiley & Sons publisher, 1994.

NMSU, "Software Metrics Toolset System Project Management Plan (SPMP)", EE490/590 Software Systems Engineering, Spring 1997.

NMSU, "System & Software Requirements Specification for the Metrics Toolset", EE490/590 Software Systems Engineering, Spring 1997.

NMSU, "Users Manual for the Software Metrics Toolset - Draft", EE490/590 Software Systems Engineering, Spring 1997.

Paulk, Curtis, Chrissis, Weber, "Capability Maturity Model, Version 1.1", IEEE Software. July 1993.

Pressman, R.S.,"Software Engineering, A Practitioners Approach", McGraw-Hill, Inc., 1992.

White, S., "Software Metric Toolset Users Manual", NMSU, 1999.

Wieringa, R.J., "Requirements Engineering, Frameworks For Understanding", John Wiley & Sons Publisher, 1996.

Supportability Assessment and Evaluation During System Architecture Development

Line H. Johannesen
ILS Manager
Kongsberg Defense and Aerospace
Kongsberg, Norway

Dinesh Verma, Ph.D.
Systems/Supportability Strategist
Lockheed Martin Undersea Systems
Manassas, Virginia, USA

Abstract. The purpose of this technical paper is to present a framework for the evaluation of system architectures from a supportability and logistics perspective. A two-pronged approach was implemented. The initial focus was on investigating the extent to which this issue had been addressed in the literature. Accordingly, this paper also presents a literature survey focused on the assessment and evaluation of system architectures in general, and their assessment and evaluation from a supportability perspective in particular. As part of the second thrust, leading system engineering practitioners and architects from the aerospace industry were interviewed. In this case, the objective was to synthesize the heuristic and experiential aspect of system architecture assessment and evaluation.

The above two thrusts, theoretical and heuristic, led to the development of a domain independent evaluation framework represented in the form of an attribute hierarchy. The input information synthesized by this research, which lead to the evaluation framework development is presented in this technical paper. The Analytic Hierarchy Process (AHP) methodology is suggested as the preferred approach for the relative evaluation of alternative architectural approaches. Finally, extensions to this framework for increased applicability within specific domains are addressed.

THE PROBLEM SETTING

The domain of systems engineering has been characterized by accelerating interest in the past two decades. This becomes evident from the references included with this study, the launch of the International Council on Systems Engineering, the launch of three new systems engineering standards in the last five years (EIA632; IEEE-P1220; EIA731), and the setting up of systems engineering working groups in multiple technical societies (SOLE-The International Society of Logistics; ASNE-American Society of Naval Engineers; ASME-American Society of Mechanical Engineers). The design phase of the system life cycle is finally being recognized for its potential impact on the development of truly efficient and effective products, systems, and structures that more closely track customer requirements and needs [Shapour, et. al., 1987; Winner, et. al., 1988]. This recognition, and continuing budget reductions, have lead to the development of concepts such as Integrated Process and Product Development (IPPD), Modernization through Spares, Application of Commercial-of-the-Shelf (COTS) Technologies, and the application of Cost as an Independent Variable.

Studies within the US Department of Defense suggest the increasing allocation of defense budgets to operate and sustain legacy systems, as shown in Figure 1. This inhibits the ability to capitalize in new weapon systems or to upgrade and modernization of legacy combat systems.

Blanchard and Fabrycky [1999] highlight the lag between cost commitment and realization, to emphasize the impact of design decisions on system operation and sustainment cost. This idea is reflected in Figure 2. The anticipated life cycle costs for a surface combatants fleet, Figure 3, further validates the idea proposed in Figure 2.

Today, *there is a demand for bolder and more rapid improvements in the total cost of system ownership*. As such, the technical risks faced by the designer are now greater, as are the stakes. These demands result, not only from an on-going reduction in available resources, but also because of changing requirements driven by

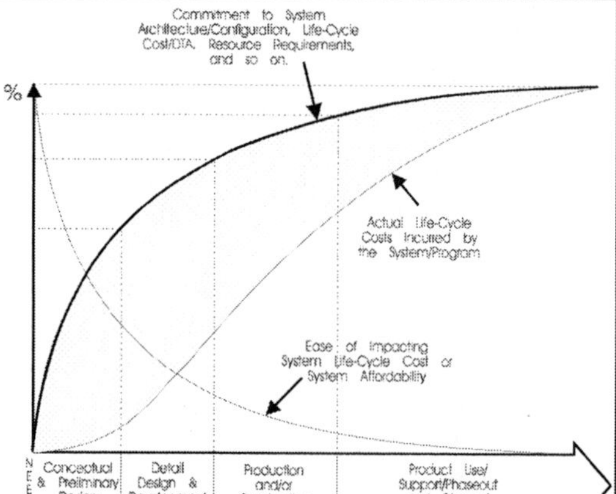

Figure 2. Commitment to system life-cycle cost and configuration.

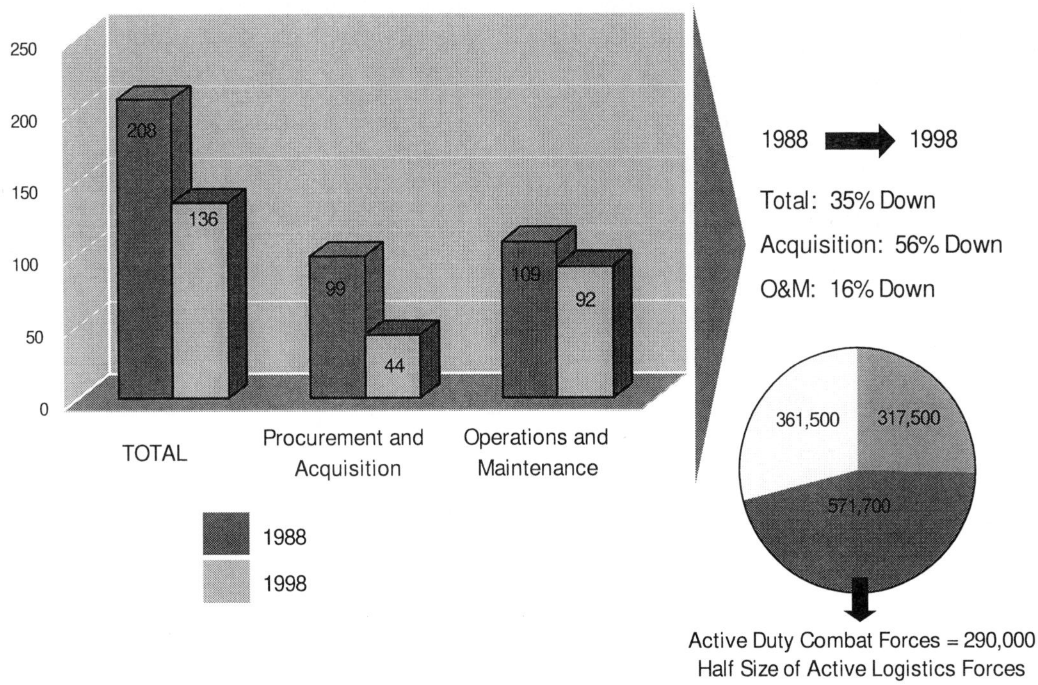

Figure 1. Budget Allocation to Sustain Legacy Systems [Plunkett & Verma, 1999].

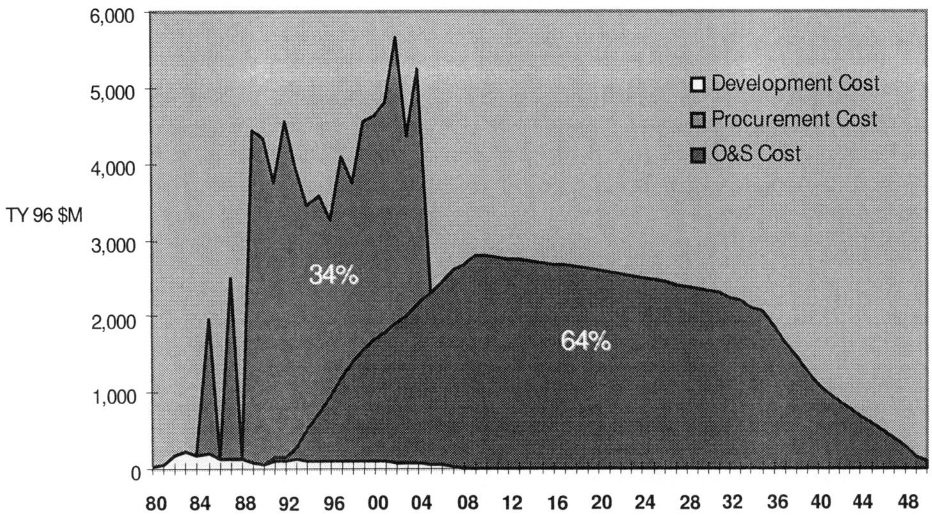

Figure 3. Life Cycle Cost of US Navy Surface Combatants [Plunkett & Verma, 1999]

changing missions (e.g., from missions in deep blue waters to missions in littoral, shallow waters), changing threats, and the trend towards joint, multiple nation, operations.

INTEGRATED PROCESS AND PRODUCT (IPPD) PRINCIPLES

In order to facilitate the realization of radical reductions in the cost of system acquisition and operation, the system design process is facing increasing scrutiny resulting in the formulation of concepts such as the Integrated Product and Process Development (IPPD). This approach is analogous to the concurrency in system engineering proposed by Blanchard and Fabrycky [1999].

They suggest the consideration of three concurrent life-cycles as part of the overall system engineering process, illustrated in Figure 4. These life cycles track (a) design and development of the primary product, (b) design, development, and installation of the manufacturing facility, and (c) design, development, and deployment of a maintenance and support capability for the deployed product and the manufacturing facility. This concurrency or "totality" during system design makes design more rigorous, comprehensive, and complex.

The fundamental thesis of the IPPD process is that a structured, disciplined, and properly managed, systems engineering process is essential for the successful development of effective systems (products and/or processes). Here systems engineering is defined as the application of efforts to [Blanchard, Peterson, and Verma, 1995]:

1. *transform an operational need into description of system performance parameters and a preferred system configuration through the use of an iterative process of functional analysis, synthesis, optimization, definition, design, test, and evaluation;*
2. *incorporate related technical parameters and assure compatibility of physical, functional, and program interfaces in a manner that optimizes the total system definition and design; and*
3. *integrate performance, producibility, reliability, maintainability, manability, supportability, and other specialties into the overall engineering effort.*

The system life cycle begins with the identification of a functional need or operational deficiency. More often than not, system operational deficiency can be articulated in terms of the cost of system ownership, rather than any particular prime mission performance parameter or attribute. This need is translated into system level requirements through the utilization of tools such as Quality Function Deployment and Input-Output matrices. The requirements definition process is then followed by the conceptual design phase (involving the synthesis and selection of system-level conceptual solutions) and the preliminary design phase (involving the modeling of expected system behavior, the allocation of system level requirements to conceptual sub-systems, and their subsequent translation into detailed design specifications). The system architecture, depicting the functional, operational, and physical packaging of the selected approach of system concept is developed during the preliminary design phase. Preliminary design is followed by detailed design and development which, in turn, leads to the actual production and/or construction of the product or structure. The product or structure is then deployed, installed, operated, and maintained. At the end of its operational (design) or economic life, the entity is either re-engineered to satisfy an evolving need or requirement, or properly retired and recycled.

A simplified schematic of the systems engineering process is depicted in Figure 5, along with primary outputs from each process phase.

The fundamental requirement from a "design for supportability" perspective is to establish methods, tools, metrics, and indicators that allow the assessment of system design during all the systems engineering phases, with a particular emphasis on conceptual and preliminary design phases. Therein lies the focus of this research endevor and this technical paper.

STATE OF RESEARCH IN PRELIMINARY DESIGN AND ARCHITECTURE EVALUATION

Systems engineering activities may be classfied into design synthesis, analysis, and/or evaluation oriented activities. These activities are iterative and also continuously changing in scope with the progression and evolution of the system engineering process. Design synthesis, analysis, and evaluation during conceptual and preliminary stages must contend with a high level of uncertainty. In order to capitalize on the opportunity to influence design, methods and metrics must be developed that will allow us to assess the "goodness" of early system designs during the early system design phases.

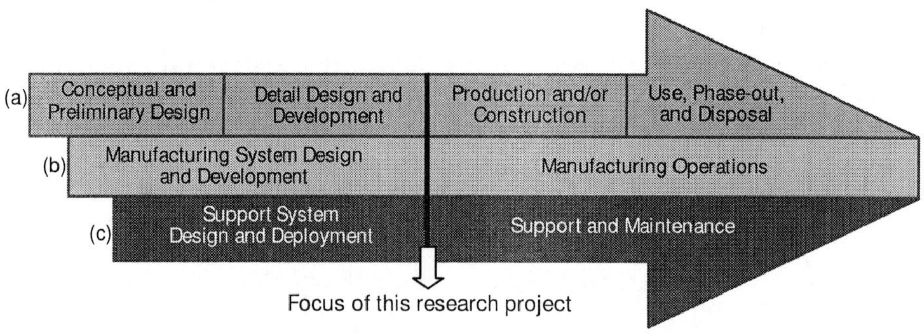

Figure 4. Concurrency in system design and development.

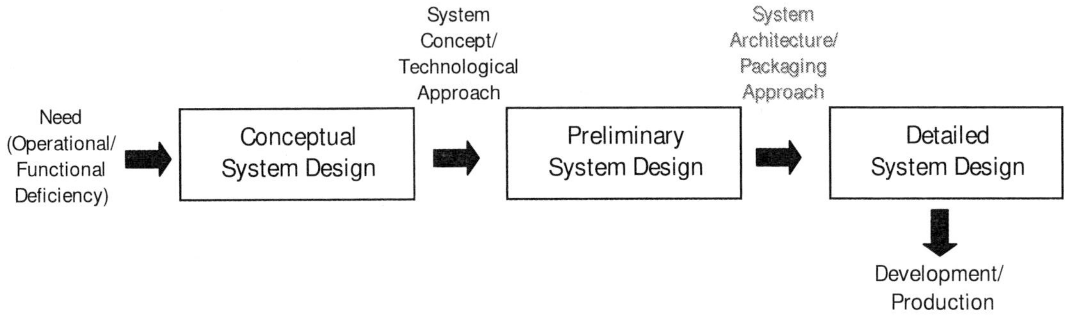

Figure 5. Schematic of the Systems Engineering Process.

A literature survey was conducted to assess the extent of research and application in the evaluation of early system designs, with a particular focus on preliminary design and system architecture. A system architecture development methodology, enhanced by sound supportability evaluation, can enable the realization of systems that meet user needs while reducing the total cost of system ownership.

A study of the literature suggests that the applicability of many traditional methodologies and optimization procedures to design evaluation is often limited due to the qualitative nature of certain design goals, requirements, and criteria. This limitation is particularly evident during system architecture development. Vastly different evaluation methodologies have been proposed [Dixon, et. al. 1989; Fabrycky, 1994; Knosala and Pedrycz, 1987; O'Grady, et. al. 1991; Ostrofsky, 1977; Thurston, et. al. 1993]. These have been developed to primarily address the late preliminary and detailed design phases of the system engineering process. Pugh [1983, 1990] has conducted research in the development of a conceptual system design methodology along with an associated evaluation methodology. This research has been extended by Verma [Verma and Fabrycky, 1995; Verma and Knezevic, 1996; Verma, et.al., 1999] through the application of fuzzy concepts to evaluate system concepts. Rechtin [1991, 1994] and Maier [1994, 1996, 1996a] have build a methodology built on heuristics for architecting systems during the early preliminary system design phase [Rechtin and Maier, 1996]. Maier [1996] has also constructed evaluation criteria for the evaluation of system architectures in the transportation domain. Talbot [1996] has created a taxonomy of system design evaluation criteria and associated indicators, without specific reference to the system architecture development phase.

Evaluating engineering designs continues to be the focus of many research groups. However, these efforts have been targeted to the evaluation of designs during the later stages of system development. There is extensive reference in the literature to the evaluation of detailed designs with regard to manufacturing and assembly.

Boothroyd and Dewhurst investigated the linkage between detail design configuration and the likely time and cost for subsequent assembly [Boothroyd, 1988]. Ulrich, et. al., attempted to correlate the assembly time saved through parts consolidation with the consequent impact on the time and cost to manufacture [Ulrich, et. al., 1991]. O'Grady and Young have conducted research to evaluate preliminary designs from the perspective of manufacturing unacceptability [O'Grady, et. al. 1991; Young, et. al. 1991]. They have proposed an artificial intelligence based approach as a means of tracking production constraint violations during the design and development process.

Neville conducted research to evaluate mechanical structures for stiffness and weight [Nevill, 1990]. Lee and Gilmore considered uncertainties in stochastic Kinematic chain design (including tolerances on link length, radial clearance, and random pit center location) through probabilistic model formulation [Lee and Gilmore, 1989]. Dhingra and Rao used fuzzy set theory to analyze kinematic/dynamic characteristics of high speed planar mechanisms [Dhingra and Rao, 1989].

Thurston, et. al., proposed utilization of multi-attribute utility theory to compare the overall value of alternative design configurations as a function of the levels of multiple performance characteristics of a manufactured item. They apply sensitivity analysis as a mechanism for modifying designs and to enhance overall utility to decision makers [Thurston 1991; Thurston, et. al. 1991; Thurston, et. al. 1992; Thurston, et. al. 1993].

Mistree, et. al., propose extension of goal programming and mathematical programming concepts to formulate a hybrid model [Mistree, et. al. 1992]. They utilize an adaptive linear programming approach to solve compromise decision support problems. This approach has been applied to some extent to preliminary designs.

Extension of the basic approach is possible through fuzzy set theory to bypass the requirement for "*precisely defined information and relationships between subsystems*" [Allen, et. al. 1990].

Otto, Antonsson, and Wood suggest application of fuzzy logic to evaluate preliminary mechanical designs [Otto and Antonsson, 1991; Wood and Antonsson, 1990]. They have analyzed the vagueness of parameters in the design of a mechanical frame structure [Wood, et. al., 1989].

Accordingly, there is sufficient validation in the literature relative to the utility of an evaluation methodology based on relevant indicators and metrics for the evaluation of early system designs [Verma and Johannesen, 1999; Verma and Giffin, 1997]. However, there is little evidence in the literature of research with regard to the development of a evaluation framework to assess system architectures from a supportability perspective. The ultimate goal of design evaluation is to isolate the "best" or "most desirable" alternative. However, this evaluation activity must be compatible with the corresponding engineering design process for maximum effectiveness. The significance and impact (on the overall system life cycle) of early design decisions has been fairly well conceptualized and documented [Fabrycky and Blanchard, 1991; Osborn, 1991; Nickelson and Belson, 1991]. In keeping with this imperative, *architecture evaluation from a supportability standpoint is the focus of this research.*

A system architecture evaluation methodology, complete in its consideration of the system life cycle, should facilitate the design and development of products more responsive to user/consumer needs and requirements, while reducing the total cost of system ownership. Further, development of this evaluation methodology should contribute to the evolving theory of system design.

EVAUATION FRAMEWORK DEVELOPMENT

Subsequent to conducting a literature search, leading practitioners and system architects were interviewed. The interview focus was to synthesizing heuristics and guidelines for evaluating system architectures from a supportability perspective. A summary of the input synthesized in these interviews, along with the data gleaned from the literature survey is presented in Table 1. This information was later refined and structured into an evaluation framework/attribute hierarchy for implementation within a commercially available Analytic Hierarchy Process (AHP) shell, Expert Choice™[1]. As such an additional focus during the creation of the attribute hierarchy was on maximizing the extent of decoupling between the attributes and the sub-attributes, consistent with AHP assumptions. A "screen shot" of the evaluation template is shown in Figure 6.

[1] Expert Choice is a trademark of Expert Choice, Inc.

CONCLUSIONS

The most significant goal of this research has been to make a contribution to the on-going evolution of the field of system architecting. Specific achievements include:

1. Synthesis of the theoretical research to evaluate preliminary design and system architectures;
2. Synthesis of heuristics and their translation into attributes and sub-attributes to evaluate system architectures; and finally
3. Development of an evaluation framework for evaluating system architectures.

Development of the evaluation framework, in the form of the attribute hierarchy, included removal of redundancy and an attempt to enhance the extent of de-coupling across the attribute hierarchy. Further, ways of measuring the attributes and sub-attributes to ensure domain independence were focused. The evaluating framework is now represented in the form of a domain independent attribute hierarchy and associated measurement mechanisms. The measurement mechanisms are quantifiable to the extent possible, but due to the early state of the design process focus in this research, some of the measuring mechanisms are represented as questions and are subjective in nature.

The attribute hierarchy can serve as a useful checklist for system architects. However, to bring additional formality to the evaluation process this framework been been implemented within a commercially available AHP (analytic hierarchy process) engine to facilitate adaptation to specific domains. The model can be used to assess the relative "goodness" of architectural alternatives within an environment characterised by imprecise information, heuristics, and qualitative judgement. Furthermore, the inherent focus on making this framework generic should allow its application across diverse problem domains and to systems of varying complexity.

REFERENCES

[Allen, et. al., 1990] Allen, J. K., R. S. Krishnamachari, J. Masetta, D. Pearce, D. Rigby, and F. Mistree, "*Fuzzy Compromise: An Effective Way to Solve Hierarchical Design Problems*", **Proceedings, 3rd Air Force/NASA Symposium on Recent Advances in Multidisciplinary Analysis and Optimization**, SFO, CA, Sept 1990.

Table 1. Input for the Assessment of System Architectures from a Supportability Perspective.

Theoretical Investigation	Heuristics and Guidelines Identified in the Interviews
• **Group** strongly **related** elements, **separate** elements that are unrelated • Choose components to be implemented independently of the internal implementation of all others • In partitioning, choose elements to be as independent as possible; i.e, low external complexity, high internal complexity • **Functional and physical** structuring should match • Cohesion-SW • Coupling-SW • Modifiability -SW • Design complexity	• Component De-Coupling/ Cohesion (Functional Dependence (Minimisation), Short (Real)/Time Requirements, Physical Decoupling) • Minimisation of Dependant Failures • Ease of Technology Refreshment and Insertion • Upgradeability (Backward Compability, Hardware/ Software Independence, Standard Interfaces, % Capacity Utilisation, Extensibility) • Orthogonality (non-overlapping functionality)/Level Modularity • Layered (replace a layer without affecting others) vs. vertical • Information Hiding; Explicit vs. Implicit interfaces • Complexity (Coupling – Cohesion)
	• Physical Commonality (# Unique LRU's) • Functional Commonality (# Unique CSCIs and HWCIs) • Operational Commonality (Common Operation/ Maintenance Training Requirements) • % Reuse From Other Sub-systems/Program/Platforms • Number of Implementing languages/Unique Protocols • Commonality at a layer • Familiarity (Procedures, displays, vendors, FM/FL/ Diagnostics, Conops, % of Unique Training, Reuse)
• Use **open** architectures. • Successful architectures are **proprietary, but open**. • Use of COTS comp. (HW)	• Standards for System Elements • Standards for Element Interfaces (External and Internal) • Modularity of the standard/Live or Dead Standard • Multiple vendors for system components • Mainstream standard/market share • Openness - Possible diversified control; Components might work independently) • Compliance

[Blanchard and Fabrycky, 1999] Blanchard, B. S. and W. J. Fabrycky, **Systems Engineering and Analysis**, Third Edition, Prentice Hall, Inc., Englewood Cliffs, New Jersey, 1990.

[Boothroyd, 1988] Boothroyd, G., "*Making it Simple: Design for Assembly*", **Mechanical Engineering**, February 1988.

[Dhingra and Rao, 1989] Dhingra, A. K. and S. S. Rao, "*Integrated Optimal Design of Planar Mechanisms Using Fuzzy Theories*", **Proceedings, 15th Annual Design Automation Conference**, ASME, Montreal, Canada, 1989.

[Dixon, et. al., 1989] Dixon, J. R., M. J. Guenette, R. K. Irani, E. H. Nielsen, M. F. Orelup, and R. V. Welch, "*Computer-Based Models of Design Processes: The Evaluation of Designs for Redesign*", **Proceedings, NSF Engineering Design Research Conference**, Amherst, Massachusetts, 1989.

[Fabrycky, 1994] Fabrycky, W. J., "*Models and Indirect Experimentation for System Design Evaluation",* **Systems Engineering**, Vol. 1, No. 1, July - September, 1994.

[Fabrycky and Blanchard, 1991] Fabrycky, W. J. and B. S. Blanchard, **Life-Cycle Cost and Economic Analysis**, Prentice Hall, Inc., Englewood Cliffs, New Jersey, 1991.

[Knosala and Pedrycz, 1987] Knosala, R. and W. Pedrycz, "*Multicriteria Design Problem - Fuzzy Set Approach*", **Proceedings, International Conference on Engineering Design**, ASME, Boston, August 1987.

[Lee and Gilmore, 1989] Lee, S. J. and B. J. Gilmore, "*The Determination of the Probabilistic Properties of Velocities and Accelerations in Kinematic Chains with Uncertainty*", **Proceedings, 15th Annual Design Automation Conference**, ASME, Montreal, Canada, 1989.

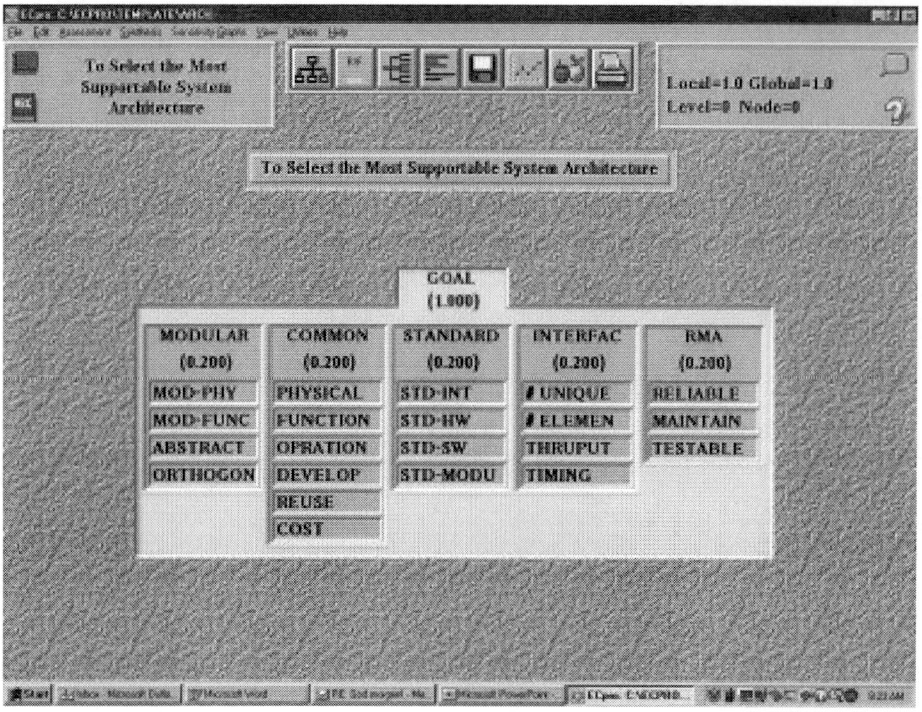

Figure 6. Attribute Hierarchy to Evaluate System Architectures from a Supportability Perspective.

[Maier, 1996] Maier, M. W., *"Systems Architecting: An Emergent Discipline"*, Proceedings, **IEEE Aerospace Applications Conference**, 1996.

[Maier, 1996a] Maier, M.W., *"On Architecting and Intelligent Transport Systems"*, **IEEE AES Transaction**, October 1996.

[Mistree, et. al. 1992] Mistree, F., O. F. Hughes, and B. Bras, *"The Compromise Decision Support Problem and the Adaptive Linear Programming Algorithm"*, **Structural Optimization: Status and Promise**, M. P. Kamat (Editor), AIAA, Washington D.C., 1992.

[Nevill, 1990] Nevill, G. E., *"Guiding Iterative Processes for Preliminary Design"*, **Proceedings, NSF Conference on Design and Manufacturing Systems Research**, Arizona State University, January 1990.

[Nickelson and Belson, 1991] Nickelson, D. and D. Belson, *"Measuring the Economic Impact of Concurrent Engineering"*, **Proceedings, CALS Expo '91**, Phoenix, Arizona, December 1991.

[O'Grady, et. al., 1991] O'Grady, P., R. E. Young, A. Greef, and L. Smith, *"An Advice System for Concurrent Engineering"*, **International Journal of Computer Integrated Manufacturing**, Vol. 4, 1991.

[Osborn, 1991] Osborn, L. A., *"Commercial and Military Business: Synergistic Partners"*, **Proceedings, CALS Expo '91**, Phoenix, Arizona, December 1991.

[Ostrofsky, 1977] Ostrofsky, B., **Design, Planning, and Development Methodology**, Prentice Hall, Inc., Englewood Cliffs, New Jersey, 1977.

[Otto and Antonsson, 1991] Otto, K. N. and E. K. Antonsson, *"Trade-Off Strategies in Engineering Design"*, **Research in Engineering Design**, Springer-Verlag, New York, 1991.

[Pugh, 1983] Pugh, S., *"Research and Development - The Missing Link - Design"*, **Proceedings, International Conference on Engineering Design**, Copenhagen, August 1983.

[Pugh, 1990] Pugh, S., **Total Design: Integrated Methods for Successful Product Engineering**, Addison-Wesley, Inc., New York, 1991.

[Rechtin, 1994] Rechtin, E., *"Foundations of Systems Architecting"*, **Systems Engineering**, Journal of the International Council on Systems Engineering, Vol. 1, July 1994.

[Rechtin, 1991] Rechtin, E., **Systems Architecting: Creating and Building Complex Systems**, Prentice Hall, N.J., 1991.

[Rechtin and Maier, 1996] Rechtin, E. and M.W. Maier, **The Art of Systems Architecting**, CRC Press, 1996.

[Shapour, et. al., 1987] Shapour, A., J. Naft, M. Pecht, and K. Richter, **Decision Support Requirements in a Unified Life-Cycle Engineering (ULCE) Environment**, Draft Report, Institute for Defense Analysis, September 1987.

[Thurston, et. al., 1993] Thurston, D. L., A. Locascio, R. Ragavan, R. Sun, and Y. Q. Tian, "*Multi-attribute Decision Methods for Engineering Product Design*", **Proceedings, NSF Design and Manufacturing Systems Conference**, Vol. 1, Charlotte, North Carolina, January 1993.

[Thurston, 1991] Thurston, D. L., "*A Formal Method for Subjective Design Evaluation with Multiple Attributes*", **Research in Engineering Design**, Vol. 3, No. 2, 1991.

[Thurston, et. al., 1991] Thurston, D. L., J. V. Carnahan, and T. Liu, "*Optimization of Design Utility*", **Proceedings, ASME Conference on Design Theory and Methodology - DTM '91**, Miami, Florida, September, 1991.

[Thurston, et. al., 1992] Thurston, D. L., Y. Q. Tian, R. Sun, and A. Locascio, "*A Value-Driven Design Process for Mechanical and Structural Systems*", **Proceedings, NSF Design and Manufacturing Systems Conference**, Atlanta, Georgia, January 1992.

[Ulrich, et. al., 1991] Ulrich, K., D. Sartorious, S. Pearson, and M. Jakiela, "*A Framework for Including the Value of Time in Design for Manufacturing Decision Making*", Working Paper WP #3243-91-MSA, **Sloan School of Management**, MIT, Cambridge, February 1991.

[Verma, et.al., 1999] Verma, D., C. Smith, and W.J. Fabrycky, "*Fuzzy Set Based Multi-Attribute Conceptual Design Evaluation*", Manuscript accepted, **Systems Engineering**, Journal of INCOSE, Vol. 2, No. 4, December 1999.

[Verma and Johannesen, 1999] Verma, D. and L.H. Johannesen, "*Supportability Engineering and Logistics Optimization/Planning Trends and Challenges: A System Integrator's Perspective*", **Proceedings, International Logistics Congress**, University of Exeter, May 1999.

[Verma and Knezevic, 1996] Verma, D. and J. Knezevic, *Development of a Fuzzy Weighted Mechanism for Feasibility Assessment of System Reliability During Conceptual Design*, **International Journal of Fuzzy Sets and Systems**, Vol. 83, No. 2, October 1996.

[Verma and Fabrycky, 1995] Verma, D. and W.J. Fabrycky, "*Development of a Fuzzy Requirements Matrix to Support Conceptual System Design*", Proceedings, **International Conference on Engineering Design**, Prague, Czech Republic, August 1995.

[Winner, et. al., 1988] Winner, R. I., J. P. Pennel, H. E. Bertrand, and M. M. G. Slusarczuk, **The Role of Concurrent Engineering in Weapons System Acquisition**, Report, Institute for Defense Analysis, December 1988.

[Wood, et. al., 1989] Wood, K. L, E. K. Antonsson, and J. L. Beck, "*Computations with Imprecise Parameters in Engineering Design: Background and Theory*", **Transactions of the ASME of Mechanisms, Transmissions, and Automated Design**, Vol. 111, December 1989.

[Wood and Antonsson, 1990] Wood, K. L., and E. K. Antonsson, "*Modeling Imprecision and Uncertainty in Preliminary Engineering Design*", **Mechanical Machine Theory**, Pergamon Press, Vol. 25, No. 3, 1990.

[Young, et. al., 1991] Young, R. E., A. Greef, and P. O'Grady, "*An Artificial Intelligence-Based Constraint Network System for Concurrent Engineering*", Technical Report TR-91-03, Department of Industrial Engineering, **North Carolina State University**, North Carolina, January 1991.

BIOGRAPHICAL SKETCHES

Line H. Johannesen received the M.Sc in System Operational Effectiveness from the University of Exeter, UK in 2000, and the MSc in Economical and Industrial Management from the University of Trondheim, NTH in 1995. She is now an Integrated Logistics Support (ILS) Engineer at Kongsberg Defence & Aerospace, Norway, where her duties include the development of ILS concepts/processes, for complex missile systems.

Her professional activities and research emphasize systems engineering with an emphasis on conceptual design evaluation, system architecture, design decision-making, life cycle costing, and supportability engineering.

Line H. Johannesen has co-authored a technical paper, "Supportability Engineering and Logistics Optimization/Planning Trends and Challenges: A System Integrator's Perspective" (1999), and is a member of SOLE and INCOSE. Within SOLE, she is the co-chair of the recently established Systems and Supportability Engineering Working Group.

Dinesh Verma received the Ph.D. and the M.S. in Industrial and Systems Engineering from Virginia Tech. He is the Systems and Supportability Strategist at Lockheed Martin NE&SS, in Manassas, Virginia, while concurrently serving as a Research Fellow at the University of Exeter, United Kingdom.

Prior to joining Lockheed Martin, Verma worked as a Research Scientist at Virginia Tech and managed the University's Systems Engineering Design Laboratory. While at Virginia Tech and afterwards, Verma served in a consulting capacity with numerous companies to include Eastman Kodak, United Defense, PSI, and Motorola.

Verma has authored over 75 papers, monographs, and co-authored two textbooks: *Maintainability: A Key to Effective Serviceability and Maintenance Management* (Wiley, 1995), and *Economic Decision Analysis* (Prentice Hall, 1998).

Legacy System Evolution to an Enterprise-Wide Architecture Framework

Yves Lacerte
Architecture Technology Corporation
P.O. Box 24859
Minneapolis, MN 55424

Abstract. A consequence of the maturation of a domain is that more and more systems within the domain are being built by different organizations. These existing systems influence the development of any future system within that domain. As this maturation proceeds, pressure grows for a common enterprise-wide framework. Manufacturers of complex software-intensive systems are responding to that challenge. These manufacturers strive toward a set of reusable assets forming a common framework that will be the basis of future domain specific software-intensive systems. This long-term corporate strategic goal needs to consider ongoing maintenance of legacy systems, as well as near-term system development efforts.

Ultimately, evolutionary paths of legacy systems, of systems currently under development, and future systems, need to be made compatible.

This paper is organized as follows. The first section describes an enterprise-wide framework and associated benefits. The second section presents notions related to system evolution. The last section discusses a strategy to evolve domain-specific legacy systems.

ENTERPRISE-WIDE FRAMEWORK

Introduction. Modern large distributed software-intensive systems have the need to do some form of fault isolation and fault management. A strong case can be made that all systems within a domain have similar requirements in that area. It therefore is economically viable that a unique solution be applied across a specific domain on a range of computing platforms. That argument can be easily generalized to other system wide functionality.

A framework is a partially completed system that forms the backbone of a system via a set of cooperating patterns and a reusable infrastructure. System frameworks are very valuable for developing software-intensive systems. Frameworks capture the common facilities required by all the applications of the domain in such a way that they can be reused as is, specialized as appropriate, or easily replaced if necessary. Frameworks emphasize design reuse over code reuse.

Much of the infrastructure among applications in a domain is the same. Building infrastructure software is difficult, full of risks, and expensive. Getting it right is often the hardest part and the most critical. Up to 60% of an application is common code that can be reused if properly structured. Examples are: means for starting and ending tasks, task and resource scheduling, methods for implementing and executing state machines, and ways of implementing associations. Use of a domain-specific framework greatly facilitates the development of an application.

The enabling technology is object-oriented technology. Advantages of an object-oriented approach are:

- Improved problem domain abstraction
- Improved scalability
- Better support for reliability and safety concerns
- Improved facilities for reuse
- Excellent modeling support (UML)
- Improved stability in the presence of changes
- Improved support for concurrency

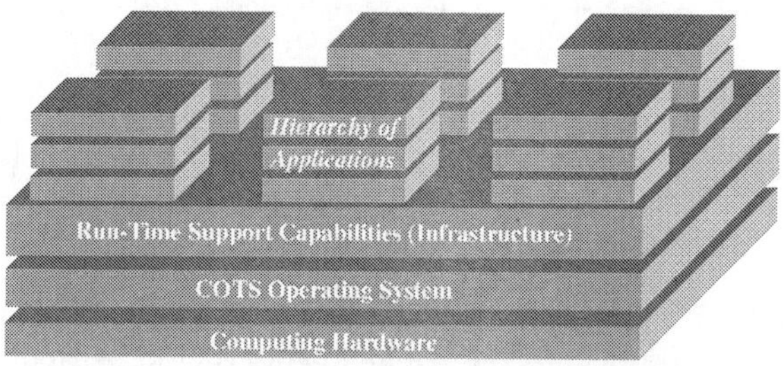

Figure 1. An Object-Oriented Framework

Constructing Frameworks. Frameworks should be constructed as a set of layers (Figure 1). This allows the framework to be portable in two ways. By allowing the lower abstraction layers to be replaced, the framework may be easily ported to different target platforms. The lower abstraction layers contain the abstractions of the underlying operating system and hardware components. Frameworks also abstract away the application details at the higher levels of abstraction. This permits the same framework to be used in a variety of applications and significantly reduces development risk

The framework should provide a library of domain-specific components. A component is a run-time entity that encapsulates and provides a cohesive set of services. The Operating System (OS) Services abstraction should permit applications to be written in an OS-independent fashion (i.e., portable). Specialized components specific to the domain should be provided: Hardware Access Services, System Services, and Communication Services.

The framework should have service components that are plug-replaceable by similar components, is portable to different platforms, provides a consistent set of services to various applications, and meets the performance and resource constraints of the applications within its domain.

The framework should leverage the large investment industry has made in developing and implementing "open systems" technologies and standards-based technologies that are in widespread use. Table 1 provides a sample list of such standards.

Services	Standards
Human Computer Interface (HCI)	X, Motif, Custom Style Guide
Data Exchange and Access	FTP, ASCII, CGM, JPEG, MPEG, HTML
DBMS	ODMG, Relational/SQL
File Management	NFS, POSIX file access
Communications	Internet Protocol Suite, Ethernet, ATM, SONET, ISDN, B-ISDN
Operating System	POSIX
Security	DCE/Kerberos, FIPS 186/46-2
System Management	SNMP, SNMPv2, CMIP/CMIS
Distributed Computing	DCE, CORBA
Programming Language	C++, Ada, Java

Table 2. Standards

Since it is expected that the framework will evolve in increments over a relatively long period when measured in terms of product cycles and rate of technological advance, the subsystems and components acquired earlier in the process will tend to establish constraints on later increments that must inter-operate. Therefore, when a new standard is preferred over one that is in use, the transition will have to be planned carefully, taking into account the other applications that might be affected.

When developing a framework, the following issues must be considered:

- The maturity of selected technologies (e.g. object technology)
- The maturity of supporting technologies (e.g. network management)
- The maturity of development environments (e.g. tools to automate software development)
- The learning curve of the company, both technical and managerial, in the use of new technologies and the associated development processes
- The learning curve of customers who may not fully understand the contractual, technical, and business approaches underlying the framework.

Architectures affect organizations as much as organizations affect architectures. Many organizations today recognize that a system framework is the result of significant investment. It makes sense to exploit a good system far beyond the single need that necessitated it. Forward thinking organizations consider their frameworks to be capital assets, to be maintained and reused as much as their buildings or their staff.

Strategic Frameworks. The long-term strategic goal is to formulate an enterprise-wide framework, arrived at jointly by government and industry. The joint government-industry group would assess future operational requirements in order to gain insight into future system usage. Consequently, the framework will be defined with expected growth in system usage, and evolution of the domain.

Benefits. The benefits to the acquirers of long-lived systems, such as DoD and FAA, are more off-the-shelf products, shorter development cycle, reduced acquisition costs, and ultimately reduced maintenance costs.

Builders of these long-lived systems will benefit from a reusable framework in terms of reduced development risks and reduced construction costs, which may translate in higher profit margins and reduced time to market, which may result in more contracts in a given time period.

The framework will assist in maintaining system interoperability over time if the framework is upgraded as a whole. It will free the application developer to concentrate efforts on enhancing operational functionality rather than building common infrastructure services.

Despite the desirability of a common framework, the natural course of events tends toward a proliferation of infrastructures. The need to modernize in manageable increments can lead to the acquisition of stand-alone systems with unique infrastructure components, if a long-range plan for a common framework is not developed and integrated with all acquisition programs. Short-term priorities, such as end of life issues and the demand for early benefits, often result in acquisitions that accelerate baseline proliferation, rather than arrest or reverse it.

Vendor Independence. Organizations acquiring large, long-lived systems need to be vendor independent. The key to vendor independence is the degree to which applications and infrastructure components can be replaced or upgraded by multiple vendors. This independence can be achieved by the development and enforcement of a set of APIs between domain-unique applications and infrastructure components. The incorporation of widely accepted industry standards to the maximum extent practicable would provide significant benefits. APIs should be developed at a level of abstraction sufficient to hide the implementation of infrastructure functions from the applications, to minimize the amount of perturbation to the applications from technology refresh of infrastructure components and vice versa.

SYSTEM AND COMPONENT EVOLUTION

Stable Evolution. The contents of systems and components of systems shift with time—today's applications and standard protocols will be tomorrow's legacy. It is necessary that systems evolve through a series of "stable intermediate forms". A long-lived system has at least 4 coexisting models: a model of the legacy components, a model of the current system, the emerging latest-and-greatest model and a model of the final solution that makes use of an enterprise-wide framework. Each model represents a stable evolutionary step.

Consider the case of evolving an operational Air Traffic Control system. At no time should an existing system be replaced with a system providing decreased functionality or reliability. Thus the present capabilities of the system must never be compromised, but only improved.

Air Traffic Control systems must provide highly reliable continuous operations. All transitional architectural stages between the current system and the target architecture should provide mechanisms to avoid compromising the reliability of the future system in comparison to the reliability of the current system. There should be a long-term approach that makes transition considerations an integral part of any architecture evolution.

Software reliability, although difficult to predict, is known to be a function of its maturity. Since it is a practical impossibility to test all possible input conditions and software states for most software systems, latent defects that are manifested in unforeseen or unlikely software states may not be detected during Operational Testing and Evaluation (OT&E). A software system that has been rigorously tested and verified is generally highly reliable; but to achieve an extremely high level of software reliability, requires several years of execution in the actual operational environment for which the system is intended. The result is known as the software reliability growth curve, shown in Figure 2.

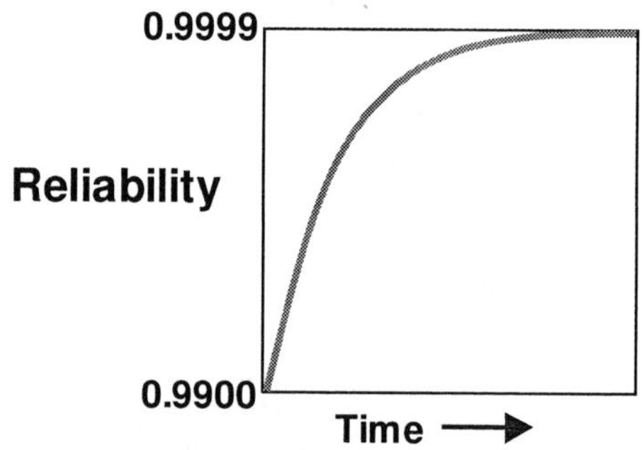

Figure 2. Reliability Growth Curve

This is a generalized representation which shows that the reliability of software will increase relatively sharply after it is deployed, grow more slowly as it matures, and eventually reach a point where it is relatively stable.

Dimensions of Component Evolution. A distributed system is made up of components that need to communicate with one another. In a long-lived system, components with varying degrees of maturity will coexist. Components will be shared across systems, be developed by different organizations, at different times, and with different tools. At any given time, components will be updated, and new components and capabilities will be added to the system. Finally, the choice of platform, the level of available technology, and current fashion in the software community all contribute to a chaotic evolution. Component evolution can be characterized as having four dimensions.

A component's interface may evolve to support new features. To ensure a stable evolution, backward compatibility must be addressed; i.e. a mechanism whereby old clients can continue to use the old interface and new clients can take advantage of the new features.

A component's implementation may evolve to a new hardware platform or a new programming language. To ensure a stable evolution, there must be a mechanism that insulates other components from these changes in the implementation yet maintains the semantic guarantees of the interface.

Communication protocols may evolve. To ensure a stable evolution, it must be possible to change or add communication protocols without rendering existing components inaccessible.

Inter-component communication models may evolve because of their applicability to a particular application. It must be possible to implement components to a new model without limiting the choice of protocols, and without sacrificing interoperability with existing components written to other models.

STRATEGIC EVOLUTION

Maintaining And Evolving A Legacy System. The essential features of legacy systems are: 1) Physical characteristics vary widely, 2) they are critical to an organization, thus the need to adapt to an organization, and 3) it is difficult to modify the software, which implies a high cost associated with the change. Maintenance of a legacy system can be characterized as: 1) defects correction, 2) re-hosting to new operating environments and 3) incremental functional improvements.

Systems that are currently in development or are about to go into development are easier to evolve if modern system and software architectural techniques are employed. For the purposes of this discussion, these systems will have the same concerns as legacy systems as soon as they are fielded.

Many organizations barely meet current software maintenance needs, with little resources to chase long-term visions. A conscious strategic direction is necessary to allow the migration of architecturally significant applications and infrastructure toward a common enterprise-wide framework such as the one discussed in the previous section. Figure 3 shows where the migration of legacy systems and systems currently under development can fit in the overall strategy.

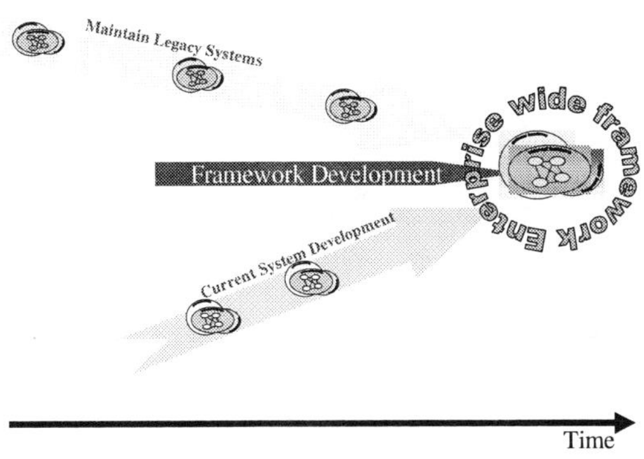

Figure 3. Evolution Strategy

A two-pronged strategy to evolving a legacy system is considered: short term evolution and long term evolution. There may be some overlap between short-term and long-term evolutionary strategies, and both strategies may need to be executed simultaneously. For example, re-hosting to new operating environments and incremental functional improvements fit in both categories.

Short-term evolution is based on low-risk technology insertions. It consists of incremental enhancements to the system that are easiest to change, and give the largest benefits to the system users. Typically, this consists of enhancements to external interfaces, followed by enhancements to human-machine interface (HMI), and finally to addressing internal communications problems.

Longer-term evolution issues are related to assessing what the problem domain will look like in the future, and how the system will be used to meet the future demands of the domain. Long-term evolution consists of the definition of an enterprise-wide framework, and the incremental introduction of the framework into current evolutionary work.

Decisions regarding which areas of the legacy system to evolve, and which portions of the framework to introduce, should consider the impact on system integrity.

Assess Current Architecture. Given a set of maintenance requests, and a set of evolution requests, an assessment of the required changes to the legacy system must be made. Initially, the extraction of the architecture of the legacy system may be needed. It is not expected that legacy systems can be readily evolved to a common framework. Those things about the system that are hardest to change are likely to be internal to the system. Therefore, the enhancements should be more at the system's periphery first. A detailed architectural analysis of the legacy system will determine if a legacy component can be salvaged, or replaced outright. Architectural mismatches should also be uncovered.

Implementation. As legacy systems are migrated to a system framework, a disciplined approach must be adopted to minimize architectural mismatch. A number of architecture patterns have been developed to help deal with these problems. Techniques include wrappers, bridges, and mediators. A wrapper can be thought of as yielding an alternate interface to a legacy component – one that is consistent with the framework. A bridge translates between the interface mechanism of some legacy component and the required interface mechanism of the framework. Finally, mediators exhibit properties of both bridges and wrappers. Mediators include a capability that supports runtime determination of the type of translation that is required for a component.

External Interfaces. The first area of focus when evolving a system is the reduction of the complexity of the external interfaces. Typically, for embedded systems such as flight software and weapon systems, interfaces are tightly coupled. For operational, non-embedded systems, such as air-traffic control systems, there are multiple interfaces with other systems. In both of these examples, the trend is toward an increasing number of interfaces, and increasing complexity in terms of bandwidth, speed, and reliability. The path of evolution is toward more open, more distributed and more object-oriented software.

Human Machine Interface (HMI). The second area of focus is the HMI. A common HMI makes systems more interoperable which in turn reduces the amount of user training required. As user interactions with the system become more complex, new HMI techniques such as touch screen, and 3D speech may be required in order to simplify the interactions, make them faster, less error prone, and ultimately safer.

Internal Communications. The next area of focus is internal communications. The idea here is that a common set of mechanisms should be used internally to communicate between computers, and within computers. Application software will be greatly simplified if it can be made unaware of where the application resides. There exist COTS products that essentially perform these functions, CORBA being the most notable. There are also software patterns (e.g. Proxy and Publisher) that are well documented in the open literature.

Introduce Framework Elements. The next step is the incremental introduction of portions of a common framework, as they become available.

CONCLUSION

This paper has demonstrated the benefits of an object-oriented common infrastructure to both acquirers of large software intensive systems and to the builders of these systems. This paper also demonstrated that the issues associated with the controlled migration of a legacy system require significant resolve from both sides. At the very least, more cooperation between industry and government will be needed.

REFERENCES

Bass, L., Clements, P., Kazman, R., *Software Architecture in Practice*, Addison-Wesley, 1998

Douglass B. P., *Doing Hard Time: Developing Real-Time Systems, with UML, Objects, Frameworks, and Patterns*, Addison-Wesley Longman, Reading, Massachusetts, 1999

Gamma E. et al , *Design Patterns*, Addison-Wesley, Reading, MA, 1994

Jacobson, M. Griss, and P. Jonsson, "*Software Reuse: Architecture, Process and Organization for Business Success*, Addison-Wesley Publishing Co., Reading, MA, 1997

Joint Technical Architecture - Army, Department of the Army, Version 5.5, 1998

Moore, K.E., Kirshenbaum, E.R, "Building Evolvable Systems; The ORBlite Project" , *HP Journal*, February 1997

Plachy, E.C, Hausler, P.A., "Entreprise Solutions Structure", *IBM Systems Journal* 38, No. 1, pgs 4-11, 1999

BIOGRAPHY

Yves Lacerte is a consulting systems engineer. He is a member of the International Council of Systems Engineering (INCOSE). He holds a BS and MA in Applied Mathematics from California State University.

The House of IPD – Integrating the WHY's, WHAT's, and HOW's for Successful Systems Development

Stefan Wenzel, Herbert Negele, and Ernst Fricke
Fachgebiet Raumfahrttechnik (Institute of Astronautics), Technische Universität München
Boltzmannstr. 15, 85748 Garching, Germany

Abstract. To be successful in a highly dynamic environment, with increased global competition, shorter life cycles, more demanding customers/users, and more complex products, different industries should take advantage of learning from each other's problems and solutions. For example, practices like QFD, Taguchi, CAX, Robust Design, or DFX that are applied (successfully?) in daily practice within automotive industries, could be used more efficiently in the space domain. On the other hand, commercial companies can learn from aerospace industries' traditional strengths, in the areas of requirements engineering, modeling and simulation, or systems engineering. A variety of potential synergies exists that should be exploited to the greatest possible extent. But what method or tool should we use, and when?

For an effective application of methods and tools in product development, a comprehensive framework is needed, which supports the selection, coordination, and assessment according to domain- and company-specific needs and constraints. Unfortunately, tools and methods often are used because it is popular to use them, but not because they ideally support the solution of specific problems. Therefore, in this paper a systematic approach is proposed on how methods and tools can be selected for a successful product development system, independent of the industrial sector of a company, but dependent on its problems, market constraints, and declared goals.

A structured model, the House of IPD, was derived from the analysis of different product development processes at commercial companies in Germany, England, and the US (Wenzel & Bauch 1996). In the House of IPD, the interdependencies and relations between goals and problems, essentials/ processes, and practices can be structured. It is possible to visualize in a matrix, how and to what extent the practices (HOWs) contribute to the realization of certain essentials (WHATs), and which essentials support which goals or solve which problems (WHYs).

INTRODUCTION

Today's markets have been formed by three different but strongly interrelated trends.

- **Globalization** results in stronger competition, distributed processes. This effects even niche markets and small or medium sized companies.
- The concurrent development and implementation of new competitive **Information- & Communication-Technologies**, which are at the same time a result and prerequisite of globalization.
- Expansion of **Embedded Intelligence (Knowledge)** in processes, organizations, products, and services.

These trends contributed to the increased complexity of product development environments. So all kind of markets have been changing quickly in the last years, including space, automotive. Each market sector has its own combination of problems and constraints, which are assumed to be unique to that market. Nevertheless, due to ongoing changes in these markets, problems formerly typical for the space sector become also typical for the automotive sector and strengths needed to survive in the automotive market becomes necessary for space companies. A successful engineering of systems for these markets requires effective and efficient solutions and overcoming specific problems and constraints.

Comparing space and automotive industries, they have two major features in common: both develop complex and hybrid products and they are integrators of subsystems drawing on a broad range of technologies (ISU 1997). But space and automotive markets differ in many aspects, resulting in differing market problems and constraints. For example, typical for the automotive industry is a highly competitive, purely commercial, global market with an immense number of different customers. Therefore, the automotive industry developed processes, methods, and tools in order to know its markets and customers, and their needs. The automotive industry generally knows WHAT to do to meet "fuzzy" customer needs and also HOW to do it. Now, with the increasing commercialization of space markets, space companies have to tackle problems that the automotive industry is already used to.

On the other hand, cars are getting more and more complex and hybridized. The number of electrical and electronic parts in a car is increasing and will increase much more in the future, especially in the areas of guidance assistance, entertainment systems, electronical control of engine or brakes, and other safety related functions. Automotive development is following a trend here akin to the direction of satellite development, which was also experienced by airplane development already (Gartz 1997). Managing this increasing complexity and hybridization and the related processes is a problem where automotive industry may learn from space industry.

But within this transition there is also the inherent risk, that methods and tools are seen as universal remedy. But if tools and methods are not adjusted to the specific needs they lack efficiency and effectivity. In the following, we'll focus on this aspect in more detail.

SOLUTIONS, METHODS AND TOOLS

Overcoming Problems with the Right Solutions. A wide variety of different practices, methods and tools can be found in practice which are mostly used in automotive as well as in space or other industries (Figure 1). They are supposed to support the achievement of the goals and to provide solutions for the problems of the respective development processes.

Methods describe **HOW** we should do what we are doing and tools are means (often, but not necessarily, computer-based) that should help us to accomplish the HOWs faster, better, and cheaper. Therefore, a tool without an adequate method and environment is rarely of much help, whereas methods can't be applied very efficiently without adequate tools. An example is, a method to enhance the product development process (or specific parts of it) could be to conduct product assessments with the help of proper metrics. A tool that collects and updates all relevant data needed to quantify the metrics could be used to implement the method more efficiently.

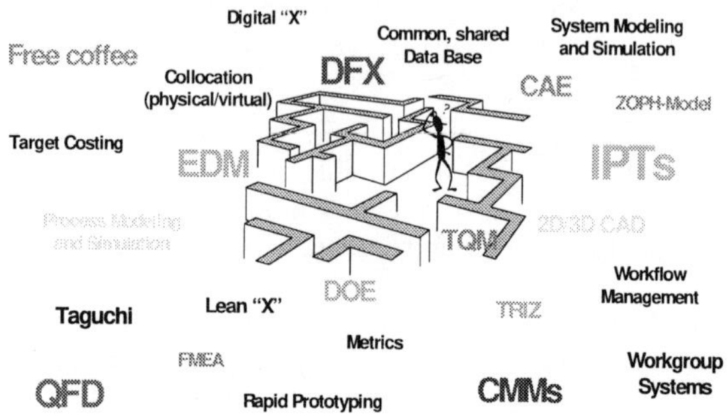

Figure 1. New methods and tools as universal remedy for all the problems?

Within a study at the Institute of Astronoutics we analyzed the value of specific essentials, methods and tools to reduce time to market and its dependency to certain environments (Youzbachi & Kader 1999). We tried to answer the question: What are proper strategies, methods, tools, and actions to reduce time to market for an individual company working in its specific environment?

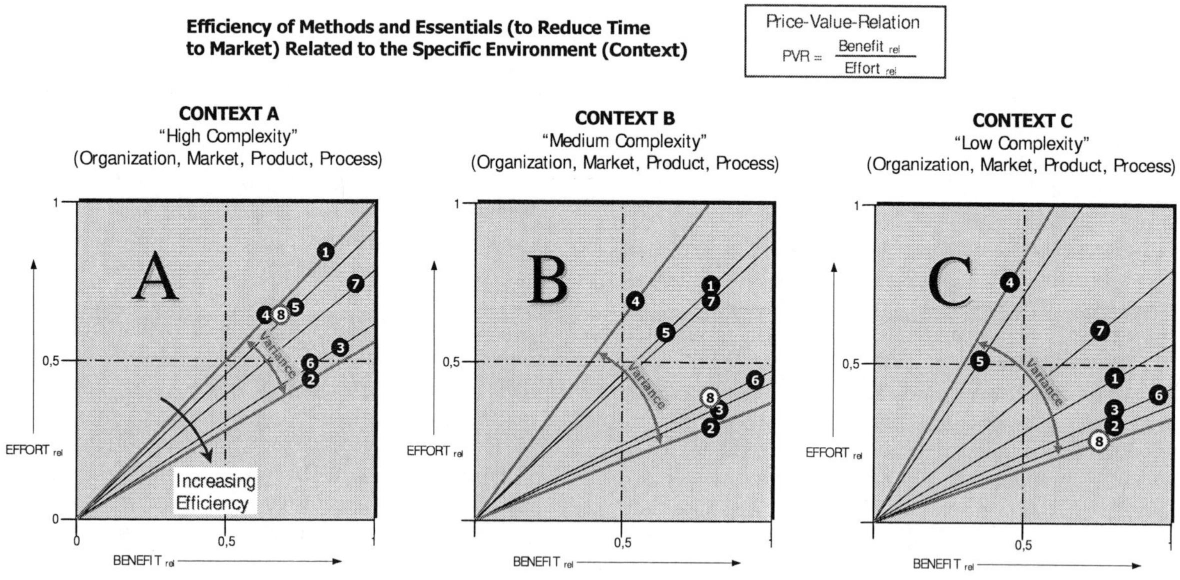

Figure 2: The efficiency of selected methods related to the specific environment (context)

Therefore, nine different companies have been interviewed. As a result, we could distinguish the development processes and their context in three different categories (environment A, B, C). In the next step, we worked out eight essential functions, necessary to reduce time to market. These were then evaluated in terms of effort and benefit by the engineers and project managers responsible. After relating the "price-value-relation" to the three environments, we could derive the following results (figure 2):

- The efficiency (price-value-relation) of a specific Method (e.g. concurrent engineering) depends on the specific environment (context) of the development system analyzed. For example, compare Method "8" in figure 2 altering in within the three environments A, B, C.
- Also the variance of the efficiency of the methods analyzed, depends on the environment (Figure 2)
- Complex environments require complex solutions
- Small sized companies with less complex organizations have in contrast to large, complex companies a larger variance in the efficiency.

Inefficient Use of Methods and Tools
Unfortunately, the best methods and tools lose impact when they are not used effectively and efficiently. This insufficiency is generally a result of the usage of wrong, too many, or not embedded and adjusted means (Wenzel & Bauch 1996). On the other hand, the benefits connected with new methods and tools, such as machines, computers, QFD, CAD, or Rapid Prototyping are usually multitudinous. They are often seen as the universal remedy for all kind of difficulties. Benefits expected are, for example:

- The "reduction" of complexity
- Cost and time savings, higher productivity
- Better quality and accuracy
- Reproducibility and reuse
- Higher flexibility
- Early verification

But the expected benefits usually do not come true without an early investment of time, money and resources (Figure 3). The pay back for these new means is similar to new products. Money has to be invested to buy new means or the appropriate knowledge. But with the acquisition of the tools, only the first step is done. The means have to be adapted to the specific requirements of the users and people have to get acquainted with and to learn how to use new processes, rules and tools. This takes mental setup time and attention. This time is often not honestly considered, rather by "sunshine-commitments". The maximum benefit is highly connected with the rate of acquaintance. The more the users are familiar with the methods and tools, the higher is acceptance and efficiency, and the lower are mental barriers and setup times.

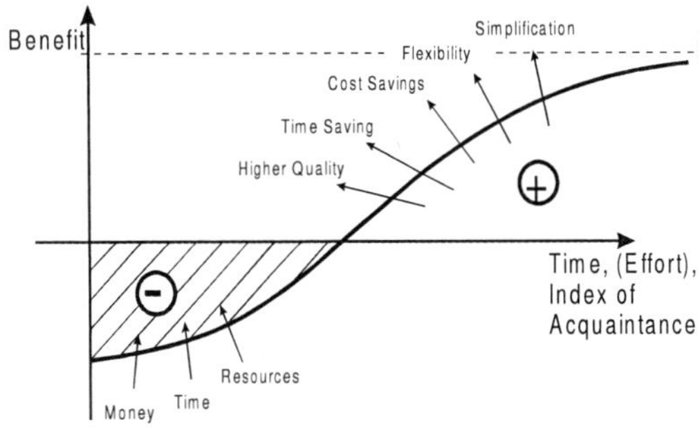

Figure 3: Tools & Methods: Investment and Benefit

The problem can be clearly illustrated with an example many people have to deal with at work or privately. It's the difficulty we have with the continuous upgrading of application programs for personal computers. Some perceived benefits associated with a new word processing program are: better user-ergonomics ('just a mouse click'), faster processing, better connectivity to other applications, and more features (e.g. integrated graphics program). But, in order to make a profit from these improvements, the user has to upgrade to a more powerful system and invest money for buying the program. Before (s)he is able to improve the processing time, (s)he has to install the program and invest learning-time to get acquainted with the new program. Thus, there is a setback in efficiency, although *this aspect is to be improved.* This kind of paradox is qualitatively visualized in Figure 3. After a learning- or acquaintance-time, depending on previous experience and the need to learn, the investment pays back and overall efficiency improves.

If the capacity of an individual or an organizational unit is assumed to be constant, the total amount of its activities can be categorized:

- "Effective Performance", which supplies the required results (e.g. creation of a drawing),
- "Supportive Activities", which are necessary to achieve the effective performance (e.g. looking through already existing drawings), and
- "Blind Performance", which is useless for the fulfillment of the tasks (e.g. waiting for drawings until they are mailed).

New means typically aim at improving the ratio between these kind of activities. But, with the introduction of a new method or tool, the blind performance does not necessarily decline at the beginning. Rather, the effort to get acquainted with the new processes reduces the effective performance and increases the support activities. After a certain time the users get more and more familiar with the new tools and the ratio between effective and blind performance improves: The "Break Even Point" is reached when the effective performance is on the former level. From now on, the tools and methods reduce the blind-performance up to a certain degree of saturation (Figure 4).

Often the actual benefits are not as drastic as expected, as people are reluctant or get tired of methods/tools. Reasons for these obstacles are:

- **Wrong methods and tools:** Methods and tools are not universal remedies though they often are promoted as such. They only can serve as a support to better carry out the right processes in the proper environment.
- **Competing and overlapping**: In many companies several different means are applied to similar tasks. This does not have to be a drawback necessarily, since it can enhance flexibility and reinforce decision-making. On the other hand, it can lead to competition between organizational units using and promoting different methods and tools (e.g. a PDM-tool), and result in reduced efficiency.

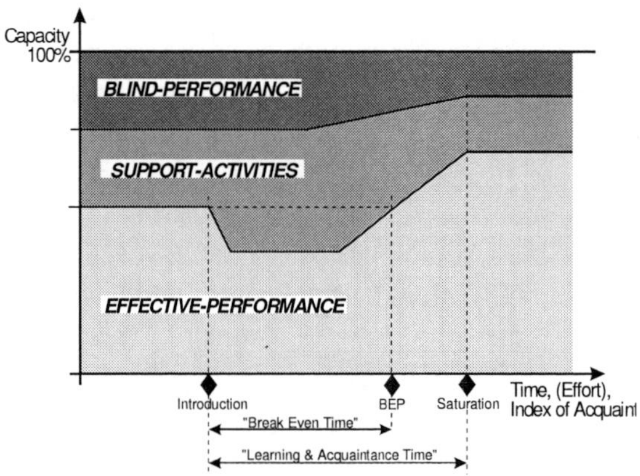

Figure 4. Setup Time for New Methods and Tools (qualitative)

- **Not embedded, adjusted, and integrated:** Means should be adjusted to the specific environment and processes of the company, in order to avoid unnecessary ballast. Another problem, especially with computer-based tools, is the lack of integration and interoperability, e.g. data exchange between different tools is not possible.
- **Wrong environment:** In many companies the introduction of new methods and tools is seen as a major threat to people who will have to change their way of working. This kind of antagonistic atmosphere kills many promising attempts to introduce new solutions.
- **Not user-oriented:** Supporting means often are developed without closely involving the later users of these means. Therefore, they tend to be too theoretical, too sophisticated, too difficult to learn and use or just inadequate for what users *really* have to do.
- **Not accepted:** Methods and tools which are not accepted will not be used. They need to be promoted by management and embedded into a supportive framework, such as infrastucture, processes and rules.
- **Too many:** A host of tools and methods means too much effort for integrating, learning, supporting, and maintaining all the different means. Less is more and a few well-known and utilized means are certainly better than a lot of unused.

THE HOUSE OF IPD

Just the availability of a lot of different solutions, practices, methods, and tools does not yet help to overcome problems and to enhance effectivity and efficiency in product development. The crucial thing is to select and implement the *right mix of solutions* and means that fit best into a particular product development system with its specific problems, constraints, goals, processes, organization, products, and environment. It was observed that some companies just knew that certain methods and/or tools (e.g., a specific simulation tool) were successfully applied in other companies or departments, and then thought using these methods/tools would solve their problems as well. Just taking over solutions from others without looking at the special situation and adapting them to specific needs rarely will yield great results. In order to support a systematic selection and implementation of the right solutions and practices for successful in systems development the **House of IPD** is proposed.

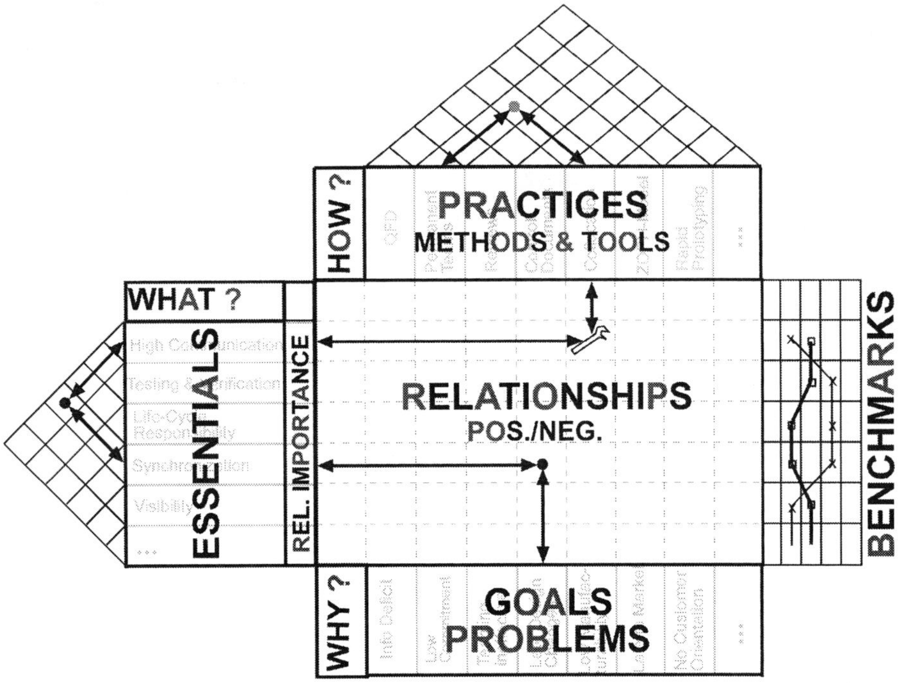

Figure 5. Structure of the House of IPD

Fundamental Structure The House of IPD was developed as a methodical approach to structure the interdependencies and relations between goals, problems, essentials, methods, and tools for the specific use in practice (Wenzel et al. 1997). In analogy to the House of Quality (Hauser & Clausing 1988), it is possible to visualize in a matrix, how and to what extent, the practices, methods, and tools (HOWs) contribute to the realization of certain essentials (WHATs) and which essentials are related to certain goals or problems (WHYs). Figure 4 provides an impression of how this matrix looks like in principle and gives examples for possible relations. In the matrix, HOWs are connected with WHATs by a small spanner symbol, whereas WHYs and WHATs are interrelated with dots.

Depending on industry or line of business, adequate essentials or processes can be defined and assigned a relative importance for the realization of the goals set, or the elimination of the problems occurring during the development process. After the definition of the most important essentials, proactive or corrective action can be initiated by the implementation of selected practices. These practices enable the essentials and should be "hands-on" methods or tools for the use in day-to-day development work. Also, the specific environment in which practices are to be implemented, with associated constraints have to be regarded (e.g., tools already used, available resources, software and hardware issues, skills of concerned people).

In order to analyze and visualize how strong (e.g., high–medium–low) each essential and practice affects another (positive/negative), they should also be related among themselves. This aspect is exemplarily shown in the roof of the house and in the triangle on the left. In a similar way this can be done for problems (problem net), goals (goal net), or problems versus goals in the "basement" It is important to carry out these steps, as the combination of certain essentials or practices can promote or sometimes hinder the impact expected. Thus, a specific mix of the "right" practices can be put together for each project. In order to improve the development system continuously, its performance can be measured along with the fulfillment of the most important essentials. This benchmark is placed on the right side of the house.

WHATs – Essentials for Successful Integrated Product Development Companies have to excel in several key aspects — Quality and Cost to market, Effectiveness and Efficiency, Time to market and Flexibility — if they want to be and remain economically successful. In order to reach this objective a set of **17** essentials has been defined that describe basic success factors (WHATs) for new product development (Wenzel & Bauch 1996). The essentials are an "answer" to the goals and problems typically found in today's product development environments (Clark & Fujimoto 1991, Wheelright & Clark 1992, Clausing 1994, Negele & Fricke 1997) and were derived from the results of several case studies of different product development processes at commercial companies in

Germany, England, and the US. With the realization of the essentials, the crucial aspects of Integrated Product Development are taken into account. The essentials are listed below. A short description of each essential is given in Wenzel et al. (1997):

- **High Communication Density**
- **Life Cycle Responsibility**
- **2D-Integration (organization: horizontal&vertical)**
- **Synchronization**
- **Clear Goals, Rules and Roles**
- **Testing & Verification**
- **Big Loops: "Lessons learned"**
- **Early and Fast Check of Profitability and Risk**
- **Cost, Time and Resource Visibility**
- **Metrics in the Loop**
- **Balancing Technology and Product Development**
- **Clear Supplier and Partner Strategy**
- **Robust Design and Customization**
- **Customer Focus and Stakeholder Integration**
- **Integration of MIT (methods, information, tools)**
- **Education and Training**
- **Capable Systems Engineering Environment**

Further Potentials The essentials listed above are one attempt to describe the WHATs for successful product development. But, the generic structure of the House of IPD can be applied to varying fields, e.g. business processes other than product development, like production or maintenance, and at different levels, e.g. company-level, project-level, or subproject-level. With adjusted essentials (processes) the expansible framework also can be employed for the "big picture" Systems Engineering or Project Management ("House of SE" or "House of PM") as well as for a more focused view of specific aspects, e.g. Change Management. For a "House of SE", e.g. the 19 different focus areas of the Systems Engineering Capability Model SECM (EIA/IS 731-1 SECM) could be used as WHATs.

Similar to the QFD method, several linked matrices or houses can be used to make visualization and application easier. Furthermore, a time dimension can be added. In different phases of, e.g., product development different problems/goals are dominant and corresponding methods and tools will have to be used. Specific houses can be established for the main phases of the product development process, thus focusing process capability assessment. To avoid dozens of different matrices, all information can be kept in a software tool that provides criteria (hierarchy level, phase, focused process, etc.) for flexibly filtering out and visualizing the matrices and information one needs.

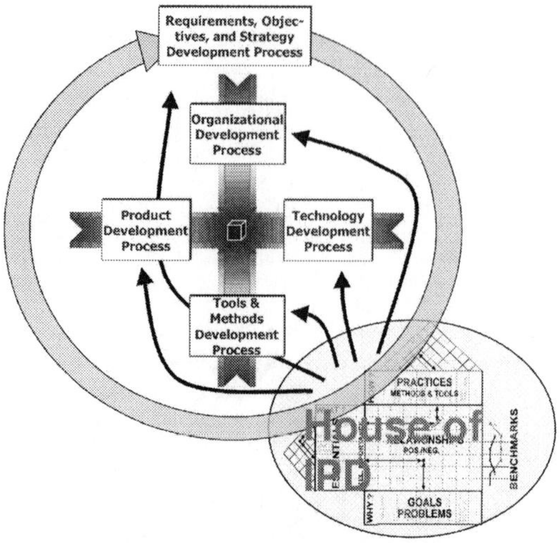

Figure 6. Five key development processes

APPLICATION OF THE HOUSE OF IPD

In a product development system it's not just the product itself that has to be developed. Each new product (generation) is the result of a product development process, which is intertwined with the development of new and robust technologies and conducted by a particular organization using specific tools and methods. Often, it is also crucial to "develop" the adequate organization (e.g., right team or functional structures, roles, etc.) and resources (e.g., skills, methods, tools, etc.). These four aspects (product development, technology development, methods & tools, and organization) are usually embedded in the specific project goals and the company's strategy, which also have to be developed effectively (Figure 6).

As indicated in Figure 6, the House of IPD can be used to structure the WHYs, WHATs and HOWs of all five key development processes, since the defined essentials include and integrate aspects applicable for all of them. Within this scope, this paper focusses on the methods&tools development process.

In practice the following procedure proved to be effective when the House of IPD is applied to methods&tools development:

- Analysis of the product development system
- Understanding and classification of problem situation, identification of key problems, definition of goals
- Tailoring of essentials according to type of development system (adaptation to special constraints and requirements of given product development system and its environment)
- Weighting and prioritizing of essentials based on identified key problems/goals
- Assessment of performance for each essential (if necessary re-prioritizing of essentials)

- Identification and prioritizing of gaps/weaknesses
- Selection and coordination of adequate practices, methods and tools to overcome the gaps/weaknesses

The practical application of the House of IPD is illustrated by means of a simplified example drawn from a project with an automotive supplier. For an easier understanding the information contained in the example House of IPD is split up into two steps (Figures 7 and 8). In the basement of the House in Figure 7 several problems found in a given product development system are listed. In our example, two of the main issues were:

- Over-engineering, leading to increased product costs,
- Insufficient customer satisfaction, leading to lower sales volumes than planned.

These problems provide the WHYs for corrective action. By tracing the WHY-WHAT-relations (dots) in Figure 7 we can find the areas that should be focused on in order to improve the development system, from the list of WHATs. Here, this trace would lead to (using the 17 essentials listed above):

- High communication
- Balancing technology and product development
- Customer focus
- ...

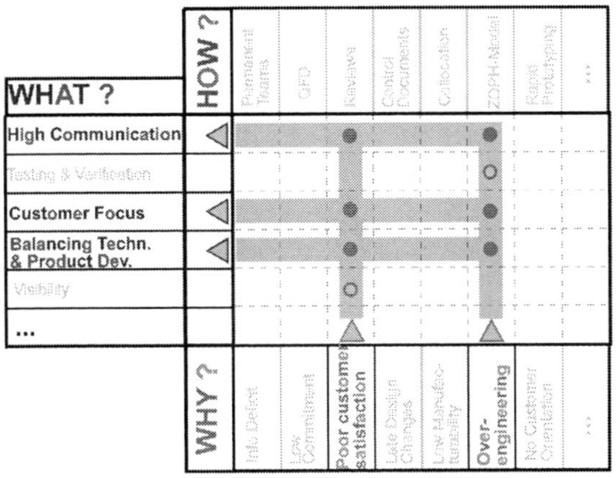

Figure 7. Step 1 – Tracing WHY-WHAT-Relations

Knowing WHAT has to be done in order to overcome these problems, in the next step, the HOWs can be identified. This includes the practices, methods, and tools that support an practical implementation of the related WHATs.

This step is shown in Figure 8. By tracing the WHAT-HOW-relations (spanners) we can find a method in the matrix that supports all of the identified essentials: Quality Function Deployment (QFD). Of course, in the real project, many other possibilities to overcome poor customer satisfaction and over-engineering were identified and looked into in detail, but here we just wanted to explain the application of the House of IPD in principle. Also, in addition, the specific environment was taken into consideration, e.g., which organizational structures existed in the company, which methods and tools were already used, which information technology (hardware and software) was available, human and political factors, and many more.

In daily practice, with the House of IPD a project manager is able to filter from the "complete" row of practices the specific solutions which best solve the problems with regard to a balance of effort/cost and benefit. Furthermore, it is not sufficient to just select and implement any or all of the practices found in related columns. Mutual dependencies and impacts of methods and tools have to be considered in order to get a coordinated mix of practices. For example, collocation and permanent teams have a positive impact on each other. Hence, it would be recommendable to implement both at the same time. This coordination of methods and tools is supported by the information contained in the "roof" of the House of IPD (see Figure 5).

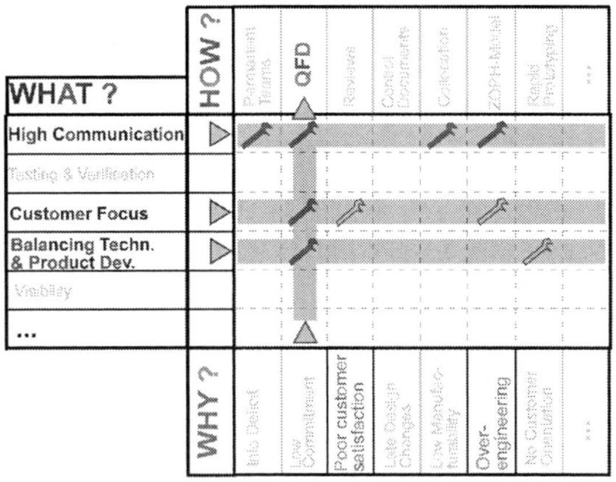

Figure 8: Step 2 – Tracing WHAT-HOW-relations

THE HOUSE OF IPD SOFTWARE-TOOL

For the practical application of the House of IPD a software tool was developed that supports capturing, structuring, combining, and visualizing the WHYs, WHATs, and HOWs and their various interrelations in several matrices (Figure 9). The implementation of an easy-to-understand, spreadsheet-like, graphical user interface makes operating it quite easy. Each of the five individual matrices

(WHY-WHY, HOW-HOW, WHAT-WHAT, WHY-WHAT, WHAT-HOW) can be edited and visualized separately or in the aggregate view (Figure 8).

Relations can be entered very efficiently by just clicking into the matrices and can be rated if there is a positive/negative impact (++, +, -, --). Search criteria for tracing the interdependencies between different matrices can be selected, e.g., which kind of relations the search algorithm should look for, and executed in two directions:

- "Forward or synthesis approach" (as described above): select one or several WHYs ⇨ find related WHATs ⇨ find HOWs related to found WHATs
- "Backward or analysis approach" for analyzing what essentials (and related goals/problems) the present methods and tools support according to the House of IPD and compare with actual goals and problems: select one or several HOWs ⇨ find related WHATs ⇨ find WHYs supported by found WHATs

Thus, combining both approaches the House of IPD model can be tested, verified and gradually improved.

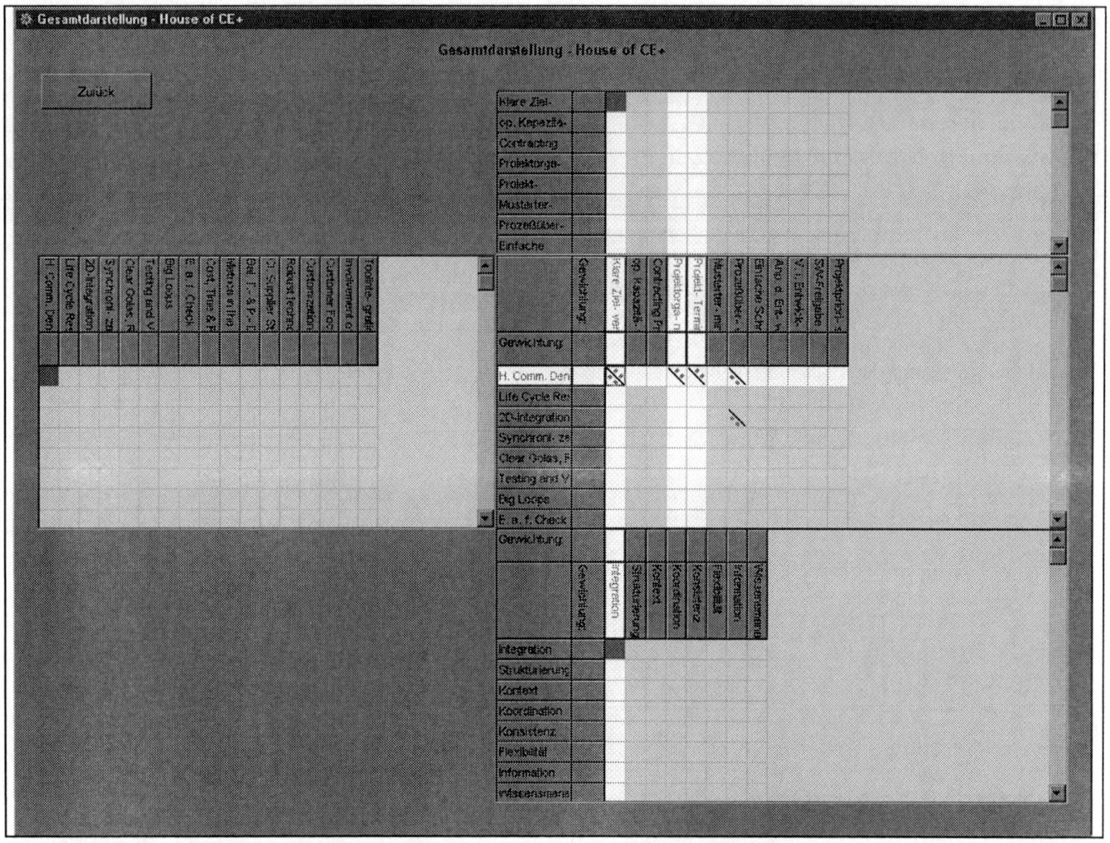

Figure 9: Implementation of the House of IPD in a computer-based Tool - Screenshoot

CONCLUSIONS

It was shown that many different problems can hinder an effective and efficient usage of practices, methods, and tools in system development. In order to successfully support product development, it is necessary to have appropriate and specific answers to the specific problems and other given constraints. These answers should encompass **what** to do and **how** to do it. Therefore, the House of IPD, a comprehensive and systematic approach was presented to enable the structuring and tracing of interdependencies and relations between the problems and goals of a company (or for a certain process, etc.), necessary essentials which show what to do, and possible methods and tools which support these essentials. Applying this approach helps to find the right mix of methods and tools for a company's specific mix of problems and goals in a systematic, understandable manner.

In order to identify synergies and potential for learning from each other, different Houses can be compared for different industry sectors, e.g., automotive and space industry or different projects/departments within a company. Thus, a systematic approach to transferring well-tried solutions for comparable problems can be provided. Future research steps will focus on the refinement of the essentials for different application contexts and the integration of cost-effectiveness of methods and tools into the House of IPD. Also, the computer-based tool introduced briefly will be applied to practical projects in different companies, and consequently improved according to user feedback.

REFERENCES

Clark, K. B.; Fujimoto, T. (1991): Product Development Performance: Strategy, Organization, and Management in the World Auto Industry, Harvard Business School Press, Boston, Mass.

Clausing, D. (1994): Total Quality Development: A Step-By-Step Guide to World-Class Concurrent Engineering, ASME Press.

Gartz, P.E. (1997): Commercial Systems Development in a Changed World, IEEE Transactions on Aerospace and Electronic Systems, 33, 2, 632-636.

Hauser, J.R.; Clausing, D. (1988): The House of Quality, Harvard Business Review 66, No. 3, pp. 63-73.

ISU (1997): Technology Transfer-Bridging Space and Society, Design Project Report of the Summer Session Program '97, International Space University, Houston.

Negele, H.; Fricke, E.; Wenzel, S. (1997): The House of CE+ — A Systematic Approach To Comprehensive Engineering of Product Development Systems, Advances in Concurrent Engineering, Proceedings of CE97: Fourth International Conference On Concurrent Engineering: Research and Applications, Oakland University.

Negele, H.; Fricke, E. (1997): Interrelating WHYs, WHATs, and HOWs for Successful Systems Engineering. Proceedings of the 1st Joint ESA/INCOSE Conference on Systems Engineering, 11-13 November 1997, ESTEC, The Netherlands.

Wenzel, S.; Bauch, T. (1996): Concurrent Engineering and More – Essentials for Successful Product Development from International Case Studies, Masters Thesis. Fachgebiet Raumfahrttechnik. Techn. Univ. München.

Wenzel, S.; Bauch, T.; Fricke, E.; Negele, H. (1997): Concurrent Engineering and More – A Systematic Approach to Successful Product Development, Proceedings of the 7th International Symposium of INCOSE.

Wheelwright, S.; Clark, K. (1992): Revolutionizing Product Development – Quantum Leaps in Speed, Efficiency, and Quality; New York.

Youzbachi, S.; Kader, M. (1999): Methoden und Tools zur Reduizierung der Produktentwicklungszeit, Internal Study. Fachgebiet Raumfahrttechnik. Techn. Univ. München.

BIOGRAPHIES

Stefan Wenzel is Research Assistant and PhD candidate at the Institute of Astronautics at the Technical University of Munich. He received his master's degree in mechanical engineering from the Technical University of Munich in 1996. He has been working in the Systems Engineering field for several years, with special focus on concurrent engineering, integrated product development, and process modeling. From 1997 to 1998 he participated in a 15 month management trainee program at "Energie Baden-Wuerttemberg (EnBW)" and the "Executive Development of the State of Baden-Wuerttemberg".

Herbert Negele recently started working for BMW AG. He received his master's degree in aerospace engineering in 1993 and his Ph.D. in systems engineering in 1998 from the Technische Univerität München. Till November 1998 he worked as an Assistent Professor at the Institute of Astronautics in the field of systems engineering with special focus on systems modeling and simulation, integrated product and process development, and management. Herbert was a founding member of the German Chapter of INCOSE and serving as its Vice President in 1997 and 1998.

Ernst Fricke is Assistant Professor at the Institute of Astronautics at the Technical University of Munich. He received his master's degree in aerospace engineering from the Technical University of Munich in 1994 and his Ph.D. in Systems Engineering from the Technical University of Munich in January 1999. His research focuses on managing changes and evolution in product development.

What the Lessons Learned from Large, Complex, Technical Projects Tell Us about the Art of Systems Engineering

Stephen C Cook
Systems Engineering and Evaluation Centre
University of South Australia
The Levels Campus, Mawson Lakes
SA 5095, Australia

Abstract. This paper examines the literature to identify the lessons that have been learned from a selection of the thousands of projects that have been conducted over the last 15 years or so. The first purpose of this review is to establish a value-for-money argument for the application of systems engineering. The review is also intended to provide guidance on the application and development of systems engineering methodologies. To provide a context, the paper opens with a definition of systems engineering, a description of key concepts and a brief discussion on supplementary methodologies. This is followed by a discussion of the lessons learned by NASA, the UK Ministry of Defence, and the UK and USA software development industries. The paper closes with discussion that concludes that systems engineering is a cost-effective way of ameliorating schedule, performance and user-acceptance risk for large, complex, technical development projects. It also concludes that the lessons learned indicate the need for more than good processes; there is a growing need to understand and manage the socio-political issues associated with creating and successfully fielding a complex, technical system.

INTRODUCTION

Those who have been accustomed to the application of systems engineering principles and methods to large, complex, technical projects find it hard to envisage tackling a substantial project without a well-established systems engineering framework and set of processes. The value of systems engineering to such practitioners is axiomatic. There are many, however, who view the effort required to produce even a minimal number of process products, (plans, documents, models, etc) as being excessive, especially in smaller projects. This raises the question of the cost effectiveness of systems engineering.

A direct approach to examining this issue, such as comparing the outcomes of projects that did use systems engineering against those that did not, was not attempted because it was felt that to assign projects into one camp or the other would be overly simplistic. Even if the continuum of process sophistication were recognised, a complex judgement would be needed to assign a process maturity index to each project. Moreover, it is unlikely that it would be possible to gain access to the data needed; such information is notoriously hard to obtain for obvious reasons.

Given the issues raised above and the limited timescale for the study, the approach taken has been to review the lessons learned from large, complex, technical projects to determine the extent to which the application of systems engineering would be of benefit. In order to place this review on a clearly defined baseline, the paper opens with a definition of systems engineering and a list of the key characteristics of the contemporary view of this field of endeavour. The review follows, along with some comments on the initiatives being undertaken by systems development authorities around the world. The paper concludes with a summary of salient issues and an overall conclusion on the value of systems engineering.

WHAT DO WE MEAN BY SYSTEMS ENGINEERING?

The background of systems engineering. SE gained recognition as a discipline following the Second World War. The increasing cost and technical complexity of development and acquisition programs in the 1950s and 1960s stimulated the need for a methodology to handle the technical and managerial complexity of large projects. Some of this recognition was no doubt due to large program failures that could have been avoided, or at least mitigated through the use of systems engineering (M'Pherson, 1980; DSMC, 1983). In the 1990s, systems engineering received increased attention as ways are sought to reverse the trend of increasing project failure, particularly in large software-based systems.

Systems engineering had it origins in defence and aerospace sectors, particularly in the United States of America and the United Kingdom. A scan of the recent proceedings of the Annual Symposia of the International Council On Systems Engineering (INCOSE) shows an increasing trend to apply systems engineering to a wider range of industries. The cancellation of US military standards a few years ago increased the rate of evolution of systems engineering and the latest standards are now strongly driven by industry concepts of best practice.

The key characteristics of systems engineering. Systems engineering is an interdisciplinary approach and means to enable the realization of successful systems (Robertson, 1998). Above all, systems engineering is a systems methodology, which means that it:

- Encourages holistic thinking (considering the entity as a whole, its internal arrangement, and its properties).
- Recognises the key characteristics of a system:
    - a hierarchy of subsystems;
    - the emergence of behaviour at particular levels of the hierarchy that cannot be decomposed to lower layers;
    - the interfaces, in particular, communication and control between and across layers in the hierarchy.

Systems engineering can also be considered as a (human activity) system in its own right: one that creates, modifies and supports, large, complex, technical systems.

Systems Engineering not only looks across a wide number of disciplines, it also should take a life-cycle-balanced approach to systems solution formulation.

Systems engineering should not be considered merely a set of procedures to be followed. Rather, it is methodology that should be thought of as a way of thinking that encompasses a set of competencies and a set of processes that can be invoked as needed, each of which can be achieved through a range of methods. An important aspect of systems engineering is the selection and tailoring of the processes to suit each project.

There has been tremendous progress in systems engineering development over the last decade. The increasing complexity of projects and the increasing incorporation of software into system solutions has driven much of this. Many new standards have appeared. As have many capability maturity models (Gabb, 1999; Sheard and Lake, 1998) that aim to determine the capability of a organisation to undertake the processes needed to successfully conduct systems engineering. The latest standard ANSI/EIA-632, which was released last year, lists 13 processes needed to engineer a system. These indicate that systems engineering has expanded its breadth beyond that of a purely technical discipline. Henceforth, when talking about *contemporary* systems engineering we mean the range of processes needed to engineer a system.

Systems engineering can be considered a meta-discipline that coordinates and interacts with other related disciplines such as project management, development engineering, integrated logistic support, test and evaluation, configuration management and software engineering.

Systems engineering does not exist in isolation to the culture and processes of an organisation. The encapsulation of the project environment by the enterprise environment is particularly salient as it is the latter that ANSI/EIA-632 addresses. Without a rich enterprise environment, project environments can be expected to be sparse and highly variable.

Complementary methodologies. It is useful to state that systems engineering is only one of a number of systems methodologies that are used to tackle systems problems. While we believe it is the most comprehensive and the one best suited to the type of large, complex, technical projects that are encountered in the defence, aerospace and software industries, it does have known limitations. Systems engineering fits into the class of *hard* systems methodologies: ones where the methods of science, engineering and mathematical analysis underpin the problem solving approach and it is known to work well when the following conditions are met (Cook et al., 1998):

- Systems objectives can be defined at the very beginning of the project.
- All parties can envisage the expected system solution.
- The process can be summarised as moving the system in question from its initial condition S_0 to an end state S_1.
- The environment (technology, organisational, social policy) is stable.
- Objectives are shared among stakeholders.

When some or all of these conditions are not met then supplementary approaches are indicated. Some of these are extrapolations of traditional practice while others are based on the alternative methods of reasoning found in the soft sciences. These can be useful for the following reasons:

- Their primary interest is in changing organisational culture and gaining commitment from participants to a particular course of action.
- They recognise the importance of values, beliefs and philosophies.

- They use an interpretive approach to tackle systems problems.

Soft system methodologies are gaining popularity for systems developments; particularly for those information systems that impact on the way an organisation conducts its business and consequently its internal organisation and power structure. Soft systems methodologies do not replace systems engineering methods but can augment them to better achieve certain goals such as improved requirements elicitation, stakeholder support, user acceptance, and management effectiveness. Interested readers are referred to Checkland and Holwell (1998) for a comprehensive coverage of the applicability of these methods and the difference between the hard and soft traditions.

The purpose of introducing soft systems approaches is to provide background for the succeeding analysis of systems engineering lessons learned. We will provide opinion on which issues can be successfully tackled by contemporary systems engineering and which will need augmentation from soft systems methodologies.

LITERATURE REVIEW

The practice of system engineering has evolved over the years to reflect contemporary factors and organisational priorities. The literature review concentrates on the last 15 years; a period typified by increasing project complexity and a greater emphasis on project through-life cost and more enlightened approaches to risk management.

Lessons learned by NASA. NASA (1989) lists a huge number of areas where mistakes have been repeatedly made in projects. Listed below are some of the more salient ones for methodology research:

a. Lack of clear definition of requirements early in system design phase. This included:
   - Starting designs before the requirements were known.
   - Vague specifications.
   - Design from the bottom-up rather than the top-down.
   - Incomplete documentation of requirements.
   - Lack of early and thorough requirements analyses prior to the start of a design.

b. Poorly defined technical interfaces between subsystems and other subsystems/spacecraft. This included:
   - Failure to understand interface requirements.
   - Too narrow a focus within the discipline/subsystem level, omission of a systems viewpoint or systems engineering awareness by the discipline engineer.
   - Incomplete interface definition.
   - Failure to update interface documentation.

c. Inadequate test planning during the system design phase, including:
   - Not seeking out expert advice (from within NASA) early to develop verification plans.
   - Lack of early test planning and test procedure development.
   - Inadequate consideration early in the systems design phase of how large amounts of data will be reduced, analyzed and reported.
   - Inadequate consideration of testability to assure that the design can be tested to demonstrate specification compliance.

d. Failure to think the design through to completion of integration. This included:
   - Inadequate consideration of accessibility/maintainability early in the design.
   - Inadequate consideration of handling and transportation requirements.

e. Insufficient attention paid to mission operations on hardware/software design requirements.

Each of these can be ameliorated by simply following traditional systems engineering principles and practice as espoused from the early 1980's onward (DSMC, 1983).

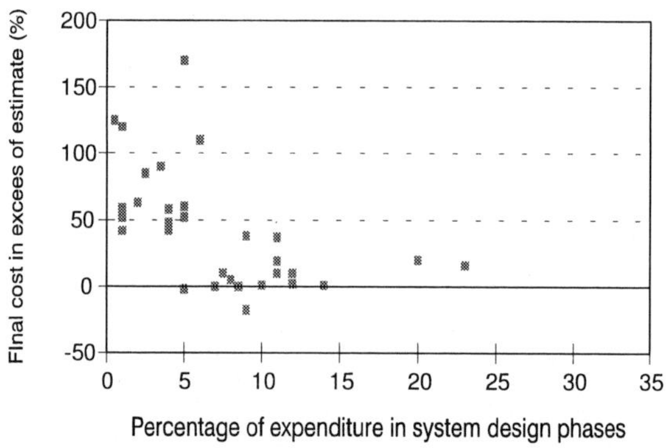

Figure 1 Scatter plot of cost overrun versus expenditure in systems design phase NASA (1995).

An important lesson from NASA is that if the expenditure on the system design phases (up to and including the preliminary design phase) is less than 5% of the estimated cost of the project, vast cost (and schedule) overruns can be expected, see Figure 1 reproduced from NASA (1995). This percentage appears elsewhere in the systems engineering literature (M'Pherson 1990, DSMC, 1983). In fact, one of the tenets of the Downey procedures, employed by the UK Ministry of Defence since the late 1960s, is that "up to 15% of the estimated total development cost may need to be spent on project definition in order to reduce risk"

(DERA, 1996). The same source quotes that this level of investment has rarely been seen in practice and cites this as one reason for disappointing project outcomes.

A point to be made here is that the money must be spent completing the tasks that are expected of these phases (ANSI/EIA-632, 1999; Blanchard and Fabrycky, 1998); not simply creating nugatory process products.

Lessons learned by UK Ministry of Defence in military system development. The following information was extracted from MOD (1998).

The UK National Audit Office 1997 Review showed that the top 25 major equipment programs had an average slippage of 35-40 months and an annual cost growth of 7-9%. (This excluded the Eurofighter and Trident projects, if these were to be included then the cost growth was -2%). The following causes of cost escalation were identified:

- Estimating inaccuracies (£130m).
- Changes to equipment specifications (£180m).
- Defence industry inflation running higher than general inflation (£340m).
- Changes in program numbers or required timetable of introduction (£400m).

Schedule slippage was attributed to the following:

- Technical difficulties (33%).
- Budgetary constraints (25%).
- The need to redefine the project (19%).
- Difficulties associated with international collaboration (15%).

In all fairness, the baselines against which the projects were judged were set early in the procurement cycle, often at the feasibility stage, when the technological solution was still uncertain.

Projects missed on average, 40% of program milestones and 10% of projects failed to meet key technical requirements.

The Learning From Experience initiative identified the following shortcomings:

- Ineffective co-operation between stakeholders.
- Over-optimism in predicting time and cost.
- Insufficient appreciation of technical and commercial risk.
- Ineffective incentivisation of suppliers.
- Insufficient investment at the Project Initiation stage.

Similar to the US and Australia, UK defence procurement has seen significant change over the last 15 years. Further improvements are planned as part of a major change program known as Smart Procurement that builds upon the application of Downey principles (waterfall systems development model with 15% expenditure on systems definition, (DERA, 1996)) to engender speedier, more coherent and interactive processes. The key for the proposals is to adopt a through-life systems approach to procurement, allied to improved commercial practices and measures related to personnel, training and information systems. The following bullet points highlight the initiatives of Smart Procurement and illustrate its breadth (MOD, 1998; MOD, 1999, Cranfield, 2000).

The MOD intends to:

a. Adopt a through-life systems approach with :
   - A formal Project Initialisation Phase to replace the Pre-Feasibility Phase of the Downey cycle: the intention is to identify and engage stakeholders and establish an applied research program.
   - Co-operative stakeholder involvement: elimination of organisational and non-constructive interfaces between stakeholders.
   - Concurrency and enlightened approval strategies.
   - Improved requirements management termed Smart Requirements that sees the evolution of the User Requirements Document in parallel with System Requirements Document.
   - Improved estimating and predicting.
   - Incremental acquisition.

b. Employ improved commercial practices that:
   - Incentivise performance.
   - Embrace partnering.
   - Bear down on Defence inflation.
   - Use past performance as an evaluation criteria.
   - Incorporate teamwork in pricing and alternative price control methods in place of free-market economics.
   - Reduce the procurement overhead.

c. Institute remedies for unsatisfactory performance.

d. Pay attention to personnel and training (MoD already sponsor an MSc in Defence Systems Engineering at University College London).

e. Utilise uniform information management systems.

f. Apply benchmarking and continuous business improvement.

The lessons learned indicated that improvements could be made to the implementation of many of their systems engineering processes. They also highlight many non-process related factors that they are also addressing through Smart Procurement: they are dealing with both the hard and the soft issues. It is important to note that they are tuning their systems engineering processes to reflect contemporary systems and management thinking and not abandoning them.

Lessons learned from large UK civil software-based system developments. Jackson, (1997) reports on a

Outcome	Description	Percentage of Projects
Type 1, project success	Project completed on time, on budget, with all features and functions as initially specified.	16.2 %
Type 2, project challenged	Project completed but over budget, over time, with fewer features and functions than initially specified.	52.7 %
Type 3, project impaired	The project was cancelled at some point during the development cycle.	31.1 %

Table 1 Project outcomes from The Standish Group (1995).

UK study of information technology investments across 14,000 organisations that:

- 80-90% of systems did not meet their goals.
- About 80% were delivered late and over-budget.
- Around 40% of developments failed or were abandoned.
- Under 40% addressed training and skills requirements.
- Less than 25% fully integrate business and technology objectives.
- Only 10-20% meet their success criteria.

While it is hardly comforting to know that the civil sector also has great difficulty realising successful software projects, this information can be used sagely to budget for software developments. Jackson, who is a management professor in the UK, takes a soft systems approach to information systems development along with other notable protagonists (Checkland and Holwell, 1998, Hitchins, 1993). These people are of the opinion that traditional systems engineering approaches are not wholly appropriate to information systems because the problems of this type are messy, ie poorly defined, subject to conflicting viewpoints, and need to be undertaken in a changing environment. These changes include implementation technology, user needs, and cultural perception of what constitutes an acceptable computer application. Given the miserable software success rate reported, this view should not be ignored.

Lessons learned from large USA civil software-based system developments. The Standish Group (1995) undertook a similar study in the USA. They received responses from 365 organisations covering some 8,380 applications in banking, securities, manufacturing, retail, wholesale, health care, insurance, services and local, state and federal organisations. They divided project outcomes into three categories as shown in Table 1.

There is a remarkable similarity to the profile observed in the UK. Usefully, the Standish report offers some analysis on the reasons for projects falling into each category and generalises them into a Success Criteria Metric that can be used to establish probable project success. They then apply this to four case studies to show its strong correlation to known project outcome. The Standish success-potential metric appears below in Table 2.

The score shown in the points column of Table 2 was derived directly from survey responses and relates to the percentage of projects where this criterion determined the fate of the project.

Index	Success Criteria	Points
1	User involvement	19
2	Executive management support	16
3	Clear statement of requirements	15
4	Proper planning	11
5	Realistic expectations	10
6	Smaller project milestones	9
7	Competent staff	8
8	Ownership	6
9	Clear vision & objectives	3
10	Hard-working, focussed staff	3
TOTAL		100

Table 2 The Standish project success potential metric (The Standish Group, 1995).

Criteria 3, 4, 7,and 9 have always been covered by traditional (pre-1990) systems engineering. Criterion 6 is a practice issue that can be incorporated into the project planning. Criteria 1 and 8 certainly feature in contemporary systems engineering thinking (EIA-632, 1999) and together with criterion 2 form the core concerns of the soft systems approach (Checkland and Holwell, 1998). Thus it is fair to say that by adopting SE principles and by applying some soft systems practices, one's project has a good chance of becoming one of the elite 16%.

In addition to the survey reported above, The Standish Group conducted interviews with various IT managers to shed further light on why projects are beset with problems. While most comments echoed the findings of the survey, the problem of competing priorities emerged as an important issue; in particular when this stemmed from an unresourced re-organisation.

We conclude that the application of systems engineering could improve a high proportion of software-based project outcomes. The application of soft-system approaches would also be appropriate in managing project expectation and the management issues reported above.

Lessons learned from large USA Federal software development. Gabrig (1993) reports in the second paragraph of his paper a similar situation for US Federal Government Software contracts to that reported by the civilian sector.

The paper highlights the following points

- When using the waterfall model, if there is a failure in any phase it propagates through to the end.
- Be vigilant in trapping faults in the review processes.
- Follow the established procedures and, in particular, get the requirements correct.
- Use well established software suppliers who have experience in projects of similar size, complexity and type.
- Fixed-price contracts have a detrimental effect on the ability of the parties to work as a team and hence on the value of the final product.

The first three points would are addressed by systems and software engineering practice (Sommerville, 1996). The fourth point is established quality management practice that is all too often forgotten or overridden by other factors. While Gabig's paper contains little quantitative information on the money that can be saved from the appropriate application of systems engineering principles and practice, the last paragraph sums up the difference in about the same terms as the other references:

> "Perhaps the foremost lesson learned by the Federal government has been that without a disciplined and methodical approach to software development, a large project can easily degenerate into an amorphous and overwhelming task. The vast majority of successful large software development projects within the Federal government have been guided by the waterfall model which provides a sequential approach to the software development process."

Lessons learned from aircraft development case studies. Moody et al., (1997) define two key metrics for projects: design difficulty and resources employed. As might be expected they are able to show that as design difficulty increases so does the resources required. When successful projects are plotted on a graph with these two parameters as the axis, they show that successful projects tend to cluster along a line with positive slope. In Chapter 32, Moody et al. show that this relationship is confirmed for a case study involving six successful aircraft developments. They also extend their method to plot project performance (based on technical, cost and schedule performance) against systems engineering fundamentals (based on the adequacy of a number of well-established systems engineering activities). Figure 2 reproduced from that book shows two lines, ones for civil aircraft and the other for military. With only six points no strong conclusion can be made but both lines indicate that an improved score in systems engineering fundamentals yields improved project performance. The separation between the two lines led Moody at al. to speculate as to the cause. While they suggest that it might be caused by inherent differences between they way the two sectors do business, it was noted that the military developments had marginal cost and schedule performance. They speculate that this suggests that the development process for government aircraft is more prone to cost and schedule difficulties. This assertion would need to be considered in the light of the greater degree of scrutiny government projects receive.

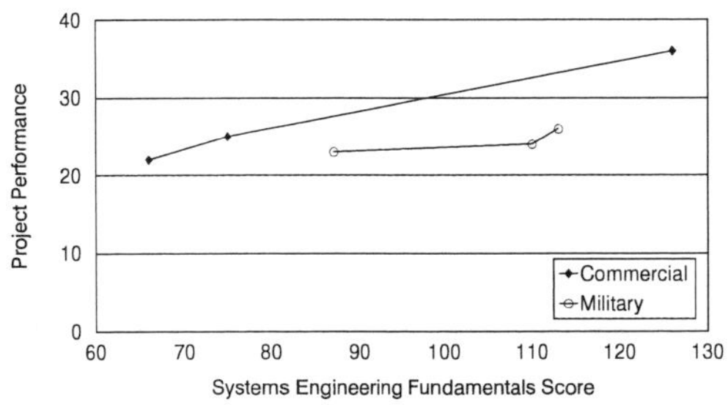

Figure 2 Project performance score versus systems engineering fundamentals (from Moody et al., 1997)

DISCUSSION

The literature reviewed held consistent messages for both hardware- and software-dominant systems. The key points are shown below group under three headings.

Guidance for systems engineering practitioners.

1. It is imperative to understand what is needed and to gain user and other stakeholder engagement before embarking on a project and to retain it throughout the life of the project.

2. The user focus must be captured in a clear, traceable and testable set of requirements with an adequate process to manage inevitable evolution and change.

3. A whole-of-life perspective is important both to create and implement appropriate system engineering methods and to identify and measure the benefits of the approach.

4. System Engineering processes and the application of standards must be tailored to the task in hand.

5. Select partners or subcontractors with a sound enterprise environment honed on projects of a similar scale and complexity. This may sound obvious but failure to heed this advice has been the cause of many project failures.

6. Attention to interface definition and management is vital for project success.

Guidance for systems engineering planning.

1. Adherence to systems engineering principles and processes across an organisation will save money. Many troubled projects cite reasons for their difficulties that should have been avoidable through the application of systems engineering. Thus systems and software engineering are a good investment and the organisation should develop an environment whereby their use becomes part of the work culture.

2. Insufficient investment in the early design phases (5 to 15%) is likely to lead to project cost overuns of between 50% and 100% for both hardware and software projects. It is better to plan to expend the time and resources during the early phases of a project than to find out that the conceptual design was inadequate the painful, expensive way.

3. The planning for systems technical evaluation (test and evaluation) albeit through modelling, simulation, analysis, or testing needs to be undertaken in the conceptual design phase. Test and Evaluation Master Plans (TEMPs) provide important guidance to all concerned on what the users consider are the important criteria for the system and how the system should be evaluated against them.

4. It is important to undertake planning against realistic expectations based on sound experience.

Guidance for process development.

1. The probability of project success (lowness of risk) is strongly related to the quality of the processes employed to engineer a system. Development of an enterprise environment is a worthwhile investment.

2. Development of processes that encapsulate soft systems approaches will encourage user involvement and stakeholder buy-in.

3. Improved commercial practices that appreciate the need for teamwork and flexibility need to be evolved from the present fixed-price arrangements that are proving to be counterproductive.

CONCLUSION

A common theme that emerges from the review material is that the application of systems engineering principles and practice will deliver better systems faster and more cost-effectively than ad-hoc, non-systemic alternatives. There was good agreement on the areas that require improvement. These can be addressed by a combination of contemporary systems engineering methods and soft systems methodologies.

The framework provided by EIA-632 provides a rich and appropriate enterprise environment in which to develop large, complex, technical systems. One that allows practitioners the scope to select from a range of alternatives those processes and methodologies which best suit their industry sector and the scale of the project in hand. Such a framework permits the integration of the hard and soft systems traditions.

ACKNOWLEDGMENT

An earlier version of this paper appears as part of the final report written for the Defence Acquisition Organisation as a deliverable for CAPO: C003/99. The financial support for this research and permission to publish are gratefully acknowledged.

REFERENCES

ANSI/EIA-632, *Processes for Engineering a System*, Electronic Industry Alliance, January 1999.

Blanchard B. S., & Fabrycky W. J., *Systems Engineering and Analysis*, 3rd Ed., Prentice Hall, 1998.

Cook S C, Sydenham P H, Harris D D and Harris M B, Lecture Notes for *Principles of Systems Engineering*, December 1998, University of South Australia. S.,

Checkland, P., and Howell S., *Information, Systems and Information Systems*, Wiley, Chichester, ISBN 0-471-95820-4, 1998.

Cranfield, *Systems Engineering for Defence: Smart Procurement the Systems Perspective*, Proc of the 3rd Annual Systems Engineering for Defence Conference, DERA/Cranfield University, Schrivenham, UK, 15-16 February 2000.

DERA, *The MoD's Downey Procedures*, 1996, DRA/LS(CS)/SYS_ENG/TG0/CMR/96/1

DSMC, *Systems Engineering Management Guide*, Defence Sysrtems Management College, Fort Belvoir, Virginia, USA, 1993.

EIA/IS-731.1, *Systems Engineering Capability Model (SECM),* Electronic Industries Alliance, January 1999. [www.geia.org/eoc/G47/eiag47.htm]

Foresight, *Building Integrated Systems*, The report of the Defence and Aerospace Foresight Panel Technology working Group, IEE, 1997, ISBN 0 85296 925 2.

Jackson M.C., "Critical Systems Thinking and Information Systems Development", *Proc of the 8th Australasian Conference on Information Systems*, 1997.

Gabb A.P. "System Engineering & Software Engineering Standards and Model," [On line accessed 10 March 1998], URL: http://www1.tpgi.com.au/users/agabb/

Gabrig J.S., *Lessons Learned from large Federal Software Development Contracts*, [Online accessed 25 Aug 1998], URL: http://www.venable.com/business/gabig.htm

Hargreaves G., *A Comparison of the Australian and UK Defence Procurement Systems for Major Projects*, MSc Dissertation, Defence Systems Engineering Group, University College London, September 1998.

Martin, James N., Overview of the EIA 632 Standard - "Processes for Engineering a System" (TUTORIAL G), 30 September 1998. [On line accessed 11 March 1999] URL: www.geia.org/eoc/G47/eia632.htm

M'Pherson P. K., "Systems Engineering: an approach to whole system design," *The Radio and Electronic Engineer*, 1980, Vol. 50, No 11/12, p545-558.

MOD, Strategic Defence Review Study 2F3/7 Smart Procurement, PPB/P(98)2, 19 January 1998, UK Ministry of Defence.

MOD, *The Acquisition Handbook - A Guide to Smart Procurement*, 2nd edition, August 1999. [On line accessed 23 February 2000], URL: http://www.mod.uk/policy/spi/handbook/front.htm

Moody J.A., Chapman W.L., Van Voorhees F.D. & Bahill A.T., *Metrics and Case Studies for Evaluating Engineering Designs*, Prentice Hall PTR, Upper Saddle River, NJ, 1997.

NASA, *NASA Systems Engineering Handbook*, SP-6105, June 1995.

NASA, *Space Engineering Lessons Learned*, Engineering Directorate, Nov 1989, [Online accessed 25 Aug 1998], URL: http://home.erols.com/ee/sysengll.htm

Robertson T.C. (Ed), Systems Engineering Handbook, INCOSE, Jan 1998.

Sheard S.A. and Lake J.G., "Systems Engineering Standards and Models Compared", Proc of INCOSE Annual Symposium, 1998.

Somerville I., Software Engineering, Fifth Edition, 1996, ISBN 0-201-42765-6.

The Standish Group, *Chaos*, The Standish Group, 1995, [Online accessed 24 March 1999], URL: http://www.standishgroup.com/chaos.html

ABOUT THE AUTHOR

After graduating in Electronics Engineering from the South Australian Institute of Technology in 1977, Prof Cook commenced work as a telecommunications equipment design engineer in the UK where he also completed an MSc in Computer Science at the University of Kent. On his return to Australia, he worked in the defence electronics industry until 1988 when he joined the Defence Science and Technology Organisation (DSTO) as an Engineer Class 5 responsible for radio communication research. In addition to his management role, he became an active contributor to the fields of radio system performance monitoring, high frequency radio systems design, multi-mechanism adaptive radio technology, modelling and simulation of military information networks, and engineering design automation. Prof Cook completed a PhD in 1990 in Measurement Science and Systems Engineering at the City University London. In 1994 he was promoted to Senior Principal Research Scientist responsible for the management and scientific leadership of the Military Information Networks Branch of DSTO. Prof Cook joined the University of South Australia as the Foundation Professor of Systems Engineering in 1997. Prof Cook has contributed to three books and has published over fifty refereed journal and conference papers.

An Application of the CEaVa Method

Bob Larsen
Major, US Army
9320 Winbourne Rd
Burke, Va 22015
Phone: (703) 425-0044
EMAIL: larsenva@erols.com

Dennis Buede
Professor, George Mason University
Dept. of Systems Engineering and Operations Research
Fairfax, Va. 22030
Phone: (703) 993-1727
Fax: (703) 993-1706
EMAIL: dbuede@gmu.edu

Abstract. In the complex world of developing requirements and eliciting user needs, engineers build billions of dollars of products that are wrong on delivery, because they solved the wrong problem. The problem statement does change, because the environment (i.e., schedule, technology, people, or politics) changes. The Continuous Early Validation (CEaVa) refinement method will stabilize the problem statement (i.e., critical requirements or KPPs), which will enhance the probability of building the right product. We will highlight the a $200 M cost savings from a multi-billion dollar Army Information Technology system case study that utilized the CEaVa method.

INTRODUCTION.

In a world of constant change in product development, when should the industry embrace a change in the system life cycle process to ensure we are developing the right products? Research indicates that 31% of the Information Technology (IT) projects will be cancelled prior to completion. In 1995 and 1996, $81 Billion and $100 Billion were spent on cancelled projects (Standish Group, 1996). Since the software industry is a sub-set of the system engineering discipline and has failure rates as high as 80%, the engineer must conduct business in different ways to succeed. To put this issue into perspective the reader needs to consider that large software systems cost far more to build and take much longer to construct than the office buildings occupied by the companies that have commissioned the software. Extremely large software systems in the 100,000-function point size range can use more resources than building a domed football stadium, a 50-story skyscraper, or a 70,000-ton cruise ship (Jones, 1998).

Modern organizations are attempting to improve the quality of their products. The methods and concepts are endless. The techniques proposed include Total Quality Management, Business Reengineering, Continuous Process Improvement, and Concurrent Engineering. However, in the complex world of developing requirements and the difficulty with eliciting user needs, engineers are building billions of dollars of products that did not solve the right problem. Continuous Early Validation (CEaVa) has great potential in correcting this dilemma. The tool should be applied at critical junctures of a program over time to validate and refine changes to the problem statement (i.e. critical requirements).

The purpose of this paper is to highlight a $200M cost savings with the application of CEaVa method. The case study demonstrated how the CEaVa method assists in answering the question-- **are we producing the right product?**

BACKGROUND.

The goal is to build a product that has a higher probability of meeting the user needs in a complex environment. The complex environment is made up of ever-changing requirements, constant change of personnel, conflicting organizational needs, organizational changes, and the technology itself. In this environment, the ability to change continuously is a "core" capability of successful firms. The bottom line is to successfully build the right product with collaboration, cooperation, and communication instilled as the core competence of a system life cycle team and stakeholders. The industry has tried many techniques, but the techniques are still falling short of producing timely and correct products.

To make the process even tougher, product life cycles have shortened dramatically, forcing companies to develop and commercialize new technologies faster than ever. Organizations are also subject to turnover of personnel, changing priorities, and complicated technical issues. As a result, the engineers must try to control the variances of the initial concepts. This is where the leader needs to have alternative actions ready to assist the project and adjust as needed. The use of the Continuous Early Validation technique is an approach that can assist engineers and customers.

FRAMEWORK OF CEaVa.

Continuous Early Validation (CEaVa) is a method that increases the likelihood of producing the right product. Many systems are being produced that are not used or useful on delivery, because the wrong problem was solved. This is common due to the changes in the environment.

The CEaVa method provides a mechanism to validate the system early to ensure the right problem is being solved. The method develops visibility of potential disconnects among stakeholders' needs, original written requirements, organizational policy, and derived requirements. The CEaVa method will validate the external and internal consistency of the problem statement. The review checks the relationship to the environment (i.e., technology, political, and schedule). Additionally, the CEaVa method provides a process to facilitate consensus resolving the potential disconnects with decision analytical reasoning for trade-off analysis of the system engineering aspects of the development.

CEaVa's goal is to stabilize the problem statement, which will increase the overall probability of producing the right product. CEaVa is a consistency checking/refinement method that stabilizes the problem statement. It is a method that should be applied continuously throughout the development of a system.

The CEaVa Method can be used in any life cycle process. The method can be used continuous through the life cycle, creation of requirements, or for the preliminary design phase. The method was developed to adapt to the needs of the stakeholder or developer. The application of the tool is depicted in Figure 1. CEaVa is overlaid (four diamonds) on the process to increase the likelihood the right problem is being solved, which leads to the right product being developed. The CEaVa method steps highlight potential disconnects that need further examination by the critical stakeholders. A more detail discussion of the method can be found in the 1999 INCOSE Proceedings (Larsen and Buede, 1999).

The method tries to ensure that the engineers are solving the right problem prior to building the system. The method institutes necessary and sufficient checks on problem definition at all levels of abstraction to ensure that all problem definitions are identical. This process tends to help stabilize the problem definition.

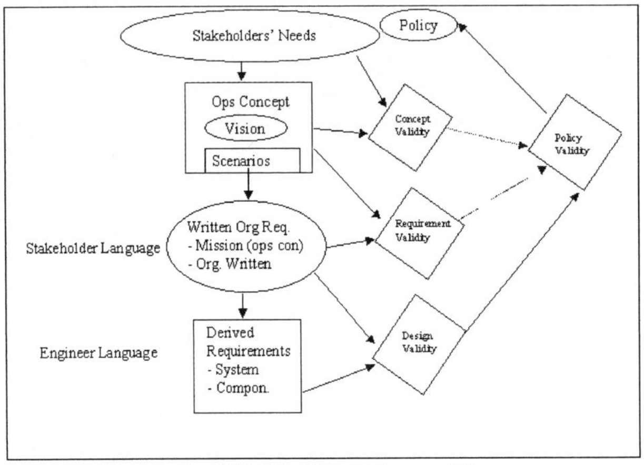

Figure 1. CEaVa Dependency Diagram

There are four components to the CEaVa Filtering Method (more details can be found in Larsen and Buede, 1999):

Component a: Conceptual validity is the correspondence between the stakeholders' needs and the operational concept. Conceptual validity needs to be established at the outset of the design process via interactions among the systems engineers and the stakeholders; however the systems engineer cannot assume that once the needs are established there is no more work to be done. Stakeholders' needs change and the operational concept must change with those needs. Conceptual Validity within CEaVa provides a mechanism to track these changes and ensure they are captured.

This step will ensure the high level expectations of the system are understood. The next part of this step is to ensure the developer and stakeholders are in agreement on the preliminary external system diagram and objective hierarchy. This is the first sub-step to establishing the relationship of performance/capability and schedule/cost. The first developments of these products are important to the rest of the process.

Component b: Requirement validity is the assurance of correspondence between the operational concept and the originating requirements. The validation occurs by establishing that the originating requirements have neither introduced new issues nor left issues out of the operational concept, thus causing the design of a different system than envisioned in the operational concept.

Component c: Design validity addresses the congruence between the originating requirements and the derived requirements. The derived requirements begin with the Systems Requirements Document, evolve to subsystem and component specifications and culminate in CI specifications. Engineering models are used to transform requirements on one or more variables to requirements on parameters that have a functional relationship with these variables.

The goal is to ensure the engineering language of the requirement fits on top of the stakeholders' language of the requirement (consistency and coherency) like an Egyptian pyramid. As the stakeholders' needs change, these changes must be filtered down through the derived requirements, shifting the pyramid appropriately.

Component d: Policy validity compares potential problem solutions to the organizational policies relating to the system. Policy Validity consists of scope, domain, and procedures cross-checking to the potential problem solution.

Lastly, policy validity will finalize the objectives hierarchy and complete the final tradeoffs of the features relative to the environmental realities of the system (i.e., schedule and cost). The trade-off process was modified from the DOD process for Cost as an Independent Variable (CAIV). The purpose of the CAIV process is to reduce the life cycle cost of new and fielded systems. CAIV is based on the realization that true military worth is dependent on operational capability, timeliness, and affordability. CAIV has been generalized to include cost, time and key personnel; Policy Validity incorporates CAIV.

The objective of CAIV is to deliver superior, not inferior, products to the user that meet or exceed expectations (requirements). CAIV is often called the "best value" approach to system development. Through CAIV we will be able to maximize our investment resources across the total spectrum of our systems.

Potential Benefits of CEaVa. The reasons for concern about improving the process are compelling. Everyone who is involved in designing an airplane agrees building the product right is important. Similarly, the IRS should not make errors, nor should software that controls air defenses, steers ships, runs banks, and so on. System and products have enormous impact on almost everything we do, and this impact will only increase in the future. There are nine benefits for using CEaVa. These will probably vary somewhat depending upon application, methodology emphasis, and type of system.

(1) Early detection of errors. One hundred times more expensive to fix a delivered error than one caught early (Boehm, 1987).

(2) Life cycle savings by easier maintenance. Every dollar of development will cost two for maintenance (Boehm, 1987).

(3) Much higher level of user satisfaction. Stakeholders are involved in another phase of the system life cycle.

(4) Reduced development risk. The time to conduct proof of concept is dramatically reduced. This is an important attribute in building the right product in a complex environment.

(5) Improved communication and project visibility. Stakeholders are involved in assessing validity of several aspects of the product development prior to large expenditures of resources.

(6) Increased probability of building the right product. A formal stakeholder review of the system problem statement relative to its environment will accomplish this.

(7) Increase ability to deliver functionality. Stakeholders refine their needs by using this procedure and offering feedback.

(8) Incorporates a rigorous learning and discovery process into the development process. Since we know we are operating on incomplete information whenever we start the product development process, CEaVa encourages us to discover inconsistency.

(9) Continuously encourages stakeholder involvement. Stakeholders are involved in the solution development that encourages ownership and commitment, and a level of cooperation.

The objective is to nudge forward the process of discovering goals along the way to induce the largest number of people possible to quickly engage, to try something; to maximize the odds of serendipity.

-Tom Peters

There are no silver bullets to solve the design problem associated with a system's life cycle. It may turn out to be impractical to test for consistency in all CEaVa items in detail. However, we believe by employing a checking method that takes into consideration sources of inconsistency leads to a better understanding of the gaps and represents the constraints for the product. This will result in a better representation of user needs. This technique will provide a higher probability of success, because it focuses on testing the system earlier based on key attributes of the user's environment. The first case study of this research demonstrated the value added.

Case Study Analysis. We selected qualitative analyses, case study approach, because this method allowed author one to become a part of the process. Author one was an active learner, so that he was able to provide insights of the use of CEaVa from a participant point of view. Case studies are particularly valuable when the evaluation aims to capture individual differences or unique variations from one program setting to another, or from one program experience to another (Yin, 1994).

The benefits of the case study approach are that it emphasizes people in the process of discovery and the studies the issue in its natural setting. Since a major part of what is happening is provided by people in their own settings, author one was able to work in those settings rather than impose upon them a preconceived or outsider's scheme of what they are about. It is the observer's task to find out what is fundamental or central to the people or world under observation (Lofland, 1984).

We used a modified Multiple-Case, Replication Design, which is an important technique for theoretical replication (Yin, 1994). The logic for this choice is that this approach uses evidence from multiple cases, making the results more compelling and the overall study more robust (Heriott and Firestone, 1983). After completion of case one, author one used the results of a second case to validate the value added by the overall methodology. Replication may be claimed with two or more data points (Yin 1994).

BACKGROUND OF CASE ONE.

The first case study of this research is Force XXI Battle Command Brigade & Below (FBCB2). The FBCB2 is both a system and a concept that will provide horizontal and vertical integration of data and information generation and processing capabilities of individual soldiers, weapons, sensors, and support platforms (refer to Figure 2).

Aggregation of individual subsystems with linkage to all Battlefield Operating Systems (BOS) will establish a computerized digital network resulting in one homogeneous battle command operational architecture throughout all facets of the brigade structure. The FBCB2 is a computer system supported by existing communications, sensors, and electrical power sources that will seamlessly interoperate with and exchange appropriate data/information with all Army Battle Command Systems (ABCS). This includes FBCB2, Maneuver Control System (MCS), All Source Analysis System (ASAS), Advanced Field Artillery Tactical Data System (AFATDS), Combat Service Support Command/Control System (CSSC2S), and Forward Area Air Defense Command/Control Intelligence System (FAADC2IS).

Force XXI Battle Command Brigade & Below (FBCB2)

FBCB2 is a joint interoperable, digital, battle command information system for brigade level and below commanders. It is designed to provide dismounted/mounted combat elements with near real-time, integrated battlefield information. This information will enhance the ability of tactical commanders, while on the move, to better synchronize their forces, achieve agility, and gain a "feel" of the battlespace through improved situational awareness and better combat awareness reporting.

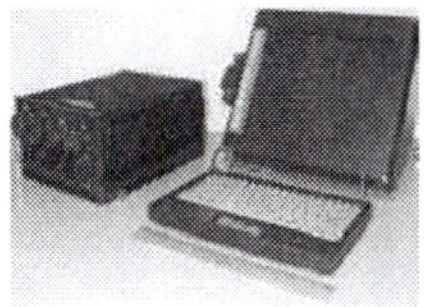

Figure 2. CEaVa Case One

FBCB2 supports the commander and staff in applying the command techniques essential to achieving victory during warfighting operations. FBCB2 amplifies the combat effectiveness of maneuver forces creating a synergistic effect on mobility, lethality, and survivability coupled with better-informed commanders.

The first author conducted a quick look with the CEaVa method to the life cycle process for FBCB2. The method highlighted several disconnects from concept, requirement, design, and policy validity.

The PM and user requested that the first author facilitate two workshops to review the status of the system. The first author applied the detailed application of the CEaVa method to facilitate a review of the disconnects from the quick look. The authors believed the CEaVa method highlighted that the FBCB2 stakeholders should refine a few items. The Army analytical agency assisted in validating the knees in the curve on key attributes of the system. Modeling and Simulation analyses, with good military judgment, did refine/stabilize the objectives and threshold for key features of the baseline system and determine the metrics for future iterative versions with the CEaVa approach. For example, why 95% vs. 80% for a performance attribute of a system? What is the impact to the systems successfulness meeting one value over another value by 2000 or 2004?

Details of the Application.

Concept Validity identified disconnects with the stakeholders needs and what was developed as the high level operational concept. For example, "the FBCB2 participants, five years ago, spent more time developing the Key Performance Parameters (KPPs), than ensuring they had identified the high level operational needs in priority order of the system, " stated a user representative who participated in the CEaVa workshops. Three of the user representatives and two of the PM representatives enjoyed the use of this structured methodology. The participants misunderstood the KPPs importance when they developed these parameters for the system. The participants admitted they were trying to determine measurements of how the system should operate vs. what the system should do. CEaVa sub-set one assisted in identifying this shortcoming. The users have a better appreciation of what KPP should be and not be. The stakeholders need to ask themselves, "Do I want to kill the program, because it failed a KPP?" The CJCS language is specific, if the level of performance at IOT&E does not meet the threshold KPP, it warrants killing a program.

Requirement Validity identified disconnects with the original vision statement and what was written in the originating document. For example, the operational concept stated the use of COTS type products. Whereas the originating requirements identified that the Mean Time Between Failure (MTBF) of the system should be over 900 hours. The average computer is built for 400-500 hours. During workshop One the stakeholders realized they were not looking at what it would cost to specify such a 900 MTBF requirement. However, the developer never brought it up as an issue until the Program Manager (PM) reviewed the system in development with CEaVa. We determined the cost of such a requirement would add an additional $5-7,000 per system. Presently, the system overall cost requirement is set at $25,000 per system. This requirement would severely break the overall cost requirement ceiling. On 23 July, 1999, the user representative changed the written requirement to match the operation concept of using COTS as much as possible and changed some of the KPPs to incremental thresholds over time.

Design Validity identified disconnects with the contractor's written document and what was written in the originating document. For example, the cold storage requirement in the originating requirements was set at –50 degrees Fahrenheit. As part of CEaVa, the method identified the contractors requirement was set at –25 degrees Fahrenheit. After much discussion the developer and the project manager realized they made an independent decision without user involvement. The developers stated this would require someone to develop special glass. The PM estimated the cost of ensuring that the originating requirements could be met with an approximate cost of $7-9,000 per system. The schedule implication could have caused delays of years to produce this requirement in mass quantity. The first shipment of 5,000 appliqués is due in the year 2000. In July 1999, the user changed the originating requirement to –25 Fahrenheit degrees.

During the first workshop the application of policy validity identified the need for the development process for FBCB2 be iterative, so that the soldiers can reshape how the Army will fight with FBCB2 and the design would evolve. Throughout the spiral development of FBCB2, the ability to achieve the written requirements and KPPs were not assessed based on Cost as an Independent Variable (CAIV). CEaVa was the mechanism that forced the stakeholders to look at how the variables are related to the overall need of the system for the Army's digitization effort. Through the application of CEaVa, it was evident to the stakeholders that some of the requirements were very challenging, and that fielding some attributes of the requirements was uncertain. The workshops tended to focus on what level of performance are needed at scheduled times. By 23 July 1999 the user updated the written requirements to the reflect technology and schedule reality.

The FBCB2 case study demonstrated that CEaVa increased the likelihood the right problem is being solved, which leads to the right product being developed. The PM believed the goodness of insuring the written requirements reflected the reality of technology limitation would benefits soldiers for years to come. The PM estimated a cost saving of $200M and a two-year schedule slippage. The goals of the process that were accomplished were:

1. Interpret stakeholders' needs. By the use of the CEaVa method the engineer increased the likelihood he was following the stakeholders' logic on the needs of the system. For example, the COTS compliance vs. the Army's standard of cold weather requirement discussed earlier.

2. Map decomposition of requirements. By the use of steps two and three of the CEaVa method the interested parties validated the consistency of the translation of the requirements. For example, the method highlighted a disconnect with the Mean Time Between Failure.

3. Identify trade space items (deferred requirements/features for next version). The use of the CEaVa method demonstrated that the stakeholder would have the opportunity to validate the key features of the system compared to the schedule and resources available. By the end of the process all participants should be able to identify what features to defer for a later version due to schedule and cost consideration. In the past this system never utilized this goal

due to the difficulty to understand DoD explanation how to utilized it.

4. Match stakeholder expectations to engineer system design. The four CEaVa steps increased the confidence of stabilizing of the problem statement by stepping through the components of the method. After the CEaVa review there was consensus developed on what were realistic expectation for the system by year. The result was the 23 July 1999 update to the written requirements that reflected technology and schedule implications.

All stakeholders agreed this framework provided them information they need to make a timely decision for their program. This case demonstrated the power of this method. As M. Singer, TRW senior system engineer stated, "this method is a natural extension of Barry Boehm work." The formal structure allows stakeholders the opportunity to visualize the critical aspects of the system relative to its environment. Then they can make decisions relative to the problem statement—Am I solving the right problem? If the answer is yes, their confidence about getting the right product at the end of the life cycle increases.

CEaVa BENEFITS FOR FBCB2.

The CEaVa method assisted stakeholders review the program relative to its environment (i.e., schedule, technology, and availability). Highlighted benefits were:

(1) Provided clearer understanding of Cost As An Independent Variable, so that the stakeholders could review feature of the system relative to the schedule.

(2) Improved communication between user representative and developers. Assisted in bounding feasible achievable solutions to understand the trade space.

(3) Assisted in reviewing the critical parameters, so that the stakeholders could understand the knees in the curve for goodness.

(4) Provided the formal framework to provide a timely review of the system.

(5) The user representative refined their written requirements, so that the system could increase the likelihood of building the right product for the soldiers and the leaders. Additionally, the change will assist in increasing the greater likelihood of passing the next test event.

(6) Detected disconnects of requirement decomposition, so that the stakeholders could visualize the issues relating to these areas.

SUMMARY.

In a complex world of developing requirements and eliciting the user needs, engineers are spending billions of dollars developing products that are not meeting user needs, because the engineers solved the wrong problem. The system life cycle developers must ensure the customer is satisfied prior to designing elaborate diagrams and building the product. We can accomplish this task with the use of a CEaVa method with any development life cycle process. The four components of CEaVa will interpret stakeholders' needs, maps decomposition of requirements, trap false requirements or misunderstandings, identify trade-off items (deferred requirements/features for next version), and match stakeholder expectations to engineer system design. Additionally, we believe CEaVa will increase the overall probability of producing the right product, save resources, and provide for a happier customer.

In conclusion, CEaVa is a mirror-like method that helps see detail, which might otherwise be missed and reflects many attributes of the system to which it is applied. It is our sincere hope this research leaves the reader with an awareness of the great potential that CEaVa offers. Any technique that can offer so much benefit surely has a place in future product development.

REFERENCES

Boehm, B.W., *Improving Software Productivity,* IEEE Computer Society, 1987.

Buede, D., *The Engineering Design of Systems: Models and Methods*, Wiley, 2000.

Davis, A.M., *Software Requirements*, PTR Prentice Hall, NJ, 1993.

Grady, R.B., *Sucessful Software Process Improvement,* Hewlett-Packard, 1997.

Heriott, R.E., & Firesone, W.A., *Multisite Qualitative Policy Research: Optimizing description and generalizing*, Education Research, 1983.

Jones, C., *Project Management Tools and Software Failures and Successes,* 1998.

Larsen, R. and Buede, D., *An Early Validation Plug and Play Module*, INCOSE Proceedings, 1999.

Lofland,J., *Analyzing Social Settings Wadsworth*, 1984.

Standish Group, *Chaos*, 1996.

Yin, R.K, *Case Study Research Design and Methods*, Sage Publications, 1994.

Bob Larsen, a systems analyst/engineer who commanded a firing battery with the 101st Airborne Division (Air Assault) and a Target Acquisition Battery with 2nd Infantry Division.

He worked at TRAC-WSMR where he assisted in the developing new techniques and systems to attack SCUDS. Also, he developed insights in the modelling for the Army's long range Tactical Missile System for a MS III decision. He presented numerous papers, briefs, and wrote an article that was published in the Field Artillery Journal in 1995 dealing with attacking SCUDS in the future. He worked on the Army Staff for two years while working DoD Deep Fires and Joint Requirements for the 1996 QDR. In March 1998, he was published in Army Magazine on the Joint Force Structure. In 1999, Bob co-authored a paper that he presented at the International INCOSE Conference. Bob is currently completing his Ph.D. at George Mason University, Virginia.

Dennis M. Buede received the B.S. degree in aerospace engineering from the University of Cincinnati and the M.S. and Ph.D. degrees from the Engineering-Economic Systems Department of Stanford University. He currently serves as a Professor of Systems Engineering and Operations Research at George Mason University. He is also the Chair of the Education and Research Technical Committee of INCOSE.

International Space Station Integrated Verification Process

Bill R. Haskins
Boeing Space and Communications
2100 Space Park Drive
Mail-Stop HS-21
Houston, TX 77058

ABSTRACT

The International Space Station (ISS) verification challenge was developing a process that ensured the verification of lots of requirements for a very complex system. The ISS integrated verification process was developed to provide a disciplined engineering approach for the verification of the ISS specification requirements and to provide a traceable archive of verification data needed to sustain ISS operations. The ISS integrated verification process has proven itself to be a tried and true structured process that can be adapted to any type of simple or complex system.

INTRODUCTION

The ISS consists of a manned orbiting facility and a ground based system. The manned orbiting facility will be generated by multiple flights over a number of years and accommodates engineering research, microgravity research, and life and natural sciences research. The ground based system provides support to the manned orbiting facility that includes services (e.g., resupply, communications) and personnel.

Since the ISS program consists of multinational organizations with differing interpretations of terminology, integration and verification definitions, as used within this paper, are:

1. Integration – The act of mating hardware and/or software components, subsystems, systems or elements at their respective interfaces and verifying the compatibility and proper operation of the integrated unit.
2. Verification - A set of activities performed to ensure that facilities and hardware/software products comply with the specification requirements imposed upon them.

VERIFICATION ROLES & RESPONSIBILITIES

The ISS verification program is managed by the Boeing and NASA Test and Verification (T&V) Team, as defined in the (Program Master Integration & Verification Plan, 1995). The T&V team leads the verification of the ISS system, providing direction and coordination with other program participants (Shuttle, International Participants, etc.), and is responsible for verifying the ISS system is a fully functional manned orbiting platform. The T&V team is also responsible for ensuring the ISS program verification processes are understood, these processes are properly implemented, and for reporting the overall progress of this implementation.

VERIFICATION PROGRAM APPROACH

The basic ISS verification program philosophy is to integrate and test on the ground, what we fly, before we fly, within the constraints imposed by geography, cost and schedule. The verification approach supporting this philosophy requires accomplishing the following objectives:

1. Conduct testing at the lowest possible levels and complete specification compliance verification prior to shipment of the element/component from the factory. This means that specification requirement compliance starts at the lower levels and builds to the higher levels within the ISS program.
2. Confirm that the elements/components comply with ISS program specification requirements and function properly as integrated units.
3. Certify that the elements/components will successfully interface with the planned assembly stage; interface with all subsequent stage assemblies; and meet its' contribution to final on-orbit configuration performance.

INTEGRATED VERIFICATION PROCESS

Each of the organizations responsible for development of an element/component is responsible for the verification of that element/component to its specified requirements. The International Participants (IPs) are responsible for the verification of their segments (e.g., integrated elements) and elements/components. The Government Furnished Equipment (GFE) providers and U.S. development sites are responsible for the verification of their elements/components. Boeing

Houston is responsible for the verification of the ISS system and U.S. on-orbit segment (e.g., integrated U.S. elements) requirements and has developed the ISS integrated verification process to verify these requirements. Each of the IPs, GFE providers, and U.S. development site's verification processes are compatible with the ISS integrated verification process. The ISS integrated verification process is also used to verify the stage unique requirements. Boeing has developed stage unique requirements to define the functional interim configurations for each stage. The stage unique requirements ensure that each stage is safe, survivable, and assembleable, and is within the capabilities of the design. If analyses find that this is not possible for specific stage configurations, then stage unique requirements are allocated to the U.S., IP, and GFE element specifications. This ensures the element can support all of the interim stage configurations, from the time the element is launched, until the final ISS on-orbit assembly complete configuration.

The ISS integrated verification process is broken up into 5 major steps, as shown in Figure 1.

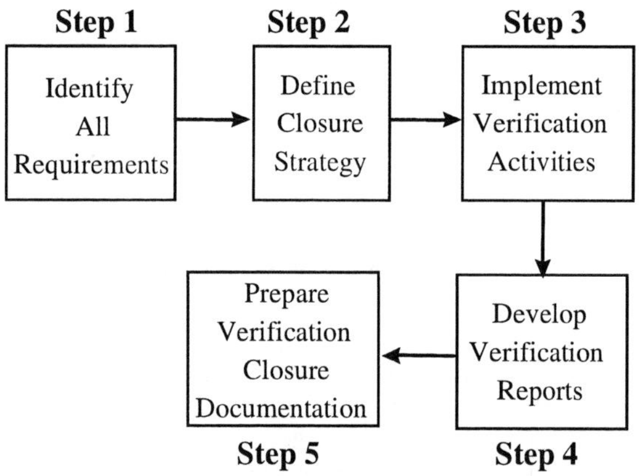

Figure 1. ISS Integrated Verification Process

Step 1 – Identify All Requirements. Traceability/allocation is established for the ISS specifications Section 3 requirements. Higher-level to lower-level requirement traceability is evaluated and documented to ensure 100% requirement traceability/allocation to the lowest level of verification implementation. Boeing Houston is responsible for establishing and maintaining the traceability of requirements in the ISS specifications from the top-down (e.g., allocation) and from the bottom-up (e.g., compliance) to the specification requirement closure documentation. The Program Verification Information System (PVIS) oracle database captures and maintains the requirements/traceability data and associated verification compliance/traceability data, and provides the required configuration control based on the ISS specification tree, as shown in Figure 2.

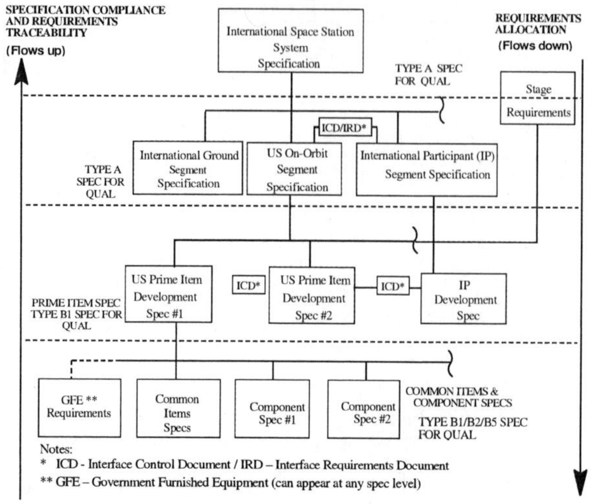

Figure 2. ISS Specification Tree

The PVIS database provides an auditable, traceable trail for closure of the system, segments, elements, and components requirements. Once the traceability/allocation of the requirements has been established, Step 1 of the integrated verification process is initiated.

Step 1 is the check and balance which assures the initial ISS system, U.S. on-orbit segment, and stage unique requirement allocation is correct. Each requirement is specifically assigned to a subsystem/technical team, and the applicable stages for each ISS requirement are identified. To accomplish this, a Verification Responsibility Matrix (VRM) is developed, as shown in Figure 3.

DOC ID	PARA ID	RESP TEAM	PARA TITLE	REQ TEXT	STG 1AR	STG 2A	STG 1R	STG 2A.1	STG 3A
ISS	3.2.1.1.1.1	ECLS	Capability: Control atmospheric pressure.	a.The on-orbit Space Station shall maintain the..	X	X	X	X	X
ISS	3.2.1.1.1.2	ECLS	Capability: Condition atmosphere.	a.The on-orbit Space Station shall maintain the..	X		X		
ISS	3.2.1.1.1.3	FCS&I	Capability: Light station.	a.The on-orbit Space Station shall control the..	X	X	X		
ISS	3.2.1.1.1.4	SMC	Capability: Respond to loss of function.	a.The on-orbit Space Station shall automatically recover...	X	X	X	X	X
ISS	3.2.1.1.1.5	SMC	Capability: Control station.	a.In response to an operator initiated command or..	X		X		

ECLS – Environment Control Life Support
SMC – Station Management & Control
FCS&I – Flight Crew System & Integration

Figure 3. Verification Responsibility Matrix

The VRM identifies each requirement in the ISS system, U.S. on-orbit segment, and all stage unique requirements. The VRM also identifies the applicable stages for each requirement. PVIS traceability reports are used to identify the applicable stages for each ISS system and U.S. on-orbit segment requirement, based on the elements/components that are being launched on a stage by stage basis. The applicable stages for the stage unique requirements are determined by the capabilities/operations required to ensure that each stage is safe, survivable, and assembleable.

The T&V team works with each subsystem/ technical team to determine the correct ownership of each requirement for verification compliance responsibility. Since each of the ISS specification requirements is traced to lower level specifications, subsystem/technical team requirement ownership is assigned at the ISS system level and verification responsibility is flowed down to the lower level specifications.

After the ISS system, U.S. on-orbit segment, and stage unique requirements have been assigned requirement ownership, the specification traceability is compared against the existing functional decomposition to determine if the functionality has been decomposed to the lowest applicable and verifiable level. This ensures all applicable ISS specification requirements have been identified to bound the scope of the verification activities. These steps, conducted by the subsystem/technical teams, validate that the requirements are in place to begin Step 2 of the integrated verification process. These steps also identify any specification requirement discrepancies.

The subsystem/technical teams also evaluate the ISS system, U.S. on-orbit segment, and stage unique requirements to identify any applicable reference requirements (e.g., interface, shuttle, environmental, structural requirements, etc.) that are invoked by the specification requirements. Reference requirements are verified the same as specification requirements.

Step 2 – Define Closure Strategy. To provide compliance for each ISS system, U.S. on-orbit segment, and stage unique requirement, a verification closure strategy must be defined and implemented. Verification Logic Networks (VLNs) are developed to graphically represent the verification closure strategy, and constitute a plan by which the stage verification activities can be executed. Test and Verification Requirements (TVRs) are developed to define each stage verification activity. Each TVR in the VLN must provide sufficient detail (e.g., objective, success criteria, conditions, etc.) to execute the verification activity and establish a relationship to other verification activities. An example of the VLN framework is shown in Figure 3.

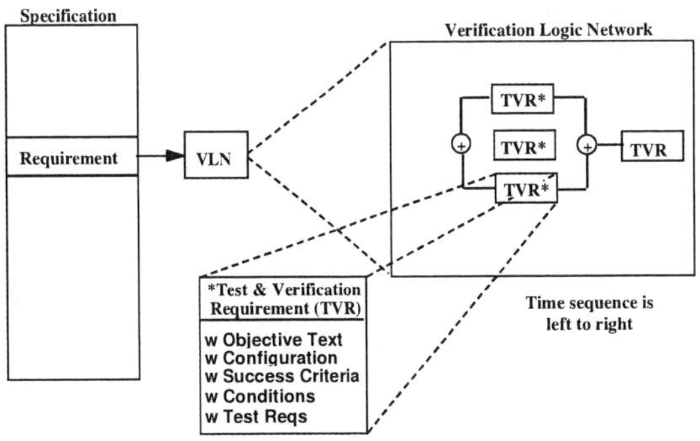

Figure 3. Verification Logic Network

The VLN has to demonstrate the path or logic flow for interconnecting each specified verification activity for each staged assembly. The VLN structures the verification activities from the lower levels to the higher levels of verification within the ISS program. The applicable verification methods that are used to verify each ISS system, U.S. on-orbit segment and stage unique requirement (e.g., test, demonstration, analysis, inspection, or any combination of these methods) is identified by each TVR in the VLN. VLNs identify prerequisite TVRs and identify the inter team-to-team dependencies, which ensure horizontal integration across teams. Verification input products, required to support implementation of the TVRs, are also identified on the VLN. When each specified TVR has been satisfied in the VLN, then the applicable ISS system, U.S. on-orbit segment, and stage unique requirement is satisfied. A detailed VLN example is shown in Appendix A, Figure A-1. To ensure that each VLN is developed with the same level of detail and content, each VLN is assessed against the VLN Quality Checklist, as shown in Appendix B, Table B-2.

TVR development requires each subsystem/ technical team to identify the following data:

1. Technical information and specific conditions for verifying the applicable ISS system, U.S. on-orbit segment, and stage unique requirements. This information can be used as inputs to the TVR's success criteria, conditions, etc.
2. The type of TVR (e.g., analysis, inspection, test, or demonstration) required and the applicable configuration for the TVR. Master TVRs are developed for requirements that have the same verification closure strategy for every stage through assembly complete.
3. The specification requirement technical baseline that the TVR is developed against.
4. Applicable reference requirements invoked by the specification requirements.

To ensure that each TVR is developed with the same level of detail and content, each TVR is assessed against the TVR Content Standard Checklist, as shown in Appendix C, Table C-1.

After the VLNs and TVRs have been successfully assessed against the VLN Quality Checklist and TVR Content Standard Checklist, the VLN/TVR package is sent out for a 21 day external review, so other organizations can review the VLN/TVR package and provide comments. If comments are received, then the resolution of the comments is negotiated with the comment provider and incorporated into the VLN/TVR package. Once the VLN/TVR package has been updated, or if no comments have been received, then the VLN/TVR package is ready for baselining. The VLN/TVR package is required to be concurred/signed off by the Boeing/NASA subsystem/technical team that is responsible for the VLN/TVR package. The VLN/TVR package is required to be baselined through the Test & Verification Control Panel (T&VCP). The T&VCP, which is chaired by a Boeing and NASA verification representative, authorizes implementation of the VLN/TVR package.

Step 3 – Implement Verification Activities. After the VLN/TVR package has been baselined, then the implementation of the TVRs is performed. Issues may surface before, during, and after TVR implementation. The implementing organizations require that these issues be resolved in order to permit completion of the TVR. The subsystem/technical team responsible for the TVRs, require that these issues, and subsequent resolution, be recorded and traced back to the TVR to show accurate and complete verification closure.

Issues during TVR implementation may be associated to implementation of the TVR, performance of the flight or test article, or failure of the hardware/software. Issues may also occur after a TVR has been completed. These can be caused by engineering changes that affect the hardware/software. These issues must be resolved before the TVR is considered closed.

Step 4 – Develop Verification Reports. After the TVRs have been implemented, verification reports are developed to address the implementation of the TVRs. The verification reports contain the following types of data:

1. The specific TVRs, addressed by the verification report, are identified.
2. The results of the tests, demonstrations, inspections, and/or analyses performed per the TVRs are documented and summarized.
3. Any noncompliance to the TVRs is identified and documented in problem reports.
4. Actions are recommended to either close the TVRs, re-verify/re-implement the TVRs, or issue waivers or exceptions against the TVRs.

The verification reports serve as backup data to the formal verification closure documentation.

Step 5 – Prepare Verification Closure Documentation. After the verification reports have been developed to address the implementation of the TVRs, the verification closure documentation is prepared to show compliance with the applicable ISS specification requirements contained in the VLN/TVR package. Preparation of verification closure documentation establishes the operating processes used by the ISS program for the preparation, review, and acceptance of verification documentation, for closure of specification requirements using data obtained and reported during the implementation of the TVRs. Specifically, the verification closure documentation requires the following activities to be performed to implement the final step of the ISS integrated verification process:

1. All applicable verification reports, associated with the TVRs for a specific VLN, are assessed to confirm compliance with the ISS system, U.S. on-orbit segment, and stage unique requirements contained in the VLN.
2. Verification Closure Notices (VCNs) are prepared to identify the specific VLN; applicable ISS system, U.S. on-orbit segment, and stage unique requirements (e.g., paragraph number, paragraph title and requirement text); applicable TVRs and associated verification reports; and any issues, waivers or exceptions.
3. VCNs are required to be concurred/signed off by the Boeing/NASA subsystem/technical team, that is responsible for the compliance of the specification requirements identified on the VCN, to justify formal closure of the requirements.
4. Stage specification compliance reports are prepared and delivered to NASA to justify compliance of all applicable ISS system, U.S. on-orbit segment, and stage unique requirements for a specific stage. The data contained in the specification compliance report is the same type of information contained in the VCNs.

These activities are required to document specification compliance and to provide a traceable archive of data needed to sustain ISS operations.

CONCLUSIONS

Summary. The ISS integrated verification process has proven itself to provide a structured and disciplined engineering approach that ensures the verification of the ISS specification requirements. The ISS integrated verification process can be adapted to verify any type of simple or complex system.

Lessons Learned. Implementation of the ISS integrated verification process over the past couple of years has resulted in a number of lessons learned. The following lessons learned have allowed the integrated verification process to become a streamlined process, that preserves the traceability from Step 1 through Step 5, yet significantly reduces manpower and resources:

1. Baseline the stage VLN/TVR packages incrementally by subsystem/technical team, instead of baselining an entire stage at one time, and provide the VLN/TVR packages electronically for review, versus hard copy. This has accelerated the review and baseline process for the stage VLN/TVR packages by over 400%.
2. Use lower level verification planning and lower level VCNs to close ISS system, U.S. on-orbit segment, and stage unique requirements, if requirements do not require integrated verification activities and are simply a "roll-up" of lower level verification data. This has resulted in a 65% savings in labor hours and documentation, since integrated TVRs and Stage VCNs are not required to be developed or baselined.
3. Shift VLN development focus from stages to total assembly complete strategies. This has significantly reduced the amount of documentation, and the subsystem/technical team only has to develop/track a single VLN versus developing/tracking a VLN for every stage (e.g., approximately 40 stages would equal 40 different stage VLNs).
4. Develop a standard VLN checklist and TVR checklist. The VLN Quality checklist and the TVR Content Standard checklist were developed to ensure that each VLN/TVR has the same level of detail and content across all subsystem/technical teams.
5. Implement a review each week to discuss delinquent verification planning and closure. This has resulted in identifying and resolving "roadblocks" which has significantly accelerated the planning and closure of the ISS specification requirements.
6. Develop master TVRs for requirements that have the same verification closure strategy for every stage. The applicable stage effectivity is identified in the TVR. Once the master TVR is baselined, it does not require rebaselining for future stages, unless the content changes in master TVR. This has eliminated the development of duplicate TVRs for each stage, since only one master TVR is required that addresses all applicable stages.
7. Obtain both contractor and customer subsystem/technical team concurrence on the lower level verification planning. This ensures that there are no surprises during implementation and closure phase.
8. Obtain both contractor and customer subsystem/technical team concurrence on the compliance to all ISS specification requirements. This ensures that all ISS requirements are reviewed/concurred for compliance by the subsystem/technical teams.

REFERENCES

D684-10020-1, *Program Master Integration and Verification Plan*. Revision A, 1995.

BIOGRAPHY

9 ½ years experience as the International Space Station technical lead of the Test & Verification team. Responsible for the implementation of the ISS integrated verification process for the ISS system, U.S. on-orbit segment and stage unique requirements for each stage. Authored major sections of the Program Master Integration & Verification Plan and developed detailed implementation instructions for each step of the ISS integrated verification process. Also authored the Program Verification Information System database document to define the requirement and verification traceability/compliance process to ensure an auditable, traceable trail for closure of the ISS specification requirements.

APPENDIX A

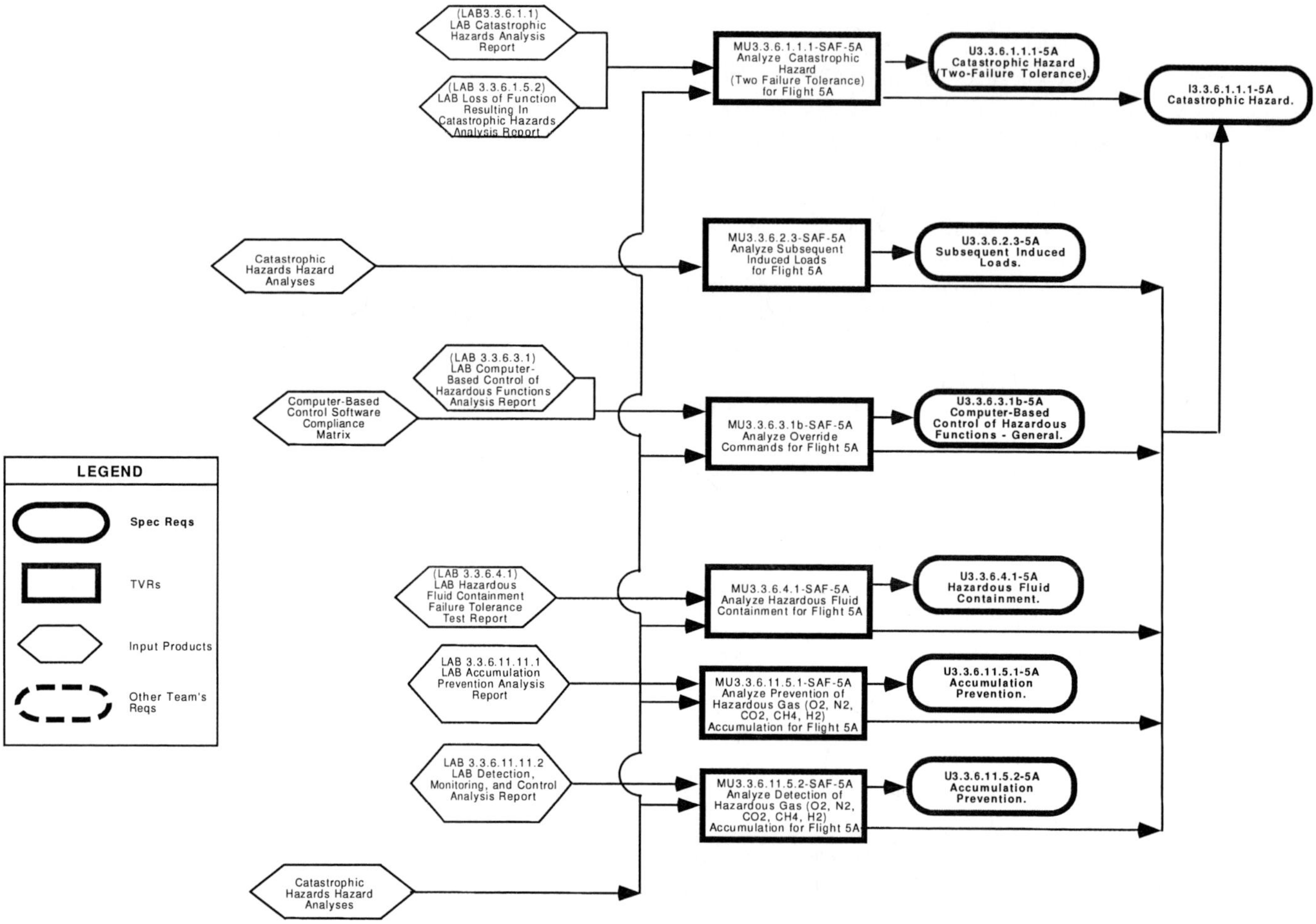

I 3.3.6.1.1.1-5A CATASTROPHIC HAZARDS

Figure A-1. VLN Example

APPENDIX B

	Quality	Criteria
1	Does the VLN have sufficient level of "technical depth" which has been defined to verify the applicable system, segment, or stage unique requirements?	The VLN represents a clear picture of how the verification of the requirements increase in complexity as the logic flows from left to right and from top to bottom). The VLN flow is an acceptable approach, with the right level of technical depth, given programmatic, schedule, and resource limitations.
2	Does the VLN exhibit that the most "cost effective" approach has been taken to verify the applicable system, segment, or stage unique requirements?	The VLN's most "cost effective" approach has been achieved by optimizing risk versus verification methods (i.e. Opportunities have been optimized for co-sponsored tests; risks associated with verifying the requirements have been evaluated to determine if a test/demo is required or if an analysis/inspection is sufficient; and the current set of changes have been evaluated to determine if any proposed tests/demos have already been costed, to ensure no repeated stage verification activities occur).
3	Does the VLN exhibit that all of the required stage integration verification input products are identified to support verification of the applicable system, segment, or stage unique requirements for this stage?	The VLN identifies the complete set of required stage integration verification input products (i.e. verification reports, drawings, models, etc.) that are required to be provided, before the HW/SW are launched, to support the verification of the applicable system, segment, or stage unique requirements
4	Does the VLN exhibit that all required inter team-to-team dependencies, (i.e. power dependencies on thermal reqs, reliability dependencies on logistics reqs, etc.), have been addressed to account for any required "horizontal integration" across teams, and have the applicable teams concurred with the other team's VLN approach?	The VLN identifies the required inter team-to-team dependencies as inputs to the applicable requirement's verification, to support "horizontal integration" across teams.
5	Does the VLN exhibit that the appropriate verification methods, (i.e. analyze, inspect, demonstrate, or test), have been identified for each of the verification planning activities?	The verification methods selected for the verification planning activities are logical, technically correct, and correctly identified in the TVRs.
6	Does the VLN exhibit that all of the appropriate/applicable requirements, specified in the "reference documents", have been reflected on the VLN?	The applicable reference document requirements (i.e. shuttle, environments, structural, etc) where applicable, are reflected on the VLN as "requirement constraints". Need to identify Reference Document ID and applicable Paragraph #'s.
7	Does the VLN exhibit that all of the applicable interface requirements have been correctly identified on the VLN and is the verification sufficient to verify that all element level external interfaces will correctly fit/form/function when mated with its joining interface.	The VLN identifies the applicable interface requirements and the TVRs sufficiently verify the fit/form/function of the applicable external interface.

Table B-1. VLN Quality Checklist

APPENDIX C

ATTRIBUTES	TVR CONTENT STANDARD CHECKLIST
STAGE EFFECTIVITY	The stage effectivity identifies all applicable stages through the final stage. Identify the applicable stages for the TVR, i.e.; 1AR, 2A, 1R, 2A.1, 3A, 2R, etc.
TVR NUMBER	The TVR Number is a structured identifier "SMART" number consisting of the Doc ID, Para #, Resp. Org, Stage #, and Revision ID. For Doc ID, use I = System, U = Segment, or A = Stage. For Para #, use applicable paragraph number and a = first shall, b = second shall, c = third shall, etc. (i.e. 3.2.1.1.1.18a, 3.2.1.1.1.18b, etc.). For Resp. Org, use the correct acronym for the applicable subsystem/technical team (i.e. ECLS, SMC, FCS&I, etc.). For Stage #, use the applicable stage number based on the launch sequence. For the Revision ID, use a "-1" for the first revision after the TVR has been baselined, a "-2" for the second revision, etc. Master TVRs must contain the letter "M" as the first character in the TVR number, i.e.; MI3.2.1.1.1.1a-ECLS-2A-1.
TVR TITLE	The TVR title should identify the verification method, short title of verification requirement for each stage, and applicable stage number. Don't just restate the function/capability. Use Analyze for all Analysis/Assessment TVRs. Use Inspect for all Inspection TVRs, Test for all Test TVRs, and Demonstrate for all Demonstration TVRs.
OBJECTIVE	The objective must be specific, and define exactly "WHAT" verification activity must be performed to verify the given requirement for the given stage. Do not just restate the design requirement. The objective must include how the required input products are going to be used as part of the analysis, inspection, test, etc. Reference documents must identify the applicable paragraphs/sections. Non - Baselined reference documents must include a date/Reference letter.
SUCCESS CRITERIA	The TVR success criteria must be "QUANTITATIVE" value, not "SUBJECTIVE" judgment. Define the criteria so that the only results that can be reached is "Pass or Fail". This should include: Upper and lower limits, No greater than, No less than, bounded by theoretical curves, discreet values, quantitative success, and identify specific parameters. The criteria should be written so that the same results can be replicated at anytime in the future - repeatable.
CONDITIONS / CONFIGURATION	Identify any "Special" or "Unique" conditions/configurations that are required to implement the TVR, i.e. environmental conditions, safety conditions, reliability conditions, fidelity of hardware/software, specific test configurations, etc. In the event that the configuration departs from the pre-published system architecture verification plan, or contains subsystems of lower fidelity, a statement of the precision of that deviation on the outcome of the data should be noted. Any formal paper work, approved by NASA, that pre-declares these differences should also be listed for traceability purposes.
PREREQUISITE TVR CONSTRAINTS	Identify any prerequisite constraints (i.e. lower level TVRs or other verification activities) that are required to be satisfied before the current TVR verification activity can be started and/or implemented. Other TVRs, shown on the VLN as inputs, should be identified as prerequisite constraints.
REQUIRED VERIFICATION INPUT PRODUCTS	Identify the verification input products, (i.e. structures data, power quality data, drawings, models, etc.), that are required for implementing the TVR verification activity. Give a brief description of the input product(s) required. The Segment/Element specification and paragraph numbers should be identified in parenthesis at the beginning of the required verification input product, (i.e.; Node1 3.2.1.1) Node1/PMA1 interface current/pressure correlation analysis data.
VLN NUMBER	The VLN Number identifies the applicable System specification paragraph number and the stage number for a given stage, i.e.; I3.2.1.1.1.1-1AR, I3.2.1.1.1.1-2A, etc.

Table C-1. TVR Content Standard Checklist

Development of Systems Engineers: A Structured Approach Based Upon International Experience

Michael B. Harris
Systems Engineering and Evaluation Centre
F2-36, The Levels Campus,
University of South Australia,
Mawson Lakes, SA, 5095,
AUSTRALIA

Abstract. The Systems Engineering and Evaluation Centre (SEEC), a dedicated research group within the University of South Australia, has been involved with an international Graduate Engineer Trainee Programme for several years. This experience has strengthened the observed enterprise-level advantages of Systems Engineering training based upon appropriate education and work experience tailored for select individuals. The lessons learned from this involvement have been gathered as the basis for a structured approach for the development of Systems Engineers.

INTRODUCTION

Systems Engineering is still an emerging discipline and is a relatively newcomer in education as well. (For instance Sydenham (1998) suggested there was only '20-30 maybe more' postgraduate degree awards and possibly over a 100 courses offered across the world in the name of Systems Engineering.) Engineering organisations search for staff training paths to guarantee their enterprise's financial and technical future, and yet the training and development needs to form Systems Engineers are usually poorly defined. Much of the current difficulty stems from the nature of Systems Engineering as a broad discipline which extends beyond the traditional, easily-defined professional engineering areas.

Naturally, the ability for an organisation to form Systems Engineers is directly correlated to the size of the organisation, the training budget available and the impetus provided by senior management. Corporations usually rely on a process of 'osmosis' of the corporate procedures and culture by the engineering staff to develop the Systems Engineers required in the medium to long term. This approach leaves any shortfalls in Systems Engineering to be filled by a deliberate 'buy-in' of expertise.

WHY SYSTEMS ENGINEERING IS DIFFERENT

Many organisations find it difficult enough to recruit and train engineers in the required disciplines, so why complicate matters with longer-term considerations of developing Systems Engineers? The answer lies in the difference in the foundation between Systems Engineering and the traditional design engineering disciplines.

Aslaksen and Belcher (1992) provide a general definition of Systems Engineering as an understanding of three components:

systems science - employing analysis techniques for resolving large-scale issues;

systems methodology – being able to move swiftly from one disciplinary area to another and thus being able to bring many sources of knowledge to bear on problem-solving; and

systems management – successful interaction of 'hard' (algorithmic) and 'soft' (behavioural) techniques to resolve large-scale issues.

They proposed several insights as directly relevant to a graduating engineer, particularly that Systems Engineering is a distinctive discipline which complements and extends the technical design basis of the chosen engineering discipline, and requires judgement of what is essential and superfluous data to provide a logical approach to projects.

The traditional design engineering disciplines provide the graduate engineer with a 'bottom-up' approach to their role in a project whereby they are designing a building block in the equipment or system. Systems Engineering on the other hand, takes a 'top-down' or 'big picture' approach, analysing the system in a holistic manner searching for suitable partitions and concentrating effort on the interfaces of the partitions. As Aslaksen and Belcher (1992) quite succinctly point out, many systems are so complex that the most important problem to be solved may in fact be deciding the method of handling all the variables and interactions. This is especially true when some of the system's variables include components (such as the human operators) which cannot be characterised in engineering terms or stated accurately as technical requirements.

Systems Engineering is not an end in itself, but usually only exists as a technical management process in a project environment. Indeed, Kasser (1996) concluded that Systems Engineering is a discipline 'created to compensate for the lack of strategic technical knowledge and experience by middle and senior project managers'. If this is correct, then education has only provided part of the answer to organisations' needs, and a real need exists to 'form' technocrats possessing technical credibility, a holistic view and management experience. While avoiding a detailed discussion of the merits and interfaces of the various disciplines represented in a technical enterprise, a guide to the perceived relationship between Systems Engineering and other directly related disciplines is presented graphically in Figure 1. It is important to note that Systems Engineering includes some elements of management, and is greater than the sum of the parts (for example the design contributions from the engineering specialties and the feedback provided by Test and Evaluation). It was pleasing to note that this facet was considered by Faulconbridge and Ryan (1999) when developing a Systems Engineering Body of Knowledge (SEBOK). One of the four main areas within their proposed SEBOK framework is Related Disciplines.

THE NEED TO DEVELOP SYSTEMS ENGINEERS

As the complexities of Systems Engineering become clearer for engineers and management, so does the need to develop Systems Engineers from the pool of trained engineers. Brown (1999) proposed that, 'INCOSE must champion the concept that SE is the art and science of harmonising content across disparate disciplines with process'. The science of Systems Engineering and its processes is readily taught in a suitable course. The art of harmonising is not so easily taught in a course, and so is a skill that must be learned from experience. Although formal education can provide the principles of Systems Engineering, more than this is needed to form

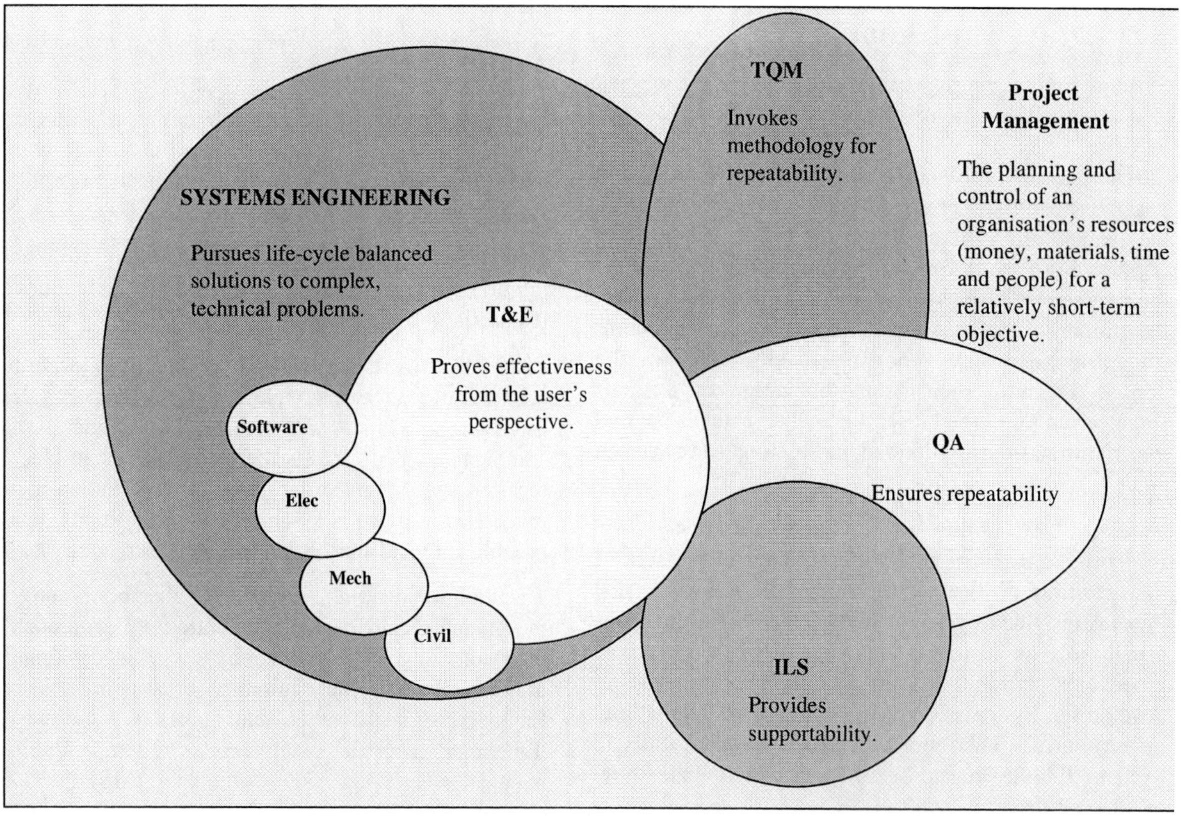

Figure 1. Relationship of Systems Engineering to Other Disciplines

Systems Engineers as they must gain the experience, individual growth and requisite 'ageing'.

Post-Graduate Education. At SEEC, the approach to Systems Engineering education is based upon this notion that a Systems Engineer is developed not just through formal training alone but requires artificial 'ageing' (i.e. professional and personal maturation) as well. Full-time post-graduate students are discouraged, as the Systems Engineering course in itself is considered insufficient. Rather, SEEC encourages employed engineers to undertake post-graduate study part-time, to allow them to pursue both their career and continuing education goals. In the case of determined full-time students without the necessary life experience, engineering maturity or industry background, SEEC seconds the student to industry for work experience to gain the industry relevance for further academic pursuit. Either way, the benefit to the university is that students are placed in the real-world 'laboratory'. As noted by Cook (1999), it is difficult to have a 'Complex System Industrial Laboratory' out the back of the faculty producing say, the next generation aircraft for instance.

In this respect, the need to develop Systems Engineers is not unlike the need to develop trained engineers in the first instance. The approach to 'ageing' a Systems Engineering candidate is akin to the work experience requirements of most undergraduate engineering courses.

Cultural Differences. Several secondary needs to form Systems Engineers are provided by the emerging nature of the discipline itself. For example, to achieve the international acceptance of Systems Engineering as a distinct discipline which INCOSE is striving for, Brown (1999) suggested that cultural differences need to be overcome. These cultural differences are not just the obvious differences in thinking and social life stemming from racial or regional cultures but also the cultural differences between the engineering disciplines and between enterprises (government versus commercial). One possible solution to this hurdle is to provide international experience as part of the development process. As an example of this need having been identified in industry, the Australian Submarine Corporation (ASC) is considering such a step, realising the likely benefits of having some of it junior engineers seconded to British shipyards to experience alternate approaches in a different engineering culture. ASC also considers an indirect benefit may also be borne from the accelerated maturation of the individuals as an indirect result of living and surviving outside their 'comfort zone' in a foreign culture.

CEA Technologies' Experience. In 1997 CEA Technologies, a radar firm headquartered in Canberra, Australia, trialled an in-house international scheme by sending a senior software design engineer on short-term attachment to its shop-front in San Diego, USA. This experiment was a great success, as the engineer got some life experience he was after, the American customers were well impressed by the on-site software support, and he brought back to the design house a wealth of customer-related and field-use lessons. The field support and marketing experience also developed a systems approach in the engineer, extending his design appreciation well beyond the code design aspects of the company's products. Management realised the marketing benefit more than compensated for the travel costs, and moreover that the development of systems thinking at a level below the Project Managers was of great benefit to the design effort and maintaining the competitive edge.

The company now has a regular cross-Pacific short-term placement programme for its engineers. Interestingly, the programme has been extended into non-engineering areas, such as short-term exchange of accounts department staff to provide a 'systems thinking' approach to other business units of the company.

Defence Workshop Proposed Model. At the Systems Engineering Society of Australia (SESA)/Department of Defence Workshop held in Canberra, Australia (1997), the need to develop Systems Engineers was discussed with several points recorded which tend to agree with the observations above. Indeed, the providers of Systems Engineering training were put on notice to consider the impact of social and cultural influences on engineering-related activities, along with the primary proposal that Systems Engineering training begins during the undergraduate specialisation education phase. The Workshop considered the most appropriate model to form competent Systems Engineers is:

1. An introductory Systems Engineering subject contained in the undergraduate engineering course.

2. Suitable work experience and on-the-job training to expose the new graduate engineers to a Systems Engineering approach to engineering and engineering management endeavours.

3. Specific post-graduate courses in Systems Engineering attended in short-course or long-course modes.

Lockheed-Martin Training Programme. The experience of Lockheed-Martin (USA) in implementing an in-house Systems Engineering programme provides interesting lessons regarding the importance of personal 'fit' and the influence of mentors. In his description of Lockheed-Martin's programme to develop Systems

Engineers, Kaufman (1997) admitted the success of the development process is highly dependent upon the personnel development and mentoring outcomes. Personnel development is based upon a value judgement of the 'right' set of experiences needed for each individual, and so nearly qualifies for the title 'Personal Development'. Mentoring was achieved by pairing a junior engineer with a senior engineer, with the purpose to transfer both technical and importantly, cultural knowledge, and to guide the personnel development steps.

MoD Graduate Engineer Trainee Programme. The U.K. Ministry of Defence (MoD) is sufficiently resourced to be able to form the civilian Systems Engineers it needs under its own programme - the Graduate Engineer Trainee Programme. The MoD recruits engineers with an Honours degree in a discipline suitable to the MoD's field (electrical, electronic, communications, mechanical, aeronautical, naval architecture or computer systems) and places them on a two-year professional development scheme. Notably, the eligibility criteria are based upon extra-curricular interests and demonstrated leadership potential as well as strong academic achievements.

In the U.K., the Standards and Routes to Registration (SARTOR) scheme is used to accredit engineers in line with the European Union guidelines. The MoD adds value to this by complementing the strict engineering discipline experiences with training to provide the engineers with the people, management and communications skills necessary to be a competent Systems Engineer in the MoD. The programme is broken into three phases:

1. *Induction Phase.* A weeklong Induction Course bridges the gap between university student life and the Graduate Engineer Trainee Programme. Each engineer is paired with a mentor, a volunteer Systems Engineer to guide the engineer through the programme.

2. *Work Experience Phase.* The main aim of this phase is to gain the work experience needed to qualify as a chartered engineer. Each work placement has a specific thrust, to cover the modules in the chartership logbook:

- Project Management
- Production, Research
- Design and Development
- Installation, Test, Commissioning, Repair and Maintenance.

The work placements are typically of three months duration and may be in commercial enterprises, defence industries or MoD units. Each placement is a 'personal fit' for each individual based upon the guidance of their mentor. There is no set order for the type of placements. During this phase, each trainee will also attend a four-week Systems Engineering course at the Royal Military College of Science.

Each trainee has the option to have one of the work placements overseas, in Germany, the United States of America or Australia. The benefit as cited by the MoD, is the opportunity to experience an engineering culture different to the British and therefore realise there are alternate methodologies successfully in use. Such a placement also accelerates personal growth and assists with the artificial 'ageing' needed for a Systems Engineer. About 80% of the trainees take up the offer of an overseas placement.

3. *Transfer Phase.* In this phase the trainee is on probation for up to three months in their first MoD position to allows on-the-job training and hand-over to bring the engineer to 'job standard' for their first real position.

SUGGESTED DEVELOPMENT APPROACH

The proposed template for developing Systems Engineers is an amalgam of the models discussed above. Figure 2 graphically summarises the proposed template.

Undergraduate. An introductory Systems Engineering subject is needed in undergraduate engineering degrees, and should be a core subject offered to final year undergraduates. This subject could be based upon one of the available Systems Engineering standards to lay the foundation of top-down processes and multi-disciplinary thinking. The details of this are well outside the scope of this paper, but have been addressed in part by the Educational Measurement Working Group of INCOSE (Sydenham, 1999) and the proposed SEBOK (Faulconbridge and Ryan, 1999).

Induction Phase. A short induction course is used to introduce the newly recruited engineers to the organisation's engineering processes. The individual engineers are paired with a mentor who plans the in-house work experience modules in the various areas or departments to ensure the right 'personal fit' for the engineer.

Training Phase. The training phase is used to gain experience in the organisation and qualify in most of the charter requirements of the professional body, as appropriate. The modules should follow the guidelines of the professional body, or at least follow the main Systems Engineering process steps.

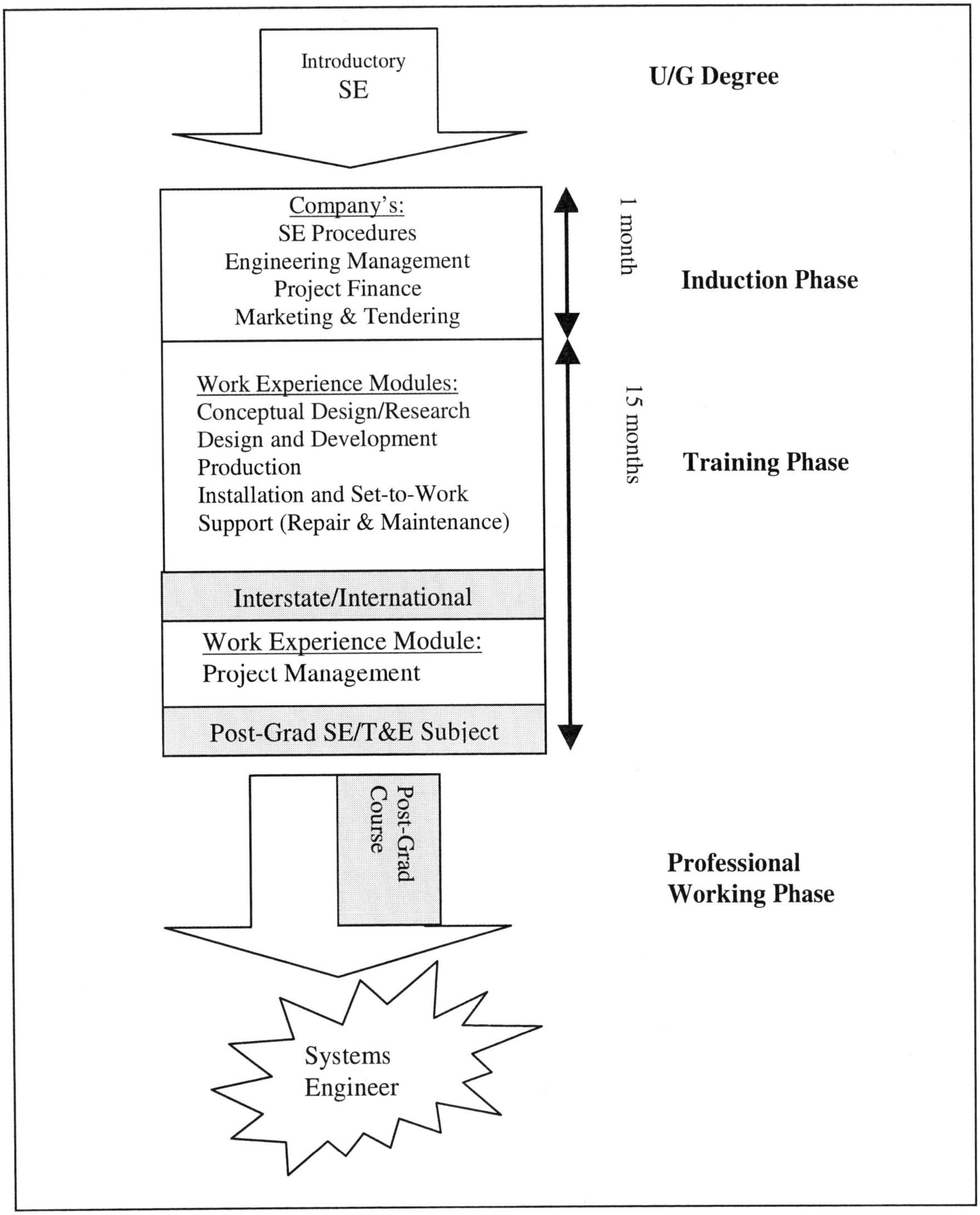

Figure 2. Proposed Template for Development of Systems Engineers

One of the modules should be conducted as a work placement interstate or overseas if resources allow. Placements with customer organisations (particularly end-users) or suppliers and sub-contractors should be encouraged, for reasons of good commercial sense and maintenance of business links. Particularly in small to medium sized enterprises lacking suitable functional areas for some of the modules, the use of business partners in the supply chain will allow work experience modules to be achieved while retaining linked benefit to the parent organisation.

The Project Management module and attendance on a Systems Engineering subject should be the last two activities of the Training Phase, to ensure the engineer has sufficient experience and maturity to get the most out of these modules. The post-graduate Systems Engineering or Test and Evaluation subject can be studied in part-time semester mode or in short course mode to suit availability, resource and scheduling concerns.

Professional Working Phase. This phase is simply the normal working life of a design engineer. Concurrently, a post-graduate award course (Masters or PhD) should be started early, as part-time awards can take up to six years to complete. The part-time study will provide the formal education in Systems Engineering to complement the evolving engineering experience and professional 'ageing', quickly leading to a Systems Engineer ripe for promotion.

A NICE IDEA, BUT

The author appreciates many firms and individuals cannot afford the luxury of the suggested approach to forming Systems Engineers. What are the options? Other approaches are considered to fall within the following categories:

- status quo (do nothing)
- rely on formal Systems Engineering education only
- have a planned induction programme within the organisation
- authenticate Systems Engineers.

The status quo approach is considered dangerous for the health of a business, as a technical organisation's competitiveness will be based in part, upon its ability to attract and retain competent technical staff including Systems Engineers. The training and development culture of a firm will continue to be a discriminating factor for individuals deciding to join, stay or go.

To rely upon engineers formally educated in Systems Engineering ignores the artistic aspect of Systems Engineering and the need to develop Systems Engineers through enterprise-level experience and artificial 'ageing'. The science of Systems Engineering is only half of the picture, and if an organisation does not develop the artistic side, then it will be left to utilise inferior Systems Engineers or else recruit the expertise at considerable cost.

A well planned induction programme may provide a enterprise view to the newly recruited staff, but in itself cannot provide the ongoing development to guide the individual in tune with their experiences, ability and needs. Importantly, such programmes can be too inwardly focussed, allowing the organisation in time to lag behind best practice. This lesson has been learned by the MoD and others such as ASC.

Authentication of Systems Engineers has been hotly debated in INCOSE for many years. The start point of describing an agreed body of knowledge for the discipline has yet to be achieved. Sydenham (1999) noted that optimal staff formation paths for Systems Engineering have yet to emerge and outlined INCOSE's efforts to identify the maturity of the three responsible sectors (academic, professional society and industrial). Efforts to accredit Systems Engineering education fail to progress due to many institutions unwilling to support mandatory accreditation and other problems associated with accreditation at international level (Sydenham, 1998).

CONCLUSION

Systems Engineering is more than a technical extension of the engineering disciplines, as it requires judgement and maturity to assess complex problems from a top-down view. A brief consideration of the relationship of Systems Engineering with other disciplines showed a reasonable overlap with management disciplines, confirming the multi-disciplinary nature of Systems Engineering.

The need to form Systems Engineers was derived from the perception that Systems Engineering is an art as well as a science. The artistic aspect is difficult to teach and so needs a structured experience-based programme supervised by a mentor. On-the-job training is stressed, complemented by formal Systems Engineering education begun early in an engineer's formative years.

The U.K. Ministry of Defence's Graduate Engineer Trainee Programme was presented as the main case study in which Systems Engineer development has been successfully used suitable work placements. Such work placements, particularly if one is cross-cultural by being with another firm, interstate or even international, add significant value and accelerate the professional 'ageing' of the engineers by exposing them to alternate engineering practices, cultural differences and character-building life experiences.

An approach for the structured development of Systems Engineers was proposed based upon early induction of Systems Engineering and work experience modules in the various phases of Systems Engineering. As a foundation, an introduction to Systems Engineering is needed in final year undergraduate degrees to set the scenario for systems thinking. Systems Engineers can then be developed from graduates through a structured process of Induction to the organisation's engineering processes, a deliberate Training Phase guided by a mentor, and study during the Professional Working Phase. During the Training Phase a business partner in the supply chain (an end-use customer or prime supplier) should be used for an interstate or international work placement for one of the training modules. A core subject of a post-graduate Systems Engineering course should be studied towards the end of the Training Phase also. Continuation of the post-graduate course needs to be strongly encouraged, to ensure the education foundation complements the build-up of experience, leading to a Systems Engineer in a timely fashion.

REFERENCES

Aslaksen, Erik and Belcher, Rod, *Systems Engineering*, Prentice Hall, 1992

Brown, Phil, 1999, 'SE Education & Research: A Global View', *Systems Engineering Society of Australia Newsletter*, No. 20, March, pp 3-4

Cook, Stephen, 1999, 'Systems Engineering Activities between Australian Academia and Industry', *Systems Engineering Society of Australia Newsletter*, No. 20, March, pp 12-13

Department of Defence, *DAO Strategic Plan 1998 – 2001*, [Online, accessed 4 Mar 1999]. URL: http://defweb.cbr.defence.gov.au/dao/strat/strat98.htm

Faulconbridge, Ian and Ryan, Mike, 1999, 'A Framework for Systems Engineering Education' in *Proceedings of SETE99 Systems Engineering, Test and Evaluation Conference*, Adelaide, Australia

Kaufman, Mark, 1997, 'Internal Development of Systems Engineers', in *Proceedings of INCOSE 97 Technical Program*, Los Angeles, USA

Kasser, Joseph, 1996, 'Systems Engineering: Myth or Reality', in *Proceedings of the 6th Annual International Symposium of the NCOSE*, Boston, USA

SESA/Defence Workshop, 1997, 'Systems Engineering Education, Training and Accreditation – Points Raised in Workshop', *Systems Engineering Society of Australia Newsletter*, No. 15, December, Annex E

Sydenham, Peter, 1998, 'Maturation and Assessment of Systems Engineering Educational Programs', in *Proceedings of SE98 Technical Papers*, Canberra, Australia

Sydenham, Peter, 1999, 'Operational Approach to Staff Formation for Systems Engineering', in *Proceedings of SETE99 Systems Engineering, Test and Evaluation Conference*, Adelaide, Australia

U.K. Ministry of Defence, *Graduate Engineer Trainee Programme* [Online accessed 10 Aug 1999] URL: http://www.desg.mod.uk/gto/eng/eng.htm

BIOGRAPHY

Michael Harris BSc (Hons), MSc (mvt) served in the Australian Army with several postings in Australia and overseas managing the T&E of armoured fighting vehicle systems and training simulators. His practitioner experience also includes development and evaluation of electronic warfare systems with CEA Technologies (Canberra, Australia). In his current position with the Systems Engineering and Evaluation Centre, Michael has consulted in T&E to Australia's Defence Department. He also manages the Centre's short course programme and the Australian involvement in the U.K. Ministry of Defence's Graduate Engineer Trainee Programme.

Electronic Systems Engineering (E-SE): Exploiting Internet Technology
– or –
A Project Portal Primer

Lawrence D. Pohlmann, Ph.D.
Strategics Consulting
Reston, Virginia

Abstract. Is it time for E-SE? Exploitation of internet technology by systems engineering (SE) will surely play heavily in our 'New Century of Opportunity.' This paper addresses the use of internet technology for supporting: a) systems engineering on a project, and b) systems engineering process improvement in an enterprise. The paper is intended to assemble a set of concise and potentially useful guidance into one place.

Principles behind the popularity of the web are discussed. These are related to the needs of project and enterprise systems engineering and program management activities. Potential dimensions of web use are described and related to the concept of a 'project portal.' A candidate project managers' wish list is presented. Lastly, a few comments are offered on futures of E-SE. We may indeed be entering the age of E-SE!

BACKGROUND

Internet technology is a significant phenomenon of the recent 'Decade of Progress.' In 1990, uses of hypermedia concepts were relatively rare. Almost no one foresaw the explosive growth in the use of internet technololgy – or the breadth and diversity of use that has become common today. As we enter this new millennium, most technology forecasters see the internet as playing an ever increasing role in many aspects or our work, as well as in our leisure and home life.

Motivations. Why this paper? Why now? In spite of the extensive progress that has been made in the use of internet technology, we seem to have just begun to address how to really use the technology to pursue 'world class systems engineering' in the words of the INCOSE charter. We are still in the 'unrestrained youth' stage in the words of Worden (1997).

While, indeed, a variety of progress on E-SE will sort of just happen – much as the growth of the web has happened – it also seems evident that we have tremendous opportunities to systems engineer E-SE. A need was perceived to assemble into one place a useful, concise primer of information about E-SE.

Focus of Paper. There are, of course, a number of possible dimensions of E-SE. Tools for computer assisted analysis, planning, scheduling and data management have been used for years. Similarly, there is extensive ongoing work in web-based tools for requirements management, systems modeling, and simulation. This paper is focused exclusively on describing potentially desirable characteristics of project web sites – characteristics that are deemed to faciliatate effective and efficient SE. This author is strongly of the opinion that a well-engineered project web site or "project portal" is an essential element of E-SE.

My Perspective. My perspective derives from: formal training in cognitive pscyhology and human information processing; experiences in computer programing and use – including development and use of web-based systems; experiences in human engineering, software engineering, and systems engineering; people and project management across a wide variety of contexts; and a deep and ongoing interest in process improvement. My interest is in looking for ways to make the life and activities of SE practitioners and managers easier, more effective, and more efficient.

Why Should We Care About E-SE? One of the authors' customers stated repeatedly and emphatically over an extended period "We will be increasingly using the web as our way of doing business." At the 1997 INCOSE symposium, an SE tool vendor proudly proclaimed "We're Web'ified." Many more of the SE tool vendors have migrated to increased web use and advocacy. The media are full of references to e-business and e-commerce. In the words of a recent popular commercial "You're E, or You're Out!"

It seems eminently reasonable to apply this same logic to SE. More and more companies are seeing efficient and effective SE as essential to remaining competitive in the 'New Century of Opportunity.' Therefore, isn't it likely that the company that doesn't seek to embrace and extend E-SE may rapidly become disadvantaged in SE practice and value added – and thus become less competitive?

THEORETICAL FOUNDATIONS FOR THE POPULARITY OF THE WEB

There are a number of legimate reasons why the web is popular. Dr. James Burke, the narrator for the "Connections" series on PBS television, proclaimed in a 1990: "For the first time in history, we are beginning to see computational support for the way people actually think" (Burke, 1990). He was discussing then-emerging hypermeida technology. He did not know he was talking about forthcoming internet technology and the world wide web. No one anticipated the extent or variety of web growth that has occurred in the 1990's.

It is relatively easy to identify a number of psychological principles, practical factors, and enterprise objectives, which can be collectively labeled the foundations for the popularity of the web. Understanding these can help us to make the right decisions in the design and development of project portals.

Psychological. There are a number of principles of human perception and information processesing that contribute to the web's popularity. These include internet technology's support for, but not limitation to:

- Information grouping and chunking
- Reasoning and data access by association
- Easy and fast navigation among levels of abstraction
- Being able to save your place, and return later
- Being able to retrace your steps
- Being able to interrupt and continue
- Enabling you to vary the sequence of data examination and review, i.e., you can work in your own style
- Enabling data relationships to be stored with the data – something that is impractical to impossible with paper documents, and with many databases
- Facilitating cognitive information mapping – that is the internal modeling of where things can be found

Practical. There are also a number of vary practical factors that make internet technology attractive; these include, but again are not limited to, being able to:

- Arrange it your way – yet stay within a common architecture and framework
- Navigate easily and quickly among related information stored in diverse locations – e.g., customer perspectives, requirements documentation, design specifications, change proposals, and test plans
- Establish multiple perspective dependent "starting points" and/or views. Various work teams and individuals can use these simultaneously. These starting point link lists can, for example, be based on:
  - Subsystem or component
  - User roles
  - Level of abstraction
  - Source or location of data
- Easily structure and restructure data and information relationships and associations
- Provide immediate publication and distribution – in several media – at very low cost
- Work and release incrementally – if not almost continuously. While this as a mixed blessing, a few guidelines can keep the process coordinated.
- Automatically notify a pre-identified group of people when a set of specific information is changed
- Collaborate in new ways, and with new efficiencies

Enterprise. Internet technology also appeals to the enterprise in that it has the potential to satisfy a number of corporate process improvement objectives. Some of these are support for:

- Simultaneous and nearly instantaneous information dissemination at comparatively low cost
- Much greater exploitation of single entry, single location storage of data elements. This can have tremendous impacts on document maintenance and version management. In the same vane, a level of change history content can be made directly and easily accessible
- Easier to use and maintain reuse repositories for processes, policies, procedures, lessons learned, and design process results and artifacts
- Easy and rapid propagation of processes, lessons learned, and process changes and improvements
- Ease of use – resulting in avoidance of at least some training costs
- Promoting consistency of documentation style
- Relatively easy and inexpensive data archiving and purging when necessary
- Relatively easy partitioning of data and data access across different sets of stakeholders with varying needs to know – with ease and relatively low cost
- Significantly reducing the time and expenses required for software tool maintenance and updating
- Routinely and frequently engaging in collaboration among geographically dispersed participants at a rich enough bandwidth that some otherwise necessary travel may be avoided

In Conclusion. When one stops to examine these types of foundations, is it really any wonder that the exploitation of internet technology has been experiencing explosive growth? Is it not easy to see extensive opportunities for E-SE?

The chances of project portal success – defined in terms of value added – are enhanced if we remain aware of the types of principles and factors mentioned above. These will be useful when identifying E-SE objectives, plans, and implementation approaches.

DIMENSIONS OF E-SE

There are a number of dimensions of web use on a project that can support effective and efficient SE. Matching specific dimensions of use to SE roles as defined by Sheard (1996, 2000) or Ring (1999) is a potential topic for another paper, or an exercise for the reader. While portal dimensions of use may be categorized in many ways, for purposes of this paper, typical dimensions of use include:

- Building and maintaining a shared vision of program objectives, products, processes, and progress
- Providing project orientation and training. We can certainly expect more internet-based training (IBT) in the future – at many different levels of granularity and topic depth.
- Providing resource libraries – e.g., for company and project policies and processes
- Supporting routine project processes – e.g., announcements, coordination memos, newsletters and releases, scheduling, calendaring, action item management, meeting agendas and minutes. We can expect increasingly capable and easy to use tools to continue to evolve for these uses. Not all of these are the sole purview of SE.
- Facilitating project coordination and supporting for collaborative work. This can occur in many ways. Net meetings, webcasts, desktop video conferencing are all within the state of the art – and are becoming easier and more affordable.
- Publishing and disseminating project products – ranging from simple, daily project announcements and news releases to major project document releases, such as plans, requirements documents, and design specifications
- Serving as the work products repository for the project – undoubtedly the largest and probably most important type of use on most projects
- Providing visibility to the relationships among products and among data within those products can be established – a visibility which can be easily established and easily updated
- Providing project publicity – promoting appropriate awareness about the project to customers, the (prime/subcontractor) development team, and the public

The value of having an easy-to-use project product repository – with embedded product and data relationships that are relatively easy to establish and maintain – should not be underestimated. This ability alone can contribute significantly to preventing or some of the historically troublesome and costly problems.

Everyone can now know, or at least have a better idea of, where the desired data is; and they can more easily find it. Many version management problems can disappear; it is now also much easier to maintain the integrity of data relationships. For example, it can be relatively easy to identify the potential impacts of a change in one data element, e.g., a specific requirement. The time lags and costs for project document distribution can virtually eliminated. For example, multiple, simultaneous accesses from geographically distributed locations (e.g., for review and comment) are now trivial. Collection and consolidation of customer and/or peer review comments is greatly facilitated.

In Summary. As web use increases a number of potentially high value advantages can accrue. SE resources can become more focused on higher value tasks, and less devoted to time consuming data management and routine coordination activities.

THE PROJECT 'PORTAL'

This section discusses the concept of the 'project portal', suggests some useful site metaphors, and talks about portal content. It ends with a discussion of some implementation issues and concepts.

Why "Portal"? The traditional definition of portal is "door, entrance; especially: a grand or imposing one" (Dictionary). The term has been adopted by the internet technology industry to mean a relatively concise, convenient gateway for accessing a variety of useful, interesing, or entertaining data – wherever that that data is located.

This portal metaphor is useful for E-SE. We define a "project portal" as a gateway to the collection of project data and data resources. That is, the portal can be viewed as the access mechanism to all of the information that has high utility for the project – wherever that data is located. The portal concept is applicable for almost all system development projects.

Project Portal Premises. Five basic premises are offered for project portal design and implementation:

- Content is king – After the novelty wears off, content will determine the utility of the site. Avoid the type of "Cute" and "clever" that are likely to get old quickly. Use animation very sparingly.
- Follow the life cycle – The project portal must mature and evolve with the project. The nature of the content and structure will migrate over time with the needs of the various phases of the project.
- Keep it simple – for example don't duplicate information, link to it, or abstract and link
- Accommodate a range of users and stakeholders – while the primary intended audience may be well-informed, frequent visitors to the site, plan the site to be easy to use for new or infrequent users. Provide site guides and maps to help then understand how the

site is structured. Recognize that different stakeholders will be interested in different data.
- It's only a tool – an important and essential tool, but still only a tool. Be wary of the portal becoming a project with a life and set of objectives of its own.

Mind Your Metaphors. It is often appropriate to use a metaphor when structuring the content and style of a section of the project web site. Use a structure metaphor appropriate for the intended audience, the type of information and expected use of the content. Some of the commonly used site metaphors include:
- Tour – has interesting places to go, with maps, guides, and lists of interesting characteristics or features of the places visited
- Library – contains resources, books, indexes, links or pointers to related information that may be useful
- Data Log – includes a record of events, normally organized chronologically
- Book – consists of a table of contents, several chapters, one or more indexes, and possibly appendices
- Model – is organized as a hierarchical structure, often includes component details from multiple viewpoints and/or from multiple levels of abstraction
- Classroom – is made up of courses, sessions, and mentoring help. May include a number of job aides such as guidebooks, checklists, concise tutorials, etc.
- Professional network – is a network structure that provides ways to find and access colleagues with similar problems, or ways to get to 'the company expert' on topics or problems of interest.

For example, the 'Tour" metaphor may be particularly useful for the publicity part of the portal. It is also well suited to a project that is in the pre-system definition or concept exploration phase. Thus, each concept alternative may be viewed an 'interesting place to go' and having a variety of unique interesting features which are described at varying and appropriate levels of detail.

Style. What about site style and format? The comment "Temperate temperance is best . . ." (attributed to Mark Twain) is appropriate. A modest amount of style guidance is probably sufficient. The style guidance should make it easy to do the right thing. Excessive style and format guidance results in too much time devoted to compliance, and less devoted to higher value activities by the project staff. Seven simple guidelines on style are offered.
- Strive for minimal policy and guidance on style
- Evolve toward a set of enterprise-maintained style guidance that facilitates commonality of core portal functions across projects. (Recognize that other portal design aspects and guidance will also evolve).
- Emphasize fundamentals, e.g.,
  - Page and content identification and labeling
  - Navigation basics
  - Consistency of structure and format within sections – and possibly to appropriate project plans
  - Credits – page content owner, curator, last update
- Establish easy-to-use templates for common types of information – e.g., meeting agendas and minutes, process descriptions, news and announcements, and project reports and documents
- Facilitate web site internal consistency via libraries of elements for reuse – i.e., by having available the necessary backgrounds, buttons, icons, navigation aids that should be routinely used
- Recognize and use applicable site metaphors
- Be rigid on only a few items (e.g., corporate identity matters, and links to corporate/division home pages), provide guidance on other 'important' items (e.g., preferred approaches to page identification and standard navigation concepts), and be flexible on the rest. Make it easy to understand what is expected.

Typical Types of Content. What kinds of data should be accessible via the project portal? Content requirements (and desirements) will vary with the nature, scope, and unique requirements of the projets, as well as with the size and experience of the team and the stage of the lifecycle. Plan for intended content and structure, but also be flexible enough to let content evolve. Periodically reassess whether the types of content are adding value.

The list below is not intended to imply that SE practitioners on the project are responsible for all of the types of data listed. They may however have an interest that these data are generated and posted – thus facilitating the variations of SE and program management coordination that contribute to program success.

Types of suggested project portal content include:
- Project orientation and training materials
  - System vision
  - Concept of operations
  - Project or program objectives
  - Links to customer sites that can provide project perspective and requirements understanding
  - Top level requirements and MOEs
  - Project background and history
  - Customer and project organization data
  - Team members and roles, prime contractor and subcontractor statements of work, who's who lists
  - Authoring and posting guidance and templates
- Project plans and status
  - Project management plans, e.g., risk management plan, SEMP & IMP (if appropriate)
  - Project news
  - Meetings & Minutes

- Schedules and calendaring
  - Process guidance – at multiple and appropriate levels of granularity
- Project generated documents and results – all appropriately inter-linked together
  - System objectives and concept of operations
  - Requirements data
  - Design data – generally includes a variety of types
  - Testing data
  - Glossary and acronyms
- Navigation aids
  - Site maps and guidance on using the site
  - What's new?
  - Starting points
  - Frequently asked questions (FAQ)
  - Capabilities for searching the site
- Add-My-Information mechanisms

Add My Information. This feature is singled out because of its importance. An essential capability for widespread use is that individual users <u>must</u> be able to post – autonomously and easily – the project data and information that they have generated. Data should go into a relatively well-defined project web site structure. Fortunately, as web tools continue to evolve, this aspect is getting easier. Soon easy-to-use web posting tools will be routinely included in standard office automation tool suites. This add-my-information capability should follow three basic principles:

- Support all of the standard information formats required by the project
  - Typically these include specifications, agendas, minutes, presentations, spreadsheets, reports, correspondence, forms, photographs, and model and design data. May increasingly include animation, audio, and video data element
- Make it easy to find where to put our data; and make it easy to put it there. This may mandate not only describing the posting capabilities inherent in the site, but also making available useful online guidance and training on the posting process.
- Minimize the administrative burden on the individual participants. For example, when new information is posted, it may be desirable that an identifier for the added information is automatically added to the "What's New?" section of the project portal.

Project Portal Implementation Concepts. The project web site itself will be a mini-project that must be systems engineered; therefore we need to follow basic systems engineering principles.

- Vision==>ConOps==>Reqs==>Plan==>Design
- Identify your customers – there are normally multiple levels of external and internal customers for the site. They will have data needs that differ in nature, granularity, and level of abstraction. The content and access needs of these stakeholders may vary.
- Support your processes
  - Provide process documentation and guidance
  - Provide process training – or links to where training at multiple levels of depth and sophistication can be found
  - Help to solve process problems
  - Have a place to collect process improvement suggestions and lessons learned
- Plan for, expect, and be satisfied with controlled, prioritized growth – not every capability of the portal needs to be implemented at the same time
- Be constantly aware that "Content is King!"
- Always strive for valued added

This last point is stressed. The project portal concept should go far beyond being a simple data storage repository and access mechanism. Thus, it is essential to define and understand the nature of potential types of value that can be added. At the same time, the project portal is really only another tool, although a very important one. Thus, portal development needs to avoid the portal becoming a major goal in and of itself – and thus ending up as a resource sink, and not producing the expected nature or extent of value added.

Regarding content, adhering to a few principles for the management of project data seems appropriate.

- Make sure the data is needed to support the project objectives and processes
- Make the data easy to find
- Make the data ease to use
- Make it easy for any authorized project participant to put new data in the most appropriate place
- Strive to keep data appropriately current – and provide ways to distinguish old data from current data
- Ensure that each type of specific data has an owner
- Make sure the data evolve appropriately with the project. For example, do not continue to collect and post metrics that were important earlier, but that are not relevant to the current phase of the project.

PUBLISHED CASE STUDY DATA

The INCOSE SE & the Internet Interest Group has begun to assemble a set of potentially relevant case studies. Emphasis is on papers and web sites that provide guidance, results, or lessons learned about the structure, implementation, or use of project web sites. An annotated list of these will be available on the Interest Group's web site. Selected examples are cited.

The early work on the HornetWeb for supporting requirements specifications management for the F/A-18 E/F (see Kepchar, 1996, and Scheurer and Kepchar, 1997) was an excellent example of extensive, high value use of a project web site. It involved integration of web tools, a requirements database, and data publishing/print tools. The effort demonstrated very positive benefits of more complete, precise, and timely coordination of specification changes, as well as signficant cost reductions in specificatons related document distribution. Positive impacts on customer relationships and customer satisfaction were also noted.

Van Gaasback and his colleagues (1998) discuss ongoing development at Northrup Grumman of web-based approaches for issue closure, action tracking, and overall program "health visibility." Worden (1998) discusses internet-based distance learning concepts and tools. Jones and Arunski (1998) discuss use of an SE web site for process- and lessons learned-related communications and networking among 700+ systems engineers within the Raytheon Systems Company. Several of their lessons learned are provided.

Mackey and Bagg (1999), in decsribing a NASA web-based lessons learned repository, discuss six categories of issues, including political, legal, security, access, technical deployment, and quality. Another important aspect of the work by the Mackey team is the use of a case-based reasoning (CBR) tool as part of the site. This work may lay some of the foundation for much broader use of CBR techniques for E-SE.

Collins and North (1999) discuss the design, implementation, and management of a SE database for a large project in the United Kingdom. Although they did not emphasis web-based concepts, their conclusions on useful content and organizational issues are equally applicable to web-based project portals. Myers and Verma (1999) discuss specific tools and implementation concepts for a web-based Product Data Management system and environment. Their context was promoting multidisciplinary collaboration for implementing cost-as-an-independent-variable (CAIV) concepts in COTS integration intensive systems.

One of the more interesting case studies to date was recently done by Brown and Lavender (1999). This case is interesting for two reasons. First, it is a second-generation case in that the work was initiated after seeing a demonstration of the HornetWeb discussed above. Second, they attempted to compute cost avoidance as a return on investment selected features of their project portal development work. One natable cost avoidance result was more than $4 million per year for an extended period. This, and other similar feature benefit analyses resulted in "eye catching ROIs" of from hundreds to several thousand percent.

Several E-SE-related case studies were presented at the recent INCOSE Mid-Atlantic Regional Conference (see www.incose-marc.org). For example, Myers and his colleagues (2000a, 2000b) discussed collaborative engineering environments. Kasser (2000) described a series of efforts in web-based conferencing. Romano and Crannell (2000) identified approaches for improving the requirements definition and validation process. Shurn and his colleagues (Chipman et al, 2000) discuss a long running effort at developing web-facilitated supply chain management.

Conclusions. Project web sites work! And they add value in a number of ways! There is a growing body of evidence on the value of project web sites – and on lessons learned in their design and implementation. Examples of specific E-SE contributions to faster, better, and cheaper SE and systems development are becoming numerous and easy to find.

A PROJECT MANAGER'S WISH LIST

In thinking about enterprise support of project web sites, one useful approach is to build and maintain some type of project managers' wish list. If you are a manager about to take on a new project, what kinds of web site related capabilities would you like to see readily available from your enterprise?

On the basis of numerous discussions about project web sites, ten concepts are offered as a point of departure for such a list. These can help to drive web exploitation strategy, planning, and implementation.

The Enterprise Already Embraces the Internet. Achieving management buy-in and willingness to commit resources is always a continuing challenge. It would be desirable if the major culture changes toward viewing the web and E-SE as essential for competiveness have already been accomplished. The appropriateness of the motto Microsoft used as they shifted to increased emphasis on internet technology comes to mind: "Embrace and Extend!"

Enterprise-based Incremental Evolution. In recognition of the potential importance, utility, and value added of good project web sites, the enterprise has established a reuseable architecture and set of suppoting tools. There is continuing planning and investment for incremental improvement in project web site development and use. Some companies have established webmaster councils or working groups toward this end.

We're Already Wired. Infrastructure is a concern. It can be costly. It has a lead time. Thus, a program manager can be expected to wish that the project facilities are already wired with sufficient bandwidth to support intended uses of the project portal.

Start Early – Before Award, Usually Before Bid. When should a project portal be created? The existence of a project web site can help E-SE activities even early in the business development cycle – long before there is a request for proposal, certainly before award. Thus it is important that the enterprise encourages, expects, and possibly even demands that a project web site be established early.

Up in a Day, Robust in a Week, Always Up to Date. It should be possible to bring up a basic project portal in a day. This is not unreasonable if the enterprise has an overall site template that just needs to be hosted and populated. Not all links need to be active immediately, but the framework of what will come can be made operational very quickly. Posting and linking of existing project data to date onto the site should only take a few more days. From that point on, portal content can continue to evolve as the project requires. The portal will be most useful if it is up to date. The goal should be near real time (e.g., daily) posting of key accomplishments and important data.

Authoring Tools, Templates, and Guidance for Each Data Type. It is desireable that the enterprise has identified common data types that will normally be created on projects. The goal is to have the tools, templates, and guidance to use them available for each of these data types. This could be a task for the enterprise's 'webmaster council.' This guidance should evolve over time as the enterprise and the projects learn the types of guidance that are the most useful.

Nearly Self-Organizing. There should be enough guidance on the web site that it is easy for an authorized project participant to get his or her data posted in a logical place and linked appropriately to related data. Another webmaster council task?

Commonality Aspirations. As stated above, the different customer sets for the project portal will have differing data content and access needs. It would be desirable if the enterprise employed a common approach across projects. While it is also recognized that different customers and different sets of team members may impose some constraints in this regard, the goal should be maximum commonality of approach.

Relative Tool Independence. It is generally desirable that the project portal is relatively independent of specific tools and tool vendors. The technology is moving to rapidly to become locked into a long-term relationship with any tool vendor. There may be exceptions.

Structural Agility. The structure of the site may need to evolve with project. Sufficient flexibility should be designed into the portal so that when restructuring is necessary, it is not prohibitively expensive.

FUTURES

It seems appropriate to end with a few brief comments on futures. While one could focus entirely on futures, this paper concludes with three predictions, two challenges, and one grand opportunity.

Three Predictions. Three predictions are offered:

- While, increased E-SE is seen as inevitable, the rate of value growth of E-SE will be dependent on how much we SE the E-SE capabilities and process.
- The efficiency of E-SE will depend in no small way in understanding and using some of the principles of data management that have long been espoused by data management professionals.
- We will see plateaus of web use and exploitation. A typical sequence of these may be: Novelty ==> Limited Use ==> Routine Resource ==> Essential Tool ==> Strategic, Managed Resource.

Two Challenges. As some of my military friends would say, we are in a target rich environment. There are many ways to exploit internet technologies for achieving better systems engineering. Two primary challenges are:

- Deciding on a set of priorities and sequence of E-SE development that will provide high leverage
- Ensuring the right types of mutual understanding and collaboration among SE practitioners, process improvement experts, data management practitioners, and human factors engineers. Only through such collaboration will the truly most effective and efficient approaches to E-SE be identified and developed.

One Opportunity. The 'New Century of Opportunity' will be full of opportunities for SE practitioners, INCOSE, and the companies that will all use SE to do good things. It seems inevitable that SE processes will continue to be improved, refined, and extended to less additional domains. In the context of E-SE, the opportunity is:

- We have recently entered the optimal window of opportunity for using SE to develop and evolve E-SE concepts and capabilities. It would good to aggressively use this opportunity.

Doing so could help the practitioners of SE, could help entire projects, could help the companies that believe in and use SE, and could result in better products as a result of the exploition of internet technologies for E-SE. May we vigorously pursue this opportunity!

REFERENCES

Brown, Phillip J, and Lavander, Jack K., "Exploiting Web-Based Technology to Foster IPDT Productivity," *Proceedings of INCOSE,* 1997

Burke, James. "The Death of Descarte." Unpublished Presentation, Seattle, 1990,

Chipman, Richard, Laskey, Kenneth J., Paul, Arthur S., and Shurn, Todd E., Missile Industry Supply-Chain Technology Initiative," *Proceedings of INCOSE Mid-Atlantic Regional Conference,* 2000

Collins, Rob, and North, Lee, The Design Implementation and Management of a Systems Engineering Database," *Proceedings of INCOSE, 1999.*

[Dictionary] Merriam-Webster's Collegiate Dictionary. www.m-w.com/netdict.htm

Kasser, Joseph, "A Web-Based Asynchronous Conference: A Case Study," *Proceedings of INCOSE Mid-Atlantic Regional Conference,* 2000.

Kepchar, Kenneth J., "Automating the Spec Management Process," *Proceedings of INCOSE,* 1996.

Mackey, William, and Bagg, Thomas C., "Systems Issues Related to Implementing on the Internet," *Proceedings of INCOSE,* 1999.

Myers, Kenneth N., and Verma, Dinesh, "System Design to Affordability In a Collaborative Systems Engineering Environment," *Proceedings of INCOSE, 1999.*

Myers, Kenneth N., and Nguyen, Mimi, "Exploiting the Collaborative Engineering Environment as a Critical Resource Multiplier," *Proceedings of IN-COSE Mid-Atlantic Regional Conference,* 2000 (a).

Myers, Kenneth N., and Beckley, Jennie, "A Web-Centric Collaborative Engineering Environment For Product Centered Lifetime Support," *Proceedings of INCOSE Mid-Atlantic Regional Conference,* 2000 (b).

Pohlmann, Lawrence D., "Internet Technology Will Change the Practice of Systems Engineering," Presentation for the Washington Metropolitan Area Chapter of INCOSE, October, 1997. [Also presented to the Chesapeake Chapter of INCOSE, March, 1998.]

Ring, Jack, "'They' Call It Knowledge Management," *Proceedings of the Thirteenth International Conference on Systems Engineering,* 1999

Romano, Joseph J., and Crannell, Mary E., "Improving Requirements Synthesis Using Group Decision Support And Virtual Teams," *Proceedings of INCOSE Mid-Atlantic Regional Conference,* 2000

Sheard, Sarah A., "Twelve Systems Engineering Roles," *Proceedings of INCOSE,* 1996.

Sheard, Sarah A., "Systems Engineering Roles Revisited," *Proceedings of INCOSE Mid-Atlantic Regional Conference,* 2000.

Romano, Joseph J., and Crannell, Mary E., "Improving Requirements Synthesis Using Group Decision Support And Virtual Teams" *Proceedings of INCOSE Mid-Atlantic Regional Conference,* 2000

van Gaasbeek, James. R., Sunday, David A., and Manuel, Gregory C. "Improvement of Systems Engineering on a Mature Program," *Proceedings of INCOSE,* 1998

Worden, Gregory, "A simplified and Evolutionary Hypermediacy Model For Project Management," *Proceedings of INCOSE,* 1997.

Worden, Gregory, "The New Academia: Computer-Based Distance Learning. Case Study," *Proceedings of INCOSE,* 1998

BIOGRAPHY

Dr. Lawrence D. Pohlmann provides consulting support for systems and organizational development. During his 30-year career, he has conducted high technology research and development for complex systems in industrial, government, and academic settings. He has applied and extended systems engineering techniques in several applications domains.

His degree is in Information Processing and Experimental Psychology; he has taught and conducted research in academic settings, and has been a systems engineering mentor. In business settings, he has applied SE to internal process design and improvement for a variety of business processes, including systems engineering, software engineering, ergonomics, business development, and business systems.

Dr. Pohlmann is a founding member of INCOSE, has initiated and managed a number of the technical working groups, has served in elected leadership positions, and developed the first Strategic Plan for the Council. He was recently the Technical Chair for the INCOSE Mid-Atlantic Regional Conference (see www.incose-marc.org).

Email: pohlmann@incose.org

Cognitive and Personality Characteristics of Successful Systems Engineers

Moti Frank
Technion – Israel Institute of Technology
Technion city, Haifa 32000 Israel
Judea and Samaria College
Ariel 44837 Israel

Abstract. According to the title, an extensive research was conducted with an objective to identify the characteristics of engineers with high 'engineering systems thinking' thinking skills and the processes by which it is acquired. The main question of the research was "what are the qualifications (knowledge, skills and aptitudes) required from systems engineers?" The General Systems Theory (GST) and the SCAW Model (Systematic Curriculum Alignment and Watch Model) for curriculum design of engineering disciplines constitute the theoretical frame of the research. Eighty-three categories were found in 28 interviews, 14 lectures and 2 observation sites which may be assorted as follows: Ten categories referring to the definition of engineering systems thinking. Four categories deal with various types of systems thinking. Fifteen categories relate to knowledge required from systems engineers. Thirty-one categories cover the skills demanded of systems engineers. Fifteen categories explore the personal aptitudes demanded of the systems engineers. Lastly, eight categories examine processes through which the system thinking capability is developed.

THE RESEARCH RATIONALE

Introduction. One of the noteworthy findings in a research performed at the Technion – Israel Institute of Technology (Frank, 1996) was that as technological systems grow larger, more complex and inter-disciplinary, the demand increases in the electronics and hi-tech industries for engineers with a capability of systems thinking as well as the recognition of Systems Engineering as an appropriate academic discipline.

In this context, a question is raised: what is 'engineering systems thinking', and whether it is a capability or skill that can be acquired in an academic institution? Attempts to interpret the findings of above research indicated that although the term 'engineering systems thinking' is commonly used in the engineering community, the research-engineering literature has no formal definition for this term. Different engineers who were asked to define engineering systems thinking came up with different answers, most of which were based on examples from their current practice.

Following the widespread use of the term 'systems thinking' in the engineering community, and realizing the immense importance of the subject, and in the wake of the findings of above-mentioned research, it was decided to study this subject within the framework of a doctorate research (Frank, 1999).

As seen below, the General Systems Theory (GST) and the SCAW Model (Systematic Curriculum Alignment and Watch Model) for curriculum design of engineering disciplines (Waks, 1995) constitute the theoretical frame of the research.

We discuss here man-made technological systems. Specifically, the research deals with hardware-software integrated systems, the main discipline in them are being electronics. Examples for the said systems may be found in the computer network of a large bank, state cellular telephone net, avionics system of an advanced fighter aircraft and so on. Systems engineers are involved in each stage of these systems' life cycle, whose function is to "see" the entire project by holistic thinking and bring it to its successful conclusion. This research deals with these engineers. All hi-tech organizations maintain today the function of a "system engineer" in most of the teams of the technological systems development projects.

It should be stressed that the term "system" applies to both simpler electronic systems, such as the facsimile, and to more complex systems (mega-systems). The term is also used in other engineering disciplines. Indeed, in this research we deal mainly with systems from the electronic engineering field, but the research results might be generalized to other disciplines also.

The main idea underlining this research was to identify the cognitive and personal characteristics and abilities of engineers having a high 'systems thinking' thinking skills. In particular, the discrimination between those endowed with such skills and those who are not was studied. It was assumed that a curriculum for constructing an 'engineering systems thinking' may be developed on the basis of those characteristics. For purposes of this research, a systems engineer with high 'systems thinking' thinking skills is one who was evaluated as such by most of his/her peers and supervisors.

The Research Objective and the Research Questions. The research was about 'engineering systems thinking'. The research objective was to identify the characteristics of engineering systems thinking and the processes by which it is acquired. Bearing in mind this objective, the following main questions were formulated: (1) what are the aptitudes (knowledge and skills) to be possessed by systems engineers? (2) What are the processes by which the engineering system thinking is acquired? (3) What are the personal aptitudes and abilities characterizing engineers with a capability of engineering systems thinking?

This study also sought to point out the relationships between different system terms, system engineering and system thinking concepts and between the different opinions of practitioners on the required skills of successful systems engineers.

LITERATURE REVIEW

The General Systems Theory – GST. During recent times, scientists, philosophers and mathematicians tried to construct a theory that could unite the various scientific branches. The product of these efforts - The General Systems Theory - constitutes a powerful frame for the understanding of the world around us in both natural and man-made systems.

In the research literature, Bertalanffy is commonly referred to as the founder of the General Systems Theory - GST. In the introduction to his book (Bertalanffy, 1968), the author writes:

"The notion of systems has been used long ago by man to describe complex mechanisms of the universe which consist of objects and relations".

Bertalanffy argued that the theory's objectives are to learn and identify the integration processes existing in sciences, in nature and in society and develop universal uniform principles, implementable in all sciences and in scientific education. In his opinion, due to technological progress, the problems arising are so complex that the traditional analytical-linear analysis methods are insufficient. Therefore systemic analysis methods are needed in economy, industry, education, urban planning, society and organizations.

According to Shenhar (1991), the General Systems Theory - GST contains a system of arguments, based on inter-disciplinary comparisons which by applying it to one specific scientific field, assist in solving problems and in explaining phenomena and processes in the said field. In an article by Katz and Kahn (1966), reviewing the common characteristics of the open systems and discussing the application of the open systems theory in the analysis of social organizations, one could find many examples of these comparisons.

According to Matthews (1992), the basis of Bertalanffy's theory is "similarity of all systems". Craczyk (1993) also stresses the ability to compare systems from different disciplines:

"It is not a single discipline but a collection of knowledge from many fields, its main focus is the similarities found in systems of al kinds. This emphasis on homogeneity allows systems models to be applied to many different situations".

GST could facilitate the analysis of complex problems and provide a macroscopic and holistic point of view while referring to a large number of aspects. The theory enables to examine the interaction between the system's elements, and it may be applied in the analysis of the entire system, its sub-systems and the interactions between the whole, its parts and the environment.

What is a System? Many definitions may be found in the literature, of the term "system". I will settle here for Otenberg's (1995) definition, given in the Internet site of INCOSE:

"What is a system? This is not such a simple question to answer. Philosophers have been working on this one for along time! For the sake of simplicity, let's just say that a system is a group of interacting interrelated or interdependent elements that together form a complex whole. All the parts of a system are related to the same overall process, procedure, or structure, yet they are all different from one another and often perform completely different functions".

Systems Engineering. According to Ottenberg (1995), systems engineering is a discipline, combining management and design approaches for the purpose of structuring and thereby designing large and complex interdisciplinary systems, by the following principles:

A. Top - down design.
B. Bottom-up integration.
C. Each system has a life cycle.
D. The customer and/or user's involvement is important and central.
E. The engineering designing takes into account optimum considerations.

Here is a quote from the Internet site of The Institute for Systems Research (http://www.isr.umd.edu):

"Real world engineering projects typically require the systems-level cooperation of experts from several engineering disciplines... Systems engineering is a discipline that develops and exploits structured, efficient approaches to analysis and design to solve complex engineering problems... systems engineering focuses on methodology rather than physical manifestations of science and engineering hardware.... Industrial demand for systems engineering is so strong and pervasive that systems engineering is highly focused on applications and the rapid exploitation of tools and methods for problem-solving, while the research engine for systems engineering, primarily in universities, must concentrate mostly on the complex mathematical methods and algorithms needed at the basis of these tools.... Systems engineering finds its focus in formulating analysis and synthesis ways for problems involving multiple aspects of the real world... Systems engineering is embodied largely in computer-based representation...these methods include such elements as system response functions, trade-off analysis, specifications and performance metrics, optimization methods... Marginal and sensitivity analysis... Programming, scheduling, control, databases... Cost estimation, decision analysis, modeling and simulation, and software environments and tools".

Systems Thinking. The method by which a complex problem is dismantled to components allegedly facilitates handling complex assignments and questions, but when doing so we lose the perception of the larger whole. According to Senge (1994), systems thinking is a discipline for seeing the whole. It is a framework for seeing interrelationships and repeated events rather than things, for seeing patterns of change rather that static 'snapshots'. It is a set of general principles, specific tools and techniques that have developed in recent years. Systems thinking is the perception of the "constructs" underlying complex problems and the distinction between changes that might cause significant improvements by minimum effort (the principle of leverage). The structure of our language does not allow one to describe a situation in which A causes B, when B causes A and both keep continuous interaction with C and D. Systems thinking offers us, for this purpose, a language that expands, changes and shapes our ordinary way of thinking in regard to complex issues.

According to O'Connor & McDermott (1997), systems thinking is:

"... Our normal pursuit from a cause and effect perspective is to try and find where the fault lies. A systems thinking perspective, however, enables us to understand... why simply faultfinding is such a futile activity. Systems thinking enables one to progress beyond simply seeing evens to seeing patterns of interaction and the underlying structures that are responsible for the patterns... Systems thinking looks at the whole, and the pats, and the connections between the parts, studying the whole in order to understand the parts. It is the opposite to reductionism..."

While according to Kim (1995), systems thinking is:

"Systems thinking embodies the idea that the interrelationship among parts relative to a common purpose of a system are what are important".

"You know that you can speak the system's language skillfully.... when it becomes second nature, when you find yourself thinking in it, when you don't have to translate a causal circle or an archetype into English to figure it out.... If you start thinking differently, you see things differently and all your actions start to change" (Senge et al, 1994, p.88).

METHODOLOGY

The research stages. The research was run in three stages. The first stage was a pilot research, in which 11 in-depth, open, non-structured and non-standard interviews were held with key figures. The second stage comprised tens of hours of the-observer-as-participant' observations in two hi-tech companies, 17 semi-constructed interviews and content analysis of 14 lectures that were given in a seminar on systems engineering. In the third stage of the research, a survey has been conducted based on a pilot questionnaire (N=31) and a final questionnaire (N=276). The qualitative paradigm was found to be suitable for the first and second stages mainly because the research examines processes in the natural environment where the subjects operate. The number of interviews and observations at the first and second stages was not set in advance. The criterion to conclude the data collection was saturation; adding more subjects did not add significant new findings.

The research cycle. The research structure has developed during the data collection, with no prior assumptions. There was no definition of the systems thinking at the beginning of the research. It was unclear what the criteria should be for selection of the subjects. A quantitative research was unsuitable because at least at the beginning, it was not specified what should be measured. So, a spiral layout was used – one that begins with an unknown, collects some data, updates and corrects and so on. The selection of the first subjects was based on two prime criteria: (1) Senior systems engineers possess systems thinking capability. (2) Supervisors' opinion is a valid information source.

The research continued with a slow progress of constant examination of the hypotheses and updating them as necessary. The definition of the systems thinking was evolved in the course of the research.

The data analysis strategy. The data analysis strategy was "content analysis": definition of the analysis units, setting **the categories** (outstanding repeated elements) and examination of frequencies.

MAJOR FINDINGS

Eighty-three categories were found in 28 interviews, 14 lectures and 2 observation sites that may be assorted as follows:

A. Ten categories referring to the definition of engineering systems thinking.

B. Four categories deal with various types of systems thinking.

C. Fifteen categories relate to knowledge required from systems engineers.

D. Thirty-one categories cover the skills demanded of systems engineers.

E. Fifteen categories explore personal aptitudes demanded from systems engineers.

F. Eight categories examine processes by which the system thinking capability is developed.

Categories Referring to the Definition of Engineering System Thinking:

(1) Understanding the whole – comprehends the whole system and the overall picture. Understands how each element operates as part of the entire system. Understands how the sub-systems link to the system.

(2) Synergy - regards the whole as larger than the sum of its parts and is able to identify the advantages stemming from the integration of the sub-systems.

(3) Comprehensive conception (not only in the engineering aspect) - understands and is capable of describing the system in all relevant perspectives. On the upper level - technological, economic, managerial, social aspects. On the system level – electrical, mechanical and operational aspects. On the engineering level - capable of examining the subject from various perspectives.

(4) Overall understanding of a new system - understands generally a system upon its presentation.

(5) Modifications - understands and is capable of anticipating all the implications of modifications entered in the system.

(6) Complexity - understands and is capable of describing the operation of complex systems.

(7) Interaction - understands and is capable of describing the interactions (some of its covert) and the hierarchical connections between the sub-systems (and between the system and systems around it).

(8) Analysis - capable of following signals and processes from the input through all the sub-systems and the interfaces to the output. Capable of delving from the whole down to the details and analyzing the systems by dismantling the whole to its components.

(9) Synthesis - capable of giving engineering solutions and designing from end to end. Capable of assembling sub-systems into a system.

(10) System failures and problems - capable of locating system malfunctions diagnosing the failure and outlining the solution.

To summarize:

A system engineer must be capable of anticipating, understanding and detailing all the implications (including the side effects) of the modifications, engineering as well as non engineering, both those initiated by the contractor and those required by the customer after the system has been handed over or after "closing" the design. On many occasions that system engineer must be capable of handling all the modification stages, commencing from the submission of the idea through the approvals to the controlling and the documenting of the modification.

Categories Referring to the Different Types of Engineering Systems Thinking. The different types of the engineering system thinking may be classified as follows:

(1) Classification by the function in which the systems thinking is required - distinction between a head of project (program manager), systems engineer, marketing manager and integration engineer.

(2) Classification by the stage of the project in which the engineering systems thinking is required - distinction between the systems thinking required in the pre-sale stages, the competition, the marketing and the writing of proposals, and the type of systems thinking required at the various development stages.

(3) Classification by the application of the system - distinction between the systems thinking required when handling a system with a customized solution and the one required when dealing with a system designed for large production series after analyzing the market needs.

(4) Classification by hierarchy - every level requires engineering systems thinking suitable for the said level. Inasmuch as the system designed by the engineer is higher in the hierarchy, so the systems thinking required is broader.

Categories Referring to the Knowledge Required from the System Engineer. The category "inter-disciplinary engineering knowledge" is the most frequent category:

The system engineer has to have a thorough knowledge in at least one major engineering field (in our case, the "anchor" field is that of electrical/electronics engineering), has to be familiar with systems and technologies relevant to this function and have basic knowledge in other related engineering topics:

* Additional branches in electrical engineering.
* Industrial and management engineering.
* Mechanical engineering.
* "Support engineering" such as QA etc.
* Computerization, software, software engineering and hardware-software integration.
* Logistics.
* "Project Management."
* Familiarity with project stages or a system's life cycle.
* Familiarity with risk and uncertainty factors, familiarity with risk management methods.
* Familiarity with follow-up and control systems for projects.
* Familiarity with costs estimation models, such as "life-cycle-cost" model.
* Familiarity with methods of project scheduling.

Categories Referring to the Skills Required from the Systems Engineer.
The system engineer must be capable of:

(1) Learning or analyzing the customer's or market's needs - understanding and describing the customer's needs and organizational assignment or understanding and analyzing the market needs. Usually he/she is required to understand the needs even better than the customer himself.

(2) Characterizing or preparing the initial requirements specifications - capable of learning and understanding and/or preparing and phrasing the requirements/preferences of the customer/user/market/operator. Understanding customer demands also in terms of price, quality, reliability, supply conditions and service. Understanding the customer's limitations and capabilities.

(3) Leading an applicability or feasibility study - capable of leading an applicability or feasibility study (by the initial requirement specs), and of preparing blueprint for a feasibility study that also contains realizable alternatives. For each alternative the engineering significance implications have to be detailed, as well as the estimated realization timetables and the required resources.

(4) Preparing final requirements specifications - based on the feasibility study results selecting an alternative and preparing final requirements specification.

RFI and RFP - preparing Request for Information and Request for Proposal.

(5) "Translating" the needs and requirements into technical specifications - knowing how to detailed requirements (to sub-systems); "translating" the needs and requirements to system or functional technical terms.

(6) Describing the goal, objectives and uses of the required system - understanding and describing the goal, objectives and uses of the required system (or the solution it could provide).

(7) Defining and designing a MMI - Man-Machine-Interface document - understanding how the system functions with the operator (sees the human element - the person is part of the system). Familiar with the operation environment.

(8) Carrying out preliminary design of the system - defining the main building blocks and their interaction; executing preliminary design of the concept and preparing the "block diagram"; participating or preparing a Preliminary Design Review - PDR (all or in part) to confirm the overall design

(9) Defining or designing the system architecture - performing an architectural

design, a physical design with setting the physical location of each of the sub-systems.
(10) Using systems design considerations - familiar with and capable of offering systems design considerations, such as: decentralized or centralized design, client-server architecture, minimum inter-model linkage and dependence, simplicity, minimum interface between sub-systems.
(11) Using tools designated for systems design - familiar with and know how to use specific systems tools.
(12) Characterizing, using and structuring simulations - characterizing, using and building system simulations, while being familiar with the advantages and the limitations.
(13) Integrating and combining experts of different disciplines - integrating and combining several systems engineers experts in different disciplines. For this purpose, the systems engineer needs inter-disciplinary knowledge (category 4.1), organizational and management capability (category 6.6.), and the ability to parallel disciplines (category 6.8). Taking part or preparing a Critical Design Review (CDR - all or in part) to confirm the detailed design.
(14) Carring out interface design - familiar with types of interfaces and is capable of performing interfaces design between sub-units. Familiar with and capable of using MUX BUS standard, interface components (UART, USART) and standards such as RS 170, RS 232, RS 422.
(15) Preparing or checking wiring and installations drawings - preparing or examining wiring and installations drawings while being familiar with the types of wires and cables, wire markings, copper wire, braids, coaxial cables, optic fibers, types of connectors and plugs, bonding, shielding, grounding, back-shells, insulations, filters, etc.
(16) Characterizing, designing or performing inspections, tests and integration runs - designing and/or performing inspections, tests and integration. Designing and/or executing laboratory tests, field tests (flights tests), environmental conditions tests, safety of flight tests, and tests towards the release of software versions. Design/execute/supervise Qualification tests. Familiar with and capable of using inspection/tests instruments and system diagnostic tools. Capability of performing "by similarity" verification. Familiar with system malfunctions/failures analysis tools such as Fault Trees, SASDM - Structured Analysis and Systems Design and FMEA - Failure Modes and Effects Analysis (Waring, 1996, p.116, 117,271).
(17) Performing engineering optimization - capable of using trade-off considerations (including refraining from over design). Familiar with engineering limitations and constraints. Mutli-discipline optimization - conciliating between the conflicts of interests of the different disciplines. Familiar with and capable of using redundancy considerations.
(18) Performing economic optimization - capable of using cost effectiveness both when selecting the most appropriate alternative for meeting the requirements and during the various design stages, or maximum benefit considerations under the constraints of a given budget (design to cost).
(19) Checking (or writing) hardware, software and system development specs.
(20) Defining the system's boundaries - capable, when necessary, to limit the size of the system, thus to allow coping with it (sometimes setting the boundaries is arbitrary). Setting the proper boundaries allows one to limit the complexity with which one has to cope. The optimal control span for the system engineer is between 5 and 9 sub-systems but no more than 12 (Waring, 1996, p.36). Inasmuch as the system engineer's level is higher in the hierarchy, so the basic elements (sub-systems) with which he deals are more complex.
(21) Characterizing, defining, examining, testing or designing the system inputs and outputs - Capable of designing the system interfaces with the systems around it.
(22) Forecast or anticipate the long-term future - has the vision/foresees the future/has long-term technological market/needs perception. Has organizational/project vision.
(23) Anticipating future modifications in the system and their implications. Capable of anticipating difficulties/problems. Capable of handling unforeseen problems. Capable of thinking and planning in advance. Capable of foreseeing and planning in advance the upper limit of the system's size and performance, while taking into account resources, manpower, infrastructure and time tables (each system has an optimal size).
(24) Using economic and business considerations – aware of basing the solution or proposal for the customer on non-engineering aspects such as business or economic considerations, profit considerations, business advantages feasibility analyses. Has a systems business perception. Reuse (both of business considerations and in order to reduce risks) - products/assets/existing infrastructures/that have already been developed/ that have already been financed/ that may be used.

(25) Regarding also non-engineering considerations – i.e. reliance of the solution or proposal for the customer on non-engineering considerations such as "political" and organizational considerations, personal wishes, personal aspirations, the deciding person's personality, management styles, the involved persons attitudes.
(26) Examining and suggesting considerations for integrating partners or sub-contractors - capable of examining and offering considerations for the integration of partners or sub-contractors (out-sourcing). Capable of working with partners, sub-contractors and/or chief contractors in all aspects.
(27) Designing by standards - familiar with and is capable of designing by official standards.
(28) Carrying out a design, compatible with different systems - knowing how to link to existing systems. Capable of performing a design, compatible with adjacent systems. Capable of performing a modular design by integrating open sub-systems and/or existing products.
(29) In defense industries - compatibility with commerce products and use of standard software tools and platforms.
(30) Using standard protocols or algorithms - familiar with and understanding of using standard protocols and algorithms. Dealing with protocols demands by definition a systems thinking capability
(31) For those engaged in communication - familiarity with leading protocols.

Categories referring to the Personal Aptitudes Required from Systems Engineers:

(1) Ability to work in a team - inasmuch as the systems become more complex and dynamic, one system engineer is no longer sufficient, even as competent as could be, to understand and see it all. By its nature, systems thinking requires various perspectives to be reviewed, therefore teamwork is required, giving some perspectives. When setting up a team one has to make sure that all system functions are represented.
(2) Good human relations – maintains good human relations and the ability to communicate on all levels and is able to establish trust relations with the customers, the ordering parties, the vendors and the sub-contractors.
(3) Auto-didact capability - capable of lifelong learning, by himself, capable of learning whatever is required for the job, capable of also learning other disciplines, knows how to produce assistance by the people around him, participates in the "learning organizations" activities, reads a lot, updates himself constantly. Makes sure to be exposed to relevant information.
(4) Wishes to engage in systems topics.
(5) Knows how to raise pertinent questions.
(6) Does not get stuck in details - understands at the upper level and is capable of continuing even without understanding the details. Capable of understanding the whole without understanding all the details. Feels comfortable with ambiguity and uncertainty.
(7) Parallelism, analogy, transfer, relation and comparison between different discipline systems - Capable of comparing and paralleling different disciplines. Has the ability to learn, infer and draw conclusions from one discipline and apply it to another, capable of relating and finding resemblance and common ground between different disciplines, and of projecting from his prime specialization to other disciplines, related to the project/system handled by him.
(8) Knows what's what - capable of non-uniformly observing and discriminating between the major and the minor. Has the ability to simplify - the ability to filter out the redundant, unnecessary information and "noises" in order to understand the picture.
(9) Evaluates different approaches on the way to the goal.
(10) Creativity:
Lateral thinking - has creative talent/lateral thinking
Capable of divergent thinking (but also convergent thinking when necessary).
Capable of heuristic thinking (but also algorithmic thinking when necessary).
Capable of filtering ideas arriving from below.
Capable of contributing in brainstorming discussions.
Innovation - capable of offering implementable creative/innovative solutions. Rendering a creative concept into a realistic one.
Inquisitiveness and curiosity - has broad interests. Does not settle for what is told to him.
Imagination - has broad thinking. Does not get "locked", nor is he "afraid" to think. Capable (and is not afraid to) cope with (new) areas outside his expertise.
Thinks about opportunities, initiates - does not stop at what he is doing (and the short-term requirements). Constantly watches/thinks what is related/how to improve/expand. Dares. Willing to take risks. Deems failures, problems and screw-ups challenges and a lever for development, and not as the end of the road.

(11) Organizational and management capability - a systems engineer acting as a project manager as well as a senior system engineer has to have:
Management-organizational capability. Technological leadership capability. Project management capability. The ability to activate and motivate people.
Capable of building, controlling and managing project work plans, timetables and costs. Capable of bringing all sub-activities to a successful conclusion of the project. Familiar with "MS-Project" programs in order to build work plan, and TOC (Theory Of Constraints) to update the work plan. Capable of identifying and dealing with bottlenecks.
Capable of managing discussions, meetings and IPTs - Integrated Program Teams.
Capable of resolving organizational, "political" and logistics problems.
Capable of presenting and/or analyzing alternatives.
Capable of expressing and presenting a subject.
Capable of holding Win-Win technical and economic negotiations.
Capable and willing to manage. Capable of building, operating, leading, running and motivating teams. Knows how to lead decision-making processes by a team. Has the ability to set priorities and allocate resources accordingly. Capable of selecting/deciding between alternatives. Has decision-making capability. Capable of conveying appreciation as well as constructive criticism to his subordinates.
Organizational structure of a project and task assignments - capable of dividing the project's work or the customer's requirements to sub-projects and assigning them for execution purposes to suitable teams in the plant, or to sub-contractors.

Categories Referring to the Ways by which Systems Thinking is Acquired

According to subjects in the research, engineers who have some innate potential, could acquire or improve their capability of engineering systems thinking by the following processes (all or in part):
(1) Accumulating experience and performing breadth functions and a variety of functions and positions (including positions requiring integrative systems thinking and functions requiring mutli-discipline occupation).
(2) Rubbing shoulders with engineers with high 'systems thinking' thinking skills and learning from their experience.
(3) Accumulating experience in positions requiring systems thinking.
(4) Working as a development engineer in an position requiring familiarity with various systems and different technologies.
(5) Constant self-education, while using professional magazines, databases, Internet, study days, conventions and the assistance of other engineers.
(6) Systems thinking may be acquired or improved by active learning, according to the principles of the Constructivist approach. The curriculum for constructing 'engineering systems thinking' has to include:
* Creating awareness of the General Systems Theory principles, the systems thinking principles, the tools and methods of system engineering and the open systems approach.
* Acquiring knowledge as specified above.
* Acquiring skills as specified above.
* Acquiring personal capabilities as specified
* Analyzing "true" systems while analyzing the system design considerations and the development documents.
* Selected topics in systems engineering.
* Simulations and "manager games".
* Team experiences and practices.
* Performing systems projects in teams.

Conclusions-The Research Importance

On the theoretical level the research results:
1. Contribute to the theoretical body of knowledge in the field of the General Systems Theory.
2. Point at a theoretical basis for the acquisition processes of engineering systems thinking.
The first stage of an engineering curriculum design is an analysis of the graduate's activities (knowledge and skills upon graduation), and therefore, on the practical level, based on the answers to the research questions, one could:
1. Design curriculum for constructing 'engineering systems thinking'.
2. Design the learning environment.
3. Formulate the principles/laws of the engineering systems thinking.

References

Anandalingam, G. Systems Engineering. In: *What is Systems Engineering*. University of PENN: http://www.seas.upenn.edu/sys/wise.html, 1997.

Bertalanffy, L.V. *General System Theory: Foundations, Development, Applications.* N.Y.: George Braziller, 1968.

Case, R. *What is Systems Engineering?* in: International Council on Systems Engineering: http://www.incose.org/whatis.html, 1997.

Chen, D. & Stroup, W. General System Theory: Toward a Conceptual Framework for Science and Technology Education for All. *Journal of Science Education and Technology,* Vol. 2, No. 3, pp. 447-459, 1993.

Dorny, C.N. Systems Engineering. In: *What is Systems Engineering*. University of PENN: http://www.seas.upenn.edu/sys/wise.html, 1997.

Frank, M. *Evaluating Outcomes of an Engineering Curriculum,* unpublished M.Sc. thesis, Department of Education in Technology and Science, Haifa: Technion - Israel Institute of Technology, (in Hebrew, abstract in English), 1996.

Frank, M. *Engineering Systems Thinking – Characteristics and Learning Processes,* unpublished Ph.D. thesis, Department of Education in Technology and Science, Haifa: Technion - Israel Institute of Technology, (In Hebrew, abstract in English), 1999.

Graczyk, S.L. Get With the System: General Systems Theory for Business Officials. *School Business Affairs.* Vol. 59, No. 2, pp. 16-20, Feb 1993.

Katz, D. & Kahn, R. Organization and the System Concept. In: *Social Psychology of Organizations.* Pp. 14-29. N.Y.: John Wiley and Sons, 1966.

Likert, R. The Method of Constructing an Attitude Scale. In Fishbein, M. *Readings in Attitude Theory and Measurement.* N.Y.: Wiley, 1967.

Matthews, C.O. An Application of General System Theory (GST to Group Therapy. *The Journal for Specialists in Group Work,* Vol. 17, No. 3, pp. 161-169, 1992.

O'connor, J. & Mcdermott, I. *The Art of Systems Thinking*. S.F.: Thorsons, 1997.

Ottenberg, M.A. What Is A System. http://www.clark.net/pub/nhp/nge/intro/what_sys.html

Senge, P.M. *The Fifth Discipline: The Art and Practice of the Learning Organization,* N.Y: Doubleday, 1994.

Senge, P. et al. *The Fifth Discipline Fieldbook.* N.Y.: Doubleday, 1994.

Shenhar, A. On System Properties and Systemhood. *Int. Journal of General Systems,* 18 (2), pp. 167-174, 1991.

Waks, S. *Curriculum Design from an Art towards a Science.* Hamburg: Tempus Pub. 1995.

Waring, A. *Practical Systems Thinking*. Boston: Thomson Business Press, 1996.

Systems Engineering is Not Just Engineering—Or is It?
A Critical Look at the Scope of our Profession

James N. Martin
Raytheon Company
james.martin@incose.org
PO Box 660246, MS 8497, Dallas, Texas, 75266, USA

Abstract. It is commonly perceived that systems engineering is merely another branch of engineering. Of course, in many ways this is true. But there are some unique aspects of systems engineering that are not relevant to "regular" engineering. This paper will describe these differences. By understanding these differences, it will help the practitioner of the systems discipline to perform the requisite tasks in a more effective manner. For systems engineering to develop into a more mature discipline, it is essential that all key attributes of the practice be understood. This paper will attempt to describe these key attributes.

BACKGROUND

Professional Licensing. The Texas Board of Professional Engineers is considering whether Systems Engineering is a discipline that needs to have its own professional engineering examination. So, the Board asked INCOSE for help in answering the question:

"Is Systems Engineering a Discipline?"

Four members of INCOSE presented a briefing to the Texas Board on September 10th, 1999—Karl Arunski, Phil Brown, Dennis Buede, and James Martin. (This paper is derived from that briefing.) The briefing [Arunski et al. 1999] had four parts:

(a) What is Systems Engineering?

(b) History of SE and of INCOSE

(c) Is SE a separate engineering discipline?

(d) Future steps

Paper Focus. The purpose of this paper is to expound upon the notion that Systems Engineering is *more than just engineering*. The objective is not to establish a single "definition" of Systems Engineering, but rather to describe special attributes of Systems Engineering that make it different from "regular" engineering. What is meant by "regular" engineering is those engineering disciplines that are normally taught in industry and in engineering colleges throughout the world.

Functional Disciplines. Almost all college-educated engineers have a good feeling for what constitutes what I will call in this paper "functional disciplines" such as Mechanical Engineering, Electrical Engineering, Chemical Engineering, Civil Engineering, Software Engineering, and so on. This is often the title of the college degree granted to a student and usually corresponds to the name of a college department.

Technology Domains. There is another type of "regular" engineering which has to do with "technology domains." Most of this knowledge is gained "on-the-job" based on the particular product line and industry that the engineer's employer is involved with. Examples of technology domains are avionics, computers, communications, structures, petrochemical processes, ceramic materials, image processing algorithms, pilot training, etc.

Specialty Concerns. And a third type of "regular" engineering is sometimes called "specialty engineering." Examples of specialty engineering are safety, reliability, maintainability, human factors, logistics support, environmental, producibility, product liability, etc. Now "specialty" does not exactly sound like it is "regular," does it? But for the purposes of this paper I will group the specialty engineering domains into the category of regular engineering. This is mainly so that I can show how Systems Engineering relates to these three types of "regular" engineering.

INTRODUCTION

A Unique Role. For this paper I will first define what is meant by "system." Next I will contrast systems engineering with so-called "component" engineering. Then I will show how systems engineering has a unique role in the product development activity. By doing this, I will be able to show some of the unique elements, along with the special value, that comes when systems engineering is present on a development project.

Integration of Project Elements. Then I will describe the special role that systems engineering has in integrating different elements of the development project. In order to perform this integration role, the systems engineer will need to draw upon knowledge and experience in areas that are not normally needed by other engineers.

Ethics and the Systems Engineer. Systems engineering has unique ethical issues when compared to other engineering disciplines. These will be described as they relate to the role of systems engineering on a project and within an enterprise. Some of the ethical issues have to do with the conflict between needs of the project versus needs of the enterprise.

Systems Engineer? I need to caution the reader that the person who performs the systems engineering tasks and has the associated responsibilities is not necessarily a "systems engineer." Why is this? First, there are many industry and business domains where there is no history of using the title "systems engineer." Second, even in companies or other enterprises that employ that title, the scope of systems engineering is so broad that engineers (and even non-engineers) of all stripes will be responsible for the systems engineering on a project.

When I use the phrase "systems engineer" in this paper, I do not necessarily mean a person with the officially assigned title of systems engineer. In fact, there are many systems engineers who do not in any manner perform systems engineering (as described in this paper). Systems engineering does not a systems engineer make.

WHAT IS A SYSTEM?

Definition of a System. The NASA Systems Engineering Handbook [NASA 1995] defines a system as follows:

> A system *is a set of interrelated components which interact with one another in an organized fashion toward a common purpose.*

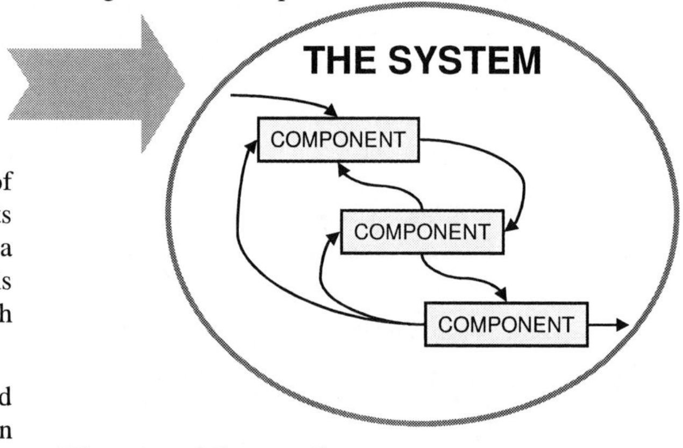

So this gives some hints as to what are the main goals of systems engineering. First, *organize* the components (and those working on these components) in such a fashion that the system *purpose* (or mission) is effectively and efficiently achieved. Second, establish and maintain a clear *vision* of the system's *purpose*.

System Components. Notice that the system is defined to consist of *components*. They further go on to explain that each of these components can itself be a system. At some point the development project will go outside the project to procure the lowest-level component in a system. It is this lowest-level component of a project's system where the majority of the non-systems engineering occurs.

For the purpose of this paper, I will call this "component" engineering. (At the beginning of this paper I called it "regular" engineering. But given the definition above for a system, you can see how it is logical to call this *component engineering* in order to contrast it with true systems engineering.)

Role of Component Engineers. "Component" engineers are certainly involved at higher levels of the system but their primary responsibility at these higher levels is to support the systems engineer with special knowledge of and experience with their own functional discipline (e.g., mechanical), technology domain (e.g., avionics), or specialty concerns (e.g., safety). Those working in the functional and technology domains are sometimes referred to as "design engineers."

Design engineers tend to become specialized in a few narrow fields of their specialty. They are often rewarded for the depth of their expertise in a particular area. In contrast, systems engineers must be broad in their knowledge and experience. If they don't have the particular knowledge they need, they will depend on the design specialists. But sometimes they must learn enough of a field to understand the architectural and performance implications.

Be aware that an individual engineer on a project may actually be *both* a systems engineer and a component engineer. There is nothing wrong with this, but merely a recognition of reality. This "double hatting" can sometimes cause a conflict of interest, so it is important to understand when this occurs and to ensure that ethical dilemmas do not occur. More often, the systems engineer will transition from that role to the role of component engineer later in a project, and then sometimes switch back to systems engineer during the integration and test phase.

Diversity of System Components. It is important to realize that a system does not merely consist of hardware and software (this is the common perception among most engineers). The actual components (the things that interrelate to give a system its useful behavior) can be as diverse as:

(a) Persons and organizations

(b) Software and data

(c) Equipment and hardware

(d) Facilities and materials

(e) Services and techniques

SYSTEMS ENGINEERING AND SCIENCE

Scientific Basis. All engineering is concerned with the application of knowledge and concepts from science and mathematics. It is useful to see how systems engineering relates to science:

> ***Science determines what IS...***
>
> ***Component engineering determines what CAN BE...***
>
> ***Systems engineering determines what SHOULD BE.***

Necessity is the Mother of Invention. As should be evident from the phrase "should be," this involves a concern for the *need* or *expectation* of somebody. Or this need could be derived from a known constraint (cost, schedule, physics, politics, etc.). The component engineer will design a solution based on what someone else has told him is needed (i.e., what characteristics *should be* designed into the component). This is usually accomplished through the specification of design requirements for that component.

SYSTEMS ENGINEERING SCOPE

Definition of Systems Engineering. The NASA Systems Engineering Handbook [NASA 1995] defines systems engineering as follows:

> *Systems Engineering is a robust approach to the design, creation, and operation of systems.*

Systems Engineering Activities. The NASA handbook goes on further to say that systems engineering consists of the following activities:

(a) Identification and quantification of system goals

(b) Creation of alternative system design concepts

(c) Performance of design trades

(d) Selection and implementation of the best design (balanced and robust)

(e) Verification that the design is actually built and properly integrated in accordance with specifications

(f) Assessment of how well the system meets the goals and objectives

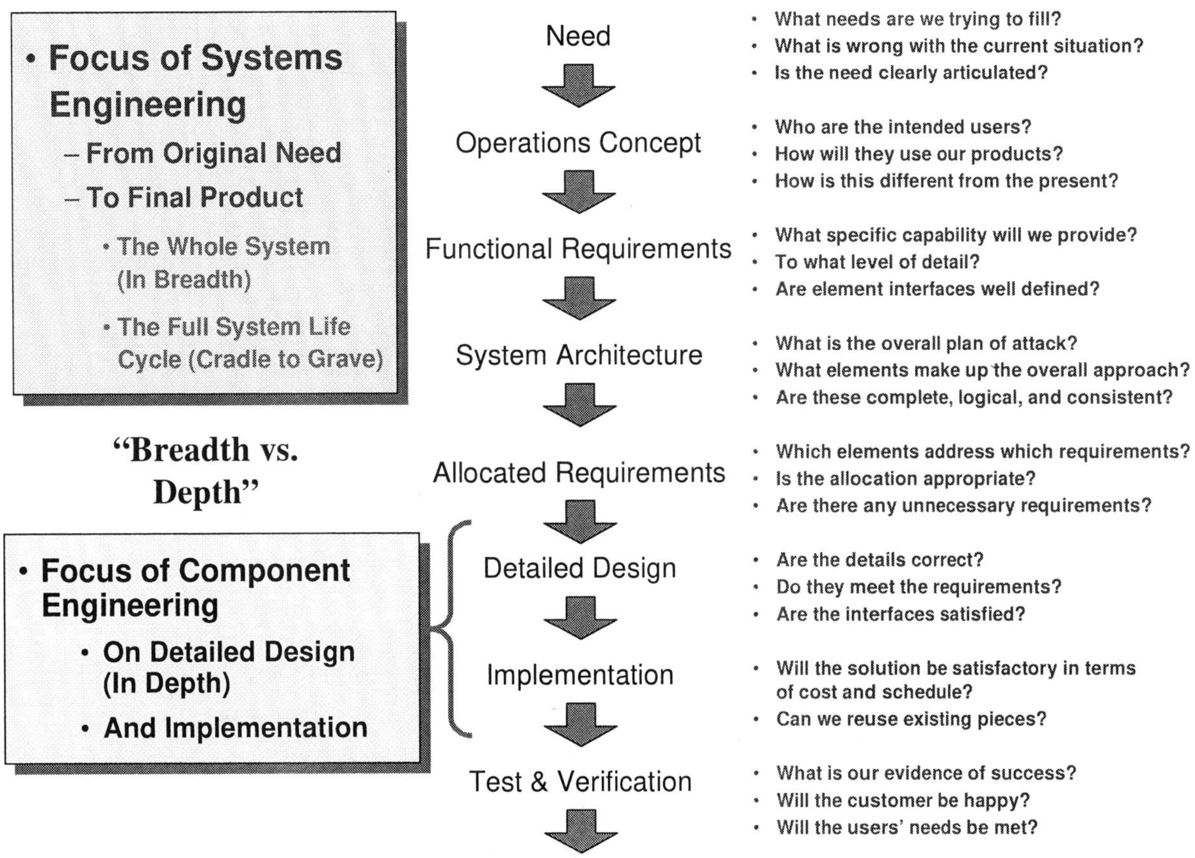

Systems Engineering Focus. Another way to look at this is to determine the questions that need to be answered by systems engineering in performing their tasks. The figure on the previous page shows the typical questions that will be asked by a systems engineer throughout the development life cycle of a product [Martin 1996].

Notice that the focus of systems engineering is from the original need all the way through to the final product. Also, there is a concern for the full system life cycle from initial concept to final disposal of the system or its waste by-products. This is in contrast to component engineering which focuses on the detailed design and implementation of their piece of the system.

Roles Relative to System Hierarchy. Another aspect of systems engineering is the "level" of responsibility within the system hierarchy during the stages of development. The special domain of systems engineering is illustrated in the figure below.

The "Vee" Model of System Development

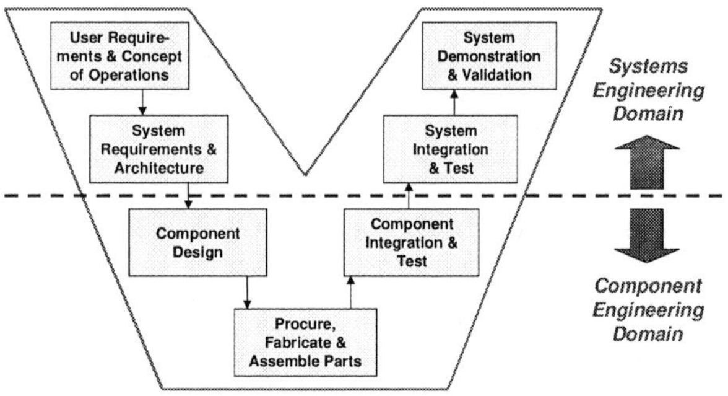

Systems Engineering Domain. This domain includes the up-front tasks of defining the user requirements and the concept of operations, and then from this deriving the system requirements and architecture. In the back-end of this development cycle, systems engineering is responsible for integrating and testing the aggregate of components and then demonstrating the system behavior under real-world conditions to real users to validate that the product actually meets their needs and expectations.

The component engineering effort involves the more traditional engineering tasks of component design, procurement, fabrication, assembly, integration and test. This does not mean that component engineers are not involved in the top-level aspects of systems development. But instead it means that systems engineering is in the lead with component engineering in a support role. Likewise, systems engineering is in a support role in the component engineering domain.

SPECIAL CONTRIBUTIONS

Focus on the Right Things. Systems engineering brings two elements to a development project that are not usually present [Harwell 1997]. First, they bring a disciplined focus on:

(a) The *end product*,

(b) Its *enabling products*, and

(c) Its internal and external *operational environment* (i.e., a system view).

The end product, of course, is the thing that performs the system mission. The enabling products are what enable the developer to produce, test, deploy, install, operate and support the end product. The operational environment involves the interactions that cross the system boundary.

Focus on the End Goal. Second, they bring a consistent *vision* of *stakeholders' expectations* independent of daily project demands (i.e., the system's purpose or mission).

SPECIAL ROLE

Integration of Technical Effort. Systems engineering has a special role to play in the development cycle. They must integrate the technical efforts across the development project in three areas:

(a) Functional disciplines

(b) Technology domains

(c) Specialty concerns

These three areas were described in some detail on the first page of this paper. The figures below illustrate this concept by showing how systems engineering spans across the various categories in each area.

Physical Integration. The task of "engineering" integration is in addition to the responsibility for "physical" integration of system components shown on the Vee diagram to the left. Both types of integration are essential to project and business success.

Integration Across Functional Disciplines

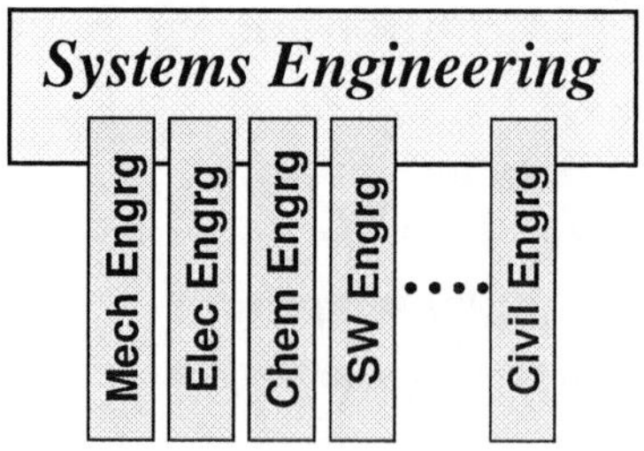

Integration Across Technology Domains

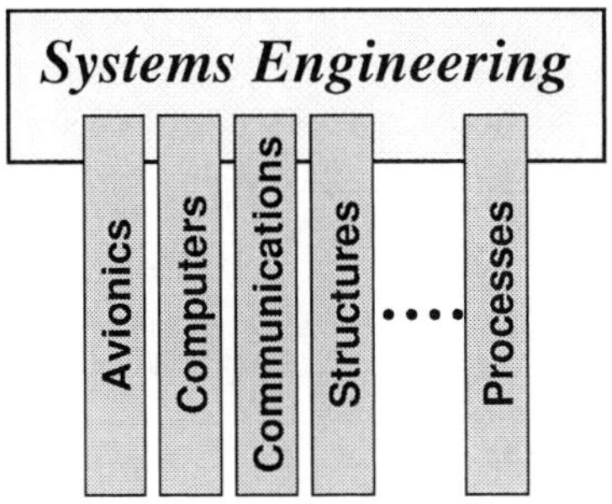

Integration Across Specialty Concerns

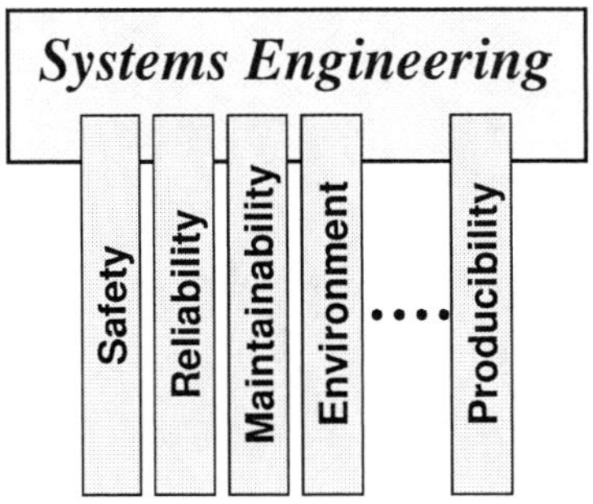

RELATION TO PROJECT MANAGEMENT

With this notion of engineering integration discussed above, it may appear that there is an inherent conflict between systems engineering and project management. In practice, this conflict often leads to confusion over roles and responsibilities and, as a result, the project suffers in terms of low morale, lower productivity, and inferior quality product.

In reality there should be no conflict. There is a need for both project management and systems engineering on development projects. The project manager should focus on the acquisition of resources (people, tools, facilities, funds, etc.) and protection of these resources from competing projects. He acts as the chief spokesman to upper management as to the importance and criticality of the project and how it fits into the overall strategic intent of the enterprise.

The systems engineer, on the other hand, is responsible for the efficient and effective use of these resources (working closely with the program manager), in addition to making sure the system meets the needs and expectations of stakeholders. Roughly speaking:

> ***Project Management ensures that the trains run on time…***
>
> ***Systems Engineering ensures that the trains run at all.***

SCIENTIFIC BASIS OF ENGINEERING

Soft Sciences. All engineering is based on mathematics and various fields in the physical sciences. As shown in the figure below, systems engineering is different since it also relies on the other fields of "soft" sciences such as the management sciences and social sciences.

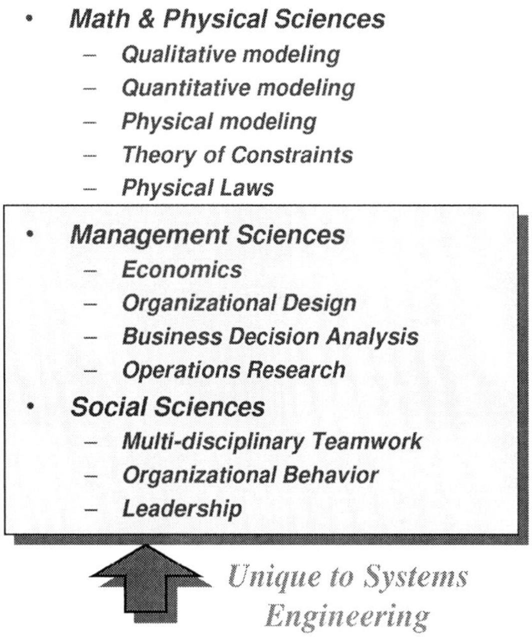

Management Aspects. Due to the responsibility of integrating the various elements of a project (as illustrated in this paper), systems engineers must rely heavily on management techniques to accomplish this feat. Such areas as economics, organizational design, business decision analysis, and operations research become of paramount importance.

Business Aspects. These management techniques are also important since the job of balancing the concerns of all stakeholders will include the business aspects of a project. So, it is essential that the business and technical issues be fully addressed. This requires a knowledge of the impacts of technical decisions on the marketability and business viability of a product.

People Aspects. Likewise, since the tasks to be integrated are performed by people and groups of people, the techniques of social science are critical to the systems engineer's job. This depends on the special areas of multi-disciplinary teamwork, organizational behavior, and leadership techniques.

Teaching the Soft Side. Because of the dependence of systems engineering on these "soft" disciplines, it is very difficult to teach systems engineering, and many engineers do not want to deal with the business and people issues that go with the job.

ETHICAL CONSIDERATIONS FOR THE SYSTEMS ENGINEER

Ethics is a system of principles governing morality and acceptable conduct. Morality is, of course, making decisions about right and wrong. All of engineering is concerned with ethics since they make design decisions that can affect the well-being, if not the life, of people and organizations.

However, systems engineering has some special ethical concerns that are not normally encountered by most other engineers. These special concerns deal with the following three areas.

(a) Achieving balance between inherent conflicts,

(b) System optimization, and

(c) Customer interface.

Achieving Balance. Inherent conflicts occur in systems engineering since many factors must be balanced against one another as various trade-offs are made to optimize performance of the system. Typical factors to consider when balancing the system are shown in the figure below.

System Optimization. Systems engineering is all about optimization. But more than just optimization is important; the system must also be *balanced* and *robust*. Balance is achieved through proper consideration of all the factors discussed above. This balance must be gained using "value functions" from each of the stakeholders. Sometimes these value functions cannot be accurately quantified and it is incumbent on systems engineering to realize when and how to quantify these parameters. Robustness for a system means that functionality and performance is not overly sensitive to errors—such as errors in analysis, design, test, or operation. During the system optmization process, conflicts of an ethical nature may arise in the three areas shown in the figure at the bottom of this page.

Customer Interface. Systems engineering is often responsible in a significant way for the interface to the customer and to the expected users of the product. They need this interaction so they can get a clear picture of the constraints of the customer (cost, schedule, acquisition rules, etc.) and the needs and expectations of users and operators (usability, functionality, and performance). This often leads to ethical dilemmas when dealing with the issues shown below.

- **Achieving balance between inherent conflicts**
  - **System Functionality and Performance**
  - **Development Cost and Recurring Cost**
  - **Development Schedule (Time to Market)**
  - **Development Risk (Probability of Success)**
  - **Business Viability and Success**
- **System Optimization**
  - **Subsystems often suboptimal to achieve best balance at system level**
  - **Ultimate system purpose must prevail against conflicting considerations**
  - **Long-term considerations (e.g., disposal) may drive technical decisions**
- **Customer Interface**
  - **Often must act as "honest broker"**
  - **Carries burden of educating customer on hard choices**
  - **Must think ahead to the next customer and next application**
  - **Must "challenge" all requirements**

SYSTEMS ENGINEERING AS A DISCIPLINE

Recognition. Is systems engineering recognized as a discipline throughout the industry? Not yet. In this field, there are currently only 47 graduate college departments in the United States (21 undergraduate and 23 graduate programs). [Arunski et al. 1999] There are an increasing number of books on the subject, but nowhere near the number as for other established engineering disciplines. INCOSE now represents the profession, but it was established only ten years ago.

Engineering Disciplines. There are various attributes of a mature engineering discipline [Arunski et al. 1999]:

(a) Accepted set of definitions
(b) Organized body of knowledge
(c) Scientific foundations
(d) Products
(e) Goals
(f) Primary design factors
(g) Professional society
(h) Means of scholarly discourse

The field of systems engineering is still developing, and many would say that all the attributes of maturity are not yet well established and documented.

Evolution of Engineering Disciplines. The emergence of any particular discipline is driven by the needs of society. About 2500 years ago, large social groups were becoming organized and there was a need to create large buildings and public facilities. From this need arose Civil Engineering. Likewise, when societies needed to conduct trade and commerce across the large expanse of oceans, the need for Marine Engineering emerged. Usually these started as a home-grown "craft industry," and then there was more widespread adoption through colleges and other teaching institutions.

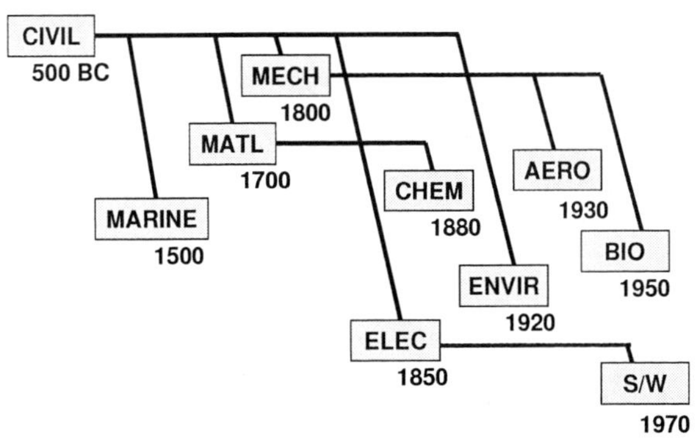

As can be seen above, the various disciplines of engineering came about at different times [Honour 1999]. Note that Systems Engineering is not yet shown as a well-recognized discipline in the industry.

SYSTEMS LEADERSHIP

It should be obvious to the reader at this point that systems engineering is more than just engineering. It involves a good deal of knowledge and skill from the management domain. But this is still not enough. The missing ingredient is *systems leadership*.

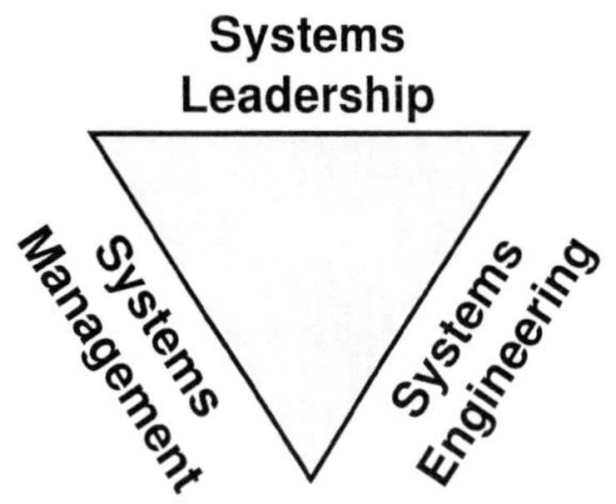

Managers think about control mechanisms and the "how-to's" of accomplishing project tasks. *Leaders* think about dreams, missions, strategic intent, and purpose. Here's another way of looking at this:

Managers do things right…

Leaders do the right things.

Different Goals and Objectives. Another difference between leadership and management is the *object* of their actions.

(a) Systems leaders deal with people and emotions.

(b) Systems managers deal with resources, organizations, tools, process, and other project elements.

(c) Systems engineers deal with technology and things.

Separation of Concerns. There is a broad spectrum of issues to be dealt with when engineering a system. It is sensible that these various concerns be partitioned effectively according to the different knowledge and skills of each person. Shown below is a typical division of responsibility between systems engineers, managers, and leaders. Notice that they address separate questions, or different aspects of the problem. (Many systems engineers are required to act in more than one of these roles at the same time—a rare skill indeed!)

Who	Questions	Results
Engineers	What? How Well?	Functions & Performance
Managers	How Much? When?	Cost & Schedule
Leaders	For Whom? Why?	Purpose & Vision

THE EXTRA VALUE OF SYSTEMS ENGINEERING

Systems engineers are most often recognized as the source for the system architecture and requirements. As you can see from the discussion in this paper, requirements and architecture are not the only products of the systems engineering effort.

The value added is more extensive and not always fully appreciated. According to [Ring 1999], systems engineering adds value to a project in three key ways:

(a) Languaging the project,

(b) Imagining and structuring the solution, and

(c) Converging creativity to closure.

Languaging the Project. Giving all participants a common language for communicating about Problem, Solution and Project Plan. The key components are: a) identifying the Problem Space and Solution Value, b) providing multiple views vs a single taxonomy, and c) promulgating systems engineering practices (EIA 632 or appropriate).

Imagining and Structuring the Solution. Clarifying not only the elements and their interrelationships that comprise the system but also the Stimulus<>Response expectations of the problem, the solution and even the project. The key components are: a) risk mitigation, b) looking beyond cause-effect to include many other types of relations, and c) selection of allocation to components....this is best accomplished by evolving the image of the solution through a series of semantic levels, finally reaching a physical, deliverable manifestation.

Converging Creativity to Closure. Devising a context sensitive protocol for incremental convergence and overseeing the sequential process of "freezing designs and reconciling business" across hundreds of implicitly related design choices. The key components are: a) convergence to technology, b) convergence to the social system executing the project, and c) convergence to sponsor-realized value.

—Adapted from [Ring 1999].

CONCLUSIONS

Onwards to a Full Discipline. I have attempted to take a critical look at the scope of the systems engineering profession. There are some who say that systems engineering is merely a way of thinking. Yes, but it is much more than that.

Until we understand the complete scope, there is little hope that we can do the necessary things to ensure full development into a mature engineering discipline.

Breadth vs. Depth. There is a basic notion that systems engineering must handle the full breadth of the system. The system must be partitioned into knowable and actionable chunks. The greatest danger a systems engineer faces is not knowing when to stop plunging into details, and when to start trusting the experts on the project. This involves more than just technical skill.

Systems Engineering is Unique. Systems engineering provides several *unique contributions* to the success of a project and a business enterprise:

1) **Unique Focus**
   a) End product and system purpose
   b) Stakeholder needs and expectations
   c) Full system life cycle
      (Conception through Retirement)
2) **Unique Approach**
   a) Integrates disciplines and technologies
   b) Balances conflicting considerations
3) **Unique Methods, Tools, and Models**
   a) System analysis and simulation
   b) Assessment of performance and risk
   c) Organization and management of information and requirements
   d) Verification and validation

The Challenge and Opportunity. The International Council on Systems Engineering has a great opportunity to advance the profession of systems engineering to a full engineering discipline. This is a worthy challenge for the 21st century.

REFERENCES

Arunski, Karl, P. Brown, D. Buede, and J. Martin, "Systems Engineering Overview." Unpublished briefing, 1999.

Harwell, Richard, *Systems Engineering.* A brochure jointly published by INCOSE and AIAA, 1997.

Honour, Eric, "Characteristics of Engineering Disciplines." Int'l Conf on Sys Engineering, 1999.

Martin, James, *Systems Engineering Guidebook.* CRC Press, 1996.

NASA, *Systems Engineering Handbook.* Ed., Robert Shishko, NASA, 1995.

Ring, Jack, " 'They' Call it Knowledge Management." Int'l Conf on Sys Engineering, 1999.

BIOGRAPHY

James Martin is a senior principal systems engineer at the Raytheon Company working on telecommunications products and services, and was previously with AT&T Bell Labs. He led the effort to develop ANSI/EIA 632, the US national standard for "engineering a system." He authored a book by CRC Press entitled "Systems Engineering Guidebook." Mr. Martin graduated with an MS from Stanford University and a BS from Texas A&M. He is an elected Fellow member of INCOSE.

Germany's V-2 Rocket Program

and the Application of Systems Engineering

T. Scott Ankrum
University of Maryland University College
Adelphi, Maryland 20783

Abstract. During World War II, Nazi Germany rained terror down on London and other European cities with the World's first guided ballistic missile. Was that a marvel of systems engineering, before the term was even invented, or were other factors at work? The V-2 rocket was taken, by Nazi Germany, from an unproven concept to mass production and use, even while the nation was under severe political and economic stress. In this paper, the progress of the V-2 program is traced, from concept to production and use, while highlighting the major problems and milestones. How the major elements of systems engineering were incorporated into the program, or not, is examined. Were the concepts of systems engineering known at the time, even if the term was not? If not, would an understanding of systems engineering have made a difference to the V-2 team, given the circumstances of war, politics and economics at the time?

PROBLEM STATEMENT

The years between the world wars saw Germany struggling for identity and respect. The Treaty of Versailles severely restricted Germany's armed forces and what it could do for weapons development. Hitler was building his armed forces by working around the Versailles restrictions and sometimes defying them. Army Ordnance, the artillery organization, was anxious to advance beyond the Paris Gun, a large, unwieldy artillery piece used to bombard Paris in World War I. From their experience with the Paris Gun, they felt that artillery technology was approaching the limit of its range. The Treaty of Versailles restricted what Germany could develop, but it did not mention rockets. To re-emerge as a world power, Germany had to surprise the world with a weapon technology that was so innovative that it would intimidate potential enemies. Those three statements can be viewed as the problem statement, from the systems engineering viewpoint. The idea was for the rockets to take over beyond the range of the largest artillery. Later, they were also viewed as replacing bomber aircraft for shorter ranges. From there, a high-level set of requirements for a rocket weapon emerged.

- It shall be a single-stage vertical launch vehicle, to minimize weigh.
- It shall deliver 100 times more explosive power than the Paris Gun, or 1,000 kilograms.
- It shall have twice the range of the Paris Gun, about 250 kilometers.
- As to accuracy, 50% the warheads shall fall within a circle equal to 0.2% to 0.3% of the range, about 1/2 to 3/4 of a kilometer.
- The vehicle and its launcher shall fit in a standard European rail tunnel and it shall not exceed the maximum width for road vehicles.

The accuracy requirement was never met. The last requirement shows an obvious intent for mobile launchers. These requirements look like a good systems engineering basis for a project, except that they were defined in March of 1936, after the first three preliminary rockets had been built and tested, and by the rocket developers themselves. (Dornberger, 1954, 1955, 1963) (Neufeld, 1995)

HISTORICAL BACKGROUND

The German army did not begin rocket development from nothing. Independent scientists had been working on rocket engines since the 1920's. An organization called the Society for Space Travel (VfR in German) was using a test site they called Raketenflugplatz (literally "rocket flying place") in suburban Berlin. These independents varied in their professionalism. More than one rocket engine exploded with fatal results, due to poor safety precautions. To secure funds, sensationalism sometimes took precedence over science, as exemplified by Hermann Oberth's failed attempt to coordinate the launch of a rocket with the opening of Fritz Lang's movie Frau im Mond (The Woman in the Moon) in 1929. (Neufeld, 1995)

THE PEENEMÜNDE FACILITY

Work was gradually brought under the control of Army Ordnance. The army offered funds to support the scientists' work and the army needed their expertise. The rocket scientists worked under General Karl Becker and Dr. (later General) Walter Dornberger, who headed the rocket project through most of its life. The army first used its Kummersdorf proving ground near Berlin. The project was small at first and budgets were meager. Later, when army Ordnance determined that rocket development deserved bigger accommodations, land at the Baltic coast resort of Peenemünde was purchased, and planning began to construct the necessary facilities. At this point, the Luftwaffe (air force) became jointly involved in the rocket project and put up some of the money needed for purchase and development of Peenemünde. The Lufwaffe later left the project entirely in the Army's hands and worked on its own projects at the other end of the facility. Peenemünde was to be both a development facility and a production plant. Army Ordnance wanted "everything under one roof", development, testing, subsystem development and manufacture would all be together. Many more scientists and engineers would be needed, most of whom were recruited through personal contacts. The scientists and engineers were paid civilian salaries, except for officers, even though they were in the army. Rank played no part in the reporting structure. Only a few subsystems would be contracted out to industry, and some basic research would be contracted to universities. The location was remote, which helped with rocket safety and security, but the facility needed a lot of work to be of any value. The initial budget problem for Peenemünde was solved because the Army and Luftwaffe competed with their offers of money for the facility. (Dornberger, 1955) (Huzel, 1962) (Neufeld, 1995)

KEY TECHNOLOGICAL HURDLES

Several basic technological hurdles stood in the way of the German rocket developers. An overview of these is provided in Table 1.

Several combinations of fuel and oxidizer were tried. Fuels included diesel oil, alcohol and hydrogen. Liquid oxygen and hydrogen peroxide were considered as oxidizers. A hypergolic (self-igniting) combination of nitric acid and vinyl isobutyl ether was also tried. Manufacturing methods and handling these materials were known at the time, so that part was an engineering issue. The thrusts and temperatures when combining them in a rocket engine, though had to be determined through the scientific method of experimentation. The final combination was an alcohol-water mixture and liquid oxygen. (Dornberger 1955) (Neufeld, 1995)

The rocket engine itself presented several major challenges. Getting the fuel to the engine was first done with pressurized nitrogen tanks, but tests proved that as the fuel and oxidizer were depleted, pressure dropped off, and constant pressure was required. Turbo-pumps were used instead, with good success. Here again, testing was required to fill a gap in engineering knowledge. Getting the fuel and oxidizer to mix thoroughly and burn completely in the combustion chamber proved a troublesome issue. Dr. Walter Thiel is credited with several innovations that accomplished this. Combustion chambers were, at first made longer and longer to give the fuel and oxidizer enough time to mix and burn. Eventually, Thiel added eighteen premix chambers and efficient spray injectors, allowing him to change to a spherical combustion chamber, which he had determined to be the most efficient. Combustion chamber burn-through was a frequent problem until it was encased in a cooling flow of the alcohol fuel. Finally, earlier testing had always used a nozzle angle of ten to twenty degrees, but Thiel showed that a thirty-degree nozzle angle produced much greater thrust because of reduced friction between the exhaust gasses and the nozzle walls. Tests, trial and error were needed to find these answers. No engineering formulas paved the path for these early rocketeers. (Dornberger 1955) (Neufeld, 1995)

The guidance system seemed to have the best engineering basis to start, but it had a long way to go. A purely inertial guidance system, based on gyroscopes was planned. Gyroscopes were already used for airplane auto-pilots, but the rockets presented new problems. A stable platform, based on gyroscopes on three axes was eventually used. Separate accelerometer gyroscopes were tried at first. Getting the rocket to tilt toward its target after the initial vertical flight presented another problem. External guide beams were also experimented with, but these were deemed to make the rocket vulnerable to enemy jamming. Being ballistic after engine cutoff, the rocket needs to have "arrow stability". That is, its center of pressure from air resistance needed to be behind its center of gravity. The problem this presented for guidance was that the controls had to be fairly strong to overcome the stability and steer. It also had to steer consistently at any speed, subsonic and supersonic. The solution was to put steering fins in the exhaust stream. Most of these were engineering issues, but only after their problems manifested themselves in tests. An electrical engineer, Helmut Hoelzer applied engineering principles to develop a mixing device for the electrical signals from the stabilizing gyroscopes. Differentiating the motion signals provided velocity, allowing the rate gyroscopes to be eliminated. Finally, the tilt to target was provided by a clock motor that tilted one gyroscope axis in the direction of the target. "The control mechanism of the rocket then seeks by means of the vanes to keep the rocket's longitudinal axis parallel to the axis of the gyroscope." This tilts the rocket toward the target. The question remains, does applying known engineering principles from different disciplines, in new combinations, to solve new problems, amount to engineering? (Dornberger, 1955) (Ehricke, 1950 c) (Neufeld, 1995) (Steinhoff, 1986)

Technological Hurdle	Engineering Basis Available
fuel and oxidizer	An engineering basis existed for producing and handling each liquid, but no data existed on the results of combining them.
fuel delivery	Pumping something as cold as liquid oxygen was a new problem.
rocket engine	Independent experimenters had built engines, but no systematic configuration studies had ever been done.
guidance system	A basis existed in airplane auto-pilots, but these were crude and imprecise compared to what the rocket needed.
supersonic aerodynamics	Only firearm and artillery projectiles had traveled faster than sound, and no work had ever been done to optimize their shape.

Table 1. Technological Hurdles

When it came to aerodynamics, the German rocketeers had little engineering knowledge to lean on. No vehicle had ever before exceeded the speed of sound, and this rocket was expected to fly at several times the speed of sound. Systematic wind tunnel tests were performed. When a wind tunnel was not available, some scientists resorted to dropping a model from an airplane, and photographing its decent. These tests were performed to determine the optimum fuselage shape and the shape of the fins, the fins that gave the rocket its "arrow stability". (Dornberger, 1955) (Neufeld, 1995)

Most of the aforementioned subsystem developments took place somewhere along the progression of rockets beginning with the first designated Aggregate-1, Assembly-1 in English and A-1 for short. They grew in size and power through the A-2 and A-3. The A-3 was a complete failure, but those failures taught lessons that helped the team improve the guidance system. The A-4 was to be the first model to be mass-produced and deployed. The German propaganda office renamed the A-4 to V-2, for Vengence-2. (The V-1 was a separate project and is described below.) While the A-4 was being planned, but before its design was complete, the development team decided they needed another test step, in a smaller scale. The A-5 was built first to test the engine and guidance system on a smaller scale. There was, apparently a plan, but none of the sources makes reference to any overall plan. Each new model was likely designated and planned during testing of the immediately previous model. The fact that no overall plan laid out the progression of A-1 through A-4 indicates that the rocket project was more science than engineering. (Dornberger, 1955) (Neufeld, 1995)

THE DESIGN

The ultimate design of the A-4 or V-2 included some innovations that cannot be described within any one subsystem. Early rocket designs put the engine and nozzle above the fuel and oxidizer tanks, which was presumed to give greater stability. As larger engines were built, however, that design risked heating the tanks excessively with the exhaust gases, and it left the fuel and oxidizer lines exposed. The V-2 had its tanks above the engine, gaining its stability with its fins. A major problem with the combustion chamber was how to keep it from melting. That problem was solved by enveloping the combustion chamber in a flow of the alcohol fuel. See Figure 1 for a cut-away diagram of an A-4. So, overall system design issues were addressed by the team, but these were attacked more with the scientific method of experimentation that with the engineering method. (Dornberger, 1955) (Neufeld, 1955)

INNOVATIONS AND FIRSTS

Several innovations or "firsts" came out of Germany's V-2 Program. It was the world's first guided ballistic missile. Guided and ballistic because it was guided during its powered flight and ballistic thereafter. Although many experimenters successfully fired liquid fuel rockets first, this was the first practical use of that technology. This was the first time any man made craft traveled faster than the speed of sound, and the V-2 traveled several times the speed of sound. Finally, it was the first man made vehicle to leave the Earth's atmosphere, reaching an altitude of 50 to 60 miles on a normal trajectory, 117.44 miles when sent straight up. (Dornberger, 1955)

The analog computer was a side benefit of the V-2 program. As part of the guidance system, electronic circuits were developed to mix the signals from the gyroscopes and ground signals. That involved the operations of addition, subtraction, integration and differentiation. It was a small step from that circuit to an independent electronic analog computer, which was used for calculating and simulation rocket trajectories.

(Neufeld, 1995) (Steinhoff, 1972)

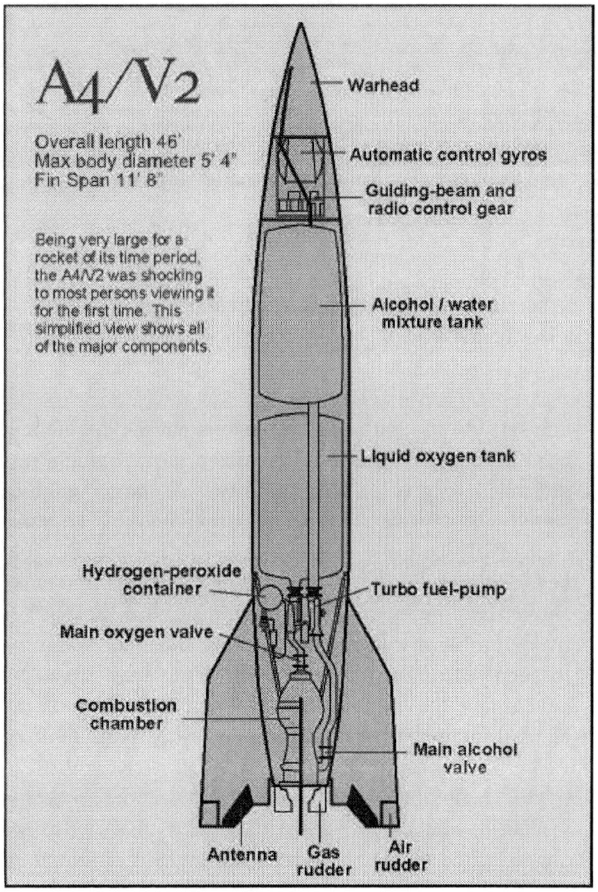

Figure 1. Cut-away view showing overall design

RESOURCE ISSUES

Before the war, the Army Ordnance rocket project was a minor one. When war was imminent and after it started, Dornberger and his lead scientists expended a lot of effort convincing their government that the rocket would be an important toll in the war effort. Through most of the war, the development effort held Germany's top priority, whatever that was. The priority system under Adolf Hitler was not well managed. He left his generals free to compete for resources and the result was that projects piled up on the top priority until Hitler would create a new higher priority. Then, the process repeated. (Dornberger, 1955) (Neufeld, 1995)

Although the development effort weathered these fluctuations well, building the production plant held second priority for a long time. Like most nations at war, Germany suffered from many shortages, so second priority projects did not get any resources. Shortages in steel, coal and gasoline, among other things, kept construction of the rocket production factory at Peenemünde at a very slow pace. Shortages affected development less directly. The government issued orders, at various times, to replace some exotic materials in the rocket with more common ones. This, of course, disrupted the engineering process as the developers tried to change designs to use steel instead of aluminum, for example. (Dornberger, 1955) (Neufeld, 1995).

CLIMACTIC TEST

On October 3, 1942 at 3:58 PM, the first successful launch of a V-2 rocket or A-4, as it was called at the time, was executed. The rocket motor burned for about 58 seconds, a little short of the programmed one-minute burn. That gave it a maximum speed of 3,300 miles an hour, or almost four and a half times the speed of sound. The rocket reached an altitude of 50 miles and came down 120 miles down range, after 295 seconds. (Klee & Merk, 1965) (Neufeld, 1995)

PRODUCTION

The initial production factory was right at Peenemünde. The idea was to continue the concept of "everything under one roof" by having production next to development. Some obvious advantages include shared test stands and launch facilities, and drawing on the developers' knowledge during manufacture. Still, some subsystems, such as the gyroscope stabilized platforms and the fuel turbopumps were contracted out to industry, where the necessary precision manufacturing facilities existed. (Dornberger, 1955) (Neufeld, 1995)

The plan for the production plant called for 5,000 workers, and they had to be housed at Peenemünde, like the developers. That meant housing had to be built, in addition to the plant. Since the housing could not be close to the factory and test facilities, they planned on an electric train for commuting. To power the train, a bigger electric generating plant had to be built, and to support the bigger generator, a bigger harbor would be needed for off-loading that much more coal. This is just a glimpse at the kinds of issues involved in building the production factory. (Dornberger, 1955) (Neufeld, 1995)

Even while the Peenemünde factory was being built, its purpose changed back and forth between being a full production facility and a pilot production facility. As a pilot production factory, its purpose would be to manufacture a small number of rockets to prove out manufacturing issues and to supply the developers for the latest phases of testing. Other manufacturing plants were planned at existing industrial companies, three of which eventually went into production of the rocket: Zeppelin Company in Friedrichshafen, Rax-Werke in Wiener Neustadt, Austria and DEMAG in Berlin-

Falkensse. After bombing raids on Peenemünde, all production was moved to underground tunnels near the city of Nordhausen in Thuringia, in the Harz Mountains of central Germany. That was called the Mittelwerk or Central Works. There, production reached a peak of 600 to 700 rockets a month. (Dornberger, 1955) (Neufeld, 1995)

Labor was handled in a way that might be called different. Before the war, construction workers for the development facility had been hard to come by. Because of security, only German citizens could be used. Once war broke out, security was less of an issue than schedule, so foreign workers were employed as well. For building the factories, especially the Mittelwerk, and later, in the manufacturing process itself, prisoners of war and concentration camp prisoners were used. Given the political situation, it is not clear that those in charge of the rocket program were given much choice, but the decision to use slave labor was not forced on them either. From a systems engineering perspective, that type of labor lowers costs, but introduces the risk of sabotage. Sabotage was a reality at the Mittelwerk, however, not on a scale that would suggest any organized plan, either internally or externally led. (Dornberger, 1955) (Neufeld, 1995) (Piszkiewicz, 1995).

DEPLOYMENT & OPERATION

It was very late in the war by the time the rockets were put to use. "The first V-2 fell at 6:43 PM. September 8, 1944 at Chiswick [Britain], the second 16 seconds later at Epping." (Dornberger, 1955) Actually though, most of the rockets were aimed at Antwerp, Belgium, an Allied staging area for their advance into continental Europe. About 4,300 V-2s were launched operationally. (Neufeld, 1995) (Dornberger, 1955)

The troops chosen to fire the rockets in the field got training from some of the developers. The training facility was first established at K slin on the Baltic coast. It was later moved to Blizna. Technically oriented soldiers, such as engineers and craftsmen were well represented in the launch crews selected. As a result, many practical suggestions came from them after some experience. (Dornberger, 1955) (Ehricke, 1950 a)

Early on, Hitler had wanted to launch the V-2 rockets from hardened bunkers in the field. Construction began on a few, but bombing and other problems made them unusable. Dornberger and his rocket team had always pushed the idea of mobile launchers. Railroad mounted launches were developed, but truck mounted launchers were what actually got used. These mobile launchers were called Meillerwagens. Railroads are easy targets for bombing, but the truck-mounted launchers could do their deed and be gone before any Allied action could hurt them. A significant amount of planning must have gone into the deployment phase. Besides the mobile launcher, each launch unit required support equipment, like a generator, the trained crew, spare parts, fuel and liquid oxygen. The missile batteries were divided into Group North and Group South. A total of six army sections, composed of one to three batteries each were assigned V-2 launch duties. (Dornberger, 1955) (Klee & Merk, 1965)

In practice, the rockets did not perform as well as hoped. The precision should have been measurable in yards, but was closer to miles. A large percentage of the rockets launched in the training field failed on the launcher and many of the remainder exploded during decent. The problem was partly alleviated by reinforcing the fuselage midsection. (Dornberger, 1955) (Ehricke, 1950 b).

PROBLEMS MOST PROJECTS DO NOT HAVE

The V-2 program had all of the problems that most systems engineering projects have, plus a few more. Sabotage has already been mentioned, and that is not often a significant risk on a project. A bigger problem for the V-2 program was bombing by the British and the United States Air Corps. That was the reason that manufacturing was moved from Peenemünde to the Mittelwerk. Even though the bombing raids only cost them a few weeks, many workers and a few developers were killed in the raids. Very little damage was done to the project, but the bombing raids compelled the development team to move. (Dornberger, 1955) (Neufeld, 1995)

EVALUATION

The V-2 program is a good example to test for the use of systems engineering because it starts with a concept, then requirements and takes them through development, testing, production and deployment in a practical situation. German Army Ordnance started with a problem statement, as defined earlier. That was refined into a short list of high-level requirements. That was a good systems engineering beginning, but the process seems to have stopped there. There is no evidence in the V-2 literature that lower level, specific requirements were defined, or that that requirements were traced forward to subsystems and components. Also in line with systems engineering, each rocket had an overall weight limit, as limited by its engine thrust. It is not clear that the subsystems and their components were systematically allocated portions of these weights. Other, non-allocable limits were traced downward though. For example, the team responsible for stability and control had to work with a given fuselage size and shape, and could only manipulate the configuration of fins and exhaust vanes.

Did the rocket team perform design analysis and optimization? They did some, for example the extensive wind tunnel and drop tests for the fuselage and fins, and extensive testing was done to optimize the combustion chamber and fuel injection before a design was implemented. The analog computer modeling can also be cited as design optimization. On the other hand, some design decisions had to be altered after actual use proved them a poor choice. The original fuel delivery system was compress nitrogen. That proved to be not consistent enough and was replaced by turbopumps. The guidance system on the A-3 proved to be totally inadequate and was upgraded during the A-5 tests. The conclusion for design analysis and optimization has to be that it was partially performed.

Testing is a phase that was very systematic. The V-2 team tested each subsystem systematically, and when they launched a rocket, they knew what new features were at risk for failure. Although no document like a test plan was mentioned it is clear from the scale of most of their tests and because each person involved in each test knew what to watch for, that tests were well planned. When testing engines for example, there were requirements for so many pounds of thrust or a certain maximum exhaust temperature that needed to be met. The wind tunnel tests did not appear to have specific numerical requirements to meet, but those tests were conducted systematically with the aim of identifying optimum configurations and shapes. Even modeling was used. Helmut Hoelzer's electronic analog computer was used to calculate and simulate trajectories. What testing lacked was change control. Many design changes were made right on a rocket's test stand and not documented. (Neufeld, 1995)

Once production was started, the need for change management became apparent. No fundamental changes were made to the rocket design after production started, and only the guidance system received significant modification, but a total of 65,000 engineering changes were made by the end of the war, which is a number consistent with aircraft development of the day. Several effective steps were taken to manage design changes after production started. A "Production Supervision" team of development engineers was assigned to supervise the incorporation of changes at the production plants. A "Drawings Change Service" was established. It probably functioned something like a change control team, being responsible for all changes to design drawings. Finally, changes were released to the production plants in blocks, rather than as they were developed. (Neufeld, 1995) These change management elements worked well, but they were not part of any original plan. They were invented after their need became apparent. In fact, elements of a baseline, necessary to change control were not in place until very late. A complete parts list for the A-4 (V-2) did not exist until mid 1944, and comprehensive design drawings were only available in early 1944, but before production started. (Neufeld, 1995) (Huzel, 1962) Apparently, the principle of change management had to be learned as part of the project. Maybe these were known principles at the time, but they were new to this team. Neufeld (1995) also points out that none of the engineers hired for the program had any manufacturing experience.

Work on actual production facilities had begun well before development and testing settled on a final design for the rocket. Was that taking an irresponsible risk with the resources required to build production facilities? It seems more reasonable to see it as the result of confidence and wanting to have everything ready when it is time to start production. A good systems engineer would not wait until the rocket design was ready before beginning to build its factory.

The biggest mistake that can be seen can only be seen when viewing the system at its highest level. The V-2 system worked. It delivered its prescribed payload over the required distance, although not with the accuracy required. Even if the accuracy requirement had been met, though, that weapon would not have had a significant effect on the outcome of World War II. The scientists and engineers did their job. The rocket system worked, but at the war level, the system did not work. Is it fair to ask a systems engineer to examine systems at the level of a world war? Dornberger and von Braun were eager to have their project funded, but they originally envisioned the rocket as a battlefield weapon, like long-rang artillery. Hitler was anxious for a war-winning weapon. He wanted an answer to the Allied bombing of German industry and civilians. Somehow, the size of the warhead that could be delivered, and the number of rockets required to have a significant effect were lost on the decision-makers. Not until the nuclear warhead could be married with the ballistic missile would the missile make strategic sense.

Normally, the final phase of a systems engineering project is retirement and disposal of the system. This should be included in the plans. No retirement and disposal plans are evident in the sources, and this is understandable for a weapon developed during wartime. There was, however, a retirement and disposal performed. Allied bombers initiated the retirement phase when they forced the evacuation of Peenemünde. At the end of the war, American, Soviet and British forces executed the disposal phase when they removed both the equipment and the developers to their own countries. The American operation, called "Operation Paperclip" got the most developers and enough parts for several V-2 launches back home. (Huzel, 1962) Table 2 summarizes the V-2 team's use of systems engineering techniques.

Systems Engineering Technique	Used	How the V-2 Team Addressed it
define the problem	yes	See the section Problem Statement, above.
system feasibility analysis	no	Early in the project, the scientists only had faith that they would succeed.
system operational requirements	yes	See the section Problem Statement, above.
maintenance and support	late	By the time production rockets were available, there was a complete plan, but not early in the project.
technical performance measures	yes	This is evident for at least some subsystems: guidance, engine and aerodynamics, for example.
functional analysis	no	The overall design was created by experimental trial and error.
allocate requirements to subsystems	yes	Not explicitly stated in the sources, but the subsystem teams seem to have been given requirements.
requirements traced through implementation and test	no	There is no evidence of detailed requirements being defined or traced. They could not have been known because of the new technologies.
system synthesis, analysis, and design optimization	partial	Many design decisions were changed after they. Others were implemented only after extensive trade-off studies and model testing.
risk management	no	There was more scientific method than engineering method. Problems were dealt with as they came.
design integration	no	Integrating a design before any rocket was built was not possible with some many unknown technologies.
systematic testing	yes	This is evident in several places, sometimes as part of the scientific method, sometimes as part of engineering.
production	yes	This was extensively planned, and even begun before the developers were satisfied.
change control	late	This was successfully implemented, but only after they learned it during production.
operational use and sustaining support	yes	It is evident that equipping the mobile launchers and the aborted bunker launch facilities was well planned.
retirement and material disposal	no	No planning was done for this, but it was done.

Table 2. Relevant Systems Engineering Techniques

CONCLUSIONS

Many aspects of the V-2 program are in line with the principles of systems engineering, but many more aspects contradict those principles. What stands out most is the number technological areas in which the rocket team needed to pioneer. The liquid fuel rocket engine itself, fuel and oxidizer, guidance and supersonic aerodynamics were all new technologies. Little or no engineering basis existed for the team to build on. They were heavily dependent on the scientific method to answer many questions before they could begin their engineering work. There were many systems engineering points missed, but mostly this was not an engineering project. It was a large scientific experiment or a series of scientific experiments. Systems engineering was not used and could not have been used on the V-2 program as a whole.

The political situation also affected the use of systems engineering. Their customer, the German government and Dornberger's Army superiors, where not interested in defining the requirements, but Dornberger and his team defined the requirements themselves. They knew the importance of that aspect of systems engineering. Under the pressures of war, many things were rushed and some shortcuts were taken. Without the war, however, there would have been no significant resources available for such a program.

It is apparent that, after the scientific questions were answered, most aspects of systems engineering were applied at the subsystem level. Each had its requirements, and the interface parameters with which that subsystem team had to work. It has been noted that whole rocket system drawings did not appear until late in the project, when production was nearly ready to begin. One can infer from that statement that subsystem drawings were maintained prior to that time.

It is difficult to fault the German rocket developers for their systems engineering lapses. They used the scientific method where it applied, and they used the engineering method where it applied. This was a successful and well-run project.

REFERENCES

Ambrose, S. (1997). *American Heritage New History of World War II.* New York: Viking.

Collier, B. (1965). *The Battle of the V Weapons.* New York: William Morrow & Company.

Dornberger, W. (1954). "European rocketry after World War I." *Journal of the British Interplanetary Society*, 13, 245-262.

Dornberger, W. (1955). *V-2.* (J. Cleugh & G. Halliday, Trans.). New York: Viking.

Dornberger, W. (1958). "The Lessons of Peenemünde." *Astronautics*, 3, 18-20 (58, 60).

Dornberger, W. (1963). "The German V-2." *Technology and Culture*, 4, 393-409.

Dungan, T. (1999 August 29). *The A4/V2 Resource Site.* "The V-2 Rocket," [on-line]. Available: http://www.geocities.com/CapeCanaveral/Lab/9711 / [1999 September 4].

Ehricke, K. (1950). "The Peenemünde rocket center, part 1." *Rocketscience – The Journal of the Detroit Rocket Society, Inc.* 4, 17-22.

Ehricke, K. (1950). "The Peenemünde rocket center, part 2." *Rocketscience – The Journal of the Detroit Rocket Society, Inc.* 4, 31-35.

Ehricke, K. (1950). "The Peenemünde rocket center, part 3." *Rocketscience – The Journal of the Detroit Rocket Society, Inc.* 4, 57-63.

Ehricke, K. (1950). "The Peenemünde rocket center, part 4." *Rocketscience – The Journal of the Detroit Rocket Society, Inc.* 4, 81-88.

Garli|ski, J. (1978). *Hitler's Last Weapons: The Underground War Against the V-1 and V-2.* New York: Times Books.

Huzel, D. (1981). *Peenmünde To Canaveral.* Westport, Ct: Greenwood Press.

Kennedy, G. (1983). *Vengeance Weapon 2.* Washington, DC: Smithsonian Institution Press.

Klee, E. & Merk, O. (1965). *The Birth of the Missile: The Secrets of Peenemünde.* (T. Schoeters, Trans.). New York: E. P. Dutton & Co., Inc.

National Air and Space Museum. (1997 July 7). "Space Race: Military Origins of the Space Race," [on-line]. Available: http://www.nasm.edu/GALLERIES/GAL114/spaceRace/sec200/sec210.htm [1999 September 26].

Neufeld, M. (1995). *The Rocket and the Reich.* New York: The Free Press.

Overy, R. (1995). *Why the Allies Won.* New York: W. W. Norton and Company.

Piszkiewicz, D. (1995). *The Nazi Rocketeers: Dreams of Space and Crimes of War.* Westport, Ct: Praeger.

Piszkiewicz, D. (1998). *Wenher von Braun: the Man Who Sold the Moon.* Westport, Ct: Praeger.

Public Affairs Office, White Sands Missile Range, US Army. (1999 August). "V-2 Rocket at White Sands," [on-line]. Available: http://www.wsmr.army.mil/paopage/Pages/V-2.htm [1999 September 4].

Steinhoff, E. (1986). "Development of the German A-4 guidance and control system 1939-1945: a memoir." *History of Rocketry and Astronautics: Proceedings of the Third through Sixth History Symposia of the International Academy of Astronautics*, 203-215.

von Braun, W. & Ordway, F. (1976). *The Rockets' Red Glare.* New York: Anchor Press / Doubleday.

Wade, M. (1999 June 10). *Encyclopedia Astronautica*, [on-line]. Available: http://solar.rtd.utk.edu/%7Emwade/lvs/v2.htm [1999 September 4].

Waligorski, M. (1999 February 18). "German Rocketry - V-2 in Detail," [on-line]. Available: http://www.hotel.wineasy.se/ipms/stuff_eng_detail_a4.htm [1999 September 26].

BIOGRAPHY

T. Scott Ankrum is a software designer, project manager and developer with over 22 years of experience in many aspects of computing, from mainframe systems to Graphical User Interface development and client/server design. He has managed projects and led development teams, and has been personally involved in software development from requirements definition to final testing. He has worked mostly in information systems development and maintenance. Mr. Ankrum holds a B.S. degree in Computer Science from American University and is currently pursuing a Master of Software Engineering degree at the University of Maryland. He is a member of the Association for Computing Machinery (ACM).

An Approach to Develop a Systems Engineering Curriculum For Human Capital and Process Improvement

Gregory D. Burke
Deputy Director, FAA Office of Air Traffic Systems Development
Washington, DC

Michael J. Harrison
Program Director, FAA Architecture and Systems Engineering Directorate
Washington, DC

Robert E. Fenton
Manager, Systems Engineering Optimization
TRW Federal Enterprise Solutions
Washington, DC

Dr. Paul G. Carlock
Chief Systems Engineer
TRW Federal Enterprise Solutions
Washington, DC

Abstract: This paper describes the approach taken by the U.S. Federal Aviation Administration (FAA) to develop a Systems Engineering curriculum. The curriculum is designed and intended to support broader Agency initiatives for improving workforce professionalism, as well as product development and in-service operations life-cycle processes. It focuses not only on the knowledge base needed to perform satisfactorily as a systems engineer in the FAA, but also on the behavioral competencies needed for effective interactions in the FAA's team-intensive system development environment. The required knowledge and behavioral competencies were defined first, and then an integrated professional development approach was conceived that stresses the acquisition of needed skills and competencies through a combination of on-the-job assignments and experiences, formal education and training courses, and self-guided learning. The FAA's curriculum development approach provides a useful model for other organizations with similar goals and objectives to consider.

Introduction: As with most Federal Agencies, the Federal Aviation Administration is under pressure to do more with less. Notwithstanding the spiraling growth in U.S. air transportation requirements, the Agency has not and does not expect to receive comparable increases in its human resources. Instead, it is seeking to maximize its effectiveness and efficiency within relatively fixed resources.

Two particular strategies are part of this overall economization thrust: streamlined processes and workforce development. The Systems Engineering Curriculum largely is embedded in the workforce development initiative. Since the systems engineering process itself is integral to better product development and support, however, there is a collateral improvement in process performance directly expected from the workforce development activity. Specifically, the Systems Engineering Curriculum will provide the intellectual source material needed to develop the best processes, and subsequently will teach the workforce in the reengineered processes that will flow from the other ongoing process improvement activities.

THE U.S. NATIONAL AIRSPACE SYSTEM

Systems Engineering expertise is critical to safe and effective operation of the National Airspace System (NAS). U.S. aviation operations constitute over 60% of global traffic flows. As Figure 1 shows, the 55,000 daily flights are tracked, processed, and controlled by more than 30,000 facilities and 17,000 air traffic control personnel. Thus, the NAS is a very complex collection of systems, procedures, facilities, and people, working together as a single system to ensure safe and efficient operations.

Figure 1: The U.S. National Airspace System

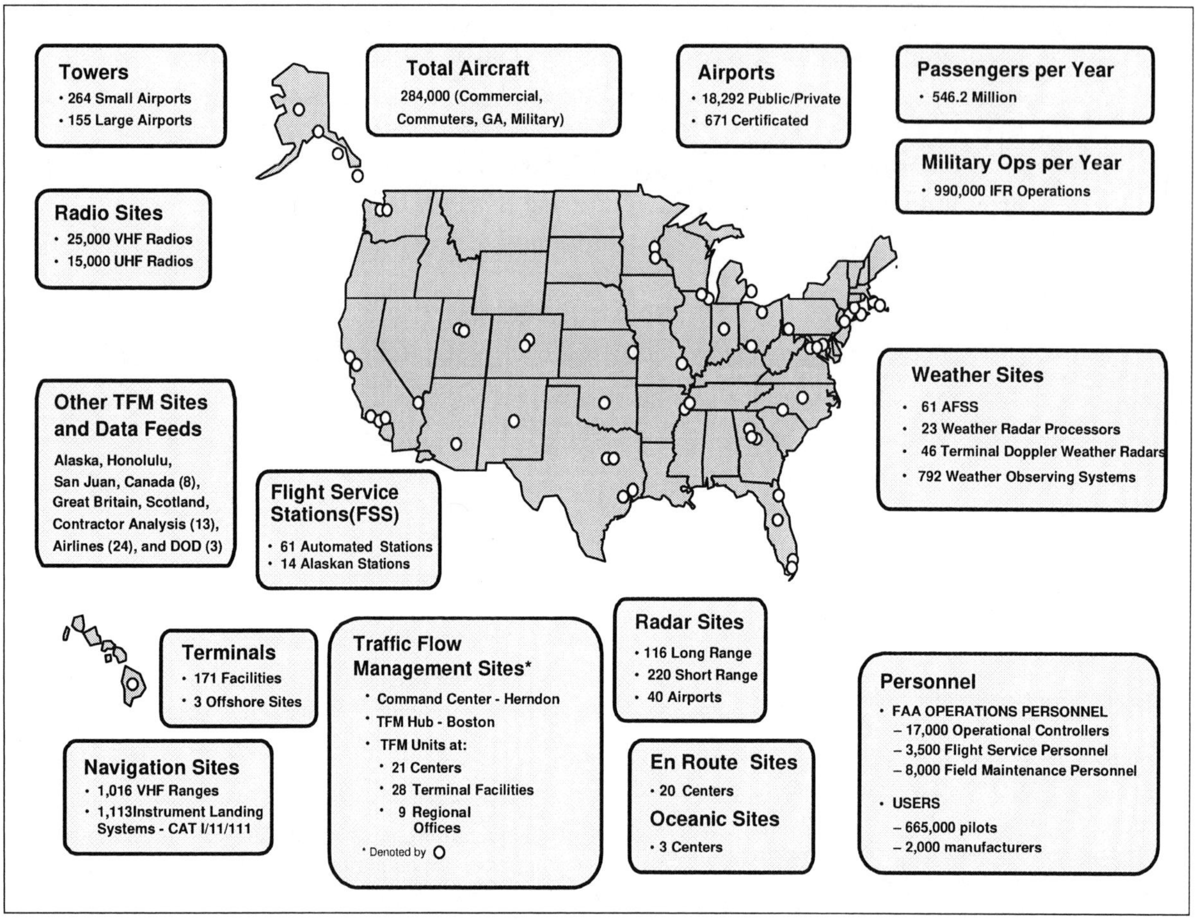

THE FAA HUMAN CAPITAL MANAGEMENT PROGRAM

Background: Two initiatives in the 1990s focused on the need for better FAA human captial management. The first initiative was Vice president Gore's National Performance Review, which recommended personnel reform as one way to improve the FAA's productivity, efficiency, and responsiveness. The second impetus was a major study by the Office of the Secretary of Transportation, which resulted in a legislative proposal for the creation of a U.S. Air Traffic Services (USATS) Corporation, partially to overcome the inflexibility of the FAA's personnel system.[1] While the Congress rejected the Corporation idea, it did empower the FAA to pursue personnel reform within a governmental framework. The Human Capital Management Program responds to that Congressional authorization.

Features of the Human Capital Management Program: Figure 2 illustrates the three major components of the ARA Human Capital Management Program, all designed to support the achievement of major organizational objectives in the ARA Performance Plan.

The Performance Management Program is a performance management and appraisal process using Management-by-Objectives techniques to measure individuals' annual contributions to broader organizational goals. It enhances productivity and performance by requiring managers to provide ongoing coaching and feedback, reward high performance behavior, and focus on results. The Acquisition Workforce Learning System (AWLS) is a framework to assist ARA employees in identifying their training and development needs and in locating and prioritizing the

[1] *Air Traffic Control Corporation Study,* Report of the Executive Oversight Committee to the Secretary of Transportation, May 1994.

learning opportunities to best meet those needs. Primary AWLS initiatives focus on intellectual capital investment planning, competency-based curricula development (including the systems engineering curriculum), individual development planning, learning support groups for managers and employees, and performance consulting with managers and work teams.

Figure 2: Relationship of ARA Performance Plan and Human Capital Management Program

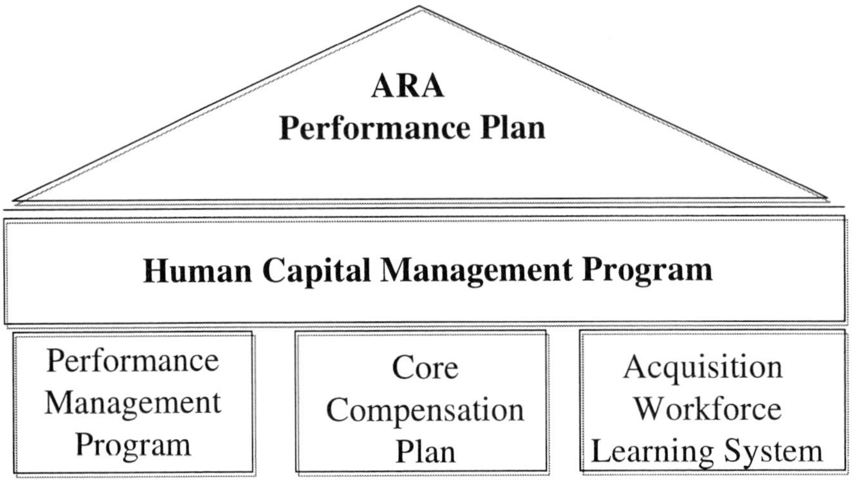

Intellectual Capital Investment Plan: Intellectual capital investment planning involves (1) the analysis of required knowledge, skills, and competencies needed now and in the future to meet organization goals, and (2) the development of approaches to eliminate the gap that may exist between future needed skills and those skills that the current workforce already possesses.

The FAA is focused on intellectual capital investments that make its workforce more capable across a range of requirements:

1. Ability to make both incremental and major changes
2. High quality and innovative nature of management and leadership
3. Ability to exploit Information Technology for knowledge sharing and reuse
4. Ability to create products economically by having a diversity of market-sensitive general knowledge and necessary expert knowledge
5. Ability to react to both short-term and forecasted long-term customer demands.

Each year, an Intellectual Capital Investment Plan (ICIP) is issued that describes the corporate investments the FAA will make to assist employees in preparing themselves to meet business objectives. Moreover, it outlines ARA's top priorities for developing its workforce and summarizes the corporate resources that are available to assist individual employees in developing themselves to meet the challenges of the future.

Curricula Development: To implement the ICIP, curricula are being developed to serve as road maps of required skills and competencies, as well as the learning opportunities to acquire those skills and competencies. Two types of curricula are being developed:

(1) **ARA Core Curriculum**—This curriculum is for all ARA employees, irrespective of their particular specialty. It addresses both the behavioral competencies (business behaviors) and technical knowledge that contribute to

Table 1: Desired Behavioral Core Competencies in ARA

• Adapting to change	• Planning and Prioritization
• Analytical Thinking	• System Thinking
• Communicating	• Teamwork / Collaboration
• Customer Focus	• Create a High-Performance Climate
• Decision Making	• Industry Expertise
• Drive for Results	• Influence and Negotiation
• Interpersonal Insight	• Innovation and Continuous Improvement
• Organizational Knowledge	• Networking
• Ownership and Accountability	• Strategic Orientation / Vision

■ = These competencies may not be required uniformly across the entire ARA workforce.

successful performance in the ARA workplace. The behavioral competencies are summarized in Table 1. Core courses will be designed to meet ARA unique learning requirements.

(2) **Role-Specific Curricula**—These curricula will address the knowledge elements and behavioral competencies needed for a particular technical or functional role or discipline, such as systems engineering, beyond those covered in the core curriculum. Over time, several distinctive curricula will be completed, representing the broad range of specialty jobs performed in ARA (e.g., contracting, administration, business management, etc.). Initially, however, four role-specific curricula have been developed, which were selected for the reasons shown in Table 2. These curricula will meet the immediate needs for these high-priority jobs, as well as furnish the roadmap for the remaining curricula. Currently, the four curricula are being integrated to ensure consistency and non-overlapping coverage, with particular attention being paid to the interplay between the Systems Engineering curriculum and the Project/Program Management curriculum.

Table 2: Initial ARA Role - Specific Curricula

Role	Constituents	Rationale
Project / Program Management	352	•Largest role constituency •Identified as highest priority •Existing Project Management Body of Knowledge (PMBOK)
Leadership and Management	246	•2nd largest role constituency •Synergy with Project Management
Software Engineering	91	•Effort already underway by Chief Information Officer •Existing BOK.
Systems Engineering	111	•Training effort already underway by Office of System Architecture and Investment Analysis. •Prior establishment of FAA Systems Engineering Council to improve SE performance

THE FAA PROCESS IMPROVEMENT PROGRAM

Acquisition Focus: Throughout the FAA, there are many initiatives underway tied to process improvement. Only one such initiative is described here, under the general topic of Acquisition Reform. As indicated previously, the FAA is capitalizing on its newly-delegated reform authority to reengineer its processes to support improved effectiveness and efficiency. Probably the leading process improvement initiative is Acquisition Reform. The new FAA Acquisition Management System strives for a 50 percent reduction in acquisition cycle time and a 20 percent reduction in acquisition costs.[2]

There are four key elements under acquisition reform. Financial management reform emphasizes life-cycle costs, analysis, and accountability, and includes the development of a robust Cost Accounting System. Cultural Change emphasizes workforce competency and improving individual and organizational effectiveness; the Human Capital Management Plan flowed from this strategic goal. Measures Implementation establishes key metrics for time, cost, quality, and performance; these are contained in an Executive-Level Metrics set and in subsidiary metric systems. Acquisition and Procurement Process Improvements use an Integrated Capability Maturity Model (the FAA-iCMM) to improve the way FAA manages, engineers, and acquires software-intensive systems across all phases of the FAA acquisition life cycle. Since processes are operated by people, it is not surprising that the FAA-iCMM and the Intellectual Capital Investment Plan are closely tied.

The FAA-iCMM: To simplify and streamline its acquisition process improvement effort, FAA developed the first major integrated Capability Maturity Model.[3] The FAA-iCMM integrates the Systems Engineering Capability Maturity Model (Version 1.1), the Software Acquisition CMM (Version 1.01), and the CMM for Software (Version 1.1) into a single, continuous representation with a recommended staging. Table 3 shows the Process Areas (PA) and the recommended staging for the FAA-iCMM. Under FAA's plan, 75% of selected Integrated Product Teams will achieve maturity level 2 by December 1999. ARA and its major internal customer, the Associate Administrator for Air Traffic Services (ATS), have

[2] *The 1998 FAA Strategic Plan.* May 20, 1998

[3] Ibrahim, Linda, et al, *The Federal Aviation Administration Integrated Capability Maturity Model (FAA-iCMM),* Version 1.0, November 1997 (http:www.faa.gov/aio)

Table 3: FAA Integrated Capability Maturity Model

Process Areas

Maturity Level 2

Lifecycle / Engineering Processes
- PA01: Needs
- PA02: Requirements
- PA05: Outsourcing
- PA08: System Test and Evaluation
- PA09: Transition

Management / Project Processes
- PA11: Project Management
- PA12: Contract Management

Supporting Processes
- PA15: Quality Assurance and Management
- PA16: Configuration Management

Maturity Level 3

Lifecycle / Engineering Processes
- PA03: Architecture
- PA04: Alternatives
- PA06: Software Development and Maintenance
- PA07: Integration

Management / Project Processes
- PA13: Risk Management
- PA14: Coordination

Supporting Processes
- PA17: Peer Review

Organizational
- PA20: Organizational Process Definition
- PA22: Training

Maturity Level 4

Lifecycle / Engineering Processes
- PA10: Product Evolution

Supporting Processes
- PA18: Measurement

Maturity Level 5

Supporting Processes
- PA19: Prevention

Organizational Processes
- PA21: Organization Process Improvement
- PA23: Innovation

Generic Practices

Capability Level 1: Initial: Performed Informally

Capability Level 2: Repeatable: Planned & Tracked
- 2.1 Establish policy
- 2.2 Allocate adequate resources
- 2.3 Assign responsibility
- 2.4 Ensure training
- 2.5 Document the process
- 2.6 Plan the process
- 2.7 Use a repeatable process
- 2.8 Management configurations
- 2.9 Assess process compliance
- 2.10 Verify work products
- 2.11 Measure process
- 2.12 Review status
- 2.13 Take corrective action

Capability Level 3: Defined: Well Defined
- 3.1 Standardize the process
- 3.2 Use defined process
- 3.3 Perform reviews with peers
- 3.4 Coordinate with affected groups

agreed to a common goal of institutionalizing mature lifecycle processes that enable high quality solutions to Agency and user needs, predictable cost and schedule, and increasing productivity. This goal will be achieved by improving process capability using the guidance of the FAA-iCMM.

The FAA is currently updating the FAA-iCMM to reflect the latest versions of the parent CMMs from which the FAA-iCMM was derived. Moreover, it is considering expanding the content of the FAA-iCMM to incorporate additional disciplines.[4]

The FAA Systems Engineering process is effectively embedded in the FAA-iCMM, since the FAA-iCMM incorporates the Systems Engineering CMM. Systems Engineering transforms operational needs into cost-effective solutions, a vitally important activity for the FAA. Accordingly, a major part of the FAA process improvement effort will occur through strengthening of its systems engineering process.

THE FAA SYSTEMS ENGINEERING CURRICULUM

Relationships: As the preceding sections describe, the systems engineering curriculum development is closely related to the objectives of the human capital management plan and to the FAA- iCMM-based process improvement effort. The ARA Core Curriculum provides Systems Thinking / Systems Engineering training for ARA employees depending on job performance needs. FAA has a major stake in having the best possible systems engineers in its workforce, and the best possible systems engineering process to orchestrate and revitalize its major acquisition activities.

Figure 3: Example Systems Engineering (SE) Role Profile for Senior Engineer

Role Title: Systems Engineering										
Role Category: Senior Engineer										
Major Focus: Provides specialized professional technical support in specific technology or function (e.g., electrical engineering, surveillance)										
Key Responsibilities					**Key Tasks**					
Technical Expertise in NAS – related area					Oversees or performs engineering trade studies					
					Provides specialized technical advice and consultation					
System Requirements / Acquisition Support					Leads or participates in IPT to develop / acquire new system					
Program Management Support					Skilled in program and engineering management tasks					
Core Competencies	**Competency Target**				**Role Specific Knowledge**	**Mastery Target**				
Adapts to Change	1	2	3	4	Generic SE Process	1	2	3	4	
Analytical	1	2	3	4	FAA Three-level SE Process	1	2	3	4	
Communication	1	2	3	4	Tailoring the SE Process	1	2	3	4	
Customer Focus	1	2	3	4	Integrated product & process development	1	2	3	4	
Decision Making	1	2	3	4	Measuring SE Capability	1	2	3	4	
Drive for Results	1	2	3	4	Risk Analysis and Management	1	2	3	4	
Interpersonal	1	2	3	4	SE Specialties	1	2	3	4	
Organizational Knowledge	1	2	3	4	SE Management	1	2	3	4	
Ownership and Accountability	1	2	3	4	SE Tools	1	2	3	4	
Planning and Prioritizing	1	2	3	4	SE Methodologies & Techniques	1	2	3	4	
Systems Thinking	1	2	3	4	Cost Analysis	1	2	3	4	
Teamwork/Collaboration	1	2	3	4	System Life Cycles	1	2	3	4	
Role-Specific Competencies	**Competency Target**				Operational & Systems Requirements	1	2	3	4	
Create High Performance Climate N/A	1	2	3	4	Problem solving	1	2	3	4	
Industry Knowledge	1	2	3	4	FAA System Domains	1	2	3	4	
Influence and Negotiation	1	2	3	4		1	2	3	4	
Innovation and improvement	1	2	3	4		1	2	3	4	
Networking	1	2	3	4		1	2	3	4	
Strategic Orientation/Visioning	1	2	3	4		1	2	3	4	

Key Features of the Systems Engineering Curriculum: The new curriculum has five primary features that define its composition and thrust:

(1) It treats both required behavioral competencies and technical/organizational knowledge and skills. The behavioral competencies are intrinsic to the consultant-type and technical roles of all ARA employees. As a result, the

---

[4] Ibrahim, Linda. *Using an Integrated Capability Maturity Model- The FAA Experience.* Proceedings of the Tenth Annual INCOSE Symposium, July 2000.

integration of technical, conceptual and business-related knowledge and skills in the context of ARA-unique work processes is being stressed, because it is essential to achieving employee effectiveness. Figure 3 is a typical "role profile" extracted from the curriculum, showing the desired development needs of an FAA Senior Engineer. The definitions for each of the four "mastery targets" for role-specific knowledge are shown in Table 4. The desired competency and mastery targets for all role profiles were established by the FAA Systems Engineering Council. The targets represent their views as to what level of systems engineering and behavioral expertise is required for all FAA engineers to perform satisfactorily in their jobs. Achievement of these targets will be measured through satisfactory completion of on-the-job assignments, training or education, and other directed learning experiences.

(2) It covers both generic and FAA-specific systems engineering processes and techniques. The basic intent is to provide both systems engineering "education" (the generic techniques) and "training" (the specific FAA practices and processes to be applied in the day-to-day jobs of the engineers). In particular, a central focus of the curriculum is the FAA three-level systems engineering process, depicted in Figure 4 and described in a recent INCOSE paper.[5] In this way, FAA engineers may understand the broad context of systems engineering, synthesize potential new best practices from a study of generic practices, and apply them in their FAA-iCMM process improvement efforts to upgrade FAA's performance continuously.

(3) It draws heavily on the concepts and material from professional organizations (INCOSE, IEEE, EIA, etc.). For example, it uses the ANSI/EIA-632 Standard in describing the generic Systems Engineering process. The FAA three-level process is then described as an adaptation of the ANSI/EIA-632 Standard to the special environment in which FAA operates.

(4) It ties directly to the normal expected career progression of systems engineers in the FAA. The curriculum reflects the competencies and knowledge requirements as an engineer moves from entry-level through journeyman and on to mastery as a Chief Systems Engineer.

Figure 4: The FAA Three-Level Systems Engineering Process

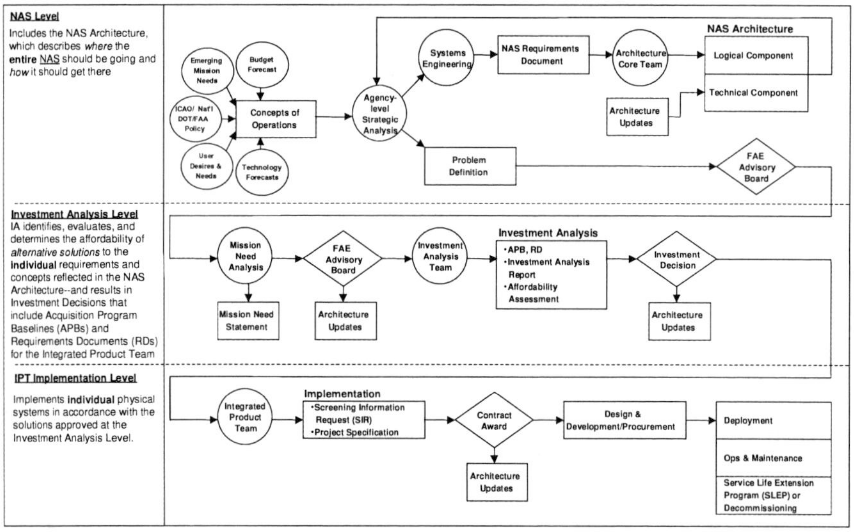

The FAA Three-Level systems engineering process is a key learning objective of the new FAA Systems Engineering Curriculum. The FAA Acquisition Executive (FAE) Advisory Board has a major role in overseeing systems engineering work at the NAS and Investment Analysis levels.

(5) It excludes the domain-specific technical knowledge also needed to function as a systems engineer in FAA. This domain knowledge (e.g., electrical engineering, telecommunications, navigation, etc.) will be acquired separately, predominantly through previous professional education and other FAA curricula.

---

[5] P.G. Carlock, J.A. Scardina, S.C. Decker, R.E. Fenton, C.W. Pate. *Agency-Level Systems Engineering for "Systems of Systems."* Proceedings of the Ninth Annual INCOSE Symposium, June 1999.

Table 4: Definitions of Systems Engineering Mastery Targets

1. **Awareness** – Provides a general, informed explanation; identifies resources (human/literature/information) that provide a greater depth of knowledge of system engineering as a discipline, as well as its application within the FAA.

2. **Understanding** – Explains systems engineering through definition and example, including the effort needed to perform systems engineering workmonitors progress and evaluates quality of results achieved.

3. **Execution** – Applies the systems engineering knowledge and learned experience to produce quality systems engineering products/service results; analyzes and/or evaluates systems engineering methods and techniques to achieve results.

4. **Mastery** – Instructs and mentors others about the best systems engineering practices and/or new developments. Provides expert advice and consultation on systems engineering techniques and practices gained from learned experience.

Curriculum Content: Table 5 summarizes the technical portion of the curriculum content. There are 15 major knowledge areas to be covered. Within each knowledge area there are several knowledge elements. For each knowledge area, the desired knowledge is staged through four mastery targets. Figure 5 shows one example of this staging for the "FAA Three-Level Systems Engineering Process" knowledge area.

Conclusions: The FAA is embarked on an ambitious voyage to improve its human capital and its processes. The Systems Engineering Curriculum is a key component of both initiatives. Now that the curriculum itself has been defined, tailored and generic systems engineering training is being developed and delivered to the workforce to implement the desired improvements. Nonetheless, this is a new initiative, barely a year old. Next year, we will follow up this paper with the "lessons learned" from the curriculum roll-out, and any changes needed to address unforeseen problems. The approach outlined in this paper may serve as a model for other organizations faced with similar development needs in their own environment.

Table 5: FAA Systems Engineering Knowledge Areas

Generic Systems Engineering Process and its Relationship to Project/ Program Management Process
- Defining Needs/ Operations Analysis and Research
- Concept of Operations
- Requirements Development
- Functional Analysis and Allocation
- System Architecture Synthesis
- System Analysis
- System Engineering Product Control
- System Engineering Process Control
- System Implementation Support

Relationship to Program/ Project Management

The FAA three-level Systems Engineering Process
- Differences between "generic" and "agency-level" / "system of systems" systems engineering
- The FAA 3-level SE Process
- FAA NAS-level systems engineering
- FAA IA-level systems engineering

FAA Implementation-level systems engineering

Tailoring the Systems Engineering Process
- What needs to be done?
- How to do it?

Systems Engineering and Integrated Product and Process Development
- Concurrent Engineering/ IPPD
- Overview of IPPD
- Systems Engineering in IPDS
- FAA organizationl roles and responsibilities

FAA organizational interface

Measuring Systems Engineering Capability
- Background; SE Capability models (e.g., EIA/IS 731)
- Relationship of SE models to FAA iCMM

Relationship of FAA SE process to FAA iCMM

Risk Analysis and Management
- Risk Identification
- Risk Assessment (Probability, severity, urgency)
- Risk Handling/ Mitigation

Risk Tracking

Cost Analysis and Management
- Life Cycle costing
- Functional Economic Analysis
- Work Breakdown Structure
- Cost Estimating Approaches
- Design to Cost
- Activity Based Costing
- Cost and Effectiveness Analysis

Cost /Benefit Analysis

Systems Life Cycles
- Research, Development, Test and Evaluation
- Systems Acquisition Life Cycle
- Planning and Marketing Life Cycle
- Software Acquisition Life Cycle

New Trends in Life-Cycles (e.g., COTS)

Systems Engineering Specialties Areas
- Systems Engineering Process
  - Information Architecture and Engineering
  - Requirements Engineering
  - Transition engineering
  - Configuration Management
  - Risk Engineering
  - Verification and Validation
  - Interface Management
- Specialty Areas / Products
  - Human Factors Engineering
  - Safety Engineering
  - Reliability Maintainability, and Availability
  - Information Security Engineering
  - Test and Evaluation
  - COTS-based Systems Engineering
  - Facility Systems Engineering
  - Aerospace Systems Engineering

Systems Engineering Management
- Evolution of Systems Engineering Structure and Organization
- Key systems engineering management (SEM) processes tools, and skills
- Activities and roles of the Systems Engineering Manager
- SEM Measures of success
- Managing the process in FAA

Selected Systems Engineering Methodologies and Techniques
- Architecture Development
- System architectures/decomposition/ WBS
- Requirements allocation
- Trade Studies
- Performance Analysis
- Information Engineering
- Data Modeling
- Prototyping
- Simulation and Modeling

Automated Systems Engineering Tools-
- Instruction on standard tools; how/when used, strengths/weaknesses
- Architecture database, CATS
- FAST
- DOORS
- COCOMO, SLIM

NASPAC, CODAS, PMAC

Operational and System Requirements
- What are requirements?
- Differences between operational and systems requirements
- Requirements Development Process
- Tools for Gathering Requirements
- Characteristics of a good requirement

Examples of good and bad requirements

FAA Systems Engineering Domains
- Air Traffic Management; service - level requirements
- Regulation and Certification; service - level requirements
- Aviation Security; service - level requirements
- Airport development; service - level requirements

Problem Solving
- Generic approach to problem solving
- Its adaptation to FAA environment

Figure 5: Example of Staged Knowledge

The FAA three-level Systems Engineering Process	Awareness	Understanding	Execution	Mastery
- Differences between "generic" and "agency-level" / "system of systems" systems engineering -The FAA 3-level SE Process -FAA NAS-level systems engineering -FAA IA-level systems engineering -FAA Implementation-level systems engineering	Familiar with the FAA 3 level SE process and roles/responsibilities of each level	Understands the model to apply to his/her own work in one or more SE levels	Executes the SE efforts in a major analytical effort in any one SE level (e.g., major investment analysis)	Operates the SE efforts in all 3 SE levels for a major organization (e.g., IPT)

Example of the desired staging of knowledge as an engineer progresses from "Awareness" to "Mastery"

Designing a Systems Engineering Educational Program Using Academic/Industry Collaboration

Mark A. Turnquist
Cornell University
School of Civil and Environmental Engineering
Ithaca, NY 14853

Raffaelo D'Andrea
Cornell University
Sibley School of Mechanical and Aerospace Engineering
Ithaca, NY 14853

Albert R. George
Cornell University
Sibley School of Mechanical and Aerospace Engineering
Ithaca, NY 14853

Peter Jackson
Cornell University
School of Operations Research and Industrial Engineering
Ithaca, NY 14853

Linda K. Nozick
Cornell University
School of Civil and Environmental Engineering
Ithaca, NY 14853

Donna Rhodes
Lockheed Martin Federal Systems
Owego, NY 13827

Robin Roundy
Cornell University
School of Operations Research and Industrial Engineering
Ithaca, NY 14853

Bart Selman
Cornell University
Department of Computer Science
Ithaca, NY 14853

Christine A. Shoemaker
Cornell University
School of Civil and Environmental Engineering
Ithaca, NY 14853

Robert J. Thomas
Cornell University
School of Electrical Engineering
Ithaca, NY 14853

Abstract. In concert with a fundamental precept in systems engineering, that system design should be driven by customer requirements, Cornell University is collaborating with industry in the development of a Master of Engineering program in Systems Engineering. This paper describes the underlying philosophy of Cornell's program, the collaborative process through which it has been developed, and the resulting curriculum, with a particular focus on the interaction between Cornell and Lockheed Martin Federal Systems (LMFS).

INTRODUCTION

A basic tenet of systems engineering is that system design should be driven by customer requirements. An educational program is certainly a system, and in creating the Master's program in Systems Engineering at Cornell University, there has been an active process of engaging some of the major customers of the program – companies that need access to such a program for their current engineers and who will also hire other graduates of the program – to define the requirements and help focus the program direction.

This paper describes the process that has been followed to define Cornell's program, with a particular focus on the interaction between Cornell and Lockheed Martin Federal Systems (LMFS). Cornell has brought to this collaboration an underlying educational philosophy for Master's degree education. The industrial partners, including LMFS, have provided the applications focus for that philosphy. Together, we are forging an innovative educational solution. We believe that publicizing this process can provide useful information for other universities and companies that are seeing the need for systems engineering education, and trying to create effective solutions to that need.

PROGRAM DEFINITION

The Need. Many of the most important problems being faced by our society are systems problems. Technological change drives shorter system life cycles as well as the need for more effective development of manufactured products, services, military systems, software systems, etc. At the same time, we are increasingly concerned about our environment as well as the basic infrastructure systems of our society that provide among other things, electricity, water, gas, telephone and communication services.

Our advancing society demands systems of increasing complexity. These systems are often designed to perform complicated functions with minimal and/or simple inputs from the person(s) using them. For example, we expect the cellular phone system to "find us" when someone calls our number, regardless of what cell we happen to be in. As another example, automated automotive suspension systems "tune" themselves to changes in road surface as we drive, with only a twist of a single knob from the driver to indicate whether a "sport" or "touring" ride quality is desired. To meet customer expectations for reliable performance of complex systems, a wide variety of complicated elements have to work together correctly.

Educating engineers to deal with systems engineering problems is a critical need, as is the development of new systems engineering methods and tools. These needs can be addressed through both teaching and research at a major research university like Cornell.

Functional Requirements. Our most basic functional requirement is to educate "T-shaped" engineers – that is, engineers who have both depth in an engineering discipline (the vertical part of the "T"), and the breadth to see across disciplinary boundaries and be able to fit the pieces of a system together (the horizontal part of the "T"). The Master of Engineering program at Cornell, as a professionally-oriented degree, is an ideal venue to increase both the depth and breadth of an engineering education, and to develop graduates who are well-adapted to take on systems engineering challenges in subsequent jobs. One of the unique aspects of Cornell's M.Eng. program is the project experience that is required, and the projects offer an exceptional opportunity to build teamwork and systems engineering skills in our graduates.

The strong multi-department support that has characterized the systems engineering development effort at Cornell provides a means through which we can improve on the single-department focus of several other universities (e.g., systems efforts within departments of industrial engineering at several universities, within departments of electrical engineering at others, or in the creation of separate systems engineering departments). We believe that systems engineering should be an explicit cross-disciplinary program, "matrixed" (in an organizational sense) with existing engineering departments, rather than either being contained within one of those departments, or defined as its own departmental "silo."

The status of systems engineering as a cross-disciplinary program in the College of Engineering creates the opportunity for core courses to be co-taught by faculty from different engineering departments, leading to important cross-fertilization of ideas among the faculty as well as the students. It also emphasizes the breadth of application of the central ideas of systems engineering, and creates an incentive for the program to be continually in touch with advances in the various disciplinary fields as well as with advances in systems engineering methods and techniques.

Conceptual Design. Our educational philosophy embraces both contextual learning (learning in context) and teamwork. It is our conjecture that students learn systems engineering best by induction, reasoning from the specific to the general. Systems engineering concepts in the abstract are of little value unless the student can relate the concepts to practical experience. Consequently, we place a heavy emphasis on contextual learning by motivating the abstractions with case studies, illustrating the methodologies with application, and integrating the learning through structured projects.

For example, a team project in the first core course in the program (Applied Systems Engineering I) requires a team of four students who have different disciplinary engineering backgrounds to create a proposal for a hybrid (solar-gasoline) powered cruising boat for a charter service on New York's State Canal System (what was once the original Erie Canal). This project requires an integrated conceptual design of subsystems for solar energy collection, on-board electric power storage, shore-based recharging, and a gasoline-powered engine for back-up and peak power use, as well as shore facilities and tour packages that make economic sense as a business enterprise. The team as a whole must understand the requirements for the complete system, how those requirements are derived, and how the work that each individual does on one or another of the subsystems fits into the overall picture.

This type of project activity emphasizes our view that in the professional world into which our students will graduate, work is organized around teams of specialists with diverse skills. Hence, we make teamwork an intrinsic part of the curriculum and challenge the students to excel at communication and coordination.

A master's level program in systems engineering should be available to both on-campus and off-campus students. Our program design involves integrating on-campus and off-campus activities and studies, and therefore involves both substantial "distance learning" components and on-campus "laboratory" exercises for off-campus students.

IMPORTANCE OF INDUSTRY/UNIVERSITY COLLABORATION

Collaboration between industry and universities has become increasingly important to achieve common goals:

1. Further the development of systems engineering;
2. Grow tomorrow's engineering workforce;
3. Combine resources to achieve advanced research objectives; and
4. Ensure educational experience is aligned with future engineering challenges.

In the past, many companies felt they could afford to satisfy educational needs for their engineering staff by creating and conducting comprehensive internal education programs. However, streamlined organizations, attention to affordability, and the complexity of education required by today's engineering professionals are driving companies to abandon the goal of providing most or all of the continuing engineering education from within. While consultants and commercial education providers can fill some of the training needs, universities are best suited to providing a full educational experience and the means to ensure young engineers expand their base knowledge by obtaining advanced degrees.

From the other side, universities are finding collaboration to be critical to ensuring their programs are relevant to the needs of students from industry. As universities better understand the needs of industry, they can provide students with improved educational offerings that employers are seeking. Industry can also provide universities with access to case studies, funding for mutually beneficial research projects, and industry internship experiences for both faculty and students.

IMPLEMENTING THE COLLABORATIVE PROCESS

The relationship between Cornell University and LMFS-Owego is an excellent example of successful collaboration in the formation and growth of a systems engineering program. This relationship has evolved from initial contact to a more formal relationship:

- Initial Meeting. In the early stages of developing a systems engineering specialization in its M.Eng. program, Cornell initiated an information exchange with LMFS-Owego. The initial meeting involved presentations from each side: Cornell presented the approach and strategy for the systems engineering initiative within the College of Engineering. LMFS-Owego shared its engineering educational needs and current educational programs. In this stage, LMFS-Owego was able to convey key needs to Cornell.
- Industry Exchange Meeting. The initial meeting grew to a multi-participant exchange meeting with several other companies involved. Industry participants were presented with the details of the Cornell strategy and curriculum plans, and were briefed on student projects. Following these sessions, industry representatives met in a facilitated session to develop industry comments on the program. At this point in time, LMFS-Owego was able to influence the program in early stages to better meet its future needs.
- Industry Advisory Meeting. Following this meeting, Cornell created a more formal Industry Advisory Board. Industry comments from the previous meeting were used to improve upon the initial program design. For example, industry recommended Cornell do some "benchmarking" against similar programs in other universities, which resulted in findings that were of considerable interest to both the university and involved industry participants. LMFS-Owego benefited from discussions with Cornell and other companies on various topics – for example, discussions on common educational needs, key skills needed by systems engineers, and the need for case studies as part of the educational experience. These meetings are continuing with an expanding participant base. LMFS-Owego is a contributor to the formation of Cornell's systems engineering program, and is a beneficiary of the results this program yields. The opportunity to dialogue with industry peers in a non-competitive situation is also extremely beneficial.

LMFS is also gaining secondary benefits from its collaboration with Cornell. By assisting Cornell in the development of case studies, LMFS is forced to take a more introspective look at itself, and thereby captures lessons learned and best practices in a manner that provides benefit to future programs. Collaboration also permits preferred access to top-notch students through involvement related to internships and sponsored research.

Table 1 summarizes the exchange involved in the university/industry collaboration.

CURRICULUM ELEMENTS

The systems engineering curriculum that has resulted from the interactions between Cornell and its industrial partners focuses particular attention on eight major elements:

- Requirements analysis
- Functional, behavioral and structural analysis
- Simulation, optimization and multicriteria decision making
- Risk assessment and management
- Life cycle analysis
- Teamwork and project management
- Information flow in systems
- Feedback control.

These elements are closely related to the set of "core" subject matter for systems engineering identified

	Industry Provides to University	***University Provides to Industry***
Educated Workforce	• Present/future skill needs for engineers • Internship opportunities	• Delivery of degree programs and continuing education courses • Internship candidates
Applicatio n	• Case study information	• Formalized case studies embedded in courses
Research	• Research funding/priorities	• Conduct of research projects and resulting innovations
Formal exchange	• Participation in the university sponsored Industry Advisory Board	• Opportunity to influence curriculum • Opportunity to learn about peer company education needs/plans

Table 1. Summary of collaborative exchanges.

by INCOSE (Panitz, 1997), but include additional emphasis on modeling (especially optimization models), information flows in systems, and feedback control, reflecting particular expertise and experience among the Cornell faculty.

The approach we are taking to functional, behavioral and structural analysis emphasizes connections between traditional tools (functional flow block diagrams and N^2 diagrams, for example) and the object-oriented perspective that is widely favored in software engineering (Oliver, *et al.*, 1997). Making these connections is important for students who will become system engineers and who will need to communicate effectively with both hardware engineers and software engineers.

We place particular emphasis on optimization and multicriteria decision making because decisions on tradeoffs in system design are at the heart of effective system engineering. The underlying goal is nearly always to make the "best" decisions (hence the focus on optimization), and there are nearly always multiple, often conflicting, criteria that must be included in the decision. Emphasis on these topics provides the students with the ability to structure decision-making problems they will face, as well as specific tools to help resolve some of those problems.

The first five of the eight elements listed above are emphasized across a two-term course sequence in Applied Systems Engineering. These two courses are team-taught, and include faculty from all five of the major participating departments (civil & environmental engineering, electrical engineering, mechanical & aerospace engineering, operations research & industrial engineering, and computer science).

Our approach to teaching teamwork and project management skills uses a team-taught course with one faculty member who is an engineer and another who is a sociologist. This has yielded a project management course that places equal emphasis on the "technical" skills of project management (planning, scheduling, budgeting, etc.) and the "people" skills (team-building, motivation, conflict resolution, etc.). The result is an innovative and comprehensive view of project management that serves students very well.

Finally, our emphasis on feedback control and information flows in systems reflects the growing sophistication of manufactured products and services in the commercial sector, as well as defense-related systems. Almost all types of systems are using greater software-hardware integration, and a growing proportion of total system cost is devoted to automated sensing, information management within the system, as well as automated control of system functions. These topics are addressed through a variety of elective courses.

THE ROLE OF PROJECT EXPERIENCES

Systems engineering is a set of skills that must be learned by practicing, using case studies and project experiences as an integral part of the educational program. The Master of Engineering degree at Cornell has a requirement for a substantial project experience, and this project experience is vital for students in systems engineering. There are several team project activities each year, but one example can serve to illustrate the important integrative role that these projects play.

In the 1998-99 academic year, a Cornell team first entered the International RoboCup Competition, where teams of robots play soccer against one another. The competition has basic rules about allowable size of robots, for example, and rules of play (e.g., robots cannot "shelter" the ball). However, the rules leave wide latitude for creative design of both the robots themselves and the larger system (including global vision of the field and strategy controllers, for example) that makes up the complete team effort for effective competition.

A total of 24 students participated in this effort, in two teams of 12. Each student team designed and built a team of robots, to compete against each other, but the two teams collaborated in design of the global vision system, in anticipation of forming an effective Cornell entry in the international competition. The teams went through a careful systems engineering effort during the fall semester of 1998, doing requirements analysis, functional and behavioral analysis, simulation to test out different conceptual designs, etc. Actual construction of the robots began in February, 1999. By early May, competitive intramural games were played between the two teams, and decisions were made on final modifications prior to the international competition in Stockholm, Sweden, in late July.

The careful systems approach used by the Cornell team paid dramatic dividends, when in their first year of entering the competition the Cornell team emerged as the World Champion, defeating teams from South Korea, Singapore, New Zealand, Portugal, and Germany en route to the championship. This kind of project experience allows the students to "live" the process of systems engineering, putting the otherwise abstract tools into practice, and seeing the effects in a direct and dramatic way.

There are also other projects that are directly sponsored by industrial partners that allow students to engage in activities that have a direct and meaningful impact on real operations in those companies. These projects take on a different "flavor" than the RoboCup project, for example, and they are also important models for systems engineering project activities.

SUMMARY AND CONCLUSIONS

We have described the effort by Cornell University and several industrial partners to jointly develop a systems engineering educational program that contains several innovative and effective features. We have focused particularly on the interaction between Cornell and Lockheed Martin Federal Systems (LMFS). Cornell has brought to this collaboration an underlying educational philosophy for Master's degree education. The industrial partners, including LMFS, have provided the applications focus for that philosphy. Together, we are forging an innovative educational solution.

The curriculum that has resulted from this collaborative process contains the elements identified by INCOSE as the "core" material for systems engineering programs, as well as additional emphasis on material that reflects particular expertise among the Cornell faculty. One of the hallmarks of the program is a strong concentration on project activities as being central to systems engineering education.

We believe that publicizing this collaborative process and its outcome can provide useful information for other universities and companies that are seeing the need for systems engineering education, and trying to create effective solutions to that need.

REFERENCES

Panitz, Beth, "Training Technology's Maestros," *ASEE Prism,* November 1997, pp. 18-24.

Oliver, D.W., T.P. Kelliher and J.G. Keegan, Jr., *Engineering Complex Systems with Models and Objects*. McGraw-Hill, New York, 1997.

BIOGRAPHIES

Dr. Mark Turnquist is a professor of Civil and Environmental Engineering at Cornell University. His research interests are in large-scale network optimization for logistics, transportation and production systems. He received his B.S. from Michigan State University in 1971, and S.M. and Ph.D. degrees from MIT in 1972 and 1975, respectively.

Dr. Raffaelo D'Andrea is an Assistant Professor in the Sibley School of Mechanical and Aerospace Engineering at Cornell University. His research interests are in theoretical, computational, and experimental issues associated with the control of mechanical and aerospace systems. He received his B.Sc. From the University of Toronto in 1991 and his M.S. and Ph.D. from the California Institute of Technology in 1992 and 1997, respectively.

Dr. Albert George is the J.F. Carr Professor of Mechanical and Aerospace Engineeering at Cornell University. His research interests are the aerodynamics of aircraft and ground vehicles. Aeroacoustic noise mechanisms and the aerodynamic performance and design of aircraft, automobiles and fans are particularly emphasized. Other interests involve manufacturing systems. Dr. George received his B.S. and Ph.D. degrees from Princeton in 1959 and 1964, respectively.

Dr. Peter Jackson is an Associate Professor of Operations Research and Industrial Engineering at Cornell University. His research interests are in material logistics in manufacturing systems. He is also an expert in the development of experiential games for education. His games are in active use at several corporations for training as well as in current courses taught at Cornell. He receievd his B.A. from Western Ontario University in 1975 and his M.S. and Ph.D. from Stanford in 1980.

Dr. Linda Nozick is an Associate Professor of Civil and Environmental Engineering at Cornell University. Her research interests are in the development and effective use of mathemeatical models to design and operate systems. Particular systems of interest are manufacturing, transportation and health care systems. She received her B.S. from George Washington University in 1989 and her M.S. and Ph.D. from the University of Pennsylvania in 1990 and 1992, respectively.

Dr. Donna Rhodes is Senior Manager of Systems Engineering Technology at Lockheed Martin Federal Systems in Owego, New York. She consults with numerous projects on systems engineering practices, technologies, and methods, and oversees the engineering excellence program. She is President of the International Council on Systems Engineering (INCOSE) and is an Associate Editor of the INCOSE journal, *Systems Engineering.* Dr. Rhodes has had an active role in evolving the practice of systems engineering over the past decade through corporate and inductry involvement. She has authored over 30 technical papers, and co-authored many corporate and industry standards and guidebooks on Systems Engineering. Dr. Rhodes received her M.S. and Ph.D. in Advanced Technology/Systems Science from Binghamtom University.

Dr. Robin Roundy is an Associate Professor in Operations Research and Industrial Engineering at Cornell University. His research interests are in the development of algorithms for decision-making in supply chains, manufacturing and distribution systems. His current research efforts are focused on capacity planning in the semiconductor industry and on issues of supplier integration. He received his B.A. and M.A. from Brigham Young University in 1978 and 1980 respectively. He received his Ph.D. from Stanford in 1984.

Dr. Bart Selman is an Associate Professor of Computer Science at Cornell University. His research interests are in artificial intelligence and computer science including tractable inference, knowledge representation, search, constraint satisfaction, planning, scheduling, default reasoning, and natural language understanding. He has a M.Sc. and a Ph.D. in Computer Science from the University of Toronto and a M.Sc. in Physics from Delft University.

Dr. Christine Shoemaker is a Professor of Civil and Environmental Engineering at Cornell University. Her research interests are in the development of numerically efficient optimization algorithms for large-scale problems and the application of optimization and modeling procedures to problems arising in environmental management. A major empahsis in her current research is on groundwater contamination and remediation. She received her B.S. from the University of California at Davis in 1966 and her M.S. and Ph.D. degrees from the University of Southern California in 1969 and 1971, respectively.

Dr. Robert Thomas is a Professor of Electrical Engineering at Cornell University. His research interests are in the area of analysis and control of nonlinear continuous and discrete-time systems with applications to large-scale electric utility systems and electromechanical-drive systems. He received his B.S.E.E., M.S.E.E. and Ph.D. degrees from Wayne State University in 1968, 1969, and 1973, respectively.

Creativity and Innovation in the Systems Engineering Process

Dr. David H Cropley
Systems Engineering & Evaluation Centre
University of South Australia
Mawson Lakes, SA 5095
Australia

Professor Arthur J Cropley
University of Hamburg
C/- 120 South Terrace
Adelaide, SA 5000
Australia

Abstract. The systems engineering process, applied across a typical system life-cycle model, features design, or synthesis, as a core element. Creativity and innovation are required, to varying degrees, in all successful synthesis activities in systems engineering. The process of creativity and innovation in systems engineering is, however, poorly understood and is not adequately fostered. Educational institutions also place little emphasis on creativity and innovation in undergraduate teaching. This deficiency results in an engineering culture that is frequently resistant to the factors which promote creativity and innovation. This paper presents a phase-model of creativity which maps onto the process of synthesis in the systems engineering life-cycle. The paper serves as a framework for fostering creativity and innovation in systems engineers, at all levels, as well as for embedding a creativity culture in the systems engineering process.

INTRODUCTION

The nature and role of creativity and innovation has received only modest attention over a long period of time, in engineering education literature. Cropley, Priest and Cropley (1997) and Cropley and Cropley (1998) provide an overview of relevant literature. Examples of attempts to place a formal structure on creativity training for engineers are rare, but include Bailey (1978) and Hanson (1987). At the same time the important roles which creativity and innovation have to play in engineering generally, and systems engineering specifically, cannot be doubted. Bollay (1970) states: "Actually, in most systems engineering projects the most difficult phase is the system *synthesis* rather than the analysis. Systems synthesis requires the greatest ingenuity in finding promising new concepts and will ordinarily require both technological inventions as well as organisational innovations. This system synthesis phase also requires the use of judgment and good sense, so as to achieve a system which represents a major advance but is not hopelessly difficult or unreasonably expensive and time consuming to develop".

Much of the modern interest in creativity in engineering resulted from the "Sputnik shock" that followed the success of the Soviet Union in launching Sputnik 1 in 1957. Despite legislation in the United States (National Defense Act) to rectify perceived faults in the training of American engineers in creative skills, little progress seems to have been made in embedding creativity and innovation as a recognised component of formal engineering education (Cropley and Cropley, 1998).

Current practice suggests that creativity and innovation (C&I) is largely regarded as a black art, possessed by some, and not by others. Companies may pay lip service to the need for C&I, or may even regard themselves as paragons of C&I, yet frequently this is the result of individual 'champions' rather than a systematic, cultural adherence to C&I in work practices and education.

Many and varied forms of C&I training and models exist. Systems engineers may be familiar with the TRIZ methodology (Williams, 1984, the acronym translates as Theory of Inventive Problem Solving) originating in the Soviet Union in the 1950's. Others may have experience of the concepts and methods of proponents such as Edward De Bono, or of techniques such as brainstorming and synectics. Given the important role of C&I in the synthesis of systems, and its consequent key role in the systems engineering process, it is important to identify a key shortcoming of many existing techniques. This deficiency, identified in Cropley (1995) is that most current methods for developing skills in C&I focus only on "cognitive skills" (skills related to thinking). The model of creativity presented in this paper builds on this, but stresses also the importance of non-cognitive factors (social, motivational, etc.) in creativity training. As stated in Cropley and Cropley (1998), "there is something incongruous about trying to foster interest in seeking the novel, unknown and unexpected by requiring people to learn set techniques off by heart".

This paper presents a model of creativity and innovation that can be applied to both the education of engineers (systems and otherwise) and to the systematic promotion of creativity and innovation in systems engineering.

A MODEL OF CREATIVITY AND INNOVATION FOR SYSTEMS ENGINEERING

Two aspects of creativity are relevant to the systems engineering process. The first is the identification of those psychological elements of creativity which adequately model the cognitive factors (related to thinking) and non-cognitive factors (relating to social influences and personality characteristics) associated with creativity. These psychological elements are of importance to systems engineering because they point the way to the development of a paradigm that can be overlaid on individual stages in the generic SE process. A "creativity process" overlay could be applied at any stage involving 'synthesis' activities, and would stimulate enhanced creativity and innovation in the engineering of complex system solutions.

The underlying activities at each of the stages, described more fully in Blanchard and Fabrycky (1998), or the INCOSE Systems Engineering Handbook (INCOSE, 1998), include processes of synthesis (of system-level solutions, of functional solutions, of physical solutions, and of innovative production methods) as well as analysis, testing and support. The greatest scope for creativity and innovation is found in the earliest stages of the systems engineering process life-cycle, in conceptual design. The emphasis here is on describing *what* the system must do, not *how* it must do it. As the process progresses the opportunity for creativity decreases with increasing definition of *how* the system must meet its requirements. This sequence repeats itself at lower levels in preliminary and detail design, always moving from lower degree of definition of the solution (focussed only on *what* the system, sub-system or components must do) to a higher degree of definition (the *how*). The dangers presented by implementation-specific requirements, at any level of abstraction, are thus borne out by the creativity process model. It is highly likely that the problem for which a solution is sought has no precedent, requiring completely new solutions and previously untried integration of disciplines and concepts. Requirements, at the system level, which constrain solution options at this point kill off the opportunity for creativity and innovation, and block the attendant benefits that these frequently bring.

From the psychological point of view, the essence of creativity is production of novelty (Cropley, 1999). Innovation requires the further step of inserting the novelty into a functioning system, for instance a research and development environment, in such a way that it works. It is, in a sense, applied creativity. Innovation thus results from a combination of factors: deep technical or specialist knowledge and appropriate management attitudes and skills, to be sure, but also 'creativity' factors. For the purposes of the present paper we must assume that engineers participating in a design process embedded in the engineering of a complex system are technically competent. The area of potential weakness in the creative process of system synthesis and problem solution that we wish to emphasise here is that of gaining and developing the 'creativity' skills, and using them in a positive and supportive environment.

Cropley and Urban (in press) show that, psychologically speaking, creativity can be regarded as having four facets: cognitive aspects (thinking skills and knowledge), motivational aspects, personality factors, and social influences. They distinguish between thinking aimed at finding the single, best, "correct" answer to a standard problem in the shortest time (convergent thinking) and thinking aimed at redefining or "discovering" problems and solving them by means of branching out, making unexpected associations, applying the known in unusual ways, seeing unexpected implications, and the like (divergent thinking). Facaoaru (1985) showed that engineers regarded as highly successful were skilled at both divergent and convergent thinking. Divergent thinking requires motivational states such as willingness to take risks, tolerance of ambiguity, and the courage of one's own convictions, as well as personal properties such as openness, flexibility and nonconformity. In order to lead to innovation, novel ideas must be communicated to other people, who must in turn be willing to accept the unexpected or unconventional, respect the inspired failure, give credit for attempting to break away from the everyday. All of this is accompanied in the mind of the person striving to achieve effective novelty by feelings and emotions such as excitement, hope, or satisfaction.

Cropley and Urban (in press) have developed a model of creativity based on this analysis. They expand Wallas's (1926) phase model of creativity to include seven phases in the emergence of a novel (creative) product: To Wallas's four phases of Information, Incubation, Illumination and Verification they have added a phase of Definition (or Activation) before Information, and phases of Communication and Validation after Verification (see figure 1). In the present paper we will refer to the first phase as "Preparation", since this fits better with an SE approach. These terms are used in a psychological context. The emergence of a creative product (or system), is seen as a process, usually involving all seven phases. In the various phases, different psychological factors predominate, for instance in the phase of Incubation convergent thinking and goal-directedness may be most important. In the phase of

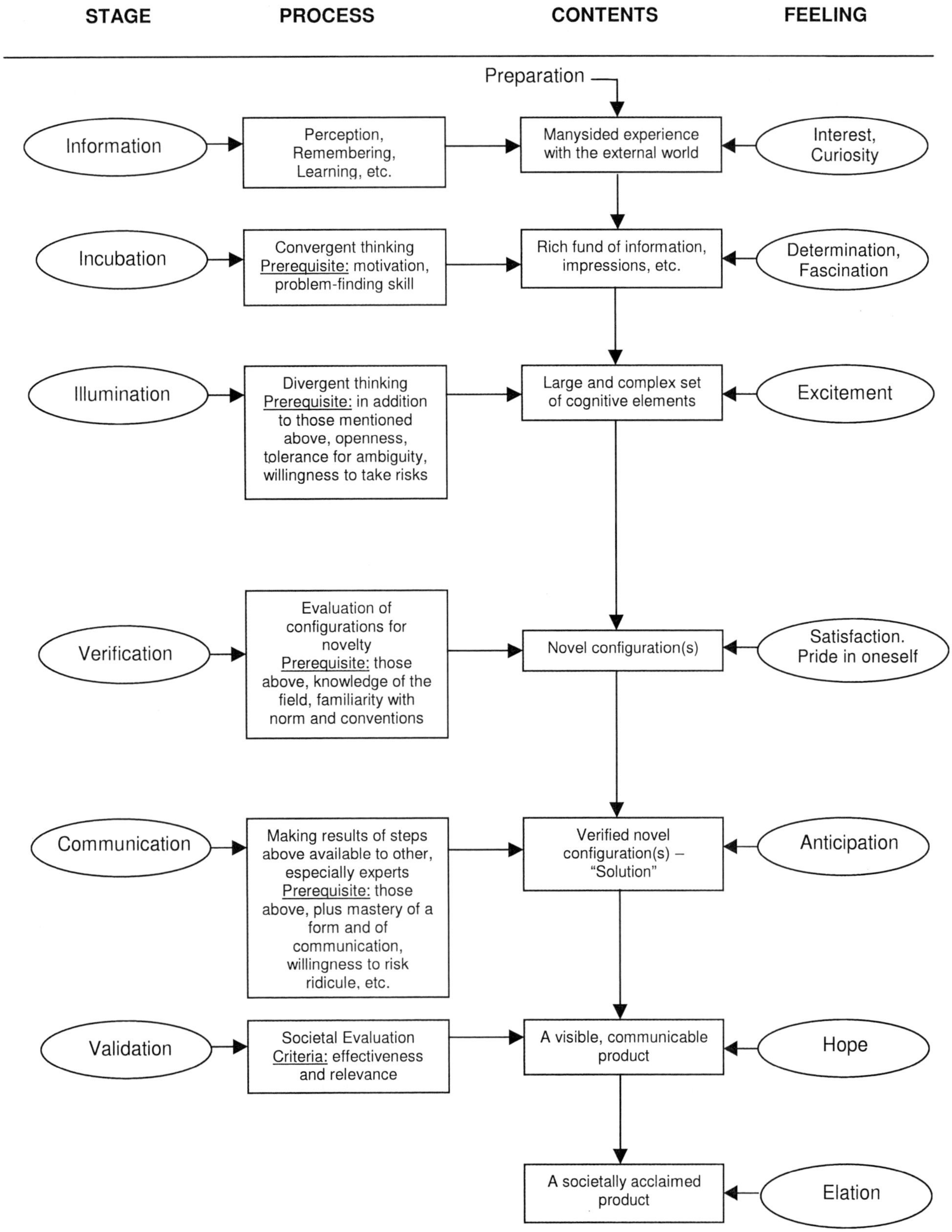

Figure 1. The Creativity Phase Model

Illumination, by contrast, divergent thinking, requiring openness and tolerance for ambiguity, predominates.

The output of each phase serves as the content of the next. For instance, the novel ideas generated in the phase of Illumination are the material worked on in the following phase of Verification, where once again convergent thinking is predominant. Each step is accompanied by appropriate feelings such as fascination (Incubation), excitement (Illumination) or hope (Validation). Our view is that this phase model of creativity can be applied to many stages involving synthesis in the SE lifecycle.

CREATIVITY PHASE MODEL STAGES

In order to draw parallels between the creativity phase model and the process of system synthesis, it is necessary to first describe the phase model stages in more detail. The general flow of the model is that processes (cognitive) and feelings (non-cognitive) act on some content (see figure 1) resulting in new content. The phase model flows from top to bottom, and from left and right, into the centre (contents), to the next stage.

Stage 0 (Preparation). This stage is important, both from a psychological model perspective, and in terms of the activities which are associated with system synthesis. The preparation stage acknowledges that creativity does not take place in isolation from other specific design activities, but requires a continual building of 'latent' knowledge in the mind of the engineer. This may be exemplified by considering a child who travels to school each day on a bus, over a period of time. Without conscious thought, the child builds latent knowledge about aspects of driving, instrument panels and customer service, for example. Years later that child becomes a design engineer for an automotive firm. It may only be at this stage that the latent knowledge is put into effect, when the engineer consciously, or unconsciously utilises the latent knowledge to design a new automobile. The preparation phase offers the opportunity to gather latent knowledge of both a generalist, and specific nature, which may be used at some future point in time. The output from this stage is a rich source of latent knowledge, or a many-sided experience of the external world.

Stage 1 (Information). This stage applies cognitive processes such as perception, remembering and learning, as well as non-cognitive factors such as interest and curiosity, to the rich source of latent knowledge derived from stage 0, in the context of a particular problem. These early stages highlight the role that deep professional knowledge has to play in creativity. In other words, it is apparent that creativity is not the result of divine inspiration, dreams or a predisposition to artistic skills. Rather it comes from preparation and knowledge of a particular field, and the harnessing of that knowledge for a purpose.

Stage 2 (Incubation). The incubation stage refines and redefines a particular problem. Convergent thinking skills, requiring motivation and awareness of a problem, together with non-cognitive factors such as determination and fascination, act on the fund of information and impressions. Convergent thinking, focused on recognising, recalling, reapplying and conforming, is important in generating the large and complex set of cognitive elements that results from the incubation stage, all in the light of an acknowledged problem.

Stage 3 (Illumination). The illumination stage applies divergent thinking, characterised by synthesis, transformation, inference, construction and context shifting, to the large and complex set of cognitive elements derived from stage 2. In order to successfully engage in this stage divergent thinking requires openness, tolerance for ambiguity and willingness to take risks as further characteristics of the creator. These are encouraged by positive emotional states such as excitement. This stage results in novel configuration(s).

Stage 4 (Verification). This stage seeks to evaluate the novel configurations derived from stage 3. As a prerequisite to this stage are knowledge of the field (professional knowledge) as well as familiarity with norms and conventions. Non-cognitive factors influencing this stage are satisfaction and pride. This stage results in verified novel configuration(s), or a "solution".

Stage 5 (Communication). Once derived, the solution(s) must be communicated to others, in particular experts. This stage requires the ability to communicate effectively, in addition to non-cognitive aspects such as a willingness to risk ridicule. The stage will be accompanied also by emotions such as anticipation of positive or negative feedback.

Stage 6 (Validation). The visible, communicable product or system which results from stage 5 is subjected to societal evaluation, examining it especially for effectiveness and relevance. These terms relate to the degree to which the product or system fulfils its objectives. Non-cognitive factors such as hope accompany this stage. Successful evaluation results in an acclaimed product or system, with consequent feelings of elation and success in the developers.

The phase model of creativity is subject to additional

influences not shown in figure 1. The process may be iterative at many stages, with both process loops, and temporal loops overlaid on the model flow. For example there may be multiple iterations around stages 2 (incubation) and 3 (illumination) as ideas are developed and refined. Alternatively there may be jumps from one stage to another which take place over longer periods of time, perhaps when new knowledge results in the ability to make progress in an earlier stage.

The creativity phase model represents a robust psychological model of creative processes. The present paper seeks now to map the stages of system synthesis onto the creativity phase model in order to shed light on the role of creativity in systems engineering. In anticipation of the following sections, it will be possible to formulate a synthesis phase model combining the stages of creativity, and their cognitive and non-cognitive factors, with the stages of system synthesis derived from the systems engineering process. This will not only serve to assist in facilitating the synthesis process, but will also indicate how creativity in system architecture synthesis may be fostered and improved.

SYSTEM ARCHITECTURE SYNTHESIS

The INCOSE Systems Engineering Handbook (INCOSE, 1998) provides a concise summary of the stages of system architecture synthesis, and the place of this activity in the wider systems engineering process. This activity may take place at different levels of the system hierarchy as the system evolves from concept through to operations.

The processes of requirements analysis and functional analysis provide the synthesis stage with a definition of a set of functions which are necessary to carry out the system's mission, and a quantification of how well those functions must be carried out and with what constraints. In simple terms the individual or team conducting the system synthesis must choose the system elements with appropriate characteristics, in a suitable arrangement to satisfy the functional architecture and requirements. System architecture synthesis has as its goal the derivation of the optimum system architecture, within constraints of time, manpower and so forth.

Two parallel system architecture synthesis activities are described in the INCOSE SE Handbook, these are shown in figure 2, drawn from the INCOSE handbook.

First is the definition and refinement of system element alternatives. Second is the synthesis of multiple system architectures. Two approaches are identified for proceeding to the selection of a preferred system architecture. A bottom-up approach identifies a menu of system element options and develops from these candidate architectures. This approach introduces constraints on the choice of architectures, but may also stimulate architecture options resulting from novel combinations of elements. A top-down approach develops candidate architectures which may then be populated by alternative elements. This approach may be driven either by convergent thinking which focuses on existing practices, or by divergent thinking which focuses on the production of novelty. Typically some hybrid of the bottom-up and top-down approaches will be adopted. Once selected, the system architecture must be further refined and integrated to ensure the ability to function in the intended environment, in an integrated manner.

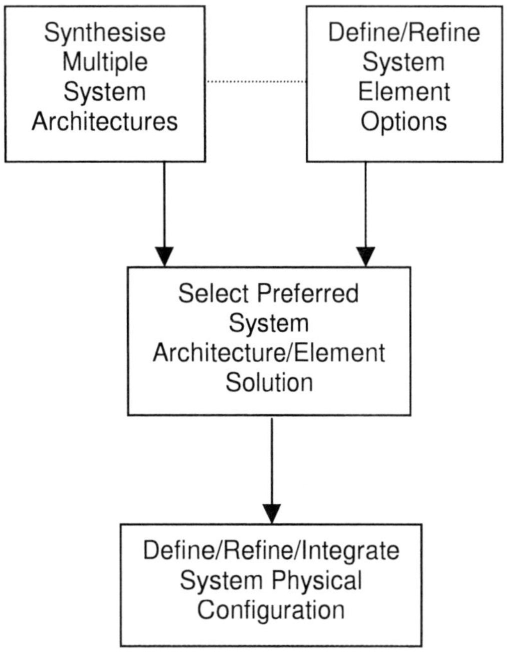

Figure 2. The systems synthesis process

APPLICATION TO SE PROCESS

Previous sections have summarised the phase model of creativity and the general system synthesis process. The manner in which the phase model may be applied in a typical system synthesis stage in the systems engineering process is now described. This section will examine the creativity phase model and the various stages of system synthesis in order to identify a mapping of the synthesis activities onto the phase model.

System synthesis may be broken down into identifiable, discrete activities. In order to demonstrate the mapping of synthesis to creativity phases, it is necessary to examine one stage of system synthesis. The synthesis activity chosen for this purpose is the 'definition and refinement of system element options', as described in the INCOSE System Engineering Handbook (see figure 2).

The targeted synthesis activity has 6 defined steps. These are summarised as: (1) *Create list of system elements.* For example, the 'system' is a warship, elements are communications, navigation, weapons, etc. (2) *Identify element option descriptors for the list of system elements.* This defines the parameters which will help to select suitable element options. (3) *Define the design space envelope.* Sets the boundaries on the design parameters listed in step 2. (4) *Develop a process to generate a range of element options.* This is the core 'creative' activity in this particular synthesis process. The list of element options may be diverse and include elements not strictly within the envelope. This step seeks to explore the full range of possibilities. The INCOSE Systems Engineering Handbook identifies the use of creativity methods in this step. Those recommended fall into the category of 'cognitive' methods. In other words no consideration is given to the wider process of using such creativity methods, or to 'non-cognitive' factors. (5) *Select element options to populate the design space.* This activity seeks to narrow the list from step 4 to those elements that can satisfy the requirement of the design. The INCOSE Systems Engineering Handbook recommends challenging the requirements in order to ensure that the best solutions are identified and chosen from the list in step 4. (6) *The element choices are described in greater detail to support the continuing synthesis process.*

Each stage of the creativity phase model is now examined, in relation to the steps discussed for system synthesis, in order to identify a mapping of synthesis to creativity phase.

Stage 0 (Preparation). This 'pre-synthesis' stage corresponds to the building of latent knowledge in the mind of the systems engineer. Occurring before the formal synthesis steps listed in the previous section, it is nevertheless important to the effectiveness of the engineer in later 'creative' stages of synthesis.

Stage 1 (Information). This creativity phase corresponds to steps 1 and 2 of the synthesis process described. The creation of a list of system elements, and element option descriptors, requires the application of cognitive and non-cogntive factors to the latent knowledge resulting from the preparation stage. The result is a rich fund of information (system elements and element option descriptors) relevant to the synthesis process, which will drive the latter stages of the synthesis.

Stage 2 (Incubation). Acting partly in overlap with the previous stage of creativity, the incubation phase utilises convergent thinking skills to generate the large set of cognitive elements (the design space envelope and design parameter boundaries) which form the basis for applying the divergent thinking required in the next stage/step. Step 3 is central to refining and redefining the particular problem in hand in the synthesis process.

Stage 3 (Illumination). Step 4 in the synthesis process, generating a diverse set of element options, maps to the illumination phase. In addition to the cognitive techniques required to stimulate the creative process, close awareness of the non-cognitive factors, such as openness and risk-taking must be recognised and fostered.

This stage demonstrates with particular force the value of applying the psychological stage model. An engineering environment that ignores non-cognitive factors such as openness and risk-taking steers solution options, even if unwittingly, in a "safe" direction. This occurs at a point where the opening up of the synthesis process is particularly important, and may even condemn it to following pathways that are in principle familiar, and are thus only capable of producing small variations in the destinations reached.

Stage 4 (Verification). The verification process maps to the population of the design space stage of synthesis (step 5). Professional knowledge and familiarity are needed to select the appropriate 'novel' solution from the list of candidates.

Stages 5 & 6 (Communication & Validation). These stages in the creativity phase model overlap to some degree with follow-on activities in the synthesis process example described. In addition, the final step of the synthesis process (step 6), which requires communication of the element choices to latter stages of synthesis, maps to these creativity stages. Of key importance in these stages are non-cognitive factors such as risk-taking, and also professional skills in communication.

The preceding example, focused on a subset of the synthesis process, illustrates the application of a creativity phase model to the synthesis process. A key feature of the creativity phase model is its generality, as well as its interface to pre-synthesis and post-synthesis activities. The creativity phase model encapsulates the activities of the synthesis process and also guides the requirements for cognitive and non-cognitive skills needed to achieve success in synthesis processes.

The mapping described in this example is illustrated in figure 3. This diagram illustrates the mapping of creativity phase model stages to corresponding activities in the synthesis activity 'definition and refinement of system element options'. Similar mappings can be made to other key SE activities, including the definition and development of system-level requirements, as well as architecture synthesis, selection of architectures and elements, and the definition of system physical configuration.

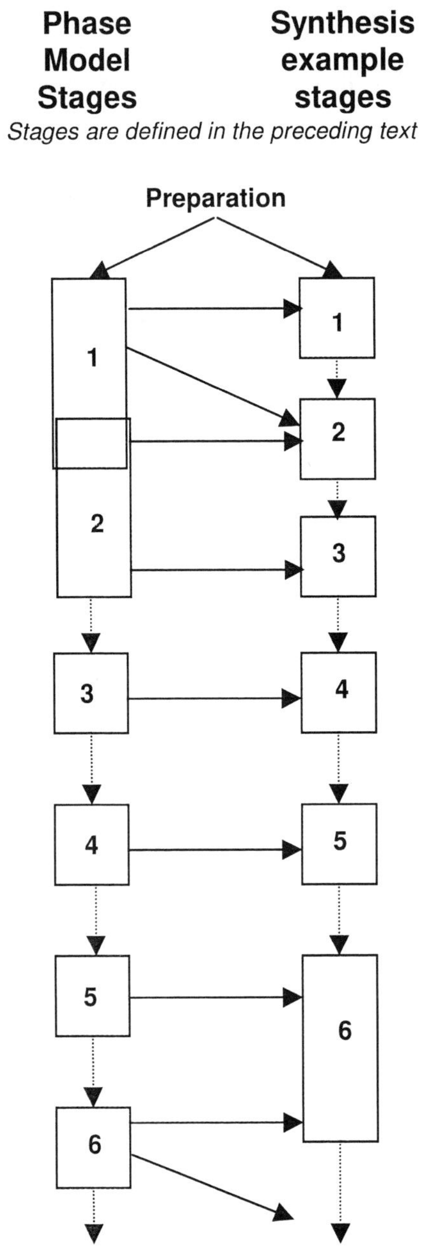

Figure 3. Phase Model to Synthesis Mapping

MANAGING FOR C&I IN ENGINEERING

One of the primary features distinguishing the phase model of creativity from other techniques and methods is the importance of non-cognitive factors in the fostering and development of creativity and innovation. While engineers can be taught skills which may assist in stimulating and producing creativity, unless these activities take place in a supportive environment, it is likely that the desired result will not be achieved.

The manner in which the C&I process is managed is therefore of central importance in a program designed to foster creativity in engineering activities. This is concisely captured by Kitsopoulos (1994) who states: "The ability to innovate is one of the main factors that distinguish successfully led enterprises from mediocre ones".

It is possible to state areas in the synthesis process where management functions should be employed to specifically foster the cognitive skills and the non-cognitive characteristics needed to ensure success. Some of these have already been suggested. They may be summarised as follows: (a) Pre-synthesis activities of engineers must seek to generate a wide and varied body of latent knowledge to feed the creative aspects of the synthesis process. Engineers must be given the means and opportunity to build this latent knowledge. (b) Professional knowledge and ability contribute vitally to creativity. Engineers must build specialist knowledge on a continuing basis to feed creativity. (c) Engineers must be made aware of cognitive skills. They must be trained in divergent thinking techniques. These may span a variety of 'creativity techniques'. (d) Engineers must be able to apply these cognitive skills in a supportive, extrinsically rewarding environment. They must feel comfortable thinking divergently, and being seen to think divergently, at the appropriate time. (e) Engineers must develop tolerance for ambiguity, openness and other similar non-cognitive characteristics. (f) The system in which they work must support the feelings which drive many of the creativity phases. Thus the engineer's pride, excitement, curiosity, etc. must be nurtured at the appropriate phase of creativity.

By fostering these aspects of the creative process managers of the systems engineering process can ensure that their 'synthesizers' are equipped with the skills, characteristics and environment in which their activities can flourish in a manner which will bring greater rewards to the system solution.

SUMMARY

In this paper we have presented a recognised model of creativity which encompasses both cognitive and non-cognitive skills and factors. This has been applied to the process of system synthesis embedded in systems engineering. A specific example of the mapping of the creativity phase model to system synthesis has been developed for the definition and refinement of system element options. This paper shows the utility of the phase model as a means for guiding and fostering creativity and innovation in system synthesis. Areas of C&I which require management support have been identified.

REFERENCES

Altshuller, G. S., *Creativity as an Exact Science: The Theory of the Solution of Inventive Problems.* (Translated from the Russian by Anthony Williams.) Gordon and Breach, New York, 1984.

Bailey, R. L., *Disciplined Creativity for Engineers*, Ann Arbor Science Publishers Inc., Michigan. 1978.

Blanchard B. S. and Fabrycky, W. J., *Systems Engineering and Analysis.* Prentice Hall, 3rd Edition. 1998.

Bollay, W., 'University projects in systems engineering', *Engineering Education*, April 1970, pp. 803-805. 1970.

Christiaans, H. H. C. M., *Creativity in Design – The role of knowledge in designing.* Lemma BV, Utrecht, Holland. 1992.

Cropley, A. J., 'Kreativitaet' [Creativity], in M. Amelang ed. *Encyclopedia of Psychology Vol. VIII, Differences in Behaviour and Performance, Part 2 Differential Psychology and Personality Research (pp. 329-373),* Hogrefe, Goettingen. 1995.

Cropley, D. H., Priest, S. and Cropley, A. J. 'Fostering Creativity and Innovation in Engineering Students', *Australasian Association for Engineering Education*, 9th Annual Conference, December 1997.

Cropley, D. H. and Cropley, A. J. 'Teaching Engineering Students to be Creative – Program and Outcomes', *Australasian Association of Engineering Education*, 10th Annual Conference, September 1998.

Cropley, A. J., 'Creativity and cognition: Producing effective novelty', *Roeper Review*, *21*, 253-260. 1999.

Cropley, A. J. & Urban, K. K. in press, 'Programs and strategies for nurturing creativity', In K. Heller, F.Moenks, R. J. Sternberg & R. Subotnik (Eds.), *International handbook for research on giftedness and talent.* Oxford: Pergamon.

Hanson, T. F., *Engineering Creativity*, T F Hanson, Newhall, CA, 1987.

INCOSE, *Systems Engineering Handbook*, Release 1.0, INCOSE. 1998.

Kitsopoulos, S. C., 'Leadership Connections: Communication, Diversity and Creativity', *Proc IEEE 1994 Intl Eng Man Conf*, pp13-17.IEEE NY. 1994.

ABOUT THE AUTHORS

Dr David Cropley, PhD: is a lecturer and researcher with the Systems Engineering and Evaluation Centre (SEEC) at the University of South Australia. With a background as an officer in the Royal Navy, he is currently working on projects including combat systems architecture studies, high level architecture applications and systems engineering processes. Included in his interests is the teaching of creativity to engineers and its role in systems engineering.

Prof Arthur Cropley, PhD: is Emeritus Professor of Educational Psychology at Hamburg University. Prof Cropley has been active in the field of creativity for over 35 years, and has extensive experience of research in this field. He has also delivered many in-house training courses to a variety on firms and government organisations in Germany. Professor Cropley was appointed as an adjunct professor in the School of Physics and Electronic Systems Engineering, University of South Australia, in 1998, to assist in developing creativity training in undergraduate engineers.

AP-233 Architecture

Erik Herzog, Anders Törne
Real-Time Systems Laboratory
Department of Computer and Information Science
Linköpings Universitet
E-mail: {erica, andto} @ ida.liu.se

ABSTRACT

This paper outlines the information model architecture of the current working draft, WD4, of ISO 10303 – 233 (AP-233) standard proposal. The objective is to communicate how the architecture of the information model permits the exchange of systems specifications between computer based systems engineering tools. The model architecture makes no assumptions on the complexity of the information exchanged and does not require specific tool capabilities. The paper also illustrates how supplemental information, in particular configuration management and process information, is handled in the information model. We believe that capturing and maintaining this information is crucial for industrial applications and hence for industrial adoption of AP-233 by the systems engineering community.

INTRODUCTION

Over the last decades computer based tools have been introduced to facilitate the systems engineering processes. There are tools for assisting engineering in virtually every aspect of the engineering process from requirement elicitation and analysis, over functional or object oriented analysis, synthesis and verification to configuration management. It is not uncommon for a tool to provide many services covering more than one aspect of systems engineering.

Despite advances in tool capabilities there exist numerous situations where information exchanges across tool boundaries are valuable. E.g., exchange of specifications between organisations using heterogeneous tool sets, exchange of specifications from legacy to modern tools, exchange of specifications to tools that provide more advanced modelling or analysis capabilities than the originating tool.

Data exchange capabilities of contemporary tools are, with some notable exceptions, weak. It is not uncommon that information entered in one tool has to be re-entered manually into another. Needless to say this is highly inefficient and error prone.

Since 1996 the authors have been involved in two projects, SEDRES[1] and SEDEX[2], identifying the core information elements of systems engineering with the objective to develop a data exchange standard for system engineering tools within the ISO 10303 (STEP) framework. Earlier results from these activities are reported in, e.g., (Johnson et al., 1999). The main element of the standard proposal is an information model that defines entities for the main information elements of systems engineering along with attributes and inter-relationships. The information model defines, in conjunction with infrastructure defined in the STEP framework, common exchange formats for data exchange between tools used in the systems engineering process. The model is detailed and formally well defined as it is intended for tool data exchange. The focus is on representing tool information in a format suitable for efficient data storage rather than representations replicating the information presented to a tool user.

System engineers from the industries active in the ISO working group as well as in the supporting projects have contributed to the requirement definition process and have reviewed the model throughout the development. In this process it has become more and more evident that different contributors have different views on the information created/handled by systems engineers. Systems engineers at different organisations can have a general agreement on the nature of systems engineering, but stress different aspects of systems engineering and base their contributions on different systems engineering processes.

The heterogeneous nature of systems engineering puts additional requirements on the structure or architecture of the information model beyond pure information entities. Only coarse assumptions on the systems engineering process or the tools in use can be made. Consequently, AP-233 makes no attempt to comply with restrictions in existing methods or to define a new system engineering method.

Specifications that are exchanged via the format defined by the information model may be of varying degree of complexity and completeness. It may cover virtually innumerable subsets of the large information set supported by the information model. Consequently,

[1] SEDRES – ESPRIT Project 20496, 1996 - 99

[2] SEDEX – funded by the Swedish National Board for Industrial and Technical Development. Project no. IPII-98-06292

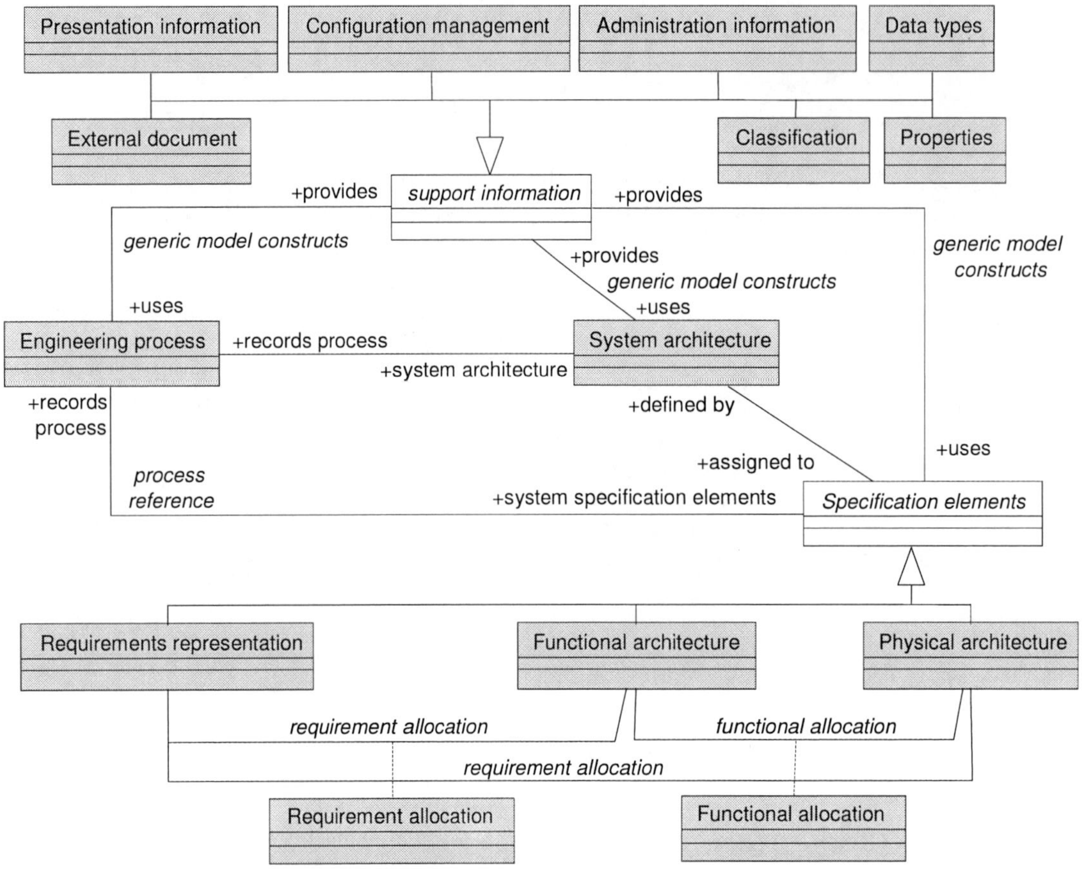

Figure 1, information model, conceptual view

the information model must not impose any penalties for specifications that are incomplete. It must offer the same level of service to all specifications regardless of complexity or completeness, while offering a well-defined semantics for systems engineering data.

In this paper the model architecture selected for AP-233 to comply with the requirements outlined above is presented. The focus is exclusively on the information model. A broader summary of recent and future SEDRES and AP-233 activities are outlined in a companion paper (Johnson et al., 2000). A second companion paper (Pandikow et al., 2000) presents a study on the prospect of incorporating object oriented systems engineering concepts into AP-233.

The rest of this paper is outlined as follows. There is an overview of the information model scope and architecture, followed by an example illustrating the smallest required elements in an exchange. The example is extended gradually to illustrate capabilities supported by the information model. Special attention is paid to capturing configuration management and process related information. This is followed by a comparison of the scope of AP-233 against those of established systems engineering standards. The paper is concluded with a summary and outline of future work.

INFORMATION MODEL OVERVIEW

In this section, the background and scope of the AP-233 information model is outlined. The objective is that the information model shall provide the structures for capturing and tracing system requirements from early user requirements through design and realisation over all life cycles of a system. General information on the information model and the results are available in, e.g., (Johnson, 1998), (Herzog and Törne, 1999) and (Herzog and Törne, 2000).

To determine what information is relevant for the domain and its structure a literature survey have been performed, e.g., (Blanchard and Fabrycky, 1998), (Oliver et al., 1997), (Martin, 1997), (Stevens et al., 1998), (Hatley and Pirbhai, 1987) and (Sommerville and Kotonya, 1998). We have interviewed system engineers at organisations involved in application protocol development in the AP-233 working group and in the supporting projects[3]. Copying elements of the information model directly from tools has been avoided, as this could have jeopardised the model's tool independence. The task to formalise the information model has been iterative in nature and has included a

[3] SEDRES, KARE (ESPRIT 28916) and SEDEX.

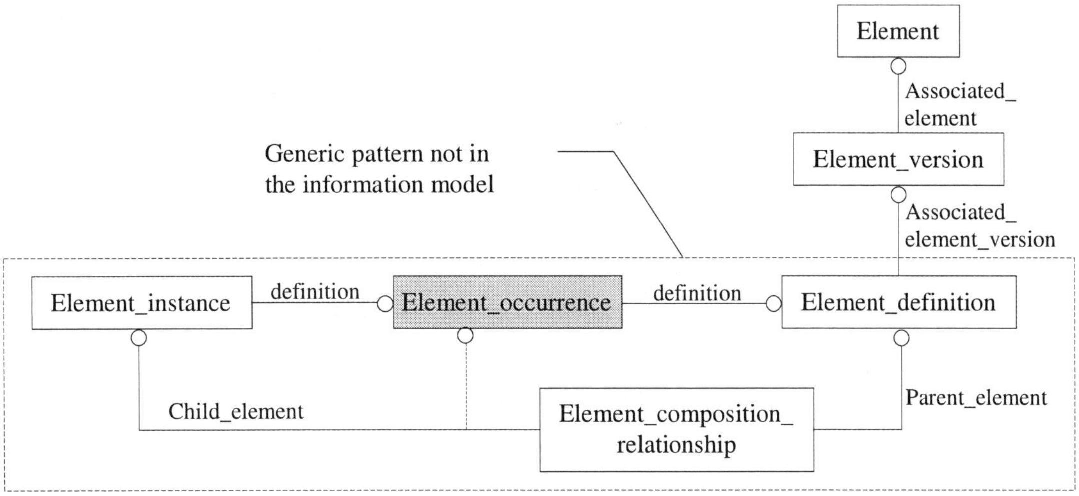

Figure 2, information model basic pattern

substantial degree of harmonisation due to the size and heterogeneity of the domain.

The industrial partners involved in the respective projects have reviewed the resulting models for completeness and industrial applicability. Interface development and real tool data exchanges as outlined in (Johnson et al. 1999) have validated substantial parts of the model. Although the interfaces developed have been of prototype quality the results are promising and the implementation of tool interfaces has uncovered a number of modelling issues that have been fed back into model development.

The information model is expressed using a formal language, EXPRESS (ISO10303, 1994.a). It is based on an extended entity relationship formalism supporting object orientation concepts and specification of constraints on data and relationships. The fact that EXPRESS is rigorous language is very important as it allows formal checking of model correctness and automation of substantial portions of tool data exchange interface implementation.

Figure 1 shows a conceptual view of the AP-233 information model in UML syntax. In the figure each shaded box represents a group of related entities. Opaque boxes are generalisations inserted to preserve clarity and for supporting relationships that are valid for all element of the generalisation. The main groups of the model are:

- *System architecture*, representing the building blocks for grouping all information valid for a system, partial view of a system or system interface. There is also support for representing the system hierarchy structure.
- *Specification elements*, defining the basic building blocks for representing requirements, functional and physical architecture.
- *Requirement* and *Functional allocation*, defining the mechanisms for tracing requirements to functions (including behaviour) and physical architecture elements and functional architecture elements to physical architecture elements respectively.
- *Engineering process*, defining the building blocks for representing activities in the systems engineering process and associating specification information to the activity the originate/relate to.
- *Support information*, representing the building blocks for representing supplemental systems engineering information. This large group is composed of groups for representing configuration management information, visual layout information, mechanisms for referencing external documents, administrative information, data types and properties.

The relationships between the groups are outlined below. The elements of the *Engineering process* group can be used to capture the systems engineering process for a project and relate *Specification elements* and *System architecture* information to the process phase they were created/referenced in. *Specification elements* provide the structures to define requirements, functional and physical architecture of systems represented by elements of the *System architecture* group. The *Support information* group provides information that can be applied to elements in the other groups.

NOTATION

This section presents the graphical information-modelling notation, EXPRESS-G (ISO10303, 1994.a) used in the STEP community and in the figures in this paper, e.g., Figure 2. Boxes represent entities, the enclosed text is the entity name/label. Lines represent relationships and basic attributes. The label close to the line defines the name of the relationship. The ring at one end of a line represents the sink of the relationship. Instantiated models are presented using the same notation with the addition that a filled triangle in the lower right corner of a box indicates an instance of a particular entity, e.g., the object of type *textual_requirement_definition* in Figure 3.

This section presents the basic modelling philosophy applied to the core systems engineering entities of the information model. With core entities we mean the entities for representing requirements, functional architecture, physical architecture and data types. Although these are different concepts, they are modelled using the same basic pattern. The structure is illustrated in Figure 2. Fictitious entity names are used as a similar structure is used in many places in the information model. For clarity no entity attributes are presented in the figure.

THE CORE ENTITIES

The entity *element_definition* (*element* can be substituted with, e.g., *requirement*, *function*, *physical*) provide the definition of an element. In case of a requirement it could be a definition of what is required - in plain text or in a more structured format. *Element_instance* is the use of an *element_definition* in a particular context. Separating use and definition of an object allow for inclusion of the context independent information in many system specifications, or in multiple versions of the same system specification. Context dependent information such as name, identifiers, relationships to other objects is associated with *element_instance* objects. The entity *element_composition_relationship* is the mechanism for creating a part-of structure. For each object added to a composition a new *element_composition_relationship* object is instantiated.

In cases where it is necessary to uniquely identify an object in a composition then the basic pattern is extended with an intermediate *element_occurrence* entity that supports representation of the hierarchy structure. This allows the *element_instance* to capture relationships that are unique to a particular object in a composition. The extension is shaded in Figure 2.

The entities *element_version* and *element* provide the functionality for version management. Each *element_definition* object has version information attached and each *element_version* object belongs to a single *element* object that groups all versions of a specification element. The selected pattern is motivated by the desire to support advanced concepts such as reusability of specification elements and version management. It also provides a consistent data exchange pattern for all tools.

The modelling pattern used is advanced. When mapping from elements in a tool's meta-model to the structures in the information model there are likely to be cases where tool interfaces have to generate objects to be compliant with information model. For data exchange this is not a problem as long as there exist a non-ambiguous reverse mapping. Experience from the SEDRES project indicates this is generally the case. For instance, the information model enforces version management capabilities. This *information* can be generated even if a tool does not possess version management capabilities, i.e., all elements in a specification are considered to be of version 1.

EXAMPLE

This section presents an initial data exchange example. The example is extended throughout the paper to illustrate the architecture of the information model. Due to size considerations we only consider the smallest of examples – a single requirement expressed in plain text.

Mapping the requirement onto the structures defined by the information model would result in a *textual_requirement_definition* object with the associated version management information as illustrated by the structure enclosed in the dashed rectangle in Figure 3. Such a definition represents a requirement fragment taken out of context that may be of interest to a receiver, e.g., for exchange or constraints common to all systems. The example does not indicate a requirement for a particular system. To put the requirement into a system context a *requirement_ instance* object must reference the *textual_requirement_definition* object. The *requirement_ instance* in turn may be associated with a specific system specification.

THE SYSTEM VIEW

Exchange of context independent information fragments are sufficient in some cases, but generally the value of information exchange is substantially higher if the data exchanged retain context information in the transfer. The exchanged elements should contain information indicating the system or system viewpoint they are relevant for. In the information model the *system_view* entity acts as a container for all specifications relevant to a specific system.

Three specific system views are defined:

1. *System_definition*, defines the specification of a complete system.
2. *Partial_system_view*, defines a particular view point, scenario or mode of the system under specification. A *system_definition* may be composed of any number of *partial_system_view* objects.
3. *System_system_interface_view,* defines an interface centred view between a number of interacting systems.

A system view object may collect any number of requirements, a functional architecture, a physical architecture description associated, as well as associated traceability information.

The *system_system_interface_view* provides a dedicated view for specifying the interface between

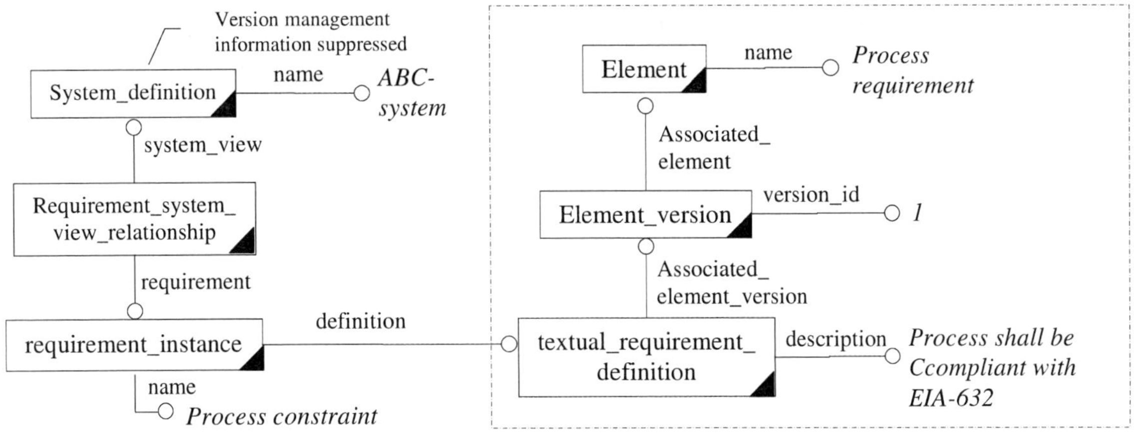

Figure 3, relating requirements to a system specification

groups of systems and is the equivalent of an interface control document. Just as for any system view object the interface may be expressed in terms of requirements, functional architecture, physical architecture, associated documents or any combination of the above elements.

Version management is supported for system views just like for requirements and functions. This provides the capability to form baselined system specifications. The model defines a system baseline candidate to be *system_definition* object with all relevant specification elements associated. Associating approvals to a baseline candidate indicates baseline acceptance.

EXAMPLE

Figure 3 illustrates how the relationship between engineering data and a system specification is established in the information model. In the example the process requirement presented previously is assigned as a requirement to a specific system. Two entities are required to link the requirement to the system. The *requirement_instance* object provides contextual information for a requirement, e.g., for capturing a contextual name and comments as well as capturing relationships across requirements and to other elements of a system specification. The *requirement_system_view_relationship* object represents the actual assignment of the relationship. The use of an entity to represent the relationship illustrates the modular architecture of the information model. A system view object is complete regardless of how many elements are assigned. For a *requirement_instance* object it does not matter whether it is associated with zero, one or more system view objects.

CONFIGURATION MANAGEMENT

This section presents how the information model supports process and configuration management information. The services offered in this area go beyond modelling data but they are vital to capture and record the systems engineering process.

The model defines entities for representing projects and activities. A project is a representation of a completed, active or planned project of arbitrary size and complexity. It consists of a network of interrelated activities that in turn may be further decomposed into sub-activities. Relations between projects can also be defined. The purpose of the model is to relate specification elements to the process step where they were produced or referenced. Information may be designated as input to, output from or referenced from an activity. In addition, the model provides for the recording of stakeholders in the activity, planned and actual start and completion dates.

The activity management model is further extended to support work management. There are two basic entities for this in the model. A *work_request* is a formal request that some specified work shall be carried out, e.g., a request for change. A *work_request* object is associated with all design objects that are involved in the requested activity. A *work_order* is the authorisation of an activity. The *activity* object resulting from the *work_order* maintains the relationship between a *work_request* and a *work_order* as an *activity* may refer to the *work_request* objects that prompted the activity. An *activity* may resolve zero to many *work_requests*. When an *activity,* authorised by a *work_order* object, is carried out, it can be expected that new specification elements are created as a result of the activity. Some of these may be new versions of existing elements. The described capabilities together with version management support in the information model enables traceability of both process and engineering data.

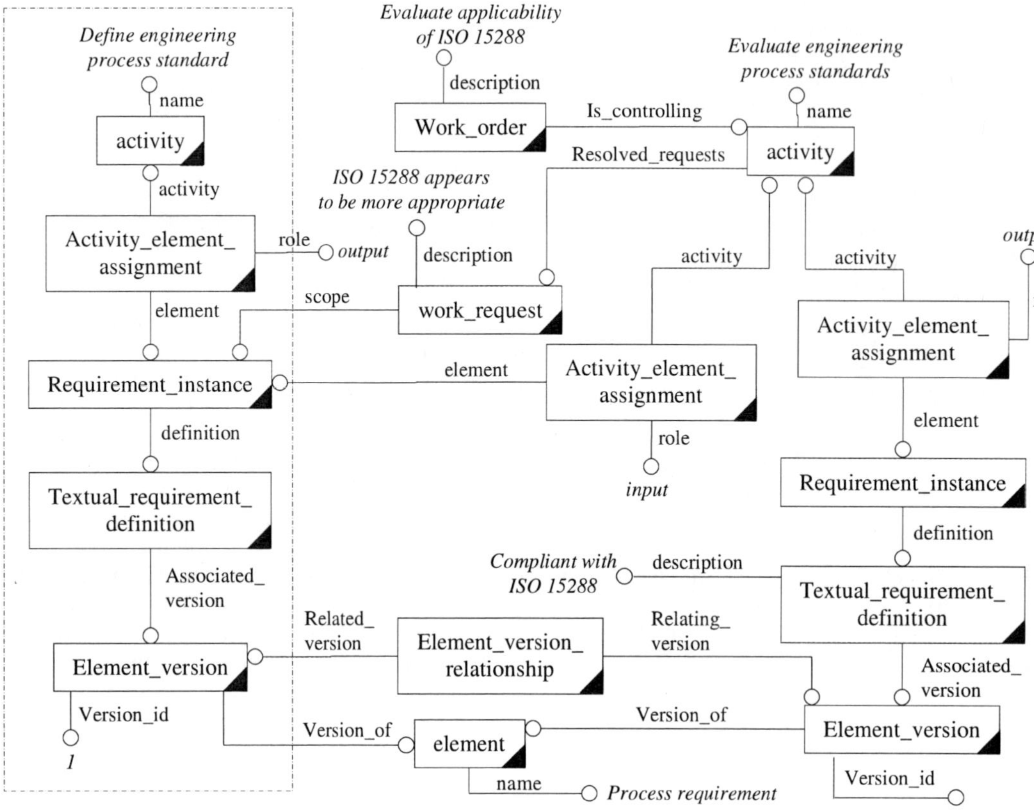

Figure 4, Work and activity management

EXAMPLE

This section illustrates the how the concepts representing version, work and activity management are related in the information model. It starts out from the example requirement, which presumably was the output from an analysis activity. The initial objects are enclosed in the dashed rectangle in Figure 4. A *work_request* (Figure 4, centre) object assigned to the original *requirement_instance* object indicates that some system stakeholder requires a modification to the requirement constraining the engineering process for a system. The requestor questions whether EIA-632 are the appropriate process for the particular system under development. In the example the request for an evaluation of alternate standards is granted. Consequently a *work_order* (Figure 4, top right) object is instantiated along with an *activity* representing the evaluation activity. The attribute *resolved_requests* of the new *activity* indicate the set of *work_requests*, in this example a single one, who shall be resolved by the activity. A single object is declared as input to the new activity – the original *requirement_instance* object. For the sake of the example it is assumed that ISO 15288 is judged to provide a more appropriate process description for the system under specification. Thus a new requirement that prescribes the use of ISO 15288 is created as a result of the activity. The *activity_element_assignment* object creates the link between the activity and the new requirement. It would also capture the motivation why a new version of the original requirement was created. From a version management viewpoint the new requirement is treated as a new version of the original one. Finally, note that in this example there is important information not captured. E.g., the assignment of the requirements to a system view as illustrated in Figure 3, and information regarding the validity of the objects: approvals, possible/estimated effectivity (see below), date, stakeholder and author information – these information model concepts are outlined in the following sections.

An important aspect of the example in Figure 4 is that it shows the modular architecture of the information model. Design data, such as requirements, are orthogonal to elements capturing engineering process related information. Thus the information model offers but does not prescribe the use of the outlined capabilities.

APPROVAL AND EFFECTIVITY

The information model also contains elements to indicate that a specific element object has been awarded an approval of some kind – an *approval*. The information model is intentionally vague on the semantics of an approval. It is assumed to be organisation specific. Nevertheless, the ability to represent that a specification or a portion thereof has passed some sort of approval procedure is an important aspect of to model.

There is also support for recording the temporal validity of an object. In the information model the concept is named *effectivity*. It records an open-ended or closed interval in time and is assigned to an object. The interval represents the open or closed time interval an object is being valid for inclusion in a system specification or can be used as a base for system realisation. A design object may be both approved and effective. The difference between approval and effectivity is that the effectivity of an element may be constrained by a time period or by an event. An approval on the other hand, cannot be revoked. An object can be approved in a specific system context, but shall not be included in new system specifications if it is not any longer effective.

ADMINISTRATIVE INFORMATION

This section outlines how administrative information is handled in the information model. This includes date and time information, person and organisational information. The structure for assigning this information is similar to that presented in previous sections. To assign a person in the role of author/creator/stakeholder to a design object, a relationship is instantiated between the design object and the object representing the person. A role attribute on the relationship indicates that for the specific relationship the person shall be regarded as author of the object.

The benefit of this architecture is that the model does not prescribe where administrative information shall be attached.

RELATIONSHIPS TO SE STANDARDS

This section outlines the relationship between AP-233 and existing systems engineering process standards, e.g., IEEE1220 (Ptack, 1998) and EIA 632 (Martin, 1999). It is our understanding standards above are dealing with guidelines on how systems engineering shall be performed and organised to achieve optimal results. The aim of the AP-233 data model and standard is to make the process more efficient by enabling data exchange between systems engineering tools. In performing this AP-233 may simplify the process of engineering a system, but it is not a remedy for a poor process.

There are, however, some common areas. AP-233 includes capabilities to represent process, but makes no assumption what this process may look like. This capability can be used to define a desired engineering process and to indicate planned output for each phase. The same capability can also be used to record the actual engineering process for a project. E.g., how work requests and work orders result in activities not planned for in advance. This facility may be used to analyse how effective the engineering process is when applied to a project. Such an analysis may provide insights on what parts of the process went smoothly and where and why problems were encountered. Information that can be carried over to future projects.

RELATED WORK

In this paper we have presented key aspects of the architecture of the current working draft of the AP-233 information model. This is not the only published system engineering information model. There are models published by Jackson (Jackson, 1994) and Oliver (Oliver, 1994) that are similar in scope to the AP-233 model – but the AP-233 model is substantially more detailed as it is explicitly developed for data exchange. There are also many similar projects within the ISO 10303 framework, but mainly for different aspects of mechanical engineering. Some, e.g., AP-203 (ISO 10303, 1994b) has reached international standard level. Others are at less advanced levels of maturity. The complete list of application protocol projects is available at the SOLIS web-server (SOLIS, 1999) at NIST (National Institute of Standards and Technology).

Configuration management capabilities, similar to those outlined in this paper, are available in modern systems and requirements engineering tools, e.g., RDD.com and DOORS. Yet, there is a difference in how the concepts are modelled. In a tool specific environment the tool designers have control of the database schema and can decide how different concepts relate. In the AP-233 model only some basic assumptions on tool capabilities can be made and hence the approach results in a model that is more modular.

SUMMARY AND FUTURE WORK

In this paper we have presented the architecture of the 4th working draft of the AP-233 information model. For the concepts presented, the architecture imposes minimal cross dependencies. Information mapped onto the structures defined in the information model is, from the model's point of view, complete and self-sufficient, regardless of the level of completeness conveyed to a systems engineer. This is an important aspect for model acceptability as it allows users with different data exchange requirements to use the model at equal terms. The examples presented have also indicated the many dimensions of systems engineering information handled by the information model and indirectly the complexity of the information handled by systems engineers.

It is our belief that the AP-233 information model is approaching completeness. Nevertheless, it will take substantial time before AP-233 becomes an international ISO standard. Realistically the international standard level will be attained in 2002, at the earliest. Most of the remaining work is specific to ISO 10303 – harmonisation with related application protocols, development of STEP integrated modules and in documentation specific areas. But there are areas in the model that shall be improved and extended. Comments and other contributions from INCOSE members are most welcome and are vital for the success of AP-233.

ACKNOWLEDGEMENTS

The authors gratefully acknowledge the hard work of participants in the supporting projects. The financial support from the European Commission and Swedish National Board for Industrial and Technical Development is also gratefully acknowledged.

REFERENCES

Blanchard, B. and Fabrycky, W.. *Systems Engineering and Analysis.* Prentice Hall International Series in Industrial and Systems Engineering. Prentice Hall, 3rd. edition, 1998.

Hatley, D. and Pirbhai, I. *Strategies for Real-Time System Specification.* Dorset House, 1987.

Herzog, E. and Törne, A. Towards a Standardised Systems Engineering Information Model. *Proceedings of the 9th annual international symposium of INCOSE*, vol. 2, pages 909–916. INCOSE, 1999.

Herzog, E. and Törne, A. Support for Exchange of Functional Behaviour Specifications in AP-233. *Proceedings 7th IEEE International Conference on the Engineering of Computer Based Systems.* pages 351–358, IEEE Computer Society Press, 2000.

ISO 10303. *Industrial Automation Systems and Integration - Product Data Representation and Exchange - Part 11: Description Methods: The EXPRESS Language Reference Manual.* ISO 10303, 1st. edition, 1994.

ISO 10303. *Industrial Automation Systems and Integration - Product Data Representation and Exchange - Part 203: Application Protocol: Configuration Controlled Design.* ISO 10303, 1st. edition, 1994.

Jackson, K. An Information Model for Computer Based Systems. *Tutorial and Workshop on Systems Engineering of Computer-Based Systems*, pages 32–43. IEEE Computer Society Press, 1994.

Johnson, J. The Sedres Project: Producing a Data Exchange Standard Supporting Integrated Systems Engineering. INCOSE 1998.

Johnson, JFE, et al. The Future Systems Engineering Data Exchange Standard AP-233; Sharing the results of the SEDRES Project. *Proceeding of the 9th annual international symposium of INCOSE*, volume2, pages 923–931. INCOSE 1999.

Johnson, JFE, et al., The Maturing Systems Engineering Data Exchange Standard AP233 & Your Role, Accepted for publication at the INCOSE 2000 symposium, 2000.

Martin, J. *Systems Engineering Guidebook.* CRC Press, 1 edition, 1997.

Martin, J., editor. *EIA-632 Processes for Engineering a System.* ANSI/EIA-632-1998. EIA, 1999.

Oliver, D. A Draft Integration of Information Models: Complement model and Oliver Model. *Tutorial and Workshop on Systems Engineering of Computer-Based Systems,* pages 44–69. IEEE Computer Society Press, 1994.

Oliver, D., Kelliher, T., and Keegan, J. Engineering Complex Systems with Models and Objects. McGraw-Hill, 1st. edition, 1997.

Pandikow et al., Integrating Systems and Software Engineering Concepts in AP-233. Accepted for publication at the INCOSE 2000 symposium, 2000.

Ptack, K.R., editor *IEEE-1220 Standard for Application and Management of the Systems Engineering Process.* IEEE Press. 1998.

SOLIS. The STEP project. http://www.nist.gov/sc4/www/stepdocs.htm, 1999.

Sommerville, I. and Kotonya, *G. Requirements Engineering Processes and Techniques.* Wiley, 1998.

Stevens, R., Brook, P., Jackson, K., and Arnold, S. *Systems Engineering Coping with Complexity.* Prentice hall, 1st. edition, 1998.

AUTHOR BIOGRAPHIES

Erik Herzog is a Ph.D. student at the Real-Time Systems laboratory at the department of computer and information science at Linköpings Universitet, Sweden. His research interests include Systems engineering, specification methods, information modelling and, tool integration techniques. He is also a nominated technical expert to ISO TC184/SC4/WG3.

Anders Törne, Ph.D., is an associate professor at the Real-Time Systems Laboratory at the department of Computer and Information Science, Linköpings Universitet, Sweden, and also managing the Linköping office of Carlstedt Research & Technology. His research interest covers design of real-time and embedded systems, systems engineering, and high-level specification languages.

The Maturing Systems Engineering Data Exchange Standard AP-233 & Your Role

Dr Julian Johnson
BAE SYSTEMS,
W365B, Warton, Preston, PR4 1AX, UK

Erik Herzog
Dept of Computer and Information Science, Linköpings Universitet, S-581 83, Linköping, Sweden

Dr Sylvain Barbeau
Aerospatiale Matra Lanceurs,
67 Route de Verneuil, 78 133 Les Mureaux, France

Michael Giblin
BAE SYSTEMS,
W365B, Warton, Preston, PR4 1AX, UK

ABSTRACT

The data exchange standard identified as AP-233, 'systems engineering application protocol' is to be established within the framework of ISO 10303, "STEP", the Standard for the Technical Exchange of Product Data.. The standard activity was initiated, and much initial technical work was pursued, by the European research project SEDRES. The work within AP-233 has continued, building on the work of SEDRES, with a global industrial representation. This paper gives a status report on the AP-233 activity. A follow-on project SEDRES-2, with expanded consortium, is well underway. The essence of the SEDRES-2 mission statement is: *to extend, validate and standardise the Systems Engineering (SE) data model and nurture its practical implementation and multi-sector exploitation as a key enabler for industry.* This paper explains the objectives, approach, time scales, and extended data scope of the SEDRES-2 project, and gives a preview of early results from this next stage in achieving a comprehensive, workable systems engineering data exchange standard. Finally, it explains the significance of AP-233 to your work, and what you can do to contribute to achieving the goal of a supported and adopted SE data standard.

INTRODUCTION

Any large project in recent years will have been defined and created not by a single company or organisation, but by many organisations working together in an integrated and co-ordinated way. Products such as EF2000, Ariane 5 and the Channel Tunnel link all represent projects where systems engineering (SE) has played a significant role in their successful development.

The scale and complexity of such projects, and the requirements for development time and limited budgets also dictate that the recent generations of systems engineering and design tools have to be exploited to the full. Indeed, not only are there systems engineering tools supporting the management of customer requirements, the emerging design, and the evaluation of alternative solutions, but there are also a large number of other design tools used by other engineering disciplines involved in the design process, including but not limited to: control engineering, structural engineering, electrical engineering, power generation and distribution and hydraulics.

Interoperability with these disciplines is most desirable to increase quality, and reduce time and cost of the systems engineering process. In this paper, the approach of neutral design data exchange as a way of achieving design data exchange is explained, and its advantages and future potential explored. The objectives of the SEDRES project (SEDRES stands for Systems Engineering Data Representation and Exchange Standardisation) and its achievements are explained. The current status of the data model which is being extended by the AP-233 "systems engineering" activity will be described. Finally, future work in AP-233 and details of the work in the SEDRES-2 project will be outlined.

NEUTRAL DATA EXCHANGE

What then is neutral data exchange, or more specifically standards-based neutral data exchange? The goal of achieving improved interoperability between design tools can be solved via a set of tool-to-tool exchange interfaces. However, a standards-based approach to design information exchange has a number of advantages, both to the organisations that use multiple design tools within a systems engineering process, but interestingly also to tool vendors. Figure 1 illustrates informally the contrast between pursuing a tool-to-tool interface approach and a standards-based approach to achieving improved interoperability, with a given set of tools[1].

From the potential need for the N(N-1) number of interfaces illustrated in the upper part of the figure, we move to the much more manageable situation of 2N potential interfaces. This means a smaller number of interfaces to develop and maintain, and increased flexibility in the use of the design tools.

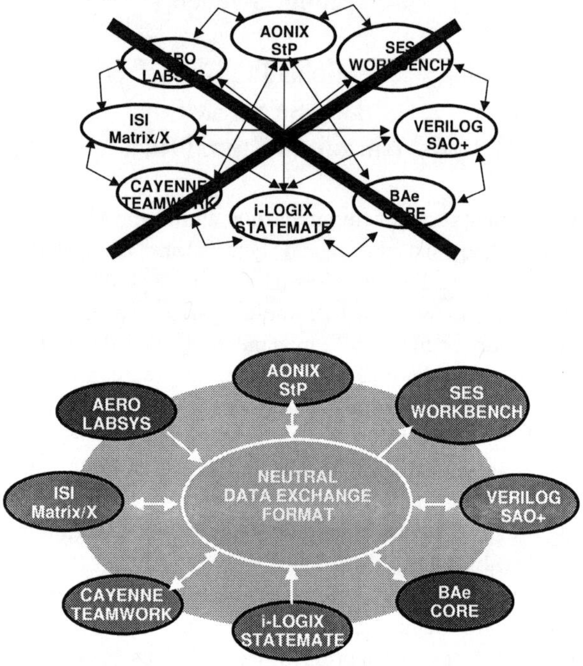

Figure 1: Advantages of standards-based exchange

Neutral design data exchange also opens up other opportunities. In addition to just achieving design data exchange via a standard format, that capability opens up the possibility to store design data in a tool-neutral format, which has particular significance, when one considers that operational life times of 40+ years are not uncommon for many systems engineering products. In addition, the abilities to pull subsets of design information from multiple design tools opens up the possibilities (with additional utilities) of performing consistency checking in a more comprehensive way than is possible with individual tools. It also makes it possible to gain 'views' of the design in ways that the existing design tool set cannot give.

The following sections explain how this vision of standards-based design data exchange is being realised, building on the work of the SEDRES project, through the related standardisation activity identified as AP-233, and most recently by the follow-on project SEDRES-2.

SEDRES-1

The European Commission co-funded project 20496, 'SEDRES', has made significant progress in producing a neutral data exchange standard based on STEP (Standard for the Technical Exchange of Product Data, ISO-10303), embracing systems engineering design data. Co-funded by the European Commission and running from 1996 to March 1999, SEDRES was initiated by Aerospatiale (France), Alenia (Italy), British Aerospace (UK), DASA (Germany) and Saab (Sweden). Also contributing are the Universities of Loughborough (UK), Linkoping (Sweden), and the Australian Centre for Test & Evaluation.

The objectives of SEDRES were to produce:

- A draft workable Systems Engineering data exchange standard;
- Progress with this standard in the ISO forum;
- A set of prototype data exchange tool interfaces for a number of tools & demonstrate;
- A method of use, based on concurrent engineering & Integrated Product Development.

Achievements. By the time SEDRES completed in March 1999, it had achieved the majority of these objectives. It had:

- produced three increasingly mature data exchange information models (successfully known as SEDRES Capability/1, /2 and Final Proposal). The main building blocks of each version are illustrated in Figure 2;
- produced prototype interfaces for several different Commercial Off the Shelf (COTS) tools used in systems engineering;
- kicked off a healthy and vibrant parallel standardisation activity within the ISO STEP community (ISO, 1994), following a successful international ballot at the end of 1997, with 12 countries voting YES.

Details about the data models, the prototype interfaces and early evaluation results, have been reported in earlier papers (Johnson 1997, 1998, Johnson et al,, 1999, Herzog and Törne 1999 , Harris & Candy 1999).

POST SEDRES-1 DEVELOPMENT

During 1999 the AP-233 data model has been extended further under supervision of the ISO working group. The main contributions originate from the SEDEX project performed at Linköping University and

[1] The tools listed here represent ones used in the SEDRES-1 project, and it is not intended to represent any endorsement of these tools.

from European research project 28916 'KARE'. The main focus of contributions have not been to extend the scope of AP-233 but to improve the capabilities of the data model further. Improvements are especially in the areas of systems architecture, functional behaviour representation, configuration management and property representation. The relationships to object oriented analysis and design methods has also been investigated.

MODEL PHILOSOPHY & SCOPE

Model Philosophy. The basic philosophy behind the SEDRES data models has been:

- To focus on semantic-level rather than document level information;
- To embrace a significant subset of the entire systems engineering domain;
- To adopt a STEP style of modelling (although Capability/1 and /2 models only approximate to a strict STEP style);
- To avoid being design tool specific;
- To avoid prescribing any specific systems engineering process, but cogniscent of standards such as EIA 632 (Martin 1998);
- To support a concept which is termed 're-use', having part of a design which is defined once but appears in multiple contexts (analogous to use of a software subroutine or object).

The main elements of each model version appear in figure 2, and are summarised in the following paragraphs.

Systems architecture - provides an entity to represent the system (or systems), to which other model elements can be related and covers relationships between systems, as well as definition of lifecycle, mode or stakeholder views on a system.

Requirements - covers structured or unstructured requirement statements, be they functional, architectural, operational aspects or system properties (safety or legislative requirements, performance, cost, etc.); relationships to requirements are also covered.

Functional - comprises entities to model the system functions, functional hierachy, flows between functions, and the functional context.

Behaviour - embraces detailed timing, sequencing and event-based behaviour. These include: data driven behaviour specifications; finite state machine concepts; a procedural or functional chain approach; a synchronous behavioural model. A 'black box' or 'stimulus-response' form is also being considered.

Configuration Management - covers the concepts needed to manage and control the different design items, including: authorship and ownership, authorisation, work management, development process reference, item versions, product variants, item maturity through the product's lifecycle. This will build on the STEP Product Data Management (PDM) Schema work.

Graphics (Visual presentation) - covers concepts such as diagram object shape, connections, and placement within the diagram, supporting transfer of the visual layout of SE notations such as: data flow diagrams, statecharts, functional flow block diagrams.

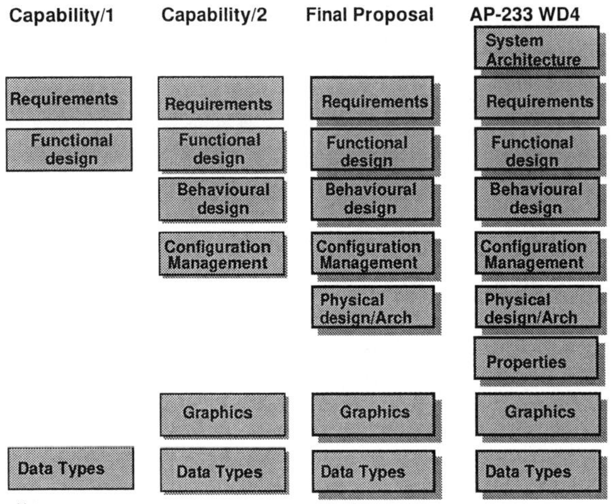

Notes:
Configuration Management essentially means Product Data Management, including aspects of process context, item identification, versioning, authorship, maturity/approval

Figure 2: Evolution and elements of SEDRES data model

Properties – covers representation of numerical calculated, assessed or measured attributes of systems, physical elements or functions. Examples include cost, weight and execution time.

Physical Architecture - covers a simple node-&-link type approach for capturing architectures, where the node-elements and connect-elements are instantiated for different technology elements. This generic approach enables the data model to support physical component topologies (interconnections without details of physical placement) for a variety of basic implementation technologies. Allocation from functions to architectural components is also supported.

Data Types – includes: strings, dates, bound (for instance Day-of-Month [1..31]) and unbound number types, compound data types or aggregations. This area will be aligned with the existing data type building blocks available within the existing STEP architecture.

The final data model from SEDRES-1 is described in more detail in (Johnson et al, 1999; Herzog and Törne 1999). The current 4th Working Draft is described in Herzog and Törne 2000.

STEP & AP-233

STEP is the shorthand name for ISO standard 10303, "Standard for the Technical Exchange of Product data" (ISO, 1994). STEP is briefly described in (Johnson et al, 1999), a more complete overview and history is available in (Kemmerer 1999), and more information is available at a number of sources (for instance, in the web site www.ukcic.org/). The advantages of basing a design data exchange standard for systems engineering on the STEP technology have been described in (Johnson et al, 1999). Each of the main data transfer standards for different application domains are called Application Protocols, hence the term AP-233.

Any person or organisation can contribute to the technical discussions within AP-233 provided they can fund their attendance at the international meetings, however voting at the ballot stages for ISO standards is always organised on a country basis. The AP-233 working group has many active participants, including organisations from the countries in the SEDRES consortium, organisations such as NASA and Lockheed Martin from the USA, and active participation from Australia.

FUTURE WORK & AP-233 DEVELOPMENT

AP-233 Development. Throughout 1999 much effort in the ISO working group was directed towards reaching consensus on the scope of AP-233. Remaining work is to complete or start work in the following areas:

- The textual Requirements document communicating the scope of AP-233;
- The STEP-style process model, or AAM (Application Activity Model);
- The refined data model, or Application Reference Model (ARM); this is essentially a data model expressed using terminology to which practicing systems engineering should be familiar;
- The creation of the integrated data exchange model, the Application Interpreted Model (AIM); the AIM 'interprets' the ARM using a number of existing STEP building blocks and becomes directly implementable;
- Conformance level statement and Abstract Test Suite (ATS). The former defines a tool interface testing framework, while the ATS contains details of individual test cases for testing interfaces.

At the time of writing (March 2000) there is substantial progress on the first three items above, with the 4th Working Draft reaching maturity. Development of the last two items will be initiated in the SEDRES-2 project with the aim to produce the first Committee Draft during 2001. Other materials will also be produced, leading up to an International Standard in 2002

Related work. Part of the AP-233 work is to relate it to other areas of STEP development, and to other relevant standards & projects, such as ANSI/EIA-632-1998 and ISO/IEC 15288 CD2.

The working group will liaise with groups developing related standards, such as STEP AP210: Electronic Assembly, Interconnect and packaging Design; PDM Schema work and the process of modularisation; AP214: Core Data for Automotive Mechanical Design Processes and AP203: Configuration Controlled 3D design of Mechanical Parts and Assemblies. It will also liaise with other groups on a national and international basis, including the INCOSE working groups such as the Tools Integration and Interoperability Working Group, and the Model Driven Systems Design working group.

Formal liaison has been established between AP-233 and INCOSE at an organisational level, with an agreement between ISO SC4/TC184, the Committee overseeing the AP-233 development, and an INCOSE individual (Dr David Oliver) in place to oversee the liaison. Formal liaison also exists between the SEDRES-2 project and the PLCS (Product Life Cycle Support) project. PLCS is aiming to produce a standard to faciliate the definition and exchange of design and support data focussed on the through-life support of a product.

SEDRES-2: Consortium & objectives. The existing SEDRES-1 partners have succeeded in getting a follow-on project, SEDRES-2, in operation with an extended consortium. Additional partners are: Eurostep Ltd (UK), a specialist consultancy company focusing in the area of standards, information management and technology, active in several areas of STEP; Technical University of Clausthal (Germany), with experience of engineering design, data management, advanced computer-aided information systems and again active in ISO STEP standardisation activities; SIA (Societa Italiana Avionica; Italy), a systems & software engineering company experienced in the design of real time control systems. These participants strengthen the consortium as the data model is further extended, validated and taken through the later stages of the ISO process.

The objective of SEDRES-2 is set against the ultimate concept of achieving a distributed environment supporting systems engineering (SE), and building on the results of the SEDRES-1 project. SEDRES-2 aims to extend the data model against the remaining key SE technical areas and refined approach on product data management, and to evaluate resulting data exchange, via practical demonstration and industrial case studies, ultimately across several industry sectors. Important aspects of the project are:

- the work is complementary to the AP-233 work;
- the technical data scope is extended over that covered in SEDRES-1, including architecture, object orientation, selected system properties and design trade study aspects;
- development work will produce an extended set of prototype tool interfaces;
- some work will involve investigating shared design repositories, rather than simply data exchange;
- The start-up of SEDRES.*network*

SEDRES.*network* is a proactive organisation to maintain a generic systems engineering view of AP-233 across a mix of stakeholders, including: partners involved in industry sectors other than aerospace, embracing (potentially) automotive, rail transport, telecommunications, & process industries; design tool vendors; the ISO community.

Timeframe, Validation Scenarios, prototyping. The SEDRES-2 project started in January 2000, and initially planned to run over 18 months, with broadly three phases:

1st semester	Requirements refinement, Validation Scenario definition, data modelling, technology scoping
2nd semester	Interface development, validation environment development, testing, evaluation preparation
3rd semester	Validation scenario execution, evaluation, final report

The project will define two Validation Scenarios (VS's), one aircraft related and the other tackling the space domain.They will be representative of a real design and an industrial organisation working collaboratively and concurrently. The concept of the VS is crucial to ensuring both the refined requirements on AP-233 can be related to a real situation, and that a vehicle exists for doing a meaningful evaluation of the SEDRES/AP-233 data exchange capability.

Both validation scenarios are defined by the following features:

- the application context,
- the phases and activities of the system engineering process being addressed,
- the technical data handled,
- the system engineering environment used in the scenario (tools & infrastructure),
- the evaluation requirement, and
- the success criteria regarding the performance of this Validation Scenario.

The data modelling activities will refine existing work, and create appropriate new elements corresponding to the technical data scope identified earlier.

The prototyping activities will produce one or both interfaces for many different tools used to support SE activities, and in general will embrace the data coverage appropriate to that particular tool. At the time of writing the exact set of tools that will be used for prototyping is not decided, but it is likely to involve (in additional to internal tools) many of the following commercially available tools: Cradle, DOORS, MATRIXx, RDD-100, SCADE, SES-Workbench, Software-through-Pictures, Statemate, Teamwork.

Evaluation. The implementation of a SEDRES-like capability for model data exchange brings with it major implications for the way system engineering can be carried out, including human and business aspects. The evaluation area will build on the existing achievements within SEDRES-1 and other projects, especially in the user-system evaluation area. There will be an emphasis on business efficiency measures with respect to team working and quality of life factors, a process involving both evaluators and industrial partners.

The evaluation approach is structured in 5 main steps:

1) the definition of the evaluation objectives,
2) the set-up of the evaluation process,
3) the integration of the evaluation environment,
4) the evaluation during the performance of the Validation Scenarios,
5) the exploitation of the results against the evaluation objectives.

It should therefore be possible to gain insight and potentially quantifiable results into the effectiveness with which SEDRES/AP233 supports the individual systems engineering activities that involve design data exchange, and into the wider team work and quality of life factors.

Contribution to AP-233. Contributions to the AP-233 standardisation and document activities (items listed earlier) will be being made throughout the project time frame, as the SEDRES-2 partners continue to provide the majority of the resources to bring AP-233 to completion.

IMS potential. IMS, or Intelligent Manufacturing Systems, (see www.ims.org) "is an industry-led, international Research & Development Program established in 1995 to develop the next generation of manufacturing and processing technologies". Many companies and research institutions from Australia, Canada, the European Union, Japan, Switzerland, and the United States have undertaken co-operative technology development to share costs, risks and expertise in areas associated with design and manufacture where there is clear mutual benefit. With over 250 companies and over 200 research institutions currently active across an array of almost 20 active IMS projects, IMS is a proven program that could be of significant value to support AP-233 involvement. Additional funding could, for instance, help support international trials of distributed SE activities across multiple trading blocks, say across the USA, Europe and Australia. Enquiries will be made about the feasibility of IMS for such 'top-up' funding.

AP-233 AND YOU

This section explores the significance of AP-233 to you, as a practising systems engineer. It outlines several of the obstacles that can jeopardise the completion of an ambitious standard such as AP-233 and what can be done to overcome such obstacles.

Significance to Systems Engineers. The very nature of systems engineering – a broad, 'glue' discipline - means that communication with many stakeholders involved in the development of complex products lies at the heart of the discipline. Systems engineers interact with customers, both users and procurers, neither of which may be particularly technically literate. Systems engineers interact with many engineering disciplines, including those for: electrical, electronics, control, hydraulic and pneumatic engineering, software engineering, etc. Typically such engineering disciplines use their own notations, conventions and design tools which have been developed or evolved to support that specific area of technology. The industry must move to a situation where the requirement and design information that systems engineers need to perform their design assessments, trade studies or design verification activities is readily to hand and easily accessible. The output from SE activities can be easily and readily communicated to the individual engineering disciplines, partners or sub-contractors for validation and subsequent development. The SE environments that can be assembled with a combination of interoperable commercial off the shelf design and systems engineering tools will make this vision achievable. AP-233 is a significant contribution to achieving that vision.

Obstacles to achieving industrial uptake. The obstacles to adoption of the emerging AP-233 can be viewed from at least two primary stakeholder groups, users and tool vendors, and in each case there are technical and business issues to be addressed.

For user organisations, users span a spectrum from practising, 'technically-deep' systems engineers at one end, to engineering managers and financial stakeholders at the other. Their technical reservations can include views that a neutral data exchange standard is neither relevant and nor possible. The view that it is not relevant may come from a particularly parochial point of view, either because managers may not be aware of the breadth of technical interactions that systems engineers engage in, or because a particular engineer's experience is itself closely 'focused'. The business scepticism may come from a number of factors. The narrow view may suggest a weaker business case than a wider picture of the need for data exchange would give. The weak business case for neutral data exchange could also come from insufficient concrete information about the cost of developing and maintaining ad-hoc tool-tool interfaces, or of the difficult-to-measure costs associated with poor information access for systems engineers.

For tool vendors there are some similar issues. It is a curious but perhaps not surprising observation that each tool vendor always appears to believe that his own tool is at the 'centre of the systems engineering universe'. This is rarely the case in actuality, since the tool being used is dictated by what the engineer needs to do at the time. However, this point of view will explain to some degree the apparent reticence of tool vendors to perceive the real need for tool interoperability. The technical criticism that a neutral standard is not possible may be a hang-over from earlier attempts, for instance, CDIF, the CASE Data Interchange Format. Despite being sound technically, it failed to be adopted more for non-technical reasons (such as insufficient buy-in from large user and tool vendor communities) than for technical reasons. The business case view for tool vendors for adoption of AP-233 has similar issues as for users: will AP-233 be the dominant standard (in this domain)? What will it cost to develop and maintain interfaces (compared with ad-hoc approaches)? Is there a market, will the same interface be appropriate across industry sectors? Is there a sound business case for users of the tool to buy AP-233 support, perhaps as an add-on module?

Overcoming obstacles. Achieving success for AP-233 is about tackling these technical and business obstacles. Tackling the business obstacles is about changing perceptions, and that is done by sound models and good evidence. For business users it is about ensuring there is a sound business case that indicates explicit commercial advantages to achieving good integrated design environments, brought about by tool interoperability which itself can be achieved by exploiting a neutral standard based tool interface strategy. What are your current organisation's costs associated with a non-integrated systems engineering environment? A recent scientific probe to Mars was lost when, after months in transit, it plunged into the Martian atmosphere, rather then going into orbit – all because the fact that different units of measurement used in different parts of the spacecraft design had not been picked up and tracked explicitly. In this case there was a very explicit cost, which was the cost of a lost mission. Many of the costs associated with lack of integrated support for systems engineering are considerably more subtle. To build sound business cases requires sound metrics on current practice and costs.

But it is not simply a project-internal view that is necessary. For the tool vendor community, the market for such tools is the primary business driver. The tool developments are taken in certain directions led by market and customer research which indicate (to each vendor) the direction that they believe to be most profitable in the short and long term. Requirements for tool interoperability and standards-based tool interfaces from one industry sector may have little significance, if other industry sectors have different requirements. However, if all the major industry sectors into which a design tool is sold have common and agreed requirements for standards-based interfaces, the majority of the market is represented, and vendors have a clear strategic direction.

The technical reservations can be tackled in a number of ways. In the SEDRES programmes, emerging data models have been validated by prototyping design tool interfaces on such data models, and demonstrating that useful data exchange can be achieved. Further, early evidence of comparative manual versus SEDRES-based data exchange provides evidence that feeds the standards-based data exchange business case. Since SEDRES/AP-233 are based on STEP technology, evidence from other areas, such as the structural and geometric design domain, can show what mature design data exchange can do. The AP203 Application Protocol for STEP is now sufficiently mature that it far exceeds the capabilities of its predecessor IGES (Initial Graphics Exchange Specification), is in production use by a number of large organisations, and CAD tools are now achieving conformance accreditation for AP-203 (the first was for the CAD tool CATIA (see the Press Release of 8 April 1999 available on http://pdesinc.aticorp.org).

What you can do. What you can do to contribute to the development of AP-233 depends both on your current view as to the value of AP-233 to your work as a systems engineer and to your role as a stakeholder, user or tool vendor.

If you remain sceptical about AP-233, it might be because you consider it to be irrelevant, it does not have a sound business case, or it is not technically feasible. Make your views known to the authors and the participants in AP-233. It is important that such views are understood and can be addressed. For instance, if your view is that AP-233 is not technically feasible, evidence to demonstrate the contrary can be provided; examples of early exchanges already exist on the SEDRES web site (www.ida.liu.se/projects/sedres/).

If you are already convinced of the need for AP-233 and of its technical and business feasibility, there are active steps you can take to contribute:

1. Make yourself aware of the ongoing progress being made within the AP-233 and SEDRES communities, primarily by maintaining awareness of the SEDRES-2 home page (www.sedres.com) and up-to-date news. Gain some familiarity with the emerging data model, scope and capabilities. Make contact with your INCOSE-AP-233 liaison and national AP-233 representatives. Consider becoming an independent industrial reviewer.
2. Consider in what way AP-233 can be exploited in your organisation. What opportunities for creating, or replacing existing, tool-tool bridges exist? How many tool-tool interfaces do you currently support? Can you see replacing these by AP-233-based interfaces, thereby reducing support costs and increasing flexibility?
3. Are there opportunities for utilising AP-233 with the interactions outside your organisation? How do you currently interact with your customers, with exchange of requirements and conceptual designs? How do you interact with your partners? With your equipment suppliers? Lobby your customers, partners and equipment suppliers to consider experimenting with AP-233 interfaces.
4. Lobby your systems engineering tool vendors. When will they have prototype AP-233 interfaces available? Surely support for AP-233 import interfaces is in their business interest, enabling data to be imported into their tool?
5. Do you have contacts into multiple industry sectors, perhaps because you provide sub-systems or systems engineering tools to multiple industries? Raise awareness of AP-233 with your contacts.

AP-233 is now at a point where it is refining the technical details and reaching industrial concensus. The emphasis on effort to achieving industrial adoption must now be extended beyond the technical, to the business and market aspects of adoption. In the authors view there is no doubt that a neutral systems engineering standard can be made to work, and will provide significant opportunities and benefits.

CONCLUSIONS

This paper has provided a summary of the need for a comprehensive systems engineering data exchange standard, and given a view of how this is an enabler for a longer term vision. It has reported the objectives and achievements of the SEDRES-1 project. It has given a view of the progress and intentions within the AP-233 development. It has explained the objectives and approach of the follow-on project, SEDRES-2. Finally it has outlined a number of the obstacles that can jeopardise the adoption of a neutral design data exchange standard such as AP-233, and proposed a number of activities that systems engineering practitioners and tool vendors can pursue, to ensure that full industrial adoption is achieved

REFERENCES

Harris, D & Candy L, Evaluation in the SEDRES Project: Measuring the Effectiveness of Model Data Exchange between Systems Engineering Tools, in *Proceedings of the 9th Annual International Symposium of INCOSE*, INCOSE, 1999.

Herzog, E & Törne A, Towards a Standardised Systems Engineering Information model, in *Proceedings of the 9th Annual International Symposium of INCOSE*, INCOSE, 1999.

Herzog, E & Törne A., AP-233 Architecture, accepted for publication at the 10th annual international symposium of the International Council on Systems Engineering, 2000.

Kemmerer, S. (ed.), STEP – The Grand Experience, NIST Special publication 939, 1999.

ISO, ISO 10303–1, *Industrial automation systems and integration - Product Data Representation and Exchange - Part 1: Overview and fundamental principles*, ISO, 1994

Johnson, JFE, SEDRES; Extending STEP from Structural Definition to Product Functionality, in *Proceedings of CALS Europe 97*, Frankfurt, 1997.

Johnson, JFE, The SEDRES Project; producing a data exchange standard supporting integrated systems engineering, in *Proceedings of the 8th Annual International Symposium of INCOSE*, INCOSE, 1998.

Johnson, JFE, Luise F, Loeuillet J-L, Inderst M, Nilsson B, Torne A, Candy L, Harris D, The Future Systems Engineering Data Exchange Standard AP-233; Sharing the results of the SEDRES Project, in *Proceedings of the 9th Annual International Symposium of INCOSE*, INCOSE, 1999.

Martin, JN, Overview of the EIA 632 Standard: Processes for Engineering a System, in *Proceedings of the 8th Annual International Symposium of the INCOSE*, INCOSE, 1998.

ACKNOWLEDGEMENT

The SEDRES-1 and SEDRES-2 projects are funded jointly by the participating industrial partner companies and the European Commission. The financial support from the Swedish National Board for Industrial and Technical Development (NUTEK) is also gratefully acknowledged. The authors gratefully acknowledge the hard work of the other project participants.

BIBLIOGRAPHIES

Dr Julian Johnson obtained a BSc and PhD in Physics (Space Science) at Kings and University College, London, respectively. He worked for 8 years as a research scientist at the Universities of London and Southampton in the UK and at NASA/MSFC in the US. In BAE SYSTEMS since 1987 in technical & management roles, most recently as Product Data Management Technologist, he is the SEDRES Technical Manager.

Dr Sylvain BARBEAU obtained his PhD on system engineering methodology for use in an industrial context and is a graduate from Nantes Electronic Institute (IRESTE). He has worked in AEROSPATIALE on several programmes such as the M-51 on the design of the electrical ground segments and development of various missile digital mock-ups. He took part in the development of a C3I system during the design of the overall system mock-up. In the SEDRES project he is responsible for the data model development, and is Project Leader of the ISO AP-233 SE working group.

Erik Herzog is a Ph.D. student at the Real-Time Systems laboratory at the department of computer and information science at Linköpings Universitet, Sweden. His research interests include Systems engineering, specification methods, information modelling and, tool integration techniques. He is also a nominated technical expert to ISO TC184/SC4/WG3.

Michael Giblin Graduated from Paisley College of Technology in 1987 in Computing Science and joined BAE SYSTEMS. He has worked on the development of in-house SE design tools, and subsequently information modelling of SE design tools and data and their interrelationship. He has been involved in the prototyping of design tool interfaces for data exchange. He is the UK expert in the ISO AP-233 SE Working Group.

Integrating Systems and Software Engineering Concepts in AP-233

Asmus Pandikow, Erik Herzog, Anders Törne
Real-Time Systems Laboratory
Linköpings Universitet
581 83 Linköping, Sweden
E-mail: {asmpa, erica, andto}@ida.liu.se

ABSTRACT

This paper presents ongoing work to extend the ISO 10303-233 (AP-233) systems engineering information model in order to integrate software-engineering concepts. The work is motivated by the increasing importance of software in contemporary systems and the gap between systems and software engineering's specification methods. Encoding entities supporting modern software engineering attains two objectives. Firstly, the model could be used for exchanging software specifications in addition to system specifications. Secondly, relationships between entities representing software and system concepts can be encoded which allows for traceability between requirements expressed in a systems specification and the software design specification.

INTRODUCTION

Requirements on and specifications of systems and software have traditionally been expressed in text, often augmented with illustrations in different formats. As long as this was the predominant method there were no explicit information exchange problems between system and software engineers. Expressing requirements and specification in natural language has distinct drawbacks, as most, if not all natural languages are ambiguous by nature. It is very difficult to express requirements in a format that cannot be misunderstood or misinterpreted. Furthermore, textual specifications cannot be simulated or verified formally. Consequently, it is not possible to make any statements about the correctness of such a specification.

Both the systems and software engineering communities have acknowledged the drawbacks of using natural language in specifications, but different methods have evolved in the respective communities. Systems engineering has adopted a function-centered approach as described in, e.g., (Hatley and Pirbhai, 1987) and (Oliver et al., 1997), while software engineering preferred the object-oriented approach. The result is a situation where moving information between the domains has become difficult. There exists a gap between the models at system and software levels, as described in (Cocks, 1999). As a consequence, decisions in the software development phases cannot be directly traced from the systems engineering point of view and vice versa. This might lead to mismatching specifications and hence result in software that might not be compliant with the original system requirements.

AP-233 is the reference within ISO 10303 (STEP) to a standardization project for systems engineering data exchange. The main aspect of this project is to create an information model that encompasses the main systems engineering information elements.

In this paper we describe ongoing work to interlink the systems engineering process and the software engineering process and to integrate object-oriented concepts into the existing elements of the current working draft of the AP-233 information model. An up-to-date overview of the AP-233 project is available in (Johnson et al., 2000) and the architecture of the AP-233 information model is presented (Herzog and Törne, 2000).

The rest of this paper is outlined as follows. The next section provides further motivation for the need to integrate object-oriented concepts with the systems engineering process and sketches the scope of the integration work. The subsequent sections describe the process of object-oriented software engineering followed by a brief description of the elements of the AP-233 information model. More information on AP-233 is available in (Herzog and Törne, 1999a), (Herzog and Törne, 1999b) and (Johnson, 1998). The object-oriented concepts are then compared to the matching parts of the AP-233 model and the degree of equivalence is identified. This is followed by a discussion of the integration work performed. A conclusion and an outline of future work finish the paper.

THE NEED TO INTEGRATE SE AND OO

In many domains, systems engineers are concerned with systems having substantial parts of their functionality implemented as software.

The increasing capacity of computer systems and the flexibility of software facilitates the realization of more system functions as software and hence increases a system's software/hardware ratio. The fact that different analysis and design methods for software and systems engineering are employed, makes it difficult to convey information from the system engineering process to the software engineering process. This also applies to the feedback from the software engineering process, which is delivered to the encompassing system engineering process.

Inherent software intensive domains, such as telecommunication, have started to look at their products as part of the encompassing system. This implies the same problem as mentioned above: conveying information between different processes, using different concepts and different notations.

Object-oriented software engineering has emerged as the dominant software engineering method. Combining the methods of object-oriented software engineering and system engineering would improve the information exchange between the engineering processes and hence improve the overall process.

We are involved in the development of AP-233 and believe that this provides an opportunity for integrating systems engineering and object-oriented concepts in order to achieve the objectives stated above. Including concepts of software engineering in the AP-233 information model will then provide the means for maintaining traceability of design decisions and their consequences throughout the complete engineering process, including software engineering. It may also improve the overall process by increasing the common understanding of the system to be developed.

One has to be aware of the fact that object-orientation originates from software engineering and is not originally intended to directly represent objects of the physical world as concepts like inheritance do not exist there. Nevertheless, the object-oriented approach might be used for representing physical structure and logical relationships between physical objects. In this paper we focus on the integration of object-orientation to support the flow of information from systems engineering to software engineering.

OBJECT-ORIENTED CONCEPTS

As object-oriented concepts originate from software engineering and as software is always only a part of the system to be developed, the early object-oriented methods such as (Booch, 1991) and (Rumbaugh et al., 1991) do not cover all aspects of the software's entire lifecycle. For example, requirements management and post-productive activities such as maintenance and disposal were usually expected to be covered by the methodology of the encompassing project.

The Unified Modeling Language UML (Booch et al., 1996) emerged from the major object-oriented methods by (Booch, 1994), (Rumbaugh et al., 1991) and (Jacobson et al., 1992). It is the first object-oriented notation that allows engineers to informally capture requirements (beginning with the help of Jacobson's "use cases") and also addresses aspects of physical architecture (in its implementation diagrams).

As the UML incorporates all important object-oriented concepts and as the Object Management Group (OMG Web Site, 2000) accepted it in 1997 as a standard, our further discussions and integration efforts are based on the current version 1.3 of the UML (OMG UML Specification, 1999).

The ideal object-oriented software engineering process can be described through three sequential phases: system analysis, design and implementation. Object-orientation provides basic concepts, which can be homogeneously used throughout all phases of the process. The basic concepts are class, object, attribute, operation, message, inheritance and polymorphism, see (Balzert, 1996) or (Muller, 1997) for an introduction. The main phases of the object-oriented software engineering process are further outlined below:

Analysis phase. Identifying the elemental use cases and the global logical packages of the system is the first step within the analysis phase of object-oriented software engineering. This is supported by the UML concepts for use cases and a system's static structure.

Completing the static model of a system (identifying classes, their associations and subsystems) and subsequently creating the dynamic model (detailed use cases and behavior descriptions) are concluding the analysis work. The UML provides additional concepts for this: use cases can be elaborated as message sequences and collaborations between objects. Moreover, state machines, activity diagrams and class operations can be used to describe behavior.

Design phase. In the design phase the system model from the analysis phase is further elaborated to gain a closer mapping to the final software. The analysis concepts are generally kept and only extended by details that allow for tailoring the model for implementation purposes. For this, the UML provides for example class templates, detailed interface and association descriptions as well as overloading and several kinds of polyphormism for class operations.

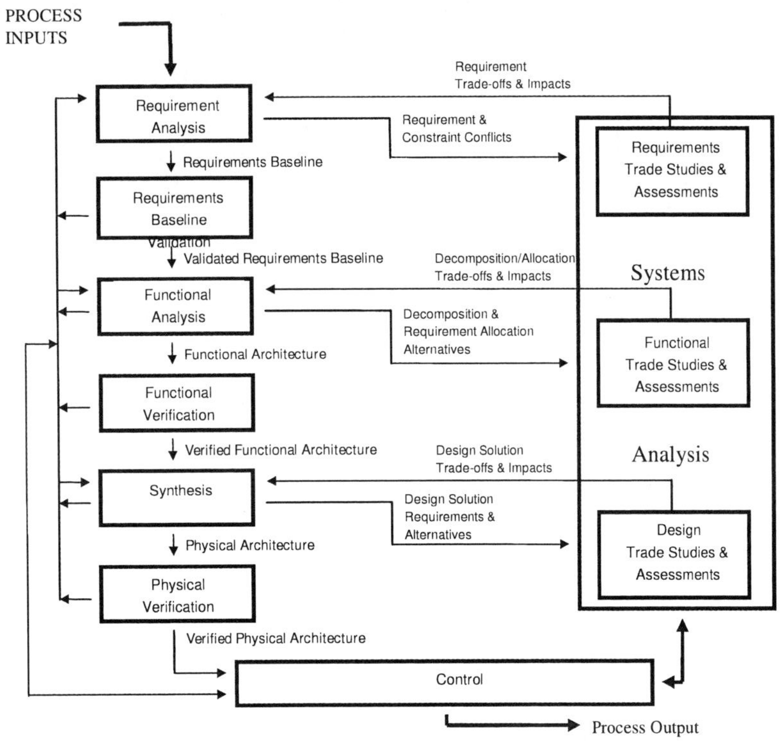

Figure 1: The IEEE 1220 Systems Engineering process

Implementation phase. Implementing the model, which emerged from the design phase in an object-oriented programming language, is the final phase of the object-oriented software engineering process. The UML supports implementation by a view of the components of the software, their interfaces and relations. It also provides a notation for the run-time deployment of software components among the system's hardware components.

UML in software engineering. The UML supports the software engineering phases with several notations, each giving a different view of the modeled system. One notation alone is not sufficient to describe the complete system and the notations usually do not require formal rigor. Instead, they permit the inclusion of semi-formal and informal elements, which allows modeling at different levels of granularity. This might lead to difficulties in interpreting and exchanging the model as it may contain ambiguities.

AP-233 CONCEPTS

The current AP-233 working draft information model, supports the core elements produced in a system engineering process based on structured analysis (Hatley and Pirbhai, 1987). The model itself is process independent, but there is a close relationship to the design elements mentioned in the process description in IEEE 1220 (Ptack, 1998). The engineering process is illustrated in Figure 1.

In the information model there is extensive support for the representation of requirements, functional and physical architectures. There are entities defined for maintaining traceability of how a system evolves.

The assumption in AP-233 is that the main elements of a complete specification for each life cycle of a system may be one of more of the following:

1. The set of requirements defining what a system shall perform, how well it shall be performed etc.
2. A functional architecture defining the functions, formally or informally, a system shall perform, including how it communicates with elements outside the system. The functional architecture may also contain elements for defining the dynamic behavior of a system, e.g., finite state machines, causal chains or formal statements.
3. A physical architecture defining the physical and/or logical architecture of the system under specification.
4. Traceability relationships defining traceability from requirements to elements in the functional or physical architecture.

5. Allocation relationship defining how elements in the functional architecture are mapped onto physical elements.

The main elements of the model are illustrated below in Figure 2 and different aspects of the model are further outlined in, e.g., (Johnson, 1998), (Herzog and Törne, 1999a) and (Herzog and Törne, 1999b).

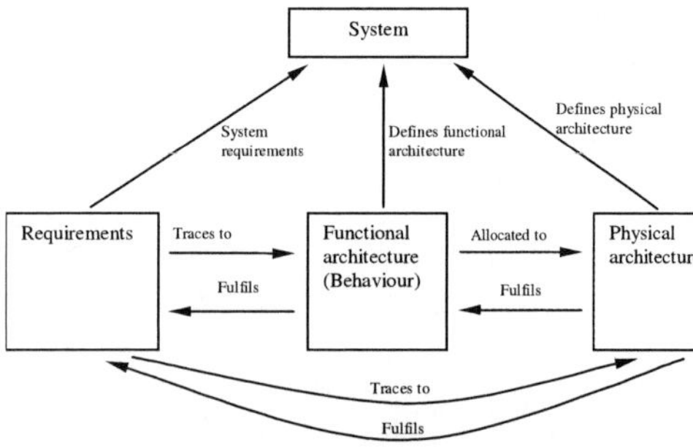

Figure 2: Information model, conceptual view

In addition to the elements presented above the information model supports representation of presentation information, version and configuration management and a wide variety of administrative information as described in (Herzog and Törne, 2000).

COMPARISON

Approach. To prepare the integration of object-oriented concepts into the AP-233 information model, we have started with comparing object-oriented concepts and their corresponding equivalents in the AP-233 information model using the following approach:

- Create a meta-model of the UML
- Identify semantically equivalent parts of the UML and the AP-233 model
- Compare the matching parts of both models and determine their degree of equivalence

The purpose of the comparisons is to support the identification of opportunities for integrating the models.

UML meta-model. The UML meta-model has been partly based on the existing meta-model in (OMG UML Specification, 1999). It has been captured in EXPRESS, just as the AP-233 information model was, in order to facilitate the integration efforts by an equivalent representation with respect to the modeling language.

UML constructs have been modeled in accordance to the modeling style selected for AP-233 in order to gain maximum congruence.

Equivalents. Table 1 gives an overview of the UML notations and how they roughly map to equivalent parts of the AP-233 information model.

UML Notation	AP-233 equivalent
Static structures	Packages, partially types, data items
Use cases	Partially in system views
Sequences and Collaborations	Partially causal chains
Activities	Causal chains
Statecharts	Finite state machines
Components and deployment	Physical architecture

Table 1: UML notation mapping

The mapping of single concepts of the UML notations to semantically equivalent concepts of the AP-233 information model is shown in Table 2.

AP-233	OO (UML)
Project management	(no equivalent)
Configuration management	(no equivalent)
Version management	(no equivalent)
Requirements	(no direct equivalent) Partially in use cases
System / sub-system	(no direct equivalent) Partially packages, classes and components
Partial system view	Partially in use cases
Functional analysis / breakdown	in classes
Causal chains	(no direct equivalent) Partially as message sequences object collaboration
Physical system structure	Partially in components and deployment
Data types	Data types, except class
State machines	Statecharts
Petri nets, causal chains	Activities and their transitions
(no equivalent)	Classes, objects and associations between them
(no equivalent)	Interactions between classes and objects

Table 2: Concept mapping

Global interconnections within the AP-233 model, such as version management and traceability had to be excluded from the mapping, as these are not supported by the UML.

Comparison. For each equivalence in comparison we evaluated whether they represent the same idea or if they represent genuinely different concepts.

Comparing the corresponding parts of the two models resulted in the following equivalence classes:

- Full equivalence
- Partial equivalence
- No equivalence

Full equivalence means that the respective UML concept can be represented by the corresponding AP-233 concept. Small extensions to the AP-233 model may have to be inserted in order to fully capture the UML characteristics. These extensions may in turn also be beneficial for systems engineering methodologies and for the systems engineering process.

Partial equivalence indicates that only some of the major characteristics of an UML concept can be found in the AP-233 equivalent. The AP-233 model would have to be extended substantially to be able to capture the UML counterpart.

No equivalence denotes that an UML concept cannot be identified in the AP-233 information model or that the corresponding concepts are semantically completely different and hence new model entities have to be created.

Table 3 summarizes the UML concepts grouped into the presented equivalence classes.

UML Concept	Equivalence class
Statecharts	Full equivalence
Activities & transitions	Full equivalence
Classes	Partial equivalence
Objects	Partial equivalence
Component view	Partial equivalence
Deployment view	Partial equivalence
Use cases	Partial equivalence
Class associations	No equivalence
Message sequences	No equivalence
Object collaborations	No equivalence

Table 3: Equivalence classes

For the cases of full or no equivalence the modeling solutions are obvious: AP-233 entities, which support fully equivalent UML concepts have possibly only to be adapted to the flavor of UML. Entities for capturing the cases of no equivalence have to be created and linked to existing context entities and global mechanisms of the AP-233 model.

Partial equivalencies require a more thorough investigation of possible integration alternatives in order to retain the semantics and modeling characteristics of both the UML and the existing AP-233 model. The following paragraphs describe the above mentioned partial equivalencies in more detail.

The UML class concept incorporates class operations and attributes, which partially can be compared to the existing AP-233 notions of functions, data items (variables) and their definition in data types. Also objects as instances of classes have similarities with the AP-233 data items and their definition in a data type. Thus, the AP-233 model provides some of the elements of a class but not a composite data type that combines them, i.e. the class as a data type is missing. See also the integration example further down.

The implementation notations in the UML, i.e. the component view and the deployment view, can for the most part be represented by AP-233 entities for physical architecture. However, the possibility of having incomplete component interface definitions is not included in the AP-233 model and the run-time character of the UML deployment view does not semantically match the AP-233 model.

The notion of use cases can for the greater part be represented by AP-233 entities for a partial view of a system, i.e. a perspective only including certain aspects of the system. Nevertheless, for the UML actors there is no semantically equivalent construct available in the AP-233 model.

INTEGRATION

We are currently integrating UML concepts into the AP-233 information model. We have decided to focus on some characteristic object-oriented concepts first and integrate the remaining parts after having gained experience from the first integration efforts. Use cases, classes and objects, associations between classes and statecharts have been selected for this, as they include at least one concept of each equivalence class in our integration taxonomy.

The integration of partial equivalencies such as classes and objects has to be carefully examined with respect to interference with AP-233 constructs. For example, to integrate the class concept we have extended the existing AP-233 data types with a new data type "class", e.g. we consider a class to be a data type, which also can be found in other object-oriented notations such as programming languages.

To avoid side effects we have decided to introduce a new abstract super type for the class data type and the existing traditional AP-233 data types, as shown in figure 3.

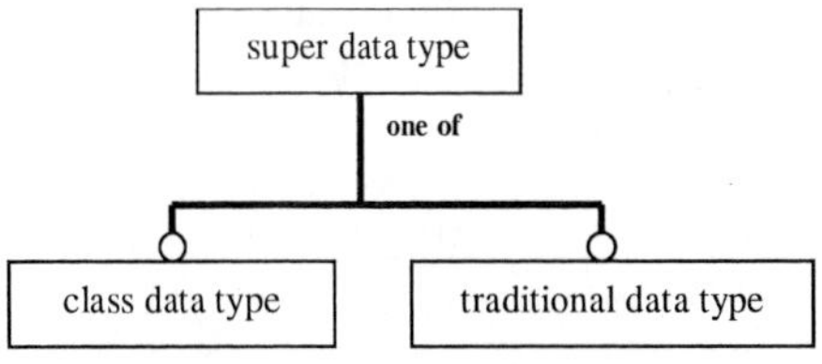

Figure 3: Integration example

The traditional data types again represent the traditional usage of data types within the AP-233 information model, whereas the object-oriented usage refers to the super data type. This means that an object-oriented data instance can either be of type class or of one of the traditional data types.

Once UML concepts are integrated in the information model, they are supported by general AP-233 concepts such as version and configuration management. Moreover, the information model can also be extended to link concepts which are already part of the information model to relevant UML concepts. For example, requirements can then also be associated with elements in the object-oriented model such as classes and objects.

This allows for the inclusion of object-oriented elements into the tracing capabilities of the AP-233 information model. Decisions taken in the software engineering phase can then be traced from a global systems engineering point of view.

CONCLUSIONS AND FUTURE WORK

It is likely that in the future software will take over even more functionality, which has so far only been realizable with hardware. Also additional tasks might be realized with the help of software, which increases the proportion of software in systems.

This development is an indication that it would be beneficial if systems engineering methods could be extended to incorporate advanced software-engineering methods. A desirable consequence is that paths for smooth information exchange between systems and software engineering could be established.

It has not been decided whether object oriented concepts as outlined in this paper shall be included into the AP-233 standard proposal. Regardless of the decision made it is important to close the gap between software and systems engineering methods – both from a method and a data exchange point of view.

We intend to continue integrating UML concepts into the AP-233 information model in order to identify examples of design data exchanges between traditional systems engineering tools and object-oriented tools supporting the UML as well as between object-oriented tools.

ACKNOWLEDGEMENTS

The authors gratefully acknowledge the hard work of participants in the supporting projects. The financial support from the European Commission for the SEDRES project (Esprit 20496) and Swedish National Board for Industrial and Technical Development (NUTEK) for the SEDEX project (Project no. IPII-98-06292) is also gratefully acknowledged.

REFERENCES

Balzert, H.: *"Methoden der objektorientierten Systemanalyse"*, Spektrum Akademischer Verlag, 1996.

Booch, G.: *"Object-Oriented Design with Applications"*, Benjamin / Cummings Publishing Company, 1991.

Booch, G.: *"Object-Oriented Analysis and Design with Applications"*, The Benjamin / Cummings Publishing Company, 1994.

Booch, G., Rumbaugh, J., Jacobson, I.: "The Unified Modeling Language for Object-Oriented Development", Rational Software Corporation http://www.rational.com/uml, 1996.

Cocks, D.: "The Suitability of Using Objects for Modeling at the Systems Level" in the *"Proceedings of the Ninth Annual International Symposium of the International Council on Systems Engineering"*, pages 1047-1054, INCOSE, 1999.

Hatley, D. and Pirbhai, I.: *"Strategies for Real-Time System Specification"*, Dorset House, 1987.

Herzog, E. and Törne, A.: "A Seed for a Step Application Protocol for Systems Engineering" in *"1999 IEEE Conference and Workshop on Engineering of Computer-Based Systems"*, pages 174–180, IEEE Computer Society Press, 1999.

Herzog, E. and Törne, A.: "Towards a Standardised Systems Engineering Information Model" in the *"Proceedings of the Ninth Annual International Symposium of the International Council on Systems Engineering"*, pages 909-916, INCOSE, 1999.

Herzog, E. and Törne, A.: "AP-233 Architecture" in the *"Proceedings of the Tenth Annual International Symposium of the International Council on Systems Engineering"*, INCOSE, 2000.

Jacobson, I., Christerson, M., Jonsson, P., Övergaard, G.: *"Object-Oriented Software Engineering - A Use Case Driven Approach"*, Addison-Wesley, 1992.

Johnson, J.: "The Sedres Project: Producing a Data Exchange Standard Supporting Integrated Systems Engineering" in the *"Proceedings of the Eighth Annual International Symposium of the International Council on Systems Engineering"*, INCOSE, 1998.

Johnson, J., Herzog, E., Barbeau, S. and Giblin, M.: "The Maturing Systems Engineering Data Exchange Standard AP-233 & Your Role", in the *"Proceedings of the Tenth Annual International Symposium of the International Council on Systems Engineering"*, INCOSE, 2000.

Muller, P.-A.: *"Instant UML"*, Wrox Press Ltd., 1997

OMG UML Specification: "OMG Unified Modeling Language Specification", version 1.3, Rational's UML Web Site at *http://www.rational.com/uml/*

resources/documentation/, Rational, 1999.

OMG Web Site: Internet homepage of the Object Management Group at http://www.omg.org, OMG, 2000.

Ptack, K.R. (editor): *"IEEE Standard for Application and Management of the Systems Engineering Process"*, IEEE Press, 1998.

Rumbaugh, J., Blaha, M., Premerlani, W., Eddy, F., Lorensen, W.: *"Object-Oriented Modeling and Design"*, Prentice Hall, 1991.

SEDRES Web Site: Internet homepage of the SEDRES-2 project at http://www.sedres.com, SEDRES-2 project, 2000.

BIOGRAPHIES

Asmus Pandikow is a Ph.D. student in the Real-Time Systems Laboratory in the Department of Computer and Information Science at Linköpings universitet, Sweden. His research addresses software engineering, systems engineering, information modeling and tool integration.

Erik Herzog is a Ph.D. student in the Real-Time Systems Laboratory in the Department of Computer and Information Science at Linköpings universitet, Sweden. His research include Systems engineering, specification methods, information modelling and tool integration techniques. He is also a nominated technical expert for ISO TC184/SC4/WG3.

Anders Törne, Ph.D., is an associate professor in the Real-Time Systems Laboratory in the department of Computer and Information Science, Linköpings universitet, Sweden, and manager of the Linköping office of Carlstedt R&D. His research interests are the design of real-time and embedded systems, systems engineering, and high-level specification languages.

An International Standard for the Description of Systems – The Telecommunication World has one

Ruediger Kaffenberger
Marconi Communications
Marconi Communications GmbH
Gerberstrasse 33
D-71522 Backnang

Abstract. The development of large system requires the participation of many people. People, that speak different languages and that adhere to different cultures, have to work together. Sometimes it is even on the small scale difficult to communicate ideas about the architecture or design principles of a system among all team members, but in a true international setting this task can become a nightmare.

Telecommunication systems from all around the world have to work together to form the global communication network we enjoy today. The international standards body has to communicate the rules for the design of communication systems to all its international members. Consequently a modelling language has been developed, that is able to describe a telecommunication system without implying a certain implementation. In this paper, an impression of this modelling language will be given and some ideas for a possible use in other application domains will be presented.

INTRODUCTION

Structure of this Paper. First the history and rationale of the effort that has lead to the description language as defined in (ETSI 1999) will be presented. A discussion of the main features follows. It contains the original definitions given in (ETSI 1999) as well as generalisations of these definitions. The aim of the generalisations is to extend the usability of the modelling language for other systems. The last part is an examination of how well the modelling language is suited in a general systems context.

History. Telecommunication systems of different origins at all times had to be compatible in some way to allow the unhindered information travel across boundaries or to allow the exchange of equipment supplied by different vendors. This compatibility at the interfaces was ensured by a large set of national and international standards. In the late 1980s the development of a new generation of long distance high capacity transport networks was started, the Synchronous Optical Networks (SONET) in the US and its European equivalent Synchronous Digital Hierarchy (SDH). The new systems required more than only a description of the signals at the transmission interfaces.

More flexible systems. The new systems were to have much more flexibility in the way their transport capacity could be allocated to different connections and services. To achieve this greater flexibility the new systems had to incorporate a sophisticated network management system.

Network Management Independent from the Transmission Equipment. The telecommunication networks business insisted not only on having the ability to use the transmission equipment of different vendors in their networks but to have a free choice among the network management systems on the market too. This required a much deeper specification and standardisation of the new telecommunication systems than that was the case in the past. The difficulty was, to produce a detailed description of the system without imposing a certain implementation. The International Telecommunications Union (ITU) produced the recommendation G.783 (ITU 1992) that describes the concept of SDH. The description uses three kinds of „functions“: „termination“, „adaptation“ and „connection“. These three kinds of function represent all transformations to a signal that are needed to describe the functionality of a telecommunications system. The European Telecommunication Standards Institute (ETSI) has taken up this concept for the European standard EN300-417-1 (ETSI 1999) and has refined it. ETSI introduces graphical symbols for the „functions“ and rules for the succession of the „functions“. Instead of the term „signal“ the more general term „information“ is used.

THE CONCEPT

A Telecommunication Example. Figure 1 shows a simplified part of a telephone connection as an example. The telephone receiver converts and combines speech and dial information into a physical representation suitable for the telephone line (Functions S_T to T_T).

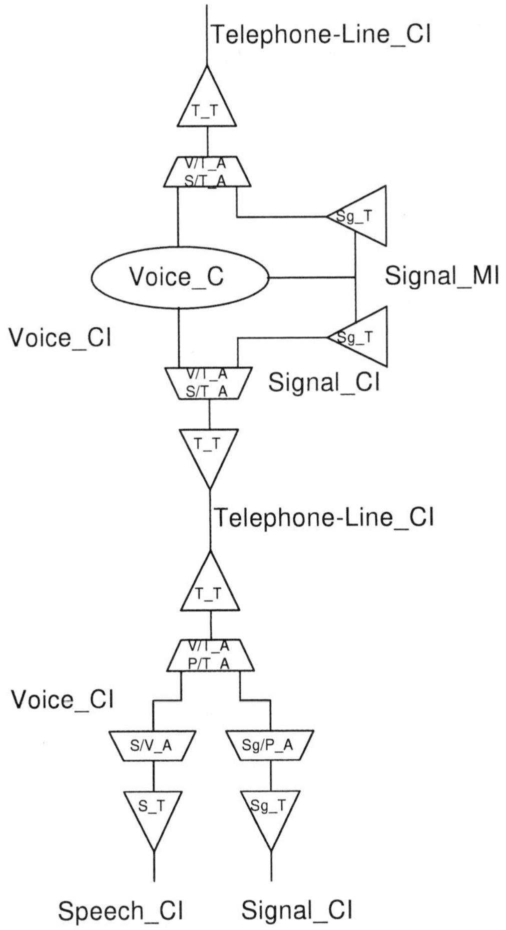

Figure 1. Part of a Telephone Connection

At the exchange office speech and dial information are separated and the dial information controls to which receiving line the voice signal is routed by the telephone switch (Functions T_T ... Voice_C ... T_T).

Functional Blocks – „Functions". (ETSI 1999) describes a function as the following: *'A "process" defined for digital transmission hierarchies (e.g. Plesiochronous Digital Hierarchy (PDH), SDH) which acts on a collection of input information to produce a collection of output information. A function is distinguished by the way in which characteristics of the collection, or of members of the collection of output information differ from characteristics of members of the collection of input information."*

The following generalisation of the above definition allows a broader range of use: The functionality of the system is described by a series of transformations of the „information" (see below) between the point it enters the system until it leaves the system. Each transformation is accomplished by a „functional block" or in this context short a „function". Each function alters only one essential property of an information.

Abstract Information – „Information". Every thing that flows from one functional block to another is described as an (abstract) „information". An information has three essential properties: structure, content and direction (Figure 2). These properties are defined only as deep as necessary to be unambiguous.

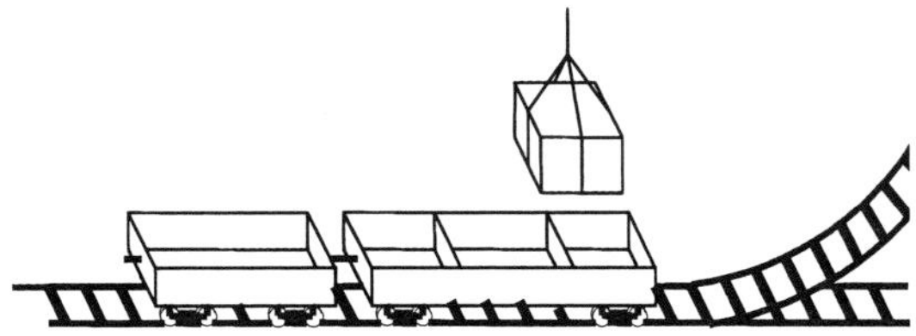

Figure 2. Structure, Content and Direction

Information flows that share a common structure are described by one (abstract) information and share a common label (name).

Hierarchy – Layers and Functional Decomposition. Hierarchy is used in the form of „layers" and of „functional decomposition":

Layers. (ETSI 1999) defines layers as follows: *'A concept used to allow the transport network functionality to be described hierarchically as successive levels; each layer being solely concerned with the generation and transfer of its "characteristic information".*

client / server layer: Any two adjacent network layers are associated in a client / server relationship. Each transport network layer provides transport to the layer above and uses transport from the layers below. The layer providing transport is termed a "server", the layer using transport is termed "client".'

More general, layers are a way to classify information by the way in which the information is transformed and to classify functionality by the kind of information it transforms. This classification reduces the complexity of the description:

Often different information is subsequently treated alike or at least in a similar way. This similar treatment can be called a service. All information items that use a common kind of service belong to the same layer, the client layer. All functions that implement a kind of service also belong to a common layer, the server layer. The information that emerges from the server layer may use the service provided by another layer.

Consequently it becomes the client to this layer. As an example Figure 3 shows a two layers stack. Both applications, telephone and internet, use functions supplied by the transport layer.

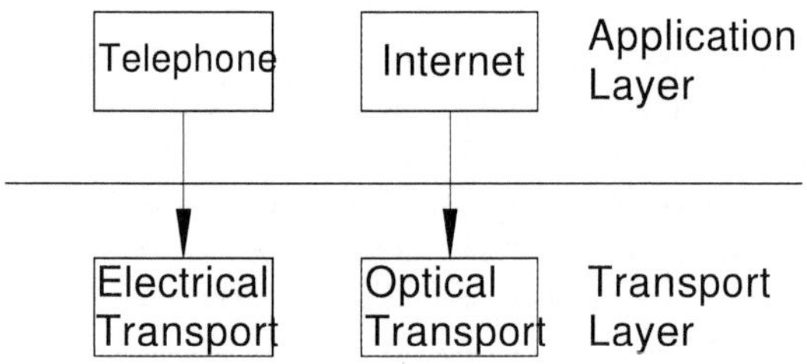

Figure 3. Client Layer and Server Layer

Functional Decomposition. The general building bock of a system in ETSI's notation is the "atomic function". It is defined as follows: '*A "function" which if divided into simpler "functions" would cease to be uniquely defined for digital transmission hierarchies. It is therefore indivisible from a network point of view.*'

(ETSI 1999) defines functional composition by "compound functions" and "major compound functions": '*compound function: A "function" which represents a collection of "atomic functions" within one layer.*

major compound function: A "function" which represents a collection of "atomic functions" and/or "compound functions" within more than one "layer".'

In essence, a functional block can contain a set of other functional blocks. This is very useful for functional decomposition, because often transformations require several steps. Frequently it is not desirable to show all these steps and to explain them. Either it would be confusing if all these transformation steps would be presented or the exact transformation steps are yet unknown.

INFORMATION

Telecommunication systems transport information. This information is usually carried by electric or photonic signals. In order to facilitate this information transport the systems also use additional information. This information is generated somewhere inside the system and is consumed inside the system too. There are many ways how the information transport inside the system is accomplished: information is carried by physical signals, by manipulation of register contents, by function calls etc. What mechanism actually is used depends on the specific implementation. A high level functional description shall not address these implementation details while a design description must address them explicitly. This is accomplished by the concept of abstract information:

Its three properties, structure, content, and direction (see Figure 2) define every information.

Structure. Structure is the syntax element of information. Structure allows to distinguish between individual information elements that make up an information. The content of an information element may be interpreted differently depending on the identity of the information element. An information element can be distinguished by its position in the information stream or by some mark. Furthermore all physical properties of a signal can serve as structure elements of an information. Examples are frequency, phase, and power level.

Content. Content is the semantic element of information. Content is encoded with the use of structure elements. A single structure element may contain meaningful information (here information is used in the common sense) or a set of elements is needed to convey the meaning.

Direction. The concept is based on a model, where abstract information flows through the system and is transformed by a sequence of functions. Thus information has a direction. It originates at a certain function and will be consumed by another connected function. This connection may be static or there may be a set of suitable functions and one of them has to be selected. In the first case the direction property of the information is fixed and in the latter case it has to be modified by a function.

FUNCTIONS

Termination Functions. (ETSI 1999) defines a "trail termination function" as follows: '*An "atomic function" within a "layer" which generates, adds, and monitors information concerning the integrity and supervision of "adapted information".*'

A general definition is, termination functions transform the content of one ore more structure elements of an information. There are „termination sink functions“ that consume bits of information content and „termination source functions“ that generate information content. Both functions can be combined to a bi-directional termination function. If the content of an element in the information's structure element has been consumed by a termination sink function it is no longer valid. The content of an information's structure element is only valid after it has been filled in by a termination source function.

Figure 4 shows the three graphical symbols for the termination function as used by ETSI (ETSI 1999). The left symbol denotes a bi-directional termination function, the symbol in the middle denotes a termination sink function and the right symbol denotes a termination

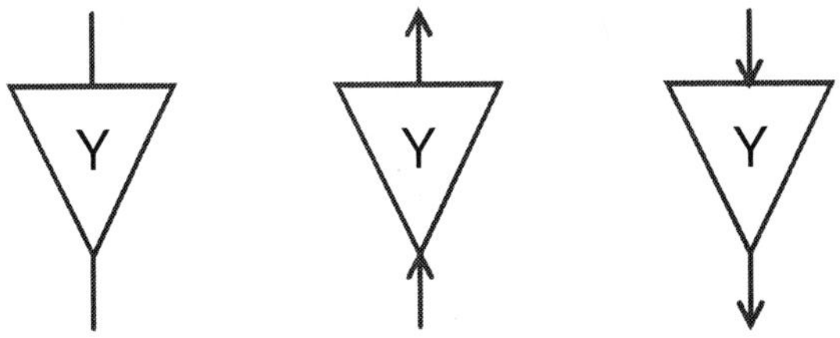

Figure 4, Graphical Symbols for Termination Functions

source function. The label of a termination sink function will have a "_Sk" appended while the label of a termination source function will have a "_So" appended. The functions shown in Figure 4 terminate a Y-information.

Adaptation Function. (ETSI 1999) presents the this definition of an adaptation function: *'An "atomic function" which passes a collection of information between layer networks by changing the way in which the collection of information is represented.'*

The general definition is, adaptation functions transform the structure of an information. This can be done in several ways. All physical properties of the signal that carries the information can be altered. Examples are frequency conversion or all kinds of modulation. On the higher layers the structure of an information is determined by the ordering of the individual information elements. Adaptation functions add or remove elements and change their grouping. Frequently several information streams are combined or an information stream is split into a multitude of information streams.

Figure 5 shows the three graphical symbols for adaptation functions as presented in (ETSI 1999). As with the termination functions there are bi-directional functions(left), sink functions (midle), and source functions (right).

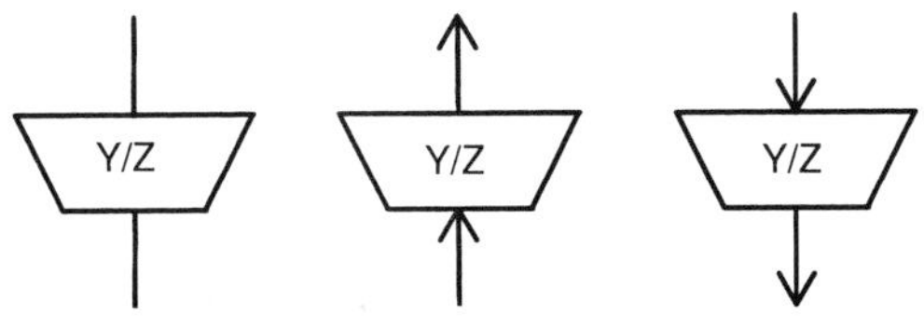

Figure 5. Graphical Symbol for Adaptation Functions

Connection Function. The ETSI definition of a connection function: *'an "atomic function" within a layer which, if connectivity exists, relays a collection of items of information between groups of atomic functions. It does not modify the members of this collection of items of information although it may terminate any switching protocol information and act upon it.'*

The respective generalisation is, connection functions transform the direction property of an information. With every information there is a source function and a sink function associated. There are cases where one of these associations changes over time. A connection function controls which one out of a set of source functions or sink functions is associated with an information as its source or sink respectively. If the associations are static then a connection function can not be applied.

Figure 6 shows the graphical symbols for connection functions. The left symbol denotes a unidirectional connection function; the right symbol

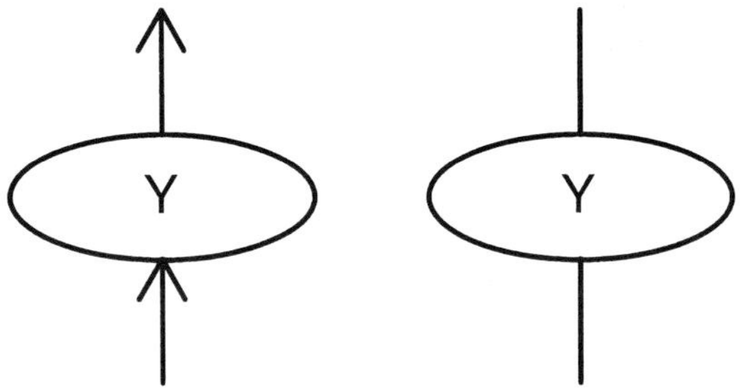

Figure 6. Graphical Symbols for Connection Functions

denotes a bi-directional connection function.

RULES

Conventions for the information. The information that leaves a function differs somehow from the information that enters the function because of the transformation. The information on one side of a function is called "Characteristic Information"; the information on the opposite is called an "Adapted Information". The definitions in (ETSI 1999) are: *'Characteristic Information (CI): A signal of specific rate and format which is transferred within and between "sub-networks", and presented to an "adaptation" function for "transport" by the server layer network.'*

Table 1 shows the relation between the kinds of information and functions.

Access Points and Connection Points. Access points and connection points denote the interfaces between functional blocks. In (ETSI 1999) the definition is as follows: *'Access Point (AP): A "reference point" where the output of an "adaptation" source function is bound to the input of a "Trail Termination source", or where the output of a "trail termination sink" is bound to the*

Function	Input	Output
Termination source	Adapted information	Characteristic information
Termination sink	Characteristic information	Adapted information
Adaptation source	Characteristic information	Adapted information
Adaptation sink	Adapted information	Characteristic information
Connection	Characteristic information	Characteristic information

Table 1. Relation between Information and Functions.

input of an "adaptation" sink function. The "access point" is characterized by the adapted client layer "characteristic information" which passes across it. A bi-directional "access point" is formed by an associated contra-directional pair.

Connection Point (CP): A "reference point" where the output of a "trail termination source" or a "connection" is bound to the input of another "connection", or where the output of a "connection" is bound to the input of a "trail termination sink" or another "connection". The "connection point" is characterized by the information which passes across it. A bi-directional "connection point" is formed by the association of a contra-directional pair.' Figure 7 illustrates these definitions. As stated above, the

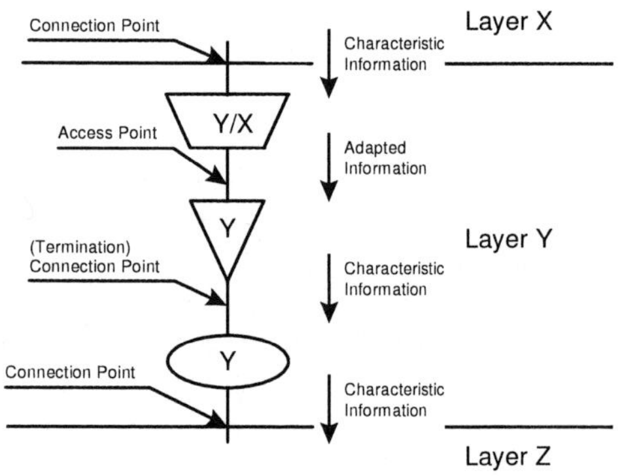

Figure 7. Access Points and Connection Points

characteristic information travels through a connection point over the boundary between layers. All three essential properties of a characteristic information have to be fully defined, because a characteristic information is visible from outside its layer. In contrast the information that travels over an access point is a characteristic information of a client layer (layer X in Figure 7) that has been adapted to the specific needs of the server layer (layer Y in Figure 7). It is called an adapted information (AI). An adapted information is internal to its layer.

The layers of the telecommunications world are equivalent to the sub-systems in other domains. Consequently connection points are equivalent to sub-system interfaces and a characteristic information is equivalent to a sub-system interface specification.

Function Binding. There are rules for the binding of functional blocks. Figure 8 shows the rules for

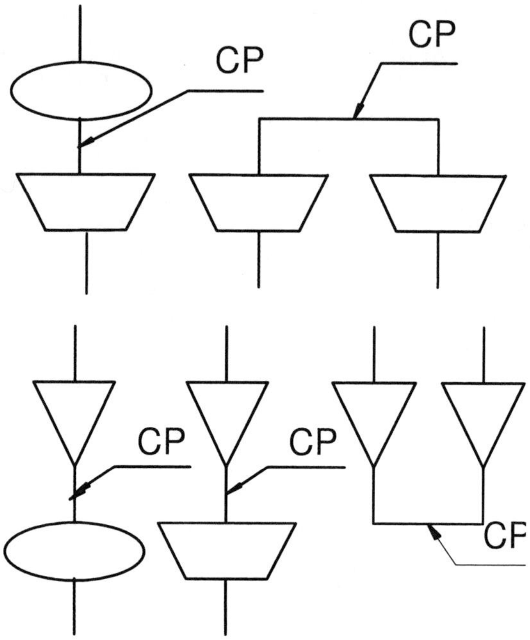

Figure 8. Function Binding at a Connection Point

functions that are bound at connection points, while Figure 9 shows the only way to bind functions at an access point. This rule enforces that an access point is only internal to a layer.

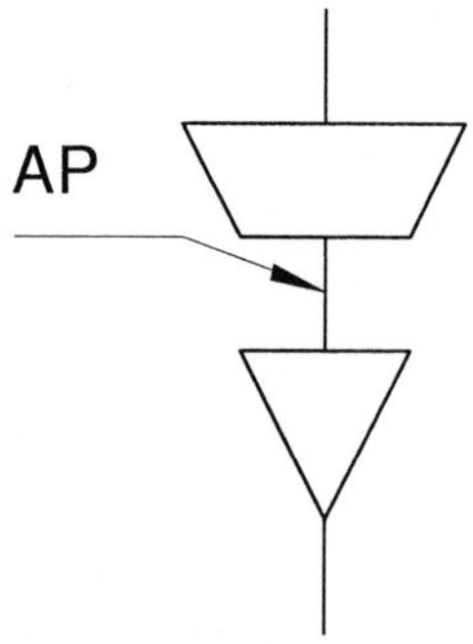

Figure 9. Function Binding at an Access Point

Functional Composition / Decomposition. As mentioned earlier, sometimes it is better to represent a set of bound functions by a compound function or a major compound function. Figure 10 shows how atomic functions may be combined into a compound function. The same rules apply to major compound functions, but they will include functions that belong to more than one layer.

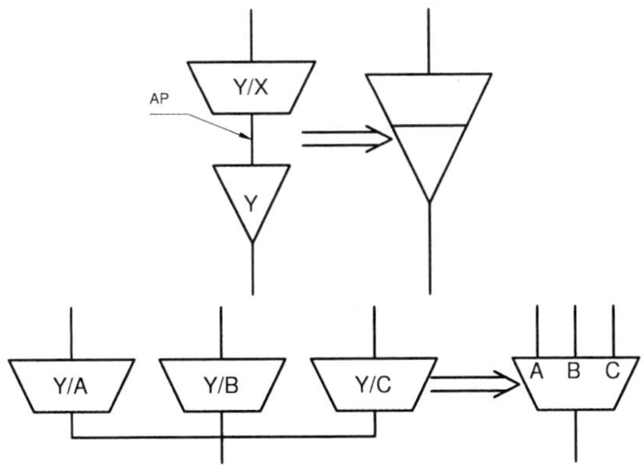

Figure 10. Rules for Compound Functions

MORE INFORMATION

Management Information. Up to this point only that information that is the subject of the transformations by the functional blocks has been presented. Characteristic information and adapted information only would be sufficient if all the transformations were purely static. Usually this is not the case and the functions need additional information about the variable parameters. This information is supplied by some control system and is called management information. The functions not only consume management information but produce it too. They generate status information and extract management information that had been inserted by some remote companion function.

Remote Information. The nature of most telecommunication systems is that the connections are bi-directional and many control mechanisms use this feature, for example to learn about the transmission quality as perceived at the remote side of the communication link. Remote information is usually produced by a termination sink function and relayed to a peer termination source function for inclusion into the data stream to the remote station.

Generalisation. Management information and remote information as presented above are specific to telecommunication systems. In a more general setting they have to be replaced:

Management information is generalised as "information from outside the system boundaries that modifies the behaviour of the system or information about the current state of the system that it generates and supplies to instances that are outside the system boundaries." Examples are user commands and status indications.

Peer-to-peer information is a generalisation of the remote information. Peer-to-peer information is exchanged between functions of the same layer. It conveys status information between collaborating functions.

ADVANTAGES OF THE SPECIFICATION METHOD

Summary of the Method. The specification method presented here uses graphical symbols and formalised textual descriptions of the functional blocks the symbols represent. Each of the three kinds of functions transforms one property of the information elements that travel through the system. There are rules that constrain how the functional blocks can be bound together. Functional blocks and information are labelled in a systematic way.

Advantages. The graphical representation of a system allows for quick comprehension of the overall working of the system. Especially the differentiation of the functional blocks and their representation through different symbols promotes the quick comprehension. The binding rules enforce that functional blocks interface only at points where the characteristics are well defined. The rules for functional composition / decomposition enforce consistency of the interfaces. While not hindering the manual production of the specification, the formalisms of binding rules and naming rules for functions and information elements open the opportunity for automated verification of completeness and consistency. The use of graphical symbols in combination with the rules mentioned, significantly reduces the ambiguity of the textual descriptions of the individual functions.

POSSIBLE USE IN OTHER DOMAINS

Information Processing. Because they deal with information elements too, the generalisations as presented here should be sufficient to use the specification method successfully in the domain of information processing systems.

Material Processing. The method as presented until now was based on the three essential properties of an information that the system processes. If it is to be used for the specification of a material processing system, an assembly line for instance, analogies between information and material have to be found. Table 2 shows such a mapping.

Information Domain	Material Domain
Structure	Spatial Distribution
Value	Characteristic Shape
Direction (of Information Flow)	Direction (of Material Flow)

Table 2. Analogies Between the Properties of Information and Material

Adaptation functions would be used to prepare the materials so that they can be processed subsequently. Termination functions would represent the process steps that put the different elements together and thus give the products the desired shape. Connection functions would denote alternatives in the material flow, for example if different sub-assemblies can be used in a following processing step.

A Very Different System. More far fetched analogies have to be employed if the method is to be used to specify a system very different from a telecommunications system, a pocket knife. This example has been used in (Oliver 1997) and thus allows a direct comparison of the modelling methods.

Termination functions would be used to describe the primary functions of the system's components, while adaptation functions would describe the means that are necessary to integrate the different functions. Connection functions would be used to describe the different bindings between primary functions the system provides. Figure 11 shows the knife and its formal graphical representation.

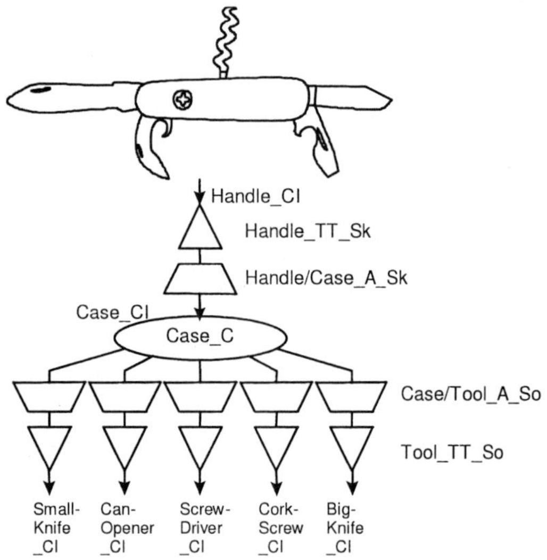

Figure 11. A Pocket Knife

The knife has two primary functions: first the handle that conveys the forces of the user's hand to the knife's blades and houses the blades that are not in use; second the blades that perform functions like cutting something, pulling a cork, or driving a screw.

The blades and the handle have to interface to integrate their functions. Adaptation functions represent the mechanisms of the joins between blades and the handle.

The knife has several blades. A connection function is used to describe the different bindings between the primary functions of the system, in the case of the knife that is whether and how the different blades can be used in conjunction.

Very General Definitions. The pocket knife example leads to some very general definitions:

A termination function represents a primary function of the system. The characteristics of this function are defined by primary (user) requirements.

An adaptation function represents an auxiliary function of the system. It is necessary if multiple and / or different primary functions (or requirements) of the system have to be integrated. The characteristics of an adaptation function are defined by secondary (system) requirements.

A connection function represents a choice in the binding between primary functions. It describes in which way primary functions can be combined. The binding characteristics would be defined by a combination of primary and secondary requirements.

A comparison with Functional Flow Block Diagrams (FFBD) and Object Modeling Technique (OMT) as used in (Oliver 1997). In (Oliver 1997) FFBD are used to describe the behaviour of the system and Object Modeling Technique (OMT) for the architectural aspects of the system. The functional blocks of (ETSI 1999) incorporate parts of the functionality of both FFBD and OMT: While a block of the FFBD represents one function performed by a certain processor (a knife blade for instance) a functional block represents the full set of functions a certain processor performs. Processing details like recursion can not be shown as in a FFBD. If we look at the architectural aspects, a functional block represents a processor object and the bindings shown in the diagrams represent relations like *uses* or *is used* relations. There are no means to show composition relationships as this is the case in OMT. Relationships of the *is a* type beyond the three top classes can only be shown through the choice of a function's label.

FUTURE WORK

In the preceding section some ideas were given, how ETSI's specification method could be generalised for the use in other domains. These ideas are currently very sketchy. From the above comparison with the diagramming methods presented in (Oliver 1997) it can be seen that the method of (ETSI 1999) is most suited for the description of the functional architecture of a system. One very valuable advantage of the method is, that user requirements (represented by characteristic information) and system requirements (represented by adapted information) and the functions that realise these requirements are easily distinguishable through the different graphical symbols.

To apply the method for a wider range of domains, a lot more work has to be done to transform all elements of the presented specification method into a consistent general form, but easily comprehensible and testable specifications should be worth the effort.

REFERENCES

International Telecommunications Union, *Recommendation G.783*, 1992.

Oliver, David W., Kelliher, Timothy P., Keegan, James G. Jr., *Engineering Complex Systems with Models and Objects*, 1997

European Telecommunications Standards Institute, *European Standard EN300-417-1-1*, 1999

BIOGRAPHY

Ruediger Kaffenberger works as a systems engineer since 1992. He is now with the Optical Networks Division of Marconi Communications, where his responsibilities include the definition of the architecture of future SDH systems. In previous positions Ruediger Kaffenberger developed the requirements for application specific integrated circuits, designed single board computers, multi-processor systems, and hard real-time software.

Ruediger Kaffenberger received a M.S. degree in Electrical Engineering from the Universität Stuttgart. He is a founding member of the INCOSE German Chapter, a member of the IEEE and the IEEE Computer Society.

Systems Engineering:

From Process towards Profession

Stuart Arnold
SEC, DERA
Fort Halstead, Sevenoaks,
Kent TN14 7BP
England

Abstract. Systems engineering competence is concerned with people, their development and how they make skilled engineering contributions to meet society's demanding need for quality system products and services. System life cycle processes, currently the subject of international standardization efforts, are used as a basis for developing a systems engineering competency framework. The value of this approach is seen to lie in the adoption of commonly agreed processes whose combined scope better matches the concept of systems engineering as a discipline. The progressive development of objective and assessable attainment levels for each life cycle process, based on a simple competency model, is seen as a route to structuring the development and achievement of recognised levels of individual systems engineering professionalism.

INTRODUCTION

This paper explores one way of thinking about the discipline of systems engineering and how competence in it might be described, structured and assessed. It considers competence using a process description of systems engineering and explores how current developments in the codification of system life cycle processes can provide a structure for thinking about systems engineering competence. Based on the approach described, frameworks could be constructed to guide practitioners towards greater levels of systems engineering proficiency and professionalism.

THE CHANGING FACE OF SYSTEMS ENGINEERING

The challenge. The systems engineering picture is changing. Gone is the myth of simplistic sequence. It has given way to more realistic life cycle representations, where linearity is mapped creatively into hierarchy - in system architecture, in projects and in technical processes.

Nor do we still just talk about avoiding throwing problems and costs over the wall, we actively practice ways to stop this, by thinking and managing whole life; increasingly we are judged by our success in this.

Gone is the emphasis of systems engineers in development making all the system decisions. Indeed, there are those who disapprove of the term systems engineer, arguing that many people across many functions in organizations practice systems engineering, even if to a limited extent, during the lifetime of a system.

Staged life cycle management is now commonplace and driven by the opportunity, problem and risk mitigation decisions that are informed by simulations, synthetic environments, evolutionary developments and incremental delivery programs.

The principles of integrated project teaming within organizations and the practices of extended enterprise trading between organizations are enabling new, more effective ways for conducting cooperative system engineering.

The opportunity. Taken together, these factors are profoundly influencing systems engineering as a discipline and are challenging whether existing process descriptions fully serve the community, the organizations that are trading systems and the systems engineering practitioners.

There is evidence of that worn cliché, a paradigm shift, being alive and well, and disturbing established boundaries and descriptions of systems engineering.

There is, once again, re-evaluation of systems engineering - what is it, how do we do it, who does it, and when in the system life cycle?

Yet with the diversity of contributors to current systems thinking and practice, common consent on these issues is illusive; the path of systems engineering standards illustrates that.

Wherever the balance of these issues lies, it seems clear that there are current challenges to past models of systems engineering, with new opportunities to refine the meaning, scope and codification of systems engineering as a discipline. From this comes a fresh opportunity to tackle some of the bedrock issues of systems engineering competence and professionalism.

ASPECTS OF SYSTEMS ENGINEERING

Three points of view. Along with its increased usage in an ever wider set of contexts, the term systems engineering has acquired a growing range of meanings. Three key ways of using the term – referring to engineering processes, organizational capability and professional discipline – have contexts of use that can introduce differences in the scope and semantics of the term systems engineering.

Engineering Processes. Process is a traditional way of defining systems engineering. A single process, standardising the scope, purpose and a set of development actions, has been traditionally associated with systems engineering [1,2].

Recently, this development-centric view has been giving way to the concept of engineering actions at a system level of thinking practiced throughout the life cycle [3,4]. This wider approach places systems engineering more usefully and effectively within the totality of business processes. It firmly recognises systems engineering as a primary aspect of the business of trading products and services, i.e. trading systems. It is also contributing to a shift in the use of the term systems engineering.

Organizational Capability. The concept of continuous quality improvement is fundamentally built on the notion that processes, their identification, their codification and their managed improvement, are an essential contributor to business success. As a result, capability improvement programs are sweeping through organizations, and models that allow assessment of how processes are performed and effectively employed are in vogue. Systems engineering is a particular focus of attention [5,6], and a strong interest in maturity models is an active influence on systems engineering process definition and use.

Professional Discipline. As the value of systems engineering to society increases, so there is a corresponding increase in the need to attract able staff, to develop them according to best practice and to ensure that they meet ever more demanding responsibilities placed on them by society. The competence of the individual is key to orgainizational success and key to a healthy systems engineering profession.

Just as capability models have multiplied, so competency frameworks are in in vogue. Educational attainment, relevant experience, accreditation and certification are issues of growing importance to systems engineering. The frameworks and common understanding necessary to achieve these goals can draw firmly on the codification of process and the quality concepts that underpin capability assessment.

A WIDER BUSINESS VIEW

Process Models. The value of process definition in systems engineering is long-standing and its formulation over decades is well documented. The goals over this time have been, and remain, clear cut. They are to build widely accepted models of systems engineering that can be used for technical cooperative action, that use common language for clarity of communication, and that enable common understanding by those collaborating to meet inter-organizational agreements and intra-organizational commitments.

It is well recognised that products and services are now more complex, have wider scopes of operation and draw on an increased range of implementation technologies than in the past. Not surprisingly, this growing system complexity is matched by growing complexity in the technical contributions. This is compounded by the interactions of larger numbers of coordinated suppliers, who span national and cultural boundaries, and who now must meet the needs of global markets for their products and services.

These demands of international trade are major drivers in systems engineering thinking and are currently strongly influencing process definition. The result will be to set more clearly the system technical processes in the context of business processes and to explain their role in an organization's actions throughout the life cycle. To this end current international standardization initiatives are building a process picture, centred on systems technical processes, that more effectively guides system technical contributions by diverse organizational functions at different stages of the life cycle [4].

Systems engineering in context. This broader view

sees the systems technical processes as a stratum in a continuum of business processes. Their context is the social domain that creates the need for systems and establishes the laws, trading conventions and social mores that govern acceptable ways of creating and using systems.

Within this social domain sits the organization and its business processes, Figure 1. The hierarchical structure seen in this view of processes exists by virtue of managerial responsibility for process; the sequence of use is independent of this structure.

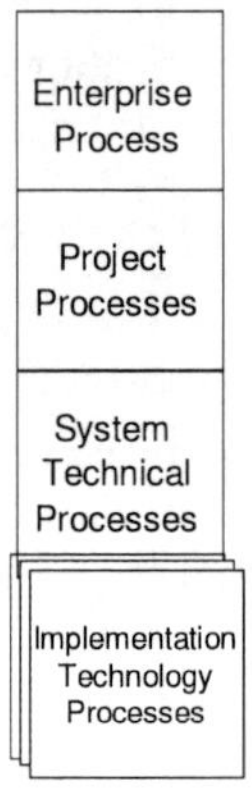

Figure 1. An Organization's Business Processes

Uppermost is the responsibility to customers and organization stakeholders. This is managed at the enterprise level through the strategic deployment of assets into infrastructural capability, including implementation technologies and enabling resources, and into individual projects engaged in conceiving of, creating, utilizing and retiring systems. The overall responsibility for life cycle management resides at this enterprise level.

Subordinate to the enterprise level is the project level, where management is concerned at a more tactical level with achievement criteria that ensure continual progress against technical, schedule and cost requirements, and ensure continued enterprise support at the major decision (stage) gates. The project is the context for the system technical processes.

A hierarchy of projects, possibly spanning different organizations, may exist. These projects are concerned with the subsystems and components that comprise the system architecture. Similarly, sequences of projects, again in potentially different organization, may be responsible for the changing nature of the system life cycle as it moves from stage to stage.

Within the project, the system technical processes are conducted. These processes address the engineering actions at the system level across the whole life cycle. They are a common set that provide for the engineering of the system and they may be employed at any point in time.

Underpinning this system technical level are the implementation technologies, where the desired component are designed, built and tested by employing processes applicable to specialist fields, e.g. software engineering, human factors.

Placing the individual in the model. The diversity of technical and managerial contributions throughout a system's life means that life cycle processes must possess flexibility and generality. Their modularity, granularity and cohesion need to be carefully selected in order to permit the building of life cycles that are themselves complex systems (of processes). Consequently, the description of life cycles, built through stages and from processes, is of necessity a creative action.

Each organizational function has its own perspective on a system's life cycle model and each contributor projects themselves into the process model. Model creators tend to place themselves at the centre of their model and reviewers expect to see themselves in the model's description. Process models are thus moulded to fit conflicting demands. As a result, abstraction levels can become uneven and boundaries of validity become distorted. Different models built from different foci of interest lack compatibility in regions that are common.

Against this background, the selection of processes is, overall, a compromise. Their description of the complexity of real world organization's characteristics and behaviour is an unavoidable simplification. Nevertheless, the scopes and grouping shown in Figure 1 goes some way to including practical organizational factors that directly impinge on the execution of the technical processes. Without this, the complex patterns of systems engineering action would be less well represented.

The emerging International Standard ISO/IEC 15288 recognises these issues and is moving toward describing technical processes in a way more in keeping with the concept of systems engineering as a discipline, by setting them in a business process context, rather than as a single, self-contained, development-centric process. This Standard offers individuals the opportunity to place themselves in the wider picture of system creation and use, see Figure 2. It lays a helpful foundation for a more useful description of the discipline of systems engineering, allowing competence and professional development to be mapped to an internationally agreed process framework.

CAPABILITY OF ORGANIZATIONS

Process Maturity. Capability is to the organization as competence is to the individual and both depend upon process definition.

Importantly, the maturity of an organization's systems engineering environment influences attainable levels of professionalism and in this regard process maturity is important to both an organization's capability and its employees' development and retention of systems engineering competence.

The explosion of process maturity models has led to many perspectives of broadly similar process models, offering differing levels of abstraction and differing foci of interest. Duplication, contention and competition are an almost inevitable consequence of the rush to provide capability models that serve particular organizational perspectives.

As with any model, each has its strength, each has its limitations. The overlaps in capability process models clearly illustrate that boundaries drawn around areas of interest can be both difficult to define, unhelpfully contraining and lead to distortions of abstraction level. Restricting models for systems engineering capability to the technical dimension is unsatisfactory and a softening of this boundary, in order to achieve a better balanced picture, permits technical decisions and actions to be meaningfully set in the context of project and business decisions and actions.

The step from process-based definitions of organizational capability to process-based competence of the individual is a natural one. People perform processes to act on systems throughout their life cycle and they typically do this within the context of organizations, Figure 2.

PROCESS - A BASIS FOR PROFESSIONAL COMPETENCE

Defining competence. At its simplest, competence may be viewed in terms of two dimensions or axes. One axis defines the process, or set of processes, considered relevant to the discipline of interest. The other axis establishes the level of proficiency attained, typically using a progression of increasing-value cardinal points that are defined in terms of attainment or performance criteria.

Since competence is typically considered in terms of the total quality of service delivered by the individual, it is normally assessed in the context of its delivery. For system engineering, the most common context continues to be that of trading enterprises and the projects within them. This strengthens the need to also consider those processes that establish the context for the system technical processes. Consequently, the system life cycle processes currently being standardised internationally appear to be an appropriate set to work with [4].

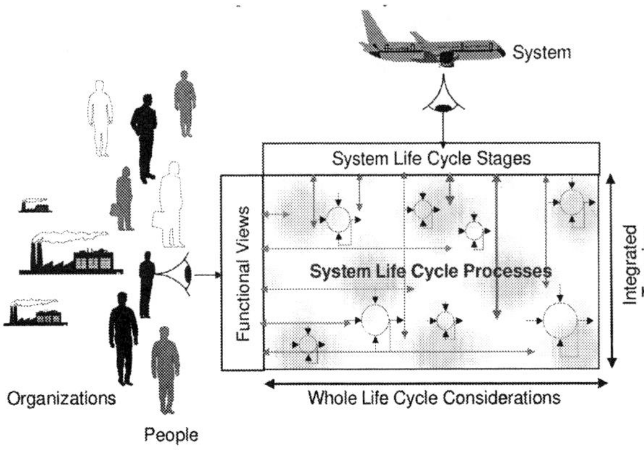

Figure 2. People in organzations apply systems life cycle process to systems

Using this line of reasoning, systems engineering competence can be defined as 'the ability to conduct system life cycle processes at a defined level or profile of levels' (see the top of Figure 4). Although this definition simplifies competence by omitting important psychological and sociological aspects, these aspects are for the most part not peculiar to the systems engineering professional and are well covered in many competence models.

This definition highlights an important concept - that a constant level of attainment across life cycle processes is neither necessary nor achievable by the individual, in order to reach a particular level of competence. The important issue is that a relevant profile of process accomplishment is achieved by the individual.

Competence profiles. The notion of profile is important. However, a single, smooth profile is to some extent an oversimplification. It assumes that a set of processes can be arranged in some meaningful, linear sequence and lead to a readily interpretable or recognizable profile. Whilst the classification in Fig 1 suggests a linear process sequence, it is actually a sequence of process groups arranged hierarchically according to management responsibility, i.e. enterprise management, project management, system technical (or system engineering) management and engineering specialism management. Within each group, meaningful linear distribution of life cycle processes along a single axis is more difficult to achieve. Typically, processes are presented in these categories according to some logical relationship, though competence profile is not normally an influence.

Setting aside this difficulty, the concept of profiles still assists understand. Figure 3 presents profile in a stylised way [7], showing normal distribution profiles centred on each of the four process groups in Figure 2. For simplicity, four titled disciplines have been associated generically with each process group. Though a gross simplification, this representation of competence profiles illustrates important issues.

Figure 3 conveys the idea that to some extent any discipline in an organization may span all system life processes, even though the level of attainment in any one process may only amount to awareness rather than a practical understanding.

Figure 3 also illustrates that there may be significant shared execution of life cycle processes between disciplines. It shows, stylistically, the shared common ground (shaded) between project managers and systems engineers. This is not an issue of encroachment but the natural state of affairs in a healthy organization.

Figure 3 similarly conveys the need for specialist engineers engaged in implementation technologies to have a clear understanding of the systems engineers focus: the systems technical processes. Thus all specialisms, such as the software engineer, human factors specialist and electronics engineer, rely on some level of proficiency in systems technical processes. In short, many people in an organization should possess some level of systems engineering competence, even if only at an awareness level, for the organization to communicate and cooperate effectively.

Figure 3 also illustrates the value of breadth in profiles in order that the summation of peaks presents a uniform level of total organizational competence.

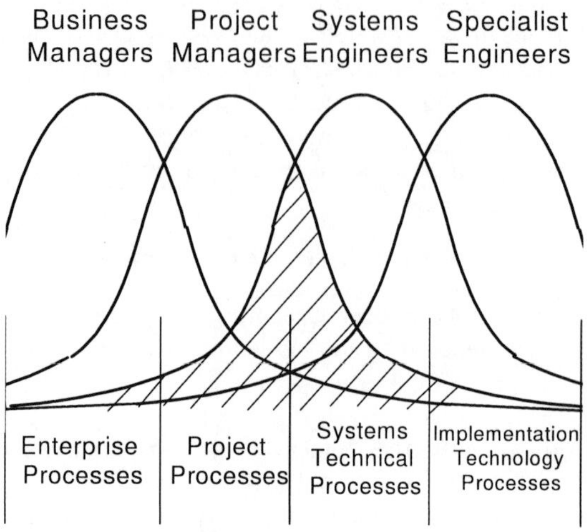

Figure 3. Stylised Competence Profiles

THE INGREDIENTS OF COMPETENCE

Objectivity in competence. In order to tackle the problem of objectivity in the quantification and assessment of levels of competence attainment, it is helpful to consider the attributes that comprise an individual's ability to perform processes. Devising parameters than can be ascribed to these attributes is an important step towards objective assessment of competence and professionalism.

Figure 4 presents a simple and practical model for considering systems engineering competence [7]. It shows ability to be composed predominantly of four constituent attributes:

- Aptitude
- Knowledge
- Experience
- Skills

Aptitude. Aptitude is a quality of the individual, principally formed from innate personal characteristics (nature) and modified over time by the net impact of social conditioning (nurture). Normally, it can only be modified to a limited extent and is thus, to a first approximation, a given. Systems engineering aptitude draws on an individuals propensity to perform, for example, abstraction handling, structured reasoning, dealing with risk, perception of need, holistic thinking. Aptitude assessment of the individual and measurement

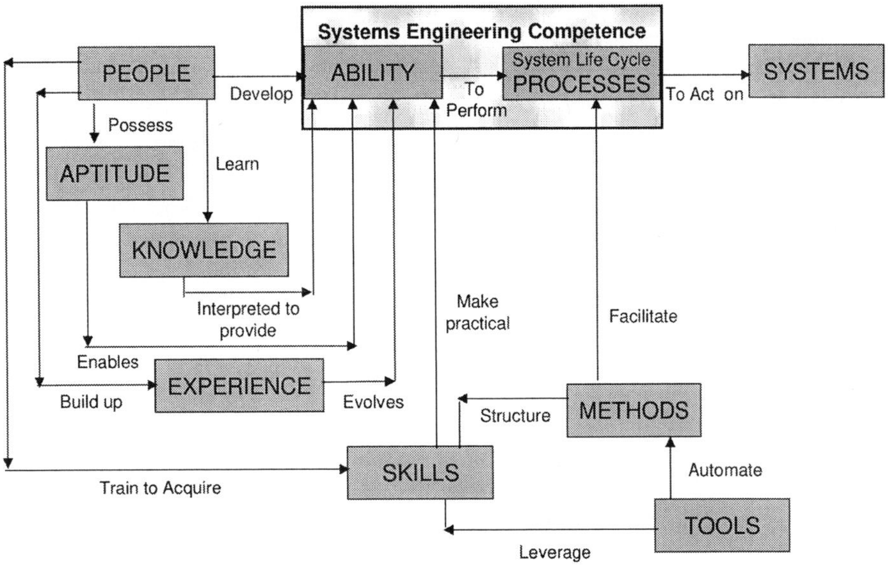

Figure 4. Competence: the ability of people to perform process

of 'the right stuff' for systems engineering is not well understood and currently unreliable. Better understanding and quantification of these factors will enable more objective assessment of the aptitude component of ability.

Knowledge. An individual's systems engineering knowledge is the outcome of gathering, structuring, retaining and accessing the accumulated body of systems engineering information. It is gained partly through formal education, often with limited practical context, and partly through training in the course of employment.

Most education is conducted according to well structured formats, though systems engineering education appears to lag both in both quantity and quality in comparison will many other disciplines. Education is concerned with conveying an understanding of systems engineering knowledge. However, levels of achievement in systems engineering education are substantially objective, typically with attainment classification and often independently assessed.

Training introduces a practical side to systems engineering knowledge, though in many organizations this still lacks good structure, availability and relevance to individual needs. Active planning and a supportive organizational culture – all parts of the capability picture – are fundamental. Again, training in systems engineering lags other disciplines.

The linking of defined education and training programs to levels of formal engineering accreditation is beginning to guide academia and organizations towards coordinated contributions to the career development of tomorrow's systems engineering professionals.

Experience. Systems engineering experience is built up through personal participation by the individual in the day-to-day conduct of systems engineering. It has been a traditional and major contributor to the development of systems engineering ability and remains the single biggest influence in professional development.

Objective assessment of experience is notoriously difficult. Nevertheless, experience factors, such as involvement in systems having diverse application domains, different life cycles, varying levels of complexity, size and formality, mean that parameters can be devised to assist auditable quantification of attainment in systems engineering experience.

Skills. Systems engineering skills are acquired as a result of practical execution of life cycle process by the individual. This execution increasingly depends on methods and tools.

Method is the detailed structuring of tasks and the use of proved techniques to introduce practicability, and also repeatability, of process execution from individual to individual. Tools provide the leverage necessary to cope with the quantity, detail and discipline of the methods employed.

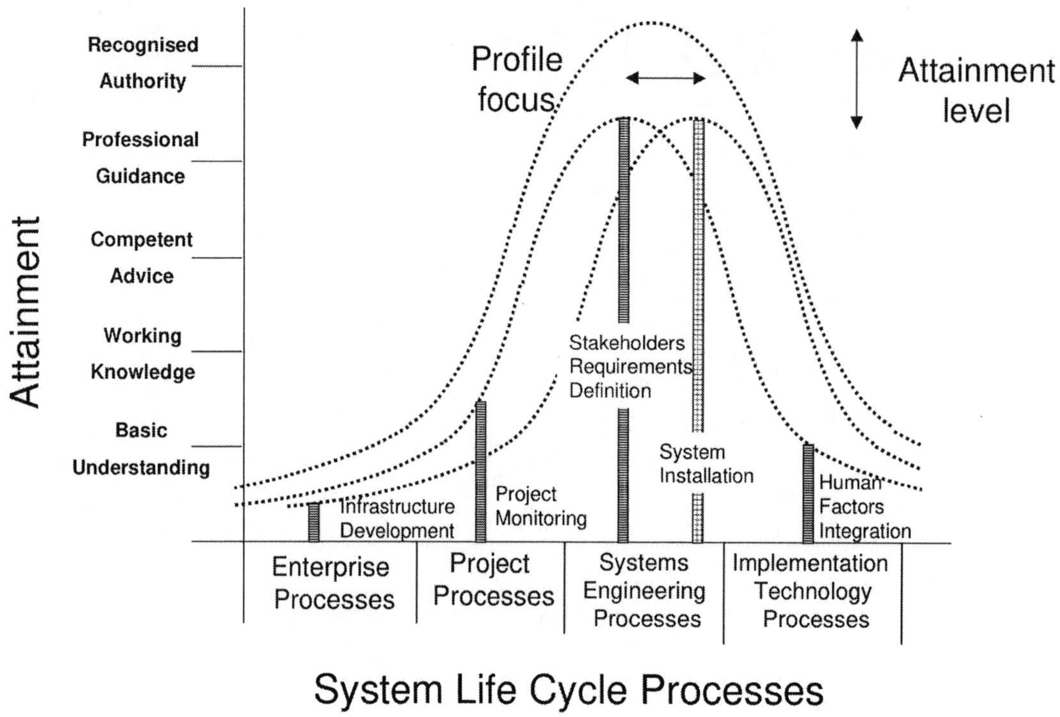

Figure 5. Competence - merging profile focus and attainment levels

Skill is thus substantially a measure of the effectiveness and reliability of processes execution achieved by an individual. Measuring the quality of delivered process outcome, according to defined process achievement criteria, is a function of method and tool selection ability for given system life cycles and the quality of their application.

SYSTEMS ENGINEERING COMPETENCY FRAMEWORKS

Objective measurement. In principle, and to some extent in practice, each of the foregoing components of ability can already be paramaterized and quantified. This requires measurement methods to be selected for each contributing factor of each ability attribute, whilst at the same time keeping in mind the different nature of individual system life cycle processes. Once defined and agreed, this approach maximises the objectivity that is essential for consistency, repeatability and for audit.

A wholly objective frame of reference for characterising each attribute of an individual, as it relates to each and every life cycle process, is a desirable but unlikely goal. There may be significant uncertainty associated with objective scales and impartial measurement techniques. Some value judgement appears unavoidable and dispassionate assessment based on trained interpretation is the surest way to counter this weakness. This presents similar challenges to those experienced in capability maturity assessment.

Quantifying attainment. An example of a quantitative scale for competence attainment is illustrated in Figure 5. Here the selection is of five cardinal points or bands.

This approach has evolved from the thinking behind continuous quality improvement and capability modeling. Whilst in principle the scale could be continuous, bands or steps of advancing ability convey the notion of recognisable and attainable steps of progressive advancement. Attainment steps avoid the weakness of identifying instantaneous values on continuous a scale, where a particular value is likely to have high uncertainty bounds and be difficult to describe.

The five bands in Figure 5 have titles that correspond to general levels of professional standing and they span the whole range of systems engineering competence in a fairly practical and understandable way. The scale in Figure 5 can map into the organizational context, placing individuals at recognizable levels of influence and expertise. These levels are essentially steps on a professional ladder and could be viewed as being prerequisites to perform particular systems engineering roles or to make systems engineering contributions in particular organizational functions.

Figure 5 illustrates, stylistically, how attainment profiles have shifting foci or emphasis in their histogram patterns. It shows two profiles of systems engineering attainment centred on the stakeholder requirements definition and on the system installation processes defined in ISO/IEC 15288. Levels of attainment in the other life cycle processes would contribute to the description of a complete profile. A generally higher level of attainment, as shown, raises the profile to correspond with higher overall competence.

Professional Accreditation. The attainment scale in Figure 5 also has meaning in society, where accreditation and certification are becoming important issues in the practice of system engineering. Systems engineers have particular social responsibilities in specific areas such as health and safety, security and the environmental impact of systems. This is attracting pressure for greater regulation. More generally, as society's expectations continue to grow, the obligations and accountability of systems engineering professionals will require better-defined and regulated professional performance and codes of conduct.

There are very many possible profiles, most of which will have histogram bars that graphically convey limited meaning without considerable interpretation. Thus, there is value to society, the organization and the individual, if a single attainment value for the profession of systems engineering, rather than a perplexing profile, can be achieved through further simplification of this data. The competence parameter now reduces to a single value estimation that is relevant, for example, to assessment of overall professionalism by a professional body, or certification by a regulating authority, such as a National or State public or professional authority. In this case, alternative terms such as novice, practitioner, professional, expert and consultant might need to be equated to the five steps. Such a single attainment value for the single discipline of systems engineering would result from some agreed fusing of histogram values. Integration under the profile or a defined set of values within profile bounds would achieve this.

CONCLUSION

A systems engineering competency framework, based on a common model of the discipline of systems engineering, would bring better structure and underpinning rationale to professional development, individual attainment and certification/accreditation. The strong element of subjective assessment typically found in most competency frameworks is countered, though not eliminated, through the adoption of an internationally developed description of processes that span both the system life cycle and the organization, and by employing a simple model of competence. These simplifications aid objectivity and assist in the understanding and development of competence for the systems engineering professional.

REFERENCES

[1] MIL-STD 499B, www.incose.org

[2] IEEE 1220, *Standard for Application and Management of the Systems Engineering Process,*IEE, 345 East 47th Street, New York, NY10017, 1999

[3] ANSI/EIA Standard 632,EIA, Arlington, Dec 1999.

[4] ISO/IEC15288 CD2, Life Cycle Management – System Life Cycle Processes, ISO,1, rue de Varembe, CH-1211 Geneve 20, Switzerland

[5] EIA Interim Standard 731, Parts 1,2 *Systems Engineering Capability,* EIA, Arlington, Dec 1998.

[6] ISO/IEC TR15504, Information technology – Software process assessment – Parts to 9, ISO,1, rue de Varembe, CH-1211 Geneve 20, Switzerland 1998

[7] Setting Standards For Systems Engineering, S.Arnold, Systems Engineering for Defence Conference, RMCS Shrivenham 20-21 January 1999.

BIOGRAPHY

Stuart Arnold is Systems Engineering Manager in DERA's Systems and Software Engineering Centre. Stuart experience draws heavily on many years of international industrial experience working for Philips in development, manufacture and product support. Before moving into government service, he was Software Engineering Manager for Thorn EMI Sensors. Stuart's recent contributions to the discipline of system engineering include his contributions to IEEE1220(1999) and EIA 632(1999). He is currently the Editor of ISO/IEC 15288.

An Ontology For Standards

J. R. Velman
E. R. Widmann
Hughes Space & Communications Company
PO Box 92919
Los Angeles, CA 90009

Abstract. The paper continues the exploration of standards that the authors initiated in [1] and continued in [2] and [3]. It provides an ontology for standards—a specification of the things and relationships relevant to the topic of standards. The ontology is presented using the ISO standard graphical language, EXPRESS-G. It uses concepts from mathematical logic to clarify the content, meaning, and use of standards. Characteristics and elements of standards that are independent of any particular usage of the standard are defined. The subject matter of standardization is classified and a taxonomy is presented. Instances of earliest use of each part of the taxonomy are described. The means of establishing standards is discussed, together with the question of voluntary versus mandatory compliance. The paper closes with a set of conclusions regarding management process standards. The paper concentrates on those aspects of standards of importance to systems engineering, and includes numerous illustrative examples.

INTRODUCTION

What and Why. *Ontology* is the branch of metaphysics that deals with "the nature and relations of being" [4]. In recent years, the concept of ontology has been adopted by the knowledge representation community to refer to an *explicit* specification of the things and relationships that are relevant to a particular topic [5]. This paper uses the term *ontology* in this latter sense.

Figure 1 shows a very brief definition of an ontology, and some key reasons why the authors deem it useful to set forth an *explicit* ontology for standards. Not least of these reasons is the fact that, in the absence of an *explicit, documented* ontology, each person brings his or her own *implicit* ontology to the discussion of a topic. Different people may have very different *implicit* ontologies that structure their communications. These differences may not be obvious from the vocabulary itself, and miscommunication results.

An ontology that is documented explicitly provides a focused view of a subject. As with any focused view, it shows some aspects of the topic with sharp clarity while other aspects are blurred or omitted entirely. Thus an ontology highlights the aspects of a subject that are relevant to a particular purpose. This paper sets forth an ontology that highlights features of standards that are important for systems engineers to consider when reviewing draft standards, writing standards, or applying standards in the practice of systems engineering.

What is an ontology?

A specification of vocabulary for some topic

A specification of relationships that hold among terms for the topic

An identification of relevant aspects of a topic

Why an *explicit* ontology?

To help understand some area of knowledge better

To help people communicate about the subject

To replace differing implicit ontologies people have without knowing it

Figure 1. What and Why

Background. During the past few years there has been an increased interest and concern with standards. Within the systems engineering community, this has been demonstrated by the review, balloting and subsequent release (at the end of 1998) of ANSI/EIA-632-1998 *Processes for Engineering A System* [6] and EIA/IS 731 *Systems Engineering Capability* [7].[1] These standards are instances of the class of standards that the authors called *management process standards* in [2].[2] The recent review, and numerous comments, by many members of INCOSE, of the committee draft ISO/IEC 15288 CD 1, *Life Cycle Management—System Life Cycle Processes* [8][3] has given further evidence of the strong interest in standardization by members of the systems engineering community. [6], [7], and [8] are all instances of *formal consensus standards* that are issued in a formal style and are developed using a defined consensus process by officially sanctioned standards-making bodies; they all are standards for human activity processes intended to achieve certain goals. In addition to these types of standards, standards of all kinds are of

[1] EIA is the Electronic Industries Alliance

[2] The authors of the present paper participated, as authors, in the development of these two standards.

[3] ISO is the International Organization for Standardization, and IEC is the International Electrotechnical Commission.

importance to systems engineers because they are a ubiquitous source of stakeholder requirements. Standards, as a source of stakeholder requirements, impact the conceptualization, development, production, test, deployment, operation, support, and retirement of systems.

Content and Organization. This paper continues the exploration of standards that the authors initiated in [1] and continued in [2] and [3]. The ontology provides a new and expanded technical answer to the question "What is a standard?" A central feature of this ontology is that a standard provides a *theory* in the technical sense used in modern logic. This perspective gives very clear meanings to the terms *normative*, *informative*, and *conforming*, which have often been the source of confusion. It also provides insight into the roles of the scope statement and of definitions that are found in many standards documents.

The ontology identifies and describes several observable properties of a standard that condition its use and understanding. A first level taxonomy of standards by subject matter was presented in [1], [2] and [3]. This taxonomy is reprised in this paper, related to types of standards identified by ISO/IEC, and the results are incorporated into the ontology.

A short paper such as this can, in reality, only present an outline of an ontology for a subject as broad as that of standards. The outline provides a solid base for immediate application and future refinement.

In addition to the presentation of the elements of the ontology, a number of examples are given to illustrate the concept of a standard as the basis of a theory and the other aspects of the ontology. The subject matter taxonomy is illustrated with examples of some of the earliest uses of standards in each category. After a discussion of the issue of mandatory versus voluntary compliance, the paper closes with an expansion of the conclusions presented in [2] with respect to management process standards.

PRESENTATION OF THE ONTOLOGY

The ontology is presented as a description of the information needed to describe the "things and relationships" relevant to a standard. The EXPRESS-G graphical language is used to present the ontology because of its power and versatility. EXPRESS-G is the graphical subset of the ISO Standard EXPRESS language [9], which was developed as a formal information requirements specification language.

Following the EXPRESS vocabulary, the principle "things" in the ontology are referred to as *entities*. An entity is characterized by it's *attributes*. In the full EXPRESS language attributes can be any of several types. The elementary types include numbers or strings of text. The only built in information structures that are more complex than these are aggregates (sets and lists, for example), selections, and enumerations. When more complex structures are required, these are achieved by means of *attributes* that are themselves *entities*. This enables the specification of very complex information structures, and facilitates hierarchical decomposition. The only attributes used in this paper are entities, *selections* among possible entities, or *sets* of attributes of one of these types.

The characteristics and elements of a standard itself are presented in the next section as an EXPRESS-G *schema*. A *schema* is a set of related entities, considered as a whole.

In representing the "things and relationships" concerned with *interpretation* of a standard and *conformance*, an EXPRESS-G diagram that shows relationships between different schemata is used.

In this paper, the terms *entity*, *attribute*, *schema*, will only be used in their EXPRESS-G sense.

ATTRIBUTES OF A STANDARD

Figure 2 shows an EXPRESS-G schema for a standard. The two primary attributes of a standard, in our ontology, are its *characteristics* and its *elements*. These represent two separate views of a standard. The *characteristics* determine the object of standardization (subject), and condition the use of a standard in various ways. The *elements* are functional components of a standard. The term *element* has been adopted from [10], where the elements are formally specified for ISO and IEC standards. These functional components exist either implicitly or explicitly for anything that may be used as a standard, whether formal or informal. In the following discussion, the terminology is ISO/IEC terminology as given in [10] and [11].

A number of ambiguities were found in [10] and [11] while developing the EXPRESS-G diagrams. This is an all too common result when a standard is expressed in natural language without using some formal language (such as EXPRESS or a language based on symbolic logic) to check for consistency.

CHARACTERISTICS

The characteristics are *subject* matter, type of *consent*, the *authority* issuing the standard, and its *style* of presentation.

Subject Matter of Standards. The *subject* of a standard is classified into of one of the three classes defined in the taxonomy of [1], [2], and [3]. The ISO/IEC directives and guides, [10] and [11], also address the subject matter of standards, and describe a number of different types of standards. These type descriptions are useful, but there is significant overlap among types, so they are not a suitable basis for a taxonomy. In the following, the taxonomy is presented first, then a map-

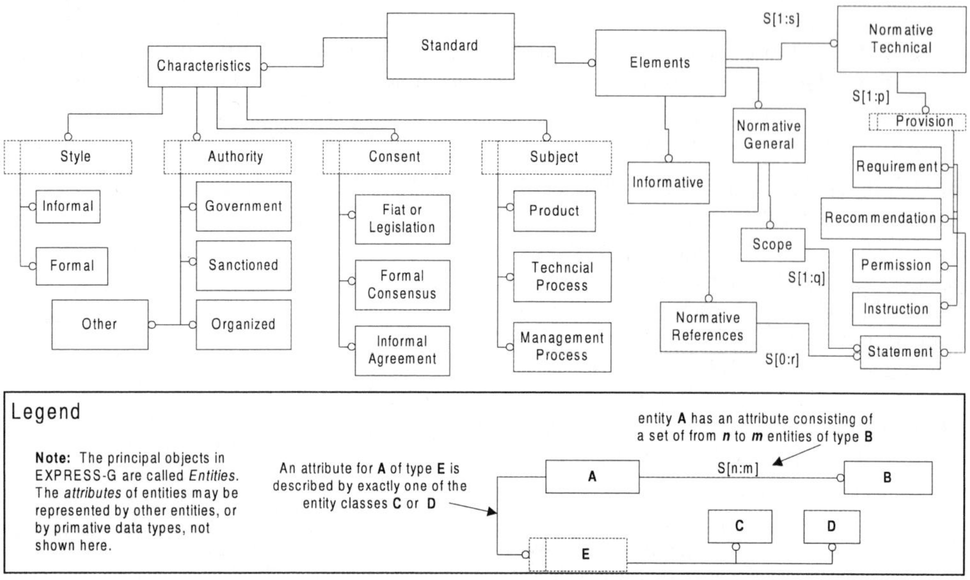

Figure 2. EXPRESS-G Diagram of the attributes of a standard

ping of the ISO/IEC types into the taxonomy is given.

Taxonomy. The classes of subject matter in the taxonomy are as follows:

Product Standards. A product standard defines particular functions, measurements, features, and perhaps test criteria for a product. The product must demonstrably possess these measurements and features, perform these functions, and pass these tests to conform to the standard. These standards tend to be the easiest to comprehend, and the most common.

Technical Process Standards. These standards specify a manufacturing process, a test process, or the like. A technical process standard specifies the exact measurable steps that must be taken to manufacture a specific product, perform a test, or produce a material.

Management Process Standards. These concern human activities, and are modeled after the technical process standards. Due to the complexity of the processes involved they are much more ambiguous and imprecise in their formulation and application.

ISO/IEC Types. ISO/IEC addresses potential areas of standardization in a "Note" under the definition of standardization in ISO/IEC Guide 2, [11]. It states that the expression "product, process or service" has been adopted to encompass the subject of standardization in a broad sense, and should be understood equally to cover, for example, any material, component, equipment, system, interface, protocol, procedure, function, method or activity. This convention is followed in this paper. The types listed in [11] are:

Basic standard. "....has a wide-ranging coverage or contains general provisions for one particular field." This would be a theory of that field, for example, the engineering of systems. According to [11] "a basic standard may function as a standard for direct application or as a basis for other standards."

Terminology standard. "... is concerned with terms, usually accompanied by their definitions, and sometimes by explanatory notes, illustrations, examples, etc."

Testing standard. "... is concerned with test methods, sometimes supplemented with other provisions related to testing such as sampling, use of statistical methods, sequence of tests."

Product standard. "... specifies requirements to be fulfilled by a product or a group of products to establish its fitness for purpose."

Process standard. "... specifies requirements to be fulfilled by a process to establish its fitness for purpose."

Service standard. "... specifies requirements to be fulfilled by a service, to establish its fitness for purpose."

Interface standard. "... specifies requirements concerned with the compatibility of products or systems at their points of interconnection."

Standard on data to be provided. "... lists characteristics for which values or other data are to be stated for specifying the product, process or service."

Figure 3 shows the relationship of the types of standards listed in [11] to the authors' taxonomy.

Earliest Instances. Product standards are probably the longest used, and therefore oldest, standards because they directly facilitate human commerce. They are also the most numerous of the standards. Product standards were in use as long ago as 7000 B.C. when

Product Standards
Basic standard
Terminology standard
Product standard
Service standard
Interface standard
Standard on data to be provided
Technical Process Standards
Basic standard
Terminology standard
Testing standard
Process standard
Standard on data to be provided
Management Process Standards
Basic standard
Terminology standard
Testing standard
Process standard

Figure 3. Mapping of ISO/IEC Standard Types into the Authors' Taxonomy

cylindrical stones were used as units of weight in Egypt [12]. Standardized measurement of the passage of time by ancient calendars began some 5000 years ago, when the Sumerians in the Tigris-Euphrates valley developed "a calendar that divided the year into 30-day months, divided the day into 12 periods (each corresponding to 2 of our hours), and divided these periods into 30 parts (each like 4 of our minutes)." [13] Money, particularly coinage, was employed as a standard unit of exchange by many ancient civilizations, thereby enhancing the conduct of commerce over the previously used method of barter.

Technical process standards are the next oldest of the standards within this taxonomy, and the second most numerous. Probably one of the earliest instances was found in Eleusis, Greece, in 1893, on an inscribed stone that dated to the 4th century BC. It "cited a decree regarding the manufacture of bronze fittings for the erection of a new stoa (portico) which became the Philonion Stoa. The bronze specified was copper/tin in a ratio of 11 parts copper to 1 part tin," [14].

Management process standards are the newest, and least numerous, of the standards within this taxonomy. The first standards in this area were those that addressed the discipline of systems engineering. While a number of books were written on this subject in the 1950's and 1960's, the first "official" standard in this area was published in 1965 as AFSC Manual 375-5 *Systems Engineering Management Procedures*. This was followed by MIL-STD-499 (USAF) *Systems Engineering Management* in 1966.

Style of Presentation. The style of presentation is classified as either *formal* or *informal*, although there is no objective boundary between the two.

The degree of formality of presentation is judged by the language and organization of the standard. The standard achieves a higher score if these follow a plainly evident pattern that enables the reader to unambiguously identify:

1. What the standard is a theory of;
2. What are its assumptions and boundaries;
3. What is the special vocabulary used;
4. Which part(s) of the presentation is intended to convey the theory; and
5. Which part(s) of the presentation are intended to aid the user in identifying an intended interpretation.

A pattern may be plainly evident either if the standard is a part of a body of standards that follow a documented pattern as are the ISO standards, which follow [10] and [11]. Alternatively, a pattern may be evident due to a clear internal explanation.

Standards that are less formal than those in the ISO family include descriptions of best practices that become adopted as standard in some sense. Another example of an informal standard is the almost universal adoption of Microsoft Word as a standard for exchange of textual data. (Here the standard we refer to is "Use MS Word for electronic exchange of textual material," rather than any standards that may or may not exist for the structuring of the binary files produced by Word.)

The Authority Establishing the Standard. There are several categories of authorities that should be considered as being substantially different, both in intent and effect. For our purposes, the authority is a selection from the following:

Government. This refers to any of various governmental bodies including legislatures, regulatory agencies, and intergovernmental associations that produce certain treaties.

Sanctioned. This refers to officially sanctioned bodies that are not governmental bodies. The officially sanctioned bodies include ISO, ANSI, and other national standards organizations, where these are not actual government agencies. In the US, this includes industrial and professional organizations certified by ANSI to produce American National Standards (for example, the AIAA, IEEE, and EIA).

Organized. Organized entities that are not officially sanctioned include individual corporations or corporate bodies (e.g. Microsoft and the SEI at CMU), and industrial consortia (e.g., EPIC, and the Telecommunications Industry Forum).

Other. This category is required because the previous three are not all inclusive. There are so many other ways standards can arise that it is not practical to attempt to list them all. Examples of this fourth category are standards that arise from folklore or common usage, or from individuals acting alone.

The Type of Consent Obtained. Again, there is not a continuous scale here, but there are several observably different approaches. The categories chosen as important for systems engineering purposes are the following:

Fiat or legislation. Standards adopted by fiat include standards promulgated by regulatory bodies, but also include standards published by industrial organizations, as for example, the Microsoft description of the Rich Text Format. Although legislative bodies or government agencies often utilize expert opinions in drafting the standards they promulgate, they need not. Another example of a standard by fiat is the standard issued by a symposium committee for the format and transmittal medium for papers submitted to the committee.

Consensus. This is defined as a documented, established procedure utilizing balloting, subject matter experts, and comment resolution. Consensus is the way standards are developed by ISO, and many other standards making bodies. In these cases, consensus does not necessarily mean "everybody agrees." There are rules concerning public review and disposition of comments received during a review. The rules for achieving a passing ballot require votes by a certain percentage of those eligible, a certain percentage of affirmative votes, and a certain upper bound on the number of negative votes.

Informal agreement. These are standards that arise when a group of people do things in a certain way "because it is a good idea."

COMMON COMBINATIONS OF CHARACTERISTICS

Some combinations of characteristics that are particularly common are shown in Figure 4, and explained here. In the figure, the most frequently occurring "type of consent" property is shown in its relation to the "authority" and "style" axes. This figure is of course an abstraction and an approximation. Not all standards representing a given combination may be in one of the categories shown, but these are the most important.

Formal Consensus Standards. These standards are developed according to documented, i.e., standardized, procedures. These procedures allow for review, comment resolution, and voting by subject mater experts. These also adhere to formal requirements for the style and wording of documents.. Formal consensus standards making bodies include ISO, IEC, professional organizations (e.g., AIAA, ASME, IEEE), and industry groups (e.g., EIA).

Standards established in this manner are often considered *voluntary* because, in and of themselves, they impose no obligations regarding their use. However, if a formal consensus standard is referenced in a contract or government regulation, the distinction of "voluntary" disappears and compliance with the standard becomes *mandatory*. An important example of such a standard is the American Society of Mechanical Engineering (ASME) Boiler Code, which was first issued in 1914. The ASME Boiler Code is possibly the most widely used voluntary standard in the world; it is mandatory in the United States and many other countries [12]. According to [12], "Probably no other single standard in America has done more for national safety than the ASME Boiler Code."

	Authority			
Style	Government	Sanctioned	Organized	Other
Formal	Fiat	Consensus	Fiat or Consensus	*Unusual*
Informal	Not Applicable	Not Applica-ble	Fiat, con-sensus, or general agreement	General agreement

Notations in cells indicate the type of consent usually associate with that combination of Style and Authority

Figure 4. Relationships Between Properties of Standards

Formal Non-Consensus Governmental Standards. These standards are established in accordance with the procedures developed by governmental agencies, for example, the United States Military Standards, and those developed by governments for regulatory purposes. Standards established by legislation can also be grouped into this category. These standards are often developed with the same rigor in terms of style, format, and content as the Formal Consensus Standards.

However, these standards are generated without the benefit of voting by subject matter experts, and sometimes without consultation with experts, hence the term *non-consensus*. These standards usually impose a legal obligation to conform, and are thus *mandatory* standards.

Informal Standards. These standards may be established by simple agreement (implicit or explicit) of a group of people to do things in a certain way "because it is a good idea," or because someone does something a certain way, and others imitate a good example. These standards are not presented in a rigorous style, and format, and there may be no "official" documentation.. For instance, there is no legislation or written agreement standardizing the number of keys on a piano, yet all pianos have a "standard" number of keys.

The following quotation illustrates the case of a group of manufacturers developing a standard [15]:

> "Anti-shoplifting alarm tags would be standardized and their attachment to goods shifted to manufacturers from retailers under a project a group of big firms is undertaking." "The group [of three firms] has formed the Consumer Products Manufacturers'

Consortium to develop a standardized…"

An extreme example of a standard that simply caught on, is found in the ubiquitous smiley face used in email to denote humor, and expressed as: :-). According to [16], this was invented by one Scott Fahlman on the Carnegie Melon University bulletin board about 1980.

ELEMENTS OF STANDARDS

As shown in Figure 3, there are several kinds of elements of a standard. The function of the *normative elements* is to convey the nature of the class of objects of standardization, situations where the standard can be applied, and the properties that an instance of an object of standardization must have in order to *conform* to the standard. The function of the *informative* elements is to provide informal additional information that will help the user interpret the standard.

The normative elements are further categorized as being either *normative technical* elements, or *normative general* elements. In an informal standard it may be very difficult to identify the different elements.

Following the ISO/IEC usage, the current ontology identifies attributes of normative elements called *provisions*.

Provisions.. Each provision is a linguistic element of one of the five types described in Figure 5. The requirements, recommendations, and permissions are distinguished, in the standard language of ISO/IEC, by the verbal moods *shall*, *should*, and *may*, respectively.[4] Instructions are given in imperative mood, and statements are made in declarative mood.

Normative General Elements. The formal ISO/IEC style requires a standard to contain an element defining the *scope* of the standard—this serves to identify an *intended domain of interpretation* (IDI) of the standard in the real world. Ideally, the specification of the IDI is completely unambiguous. The variety of things included in the IDI can be very broad, including, for example: suppliers, parts, dimensions, processes, events, deliverables, and even human emotions.

In addition, these elements can contain *normative references*, which are references to other documents that are made a part of the standard by reference in its other provisions.

Normative Technical Elements. The provisions of the *normative technical* elements are assertions concerning the objects in the IDI and the relationships among them.

1. A *requirement* is a provision that conveys criteria to be fulfilled. In an ISO/IEC standard, requirements are known by their use of the verbal form "shall." Prohibitions are indicated by "shall not".
2. A *recommendation* is a provision that conveys advice or guidance. It indicates that among a number of possibilities, one is particularly suitable. (It is not necessary for the standard to list the alternatives). The ISO/IEC required verbal form for a recommendation uses the use of the word "should." The form "should not" constitutes a recommendation not to do something, rather than a prohibition.
3. A *permission* is a provision that expresses a course of action (or its result) that is permissible within the limits of the standard. Permission is indicated for ISO/IEC standards by the verbal form "may," and is to be contrasted with statements of possibility or capability that use the form "can."
4. An *instruction* is a provision that conveys an action to be performed, and for ISO/IEC standards it is designated verbally by use of the imperative mood. Instructions can be used, for example, to describe the steps to be taken in carrying out a test. A specific example would be "Switch on the recorder".
5. A *statement* is a provision that conveys information. Possibly the most common example is a definition contained in the *terminology* element of a standard. Simple declarative statements convey these. One special verbal form applies to statements that denote possibilities or capabilities, and that is the verbal form "can." Statements can be used, for example, to describe physical environments or operational contexts, and to describe the characteristics of processes when these characteristics aren't part of a direct requirement, but are defined for reference purposes. The *scope* element of an ISO/IEC standard contains statements, and the scope "shall not" contain requirements.

Figure 5. Provisions of a Standard

Ideally, the properties and relationships are unambiguously observable

Some of the normative technical provisions can be *definitions.* The definitions are used to clarify the intended interpretation of the standard, or to simplify the language of the other assertions.

Informative Elements. Finally, a standard can have *informative* elements, which also are there to clarify the IDI and relationships, and possible ambiguities due to expressing the provisions in natural language. Because of the formality and conciseness of the provisions of a formal standard, it is often difficult to understand their meaning without further explanation or example.

In addition, the use of a standard is often aided by an understanding of how it fits into the context of related standards, what its history is, and the reasons for its preparation. Information of these and related types are given in the informative elements of the standard. [10] specifies certain required and certain optional informative elements for ISO/IEC standards. The required informative elements include a title page[5] and a foreword, each of which has special requirements on its

[4] The ISO/IEC guides and directives cited do not specify *permission* as a type of provision. However, they do specify the verbal form used for permissions in the same context as the specification of the verbal forms used for the other provisions. The present authors have resolved this ambiguity in favor of *permission* being a type of provision.

[5] The title itself, however, is normative.

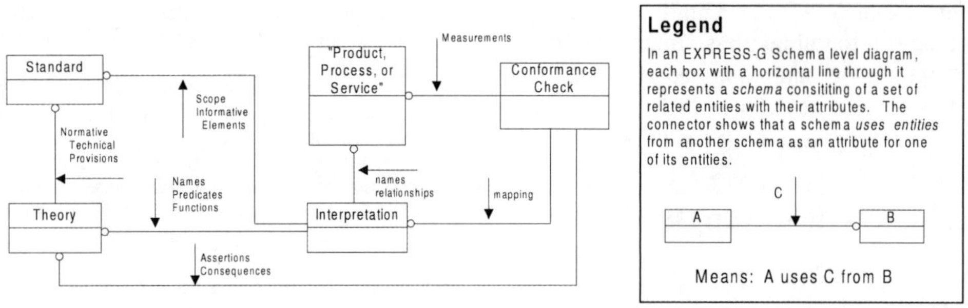

Figure 6. EXPRESS-G Diagram for Interpretation of a Standard

form and content.

MEANING OF A STANDARD

In [1] and [2], a standard was characterized as presenting a model that the object of standardization should emulate. While this is a useful view, it is difficult to make precise. The current ontology is based on the use of a *formal logical theory* as a step in establishing the meaning of a standard.

Why the Use of Mathematical Logic Is Important. One may ask: is the use of formal languages and theories necessary, or even useful? A definite positive answer is given in [17], which describes the design of a processor that required use of the IEEE 754 standard for binary floating point arithmetic. When this standard was translated into a specification language based on logic and set theory it was found that the standard was both ambiguous and inconsistent. These faults were attributed to the use of natural language in the standard. By formulating the standard mathematically, these faults were made more apparent.

It may not always be practical to express a standard in a formal language. However, if a standard were formulated with the understanding that it should be possible (if tedious) to express it in a formal language of logic, many errors and ambiguities could be avoided.

Modern mathematical logic was developed in the late nineteenth and early twentieth century for the purpose of unambiguous representation of relationships and propositions, and reasoning about them. Currently it is being used as a basis for knowledge representation in diverse fields including law and medicine. It is ideally suited as a basis for understanding, analyzing, and formulating standards.

Use of mathematical logic. The use of such a theory is diagrammed, using an EXPRESS-G schema level diagram, Figure 6. Here, major elements are schemata, similar in form to the schema shown for a standard in Figure 3. The schema icon (box with a solid horizontal line through it) in the upper left of Figure 6, labeled "Standard" represents the entirety of Figure 3. The entity level diagrams for the other schemata in Figure 6 are not given in this paper.

The schemata in Figure 6 are related by means of entities in one schema being used as attributes by an entity in another schema. The names of the specific attributes are shown next to the arrows perpendicular to the connectors, in accordance with ISO 10303-11[9].

Referring to Figure 6, the application of logic to the field of standardization consists of the following steps:

1. The assertions of the *normative technical provisions* are converted into formal assertions in a language based on symbolic logic to obtain a formal *logical theory.*
2. The vocabulary of the formal logical theory is *interpreted*—that is, harmonized with names and relationships in the real-world IDI (a product, process, or service), using the *scope,* and *informative elements* of the standard. This results in a *mapping* between the theory and the real world; this is an *interpretation* of the *theory.*
3. In performing a *conformance check*, the *mapping* is used to compare assertions and consequences of the *theory* with measurements of the real world IDI. If the IDI satisfies the theory, it is said to be a *model* of the theory.
4. If the IDI is a *model* of the *theory*, it *conforms* to the standard.

In these statements, the terms *theory, interpretation, and model* are used in precise technical senses that have been time tested in applications of mathematical logic.

The reader should note that the sense of the term "model," used here, is different than the sense used in [1] and [2]. While this may result in some confusion the increase in precision makes this worthwhile.

Translating a standard into formal language. In order to apply mathematical logic to interpret a standard, a special formal language is designed and tailored to the IDI. The language will have a vocabulary consisting of *names* of things in the IDI, *variables* (such as X, and Y) that can be used to denote things in the IDI, and *functions* that can also be used to denote things in the IDI. The description of a function is somewhat complex, and is be deferred to a later paragraph.

Asserted relationships in the IDI, and asserted properties of things in the IDI are represented by *predicates*. Symbolically, a predicate[6] representing a property is just a name denoting the property followed by a name, function, or variable in parentheses denoting the thing that has this property. Similarly, a predicate representing a relationship is symbolized by a name denoting the relationship followed by a parenthesized list of the names, variables, or functions that represent items that are related to each other in this way.

In representing something from the IDI a *function* can be used in a way that is similar to use of the phrase "the man who came to dinner" in natural language. This phrase refers to a specific man, but not by name. For example, validated requirements sets might be things in the IDI. Such sets might be needed for different objects. The requirements may come from many different stakeholders. Thus a particular validated requirements set is a *function* of the particular stakeholder and the particular object. The term *v_r_set(X,Y),* might be chosen to represent this, meaning "the validated requirements set for Y due to stakeholder X." Note that this is *not* a predicate. Predicates have arguments that are from the IDI and values of *true* or *false*. Functions have arguments from the IDI, and values *in* the IDI.

Standard logic provides certain logical connectives, as shown in Figure 7,[7] and rules for assembling strings of predicates into sentences. It also it provides means of establishing the *logical consequences* of any set of assertions—sentences that are taken to be true as a basis for a certain theory. (The assertions may be referred to sometimes as axioms, or as postulates.)

[6] The symbols for relationships such as *shall_define(.,.),* or *system(.)* are referred to as predicate symbols (predicates, for short). This is because they serve the same grammatical function as predicates in natural language. The expression, *system(X),* translates to the English sentence "X is a system." In this sentence, X is the subject and "system" is the predicate. The word *is* is a copula—a word that links subject and predicate. In some languages the copula is omitted when the grammatical proposition is a simple linkage of subject and predicate.

It is generally a good idea to give the predicates in our language names that have mnemonic value. Often the nicest mnemonic values would be short phrases in natural language, such as "has interest in." For clarity it is also important that predicates have names without blank spaces in them. One standard way of achieving this is to use an underscore in place of a blank, as in "shall_define." Similar conventions are standard for the symbols representing "things" in the domain of interpretation.

[7] While there are standard symbols for these concepts, they will be unfamiliar to most readers of this paper and we shall use familiar English words in bold face.

Symbol	Meaning
and	(A **and** B) is true when A and B are both true.
or	(A **or** B) is true when at least one of A and B is true. Note that this is an inclusive *or.*
not	**not** E is true when E is false, and false when E is true.
implies	From A is true **and** (A **implies** B) is true, then B is true.
iff	**iff** is if and only if. (A **iff** B) is equivalent to (A **implies** B) **and** (B **implies** A).
For_all	**For_all** X E(X) is true if E(X) is true no matter what name of an object in the IDI is substituted for X.
Exists	**Exists** X E(X) is true if there is *some* name that can be substituted for X that will make E(X) true.

Figure 7. Logical Terminology Used in This Paper

Once the user of logic has established a vocabulary, and asserted some logical sentences as true, the resulting system can be tested for consistency; if it is consistent it can be used as the basis of a *theory*. The *theory* is the entire set of logical consequences of the assertions as determined using commonly accepted rules of inference and logical axioms.

Interpretations, Models, and Conformance. A standard asserts generic properties and relationships for the IDI. In order to find out if a particular instance of a product, process, or service conforms to the standard it is necessary to define a mapping of the language of the standard to the real world instance.

In mathematical logic, an *interpretation* is just such a mapping. An interpretation identifies names in the theory with objects in the domain of interpretation, predicates in the theory with properties or relationships of objects in the domain of interpretation. The assertions of the theory, in this way, become assertions about the domain of interpretation. If the assertions that are the basis of the theory are all *true*, then the *interpretation* is said to be a *model* of the logical theory.

The application of this approach to the field of standardization is straightforward in principal. What is needed, having established the formal language, is the mapping from the formal language to the instance, and tests to determine whether the assertions of the theory are *true* in the real world instance.

In application, this process of *interpreting* the standard may be quite difficult, depending on how well the standard is written. It may be difficult to determine whether a particular thing corresponds to a certain name in the formal language. The term *system* may be an example of this. *Stakeholder* may be another. Once names have been assigned, determination of the truth of the assertions may require complex tests and measurements to be performed.

If these assignments and measurements can be

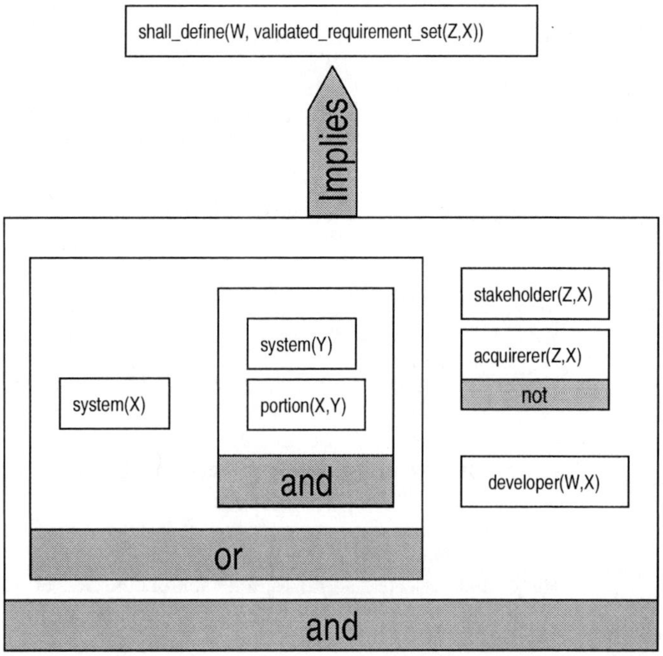

Explanation: The word in the grey region of each box shows the logical connective that modifies or joins the expressions in that box; a box with no connective represents a single predicate. The predicate meanings are:

- **developer(W,X)** means W is the developer of something called X
- **shall_define(W,U)** means W shall define U; in this case, U is a
  - **validated_requirement_set(Z,X)** which is a funtion that stands for the requirements for the item X, as defined by Z, in validated form
- **system(X)** means X is a system
- **portion(X,Y)** means X, the thing being developed, is a portion of Y
  - in this case, **system(Y)**
- **stakeholder(Z,X)** means Z is a stakeholder in X, the thing being developed.
- **acquirer(Z,X)** means Z is the acquirer of X, the thing being developed.

Figure 8. ANSI/EIA-632-1998 Requirement 15

made, and the assertions are true, then the instance is a *model* of the theory, and can be said to *conform* to the standard.

It is the duty of the formulators of a standard to ease this process by the precision, clarity, and completeness of provisions. Well formed definitions and other *statements* in the provisions help establish the mapping. In order to ensure that the truth of the assertions can be evaluated, [18] specifies that "only such requirements shall be included as can be verified." Moreover, [10] requires that each requirement in a standard must contain "either a reference to the test method for determining or verifying the values of the characteristic, or the test method itself."

An Example of Expressing a Requirement. In order to clarify the steps used in translating a requirement of a standard into a sentence of logic an example from [6] is presented here. As just noted, a first step is to establish a vocabulary. There are many ways of doing this, and it should be done for a standard as a whole, rather than for a single requirement. This is not practical in a short paper, so some *ad hoc* assignments of the vocabulary for things and relationships are made, recognizing that they are not necessarily optimal choices.

Consider Requirement 15 from [6], which asserts:

> "The developer shall define a validated set of other stakeholder requirements for the system or portion thereof."

It is necessary to look at the context of this assertion in order to assign a formal vocabulary for it's objects, properties, and relationships. First, the "other stakeholder" must be interpreted by comparison to Requirement 14 of [6], which is identical to 15 except that it calls for a validated set of *acquirer* requirements. Thus, an "other stakeholder" is some stakeholder that is not the acquirer. Second, it is necessary to refer to Clause 6 of [6], "Application key concepts." These key concepts show that requirement 15 is intended to be applied in a hierarchical building block framework. In this framework, a single project could contain many different systems (as defined in [6]), and there may be a number of different developers. We therefore take "developer" to refer to every developer in the domain of interpretation. Likewise, "system," and "portion thereof" mean "every system" and "every portion thereof."

The reader may find it helpful to refer to Figure 8 in following the analysis.

This requirement has a top-level relationship with predicate symbol *shall_define(W,Z)*, meaning "W shall define Z." There are conditions on W and Z, however. The W here has the property of being the *developer* of a "system or a portion thereof." This can be written as *developer(W,X)*, where W varies over all the developers, and X varies over all the things being developed.

The later, are instances of "system or portion thereof." This may be represented by the compound expression *(system(X)* ***or*** *(portion(X,Y)* ***and*** *system(Y))*. These expressions serve to fully identify the developer in relation to the thing being developed.

Next consider the stakeholder. The stakeholder

relationship is of the form "Z is a stakeholder in X," so this relationship has two arguments. Taking into account the fact that the stakeholder referred to is not an acquirer, this is represented by the compound expression *(stakeholder(Z,X)* ***and not*** *acquirer(X))*.

The thing that "shall be defined" is a validated set of requirements for the stakeholder and the "system or portion" under consideration. The *function v_r_set(W,Y)* can be used to represent this item uniquely, as described previously.

We now have all the parts, and can assemble the full statement of Requirement 15. It is:

> **For_all** X,Y,Z,W ((system(X) **or** (portion(X,Y) **and** system(Y))) and developer(W,X) **and** stakeholder(Z,X) **and not** acquirer(Z,X)) **implies** shall_define(W, v_r_set(Z,X)).

This says, in translation back to English, "For all X, Y, Z, and W where X is either a system, a portion of a system Y, or both, and Z is a stakeholder in X, and Z is not an acquirer of X, and W is the developer of X, then W shall define the validated requirements set belonging to X due to the stakeholder Z."

Recommended References. For a very readable introduction to the concepts of modern mathematical logic, addressed to the intelligent non-specialist,, the reader is referred to [19], which was written by one of the modern pioneers. [20] is an inexpensive and readable text at the undergraduate level.

REMARKS ON MANAGEMENT PROCESS STANDARDS

In [1] and [2], the authors examined issues related to management process standards in general, and to systems engineering process standards in particular. Possible ways to resolve these issues were proposed. In particular, the authors arrived at two conclusions regarding Management Process Standards:

1. In most cases, management process standards should be used for guidance, not for conformance.
2. Even then, management process standards should be tailored to fit the context of application.

After participating in recent reviews of standards the authors of this paper now propose a third conclusion:

3. The normative provisions of a management process standard that contain requirements and instructions should be kept to a minimum; as many axiomatic provisions as possible should be recommendations or permissions.

The basis for the two conclusions from [2] is repeated in Figure 9. These also provide a basis for the third conclusion. However, recent trends deserve special comment.

<u>Issue #1: Complexity</u>. The concepts themselves are complex and abstract, and the terms used may have many different connotations for the developers and the users of the standard. This makes it difficult to be unambiguous in describing the relationships between the concepts of the standard, and determining their application.
<u>Issue #2: Guidance</u>. The degree of optimization and definition of the concepts can lead to increased costs by rigidly complying with the standard. To better understand this issue for management process standards, it is informative to first examine the same issue applied to product standards. In formulating a product standard, many properties may be chosen arbitrarily without necessarily incurring a cost. The only important thing is that the properties are "standardized"; it is not always important for them to be optimum. For instance, there is no clear optimum between the European standard paper size of A4 [210 mm (8.27") by 297 mm (11.69")], the US commercial standard letter paper size (8.5" by 11"), and the US Government standard letter paper size (8" by 10.5"). The three standard paper sizes, however, are different measurements. By way of contrast, for a management process standard, if the process is very explicitly defined, and is less than optimum, then rigid compliance to the standard will result in an increase in costs for products and services produced using the standard.
<u>Issue #3: Imprecise Application & Measurement</u>. The contexts within which the standard would be applied are both complex and varied. The ability to make precise and accurate measurements of the properties involved is still a very immature technology and may never be as accurate as those used for product standards. Moreover, the complexity of the context of application makes it even more difficult to determine whether the process will really be "best" or, at the least, not result in undue expense, risk, or danger.

Figure 9. Issues with Respect to Management Process Standards

Both EIA 632 and EIA/IS 731 were based on a consensus process, and contain relatively small sets of requirements and instructions. EIA 632 has only 33 requirements.

An examination of the draft ISO 15288 CD 1, *Life Cycle Management – System Life Cycle Processes,* [8], reveals that it has 177 requirements. This is roughly five times the number of requirements contained within EIA 632, even though the two standards cover basically the same IDI. The draft ISO 15288 standard appears to be overly prescriptive in many areas and, if incorporated as part of a contractual relationship between a developer and an acquirer, would almost certainly lead to increased costs. It has not been objectively demonstrated that there would be a commensurate increase in verifiable benefits relative to a much less complex and prescriptive standard.

An examination of the current state of the CMMI effort in comparison to EIA/IS 731 reveals a similar growth. EIA/IS 731 has only 12 generic practices, compared to approximately twice that many contained separately in each of its two source models (INCOSE SECAM and EPIC/SEI SE-CMM). The number of Generic Practices are particularly important with regard to the complexity of a capability model since they have a multiplicative effect. That is, each Generic Practice is applied to all of the Focus Areas in the model, as opposed to the Specific Practices, which apply only to their unique Focus Area. The reduction in the number of Generic Practices was accomplished in large part as a result of the INCOSE Corporate Advisory Board's request to make the "merged" EIA/IS 731 a streamlined model, [21].

In contrast, the current state of the CMMI effort reveals substantial growth of requirement or instruction provisions. This effort has resulted in six capability maturity models: Software, Systems Engineering, and Software/Systems Engineering, each with both staged and continuous versions. It should be noted that there was only one Software and one Systems Engineering model that served as input to the CMMI effort. In the Systems Engineering continuous version of CMMI, the number of Generic Practices has grown to 22. This is almost twice the 12 Generic Practices contained in EIA/IS 731, which is acknowledged to be a base document for the CMMI effort. The number of Process Areas has grown to 26, compared to 20 Focus Areas in the EIA/IS 731. As noted above, the number of Generic Practices have a multiplicative effect upon the complexity of the continuous Systems Engineering capability model of the CMMI effort, since Generic Practices are applied to each Process Area. In the case of the CMMI effort, the number of both Generic Practices and Process Areas has increased substantially, thus further increasing the complexity. It remains to be seen whether any true benefit will accrue that is commensurate with the increased cost of compliance, should such an overly prescriptive standard become a contract requirement.

Moreover, the character of natural language together with the often ambiguous nature of human activities themselves virtually assures that a management process standard with many requirements will have substantial ambiguities and inconsistencies that will greatly exacerbate the difficulty and cost of attempting to establish conformance.

REFERENCES

[1] J. R. Velman and E. R. Widmann; "Standards: Their Significance and Potential Meaning to the Systems Engineering Community"; Proceedings of the Eighth Annual International Symposium of the International Council on Systems Engineering; Pages 157 – 164; Vancouver, British Columbia, Canada; July 36 – 30, 1998.

[2] J. R. Velman. E. R. Widmann, and G. J. Hudak; "Standards: A Perspective and Some Future Directions for the Systems Engineering Community"; Proceedings of the Ninth Annual International Symposium of the International Council on Systems Engineering; Brighton, United Kingdom; June 6 – 10, 1999.

[3] J. R. Velman and E. R. Widmann; "Observations on Systems Engineering Related Standards"; Proceedings of Thirteenth International Conference on Systems Engineering, Las Vegas, Nevada, August 9-12, 1999.

[4] Webster's Ninth New Collegiate Dictionary, MERRIAM-WEBSTER INC., Publishers; Springfield, MA; 1985.

[5] R. Davis, H. Shrobe, and P. Szolovitis; "What is Knowledge Representation?" AI Magazine, 14(1):17-33. 1993.

[6] ANSI/EIA-632-1998, Processes for Engineering a System; Electronic Industries Alliance; Arlington, VA; December 1998.

[7] EIA Interim Standard 731, Systems Engineering Capability (EIA 731.1, Part 1: Model, EIA 731.2, Part 2: Appraisal Method), Version 1.0; Electronic Industries Alliance; Arlington, VA; December 1998.

[8] ISO/IEC 15288 Committee Draft 1, Life Cycle Management–System Life Cycle Processes. ISO/IEC JTC1/SC7 N0285, Secretariat: Canada, July 1999.

[9] ISO 10303-11, Industrial automation systems and integration—Product data representation and exchange—Part 11: Description methods: The EXPRESS language reference manual.

[10] ISO/IEC Directives, Part 3; "Rules for the Structure and Drafting of International Standards"; Third Edition, International Organization for Standardization, and International Electrotechnical Commission; Geneva, Switzerland; 1997.

[11] ISO/IEC Guide 2; "Standardization and related activities – General vocabulary"; International Organization for Standardization, and International Electrotechnical Commission; Geneva, Switzerland; 1996.

[12] Maureen A Breitenberg; "The ABC's of Standards-Related Activities in the United States"; National Institute of Standards and Technology, Gaithersburg, MD; NBSIR 87-3576; 1987.

[13] "A Walk through Time"; A NIST Physics Laboratory Presentation; URL: http://physics.nist.gov/time; National Institute of Standards and Technology, Gaithersburg, MD; August 1997.

[14] Maureen A Breitenberg; "The ABC's of Certification Activities in the United States"; National Institute of Standards and Technology, Gaithersburg, MD; NBSIR 88-3821; July 1988.

[15] Tara Parker-Pope; "Consortium to Develop Security Tags For Items Sold in Groceries, Drug Stores"; Wall Street Journal; Dow Jones & Company; Page B3; March 19, 1999.

[16] The On-Line hacker Jargon File, version 4.0.0, 24 JUL 1996, URL: http://www.tuxedo.org/~esr/jargon/.

[17] J. Gibbons; "Formal Methods: Why Should I Care? The Development of the T800 Transputer Floating-Point Unit"; Proceedings of the 13th New Zealand Computer Society Conference, Pages. 207-217, 1993.

[18] ISO/IEC Directives Part 2; "Methodology for the development of International Standards"; Second Edition, International Organization for Standardization, and International Electrotechnical Commission; Geneva, Switzerland; 1992.

[19] Alfred Tarski, Olaf Helmer (Translator); Introduction to Logic and to the Methodology of Deductive Sciences; Dover Publications; May 1995.

[20] Stolyar, A. A.; Introduction to Elementary Mathematical Logic; Dover Publications; New York; 1983.

[21] E. R. Widmann; "Key Features of the 'Merged' EIA/IS 731-1 Systems Engineering Capability Model"; Proceedings of the Eighth Annual International Symposium of the International Council on Systems Engineering; Pages 597 – 604; Vancouver, British Columbia, Canada; July 36 – 30, 1998.

BIOGRAPHIES

J. R. Velman, Ph.D. is in the Technology Planning organization of Hughes Space and Communications Company. His areas of responsibility include management of the company's participation in international and national standardization activities that may affect the company's business. Previously, he was Manager of the Systems Design Laboratory of Hughes Space and Communications Group. During his 37 years at Hughes, he has contributed to many space systems programs. His work on spacecraft attitude dynamics and control has been widely referenced. He also has contributed to Hughes support of General Motors automotive systems engineering, and was one of the presenters for the Hughes Systems Engineering Seminars to GM Europe. Prior to joining Hughes, he worked on space systems studies at Northrop, and missile systems engineering at Bendix. He is a member of the Standards Executive Council of the AIAA and of the US TAG for ISO TC20 SC 14, Space Systems and Operations. Until recently, he was the Chair of the INCOSE Education and Training Technical Committee, a member of the Technical Board, and a member of the ANSI/EIA-632 Technical Committee. He was the chair of the INCOSE Standards Task Force, and is currently co-chair of the INCOSE Standards Technical Committee and the Hughes representative to the INCOSE CAB. Dr. Velman is an INCOSE Fellow.

E. R. Widmann is in the Satellite Systems Engineering Operation of Hughes Space and Communications Company (HSC). He is currently involved with an effort to improve the management of requirements across several product lines of commercial communications and government satellites in order to achieve increased efficiencies. Previously, at Hughes Aircraft Company (HAC), now Raytheon Systems Company since December 1997, he served as a systems engineering manager on a number of electro-optical product development efforts for both land and airborne applications. He was also a key participant in systems engineering process activities, serving as the: (1) HAC-wide systems engineering representative for improving the HAC-developed, common Product Development Process (PDP) and (2) HAC-wide systems engineering lead responsible for deployment of a common systems engineering process, which was an integral part of the PDP. He also supported process-related activities associated with the transition of Hughes Aircraft Company to the Raytheon Systems Company. Prior to joining HAC, he was an officer in the US Army and spent four years in the Office of the Secretary of the Air Force, Office of Special Projects, and two years at the US Army Satellite Communications Agency. Mr. Widmann is currently a Member of the Technical Board of INCOSE, where he is Chair of a special Technical Board Team to develop *The Taxonomy of Systems Engineering Competency*. He previously served as a Member of the INCOSE Technical Board and Chair of the INCOSE Measurement Technical Committee from 1995 to 1998. He was the Chair of the INCOSE Capability Assessment Working Group from 1992 to 1995, where he organized and significantly contributed to the development of the INCOSE *Systems Engineering Capability Assessment Model*. He was the Associate Chair (US) of the INCOSE Standards Task Force from 1997 to 1998. He was the lead INCOSE representative on the EIA SECM Working Group and a co-author of the EIA/IS 731 *Systems Engineering Capability*. He is currently the HSC representative to the EIA G-47 (Systems Engineering) Committee and the HSC alternate representative to the INCOSE Corporate Advisory Board. Mr. Widmann has published extensively on systems engineering subjects. He has a M.S. Degree in Electrical Engineering from Purdue University and both a B.S. Degree in Electrical Engineering and a B.A. Degree with a concentration in Physics from Rutgers University.

Testing—Let Me Count the Ways: Taguchi versus Combinatorial Design

Jerry Huller
Raytheon Company
16800 East CentreTech Parkway
DN, Bldg. 485, M/S 6109
Aurora, Colorado 80011-9046 USA
cjhuller@west.raytheon.com, j.huller@ieee.org

How do I test thee? Let me count the ways.
I test thee to the depth and breadth and height ....
(with apologies to Elizabeth Barrett Browning.)

Abstract. Testers face the challenge of doing as much testing as possible within the available, and usually constrained, schedule. It is not practical to exhaustively test all combinations of system test cases. There are methods that generate a small subset of test cases that provide good coverage of the test domain. This paper discusses the author's experience with two such methods—Taguchi (orthogonal array) techniques and the Combinatorial Design Method (CDM). The CDM has proven to be more flexible for system level testing of commercial satellite ground systems.

INTRODUCTION

This paper will briefly describe the business market and the configuration of a typical ground system, also known as a ground station. The elements of redundancy will be described. The need for testing of the redundant combinations leads to a discussion of techniques for identifying test cases. The Taguchi techniques, which the author learned about at an INCOSE tutorial, are reviewed. A specific example and a general example are presented. The author's experience with limitations of the techniques is briefly discussed. The Combinatorial Design Method is then described. A specific example for a recent ground system is given. The author's experience with this technique is described.

THE FUTURE IS UP

Despite some setbacks in 1999 for the mobile telephone satellite industry, the satellite business should continue to boom. John Pike of the Federation of American Scientists has noted that the commercial space industry has been growing at about 10 percent a year for the last two decades, and he expects the trend to continue (Space Business News 1998). The Teal Group predicts that almost 1,500 commercial communications satellites valued at $126.8 billion will be launched from 2000 through 2009 (Aerospace Daily 1999).

These new satellites will require new ground systems or upgrades to existing ones. Raytheon Company is a major, global provider of hardware and software solutions for commercial customers who operate satellite ground systems. Historically, these multi-million dollar projects have been characterized by short duration (approximately twelve to eighteen months, depending on the launch date for the satellite), reuse of code and previous system architectural designs, redundancy, tailoring of the design to satisfy international customer needs and constraints, and a small, core team (7-16 people).

A GROUND SYSTEM

An example ground system consists of three sites, as depicted in Figure 1. One site is the primary Satellite Control Center (SCC). Operators in the SCC control and monitor one or more orbiting satellites. A backup SCC at another site provides redundancy for satellite control. Co-located at the backup SCC is the primary Telemetry, Command, and Ranging (TCR) site. The TCR site contains the hardware, including antennas, for communicating with the satellites. A backup TCR site provides redundancy.

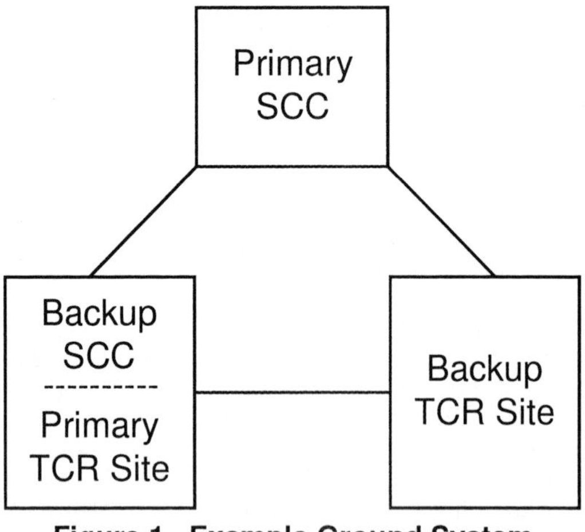

Figure 1. Example Ground System

A simplified block diagram of a ground system is shown in Figure 2. The Computer subsystem consists of the file servers, workstations, and local area network (LAN) that run the application programs for controlling and monitoring the satellite and associated ground equipment. The Baseband subsystem consists of baseband units (BBUs) and time code devices, such as Global Positioning System (GPS) units, for time stamping the telemetry data. The BBU is used to generate commands or ranging signals, which are sent, to a satellite, and to process telemetry or ranging signals which are received from a satellite. The term *baseband* refers to the frequencies used by a BBU. The Radio Frequency (RF) subsystem consists of hardware to uplink and downlink signals to and from a satellite via the Antenna subsystem. Typical antenna sizes for commercial communications satellites are 9–13 meters in diameter. The Site Communications Network subsystem contains the hardware and communications links, such as leased telephone lines, to interconnect the SCC and TCR sites.

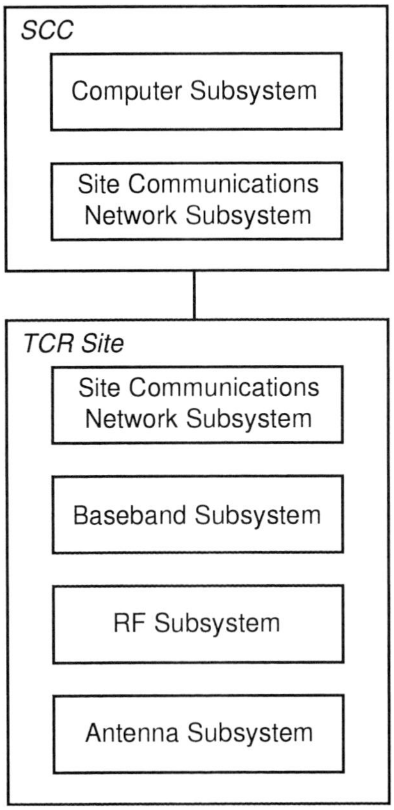

Figure 2. Ground System Subsystems

The application software in an SCC provides such capabilities as the following: commanding a satellite, processing telemetry, determining the range to a satellite, statusing and controlling the ground hardware to support satellite operations, monitoring the status of satellite subsystems, performing maneuvers to keep the satellite in its designated orbital location (referred to as stationkeeping), and operator training via a simulated satellite. The application software generally resides on a file server and is accessed via client workstations in the SCC.

To meet availability requirements for a ground system, redundant equipment is provided. As described earlier, the SCC and TCR sites have backup locations. The Site Communications Network subsystem provides multiple communications paths for the data between an SCC and its TCR site. For example, as shown in Figure 1, data from the primary TCR site can be routed to the primary SCC via the backup TCR site if the communications link between the primary SCC and primary TCR site becomes nonoperational.

Within the primary SCC, there is typically a primary server and a backup server. At the backup SCC, there is a remote server. The same software is installed on all servers. Key operational data is backed up from the primary server to the other servers, so that any server can assume operational control within a short time period.

All workstations in an SCC are redundant. A workstation can run any of the application programs.

The primary and backup TCR sites often contain identical equipment for the Baseband, RF, and Antenna subsystems. However, the antennas may be different sizes or models within the Antenna subsystem. Within each Baseband subsystem, a spare time code unit and a spare BBU are usually provided. For an SCC controlling two satellites, the Baseband subsystem may include three BBUs. One BBU is dedicated to each satellite, with the third serving as a redundant backup for either satellite. The RF subsystem contains redundant hardware for uplinking and downlinking signals to and from the satellite via the online antenna.

Redundancy is also provided in communications between the ground system and the satellite. Two telemetry streams at different frequencies are typically provided.

To summarize, redundancy is provided in the following:

- SCC sites
- TCR sites
- File servers at the SCCs
- Workstations at the SCCs
- Communications links between the sites
- BBUs at a TCR site
- Time code units at a TCR site
- Uplink hardware at a TCR site
- Downlink hardware at a TCR site
- Telemetry streams from the satellite

It is evident that there are many combinations of

equipment units along the signal path from a ground system operator to the satellite and back. These combinations are referred to as *data paths* in this paper.

THE PROBLEM

The system tester is faced with the challenge of showing that typical satellite operations can be performed with any of the data paths that an operator could choose. This has the added benefit of showing that single failures of equipment do not inhibit satellite operations. However, demonstrating proper functionality is not the only reason for this testing. Exercising the different data paths also serves as an excellent checkout of the hardware and software during system integration and test. This provides a high degree of confidence in the system prior to formal testing.

Exhaustively testing all combinations and data paths is just not practical in today's fast-paced commercial marketplace. An efficient way of generating a minimal number of test cases that provide "good" coverage of the test domain is needed.

TAGUCHI TECHNIQUES

The author learned about Taguchi techniques at a professional tutorial conducted during the INCOSE 6th Annual International Symposium in Boston, Massachusetts, USA. Taguchi techniques are usually associated with the robust design of experiments—to determine near optimal combination of design parameters. (Phadke et al. 1996) showed that the techniques can be extended to testing. Instead of developing a near optimal design solution, a tester uses these techniques to generate a quasi-optimal set of test cases. The references in (Cohen et al. 1996) describe several applications of Taguchi techniques to testing.

Consider the following example. You want to conduct a test of telemetry processing. You have several choices for the test configuration, depending on the TCR site, the BBU unit, and the satellite telemetry stream selected. Each of these choices, or factors, has two levels. The TCR site can be Site 1 or Site 2. The BBU unit can be BBU 1 or BBU 2. The telemetry stream can be Stream 1 or Stream 2. An exhaustive test, also known as a full factorial test, would consist of 2*2*2 = 8 test cases.

Genichi Taguchi developed a family of fractional factorial experiments using orthogonal arrays. Fewer experiments are required with these arrays—without sacrificing statistical validity. For the above example, the Taguchi technique would be to use the L4 orthogonal array shown in Table 3 (the *4* indicates that the array has 4 rows, which implies four test configurations or test cases). Fifty percent fewer, or only four test cases, would be needed to show that any telemetry stream, any BBU, and any TCR site provide the capability to process telemetry data from the satellite.

Test Case	TCR Site	BBU	Stream
1	1	1	1
2	1	2	2
3	2	1	2
4	2	2	1

Table 3. L4 Orthogonal Array for Telemetry Example

The L4 array contains all pairwise combinations of the three test factors. The array is orthogonal; that is, the columns are mutually orthogonal. For any pair of columns, all factor levels occur, and they occur an equal number of times. In other words, there are the same number of test data points for each level of each factor. The columns in Table 3 show two tests under the first level of the factor (Site 1, or BBU 1, or Stream 1) and two tests under the second level of the factor (Site 2, or BBU 2, or Stream 2). Orthogonality, reflected by the proportionally balanced columns, allows the factors to be evaluated independently of each other. In some sense, the test points are distributed uniformly across the test domain.

The technique is applicable to factors with three levels (in other words, test parameters with three possible values). An example of the L9, three-level, array is shown in Table 4. To fully test all factors and levels would require 3*3*3*3 = 81 test cases. The Taguchi technique generates only nine test cases, an 89% reduction. For example, test case #8 would consist of a test configuration where Factor One has value 3, Factor Two has value 2, Factor Three has value 1, and Factor Four has value 3.

Test Case	Factor One	Factor Two	Factor Three	Factor Four
1	1	1	1	1
2	1	2	2	2
3	1	3	3	3
4	2	1	2	3
5	2	2	3	1
6	2	3	1	2
7	3	1	3	2
8	3	2	1	3
9	3	3	2	1

Table 4. L9 Orthogonal Array

Books such as (Ross 1998) and (Phadke 1989) describe the Taguchi techniques and provide examples of orthogonal arrays. (Ross 1998) gives guidance on modifying the basic orthogonal arrays to accommodate a mixture of two-, three-, and four-level factors.

The author has used the Taguchi techniques as a

starting point for data paths testing for two satellite ground systems. Two problems were found in applying the techniques. The first difficulty was that the number of test factors and test levels sometimes did not match any of the classic orthogonal arrays. The alternative was to modify the basic arrays. However, this was easier said than done. The guidance on adapting the basic arrays to the test situation seemed cumbersome, abstract, and time-consuming. An advanced knowledge of statistics would have been necessary to complete the task. Instead, engineering judgement was used to tailor and condense a larger orthogonal array.

For ground system #1, there were five factors. The first could assume any of three values (e.g., primary server, backup server, or remote server). The remaining four could assume any of two values. However, there was no orthogonal array with these characteristics listed in the reference books. An L8, two-level, array with seven test factors (test parameters) was selected as the starting point. The last four columns (factors) of the array contained the two values that could be assumed by those factors. Engineering judgement was used to condense the first three columns, which showed either of two values, into one column (factor), which showed any of three values, as depicted in Table 5. This modified, no-longer-orthogonal, L8 array with five factors produced eight test cases.

Before:

Factor One	Factor Two	Factor Three	Factor Four	...	Factor Seven
1	1	1	...	...	...
1	1	1	...	...	...
1	2	2	...	...	...
1	2	2	...	...	...
2	1	2	...	...	...
2	1	2	...	...	...
2	2	1	...	...	...
2	2	1	...	...	...

After:

Factor One′	Factor Four	...	Factor Seven
1	...	...	...
1	...	...	...
2	...	...	...
2	...	...	...
3	...	...	...
3	...	...	...
1	...	...	...
1	...	...	...

Table 5. Depiction of Test Factors and Their Values for Ground System #1

The second problem with the Taguchi techniques was the realization that not all test factors will be independent. This limits the application of orthogonal arrays. For ground system #2, there were seven factors, all with two levels. This implied use of the L8, two-level, array. However, analysis of the resulting array revealed an incompatibility problem. This occurred, because two of the factors, the BBU for satellite 1 and the BBU for satellite 2, had a critical dependency. This ground system controlled two satellites. There were three BBUs at the TCR site. One BBU was dedicated to each satellite, while the third was a redundant backup for either. Using the L8 array would have resulted in two test cases where the same BBU was used for both satellites at the same time; see test cases #3 and #4 in Table 6. That would be an invalid test configuration. Two of the rows in the L8 array had to be arbitrarily modified, which destroyed the orthogonality of the test matrix, with some loss of rigor in the application of the Taguchi technique.

Test Case	...	BBU for Sat. 1	BBU for Sat. 2	...
1	...	BBU 1	BBU 3	...
2	...	BBU 1	BBU 3	...
3	...	***BBU 2***	***BBU 2***	...
4	...	***BBU 2***	***BBU 2***	...
5	...	BBU 1	BBU 2	...
6	...	BBU 1	BBU 2	...
7	...	BBU 2	BBU 3	...
8	...	BBU 2	BBU 3	...

Table 6. Problem with Taguchi Technique for Ground System #2

COMBINATORIAL DESIGN METHOD (CDM)

The author subsequently discovered an approach that circumvents the limitations of the Taguchi techniques while remaining systematic and highly flexible. That approach is the Combinatorial Design Method (CDM), as described in (Cohen et al. 1996).

In the CDM, the tester generates test cases that cover all pairwise, triple, or *n*-way combinations of test parameters (test factors). Covering all pairwise combinations means "that for any two parameters *P1* and *P2* and any valid values *V1* for *P1* and *V2* for *P2*, there is a test in which *P1* has the value *V1* and *P2* has the value *V2*" (Cohen et al. 1996). The Telcordia Technologies (formerly Bell Communications Research) experience is that pairwise coverage is sufficient for good code coverage and checking the interactions of system functions (Cohen et al. 1996).

This method also allows the tester to specify constraints on the test parameters. This prevents vacuous test scenarios or impossible relationships among the test parameters.

Consider the following example from a recent project that the author worked on. There are four primary test parameters that represent redundant elements of the ground system. A fifth parameter, called FMRT, is included to test a special capability of the satellite. For all test cases, a common set of tests is run to demonstrate key functionality of the ground system. The test parameters and their values are shown in Table 7.

Test Parameters	*Values*
BBU Unit	Primary TCR Site - Primary BBU Primary TCR Site - Backup BBU Backup TCR Site - Primary BBU Backup TCR Site - Backup BBU
Real-time (RT) Server	SCC Primary SCC Backup SCC Remote
Ground Status and Control (GSC) Server	SCC Primary SCC Backup SCC Remote
Telemetry Stream	Stream 1 Stream 2
FMRT Testing	Yes No

Table 7. Test Elements for Ground System Example

Other considerations eliminated time code servers and RF equipment as test parameters for the redundancy testing. All test parameters are independent in this example.

Exhaustive testing would consist of 144 test cases. However, testing based on the CDM consists of only 12 test cases, or data paths, a 92% reduction, as shown in Table 8, Data Paths Configuration Table.

The table shows all pairwise interactions between the test parameters. Each level, or value, of a particular test parameter appears in a test case with every value of the other parameters. For example, consider the parameter value "Primary TCR Site - Primary BBU." It is tested with SCC Primary RT Server (test case #1), SCC Backup RT Server (test case #9), and SCC Remote RT Server (test case #10). It is also tested with SCC Primary GSC Server (test case #1), SCC Backup GSC Server (test case #9), and SCC Remote GSC Server (test case #10). Likewise it is tested with parameter value Telemetry Stream 1 (test case #1) and Telemetry Stream 2 (test case #9, or #10). And finally the parameter value is paired with (test case #1, or #10) and without (test case #9) FMRT Testing.

The author's experience with using pairwise coverage in the CDM is that customers are pleased with the scope and breadth of the functional testing. Another project that has used the CDM has reported similar results.

Additional Details. Some information on the theory behind CDM and descriptions of other authors' experiences with the CDM are available in technical papers cited at Telcordia's website, at Uniform Resource Locator (URL) `http://aetgweb.argreenhouse.com`. (Cohen et al. 1996) is a primary reference. The author has described cost and schedule savings associated with the CDM, for the ground system example shown in Tables 7 and 8, in (Huller 2000). Topics for further investigation are also identified in the paper.

Comparison. The Taguchi techniques and the CDM are related. The orthogonal arrays of the Taguchi techniques are combinatorial design methods for pairwise coverage, but with the restriction that every pair of values must occur exactly the same number of times. As noted in (Cohen et al. 1996), this makes orthogonal arrays impractical for testing. For example, for a system with 100 parameters with two values each, the Taguchi techniques require at least 101 test cases, while the CDM covers all pairs with ten test cases.

While the orthogonality criterion is necessary for the statistical analysis associated with Taguchi techniques, it is not critical for the generation of test cases. In fact, it can be a handicap, as the previous discussion of problems with the Taguchi techniques shows. Statistical bias is not relevant, because the author's test cases require a 100% pass rate.

The author has recently used the CDM to successfully (re)generate test cases for the ground systems associated with Tables 5 and 6 earlier. The CDM easily handled the BBU constraint associated with Table 6.

Data Path Number	BBU Unit	RT Server	GSC Server	Telemetry Stream	FMRT Testing
#1	Primary TCR Site - Primary BBU	SCC Primary	SCC Primary	Stream 1	Yes
#2	*Backup TCR Site - Primary BBU*	SCC Backup	SCC Backup	Stream 2	Yes
#3	*Backup TCR Site - Backup BBU*	SCC Backup	SCC Primary	Stream 2	No
#4	*Backup TCR Site - Backup BBU*	SCC Primary	SCC Backup	Stream 1	Yes
#5	*Backup TCR Site - Primary BBU*	SCC Primary	SCC Primary	Stream 1	No
#6	*Backup TCR Site - Primary BBU*	SCC Remote	SCC Remote	Stream 1	Yes
#7	*Backup TCR Site - Backup BBU*	SCC Remote	SCC Remote	Stream 2	Yes
#8	Primary TCR Site - Backup BBU	SCC Backup	SCC Backup	Stream 1	Yes
#9	Primary TCR Site - Primary BBU	SCC Backup	SCC Backup	Stream 2	No
#10	Primary TCR Site - Primary BBU	SCC Remote	SCC Remote	Stream 2	Yes
#11	Primary TCR Site - Backup BBU	SCC Remote	SCC Remote	Stream 1	No
#12	Primary TCR Site - Backup BBU	SCC Primary	SCC Primary	Stream 2	Yes

Note 1: The SCC remote server is at the backup SCC. The other servers are at the primary SCC.

Note 2: The data paths (matrix rows) have been reordered to facilitate testing of transitions between servers, and partly for convenience for test setup.

Table 8. Data Paths Configuration Table

CONCLUSION

The CDM provides a systematic approach to generating a reasonably small number of test cases that provide good coverage of the various data paths in a commercial satellite ground system. The method is flexible and allows constraints or relationships among the test parameters to be accounted for. Training in statistics is not required to use the method.

The CDM has been successfully used to determine system test cases for data paths testing. Tester and customer satisfaction has been high.

REFERENCES

Aerospace Daily, June 21, 1999. This updates the article in Aerospace Daily, September 15, 1998. Aviation Week Group, McGraw-Hill Inc.

Cohen, D.M., Dalal, S.R., Parelius, J., and Patton, G.C., "The Combinatorial Design Approach to Automatic Test Generation." *IEEE Software*, September 1996, pp 83-88.

Huller, J., "Reducing Time to Market with Combinatorial Design Method Testing." Proceedings of INCOSE Colorado 2000 Conference, (Denver, CO, March 26-28, 2000), pp 51-57.

Phadke, M.S., *Quality Engineering Using Robust Design*. Prentice Hall, Englewood Cliffs, 1989.

Phadke, M.S., Clausing, D.P., and Cohen, L., "Tutorial #4: Systems Engineering: A Competitive Advantage in the Commercial Markets." Sixth Annual International Symposium of the

International Council on Systems Engineering (INCOSE), July 8, 1996.
Ross, Phillip J, *Taguchi Techniques for Quality Engineering*. McGraw-Hill, New York, 1988.
Space Business News, September 2, 1998. Phillips Business Information, Inc.

BIOGRAPHY

Jerry Huller is currently a Senior Test Engineer at Raytheon Company in the Command, Control, Communication, and Information Systems business unit. He holds a B.A. in Mathematics from Davidson College and an M.A. in Applied Mathematics from the University of Maryland, College Park. Jerry has over 18 years of experience in defining system/software requirements, quality assurance testing, systems engineering, and customer technical support for military and commercial programs. For the past 4 years, he has served as Integration and Test Lead for several commercial satellite ground system projects. Jerry is a member of the INCOSE Verification and Validation Interest Group and is active in the Colorado chapter of INCOSE.

Case Study in Effective Government-Contractor Partnering

John A. Thornton
Space and Naval Warfare Systems Command
4301 Pacific Highway (OT-1)
San Diego, CA 92110-3127

Heide A. Kinsinger
Lockheed Martin
9500 Godwin Drive
Manassas, VA 20110

Michael A. Luczak
Raytheon Company
Naval and Maritime Integrated Systems
1847 W. Main Street
Portsmouth, RI 02871

Abstract. Any Department of Defense (DoD) acquisition program manager would argue for more funding and more schedule as a rationale for successful program execution, claiming his or her program is on a "fast track". At the same time, the days of having relief provided due to cost overruns and schedule delays are becoming history, and such perils unquestionably increase the risk of unwanted scrutiny of programs. These realities have challenged program managers to seek new and innovative ways to manage their programs. The government and contractor program managers for the Space and Naval Warfare System Command's Advanced Deployable System (ADS) Program have responded to this challenge by developing an effective government-laboratory-contractor partnership, and utilizing this efficient relationship in virtually every facet of program planning and execution. The case study presented in this paper discusses how the ADS Underwater Segment (UWS) has used this partnership in planning and executing its 42 month program, which was completed on time and under budget. It provides lessons learned from this management experience for consideration by other program managers interested on embarking on such a path.

INTRODUCTION

Program Definition. The Advanced Deployable System (ADS) is a wide area, rapidly deployable, acoustic undersea surveillance system designed to operate in littoral waters in support of joint operations. Its core mission is to provide the Joint Task Force Commander (JTFC) with real-time, accurate, and reliable undersea surveillance of advanced nuclear and modern diesel-electric submarines, surface shipping, and mine-laying activities.

Program Definition. The ADS Program has been tasked with the combined challenges of developing system which establishes undersea surveillance within a few days of a Fleet Commander's request (a new mission), operates in shallow littoral ocean areas (a new environment), deploys light weight undersea fiber optic cables from the confined spaces available on non-dedicated platforms (new technology), and uses only a few operators to monitor the system (sharply reduced manning levels). In addition to responding to these challenges, the program was required to demonstrate the utility of its system by deploying a prototype in a major Fleet exercise, an exceedingly ambitious undertaking in such an early program phase. Finally, the program was challenged with the difficulties associated with midstream, cross-country relocations of the government program office and the major subcontractor (responsible for 75 percent of the effort).

Methodology. To most effectively develop a system which met the ADS operational requirement with its many unique challenges, the Navy and contractor program managers recognized the need to carefully craft their program to maximize the value-add of the resources available to them. They agreed that the best way to do this was to commit to a government-contractor partnership in an Integrated Product and Process Development (IPPD) environment. For this program, IPPD has been implemented by: breaking down the traditional, inefficient government-contractor barriers through the effective use of government-contractor Integrated Product Teams (IPTs) truly empowered with decision-making authority, committing a significant amount of up-front effort and resources to establish a clear and executable baseline, and following a disciplined, integrated systems engineering-business approach to development. It was also recognized that the IPTs would have to be an integrated team in practice as well as in name.

Team Players. The major players who played a role in the ADS development described in this paper included the Navy's ADS Program Office (under the Space and Naval Warfare Systems Command (SPAWAR)), and its principal government laboratory,

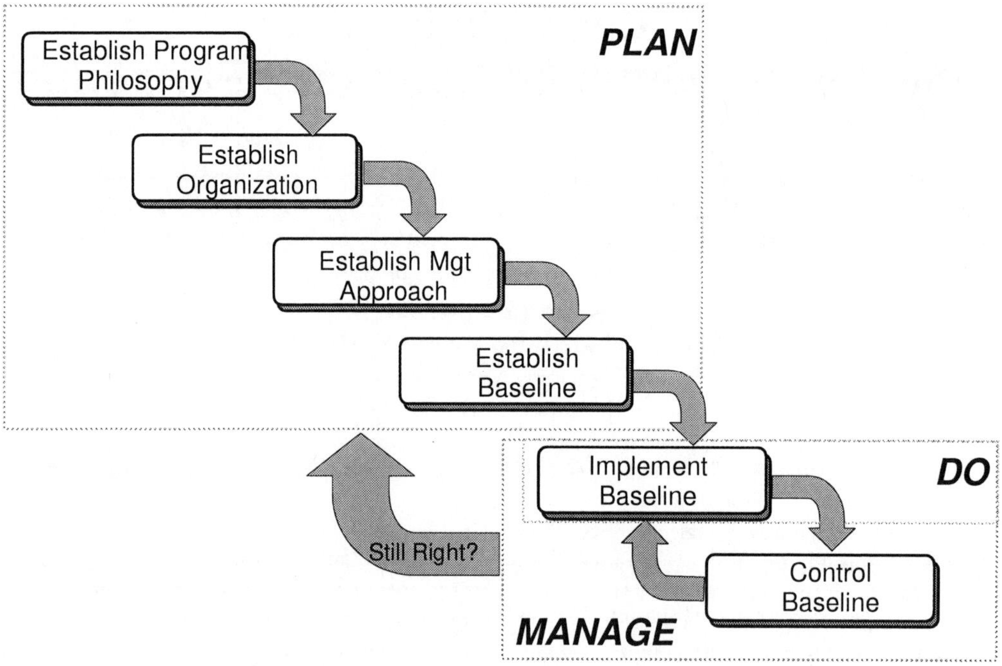

Figure 1. Steps in Program Planning and Execution

SPAWAR Systems Center (SSC); the prime contractor, Lockheed Martin Undersea Systems, and its principal subcontractor, Raytheon Naval and Maritime Integrated Systems; and a number of government laboratories and support contractors.

This paper describes how the ADS Program's Underwater Segment implemented an IPPD methodology during its 42 month, Program Defintion and Risk Reduction (PD&RR) Phase, which completed on schedule and under budget. Its conclusions describes a number of approaches which went particularly well, as well as a number of areas which need refinement as the program enters its next phase of development.

STEPS TAKEN TO IMPLEMENT IPPD

This section of the paper describes the major steps taken in program planning and execution. These steps are in the form of Deming's circle of quality (for ADS, "plan-do-manage") as shown in Figure 1. The following paragraphs summarize the concepts and activities of each step. A detailed treatment of these steps can be found in (Luczak and Thornton, 1997).

Establishing the Program Philosophy. Prior to program initiation the Navy program manager introduced his government team to the government-contractor relationship which he would expect for this phase of the program. Part of this introduction included his well-disseminated program vision which read:

"The contractor is the key to our success. We intend to work cooperatively to develop an affordable shallow water surveillance capability. The government team will strive to ensure the contractor understands the requirements. The government team will provide added value to the contractor's efforts."

The ADS vision essentially signalled a need for program personnel to rethink and change the way they had been accustomed to developing systems, including the vital government-contractor relationship. This vision was part of discussions during the initial government-contractor interaction, and together with a number of program "guiding lights" provided the basic foundation for the program's government-contractor relationship. Among others, these "guiding lights" included:

- *"Do What Is Right". This was meant to break the inclination of doing things the way they have always been done and to undertake work only after the objectives of an effort were understood, and when the effort was believed to add value to the Program.*
- *"Program First – Contractor First". The ADS Program must have the highest priority in all ADS team member's work and all effort must first serve the program. Since ADS is the highest priority and the contractor is the key to our success, the ADS contractor will come first. Everyone will work to make the contractor a success.*

- *"Requirements Definition". By the Integrated Baseline Review (IBR), the ADS team will define the physical and operational requirements for ADS as well as contractor Statement of Work (SOW) requirements. At a minimum, the rationale and the owners of all requirements will be identified.*

The joint government-contractor team agreed early-on that a properly implemented IPPD methodology would be the most effective way to carry out this program philosophy.

Establishing the Organization. The next step in the IPPD process was to determine the team composition which would best serve the development. The consensus was that IPTs would be the main focus of the team structure. Basic principles which governed the formation of the IPTs included:

- Joint government-contractor teams
- Multi-disciplinary
- Product-oriented; organized on subsystem level
- All members are workers (i.e., no "checkers")
- Collocation at the site where work was performed
- Best resource for the job, affiliation (i.e., government or contractor) transparent
- Responsible for ALL decisions within the baseline

Within two months of program inception, a professionally facilitated team launch/training session was used to define team roles and responsibilities and to provide definition of preliminary processes to be used by the IPTs. The session included participation by all members of the team and was effective in quickly building team cohesion. At the time of the team launch we formed into four teams based on our best guess of what team structure would effectively meet our needs. The team launch session validated this structure and it is shown in Figure 2 .

One of the four teams, the Systems Engineering and Management Team (SEMT), was directly responsible to the program managers for delivering the UWS Product on schedule and within budget, and to an agreed upon level of performance. This leadership team also included leads from the subsystem IPTs and was co-chaired by a government and a contractor representative.

The SEMT reported to an Executive Steering Group which consisted of the government and contractor program managers and senior technical leads. This relationship facilitated the proper interface between the Underwater Segment and other ADS Program IPTs and working groups.

The other three teams were organized as IPTs at the subsystem level (i.e., Wet End Hardware, Installation, and Mission Planning subsystems). Two of the teams were chaired by contractor personnel, and the other by a government laboratory engineer. Each subsystem IPT was empowered to make ALL decisions affecting its product within the cost, schedule and performance baseline. In other words, the SEMT provided the foundation and direction to the team and the subsystem IPTs provided the building blocks for the system.

Following the team launch, the SEMT continued refinement of the systems engineering and management processes and ultimately documented them in a joint-government-contractor Management Plan (equivalent of the traditional SEMP and Program Plan).

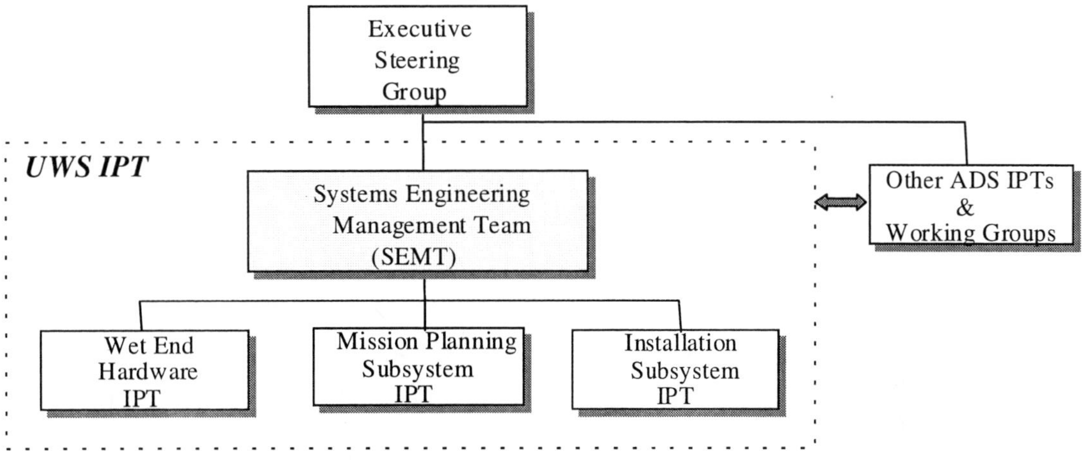

Figure 2. UWS Team Structure

Establishing Management Approach. The management approach used to implement the IPPD methodology consisted of two major elements: IPTs – the people, and the Integrated Development Process (IDP) – the disciplined approach. A primary premise of this approach is a holistic concept whereby management and technical disciplines are brought together to produce the product in an integrated government-contractor team environment. For this approach to be effective it requires allegiance to the product as opposed to organization or discipline.

The IDP is illustrated in Figure 3. The SEMT is the heart of the IDP. The SEMT is responsible for defining the inputs to the program in the form of product requirements and process requirements, and the expected outputs from the process, as well as the implementation of the leadership techniques, management activities, and technical direction efforts.

Figure 3 provides a summary of the SEMT activities which are included in the IDP. Specific details of these activities can be found in (Castor, et.al., 1998).

Definitions of the three principal areas of emphasis are:

- *Leadership techniques* are those quality methods which are enablers for implementation of a truly effective management strategy. These methods are applied during all management activities and technical direction efforts.
- *Management activities* are those activities necessary to establish, implement, and maintain the organization, the program baseline, and the development process.
- *Technical Direction efforts* are those efforts necessary to establish, implement, and maintain the product baseline, monitor technical performance, and ensure that the segment is integrated into the total system. These efforts are guided by agreed-upon, documented processes.

Before the IDP could begin in earnest, the subsystem IPTs and the SEMT had to reach concurrence on the inputs and outputs of the process. That effort was grueling, time consuming, and often frustrating. However, at each iteration, the output of that effort was consistently a clearly defined product and well understood responsibilities and expectations.

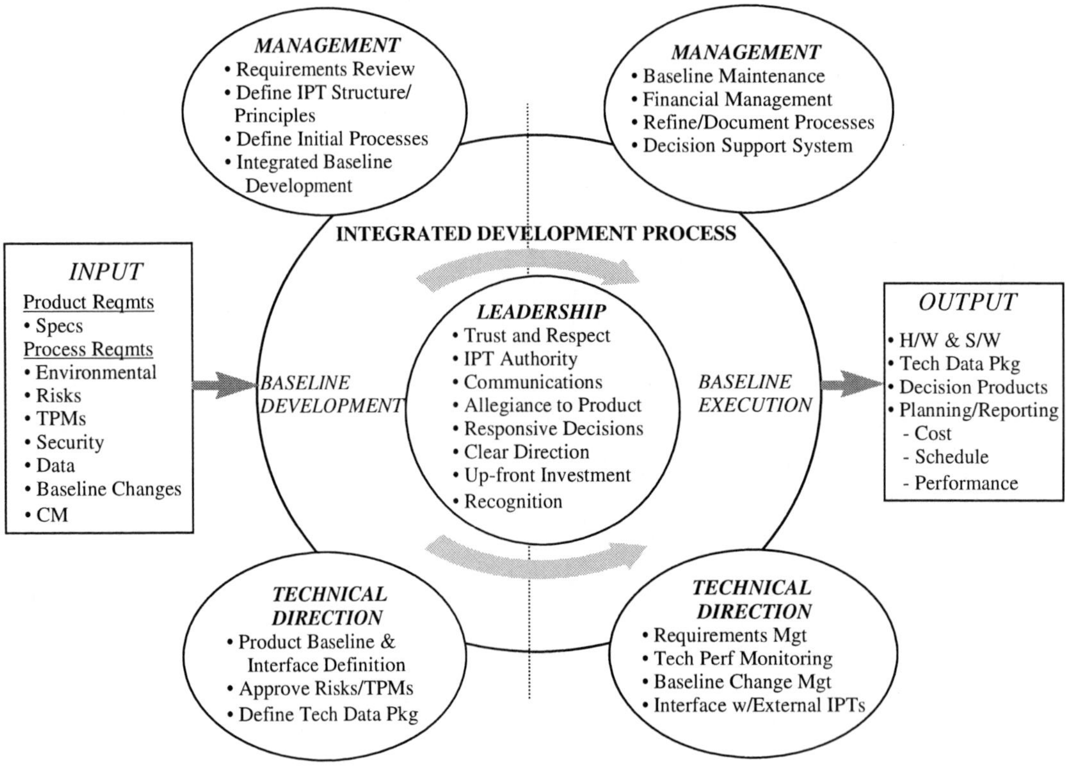

Figure 3. The Integrated Development Process (IDP)

Establishing the Program Baseline. The first major milestone following the Post Award Conference was the System Requirements Review (SRR). The review focused on definition of the product requirements and agreement by all parties on the requirements baseline. It was the first real test of the effectiveness of the IPT structure. The government-contractor team resolved all major issues during the preparations for the review and very few action items resulted. The review turned out to be more of a report to the government and contractor program managers on what had been accomplished and what was planned, as opposed to the traditional SRR which requires substantial program manager decision-making and direction.

The next major milestone was the Integrated Baseline Review (IBR). The purpose of the IBR was to establish the cost, schedule and performance baseline (or, the plan) for the program phase. The baseline was an agreement by all parties, government and contractor, on the specific tasks, resources and completion criteria for the program. In order for the government to have shared ownership of the baseline, its resources as well as the contractors' were included in the plan.

The IPTs had people from many different backgrounds used to doing business in a number of different ways. As such, we considered it important to kickoff the IBR with a professionally facilitated training session which defined the expectations in terms of the process, established the rules for planning, and described the process whereby an effective plan is developed and implemented.

The SEMT set the overall framework for the IBR by defining the overall program structure, milestones and constraints. The Subsystem IPTs then created their own detailed schedule of tasks. For each task, they identified the required resources which included an estimate of the hours required from each government and contractor team member. The IBR effort caused the IPTs to carefully examine subsystem boundaries and products for which they would be responsible. One of the rules established by the SEMT for defining the boundaries (and determining IPT responsibility) was that the product should have a minimum number of interfaces and it should be testable and verifiable as an assembled product.

Midway through our program we were funded to accelerate the introduction of an option to the main program and began a parallel development. The IBR approach was again put into action. This approach allowed fact-facting and negotiations to be conducted simultaneously with baseline development which enabled the associated contract modification to be completed within two months of proposal submission.

Implementing the Program Baseline. Many programs are overwhelmed with difficulties in implementing the baseline. This is largely due to improper up-front planning and thus an IBR process which leads to a non-executable plan. On the other hand, the commitment our team made to the planning effort enabled ready implementation of the plan and its use as an effective management tool. Once the plan was implemented, the primary focus of the SEMT became maintenance of the baseline. This has required a review of proposed changes and evaluation of those changes relative to program goals, while doggedly protecting the program against requirements creep.

Earned Value management was a valuable tool to apply to all stages of the program. Earned Value was used to ensure that the program was on track when measured against the cost and schedule baseline. The process by which Earned Value would be taken and tracked was a major output of early planning. The Earned Value process applies to both the government and contractor IPT resources. This unique concept had many difficult implementation problems, especially at government laboratories where it was an unfamiliar approach. A principal charter of the SEMT was to continually review progress against Earned Value and make required midcourse adjustments.

Controlling the Program Baseline. Shortly after the cost, schedule and performance baseline was established, a process to control the baseline was defined. The baseline control process was a primary responsibility of the SEMT. Changes to the product requirements as a result of forces internal and external to the development effort can have a major impact on the baseline, and their effects ripple down through the requirements tree to the lowest level of the product. Both external and internal changes were reviewed by the management team to ensure that they were necessary and sufficient and that life-cycle implications had been considered. External changes (those which affected other program segments), depending on their source, were oftentimes more difficult to negotiate. However, they were all evaluated in the same manner as internal changes and recommendations were made to the program managers.

Our objectives for a configuration management process were to define an approach which was affordable and not too onerous. Our decision was to let the organization that would produce most of the drawings and perform most of the manufacturing propose the process, and then have the IPT adopt it as a whole.

Tools for Effective Communications. A unified and complete Data Management process is required to ensure that program and system design data are documented and managed throughout the development life cycle. The Data Management process approach should allow easy and quick access to in-process and approved data by all parties of the IPTs. Probably the biggest issue we faced in Data Management was coming to consensus on what types of data we needed to capture in the shared library. Our decision in this area was based on our objectives for Data Management which were to: communicate status, provide real time opportunities for review and development of specifications and the Technical Data Package, provide a historical record of why decisions were made and what trade-offs were considered in making those decisions, and provide data for life-cycle analysis of cost, supportability and reliability.

We decided to use a shared database in a Lotus Notes environment to achieve these objectives. All parties had open access to the data during the data development process. This totally obviated the need for formal contract data deliverables and the incumbent review cycles and updates typically associated with them. The database became the second of two data deliverables (as discussed earlier the Management Plan was the other).

CONCLUSIONS AND LESSONS LEARNED

There were many lessons learned from our experience in government-contractor partnering. Most of our processes worked well and have been applied the to the next phase of the program, to the extent that they made sense for the phase. Others required refinement and they have likewise been applied to the next phase.

Leadership Team.

- 👍 The commitment of the team to expend the necessary resources to establish a clear and executable cost, schedule, and performance baseline resulted in a baseline which was managed for the entire development (no re-plans).
- 👍 The SEMT's positive reaction to difficult problems created an atmosphere where there were no secrets, no surprises, and there was no fear of reprisal. This allowed for the leadership team to make informed decisions and to address problems before they became insurmountable.
- 👍 The open and honest communications in a team environment did oftentimes slow management decisions, but better decisions were routinely made since all information was known and all view points were represented.

Integrated Product Teams (IPTs).

- 👍 Government personnel being part of the product development process, as opposed to being "checkers", proved to be very efficient and effective use of resources.
- 👍 Since the focus was always on the product and what had to happen to make the product successful, conflict between organization and product was minimized, and an allegiance to product vice organization was fostered (as well as the concept "we all pass or we all fail together"). The natural tendency of people to stick close to their organization in favor of the team received little attention as the development progressed due to the successes which were the obvious result of the teaming concept.
- 👍 The ins-and-outs of most company processes were shared for the benefit of the team while due respect was provided for proprietary areas.
- 👍 All design reviews enjoyed "first-pass" success (with no dry runs or repeats), with no surprises and few action items. This is a far departure from typical DoD programs wherein the preparation and fallout of these reviews routinely consume countless resources.
- 👍 The government team members gained keen insight into the contractor world which enabled them to work more effectively as part of the development team.
- 👎 Collocation at the site where the work was being performed was valuable but proved to be difficult at best. In theory it made sense and it did have its benefits, but our approach (50 percent on-site) burnt people out. We may have been overzealous in that effort and probably could have eased back on this practice earlier than we did.

Systems Engineering Processes/Tools.

- We chose to be patient in deciding on our processes. We defined them early, iterated on them, and then documented them in a Management Plan. This plan was used on a daily basis by our team (as opposed to the traditional SEMP imposed in the front end of programs which receives limited use).
- We chose simple tools for this early program phase and they worked.
- We emphasized management of high and medium risks and did not lose our focus by expending unnecessary resources on the low risk items.
- We managed a handful of Technical Performance Measures (TPMs) which enabled focus on the key measures of development progress.
- Centrally locating program and technical data and making it accessible to all members of the team created a positive impression on everyone involved, making each rightly feel that he or she is a valued entity.

Business Processes.

- As was the case with the systems engineering processes, we iterated on our business processes before solidifying them in our Management Plan.
- Our commitment to developing a clear and executable baseline paid great benefits. The requirements for each task were well known at task initiation. The program was effectively and efficiently implemented in accordance with this plan.
- Earned Value management proved to be an effective tool for assessing progress and forecasting problems. Implementing the Earned Value system in the Navy laboratories was not without challenges.
- Management reserve was provided to the contractors to manage and was not held by the government, which is oftentimes the norm in DoD programs. Contractor management in this area was effective.
- Both the prime contractor and each subcontractor shared the same award fee scores. The government evaluated one set of award fee criteria for the contractor team and there were no separate criteria by which the subcontractors were evaluated.

Integrated Team Concept.

- Diverse backgrounds and old operating paradigms can mitigate against the success of a truly integrated team. Our experience was that professionally facilitated team building sessions went a long way in developing the government-contractor team. As the program progressed, government and contractor people collocated and working side-by-side, getting to know each other proved most valuable.
- In the latter stages of this phase, it became evident that marked efficiencies could be gained by including the entire ADS program in the IPPD methodology. The Underwater Segment approach to system development is being used for the entire ADS system during the next phase of system development. Both the government and prime contractor have identified overall systems engineers to guide the development across the program.

New Startup Program. Midway through the primary development a second, parallel development started. Many of the benefits of our first experience were applied to the program, but we could have done better in a number of management areas.

- The program expanded the responsibilities of the incumbent management team to the extent that focus on the new development was difficult to maintain and conflicting priorities diluted management effectiveness.
- We waited for almost one year before we designated a government counterpart to the contractor lead with the time available to focus on the new program.
- We fell short in our efforts to integrate a new contractor team with the same nurturing as we did with the contractors for the first program.

Finally, the authors of this paper wish to take this opportunity to acknowledge the efforts of the entire Underwater Segment team for their hard work in this unfamiliar IPPD environment. The willingness of the entire team to routinely set aside personal and organizational agendas to create a unique government –contractor relationship has been the single most important factor in the success of the program. Special thanks go to Mr. Tom Higbee, the Navy ADS Program Manager, for giving us the latitude and the encouragement to pursue this path, and to Mr. Rob Hutcheson, the Lockheed Martin Undersea Systems Program Manager, for fully embracing this approach and providing the resources to help us in this journey.

REFERENCES

Luczak, M.A. and Thornton, J.A., "An Approach to Successful Integrated Product and Process Development (IPPD)." *Proceedings of the Seventh Annual International Symposium of the International Council on Systems Engineering, Volume I* (Los Angeles, CA, August 3-7, 1997).

Castor, R.A., Hutcheson, R.T., Luczak, M.A., Thornton, J.A., "Implementation of a Government-Contractor Leadership Team in an Integrated Product Team (IPT) Environment.", *Proceedings of the Eighth Annual International Symposium of the International Council on Systems Engineering, Volume I* (Vancouver, BC, Canada), 26-30 July 1998).

BIOGRAPHIES

Heide A. Kinsinger received a B.S. (1979) in Electrical Engineering from West Virginia University. She has worked for IBM, Loral and Lockheed Martin Undersea Systems for 18 years and has 20 years experience in military hardware development engineering, systems engineering, engineering management and program management. She is currently the Lockheed Martin Deputy Program Manager for ADS.

Michael A. Luczak received his B.S (1968) in Education from State University of New York at Geneseo and his M.S. (1985) in Electrical Engineering from the U.S. Naval Postgraduate School. During the past nine years he has worked as a Senior Systems Engineer with TRW System Services Company, Lockheed Martin Undersea Systems, and at Raytheon Naval and Maritime Integrated Systems in Portsmouth, Rhode Island. His primary emphasis has been in the area of Undersea Surveillance System development. Prior to that he spent 21 years as a Naval Surface Warfare Officer.

John A. Thornton received his B.S. (1982) in Ocean Engineering from Florida Atlantic University and his M.S. (1989) in Civil Engineering from The George Washington University. He is a registered professional engineer in the State of Virginia, and has worked for the Navy for 15 years. His primary areas of interest are underwater fiber optic cables and ocean systems. He is currently the Systems Engineer for the Advanced Deployable System, a new acquisition program developing advanced acoustic sensing systems.

Towards the Development of Domain-Specific Guidelines for a Systems Engineering Framework: Commercial Aircraft

Scott Jackson
The Boeing Company
Long Beach, CA

Greg Mathers,
The Boeing Company
Seattle, WA

Mary J. Simpson
Battelle Laboratories
Richland, WA

Joseph J. Simpson
System Concepts
Seattle, WA

Cheryl Atkinson
ADSE
The Netherlands

Erwin Duurland
ADSE
The Netherlands

Ashok Jain
Honeywell Engines and Systems
Phoenix, AZ

Abstract. The Joint Commercial Aircraft Working Group (JCAWG) consists of members from INCOSE, other professional societies, major aircraft manufacturers, regulatory agencies, suppliers, and other companies in the commercial aircraft domain. JCAWG is chairing the development of a supplemental guideline for the Commercial Aircraft Transport Domain under the title of "Guidelines for the Application of Systems Engineering in the Commercial Aircraft Domain." The primary purpose of the Guidelines is to span the gap between the ANSI/EIA standard and other guidelines in the aircraft industry. These Guidelines are expected to be the forerunner for similar guidelines in other application domains.

INTRODUCTION

The application of systems engineering (SE) to commercial domains assumes that SE is an open process, that is, that it is applicable to any application domain, as long as these application adhere to fundamental principles. The International Council on Systems Engineering (INCOSE), in its approach to capability maturity models, stresses the "domain-balanced" aspect (*Insight*, 1999).

It is a stated objective of the INCOSE Systems Engineering Applications Technical Committee (SEATC) to foster the practice of systems engineering (SE) in specific domains, for example, commercial and public interest domains. In addition, (EIA 632, 1999) specifically states that that document "is not limited to specific disciplines, industry sectors, or technology domains." It is the goal of this collaboration to fill the need for domain-specific guidelines for one application, namely, commercial aircraft. The document being developed is called "Guidelines for the Application of Systems Engineering in the Commercial Aircraft Domain" (hereinafter simply called the Guidelines). Another work (Jackson 1997) addressed the practice of SE in the commercial aircraft domain. While the prior work focused on the SE process and how it would be applied to the commercial aircraft domain, these Guidelines expand on that work and capture the specifics of the SE framework in that domain. (Martin, 2000), discussing the genesis of EIA 632, states that it is expected that documents similar to EIA 632 will emerge for specific domains, such as aircraft.

(Jeffroy, et al, 1999) shows how Airbus Industrie, makers of the Airbus line of aircraft, adhere to the basic principles of SE. A basic principle of these works, as well as these Guidelines, is that aircraft and air transportation systems are systems with their own unique functions and drivers.

This paper serves two purposes: First, it describes the process by which the Guidelines were initiated and developed. Secondly, it presents and overview of the information in the Guidelines. Since the information presented in this paper represents the Guidelines when the paper was submitted, it can be expected that the final product will be more mature.

THE ROLE OF THE JOINT COMMERCIAL AIRCRAFT WORKING GROUP (JCAWG)

The JCAWG operates under the auspices of the Systems Engineering Applications Technical Committee

(SEATC) of INCOSE. The Seattle Metropolitan Chapter is the current chapter sponsor of the JCAWG. It consists of members from INCOSE, other professional societies, major aircraft manufacturers, regulatory agencies, suppliers, and other companies in the commercial aircraft domain. Geographical representation includes members from both North and South America and Europe. The "Joint" in the title reflects the group's philosophy and working agreement.

GUIDELINES *VS.* A STANDARD

An early question the JCAWG had to answer was: Should we develop a standard or simply guidelines? It was agreed that guidelines would fit our needs more than a standard. First of all, guidelines could be deployed faster. Secondly, guidelines fitted our need to make suggestions regarding frameworks for conducting SE in the commercial aircraft domain rather than agreed-to methodology which is expected of all practitioners in the domain.

A FORERUNNER FOR FUTURE GUIDELINES

Another objective of these Guidelines is to become a forerunner for similar guidelines in other fields. SEATC has, at this writing, nine working groups (WGs) and interest groups (IGs) representing different application domains, for example, telecommunications, healthcare, motor vehicles, rail transportation, etc. Each domain has its own processes, parameters, and methodologies. Hence, each field merits its own domain-specific guidelines, which individually may be very different from the commercial aircraft guidelines. Hence, a vision of SEATC is that there will some day be such guidelines for all domains.

ATTRIBUTES OF THE GUIDELINES

Some of the envisioned characteristics of the Guidelines are as follows:

- The Guidelines are expected to be lean, not exceeding 30 to 60 pages.
- The Guidelines will not attempt to explain systems engineering to the reader but will assume that the reader has access to or is familiar with other higher-level systems engineering guidelines, such as EIA 632 and IEEE 1220. It was agreed that some brief generic SE material would be acceptable as introductory material in each section.
- The Guidelines will not repeat any material found in the higher-level documents. To avoid duplication with other documents, the Guidelines will reference these other documents, where applicable.
- Examples of information to be found in the document are (a) existing process frameworks in the industry which are compatible with and complement the SE process, for example, the certification processes found in (ARP 4754, 1996), and (b) frameworks for treating particular requirements categories in to the industry, for example, (RTCA/DO-178B, 1992) for software requirements. The term "framework" is meant to imply a structure within which specific practices may be defined. These Guidelines do not intend to define those practices but rather the structure within which they may exist.
- The Guidelines will use existing terminology found in the aircraft industry, wherever possible.
- The Guidelines will not divulge any proprietary information of any organizations, such as organization-specific practices.

COLLABORATIVE AGREEMENT

One principle agreed to among JCAWG members very early was that the Guidelines should not reflect specific practices at any aircraft manufacturer. This principle is in agreement with previous products which have been produced in this collaborative manner. It is also in agreement with its scope, that is, the description of a generic framework for the domain and not specific practices. In addition, it should not be an INCOSE product, but should reflect an agreement among all the relevant professional societies. As of this writing a collaborative agreement was being reviewed by current and proposed participants. This agreement is intended to permit the broad-based perspectives to be shared within the forum of JCAWG, and transcribed into the Guidelines to reflect the total SE aspects of the domain.

The guiding principles of operation for the Guidelines are based on the understanding that all participating organizations are considered equal partners. Approval of the Guidelines will require a unanimous vote. Some of the proposed provisions of the agreement are as follows:

- All parties agree that the joint publication of this document will lead to the development and manufacture of better commercial aircraft, regardless of the organization or country of the participants.
- The joint publication will provide strength to the application of SE in the domain in which all parties are participants.
- Agreement regarding the application of SE in the domain will reduce the negative effects of differing frameworks.
- All parties are expected to benefit from the sharing of ideas.
- All participating parties assume no liability for the use of these Guidelines.

- No party is expected to exchange any proprietary or otherwise legally protected information.
- All parties have one vote. A unanimous decision is required for final approval. The Guidelines are jointly owned by all parties.
- All parties may publish the Guidelines providing they do not modify it in any way. The Guidelines will be published under a public domain copyright.

Since the agreement is being reviewed, these provisions may change.

SCOPE

As described by (Mathers, 1999) the primary purpose of the Guidelines is to span the gap between the ANSI/EIA standard and other Guidelines in the aircraft industry.

Figure 1 illustrates the envisioned scope of the Guidelines. The two parameters which define the scope are the document breadth (the opposite of domain applicability) and the treatment of certification. The list of documents shown in this chart is, by no means, meant to be exhaustive. Many other standards and guidelines exist.

Top-Level Standards. At the top level key International Standards Organization (ISO) document treat system development at the broadest level. ISO 9000 focuses on quality and customer satisfaction, while ISO/IEC 15288 introduces key concepts central to systems engineering, such as development stages. Of course, both documents are applicable to any domain. Since ISO/IEC 15288 is not yet approved, it cannot, as yet, be used as an authoritative source.

Generic SE Process Level. At the second level of breadth, several key documents are available which define the SE process in greater detail. Although the term "systems engineering" is never used in (ANSI/EIA 632, 1998), this document is the most widely accepted standard for this process. Additionally, (IEEE 1220, 1995) provides a more detailed level of the SE process. Finally, although MIL-STD-499B has been withdrawn, it was for many years the definitive standard for SE.

Domain-Specific Level. The Guidelines represent the domain-specific application of SE to the commercial aircraft domain. These Guidelines are most closely aligned with ANSI/EIA 632.

External Environment. There are several documents representing the external environment of laws and regulations pertaining to the commercial aircraft domain. These include the Federal Aviation Regulations (FARs), Joint Airworthiness Requirements (JARs), International Civil Aviation Organization (ICAO) regulations, SAE/ARP 4754 and 4761, and RTCA DO-178B and SC-180.

While ARP 4754 invokes the principles of SE in the certification process, the Guidelines accomplish two other goals:

- First, the Guidelines go beyond certification issues to address any needs that the stakeholders might identify, such as performance, economy, and passenger needs.
- Secondly, the Guidelines complement ARP 4754 by creating a framework within which the SE principles can be applied. This framework includes such factors as, but not limited to, a template for commercial aircraft functional and physical system architectures.

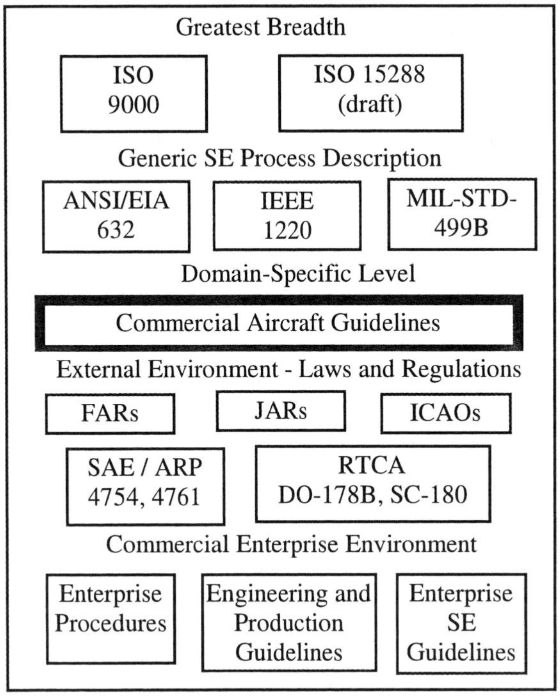

Figure 1. Levels of Systems Engineering Standards and Guidelines Which May Pertain to the Commercial Aircraft Domain

Organization-Specific Level. Finally, the fourth level consists of those documents which define the organization-specific SE practices, such as those which appear as procedures in specific aircraft manufacturers.

Note that in this figure no lines connect the various standards and guidelines. This is because there is no formal line of authority among them, due to the fact that they were produced by a variety of organizations. In spite of this, the JCAWG has agreed that the terminology and concepts found in ANSI/EIA 632 will be the primary basis for the Guidelines. Hence, the

ANSI/EIA 632 is the primary "parent" of the Guidelines.

While the Guidelines are still in draft form, the following sections provide an overview of some of the major topics covered in them.

THE AIR TRANSPORT SYSTEM AND THE COMMERCIAL AIRCRAFT SYSTEM

One of the earliest challenges of the JCAWG was to define the Commercial Air Transport System and the Aircraft System. Figure 2 maps the relationship between the Worldwide Aviation System, the Commercial Air Transport System and the Commercial Aircraft System. A system at any level may have elements owned by the aircraft manufacturer, the airline company, the airport, regulatory agencies, or other entities. All of these entities comprise the commercial aircraft domain.

Figure 2 provides a functional view of the Worldwide Aviation System architecture. It assumes that there are three top-level aviation functions:

The World Aviation System Level. There are three top-level functions at the World Aviation System level:

- Provide Air Transport. The element Things That Fly satisfies this function.
- Provide Air Traffic Management. The element Air Traffic Management performs this function.
- Provide Airport Capability. The element Places to Fly From and Return To satisfies this function.

Although the Commercial Aircraft System is the subject system of the Guidelines, the Worldwide Aviation System is shown to illustrate the context within which the Commercial Aircraft System operates. In addition, this larger system is the system with which the Commercial Aircraft System interfaces. Finally, it is necessary to show the larger system because, in some instances, functions may be allocated at a higher level than the Commercial Aircraft System itself.

The Commercial Air Transport System Level. At the Commercial Air Transport Level the elements are:

- Commercial Aircraft. This element is a subset of the Things That Fly group at the top level.
- Airports. This element is a subset of the Places to Fly From and Return To group.
- Civil Air Traffic Control. This element is as subset of the Air Traffic Management group.

The Commercial Aircraft System Level. The final element is the Commercial Aircraft System which is a part of the Commercial Aircraft group. This element consists of the aircraft and all its subsystems (propulsion, airframe, avionics, controls, etc.)

The Concept of Operational and Enabling Systems. In the preceding discussion each of the higher level elements can be seen as an enabling element to the operational system of interest, the Commercial Aircraft System.

ANSI/EIA 632 introduces the concepts of operational and enabling products. A system consists of both its operational products and its enabling products, as shown in Figure 3.

In the case of an aircraft, the aircraft itself is the

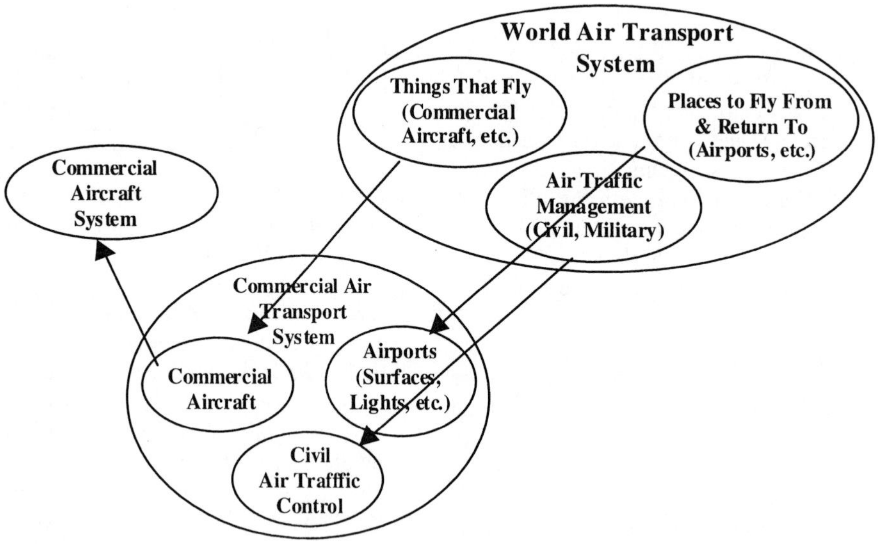

Figure 2. Partial Mapping from the World Air Transport System to the Commercial Aircraft System

operational product, that is, the element that performs the mission of the aircraft. The enabling products are the collection of elements which are necessary for the aircraft to perform this operation but do not participate directly in that operation.

There are seven types of enabling products as shown in Figure 3. Products, such as the aircraft maintenance system, which sustain the aircraft throughout its life, are called support enabling products, as described by (Geisert and Jackson 2000). Enabling products can be persons, equipment, facilities, documents, or a combination of these. The important aspect of the enabling products is that requirements can be allocated to them just as much as the operational products.

The enabling elements of the Commercial Air Transport System are many and important. These elements include, among others, the Aircraft Manufacturing Enterprise and the Ground Maintenance System. Enabling systems of the Commercial Aircraft System include the Aircraft Servicing System, primarily of which the fuel supply is a major component.

certification process dominates the verification stage. Hence, although the standard stages remain intact, the commercial aircraft domain brings its own emphasis.

AIRCRAFT STATES

The identification of states within which to define the operation of a commercial aircraft is useful for the assignment of requirements. Table 2 shows a suggested set of aircraft states. States may be defined to greater levels of detail.

FUNCTIONS

(ARP 4754, 1996) recommends that a comprehensive functional analysis be performed as part of the certification process. This analysis requires that individual subsystem functions be traceable to top-level aircraft functions. The Guidelines place these functions in a larger context, showing that the Perform Guidance function, for example, can be allocated to the Flight Deck Crew or to the Worldwide Airspace System as shown in Figure 2. The top-level functions are as follows:

- Provide and Distribute Communications
- Plan, Generate and Control Aircraft Movement
- Provide Crew, Passenger, and Cargo Environment and Services
- Detect and Analyze Aircraft Conditions for Flight
- Distribute Aircraft Information
- Generate and Manage Internal Power and Manage Systems Materials
- Provide Airframe Movement and Attachment Capability
- Provide Containment and Internal Support

In accordance with basic SE principles, functions are, to a limited extent, configuration independent. The Guidelines provide a template which enables the practitioner to allocate the functions to the proper elements of the system architecture.

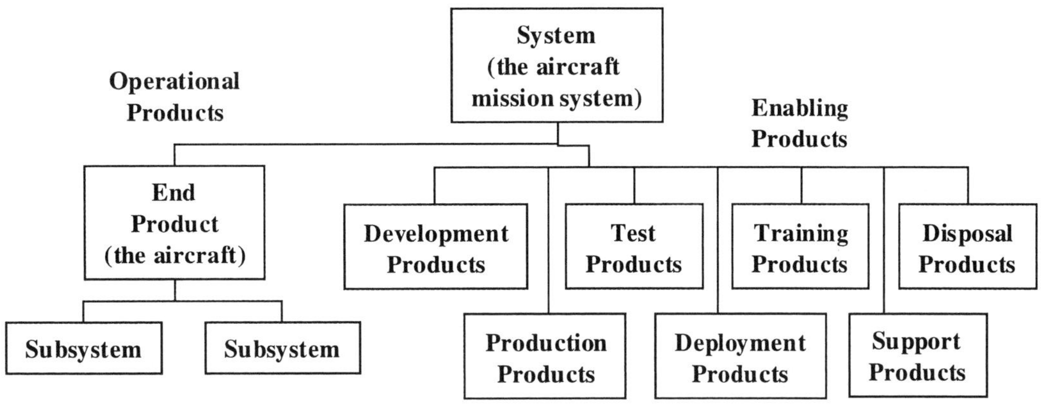

Figure 3. An Operational and Enabling View of the Commercial Aircraft System

COMMERCIAL AIRCRAFT LIFE CYCLES

Although the number of stages of development varies in different sources, there is very little difference among them. The Guidelines have recommended the six-stage model, as shown in Table 1. In addition, the Guidelines have shown the life-cycle stages at three levels: the enterprise level, the aircraft level, and the subsystem level. These level are shown conceptually in the life-cycle context diagram of Figure 4. These stages are shown correlated to the ANSI/EIA 632 model.

One of the unique aspects of the commercial aircraft domain, like any commercial domain, is that the early phases are driven by the business development activities: analysis of the validity of the business case, establishing a consortium, partnerships and the selection of strategic suppliers. The second aspect is that the

<table>
<tr><th>ANSI/EIA 632 Model</th><th colspan="2">JCAWG Guidelines Model</th></tr>
<tr><td>Assessment of Opportunities</td><td colspan="2">Assessment of Opportunities and Marketing</td></tr>
<tr><td>Investment Decision</td><td colspan="2">Investment Management</td></tr>
<tr><td>System Concept Development</td><td rowspan="2">Aircraft System Development Life Cycle</td><td>System Development and Certification</td></tr>
<tr><td>Subsystem Design and Pre-Deployment</td><td>Subsystem Development</td></tr>
<tr><td rowspan="3">Deployment, Operations, Support, and Disposal</td><td colspan="2">Production</td></tr>
<tr><td colspan="2">Sustaining</td></tr>
<tr><td colspan="2">Disposal</td></tr>
</table>

Table 1. Commercial Aircraft Life-Cycle Stages

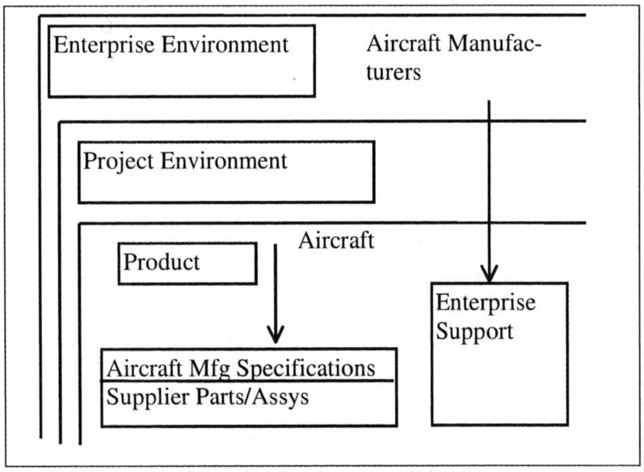

Figure 4. Life-Cycle Context Diagram

REQUIREMENTS

In the commercial aircraft domain the following focus areas are of importance:

Customer requirements. The capture of customer needs in functional form, rather than preconceived solutions, is of utmost importance.

Certification requirements. In accordance with ARP 4754, the development of functional requirements associated with the top-down functional analysis is the top priority process.

State	Sub-State	Sub-Sub-State
Ground	Maintenance	Long Term (in hangar, B & C checks)
		Short term (at ramp)
	Storage	Long Term (inactive aircraft)
		Short Term (active aircraft)
	Turnaround	
	Pushback	
	Taxi Out	
	Taxi In	
	Docking	
	Refused Takeoff	
Flight	Takeoff	
	Climb	Terminal Control
		En route Control
	Cruise	
	Descent	
	Initial Approach	
	Final Approach	
	Go Around	
	Landing	

Table 2. Aircraft States

Domain-unique requirements. Although SE requires that all requirements be addressed, the following top-level requirements receive special attention in the commercial aircraft domain:

- Safety
- Direct operating cost (DOC)
- Weight
- Reliability (especially dispatch reliability)
- Performance (range, payload)
- Fleet commonality

SYNTHESIS

The Guidelines reference traditional aircraft sizing methodologies, such as those outlined by (Corning, 1977; Raymer, 1999; Roskam; and Toorenbeek, 1988) provided those methodologies are practiced in an SE context with the appropriate functional and requirements analyses.

Commercial aircraft domain-specific aspects of trade studies include:

- Allocation of requirements to the proper level of the system architecture. For example, the Provide Guidance function can be allocated either to the Aircraft System level or to the Worldwide Airspace System level.
- Consideration of new concepts. Trade studies should allow for synthesis of new aircraft concepts, such as the High-Speed Civil Transport or the Blended Wing-Body.

CERTIFICATION

While certification is a large subject, the Guidelines do not address it as such. They point to the use of ARP 4754 and other traditional guidelines for certification. While ARP 4754 recommends the use of SE principles including a comprehensive functional analysis, the Guidelines provide a functional and architectural template for implementing the recommendations of ARP 4754. A primary goal of the Guidelines is the development of a high-level generic architecture upon to which the functions will be mapped.

SOFTWARE

Similarly, the Guidelines reference RTCA/DO-178B, for example, for guidance relative to the incorporation of software in a system. This reference recognizes that software is a part of a system whose requirements should conform to the requirements of the whole system.

SYSTEMS ENGINEERING MANAGEMENT AND CONTROL

The Guidelines address those management and control aspects peculiar to the commercial aircraft domain, including:

- Aircraft System level review. The Guidelines recommend that design reviews be held at the Aircraft Level regardless of whether the development is for a new aircraft, derivative design, or a change-based design for a specific customer.
- Supplier emphasis. The commercial aircraft domain is a supplier driven industry. The Guidelines recommend rigorous design and production control through all levels of the design including supplier sub-tiers.

CONCLUSIONS

As of this writing, a complete first draft of the Guidelines has been published and distributed among the JCAWG members for comment. In addition, when approved internally, this draft will be placed on the INCOSE web site in the SEATC and JCAWG web pages for all to see. JCAWG welcomes comments from INCOSE and members of other organizations.

We believe that JCAWG is breaking new ground in the publication of domain-specific guidelines for the a systems engineering framework. In addition, we believe that these Guidelines, in particular, fill a need in the commercial aircraft domain which has not been served, at least as comprehensively, by any other document. It is hoped that these Guidelines will contribute, in some part, in the development of new aircraft which are safer, higher quality, and which serve all the stakeholders needs.

REFERENCES

Corning, Gerald, *Supersonic and Subsonic CTOL and VTOL Airplane Design*, published by the author: College Park, Maryland, 1977.

Geisert, Madrona A. and Jackson, Scott, "The Application of Systems Engineering to the Synthesis of Enabling Products: An Aircraft Support System," INCOSE Proceedings, 2000.

IEEE Trial-Use Standard for Application and Management of the Systems Engineering Process, IEEE Std 1220-1995.

"INCOSE Position on Capability Maturity Models and the Capability Maturity Model Integration (CMMI) Effort," position paper adopted by the INCOSE Technical Board, *Insight*, Summer 1999, pp. 19, 20.

Integrated Capability Maturity Model, Federal Aviation Administration (FAA), 1999.

Jackson, Scott, *Systems Engineering for Commercial Aircraft*, Ashgate Publishing Limited, 1997.

Jeffroy, et al, "Airbus System Engineering Policy," INCOSE Proceedings, 1999, pp. 341-46.

Life-Cycle Management - System Life-Cycle Processes, International Standards Organization (ISO) and International Electrotechnical Commission (IEC), ISO/IEC 15288, 1999 (draft).

Mathers, Greg, "Systems Engineering in the Commercial Air Transport Domain," *Insight*, Summer 1999, pp. 17, 18.

Martin, James, "Processes for Engineering a System: An Overview of the ANSI/EIA 632 Standard and its Heritage," *Systems Engineering Journal*, Vol. 3, Number 1, 2000.

Processes for Engineering a System, Electronic Industries Alliance, ANSI/EIA Standard 632-1998, approved January 7, 1999.

Raymer, Daniel P., *Aircraft Design: A Conceptual Approach*, AIAA Education Series, New York, NY, 1999.

Roskam, *Aircraft Design, Parts I-VIII*, DAR Corporation, Lawrence, Kansas (darcorp.com)

RTCA, Inc., *Software Considerations in Airborne Systems and Equipment Certification*, RTCA/DO-178B, 1992.

Society of Automotive Engineers (SAE) in cooperation with the Federal Aviation Administration (FAA), *Guidelines for the Certification of Highly-Integrated and Complex Aircraft Systems*, ARP, 4754, 1996.

Systems Engineering, draft military standard, Department of Defense, MIL-STD-499B, 1992. (cancelled)

Torenbeek, Egbert, *Synthesis of Subsonic Airplane Design*, Delft University Press / Kluwer Academic Publishers, 1988 (ISBN 90-247-2724-3)

AUTHORS

Scott Jackson is a Senior Specialist in System Engineering at the Boeing Company in Long Beach, California and is a member of the Boeing Systems Engineering Working Group. He also teaches systems engineering in the University of Southern California master's program. His book *Systems Engineering for Commercial Aircraft* was published by Ashgate Publishing Limited in 1997.

Greg Mathers is a Senior Specialist in Systems Engineering with the Boeing Commercial Aircraft Group in Seattle, Washington. He is chair of the Joint Commercial Aircraft Working Group (JCAWG).

Mary J. Simpson is a Staff Engineer with the Battelle Laboratories in Richland, Washington. Formerly with the Boeing Commercial Airplane Group, she performed strategic engineering and process management analysis for the Production Systems Management Board. She was the principal author of the DOE Strategic Plan (1996) at the Hanford site. She is the former chair of the INCOSE Corporate Advisory Board.

Joseph J. Simpson an independent systems engineer with Systems Concepts in Seattle, Washington. He was formerly a Systems Engineer with the Boeing Commercial Airplane Group.

Erwin Duurland is a consultant in Systems Engineering with ADSE in the Netherlands. He was formerly with Fokker Aircraft and was a co-founder of the Netherlands INCOSE chapter. He is co-chair of the Joint Commercial Aircraft Working Group (JCAWG).

Cheryl Atkinson is a Director with ADSE in the Netherlands. She is a founding member of the Netherlands Chapter of INCOSE.

Ashok Jain is the Systems Engineering Manager with Honeywell Engines and Systems in Phoenix, Arizona. He was formerly a Scientist at the National Aeronautical Laboratory in Banaglore, India. He is a member of the Honeywell Systems Engineering Council.

Systems Engineering – Consumer and Infrastructure Approaches

Dr. Myron Kayton, President, Kayton Engineering,
P.O Box 802
Santa Monica, CA 90406

Ron Ogan, Consultant
1916 Sussex Drive
Carrollton, TX 75007

Abstract. Systems Engineering processes increase in complexity for infrastructure applications compared with consumer. The level of testing documentation, subassembly qualification and verification of simulation tools are important for infrastructure systems but are of minimal value for consumer systems. Requirements tracking and flow-down from the customer performance specifications are more detailed and costly for infrastructure systems. Infrastructure systems that are based upon stable technologies, such as buildings or utilities usually do not use Systems Engineering processes.

1. CONSUMER PRODUCTS

Consumer products have short development cycles, typically less than a year, and short life spans, typically 4-5 years. Table 1 and Figure 1 show comparisons. Testing is extensive to avoid legal action and to protect the company's reputation. Delivered documentation is often limited to a Users' Manual and Repair Manual, if outsiders are expected to do repairs.

Consumer products have high production rates, often thousands per day. Product quality is maintained by expensive periodic tests which repeat the initial Qualification Tests. Cost is the over-riding variable. Other factors are reliability, performance, and human convenience. External interfaces are usually simple, for example, reception of broadcast radio signals or transmission of standardized cell-phone radio signals. Electronic products must meet US-FCC and European specifications for radiated emissions.
There are no requirements on pulses sent into the utility power-lines, to the chagrin of the power companies. Underwriter's Laboratory certification may be done for protection against lawsuits or for marketing reasons.

Consumer products that affect safety of life are medical devices, for example pacemakers, drug delivery pumps, or radiation imaging systems. Automobiles have electronic braking systems and will soon have collision-avoidance systems that have full-authority control of the brakes. Proposals are often made to equip cars with road-following electronics. These safety systems are developed under formal controls resembling those for infrastructure projects. They require additional testing, usually by a disinterested third party. Such testing, with independently created simulations, can add 10% to the cost of the product.

2. INFRASTRUCTURE

Infrastructure systems are purchased by large bureaucracies,
usually government agencies or large corporations.
They can be:
>water supply systems
>control centers: air traffic control, battlefield,
>emergency response, or commuter-traffic.
>tax-collection systems including software
>law enforcement data systems
>military systems that range in complexity from walkie-talkies to aircraft carriers to ballistic-missile defence systems.
>aircraft
>navigation systems

These systems are usually purchased in small numbers, often just one. Engineering and test efforts cannot be amortized over a large number of units. Funding is often annual, precluding investment in high initial quality with the intention of reducing later operating costs. Infrastructure systems usually remain in service for more than 50 years and undergo several rounds of upgrade as requirement change and as parts become unavailable for repairs.

The system engineering process begins with a long period of comparative designs, ranging from simple to complex. Each is designed to the point where its cost, reliability, performance, human interfaces, and external interfaces can be assessed and compared (ref. 2). Infrastructure systems usually interface with the external world in complex ways that are defined by an "Interface Control Document". Errors in that document have resulted in catastrophes, such as the failure of the Mars Climate Observer.

The test process occurs at many levels. Devices are built and tested. Several devices are interconnected and tested as an entity. Gradually the entire system is built up and tested, often over many years. Test plans and methods of evaluation are produced by the system engineers for the hardware, software, and integrated systems.

Delivered documentation is extensive, consisting of elaborate descriptions of the system and the design process that created it. The documentation helps the teams that continually upgrade the system, long after the initial designers have retired or died.

3. SIMPLIFICATION

Consumer chips are approaching the "system on a chip" in which a small number of custom chips, supported by a few commodity chips, solve the entire problem on a few boards within a single enclosure. Design of consumer products therefore occurs on an ever shortening schedule. System engineering is mostly invested in the design of the custom chips, typically application-specific integrated circuits (ASICs). The rest is in meeting thermal and vibration environments.

Infrastructure projects, that will be in service for generations, require longer periods of system engineering. The electronic devices that make up the system use commercial components similar to those in consumer devices. Since the cost of failure of infrastructure is high, whether in loss of taxpayer time or loss of life, these systems use parts selected for reliability, for example by screening and burn-in. They may have to meet higher temperature, vibration, or radiation levels than do consumer products.

4. CONCLUSION

Consumer products are designed with a brief system engineering process that evolves into manufacturing control. Infrastructure products are designed with a lengthy system engineering process that evolves into product upgrades. The former is weak and being strengthened. The latter is overly complex, addresses paperwork rather than customer needs, and should be simplified.

Systems engineering defines initial architecture concepts and design requirements for the major components and assemblies as shown in the "Vee" process, Figure 2. The design engineers convert the concepts into hardware and software to meet the performance requirements. Systems engineering completes the process by setting the requirements for integration, test, and the validation phases.

Process	Consumer	Infra-structure
Systems Architecture	Yes	Yes
System trade off analysis	Yes	Yes
Subassembly detailed design	Yes	Yes
Subassembly Qualification	No	Yes
Test Plans	No	Yes
Simulation Tool Verification	No	Yes
System Design Verification Testing (DVT)	Yes	Yes

Table 1: Systems Engineering Process

	Typical Time in months	
PROCESS	**Consumer**	**Infra-Structure**
Need	**1**	**3**
Concept	**1**	**4**
Functional Requirements	**1**	**3**
Sys Architecture	**2**	**6**
Allocated Rqmts	**2**	**6**
Detailed Design	**8**	**16**
Implementation	**3**	**12**
Test & Verify	**3**	**12**
TOTALS-months	**21**	**62**

Figure 1. Product DevelopmentCycle

REFERENCES

1. Arunski, Karl; Brown, Phil; Buede, Dennis; Martin, James;, "Presented to the Texas Board of Professional Engineers", September 10, 1999.
2. Kayton, AES article
3. Rechtin, Eberhardt, Systems Architecting, Prentice Hall, Inc., January 1991
4. Martin, James N. INCOSE presentation, Sept.1999.

BIOGRAPHY

Dr. Myron Kayton has 45 years of experience at Kayton Engineering, TRW, NASA and Litton G&CD designing avionics, navigation, communication, and computer-controlled systems. As President of Kayton Engineering Company, he has served more than 100 clients, large and small, by creating innovative designs and analyzing their performance, cost, and failures.

Dr. Kayton is a registered electrical and mechanical engineer. He is a Fellow of the Institute of Electrical and Electronic Engineers (IEEE), was an elected member of the corporate Board of Directors, and served two terms as President of its Aerospace and Electronic Systems Society. He is the author of the standard reference text, AVIONICS NAVIGATION SYSTEMS (first and > second editions) and of NAVIGATION: LAND, SEA, AIR AND SPACE and has lectured throughout the world.

Dr. Kayton received the Ph.D. in Instrumentation from M.I.T. in 1960, the M.S. from Harvard University with a concentration in electrical engineering, and the B.S. in mechanical engineering from The Cooper Union. He is an instrument-rated pilot and holds an FAA Project Raincheck certificate in Air Traffic Control.

Mr. Ogan's education includes B.S., Physics, Oklahoma State University and M.S. Engineering, Southern Methodist University. Recently employed as a Systems Engineer under contract to Raytheon TI Systems, Lewisville, TX since 1995. Previous experience included staff engineer at Martin Marietta (now Lockheed Martin Corp.), Orlando, FL working on Electro-Optic programs and Project engineer on Space Shuttle Main Engine Controller Block II at Honeywell, Clearwater, FL. Currently Chairman and previously Program Chair, Secretary/Treasurer of the IEEE, Aerospace and Electronics Systems Society, Dallas Chapter. Elected to Senior member status with IEEE and member of INCOSE.

Figure 2 Systems Engineering "Vee" Process –Ref 4

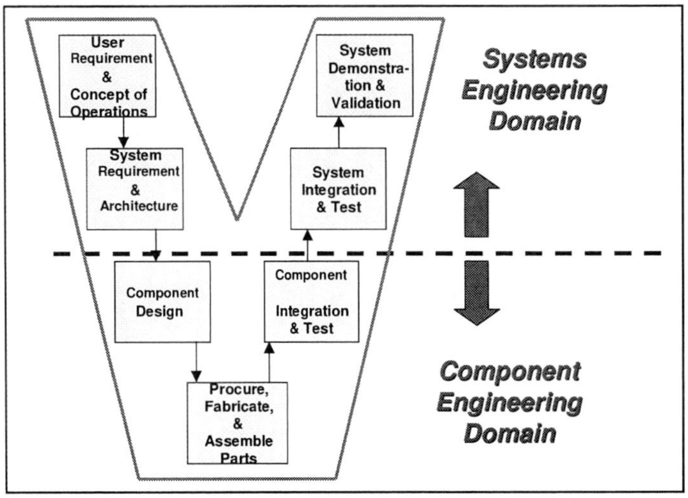

The Application of Systems Engineering to the Synthesis of Enabling Products: An Aircraft Support System

Madrona Geisert
The Boeing Company
Long Beach, California

Scott Jackson
The Boeing Company
Long Beach, California

Abstract. A system consists of its operational element, that is, the product, and one or more enabling elements. Traditional systems engineering (SE) is devoted to the formulation of requirements for and the synthesis of the operational elements with little attention to the enabling elements. A typical enabling element is the support system for an aircraft. The heart of the support system is a support data system which manages the flow of data and equipment among the various elements of the support system. This data system is the focus of this paper. However, the structure and functionality of the entire support system and relationship to the aircraft are described. The traditional SE processes are used to synthesize the data system. These include the development of a mission statement, the performance of a functional analysis, the assignment of requirements, identification of interfaces, the creation of a functional architecture, the allocation of requirements to system elements, and the selection of a final system construct. During these steps it is necessary to focus on the needs of the operational product itself, the aircraft.

INTRODUCTION

The traditional view of a system normally focuses on the operational product, for example, an aircraft. Systems engineering holds, however, that a system can be any collection of elements required to achieve a given objective. In the broader view, these elements can include products beyond the operational elements. An excellent example is that of an aircraft, either commercial or military.

If the operational product is to be developed using the traditional SE processes, then it holds that the same processes should be used for the enabling system. Furthermore, SE holds that the development of the support system should be concurrent with the operational system and that the whole system (operational and sustaining elements) should be balanced as a whole.

SE also allows that system elements may be developed when other elements are "heritage" elements, that is, existing. It is the latter case that this paper will examine.

In the aviation domain, as in other domains, the financial aspects, both recurring and non-recurring, can often exceed that of the operational elements. For this reason alone, the enabling elements deserve at least equal treatment with the operational elements.

In short, this paper treats the support system when that system is *the* system.

THE CONCEPT OF THE ENABLING SYSTEM

ANSI/EIA 632 introduces the concept of the enabling system as distinct from the operational system. A system consists of both its operational elements and its enabling elements, as shown in Figure 1.

In the case of an aircraft system, the aircraft itself is the operational element, that is, the element that performs the flight of the aircraft. The enabling element is the collection of elements which are necessary for the aircraft to perform this operation but do not participate directly in that operation. The aircraft manufacturer, is therefore, an enabling element. Enabling elements can be persons, equipment, facilities, documents, or a combination of these. The important aspect of the enabling elements is that requirements can be allocated to them just as much as the operational elements.

EIA 632 defines seven types of enabling "product sets." Each product set can contain documentation, personnel, equipment, and processes. They are as follows:

- Development Products. In the aircraft industry these consist primarily of the engineering resources belonging to the aircraft manufacturer and its suppliers.
- Production Products. These are the aircraft fabrication and assembly resources.
- Test Products. These are the aircraft ground and flight test equipment, personnel, and other resources.
- Deployment Products. These are all resources required to deliver aircraft to the customer.
- Training Products. These include flight simulators and other training resources.
- Support Products (shown in bold). These are all resources required to support the aircraft. These include the ground maintenance and servicing. In

this paper the support products are elements of the support system being synthesized.
- Disposal Products. Examples of disposal products include the equipment required to refurbish or dispose of the aircraft.

Each of these product sets can be considered to be a system into itself since each product set acts as a cohesive group to perform a unique function. In the case of the support system, it is the collection of products required to sustain the aircraft.

MISSION OF THE SUPPORT SYSTEM

The mission of the aircraft support system is to support the aircraft throughout its life cycle. This support consists of maintenance, spare parts, fuel, servicing, and aircraft modifications.

THE SYSTEMS ENGINEERING APPROACH TO SUPPORT SYSTEM DEVELOPMENT

Figure 2 illustrates the SE process used to develop an aircraft support system. Most of the elements of this process will be familiar to the reader, e.g., requirements analysis, functional analysis, and system synthesis. However, this chart emphasizes key support system aspects.

Note the use of data from current support systems as a key top-level input. This element allows the analyst to incorporate the features of existing support systems which will either (1) be mandated parts of the final support system, or (2) be elements to be traded against newly developed items.

The system modeling analysis is the primary verification approach. Within this analysis the performance of each support system element can be tested against its objectives.

Finally, note the ultimate creation of the support data system which will tie the system together.

The outputs of this model are (1) the functional model of the system, (2) the documentation of the support system description, (3) the information system architecture, (4) the system requirements, and (5) the Integrated Master Plan (IMP), Integrated Master Schedule (IMS), and System Engineering Master Plan (SEMP) documentation for support system development.

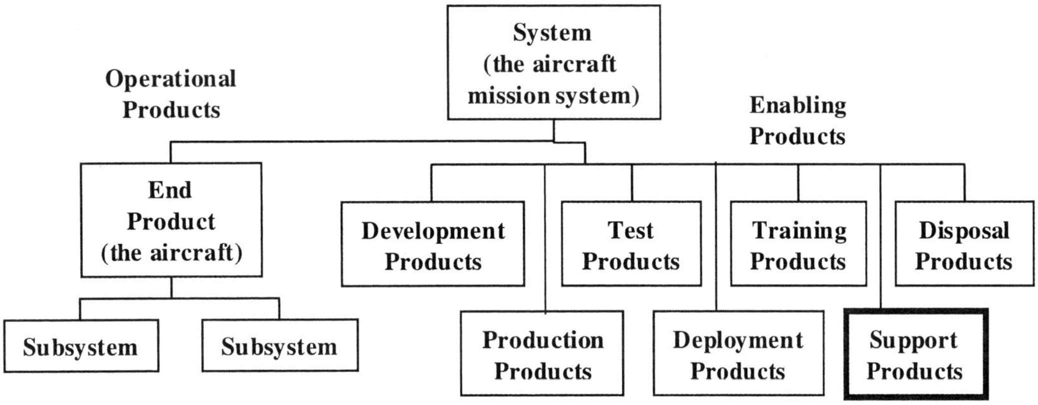

Figure 1. An Operational and Enabling View of an Aircraft System

AN AIRCRAFT SUPPORT SYSTEM

An aircraft support system is a collection of products required to maintain an aircraft throughout its life cycle. These products include the equipment, software, personnel, documentation, and facilities required to perform the support function.

ROLE OF THE OPERATIONAL SYSTEM IN THE DEVELOPMENT OF THE SUPPORT SYSTEM

Since the operational aircraft is considered a "heritage" system in the present analysis, then it must be asked what is its role relative to the enabling system, namely, the support system? There are two basic roles: (1) First, it acts as a source of requirements. After all, the role of the support system is to support the aircraft. The demands of the aircraft constitute the basic requirements for the support system. (2) Secondly, the aircraft constitutes the primary external interface for the support system. These interfaces must be clearly defined and satisfied.

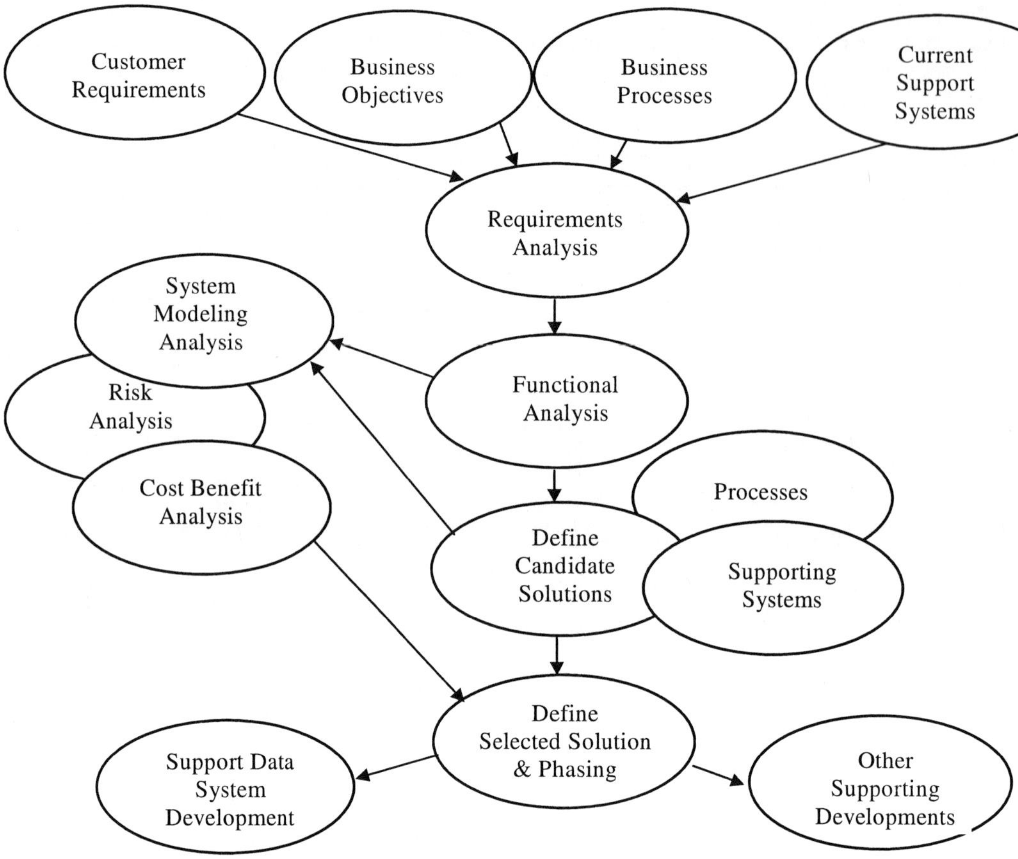

Figure 2. The Systems Engineering Approach to Support System Development

FUNCTIONAL ANALYSIS

The first step in the synthesis process is the development of the functional architecture. The functional analysis encompasses the entire aircraft system, and not just the support system, in accordance with the principle that the support system is part of a larger system. All functions are covered from the completion of manufacturing to disposal.

Figure 3 is an example of the results of the functional analysis of the entire system, including the system support. Following is a description of the top-level system functions. Although the functional descriptions include aircraft-level functions, these descriptions will focus on support-level functions. It will be seen that the majority of the system-level functions are enabling functions.

0.0 Perform Flight

This top level function forms the basis for the functional analyses.

1.0 Prepare Aircraft System for Service

This function includes all activities that occur after the manufacture of the equipment but before it is placed into service. It includes all modifications for a specific use, user or additions to the equipment that was not accomplished as part of manufacturing. It includes transport to user location, tests, modifications, and inspections necessary to prepare the equipment for service. This function is exclusively in the enabling system domain.

2.0 Perform Aircraft System Operations and Maintenance

This function includes all flight planning, preparation of the aircraft for flight or standby, taxi, takeoff, fly to destination, fly back to home base or airport, land at home base or airport, and perform aircraft post-flight operations. This function is a combination of operational and enabling elements.

2.1 Perform Flight Planning and Flight Support

This function includes reviewing weather data, optimizing flight route, selecting aircraft configuration and schedule, reviewing flight plan, and transferring system data to aircraft. This includes all planning and analysis for the overall logistic support (number of spares, support equipment, and personnel), maintenance plans for a given flight, and recommendations for resolving operational emergencies. This is a strictly enabling function.

2.2 Perform Aircraft Servicing

This function includes unloading passengers, cargo, and crew, shutting down the aircraft, cleaning, waste removal, minor repairs, installing flight support equipment, replacement of consumables, initial check-out of the aircraft, loading passengers, cargo, and crew, and start-up. This is also an enabling function.

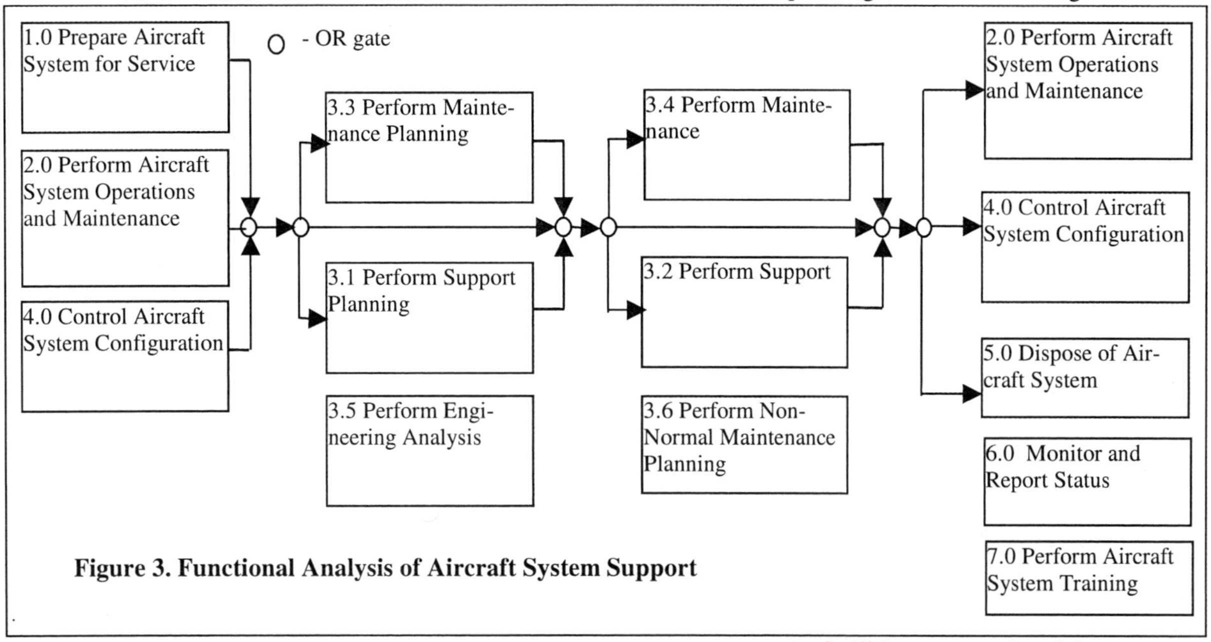

Figure 3. Functional Analysis of Aircraft System Support

2.3 Perform Pre-flight Preparations

This function contains all aircraft, crew, and passenger requirements preparation for flight, move to the taxiway, and taxi to the end of the runway including anti-icing, if needed. This is an operational function.

2.4 Perform Flight Operations

This function includes aerodynamic performance, thrust, passenger and crew accommodations, cargo capability, environmental control, communications, guidance and control, power, situational awareness, and maintain structural integrity. It includes monitoring and recording of equipment performance and fault information. This is the primary operational function.

2.5 Perform Post-Flight Operations

This function includes all activities performed during taxiing to the designated servicing/ parking area. This is the final operational function.

2.6 Perform Flight Line Maintenance Planning

This function provides for the integration, planning and scheduling for the execution of maintenance performed on the flight line such as check, refurbishment, equipment fault detection and repair, inspections and servicing, and on-wing propulsion maintenance. It includes assessing aircraft system and equipment maintenance needs, planning maintenance schedules, assigning tasks, recording maintenance actions, and planning for and scheduling the necessary spare parts, facilities, personnel, training, support equipment, technical data, and tools. This function includes the collection of operating and resource data necessary to conduct maintenance planning. This is a major support, that is, enabling, function. Some of the subfunctions of maintenance planning are as follows:

- Collect Crew Debrief Data
- Collect Aircraft System Data
- Collect Preliminary Diagnostic Fault Data
- Perform Diagnostics of Operating Data
- Recommend Maintenance Action
- Develop Maintenance Action

- Plan and Schedule Tasks
- Collect Maintenance Data
- Identify Deferred Maintenance
- Perform Flight Line Non-Normal Maintenance Planning

2.7 Perform Flight Line Maintenance

This function provides for the execution of the flight line maintenance planned and scheduled. This function includes updating of the configuration control documents of the aircraft, updating maintenance records and maintenance actions actually accomplished.

2.8 Perform Emergency Operations

This function includes the activities of all personnel, hardware, and software necessary to eliminate emergencies which may result in the loss of life, injury, or significant damage to the aircraft if immediate action is not taken.

2.9 Perform Non-Normal Operations

This function includes surges, compressions, and contingencies, and abnormal maintenance such as the recovery of an aircraft.

3.0 Support Aircraft System

This function consists of all sub-functions necessary to deliver flight capable equipment to the aircraft system. It begins when the aircraft system is operational. It includes all planning for and performance of depot and heavy maintenance. The maintenance planning and support are included in this function. This function is purely enabling and is the principal support system function.

3.1 Perform Support Planning

This function provides for the planning analyses required to define the facilities, support equipment, and provisions (spares and material) needed to support operations and maintenance of the aircraft system.

3.2 Perform Support

This function provides the support resources required to perform both flight line and periodic maintenance. It includes procurement of new spares, repair of repairables, and the overhaul or refurbishment of major components. It provides the support equipment necessary to maintain the aircraft system and assure flight readiness.

3.3 Perform Planning for Periodic Support

This function provides for the integration, planning and execution of maintenance not performed on the flight line.

3.4 Perform Periodic Maintenance

This function provides for the maintenance of the system and equipment not performed on the flight line.

3.5 Perform Engineering Analysis

This function performs sustaining engineering analyses, such as evaluation and assessment of the performance of the aircraft system to identify areas which need improvement.

3.6 Perform Non-Normal Maintenance Planning

This function provides the planning and scheduling of resources for maintenance actions other than emergency for which specific action must be taken.

4.0 Control Aircraft System Configuration

This function provides all of the aircraft system changes that are the result of maintaining or changing performance, improving supportability, or reducing the cost of ownership. It includes the functions necessary to manage all modifications of the fleet and the cost and operational effectiveness analysis necessary to identify and quantify the benefits of the change. This is an enabling function.

5.0 Dispose of Aircraft System

This function includes all requirements for identification and tracking of disposed elements, transportation and handling, support equipment necessary for material processing, personnel, facilities, technical procedures and the data required for processing items out of the inventory. This function also includes disposal methods to be consistent with environmental and ecological requirements. This is also an enabling function.

6.0 Monitor and Report Status

This function includes monitoring and recording parameters indicative of the health and status of the aircraft and its subsystems. The data recorded will be down loaded to ground receivers while the aircraft is in flight or at the end of each flight. The data will be used to support proactive maintenance, facilitate fault isolation, guide maintenance planning and scheduling, and support engineering assessment of system performance and supportability. This function is completed with the transfer of the recorded data at the end of the flight and all power is removed from the aircraft. This is another enabling function.

7.0 Perform Aircraft System Training

This function provides for operations training of the flight crew and maintenance training of the flight line (organizational) and maintenance crews, maintenance planning and support training, and sustaining engineering analysis and support training. This is the final enabling function.

It can be seen from the above discussion of the aircraft system functions that the majority of system functions are enabling functions. The only operational functions occur within Function 1.0. While the above functions can be expanded to more detail, the above discussion provides the primary functions required for an aircraft support system.

REQUIREMENTS ANALYSIS

The second step of the synthesis process is to develop the requirements associated with the functions. The requirements for the aircraft support system are process driven. Although the support system consists of equipment, people and processes, the support processes define the structure of the support system. These process requirements emanate from the users, that is, the maintenance personnel, the engineers, and planners. These process requirements include business processes. The net result will be to define current and future automation. The requirements described here focus on the aircraft support data system since the data system reflects the functionality of the entire support system.

Types of Requirements. Following are the general types of requirements which define the overall characteristics of the aircraft support data system.

General System Requirements - These requirements specify the degree to which the data system is easily expandable, upgradeable, user friendly and adaptable to operational requirements.

System Environment – These requirements describe the degree to which the data system operates in various external operational environments.

Data Environment – These requirements specify the commonality of data elements, standardized terms, and definitions.

Security Requirements – These requirements describe the identification and passwords needed for users.

Auditing Function – These requirements specify the capabilities for collecting and recording information of various type of events, such as events for audit purposes, system failures, and user attempts to secure files.

Data Integrity – These specify the capabilities for the support data system to validate the integrity of the data received and transmitted.

Report Generation – These requirements specify the reports that the support data must generate for performance reporting.

Transaction Processing – These requirement specify the capability for receiving and processing transactions from a customer to keep the aircraft flying.

Large Scale System Integration – Also included are the requirements for the support data system to interact with the internal and external elements within and outside a corporation, suppliers, and customers.

THE SUPPORT SYSTEM ARCHITECTURE

The third step of the synthesis process is to develop a system architecture to which the requirements can be allocated. The architecture of the support system is shown in Figure 4. The support system consists of the following elements:

The Maintenance System. Maintenance is the most obvious element of a support system. It consists of all the equipment, personnel, software, facilities, and documentation required to maintain the aircraft, both during routine turnaround as well as periodic servicing. The types and quantities of equipment, personnel, and so forth are the objectives of the SE analysis. It also includes plans and schedules, aircraft and support equipment maintenance work-in-progress documentation and tracking, work card instructions, links to drawings and other technical data and maintenance cost and cost history data.

The Modifications System. Aircraft are constantly undergoing modifications. These modifications can be performed for a variety of reasons such as repair, alteration, and modification to the aircraft and engines. This element identifies and tracks plans and schedules to modify an aircraft system.

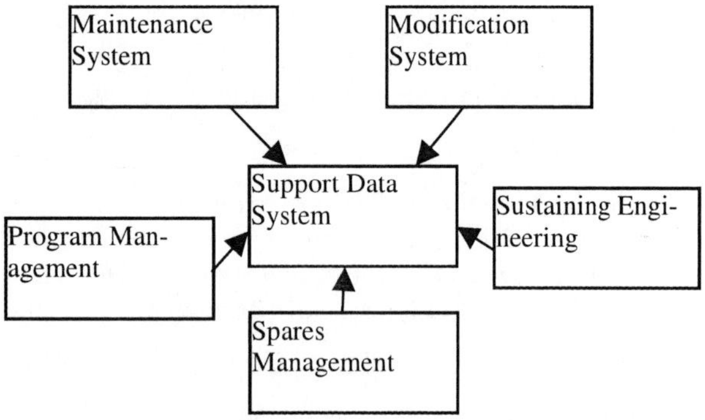

Figure 4. Aircraft Support System Architecture

Sustaining Engineering. This system performs the engineering for the modifications and other engineering functions. This system also manages the reliability and maintainability data base, aircraft structure integrity system and engineering disposition data base.

Program Management. This element controls the aircraft configuration and other management functions. It includes property management data, quality assurance data, and aircraft effectivity.

Spares Management. This system is responsible for managing the repair of repairables data base, inventory forecasting, and the allocation of spares to the various aircraft sites, and storage/warehouse locations.

Support Data System. This system controls and tracks all data among all the other elements of the support system.

BASELINE SOLUTION

The final step of the support system synthesis is to select the components to fulfill the requirements. The total support system solution, like an operational aircraft system, reflects the requirements considering a total system approach, maximum leverage of existing resources, maximum leverage of supplier technology, and new development where it is cost effective. The capability to interface with the existing legacy systems is a major consideration. Also important are system quality factors such as reliability, maintainability, availability, expandability, reserve growth capacity, expanded operation, system resource reserve capacity, facility power, grounding, floor loading, space, environmental conditions, and security.

The synthesis process begins with the functional analysis shown in Figure 3. The principle is that each function must be allocated to one or more architectural elements. These functions are then reflected in the functional architecture shown in Figure 4. The final step in synthesis is the selection and integration of the components to build the architecture. The selection of components entails trade studies considering the requirements listed above. Each trade study considers three options: existing components, off-the-shelf components, and newly developed components. However, the paramount metric for component selection is cost, with life-cycle cost being the dominant factor.

CONCLUSIONS

We have seen that SE principles can be brought to bear for the formulation and synthesis of an enabling system, in this case, the support system for an aircraft. We have also shown how these principles apply to the entire aircraft system and not just the operational element (the aircraft) or the enabling element (the support system).

This application has been implemented on the Sustainment Data System project.

More importantly it is hoped that this example will provide a stimulus for similar analyses in other domains, for example, the telecommunications or motor vehicles domains. Each domain contains its own individual operational elements (cars, telephones, etc.) and enabling elements (repair, manufacture, etc.).

Although the analysis described in this paper was based on the USAF C-17 Flexible Sustainment system, the methodology can be applied to commercial aircraft support systems as well.

REFERENCE

Processes for Engineering a System, Electronic Industries Alliance, ANSI/EIA Standard 632-1998, approved January 7, 1999.

AUTHORS

Madrona Geisert is a Specialist in Systems Engineering at the Boeing Company in Long Beach, California, and works on the C-17 Flexible Sustainment Program.

Scott Jackson is a Senior Specialist in Systems Engineering at the Boeing Company in Long Beach California. His book *Systems Engineering for Commercial Aircraft* was published by Ashgate Publishing Limited in 1997.

Denver International Airport: How could System Engineering Principles Have Prevented Disaster?

R. H. Cook
University of Maryland University College
College Park, Maryland

Abstract. The new international airport in Denver is a massively complex project that suffered from serious delays and budget overruns. It has been extensively post-mortemed in the press and trade journals, and its troubles even received a hearing before the House of Representatives Subcommittee on Aviation. This student paper, produced as part of work towards the MSWE degree at the University of Maryland University College, examines some of the airport's problems with a view to the role played by systems engineering in the conception, design, development, and installation of the airport's baggage handling system. What principles from the systems engineering discipline could have been applied, and how might they have affected the outcome of the project?

A CASE STUDY: DENVER INTERNATIONAL AIRPORT

Background: What is the DIA? The Denver International Airport is one of the largest and most technologically advanced airports in the world. But the project encountered many delays, finally opening 16 months behind schedule on Feb. 28, 1995. After an initial budget of $1.5 billion, costs eventually escalated to $5.3 billion (Dempsey, Goetz, and Szyliowicz, 1997). Lawsuits, investigations by the FBI and SEC, and accusations of cronyism and influence peddling resulted as investors saw the status of their bonds degraded to junk. Design changes and failure to recognize risks are partly to blame. Many factors contributed to the cost overruns, including the millions of dollars of interest paid on revenue bonds before the airport was open to generate any income. One failure that prevented the airport from opening on time, in October 1993, was the baggage system. It may be useful to examine the systems engineering checkpoints in the development life cycle of the baggage system, to find out where application of systems engineering principles might have helped.

Planning the Airport: System Concept Definition. The Airlines Deregulation Act of 1978 caused many airlines to adopt a hub and spoke system. Denver in 1980 was a hub for three airlines, Frontier, Continental, and United, which brought low fares and increased passenger traffic. Air travel forecasting predicted demand for a new airport based on growth rates in 1986. The FAA was concerned that Stapleton airport's problems with congestion and bad weather would worsen under the forecasted passenger increase. However, by the time the new airport was begun in 1989, Frontier had disappeared, Continental was in financial difficulty, and passenger enplanements at Denver had started to decline. The FAA had projected a total of 55 million passengers for Denver in 1995. The reality turned out to be only 31 million (Dempsey et al., 1997). The airport had originally been envisioned as a hub for three airlines. It came into being as a hub for only United. United, along with Continental and the other airlines, strongly resisted plans for a new airport. This was due to the increased cost they would have to bear along with increased possible competition for fares. Although the airlines signed agreements with Denver in September 1985 to pay a certain proportion of the costs of a new facility, their opposition later increased (Dempsey et al., 1997). United refused to agree to lease gates at the new airport until well into the planning and construction. The design changes they then requested were a cause of cost overruns. Part of the system concept definition phase of a project includes a view of the system during its operation phase. United reached agreement with the city in June 1991, requiring various concourse modifications, and insisting on a fully automated baggage system (Dempsey et al., 1997). It was traditional in the U.S. before DIA for each airline to provide its own baggage system. It was not until late 1991 that the decision was made to have an airport-wide integrated baggage system. At this time the BAE Automated Systems company (BAE stood for Boeing Airport Equipment at the company's inception) already had a contract to build a baggage system for United at DIA. Ginger Evans, the head of contruction at DIA, said that plans for the baggage system came late because the airport had expected individual airlines to build their own systems (Rifkin, 1994).

The Project Management Team and Master Plan. Dick Veazy produced a master plan for the airport in 1986. Six consulting companies parceled out some 105 technical tasks. Nine consulting firms were hired by the City to review various aspects of the plan. In 1987, the City established a Project Management Team, awarding the $34 million contract to Greiner Engineering, Inc. (an engineering, architectural, and airport planning firm) and Morrison-Knudson Engineering (a design and construction firm). According to Dempsey et al. (1997), an Airline Airport Affairs Committee existed early in the design process which among its technical subcommittees included one focused on baggage.

System Requirements for the Baggage System. United has nearly 70% of the flights at Denver. Much of the traffic does not originate or terminate in Denver, but is on its way somewhere else – Denver is a hub for United. United needed to turn its aircraft around in 35 minutes. They wanted bags to be delivered from terminal to concourse (a distance of 3400 feet) in ten minutes, and between any two gates on the 3,300-foot-long concourse in under 6 minutes. This is a competitive factor for an airline, as shown by the Munich airport's guarantee of bag delivery from plane to baggage claim in eight and a half minutes. Time on the ground moving luggage can mean lost profits. Steve Steers, senior vice president of customer service for United Airlines, was quoted as saying that United demanded an automated cart baggage system because of the distance from the terminal to its concourse (Rifkin, 1994). In fact, the alternate conveyor belt and sorter system that Concourse C was using when the airport finally opened in 1995 worked so well that the tenant airlines opposed plans to expand the automated system there (Dempsy et al., 1997). Implicit in the concept of an integrated airport-wide system is the fact that putting all the bags in one system requires higher throughput rates than would be required by individual systems alone. Thus BAE was left with what president Gene Di Fonso called "unprecedented performance requirements" due to the distances involved, the amount of baggage, the delivery times, and its complete integration (Dempsey et al., 1997). Nothing like it had been attempted before. Requirements changes had some impact on the system. After the initial $195 million contract for Denver was given to BAE in early 1992, several changes were requested by the airlines. United, wanting to reduce costs, changed its Concourse B design from two complete loops of track to one. Later, requirements were changed to relocate outside stations, add a mezzanine baggage platform, and provide Continental a larger baggage link.

Interface Identification. Some of the difficulties encountered by BAE in implementing its system were apparently due to working in a facility under construction. Overloaded motors due to power interruptions, unreliable communications for engineers, and limited access due to construction were among the problems. Access to the baggage system venues was an issue when the City of Denver and BAE were considering lawsuits against each other. The new baggage system required changes in buildings already under way, in the form of structural penetrations, redesign of the electrical distribution system, coordination with the terminal contractor for curbside baggage check-in, and a new level in the landside terminal, Level 4A, to accommodate the steel tracks of the system (Dempsey et al., 1997). Any change in the airport design, such as relocation of an escalator, could have an undesirable effect on the baggage routing. An interface area that was better anticipated, and seemed to work out well, was the software interface with the airlines' reservation systems.

A Timeline for the DIA Baggage System. The following is a condensed timeline for events in the baggage system development, taken from Auguston(1995), Dempsey et al.(1997), and Knill (1994b). Dates are approximate

April 1990. Consultants recommend carts pulled by tugs for long hauls and belt conveyors for shorter distances. United is still opposed to the new airport and has not yet agreed to occupy the Concourse B designed for them.

August 1990. After consulting with Neidle Patrone Associates (BNP), the City decides to install a tug and cart system for the entire airport.

October 1990. The City writes to the Airlines Airport Baggage Subcommittee stating that airlines' requests to build their own systems will be considered if they do not jeopardize a future integrated system.

November 1990. United hires BAE to develop a baggage handling design for the United concourse only. Continental hires BNP to implement a high-speed conveyor belt system for Concourse A.

June 1991. The decision is made to make baggage handling an airport-wide function. United recommends BAE. Requirements are defined.

August 1991. DIA issues an RFP with target completion date October 1993.

Sept. 1991. Two consortiums, Harnischfeger Engineers and Sandvik, submit proposals. BAE submits a discussion paper but because of time pressures does not bid.

Oct. 1991. The City of Denver requests and receives a

schedule and cost estimate from BAE.

Nov. 1991. The Baggage Subcommittee writes to the City expressing concern about being able to complete the baggage system by mid-1994 as called for in the master project schedule.

Jan. 1992. BAE receives a contract for beginning the baggage system.

Aug. 1992, Sept. 1992, and March 1993. The City requests changes to the baggage system.

Oct. 1993. The airport opening is delayed, partly due to the baggage system.

Dec. 1993 and March 1994. Airport opening delays.

April 1994. The media are invited to watch a baggage test that fails; Germany's Logplan company is hired to monitor and review BAE's work (Rifkin, 1994).

May 1994. Airport opening delayed indefinitely.

Aug.-Sept. 1994. Denver's mayor orders installation of a conventional cart and tug system from Rapistan Demag as a temporary backup. The original plan for the baggage system is scaled back

Feb. 1995. The airport opens. The new baggage system serves only United's Concourse B.

In sharp contrast to the intended airport-wide automated baggage system, the opening day system is an amalgam of backup cart and tug service and parts of the automated system. In order to get the system working, the loop of track assigned to Concourse C is modified and linked to Concourse B. This increases the total number of carts and reduces the number of carts per second on each track by half, to lessen their speed and also to reduce the load on the software. Problem software is avoided by modifying the design, so that the system has continuously circulating carts which can be pulled off as needed, rather than dispatching the carts from queues as originally planned. The new automated system handles only baggage originating in Denver, for United. This is because outgoing baggage can be checked at a slower rate, while incoming baggage produces a flood of bags all at once. Baggage terminating in Denver, transfer baggage, and baggage for Continental and other airlines are served by the conventional backup system. Fig.1 compares the baggage system final cost of $248 million plus $63 million for the backup system, with its original planned cost of $193 million.

Fig. 1 Planned and Actual Cost of Baggage System

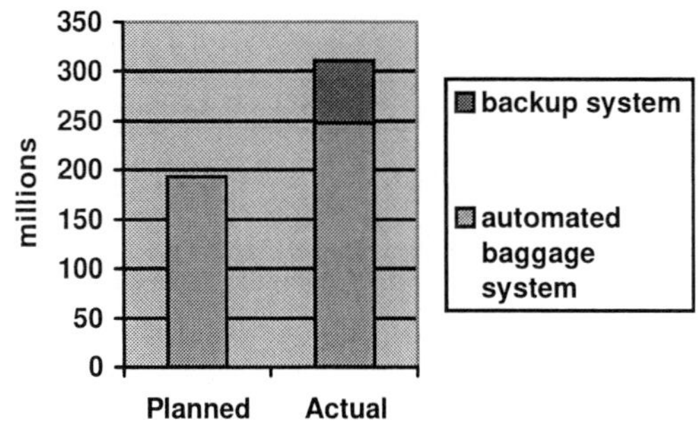

Description of Baggage System. BAE calls its automated baggage handling the Telecar system. It is like a miniature computer-controlled railroad, with 3,550 individual-bag carts (called DCV's for destination coded vehicles) running on tracks suspended from the ceiling in underground tunnels. Fins on the carts pass through slots in motors mounted under the tracks (Knill, 1994a). 5,000 of these linear induction motors pull the free-rolling carts along at up to 17 miles an hour, three to five times faster than conveyor belts. The system is designed to handle 700 bags per minute. Special larger carts accommodate skis and golf clubs. Loading and unloading occur automatically, slowing but never stopping the carts. The idea is to scan the bar-coded bag and transfer the information, along with a gate number, to a radio transponder tag on the cart. Then the bag can be individually tracked and rerouted quickly in case of a last minute gate change. Fig. 2 shows a layout of the Denver airport. The underground baggage system involves a complicated network of flows that must be tightly managed by the software (Auguston, 1994).

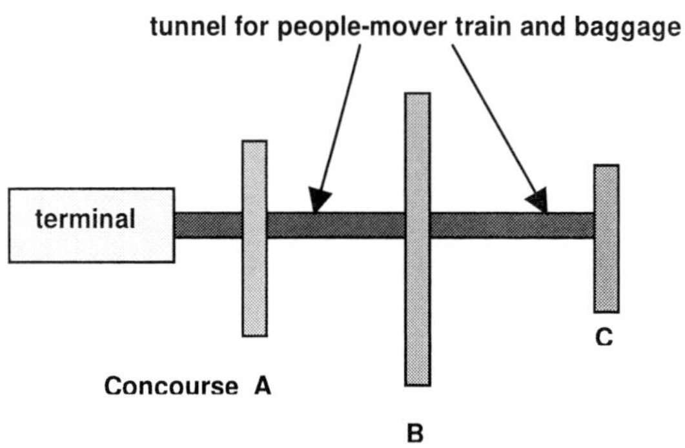

Fig. 2 Layout of Denver International Airport

the software.

System Design: Technical Risk Assessment Following a systems engineering methodology, the system design phase of a project would involve selecting a system architecture by developing alternatives and choosing the best feasible design. This stage includes technical risk analysis and mitigation plans. The DIA baggage handling system incorporated several technologies that were still to be proven, especially on a scale such as Denver's. Destination coded vehicles for single bags had been attempted and failed before in a BAE system for Pan Am at JFK Airport and in system for American at Dallas-Ft.Worth (DFW) Airport (Auguston, 1995). These systems were replaced with more conventional baggage systems. Single-bag carts were in operation successfully on a much smaller scale (184 carts to Denver's 3550) at the San Francisco Airport, where the system was built for United by Docutel. When Docutel ran into financial trouble, United asked Boeing to take over the company, which became Boeing Airport Equipment before Boeing allowed investors to buy it out. The San Francisco system uses simple tracking rather than sophisticated car management software. It does also use automatic loading and unloading, but again on a much smaller scale and at half the speed of the DIA system. And although the linear induction motor (LIM) system is a proven technology in other applications, and is used at the San Francisco Airport as well as airports in Atlanta and Singapore, LIM had never been used in an application the size and complexity of the system at DIA (Auguston, 1995). Denver used a consulting firm, Breier Neidle Patrone Associates, who reported operational and maintenance problems and high maintenance costs for the baggage systems at San Francisco, DFW and JFK (Dempsey et al., 1997). BAE was considered to be the top baggage handling company in the country, with the largest installed base of baggage handling systems and 26 years of experience. Even though most of their systems were belt conveyor or cart and tug systems, United wanted their new automated system for its concourse (Knill, 1994). The Harnishfeger consortium's bid would have used multi-bag carts with manual loading; the cart's destination would be determined at check-in; and the completion date was October 1994. Both the Harnishfeger and Sandvik bids were rejected, and BAE was persuaded to accept the job. As we have seen, the system encountered major difficulties. The mechanical problems caused luggage to be tossed and even mangled, and carts to be jammed. More magnets had to be added and modifications made to reduce vibrations, among other changes. One of the most serious delay-causing problems in the baggage handling system was the software.

The Empty Cart Management Problem. A major problem in materials handling applications such as a baggage handling system is the problem of line balancing. The goal is to provide good service to all lines. In the case of DIA, that means providing a sufficient supply of empty carts to each of the conveyor belts feeding bags into the system (Auguston, 1995). This, the software written at BAE was incapable of doing. That is due to one of the most basic tenets of software engineering: you have to understand how to solve the problem first, before you can implement the solution in software. The evidence that this was not the case with the automated baggage system can be seen in the fact that some of the original software was jettisoned. The plan of dispatching empty DCV's from a queue had to be abandoned after much trial and error, and was replaced with continuously circulating carts. How could this risk have been identified?

Handling the Risk of New Technology: Prototyping and Simulations. A version of the automated baggage handling system was prototyped in Dallas, Texas, where BAE is based (Knill, 1994b). But a prototype or simulation must be done in detail. "A cursory model does not expose the weak links in the system, which is the whole point of doing a simulation in the first place." (Richard de Neufville in Auguston, 1995). And it had been the opinion of Breier Neidle Patrone, an early consultant on the selection of the baggage system, that "with regard to the single bag DCV, considering the prototype stage, we strongly feel it is not capable of being implemented within the project schedule." (Knill, 1994e). An article by John Swartz (1997) describes his computer simulation of the DIA baggage system. Swartz`s results show a likely deadlock under loaded conditions. In fact, a year after DIA`s opening, it was still necessary to shut down the BAE baggage system being used for inbound bags when loads peaked. According to Swartz(1997), the original consulting firm also ran a simulation of the automated baggage system. Although they recommended against the single bag cart, they did not forward the simulation results to Denver or to the contactor (BAE).

Risk Mitigation: Backups and Contingency Plans. At the Pittsburgh International Airport, the US Air automated baggage system was not operational for months due to faulty bearings in a high-speed connecting conveyor (Auguston, 1994). But the passengers never knew it - conventional tug and cart systems filled the gap. By contrast, Denver waited until the airport's opening had been delayed three times - a 10 month period- before deciding to install a conventional tug and cart system for backup.

Integration and Test Plans. The Franz Joseph Strauss Airport, opened in Munich in May 1992, has a less complex system, involving conveyor belts. Technical advisors from that baggage system told Denver officials that they spent 2 years testing the system, which ran 24 hours a day for 6 months before the airport opened (Rifkin, 1994). An automated tray system at Frankfort took three years to debug. Backup equipment from a sorter manufacturer kept the system moving (Knill, 1994d). Yet in June of 1993, BAE wrote to the City of Denver that the baggage system installation would be complete by October 1993, and in September they assured the City that testing would be completed by December 1993 (Dempsey et al., 1997).

Role of Systems Engineering. In this case study, there was no systems engineering team to consider the airport as a whole, hence the failure to recognize baggage handling as a critical subsystem. There was also failure to recognize the risk of applying technologies in a scope and complexity never before attempted. Various consulting firms, including TRA Architecture, Engineering, Planning, Interiors, the firm of Neidle Patrone Associates (BNP), and Logplan, gave the City of Denver good advice. Perhaps the lack of a systems engineering team empowered to act globally on behalf of the airport was a factor in the City's failure to alter its course of action. Systems engineering for the baggage subsystem might have helped to highlight the inadequacy of the prototyping that was done, and the lack of feasibility studies. Bernie Knill, editor of *Material Handling Engineering*, analyzes it this way: "A system supplier and user who together lack understanding of, and experience in, real-time material handling software." (Knill, 1994b). One point that stands out is the mystery of software to many of the people involved in the project. As the systems architect and integration consultant for the new baggage handling tray system at Charles de Gaulle airport near Paris, Dave Tapley, said, "Industry has a habit of making mechanical choices first and then thinking that they can add complexity later through the software and controls." (Auguston, 1994). Although software has been called a craft and a creative work, as Ebert (1997) points out, all software is not the same. Techniques for approaching distinct domain specific problems would provide better quality. In particular, the software problem of this case study, empty cart management, was a known problem of the materials handling industry. Related algorithms were developed in installations such as computer-directed towline carts, automated guided vehicles and automated electrified monorails (Knill, 1994b). Perhaps here is an opening for domain engineering. Then the problem could have lent itself to standard engineering solutions, or if found to be breaking new ground, then the risk should have been apparent. It would have been the responsibility of the systems engineering team to see that this risk was properly addressed.

Conclusions. The role of systems engineering is most critical in the early, definition and design phases of a system. In Fig. 3, some of the points in the systems engineering development life cycle are shown. They are system concept defintion (SCD), requirements definition (RD), requirements analysis (RA), consideration of architecture alternatives (A), technical risk evaluation (RE) and risk mitigation plans (M). At these points in the DIA baggage system development, system engineering intervention might have headed off problems. The first priority, because of all the money invested, would have been to get the airport open on time. With the application of system engineering, that goal could have been achieved, either with a different baggage system, or with a redundant system in place to support the airport while development of the originally desired baggage system continued. DIA's automated baggage system is operating successfully today and BAE Automated Systems has gone on to complete another Telecar installation at Heathrow Airport.

Fig. 3 DIA Baggage System Case-in-point

Early concept definition prevents airport changes to accommodate baggage system (&vice versa); more time to develop system.	SCD
Analysis & quantification of user needs, i.e. speed, bags per minute, development of evaluation criteria may lead to other requirements.	RD
Requirements analysis may lead to consideration of other designs, i.e. multi-bag DCVs, belt systems.	RA
Baggage system was not like any that had been done before; does the technology exist and is it reliable?	RA, RE
Denver RFP: what are the critical technical issues?	SCD RE
Look at other airports (i.e. Frankfort, DFW, JFK, Munich, Pittsburgh) for problems, work-arounds.	RE, M
Cost/benefit analysis; $193 million for DIA vs. $34 million for Pittsburgh; what capabilities are needed?	SCD
Does cost/benefit analysis favor this configuration?	A

Can the performance requirements be satisfied by the candidate architecture: i.e. speed, distance, number of DCVs etc.	A
Is modeling and/or simulation needed to explore problems and demonstrate capabilities?	A, RE
Is there vulnerability in terms of airport opening?	RE, M

Reference list.

Auguston, K. (1994, October). A lesson in dealing with complexity. Modern Materials Handling 49(12), p.40.

Auguston, K. (1995, April). The Denver airport: now the audit begins. Modern Materials Handling 50(4), p.65.

Bozeman, J. (1994, October 10). United to simplify Denver's troubled baggage project. ComputerWorld 28(41), p.76.

Dempsey, P., Goetz, A., and Szyliowicz, J. (1997). Denver International Airport: Lessons Learned. New York: McGraw-Hill.

Ebert, C. (1997, November). The road to maturity: navigating between craft and science. IEEE Software 14, p.77-82.

Flynn, K., and Reina, P. (1995, November). Denver's baggage system finally nears finish. ENR 235, p.15.

Gibbs, W.(1994, September). Software's chronic crisis. Scientific American, pp.86-95.

Gottschalk, M. (1995, April). Denver airport finally in the bag. Design News 50(51), p.30.

Jackson, W.(1996, February 5). The star of Denver airport`s successful show is TRACON. Government Computer News 15(3), p.15. Available: Computer Database 18015092(IAC).

Knill, B. (1994a, July). Flying blind at Denver International Airport. Material Handling Engineering 49(7).

Knill, B. (1994b, August). Reality checks in to baggage handling system. Material Handling Engineering 49(8).

Knill, B. (1994c, September). New baggage handling solution. Material Handling Engineering 49(9).

Knill, B. (1994d, October). Baggage system: push comes to shove. Material Handling Engineering 49(10).

Knill, B. (1994e, November). Charges fly but bags don't move. Material Handling Engineering 49(11).

Knill, B. (1994f, December). Yes! February 28, 1995! Material Handling Engineering 49(12).

Phillips, E. (1994, August). Denver, United agree on baggage system fixes. Aviation Week & Space Technology.

Reuter, H. (1996, November). Denver's new airport has its problems. Flug Revue [Online], 6 paragraphs. Available: http: //flug-revue.rotor.com/FRheft/FRH9611/FR9611d.htm

Rifkin, G. (1994, August 29). What really happened at Denver's Airport. Forbes.

Schein, E. (1996, February 19). The Denver airport is still trying to get a handle on United baggage system. PC Week 13(7), p.14(1). Available: Computer Database 18015465(IAC).

Scott, W. (1995, February 27). Baggage system scores high on `stress test`. Aviation Week & Space Technology 142(9), p.37.

Swartz, J. (1997, January). Simulating the Denver airport automated baggage system. Dr. Dobb's Journal 22(1), p.56. Available: Computer Database 18960311(IAC).

BIOGRAPHY

Mrs. Cook has eleven years of programming experience in a commercial environment. She is currently a student in the Master of Software Engineering degree program at the University of Maryland University College.

Extending EIA-731 Systems Engineering Capability Model Appraisal Method for Safety and Tailoring the Method to Yellowstone National Park

Sam Alessi, U.S. Deparatment of Energy
850 Energy Drive, MS 1225
Idaho Falls, ID 83401
James A. Johnesee, Catherine M. Plowman
Bechtel BBXT Idaho, LLC
P.O. Box 1625, MS 3875
Idaho Falls, ID 83415-3875
Nelson Siler
Yellowstone National Park
P.O. Box 168
Yellowstone Park, WY 82190-0168

Abstract. Integrated safety management requires that safety be integrated with basic management and engineering practices. The objective of this work was to add safety to the EIA-731 Systems Engineering Capability Model Appraisal Method and thereby gain simultaneous and integrated findings. Safety appraisal information was gleaned from the Department of Energy, the Department of Interior, the Private Sector, the Occupational Safety and Health Administration, and other sources. This information was cast as a series of maturity-oriented questions and added to EIA-731. The integrated questionnaire was then tailored for application at Yellowstone National Park and the Idaho National Engineering and Environmental Laboratory. Results are not available at this writing due to delays in the scheduling of the appraisal, but will be included in a follow-up paper. The integrated Safety Systems Engineering Capability Model Appraisal incorporates general safety principles that are applicable to any industry interested in project management, systems engineering and safety.

THE PROBLEM

Yellowstone National Park has recently placed a safety manager in a senior leadership position. This is in response to fatalities and Occupational Safety and Health Administration violations. The Yellowstone National Park goal is to implement an Integrated Safety Management System, self-assessment systems, and appraisal systems that will result in the behavior change of the park employees and the management system. The problem is exacerbated by to the eroding infrastructure of the National Parks in general caused by the difficulty of obtaining infrastructure funding.

The Department of Energy Idaho Operations Office and Yellowstone National Park signed a Memorandum of Agreement to partner on issues relevant to both organizations. Through this Memorandum of Agreement, the Idaho National Engineering and Environmental Laboratory's expertise in systems engineering was proposed as a way to help address the multiplicity of Yellowstone National Park's issues in a systematic way. The first step in this approach was to observe the business and operations style of park staff and to understand priorities. This was accomplished through visits and discussions, and followed up with overview training in systems engineering principles.

The greatest need identified, due to outside pressure and an internal desire to improve, is for worker and visitor safety. In an effort to understand the current environment, the Team had the idea to simultaneously appraise the management, the work execution, the safety practices and the safety culture. To do this, it was proposed to integrate safety questions into the existing EIA-731 Appraisal Method and to then tailor the Method for use at Yellowstone National Park.

WHY USE MATURITY MODEL?

Unlike checklists and expert-driven appraisals, maturity models are more sophisticated in their use of combined quantitative and qualitative approaches. Maturity Models:

- Involve a questionnaire to provide reconnaissance measures,
- Involve focus groups and interviews for improved two-way communications and increased stakeholders involvement,
- Involve a facilitative appraisal team versus an expert judgement team,
- Provide two-dimensional benchmarks - resources and behaviors,
- Provide integrated training,
- Consider strategic planning principles.

Safety, a critical component of a mature work planning processes, provides strong support for the production of quality products and services. Existing maturity models have not adequately addressed safety issues nor has the nature of a mature and integrated safety system been well defined.

Maturity models drive improvement by identifying weaknesses relative to the process model and stakeholder comment, and then preparing and completing an action plan to satisfy the requirements stated in the model.

ELEMENTS OF SAFETY EXCELLENCE

The document *Elements of Safety Excellence* is based on the Amoco Corporation's *Template for a Safety Management System – Objectives and Indicator Measures*. These Elements provide the basis for the customer's safety program implementation.

The document *Elements of Safety Excellence* covers nine areas:

- Behavioral Skills
- Commitment and Leadership
- Communications
- Incident Investigation and Analysis
- Involvement, Roles, Responsibilities, and Accountability
- Performance Measurement and Assessment
- Policies, Standards and Procedures
- Risk Management and Evaluation
- Training

These elements are broken down into about fifty objectives with about two hundred indicators of success.

The four objectives that the Team concentrated on for the Safety Systems Capability Model Appraisal include:

- Utilize self-assessment tools and the Safety Improvement Cycle to develop actions plans for continuous improvement efforts (commitment and leadership),
- Establish methods for meaningful personal involvement in safety activities (involvement, roles, responsibilities, and accountability),
- Select relevant measures to track progress in safety activities (inputs) and in safety performance (outcomes) (performance measurement and assessment), and
- Present Senior Managers with alternative management approaches (value based, behavioral based, compliance based) to implementing and Integrated Safety Management System (training).

SAFETY EVALUATION PROFILE

The document *Safety Evaluation Profile* is based on International Paper Company's *Safety Evaluation Profile*, and was modified for use in the National Parks by a group of Safety Managers and Safety Personnel from the Pacific West Region, Grand Canyon National Park, and Yellowstone National Park.

The document *Safety Evaluation Profile* consists of eight elements:

- Demonstrated Management Leadership and Process Management
- Employee Involvement and Union Support
- Operational Analysis
- Prevention and Mitigation of Hazardous Conditions and Unsafe Work Practices
- Safety and Health Training
- Safety Programs
- Visitor Training
- Work Site Analysis

Each of the eight elements includes one or more programs. Examples include:

- Demonstrated Management Leadership and Process Management includes programs such as Accountability Systems, Action Plans, Demonstrated Management Involvement, and Safety Resources.
- Prevention and Mitigation of Hazardous Conditions and Unsafe Work Practices includes program such as Off-the-Job Safety, Preventive Maintenance Program, Project Planning, and Safety Performance Reinforcement.
- Safety Programs include programs such as the Electrical Safety Program, the Hazard Communication (right to know) Program, the Hearing Conservation Program, and the Personal Protective Equipment Program.
- Work Site Analysis includes programs such as Behavioral Job Analysis, General Work Site Inspections, and Incident Investigation and Analysis.

Safety and selected other personnel answer questions on each of the programs. The program information is then evaluated and ranked from one to five:

- One – the requirement has not been implemented.
- Two – there has been minimal implementation of the requirement, the program effectiveness has been minimal, and there are major opportunities for improvement.
- Three – there has been partial implementation of the requirement, the program is somewhat effective, and there are opportunities for improvement.
- Four – there has been full implementation of the program requirements, the program is effective, and there are some opportunities for improvement.
- Five – the program is highly effective and is an outstanding example because the continuing improvement process is on going.

The Systems Engineering Capability Model Appraisal formed the basis for the Safety Systems Engineering Capability Model Appraisal.

SYSTEMS ENGINEERING CAPABILITY MODEL

The Systems Engineering Capability Model and the associated Appraisal Method is described in EIA/IS-731.2.

The Appraisal Method compares the organization's project performance and its systems engineering capabilities, against generic characteristics and specific practices.

This Appraisal Method was selected by the Team because it:

- Reduces the barriers to organization wide process development,
- Provides a publicly accessible method to acquire capability baselines, and industry and product independent comparative information,
- Baselines the efforts and successes to date,
- Supports continuous process development, and
- Can be performed as an in house self-appraisal or conducted with the assistance of an outside organization.

The Team established the purposes of the Appraisal Method:

- To establish the organization's baseline,
- To identify specific areas for improvement based upon known deficiency areas,
- To obtain buy-in for changes in the organization,
- To confirm process improvement progress, and
- To determine the new baseline during second or subsequent appraisals.

The Team also identified these assumptions in the Appraisal Method:

- The System Engineering Capability Model, described in EIA/IS-731.1, is the standard,
- The Appraisal Team Members have been trained in basic organizational appraisal techniques, and
- The focus and tone is on self-improvement and not on audit.

The Team modified the Appraisal Method to:

- Better meet the objectives of the customer's organization,
- Include all the appraisal areas in the initial appraisal,

- Select the appraisal areas of greatest significance or those targeted for process improvement, and
- Concentrate on any cohesive unit, program or project.

The Appraisal Method continues to consist of a number of steps in four phases:
- Pre-Appraisal Phase,
- Preparation Phase,
- On-Site Phase, and
- Post-Appraisal Phase

PRE-APPRAISAL PHASE

The Pre-Appraisal Phase included these steps:
- Obtain Appraisal Sponsor Commitment - this step established the Appraisal Sponsor's commitment to the appraisal, and determined the goals and objectives of the appraisal.
- Select Appraisal Parameters - this step tailored the process and the products to meet the Park's goals and objectives.

PREPARATION PHASE

The Preparation Phase consisted of these steps:
- Plan Appraisal Details – this step produced, and obtained approval of, the Appraisal Plan.
- Familiarize Team with Appraisal Method – this step prepared the members of the Appraisal Team for performing their roles.
- Collect Questionnaire Information – this step obtained and recorded the information.
- Analyze Questionnaire - this step developed the exploration questions for the interviews and the exploratory topics for the focus groups.

At this point, the first tailoring effort took place.

APPRAISAL TAILORING

The Safety Systems Engineering Capability Model Appraisal Questionnaire still consists of three sections: a Technical Section, a Management Section, and an Environment Section.

The Technical Section is divided into seven focus areas. Examples of these areas are Define Stakeholder and Systems Level Requirements, Define Solution, Integrate System, Verify System, and Validate System. Each of these focus areas is divided into one or more theme areas.

The Define Technical Problem focus area includes the theme areas of Problem Refinement, Requirements Analysis, Requirements Quality, Requirements Evolution and Maintenance, and Feedback and Verification. The Assess and Select focus area includes the theme areas of Selection of Appropriate Decision making Techniques, Consideration of Alternatives, Evaluation Criteria, and Selection and Communication of Alternatives.

The Management Section, originally divided into eight focus areas, now has nine focus areas. Examples of these focus areas are Plan and Organize, Integrate Disciplines, Manage Risk, Management Information, Manage Configuration, and Ensure Quality.

The Monitor and Control focus area contains the theme areas of Degree of Formality, Monitoring, and Thresholds Exceeded. The Coordinate with Suppliers focus area contains the theme areas of Outsourced Work Product Identification, Supplier Selection, Work Product and Activity Definition, and Supplier Management.

The Environment Section, originally divided into four focus areas, is now divided into six focus areas. Examples of these focus areas are: Define and Improve the Process, Manage Technology, and Manage the Support Environment. The Manage Competency focus area contains the theme areas of the Learning Environment, Competency Needs, Knowledge Delivery to Programs, and Competence Assessment and Achievement.

To meet the objectives (increase the visibility of the safety process, safety leadership, and safety communications) of the Yellowstone National Park's Safety Manager, three focus areas were added to the Appraisal. These focus areas are based on the current Safety Model at the Park.

Yellowstone National Park's Safety Model strives to ensure that the safety and the safety of the processes being used to create the program. These processes include the establishment of safety goals and their subsequent measurement and analysis, and then the implementation of corrective actions to attain the goals.

In the Management Category, Section 2.9 – Ensure Safety, was added. Based on discussions with the Safety Manager, three theme areas were added to the standard Fundamentals, and Effectiveness and Utility Ratings.

- Leadership Involvement
- Safety Process
- Tools and Techniques

The Park's Safety Model is based on the fact that an effective safety management system starts with the demonstrated commitment of senior management to achieve excellence performance, along with the willingness and ability to personally lead this effort. Senior managers define what the expectations of management are (the roles), what they will do to fulfill those expectations (actions), how they will be measures and held accountable (performance outcomes), and how other can assist in this effort. In addition, there must be opportunities for others in the organization to become involved in leadership roles, including participation by all levels of employees

In the Environment Category, Section 3.5 - Demonstrate Leadership, was added. After discussing this with the Safety Manager, twenty-four theme areas were added to the standard Fundamentals, and Effectiveness and Utility Ratings.

- Establish and Communicate Vision
- Consistent Philosophy
- Self-Assessment
- Allocate Resources
- Visible Involvement
- Health Performance Indicator
- Safety Outcome Accountability
- Atmosphere
- Assess Effectiveness of Existing Safety Communication
- Behavior Training
- Behavior Observations
- Coaching
- Select Measures
- Establish Measures
- Target Levels
- Tracking and Assessment
- Audit Process
- High Quality Audits
- Encourage High Level Audit
- Utilize Audit Results
- Root Cause
- Quality of Incident Investigation
- Reporting of Near Misses
- Create Expectation

Yellowstone National Park's Safety Model is based on the belief that successful safety results depend on a free flowing, two-way communication between management and the employees. Management communicates the vision, the mission, the values, and the expectations; and provides general policy and direction regarding safety. Individuals raise issues for consideration, make suggestions, and provide feedback regarding the clarity and understanding of management's communication.

To support this belief, Section 3.6 – Communicate Effectively, was also added to the Environment Category. The Safety Manager identify two themes to add to the standard Fundamentals, and Effectiveness and Utility Ratings:

- Safety and Health Communications
- Area Quality Circles

Working together, the Team came up with the addition questions for these theme areas Examples of these questions include:

- Are work products ever evaluated against safety requirements? (level 1)
- Are safety improvement tools and equipment used to reduce incidents and improve worker safety? (level 1)
- Is management's role in safety improvement activities communicated? (level 1)
- Does management appear to believe in its safety vision? (level 2)
- Is training provided on the use of advanced safety improvement tools and equipment? (level 2)
- Is responsibility for project/work/product safety activities and program team improvements assigned? (level 2)
- Is an environment created that encourages employee participation in identifying, reporting, and solving safety issues? (level 2)
- Is process established to detect the need for safety oriented corrective actions? (level 2)
- Are the safety assurance processes evaluated for adherence to standards and policies

throughout the life of the program/project/work? (level 3)
- Are work products periodically evaluated against safety requirements? (level 3)
- Are safety lessons learned fed back into program/project/work processes for robustness of future designs? (level 4)
- Does the organization eliminate the causes of defects by changing the standard process for safety assurance? (level 4)

After this tailoring is completed, the next step is to convene a group of safety subject matter experts (from industry, the unions, and the work floor) and to reach a consensus on the question content and level, and the process maturity baselines targets for successful organizations.

Discussions with the customer also lead to the definition and description of evaluation criteria

EVALUATION CRITERIA

Four measures of success, based on the Elements of Safety Excellence formed the evaluation criteria:

- Self-assessment is line driven, using cross-functional Teams.
- Employees are involved in the development, communication, and execution of safety programs, processes and systems. The process is employee driven.
- Private providers of safety systems are invited to present their continuous improvement process to the staff.
- Baseline assessment of the safety system is established utilizing the Safety Profile Evaluation.

PRELIMINARY OBSERVATIONS AND CONCLUSION

The study has already made contributions to two measures of success:

- The Team presented the Safety System Engineering Capability Model Appraisal to the Staff
- The baseline assessment is being revised so that it is also based on the Safety Systems Engineering Capability Model Appraisal.

Results are not available at this writing due to delays in the scheduling of the appraisal, but will be included in a follow-up paper.

BIOGRAPHY

Dr. R. Sam Alessi is the Systems Engineering Program Lead at the Department of Energy, Idaho Operations Office. He is responsible for fostering the systems engineering capability achievement, assessment, and enhancement within the Department of Energy. His specific goals include improving the Idaho National Engineering and Environmental Laboratory's (INEEL's) integration and work proficiency, supporting the environmental management and nuclear energy mission areas, utilizing systems engineering to bring work to the INEEL, and helping to integrate and define the INEEL. Previously, Sam utilized systems engineering with the United States Department of Agriculture before coming to the INEEL in 1997. He has a Ph.D. in Soil Physics with continuing Systems Engineering education. He currently contributes leadership as Region I Director and Department of Energy advisory member for Academia and Government of the International Council on Systems Engineering. He is a member of the Department of Energy Wide Systems Engineering Process Group and is the Department of Energy representative on the Software Engineering Institute/Department of Defense Capability Maturity Modeling Integration Project. He has published numerous systems engineering papers, and has adjunct professor status with the University of Idaho where he teaches a graduate course on requirements inquiry.

Nelson Siler, Si as he likes to be called, is currently the Safety Manager at Yellowstone National Park. Si is a 33-year veteran of the National Park Service. His first 17 years were spent as a Field Ranger responsible for structural and wildland fire, safety, emergency medical services, search and rescue, and law enforcement at Redwoods, Crater Lake, Grand Canyon, Hot Springs, and Yosemite National Parks. For the last 15 years, Si has been a full time Safety Manager servicing at Yosemite, Sequoia, and Kings Canyon and as the Regional Safety Manager for the Intermountain Region and the Support System Safety Office in Santa Fe, New Mexico. As a Safety Manager, Si has worked with field managers in development and implementing various safety management systems and processes for employees and visitors. Si has been focused on leading safety change around a performance management system and continuous safety improvement.

Catherine Plowman has worked at the Idaho National Engineering and Environmental Laboratory since 1995. She is leading the Systems Sciences Group, and has managed the Department of Energy's Partnership in Systems Engineering Excellence. Prior to that, she worked at the NASA's Johnson Space Center in Houston, Texas, developing Space Station simulations, and providing Systems Engineering expertise to organizational development initiatives. She holds a Bachelor of Science in Aerospace Engineering and a Bachelor of Science in Computer Science from Texas A&M University, and has been working as a Systems Engineering since 1985.

Jim Johnesee is a scientist/engineer in the Systems Sciences Group at the Idaho National Engineering and Environmental Laboratory. He works with both external and internal customers in eliciting expectations; defining, describing, and validating requirements; preparing specifications and project plans; monitoring and reporting work; and verifying the results. His projects include the environmental and energy areas, and range from basic science through product deployment. He holds degrees from the United States Naval Academy, Georgia Institute of Technology, and New Hampshire College; and has worked both safety and other maturity appraisals and self –assessments for the Department of the Navy and the Department of Energy.

Propulsion Control of Aircraft: A Case Study in Systems Engineering

Robert A. Johnson
University of Maryland, University College
3818 Charles Avenue
Alexandria, VA 22305

ABSTRACT

On July 19, 1989 United Airlines Flight 232 was cruising at approximately 37,000 feet between Denver and Minneapolis when it experienced a catastrophic failure of the number two (tail-mounted) engine. At the moment of failure the engine ejected shrapnel through the tail section, destroying all three on-board hydraulic systems. The complete loss of hydraulics left the pilots of the McDonnell Douglas DC-10 aircraft without the ability to move the flight controls. In contrast to what most aviation experts would have expected as an outcome, the airplane was crash-landed at Sioux City, Iowa with 185 of the 296 passengers and crew surviving. The flight crew was able to maintain rudimentary control of the aircraft with only the use of thrust from the two remaining wing-mounted engines by independently moving their respective power levers. It was not until the final touchdown that the crew's command of the aircraft was lost due to the imprecise nature of manual propulsion control (Propulsion Controlled Aircraft [PCA], 1999).

Following the accident, the National Transportation Safety Board (NTSB) recommended that Propulsion Control of Aircraft (PCA) be evaluated as a "pilot friendly" backup system using engine thrust as the only actuating mechanism in the case of primary flight control failure. This paper examines the use of systems engineering to effectively decompose the problem, identify the solution set, and integrate the solution with the potential for improved safety and reduced life cycle costs. An overview of aircraft flight dynamics and primary control systems is provided in order to understand the basic system properties. Analysis includes physical systems as well as software systems and their interface. Finally, the use of simulation to better understand system behavior and mitigate risk while arriving at a system-based solution is examined (Blanchard, 1998). Control the aircraft in flight after a primary flight control failure and accomplish that with an interface which is intuitive to the pilot, that is the problem. The solution could only have been reached through systems engineering.

DEFINING THE PROBLEM

In the case of Propulsion Control of Aircraft, the NTSB provided the statement of need following the Sioux City crash encouraging, "research and development of backup flight control systems ... that utilize an alternate source of motive power separate from that source used for the conventional control system" (Accident Report NTSB, 1989). The National Aeronautics and Space Administration (NASA) then took the lead and proceeded toward a problem definition. NASA defined the problem in the following manner: "There is no satisfactory method onboard the aircraft for effectively controlling the aircraft with a disabled primary flight control system" (Blake, et al., 1995). NASA also stated, "Manual throttle control of engines is extremely difficult because of pilot unfamiliarity with dynamic response of the aircraft in this mode" (Blake,et al. 1995). Identifying that the aircraft's dynamic response with propulsion inputs was different than with flight control inputs was where NASA began to move from problem definition to problem decomposition.

Using the "V" Model as a Systems Life Cycle Template. NASA's published report does not indicate that they set out to use the "V" model as the specific systems life cycle methodology for their development. However, the top down/bottom up process approximates the processes NASA documented in successfully designing and testing a PCA system. Therefore, when possible, this paper will align NASA's process to the "V" model in order to support the use of the "V" model as an effective methodology to arrive at complex system solutions.

The Airplane as a System. An airplane is an exquisite example of numerous subsystems grouped together, synergistically exchanging inputs and outputs in order to achieve a single purpose – controlled flight. A conventional airplane (like most complex systems) can be decomposed into many subsystems and to do so may help define the scope of the solution. In this case, the pursuit of the System Concept Definition must include how the airplane normally flies as well as how it is made to fly with propulsion inputs only.

Primary Flight Control. The normal control of an aircraft in flight is accomplished by the pilot's manipulation of three basic control surfaces: the rudder, the elevators, and the ailerons. The ailerons are hinged panels that are integrated into the trailing edge near the outboard end of each wing. When displaced through pilot input the ailerons are deflected up on one side and down on the other, resulting in an increase in lift on one side with decrease in lift on the opposite side. This causes the aircraft to rotate about its longitudinal axis, or to roll.

The elevators are the hinged panels that are integrated into the trailing edges of the horizontal stabilizer at the tail of the airplane. The movement of the elevator surface up or down by the pilot results in the aircraft's rotation about its horizontal axis, or pitching motion, resulting in climbs and descents.

Finally, the aircraft's rudder is the hinged panel that is integrated into the trailing edge of the vertical stabilizer at the aircraft's rear. Movement of the rudder by the pilot will cause the aircraft to rotate about its vertical axis, or yaw. The pilot uses the rudder to balance asymmetric aerodynamic forces generated at the wings and to align the aircraft with the runway during takeoff and landing.

Propulsion Flight Control. Through the use of propulsion the aircraft can be controlled in flight—but in an entirely different manner. To achieve movement around the aircraft's horizontal axis, propulsion is symmetrically added to or subtracted from engines. This accelerates or decelerates both wings at the same time. Accelerating or decelerating the aircraft symmetrically will result in a symmetric increase or decrease in lift. The associated increase or decrease in lift will result in a proportional pitch up and climb or pitch down and descent, thus emulating the control of the elevator. Movement about the longitudinal and vertical axes occurs through the use of asymmetric thrust application. On the side that thrust is added initially, the aircraft yaws about its vertical axis. The yawing of the aircraft creates a sideslip favoring the presentation of the wing on the side of the added thrust and equally reducing the presentation of the opposite wing. The favored wing generates additional lift with decreased lift to the opposite wing and a resultant roll about the aircraft's longitudinal axis. Any steady state bank angle created by a roll about the aircraft's longitudinal axis will result in a turn in just the same way that a turn results from using the aircraft's ailerons.

Figure 2 (attached) helps to illustrate the normal and PCA flight control dynamics.

CONCEPT TO DESIGN

A new system connecting the pilot to the aircraft allowing the airplane to be flown with propulsion alone had its "humble beginning from a rough sketch on a TWA napkin that Dryden Engineer, Frank Burcham, drew on a flight to St. Louis for a McDonnell Douglas Aerospace (MDA) meeting" (Propulsion Controlled Aircraft (PCA), 1995). The design drawn on a napkin took the pilot's inputs and put them through a flight control computer to the two engines with aircraft response feedback provided back to the flight control computer. "The intent of the Dryden program was to develop a computer-assisted engine control system that lets a plane fly safely with engine-only power" (PCA, 1995).

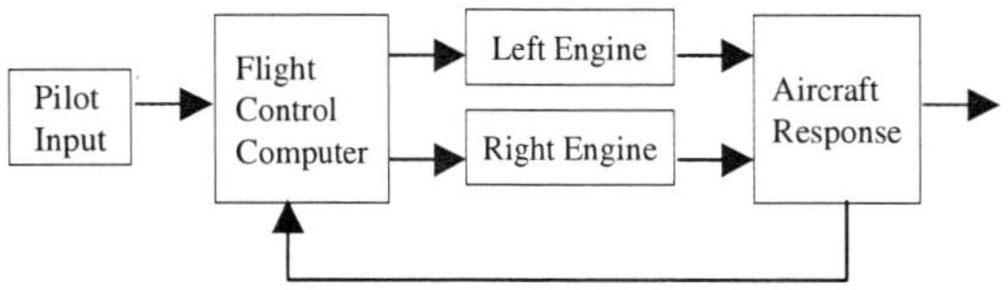

Figure 1. Burcham's PCA Design

Control Laws and Feedback Loops. In assessing an aircraft's handling qualities, the aircraft's responses are evaluated by its movements around its axes. The aircraft's movement around its horizontal axis, referred to as pitching movement, is defined in flight test as "longitudinal" flight characteristics. An aircraft's characteristics about the longitudinal and vertical axis, referred to as roll and yaw respectively, tend to be dynamically coupled in flight. Due to this dynamic coupling, in flight test they are grouped together and referred to as lateral-directional flight characteristics. "PCA control laws provide aircraft longitudinal flight control through parallel throttle movement fore and aft to control climb or descent flight path. PCA control laws provide aircraft lateral-directional flight control through asymmetric throttle movement to control bank angle" (Blake, et al. 1995). Aircraft feedback data included: track and bank angles; roll, yaw, pitch, climb, and descent rates; pitch attitude, altitude, and airspeed (Blake, et al., 1995). This feedback data is obtained through outputs from gyros and air data computers used by the aircraft's navigation/avionics subsystems. Control law structure and gains were developed using an analytical model of the aircraft and MATLAB® Control System Toolbox. NASA's use of existing subsystems highlights the need for broad technical expertise in the design process and the necessity for awareness of adjacent subsystem structure in the event that adjacent subsystems can be used in the solution set.

Keeping the Pilot in the Loop. The pilot is viewed as a vital subsystem to aircraft operation. Consideration for the pilot's operation as the user was given early in the design process through simulation and evaluation of system interface design. The pilot's inclusion early in the design process also focuses on the "user requirements" element of Concurrent Engineering (Mackey, 1999) and mitigates the risk of user-generated design changes later in the system engineering process. Although the pilot has been referred to as "non-linear, time variant and adaptive" (Ohmit, 1996), the human factors consideration made by NASA during the design phase lessened the need for the pilot to be adaptive to the system being designed.

Simulation in the Design Process. In the context that simulation utilizes "an operational model of a system to conduct experiments," it also mitigates risk and provides an environment to evaluate pilot interaction with the planned control system as well as evaluate the control system characteristics (Blanchard, 1998). Both NASA Dryden and NASA Ames Research facilities conducted piloted simulation tests relatively early in the design phase to evaluate PCA control laws, pilot interface and PCA display requirements. Early simulation can help the systems design team determine if early choices in system's requirements and design are going to lead to accomplishing what the statement of need asks. NASA's use of simulation helped refine the PCA subsystem design and led to significant improvement in the control laws, as well as the selection of the standard autopilot control interface versus a sidestick controller. Through simulation NASA also validated the choice of controller that the pilot would use to interface with the airplane in PCA flight.

Configuration Item (CI) Importance. In the context that a CI is an end item component that is "accepted, purchased, controlled and maintained" (Mackey, 1999), it may be a standard item such as a computer chip, circuit board, or software module. However, when a new system requires human interface the importance of the interfacing CI cannot be overemphasized. The systems engineer "must choose the types of systems installed on the aircraft, their operating modes, the resolutions required for each system and the operator interface required to allow the aircrew to best use the system" (Gordon, et al., 1995). It is the operator interface viewed as a CI that could (and in this case did) have its consideration brought into the system development process as early as the system design phase.

TESTING AND INTEGRATION

"In the true sense, a complete evaluation of the system, in terms of meeting the initially specified consumer requirements, cannot be accomplished until the system is produced and functioning in the operational environment" (Blanchard, 1998). In the case of PCA, NASA mitigated risk and enhanced the design process by using simulation testing early in the design process. However, to prove the concept and pave the way for industry acceptance, PCA had to be test flown.

Simulation in the Testing Process. The simulation testing that NASA initiated early in PCA development could be compared to what Blanchard refers to as "Type 1 testing" which is for the primary purpose of testing design, or in this case, control laws. Blanchard also refers to "Type 2 testing" which is accomplished later in detail design and in NASA's simulation included control law refinement and evaluation of the pilot to system interface.

Pilot Interface Testing. "The objective of pilot interface testing was to compare two PCA controllers – 1) sidestick controller, and 2) thumbwheel controller" (Blake, et al., 1995). As the sidestick controller's name implies, it uses a standard sidestick to allow the pilot to command roll rate and flight path angle rate. The thumbwheel controller consisted of a knob to control roll and a thumbwheel to control flight path angle and was, in fact, a standard autopilot control panel. The benefit gained by NASA in using pilot (user) testing allowed the subsystem design effort to bridge from system design to configuration item development while at the same time providing valuable test data for subsystem refinement.

The "Cooper Harper" Pilot Rating Scale. As important as any agreed upon system or subsystem requirement, NASA had to also quantify the level of difficulty in using PCA, not merely from the perspective of the controls manipulated by the pilot but also by the level of difficulty for the pilot to successfully control and land an aircraft using PCA. The test and evaluation standard which NASA used was the "Cooper Harper" Pilot rating scale, named for its authors: George E. Cooper of NASA Ames Research Facility, and Robert P. Harper, Jr. of Cornell Aeronautical Laboratory. The Cooper-Harper Pilot Rating Scale allows the pilot to use a corrective action loop to make an objective evaluation of an aircraft's handling qualities while executing a specific task. After completing the evaluation loop the pilot can then arrive at a numerical value which quantifies the level of difficulty in completing the task (Figure 3 attached, Cooper & Harper, 1969). The use of numerical weighting in the test and evaluation process allows the systems engineering team to make selections or determine the need for design change in a quantitative manner.

Its is important to note that the use of the rating scale is related to the pilot making an evaluation of the aircraft while performing a *specific* flight task. In a more generic sense the test and evaluation of any system that requires human interface should be performed in a manner related to the required task or tasks that will be demanded of the completed system in its operating environment. This evaluation should also be done by a member of the target population of users as was done in this case by NASA. Additionally, the ability to quantify the level of difficulty of the tasks as they are accomplished by the test population helps to reduce subjectivity in the evaluation process.

Product Integration. Although initial flight testing was successfully accomplished on NASA Dryden's F-15 test aircraft in April 1993, product integration can be considered to have been completed with the successful flights of the McDonnell Douglas MD-11 (August 1995) where a standard aircraft autopilot panel was used as the pilot-to-system interface for PCA landings. McDonnell Douglas Aircraft has developed and implemented PCA control laws for the MD-11 jet transport, but PCA has not been universally embraced by the jet transport industry as a necessary aircraft subsystem.

POTENTIAL INDUSTRY BENEFITS AND MONETARY PREDICTION

A NASA study was conducted for a 30-year life cycle of a fleet of 300 aircraft in the category of 400,000 lb. take-off gross weight. It assumed that PCA eliminated mechanical backup systems, training costs are not changed, PCA will save one aircraft during that 30-year life cycle and a five percent insurance savings is realized (Blake, et al., 1995). The results of that study are presented in Table 1.

Safety	Eliminate catastrophic accidents due to loss of primary flight control	
Economic	◆ Weight reductions	$295M
	◆ Insurance Savings	42M
	◆ Saved Airplane	110M
	◆ PCA Certification Costs	(10M)
	Total Life Cycle Savings	$436M

Table 1. Projected Industry Benefits

SUMMARY

Relating the process to the "V" model, NASA engaged the problem top-down by looking at the aircraft as a dynamic grouping of subsystems, and by evaluating user requirements. They were able to progress through preliminary and detailed design to effective testing and implementation of the system solution.

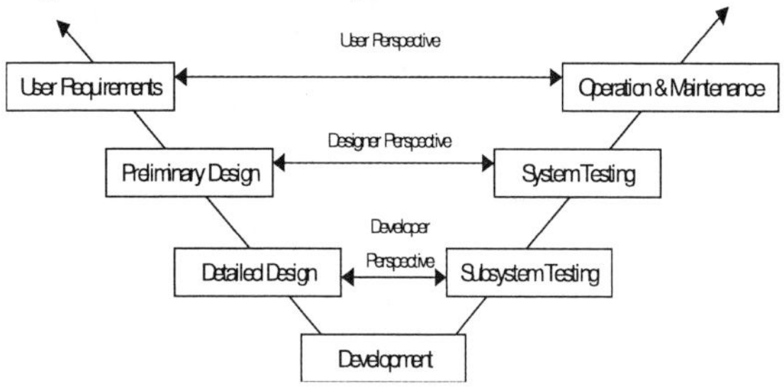

Figure 4. "V" Model(Blanchard, 1998).

As a case study in systems engineering PCA could not have been accomplished in any other manner that could have better answered the "statement of need." NASA's solution set utilized simulation to prototype and test control laws and pilot interface design. NASA carefully and scientifically proceeded through the system development process enabling them to integrate and successfully test fly PCA in F-15 and MD-11 aircraft. So then, why doesn't every transport jet flying today have some form of PCA as a backup system? It could only be suggested that it is attributable to the fact that the NTSB—and not the airline industry—identified the need. Without a perceived need on the part of the parent industry PCA may never be more than an excellent example of a problem solved through the effective use of systems engineering.

REFERENCES

Accident Report NTSB Identification: DCA89MA063, United Airlines Flight 232, Sioux City, Iowa, July 19, 1989. (1989). [On-line]. Available: www.ntsb.gov/aviation/dca/89A063

Blake, M., Bryant, D., Bull, J., Conley, J., Davis, G., Gibson, J., Hardy, G., Mah, R., & Williams, D. (1995). Piloted Simulation Tests of Propulsion Control as Backup to Loss of Primary Flight Controls for a Mid-Sized Jet Transport. NASA Technical Memorandum 110374 (pp. 1-30) [On-line]. Available: http://airlinepilots.com/safety/safety014.htm

Blanchard, B. (1998). System Engineering Management. The Use of Simulation in System Engineering (2nd ed., pp.189). New York: Wiley & Sons.

Burcham, F., Fullerton, C., Gilyard, G., Stewart, J., & Wolf, T. (June 1991). Investigation of the Use of Throttles for Emergency Flight Control. AIAA-91-2222.

Burcham, F., Maine, T., & Wolf, T.(1993). Flight Testing and Simulation of an F-15 Airplane Using Throttles for Flight Control. AIAA 92-4109-CP.

Cooper, G., & Harper, R. (1969). The Use of Pilot Rating in the Evaluation of Aircraft Handling Qualities. NASA Technical Note TN D-5153 (pp. XX-XX). Washington, D.C.

Gelhausen, P. (1993). Benefits Assessment. PCA Workshop, NASA Dryden.

Gordon, V., Landmann, M., Lenahan, T., & Masters, G. (1995). Systems Testing. U.S. Naval Test Pilot School Manual No. 109. (pp. 1-1–1-10). Naval Air Warfare Center Aircraft Division, Patuxent River, Maryland.

Mackey, W. (1999). SEAS Training Program. SSDN System Development Life Cycle Model. (Class Notes, Unpublished)

Ohmit, E.(1996). Advanced Flight Control System. Lecture Series Calspan Corporation, U.S. Naval Test Pilot School, Unpublished.

Propulsion Controlled Aircraft. (1999). [On-line]. Available: http//eudoxus.usc.edu/pca/pca.html

Propulsion Controlled Aircraft: 1995 NASA Nominee for National Invention of the Year. (1995). [On-line]. Available: www.dfrc.nasa.gov/projects/pca/index.html

Richards, R. (1993). Introduction to Flight Controls. U.S. Naval Test Pilot School Class Notes. Naval Air Warfare Center Aircraft Division, Patuxent River, Maryland.

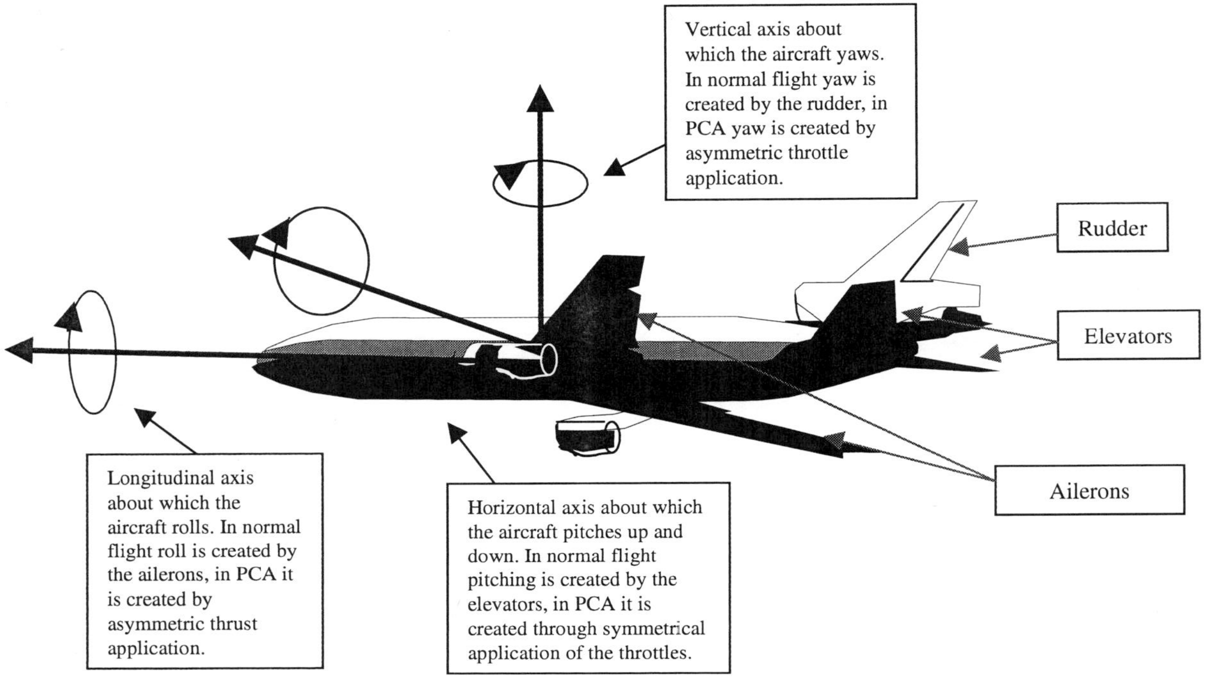

Figure 1. Flight Control Dynamics

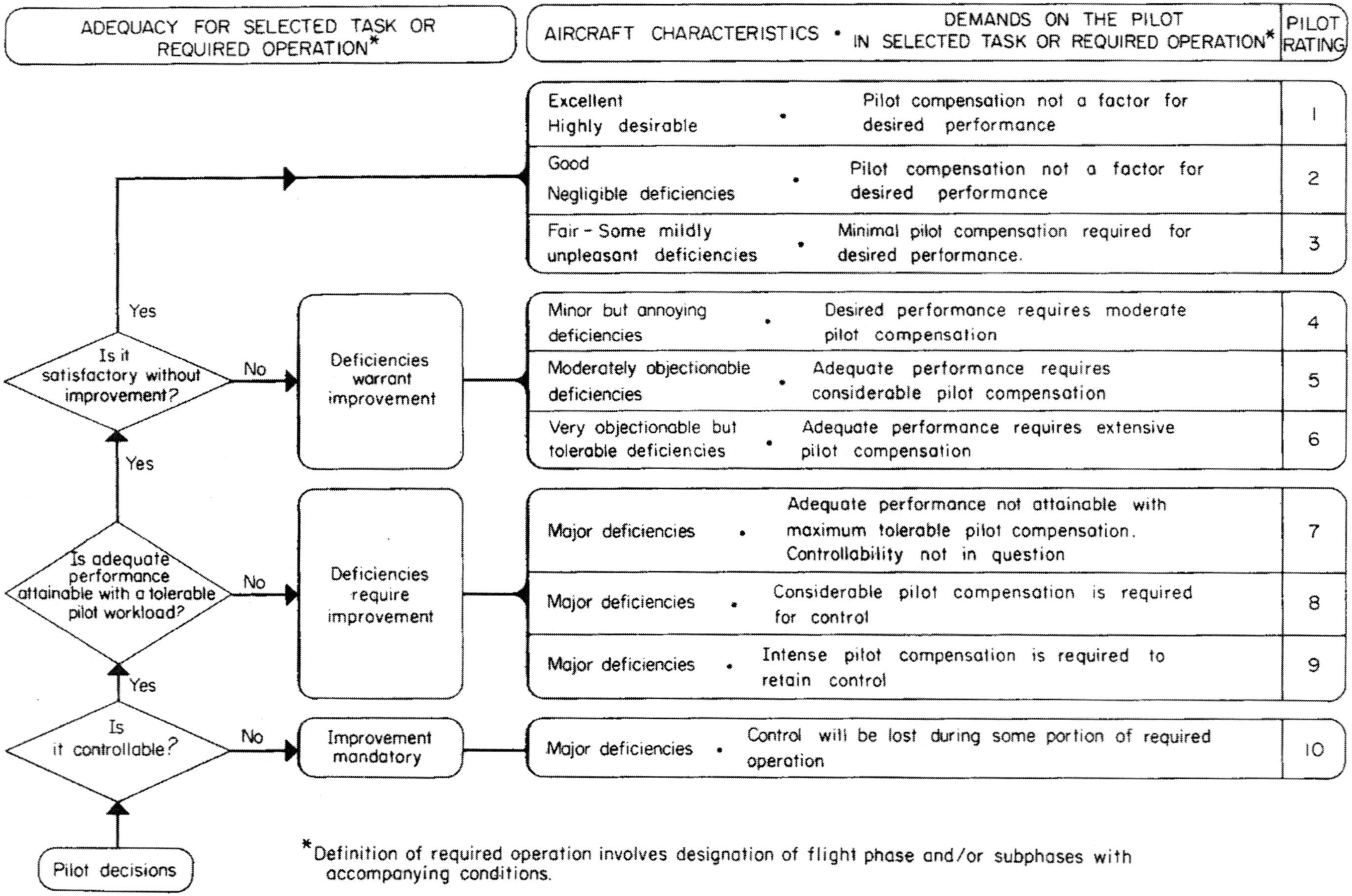

Figure 3. Handling Qualities Rating Scale

Teaming for Teaching: Producing Effective Systems Engineers for the 21st Century

Joseph Kasser
Systems Engineering and Evaluation Centre (SEEC)
University of South Australia
School of Electrical and Information Engineering
The Levels Campus, Building F.
Mawson Lakes, South Australia, 5095

Abstract. As we enter the 21st century, the demands on our technological personnel are greater than ever. Universities wishing to meet this growing demand for education in systems engineering are facing a scarcity of qualified seasoned systems engineers who can teach the topic. This gap between the need and the capability to train personnel is not an easy one to fill. This paper applies an industrial solution to the problem faced by individual universities, namely synergistic teaming to provide educational opportunities greater than those can could be provided by the individual institutions.

INTRODUCTION

As we enter the 21st century, the demands on our technological personnel are greater than ever. For example:

- Major government funded systems development has traditionally been characterized by cost and schedule overruns and other (spectacular) failures.
- Employers need effective systems engineers to meet the demands of producing modern complex systems within the constraints of schedule and budget.
- Building modern complex systems or "systems of systems" and other systems with international subcontracts and partners requires that the builders have a global perspective.

This gap between the need and the capability of the personnel is not an easy one to fill. Universities wishing to meet this growing demand for education in systems engineering are facing a scarcity of qualified seasoned systems engineers who can teach the topic. Consequently the instruction provided to students may not be at the level program directors and students desire.

This paper proposes applying an industrial solution to the problem faced by individual universities, namely synergistic teaming to provide educational opportunities greater than those can could be provided by the individual institutions.

The traditional approach of teaching theory in academia does not work too well in systems engineering because it is a field that is evolving rapidly. By the time a methodology gets into a syllabus the state of the art has moved on. In addition, while there are few proven theoretical methodologies in the field, any literature search of the field will show there are a lot of empirical approaches that have been published as symposia papers.

Luckily, the part-time or adjunct faculty teaching systems engineering tend to be senior level people who are doing systems engineering as a full time job, and are teaching part time. These people, not only teach the theory as expressed in the text books, they are in an excellent position to comment on the theories and tell their students what works and what doesn't work. In effect they have returned to the tried and true approach to teaching engineering skills, namely the master-apprentice model. This is the teaching model adopted in the Graduate School of Management and Technology at University of Maryland University College (UMUC) from teaching courses in the Master of Software Engineering and Master of Science in Computer Systems Management Degrees.

Even resorting to adjunct faculty does not provide enough qualified instructor candidates. While there are many experienced practitioners who could teach systems engineering in general they tend not to have terminal degrees[1]. The accreditation criteria for universities which requires a specific minimum of instructors with terminal degrees for teaching at the graduate level thus tends to prohibit the use of otherwise qualified instructors and significantly reduces the pool of available talent. Universities which are able to find experienced qualified practitioners with terminal degrees hire them to teach and then may find out that, while a particular person may have an excellent grasp of the subject, they cannot teach adult learners. And, as this situation is only discovered in the classroom, it becomes a lose-lose situation. The students suffer due to the lack of instruction, and the instructor goes through a bad experience.

Teaming has traditionally not been viewed as a solution to this problem because universities in a geographical area are competing for students among the same population. However the advent of the world wide web coupled with the growth of distance learning technology have made teaming a viable solution to the problem in certain situations.

Consider the requirements for successful teaming and the implications thereof.

CONCEPT OF OPERATIONS

As with any good engineering project, it begins with a vision, commonly known as a concept of operations.

A team of universities, each well known in their area (geographical or expertise) offer a joint graduate degree in systems engineering. As far as the team is concerned:

- One or more topics is/are taught only by the institution with the recognized expertise. The University of South Australia (UniSA), for example, would provide expertise in the systems engineering topics by virtue of its association with the System Engineering and Evaluation Center (SEEC) in suburban Adelaide.
- Several topics are taught by two or more institutions
- The remainder of the topics is taught by all institutions in the team.
- The team is made up of institutions well separated by distance. Each is located in an area with potential students. For example UniSA could team with an institution in England, another in the Washington DC area of the United States of America and one in India[2].

[1] A terminal degree is generally one at the Doctorate level.

The courses are offered in several formats to suit the lifestyle of the adult learner. These include:

- Traditional synchronous classroom sessions over the course of a semester.
- On-line sessions over the course of a semester via distance education in synchronous or asynchronous formats.
- Short three or five day synchronous seminars[3].
- The executive format of consecutive synchronous weekend sessions enhanced with web-assisted asynchronous extensions.

Students take courses from the institution of choice via their method of choice. In the situation in which a course is offered by more than one institution, the students will soon learn which institution and which instructors are more suited to their needs and plan their studies accordingly. This competition for students will tend to increase the quality of the courses and ensure that they remain reasonably current. For example, several students in the now terminated joint Master of Software Engineering (MSWE) degree offered by the University of Maryland at College Park (UMCP) and UMUC did express preferences as to institutions and instructors in acquiring knowledge of specific topics[4].

While each university locates instructors, the pressure on program directors to find instructors for every course is lessened.

[2] England provides entry in the European Union as well as the British defense industry. Washington DC is the location of many contractors providing systems engineering services to the U.S. Government. India is a growing area in the field of systems and software engineering and students seem to be one of its major exports.

[3] The short seminars allow for instructors to be flown to their students, in the manner in which UniSA personnel offer courses in the United Kingdom and makes use of foreign talent in Australia.

[4] It was not at all one-sided. Some students preferred UMCP, others UMUC.

REQUIREMENTS FOR TEAMS

Theoretically forming teams should not be too difficult, in practice it will be a major accomplishment. The requirements for successful teams in academia are the same as those for successful teams in industry, namely

- Each member has something to contribute and lack some capability provided by other members of the team.
- The members have compatible cultures. In the United States there tends to be two kinds of universities, the research university and the teaching university. As UMUC and UMCP found out, incompatible cultures are a major impediment towards forming a successful team.
- The institution understands the needs of, and cares for adult learners.
- The institutions provide most if not all of the systems engineering body of knowledge, or at least the subjects taught in current degrees in systems engineering.
- The full-time faculty at each institution have worked in the field successfully before entering into academia.
- Most of the classes are taught by adjunct faculty who are doing what they are teaching. If they are not doing it while teaching, then they should have done it within the last two years.
- One institution has to administer the program, the others provide the quality control. This is the principle of checks and balances.
- As important as the instruction is the access to current journals and textbooks, and databases. The ability to provide these capabilities is critical when the student body is at a distance. Providing on-line access to the data is a service provided by more and more institutions, however providing access to physical books and journals is more difficult. While several freight carriers can provide this capability overnight in the continental United States at a reasonable cost, the cost of providing the service internationally is still prohibitive. The international members of the team provide the physical materials in their geographical areas.

In practice however, teaming will not be simple. However, it is the way of the future. Experience has already shown that it requires:

- major commitments by each institution and,
- personnel in each institution committed to the vision of the team and providing their students with the best educational opportunities they can.

- The challenge in forming a successful long-lived team is that it will be a true example of engineering a complex system and may even end up as a case study in one of its classes.

OTHER BENEFITS OF TEAMING INTERNATIONALLY

Other benefits include:

- The institutions in the team are not competing for students who wish to study in the classroom.
- Students are exposed to other ways of doing things in other nations and cultures. This exposure comes from both the instructors and their classmates.
- Students in the on-line classes work in teams on projects with people. This constructivist approach to learning provides both the global perspective and the ability to interact with co-workers in distant time zones.
- Australian and British universities offer research degrees at the Masters and Doctoral levels which do not have residency requirements. By teaming with a Stateside university, the degrees would be available to the professional in the USA who does not have the time to spend in a 'residency'. This opens a new market to the offshore universities. In addition, as well as raising the effectiveness of systems engineering, making this type of degree available in the USA would, in the long term, provide a greater pool of subject matter experts with terminal degrees for teaching in the classroom.

IT IS HAPPENING

Teaming is already starting to happen. For example:

- UMUC and UMCP had a joint graduate program in Software Engineering. When the joint program terminated in May 1999, UMUC converted the degree to the on-line format while continuing the phase out of the joint students and as of September 1999 it was their fastest growing program (Kasser, et al., 1999).

- UniSA is actively collaborating with University College, London in providing courses in systems engineering.

CONCLUSIONS

Teaming for teaching systems engineering offers benefits to both institutions and students. As such it should only be a matter of time before the first such team is formed and offers world class graduate education in systems engineering.

REFERENCE

Kasser, Joseph E., Goff, D., MacKenzie, G., "*Bringing the Master of Software Engineering Degree On-line at University of Maryland University College*", SETE-99, Adelaide, Australia, 1999.

BIOGRAPHY

Dr. Kasser has more than 25 years of award winning experience in management and engineering. He is an Associate Research Professor at the Systems Engineering and Evaluation Centre at the University of South Australia. He also teaches software engineering at the University of Maryland University College via Distance Learning. He is a recipient of NASA's Manned Space Flight Awareness (Silver Snoopy) Award for quality and technical excellence. He is a Certified Manager and a recipient of the Institute of Certified Professional Manager's 1993 Distinguished Service Award. He is the author of Applying Total Quality Management to Systems Engineering published by Artech House and more than 30 journal articles and conference papers. His current interests lie in the areas of applying systems engineering to organizations and using technology to improve the practice of management.

The Role of Configuration Management in Earned Value Management

Karen G. Kehoe
Lockheed Martin Technical Operations
PSC 45 Box 1352
APO AE 09468-1352

William H. McCumber, Jr., Ph.D., P.E.
President, EagleRidge Technologies, Inc.
118 Ledgerwood Lane,
Rockwood, TN 37854

ABSTRACT

Project control is a delicate, interactive balancing act involving cumulative cost, consumption of time (schedule execution), and evolution of performance. Cost is reported to the project manager through finance; schedule status is reported through the operating departments; and performance is reported through systems engineering. Absent some unifying structure, these three essential elements of project control proceed asynchronously, independently of each other, and thus can be said to be time-incoherent. Configuration management provides the needed unification. It gives context to accomplishment; substantiates products, and reconciles cost, schedule, and content. That is what this paper is about.

EARNED VALUE

The simple idea underlying earned value management (EVM) is, "Plan your work. Then work your plan." At predefined control points, compare the expected expenditure (Budgeted Cost of Work Scheduled—BCWS) to the actual expenditure (Actual Cost of Work Performed—ACWP). At the same point, compare the actual expenditure (ACWP) to the budgeted cost of work performed (BCWP). Variances between expectation and measurement are used to focus resources on troubled areas of the project (DoD and NASA Guide to PERT/Cost, 1963).

The Office of the Secretary of Defense maintains an earned value web site for government, industry and academic users sponsored by the Office of the Under Secretary of Defense (Acquisition, Technology & Logistics) Acquisition Resources & Analysis/Acquisition Management (periodically updated—this reference last updated March, 2000).

David Christensen of Southern Utah University maintains a comprehensive list of articles, papers and books on earned value, (Christensen, 2000).

Earned value is an idea nearly a half-century old, having its roots in the Navy Polaris program and the Air Force Minuteman program of the 1950s and 1960s. It is periodically rediscovered (Abba, 1995), exploited, and eventually flounders on the shoals of parochialism.

The usual problem lies in the way in which various sponsors see EVM. Accountants prefer that costs be tiered along organizational lines; technologists prefer that costs be tiered along product aggregation lines. For the technique discussed in this paper to work, earned value must be accumulated based on a product-oriented work breakdown structure (WBS), and configuration management (CM) must start much earlier in the program development cycle than currently.

The significant shortfall in EVM is lack of time-coherent data. One must first secure (evolve/acquire over time) a known system (or subsystem) configuration at a control point, then:

- Measure the technical performance of the system.
- Calculate the cost of making the system components available.
- Determine the scheduled time used at the control point.
- Characterize the state of the "system" or acquired component maturity.

Project Evaluation

Archibald (1976) presents the following three-step process for project evaluation.

> At periodic intervals:
> 1. *Determine status* on a total project basis, of

Actual work accomplished
Current and anticipated technical results
Resources expended (time, labor, and money).

2. *Compare status to plan,* for
Schedule
Budgeted and currently estimated costs
Technical specifications to be met, both at the time of comparison and at completion of the project.
3. *Identify variances* between current or future cost, schedule or technical performance, and related plans.

At this point, the evaluation process gives way to project direction, which involves determining and authorizing appropriate actions to eliminate the variances between performance and plan.

A more detailed 32-step "Earned Value Management System Criteria" checklist may be found by clicking on Criteria from the OSD WebSite, but the basic ideas haven't changed in forty years.

CONFIGURATION MANAGEMENT

Configuration management (CM) status accounting records the known system content (Configuration Items—CIs) at the time measurements are taken. Cost information is derived from expenditures on tasks, the products of which are incorporated into formal and informal baselines. Schedule information is derived from calendar days expended to reach the control point.

In a project of any significant complexity, multiple threads of development are ongoing simultaneously. In assessing earned value of technical performance at a control point, care must be taken to only use costs accumulated along the thread leading to the specific technical performance measurement and to avoid mixing in costs derived from parallel threads. This is the essential reason for requiring a product-oriented work breakdown structure—so that CM can separate the artifacts of different threads. Modern software makes this manually tedious task a simple mouse-click on an underlying database.

Relevance and Products of Formal CM

The relevance of CM is summarized in the following process descriptions:

CONFIGURATION MANAGEMENT PROCESS

- **Planning and management**
  - **Identification**
  - **Baseline Management**
    - *Configuration Control Board*
    - *Version & Release*
    - *Change Management*
      - Change Processing and Control
  - **Build**
    - *Control*
    - *Archive*
  - **Status Accounting**
  - **Audits**

Key data products of these processes that give context to Earned Value Management (EVM) measurements are:

Planning & Management—the CM tasks, the schedule for baseline production and control points, and status reporting requirements.

Identification—the inventory of authorized configuration items and changes thereto; the historical library of acquired system assets.

Baseline Management—the plan for how the system and its constituent parts (configuration components and changes) will be analyzed, approved, assembled, and scheduled into "frozen" and quantifiable baseline deliveries at specific control points. The plan defines the evolution and acquisition of system content, the capability that will exist at formal contractual milestones, and the insertion points for incremental (internal) milestones. It is the job of the change control board (CCB) to manage baseline cost, schedule, and content in context with each other.

The Change Management aspect of updating baselines provides data critical to analyzing the status and health of the configurations. Trend analysis using change metrics can be used to characterize the function, stability, and performance of the system (i.e., form, fit, and function) at formal and informal milestones.

Build—the build report and Version Description Document of inclusive and outstanding components and changes to be delivered and installed.

Status Accounting—the correlated and integrated set of reports that relates configuration component status to past, current, and future baselines. A cumulative Baseline Configuration Cross-Reference Index defines the "health and wealth" of the system inventory as it evolves toward each control point.

Audits—the metrics from a formal review of the functional and physical characteristics of the completed and delivered "as built" baseline. This data substantiates how well components meet specified functional and performance requirements.

CM, Program Management and Systems Engineering processes can be tightly coupled by leveraging and relating the data of each. CM processes take custody of products from other disciplines, including Program Management, when detailed cost and schedule are defined as configuration component attributes and placed under formal control. A relational CM database that captures and controls the products of program processes then becomes the source of contextual reports that input to both Technical Performance Management (TPM) and Earned Value Management (EVM).

Usefulness of CM to EVM

The value of rolling Configuration Status Accounting data up into the EVM process adds another perspective: given the recorded cost and schedule expenditure, are system functional capability and performance maturing or regressing? What can be expected at the next milestone? Where should trade-offs among function, stability and performance be performed in the short term to insure progress toward a balanced "system" in the long term?

The Configuration Status Accounting Report (CSAR) is the only relational record of configuration item attributes (the whats, whys, and how well). When program and technical management use CSAR data more comprehensively, function, performance, and stability issues can be proactively addressed and resolved. If a problem is predictable from change impact analysis and fix trend data, program management and systems engineering can then project and depict the point at which cost and schedule expense are reasonable given the health and wealth of the system (inventory). Such visibility gives the customer the perception of a successfully managed program in which the costs of achieving function, stability and performance are balanced along the way.

Configuration management begs coherence among the elements of program data. The project manager knows how much time has been used from reports provided through the operating units. He or she also knows how much of the budget has been consumed from reports through finance. Only through relating to CM data are the value and quality of acquired assets associated with that expenditure of resources known explicitly. That value is determined by systems engineering using some combination of estimation, analytical, and simulation techniques on a known system configuration as recorded by Configuration Management.

EARNED VALUE MANAGEMENT

Configuration management status accounting keeps a running account of completed system hardware and software components (configuration items—CIs and CSCIs), documentation and process. At control points, the exact product for which resources have been expended is precisely known. For example, consider the situation at the control point illustrated in Figures 1 through 4.

Figure 1 is the planned relationship between budget expenditure and technical results achieved. The technical performance measurement (TPM) is targeting miss distance. The goal is to minimize miss distance; thus the measured TPM value should decrease with budget expended.

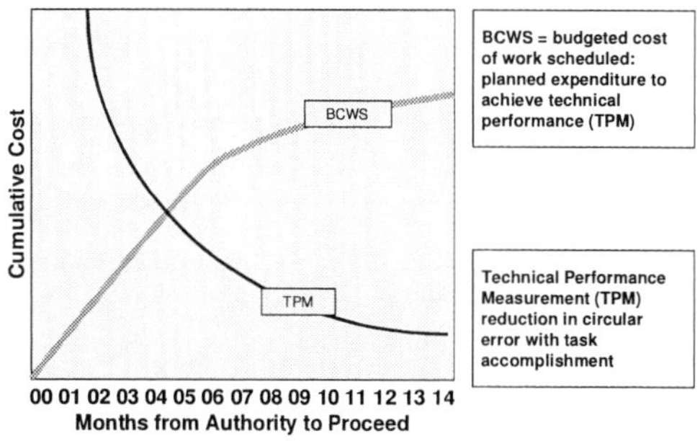

Figure 1—Budget and Performance

In Figure 2, the actual cost of work performed (ACWP) is added to the cost-performance data in Figure 1. At "Time Now," ten tasks have been accomplished. These ten tasks bring the system design to a control point where performance is evaluated. Configuration management is tasked to certify the system inventory at the point of performance evaluation. (Unless one knows what is being evaluated, evaluation is an empty exercise.) Expectation is that expending the cumulative budget up to the control point will accomplish twelve tasks. For purposes of illustration, budget each task at \$1,000. Thus twelve tasks should cost \$12,000. This is the planned result for the expenditure as read from the budgeted cost of work scheduled (BCWS). If everything is on track (and it may not be) the project has "earned" the planned value. Reality is that the actual cost of work performed (ACWP) up to the control point is (in our example) eleven thousand dollars. Eleven thousand dollars were consumed to accomplish ten tasks.

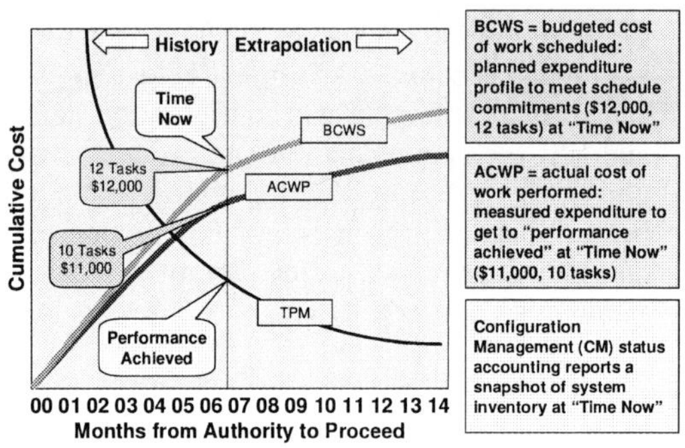

Figure 2—Budget and Actual Costs

It is important to note that only the ten tasks leading to the evaluated system inventory are relevant. Since projects are conducted with many parallel threads of tasks, tasks have been performed for which budget has been provided but that do not affect the evaluation of this TPM at this control point. Those tasks do not affect this TPM function and thus are not relevant to this evaluation.

Referring to the plan, we are behind schedule by two tasks. We have completed ten tasks against a planned completion of twelve tasks. We have spent \$11,000 to complete ten tasks, against a budgeted expectation of \$10,000. The cost to accomplish ten tasks is on the tracking curve, "budgeted cost of work performed" (BCWP).

Project Direction

The variances between plan and accomplishment are in two forms: cost variance (BCWP-ACWP) and schedule variance (BCWP-BCWS). Specifically, the

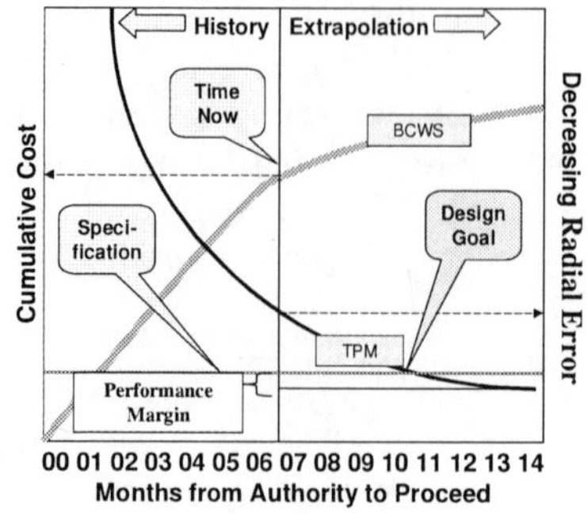

Figure 3—Add-in BCWP

actual cost of executing ten tasks to provide the system for evaluation is \$11,000; the assigned budget to reach ten tasks is \$10,000. Thus, cost variance is -\$1000.

Referring again to the plan, the planned budget to reach ten tasks is \$10,000; the planned budget to reach "Time Now" is \$12,000. The project is now two tasks behind schedule at "Time Now." The accomplishment of tasks has not kept pace with the plan. At "Time Now" the schedule variance is (minus) -\$2,000.

It is convenient to express variances in percentages. Cost variance is calculated by the following equation:

$$CV(\%) = \frac{BCWP - ACWP}{BCWP}$$

Schedule variance is calculated by the following equation:

$$SV(\%) = \frac{BCWP - BCWS}{BCWP}$$

Since both cost variance and schedule variance are negative, the project is both in a cost overrun condition and behind schedule. The project manager now has enough specific information to rationally redirect resources to tasks that narrow the gap between plan (BCWS, BCWP) and actual (ACWP).

PERFORMANCE MARGIN

Planning

In the previous discussion, it was implied that at "Time Now" the actual system performance was exactly as predicted. Realistically, performance evaluation is as variable as cost or schedule and is subject to similar analysis/corrective action.

"Time Now" establishes the control accounting point. At the control point, the targeting error technical performance measurement (TPM) is planned for the value where the TPM curve crosses the "Time Now" line. Funds have been budgeted to drive the TPM to the goal illustrated in Figure 4. Deviations from the plan at "Time Now" require reflection and re-planning whether the TPM is under-performing or over-performing. The goal is to meet the specified value for the TPM. There are no extra rewards for exceeding the goal, but there are extra penalties (cost, resources, time) attached to continuing to work on refining the TPM.

Engineers will characteristically push for technical excellence over and above the minimum necessary to meet requirements. While not as satisfying as technical excellence, performance margin (over performance) is coin-of-the-realm to the project manager. Performance margin can be traded for cost and/or for schedule. To the customer, "Give us another 60 days and $20,000 and we will give you a hundred-yard improvement in miss distance."

Figure 5 illustrates a very important aspect of earned value management. Performance margin can be traded for cost and/or schedule advantage.

Performance margin, like cost and like schedule, is coin-of-the-realm in project management trade-offs.

The design goal is reached when the TPM curve intersects the specification line. More money and time have been allocated to achieving the specified outcome (Δ cost, Δ time) that may now be reallocated to more critical tasks. Equivalently, the customer may prefer to squeeze the most performance (Δ performance) from the available cost and schedule. In any event the customer should be involved in the planning to take advantage of early achievement of the TPM performance goal. Once the TPM goal is reached, configuration

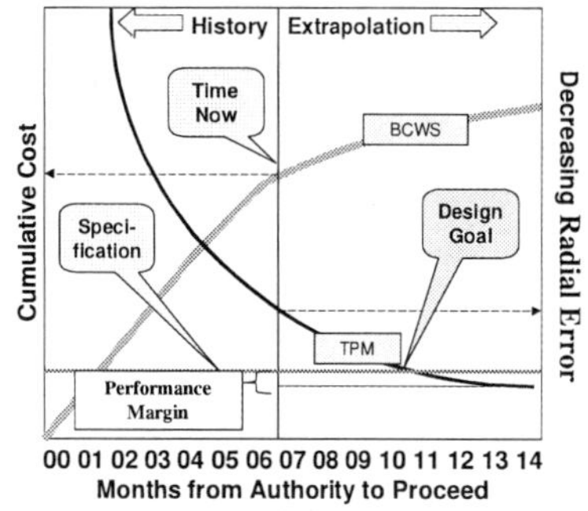

Figure 4—Design Goal and Performance Margin

management locks the system inventory. A configuration that meets the specified performance goal will now be on the shelf.

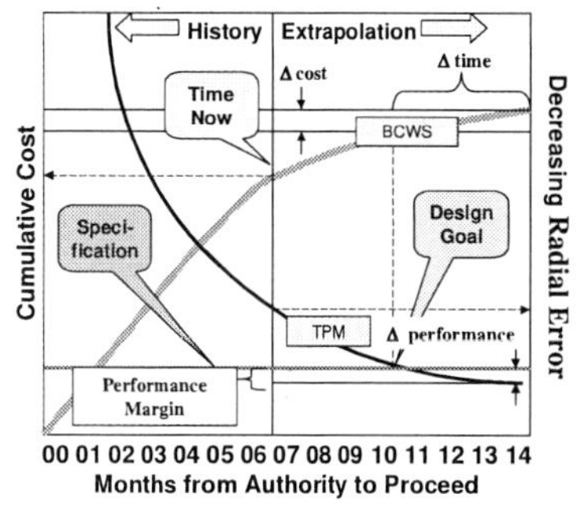

Figure 5—Balancing Performance, Cost and Schedule

OTHER STUDIES OF TPM IN EVM

Kulick (1997) writes,

> The difference between the plan and the actual measures represents a technical variance of sorts which is either bad, good, or somewhere in between depending upon the level of tolerance allowed for results which stray from the plan. Often the TPM process ends here, having performed its traditional duty of bolstering a subjective earned value assessment. This is primarily because the ability to analyze a technical measurement in terms of its variance from the plan and its relation to the established tolerance levels is relatively straight-forward, while the quantification of the variance in terms of its overall impact on the technical development process, not to mention cost and schedule, is elusive at best. ...TPM has languished in terms of the methodical development of techniques to collect and organize technical data, as well as to integrate and analyze the results within the context of other program status data.

Pisano (1998) conducted a retrospective analysis on the T45TS Cockpit-21 program, the Federal Aviation Administration's (FAA) Wide Area Augmentation System (WAAS) program, and the Navy's H-1 helicopter upgrade program and found,

> Currently-reported earned value data contains invaluable planning and budget information with proven techniques for program management, however, shortcomings of the system are its emphasis on retrospection and lack of integration with technical achievement. The TPM approach, using the techniques of risk analysis and probability, offers a promising method to incorporate technical assessments resulting *systematically* from technical parameter measurements to derive more discrete management data sufficiently early to allow for cost avoidance.

The missing coupling between EVM and TPM can be achieved by accessing CM information, as illustrated by the following example.

EXAMPLE

Weapon System Effectiveness

The key technical performance measure (TPM) at the systems level is *Weapon System Effectiveness* (E). That is the compound probability:

$$E = A_i \times R(t) \times D(r) \times T(r,\sigma) \times S(d)$$

This is composed from the following:

- Weapon system intrinsic availability. Can it be committed when needed?

  $$A_i = \frac{MTBF}{MTBF + MTR + LD}$$

  where MTBF = mean time between failures, MTR = mean time to restore function, and LD = logistics delay.

- Weapon system reliability. Will it continue to operate through mission accomplishment?

  $$R = e^{-\lambda t}$$

  where

  $$\lambda = \frac{1}{MTBF}$$

- Warhead Destruct probability at radius, *r*, from target center.

  $$D(r) = f(r)$$

  where the Destruct probability is a function of the radial distance from the target.

- Circular Error probable—the probability that the warhead will fall within a radius, *r*, of the aim point. The targeting equation is:

  $$T(r,\sigma) = 1 - e^{(\frac{-r^2}{2\sigma^2})}$$

  where r is the radial distance from the center of the target [same r as in D(r)] and σ is the standard deviation of impacts from several simulated trajectories.[1]

- Weapon system survivability—the probability that the weapon system counter measures will protect it over the mission duration.

  $$S = f(d)$$

  where survivability depends primarily on the duration (*d*) of exposure to hostile action.

First observation is that the key parameters are mean-time-between-failures (MTBF) that appears in both Availability and Reliability equations, and dispersion of the trajectory end-point, indicated by the standard deviation, σ, in the Targeting equation. This provides the first two focus areas of the system design.

Planning

Figure 6 presents the planned budget and performance for the example. Configuration management separately handles the two possible alternative solutions to the MTBF imperative, high reliability parts, and/or redundant parts. At some point early in the design a technical decision will direct the selection of approach. Until the decision is made, CM must carry both solutions in parallel.

[1] Notice that r must be non-zero for the trajectory impact probability to have meaning. The probability of hitting a point is essentially zero, so we set r from the warhead destruct radius.

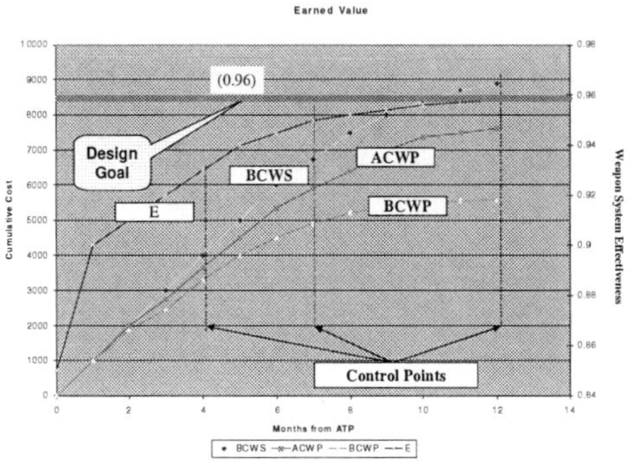

Figure 6—Planned Budget and Performance

Figure 7 is a history of the evolution of weapon system effectiveness (E) along with the earned value tracking parameters BCWS, ACWP, and BCWP. Control points are indicated at months 4, 7, and 12. Configuration management is tasked to deliver the system inventory at the control points so that performance evaluation is made against a known system. At the seven-month checkpoint the project is cost overrun with schedule slippage. At the twelfth month the parameters continue to diverge, indicating that corrective measures taken at the seventh month were not successful. Performance is tracked against the right-most vertical axis (0.84 to 0.98). All cost curves are tracked against the left-most axis ($0 to $10,000).

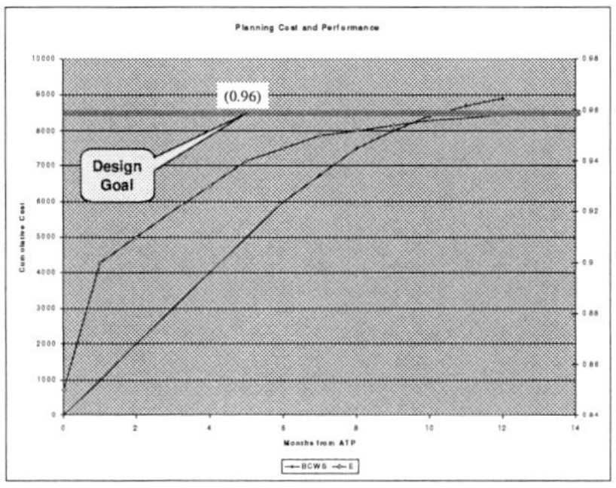

Figure 7—Evolution of Weapon system Effectiveness

CONCLUSIONS

Cost and schedule tracking is meaningless in the absence of tracking the performance of a solution and characterizing the value and maturity of the solution. Performance is achieved through execution of tasks that consume time and resources. Time and labor expended create a system design that is tested for performance. Configuration management is responsible for identifying the actual system inventory at control points. Project management is responsible for issuing direction to the operating departments that, when executed, narrows the gap between predicted and measured cost, between predicted and measured schedule, and between predicted and measured performance. Configuration management (knowing what the system consists of at any time) is the unifying concept in earned value management.

REFERENCES

DoD and NASA Guide to PERT/Cost, 1963.

Archibald, Russell D., Managing High Technology Programs and Projects, John Wiley & Sons, 1976.

Office of the Secretary of Defense Web Site, "Earned Value Management: Integrating Cost, Schedule and Technical Performance for Project Management," at URL .http://www.acq.osd.mil/pm, March, 2000.

Abba, Wayne, "Earned Value Management Rediscovered!" OSD Program Executive Officer Conference, October 1995.

Christensen, David S., "Earned Value Bibliography: Comprehensive Bibliography of Earned Value Literature," Southern Utah University, March 2000.

Kulick, Kathryn A., Technical Performance Measurement - A Systematic Approach to Planning, Integration and Assessment, *The Measurable News*, June, 1997.

Pisano, N. D., Technical Performance Measurement, Earned Value and Risk Management: An Integrated Diagnostic Tool for Program Management, NAVAIRSYSCOM, 1998.

BIOGRAPHY

Karen G. Kehoe is a Senior Staff Systems Engineer on an overseas assignment with Lockheed Martin Technical Operations Company where she is responsible for re-engineering legacy systems engineering and integration management processes for an operational program. Previously she was corporate technical consulting resource from the Lockheed Martin Software and Systems Resource Center supporting numerous Lockheed Martin companies. She has been awarded "chair" assignments on 2 IBM division headquarters technology staffs and received numerous management awards for SE process and automation solution architectures for complex aerospace weapons and satellite systems acquisition programs. She is a trained instructor of the Technical Management Plan Workshop and author of an Integrated Systems Configuration Management course. A member of INCOSE since 1992, Ms. Kehoe was the Session Chair for the Automation Design Track of the third annual NCOSE International Symposium in 1993.

Dr. William H. McCumber, Jr., is President of EagleRidge technologies, Inc., and adjunct professor in the distance learning program of the Graduate School of Management and Technology of the University of Maryland University College. Until retirement in February 1999 he was Senior Staff Systems Engineer, Lockheed Martin Software and Systems Resource Center, as lead consultant for systems engineering, architecture, course development and training. He was Technical Chairman for the 1993 Third International Symposium of the National Council on Systems Engineering. Dr. McCumber holds a BSEE from the University of Oklahoma, MSE from the University of Alabama (Huntsville) and Ph.D. from the University of Houston. He is a registered professional engineer.

A Systems Comparison of Public Perception and Policy towards Genetic Engineering in the EU and the US

Florian Kraus
Herbert Negele
Technische Universität München
Institute of Astronautics
Boltzmannstr.15, 85748 Garching, Germany

Philip L. Bereano
University of Washington
Department of Technical Communication
14 Loew Hall, Box 352195
Seattle, WA 98195-2195

Abstract. There has been a steadily increasing debate during the last years about how to regulate genetically modified organisms and their use in food processing and agriculture. As the discussion advanced, one could identify two fundamentally different positions, represented by the United States and the European Union.

The goal of this work was to figure out possible reasons for the obvious differences in public perception and policy between the EU and the US. The approach to the problem is based on Peter Checkland's "Soft Systems Methodology", which was adopted to the specific problem situation. It revealed a fair number of factors which are contributing to the different development of the situation in the EU and in the US. Nevertheless, the interaction of those reasons appears to be even more important than each single reason. Systemigrams, developed by Boardman, were used to further analyze and display those interactions in a transparent manner.

INTRODUCTION

During the last decades the world has witnessed the advancement of a variety of new and innovative technologies, each of which has a more or less substantial impact on humanity. One of those technologies is Genetic Engineering (GE), which is supposed to be one of the key technologies of the next century.

Among several GE techniques, recombinant DNA (rDNA) is the most sophisticated and powerful tool, which evolved during the seventies and was steadily improved and developed since then. There are two important areas of application for rDNA, which led repeatedly to very controversial discussions about how to apply and regulate this technology. One is the area of human genetics with applications like for example the "Human Genome Project" or cloning. The other important application of rDNA is in the area of plants and agriculture, for example genetically modified crops or the treatment of cows with "Bovine Growth Hormone". Since those two fields raise similar questions as well as fundamentally different ones, it is worthwhile to separate them and limit the analysis to one of those fields, in this case the field of plants and agriculture.

The key feature of rDNA is the capability to mix genes on the cellular rather than the organismal level. This technique enables scientists to recombine genes from dissimilar sources to produce genetically novel, transgenic organisms. Genes are transferred horizontally from one individual to another (as opposed to vertically, from parent to offspring), often making use of infectious agents as vectors or carriers of genes so that genes can be transferred between distant species that would never interbreed in nature.

This new technique opens up a more or less unlimited variety of possibilities. The biotech industry's point of view is that GE and especially rDNA will provide solutions for many of the contemporary problems. This includes:

- increased yields from modified crops, which resist pests, drought, frost and diseases
- modified strains of bacteria and higher plants that could degrade toxic wastes or mop up heavy metals to clean up the environment
- environmentally more friendly transgenic crops that would reduce the use of pesticides, herbicides and fertilizers
- increased nutritional value of foods

Nevertheless, there are numerous voices, including politicians, scientists and consumers, who constantly warn of the potential downsides GE might have. The most common concerns are:

- decrease of biodiversity
- increased use of herbicides and pesticides
- threat of the creation of superweeds

- development of resistance among pests
- incompatibility with sustainable agriculture
- creation of antibiotic resistant bacteria
- increased residues of toxins in foods
- allergenic potential of transgenic plants

Generally scientists admit a lack of understanding in terms of gene expression. Richard Lewontin, a Havard geneticist, compares an organism with a certain genetic code to an ecosystem: "You can always intervene and change something in it, but there is no way of knowing what all the downstream effects will be or how it might affect the environment. We have such a miserably poor understanding of how the organism develops from its DNA that I would be surprised if we don't get one rude shock after another" (Pollan 1998).

The key question is whether the opportunities of GE outweigh the risks. Most stakeholders agree, that the consequences of an accident with this powerful technology would be severe (see concerns above), but there is a general disagreement about the likelihood of an accident. In this case, the term accident includes unintended higher order effects. If we define risk as the product of the probability of an accident and the gravity of its consequences, this disagreement results in a fundamentally different perception of the risk of GE. Furthermore, people have a different perception of risk and a different willingness to take risks. In general, Americans appear to have a higher risk acceptance than Europeans do.

Given this general disagreement and scientific uncertainty, the key question was how to cope with this new and powerful technology, with its opportunities and its risks. The US chose a fundamentally different approach to the issue, compared to the European Union and most of the rest of the world. There is no doubt that this difference is existent, the question to be answered is: Why is there such a noticeable difference in terms of public perception and policy?

According to Dörner (Dörner 1989, Negele 1998), the human brain tends to think in linear cause-effect chains. This approach is doomed to fail when applied to a complex system, where a variety of elements are linked dynamically. Since a human society is in general an extraordinary complex system with many interrelations and uncertainties, the systems thinking approach provided suitable tools to deal with such a difficult and undefined problem situation. This paper is based on a thesis (Kraus 1999), which was the result of a cooperation between the Department of Technical Communication at the University of Washington in Seattle and the SE Group of the Institute of Astronautics at the TU München.

Given this scientific background, the paper will continue with a description of the situation in the EU and the US in terms of legal framework, attitude of the industry and public perception of the issue, followed by a short problem definition. Based on this, an approach which is based on Checkland's "Soft Systems Methodology" is applied to analyze the differences between the EU and the US. In Checkland's "Soft Systems Methodology", the analysis starts out with the definition of the problem-relevant systems. After defining a conceptual model, which represents the ideal situation, this model is compared to reality in order to identify the underlying reasons for the problem situation.

Due to the rapid development of this issue, the authors want to point out that **the rest of the paper refers to the situation in fall of 1999**. The next paragraph is meant to give the reader a brief update about the recent, most important developments in this area since then, which are not taken into consideration in the following analysis.

In Europe, the attitude and the situation in general have not changed too much. European consumers are increasingly skeptical over genetically-engineered food and food produced using industrial rearing, according to an annual survey published by the international analysts Healey and Beaker. In total, 65% of those questioned in 1999 indicated that they did not wish to purchase goods containing genetically-modified organisms (GMOs), compared with 61% in 1998 (Genet 2000).

The more interesting changes have taken place in the US. The most important turning point in the whole debate was the adoption of the biosafety protocol in Montreal on January, 29th 2000. The United States, which had blocked the negotiations in Cartagena one year earlier, has always opposed labeling and fought import bans except in cases where the product is shown to be risky. It had to make concessions on those and several other points. But there were not only changes in the international legislation but as well on the national level. In a USA WEEKEND poll from February, 12th 2000, 79% of the people questioned stated that it should not "be legal to sell genetically modified fruits and vegetables without special labels" (USA WEEKEND 2000). On February, 24th 2000, Senator Barbara Boxer (Democrat) introduced a bill to require consumer labels on GE foods. A January poll conducted by Reuters at the annual convention of the American Farm Bureau Federation showed farmers retreating from GMs: farmers plan to cut GM maize plantings by 23%, GM soybeans by 15% and GM cotton by 26%. Snack maker Frito-Lay is telling its suppliers that it will stop using GM corn.

SITUATION IN THE US

Legal Framework and Government Position. The legal framework of the US, which is the leading exporter of "Living Modified Organisms" (LMOs), stresses the "Principle of Familiarity" as basis for decision-making in the context of modern biotechnology. This means, that genetically modified (GM) products are regarded to be substantially equal to traditionally processed foods. Essentially the US does not have a binding regulation of GMOs which would limit the scope of action of the biotech companies. The attitude of the US Government is in general pro-biotech. This is reflected in the legislation and in the actions of leading US politicians.

The US Biotech Industry. In the view of the US biotech companies, the rigid European legislation appears to be an obstacle to the expansion of their business and to scientific progress. They favor weak legislation on both the national and international level in order to create a free international market without trade barriers.

Public Perception in the US. Polls carried out in the US over the last years have shown repeatedly that the majority of the American population is not aware of the fact that an estimated 60 percent of all processed foods sold in the supermarkets is genetically engineered. When told about this fact, the majority of the persons asked favors a labeling of GE products and would avoid purchasing them. Due to the lack of public attention, the skepticism of the American population towards GM foods, which becomes clear in the polls mentioned above does not have any impact on the market so far. Compared to Europe, there is little public attention to this issue so far, neither among consumers nor in the media.

SITUATION IN THE EU

Legal Framework and Government Position. The European Union is subject to the same economic considerations, which led in the US to a strong promotion of the biotech industry by the governmental agencies. However, the EU chose a completely different approach to the issue.

The viewpoint of the European Union is not totally against genetic engineering, but there is a clear skepticism towards GMOs and their deliberate release. Therefore, the EU has set up guidelines for intensive approval procedures, which are much harder and more time consuming than in the US. Thus, safety considerations prevail over economic interests in the EU.

The European Biotech Industry. Initially the European biotechnology industry resisted proposals for biotechnology directives. In 1988 the industry finally accepted the basic legislative framework. Industrialists were persuaded by warnings about European disharmonies, at both the socio-political and juridical levels (Science and Public Policy 1996).

Public Perception in the EU. In the summer of 1997, biotech food emerged as the most explosive environmental issue in Europe. Protestors had destroyed dozens of field trials of the very same "frankenplants" that are already commercially grown and marketed in the USA. Throughout Europe the public has demanded that biotech food be labeled in the market. In spring 1999, the strong reluctance of consumers to accept genetically engineered ingredients in their foods triggered a chain reaction, which is still not finished. Step by step, one major food company after the other declared to go GM free as a response to consumer pressure.

DEFINING THE PROBLEM

In the case of biotechnology it is not really suitable to talk about a problem situation. In a societal context, the perception of what the problem is strongly depends on the situation of the investigator himself. This tension of the definition of a problem is certainly given in the case of biotechnology (Figure 1). A representative of a biotech company will see the reluctance of European consumers to accept GM food as a problem whereas a NGO activist will perceive the situation exactly the other way round.

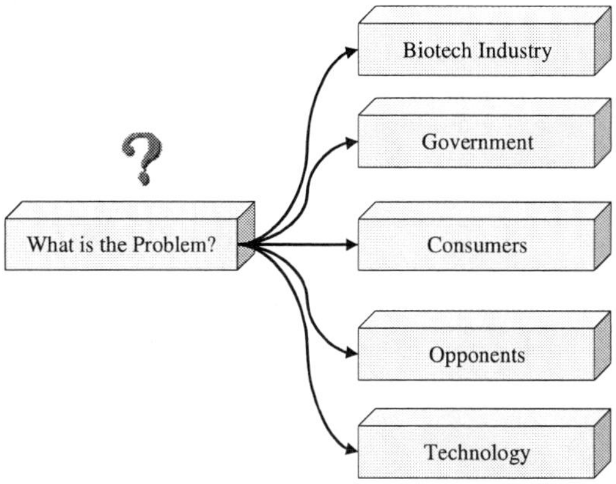

Figure 1: Defining the Problem

According to Checkland (1990), it is worthwhile to "collect as many perceptions of the problem as possible from a wide range of people with roles in the problem situation". In the case of biotechnology, there is a variety of different stakeholders with a variety of different problem definitions.

The Biotech Industry. The biotech companies have a substantial interest in the creation of a worldwide market without trade barriers and a liberal legislation on the national and international level.

The Government. The government has to ensure that there is no release of GMOs into the environment, which might have a detrimental impact on humans or the environment. On the other hand, the government has to establish a system, which provides a basis for economic growth and scientific advance. Thus, the government also has a strong incentive to promote biotechnology, which is supposed to be one of the major markets of the next millennium.

The Consumers. The basic interest of the consumers is a sufficient food supply, which has a high quality and is offered for a reasonable price. Additionally, the citizens demand that the environment they live in not be destroyed in a short or long term perspective. On the other hand, the population profits from a strong economy, which ensures material wealth and job opportunities for the citizens.

The Opponents. There is a strong group of opponents of biotechnology, which is organized worldwide. Members include farmers, environmentalists, many NGOs (Non Governmental Organizations), and civil activists as well as university professors and scientists. Their viewpoint is that genetic engineering poses a substantial risk for the people and the environment. They claim that biotechnology did so far only serve to increase the industry's profits and the corporate control of the market. The opponents of biotechnology demand a moratorium on all GMOs, until there is firm scientific evidence that these organisms do not pose any long-term risk for the environment, the human health or biodiversity in general.

The Technology. With the development of rDNA the scientists entered areas which have been out of their scope so far. This new technology offers both peerless opportunities and incomparable risks. The technology is developed well enough to manipulate the very core of life on earth, but it is not sophisticated enough to make any predictions about potential second order effects. This fact is generally admitted by both, the biotech proponents as well as the opponents.

Each of the stakeholders mentioned above has his very specific point of view and set of interests. Unfortunately, these interests can be mutual exclusive, as for example in the case of the government. It is simply impossible to both avoid any risk for the environment by establishing a rigid legal framework and promote the biotech industry. The interaction of the stakeholders' interests is shown in Figure 2. It displays the complexity of the system: to change one parameter will always affect every single other parameter.

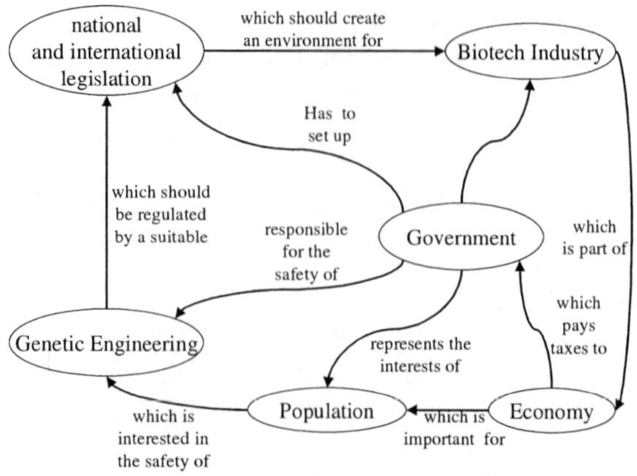

Figure 2: Interaction of Stakeholders

As shown above, the context of biotechnology is everything but simple. It is a highly dynamic and interconnected system with a variety of stakeholders and mutual exclusive interests. Hence it is reasonable to try to analyze this problem with a systems thinking approach.

ROOT DEFINITIONS OF RELEVANT SYSTEMS

The formation of opinion in a society is a dynamic and complex process, which is biased by a variety of different factors. Most of the times it is not one single factor having the main influence, but rather the combination of several factors (Figure 3) and their interactions among themselves, which eventually determines the public perception of a problem.

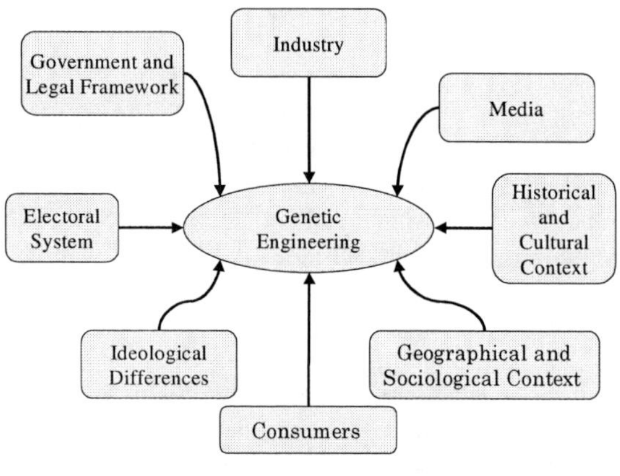

Figure 3: Relevant Systems

THE CONCEPTUAL MODEL

The design of a conceptual model for the problem of genetic engineering is subject to an initial evaluation problem. Since there is no general agreement how to handle the issue, there can be no conceptual models, which are not at least partly based on personal values. Therefore, the design of the following conceptual model is based on democratic principles rather than on issues connected to bioengineering.

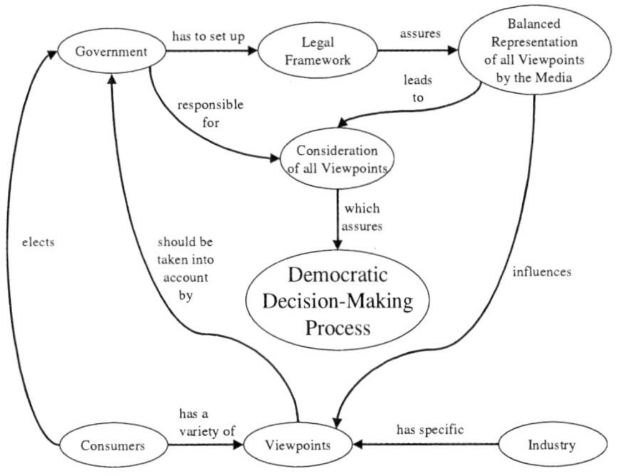

Figure 4: Democratic Decision-Making Process

Democratic decision-making (Figure 4), in contrast to bureaucratic or technocratic decision making, is based on the assumption that all who are affected by a given decision have the right to participate in the decision-making process. Participation can be direct in polls or elections or indirect through representatives. To facilitate a democratic decision making, it is indispensable to grant everybody free access to information. A sound decision is only achievable, if the full versatility of different viewpoints is discussed and presented to everybody.

ANALYSIS OF THE DIFFERENCES BETWEEN THE EU AND US

There is a variety of possible explanations, which might explain the differences between the European and the American attitude towards Genetic Engineering and its application in food and agriculture. Some of them appear to be more important than others, but the interaction of all those factors turns out to be the most important influence on the issue.

Electoral System. The common electoral system in the USA appears to be a major reason why minority viewpoints on public issues do not attract as much attention as they do in Europe. In Europe the electoral system is generally based on a proportional representation. This is not the case in the US, due to the "winner takes all principle", which allows minorities as large as 49% to be ignored.

Due to this electoral system there is very little representation of political minorities in the US Congress and thus in the political discussions broadcasted on the media. This leads to a so-called voter apathy since a substantial part of the population has the feeling, that their views are not taken into consideration. Another effect of the electoral system is the strong dominance of the two major parties, the Republicans and the Democrats.

In Europe, environmentalism started as a minority issue as well, but it would never have become so strong without the political representation of those groups in the political discussions and the resulting media coverage. This success of environmentalists was only possible because the electoral system in European nations allows the representation of minority viewpoints. Thus, concerns about GMOs are readily translated into political agendas.

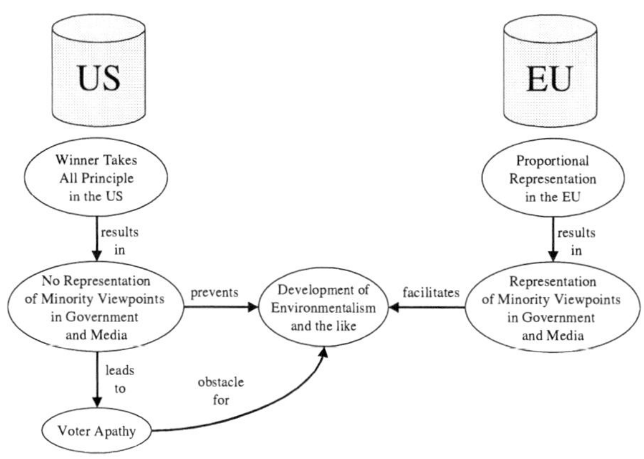

Figure 5: Differences in the Electoral System

Links between the Government and the Industry. There are strong links between the US government and the American biotech companies, which reach back into the Reagan and Bush administration. Those links may serve as an explanation for many incidents, in which the US government supported the viewpoint of the biotech industry.

As a consequence, the strategy of the FDA, which is the responsible governmental agency in the US for food safety, is not very consumer oriented. The FDA determined that whether a food had been genetically engineered was not a "material fact". About the controversial issue of labeling, James Maryansky, its biotechnology coordinator, said the FDA would not "require things to be on the label just because a consumer might want to know them" (Borger 1999).

But there is not only a visible influence of the biotech industry on domestic policies in the US, the interests of this specific industry are as well reflected in US foreign policies. There are several examples of major US politicians and governmental officials fighting for the interests of companies like Monsanto on the highest political level. In New Zealand, US ambassador Josiah Beeman appeared on national television and warned that if New Zealand tried to label genetically engineered food, trade sanctions might follow.

Due to the different political system in Europe, in which politicians do not have to rely on external funding for their election campaigns as much as politicians in the US, the links between European companies and the political level are weaker than in the US (but still existent). The industry in Europe does certainly influence the political decision making process, but not to the extent as in the US. This becomes obvious in the European regulation of biotechnology, which is a severe obstacle for biotech companies and their business. In contrary to the US, where the industry convinced the government that there is no need for a new legislation, the European legislative agencies are constantly amending and mostly strengthening the legal framework.

Representation of countervailing views in the media. The variety of different opinions reflected in the media of the United States is limited due to several reasons. Since American media are almost all privately owned, the vast majority of the US media has a very specific interest in guiding the public opinion into a certain direction. The choice of what topics are covered by a certain media, and especially how they are discussed, strongly depends on the kind of business the owners of this media are involved in. The corporations try to bias the public perception of specific issues according to their own commercial interests. The dependence of privately owned media on advertising sales further supports this process, which constrains the versatility of views represented in the US media.

Furthermore, the number of companies controlling the US media has steadily decreased during the last decades. The magazine 'The Nation' published a chart, showing the sway of four giant corporations (NBC, ABC, CBS and CNN) that control the major TV news divisions in an ever more "contracting media cosmos". "Two of these four corporations are defense contractors (both involved in nuclear production), while the other two are mammoth manufacturers of fun 'n' games. Thus we are the subjects of a national entertainment state, in which the news and much of our amusement come to us directly from the two most powerful industries in the United States" (Miller 1996). Two other companies having a considerable power in this field are Time Warner and Disney.

Due to the different media structure in Europe, such a concentration of power in the hands of a few companies is nearly impossible. Most European countries have several channels, which are publicly owned. Additionally, Europeans experience a more versatile media since it is possible almost everywhere to receive channels from the neighboring country.

The discussion about genetically engineered foods and agricultural products was started by activists in Europe, caught fire in January 1999 and caused several major food companies to go GM free. What made the difference, both the activists and the industry say, was the press coverage in the European media (Independent 1999). In contrary to this, most US newspapers and TV stations have had either zero coverage or rather pro-industry reports on the issue of genetic engineering.

History of Negative Impacts of Technology in Europe. Especially in this century, Europe has experienced a series of severe backlashes from modern technologies, which lead to a fundamental skepticism towards new techniques and technologies, which is in general higher than in the US. This caution in Europe is based on experience and reflects the willingness and the necessity to learn from this experience.

The memory of the Nazis and with them of the eugenics experiments, Hitler's plan to create a "super race" by genetic selection, is still present all over Europe and the issue of television panels. The parallel to genetic engineering of agricultural products and foods is obvious, namely the creation of super organisms by manipulating living organisms. Thus, the caution of those issues is higher in Europe than in the US where, as Brian Tokar put it, "eugenics have a smiling liberal face. It is all about choice and empowerment" (Presentation at a conference in Seattle, May 1999).

Numerous other incidents have been even more important to the Genetic Engineering field than this dark chapter of European history. Besides global environmental concerns like the Greenhouse Effect or the Ozone Hole, there have been two other incidents, which affected mainly Europe and thus increased the level of skepticism towards technology and its implications. One was the meltdown of the atomic power plant in Chernobyl and the other one was the mad cow disease (BSE) crisis in Britain. Both have been exacerbated by a series of flawed human decisions and governmental misbehavior (Rampton and Stauber 1997).

The whole discussion surrounding the economic issues made European consumers extremely sensitive about the safety of their food chain and has undermined confidence in their regulatory agencies. Until now, the US has not experienced a serious food scare on the scale of Britain's brush with BSE which would make the population similarly aware of the sensibility of an ever more interconnected food chain.

Abundance of Space and Nature in the USA. Due to the abundance of space in America, many environmental damages are kept out of sight of daily life. Power plants, waste disposal sites or incinerating plants can be built distant from the cities. Thus, the consumer is not necessarily confronted with the downsides of excessive use of resources or of high energy consumption. Additionally there are many areas in the USA, which are hardly populated and thus consist of untouched nature and intact environments. Since people travel for vacation to National Parks or other unspoiled areas they seldom experience the detrimental impacts of their lifestyle on the natural environment outside those recreational areas.

In contrary to the US, it is much harder in Europe to find such remote areas. Most of Europe is populated or at least utilized in one or another way. In January 1999 Europe had a population density of about 134 people per square mile compared to the US with only 76 people per square mile, about half. Because of the high population density in Europe, the individual is more likely to be affected by the action of others. This is true for all private people, but, in regard to GMOs, we note that it is true as well for farmers. The threat of cross-pollination of GM plants is likely to be greater in Europe because the utilized areas are smaller and fields are closer together. This poses a problem especially for organic farmers, who fear to lose their status as organic farmers, if their fields are contaminated by cross-pollinating GM crops.

The result is a more active European governmental regulation in every part of society to insure a functioning community life. The necessity of conscious planning, which is reflected in the legal framework of the society makes people think more about the importance of a healthy environment and the consequences for their lifestyle for themselves and for others.

Importance of Food Quality. On average, in Europe people attach a higher value to the quality of their food than people in the US do. Food is part of the quality of life and a lifestyle issue in general.

Even though there are supermarkets in Europe which are comparable to the ones in the US, there are as well many small markets and shops which specialize in a certain kind of grocery products. The quality of the products sold in those places is in general higher than in the supermarkets. The food is more expensive there and it takes more time to shop in three or four different places than just in one big supermarket. Nevertheless, many people in Europe are willing to invest more time and money in order to have products with a higher nutritional value and better quality.

As we can see, the notion of what food means and therefore the importance of food quality in the US is different from the attitude in Europe. Since Americans in general seem not to attach so much value to the quality of food, they do consequently not care as much about genetically engineered foods, as long as they are not more expensive than traditional foods or do not taste worse.

Different Notion of Environment. The European notion of environment is different from the one in the US. This is expressed in domestic policies, in the attitude of the governments in international environmental negotiations (like for example in Rio or Cartagena), but as well in very simple statistics about the use of resources, which reflect the behavior of the population. Americans use about twice as much energy per capita as Europeans, 10 times more than Asians and 20 times more than Africans do (National Geographic 1998). Multi way bottles or reusable yogurt glasses, which are common in Europe, are hard to find in American supermarkets.

In the US, environment is seen in general as a commodity, which can be either used or commercialized. This attitude towards nature and environment in the US makes it easier for people to accept genetic engineering, since genetic engineering merely further adapts the environment and nature to the human needs.

CONCLUSION

Since a society is a complex and dynamic system, the examination of single aspects (following the Cartesian notion of reductionism) can only reveal part of the truth. In order to understand the whole functioning of the societal and political processes, one has to look at society as a whole rather than just on single elements. Especially in this case it appears that the interaction of the different factors is at least as important as the impacts of the respective factors, if not more important. Hence it is necessary to examine the interaction of the single elements in a systems approach rather than just looking at the respective factors.

It only takes one glance on the Systemigrams below to realize the differences between the EU and the US. Whereas in the EU (Figure 6) there is a variety of factors which fire the public discourse and thus bias the whole process, whereas the situation looks quite differently in the US (Figure 7).

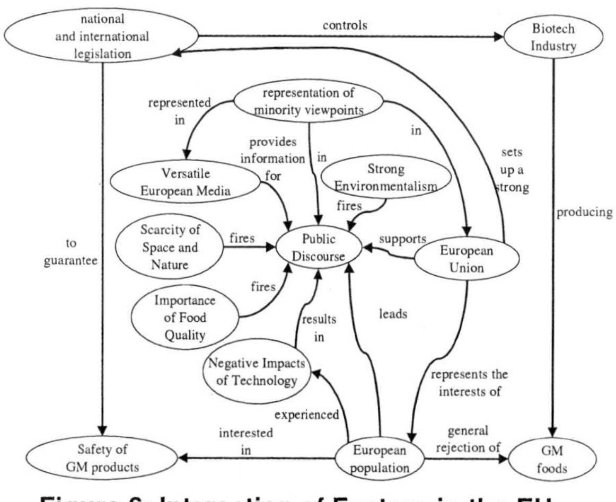

Figure 6: Interaction of Factors in the EU

Interestingly enough, even though the sinlge elements are the same in both the EU and the US, the interaction of those elements is completely different, as shown in the two Systemigrams. Therefore, the conclusion is that not the single elements and their attitude are the only decisive factors but rather the elements, their attitudes and especially their interaction. The Systemigrams prooved to be a valuable tool to display those interactions in a transparent manner.

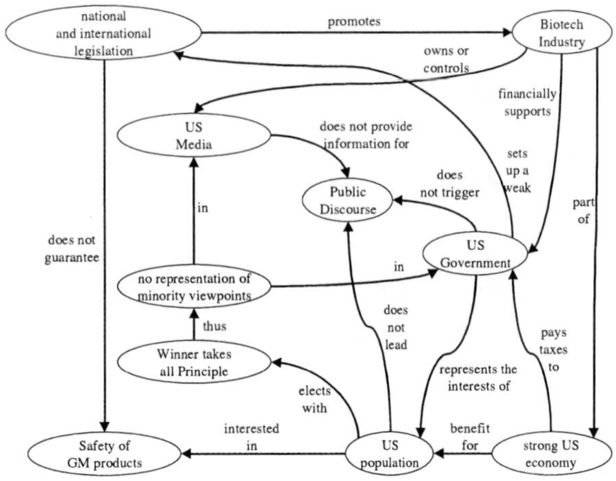

Figure 7: Interaction of Factors in the US

The systematic analysis of the problem has helped to reveal a number of theories, which may serve to explain the differences between the EU and the US. Due to the nature of social systems it is unlikely that the list of reasons is complete. More detailed research would probably uncover other possible reasons, which have been neglected in this analysis. Still, the systematic approach to the problem assured that a variety of viewpoints and arguments were taken into account, which could have been neglected easily in an unstructured approach.

REFERENCES

Borger, J. "Why Americans are happy to swallow the GM food experiment", The Guardian, London, February, 20 1999

Checkland, P., "Systems Thinking, Systems Practice", John Wiley & Sons Ltd. 1990

Dörner, C. "Die Logik des Mißlingens – Strategisches Denken in komplexen Situationen. Reinbek: Rowohlt, 1989

Genet "Consumers increasingly skeptical over GM foods", Genet Newsletter, March, 22 2000

Independent, "GM foods - Victory for grass-roots action", The Independent (London), May, 2 1999

Kraus, F., "Genetic Engineering in the EU an the US – A Systems Comparison" München: Technische Universität München, Semesterarbeit, 1999

Miller, M. C., " Free The Media", The Nation 1996, http://www.thenation.com/1996/issue/960603/0603mill.htm

National Geographic, "Population", National Geographic October 1998

Negele, H., "Systemtechnische Methodik zur ganzheitlichen Modellierung am Beispiel der integrierten Produktentwicklung", Dissertation, Fachgebiet Raumfahrttechnik, Technische Universität München, 1998

Pollan, M., "Playing God in the Garden", New York Times Sunday Magazine, October, 25 1998

Rampton, S. and Stauber, J. "Mad Cow USA – Could the Nightmare happen here?", Common Courage Press 1997

Science and Public Policy, "Biotechnology Risk regulation in Europe", Science and Public Policy, Volume 23, number 3, June 1996

USA WEEKEND " Debate results: America's newest food fight", USA WEEKEND, March 19, 2000

Meta-systems Engineering

A New Approach to Systems Engineering based on Emergent Meta-Systems and Holonomic Special Systems Theory

Kent D. Palmer, Ph.D.
Trace Studies Institute
P.O. Box 1632
Orange, CA 92856 USA
714-633-9508 palmer@think.net

INTRODUCTION

This paper introduces several different future extensions to the systems engineering discipline based on recent developments in general systems theory made by the author[1]. These recent discoveries recognize that there are many different schemas of intelligibility besides the system schema, such as the meta-system schema, the domain schema, the world schema, etc. that help us elucidate phenomena[2]. Each of these various schema calls for a different response from engineering, and thus engenders new engineering disciplines, or at least new approaches to the engineering of large scale systems. Among them are Meta-systems Engineering[3], Special Systems based Holonic Engineering[4] and Domain Engineering[5], World Engineering[6] and Whole Systems Design[7]. What is needed is a way to understand how these various kinds of schema and their associated engineering disciplines fit together into a coherent set of approaches. In this paper we will develop a theory of how this coherence of different approaches based on the various schemas of understanding might be achieved.

Keywords. Holonomics, Meta-systems, Systems Theory, Systems Engineering, Meta-systems engineering, Special Systems, Emergent Meta-systems, Whole Systems Design, Autopoietic Systems, Dissipative Systems, Reflexive Systems.

FROM SUPER-SYSTEM TO META-SYSTEM

A new trend in Systems Engineering is to begin to think about the difference between the "system of systems[8]," also known as the *super-systems,* engineering which deals with *mega-systems* or *macro-systems*, as opposed to the engineering of normal medium scale meso-systems or small scale micro-systems[9]. In fact, we might think of a whole scale of various levels of different sized systems which might call for different approaches to systems engineering due to the emergent properties that appear at the various scales. However, I would like to contrast this trend of considering *super-systems* as a special class needing peculiar methods, with another approach which instead emphasizes *meta-systems* (as another special class needing peculiar methods) and calls for the development of a particular sub-discipline of systems engineering that is not concerned with the effects of scale, so much as the effects of moving up a series of logical meta-levels from a system at any scale. This new discipline would be called **meta-systems engineering,** as opposed to systems engineering. As our basis for understanding what a *meta-system* might mean, we will take the Russell-Copi[10] concept of logical meta-levels developed in Principia Mathematica[11], which was also further developed by others such as Gregory Bateson,[12] who attempted to solve the problem of logical paradox, and we will contrast, as they do, the movement up toward higher meta-levels of logical type with the movement downward toward lower logical types. When we move to a meta-level it is very different from moving up or down a series of different nested scales of, for instance, "systems within systems within systems". As we move through the series of system levels there is a relative change of scale but at each level we are still dealing with *a system*, which is a template of understanding that we apply to certain types of phenomena. But when we move up to a logical type meta-level, i.e. to a higher logical type, then there is a strong difference in characteristics and interrelationships which cause us to understand that we are no longer dealing with a system, per se. Anthony

Wilden has written a book called The Rules Are No Game[13], which expresses this qualitative and quantitative phase change very well. A *game* is seen to be a model of an idealized system that is of a higher logical type than all the specific instances of playing a particular game. Thus if the game exists at meta-level one, then the *rules* are at the meta-level two. This is very different from moving to a different game in the ontic[14] scale, say in a "game of games of games". As you move up a level of ontic scale, one is still confronted with a game at the higher level. But when you move up an onto-logical[15] meta-level from any particular template of understanding, like the system, then you are confronted not with a game but with rules, i.e. something very different from a game which is intrinsic to the game but not the game itself. We call the rules the essence of the game. Rules describe the way you play a game and are definitely not the game itself as an abstraction$^{(1)}$ (meta-level one) or any concrete instance$^{(0)}$ (meta-level zero) of the play of the game. Rules exist at an onto-logical level$^{(2)}$ (meta-level two) beyond the game$^{(1)}$ where no players, pieces, or board exists except as terms of reference in the rules. Rules are static while games are dynamic. Rules seem arbitrary from the viewpoint of other games whose rules appear idiosyncratic or different. To take another example, the meta-level above spoken$^{(0)}$ language$^{(1)}$ is the grammar$^{(2)}$ of the language. Grammar is not a language itself but something else that describes the essence of a language by offering a set of constraints on the play of language. The idealization of a game$^{(1)}$ constrains the play of a particular game$^{(0)}$. If you go up another meta-level$^{(2)}$ one finds the categories of properties that exist which define a realm of possibility that the variation in the rules may take advantage of to define variations of the same game. For instance, a card deck is the basis for the invention of many different kinds of games of cards. The rules of different games take advantage of various aspects of the differences between the cards. With respect to language, one finds at the meta^2-level the categories of properties that constrain the grammars of all languages. These are properties like the various sounds that human beings can make with their vocal organs.

Quickly we realize that moving up to higher and higher meta-levels of onto-logical typing takes us into a very different realm from the systems of any ontic scale. Ontic systems of any scale may be characterized by an abstract gloss$^{(1)}$ that is a higher logical type than the concrete instances$^{(0)}$. At the meta^2-level one finds the rules, or constraints, that determine the essence of the system, game or language of whatever ontic scale is under consideration. If we move up to the next logical typing level$^{(3)}$ we find the meta-constraints that appear as categories of properties that determine the things that may function within a game, system or language. These meta-constraints underdetermine the lower level rule-like constraints which in turn underdetermines all possible particular instances of games, or systems or languages. What happens when we go through this exercise is that we discover that systems have essences that are constrained or determined by rules and that these rules are constrained by even higher level constraints on the categories of the properties of things that may give rise to games, or systems, or languages. Higher level general constraints on properties of things are quite different from lower level rule-like constraints on a specific system, game or language which gives rise to specific instances.

In order to be as clear as possible this can be expressed in the following way: The categories of the properties of a system, game or language, in fact any gestalt, constrain the properties of things which can be cited in the lower logical typed rules which apply to the even lower logical typed players, pieces and the board that is governed by the rules. A Castling Move in Chess is a peculiar possibility given the properties of the King and Castle and their position on the board. The properties that distinguish the board, the pieces and the sides of the board, etc. make it possible to define a Castling rule which then can define actual play. Properties of things have a higher logical type than the rules that relate things, which in turn, have a higher logical type than the things that obey or disobey those rules. Anomalies occur when there are rule violations or when there are undefined situations that appear in actual play. An ad hoc case by case judgement that deals with lapses in the rules exists at the fourth meta-level.

We mention games, systems and languages in one breath because we believe that these are variations, or representations of the same template of understanding. Games, systems and languages all have the same basic schema. Each is a gestalt in which figures (forms) are seen on a background. In Games this is obviously the pieces on the board. In language it is the word on the background of the stream of speech. Systems are more general and thus correspond more directly to the form of the template of understanding itself. A system is a gestalt composed of anything that relates a figure to a background in a "systematic way", i.e. a way that is based on rules and the properties of the things that can be within the system including exceptions. Rules, properties and exceptions define the meta-levels of the system which may be mapped down on various phenomena in existence. The system^{1} is a homoeomorphism between various phenomena^{0} that have a similar rule-based^{2} property-based^{3} and exception-based[4] configuration. We may draw this homoeomorphism between languages and games as Wittgenstein does in his famous term language-game as a form of life.[16]

THE FRAGMENTS OF BEING

In order to understand this series of meta-levels let us begin very generally and think not just of a *system,* but of any *entity*. Any entity can be designated to have Being. Being is the most general concept we can project on a thing, thereby turning it into an entity[17]. Being is a more general concept than the concept of system. Being covers all the templates of comprehension of things. It is the most general schema that we project on things. Being has traditionally four aspects: Reality, Identity, Presence and Truth. Reality is designated by judgement when we say *X is.* Identity is designated by discrimination when we say *X is X.* Presence is designated by reference when we say *X is here-now* or *This is X*. Truth is designated verification when we say *X is Y.* All of these statements are traditional ways of ascribing Being to things within the Indo-European worldview which is unique among the various historical worldviews in developing the concept of Being.

The study of the most general concept, i.e. Being, and its relation to things is called Ontology. Ontology and Epistemology are the normal constituents of Meta-physics, i.e. the philosophical description of what goes beyond physics. Epistemology tells us what we can know and Ontology talks about whether what we know is really, truly, identically present or not. In this century Continental philosophy has discovered that this most general concept, i.e. Being, is not unified but in fact is fragmented into an assortment of various Kinds of Being. An analysis of these kinds shows that the various kinds of Being are naturally composed of a series of meta-levels along the lines of those we have seen in relation to systems, games and language. Thus it becomes clear that the distillation of the meta-levels of systems and systems-like things is not a specific property of systems, but of all things designated with Being within our worldview. This ontological property of logical layering is specifically rooted in all Indo-European languages. From this we can see that it should in principle be possible to subject all the possible templates of understanding to this same kind of meta-level onto-logical analysis and thus specify their articulation at the various meta-levels of manifestation.

The series of kinds of Being has a specific and determined order that is true for all things.

Being's meta-levels	Bateson's series	Modalities of being-in-the-world	Associated Cognitive abilities
$Being^5$ meta-level ULTRA Existence	This step into non-Being is ultimately unthinkabl e	empty handedness emptiness or void	cognitive inability
$Being^4$ meta-level WILD	$Learning^4$ *Learning to learn to learn to learn*	Out-of_hand	encom-passing
$Being^3$ meta-level HYPER	$Learning^3$ *learning to learn to learn*	In-hand	bearing
$Being^2$ meta-level PROCESS	$Learning^2$ *learning to learn*	Ready-to-hand	grasping
$Being^1$ meta-level PURE	$Learning^1$ *learning as an ideal gloss*	Present-at-hand	pointing
$Being^0$ meta-level entity	Concrete $instances^0$ of learning in the world	Orientation toward things	thing

Table 1: Levels of Being

Bateson, in Steps to the Ecology of the Mind, gives an excellent example of stepping through the series of meta-levels in his analysis of the meta-levels of learning. This may be done by starting with anything in the world. Heidegger tells us what the modalities of our being-in-the-world are in relation to the various meta-levels of Being. Merleau-Ponty points out some of the cognitive abilities in relation to things that exemplify these modalities. His view may be augmented by those of Levinas[18] to help fill out this column. Some of these concepts have been filled in by the author to complete the schema[19]. What we can see from Bateson's account of the meta-levels of learning is that when we start from concrete instances of learning and attempt to define learning, what then appears is a fairly static abstract gloss that serves as a definition of a cognitive capability in humans, animals and perhaps in machines. This abstract gloss is what appears at the level of Pure Being. Learning is considered as something that may be pointed out in the world which is present-at-hand, i.e. available to us in the world.

When we go up a level and attempt to understand how we *learn to learn*, this is where the rules or constraints on learning are discovered. Various constraints need different learning strategies to overcome or to maneuver around them. Learning to learn is more than merely something we point out as a cognitive capability. It is something that we grasp in doing it. We relate to it in a fashion which is ready-to-hand, i.e. it is something we use directly to move toward the goal of present-at-hand learning. Learning to learn is like technology, it is an assorted means to an end. This meta-level is called Process Being. *Learning to learn* tells us more about the essence of learning, i.e. the constraints on learning that must be negotiated in order to learn how to learn.

When we move up to the next higher meta-level which is *learning to learn to learn*, things begin to become difficult to think about. It becomes more and more difficult to describe what is meant and to hold onto the concepts at this level. This level is called Hyper Being[20]. At this level we are relating to things via bearing and our modality of being-in-the-world is called the in-hand. It is called the in-hand because at this meta-level things transform into other things in our hands. This level defines the meta-constraints that determine the genetic unfolding of the thing which gives the thing its properties. Thus, this level defines the genetic unfolding of *learning to learn* within the world. This unfolding is something we bear and over which we have little real control. This, for instance, is described by Kuhn[21] in terms of paradigm changes in science. Scientific progress is made by continually expanding our horizon of ways of learning to learn from nature. But one has very little choice in the paradigm changes that occur because they are a social phenomena. One may accept or deny a paradigm, but little else.

Finally, at the last meta-level of learning, i.e. *learning to learn to learn to learn*, one loses control completely. This is seen as a total encompassing by the phenomena where everything is out-of-hand, i.e. out of control[22]. At this level there is no conceptual room to maneuver. Bateson calls it tantamount to personal enlightenment. This is because the constraints that determine the genetic unfolding change so that a different species of a thing is created with a different series of unfoldings. Learning^{4} is complete because a constant transformation of the meta-essence of learning is continually changing. This is thought of as something only the "gods" could bear[23]. For human beings it would be tantamount to being subjected to a regime of permanent overwhelming fundamental change. When we get glimpses of this depth of change we call it a genuine emergent[24] event that restructures our world.

From this summary of the levels of Being, as applied to Bateson's levels of learning, we can see that we move from the thing$^{\underline{0}}$ itself in the world, to a gloss$^{\underline{1}}$ of that thing at the first meta-level. At the second meta-level we find that the essence$^{\underline{2}}$ of the thing appears as the rule-like constraints that determine the use of the ideal gloss of the instances. At the third meta-level, we find the meta-constraints that determine the meta-essence$^{\underline{3}}$ properties of the things that underlay the expression of rules, which is how everything within the same category is constrained. Normally this refers to the genetic unfolding of the species of the thing. At the fourth meta-level, we find exceptions$^{\underline{4}}$ to the rules and meta-rules that defy analysis.

Let us take the example of geometry. In geometry we have a series of n-dimensional spaces that are discovered by mathematicians in spite of the fact, we can only experience directly three, or four if you consider time a dimension. The series of n-dimensional spaces are nested in a way that has wonderful coherence and integrity. Points, lines, surfaces and dimensional forms are reused over and over again to produce higher dimensional figures. This nesting of higher and higher dimensional forms can be likened to the concept of the micro-system, meso-system, macro-system, super-system, mega-system etc. At each level there is greater and greater demand for integrity and coherence within the lower level systems which is necessary for the higher level system to work as a higher level ontic system rather than a mere aggregate. However, if instead we go in the orthogonal direction of thinking about meta-systems, then we find very different objects. For instance, given various mathematical figures$^{\underline{0}}$ we might find an n-dimensional space, if we move to the meta-level we find the abstraction$^{\underline{1}}$ of the discipline of geometry. But when we go to the next meta-level we find within geometry the process$^{\underline{2}}$ of producing theorems by proofs and other activities that generate theorems about geometric mathematical objects. If we move up to the next meta-level, then we have the axioms$^{\underline{3}}$ that all our geometry is based upon. Finally if we move up to the highest attainable meta-level of Being, we find exceptions$^{\underline{4}}$ and contradictions. For instance, we really do not know about the essence of geometrical things unless we understand the process of producing proofs. In education geometry is composed of a series of static geometrical forms that we learn about in our classes on geometry. But to become geometers we must learn to do proofs. Learning to do proofs means mastering various techniques for learning about geometrical objects. When we understand proofs within the known realm of geometry then we can begin to question the axioms and postulates that define the domain of geometry. At this level we see that geometry had undergone paradigm shifts when it was discovered that the parallel lines postulate could not be proved. Geometers produced alternative geometries by allowing parallel lines to cross. It was discovered that there was a trace point of indecision[25] in the axiomatic basis of geometry itself. This point of indecision causes a process by which we learn how to learn to learn, i.e. a paradigm shift is generated within the field itself. This causes us to understand more deeply the axioms of geometry. These axioms are the meta-constraints that determine the properties of objects within the geometrical realm. They make possible the unfolding of geometrical proofs that effect the products of the proofs themselves. We define the objects of points, lines and surfaces and their properties and then take them for granted as part of our axiomatic platform. It is possible that there are exceptions or contradictions that may exist within an axiomatic system. These exceptions or contradictions exemplify the highest meta-level of Being. In geometry a contradiction might be generated by maintaining that parallel lines both cross and do not cross. We attempt to avoid such contradictions at all costs because they cause the whole discipline to collapse into chaos. An example of an exception is the dimensionlessness of a point. Everything in geometry has dimension except the point. The dimensionlessness of the point is very difficult to understand, but it is nevertheless assumed as an exception or contradiction within geometry that allows the geometrical formal system to work[26].

ONTIC AND ONTOLOGICAL HIERARCHIES

We have explored the various meta-levels of Being in order to show that this is a completely different horizon than that of the various scales of systems. We have seen that when we move in this direction we determine the essence (constraints) of the system and meta-essence (meta-constraints) of the properties of the things within the system that determine the forms that appear within the scale horizon. At the highest meta-level, exceptions in this lattice of constraints are identified, like Godellian statements for which no determination can be made as to whether they are inside or outside the formal system. Now, we will attempt to show how this onto-logical series applies to the definition of a system. This can be done by defining the horizon of scales as the ontic hierarchy. This means that it relates to the things that are designated to have Being without logical differentiation. Orthogonal to this hierarchy is another hierarchy of our ways of understanding the things in the world. We will call this the onto-logical hierarchy. It is composed of the fundamental comprehensible types of things we find. This hierarchy has the following levels:

Pure *Deterministic* *Continuous*	*Process* *Probablistic* *Stochastic*	*Hyper* *Possiblistic* *Fuzzy*	*Wild* *Propensity* *Chaotic*
pluriverse	Over-determination	coherence	incoherence
kosmos	mapping	Transform-ations	blanks
world	Showing and hiding across horizon	projection	opacity
domain	filtering	assumptions	blind-spots
meta-system	dualities	resources	catastrophes
system	rules	properties	exceptions
form	Proof of theorems	axioms	anomalies
pattern	categorization	spectra	singularities
monad	isolation	cross-over	mutations
facet	distinguishing	integrity	flaws

Table 2: Ontological Hierarchy

Notice that what appears in this hierarchy are templates for an understanding of things. A system is one of those ways of understanding, but only one among several. Systems, as Rescher has shown[27], are based on intuitions about things that come from dealing with organisms in our environment. When considered very broadly, systems have many of the properties of organisms. Here we define a system as *a social gestalt*. This is to say it is a figure-ground relation seen by a group of people, or degenerately by a single individual. The *sine quo non* of such social gestalts are traditionally other groups of animals, or degenerately single organisms, or further degenerately plants, or at the limit of degeneration physical formations. We project the "system" template of understanding onto the ontic hierarchy. We may alternatively project other templates, or schema, of the onto-logical hierarchy onto the ontic hierarchy. For different phenomena, various onto-logical hierarchy templates may be appropriate. It is a matter of aesthetics or personal preference as to which templates of understanding are projected on which phenomena[28]. Much of the confusion in science occurs because different researchers project different onto-logical templates of understanding onto the same phenomena. The ontological hierarchy as a whole gives us a good measure of our progress in formulating a systems theory and in producing a systems engineering discipline based on such a theory. The standard for systems theory in our time is the *formal structural system* which covers the layers of the ontological hierarchy from system down to pattern. A form is an element in a formalism. We construct formalisms like geometry or logic and do proofs in these disciplines. A weaker standard of comprehension is an explanation which we give when we cannot do proofs. This standard operates at the level of pattern and is called structuralism[29]. It allows us to traverse discontinuities in forms or deal with time. The weakest standard of comprehension is the description of the system. We only give descriptions when we cannot explain or prove. We combine these three different standards of comprehension and call this the scientific approach to phenomena. A good generalized example of a formal structural system is George Klir's Architecture of Systems Problem Solving[30]. Science does not deal very well with any of the onto-logical levels from the meta-system upward or below the level of the monad. However some of these ontological levels are necessary for us to understand what science itself is. For instance, every system that science studies exists in some field defined by the meta-system. We mount our campaign to understand that system by creating a discipline which studies that class of phenomena. That discipline operates in a world shared by other disciplines. All those disciplines are gathered together in the university which contains all accepted disciplines. But beyond the university there may be many quasi-disciplines or proto-disciplines that are not accepted but which exist in the general economy of all possible disciplines including magical or other non-scientific approaches to things. On the other hand the monad is the lowest element of content in a pattern. Monads are the existent that the patterns are made of which structuralism finds to be the categorizable contents of form. Facets are the ways that these monads appear to each other in different contexts. The monad is projected by science as the non-reducible level that all other ontic scale levels are reduced to. We projected qualities such as earth, air, fire and water to be atomic until Democritus realized that it was possible that there were quantal atoms. We projected these ideal quantal atoms as the lowest level of reality until we discovered fundamental particles. Eventually we gave up this level for quarks which are never seen in isolation. Eventually we may give up quarks for something even more basic. Projecting the ultimate stratum level zero of substance[31] is part of the game of science which attempts to reduce everything to that level. But in doing so Science reveals the levels of ontic emergence that segments the ontic hierarchy into various recognizable levels of phenomena which have different characteristics and different kinds of relations. Each of these ontic levels is the underdetermining basis of the next higher level. "Supervenance" is the technical term in Analytical Philosophy for the mapping down of a higher level ontic configuration onto a lower level ontic configuration. Each mapping down is partially determined by the lower level and partially non-determined. To the extent that it is not determined there is room to maneuver and room for new non-reducible properties and relations to appear which exemplify emergent phenomena.

Systems Engineering focuses on the emergent aspects that appear at any particular ontic level, however we discern it. It is interesting that systems are assemblies of physical components with specific properties and actions. These components have both functional and agent shadows. As we build up the ontic hierarchy by assembling components, we only arrive at the next higher ontic emergent level when the functional hierarchy and the agent hierarchy meet the assembly hierarchy at the same point. We normally think of function as a single kind of thing that subsumes and supports the intentions of the users of the system. Agency on the other hand relates to the various autonomous actors that work together to perform the functions. The separation of distributed agency and the gatheredness of the intention supporting uniformity of function form a spectra along a single dimension orthogonal to the dimension of physical assembly. The Agency shadows of the component is the basis for what is called the physical architecture while the Function shadows of the physical assembly is the basis for what is known as the functional architecture. When the two shadow architectures that appear within the general economy overflows, the restricted economy of the components that inhabit space and time merge at some ontic level of assembly. Then we have an emergent property appear. If some aspect of the assembly breaks, then we de-emerge[32] from this point of the articulation of emergence. The unity of the functionality of the system fragments and the agency may become uncoordinated. If there are multiple kinds of emergence that occur, then there is really a kind of function related to each kind of emergent characteristic that finds itself integrated at some level of the systems articulation.[33]

In general, given any phenomena that is considered as a system, i.e. a social gestalt, which means a gestalt for some group of people[34], then we move up to the meta-systemic level. At that level we are breaking apart that system into its constituent elements and, thus, deconstructing it so that its emergent properties disappear and the field within which those elements swim appears instead. That field sees the sub-systems as gestalts on the ur-ground of the meta-system. Any specific thing can be thought of in relation to the various meta-levels of Being. But if we take each of the templates of comprehension (cognitive schemas) up that series of steps, we will get very different results as seen in the table above. For the system which is like a language-game we will find the rules at the level of Process. Beyond that we will find the meta-rules that determine the properties of the things that are allowed within the system. Beyond that we find the exceptions and contradictions that are the violations of the property constraints and game rules.

When we explore the onto-logical meta-levels of the various templates of understanding we find some very interesting differences between the various meta-levels. Looking at the Formal Structural System as a whole we see at meta-level^2 rules, theorems and categories. At meta-level^3 we see properties, axioms and spectra. At meta-level^4 we see exceptions, anomalies and singularities. If we look carefully at these three levels we see the nesting of the levels fairly clearly. Notice that as one moves to higher meta-levels of the system, one finds rules and then properties of things within the system, and then exceptions. But when we look at forms, then there are proofs of theorems and then axioms and then anomalies. The forms are shapes of things with properties. As we advance up the meta-levels of system we approach something that feeds into our understanding of form. Similarly, when we look at pattern, then we move from categorization of contents, to spectra of qualities, then to singularities. Axioms concern the minimal elements from which the forms are built up. Those minimal elements can be categorized according to qualitative criteria as a way of approaching the actual spectra that lie below the categorizations. When we look at monads then we move from isolation, then to cross-over then to mutation. Isolation allows us to see the minimal discernable quanta of the phenomena that makes up the spectra. When we try to determine this exactly, it normally leads to a recognition of a bleeding over into other minimal discernables called cross over or tunneling between isolatable elements. The cross-over or bleeding out of minimal discernables causes us to look at how we distinguish one thing from another and thus calls into question the integrity of our minimal discernables. Cornelius Castoriadis talks about Magma[35] as the non-determinable proto-order of things beyond our projections of order. The lowest bound of the onto-logical hierarchy of templates of understanding is the ontic magma beyond all our discriminations. Deleuze and Guattari[36] talk about the rhizome of interconnections that produces a labyrinth of distinctions and produces monadic discriminations which, taken together, are impossible to organize completely. Facets and Monads are projected beyond experience to explain the fact that we comprehend determinate things within the buzzing confusion of our experience. All the things that do not fit into our projections are pushed out into Wild Being at every threshold of comprehension. It is out of Wild Being that the things that change our view of the world arise. Emergent events move through each of the levels of Being on their way into our world. They many percolate up through any of the templates of understanding. A genuinely emergent event passes through all four meta-levels[37]. Events that do not involve all four levels of Being are called artificial because they do not fully reprogram our organization of the world at some level of understanding.

A similar nesting can be seen occurring at the upper thresholds of understanding. Systems can only exist if they have the necessary resources. Resources are the meta-level beyond the duality or complementarity of meta-systems that is the meta-level of the meta-system itself. The meta-system is normally a set of integrated complementarities of complementarities that defines the environment or ecosystem that the system finds itself within and inhabits. Meta-systems cannot be fully dominated by domains but their filtering of systems is based on higher level assumptions. Domains attempt to construct a restricted economy with a unified ideal viewpoint on the phenomena with which they are concerned. Domains attempt to tighten up the filtering done by the meta-system on its constituent systems by increasing rigor. Filtering is done by the production of theories that connect phenomena in ways that are coherent for the domain. Theories are ways of looking at the phenomena which is based on implicit and explicit assumptions. The Domain is an incarnation of the general projection of the worldview on a specific set of phenomena. This projection is a reification of the showing and hiding of the world. The world establishes the horizons across which the phenomena manifest. Moving from one horizon to another is a fundamental transformation at the level of Kosmos. The kosmos is a mapping exercise that takes us beyond our direct experience and attempts to be all inclusive. These maps attempt to give global coherence to all phenomena of a certain kind. These coherences arise from the over-determinations of phenomena in the general economy that cannot be dominated completely by the kosmos and thus is called the pluriverse because it is constructed of multiple intersecting universes along the lines that David Deutsch suggests in The Fabric of Reality[38]. The highest level of understanding bumps into the incredible variety of things that exists within the universe and not one grand unified scheme can account for all the variety even if it could account for the general laws of nature that underlay the arena in which the variety interacts.

It is important for Systems Engineering as a discipline to realize that the "system" is not the only schema or template of understanding that we might apply to the emergent ontic hierarchy. The "system" fits into the "formal structural system" and this has a dual in the "world domain meta-system". These two dual templates apply to experience and are augmented by two pairs of other templates that are projected beyond experience in order to make sense of experience. Kosmos attempts to unify all the phenomena of the world through maps, and what it fails to map falls off our model of the earth into the pluriverse which is a catchall for all we do not understand about the universe. Monads attempt to supply the ultimate level of reduction at whatever ontic level that it is projected onto, whether it is organisms, atoms, fundamental particles, quarks, sub-quarks, etc… The facet governs everything that falls outside the monad's capability of reduction. Within experience there are six thresholds of comprehension[39], at least notionally. In other words this is only a model of the thresholds taken from the current literature of Science in the broad sense which includes hard and soft sciences. There are endless variations of these various thresholds in the literature. But for our purposes we can focus on these six experiential thresholds by which we can comprehend the phenomena we see "out there" in the realm of the ontic emergent hierarchy. The "formal structural system" (notice that these are mentioned in the order of their power of explanation of phenomena) is well understood[40]. What is not well understood is the inverse dual of the formal structural system that appears as the combination of the *domain world meta-system*. Notice that Systems Engineering is attempting at this point in time to establish itself as a discipline with a specific domain. The domain is a filter and the meta-system is the field which underlies this filter, while the world is a showing and hiding structure based on horizons. When we consider the environmental impact of our work on systems, then we are dealing with the meta-systemic field. What we have not yet taken on is the project of World Engineering. World Engineering would have to look at the interactions and side-effects of all possible systems that appear on the horizons of the world. World Engineering is still the stuff of science fiction[41]. If we were to take on that task then there are many things that we would have to consider within the auspices of our discipline that are not considered now. We have not taken ownership of the interspace between the systems we build. World Engineering would consider the relation between the various systems of whatever scale and would take into consideration the interaction of these systems.

SYSTEMS AND META-SYSTEMS

At this point in the history of the development of our discipline, systems engineering, we tend to focus on *systems* because there has been a good formal structural systemic basis developed by science in the last few hundred years. Systems are descriptive of any phenomena seen as a social gestalt[42]. Systems have broad applicability because they can be applied to any phenomena that is construed as a social gestalt. Thus it is an extremely malleable template of comprehension. It is also highly structured due to the fact that it consists of rules and properties at its meta-level. Proofs and categorizations have greater explanatory power but rules have greater structuring power through the modeling of constraints at both the Process Being *essence* and Hyper Being *meta-essence* levels. Axioms are arbitrary and have limited extent so that proofs have extremely narrow scope compared with structures or systems. Categorizations are also arbitrary and though they have broader extent than proofs, their extent is still extremely limited comparatively. Spectra appear to be grounded in phenomena but properties formulate the qualitative content of the phenomena so that they can be understood and incorporated into our systems as variables. Thus, in general, although the explanatory levels of systems are weak, they give us quite a bit of organizational leverage. That is why we tend to focus on this level when we turn to engineering projects and away from doing science. That is when we leave discovery work and begin building and construction.

We get a fairly high leverage when thinking about things in terms of systems and this compensates for their lack of explanatory power. It seems that there is a tradeoff between explanatory power and structuring at the meta-levels of Being. This is why we do not call our discipline Forms Engineering or Patterns Engineering. But what we fail to appreciate in many instances, is that there is something to be gained by looking at the discipline and meta-systemic levels as well. This essay suggests going one step further than usual by addressing the meta-systems level which, as it turns out, is complementary to the systems level. Meta-systems are environments, ecosystems, situations, milieu or contexts. We see them when we deconstruct the super-system and allow its subsystems to be seen within the internal environment of the super-system. The meta-system indicates the field within which the system arises and within which it interacts with other systems. Meta-systems are inherently complementary and thus not unified in the way that systems are unified. Meta-systems always contain duals, they supply the resources within the arena that the systems need to operate in order to function and interact. They provide the communication between systems within that arena. A good analogy is the operating environment within which applications run in computers, so called "operating systems," which are really meta-systems. Formally, the meta-system is to the system as the universal Turing machine is to the Turing machine. It is an environment that runs Turing machines that it reads from tape and adjudicates between them providing them resources as necessary. Meta-systems engineering is the natural complement to systems engineering. Systems engineering is concerned with the unified product that is to be built. Meta-systems theory is concerned with the environment that this product will go into and its side-effects in that environment[43]. It also considers each level of the ontic hierarchy to be a deconstructed super-system, which when taken apart, gives us a meta-systemic environment for the sub-systems to arise within and interact with each other. Thus, meta-systems engineering is what holds sway as the product is being developed. The meta-system describes the design landscape of all possible product designs and how the selected designs arise and interact within the development process. Processes live inside of meta-systems which produce systemic products. The complementarity between process and product is similar to the complementarity of the system and meta-system. The complementaity between quality and quantity are similar. Product quality is improved by measuring the process that develops that product. Whenever you find complementarities it is a sign of a meta-system. For instance, the complementarity between reading and writing of data in the Turing machine and in computer systems, is generally a sign of an interaction with that machine's environment. Environment related operations are always complementary.

Due to this complementarity between systems and meta-systems, we cannot have a systems engineering discipline without a complementary meta-systems engineering discipline. And it turns out that this is exactly the discipline we need in our time, because it is the side-effects of systems in the environment that is the fundamental problem facing our discipline. We design systems but ignore the meta-systemic implications of those systems and sometimes that leads to unintended consequences. Meta-systems, though, are not just ecosystems but also relate internally to our systems design and to the design process. Thus each supersystem, when de-emerged, turns into a meta-system for the sub-system components. It is this phenomena that leads us to consider the combination of systems and meta-systems holonomic. This is to say that together they describe what Arthur Koestler called Holons[44]. Holons are things like organs in the body that are parts from the perspective of things above them and wholes from the perspective of things below them in the ontic hierarchy. Systems, when decomposed, give us meta-systemic fields which spawn sub-systems and so on down the ontic hierarchy. In other words the ontic hierarchy is constructed out of the action of transforming from system to meta-system or vice versa. The power of the complementarity between system and meta-systemic views is that it generates the ontic hierarchy that encompasses everything that we ascribe to Being within our worldview.

Meta-systems engineering does not look at building things, but examines taking them apart. It is deconstructionist[45] in the postmodern sense. In fact, one interpretation of Postmodernism[46] is the realization that there is a general meta-systemic economy that operates outside of the historically sanctioned restricted economy of ideas, values, significance etc[47]. One of the things this postmodern viewpoint takes apart is "systems engineering" itself. When we look at systems engineering as a discipline we see that it is composed of a core related to systems theory and a periphery that is made up of many specialties that come from the various domains in which systems engineering is applied and these are integrated into the various kinds of systems we build. The sine quo non of our approach to building things is the integration of emergent effects from multiple disciplines. Thus, the set of possible domains from which we draw can be seen as the meta-system to the system we are attempting to build. Systems engineering itself is a field with many sub-disciplines making up a rich fabric of concerns. The meta-system is what mediates between the domain of systems engineering and its various sub-domains. What has hardly been imagined yet is that systems engineering encompasses all the various fields of human endeavor by which we attempt to project the template of understanding that allows us to see systems in the world. The complementary template is that of the meta-system which sees the underlying proto-gestalts of gestalts on the ur-field beneath the figure ground relations that make up the system. These two templates together allow us to define holonomics which is the study of holons and holarchies of holons. This gives rise to what is sometimes called *whole systems design*[48] which is a subfield of systems engineering that is concerned with the production of holonic systems, i.e. systems that fit into the whole and are whole themselves. The ideal of such systems are what George Leonard[49] calls *Holoidal* systems which are systems that have attributes like a hologram in which each part functions based on an image of the whole system. Holoidal systems are the opposite of aggregate systems which are blind to the wholes that they are a part of. Whole systems design is directed at understanding holoidal systems and building them such that the world is seen as nested wholes each of which is holoidal in relation to the upper level wholes of this different kind of ontic hierarchy. In this kind of hierarchy we have increased the level of coherence demanded from the meta-system coherence of fields to the coherence of domain filters or to the level of the coherence of the world itself where the horizons are seen to be coherent. As we do this the nature of the ontic hierarchy changes. Systems Engineering puts together forms so that they create coherent gestalts. Meta-systems engineering wants the sets of gestalts to be coherent. Domain engineering wants those gestalts to be coherent with respect to a selected filter of phenomena, sometimes called a paradigm. World engineering wants all the horizons upon which phenomena appear to be coherent within a worldview. What starts out as a bland composition slowly takes the form of a hologram as we go up the levels of the ontological hierarchy and imagine a different kind of engineering at each level. A Kosmic engineering, if that were possible, would ask for all the worldviews to be coherent within the universe.

Equally as we move down the ontological ladder we encounter greater and greater degrees of decohernece where monads, the minimal discernable elements, are the ultimate conceivable fragments of existence. Systems Engineering attempts to increase coherence one notch from the level of forms in the world because its structuring in the meta-levels of Being provides a big jump in terms of effective coherence. But this coherence carries with it the emergent properties that are realized by the systemic whole. It is necessary to allow a complementary de-emergence to occur which will give coherence to the set of gestalts rather than merely to the gestalt itself.

Moving from separation to gatheredness we go to even higher level notches on the coherence scale by applying the ontological hierarchy to the ontic hierarchy step by step. This takes us more and more deeply into *whole systems design*[50] as a branch of Systems Engineering. Systems Engineering should stress its foundations in Systems Theory. Unfortunately these foundations are lost to most of the "systems engineering" community because they never studied systems theory. It is strange to think that the theory of systems is not required for professionals to practice systems engineering. This is like saying that electrical engineers do not need to know the theory of electrical circuits in order to design them. Hopefully, eventually systems engineering will rediscover its roots in academic General System Theory. Then the discipline will no longer feel adrift with no scientific foundations. General Systems Theory is the meta-science of all science that treats systems in general in a scientific manner. General Systems Theory is to Particular Sciences as Mathematical Category theory is to the various Mathematical Categories, like sets, groups, lattices etc., that are the objects of various branches of mathematics. But Systems Engineering should also recognize its sister discipline, Meta-systems Engineering, which should be based on a General Meta-systems Theory that should complement general systems theory. Unfortunately, this discipline does not exist at the moment, unless we consider the study of ecosystems[51] an example of such a study restricted to how biological organisms interact within their environment. However, we can still pay attention to meta-systems within our practice, by considering the implications of what we are doing for the relevant environment and by considering the design field itself out of which our solution arises. We can also think about how the de-emergent fields within which sub-systems operate as part of the super-system.

FROM META-SYSTEMS TO SPECIAL SYSTEMS

We define holonomics to be the study of holons and holarchies both within the world and in theory. We note that through the recognition of duality there has been progress in holonomics that the reader should be aware of. What we find when we look at systems and meta-systems as a duality, is that the system is a whole greater than the sum of its parts, while the meta-system is a whole less than the sum of its parts. The meta-system has *lacks* and *deficiencies* that are exactly what is needed for the system to fit into it. We build the nested levels of our super-systems by allowing each level to unfold into a meta-system that sustains its sub-system parts. By moving back and forth between these views, we develop a holonic way of seeing the *systems of systems*. However, we should note that there is a third possibility. That is the possibility of wholes exactly equal to the sum of their parts. This brings us to the mention of Special Systems theory which should be the third discipline that is developed between the complementarity of General Systems Theory and General Meta-systems Theory. *Special Systems* deal with anomalous systems in which the whole is exactly equal to the sum of the parts. Such systems are aggregative yet still whole. There are three examples of such systems, they are called Dissipative, Autopoietic and Reflexive. Dissipative special systems are equivalent to what Ilya Prigogine[52] calls "Dissipative structures" which are negentropic. Autopoietic special systems are self-organizing and are equivalent to what Maturana and Varela define as self-producing systems[53]. Reflexive special systems are social in nature and correspond to the kind of reflexivity that John O'Malley describes in The Sociology of Meaning[54] and which Barry Sandywell describes in his Logological Investigations[55]. Each of these special systems function as a whole that is exactly equal to the sum of its parts but in different ways. The autopoietic system represents homeostatic balance through the maintenance of the system's own organization. Dissipative and Reflexive systems are a pair which are each out of balance separately but together provide a model of dynamic balance. Autopoietic systems can be seen in terms of the model of the Perfect numbers while Dissipaitve systems can be seen in terms of the model of the Amicable numbers, and Reflexive systems can be seen in terms of the model of the Sociable numbers. The perfect numbers are those rare examples where the factors of a number add up exactly to the number itself without deficiency or surplus. Amicable numbers are plentiful and are examples of two numbers whose parts add up to each other. Sociable numbers extend this same trick to groups of numbers higher than two. Perfect and Amicable numbers were known in the Greek era and were symbols of the possibility of perfect systems. Sociable numbers were only discovered in 1914 and so extend these kinds of numbers to a set that reflects the holonic properties of all three special systems. However, the special systems theory has firmer grounding in mathematics than this. The series of HyperComplex algebras give us our mathematical model for the special systems.

Meta-system	Sedenion or higher non-division Algebras This algebra has one real and fifteen imaginary numbers and loses the division property
Reflexive Special System	Octonion Algebra This algebra has one real and seven imaginary numbers and loses the associative property
Autopoietic Special System	Quaternion Algebra This algebra has one real and three imaginary numbers and loses the commutative property
Dissipative Special System	Complex Algebra This algebra has one real and one imaginary number in conjunction.
System	Real Algebra This algebra has one real number

Table 3: Types of Systems and Algebras

There are also anomalous physical systems that display the properties of these rare *special systems*. Dissipative systems are seen in nature in the phenomena of Solitons. Autopoietic systems are seen in nature in the phenomena of the Cooper pairs in superconductivity. Reflexive systems are seen in nature in the phenomena of the Bose-Einstein condensate and other macro-quantum mechanical phenomena. Given the existence of these anomalous physical examples and mathematical underpinnings, Special Systems theory is as scientific as any discipline might hope to be.

Special systems theory gives rise to a new kind of Holonic Engineering which attempts to build systems, such as self-organization, with the properties of the special systems. These are the properties of intelligent living social systems. One definition for a Holonic System is "A system which self-organizes and evolves to dynamically optimize survivability, adaptability, flexibility, efficiency and effectiveness"[56]. Holonic Manufacturing Systems[57] have this kind of ideal. Special Systems theory is the first unified theory of these kinds of systems. Holonic Engineering makes use of the Special Systems theory foundations to build systems that are in aggregate still whole, that self-organize and socially interact as intelligent agents, and which introduce order into the world through their mutual action.

Beyond the special systems themselves there is also the form of the Emergent Meta-system[58] that describes the joint action of normal entropic systems with the various special systems. Emergent Meta-systems are swarms of holonic agents that create, mutually interact, form gestalts, explore possibilities and then vote through mutual annihilation on which possibilities should be realized in the next cycle. Emergent Meta-systems Engineering looks beyond the synchronic holarchy to a diachronic holodynamic formation which designs itself in a way similar to the workings of the grouped genetic algorithm[59]. It is one thing to talk about autopoietic self-production and it is quite another to talk about self-design[60]. Self-design can only be achieved by a swarm of holoidal holons that interact to produce their own organization as a social collaboration. The individual elements collude with each other to assure their continued existence over time. Such a system assumes discontinuity instead of the continuity that our systems normally assume. Swarms of Intelligent social agents produce each other and mutually interact and then recognize their own design and elaborate the various possibilities for the development of that design until they vote which possibilities to act upon. Emergent meta-systems provide us with a model of the "ultimate" System that engineers itself as part of its functioning. The engineering of self-designing systems goes beyond autopoiesis to Autogenesis, i.e. the self boot strapping of organization that produces the self-producing system.

FUTURE KINDS OF ENGINEERING

Now that we have defined various strange kinds of engineering that appear as future possibilities, let us look at them together once more. Systems Engineering is a discipline which leverages from the System ontological template of understanding which has a great deal of structure at its meta-levels as compared with the lower level templates such as form and pattern. We can think of other disciplines such as Form Engineering and Pattern Engineering as sub-disciplines below Systems Engineering. But beyond Systems Engineering, we can also imagine Meta-systems Engineering, Domain Engineering, World Engineering. At each level we are introducing greater and greater coherence into the ontic hierarchies of the systems we build. And yet there is another dimension that we need to recognize which is the dimension of the special systems that moves out orthogonally from the duality of Systems and Meta-systems. In the special systems we find the true meaning of holonomics as the study of holons, not in the sense of holoidal systems, but in the sense of aggregates that are separate but whole at the same time because their whole equals the sum of their parts. Special systems engineering concentrates on creating intelligent social agents that organize themselves, but these agents do not design themselves. This is to say that such agents have a static essence. When we consider giving these agents a dynamic essence by creating a meta-essence that can design itself, then we can see the possibility of an emergent meta-systems engineering of systems that design themselves and thus boot strap their own order into existence through autogenesis.

All this may sound like science fiction, but it turns out that the foundations of this twenty first century engineering exists today in the form of special systems theory and emergent meta-systems theory. So let us start this new century by exploiting this future engineering that has serendipitously come to us now[61].

CONCLUSION

You can think of this paper as an introduction to several strange new kinds of engineering disciplines that may grow out of systems engineering as we know it today. It is based on recent advances in Systems Theory. Systems theory should be the foundation of our systems engineering discipline. However, too few of us know about any of the recent advances in General Systems Theory which could serve as a basis for better engineering of systems. This paper attempts to bring some of those cutting edge advances into focus by projecting the systems engineering disciplines that may emerge in this new century.

ACKNOWLEDGEMENTS

Would like to thank my mentor Ian Dallas, as well as Ben Goertzel, Onar Aam, Bob Cummings, Colin Helms and David Poole.

ABOUT THE AUTHOR

Kent Palmer is a Principle Systems Engineer at a major Aerospace Systems Company. He has a Ph.D. in Sociology concentrating on Philosophy of Science from the London School of Economics and a B.Sc. in Sociology from the University of Kansas. His dissertation on The Structure of Theoretical Systems in Relation to Emergence[62] focused on how new things come into existence within the Western Philosophical and Scientific worldview. He has written extensively on the roots of the Western Worldview in his electronic book The Fragmentation of Being and the Path Beyond the Void[63]. He had at least seventeen years experience[64] in Software Engineering and Systems Engineering disciplines at major aerospace companies based in Orange County CA. He served several years as the chairman of a Software Engineering Process Group and is now engaged in Systems Engineering Process improvement based on EIA 731 and CMMI. He has presented a tutorial on "Advanced Process Architectures[65]," which concerned engineering wide process improvement including both software and systems engineering. Besides process experience, he has recently been a software team lead on a Satellite Payload project and a systems engineer on a Satellite Ground System project. He has also engaged in independent research in Systems Theory which has resulted in a book of working papers called Reflexive Autopoietic Systems Theory[66]. A new introduction to this work now exists called *Reflexive Autopoietic Dissipative Special Systems Theory*[67]. He has given a tutorial[68] on Meta-systems engineering to the INCOSE Principles working group. He has written a series on *Software Engineering Foundations* which are contained in the book Wild Software Meta-systems[69]. He now teaches a course in "Software Requirements and Design Methodologies" at the University California Irvine Extension. He may be reached at palmer@exo.com.

ENDNOTES

[1] See "Reflexive Autopoietic Dissipative Special Systems Theory" by Kent Palmer at http://server.snni.com:80/~palmer/autopoiesis.html or http://dialog.net:85/homepage/autopoiesis.html

[2] The approach taken in this work is further elucidated by several papers by the author written for International Society for the Systems Sciences (ISSS; http://isss.org) 2000 conference in Toronto. These papers may be seen at http://dialog.net:85/homepage/ autopoiesis.html including the following titles "Defining Life And The Living Ontologically And Holonomically;" "New General Schemas Theory: Systems, Holons, Meta-Systems & Worlds;" "Intertwining Of Duality And Non-Duality;" "Holonomic Human Processes;" and "Genuine Spirtuality And Special Systems Theory"

[3] Van Gigch, John P. System Design Modeling and Metamodeling. New York : Plenum Press, c1991. See also Decision Making about Decision Making : metamodels and metasystems. Edited by John P. van Gigch ; with a foreword (metacomment) by Stafford Beer; Cambridge, Mass. : Abacus Press, 1987.

[4] Jeffrey S. Stamps Holonomy: A Human Systems Theory. Intersystems Publications, Seaside, CA 1980

[5] See http://www.cse.ogi.edu/~walton/dom_eng.html and for a bibliography see http://i90fs4.ira.uka.de/ bibliography/SE/domain.html

[6] Dyson, Freeman J.. Disturbing the Universe. New York : Harper & Row, c1979. See also Emergent Worlds Theory at http://server. snni.com:80/~palmer/emergent.htm

[7] Whole Systems Design Association at http://www.earthcorps.com/wsda/ See also Whole Systems Design course at Antioch University Seattle at http://www.seattleantioch.edu/ WholeSystem/ See Whole Systems Design (WSD) web site at http://www.arashi.com/WholeSystem/

[8] "Toward a Unified Systems Methodology for Australian Defense Systems-of-Systems" S.C. Cook, E. Lawson and J.S. Allison, INCOSE 1999 page 17; A Systems Engineering Process for Systems of Systems, Charles L. Roe, INCOSE 1999 page 20; "Architecting Principles for Systems-of-Systems", M.W. Maier 1997 on line at http://www.infoed.com/open/papers/ systems.htm

[9] By this is meant very small scale systems not micro-computer systems.

[10] Copi, Irving M.. The Theory of Logical Types. London, Routledge and K. Paul, 1971.

[11] Whitehead, Alfred North and Bertrand Russell, Principia Mathematica, Cambridge, University Press, 1910

[12] Bateson, Gregory. Steps to an Ecology of Mind. New York : Ballantine Books, c1972

[13] Wilden, Anthony. The Rules are No Game : the strategy of London ; New York : Routledge & K. Paul, 1987.

[14] Ontic is a term introduced by Heidegger in Being and Time which denotes the "beings" themselves without taking into account their Being. Ontos is the Greek word for Being. This is contrast with the Ontological which considers the Being of all beings as an Abstract gloss. Heidegger discusses ontological difference between the concept of Being (addressed by ontology) and the beings (considered ontic) that fall under that concept. See Heidegger, Martin. Being and Time. Translated by John MacQuarrie and Edward Robinson. London, SCM Press [c1962]

[15] Onto-logical expresses the fact that the concept of Being is directly related to logic which is concerned with the aspects of Being which are identity, reality, truth and presence. Rationality deals with all the aspects of Being in terms of relating our discourse to the world. Logic deals only the way that these aspects appear within the discourse itself.

[16] Wittgenstein, Ludwig, Philosophical Investigations; Translated by G.E.M. Anscombe. New York, Macmillan [1953]

[17] i.e. a thing with ontos.

[18] Levinas, Emmanuel. Otherwise than Being : or, Beyond essence. Translated by Alphonso Lingis. Hague ; Boston : M.; Hingham, MA : Distributors for the U.S. and Canada, Kluwer Boston, 1981.

[19] Specifically the idea of the In-hand and Out-of-hand modalities that continue the series started by Heidegger of present-at-hand and ready-to-hand. Also the idea of Encompassing as the highest cognitive level to augment the idea of pointing and grasping developed by Merleau-Ponty and bearing contributed by Levinas.

[20] This name is taken from what Merleau-Ponty in The Visible and the Invisible calls the hyper dialectic between Heidegger's *Process Being*, i.e. Being mixed with time, and Sartre's *Nothingness*. See Merleau-Ponty, Maurice, The Visible and the Invisible; followed by working notes., Edited by Claude Lefort. Translated by Alphonso Lingis. Evanston [Ill.] Northwestern University Press, 1968.

[21] Kuhn, Thomas S.. The Structure of Scientific Revolutions. [Chicago] University of Chicago Press 1962

[22] Kelly, Kevin, Out of Control : the new biology of machines, social systems, and the economic world Reading, Mass. : Addison-Wesley, 1995

[23] In Greek myth the gods are continually changing their form. However, when human beings in myth transform as Daphne does, for instance. It is usually permanent.

[24] Mead, George Herbert, The Philosophy of the Present. Chicago, London, Open Court publishing Co., 1932.

[25] See Derrida, Jacques. Of Grammatology Translated by Gayatri Chakravorty Spivak. Baltimore : Johns Hopkins University Press, 1976. Derrida calls these trace points "hinges" we can think of them as hinges between different possibilities.

[26] Another example of an exception is the Mobius band in which a surface only has one side or the Kleinian bottle in which the inside and outside surfaces are the same. Such anomalies challenge our intuitions about geometrical objects and teach us much in the process. For instance, the mobius strip and Kleinian bottle may be seen as lessons in the meaning of non-duality. Non-duality is a property of all holonomic systems. See Rosen, Steven M.. Science, Paradox, and the Moebius Principle : the evolution of a "transcultural" approach to wholeness Albany : State University of New York Press, c1994

[27] Rescher, Nicholas. Cognitive Systematization : a systems-theoretic approach to a coherentist theory of knowledge, N.J. : Rowman and Littlefield, 1979.

[28] Systems Engineering is a discipline whose members have a predilection for projecting the "system" cognitive template on things. A more mature discipline will recognize that this is merely one of many different fundamental types of comprehensional templates that are tools we might use to understand things.

[29] There are other kinds of pattern, namely value, sign and process. Process here means discontinuities in time while Structure means discontinuities in some plenum like space.

[30] Klir, George J., Architecture of Systems Problem Solving. New York : Plenum Press, c1985.

[31] Johansson, Ingvar. Ontological Investigations : an inquiry into the categories of nature, man, and society London ; New York : Routledge, 1989.

[32] This idea of de-emergence originates with Bob Cummings.

[33] This explanation owes much to David Poole of Altair Systems (dpoole@altaira.com) who has developed a state machine method for defining satellite and booster information systems architecture for use in ground systems.

[34] Here we ground "systems theory" and thereby "systems engineering" in a kind of social phenomenology ala Alfred Schutz and Aron Gurwitsch. Schutz considers the implications of phenomenology for sociology and Gurwitsch update's Husserl's work to add the awareness of gestalts beyond forms. A combination of the two gives us a feel for what a social phenomenology of systems should be like. See Gurwitsch, Aron. Field of Consciousness. Pittsburgh, Duquesne University Press, 1964. See also Schutz, Alfred, The Phenomenology of the Social World., Translated by George Walsh and Frederick Lehnert. [Evanston, Ill.] Northwestern University Press, 1967

[35] Castoriadis, Cornelius, The Imaginary Institution of Society. Cambridge, Mass. : MIT Press, 1987. See also World in Fragments : writings on politics, society, psychoanalysis, and the imagination edited and translated by David Ames Curtis. Stanford, Calif. : Stanford University Press, 1997.

[36] Deleuze, Gilles and , Félix Guattari. A Thousand Plateaus : capitalism and schizophrenia. Translation and foreword by Brian Massumi. Minneapolis : University of Minnesota Press, c1987.

[37] See The Structure of Theoretical Systems in Relation to Emergence. London School of Economics, University of London, Dissertation, 1982 by the author.

[38] Deutsch, David, The Fabric of Reality : the science of parallel universes-- and its implications New York : Allen Lane, c1997.

[39] From world down to pattern, because kosmos, pluriverse and monad, facet lie outside experience, i.e. are a priori.

[40] Wilden, Anthony. System and Structure: essays in communication and exchange. London, Tavistock Publications, 1972.

[41] See Dyson on terraforming the planets.

[42] Understanding the schema system as a "social gestalt" implies social construction and the social invention of systemic phenomena, which implies that systems are not objective characteristics of the phenomena but that they are projected onto the ontic substrate of the phenomena by social groups.

[43] See "Industrial Ecology and Systems Engineering – a perfect match?" O.A. Asbjornsen INCOSE 1999 page 35.

[44] Koestler, Arthur, Janus : a summing up. New York : Random House, c1978.

[45] Derrida, Jacques. Of Grammatology. Translated by Gayatri Chakravorty Spivak. Baltimore : Johns Hopkins University Press, 1976.

[46] Plotnitsky, Arkady. Complementarity : anti-epistemology after Bohr and Derrida. Durham : Duke University Press, 1994. See also Plotnitsky, Arkady. In the Shadow of Hegel : complementarity, history, and the unconscious. Gainesville : University Press of Florida, c1993.

[47] Bataille, Georges, The Accursed Share : an essay on general economy. Translated by Robert Hurley. New York : Zone Books, 1988-1991

[48] See Whole Systems Design Association at http://www.earthcorps.com/wsda/

[49] Leonard, George Burr, The Silent Pulse : a search for the perfect rhythm that exists in each of us New York : Dutton, c1978.

[50] Whole Systems Design homepage is at http://www.arashi.com/wsd/

[51] Pickett, Steward T., Jurek Kolasa, and Clive G. Jones, Ecological Understanding. San Diego : Academic Press, c1994.

[52] Prigogine, I. in collaboration with Isabelle Stengers.. The End of Certainty : time, chaos, and the new laws of nature. New York : Free Press, 1997. See also Prigogine, I.. Order Out of Chaos : man's new dialogue with nature. Toronto ; New York, N.Y. : Bantam Books, 1984.

[53] Maturana, Humberto R., Maturana and Francisco J. Varela. Autopoiesis and Cognition : the realization of the living Dordrecht, Holland ; Boston : D. Reidel Pub. Co., c1980.

[54] O'Malley, John B. Sociology of Meaning. London, Human Context Books [1972]

[55] Sandywell, Barry. Logological Investigations London ; New York : Routledge, 1996 volumes 1-3

[56] Holonic Solutions: http://www.holon.com.au/

[57] http://hms.ifw.uni-hannover.de/

[58] Emergent Meta-systems are similar to the Self Generating Systems of Ben Goertzel. See Goertzel, Ben. Chaotic Logic : language, thought, and reality from the perspective of systems science. New York : Plenum Press, c1994.

[59] See Emanuel Falkenauer Genetic Algorithms and Grouping Problems (Wiley 1998)

[60] This is like the distinction that Barry Sandywell makes between *social construction* verses *social invention*. He distinguishes between the pre-reflexive, reflective and reflexive which correspond to the dissipative, autopoietic and reflexive special systems.

[61] This same thing has been said of SuperString Theory which is billed as a next century science that fell into the 1990s. Special Systems Theory and Emergent Meta-systems theory is similarly a future systems theory that has fallen into our own time by serendipity.

[62] http://server.snni.com:80/~palmer/disab.html You may also try http://dialog.net:85/homepage/ or http://think.net/homepage/ for any of the web related material.

[63] http://server.snni.com:80/~palmer/fbpath.htm

[64] http://server.snni.com:80/~palmer/resume.html

[65] http://server.snni.com:80/~palmer/advanced.htm

[66] http://server.snni.com:80/~palmer/refauto2.htm

[67] http://server.snni.com:80/~palmer/autopoiesis.html

[68] http://dialog.net:85/homepage/incosewg/index.htm

[69] http://server.snni.com:80/~palmer/wsms.htm

Overview of a CONOPS for an SE Education Community

Jack Ring
Kennen, Inc.
Scottsdale, AZ
jring@kennen.com

A. Wayne Wymore
SANDS, Inc.
Tucson, AZ
awwymore@yahoo.com

Abstract: This paper summarizes a concept of operations (ConOps) for a Systems Engineering Education Community (SEEC). An SEEC enables those involved in performing systems engineering to improve systems engineering. An SEEC is envisioned as a vehicle for competency and proficiency growth by all practitioners of systems engineering as well as the vehicle for measuring, quantitatively, both the supply and demand sides of the SE learning community. Finally, the SEEC should be a resource for helping all members of the community make choices about the content, structure, utilization and outcomes of an SEEC.

The best SEEC is the one that produces a stream of the appropriate mix of SE practitioners for forthcoming projects at minimum cost and cycle time. Relative to current SE learning providers we estimate that cycle times must be reduced three fold and learning extent must be expanded nine fold. Also, capacity must increase two to five fold.

INTRODUCTION

The ConOps for an SEEC was prepared for the Education Measurement Working Group of the E&R TC, INCOSE. The Education Measurement WG was formed to make Systems Engineering education a proven, value-adding, activity that matures in a systemic manner. This paper presents only an overview of the ConOps for an SEEC. A more comprehensive version may be found at www.incose.org.

KEY PROBLEM

The SE community consists of three types of stakeholders; 1) SE practitioners who perform in system development projects, 2) SE practitioners who manage SE project teams and SE organizations, and 3) SE practitioners who act as principals, e.g. professors and teachers, in an SEEC. All are, or should be, practitioners of SE (PSE) and all need to improve their competencies in the practice of SE and in the transfer of SE knowledge to others.

The SE community does not have clear indicators of direction nor adequate sources of improvement. Further, the choices they do have are not quantified as to value and choice-making aids are inadequate. The key problem is the lack of a unified framework among the stakeholders for rating learning options, making choices and scoring outcomes. Although college degrees are an indicator of SE competency a degree is not a sufficient indicator of which persons and organizations can create systems effectively (Sydenham 1999). Instead, all stakeholders desire a "Consumer-Provider Rating system" that will enable:

- Project PSE's to make good choices about education providers and employers,
- Providers to make good choices about the delivery environments and experiences they offer, the PSE's they accept, the employers they serve,
- Employers/Sponsors to make good choices about which Providers to support and which PSE's are more likely to yield a good return on investment. Equally important are good choices regarding which adaptations they need to make, internally, in order to let project PSE's be most effective.

This tripartite SE community needs a rating system that; is rooted in customer value, is buffered against erroneous knowledge such as subjective or destructive judgments, and has the acuity to assess both actual performance and potential performance improvement from contemplated changes.

Note that it is not necessary for a ConOps to get embroiled in defining SE nor in prescribing SE processes. Although follow-on work spawned by this ConOps may have to grapple with those specifics, a ConOps can successfully talk about the improvements that system users need without delving into the system's internals.

AN SEEC IN OPERATION

We see an SEEC in context as shown in Figure 1.

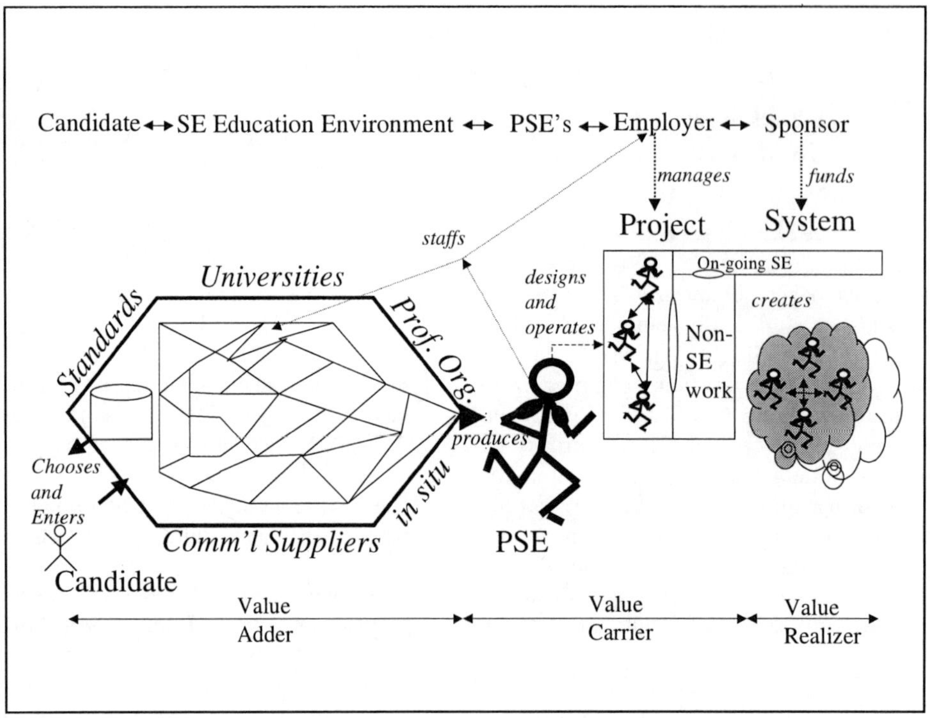

Figure 1. Context of an SEEC

The context of an SEEC starts (reading from right to left) with a Sponsor needing a new system.

Sponsor: The Sponsor funds the system, including its development. The sponsor and related beneficiaries realize value from the system after it is delivered, operated and adapted to the operational situation (Ring 98).

Employer: The sponsor typically relies on an Employer to manage the project that creates the system. The Sponsor selects the Employer who convincingly proposes to accomplish the Project "better, faster, cheaper" than competitors. Sponsors and Employers share the risks inherent in creating the system and share the rewards that flow from the value exhibited by the system when operational.

Project: The project is where time, resources, competencies, goals, status reviews and activities are mixed together and results emerge in terms of Quality, Cycle Time, Cost and Learning. For purposes of this paper a project is viewed in three parts; a front-end part consisting mostly of SE work, an on-going SE part that transcends development, deployment and adaptation, and a third part that is the non-SE work of component engineering, integration and test. Project management and other administrative tasks are not shown. Although projects vary widely, we estimate that the front-end part ought to consume about 5% of the project budget and the on-going part ought to consume another 5% to 10%. Ideally the amount of SE required is minimized as PSE's improve.**Practitioners of SE (PSE's):** As part of the overall project, PSE's, as employees or contractors, collaboratively design the SE project (perhaps documenting the scheme as a SEMP). Then PSE's operate the SE project by forming relationships with one another and with other people who are in non-SE roles on the project.

The degree to which PSE's are effective in a project setting is modulated by three factors:

- Competencies and Proficiency levels of individual PSE's.
- Collaborativeness and immunity to situations which tend to disturb and degrade individual and workgroup enthusiasm.
- SE project work climate, method and tooling. The project work climate and overall culture that is generally created by the employer and influenced by the system project's sponsor and can affect productivity and innovation by a factor of 10 or more for both the PSE's and other project members (Livingston 1982).

The results of SE work are the SE work products or artifacts. The SE artifacts inform the PSE's and the Non-SE performers on the overall project who then produce the balance of the deliverable artifacts that complete the project. Collateral outputs of the SE project embellish the SE body of knowledge. Yet other outputs of the project are by-products that may be benign or may be toxic waste (such as erroneous knowledge carried forward or a conflicting relationship that is left unresolved).

SEEC: A SEEC produces PSE's each of which will possess a profile of competencies and exhibit a proficiency level in each competency.

A SEEC must consist of at least five types (subsystems) of providers. These are: universities and other academic centers, commercial suppliers of SE learning, standards bodies, and professional organizations as well as *in situ* on-the-job-training (OJT) subsystems. These five modes of requisite variety are necessary because of the span of domain knowledge required by PSE's and because PSE's exhibit various learning styles. Each of these subsystem types are expected to overlap in subject matter but differ in the type of learning offered. Also, we foresee that many learning sessions must take place "anytime, anywhere, anyhow" as contrasted to "students on campus." Although Figure 1 does not illustrate the fact in the interest of readability, it should be noted that Projec and *in situ* can be congruent and should be if possible. That is, each project should be an SEEC subsystem.

Although academic centers are striving to create more realistic learning Communities (Axelband et al 1999), (Frey, et al 1999), (Kurstedt et al 1999), (Lang and Levin 1999) we believe that structural and cultural limits in academia will preclude universities and related laboratories from being sufficiently responsive. However, we also believe that adequate progress can be made by systemizing and harmonizing the variety of learning opportunities that already exist or will, perforce, exist.

An appropriate metaphor may be the learning community for "Top Gun" fighter pilots. Only so much can be learned in ground school, even with flight simulators. More is learned in actual flying and even more when practice is focused on various pseudo-threats. Then comes the real thing and the learning accelerates tremendously, even to the level, for some at least, of acknowledging that only a limited range of competencies have been mastered so far. Further, the scope exceeds "one person - one plane" because modern combat requires collaborative maneuvers. Learning extends to "sharing the risk and taking up the slack" for the good of the team. In this metaphor, the questions are; "How does a fledgling or advanced pilot know what experiences to pursue next?" and "Where can he/she go to gain such experiences?" and "In case alternatives exist how does he/she know which one is likely to suit his/her unique situation the best?"

SEEC adds value to PSE participants by increasing their repertoire of competencies and proficiency level in each competency.

The SEEC must span the needs not only of PSE's on projects but also of PSE's who act as employer managers and PSE's who act as principals in the SEEC subsystems. The more capable PSE's should be able to contribute effectively in any of these situations.

The value-added to a PSE is considered latent until the PSE produces artifacts. Consequently, value-added is an emergent behavior of a collaboration rather than a guaranteed effect of a resource.

Candidates: The SEEC processes Candidates to produce PSE's. A small percentage of candidates will experience the SEEC for the first time but the majority of Candidates will be alumni, that is, PSE's who are recycling through the SEEC. PSE's will recycle through the SEEC multiple times in order to augment their respective capabilities incrementally. One mode of recycle is the Real plane where the practitioner physically returns for more experiences. The more prevalent mode of recycle, however, is the Reflection plane where the Practitioner imagines, recalls and reaches deeper understanding (Schon 1987). The more advanced PSE may transit an SEEC, in real or in reflection, approximately a thousand times during a 40 year career.

Each cycle through the SEEC increases basic SE competencies and respective proficiency levels. Also, each cycle increases a PSE's personal learning power (rate of adding competencies and increasing proficiencies) as the PSE's level of awareness increases and he/she "learns to learn" (Wymore 69). Learning to learn is especially important during *in situ* sessions of direct project work.

PSE'S ADD VALUE:

Sponsor-realized value is achieved in a generative manner. The SEEC, by turning candidates into PSE's, is a value adder. The resulting PSE's are carriers of latent value and, when allowed to apply their knowledge in projects they trigger the value realization phase. PSE's add value to the project and the resulting system in three ways.

"Languages the Project" - wherein a common language is installed in (actually adopted by) all project participants as eloquently described and demonstrated by Fernando Flores in (Rubin 1999). A common language enables participants to dialog about a systems life cycle, systems terminology, work products, methods and tools for analysis and synthesis and numerous other topics (McDavid). Usually a generic language is installed first, followed by specific terms and names for each system that is the subject of a project. The generic language can be installed by academics, professional societies or standards. PSE's do the rest during a specific project by naming of phenomena regarding the problem space, the conceptual representation of the solution system and the logical representation of the same system. Measures Of Effectiveness (MOE's), risks and critical success factors (CSF's) are also discerned and named by PSE's who also elucidate the network of interrelationships and respective significances of these.

"Imagines and structures both the problem system and the solution system" - wherein the artifacts of SE are produced. In (Evans and Patterson 1998) we are reminded that the eventual solution system evolves from a conceptual understanding of the problem to a model and simulation of the problem symptoms and problem amelioration strategy. Then an initial, nearly inexplicable thought occurs regarding the solution system. It is followed by a conceptual diagram or story followed by a model and simulation followed by a set of abstractions that are interrelated in an architecture. To preclude this evolving model from becoming incomprehensible the few key determinants of system behavior and cost are identified. System development progresses to specifying and creating physical manifestations (aka components) and on to interconnected sets that finally qualify as a deliverable system. The balance of a PSE's contribution occurs subsequent to delivery. Having confirmed that the set of components exhibited acceptable behavior in the pseudo-reality of the development project, PSE's next confirm that the web of components produce acceptable behaviors in the real operational Community. Also, PSE's help discern the inevitable adaptations to interfacing systems that will further benefit the users.

"Converges risk and creativity to closure" is the third contribution of PSE's wherein the few key determinants of system success are used to guide all trade-offs and judge all design proposals and design change proposals. Here PSE's deal with numerous new ideas and suggested shortcut by other project members as well as employers and sponsors. And the PSE's must adjudicate all within the "heartbeat" of the project. Only those persons having understanding of the systems theoretic view of the design are qualified to specify the allowable sequence of design reviews and baseline reconciliations. Typically, only PSE's are thus qualified.

The resulting system, when operated to the benefit of the Sponsor completes the value realization process. But this process should not be thought of as a static model. In the interest of "better, faster, cheaper" the real question is, how can the generative process be accelerated – but with fewer resources?

SEEC INTERFACES

Without prescribing the content of the SEEC we can remark on the primary interfaces the SEEC should exhibit. Items 1 – 6 comprise an SE Body of Knowledge whereas item 7 is an SEEC capability.

1. An ontology of Systems Engineering that identifies the terminology, usage and interrelationships across the stakeholder domains
2. Principles, practices, standards, hueristics and handbooks regarding systems identification, design and engineering.
3. Career progression guidelines for planning the evolution of a PSE,
4. Bill of Learning Opportunities and a Rating Scale and Procedure.
5. Choice-making decision support protocol and aids.
6. Source material for Competency/Proficiency Development.
7. Dialog Facilitator that enables a PSE to engage in reflection and action learning.

IMPROVING PSE'S

This section describes how an SE community can: a) characterize itself, b) make mutually beneficial choices among alternative investments and relationships and c) create future learning communities that maximize the value added to each user.

Although the behavior of almost any system is more than the linear sum of the behavior of its elements, the fact remains that system behavior is still some function of the behavior of the basic elements and interrelationships. Accordingly, SE behavior can be changed only by changing one or more elements. We must focus on elements because SE is a peopled system wherein the type and intensity of relationships are emergent behaviors that we cannot presume to change directly. Improving SE must be done by improving one or more PSE's, be they project practitioners, employer managers or provider principals, and doing so in a way that causes the resulting system to exhibit improved effectiveness rather than exhibiting conflicts and diminished performance.

Barring severely constraining factors, the marginal utility of SE is improved by increasing the competencies and proficiency levels of PSE's who are the carriers of SE value to stakeholders. The marginal utility of SE practitioners is improved through experiencing the SEEC.

Participants in the SE community have numerous individual concerns but they also have three common concerns which can be the unifying framework for improving SE. These are Time, Competencies, and

Proficiency Levels.

Time = a calendar of events.

Competencies = The subjects of education and the "operators" of application. We anticipate that there are 200 to 300 distinct competencies pertinent to the whole SE community. We think the breadth of competencies is very important and often seriously understated in most SE education literature.

Proficiency Level = an indicator of value-adding potential. The degree to which each participant can apply SE competencies. Specifying proficiency levels is similarly beyond the scope of this ConOps but conceptually we expect the levels to be something like:

- SE Fellow
- SE Coach/Mentor
- SE Master
- SE Practitioner
- SE Apprentice
- SE Intern

Framework: This suggests that a three axis Competency, Proficiency, Time (CPT) coordinate system will provide an appropriate framework in which the participants can locate themselves and estimate the probable effects of transition choices. Such a framework and its use is illustrated Figure 2.

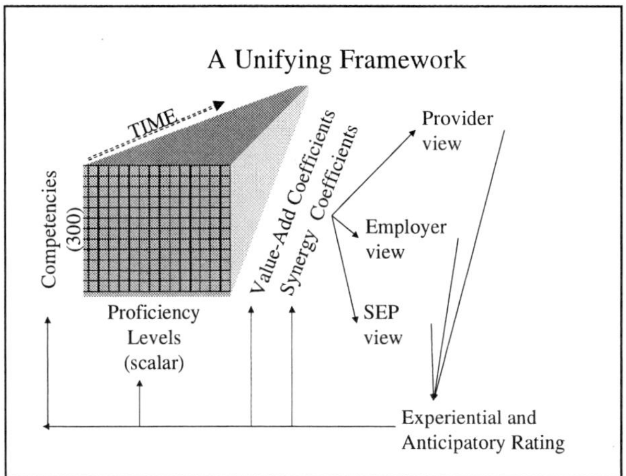

Figure 2. A Unifying Framework

Estimating Current Situations Each PSE would be located at specific coordinates in this framework and could express desired target coordinates. Each PSE's current location will be estimated by means of self-assessment, employer assessments and provider assessments.

Each PSE's learning potential could be assessed using instruments (Hermann 1997), intuition and other means. This would indicate the locus of possible future locations for each PSE.

Employers would express their current and future needs in terms of the numbers of staff required at each CPT cell. These estimates could be made by incumbent PSE's, associates, prospective PSE's, Providers and "maturity assessment services." Each employer's current profile is thus estimated for each CP cell. In addition, estimates will be made for factors related to PSE effectiveness, such as standards, paradigms, culture, risk preferences, SE make vs. buy proclivity, etc. Also, estimates will be made on the relevance (interrelationship) of these to PSE effectiveness.

Providers will register their capacity at each CPT location, describe the prerequisites as constraints and state their collaboration coefficients with respect to other providers at the cell level. Each Provider's profile of CPT offerings and MOE will be estimated by self-assessment, cross-provider assessments and PSE's (past clients, prospective clients and clients who opted for other providers) as well as assessments by employers.

Note that although PSE's and employers focus on "the ends" that is, current and future locations (states) the providers focus on "the means" that is, state transitions which comprise the value-adding process that facilitates and encourages PSE's and employers to invest in moving from a current competency-proficiency state to a new competency-proficiency state.

Estimates of provider's locations are not limited to the enterprise level of granularity. For instance, the SE specific competencies-proficiencies of provider Principals are important, also, because older and/or more advanced PSE's learn more, faster from those they respect as having "been there, done that." Also PSE's, especially younger ones, seem to learn faster from those who can affect their careers directly. This is another reason why *in situ* can be a powerful subsystem in the SEEC.

Choice Making: The respective parties will make choices about which transition actions to undertake. These decisions can be made by estimating the future expected value of each decision and then comparing alternatives and making choices.

Each PSE would estimate the marginal value coefficients expected from alternative job offerings and SEEC providers. Likewise, each employer would estimate a marginal value coefficient for each PSE's enhanced competency development. Finally, each provider would estimate a marginal value for each candidate PSE and each employer relationship.

Organizational inertia must be factored in because it will be a significant deflator of net future value. We estimate inertia of the participants as (in descending order of change proficiency):

1. PSE
2. Employer Small
3. Employer Large
4. Provider in situ
5. Provider commercial
6. Professional Society
7. Standards body
8. Provider - institution

Because this is a multi-party game each selection is likely to influence the estimate of future expected value on other alternatives. Accordingly, it is necessary to use synergy coefficients between the choices (that is, CPT cells to respective parties and respective parties to respective parties.)

The concept described herein supports local decisions but recognizes that each local decision can propagate to global outcomes

The old General's admonition that the winner is the one who comes to battle "the fustest with the mostest" notwithstanding, the SE community and their customers may not be playing in a zero-sum game. Rather, a better metaphor for the system we are seeking may be 'the community caretaking of a common good.'

Community Information Access: Estimates of coupling coefficients may be accomplished periodically, episodically and/or continuously. Regardless, the goal is adequate, accurate and timely data and updates must not be delayed for "control" purposes by any participants.

That all participants must have access to adequate, accurate and timely data is probably obvious but must be stated for completeness. This does not mean that everyone must have the authorization to see all assessments. Privacy and Intellectual Property rights can be honored by allowing for negotiated access. In fact, one participant's refusal to grant access to another participant can be a very informative act all by itself.

Decision aids: Because of the frequency and implicitness of the choice-making we suggest that the technology of software agents be evaluated for this purpose.

SEEC PERFORMANCE EXPECTATIONS

The magnitude of the current "gap" between a) the SE community capability and b) the needs of Sponsors for "better, faster, cheaper" was estimated from informal discussions with a number of practitioners regarding the degree to which their talents were used, the time and cost of educational sessions and the degree to which they were prepared to contribute on various system project scenarios. Although employers may have a different view, the PSE's unanimously agreed that the root causes of the gap today were; firstly, employers, secondly, providers and thirdly PSE's. If this is a true estimate of the situation then priority should be given to educating employer management rather than PSE's.

Certainly a more formal and comprehensive assessment of gap size should be done. As the SEEC becomes operational it will quantify the gap frequently as a normal part of its auto-alignment of itself with its context. Meanwhile, our preliminary estimates are:

- SEEC cycle times must be reduced by a three fold relative to current experiences,
- SEEC must become nine-fold more capable of adding value to PSE's during the aforementioned reduced cycle times. Note that this seemingly formidable challenge may be met simply by ensuring retention and application. This, of course, is the rationale for integrating the subsystems into a learning Community.
- Our initial estimate of community priorities for improving SE is (descending order):
  1. Employer management,
  2. Provider principals (professors, mentors, coaches, etc.) and
  3. Project practitioners.

For additional perspective on the scope and dynamics of the SEEC we estimate the following:

- PSE's constitute 2 million persons making 4 million choices per year. Less than 500,000 of them actually utilizing an SEEC subsystem for competency development experiences annually.
- Employers in 50,000 establishments making 250,000 choices per year and sending 2,000 leaders per year to utilize an SEEC subsystem for competency development experiences.
- Providers in 2,000 establishments making 4,000 choices per year and sending 2,000 principals per year to utilize an SEEC subsystem for competency development experiences.
- The SEEC must support the planning and choice making activities asynchronously. Delivery of the competency development experiences will be mass customized for anytime, anyplace, anyway utilization.

HETERARCHICAL CONTROL

No singular control point exists in this 'three-body problem' situation. PSE's cannot force employers and providers to improve any more than employers can force PSE's and providers to improve. Likewise, providers are relatively powerless to demand improvements of PSE's or employers, let alone demand collaboration from other provider subsystems. Although standards authorities may attempt to regulate all the others, as do some very large sponsors and industry associations, basic system theory says that if the gestation cycle of a standard is far longer than the duration of associated knowledge cycles then the standards are largely irrelevant when finally released. In such situations standards cannot contribute to control.

Because all relationships will be elastic and reflexive, the inescapable conclusion is that the problem of improving SE requires a system for improving the elements and interrelations in SE in an egalitarian and synergistic fashion – in other words a heterarchical system.

SE Value Web Emergence: Given the expected volume and interaction of choices the whole system may or may not exhibit any sign of stability. Whether stability emerges is not so much a function of competencies and proficiencies but whether the participants are mutually informed (Axelrod) and whether they choose to a) compete because they assume a declining returns situation or choose to b) co-align because they assume an increasing returns situation (Arthur 1990). Although the majority of current literature on collaboration stresses that the key factor is mutual trust, (Axelrod) has shown that members of a group tend toward community norms when they know that detection and punishment are likely. The necessary and sufficient conditions for co-aligning subsystems has been described in (Wymore 97).

SUMMARY

The SE community is faced with creating more complex and dynamic systems and in doing so "better, faster, cheaper." This is not just a NASA initiative but is endemic throughout the industrial, commercial and public sector.

SE practitioners must increase their respective competencies and proficiency levels regardless of whether they practice on projects, or as managers of SE teams and organizations or as principals in educational institutions, both academic and commercial.

An SEE consisting of at least five kinds of subsystems is necessary and may be sufficient depending on the degree of collaboration evidenced by the subsystems.

This tripartite community needs a common framework for quantifying their respective situations, evaluating learning alternatives, and evolving the SEEC.

The SEEC notion clearly invites a perspective shift from "the education institution" to "the education experience." Accordingly, the PSE evolves from being "student" to being "co-learner" and eventually to becoming the "learning Community."

This shift does not imply in any way that educational institutions are irrelevant. On the contrary, the need for world-class PSE's places a great challenge on such institutions to improve and expand. But it does call for understanding that the educational institutions alone cannot create the spectrum of learning Communities required by aspiring PSE's. One, not insignificant, reason is that there is far more to SE than engineering

REFERENCES

Arthur, B., *"Positive Feedbacks in the Economy."* Scientific American, February, 1990

Axelband , E., Friedman, G. Croxall, R. O-use, S., *"The Education of Mission Systems Engineers."* Proceedings of 13th International Conference on Systems Engineering, 1999

Axelrod, R. *"The Complexity of Cooperation."* Princeton University Press, 1997

Evans and Patterson, *"Perfecting the Image System Development as a Continuum of Design Decisions."* IEEE-SMC Conf. Proc., 1998.

Frey, D., Bellinger, S., and Smith, M., *"Using Hands-on Design Challenges in a Graduate Degree Program in System Design."* Proc. of 13th Intn'l Conf. on Systems Engineering, 1999

Hermann, Ned, *The Whole Brain Business Book*, McGraw Hill, 1997

Kurstedt, H., McCollom, E., White, O. and Wiswell, B. *"A Cross-disciplinary Course in Relationship Competence for Systems Engineers."* Proc. of 13th Intn'l Conf. on Systems Engineering, 1999

Lang . G. and Levin, M., *"Mulitilevel Approach to Systems Engineering Education."* Proc. of 13th Intn'l Conf. on Systems Engineering, 1999

Livingston, W., *"Friends in High Places."* Appendix 1, FES Publishing, 1982.

Ring, J., *"A Value-seeking View of Systems Engineering."* IEEE SMC 1998 Conf. Proc.

Rubin, H. *"The Power of Words."* Fast Company, Issue 24, pg 142, 1999

Schon, Donald, *"Educating the Reflective Practitioner."* Jossey-Bass, 1987

Sydenham, P., 1999, Proc. of the Australian SETE99 Conference.

Wymore, A. Wayne, 1969, *"A Model Curriculum in Systems Engineering."* Journal of Systems Engineering, Vol. 1, No. 2, April, 1969, pp. 291 – 324, particularly p. 314.

Wymore, A. Wayne, 1997, *Subsystem Optimization Implies System Suboptimization: Not!*, see www.sie.arizona.edu/faculty/wymore.html

AUTHOR INDEX

AUTHOR INDEX

AUTHOR INDEX

John Wiley & Sons
111 River Street
Hoboken, NJ 07030-5774

ISBN 978-1-5108-6245-6

CURRAN ASSOCIATES INC.
proceedings.com